HAMBLEDON HILL, DORSET, ENGLAND.

Excavation and survey of a Neolithic monument complex and its surrounding landscape

Volume 2

See you our pastures wide and lone,
Where the red oxen browse?
O there was a City thronged and known,
Ere London boasted a house.

And see you, after rain, the trace
Of mound and ditch and wall?
O that was a legion's camping-place,
When Caesar sailed from Gaul.

And see you the marks that show and fade,
Like shadows on the Downs?
O they are the lines the Flint Men made,
To guard their wondrous towns.

Trackway and Camp and City lost,
Salt Marsh where now is corn;
Old Wars, old Peace, old Arts that cease,
And so was England born!

She is not any common Earth,
Water or wood or air,
But Merlin's Isle of Gramarye,
Where you and I will fare.

Rudyard Kipling, from 'Puck's Song', *Puck of Pook's Hill*, 1906

The chalk, which I have spoken of coldly when I discussed the preservation of the Old Road, should somewhere be warmly hymned and praised by every man who belongs to south England, for it is the meaning of that good land. The sand is deserted since men learnt to plough; the Weald, though so much of its forest has fallen, is still nothing but the Weald – clay, and here and there the accursed new towns spreading like any other slime. But the chalk is our landscape and our proper habitation. The chalk gave us our first refuge in war by permitting those vast encampments on the summits. The chalk filtered our drink for us and built up our strong bones; it was the height from the slopes of which our villages, standing in a clean air, could watch the sea or the plain; we carved it – when it was hard enough; it holds our first ornaments; our clear streams run over it; the shapes and curves it takes and the kind of rough grass it bears (an especial grass for sheep), are the cloak of our counties; its lonely breadths delight us when the white clouds and the flocks move over them together; where the waves break it into cliffs, they are the characteristic of our shores, and through its thin coat of whitish mould go the thirsty roots of our three trees – the beech, the holly and the yew. For the clay and the sand might be deserted or flooded and the South Country would still remain, but if the Chalk Hills were taken away we might as well be the Midlands.

Hilaire Belloc, *The Old Road*, 1911

HAMBLEDON HILL, DORSET, ENGLAND.
Excavation and survey of a Neolithic monument complex and its surrounding landscape

Roger Mercer and Frances Healy

with contributions by
Michael J Allen, Phil Austin, Alistair Barclay, Alex Bayliss, Martin Bell, Robert Berstan, Lisa Brown, Catherine Chisham, Alison Cook, Mark Copley, Michael Cowell, Timothy Darvill, Richard Evershed, Jonathon Hather, Hillary Howard, the late Su Johnson, Glynis Jones, the late Robin Kenward, Moira Laidlaw, A J Legge, F G McCormac, J I McKinley, Stuart Needham, Alastair Oswald, Rog Palmer, C Bronk Ramsey, Michael Richards, Fiona Roe, Alan Saville, the late Isobel Smith, Rachael Seager Smith, the late Bob Smith, Elizabeth Somerville, Andrew Stott, and Nick Wells

and principal illustrations by
Silvia Stevenson and John Borland

Further illustrations by Martin Bell, Lisa Brown, Timothy Darvill, Sharon Dixon, Jane Green, Nick Griffiths, Liz James, Alastair Oswald, Rog Palmer, Joanna Richards, Philip Sinton, the late Isobel Smith, Gordon Thomas, and Karen Wicks

ENGLISH HERITAGE

2008

ARCHAEOLOGICAL REPORTS

Published by English Heritage, Kemble Drive, Swindon SN2 2GZ
www.english-heritage.org.uk
English Heritage is the Government's statutory adviser on all aspects of the historic environment

Printing 10 9 8 7 6 5 4 3 2 1

First published 2009

ISBN 978 1 905624 59 1

Product Code 51319

British Library Cataloguing in Publication data
A CIP catalogue record for this book is available from the British Library

The National Monuments Record is the public archive of English Heritage. For more information, contact NMR Enquiry and Research Services, National Monuments Record Centre, Kemble Drive, Swindon SN2 2GZ; telephone (01793) 414600

Brought to publication by David M Jones, Publishing, English Heritage, Kemble Drive, Swindon SN2 2GZ

Edited by Val Kinsler, 100% Proof
Indexed by Alan Rutter
Page layout by Val Kinsler, 100% Proof

Printed in England by by 4edge Ltd, Hockley

Contents

Volume 2

5 Molluscan and sedimentary evidence for the palaeo-environmental history of Hambledon Hill and its surroundings

Martin Bell, Michael J Allen, the late R W Smith and the late Su Johnson

5.1 Introduction

The environmental context of Neolithic monuments is particularly relevant in revealing both the differing characters of the main classes of monument and the contrasting time depths of human activity in the settings in which they were placed. The molluscan evidence from Hambledon Hill raises interesting questions about the setting of the site and the activities that took place within it and in the surrounding area. Investigations of molluscs from features on the hilltop associated with the Neolithic enclosures are combined with the study of colluvial and alluvial deposits from the surrounding slopes and valleys and their contained mollusc assemblages. Together these two investigations provide evidence for both the nature of the Neolithic hilltop environment and the development and use of the wider landscape in which the Hambledon Hill complex was set.

No buried soils were recognised on Hambledon Hill during the excavation, although possible truncated examples were identified in the post-excavation stage on site P (see 3.3.2, 3.3.4) but were not sampled. Columns of samples had been taken through ditch sediments but they did not survive, and it is reported that they were largely of vacuous chalk rubble unsuitable for mollusc analysis (R Mercer, pers comm). Nevertheless, a major residue sorting programme from flotation of samples from the Neolithic site was carried out by Professor A J Legge, and the flots were retained for further analysis. This was designed to obtain representative samples of seeds and bones. A proportion of the flots was found to contain abundant molluscs. In the absence of soil samples taken and processed specifically for molluscs from Neolithic contexts on the hill, a selection of the flots was examined by SJ and MB. This provided data about the Neolithic hilltop environments. Residues equate to the heavy fraction of a flotation sample, including bone and lithic material, recovered from the sieve and flots to the light fraction of a flotation sample, including charred plant remains, recovered from the surface of the water.

In order to provide information on the environment and land-use around the hill, R W (Bob) Smith and Martin Bell undertook an investigation of colluvial and valley sediments. These investigations included work on a Bronze Age site in Everley Water Meadow located during fieldwalking by Rog Palmer (see Ch 2). This led to further archaeological and palaeoenvironmental fieldwork at Everley Water Meadow in 1983–4; the archaeological investigation of which was largely conducted by RWS as a part of his postgraduate research (Smith 1985). Molluscan and environmental analysis for this project was conducted by MB and MJA. That study provided much information on how the landscape had evolved during the second half of the Holocene, but it was not possible to identify sedimentary increments which could be related specifically to the time of the Neolithic enclosures.

All the detailed palaeoenvironmental investigations at Hambledon Hill can now be placed into the much wider context of the Wessex chalk by comparison with recent work at Maiden Castle (Sharples 1991), Windmill Hill (Whittle *et al* 1999) and, more locally, at Whitesheet Hill (Rawlings 1994; Rawlings *et al* 2004), as well as ongoing research into the Neolithic landscape of the Allen Valley, Cranborne Chase (Allen 1998; 2000a; 2002; French *et al* 2000; 2003; 2007).

During the molluscan analysis employed here, species nomenclature follows Kerney (1999), but the broad ecological groupings are those outlined by Evans (1972, 194–203) as used in the initial analytical programme (Bell and Allen 1985).

5.2 The causewayed enclosure complex

Martin Bell, Su Johnson and Michael J Allen

A number of selected Neolithic contexts had been sampled and were processed by Professor A J Legge for other environmental evidence by flotation in a Siraf-type tank. A large number of flots were analysed for molluscs for undergraduate projects at the University of Wales, Lampeter, and latterly the University of Reading between 1992–2000. Only a representative proportion of those which produced adequate assemblages for interpretation are reported here. This analysis is based on subsamples additional to those used for student projects and all the identifications have been made by SJ and MB and are presented in Tables 5.1 to 5.3.

It must be acknowledged that assemblages solely derived from flots from flotation do not provide an ideal basis for interpretation. This method may create problems and biases that need to be made explicit at the outset. The sizes of sieves used were 1 mm and 300 μm. If the 300 μm sieve was always used for the flots then the smallest taxa that floated would be recovered, and this would be comparable to conventional analysis employing sieves of 0.5 mm mesh (cf Evans 1972).

There are some shells of this size in all the samples reported. If, however, this small sieve mesh was not always used, then some of the smaller taxa (eg *Vallonia*, *Carychium* and *Punctum*), and more fragile shells, will be under-represented. No residue was available for examination and certain types and sizes of shell which do not readily float will be under-represented, especially apical fragments of the smaller taxa and heavier and larger shells, eg *Pomatias elegans*. The range of species present in these samples, however, indicates that taxa of all sizes were represented, but that small taxa and more fragile species are likely to be under-represented.

A few samples were very large, containing thousands of shells, and these were subsampled using a riffle-type sample divider. Molluscs were extracted from the flots, identified and counted (Tables 5.1–3). These samples should be regarded as a series of spot samples which had not been taken in a column as a sequence. Samples have, therefore, been selected and arranged, not in direct stratigraphical order, but in chronological sequence, to construct chronologically sensible mollusc diagrams (Figs 5.1–3). One sequence of samples has been identified from the main causewayed enclosure and two from the Stepleton spur. Each of these sequences has been compiled from a number of samples from three to five separate ditch segments, which in some instances contained different local stratigraphies. These mollusc diagrams were produced using *Tilia* and *Tiliagraph* software.

Evidence from pits and other internal features cannot be related stratigraphically either to one another, or to the ditches. In interpreting the results we must consider to what extent differences between samples are temporal or spatial. An additional problem of interpretation is that all the samples derive from ditch or feature fills. A significant proportion of the molluscs will therefore be allochthonous, ie derived from a range of contexts which may include eroded material from earlier soils and subsoil features. An autochthonous component, which actually lived in the ditches, may reflect the ditch microenvironment rather than the wider landscape. In particular, there is likely to be a rock-rubble component that lived in scree from eroding banks or the vacuous interstices of the ditch fills (Evans and Jones 1973). We have attempted to assess this factor by indicating in Tables 5.1–3 which of the contexts sampled contained a rock-rubble component and which did not. It confirms that only a small number of rock-rubble contexts were sampled. The same tables also give some indication of the numbers of Neolithic finds in the contexts sampled by grouping them in three categories: none; some; abundant. Most of the samples come from contexts in which artefacts were abundant. This accords with information that contexts were selected for flotation if they appeared to contain promising quantities of charred plant material. Some bias towards contexts with greater evidence of human activity will therefore exist.

5.2.1 The central area

The main enclosure

The samples examined were sieved flots from the 1974 excavation of the main enclosure (Fig 3.9: segments 2, 3 and 4). In total, ten samples were examined from three adjacent ditch segments on Site A; the results are presented in Table 5.1 and Figure 5.1. The samples have been arranged chronologically in what is regarded as a reasonably secure stratigraphic sequence: samples from layers or features 13, 12, 10, 8, 7, and 2 come from segment 3 and were in stratigraphic sequence; 9 is from an adjacent segment (segment 2, immediately to the south-west); 11 is from another (segment 4, immediately to the north-east) and might be a little later than 13; samples from 5 and F1 are from cuts tied to the rest of the stratigraphy. Layer 2 is much later than the other sampled contexts and derives from the turfline sealed by bulldozing the bank in the mid 1960s. The relevant sections are illustrated in Figures 3.9 and 3.13.

This produces the following sequence from earliest to latest:

Samples from L11 and L13 – basal ditch fills in adjoining segments; the two samples are not sequential (Phase I).
Samples from L9 and L12 in adjoining segments; the two samples are not sequential but post-date layers 11 and 13 (Phase II).
Samples from L10 and L8 in segment 3 – chalk rubble fills (Phase III).
Sample from F1 in segment 3 – a pit cut into the chalk rubble fills (Phase IV).
Sample from L7 in segment 3 – slow ditch silts (Phase V).
Sample from L5 in segment 3 – slot cut into slow silts (Phase VI).
Sample from L2 in segment 3 – turfline sealed by 1960s bulldozing (Phase VIII/d).

The earliest nine samples are all thought to be Neolithic and have produced essentially comparable assemblages. They are dominated by a restricted range of species but the assemblages are relatively species-rich. Three of the most common, *Discus rotundatus*, *Oxychilus cellarius* and *Vitrea contracta*, are found in rock-rubble habitats but the sediments sampled were not vacuous rock-rubble but mixed chalk and soil fills. It is therefore possible that these predatory zonitids represent decaying plant matter, commonly found under leaf litter on a deciduous woodland floor and among leaf and dead vegetation accumulating in ditches on woodland margins (Allen pers obs, Offham Hill, South Lodge, Balksbury). The assemblages include a significant component of taxa which are not found in rock-rubble, eg *Trichia hispida*, *Carychium tridentatum* and *Cochlicopa*. A number of taxa are present in small numbers which are indicative

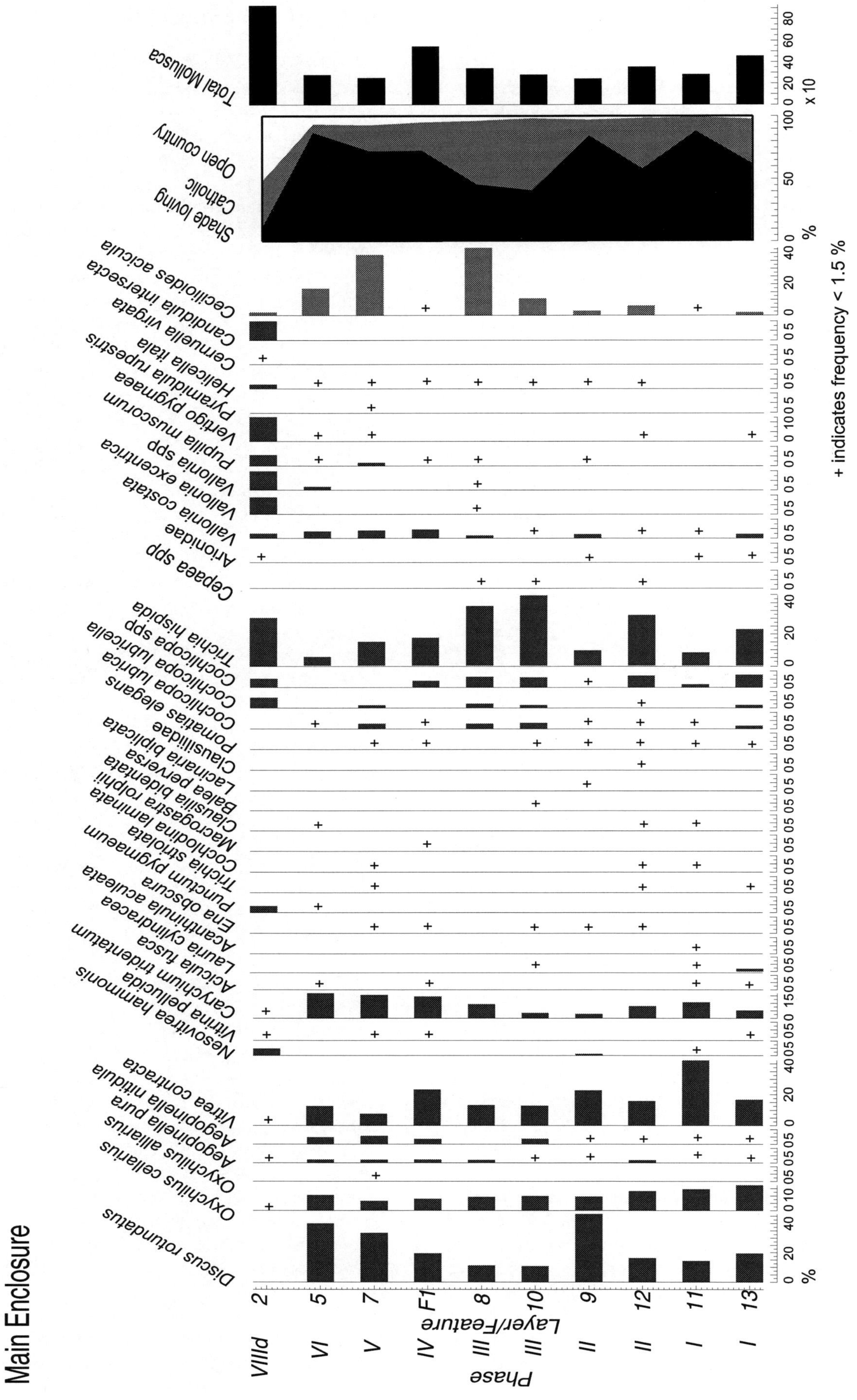

Fig 5.1 Mollusc diagram from main causewayed enclosure ditch.

Table 5.1 Main causewayed enclosure 1974 (site A). Molluscs from ditch samples and internal features

Coarse and 500μm fractions for all samples. Only F1 done by students
Key to artefacts: • (none) ⋆ (some) ⋆⋆ (abundant)
Key to rock rubble: • (none) × (some)

	Main enclosure ditch										*Internal features*			
Phase	*I*	*I*	*II*	*II*	*III*	*III*	*IV*	*V*	*VI*	*VIII*				
Segment	*3*	*4*	*3*	*2*	*3*	*3*	*3*	*3*	*3*	*3*				
Context	*L13*	*L11*	*L12*	*L9*	*L10*	*L8*	*F1*	*L7*	*L5*	*L2*	*F2*	*F6*	*F42*	*F46*
Artefacts	•	⋆	⋆	⋆⋆	⋆	•	⋆	⋆⋆	⋆⋆	⋆	⋆⋆	⋆⋆	⋆	⋆
Rock rubble	•	•	•	•	×	×	•	•	•	•	•	•	•	•
Pomatias elegans (Müller)	3	2	1	1	1	–	1	1	–	–	1	–	2	3
Acicula fusca (Montagu)	2	4	–	–	–	–	3	–	1	–	–	–	–	–
Carychium tridentatum (Risso)	23	30	28	7	10	32	79	39	46	3	3	1	2	–
Cochlicopa lubrica (Müller)	8	1	1	2	10	11	4	8	3	–	–	1	–	–
Cochlicopa lubricella (Porro)	8	–	1	–	5	9	–	4	–	58	–	2	–	–
Cochlicopa spp	35	5	25	3	17	22	22	–	–	49	2	–	–	–
Pyramidula rupestris (Draparnaud)	–	–	–	–	–	–	–	1	–	–	–	–	–	–
Vertigo pygmaea (Draparnaud)	–	–	1	–	–	–	–	3	1	117	–	19	–	2
Pupilla muscorum (Linnaeus)	–	–	–	1	–	2	1	4	1	51	–	5	1	2
Lauria cylindracea (da Costa)	8	1	–	–	3	–	–	–	–	–	–	–	–	–
Vallonia costata (Müller)	10	1	3	5	4	5	25	10	10	22	–	15	–	–
Vallonia excentrica Sterki	–	–	–	–	–	1	–	–	–	83	–	29	–	–
Vallonia spp	–	–	–	–	–	1	–	–	5	91	–	–	–	–
Acanthinula aculeata (Müller)	–	4	–	–	–	–	–	–	–	–	1	–	1	–
Ena obscura (Müller)	–	–	1	1	1	3	3	1	–	–	–	–	–	–
Punctum pygmaeum (Draparnaud)	–	–	–	–	–	–	–	–	1	38	–	1	–	–
Discus rotundatus (Müller)	88	40	57	112	30	38	106	84	111	–	48	27	94	127
Arionidae	+	+	–	+	–	–	–	–	–	+	–	–	–	–
Vitrina pellucida (Müller)	1	–	–	–	–	–	2	1	–	2	–	–	–	–
Vitrea crystallina (Müller)	–	–	–	–	–	–	–	–	–	–	–	15		–
Vitrea contracta (Westerlund)	76	119	56	55	36	45	126	19	35	9	7	22	9	4
Nesovitrea hammonis (Ström)	–	1	–	3	–	–	–	–	–	44	–	–	–	–
Aegopinella pura (Alder)	2	3	6	1	2	6	12	5	6	6	10	–	1	2
Aegopinella nitidula (Draparnaud)	4	4	4	2	4	–	19	14	13	–	–	–	2	–
Oxychilus cellarius (Müller)	78	41	46	23	27	31	43	16	29	3	10	114	20	15
Cecilioides acicula (Müller)	9	3	23	7	34	260	5	160	58	18	8	768	230	55
Cochlodina laminata (Montagu)	–	1	2	–	–	–	–	1	–	–	–	–	–	–
Macrogastra rolphii (Turton)	–	–	–	–	–	–	1	–	–	–	–	–	–	2
Clausilia bidentata (Ström)	–	1	2	–	–	–	–	–	1	–	–	–	–	2
Balea biplicata (Montagu)	–	–	–	1	–	–	–	–	–	–	–	–	1	–
Balea perversa (Linnaeus)	1	–	–	–	1	–	–	–	–	–	–	–	–	–
Clausiliidae	–	–	2	–	–	–	–	–	–	–	–	–	–	–
Candidula intersecta (Poiret)	–	–	–	–	–	–	–	–	–	93	–	1	–	–
Cernuella virgata (da Costa)	–	–	–	–	–	–	–	–	–	3	–	–	–	–
Helicella itala (Linnaeus)	–	–	1	1	1	4	1	1	1	20	–	1	–	1
Trichia striolata (Pfeiffer)	2	–	1	–	–	–	–	1	–	–	–	–	–	–
Trichia hispida (Linnaeus)	104	23	113	23	125	129	96	38	15	236	–	5	–	2
Cepaea spp	–	–	1	–	2	1	–	–	–	–	–	–	–	–
Taxa	17	16	18	15	16	15	17	19	15	16	8	15	10	11
Shannon Index	2.08	1.81	2.01	1.64	1.85	1.97	2.07	2.13	1.87	2.19	1.36	1.87	1.05	0.93
Brillouin Index	2.01	1.73	1.93	1.55	1.76	1.90	2.01	2.01	1.78	2.15	1.23	1.78	0.96	0.85
Δ_2	0.84	0.76	0.82	0.71	0.75	0.80	0.84	0.82	0.78	0.86	0.62	0.76	0.47	0.37
Δ_4	5.44	3.21	4.60	2.50	3.09	4.07	5.49	4.80	3.59	6.12	1.67	3.23	0.91	0.61
Totals	**454**	**281**	**352**	**241**	**279**	**340**	**545**	**251**	**279**	**928**	**82**	**258**	**133**	**162**

of woodland including *Acicula fusca, Ena obscura,* and the Clausiliidae (*Cochlodina laminata, Macrogastra rolphii, Clausilia bidentata, Balea perversa* and *Balea biplicata*). These give species-rich assemblages, suggestive of mature environments with only moderate Δ (delta) diversity indices, indicating a restricted habitat diversity (Tables 5.1–5.3). The rare occurrence of five Clausiliidae species tends to confirm the mature nature of the habitat and indicates the presence of woodland and probably mossy ground litter, and the anthrophobic nature of *Balea perversa* (Kerney 1999, 174) may suggest a largely unmodified woodland. In Neolithic levels the percentage of open-country taxa is low in all samples but rises through the sequences to a maximum of <5% (excluding *Vallonia costata* which can occur in both open country and woodland). This mainly comprises small numbers of *Pupilla muscorum* and *Helicella itala* in which individual species seldom exceed 1.5% in any one context. The other notably abundant species are *Carychium tridentatum* and *Trichia hispida,* the former is a tiny species and may be under-represented in these assemblages because of the sieving and retrieval practices. The latter is recorded in reasonable proportions in the Neolithic, pre-henge, woodland environment from Durrington Walls (Evans 1971).

The latest sample from this sequence (L2) represents the twentieth-century soil buried by bulldozing the hilltop in advance of cultivation in 1964. The mollusc assemblage is totally different from the earlier contexts. It is a more diverse assemblage of *Trichia hispida, Vallonia* spp, *Vertigo pygmaea* and *Pupilla muscorum* with higher diversity indices (*H'*, HB, Δ_2 and Δ_4). It includes the recent introductions *Candidula intersecta* and *Cernuella virgata.* This assemblage is consistent with the grazed grassland which is known to have existed on the hill prior to commencement of cultivation of the excavated part of the site in 1964.

Internal features

Four of the sampled internal features were identified as Neolithic because they contained artefacts (Fig 3.51: features A F2, F6, F42 and F46). None of these fills comprised vacuous chalk rubble. More detailed descriptions are available in the feature catalogue (3.3.7) and all four are illustrated in Figure 3.58:

Feature A F2 – large lobate tree (throw) hollow with chalk rubble and peagrit at base and dark brown loam upper fill with artefacts in all layers including greenstone axe fragment.
Feature A F6 – subcircular pit 1.1 m × 1 m × 0.25 m. Neolithic artefacts (pottery, flints, sarsen axe-polisher, animal bone, cereals, and nuts) in fill of brown soil, chalk lumps and flint.
Feature A F42 – probable feature 0.8 m in diameter, 0.15 m deep. Contained a small amount of pottery in fill of brown soil with large chalk and flint lumps.
Feature A F46 – kidney-shaped pit 1.90 m × 1.55 m × 0.60 m with earth and chalk fills, pottery, struck flint and charcoal concentrated in small recut with dark brown soil fill with flint and chalk. Source of molluscs within feature uncertain.

All but Feature 6 produced mollusc assemblages similar to the ditch fills with 3% or less open-country taxa (Table 5.1). In each case *Discus rotundatus* and *Oxychilus cellarius* predominate and this may reflect a rock-rubble component. *Oxychilus* can also be very common in undisturbed leaf litter in woodland and in windblown leaf litter accumulating in ditches (Allen pers obs, Balksbury, South Lodge). Feature 6 has a wider range of species including significant proportions of *Vertigo pygmaea, Vallonia costata, Vallonia excentrica* and *Pupilla muscorum,* which point to more open conditions (31%). The assemblages also differ in having low diversity indices more typical of immature communities. The artefactual evidence indicates that the feature is earlier Neolithic and, if so, may support evidence (below) from Stepleton for more open areas within the enclosures. There is, however, the possibility of some contamination and mixing in this sample since it also produced an apex of the medieval introduction *Candidula intersecta.*

5.2.2 The Stepleton spur

The samples examined were flots from the 1979 and 1981 excavations.

Stepleton enclosure

The samples are from the north side of the enclosure, from various ditch segments dispersed over 100° of the ditch circuit and a linear distance of *c* 100 m (Fig 3.81: segments 8, 12, 15–17). Consequently the stratigraphic relationships between ditch layers cannot be regarded as secure. None of these fills is regarded as vacuous rubble. The sequence of layers is as follows, all these layers are early Neolithic, fourth millennium cal BC. The relevant sections are illustrated in Figures 3.88 and 3.90:

L2A – segment 12, comprised dark black-brown humic loam with angular chalk lumps and broken flint in a pit cut into the lowest chalk rubble fill (Phase III).
L3A and L3B – cannot be separated stratigraphically. 3B – segment 15, dark grey-brown silt loam with chalk fragments and charcoal. 3A – segment 8, mid-brown silty loam with chalk lumps loose to firm (Phase III).
L3C and L3D – relationship between these two is uncertain. 3C – segment 17, dark brown firm silt loam with chalk rubble. 3D – segment 16, dark brown/black humic loam with burnt material and charcoal (Phase III).
L6A – segment 12, earliest context sampled. Dark brown silt loam with chalk fragments (Phase I).

The results are presented in Figure 5.2 and Table 5.2. The two most abundant taxa show some degree of antipathetic behaviour: *Discus rotundatus* increases and *Vitrea contracta* shows a less pronounced decrease over time. Both are characteristic of rock-rubble as is *Oxychilus cellarius* which represents 10% in the earliest layer (L6A) and less in later layers. The rock-rubble component is likely to have been greater in the earlier layers. Other abundant taxa, not indicative of rock-rubble are the Aegopinellas, *Carychium tridentatum* and *Trichia hispida* which are more common together in stable, long-grass, swards and scrub. The shade-loving species *Acicula fusca* is present in every sample and the other shade-loving taxa are *Ena obscura* and the Clausiliidae. The proportion of open-country taxa is less than 10% in all but two samples: L3D where a higher proportion is due to 17% of *Vallonia costata*, which might not be a part of the open fauna, and the latest sampled layer L2A, where the Vallonias and *Helicella itala* point to slightly more open conditions later in the life of the site.

Stepleton outworks

Samples were also examined from the inner outwork (Fig 3.81: segments 5 and 6) and outer outwork (Fig 3.81; segment 2) at Stepleton which post-date the causewayed enclosure. The results of this analysis are presented in Figure 5.3 and Table 5.2. The samples have been arranged in the following tentative sequence. The relevant sections are illustrated in Figures 3.96, 3.97, 3.99, and 3.103:

L2B – Inner outwork early Bronze Age layer. Dark brown-black burnt loamy clay with flint and chalk lumps and some pea grit (Phase VII/a).
Sample from F511 is a recut in the outer outwork. This contained Beaker pottery. Dark brown-black very humic loam with some chalk and flint (Phase VII/a).
Sample from L3C – Inner outwork. Dark grey-brown silt with charcoal and medium packed chalk lumps (Phase V/I).
Sample from L5B – Medium grey-brown silt with few chalk lumps (Phase II).
Samples from L5 and L4A are from the inner outwork, equivalent positions in the base of two adjacent ditch sections. 4A – burnt dark brown/grey silt with chalk lumps. 5 – dark grey-black silt with some pebbles and burning (Phase I).

Analytical results are shown in Table 5.2 and in Figure 5.3. The basal layers 5 and 4A contained higher proportions of rock-rubble taxa *Vitrea contracta* and *Oxychilus cellarius*; these decline through the sequence, perhaps pointing to a reduced proportion from this habitat. *Discus rotundatus* fluctuates. As in the enclosures there are significant proportions of other taxa not characteristic of rock-rubble, notably *Carychium tridentatum*, the Aegopinellas and *Trichia hispida*. A range of other shade-loving taxa includes *Acanthinula aculeata* in all samples and *Acicula fusca*, present in all but one sample. The proportion of open-country taxa is below 10% in all but the latest two samples (F511 and 2B) which contain post Neolithic artefacts. They contain significant proportions of *Pupilla muscorum* with other taxa *Vallonia costata*, *Helicella itala* and *Vertigo pygmaea*, which supports the evidence from the Stepleton causewayed enclosure for a more open environment in the later stages of the site's history.

Discrete features

Eight samples were examined from seven features excavated in 1979 and 1981 on the Stepleton spur (locations on Fig 3.108). None of these feature fills was vacuous. In three cases it is not recorded which layer was sampled so the descriptions of each layer have been included.

Feature 2A F37. Feature without any finds, not dated, and possibly recent. Fill of (i) dark brown humus with angular chalk pebbles (ii) lighter brown with higher chalk content and pebbles.
Feature 4B F155. Pit 1.36 × 1.38 × 0.35 m. Contained Neolithic pottery, flint and bone. Sample from Layer 2 – chalk fragments in cream silt.
Feature 4B F153. Pit 0.94 × 0.90 × 0.27 m. Contained Neolithic pottery and other finds. Fill of (i) dark brown loam with chalk fragments, (ii) chalk fragments in cream silt.
Feature 4B F129. Pit outside the Stepleton enclosure, 1.4 × 0.95 × 0.18 m. Many finds including Neolithic pottery, bone, flint and charcoal. Dark brown black loam with chalk fragments.
Feature 4A F3+3B. Pit 1.2 × 1.10 × 0.30 m containing Neolithic pottery, flints and animal bone. Fill of dark soil.
Feature 2A F177. Probable posthole in inner outwork rampart. Fill of (i) dark brown soil with comminuted chalk and flint, (ii) grey-brown soil with a few chalk lumps, (iii) light brown soil and chalk lumps.
Feature 2A F17. Oval pit 1.3 × 0.9 × 0.55 m in inner outwork bank area. Both sampled layers contained Neolithic pottery and flint. Lower fill light chalky matrix; upper fill medium brown humic.

The results are shown in Table 5.3. As with the ditch fills, many of the Stepleton features contain high proportions of the rock-rubble group. Three features contain low proportions of the open-country species (13% or less) comparable to the ditches: the fills of features 2A F17, 2A F177 and 4B F153. This contrasts with features with a larger proportion of open-country taxa: features 4B F155 (27%), 4B F129 (25%), 4A F3 (36%) and 2A F37 (59%). Excepting feature 2A F37, Neolithic pottery was found in these features and indicates that the enclosure interior was more open than the assemblages living in the local ditch microhabitats suggest.

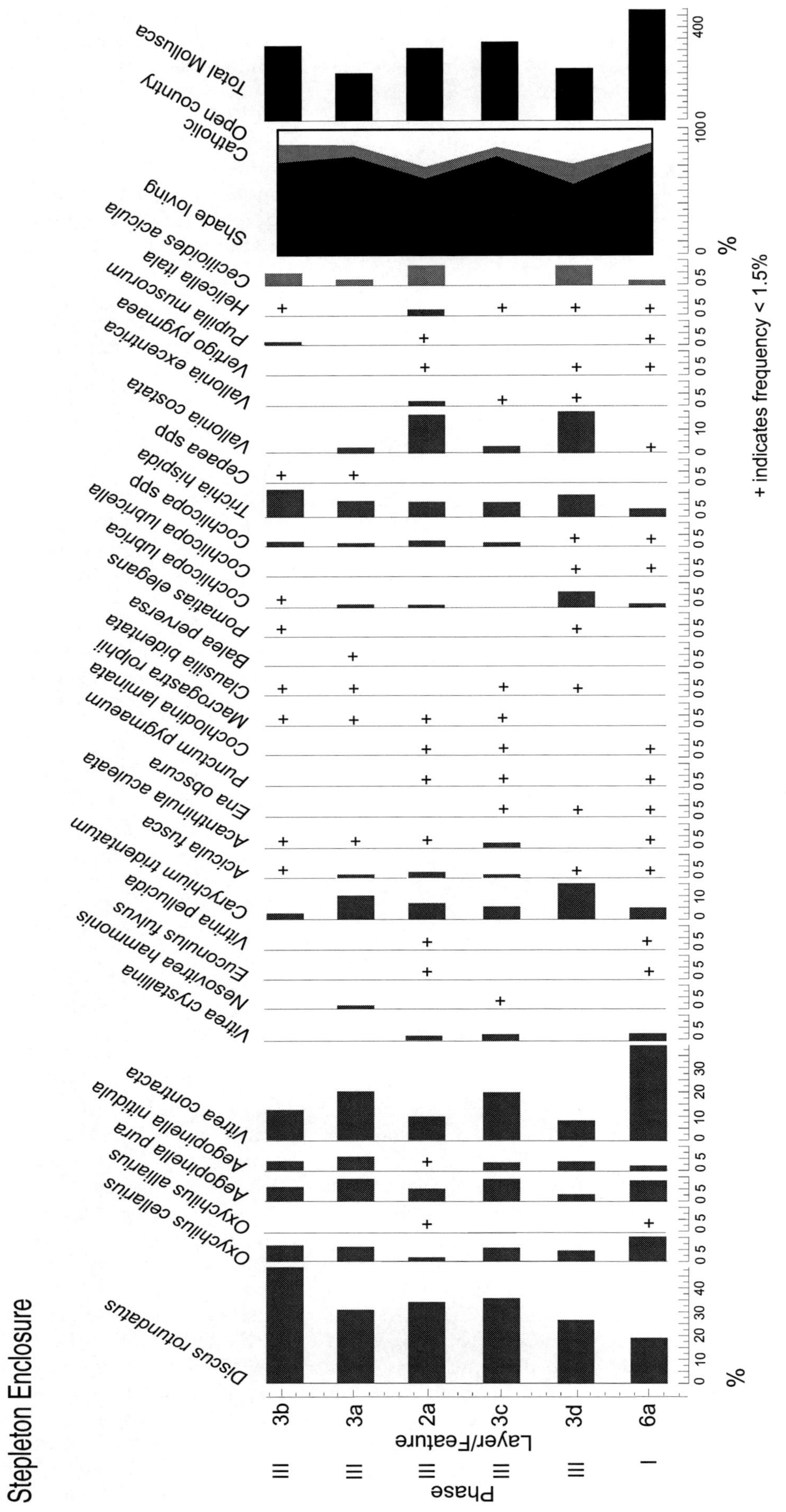

Fig 5.2 Mollusc diagram from Stepleton enclosure.

Table 5.2 Stepleton spur 1979 and 1981. Molluscs from the enclosure ditch in Area 4B and from the inner and outer outworks

Key to artefacts: • (none) * (some) ** (abundant)
Key to rock rubble: • (none) × (some)

	Enclosure ditch						*Inner outwork*					*Outer outwork*
Phase	*I*	*III*	*III*	*III*	*III*	*III*	*I*	*I*	*II*	*V/I*	*VII/a*	*VII/a*
Segment	*12*	*16*	*17*	*12*	*8*	*15*	*5*	*5*	*5*	*5*	*5*	*2*
Sample	*1*			*200*		*3*	*5*	*6*	*5*	*5*		*5*
Context	*6A*	*3D*	*3C*	*2A*	*3A*	*3B*	*5*	*4A*	*5B*	*3C*	*2B*	*F511*
Artefacts	*	**	*	**	**	**	*	**	*	*	**	**
Rock rubble	•	•	•	•	•	•	•	•	•	•	•	•
Pomatias elegans (Müller)	–	1	–	–	–	3	–	1	2	2	5	2
Acicula fusca (Montagu)	6	1	5	8	3	3	+	2	4	5	–	1
Carychium tridentatum (Risso)	22	33	18	21	20	8	16	15	49	34	22	24
Cochlicopa lubrica (Müller)	8	14	–	4	3	3	1	3	2	1	1	7
Cochlicopa lubricella (Porro)	4	2	–	–	–	–	3	2	2	2	2	–
Cochlicopa spp	4	1	6	8	3	7	3	–	6	3	1	–
Vertigo pygmaea (Draparnaud)	1	1	–	3	–	–	–	–	2	1	3	9
Vertigo pusilla Müller	–	–	–	–	–	–	–	–	1	–	–	–
Vertigo spp	–	–	–	–	–	–	–	1	–	2	–	–
Abida secale (Draparnaud)	–	–	–	–	–	–	–	–	–	–	–	1
Pupilla muscorum (Linnaeus)	2	–	–	1	–	4	–	–	12	4	63	72
Vallonia costata (Müller)	1	38	10	49	5	–	5	2	15	1	18	4
Vallonia excentrica Sterki	–	1	1	6	–	–	–	–	2	–	–	4
Acanthinula aculeata (Müller)	4	–	7	3	2	2	1	3	3	8	2	1
Ena montana (Draparnaud)	–	–	–	–	–	–	1	–	–	–	–	–
Ena obscura (Müller)	2	2	1	–	–	–	–	1	1	2	2	–
Punctum pygmaeum (Draparnaud)	1	–	2	1	–	–	–	2	2	1	1	–
Discus rotundatus (Müller)	88	58	117	103	61	152	32	88	96	121	77	51
Arionidae	–	–	–	–	–	–	–	–	–	+	–	–
Vitrina pellucida (Müller)	1	–	–	3	–	–	1	–	–	1	–	–
Vitrea crystallina (Müller)	15	–	9	6	–	–	1	11	–	–	–	2
Vitrea contracta (Westerlund)	183	18	65	30	40	39	99	73	86	51	5	53
Nesovitrea hammonis (Ström)	–	–	1	–	3	–	–	–	–	1	–	–
Aegopinella pura (Alder)	40	6	30	15	18	18	3	18	34	23	5	3
Aegopinella nitidula (Draparnaud)	10	8	11	4	11	12	6	9	16	15	11	10
Oxychilus cellarius (Müller)	47	10	19	5	12	21	98	50	34	35	6	28
Oxychilus alliarius (Miller)	3	–	–	2	–	–	–	–	–	–	–	–
Euconulus fulvus (Müller)	1	–	–	1	–	–	–	–	–	–	–	–
Cecilioides acicula (Müller)	10	20	–	28	5	17	–	–	–	1	21	179
Cochlodina laminata (Montagu)	1	–	3	1	–	–	–	2	2	2	2	2
Macrogastra rolphii (Turton)	–	–	1	2	1	1	–	–	–	–	1	–
Clausilia bidentata (Ström)	–	1	+	–	1	1	–	1	3	1	–	2
Clausiliidae	–	–	–	–	–	–	–	1	–	–	–	–
Balea perversa (Linnaeus)	–	–	–	–	1	–	–	–	–	–	–	–
Cernuella virgata (da Costa)	–	–	–	–	–	–	–	–	–	–	–	2
Helicella itala (Linnaeus)	2	2	3	8	–	2	5	7	5	11	5	22
Trichia striolata (Pfeiffer)	–	–	–	–	–	–	–	–	–	–	2	–
Trichia hispida (Linnaeus)	16	20	20	19	13	36	7	25	32	23	7	5
Helicigona lapicida (Linnaeus)	–	–	–	–	–	–	–	–	–	–	1	–
Cepaea spp	–	–	–	–	1	1	–	–	–	1	–	–
Taxa	22	17	18	22	16	17	15	20	22	23	21	21
Shannon Index	2.00	2.17	2.11	2.28	2.10	1.83	1.70	2.13	2.32	2.21	2.13	2.30
Brillouin Index	1.92	2.05	2.02	2.16	1.97	1.75	1.61	2.03	2.23	2.11	1.99	2.19
Δ_2	0.78	0.85	0.81	0.83	0.83	0.73	0.74	0.83	0.86	0.83	0.81	0.86
Δ_4	3.64	5.85	4.36	5.08	5.01	2.72	2.85	4.99	6.42	4.90	4.35	6.45
Totals	462	217	328	303	196	316	282	317	411	351	241	305

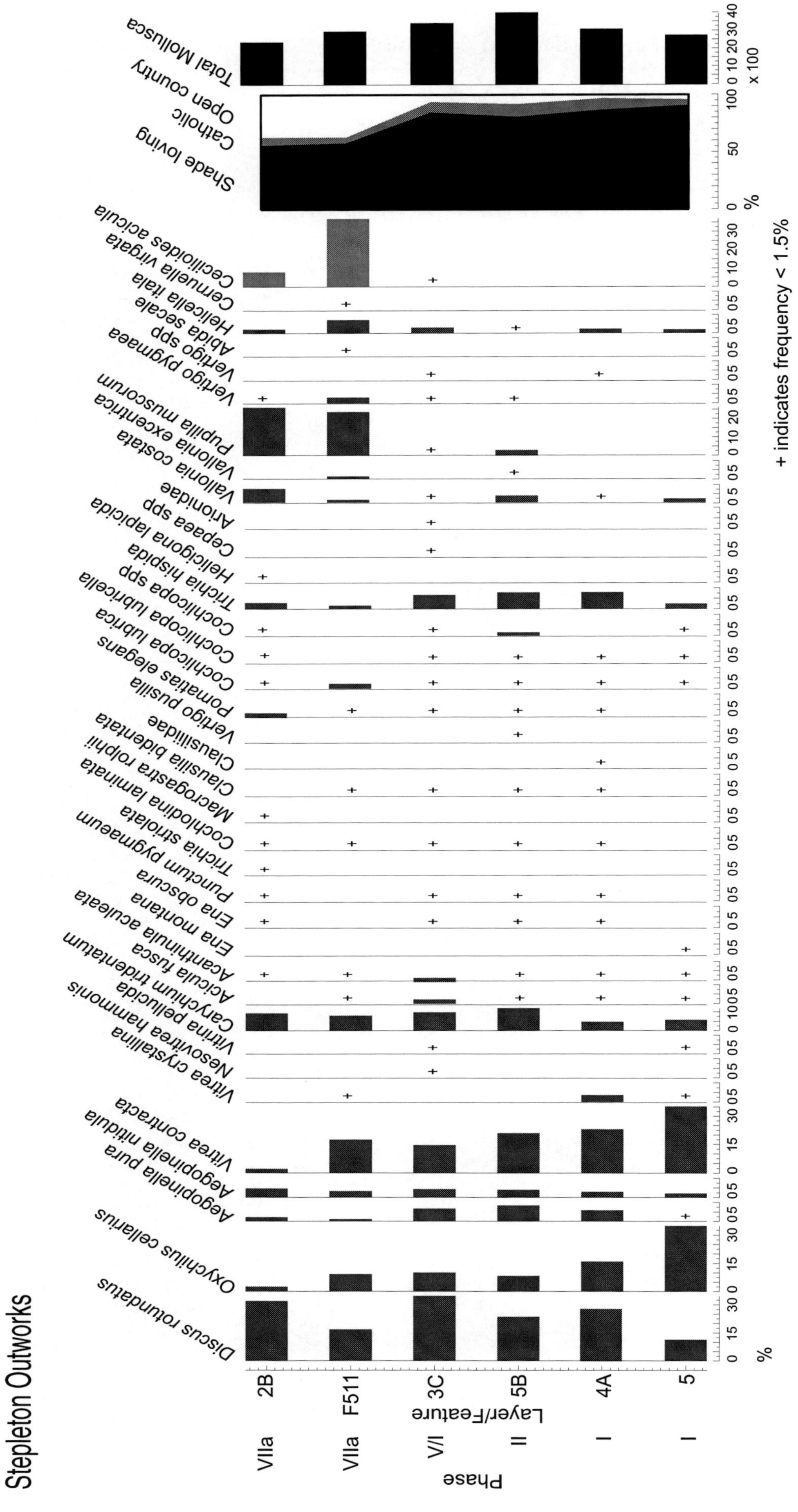

Fig 5.3 Mollusc diagram from Stepleton outworks.

Table 5.3 Stepleton spur 1979 and 1981: molluscs from discrete features

Key to artefacts: • (none) * (some) ** (abundant)
Key to rock rubble: • (none) × (some)
Sample from F17 upper mixed – some shells concreted with chalk, some with more organic matrix.
?coarse fraction only – only 1 bag found per sample
Samples from F37, F129, F153, F155, F177 originally done by students

Feature	*2A F37*	*4B F155*	*4B F153*	*4B F129*	*4A F3*	*2A F177*	*2A F17 lower*	*2A F17 upper*
Artefacts	•	**	**	**	**		*	*
Rock rubble	•	•	•	•	•	•	•	
Pomatias elegans (Müller)	–	–	–	+	–	1	5	3
Acicula fusca (Montagu)	–	–	–	–	–	–	1	3
Carychium tridentatum (Risso)	–	3	1	–	1	2	12	26
Cochlicopa lubrica (Müller)	–	3	–	–	7	–	–	2
Cochlicopa lubricella (Porro)	3	3	–	–	–	1	2	–
Cochlicopa spp	3	4	+	2	–	–	3	10
Vertigo pygmaea (Draparnaud)	3	6	3	2	5	1	–	1
Pupilla muscorum (Linnaeus)	63	9	5	2	11	4	–	10
Vallonia costata (Müller)	5	8	2	–	44	–	1	10
Vallonia excentrica Sterki	13	10	9	18	8	3	–	4
Acanthinula aculeata (Müller)	–	–	1	–	–	3	9	10
Punctum pygmaeum (Draparnaud)	–	–	–	–	–	–	1	–
Discus rotundatus (Müller)	18	18	52	36	28	63	110	161
Arionidae	–	–	–	–	–	–	+	–
Vitrina pellucida (Müller)	–	1	–	–	1	–	–	–
Vitrea contracta (Westerlund)	16	18	44	8	42	2	51	76
Nesovitrea hammonis (Ström)	–	–	–	1	3	–	–	–
Aegopinella pura (Alder)	–	–	1	–	1	–	17	21
Aegopinella nitidula (Draparnaud)	2	1	2	–	1	–	27	17
Oxychilus cellarius (Müller)	9	7	18	19	43	9	84	84
Euconulus fulvus (Müller)	–	–	1	–	1	–	–	–
Cecilioides acicula (Müller)	398	283	376	443	55	67	13	237
Cochlodina laminata (Montagu)	–	–	–	–	–	–	1	4
Macrogastra rolphii (Turton)	–	–	–	–	–	1	–	1
Clausilia bidentata (Ström)	–	1	–	–	–	–	2	–
Balea biplicata (Montagu)	1	1	–	–	–	–	–	–
Balea perversa (Linnaeus)	–	1	–	–	–	–	1	–
Candidula intersecta (Poiret)	2	–	–	–	–	–	–	–
Cernuella virgata (da Costa)	5	–	–	–	–	–	–	–
Helicella itala (Linnaeus)	12	3	–	1	9	2	–	1
Trichia striolata (Pfeiffer)	–	–	–	–	–	–	–	5
Trichia hispida (Linnaeus)	21	7	10	4	6	12	15	39
Cepaea spp	–	–	–	–	1	–	–	–
Taxa	14	17	13	10	17	13	16	19
Shannon Index	2.12	2.49	1.78	1.70	2.16	1.50	1.93	2.13
Brillouin Index	1.99	2.25	1.65	1.55	2.04	1.34	1.86	2.05
Δ_2	0.82	0.90	0.77	0.76	0.85	0.61	0.80	0.82
Δ_4	4.80	9.76	3.37	3.32	5.87	1.59	4.08	4.70
Totals	**176**	**104**	**149**	**93**	**212**	**104**	**342**	**488**

Interestingly, features 4B F153 and 4B F155 were adjacent to each other, yet their subtly different mollusc assemblages suggest that they were not contemporaneous. Feature 2A F37 did not contain Neolithic material, has a larger proportion of open-country taxa (59%) than any other prehistoric feature on the site and contained two taxa which are post-prehistoric introductions, *Candidula intersecta* and *Cernuella virgata;* it is therefore assumed to be recent.

5.2.3 The hillfort spur

The only unprocessed samples available from the hilltop were from a trench excavated in 1986 on the hillfort spur. This trench was designed to test the hypothesis that the ditch was of Neolithic date; radiocarbon dating has subsequently indicated that it is late Bronze Age/early Iron Age (2450 ± 35 BP; OxA-7776, *c* 700–400 cal BC). The samples were unfortunately very small (*c* 160–260 g) and were all from the primary ditch fill. The section shows that they were all from fine-grained sediments, rather than the vacuous chalk rubble that formed the great bulk of the fill. In seven samples examined only eleven molluscs were found and these do not provide a valid basis for interpretation. The section (Fig 3.152) suggests that the primary fill accumulated rapidly; there are alternating fine sediment and chalk rubble layers which, by analogy with the ditch fills of the Overton Down Experimental earthwork (Bell 1990; Bell *et al* 1996), could have accumulated over as little as three or four years.

5.2.4 Causewayed enclosures: discussion

The assemblages are made much more difficult to interpret by three factors noted in the introduction: (a) they are from water sieving which is likely to have distorted assemblage composition, (b) they are feature fills which will contain a proportion of earlier eroded shells and may also reflect more shady ditch microhabitats, (c) they contain high proportions of three taxa which are known to be abundant in rock-rubble. Each of these factors must be taken into consideration.

Sampling taphonomy and questions of scale

Since there were no unsieved samples from Neolithic contexts for comparison, the effects of flotation on assemblage composition are difficult to assess. Comparison elsewhere indicates that the use of flot samples can introduce a significant distortion in the abundance of some taxa (O'Connor 1977, 270). It is probable that small (eg *Carychium tridentatum*) and fragile taxa in particular are under-represented. Some taxa, possibly *Discus* and *Oxychilus*, may be over-represented as a result. Analysis separating taxa recovered from flots and from residues of standard wash-over flotation following Evans (1972) can show a marked distortion in two assemblages. Woodland assemblages from 27 samples from Handley Down Neolithic mortuary enclosure (Allen in prep) showed that open-country taxa (*Vallonia* spp, *Vertigo* spp, and *Pupilla muscorum*) were consistently more commonly present in the flots than the residues, while shade-loving taxa (*Aegopinella nitidula, Oxychilius cellarius* and the Clausiliidea) were more prevalent in the residues. This would indicate that, if anything, the more limited open-country faunas at Hambledon are over-represented as a result of the processing method adopted.

The taphonomy of assemblages from ditches and pits is well explored by Evans (1972, 321). The assemblages include life communities of snails living on the contemporaneous land surface adjacent to the ditch/pit and on the adjacent ditch side of the bank and communities living in the ditch. Shells may also be derived from older or ancient populations in the soil or subsoil through which the ditch/pit was cut. In the primary fills, assemblages living in the ditch will be very limited owing to the inhospitable conditions provided by the coarse and rapidly deposited chalk rubble. In the secondary fills where stabilisation may occur, sedimentation rates decrease, and the assemblage living in the ditch may be appreciable. At this time, however, the ditch is a much shallower feature and the assemblage will reflect both that of the ditch vegetation community and those of the adjacent ecologies (K D Thomas 1985). Only in the upper fills, often characterised by ploughwash (none sampled at Hambledon), are the assemblages likely to relate almost entirely to the local non-ditch habitat, and this is often at a time many centuries, or even millennia after the ditch was first excavated (Allen 1995a; Evans 1972, 321–28; Limbrey 1975, 290–300).

To what spatial scale do these assemblages relate? Modern analogue studies provide some indication of the spatial scale of vegetation boundaries which may be reflected by molluscan assemblages. At a woodland/grassland boundary Davies (1999) showed that woodland species extended across a *c* 5–6 m boundary zone but even within this they declined sharply. Rouse and Evans (1994) showed that in a present-day grassland environment on the ramparts of Maiden Castle distinctive molluscan assemblages were related to characteristics of vegetation structure, lime content and warmth; the assemblages displayed sharp boundaries often on a scale of *c* 4 m. Subfossil assemblages in the Neolithic soil at Easton Down picked out an environmental boundary at a scale of decimetres (Rouse and Evans 1993, fig 12). Modern analogue studies by one of us (MJA) show that species prevalent in mature woodlands at Offham, Sussex, and Butser, Hampshire (*Aegopinella nitidula, Aegopinella pura, Acanthinula aculeata* and *Clausilia bidentata*), can represent up to 10% of the grassland fauna as much as 76 m (Butser) and 215 m (Offham) from the 'source' woodland. Some of the more typical open-country species (*Helicella itala, Cernuella virgata, Candidula* spp and *Vertigo pygmaea*) formed more than 10% of the assemblage within 3 m of the woodland edge.

The accumulation of autumn and winter (November) leaves in ditches at both Offham, Sussex and Balksbury, Hampshire, provided temporary winter refuge for assemblages dominated by *Oxychilus cellarius, Aegopinella nitidula* and *Vitrea* spp. The woodland edge was 35 m and 55 m away from the sampling points. The character of the assemblages changed dramatically in the summer (July) months at Offham with the woodland component listed above representing less than 5% of the live assemblage (but *c* 45% of the dead near-surface assemblage). In ditch contexts, such as Hambledon, spatial resolution is likely to be blurred, because some of the material has been derived. However, the examples outlined do suggest that most of the molluscs are likely to relate to conditions within a few tens of metres of the sampling point. It seems unlikely that high proportions of woodland taxa would have been derived from a woodland/open country boundary more than a few tens of metres away at most.

Some indication of whether the sampled locations are broadly representative of a wider landscape, and how uniform that landscape was, may be provided by species diversity indices (cf Entwistle 1990; Entwistle and Bowden 1991). The application of species diversity indices allows us to examine several factors:

i) closeness of sampled assemblage to a likely real population; Shannon index (*H'*) – Brillouin index (HB), see Evans 1979b; Evans 1983
ii) the diversity of the ecological mosaic sampled (Δ_2 and Δ_4)
iii) the complexity or maturity of the assemblages and thus the environment they inhabited.

There are problems in using any diversity indices on molluscan assemblages derived from the excavation on Hambledon. Species diversity indices should be used only on 'total' archaeological assemblages; ie those from which we have recovered the total or near total population through careful wash-over flotation and extraction from the residues (cf Evans 1972, 44–45). Indices have been calculated for the assemblages derived from flots of sieving (Tables 5.1–5.3); these must be interpreted with caution, because of possible loss of species and bias resulting from flotation.

Interpretation – the landscape and land-use

The ditch fills may contain a significant proportion of taxa eroded from soil and subsoil contexts pre-dating Neolithic activity. The species represented may not all have lived together at one time or place. This is an additional reason for being cautious in the interpretation of the indices of species diversity. It is possible that a derived component accounts for the old woodland taxa such as *Acicula fusca, Ena obscura* and the less common Clausiliidae. There were marked differences in the character of shell preservation in some samples which suggest a reworked component, although specimens that were more eroded or stained were not more abundant among the foregoing taxa. The fragile *Acicula fusca* were often particularly well preserved.

A significant proportion of most of the assemblages is made up of the three taxa, *Discus rotundatus, Oxychilus* and *Vitrea,* which are known to form rock-rubble assemblages. As Tables 5.1–3 show, very few of the sampled contexts were actually vacuous rubble. The few contexts with vacuous chalk rubble (clast-supported sediments) produced similar assemblages to those in non-vacuous (matrix-supported) sediments. There is no marked difference in the assemblages found in chalk rubble fills and the soil-rich secondary fills, or slots associated with concentrations of artefacts and animal bone in the upper ditch fills. Differences would be expected if the predominance of shade-preferring species was the result purely of rock-rubble habitats. We conclude from these observations that the assemblage is likely to include a rock-rubble component but that the available evidence does not suggest that this is the sole explanation for the presence of these three species. They are common in leaf litter and have been noted to be particularly abundant (representing up to 68% of live assemblages), in wind-blown leaf litter in a shallow ditch (Allen pers obs, Offham November 1986). Leaf litter occurring in the autumn and winter creates a wet microenvironment which attracts a small vagrant community contrasting with the summer community (July 1987), but which is more likely to be represented as a result of increased mortality rates in the autumn and winter.

It could be argued that a combination of some of the foregoing possibilities: eg rock-rubble component mixed with other woodland taxa weathered from earlier soils, or subsoils, might explain the predominantly shade-loving character of the assemblage. In most samples there are less than 10% open-country taxa. While it is probable that the factors discussed have exaggerated the evidence for shade, it is not likely that they explain it totally. Ditch sediments forming over a 400-year period in a largely open environment, however rubbly and overgrown the ditch itself may be, would be expected to contain a much larger proportion of open-country taxa, at least in some areas. For instance the well-vegetated ditch of the Overton Down Experimental Earthwork contains few shade-loving taxa, all the more surprising because we know that subsoil features with ancient woodland shells have in this case contributed sediment to the ditch fill (Bell and Johnson 1996). The presence of such a diverse range of shade-loving taxa indicates the existence of mature shady habitats in the vicinity. The Hambledon ditch faunas are mostly similar although there is a small increase in open-country taxa during the life of the Neolithic site. The real change comes, however, with the latest layers containing Beaker and early Bronze Age artefacts, suggesting that it was then, rather than during the main period of Neolithic activity, that the main clearance of Hambledon Hill top took place.

The ditch microenvironment would have created more shady conditions locally. Comparison of the ditch and feature fills at Stepleton indicates that the interior was rather more open and there is similar evidence from feature A F6 in the Hambledon Hill enclosure. If the hilltop was an 'island' of more open conditions within a 'sea' of woodland, this may have acted as a barrier, or delay to colonisation by more xerophilous open-country taxa. This has been suggested as an explanation for the lack of open-country taxa associated with the causewayed enclosures on the South Downs (K D Thomas 1982) and Maiden Castle (Evans and Rouse 1991a). Had this been the case, however, we would expect that species present in woodland, but tolerant of open conditions (eg *Trichia hispida* or *Vallonia costata*) would show a marked increase, which does not occur. We do know that Hambledon Hill was in use for *c* 400 years between 3700–3300 cal BC (see Ch 4). It is a site that the artefact assemblages show was a nexus of social communication for a wide geographical area. Over that period of time, with so much coming and going, there would surely have been opportunities for colonisation by open-country taxa if the hilltop itself had been fully open. As it is, there is just a small increase in the proportion of open-country taxa in contexts which are later in the early Neolithic use of the site.

If we are correct in inferring the survival of trees and scrub at the time of Neolithic activity, then the possibility should be entertained that certain of the interior features originated as tree throw pits or tree hollows. A possible candidate is suggested by the lobate plan of A F2 in the main enclosure (Fig 3.58). Another treehole, containing Neolithic artefacts, lay beneath the main enclosure bank (see 3.3.2) and another may have been utilised on site B (see 3.3.7). The presence of Neolithic artefacts, especially in the upper fills of these features, does not rule out the possibility that they originally held trees. The hints here of a possible symbolic relationship between treethrow and artefact deposition are strengthened by comparable evidence from other sites (C Evans *et al* 1999).

Marked differences have been demonstrated between the two causewayed enclosures in terms of the types of activity and material culture represented (see 3.3.8, 3.5.8), but it is notable that the mollusc assemblages are essentially similar, with no suggestion of contrasting environmental settings. Nor does the limited environmental evidence from the outworks on the Stepleton spur suggest any major clearance at the time when outworks enclosed the entire hilltop. This has previously been interpreted in functional terms as an enclosure associated with cattle husbandry 'the corralling and protection of very large numbers of animals' (Mercer 1990, 29). The molluscan evidence indicates that the main extensive clearance was after this phase; late Neolithic deposits are almost absent, and it seems possible that clearance did not take place until the period of Beaker and early Bronze Age activity.

5.3 Valley sediments around Hambledon Hill

Martin Bell and Michael J Allen

During the final major season of excavation on the Neolithic site in 1982, RWS and MB commenced an investigation of the valley sediments around Hambledon Hill in a search for evidence of prehistoric environment and land-use. The approach adopted was based on that used in a study of dry valley sediments on the South Downs (Bell 1983). An attempt was made to go beyond that earlier study by trying to obtain a more spatial picture of the distribution of sediment types by numerous trenches and test pits rather than a single section. There was only enough time to investigate three landscape units. These were the dry valley sediments in Coombe Bottom, a transect of colluvial sequences from Stepleton Spur to Everley Water Meadow and more extensive work on the river valley sediments in Everley Water Meadow by RWS, which was continued by him in 1983–4 (Fig 1.4).

The field methods involved mechanical excavation to expose the Holocene sediment sequences in section, and the dating of the sequences through the position of artefacts recovered by hand excavation and facilitated by three-dimensional artefact recording The environmental conditions under which the sediments had accumulated were studied chiefly by mollusc analysis. This was based on samples taken in the field and processed by wash-over flotation and sieving down to 0.5 mm using conventional methods (Evans 1972).

5.3.1 Coombe Bottom

This prominent dry valley (Fig 5.7) runs E–W from the Iwerne valley. It has the Hambledon Hill causewayed enclosure at its head and separates the Shroton Spur, with its outworks, to the north, from the Stepleton spur, with its causewayed enclosure and outworks, to the south (Fig 1.4). It was thought that the valley may have trapped sediments derived from activity on the upland and slopes.

The sediments

Sediments on the valley floor were examined primarily by means of an L-shaped machine-cut trench (b) at NGR ST 8565 1190 (Fig 5.4). This was cut by a JCB using a toothless ditching bucket, 7 m long down the valley axis and 5 m long perpendicular to the axis. The latter arm was taken to a depth of 2 m (Fig 5.5) but only the upper *c* 0.74 m was of Holocene date. This was a dark yellowish-brown silty clay loam colluvium, with 20–40% flints and hard rounded chalk pieces. The sedimentary sequence was dated by means of artefact locations from a 2 m by 1 m hand-excavated strip (Fig 5.4). Flint artefacts and flint-gritted pottery were concentrated in the lower part of this sequence; two sherds have been identified as Neolithic, three as Beaker.

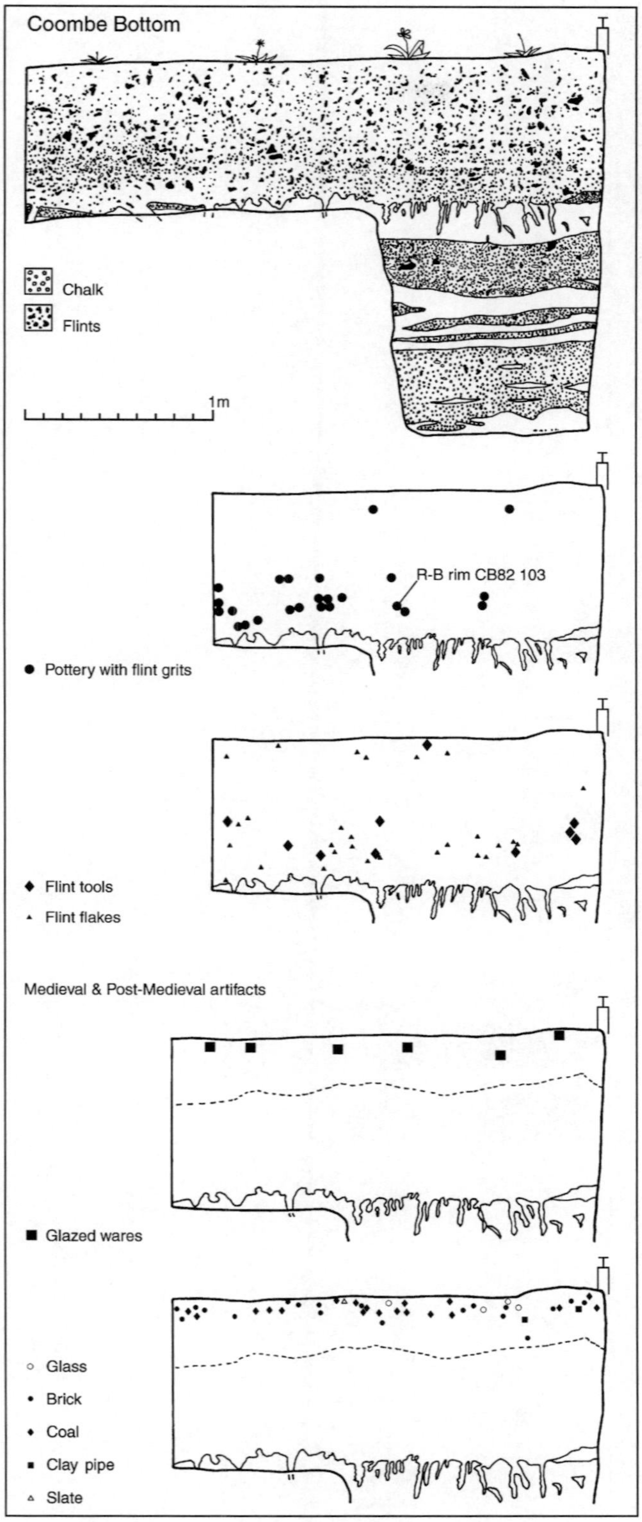

Fig 5.4 Coombe Bottom valley Trench b showing the sedimentary sequence and artefact distributions.

There was a late Iron Age or Romano-British Black Burnished Ware rim 0.20 m from the base of the Holocene sediments. Medieval and post-medieval artefacts were concentrated in the modern, plough-disturbed, layers. Thus a layer of recent ploughsoil concealed older colluvium which appeared to date largely from the late Iron Age/Romano-British periods. This contained a small number of Neolithic and Bronze Age sherds which could suggest some limited activity, perhaps involving manuring, in the valley during these periods. Alternatively these early sherds may have been eroded from hilltop contexts.

Fig 5.5 Coombe Bottom valley Trench b section. Photo Martin Bell

Below the post-glacial colluvium was a sequence of chalk meltwater deposits consisting of alternating bands of small chalk pieces in a very soft chalk marl. These deposits are analogous to those of late Devensian date reported by Kerney (1963) and Kerney *et al* (1964) from dry valleys in south-east England and from Holywell Coombe Channel Tunnel site at Folkestone, Kent (Preece and Bridgland 1998), and at Burleston Down in Dorset (Allen 1999).

The molluscs

The stratigraphy at the point sampled can be summarised as follows:

0–0.23 m. Cultivated topsoil. Dark brown (10YR 4/3) silty clay loam with 10% small flints and chalk.

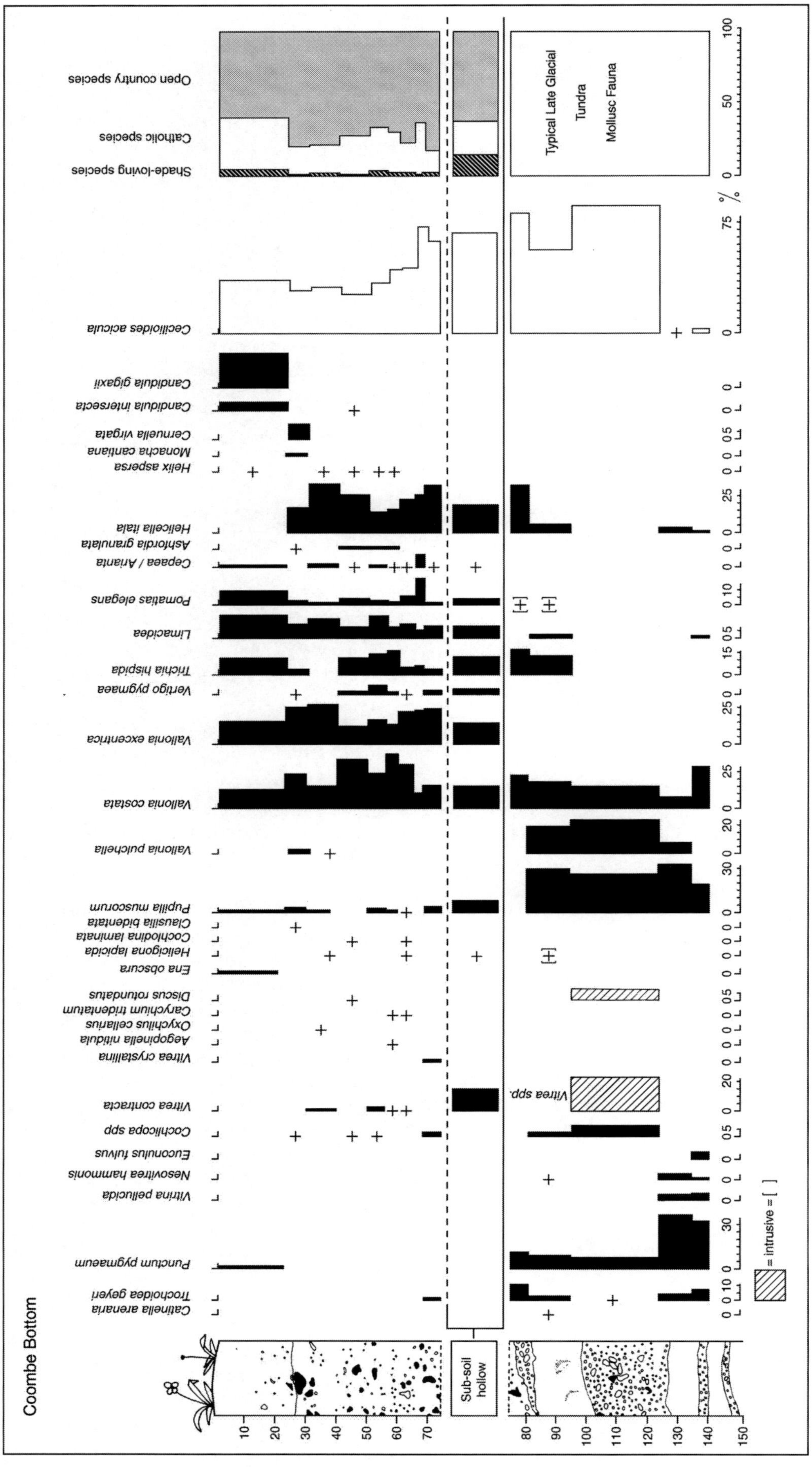

Fig 5.6 Coombe Bottom valley Trench b mollusc diagram.

Table 5.4 Coombe Bottom dry valley: table of molluscs

All totals exclude *C acicula*. [ ] = modern specimens
Note: intrusive (modern) specimens are excluded from calculations

		Chalk meltwater deposits					*Colluvium*								
	hollow	*Late Glacial*					*Prehistoric*			*Roman*		*Medieval–Post-medieval*			
Sample	*15*	*14*	*13*	*12*	*11*	*10*	*9*	*8*	*7*	*6*	*5*	*4*	*3*	*2*	*1*
Depth (cm)	*spot*	*134–140*	*123–134*	*94–123*	*80–94*	*74–80*	*68–74*	*65–68*	*60–65*	*56–60*	*50–56*	*40–50*	*30–40*	*23–30*	*0–23*
Wt (g)	*904*	*2000*	*2000*	*2000*	*2614*	*1648*	*1556*	*1571*	*1723*	*1733*	*1513*	*2000*	*2000*	*1892*	*2000*
Pomatias elegans (Müller)	1	–	–	–	+	+	1	6	5	3	4	7	2	3	4
Carychium tridentatum (Risso)	–	–	–	–	–	–	–	–	–	1	–	–	–	–	–
Carychium spp	–	–	–	–	–	–	–	–	+	–	–	–	–	–	–
Catinella arenaria (Bouchard-Chambreaux)	–	–	–	–	1	–	–	–	–	–	–	–	–	–	–
Cochlicopa spp	–	–	–	1	1	–	1	–	–	–	2	1	–	1	–
Vertigo pygmaea (Draparnaud)	1	–	–	–	–	–	1	–	1	3	9	1	–	1	–
Pupilla muscorum (Linnaeus)	2	12	8	2	6	–	2	–	1	2	4	–	2	3	1
Vallonia costata (Müller)	4	19	2	2	6	2	8	4	25	46	34	59	13	24	6
Vallonia pulchella (Müller)	–	–	2	3	6	–	–	–	–	–	–	–	1	2	–
Vallonia excentrica Sterki	4	–	–	–	–	–	12	8	20	19	25	24	23	26	7
Ena obscura (Müller)	–	–	–	–	–	–	–	–	–	–	–	–	–	–	1
Punctum pygmaeum (Draparnaud)	–	21	9	1	3	1	–	–	–	–	–	–	–	–	1
Discus rotundatus (Müller)	–	–	–	[1]	–	–	–	–	–	–	–	+	–	–	–
Vitrina pellucida (Müller)	–	3	1	–	–	–	–	–	–	–	–	–	–	–	–
Vitrea crystallina (Müller)	–	–	–	–	–	–	1	–	–	–	–	–	–	–	–
Vitrea contracta (Westerlund)	4	–	–	–	–	–	–	–	1	1	4	–	1	–	–
Vitrea spp	–	–	–	[3]	–	–	–	–	–	–	–	–	–	–	–
Nesovitrea hammonis (Ström)	–	1	1	–	+	–	–	–	–	–	–	–	–	–	–
Aegopinella nitidula (Draparnaud)	–	–	–	–	–	–	–	–	–	1	–	–	–	–	–
Oxychilus cellarius (Müller)	–	–	–	–	–	–	–	–	–	–	–	–	1	–	–
Limacidae	2	1	–	–	1	–	4	2	9	11	13	15	11	9	7
Euconulus fulvus (Müller)	–	3	–	–	–	–	–	–	–	–	–	–	–	–	–
Cecilioides acicula (Müller)	58	2	+	94	44	40	86	84	83	106	95	69	40	43	27
Cochlodina laminata (Montagu)	–	–	–	–	–	–	–	–	1	–	–	1	–	–	–
Clausilia bidentata (Ström)	–	–	–	–	–	–	–	–	–	–	–	–	–	1	–
Candidula intersecta (Poiret)	–	–	–	–	–	–	–	–	–	–	–	1	–	–	3
Candidula gigaxii (L Pfeiffer)	–	–	–	–	–	–	–	–	–	–	–	–	–	–	11
Cernuella virgata (Da Costa)	–	–	–	–	–	–	–	–	–	–	–	–	–	10	–
Helicella itala (Linnaeus)	5	1	1	–	2	3	15	9	20	21	21	49	28	18	–
Trochoidea geyeri (Soós)	–	5	1	+	1	1	1	–	–	–	–	–	–	–	–
Monacha cantiana (Montagu)	–	–	–	–	–	–	–	–	–	–	–	–	–	2	–
Ashfordia granulata (Alder)	–	–	–	–	–	–	–	–	–	2	3	3	–	1	–
Trichia hispida (Linnaeus)	3	–	–	–	6	2	2	2	4	21	20	21	–	4	5
Helicigona lapicida (Linnaeus)	+	–	–	–	+	–	–	–	+	–	–	1	–	–	–
Cepaea/*Arianta* spp	+	–	–	–	–	–	+	3	1	1	3	1	2	–	1
Helix aspersa (Müller)	–	–	–	–	–	–	–	–	–	1	1	2	1	–	+
Taxa	9	9	8	5	10	5	11	7	11	14	13	14	11	14	11
Shannon Index (H')	2.08	1.70	1.65	1.52	2.05	1.52	1.88	1.80	1.82	1.92	2.15	1.87	1.75	2.08	2.12
Brillouin Index (HB)	1.68	1.52	1.33	1.07	1.71	1.07	1.62	1.54	1.66	1.77	2.00	1.76	1.58	1.89	1.83
Δ_2	0.86	0.77	0.75	0.77	0.85	0.77	0.80	0.81	0.80	0.80	0.86	0.80	0.78	0.84	0.86
Δ_4	8.85	3.63	3.55	6.20	7.25	6.20	4.45	5.23	4.23	4.20	6.25	4.01	3.65	5.43	7.25
Totals	**26**	**66**	**25**	**9**	**33**	**9**	**48**	**34**	**88**	**133**	**143**	**188**	**85**	**105**	**47**
Magnetic susceptibility ($\times 10^{-8}$ SI/kg)	53	1	2	1	4	23	43	48	50	43	36.5	31	35	39	48

0.23–0.74 m. Post-glacial colluvium. Dark yellowish-brown (10YR 3/4) silty clay loam with 20 to 40% small and medium flints and chalk pieces.
0.74–1.90+ m. Pleistocene chalk meltwater deposits. Pale yellow (2.5Y 8/4) chalk marl with lenses of small rounded chalk pieces.

The Pleistocene sediments had low mollusc numbers (Table 5.4) and a restricted assemblage dominated by *Pupilla muscorum, Vallonia costata* and *Punctum pygmaeum*. Of special interest is the presence of *Trochiodea geyeri*, which has been extinct in Britain since the late glacial (Kerney 1999, 184), or very early Holocene, and today has a basically Central European distribution (Kerney and Cameron 1979, 183). There are various British Pleistocene records (Sparks 1953; Evans 1972) including some from Late Devensian assemblages on the North Downs (Kerney 1963) with which this assemblage, as a whole, is closely comparable. It appears to relate to Kerney's (1977) mollusc biozone Z which is equivalent to pollen zones I and II (for an outline of late Pleistocene/early Holocene zonation see Preece and Bridgland 1998, table 1.1). A few shell fragments would not be expected in biozone Z (1 apex of *Discus rotundatus*, 3 apices of *Vitrea* spp and non-apical fragments of *Pomatias elegans* and *Helicigona lapicida*). These are thought to be intrusive via earthworm burrows, which were such an obvious feature at the top of the Pleistocene sequence (Fig 5.5). Bell (1981b, 375) showed that earthworms take mollusc shells down to line aestivation chambers.

The trench did not expose the base of the Pleistocene sequence and the lower part of the stratigraphy may well repay further investigation, since similar sequences elsewhere have produced evidence of interstadial deposits of zone II (eg Burleston Down, Dorset; Allen 1999). It seems probable that the deposits investigated are of zone III date and represent extensive physical erosion within the Coombe Bottom valley in the late Devensian.

At the base of the post-glacial stratigraphy was a subsoil hollow no more than 0.2 m in width and depth. Such features frequently represent fossil tree holes and contain a woodland mollusc assemblage. However, in this case there was a small mollusc assemblage mostly comprising open-country taxa and the feature is perhaps more likely to represent an animal burrow. Mollusc taxa indicative of shaded woodland conditions are likewise very few in the overlying colluvial sequence; consequently there is no evidence for the original climax woodland soil in this valley. This is particularly striking given the predominance of shade-loving taxa reported (above) from Neolithic contexts on the hill. The sediments are so calcareous that these shells are unlikely to have been destroyed by decalcification. A more probable explanation is that the original woodland soils have been removed by erosion. Such erosion of Holocene woodland soils has been documented in parts of chalkland valleys at Itford Bottom, East Sussex (Bell 1983) and throughout much of Wessex and the area of Dorchester, Dorset (Allen 1992; 1997a).

The surviving post-glacial colluvium showed little evidence of either internal stratigraphy or molluscan evidence for ecological change. From the base the assemblage is of open-country character, the predominant taxa being the Vallonias, Limacidae and *Helicella itala. Trichia hispida* increases above 0.6 m. This group of species predominates in many colluvial deposits which are believed to derive from arable land (Bell 1983, 131). Non-apical fragments of *Helix aspersa*, a Romano-British introduction, occur down to 0.6 m, implying that the upper part of the colluvium may be Roman or later. The medieval introductions *Candidula intersecta, Candidula gigaxii* and *Cernuella virgata* are largely confined to the top 0.3 m and confirm the dating provided by artefacts.

An incipient stone horizon was noted at 0.56–0.6 m, overlain by a stone-free, worm-worked or possibly temporary stabilisation/hiatus in sediment build-up. This is confirmed by the peak in the coarse fraction (>5.6 mm) shown in the particle size histograms (archive), and the stabilisation may be reflected in the increase in molluscs per kilogram and peak in the Shannon (*H'*) index. Evidence of the relict former soil particles with higher magnetic susceptibility may be reflected in the lower portion of the Holocene sequence (Table 5.4).

Soil pits in Coombe Bottom

Five soil pits were dug using a JCB to examine sediment variation within the valley (Figs 1.4 and 5.7). Three pits ran along the lowest part of the valley axis:

Pit H. At NGR ST 8555 1190. 0–0.58 m colluvium. Below 0.58 m were Pleistocene meltwater deposits.
Pit G. At NGR ST 8579 1190. 0–0.63 m colluvium with medieval green-glazed jug handle in the top 0.24 m and a piece of unstratified Romano-British pottery. Below 0.63 m were Pleistocene meltwater deposits.
Pit A. At NGR ST 8578 1189. 0–1.14 m colluvium, at *c* 0.60 m was a post-medieval jug handle, a piece of brown glass and a medieval sherd. There were two Romano-British sherds. Below 1.14 m were Pleistocene meltwater deposits.

Two pits were dug on each side of the valley to obtain information on the cross-profile of valley sediments:

Pit E. At NGR ST 8565 1197 on the north side of Coombe Bottom. 0–0.46 m topsoil and colluvium overlying chalk.
Pit F. At NGR ST 8567 1183 on the south side of Coombe Bottom. 0–0.30 m cultivated topsoil; 0.3–1.36 m colluvium; 1.36–1.58 m possible truncated palaeosol; 1.58 m+ Pleistocene meltwater deposits.

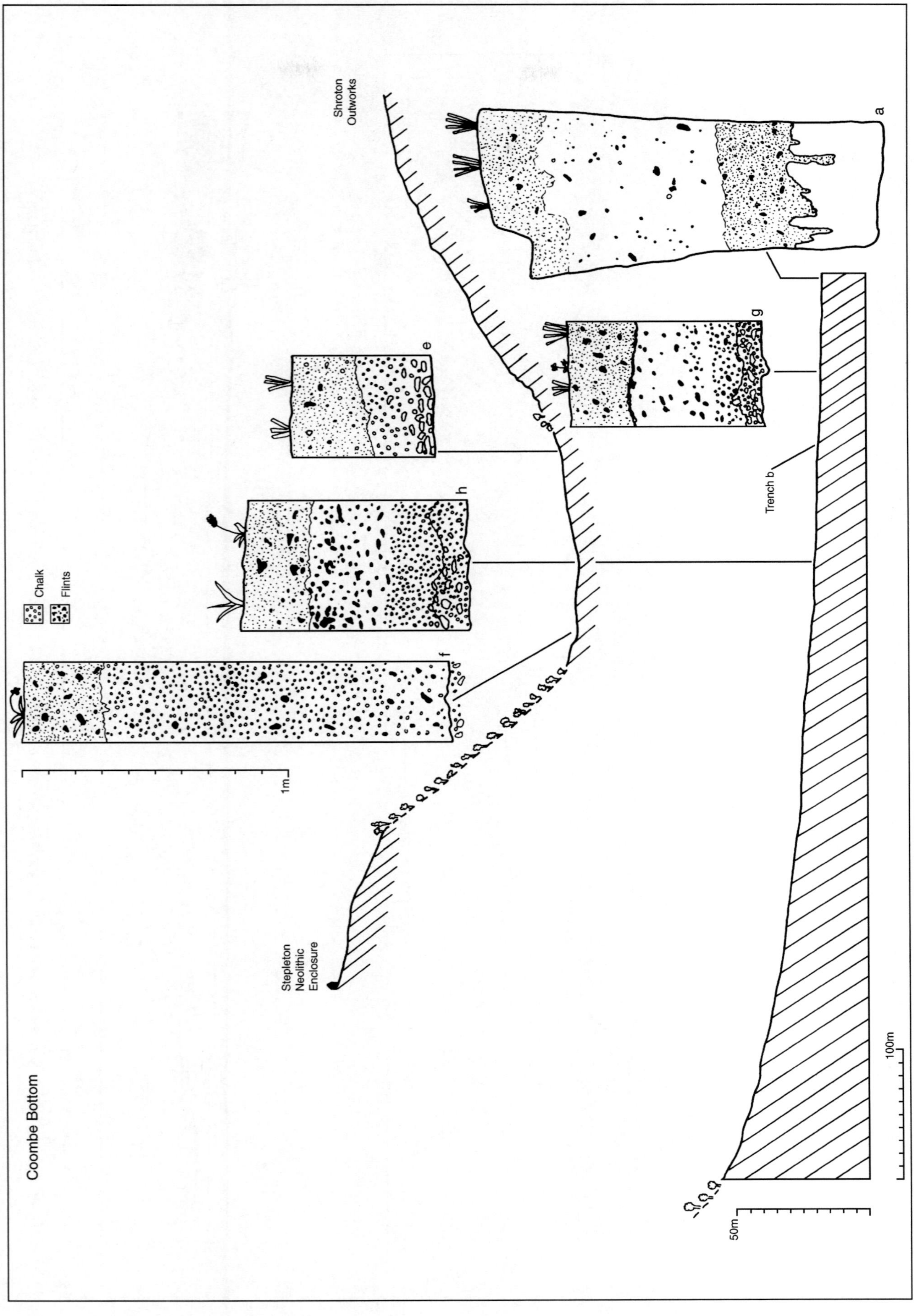

Fig 5.7 Coombe Bottom, cross and long profiles showing soil pit sections.

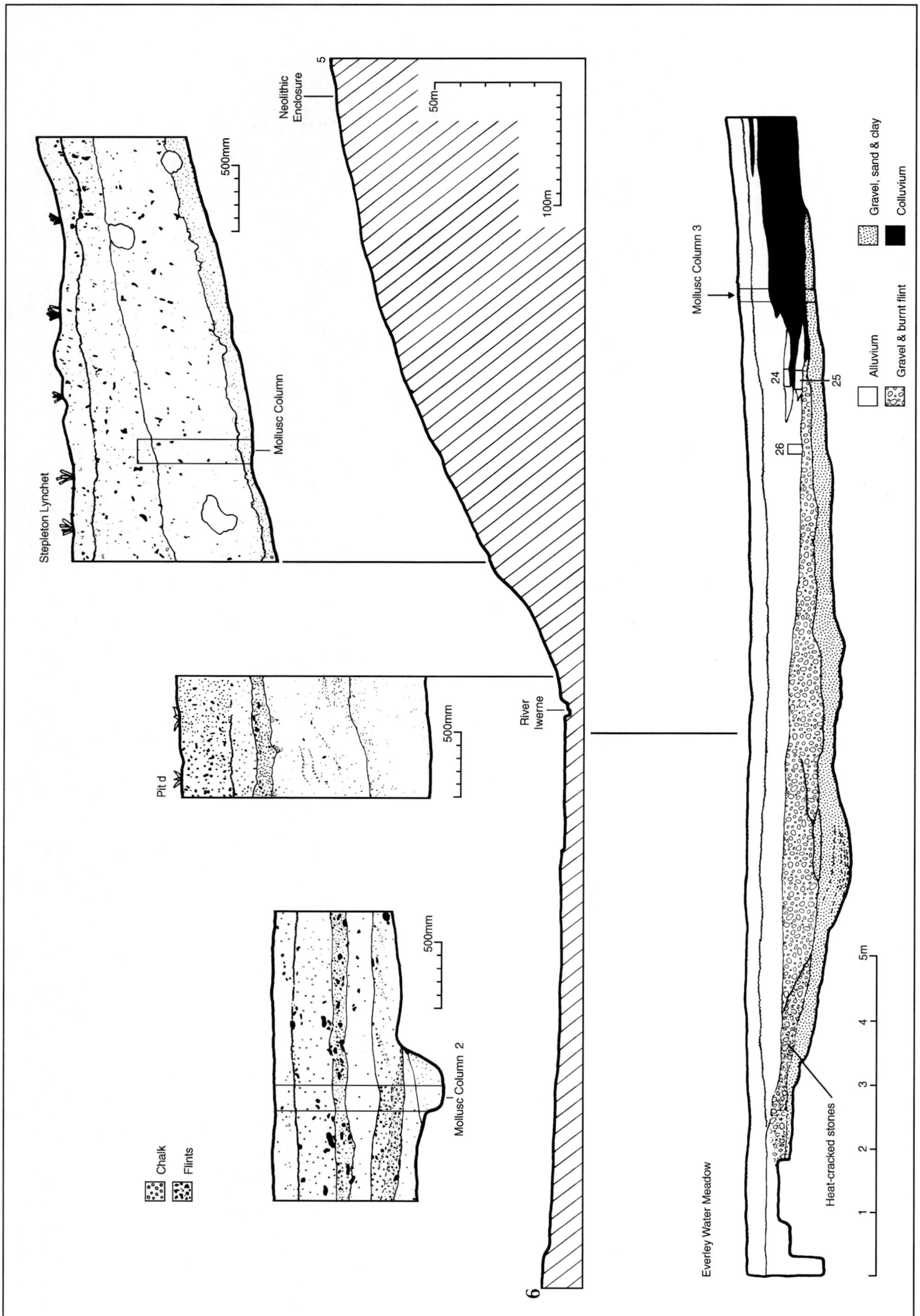

Fig 5.8 Transect from Stepleton enclosure to Everley Water Meadow in the Iwerne valley showing soil pits, mollusc column 3 and excavated sections.

The soil pits down the valley axis indicate that the sequence investigated in Trench B is broadly representative; deeper colluvium exists lower down the valley to the east, but much of this appears to be medieval or later. Ridge and furrow of probable medieval date survives on the south side of the Shroton spur on the slopes of Coombe Bottom (Fig 3.73). Pit F has revealed a much deeper reservoir of colluvium at the foot of Stepleton spur. Further evidence for eroded sediments on this slope come from a series of lynchet banks, the nearest of which is 21 m upslope from Pit F, that act as barriers to further downslope soil movement. It is unfortunate that there was no opportunity to investigate the date and environmental sequence of this colluvium in detail although colluvium elsewhere on Stepleton spur is discussed below.

5.3.2 Stepleton to Everley Water Meadow transect

A line of soil pits was dug to examine the soil and sediment profile from the slopes outside the Stepleton causewayed enclosure down to the valley floor of the Iwerne stream at Everley Water Meadow (Figs 1.4, 5.8).

Stepleton lynchet

On the east side of Stepleton spur, downslope from the Neolithic enclosure, is a series of lynchets (Fig 2.7). It was known from the excavations in the causewayed enclosures that later cultivation had taken place on these slopes. Pottery scatters in the tops of the ditch

Table 5.5 Stepleton Lynchet. Molluscs

All totals exclude *C acicula*

	Lynchet ploughwash										
Sample	*34*	*35*	*36*	*37*	*38*	*39*	*40*	*41*	*42*	*43*	*44*
Depth (cm)	*130–136*	*125–130*	*120–125*	*115–120*	*110–115*	*100–110*	*90–100*	*80–90*	*70–80*	*64–70*	*50–64*
Wt (g)	*1500*	*1600*	*1500*	*1500*	*1500*	*1500*	*1500*	*1500*	*1500*	*1500*	*1500*
Pomatias elegans (Müller)	1	1	1	8	2	1	5	1	1	2	2
Cochlicopa spp	1	–	5	2	3	2	3	1	1	2	2
Vertigo pygmaea (Draparnaud)	–	4	–	1	–	2	2	2	1	4	21
Pupilla muscorum (Linnaeus)	4	4	4	3	6	6	4	10	7	16	11
Vallonia costata (Müller)	–	4	–	1	6	10	13	22	28	15	5
Vallonia pulchella (Müller)	–	–	2	–	1	1	–	–	–	–	–
Vallonia excentrica (Sterki)	13	11	12	18	15	36	59	64	51	50	24
Punctum pygmaeum (Draparnaud)	–	1	1	–	–	–	–	–	–	–	–
Discus rotundatus (Müller)	+	2	+	1	1	+	+	1	+	+	+
Vitrea contracta (Westerlund)	–	–	–	–	1	–	–	–	–	2	1
Oxychilus cellarius (Müller)	–	–	–	–	–	1	–	–	1	–	–
Limacidae	–	–	–	–	2	–	3	1	8	4	4
Cecilioides acicula (Müller)	–	2	1	2	2	12	35	31	67	57	6
Cochlodina laminata (Montagu)	–	–	–	–	–	1	–	1	–	–	–
Clausilia bidentata (Ström)	+	1	–	–	1	–	+	–	–	–	1
Candidula intersecta (Poiret)	–	–	–	–	–	–	–	–	–	–	9
Candidula gigaxii (L Pfeiffer)	–	–	–	–	–	–	–	–	–	–	2
Cernuella virgata (Da Costa)	–	–	–	–	–	–	–	3	7	5	6
Helicella itala (Linnaeus)	2	8	15	9	13	15	21	12	20	14	4
Trichia hispida (Linnaeus)	1	1	1	+	3	1	4	3	4	6	9
Helicigona lapicida (Linnaeus)	+	+	+	+	+	+	–	+	+	+	–
Cepaea spp	1	+	+	+	1	–	1	–	1	–	–
Helix aspersa (Müller)	–	–	–	–	–	–	–	–	–	+	+
Lymnaea truncatula (Müller)	–	–	–	–	–	–	–	1	–	–	–
Mytilus edulis	–	–	–	–	–	–	–	–	–	+	–
Taxa	7	10	8	8	13	11	10	12	12	11	14
Shannon Index (*H'*)	1.38	1.96	1.63	1.60	2.10	1.62	1.57	1.57	1.77	1.86	2.24
Brillouin Index (HB)	1.10	1.65	1.40	1.38	1.81	1.44	1.44	1.43	1.64	1.72	2.03
Δ_2	0.64	0.82	0.75	0.74	0.84	0.71	0.68	0.67	0.77	0.77	0.86
Δ_4	2.00	5.53	3.36	3.09	5.72	2.58	2.32	2.12	3.37	3.52	6.73
Totals	**23**	**37**	**41**	**43**	**55**	**76**	**115**	**121**	**130**	**120**	**101**
Magnetic susceptibility ($\times 10^{-8}$ SI/kg)	17	21	24	24	25	34	23	23	29	25	20

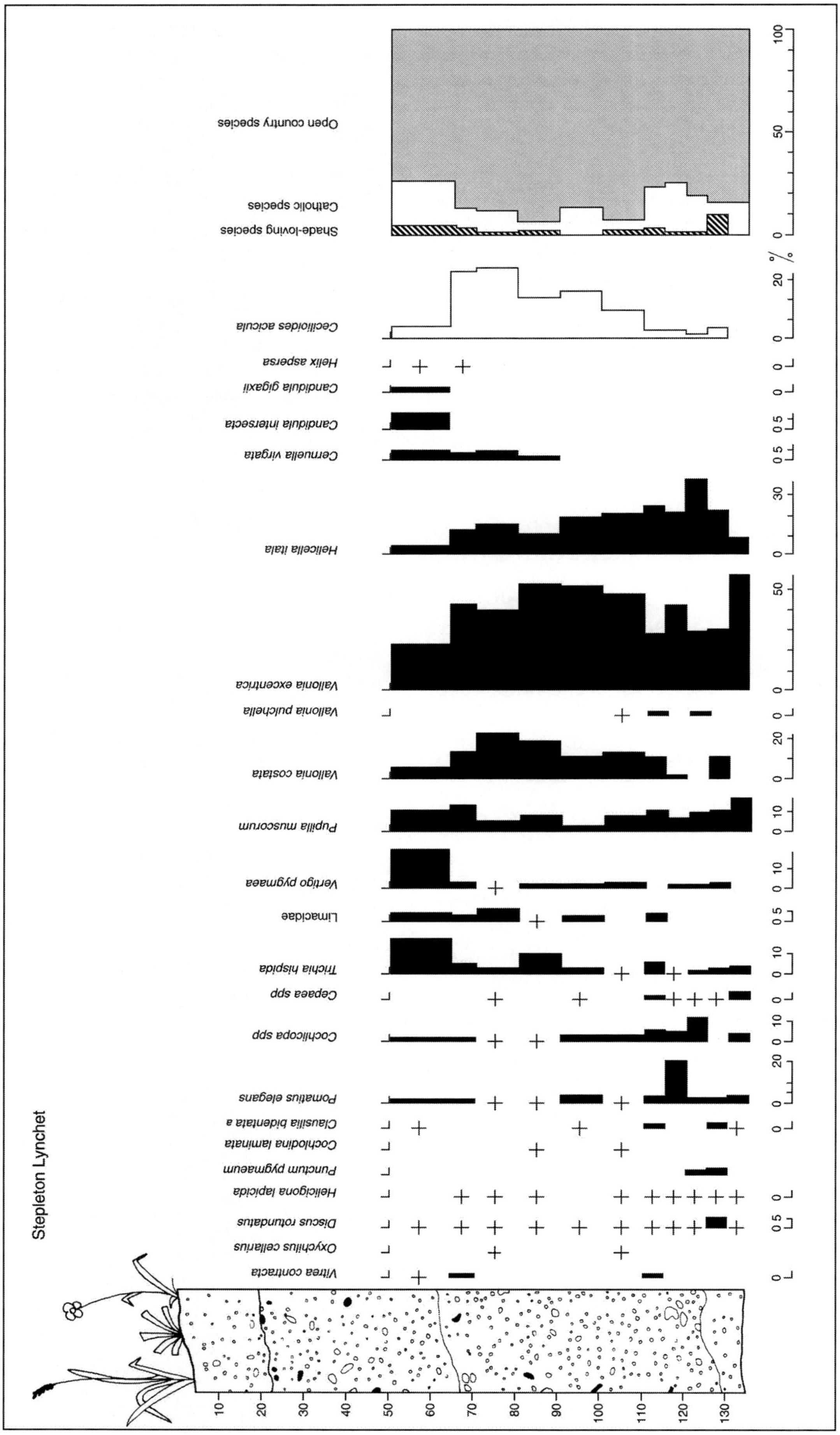

Fig 5.9 Stepleton Lynchet mollusc diagram.

fills suggested cultivation in the Bronze Age to Romano-British periods but nothing later, although ridge and furrow on the south edge of the Shroton spur has already been noted. One of the lynchets forms a very pronounced break of slope *c* 400 m east of the Stepleton enclosure and must reflect a long-standing boundary of cultivation at the top of the steep slope of the Iwerne valley. A trench 3.5 m by 1 m was dug mechanically into the top of this lynchet at NGR ST 8587 1168 (Fig 1.4). Part of the trench face was trowelled back and 163 artefacts were recorded. The datable finds were overwhelmingly late Iron Age or early Romano-British Black Burnished Ware (45 sherds) and Romano-British (27 sherds) in such abundance from a small trench to suggest the proximity of occupation. A shale armlet fragment (Fig 10.2: S36) and late Iron Age and Romano-British sherds occurred in the basal layers. There were only two prehistoric sherds and it can be concluded that the formation of this lynchet was late Iron Age and Romano-British.

Stepleton lynchet molluscs

The stratigraphy at the point sampled is summarised as follows:

0–0.22 m Cultivated topsoil, brown (10YR 4/3) silty loam
0.22–0.64 m Organic-rich recent colluvium, brown (10Y 4/3) silty loam
0.64–1.36 m Chalky organic-poor colluvium, yellowish-brown (10YR 5/6) silt loam with 35% small chalk pieces
0.136+ m Pleistocene deposit, yellow (2.5Y 7/4) marl with 70% small rounded chalk pieces

Since the upper colluvium was clearly modern, only the sediments below 0.5 m were analysed (Fig 5.9). As in Coombe Bottom, shade-loving mollusc species are very few throughout and it must be presumed that here too climax woodland soil and its contained molluscs have been removed by erosion. The lynchet assemblage is remarkably uniform, though the number of shells increases upwards. The overall impression is of unfavourable conditions and low species diversity. The assemblage is dominated by the Vallonias, particularly *Vallonia excentrica*, and *Helicella itala* with smaller numbers of *Pupilla muscorum* and *Trichia hispida*. The restricted diversity and many of the species present are typical of colluvial assemblages, although the abundance of *Vallonia excentrica* suggests grazed grassland phases (Evans 1993), as does the presence of *Vertigo pygmaea* and *Pupilla muscorum*. A modest rise in the last two species above 0.7 m may reflect an episode of more stable conditions (possibly reflected in the 4 diversity indices) between older and more recent colluvial deposits. The introduced species *Cernuella virgata* extends down to 0.9 m, but this species was almost certainly present from the late Iron Age at Maiden Castle (Evans and Rouse 1991b, 125). The other introductions, *Candidula intersecta*, *C gigaxii* and *Helix aspersa*, are confined to the recent colluvium.

Soil pit d

At the base of the Stepleton spur was a pronounced terrace-like feature on the west side of the Iwerne river forming the edge of the valley floor. It was investigated as a possible colluvial deposit by mechanical excavation at NGR ST 8600 1138. This showed (Fig 5.8) that there was only 0.67 m of colluvium, much of it disturbed by recent cultivation. The underlying sequence was Pleistocene solifluction deposits which had apparently been subsequently cut into by the Iwerne stream creating the terrace.

5.3.3 Everley Water Meadow

R W Smith, Martin Bell, Roger Mercer and Frances Healy

Introduction

Everley Water Meadow lies in the Iwerne valley at the foot of the Stepleton spur, at NGR ST 861 115 (Fig 1.4). It was selected for particularly detailed investigation of the question of prehistoric activity in valleys because field survey by Rog Palmer in 1977 had revealed a scatter of worked flint of late Neolithic or early Bronze Age date, and calcined flints. RWS was responsible for this part of the study in 1982 and this led to further investigations by RM and RWS in 1983 and 1984. RWS prepared an interim account of the investigation to 1983 (Smith 1983), which also forms one of several study areas in his PhD thesis (Smith 1985). This work is integrated here with the full results of the 1982–4 excavations, superseding interim reports by RM (Mercer 1983; 1984a; 1984b).The water meadow itself was created in the post-medieval period, apparently around the 1760s. This involved cutting a new channel for the Iwerne stream on the west side of the valley, at the base of the Stepleton slope and slightly upslope from the lowest part of the valley floor occupied by the prehistoric and subsequent channels. From this new channel, and a series of irrigation channels joined to it, some of which were found in the excavation, the meadows would have been seasonally flooded to promote lush growth for pasture.

The field was surveyed and systematically walked in 1982; the methods and results are more fully described by Smith (1983; 1985). A contour survey led to the identification of the lowest part of the valley floor at the base of the Stepleton spur, the contours suggesting the positions of several successive channels (Fig 5.10). To the east, 1–1.2 m above the channels, was a higher gravel terrace. A thin scatter of Roman, medieval and post-medieval artefacts extended over the field without concentrations and is likely to have derived from

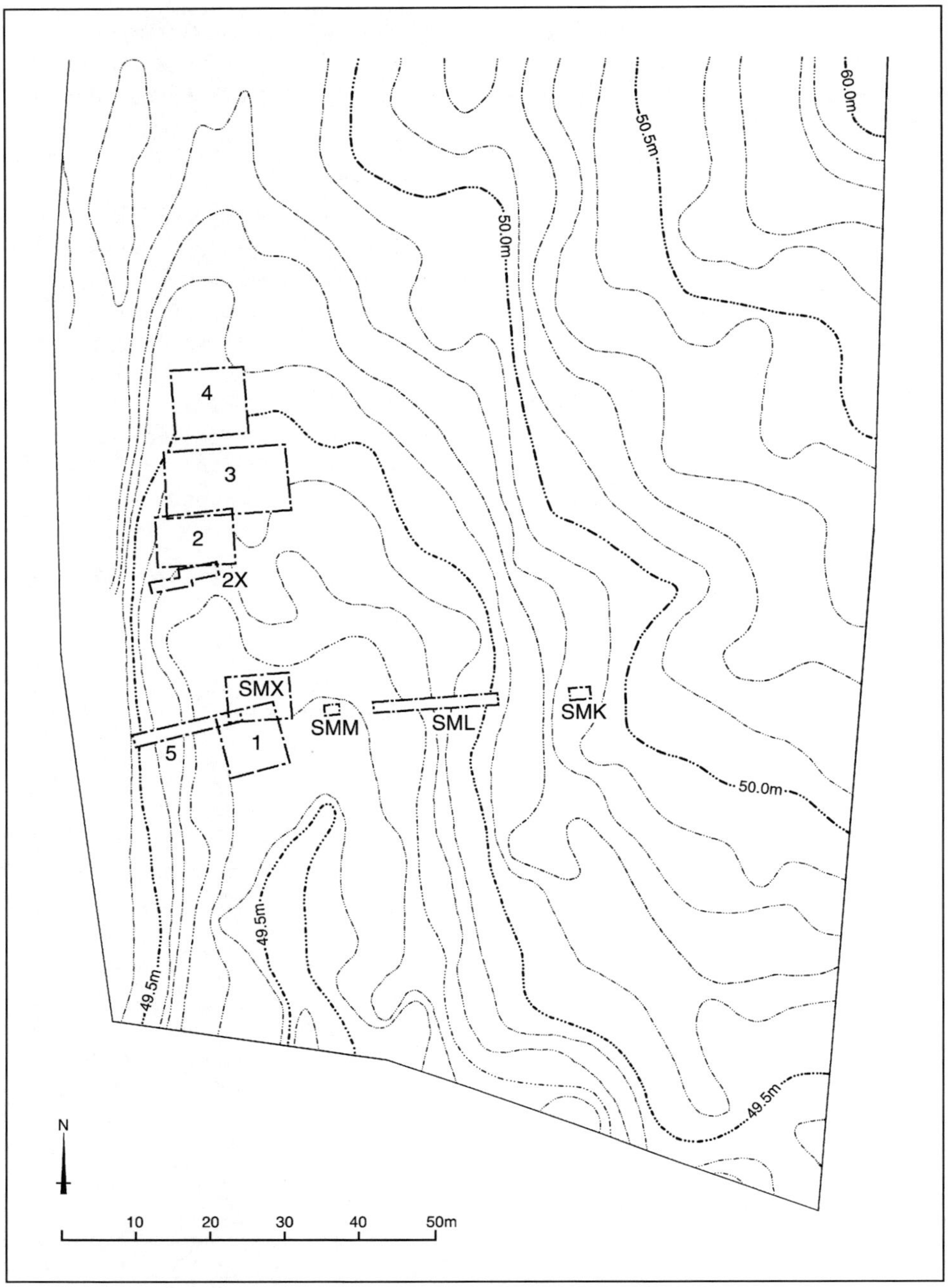

Fig 5.10 Everley Water Meadow. Contour survey and trench plan. The location of Everley Water Meadow is shown in Figure 1.4.

manuring. The pottery was made up of 4 sherds/20 g Roman and 13 sherds/89 g medieval, mainly mid-twelfth to fourteenth-century Laverstock coarsewares, with some late tenth to early eleventh-century Cheddar-type ware. The distributions of struck flint, burnt flint and iron slag were more localised. Twenty-three pieces of struck flint (see Saville 10.2.9, Table 10.60) and half-a-dozen pieces of iron slag occurred in overlapping concentrations on the gravel terrace. Calcined flints were densely distributed along the former river channel and not on the terrace. Excavation subsequently took place in two areas which, although only about 15 m apart, provided different samples of the valley bottom sediments.

The south area

Investigation started here 1982, in which season the field was known as Stepleton Water Meadow. A line of machine-cut test trenches was set out from the terrace into the area of the river channels (Fig 5.10: SMK–SMM). Selected areas were then hand excavated so that the artefacts could be projected onto drawn sections. The westernmost trench (SMN) was expanded into a larger cutting (SMX) in order to examine the palaeochannel deposits. In 1983 this area was extended again (Area 1) and in 1984 a trench was dug by machine from the edge of the already excavated area to just east of the Iwerne stream (Area 5).

Table 5.6 Everley Water Meadow. South area. Description of the sediments represented in Figs 5.11–12

The finds listed for each unit include those from equivalent layers which are not shown on the published section.
At the time of compilation (2002) the pottery from the 1983 season was missing, although preliminary identifications were available. Where sherds are quantified here they are from the 1982 season.

R W Smith's unit	*Layer(s) in Fig 5.12*	*Description*	*Finds*
Ap	1	1980s ploughsoil with alluvial content	Cu alloy coin, iron objects (mainly nails), iron slag, 4 sherds/12 g Roman, 41 sherds/123 g medieval (mainly Laverstock type coarseware, some Cheddar type Saxo-Norman wheelthrown, 1 sherd Hermitage-type sandy ware), 2 sherds/7 g post-medieval, struck flint, animal bone
F1, F2		Gullies probably relating to water meadow	
A		Unploughed alluvium	
B		Stoneline surviving in hollow, where cultivation had not disrupted pre-water meadow turfline	
C		Silt in former channel	
Dp	2	Plough-disturbed alluvial fill of depression over former channel, mixed with gravel by cultivation	Cu alloy ?pin fragment, and iron objects including at least 1 nail, iron ore, iron slag, 1 sherd/4 g Roman (samian), 19 sherds/74 g medieval (mainly Laverstock-type coarseware, some Cheddar type Saxo-Norman wheelthrown), struck flint, animal bone
D	4	Unploughed dark alluvium containing bands and flecks of charcoal. Minor features (3^n) were cut from within this layer. Feature 4^n is a silt-filled depression.	9 sherds/64 g medieval (some Laverstock type coarseware, mainly Cheddar type Saxo-Norman wheelthrown), fragment of brick or tile, single unworked fragments of Jurassic limestone and Greensand, struck flint, burnt flint, animal bone, shell (?oyster)
E		Lens of small flint and chalk gravel probably representing a stream base, interleaved with D	
F	15A–15C (=Area 1 L1)	Extensive spread of gravel, much of it calcined, in a matrix of sandy silt containing lenses and bands of darker silt	Iron nails, 1 fragment iron ore, slag, 1 body sherd/33 g in grog- and flint-tempered early Bronze Age fabric, 2 body sherds/31 g in sandy late Bronze Age fabric, 1 base sherd/8 g in flint-tempered late Bronze Age/early Iron Age fabric, samian, 3 sherds/11 g medieval (1 Laverstock-type coarseware, 2 Cheddar type Saxo-Norman wheelthrown, smaller and more abraded than BA sherds), brick or tile fragments, fragment of Syenite mould for a socketed axe (probably from Wales or the south-west – Needham, Ch 10, Fig 10.4), 2 weathered Niedermendig lava fragments, Greensand fragments, shale armlet fragment (probably lathe-turned; Fig 6.19: S37), struck flint, much animal bone (some burnt)
H	8	Gravels in a subsidiary (?storm) channel, with burnt flint	Animal bone (including the charred coracoid of a crow or rook), fired clay, iron slag, 1 fragment ?iron ore
5	F10	Rectangular pit containing a mass of heat-shattered flint mixed with charcoal and ash, cut into gravel of channel bank	3 flint flakes, 1 piercer
G, J	14, 16	Dark gravel formations on opposite sides of the channel with calcined flint (less frequent than in F=L15). Heavily stained with iron and manganese	Chisel arrowhead, uncorticated and in sharp condition (Saville, Ch 10, Fig 10.42), unidentified bone fragments Arrowhead provides later Neolithic *terminus post quem* for gravels. Burnt flint may suggest that burnt mound was already in existence upstream when they were deposited
N	13	Grey-brown flinty clay loam below gravels G. May represent traces of a previously more extensive palaeosol Also features beneath gravels in surface of Coombe Rock (not on section), some ?natural but one (area 1 F6) pit-like and containing ash, charcoal and a bone fragment	
K	18	Clean chalk mud mixed with a little sandy silt	Bone fragments extracted with molluscs
L1–2	17a–b	Grey-green mottled brown clay (17a) overlying charcoal-stained grey-green clay (17b)	
L3	17c	Charcoal-stained derived Greensand	
M	19	Iron-stained gravel interleaved with L	
L4–6	17d–j	Braids and lenses of clayey, Greensandy silts	Bone fragments extracted with molluscs from L17d
P		Coombe Rock	

Fig 5.11 Everley Water Meadow. South area (Trench SMX, Area 1, part of Area 5).

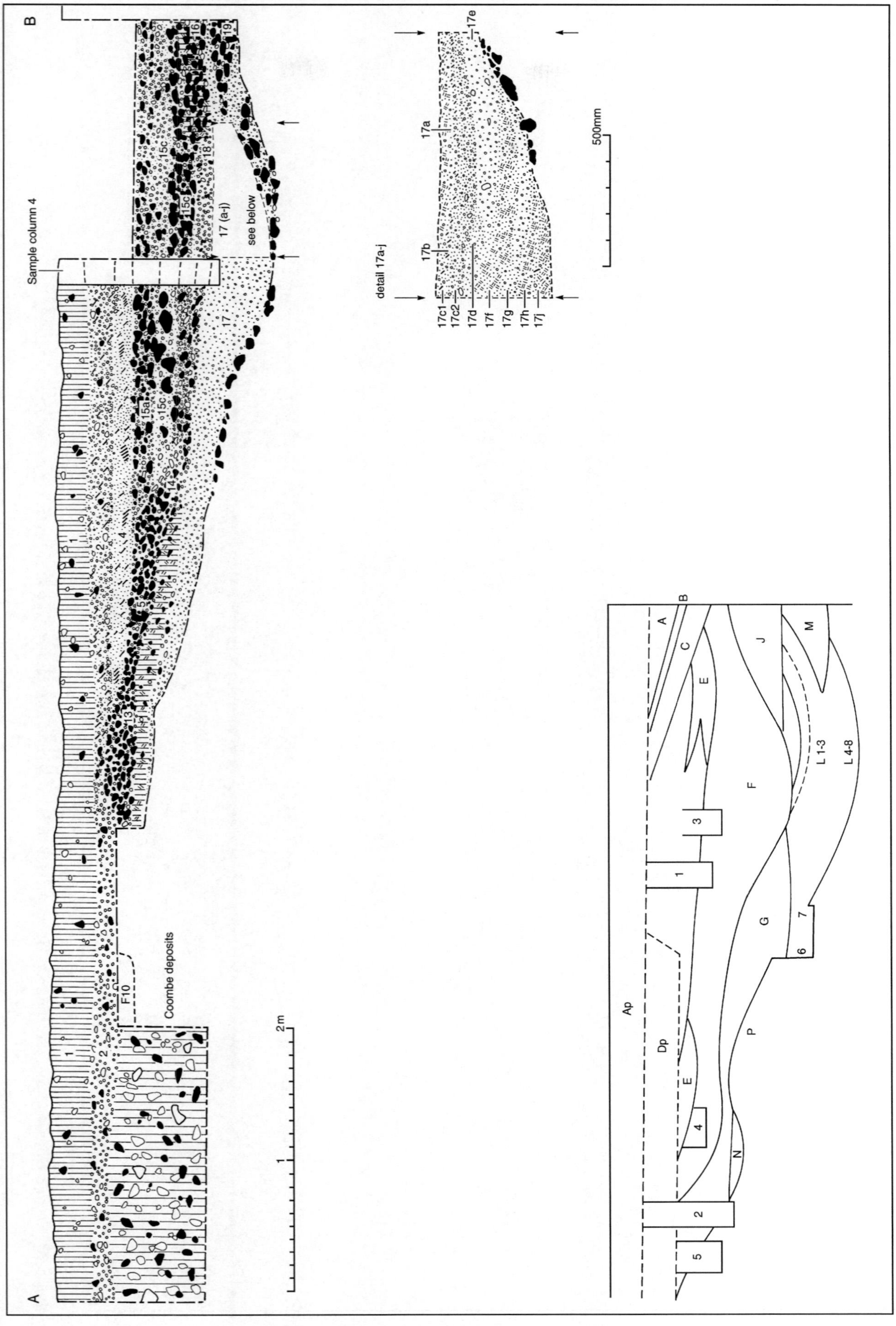

Fig 5.12 Everley Water Meadow. South area. Section and block diagram of palaeochannel deposits, showing the location of Sample Column 4. The notations on the diagram correspond to the stratigraphic units described in Table 5.6.

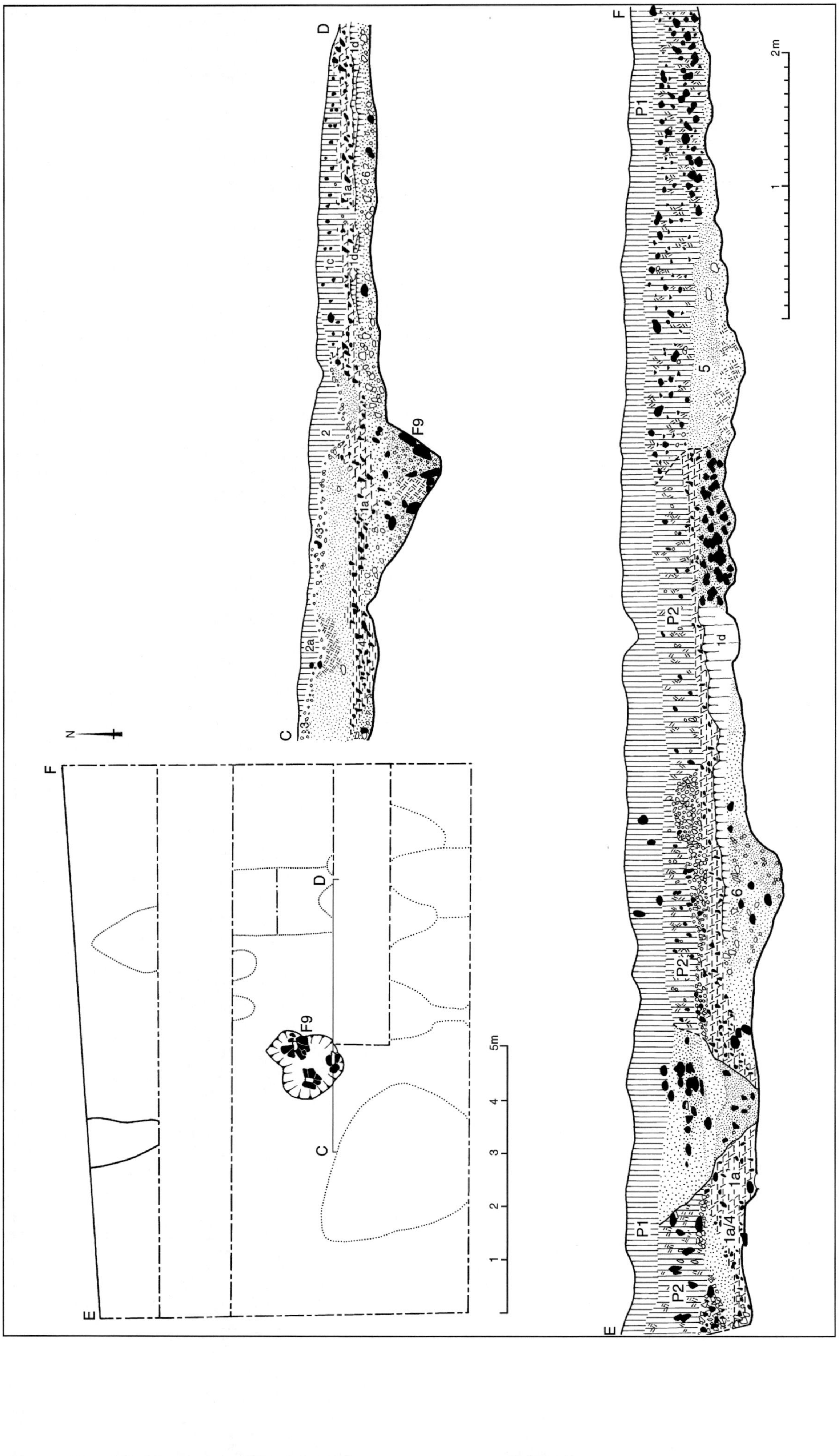

Fig 5.13 Everley Water Meadow. North area. Sections through burnt mound and plan of features in surface of gravel beneath it.

The terrace

The aim of work on the terrace was to identify an archaeological origin for the flint scatter. A ploughsoil 0.23 m thick was underlain by 0.20–0.67 m of decalcified valley gravel with a wavy and involuted lower boundary overlying Coombe Rock containing chalk and Greensand; the latter outcrops in the valley *c* 1 km north of the site (Fig 1.2). Subsequently, apparently during the late glacial, the river Iwerne cut down into these solifluction deposits. During the Holocene, decalcification and the formation of solution features occurred and the trenches also revealed evidence of root casts left by former trees, in one case with charcoal within its fill. The effects of agriculture on the terrace were severe, in places undisturbed gravels had been almost completely planed away and nowhere was there stratigraphic separation between iron nails, medieval pottery (again mainly Laverstock coarsewares) and flint artefacts discarded several millennia earlier. Hopes that prehistoric surfaces might survive intact on the terrace were not realised.

The palaeochannels

The westernmost 1982 trench was sited within the area of the palaeochannel and revealed its western bank, into which a rectangular pit was cut (Fig 5.11: F10). The pit contained a mass of heat-shattered flint mixed with charcoal, ash and a small amount of struck flint (Table 5.6). An adjoining area 8 m by 6 m was opened up (Fig 5.10: SMX), leading to the recovery of a late Bronze Age Syenite stone mould for casting socketed axes (Fig 10.4), a few sherds of late Bronze Age pottery and some metalworking slag. The conjunction of these finds suggested that there might be an industrial site at the stream edge. This prompted further investigations, in the course of which the south area was extended by further excavation in 1983. The channel, which overall was 14 m wide, comprised a series of successive intercutting stream beds. These are shown in plan and section in Figures 5.11–12. The deposits are described in detail in Table 5.6. The slag subsequently proved to be iron slag.

The long section cut in 1984 from the edge of the excavated area to just east of the present Iwerne stream (Fig 5.10: Area 5) revealed the section simplified in Figure 5.8. The alluvium was interleaved with a series of lenses of colluvium (including E), containing small rounded chalk pieces, which thickened as they approach the Stepleton slopes to the west. Modern analogues for these types of deposit are seen in the fans of sediment deposited downslope of rills and gullies during major erosion episodes on the chalk (Boardman 1992; Bell 1992). Similar Iron Age examples were recorded within dry valley sediments at Kiln Combe in Sussex (Bell 1983), and Strawberry Hill, Wiltshire (Allen 1992). The presence of small rounded chalk pieces indicates that gullies were cutting down to underlying chalk or Pleistocene deposits. Since these fans were interleaved with alluvium it is clear that an unknown proportion of the sediment derived from the slope would have been transported by stream activity and reworked as alluvium on the valley floor.

The north area

A single trench was opened in 1983 to examine the densest concentration of burnt flint (Fig 5.10: Area 2) which proved to be a burnt mound. Further trenches were excavated to the north and south in 1984 (Fig 5.10: Areas 2X, 3, 4).

Coombe Rock lay at the base of the sequence, as in the south area. It was succeeded by water-laid clays and silts, which were charcoal-stained in part of Area 2X. Patches of palaeosol survived (eg Fig 5.13: L1d) and there were several probably natural features beneath the burnt mound, of which few were known at that time in the south-west of England. Finds from the palaeosol include an end scraper on a blade with elaborate trimming on both lateral edges (see Saville, 10.2.9), and animal bone fragments (see Legge, 8.4). One pre-mound feature was clearly deliberately constructed. EWM83 F9 was a steep-sided trilobate pit measuring 1.40 m across and more than 0.50 m deep. In it were three stone-packed post sockets *c* 0.15 m in diameter (Fig 5.13).

The mound itself was much truncated by the river, by later features, especially the channels of the water meadow, and by ploughing. Its plan is difficult to reconstruct and, especially towards the edges, it is not always possible to be sure whether the deposit was *in situ* or reworked. It extended for approximately 17 m along the river, and measured at least 8 m across, its south edge lying within Area 2X and its north edge in the south-west part of Area 3, some of it remaining unexcavated to the west of Area 3. At its edges a thickness of as little as 0.02 m survived. It was deepest in a linear depression, probably a former channel, where it survived up to 0.35 m thick. It was made up of soil with a very high density of burnt flint. In Area 2, EWM83 L1A, a black layer with much charcoal and burnt flint, graded westward into EWM83 L4, in which there was much burnt flint but less charcoal. In Area 4, the deposit was divided into EWM84 L4 and L4A. In a deeper, undisturbed area was the upright lower base of a Deverel-Rimbury vessel, with the stump of its wall remaining, next to a red deer antler pick (Fig 5.14). Other finds from the mound included further Deverel-Rimbury sherds, a small amount of relatively undiagnostic struck flint (see Saville, 10.2.9), an unworked shale fragment, and unidentifiable animal bone fragments (see Legge, Ch 8). Over 180 kg of calcined flint were recovered (see Saville, 10.2.9). Charcoal from within and beneath the mound was predominantly of scrub species, mainly Maloideae and *Prunus* sp (see Austin *et al*, 6.1). Three bulked charcoal samples from within the mound were dated to 1600–1260 cal BC (3160±70 BP; HAR-6529), 1520–1120 cal BC (3090±80 BP; HAR-6530) and 1500–1120 cal BC (3070±70 BP; HAR-6531; Fig 4.20; Table 4.1).

Fig 5.14 Everley Water Meadow. North area. Pot base and antler pick in burnt mound. Scale in centimetres

The edges of the mound were directly under the ploughsoil, but most of it remained sealed by water-laid deposits. The ubiquitous alluvium was interspersed with layers and lenses of gravel and chalky material, like those in sample column 2, which are described below. Later ditches and gullies were cut through these deposits. Most of them probably related to the water meadow, notably a straight ditch surviving to 1.50–2.30 wide and *c* 0.50 m deep with shelving sides and a flat bottom (EWM84 F7), which ran on a straight north–south course through Areas 4 and 3 and into Area 2. Within this ditch in Area 4 was a subrectangular depression measuring *c* 4 m × 1.80 m, extending up to 0.20 m below the base of the ditch, with at least five postholes set around its edges. At its centre was a yet deeper ovoid area (EWM84 F7A), measuring *c* 1.80 m × 1.50 m, flanked by a single large posthole with a postpipe 0.20 m in diameter. While these features are difficult to interpret in detail, their location in the ditch suggests that they were the remains of a hatch or sluice. Most of the smaller gullies in both north and south areas ran on a similar alignment. They would seem to have been elements of a system like those described by Whitehead (1967) and Cook (1994), although the scale of the excavation was insufficient to elucidate its plan. If the structure in F7 was indeed a hatch, it would suggest that the ditch was a main or carrier. Not all the later ditches were of the same date or function. Once F7 was silted, a smaller gully (EWM84 F3) was cut through it, extending to either side and crossing it at an oblique angle. Since F3 cannot have drained into or taken water from a silted channel, it must reflect later activity. Insofar as any of the now (2004) missing pottery from these features was identified, it was of Roman and medieval date. Both are likely to have been redeposited.

The molluscs

Martin Bell and Michael J Allen

Four columns of mollusc samples were taken from areas of the site with contrasting sedimentary histories. Work has been concentrated on sample column 2 from Area 2X in the north area, immediately south of the burnt mound (Fig 5.10). Part of the Bronze Age burnt mound was intact on the channel bank and sealed a buried soil (samples 12 and 13). The channel here contained sediments with much burnt gravel and Bronze Age finds. In the south area the channel deposits contained both Bronze Age and Romano-British artefacts and parts at least of the channel fill were apparently reworked in the Romano-British and medieval periods. Here there is less certainty regarding which of the lower channel samples can be attributed to the Bronze Age (Table 5.6). Sample column 1 was collected in 1982 from a part of the channel that was subsequently shown to have evidence of Romano-British reworking; consequently this column has not been analysed. Sample column 4 from Area 1 is a sequence of samples taken from the central area of the channel in 1983 (Fig 5.12). Area 5, the machine-cut trench which extended the same cutting in 1984, produced sample column 3 through the alluvial/colluvial interface shown in Figure 5.8.

Groupings of freshwater species (moving water, ditch, catholic and slum species) follow Sparks (1961). Many of the samples come from stream channels and will be partly allochthonous, ie derived from various habitats; this needs to be borne in mind in their interpretation. In some cases the sedimentary context suggests that the molluscs will be mainly autochthonous, ie they lived *in situ*. These include an old land surface below the burnt mound (sample 12) and overbank alluvial sediments in the upper channel fills: sample column 2, 0.17–0.45 m (which also contains a colluvial component) and 0.58–0.81 m and sample column 3, 0.24–0.64 m. These assemblages can be compared with the molluscan taxocenes defined on the basis of previous studies of chalk river valley floor assemblages (Evans *et al* 1992; Davies *et al* 1996; Davies 1998).

On the mollusc diagram freshwater species have been plotted as percentages over and above the land species (Fig 5.15). The numbers of bivalves have been divided by two to give total of individuals but the bivalves (*Pisidium* spp) have not generally been identified and were mostly fragmentary. Species diversity indices have been calculated for the terrestrial component of the assemblages (Tables 5.7–5.9).

Sample column 2

The stratigraphy can be briefly summarised as follows. Glynis Jones' identifications of the charred plant remains and Phil Austin's identifications of the charcoal from each sample are appended, excluding the indeterminate fragments:

0–0.17 m. Cultivated topsoil (Ap). Brownish-black (10YR 3/2) silt loam with fine flint sand and 15% medium flint gravel. 2 fragments cf *Quercus* sp, 2 fragments Maloideae.
0.17–0.45 m. Clay alluvium with some colluvium (D). Brownish-black (10YR 3/2) clay loam mottled and gleyed. 10% medium flint gravel, 20% small rounded chalk pieces. 10 grains *Triticum* cf *aestivum,* 8 grains *Triticum* sp, 1 grain cf *Hordeum* sp, 7 grains indeterminate cereal, hazelnut shell fragments, 1 seed *Vicia/Larythus*, 1 seed *Galium aparine*, 23 fragments *Quercus* sp, 7 fragments *Corylus avellana*, 14 fragments *Corylus/Alnus*, 6 fragments Maloideae, 1 fragment *Prunus* sp, 1 fragment cf *Fraxinus excelsior.*
0.45–0.58 m. Gravel band (?E). Brown (10YR 4/4) mottled and gleyed. Clay loam with 70% stones (40% flint, 30% small rounded chalk). 3 grains *Hordeum* sp, 5 fragments cf *Quercus* sp, 2 fragments Maloideae, 2 fragments cf *Prunus* sp.
0.58–0.81 m. Clay (D). Greyish-yellow (10YR 4/2) clay mottled and heavily iron-stained on top, manganese stained and gleyed below. 2% small chalk pieces in top, stone-free below. 2 grains *Triticum* sp, 1 grain *Hordeum* sp, 4 fragments Maloideae, 2 fragments *Quercus* sp, 1 fragment *Fraxinus excelsior.*
0.81–0.92 m. Gravel containing burnt flint (G, J). Dark greyish-yellow (2.5Y 5/2) chalky gravel. 30% burnt flint and 30% rounded flint gravel. Relates to, or derived from, the Bronze Age burnt mound. A middle Bronze Age base fragment was found in this layer (L13A) nearby in the cutting. 1 grain *Triticum* sp, 1 grain *Hordeum* sp, 2 fragments *Quercus* sp, 5 fragments Maloideae or cf Maloideae, 1 fragment cf *Betula* sp, 1 fragment *Corylus/Alnus.*
0.92–1.14 m. Sandy clay (L). Yellowish-brown (2.5Y 5/3) sandy, iron-stained in places. 10% small rounded chalk pieces. Bronze Age or earlier. 1 fragment cf *Quercus* sp, 2 fragments *Corylus/Alnus*, 1 fragment cf Maloideae, 1 fragment *Prunus* sp, 3 fragments cf Salicaceae.
1.14+ m. Coombe Rock (P) with 40% rounded flint gravel, iron-stained.

In addition spot samples were also analysed:

Samples 12 and 13. A thin palaeosol (N). Very dark grey (7.5YR 3/1) horizon from below the Bronze Age burnt mound itself. 63 fragments Maloideae, 31 fragments *Prunus* sp, single fragments of *Corylus avellana, Fraxinus excelsior, Quercus* sp, *Rhamnus catharticus*, Salicaceae.

Sample 14. The fill of ditch EWM84 F7, briefly described above, with (?redeposited) medieval finds which may relate to the operation of the water meadows. 16 fragments *Quercus* sp, 2 fragments *Corylus avellana*, 1 fragment *Corylus/Alnus*, 5 fragments *Prunus* sp, 2 fragments Maloideae, 1 fragment cf *Acer campestre*, 1 fragment Salicaceae.

The results of molluscan analysis are shown in Figure 5.15 and Table 5.7. The most striking aspect of the assemblage is that the proportion of freshwater species in this column is surprisingly small, *c* 15% at the base, never more than 20% and down to 10% above 0.45 m. Furthermore, there is only limited evidence among the freshwater species for those clearly associated with *moving* water. In the bottom two samples (Unit L), below a layer of calcined flints corresponding to the burnt mound, the moving water group is represented only by single shells of *Bithynia tentaculata* and *Physa fontinalis*, and the ditch group by single shells of *Gyraulus albus* and *Ancylus fluviatalis*. More abundant were *Lymnaea truncatula* and *Lymnaea peregra* which do not demand moving water. At no point in the column is there a pronounced peak of moving water species such as would clearly indicate the base of the watercourse. Of particular interest among the freshwater assemblage is *Myxas glutinosa*, which was present until at least the Romano-British period (Unit D). Today it is a rare and endangered species found in Snowdonia and one site on the Thames, but it was once much more extensively distributed (Kerney 1999, 57).

The terrestrial assemblage is in dramatic contrast to the restricted assemblages from the broadly contemporary colluvial deposits on the other sites; it is richer and more diverse, particularly below *c* 0.58 m. The assemblage as a whole consists of shade-loving species, particularly *Carychium tridentatum, Discus rotundatus, Aegopinella nitidula* and *Oxychilus cellarius*, but no species predominates and the assemblage is most notable in terms of its variety. Of special note is the presence, again until Romano-British times, of *Vertigo pusilla* which today is restricted to a patchy relict distribution (Kerney 1999, 91) and does not occur south of Bristol though it was once more widespread. Also present is *Vertigo moulinsiana*, a species found close to rivers in calcareous areas which has declined in the later Holocene and is not now recorded in this catchment but occurs within a few miles (Drake 1999). Marsh species also occur in small numbers, eg *Succinea/Oxyloma, Vertigo antivertigo* and *Zonitoides nitidus*. There were two pronounced horizons with fewer shade-loving species, both corresponding to layers of gravel. The lower is at 0.81–0.92 m and comprised calcined flint associated with the burnt mound (Unit G). Here the decline in the proportion of shade-loving species is mirrored by an increase in species of catholic ecological preferences particularly Limacidae and *Trichia hispida*. This seems to reflect a genuine

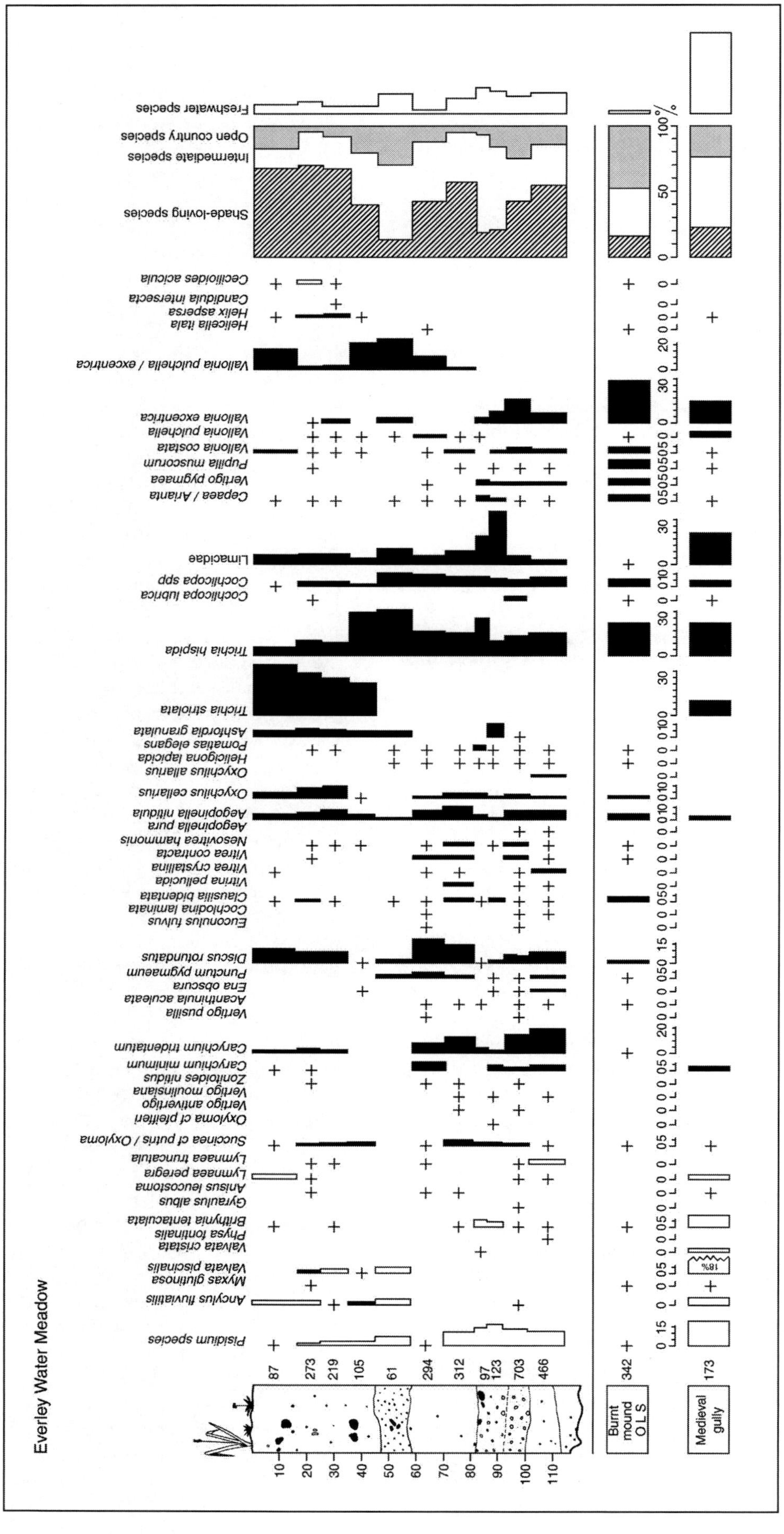

Fig 5.15 Everley Water Meadow. Mollusc Column 2.

Table 5.7 Everley Water Meadow: table of molluscs from column 2

Totals exclude *C acicula*. Species diversity is calculated on the terrestrial assemblage which is assumed to be autochthonous
+ = Taxa reported from winterbournes with intermittent flow • = Taxa reported from winterbournes with perennial flow

Sample	*1*	*2*	*3*	*4*	*5*	*6*	*7*	*8*	*9*	*10*	*11*	*12*	*13*	*14*
Context/feature												*burnt mound*		*gully*
Depth (cm)	*101–114*	*92–101*	*86–92*	*81–86*	*70–81*	*58–70*	*45–58*	*35–45*	*25–35*	*17–25*	*0–17*	*spot ols*	*spot*	*spot*
Wt (g)	*1815*	*1688*	*2000*	*2000*	*1716*	*2000*	*2000*	*1916*	*2000*	*2000*	*2000*	*6200*	*2000*	*2000*
Pomatias elegans (Müller)	5	5	1	3	1	+	+	–	+	+	–	+	–	–
Carychium minimum (Müller)	21	13	3	–	–	19	–	–	–	2	1	–	–	2
Carychium tridentatum (Risso)	67	84	2	3	33	20	–	–	5	9	2	2	+	–
Succinea cf *putris*/*Oxyloma*	3	10	2	2	11	1	–	3	5	5	1	3	–	–
Oxyloma cf *pfeifferi* (Rossmässler).	–	–	1	–	–	–	–	–	–	–	–	–	–	–
Cochlicopa lubrica (Müller)	–	19	–	–	–	–	–	–	–	1	–	1	–	1
Cochlicopa spp	29	29	6	6	23	25	5	2	8	9	1	20	–	3
Vertigo pusilla Müller	–	1	–	–	–	1	–	–	–	–	–	–	–	–
Vertigo antivertigo (Draparnaud)	–	2	–	–	1	–	–	–	–	–	–	–	–	–
Vertigo pygmaea (Draparnaud)	9	12	2	2	–	1	–	–	–	–	–	17	–	–
Vertigo moulinsiana (Dupuy)	1	–	1	–	1	–	–	–	–	–	–	–	–	–
Pupilla muscorum (Linnaeus)	3	7	1	–	1	–	–	–	–	1	–	22	–	1
Vallonia costata (Müller)	12	24	2	–	5	3	–	1	2	3	2	12	–	1
Vallonia pulchella (Müller)	–	–	–	–	4	1	1	1	1	2	–	1	–	3
Vallonia excentrica Sterki	30	108	11	3	–	–	2	–	6	1	–	106	1	11
Vallonia pulchella/*excentrica*	–	–	–	–	5	29	12	20	6	4	12	–	–	–
Acanthinula aculeata (Müller)	5	3	–	1	1	2	–	–	–	–	–	1	–	–
Ena obscura (Müller)	6	9	2	–	–	–	–	1	–	–	–	–	–	–
Punctum pygmaeum (Draparnaud)	6	7	1	–	6	11	1	–	–	–	–	3	–	–
Discus rotundatus (Müller)	30	38	2	1	36	50	2	+	17	21	8	8	–	–
Vitrina pellucida (Müller)	1	1	–	–	7	–	–	–	–	–	–	–	–	–
Vitrea crystallina (Müller)	13	3	–	–	2	4	–	–	–	–	1	–	–	–
Vitrea contracta (Westerlund)	2	11	–	–	6	6	–	–	–	1	–	3	–	–
Nesovitrea hammonis (Ström)	4	11	1	–	6	2	–	1	2	1	–	2	–	–
Aegopinella pura (Alder)	3	2	–	–	–	–	–	–	–	–	–	–	–	–
Aegopinella nitidula (Draparnaud)	28	40	2	3	27	21	1	4	14	13	3	15	1	2
Oxychilus cellarius (Müller)	9	20	2	2	12	5	–	1	19	19	3	7	–	–
Oxychilus allairus (Miller)	9	–	–	–	–	–	–	–	–	–	–	–	–	–
Zonitoides nitidus (Müller)	–	4	–	–	4	1	–	–	–	1	–	–	–	–
Limacidae	17	44	41	17	28	21	6	5	17	21	6	4	–	13
Euconulus fulvus (Müller)	–	1	–	–	–	1	–	–	–	–	–	–	–	–
Cecilioides acicula (Müller)	–	–	–	–	–	–	–	+	1	8	1	1	–	–
Cochlodina laminata (Montagu)	3	1	–	–	–	1	–	–	–	–	–	–	–	–
Clausilia bidentata (Ström)	5	4	3	1	7	2	+	–	3	4	+	12	–	–
Candidula intersecta (Poiret)	–	–	–	–	–	–	–	–	1	–	–	–	–	–
Helicella itala (Linnaeus)	–	–	–	–	–	4	–	–	–	–	–	2	–	–
Ashfordia granulata (Alder)	–	–	1	8	–	–	2	4	11	14	3	–	–	–
cf *Trichia striolata* (C Pfeiffer)	–	–	–	–	–	–	–	24	58	81	31	–	–	11
Trichia hispida (Linnaeus)	66	89	11	22	47	51	18	32	20	29	6	80	–	17
Helicigona lapicida (Linnaeus)	+	+	+	1	+	+	+	–	–	–	–	+	–	–
Cepaea/*Arianta* spp	2	5	3	3	2	4	1	–	2	1	1	14	–	1
Helix aspersa (Müller)	–	–	–	–	–	–	–	1	7	6	+	–	–	1
Land mollusc Taxa	27	29	22	16	23	24	10	13	18	21	14	20	2	12
Land mollusc total	**389**	**607**	**101**	**78**	**276**	**286**	**51**	**100**	**204**	**249**	**81**	**335**	**2**	**67**
Theodoxus fluviatilis (Linnaeus)	–	–	–	–	–	–	–	–	–	–	–	–	–	1
+ *Valvata cristata* Müller	–	–	–	1	–	–	–	–	–	–	–	–	–	4
• *Valvata piscinalis* (Müller)	–	–	–	–	–	–	3	1	5	4	–	–	–	32
Bithynia tentaculata (Linnaeus)	1	+	3	4	2	–	–	–	1	–	1	3	–	15
• + *Physa fontinalis* (Linnaeus)	1	–	–	–	–	–	–	–	–	–	–	–	–	–
+ *Lymnaea truncatula* (Müller)	17	8	–	–	–	2	–	–	1	2	–	–	–	–
+ *Lymnaea peregra* (Müller)	6	3	–	–	–	–	–	–	–	3	3	–	–	5
Myxas glutinosa (Müller)	–	–	–	–	–	–	–	–	–	1	–	1	–	1
+ *Anisus leucostoma* (Millet)	–	–	–	–	1	1	–	–	–	1	–	–	–	2
+ *Gyraulus albus* (Müller)	–	1	–	–	–	–	–	–	–	–	–	–	–	–
• + *Ancylus fluviatalis* Müller	–	1	–	–	–	–	2	2	3	7	2	–	–	9
Pisidium (valves) ÷2	49	83	19	14	33	3	4	2	5	6	+	3	–	33
Freshwater taxa	5	5	2	3	3	3	3	3	5	7	3	3	0	9
Freshwater totals	**74**	**96**	**22**	**19**	**68**	**6**	**9**	**5**	**15**	**24**	**6**	**7**	**0**	**102**
Shannon Index (*H'*)	2.73	2.64	2.27	2.25	2.61	2.57	1.88	1.97	2.42	2.35	2.01	2.20	0.69	2.04
Brillouin Index (HB)	2.60	2.55	2.00	1.98	2.47	2.43	1.64	1.79	2.27	2.21	1.79	2.09	0.35	1.81
Δ_2	0.91	0.90	0.80	0.85	0.91	0.90	0.80	0.81	0.87	0.85	0.80	0.82	0.50	0.84
Δ_4	10.23	9.22	4.25	6.02	9.91	9.16	4.43	4.45	7.10	5.81	4.19	4.77	0	5.72
Totals	**463**	**703**	**123**	**97**	**312**	**292**	**60**	**105**	**219**	**273**	**87**	**342**	**2**	**169**
Magnetic susceptibility ($\times10^{-8}$ SI/kg)	3	1	2	2	7	6	10	13	8	8	8	34	31	8

ecological change, rather than a taphonomic artefact of changed sedimentary conditions (Harris 1983). The spot sample taken from a shallow palaeosol below the burnt mound (Unit N) produced a mollusc assemblage broadly matching that from 0.18–1.01 m in sample column 2 (Fig 5.15). This correspondence also strengthens the view that the layer in sample column 2 with fire-cracked flints was indeed contemporary with the burnt mound, rather than derived from it at a later date, like Unit F in the south area. The palaeosol contains a smaller number of freshwater molluscs and more evidence of open-country species which account for 48% with only 15% shade-loving species. The predominant species is *Vallonia excentrica* which generally achieves abundance in grazed grassland (Evans 1993). The assemblage is comparable to taxocenes 1 and 6 of Evans *et al* (1992), which appear to derive from meadow or pasture subject to only occasional winter floods. It is certainly at the drier end of the spectrum of floodplain faunas, as the presence of *Pupilla muscorum* suggests (Davies 1998) and lacking in those species which Robinson (1988) found to be characteristic of regularly flooded pastures in the upper Thames catchment. Clearly there was an episode of open conditions immediately preceding, and at the time of, the burnt mound. Following this the shade-loving species again increase.

The assemblage at 0.58–0.81 m is from an alluvial clay and is likely to be mainly autochtonous. Faunas of similar composition are associated with alder and willow carrs along the banks of the river Test in Hampshire (Davies *et al* 1996).

The second layer of chalk fragments and gravel (between 0.45 and 0.58 m, Unit E) corresponds to a phase of Romano-British colluviation. It appears to mark a hiatus at which a number of changes occur, perhaps relating to an erosion episode. There are fewer molluscs but slightly more *Pisidium, Ancylus fluviatalis* and *Valvata piscinalis*, indicating a greater fluvial component. Shade-loving species decline and a number of them never become abundant again. In the gravel layer they are replaced by species of more catholic ecological preferences. The occurrence of *Helix aspersa* indicates that the sediments above 0.45 m are Romano-British or later.

Following this, some shade-loving species again increase (Unit D) but this time they are entirely dominated by a single species, cf *Trichia striolata*. This identification is given as probable because there is some uncertainly as to whether a particularly striated form of *Trichia* found in some southern British riverine sequences is *Trichia striolata* or a striated variant of *Trichia hispida* (M Robinson pers comm referring to Wallingford, and J G Evans pers comm on Runnymede). Its presence here is paralleled in the riverside sequence at Runnymede Bridge, Surrey (Evans 1980). *Trichia striolata* is abundant today in the fen environments of the Hampshire Test (Davies *et al* 1996). Also noteworthy, though less abundant, is *Ashfordia granulata*, which is also present in the underlying deposits. Today it is a species found along river banks and other damp herbage (Kerney 1999, 190); it occurs in carr and fen environments in the Test Valley (Davies *et al* 1996) but is rarely found subfossil (Evans 1972, 178).

The sediments in Unit D between 0.17 and 0.45 m contained small chalk pieces, demonstrating a significant colluvial component. It is thus noteworthy that the molluscs from this layer show little evidence of the restricted range of open-country species which we have seen in these deposits in Coombe Bottom and Stepleton lynchet. Presumably the assemblages from more favourable environments in the valley centre have greatly diluted the faunas from less favourable, arable environments upslope from which a proportion of these sediments were derived. They also contain an alluvial component and the assemblages have similarities with Taxocene 1 (Evans *et al* 1992), which appears to indicate meadow/pasture although in this case there is also evidence of shade, probably along the stream banks.

Creation of the water meadows from the eighteenth century presumably accounts for the continued presence of some freshwater species after channelling of the stream, but there is no clear species change that we can associate with the establishment of lush meadows, although evidence for this may well have been destroyed by the recent cultivation of the surface horizons (Unit Ap). A spot sample (14) from ditch EWM84 F7 east of the palaeochannel clearly relates to the upper part of the sample column 2 sequence, as the presence of cf *Trichia striolata* shows. This contained a much larger proportion of moving water species than any other sample; the ditch probably formed part of the irrigation system of the water meadows.

Sample column 3

The location of this column in Area 5 is shown in Figure 5.8, and the results are presented in Tables 5.8–9. Because the mollusc numbers are low, the results are not presented graphically. Phil Austin's identifications of the charcoal from each sample are appended, excluding the indeterminate fragments. The stratigraphy sampled is summarised as follows:

0–0.14 m. Cultivated topsoil.
0–24–0.43 m. Alluvium with a few rounded small chalk pieces.
0.43–0.64 m. Alluvium with small rounded chalk pieces. 13 fragments *Quercus* sp, 2 fragments *Corylus avellana*.
0.64–1.00 m. Chalky colluvium. 7 fragments *Quercus* sp, 2 fragments Maloideae, 2 fragments *Prunus* sp.
1.00–1.24 m. Sand with flint gravel, some fire-cracked.
1.00–1.24 m+. Coombe Deposits.

In addition spot samples were taken as shown in Figure 5.8:

Spot sample 24, a lens of chalk pieces and sand in possible channel. 3 fragments *Quercus* sp, 2 fragments *Prunus* sp, 2 fragments *Maloideae*.

Spot sample 25, sandy silt with charcoal, possible channel.
Spot sample 26, clay alluvium with some chalk pieces.

Only one sample in the series, spot sample 24, contains a substantial proportion of freshwater species (57%). This includes moving-water species *Valvata piscinalis* and *Bithynia tentaculata*, the catholic species *Lymnaea peregra* and the slum species *Lymnaea truncatula*. Thus the molluscs confirm the field impression that this lens is probably a stream-bed deposit. As regards the rest of the sequence, freshwater species nowhere account for more than 8% over and above the terrestrial total.

The terrestrial assemblage at the base of sample column 3 does not resemble the basically shade-loving assemblage in the lower half of sample column 2. However, the basal sample in sample column 3 probably corresponds to the sample column 2 sample at *c* 0.81–0.92 m since both contain burnt flints and contain comparable molluscan assemblages. That in sample column 3 comprises 30% shade-loving species, only one open-country species (*Vallonia excentrica*) and a predominance of species of catholic ecological preferences. The assemblages from the overlying chalky colluvium does not find a match in sample column 2 and almost certainly relates to the inferred erosion hiatus in that column at *c* 0.58 m. The assemblage contains very few shade-loving species and is entirely dominated by *Trichia hispida*, *Vallonia excentrica*, the Limacidae and *Vallonia costata*; an assemblage that very closely matches that from chalky, presumably arable-derived, colluvium of the Stepleton lynchet, Coombe Bottom, etc. The presence of *Helix aspersa* in this colluvium points to a Romano-British or later date.

Spot sample 24, the probable channel deposit, and the overlying sediments in the main column, produced assemblages in which cf *Trichia striolata* is overwhelmingly predominant, thus suggesting that these layers relate to the sediments above *c* 0.45 m in sample column 2. They include a smaller, though still significant proportion, of shade-loving species. Although these upper layers are basically alluvium, they contain some small rounded chalk pieces, reflecting a colluvial component the proportion of which decreases with distance from the valley side. The molluscs tell a similar story with a much larger proportion of those species already identified as typical of colluvial assemblages than in sample column 2.

Sample column 4

This column of four samples (Tables 5.8–9) was collected in Area 1 in 1983 and water-sieved in Edinburgh. Many of the samples contained only a few shells but the lowest samples from Units L and K (Fig 5.12: L18, L17) in the base of the sequence contained more useful numbers and provide some additional information. The two lowest samples contain *Trochoidea geyeri* which has been extinct since the late glacial; all other taxa present are also found in the late glacial. Above these is a sample with some post-glacial taxa. The sample from Unit K (L18) is rich in post-glacial Mollusca with a significant number of woodland taxa and may correspond to the samples below 0.92 m in sample column 2. This column indicates the survival of late-glacial chalk meltwater deposits in the base of the channel sequence.

Modern stream samples

To provide comparanda for the mollusc assemblages from the palaeochannels two samples were collected from the modern stream sediments. Sample 16 was sediment from the stream edge close to the excavation, sample 17 from the north edge of the water meadows near the outlet of Ranston Lake. The faunas are listed in Table 5.9; they are much richer in molluscs and of sharply contrasting character when compared to the earlier assemblages. There is a total of 20 freshwater taxa as compared to 11 from the pre-eighteenth-century contexts. Freshwater molluscs dominate both modern samples. Land Mollusca, which predominate in all the prehistoric samples, comprise only 2.7% of the combined land and freshwater total in sample 16, and 8% in sample 17. The logical inference to draw from this is that the creation of the water meadows and the landscape lakes and ponds which lie upstream in Shroton Park and beyond have created a very different stream regime to that which existed before the post-medieval period.

Everley Water Meadow conclusions

Martin Bell and R W Smith

The date of Unit L remains rather unclear. The mollusc samples from the base of this unit in sample column 4 turned out to be late glacial. Elsewhere the unit was thicker and rich in charcoal, especially at its surface (L17a–b). Having excavated this unit, RWS's (pers comm) view was that this unit could not all be late glacial. It may be that the sediments sampled in sample column 4 are a separate earlier deposit or that they include a derived late-glacial fauna. If that is accepted then the presence of much charcoal could relate to either natural fires or to human activity some time between the Mesolithic and the Bronze Age. Extensive Mesolithic flint scatters are known nearby to the east on the chalk escarpment at Iwerne Minster (Summers 1941) and 1 km south in the Iwerne valley at Stourpaine (Palmer 1977, 152). Some of the flintwork from the valley is likely to be of Neolithic date although it is uncertain whether any is contemporary with the causewayed enclosure complex. It is possible that, as RWS (1983) suggested, the charcoal-rich surface of Unit L points to clearance and valley floor activity at around this time.

The burnt mound excavated in Areas 2 and 3 was severely truncated, but enough of its base remained to show that it belonged to the middle Bronze Age.

Table 5.8 Everley Water Meadow: table of terrestrial molluscs from columns 3 and 4, and modern stream samples 16 and 17

All totals exclude *C acicula*. Species diversity is calculated on the terrestrial assemblage which is assumed to be autochthonous

	Column 3									*Column 4*				*Mod stream*	
Sample	*25*	*26*	*18*	*19*	*20*	*24*	*21*	*22*	*23*	*K*	*L*	*L*	*L*	*16*	*17*
Depth (cm)	*spot*	*spot*	*106–124*	*85–100*	*64–85*	*spot*	*43–64*	*24–43*	*0–24*		*top 10*	*Mid 10*	*Bot 10*		
Wt (g)	*860*	*2000*	*2000*	*2000*	*2000*	*1800*	*2000*	*1750*	*2000*					*732*	*1482*
Pomatias elegans (Müller)	1	+	2	+	2	–	4	1	+	–	–	–	–	–	1
Carychium tridentatum (Risso)	–	–	2	–	–	–	1	2	1	4	–	–	–	cf 6	–
Carychium sp	–	–	–	–	–	–	–	–	–	–	–	–	–	–	1
Succinea cf *putris/Oxyloma*	–	–	2	2	1	–	1	3	–	8	4	1	10	8	1
Cochlicopa lubrica (Müller)	–	–	–	1	–	–	2	–	–	–	–	–	–	–	–
Cochlicopa spp	1	+	6	3	2	2	4	2	2	6	–	–	–	–	1
Columella columella (Martens)	–	–	–	–	–	–	–	–	–	1	1	1	1	–	–
Vertigo pusilla Müller	–	–	–	–	–	–	–	–	–	1	–	–	–	–	–
Vertigo antivertigo (Draparnaud)	–	–	–	–	–	–	–	–	–	4	4	–	–	–	–
Vertigo pygmaea (Draparnaud)	–	–	–	2	–	1	–	–	1	–	–	–	–	–	–
Vertigo spp	–	–	1	–	–	–	–	–	–	–	–	–	–	–	–
Pupilla muscorum (Linnaeus)	–	–	–	–	–	–	–	–	–	+	4	15	6	1	–
Vallonia costata (Müller)	–	–	1	4	2	1	5	2	15	1	3	3	3	–	–
Vallonia pulchella (Müller)	–	–	–	2	1	4	4	2	4	–	3	5	3	–	1
Vallonia excentrica Sterki	–	3	6	24	44	6	2	2	12	4	–	3	–	–	–
Vallonia spp	–	–	–	–	–	–	22	13	–	–	–	2	–	–	1
Acanthinula aculeata (Müller)	–	–	–	–	–	–	–	–	–	–	–	–	–	–	1
Ena cf *obscura* (Müller)	–	–	–	–	–	–	–	–	–	–	–	–	–	1	–
Punctum pygmaeum (Draparnaud)	–	–	–	–	–	–	–	–	–	+	+	1	–	–	–
Discus rotundatus (Müller)	1	+	+	–	+	+	–	15	8	+	–	–	–	2	12
Vitrina pellucida (Müller)	–	–	–	–	–	–	–	–	–	1	1	–	–	–	–
Vitrea crystallina (Müller)	–	–	1	–	–	–	–	2	–	–	–	–	–	2	–
Vitrea contracta (Westerlund)	–	–	–	–	–	–	–	–	–	4	–	–	–	2	–
Vitrea spp	–	–	–	–	–	–	–	–	–	–	+	–	–	–	1
Nesovitrea hammonis (Ström)	–	–	2	–	–	1	2	2	1	1	–	–	–	1	1
Aegopinella nitidula (Draparnaud)	–	–	1	–	1	1	–	2	2	22	2	–	–	cf 4	4
Oxychilus cellarius (Müller)	–	–	4	–	–	1	3	5	2	–	–	–	–	–	–
Aegopinella/Oxychilus sp	–	–	–	–	–	–	–	–	–	–	–	–	–	–	2
Zonitoides nitidus (Müller)	–	–	–	–	1	–	–	–	–	4	–	–	–	–	–
Limacidae	1	–	2	3	7	6	7	3	5	5	2	1	1	3	2
Euconulus fulvus (Müller)	–	–	–	–	–	–	–	–	–	1	–	–	–	–	–
Cecilioides acicula (Müller)	–	–	–	1	–	1	2	–	1	–	–	–	–	–	1
Cochlodina laminata (Montagu)	–	–	–	–	+	–	–	–	–	–	–	–	–	–	–
Clausilia bidentata (Ström)	–	–	+	–	+	–	1	+	2	13	–	–	–	–	–
Clausiliidae	–	–	–	–	–	–	–	–	–	–	–	–	–	1	1
Candidula intersecta (Poiret)	–	–	–	–	–	–	–	–	–	–	–	–	–	3	–
Cernuella virgata (da Costa)	–	–	–	–	–	–	–	–	–	–	–	–	–	+	–
Helicella itala (Linnaeus)	–	–	–	–	1	–	+	–	–	–	–	–	–	1	–
Trochoidea geyeri (Soós)	–	–	–	–	–	–	–	–	–	4	7	9	7	–	–
Helicellids	–	–	–	–	–	–	–	–	11	–	–	–	–	–	–
Ashfordia granulata (Alder)	–	–	8	–	–	4	–	1	–	–	–	–	–	1	2
cf *Trichia striolata* (C Pfeiffer)	–	–	–	1	2	22	59	26	13	–	–	–	–	–	–
Trichia hispida (Linnaeus)	3	5	24	33	33	4	9	2	7	–	–	–	–	8	11
Helicigona lapicida (Linnaeus)	–	–	+	–	+	–	–	–	–	–	–	–	–	–	–
Cepaea/Arianta spp	–	–	5	1	+	–	–	1	–	2	–	–	–	1	1
Helix aspersa (Müller)	+	+	–	3	+	+	1	+	1	–	–	–	–	–	1
Land taxa	6	5	15	11	12	12	14	17	16	21	11	10	8	16	15
Land mollusc totals	**7**	**8**	**67**	**79**	**97**	**53**	**127**	**86**	**88**	**86**	**31**	**32**	**32**	**45**	**44**
Shannon Index (*H'*)	1.61	0.66	2.19	1.67	1.47	1.94	1.88	2.32	2.40						
Brillouin Index (HB)	0.96	0.50	1.91	1.49	1.32	1.67	1.72	2.05	2.14						
Δ_2	0.80	0.47	0.83	0.72	0.67	0.78	0.75	0.85	0.89						
Δ_4	0	1.15	5.23	2.73	2.11	3.92	3.04	6.18	8.92						
Magnetic susceptibility ($\times 10^{-8}$ SI/kg)	9	5	6	12	6	6	6	8	10	–	–	–	–	–	–

Table 5.9 Everley Water Meadow: table of aquatic molluscs from columns 3 and 4, and modern stream samples 16 and 17

All totals exclude *C acicula*
+ = Taxa reported from winterbournes with intermittent flow • = Taxa reported from winterbournes with perennial flow

Column	*Column 3*									*Column 4*				*Mod stream*	
Sample	*25*	*26*	*18*	*19*	*20*	*24*	*21*	*22*	*23*	*K*	*L*	*L*	*L*	*16*	*17*
Depth (cm)															
spot	*spot*	*106–124*	*85–100*	*64–85*	*spot*	*43–64*	*24–43*	*0–24*		*top 10*	*Mid 10*	*Bot 10*			
Wt (g)	*860*	*2000*	*2000*	*2000*	*2000*	*1800*	*2000*	*1750*	*2000*					*732*	*1482*
Theodoxus fluviatilis (Linnaeus)	–	–	–	–	–	–	–	1	+	–	–	–	–	–	–
+ *Valvata cristata* Müller	–	–	–	1	–	–	–	–	–	–	–	–	–	48	14
• *Valvata piscinalis* (Müller)	–	1	–	3	1	6	5	1	1	–	–	–	–	12	3
Potamopyrgus antipodarum (Gray)	–	–	–	–	–	–	–	–	–	–	–	–	–	2	25
Bithynia tentaculata (Linnaeus)	+	13	1	–	1	2	1	–	+	–	–	–	–	10	3
+ *Lymnaea truncatula* (Müller)	–	–	–	–	–	1	–	1	1	5	1	4	1	–	–
Lymnaea cf *palustris* (Müller)	–	–	–	–	–	–	–	–	–	–	–	–	–	6	–
Lymnaea cf *truncatula* (Linnaeus)	–	–	–	–	–	–	–	–	–	–	–	–	–	1	–
+ *Lymnaea peregra* (Müller)	–	1	1	–	1	1	–	1	1	6	–	–	–	51	–
Lymnaea cf *peregra* (Müller)	–	–	–	–	–	–	–	–	–	–	–	–	–	14	12
Lymnaea sp	–	–	–	–	–	–	–	–	–	–	–	–	–	–	1
Physa fontinalis (Linnaeus)	–	–	–	–	–	–	–	–	–	–	–	–	–	110	14
Planorbis planorbis (Linnaeus)	–	–	–	–	–	–	–	–	–	–	–	–	–	26	11
Planorbis carinatus Müller	–	–	–	–	–	–	+	–	–	–	–	–	–	+	–
Anisus leucostoma (Millet)	–	–	–	–	–	–	–	–	–	3	2	2	–	–	5
Anisus vortex (Linnaeus)	–	–	–	–	–	–	–	–	–	–	–	–	–	196	110
Bathyomphalus contortus (Linnaeus)	–	–	–	–	–	–	–	–	–	–	–	–	–	8	15
Gyraulus albus (Müller)	–	–	–	–	–	–	–	–	–	–	–	–	–	127	44
Armiger crista (Linnaeus)	–	–	–	–	–	–	–	–	–	–	–	–	–	4	–
Hippeutis complanatus (Linnaeus)	–	–	–	–	–	–	–	–	–	–	–	–	–	20	3
Planorbis sp	–	–	–	–	–	–	–	–	–	–	–	–	–	34	12
• + *Ancylus fluviatalis* Müller	–	–	–	–	–	–	2	–	1	2	4	–	–	5	19
Sphaerium corneum (Linnaeus)	–	–	–	–	–	–	–	–	–	–	–	–	–	1	–
Pisidium henslowanum (Sheppard)	–	–	–	–	–	–	–	–	–	–	–	–	–	3	–
Pisidium pulchellum Jenyns	–	–	–	–	–	–	–	–	–	–	–	–	–	5	–
Pisidium/Sphaerium (valves) ÷2	–	1	1	2	2	20	2	1	2	8	5	7	–	42	49
Pisidium sp (valves) ÷2	–	–	–	–	–	–	–	–	–	–	–	–	–	448	116
Mytlius edulis	+	–	–	–	–	–	–	–	–	–	–	–	–	–	–
Freshwater taxa	0	4	3	3	4	5	4	5	5	5	4	3	1	19	13
Freshwater totals	**0**	**16**	**3**	**6**	**5**	**30**	**10**	**5**	**5**	**20**	**10**	**10**	**1**	**1117**	**456**

The functions of burnt mounds are as yet imperfectly understood, but they are particularly common in the Bronze Age (Bradley 1978, 83) and are frequently associated with river banks and settlement. Examples have now been recorded, or are inferred, within almost all the classic Deverel-Rimbury settlements of Wessex from Shearplace Hill to South Lodge, both in Dorset. Pit F10 on the river bank a little further downstream in the south area may well have been contemporary, and the mound was almost certainly the source of the burnt flint incorporated in later deposits here. The socketed axe mould fragment and late Bronze Age sherds from gravels deposited or reworked in Roman or later times reflect activity for which no *in situ* evidence was recovered. The mould, of Syenite from Wales or the south-west, was probably used to cast Stogursey axes, the production of which spanned much of the late Bronze Age (see Needham, 10.1.4). The fragment and the sherds together hold out the possibility of late Bronze Age metalworking and settlement a little way upstream.

In prehistory the valley sediments were characterised predominantly by gravels with some sand bands and finer sediments. These deposits formed within channel-beds, and point bars of what may originally have been a braided channel system. The first evidence for significant overbank flooding, leading to the wider deposition of alluvium, is in the Romano-British and medieval periods. By this time the landscape was substantially cleared and the slopes were extensively cultivated. Significant amounts of colluvium have been shown to have reached the valley floor in the Romano-British period where reworking took place, contributing sediment for deposition as alluvium. This supports the general model that alluvium deposition on river valleys floors followed widespread clearance and extensive cultivation (Shotton 1978; Limbrey 1983; Limbrey and Robinson 1988).

In the Romano-British period the area was cultivated, following levelling or erosion of the earlier burnt mound; manuring took place at a time when some alluviation was occurring. Further cultivation occurred in the medieval period prior to the post-medieval creation of the water meadows, which comparison of the modern and palaeochannel stream faunas indicates created major change in the character of the river environment. It is striking what a small proportion of freshwater taxa, and especially the moving water group, is present in the pre-eighteenth-century channel deposits. The project sectioned the whole of the lowest part of the valley without locating (or at least sampling) ancient stream deposits which are as rich in freshwater shells as the present stream. The prehistoric stream cannot have occupied the modern course because that lies slightly upslope and we have shown that it was an artificial post-medieval cut through Romano-British and medieval colluvial deposits. This must lead us to question whether the prehistoric to pre-eighteenth-century channels did actually carry year-round moving water similar to the modern stream.

Because of the ecological interest which attaches to chalkland streams there are a number of studies which compare the present-day mollusc faunas of perennial and intermittent sections of winterbourne chalk streams. Lists comparing the mollusc taxa in the two sections have been published for the South Winterbourne in Dorset (Casey and Ladle 1976) and for the Winterbourne, a tributary of the Lambourne in Berkshire (Wright *et al* 1984). These studies provide the basis of the annotations in Tables 5.7 and 5.9, indicating those freshwater taxa found in streams of seasonal and perennial flow. Other studies of the molluscan ecology of winterbournes which have been useful for comparison are Berrie and Wright (1984) and Ladle and Bass (1981). The intermittent sections of these streams have a restricted range of taxa, usually fewer than 10. This compares with 22 freshwater taxa recorded in the present Iwerne stream and 11 taxa recorded in pre-eighteenth-century contexts at Everley Water Meadow. Of these, six taxa (marked by a '+' in Tables 5.7–9) have been recorded from the seasonal sections of winterbournes. Two of the taxa represented by several individuals, *Bithynia tentaculata* and *Valvata piscinalis*, are not recorded from sections of intermittent flow. Two (*Ancylus fluviatilis* and *Physa fontinalis*), which are found in intermittent streams in Dorset, are confined to those sections of the Berkshire Winterbourne with perennial flow (Wright *et al* 1984). Such contrasts in assemblage composition are perhaps explicable in terms of the volume and seasonality of flow in specific winterbournes. It is unfortunate that the fragmentary condition of the *Pisidium* species, and limited time, have prevented their identification, since in the Berkshire Winterbourne study there were different *Pisidium* species in stretches of seasonal and perennial flow (Wright *et al* 1984). The available evidence does, however, show that the prehistoric and early historic Iwerne had an impoverished freshwater mollusc fauna similar to that of winterbourne streams. The presence of some taxa not recorded in streams of intermittent flow suggests that, in common with many chalk streams, while flow was probably greatly reduced in late summer to early winter (Ladle and Bass 1981, fig 2) the flow probably did not totally cease.

There is wider evidence that past variation in chalk streams would have exerted significant influence on the suitability of downland areas for settlement and agriculture. It has been shown that the headwaters of the Wiltshire Kennet near Avebury did not support a perennial stream in prehistory (Evans *et al* 1993). Conversely the South Winterbourne in Dorset, which today has seasonal flow, flowed perennially in the past (Evans and Rouse 1991a). Chalk streams on the South Downs flowed at a higher level and more continuously prior to pumping of the chalk aquifer from the nineteenth century (Bell 1981a, 56–9). Lockwood (1983) has calculated the hydrological effects of deciduous woodland on stream flow, concluding that in wildwood times streams would have had a more seasonal flow with much reduced discharge in summer. However, no marked change in the freshwater mollusc fauna of the Iwerne occurred as the landscape became more open in later prehistory, nor when it was subject to widespread cultivation from Romano-British times. The major change in the character of the river seems to have taken place much later, during the post-medieval period. So marked is the change in river regime suggested by the molluscs that we should consider that water management at this time may have involved a major diversion of the Iwerne headwaters. The geological map shows an extensive area of alluvium and gravel extending west of the Iwerne and north of Hambledon Hill (Fig 1.2). It seems possible that discharge from the headwaters once flowed west into the Stour and was diverted south in the eighteenth century, but this remains speculative and has not been investigated on the ground. Diversion of the river may have been associated both with the creation of water meadows and perhaps landscaping and emparkment up the valley with the making of a small lake at Shroton, all of which would further have enhanced freshwater mollusc diversity.

5.4 Wider comparisons and discussion

Michael J Allen and Martin Bell

Introduction and limitations

The study of Hambledon Hill in the Neolithic is restricted to the hilltop environment itself. There is little evidence for the presence of activity or environments contemporary with the causewayed enclosures and outworks in the surroundings (see Ch 2; RCHME 1996). Indeed, this state of palaeoenvironmental and archaeological evidence is comparable to many other studies of causewayed enclosures on the chalk of southern England. Examples include Maiden Castle, Dorset (Evans and Rouse 1991a; 1991b), Whitesheet Hill, Wiltshire (Rawlings 1994; Rawlings *et al* 2004), Offham, East Sussex (Drewett 1977), and Whitehawk, East Sussex (Russell and Rudling 1996, 51–56). The discussion below is divided into two principal sections: that relating to the Neolithic landscape, and that relating to the later Holocene landscape.

Neolithic

The Neolithic hilltop environment and land-use

Prior to analysis of the environmental evidence the general perception of Hambledon Hill in the Neolithic seems to have been of a cleared grassland landscape. The English Nature (1987) leaflet on the Nature Reserve describes the present grassland community as existing since the time of Neolithic activity. More widely, Barker and Webley (1978) have hypothesised that causewayed camps in general were situated in grassland areas. Certain types of Neolithic site were situated in cleared areas; in the earlier Neolithic long barrows and chambered tombs were usually within clearings of modest size and were frequently places with a history of earlier activity (Bradley 1993, 45) sometimes even represented by, for instance, artefacts or features of Mesolithic date (Allen 1995b; Allen and Gardiner 2002), or evidence of Neolithic activity and cultivation. Later in the Neolithic, henges and cursus monuments were situated in larger cleared areas. Since causewayed enclosures are the most prominent foci of activity by groups which, at Hambledon Hill, at least, were clearly engaged to a significant extent in animal husbandry and crop growing (Jones and Legge, 6.2), it was not an unreasonable deduction that the site would be in a cleared landscape.

That model is not, however, supported by the molluscan evidence. The difficulties of interpreting these ditch faunas have already been discussed at length. It is the case that molluscs will largely reflect conditions local to the point of sampling. The evidence suggests, however, that we cannot discount the entire suite of shade-loving taxa as being a result of local ditch micro-environments and rock-rubble faunas. It seems improbable that such a consistent group of mainly shade-loving Neolithic assemblages would derive from shaded ditches in an otherwise open landscape. The sheer taxonomic range, inclusion of uncommon species and proportions of shade-loving taxa indicate the presence of more extensive shaded habitats. Despite the ambiguity of the recovery methods of the shells, the Shannon and Brillouin indices are close, suggesting near 'total populations', and mirror the indices from shaded habitats at Maiden Castle (Evans and Rouse 1991b). These moderate diversity indices, and constant Δ (delta) indices, suggest the presence of a large, uniform, and moderately complex local habitat more in keeping with mature woodland than many other habitats. The causewayed enclosures seem to have been situated in a landscape where significant woodland remained and clearance was only partial. The environment seems to have become slightly more open in the 400-year life of the early Neolithic site. It is possible that clearance occurred in the later Neolithic, as suggested in Chapter 3 (3.3.2); no samples of that period have been analysed and, given the continued presence of shade-loving taxa in the early Bronze Age, we consider that the main clearance of this landscape is most likely to have taken place in the Beaker and early Bronze Age periods.

Proximity and character of woodland

Less certain is the proximity of the woodland to the enclosures. We have already suggested on the basis of modern analogue studies that most of the molluscs are likely to have reflected the environment within tens of metres of the ditches. While there is no certain evidence from the molluscs that the top of the hill was fully cleared in the Neolithic, the molluscan evidence would allow the possibility that some trees remained within the enclosures. We acknowledge, however, that the existence of the enclosures makes it likely that some clearance took place, but it may not have been much more than the area of the enclosures. Given the problems of interpreting these samples, it is possible that a partly cleared area extended in places to the top of the surrounding steep slopes which are within 200 m of the enclosures. If so, that would have created a partially cleared area of *c* 50 ha (*c* 80 acres), providing vistas over the surrounding lowland. We stress, however, that the evidence points to a wooded, or partly cleared, landscape not a bald grassy hilltop surrounded by woodland.

As regards the character of the tree cover, the molluscan evidence indicates mature deciduous woodland. The assemblage includes rupestral taxa (ie those living on firm dry surfaces such as rocks and trees, Evans 1972, 399). In this case the probable habitat is trees and fallen logs; there are other taxa which are found in moss and leaf litter. This picture accords with the charcoal evidence (see Austin *et al*, Ch 6), which points to a temporary clearing at an ecotone, including mixed and pure stands of woodland, open and woodland edge areas. All this implies a much more extensively wooded environment than the mixed scrub and long grassland that is today invading the steeper slopes of Hambledon Hill and many other chalklands as a result of reduced grazing pressure from domestic animals and rabbits.

Is this local setting similar to other causewayed enclosures in southern England?

Counter-intuitive as this interpretation of the causewayed enclosure environment may seem, it gains a strong measure of support from comparison with a growing body of environmental evidence from other causewayed enclosures (Evans and O'Connor 1998, 205). Extensive mollusc analyses, from more reliable contexts and better samples, at Maiden Castle (Evans *et al* 1988; Evans and Rouse 1991b), Windmill Hill (Fishpool 1999) and Whitesheet Hill (Allen 2004), all show that woodland survived at the time of the construction of the early Neolithic causewayed enclosures. Certain contexts at both Maiden Castle and Windmill Hill showed evidence of partial and local clearance, similar to that suggested by some of the interior features at Hambledon, but there is also evidence of Neolithic regeneration at Maiden Castle. Major clearance, as at Hambledon, does not take place until the time of Beaker and early Bronze Age activity. The intensively used Windmill Hill causewayed enclosure produced more evidence of clearance, but with the possibility of surviving scrub or woodland during some phases of activity (Evans 1972; Fishpool 1999). Investigations by K D Thomas (1982) of a series of Neolithic enclosures on the South Downs were, like Hambledon, largely based on ditch assemblages, but woodland taxa were predominant throughout. Knap Hill (Connah 1965) has similarly produced a woodland mollusc assemblage. Further afield, in East Anglia, the situation at the wetland edge causewayed enclosure of Etton (Pryor 1998) was rather different. The surrounding landscape seems to have been mainly grazed grassland. A quarter, to half, of the landscape was tree or shrub covered with the enclosure apparently being more open than its surroundings, and dung beetles indicate that the enclosure was used for domesticates.

A chalk hilltop complex, possibly similar to Hambledon but less fully studied, can be seen at Whitesheet Hill, where a Neolithic causewayed enclosure is possibly flanked by other Neolithic enclosures on adjacent spurs separated by a deep dry valley (in this case Swincombe Bottom). At the centre of the complex is an Iron Age hillfort. As in the Hambledon complex, the Neolithic environmental data contemporary with the causewayed enclosure is confined to hilltop features. The deep causewayed ditch (3.8 m) is dated to 3780–3380 cal BC (4800±70 BP, BM-2784; 4820±50 BP, BM-2785) and a number of shallow pits within the enclosure have produced similar dates. Poorly preserved land snail evidence from the coarse rubbly primary fills tentatively indicates some shade but local environs which were generally open, if not comprising long grass. The ditch recut associated with Mortlake-style Peterborough Ware produced snails (Allen 2004) and pollen (Scaife 2004) indicating tall ungrazed grassland and some shrubs (snails) of hazel, oak and *Prunus* (charcoal). However, in contrast to the picture at Hambledon, the local environment (pollen) was largely devoid of trees, but the presence of both *Pteridium* and *Dryopteris*-type spores may indicate that woodland existed prior to clearance (Scaife 2004).

While these comparisons clearly show some contrasts in the environmental settings of causewayed enclosures, what is striking is how many were situated in landscapes which were partly wooded. This must lead us to reject earlier notions that these were necessarily focal points in the agricultural economy of these communities. Increasingly, causewayed enclosures are regarded as peripheral to the main foci of Neolithic land-use (Bradley 1984b, 26–7; C Evans 1988; Gardiner 1991a; Thomas 1991, 32–8; Edmonds 1993, 104; Allen 1997a, 278–9). Indeed they need not have been physically in the centre of the Neolithic 'lived-in' landscape; social meeting points may be better located on the margins of several joining social or physical landscapes, in an ecotonal location, or at the social margin. In such areas Evans and O'Connor (1998, 205) suggest there may even have been deliberate maintenance of woodland through the Neolithic.

People and trees

It has been argued that the creation of concentric causewayed enclosures reflects the boundaries between cleared and wild areas (C Evans 1988). Brown (1997) has made the important point that openings within the wildwood are not necessarily deliberate human acts of clearance. Some may reflect opportunistic utilisation of areas of natural tree throw with which we are becoming increasingly familiar from the more frequent storms of recent years, particularly that on 16 October 1987 (Bell and Walker 1992, fig 1.5). That may be a relevant model for this highly exposed hilltop location from which the molluscan record is more consistent with woodland disturbance and regrowth rather than large-scale clearance. It is particularly noteworthy that in at least one case (Hambledon AF2) we have shade-loving molluscs in a clear example of a tree-throw feature which also contained Neolithic artefacts. Comparable associations are reported by C Evans *et al* (1999) in East Anglia where a plausible case is made that these represent deliberate acts of middening in tree throw features. The point is well made that, in a forested environment, trees are likely to have been 'central to concerns, myths, classifications and values' (C Evans *et al* 1999, 241). As Davies (1988) puts it, trees stand over and against the generations in a way which demands acknowledgement. Ingold (1993) refers to trees as Chronotopes – places charged with temporality. These observations provide us with a model of earlier Neolithic activity *within* an at least partly wooded landscape which seems to be in better accord with the evidence than the traditional model of a largely cleared agricultural landscape.

How extensive was this woodland?

We cannot define how extensive were any of the woodland tracts defined above. Sampling around the base of the hillslope failed to find contexts contemporary with the Neolithic activity on the hilltop. Further afield locally there are neither sites nor environmental data with which to determine the extent, or range of this woodland. Whether it was just confined to the steeper slopes of the Hambledon complex, or whether woodland and forest extended across much of the wider landscape of the Oxford Clay of Blackmoor Vale and the Tertiary deposits and low rolling chalkland of Cranborne Chase, must remain largely speculation. Some clue as to the nature of this environment may, however, be obtained from examining both local Neolithic landscapes, eg the Allen Valley, Cranborne Chase (Entwistle and Bowden 1991; Allen 1999; 2000a; 2002; French *et al* 2000; 2003) and the Dorchester environs (Allen 1997a; 1997b) and the environment of other Neolithic chalkland monumental landscapes such as Stonehenge (Allen *et al* 1990; Cleal and Allen 1995; Allen 1997c) and Avebury (Smith 1984; Whittle *et al* 1999; Allen 2005a). These are briefly explored below.

Can we see any development of the hill-top land-use and environment during the Neolithic?

Unlike some other Neolithic monuments, there is no clear evidence for major clearance, or local woodland regeneration, as suggested at Maiden Castle, for instance. Woodland encroachment is also suggested at Offham, and at Whitesheet Hill (Allen 2004). In the Hambledon complex, however, we can tentatively suggest slightly more open conditions on the hilltop in later contexts in the Hambledon Hill enclosure and more so in the post-Neolithic Stepleton outwork samples.

The local Hambledon landscape

The Hambledon landscape produced no evidence of Neolithic colluviation and this accords with the evidence for only limited and local clearance at this time. A similar absence of Neolithic colluvium has been revealed by other chalkland landscape surveys in the South Downs, Sussex (Bell 1983; Allen 2005b), in the Maiden Castle landscape in Dorset (Evans 1991, 251; Middle Farm, Dorset, Allen 1997b), in Wiltshire around Stonehenge (Richards 1990) and in the area of the Wessex Linear Ditches Project (Bradley *et al* 1994). Areas which emerged as a major foci of later Neolithic ceremonial activity were extensively cleared during the Neolithic, as at Avebury (Smith 1984), Stonehenge (Allen *et al* 1990; Allen 1997c), and, in Dorset, Mount Pleasant (Evans and Jones 1979) and the Cranborne Chase Cursus (Barrett *et al* 1991).

Neolithic soil profiles seem to have been stripped from the valley, footslope and lowland locations later in the Holocene, perhaps associated with more extensive activity in the later Bronze Age or Iron Age. The removal of these Neolithic soils in valley locations (cf Allen 1992), may relate to periods of intensive activity (clearance, preparation of ground for construction, tillage) in the earlier Bronze Age and relate to renewed activity on the hill at this time. In common with many areas of less intensive later Neolithic activity, such as the South Downs and the Maiden Castle area, Hambledon Hill seems to have been extensively cleared in the Beaker period/early Bronze Age.

Soil erosion

It has been widely accepted that in the mid Holocene much of the chalkland carried brown forest soils (eg Limbrey 1975) for example in the Maiden Castle landscape (Evans 1991), but see Allen (2002) and French *et al* (2000; 2003). The rich dark soil with woodland molluscs found in some Neolithic features would represent remnants of this soil, which in many parts of the hill seems to have been highly calcareous. Unfortunately the Hambledon project produced no surviving Neolithic buried soils. Taylor (1960) describes a 'typical rendzina soil' beneath a bank sectioned by Bonney in 1960 and possible truncated soils were noted in the post-excavation stages from site P (see 3.3.2, 3.3.4). However, there was no evidence of a stoneless A-horizon and the profile was almost certainly truncated since it was overlain by a hump in the ploughsoil rather than by an undisturbed bank (see 3.3.2). It may therefore represent an area protected from solution and mechanical erosion below a subsequently largely eroded bank. The effect of chalk dissolution on the archaeological record – originally described by Atkinson (1957) – remains difficult to quantify because it is so often complicated by the erosive effects of tillage. It has, since the early days of the project, been accepted that the archaeological features on Hambledon Hill have been truncated as a result of this combination of processes, and estimates of between 0.30 m and 1 m are made in Chapter 1 for various areas of the hilltop. Former thicker soils of this order would be in line with the molluscan evidence for woodland cover surviving into the Neolithic. We can also approach this quantification problem by calculating back, in a very crude way, from the cross-sectional area of the colluvial deposits investigated in slope and valley bottom reservoirs (Bell 1986). Thus in Coombe

Bottom we have the product of about 0.20 m of erosion from the catchment and on a transect down the east end of the Stepleton spur from the Stepleton lynchet to the base of the slope we have a product of 0.06 m. These figures are of a similar order of magnitude to those calculated from other areas (Bell 1986; R Evans 1990). This is based only on the erosion products and does not include the effects of dissolution processes. The surviving colluvia must represent minima. We presume that the former earlier Holocene soils have been scoured out, probably at the time of Bronze Age clearance, from the Coombe Bottom valley. The full extent of colluvial deposits is unlikely to have been identified by this limited study, and it is clear from the investigation of the colluvial alluvial interface in Everley Water Meadow that colluvium has been reworked by stream action.

The wider Neolithic landscape

The interpretation of Hambledon Hill landscape provides some detail within which to understand the communities on and around Hambledon Hill. These communities, however, ranged across a much wider landscape, and thus some comparison with that wider landscape allows us to view the Hambledon data more holistically. The examination of this wider landscape examines two sets of data: firstly the as yet unpublished data from the Whitesheet Hill causewayed enclosure, and Iron Age footslope colluvium on the lower slopes of that hill, and secondly the data from Cranborne Chase. In this area the published work of Entwistle and Bowden (1991), provides a general basis, but much more detailed results are now available from the recent research by one of us (MJA) in the Allen Valley and at Down Farm (Allen 1999; 2000a; 2002; French *et al* 2000; 2003; 2007). We have compared the local landscape with similar chalkland monuments listed above, such as Maiden Castle etc; however, perhaps more pertinent to the Neolithic landscape to which Hambledon Hill related, is the detailed work on the reconstruction of the Neolithic landscape of a part of Cranborne Chase (the Allen Valley), on the edge of which Hambledon Hill lies. The head of the Allen Valley, and a concentration of Neolithic monuments therein, lies only 12 km from Hambledon Hill. Research conducted initially by Bowden and Entwistle (1991) provided the basis for more detailed research (Allen 1998; 2000a; 2002; French *et al* 2000; 2007) of detailed composite analysis of a number of Neolithic monuments and earlier Bronze Age sites (Allen 1998), which will provide maps showing the development of the vegetation mosaic in the area (cf Allen 2000b).

In the Allen Valley and on the Down Farm chalkland plateau of Cranborne Chase, we can see that the major changes in this landscape occurred not in the Bronze Age, as perceived by Barrett *et al* (1991), but considerably earlier (French *et al* 2000; 2003; 2007; Allen 2002). Land snail evidence indicates that, apart from the very early monuments (long barrows), which initially existed in clearings in woodland, many of the succeeding Neolithic monuments (cursus, henges etc), were established in a largely open landscape. Large-scale augering (French *et al* 2000; 2003; 2007) has demonstrated that the soils had become denuded and rendzinas formed by, at latest, the later Neolithic and that, in contrast to many other areas of the chalkland, neither extensive nor deep colluvial deposits exist. In many ways this equates with the Neolithic landscape of both Dorchester and Stonehenge. Indeed the mosaic pattern of vegetation postulated from high-resolution mapping of past landscapes (cf Allen 2000b) demonstrates the landscape diversity at this time.

The post-Neolithic landscape of Hambledon Hill and its surroundings

We have concluded that woodland persisted on and around the Hambledon hilltop throughout the period of the early Neolithic site. Clearance was underway by the period of Beaker and Bronze Age activity on the Stepleton Spur. The chalk upland of the hill and Coombe Bottom was cleared during the Bronze Age and some colluviation occurred. By contrast the Iwerne valley retained significant tree cover throughout the Bronze Age and, although the old land surface below the burnt mound shows that there was cleared grassland on the banks of the stream at that time, regeneration followed. The scarcity of Iron Age artefacts from the hilltop excavations, given the proximity of two major hillforts, implies that at this time the hilltop may have been given over to pasture. Possibly in the Bronze Age, and certainly by Iron Age and Romano-British times, there were fields on the Stepleton Spur. Many of the other fields on the sides of Hambledon and its spurs are likely to be of similar date, although there is evidence that some pre-date the hillfort. This was the period of greatest arable activity in the landscape, when colluvial deposits were deposited in Coombe Bottom and at the base of the Stepleton slope in the Iwerne valley. The valley floor was cleared and cultivated during the Romano-British period but the stream sides remained shaded and are likely to have retained tree cover. In post-Roman times there is some ridge and furrow on the Shroton spur and in the hillfort but the upland is likely to have been mainly pasture with arable around the valley bottom settlements, as indicated by artefact distributions pointing to arable and manuring in Coombe Bottom and the area which later became Everley Water Meadow.

The really big change in the valley floor landscape comes in the eighteenth century when the water meadows were created. These are rich pastures on which early lambs could be fattened, hay produced and then cattle maintained in the late summer (Doherty 1985). The practice created a distinctive habitat type in many river valleys in Wessex; a few still survive, for instance near Salisbury (Cowan 1982; Sheail 1971) and are important for nature conservation purposes. To create the water meadows at Everley a new channel was cut slightly upslope, and leading from this were irrigation channels. The diverse range of freshwater molluscan taxa found in the Iwerne stream today is in sharp contrast to the smaller percentage and much narrower species range of freshwater taxa found in the Iwerne channels of prehistoric to medieval date. It is concluded that the pre-eighteenth-century channels of the Iwerne carried a much reduced flow which, by comparison with the faunas of other winterbourne streams, was probably seasonal and largely confined to the wettest months of the year. The molluscs suggest that, in some years at least, the flow may not totally have ceased in summer. It seems probable that the making of water meadows, the creation of lakes and the emparked landscapes of the valley floor was associated with substantial waterwork operations, which in any case are implied by the new Iwerne channel. This may have involved the diversion of flow from elsewhere down the Iwerne channel to create the present perennial stream with its richer, more diverse, mollusc fauna.

Viewing the post-medieval landscape of the Iwerne valley with its gentry mansions, lakes and parks we may conclude that the dramatic landscape transformation of the post-medieval period owed more to the need to make a mark on the landscape, as part of social interaction, than it did to the requirements of everyday agricultural production. In that respect this most recent dramatic transformation may well be similar to the first, the making of the early Neolithic complex up on the hill, at least if the implications of the molluscan assemblages are accepted.

6 Charcoal and charred plant remains

6.1 The wood charcoal

Phil Austin, Catherine Barnett (neé Chisham) and Jonathan Hather

6.1.1 Introduction

The excavations at Hambledon Hill resulted in the recovery of a substantial amount of wood charcoal macro-remains from a diverse range of contexts, representing episodes of site use extending from the Boreal to the early Bronze Age on the hilltop and into the post-medieval period in Everley Water Meadow. While this report focuses on the period of intensive use of the hilltop in the earlier Neolithic, material from other periods was also examined and is discussed below.

Incorporated into this report are the results of two earlier investigations of the charcoal – that from the main causewayed enclosure ditch (Chisham 1994), and from pits on the Stepleton spur (Austin 1995). Some of the remaining fractions of samples originally identified by Carole Keepax in the 1970s in advance of radiocarbon dating have been re-examined as part of this investigation and the results are integrated here.

Aims

The following aims were formulated with respect to the palaeoenvironmental investigation as a whole, and the broader context of the socio-cultural interpretation of the site:

a) to provide an account of the prehistoric vegetation on and around the site complex and, where possible, investigate evidence for temporal and spatial vegetational change, and
b) to investigate the evidence for the exploitation of woody plants for their functional properties and/or non-functional (culturally associated) attributes.

Methods

Recovery, sampling, and identification

Manual recovery was practised consistently each season for each context type and accounts for the majority of charcoal collected. Charcoal finds were often lifted in bulk and subsequently sorted with tweezers under good light. Some individual fragments were picked out by hand during excavation. Wet sieving, dry sieving, and flotation of bulk samples were practised less consistently, according to resources and context, as described more fully by Jones and Legge (6.2). Contexts apparently rich in plant remains were sampled more intensively than those less obviously so. Pits, for example, were sampled more than ditches.

Comprehensive temporal and spatial coverage of the site was attempted by examining samples from discrete phases or horizons, and specific features. The contemporaneity of individual ditch segments and the phases to which the layers in them were assigned are not, however, ensured. Ditch fills are therefore regarded as more-or-less homogeneous 'Neolithic' deposits for the purposes of interpretation, except where otherwise stated. Samples from postholes or and pits classed as definite or probable (3.1.2) were selected in preference to samples from otherwise poorly defined, or possibly contaminated, contexts. Multiple samples recovered from the same feature are treated as a single sample except when a feature contained distinct contexts or stratification.

The areas and context groups from which charcoal was examined are listed in Table 6.1. Charcoal from the following context groups was not examined: the outer east and south cross-dykes, pits excavated on the Stepleton spur in 1978–80 and 1982, and the Iron Age hillfort. This material was not studied principally because either no charcoal was available for examination, fragment condition was very poor and/or the quantity of charcoal available was too small to provide any useable information, or it was judged that the information gained would not make a significant contribution to the overall interpretation.

Examination of fragments

Prior to examination each sample was passed through a nest of 4 mm-, 2 mm-, and 1 mm-gauge sieves. Although charcoal fragments <4 mm are sometimes examined, in this investigation only material from the >4 mm size category were considered for identification. Keepax (1988) suggests that examination only of fragments >3.75 mm does not significantly affect the range of taxa represented and identified. Fragments <4 mm are less likely to retain sufficient diagnostic anatomical features to allow secure identification. Anatomical features used to determine relative maturity, for example, may also be absent for the same reason (Gale 2004). Thus the amount of information available decreases as the time required to gather it increases.

All recovery techniques may affect fragment quantity and quality, thus influencing the range of taxa recovered (Smart and Hoffman 1988). Hand-picking, for example, favours the recovery of fragments

Table 6.1 Summary of charcoal samples examined – all periods

Values for indeterminate fragments are both included in the overall fragment totals and recorded separately. Counts of 'not-woody' fragments are excluded.
Totals of recorded charcoal finds are for the entire context group, not simply those parts of it from which charcoal was examined. They may include samples not containing charcoal.

Area	*Fragments*	*Indeterminate fragments*	*Taxa identified*	*Samples examined*	*Features from which charcoal examined*	*Recorded charcoal finds*	*% of samples examined*
Main enclosure pits	1130	29	8	61	17	108	56
Main enclosure bank area, site P1	25	0	5	4	2	4	100
Main enclosure ditch	1240	57	16	78		97	80
Inner east cross-dyke	131	22	6	3		8	38
Inner south cross-dyke	102	1	7	4		8	50
Long barrow	18	0	3	5		7	71
Inner south cross dyke/western outwork bank area	64	0	5	6	2	6	100
Western outwork bank area	84	0	2	2	1	2	100
Western outwork	6	0	1	1		1	100
Central area totals	**2800**	**109**	**17**	**164**	**22**	**241**	**68**
Shroton spur outwork	**140**	**1**	**3**	**4**		**31**	**13**
Stepleton spur pits	648	12	13	118	18	289	41
Stepleton enclosure	336	20	7	21		78	27
Structure in NW of Stepleton enclosure	11	2	2	4	32	40	10
Inner outwork gateway and bank area	371	13	3	9	9	38	24
Inner outwork	1538	233	14	36		121	30
Middle outwork	12	0	3	2		7	29
Outer outwork	9	0	1	1		3	33
Stepleton spur totals	**2925**	**280**	**17**	**191**	**29**	**576**	**33**
Hanford spur ?Boreal features	68	2	3	10	3	13	77
Hanford spur pits	165	27	6	22	3	77	29
Hanford spur gateway	151	2	1	11	1	13	85
Inner Hanford outwork	230	38	6	12		19	63
Outer Hanford outwork	133	16	8	10		14	71
Hanford spur 'flint mines'	102	3	6	17		36	47
Hanford spur totals	**849**	**88**	**12**	**82**	**7**	**172**	**48**
Everley Water Meadow burnt mound/old land surface	215	38	8	5		34	15
Everley Water Meadow other contexts	260	71	11	17		82	21
Everley Water Meadow totals	**475**	**109**	**11**	**22**		**116**	**19**
Overall totals	**7189**	**587**	**25**	**463**	**58**	**1136**	**41**

sufficiently conspicuous to be identified by the human eye, and large enough to be handled relatively securely, while flotation can lead to fragment loss and size reduction (Greenlee 1992). Floated material consisted of fragments predominantly falling within the <4 mm size fractions. To a lesser extent this also applied to fragments recovered through wet sieving. A large proportion of fragments from samples retrieved manually tended to fall into the >4 mm class size. Where present, fragments falling into smaller size classes from these same samples often exhibited characteristics indicative of relatively recent (post-excavation) fracturing. It follows that fragment counts for some samples may have increased since recovery, and fragments <4 mm may have derived from fragments >4 mm.

Where such suspicions existed material from the <4 mm sieves was often examined. Taxa composition in lower size ranges did not, however, differ significantly from that of material recovered from the >4 mm sieve. Because of these findings and the cursory nature of these supplementary examinations, the identifications made are not included in the overall results of the investigation. These factors, in addition to the limited amount of time available and the large amount of material to be examined, seemed sufficient to justify the decision to restrict the size range examined. However, where wet-sieved samples contained no fragments >4 mm, a decision was made to gather the limited information offered by those <4 mm and the results of these examinations are included in the results and feature in the interpretation.

Keepax (1988) recommends examination of a minimum of 100 fragments per sample (preferably 3–400) to recover the full range of taxa present. In excess of this figure it becomes progressively less likely that any taxa previously unrecorded from that sample will be identified. The policy adopted for this analysis was therefore to examine a minimum of 100 fragments per sample or feature wherever possible.

Quantification

Interpretations of charcoal assemblages are dependent on an understanding of charcoal taphonomy and the methods used to identify relationships between the charcoal assemblage and the former abundance of individual taxa. Investigations into the taphonomy of archaeological charcoal (eg Lopinot 1984; Rossen and Olsen 1985; Keepax 1988; Smart and Hoffman 1988; March 1992), demonstrate unequivocally that the relationship between archaeological charcoal and its original source, the palaeoenvironment, is a complex one. Such relationships are inferred from the relative values of fragment counts, weights, or volumes for different taxa (Smart and Hoffman 1988). While these properties can be empirically established, the values obtained may have little, if any, meaning.

It is believed, therefore, that attempts to quantify the material examined by reference to fragment numbers, weight, or volume would be potentially more misleading than it would be informative. Presence/absence analysis is, arguably, the least misleading approach available at present for the analysis of archaeological charcoal, and this is the principal method used here. Each taxon present in each context is regarded as equally significant in terms of source environment irrespective of actual quantities recorded by fragment number, weight, or volume of that species. Popper (1988, 61) defines this as the 'ubiquity' of a taxon. In essence it is a measure of the frequency of occurrence in each context type of the taxa identified. Focus on assemblage/sample composition and the archaeological context facilitates context-related variation analysis. Context-related variation has been extended to the interpretation of wood charcoal assemblages with some success by Thompson (1984) and by Cartwright (1997). This approach is implicit in the interpretative analysis of the material from this site.

Identification

Fragments were prepared following the methodology advocated by Leney and Casteel (1975) and examined under an epi-illuminated microscope at magnifications up to ×400. Identification, to the lowest possible taxonomic level (species level wherever possible), was determined with reference to the relevant literature (Schweingruber 1990a; 1990b; IAWA Committee 1989). Further reference was made to modern charcoal specimens and reference slides held at the Institute of Archaeology, University College London, when identification was in doubt.

Fragments which could not be positively identified but bore a distinct similarity to a particular taxon were recorded as 'cf' and are included in the final analysis as being of that taxon. Wood charcoal fragments for which no identification was possible, and fragments identified as non-woody charred organic material, are recorded as 'indeterminate' and 'non-woody', respectively, and included in the results as such. Quantities of 'non-woody' material are recorded only in the full list of results (in the archive) and are not included in the summary results. Binomial species names are given where a specimen could be securely identified as being a particular species or where only one representative of the genus is native. Nomenclature follows that of Stace (1991).

Differentiating members of the Rosaceae family is particularly difficult, even as uncharred wood. Members of the Rosaceae, subfamily Maloideae, for example, often cannot be determined below this level (Schweingruber 1990b). However, some of the fragments identified as such were tentatively further identified as cf *Sorbus* (whitebeams, rowan, wild service tree) or cf *Crataegus* (hawthorns). It is thought that the latter is the genus most likely to be represented. Likewise, in the form of wood charcoal, *Prunus* cannot often be confidently differentiated below genus level. Nonetheless, it was occasionally possible to identify fragments as cf *P avium* (wild cherry) or cf *P spinosa* (blackthorn). At this site it is thought that *P spinosa* is the species most likely to be represented as charcoal. Several species of both native genera of Salicaceae (*Salix* and *Populus* – willow and aspen) are likely to be represented. Occasional identifications of cf *Salix* were made. No such distinctions are made in the presentation of the results. While differentiation was normally possible, fragments recorded as *Corylus*/*Alnus* (hazel/alder) did not retain sufficient anatomical features to enable the separation of these two members of the Betulaceae. Growing conditions preferred by *Alnus glutinosa* were available nearby and it is thought that at least some of the fragments could be of this taxon. The majority, however, are likely to be *Corylus avellana* (hazel).

6.1.2 Results

In total, 7185 fragments were examined (including earlier studies) from 463 samples. Of these, 587 fragments could not be securely identified. Twenty-five taxa were identified from the site as a whole, representing a potential floristic range in excess of 40 distinct species. Table 6.1 summarises the context groups from which samples were examined. Absolute fragment counts are also shown. Table 6.2 lists all the taxa identified, arranged according to plant form, and includes suggested 'missing' taxa, identified with reference to phytosociological models such as those of Polunin and Walters (1985), Ellenberg (1988), Rodwell (1991), and Peterken (1993). Figures 6.1–3 summarise taxon ubiquity. The assemblage as a whole

Table 6.2 List of all taxa identified and of 'missing' woody taxa, arranged according to plant form

+ taxa identified in post-Neolithic samples only, * includes some shrub species, ** includes some large tree species.
Taxa not anatomically distinguishable below family/subfamily/genus are listed accordingly.
'Missing' taxa are those present in modern chalkland/deciduous woodland habitats (following Polunin and Walters 1985; Rodwell 1991) and thus likely to have been components of the former vegetation in the area, although not identified among the Hambledon samples.

Identified taxa			*'Missing' taxa*	
Large- or medium-sized trees				
Acer campestre		Field maple		
Betula sp		Birch		
Carpinus betulus		Hornbeam		
Fagus sylvatica		Beech		
Fraxinus excelsior		Ash		
Pinus sylvestris		Scots pine		
Quercus sp		Oaks		
Salicaceae				
	(*Salix* sp)	Willows*		
	(*Populus* sp)	Poplars		
Taxus baccata		Yew		
Tilia sp		Limes		
Ulmus sp		Elms		
Small trees or large shrubs				
Buxus sempervirens		Box	*Sambucus nigra*	Elder
Cornus sanguinea		Dogwood	*Ligustrum vulgare*	Privet
Corylus avellana		Hazel	*Euonymus europaeus*	Spindle tree
Corylus/Alnus glutinosa		Hazel/alder		
Frangula alnus+		Alder buckthorn		
Ilex aquifolium		Holly		
Maloideae				
	(*Crataegus* sp)	Hawthorns		
	(*Malus* sp)	Apple		
	(*Sorbus* sp)	Whitebeams**		
		Rowan		
		Wild service tree		
	(*Pyrus* sp)	Pear**		
Prunus sp		Blackthorn		
		Cherries**		
Rhamnus cathartica+		Buckthorn		
Viburnam sp		Guelder rose		
		Wayfaring tree		
Shrubs, lianas, climbers, epiphytes				
Erica vagans		Cornish heath	*Lonicera* spp	Honeysuckle
Vitis vinifera		Grapevine	*Hedera helix*	Ivy
Clematis vitalba+		Traveller's joy	*Viscum album*	Mistletoe
Rosa spp+		Dog roses*	*Rubus* spp	Brambles

is among the richest recorded for a Neolithic site in Britain. While this undoubtedly reflects the scale of the archaeological investigation, more significantly, it demonstrates the very broad range of woody plants actually available and exploited.

Description of samples/context type

Charcoal of Boreal age

Once the identifications were made, it became apparent that the charcoal assemblage from one feature (HN82 F279, then thought to be a posthole, although not a very convincing one, in the substructure of the inner Hanford outwork bank) consisted mainly of *Pinus sylvestris*, with some *Corylus/Alnus* and ?Betulaceae. This combination of taxa was atypical of Neolithic contexts on the hill and suggestive of a substantially earlier date. Two single fragments of *Pinus sylvestris* charcoal were dated to 7580–7200 cal BC (OxA-7845, 8400±60 BP) and 7600–7380 cal BC (OxA-7846, 8480±55 BP; Ch 4), confirming a Boreal age for the charcoal and perhaps for the feature. *Pinus* charcoal from another possible posthole (WOWK3 F4, apparently part of the substructure of the Neolithic inner south crosos-dyke bank) was also dated, with an older result: 8160–7590 cal BC (OxA-7816, 8725±55 BP; Ch 4). Here the associated taxon was *Corylus/Alnus*).

These measurements raise the possibility that other *Pinus* charcoal from the hill may also date from the early Mesolithic. *Pinus* charcoal was unevenly and often widely spaced. It was found without artefacts in two other nearby features on the Hanford spur (HN82 F507 and F773, in which all the charcoal was *Pinus sylvestris* except for a single *Corylus* fragment from F773, a feature similar in character to F279. These and the dated features are described and discussed in Chapter 3. Only two single fragments of *Pinus* charcoal were found in contexts with Neolithic artefacts and charcoal of temperate deciduous taxa.

Ditch deposits

Figure 6.1 shows the ubiquity of taxa in samples from the main causewayed enclosure ditch, the Stepleton enclosure ditch and inner Stepleton outwork ditch. The following description applies only to the Neolithic deposits in these ditches.

The general pattern that emerges is the predominance of *Quercus*, *Corylus* and Maloideae. *Prunus* and *Fraxinus* are also ranked high and feature prominently in most samples. This pattern is evident through all phases. Relative proportions are also generally temporally consistent, from the earliest to later deposits. Detailed discussion of individual ditch phases is generally not warranted, given the general homogeneity of the charcoal from ditch deposits. Nonetheless certain deposits do require further comment.

In the main causewayed enclosure ditch phase IV deposits were most extensive on site G (segments 16–19) with smaller quantities of charcoal elsewhere. Samples from site G were particularly rich (17 taxa), and account for the apparently higher taxon diversity of the main causewayed enclosure ditch as a whole (Fig 6.1). If these contexts are not taken into consideration, the assemblage from the main enclosure ditch is more-or-less in keeping with those from the other ditches.

Samples from the ditches of the south long barrow are small and few and probably do not fully represent the original composition of the context. Possible invertebrate damage was evident in *Corylus* fragments from the single phase I sample.

The Hanford inner and outer outwork ditches have higher proportions of taxa indicative of open conditions, particularly from basal deposits in the inner outwork, although the overall range of taxa represented is comparable to other deposits. It may be significant than the Hanford spur is spatially distinct from the core of the complex, and that at least parts of the Hanford outworks seem to have been built at a relatively late stage (Ch 4).

Possible structural remains

The Shroton outwork. Only three taxa were recovered from the ditch, *Fraxinus*, *Corylus* and *Quercus*. It is thought that their presence may relate to structural features associated with the bank. Material from the Shroton spur postholes was not examined.

The main enclosure. A possible posthole in the bank area of the main causewayed enclosure (Fig 3.7: P1 F29) contained *Corylus* charcoal.

The western outwork. Charcoal from a posthole in the western outwork bank area (Fig 3.45: WOWK2 F6) was dominated by *Quercus*, some of which was dated to *3630–3350 cal BC* (4660±40 BP; OxA-7815) and seems to confirm the presence of a post in the bank area. One fragment of *Pinus* was identified.

The inner south cross-dyke. The part of WOWK3 F4 that contained Boreal *Pinus* charcoal and some *Corylus*/*Alnus* charcoal (described above) was cut by a deeper feature, probably a posthole, which contained *Fraxinus* charcoal dated to *3650–3510 cal BC* (OxA-8861, 4780±45 BP) and *3640–3420 cal BC* (OxA-8862, 4690±45 BP).

The inner Stepleton outwork. In the gateway area of the inner outwork, samples from postholes (Fig 3.111: 3B F401, F442, F450, F502, F601B, F603, and F601) were exclusively identified as *Quercus*. The charcoal from F601B was recorded in the field as 'burnt wood *in situ*'. Charcoal from 3B F524, a posthole in the bank area a little to the east of the gateway, was identified as Maloideae. The Maloideae include a few taxa suitable for post use (eg *Sorbus aria*), and it may be relevant that the post is unlikely to have been more than 0.10 m in diameter. Charcoal from 3B F537 in the same area was identified as *Pinus*. It is uncertain, however, whether the charcoal came from posthole F537A or from a nebulous spread of material which overlay it.

The strongest evidence for the probable nature of structural wood use at the site is provided by charcoal from the phase II and III deposits (see 3.5.4). While *Quercus* and *Corylus* were ubiquitous in these contexts, other taxa less obviously associated with structural use were also present, eg *Ilex aquifolium*. Layer 4A in cutting 1 of segment 6 is particularly significant in that it seemingly represents *in situ* burning of possible structural material (Fig 3.99; Pls VIII–IX). Burnt clay and coherent charred timbers were exceptionally well preserved within a band of Clay-with-Flints, which the bank was constructed from at this point. Away from the Clay-with-Flints, charcoal from this horizon and the phase III fills, also associated with the burning and bank collapse, was less well preserved within a chalk matrix. The combination of finds and features is interpreted as representing some kind of catastrophe, probably a conflagration (Mercer 1980). *Corylus* accounts for most of the identified charcoal from this deposit. *Quercus* and *Acer* were also present in small quantities. The high occurrence of *Corylus* and low occurrence of *Quercus* in this horizon contrasts with the increase in occurrence of *Quercus* in chalk rubble fills higher up in the segment. This possibly reflects the sequence in which wooden features entered the ditch following burning and bank collapse. Seemingly *Corylus* roundwood (?wattle/hurdle work) was incorporated into the ditch followed by *Quercus* timbers from the body of the bank.

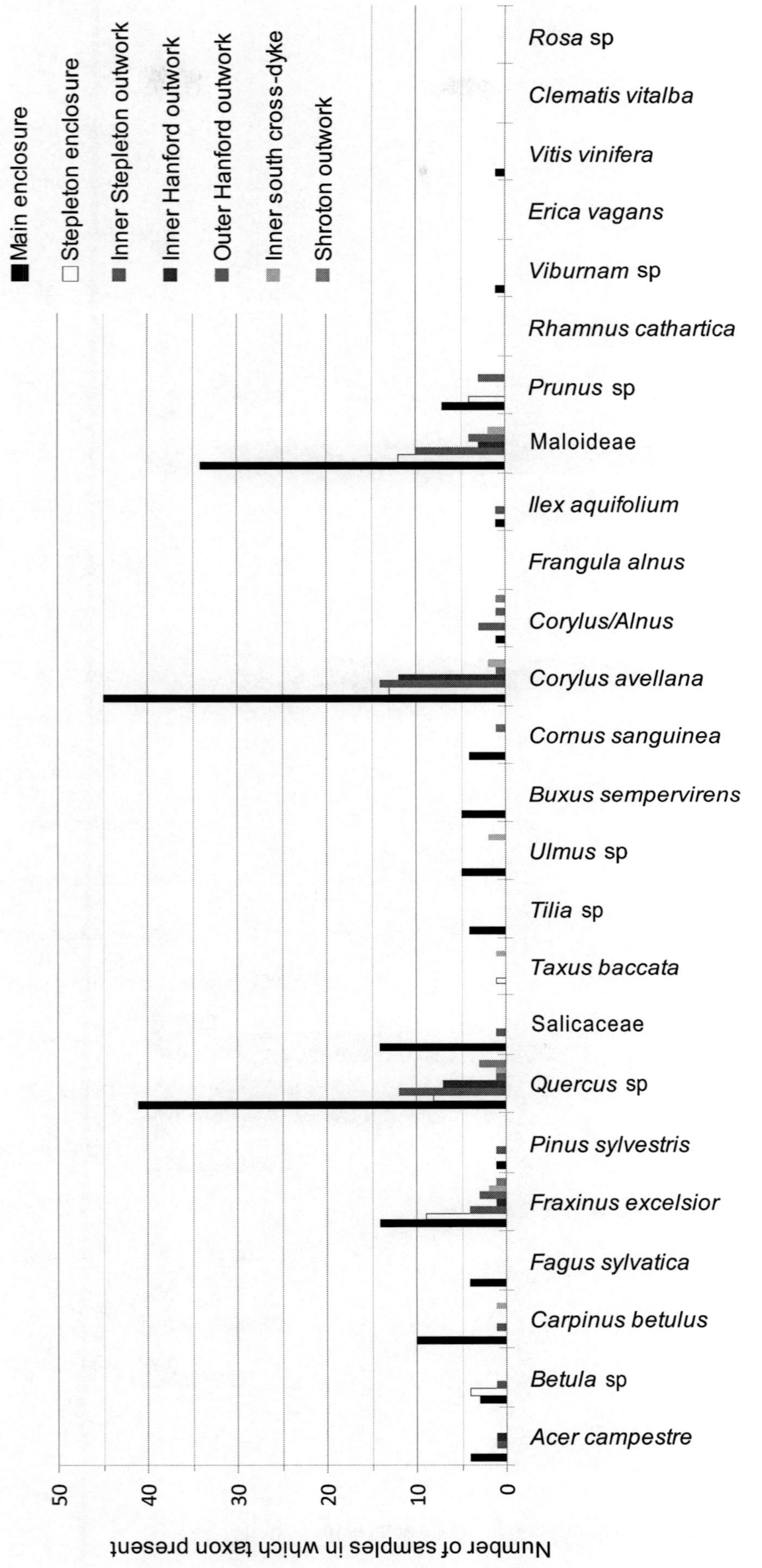

Fig 6.1 Charcoal taxon ubiquity. Banks and ditches (Neolithic contexts only).

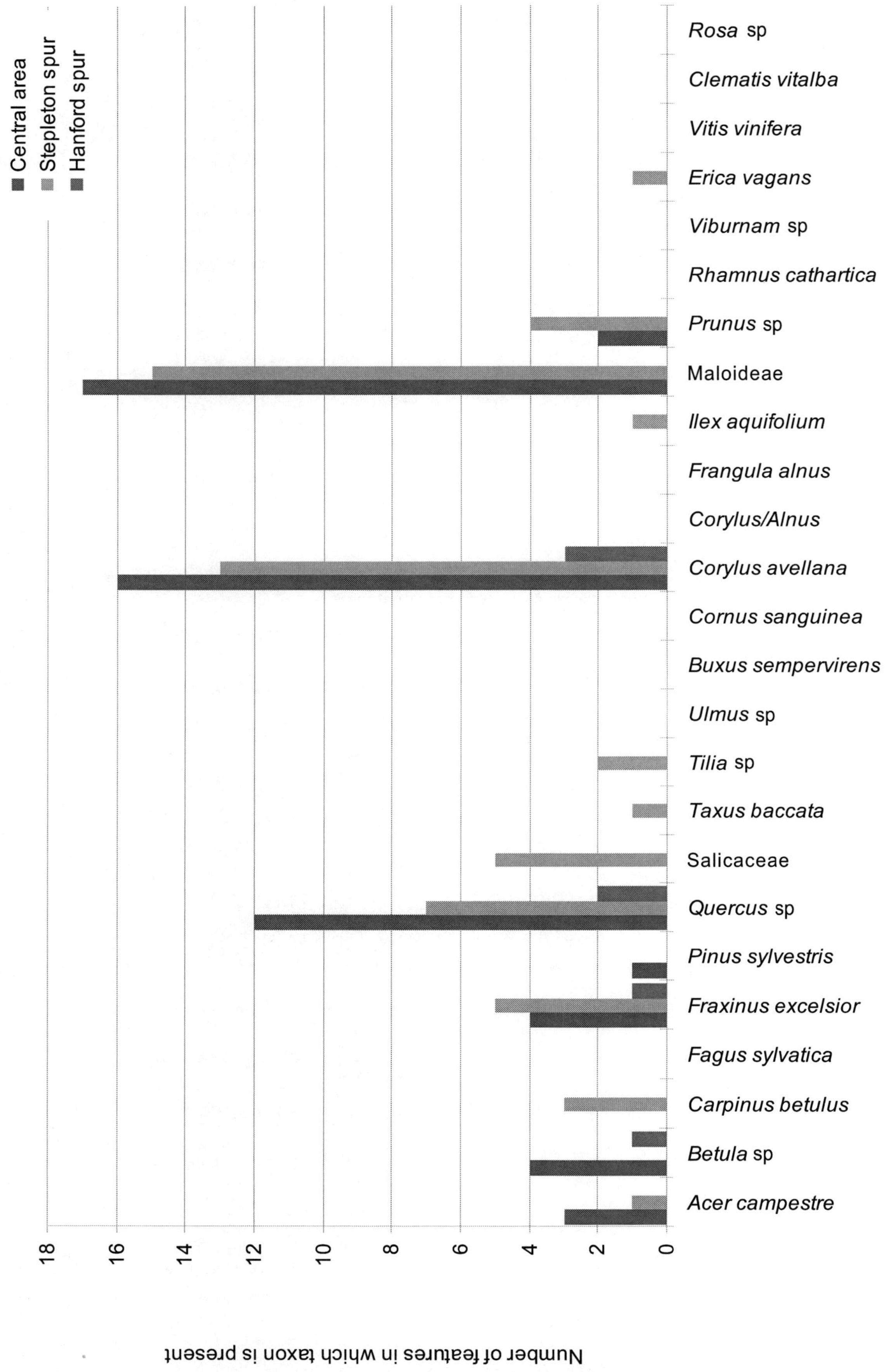

Fig 6.2 Charcoal taxon ubiquity. Neolithic pits.

The Hanford outworks. Samples from the Hanford inner outwork 'gateway' posthole HN82 F854, were composed exclusively of mature wood of *Quercus*, representing what may have been a substantial former post.

Pits

All the pits investigated were Neolithic. The results are presented in Figure 6.2. Differences in the taxon composition of pits from the different areas of the site are apparent. The charcoals from the Stepleton pits are the most diverse (13 taxa), followed by main causewayed enclosure pits (eight taxa) and the Hanford pits (six taxa; Table 6.1). The apparent disparity in the range of taxa identified from pit contexts as a whole may reflect the quantity of material examined from each area. Considerably more fragments were available, and were examined, from the 17 Stepleton and 18 central area pits than from the three Hanford spur pits.

The Hanford 'flint mines'

Charcoal samples from the Hanford 'flint mines' do not suggest any distinctive function (Fig 6.3). It may be significant that all the taxa present, particularly *Quercus*, *Fraxinus*, and *Corylus*, are good fuelwoods.

6.1.3 Discussion of the results

The following discussion is divided into two parts. The first considers the results of the charcoal analysis primarily as ecological information concerning the former vegetation on and around the site over the period it was in use. The second part focuses on anthropogenic factors as they relate to possible past human/plant relationships. This separation is for convenience only. It is not suggested that ecological and cultural considerations are at all mutually exclusive.

The nature and source of the Neolithic vegetation

The charcoal could be interpreted as reflecting a highly varied mixture of vegetation types, both in terms of structure and composition. Clear affinities between the archaeological assemblage and any one particular modern woodland type are not apparent. No single floristic association (eg a chalkland flora) can be said to dominate the Neolithic remains. What seems clear, however, is that the ecotonal location of the site complex is reflected in the richness of the charcoal assemblage as a whole.

The minimum ecological prerequisites for each of the plants identified could have been satisfied locally, perhaps even within 1 km of the site. This possibility arises because of the patchwork of soil types and geology of the area (see 1.1, 1.3). It is sufficient here to note the presence of the chalk outcrop, on which the site itself is located, the Greensand and clays to the north of the site, and the limestone to the west (Fig 1.2). Each of these offers the possibility of distinct ecological niches. The proximity of the rivers Iwerne and Stour, which flank the site to the east and west respectively, further contributes to the biotic and edaphic diversity and thus the overall potential floristic richness of the area.

The quantity of samples available from Neolithic contexts was significantly greater than from post-Neolithic contexts. While this may partly account for differences in taxon representation between Neolithic and post-Neolithic samples, it cannot be regarded as a complete explanation of the variations. Despite temporal differences in intensity of site use, it is thought that the richness of the Neolithic assemblage represents the real presence of a higher level of taxon diversity and vegetation cover, available and accessible during this period.

The most obvious feature of the Neolithic assemblage is the ubiquitous presence of *Quercus*, *Corylus* and Maloideae. Unfortunately, for the purposes of palaeoenvironmental interpretation, each of these taxa is somewhat catholic in its ecological requirements and, correspondingly, in its geographical distribution. This is evident from both the archaeological record (Godwin 1975; Keepax 1988) and more recent ecological studies (Rodwell 1991; Packham *et al* 1992). Not only can these taxa be considered poor ecological indicators, they also have a long-established history as preferred sources of fuel, and as raw materials for construction and artefact manufacture (eg Edlin 1970). Furthermore, all are potential sources of human foodstuffs in the form of, for example, nuts, berries and young shoots, and sources of livestock fodder (Rackham 1977). The most commonly represented taxa may arguably provide more information about the cultural/economic use of wood, and associated resources, than they do about the nature of the former vegetation. Nonetheless, these taxa consistently occur abundantly in samples throughout the site and over the *c* 300–400 years of Neolithic site use. In itself this can be taken to indicate their continuing availability.

The Neolithic samples contain taxa tolerant of shade – *Ilex*, *Carpinus* and *Taxus*, moderate shade taxa – *Ulmus*, moderate light-demanding taxa – *Quercus* and *Tilia*, and light-demanding taxa – *Acer*, *Betula*, *Cornus*, *Fraxinus* and *Prunus* (Edlin 1949). While *Corylus* is shade-tolerant, it requires open conditions for high nut production. The conspicuous presence of charred hazelnut shell at the site (see Jones and Legge, 6.2) indicates that some *Corylus* grew in open conditions. Some shade-tolerant taxa can also thrive in open conditions and so their presence is not conclusive evidence of closed woodland. However, the present-day ecology of many of the medium/large tree taxa (eg *Taxus*, *Fagus*) suggests that these could have been present in more-or-less pure stands. Both these produce heavy shade, under which it is difficult for other plants to survive. Similarly, other canopy-forming trees (*Quercus*, *Ulmus*, *Fraxinus*, *Carpinus*, *Tilia*, and some members of the Salicaceae and Maloideae) indicate that mixed or pure stands of woodland are likely to have been present.

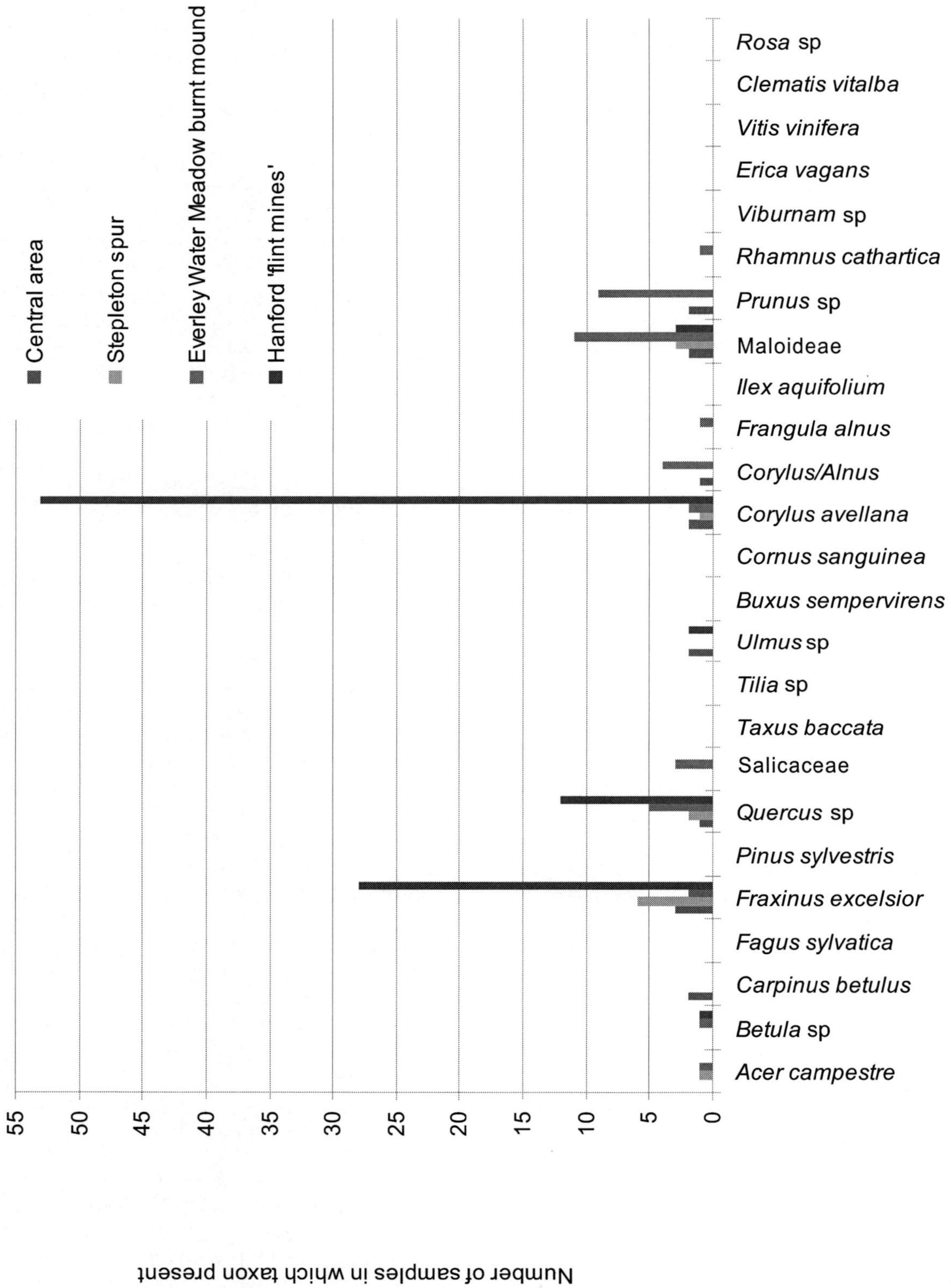

Fig 6.3 Charcoal taxon ubiquity. Beaker and Bronze Age contexts.

Many of the taxa identified are calcicoles (lime-loving) and thus could have grown on the hill itself. Whether or not this is so is difficult to demonstrate. Convincing evidence for trees growing on the hill slopes or within the confines of the site is scarce. Only one tree hollow can be confidently dated to the Neolithic (P1 F24/24A), although others may be coeval (see 3.3.7). Fragments of Maloideae, *Tilia* and *Pinus* charcoal were recovered from F24a, but are not thought to relate to the tree that grew there. Stratigraphically this feature pre-dates the main enclosure bank, and seemingly indicates that trees were growing on the hill prior to the bank's construction. No clear evidence was found for post-construction tree growth on the site, although the lack of such evidence does not exclude this possibility. It is also possible that the steeper slopes of the chalk outcrop were not cleared of vegetation until the Bronze Age, if then. *Taxus* and *Buxus*, for example, survive particularly well on the scarp slopes and coombes of modern chalklands (Smith 1980) and could have done so in the past. *Fraxinus*, *Taxus* and, less certainly identified, *Crataegus* and *Prunus spinosa*, are capable of colonising disturbed chalkland habitats as pioneers (ibid). These taxa are present in both primary and subsequent Neolithic deposits. *Pinus* and *Betula* are other potential pioneer species but do not thrive on chalk. Their presence may suggest more geographically widespread disturbance. *Viburnam*, *Alnus*, and many Salicaceae particularly prefer much damper conditions and would have flourished along the margins of local rivers.

The presence of taxa requiring open conditions (eg *Betula*) indicates that open areas and woodland edges were present. The causes, spatial distribution, and permanency of clearings are, however, less certain and cannot be determined on the basis of the charcoal evidence alone. The dynamic nature of woodland ecology may provide an adequate explanation for the presence of openings in the canopy. Mechanisms such as windthrow and the senescence of individual trees or even-aged stands are factors which contribute to the presence of openings in modern woodland habitats (White 1979) and are believed to have done so in the Neolithic (T Brown 1997). Conversely, initial anthropogenic clearance and localised thinning of existing closed woodland, may have increased the susceptibility of the remaining vegetation to natural processes of disturbance. If regenerated 'secondary woodland' is allowed to occur, its character can differ markedly from that of the original woodland in both overall composition and the relative abundance of particular taxa (Peterken 1996), especially if it is subjected to further human interference. Clearance episodes and the establishment of patches of secondary woodland could be supported by the composition of the Hambledon charcoal assemblage.

T Brown (1997) suggests that natural openings may have been opportunistically exploited and maintained by human populations during the Neolithic. While this is speculative, it is possible that site locations were partly chosen to exploit natural openings, which were subsequently much modified. However, differentiating between a natural opening not subject to significant human interference, a deliberately maintained natural opening, and clearance created solely by human agency remains problematic. It seems probable that at Hambledon both natural processes and anthropogenic clearance contributed to the presence of open areas.

Other sources of palaeoenvironmental information

The composition of the charcoal assemblage alone does not demonstrate unequivocally the form of woody vegetation associated with the site complex throughout the Neolithic (ie closed dense woodland, open light woodland, or open scrub/grassland with occasional trees). The molluscan evidence (Bell *et al*, Ch 5) suggests that the complex stood in a landscape where significant woodland remained and clearance was only partial, the environment becoming slightly more open in the 400-year life of the early Neolithic site, but undergoing more intense and sustained clearance only in the early Bronze Age. The charcoal evidence does not conflict with these conclusions. The faunal remains (Legge, Ch 8) include cattle, pig, and small numbers of wild mammals whose primary natural habitat is woodland or open woodland/woodland edge. The presence of such species strengthens the argument for extensive woodland cover and woodland margins.

Comparison with other sites

Direct detailed comparison with other charcoal assemblages is often impossible, not least because of differences in scale of excavation and charcoal recovery, and preferred method of quantification. Bearing these reservations in mind, much the same principal taxa are recorded in the charcoals from Maiden Castle (Salisbury and Jane 1940; Gale 1991), Whitesheet Hill (Gale 2004), and Offham Hill (Cartwright 1976). The Whitesheet Hill and Offham Hill charcoal assemblages are interpreted as representing initial disturbance around the time of enclosure construction followed by differing degrees of woodland regeneration. However, Salisbury's and Jane's (1940) interpretation of the charcoal from Maiden Castle proposed an open environment in the Neolithic. This assessment was severely criticised by Godwin and Tansley (1941) and subsequently by Gale (1991) in the light of her analysis of the charcoal from more recent excavations. Charcoal studies from enclosure and non-enclosure sites from the south Dorset Ridgeway project (Carruthers and Thomas 1991), and the Stonehenge environs project (Gale 1990), appear to demonstrate the persistence of extensive, but not necessarily closed or continuous, woodland in southern Britain throughout the Neolithic. Insofar as comparison is possible, the results of this investigation are thus similar to the charcoal evidence from other earlier Neolithic sites in broadly comparable geographic locations.

However, while it could be argued from the charcoal evidence that predominantly wooded environments were preferred locations for such sites (bearing in mind that woodland regeneration appears to have been allowed to occur following initial clearance episodes) this is by no means conclusive. Similarly, it does not follow that the vegetation associated with enclosures typifies more distant areas or other site types during the earlier Neolithic. These comments appear to be supported by palaeoenvironmental evidence from other sources, notably mollusc remains (Bell *et al,* Ch 5) and, less frequently, pollen (eg Thorley 1981; Scaife 1982; Scaife 1991; Waton 1982) from enclosure and non-enclosure sites. For example, away from the Maiden Castle enclosure, a broadly contemporary Neolithic pit produced a fairly open country molluscan fauna, while the later Flagstones enclosure, also in the Dorchester area, built *c* 3000 cal BC, stood in pasture (Allen 1997b, 167–74).

Vegetation change

Interpretation is complicated by the nature and temporal resolution of the archaeological evidence, our understanding of ecological processes, and difficulties in distinguishing between the effects of past human activities and those of natural phenomena. Ecological processes, for example, can operate at different scales, micro-scale fluctuations occurring within the wider context of macro-scale events and processes. The compositions of wooded ecosystems, therefore, may fluctuate at stand level, appear to remain stable for centuries at a regional, or 'landscape', level, but may undergo significant and fundamental changes at larger scales (Delcourt *et al* 1983; Sprugal 1991; Peterken 1996).

Comparison of the assemblage with the composition of modern woody plant communities, described by Rodwell (1991) and Polunin and Walters (1985), suggests minor taxa (eg *Sambucus nigra*, *Ligustrum vulgare*, *Euonymus europaeus*, *Hedera helix* and *Rubus* agg), although not identified among the assemblage, would have been present during the Neolithic along with the identified taxa. Significantly, perhaps, while these taxa have poor fuel value or are of limited economic use, their presence in samples might be expected if indiscriminate clearance had occurred; instead selection from the local area is indicated.

Only four of the 25 taxa identified were not represented in the Neolithic samples: *Clematis vitalba*, *Rhamnus catharticus*, *Frangula alnus* and *Rosa*, which came from likely Roman contexts. Neolithic samples contain the following large tree taxa not present in Bronze Age and younger samples: *Fagus*, *Taxus*, and *Tilia*. Beaker and Bronze Age samples contain four of the eleven large- or medium-sized tree taxa (Fig 6.3); later Bronze Age to medieval samples contain seven taxa in this category. Given the differences in sampling methods, quantity of samples, and the amount of charcoal recovered from contexts of different periods, it is not clear if this represents a genuine decline in the presence of large/medium-sized tree taxa from the Bronze Age onwards. Changes in the nature and intensity of site use may also be reflected. Apart from *Quercus*, *Fraxinus* is the commonest large tree taxon in post-Neolithic samples. Like *Acer*, this species is light-demanding. Both taxa often feature in open conditions, such as those presently found in scrub, hedgerows, or light open woodland and woodland margins. It may be significant that both species coppice well and, historically, have been heavily managed as such (Edlin 1970). These considerations, along with the apparent higher proportion of small tree or large shrub and shrub or climber taxa, which also require open conditions, in post-Neolithic samples, may support the argument for prolonged woodland clearance.

Comments regarding specific identifications

Buxus sempervirens. While *Buxus* is considered native to the British Isles (Stace 1991) it is rarely found as charcoal. Keepax (1988) cites only one pre-Roman find, tentatively identified by Godwin (1975) from a Neolithic context. While it can be locally abundant where suitable growing conditions exist today, it is otherwise rather scarce. It seems probable that this was also so in the Neolithic, with local occurrence indicated by its presence in the ditches.

Pinus sylvestris. Some confusion remains over the status of *Pinus* in southern Britain. It is generally regarded as native to Scotland, from where it was reintroduced into England and the southern counties following its virtual extinction by the mid-Holocene (Birks *et al* 1975). Charcoal of this taxon occurs in several samples at Hambledon, and at other Neolithic sites in the south of England (Godwin 1975; Keepax 1988). The Boreal dates for samples from two features at Hambledon, cited above, leave open the possibility of a Neolithic date for pine charcoal from other contexts on the hill, in some of which it was associated with Neolithic artefacts and more abundant charcoal of temperate woodland taxa. This is made all the more likely by pollen evidence such as that from the Hampshire Basin and other areas in the south of England (Scaife 1991) which demonstrates the local presence and persistence of *Pinus* from the Neolithic to the middle Iron Age. Earlier still, *Pinus* pollen and charcoal from a probable Mesolithic soil lens in the Fir Tree Field shaft, Cranborne Chase (Green and Allen 1997), and from massive postholes of Boreal age in the Stonehenge area (Cleal *et al* 1995, fig 25), show that pine was a component of the Boreal chalk landscape.

Vitis vinifera. A single fragment of *Vitis* charcoal was identified during Chisham's (1994) study of charcoal from the main causewayed enclosure ditch. The fragment formed part of sample HH76 67 and came from layer 9A (a phase IV deposit) in segment 17 (Fig 3.29). The fragment appears to have been part of the stem of a mature specimen, with three to four annual rings remaining. The specimen would have been mature enough to support fruit production.

The *Vitis* charcoal complements the single charred grape pip recovered from pit 4B F53 on the Stepleton spur (Jones and Legge 1987; Jones and Legge, 6.2). Despite deriving from different areas of the site the finds are more-or-less contemporary. The pip has been radiocarbon-dated to *3640–3340 cal BC* (4660±80 BP; OxA-931). While the *Vitis* charcoal is not itself dated, there are radiocarbon dates for other samples from the same context: articulating animal bone has been dated to *3570–3380 cal BC* (mean of two measurements of 4800±65 BP – OxA-7020, OxA-7021) and *3530–3390 cal BC* (mean of 4725±60 BP – OxA-7019 and 4625±65 BP – OxA-7058); and bulk charcoal samples have been dated to *3650–3390 cal BC* (4670±100 BP; HAR-2375) and *3640–3400 cal BC* (4610±90 BP; HAR-2377). Together these two finds are the earliest known record of this taxon in Britain and, for the charcoal fragment, the earliest example recorded anywhere in northern Europe.

The following questions arise from the presence of this taxon in Neolithic Britain: was *Vitis* native or imported? And, perhaps more significantly, was it being cultivated, either in its wild or domesticated form? To be attributed native status a species must have been recorded from post-glacial deposits predating the isolation of Britain from mainland Europe *c* 10,000BP (Godwin 1975, but see N Brown 1997). The find of *Vitis* charcoal is clearly too recent to fulfil this criteria. Nonetheless the absence of earlier finds does not rule out the possibility that it entered southern Britain in the early post-glacial, maintaining a minor presence which has remained undetected to date. At present it seems more likely that it was imported, either as seed or cuttings, from a source in Asia or the Mediterranean. Although there is no clear consensus, *Vitis* is generally considered native to Western Asia, and was probably first brought into cultivation in the Levant *c* 5000 cal BC. Evidence for the cultivation of this taxon in Europe is scanty, and generally later in date. The earliest examples cited by Jones and Legge (1987) are seeds of the wild variety from levels dated to between the eleventh and the eighth millennia cal BC at Balma Abeurador in the south of France (Vaquer *et al* 1986). Rausing (1990) discusses grape-pip impressions in early Neolithic sherds from three sites in southern Sweden (Mogetorp, Östra Vrå, and Moäng). The Mogetorp find may have pre-dated Hambledon by as much as 1000 years, since associated radiocarbon dates span the second half of the fifth millennium cal BC. *Vitis* pollen has also been recorded in Neolithic contexts in Denmark (Rausing 1990). The pathway by which the Hambledon specimens may have arrived remains unclear, but raises interesting questions as to the chronology and nature of contact and exchange between Britain and continental Europe.

The grape pip is described as morphologically comparable with domesticated varieties (Jones and Legge 1987; Jones this chapter). Regrettably, no such differentiation can be made for the charcoal specimen. However, given that the pip appears to be a domesticate it is a reasonable assumption that the wood was also from a domesticated variety. Much of the earlier Neolithic falls within the Atlantic period, partly characterised by the 'climatic optimum'. During this period Britain is believed to have experienced greater precipitation and higher summer temperatures than at present, by as much as 2°C (Barber *et al* 2004). This would have provided favourable growing conditions for *Vitis*, although the chalkland soils would not have been ideal. During this period other thermophilous species make a marked impression in the palynological record, notably *Tilia, Fagus* and *Carpinus* (all represented at Hambledon).

If the Hambledon specimens are domesticates, the cultivation of *Vitis* in Neolithic Britain is a strong possibility. This is strengthened by the presence of mature wood capable of fruit production. The purpose of its cultivation is open to speculation, but fruit consumption and fermentation are the obvious candidates. It seems that *Vitis* was a rare and exotic specimen in Neolithic Britain and may thus have been attributed special significance.

Erica vagans. Six fragments of *E vagans* were identified in three samples (ST81 C257, C259, C264), all from pit 4B F178 on the Stepleton spur, which was rich in Neolithic artefacts (see 3.5.6). It is believed that this find represents the only macrofossil record of this taxon in post-glacial prehistoric deposits in Britain (McClintock, pers comm). The present-day distribution of this species in Britain is confined to specific locations at the Lizard peninsula, Cornwall, where it is a significant component of 'tall' and 'mixed heath' communities. Its occurrence here is closely linked to soils overlying the Gabbro and Serpentine bedrocks. Marrs and Proctor (1978) suggest this association may be due to the specific soil conditions required to meet nutritional needs. It is also found in isolated locations in north-west Ireland, western France, and northern Spain (McClintock 1989). Given its present-day distribution, it is an apparently anomalous component of the Hambledon charcoal assemblage.

Unusually for a member of the Ericaceae, this taxon is able to tolerate alkaline soils, such as those found at Hambledon Hill. The warm and humid climate of the region where it grows today may have been matched in other areas during the Atlantic 'climatic optimum'. It is therefore possible that it grew in or around the site, probably as a component of 'Chalk heath', during the Neolithic. Evidence for heathland communities in southern Britain prior to the Bronze Age is, however, sparse, and rests mainly on the inference of clearance by Mesolithic populations. For example, pollen from Oakhanger, Hampshire (Rankine *et al* 1960) and Iping Common, Sussex (Dimbleby *et al* 1965), is interpreted as indicating woodland clearance followed by development of heathland vegetation prior to the Neolithic. Similarly, pollen from non-cultural deposits suggests that the modern heaths of east Dorset and west Hampshire may have their origin in the early Atlantic period (Moore 1962). More recently, Allen and Scaife (1991) have discussed the evidence for the creation and expansion of a predominantly heath vegetation in the Poole Basin in the late Bronze Age. They suggest that this derived from significant but limited Neolithic heath vegetation, itself perhaps deriving from late Devensian relict communities. Nonetheless, evidence for lowland Neolithic (acid) heath communities remains limited; whereas for 'Chalk heath' it is apparently non-existent. Therefore, while localised heathland may have existed, it is believed that the specific requirements for the growth of *E vagans* were not available. In the 'mixed heath' communities of the Lizard peninsula *E vagans* typically co-dominates with *Ulex europaeus* (gorse). No charcoal from this taxon has been identified from Hambledon Hill, although it was present in post-Neolithic contexts at Maiden Castle (Gale 1991). There is little to encourage speculation that *E vagans* was growing anywhere in Dorset during the Neolithic.

The favoured hypothesis is that *E vagans* was imported from Cornwall, for reasons that are unclear. Heather may have been available from sources closer to Hambledon Hill which, it is felt, would negate the need to import heather from such a distant source, unless it was valued for specific properties or attributes which are no longer apparent. Therefore, a more plausible explanation for its presence at Hambledon Hill is that it was transported incidentally, possibly along with more valuable goods or raw materials. Evidence of long distance trade in polished stone axes and pottery provides the necessary link between Hambledon Hill and the Lizard peninsula. Axeheads of rocks from the south-west were deposited on the hill, mainly inside the main enclosure (Smith, Ch 6), and their sources correlate well with the modern distribution of *E vagans*. The Gabbro-tempered pottery from pits in the main enclosure provides another connection with the Lizard peninsula (see Smith, 9.1; Darvill, 9.2). While the evidence is circumstantial, it seems highly plausible that *E vagans* was transported along with the stone axeheads and/or the gabbroic pottery.

Clematis vitalba and *Rosa*. The combined presence of *Clematis* and *Rosa* is interesting in as much as it is suggestive of hedge-like vegetation or woodland margin (although *Clematis* can also occur in closed woodland). Fragments of these taxa were identified only in a single sample from a ploughsoil in which the most abundant pottery is Roman. *Prunus*, also a common species of modern hedgerows, was also present. Sample composition and probable date, added to the presence of a Romano-British hollow way running through the inner outwork gateway, increase the possibility that the sample may represent a hedge, in a more formalised landscape.

Anthropogenic factors

Arguably one of the principal constraints encountered when attempting to reconstruct vegetation from charcoal remains is the association of wood with charcoal creation and human activities. The presence of charcoal in an archaeological context is not an incidental occurrence (unlike the presence of mollusca and pollen, for example). In practical terms human agency operates decisively at three key stages: 1) the acquisition or avoidance of wood, 2) its exposure to fire and, 3) its incorporation, or (re)deposition, into the context from which it is recovered archaeologically. Similarly, ecological constraints, actions arising from functional requirements, political concerns and cultural perceptions and beliefs may influence woodland composition, and the woods that are exploited, over a range of temporal and spatial scales and with different degrees of intensity. It is not intended to deal with these issues in great detail here. Nonetheless such factors are likely to influence the nature and composition of charcoal remains and their interpretation profoundly.

Source of the wood charcoal

In the British Isles today naturally occurring large fires are rare in wooded areas. Where they do occur it is usually due to the flammable nature of some types of ground vegetation, rather than the presence of combustible tree taxa (Packham *et al* 1992). There is no evidence that any of the charcoal at Hambledon Hill derives from non-anthropogenic *in situ* burning of living vegetation, and it is likely that human agency was the sole source of the charcoal at the site. No hearth-like features are described from Neolithic contexts. Nonetheless, it is assumed that most of the charcoal was generated in hearth-like fires, the precise function of which we can only speculate. Domestic fires, for food processing, warmth, and light; fires explicitly to burn waste, from vegetation clearance, artefact manufacture, and construction activities; and ceremonial and symbolic fires, are equally plausible.

Condition of the charcoal and possible maintenance of structures

Invertebrate damage and fungal degradation were inferred from the presence of 'bore-holes', fungal hyphae, and descriptions of the morphological characteristics of uncharred degraded wood (eg Hicken 1975; Rayner and Boddy 1988). Fungal hyphae were observed in vessels and, very occasionally, in the ground tissue of many fragments from various contexts across the site. Insect damage frequently follows fungal attack (Hicken 1975), and it is thought this further contributed to the poor condition of the fragments. The extent of decay in the original wood cannot be determined from the charcoal. Because wood charcoal is highly resistant to biological degradation (Keepax 1988), any degradation is likely to have begun prior to charring. It cannot be determined if degradation occurred prior to acquisition, during stockpiling, or *in situ* (during use). Salisbury and Jane (1940) used evidence of fungal degradation in the charcoal from Maiden Castle to infer the local collection of fuelwood. While an acceptable hypothesis for some of the Hambledon material, this possibility is less plausible when considering samples probably derived from structures, and an alternative explanation is required.

The condition of charcoal from the ditches was often poor. Fragments were frequently contaminated (sometimes severely) with calcareous deposits, occasional mineral deposits (?Fe), and other inclusions. Charcoal (especially *Quercus*) closely associated with the chalk matrix below silt horizons was particularly affected. Excepting material from the samples specified below, the condition of the charcoal from possible structural material was generally fairly good. Invertebrate damage and, perhaps, fungal degradation were less evident in fragments from postholes (mostly *Quercus*) than fragments from other contexts (mostly *Corylus*). The intrusive deposits described above were also evident in many fragments.

The lower levels in the central part of segment 6 of the inner Stepleton outwork provides the clearest evidence of *in situ* burning of structural features (see above), apparently destroyed in a single episode. Numerous fragments in samples from this deposit appeared either 'vitrified' (mostly in samples ST79 C91 and C107) or, while possibly not 'vitrified', very brittle and prone to crumbling, losing coherence when handled (ST79 C34, C35 and C39). Brittle fragments also showed signs of decay, ie invertebrate damage and/or fungal degradation (suggestive of, for example, 'white rot'). Anatomical features in 'vitrified' fragments were highly distorted and many were unidentifiable. This phenomenon is believed to be caused by rapid intense heating at temperatures in excess of 700°C (Prior and Alvin 1983). The 'vitrified' charcoal adds support to the idea of wooden features being destroyed by intense fire, perhaps during a conflagration. Charcoal from other contexts did not generally display such extreme distortion. 'Vitrified' charcoal showing comparable physical distortion has been identified from Maiden Castle by Gale (1991). The combination of these factors may support the hypothesis offered here that degradation principally occurred during use and that some structural components were perhaps nearing the end of their useful life.

Two possibilities arise from the condition of numerous *Quercus* fragments from postholes: a) the onset of decay occurred before posts were being fire-hardened prior to use, or b) posts were not fire-hardened in this way and were showing signs of degradation in use. The first possibility suggests that wood in prime condition was not available or not being used. Alternatively wood was stockpiled, or reused, and suffered degradation during this time. In this instance fire-hardening may have been employed to improve the durability of poor-quality wood. However, Whittle (1997, 158) suggests that fire-hardening in the (later) Neolithic was not 'normal practice'. The second possibility, and the one favoured here, is that wood was decaying while in use prior to burning. Similarities between the Hambledon material and descriptions of charcoal from late Neolithic posts and postholes at West Kennet (Whittle 1997) further support this conclusion.

Charcoal from a single posthole was typically made up of one abundant taxon by fragment quantity (almost exclusively *Quercus*), and commonly one or more fragments from one to four other taxa. While this may be explained simply by the accidental inclusion of stray material, alternative possibilities are that the less represented taxa are remnants of former posts, or wedges. Inconsistencies in the quality of *Quercus* fragments from the same feature may indicate that decaying posts were being replaced with the same taxon. Post replacement may have occurred in some instances, notably 3B F601, and supports the idea of maintenance of structural features.

The presence of deliberately grown barriers or boundaries might also be supported by the charcoal evidence, but remains conjectural. Taxa suited to forming protective barriers (notably *Crataegus* and *Prunus spinosa*, which are likely to have been present among the Maloideae and *Prunus*) are much in evidence in all contexts. Charcoal of these taxa recovered from ditches may represent the maintenance of such features or, alternatively, the routine clearance of invasive scrub.

Selection/avoidance and non-structural plant use

The strength of the evidence from ethnographic and historical accounts (eg Heizer 1963; Smart and Hoffman 1988; Hastorf and Johannessen 1991; Shackleton and Prins 1992), demonstrates that the selection, avoidance, or conservation, of particular woods, or woodland stands, is often a complex amalgam of ecological, functional, and non-functional considerations. For example, the relative abundance and location of specific taxa, the purpose for which the wood is intended, particular properties, such as durability or strength, or cultural associations, such as links to ancestors, may all be important factors simultaneously contributing to perceptions of what can and cannot be exploited at a given time. The probable contribution of such factors to the nature of a charcoal assemblage is generally inferred, but can rarely be demonstrated.

However, the presence of both *Erica vagans* and *Vitis vinifera* clearly suggests that alien and exotic plant resources were available, through cultural connections, and accessible, via trade networks, to the Neolithic people of Dorset. Similarly, the diversity of the assemblage and correlations between context type and taxa present, suggests that, in addition to the gathering of (dead) wood for fuel, wood was being specifically selected for other reasons, such as for construction and artefact manufacture. Also, given the supposed functions of the site, it cannot be ruled out that wood may have been gathered for less mundane reasons. Heizer (1963), for example, discusses 'ritualised' fuel gathering in which the act of gathering and stockpiling wood is part of larger ritual practices, while Hastorf and Johannessen (1991) describe the importance of symbolic associations in the choice of fuelwoods. Symbolic and ceremonial fires are well documented in northern Europe (Frazer 1923), and particular woods may have been selected for these purposes. *Betula* charcoal, for example, recovered from inside a fragmentary pot at the base of the main causewayed enclosure bank on site P1, is suggestive of symbolic/ceremonial use of particular woods, while *Corylus* and Maloideae charcoal inside one of two child skulls built into a flint cairn on the base of the adjacent ditch suggest deliberate placement.

Virtually all the trees and shrubs represented have parts of value as plant foods, medicines, poisons, animal fodder, and bedding as well as fuel (eg nuts, berries, fruits, leaves, and inner bark: Grieve 1976; Mabey 1996). Arguably, taxa considered more useful as a source of secondary products, rather than for their wood (eg *Sambucus*), may have been preserved for uses such as these, or, alongside other woods, conserved to maintain the required conditions for non-woody plants exploited for such purposes.

Exploitation of the physical properties and aesthetic qualities of many of the woods represented is historically and ethnographically well documented (Edlin 1970). The fashioning of objects designed for functional or esoteric purposes is likely to have been a common activity. Presumably some of the Hambledon charcoal originated from discarded, broken, or purposefully burnt artefacts, and as by-products of activities such as artefact manufacture. Individual trees, specific taxa, and/or particular stands may have been valued as living components of the landscape or as deadwood (on or off site), solely for their aesthetic qualities or attributed magical or spiritual properties, as documented in various historical and ethnographic accounts (Porteous 1928; Hadfield 1974; Davies 1988; Schama 1995; Rival 1998) and inference from archaeological sources (Boyd 1988). The composition of post-Neolithic samples may indicate that less desirable woods (eg *Rhamnus*) were gathered when preferred woods were absent, or inaccessible, a response discussed by Shackleton and Prins (1992).

Pits and ditches

In terms of the taxa represented, the Stepleton pits are richer than those elsewhere on the hill. They are, indeed, the only pits to contain *Erica vagans*, *Ilex*, *Taxus*, *Carpinus*, and Salicaceae. The diversity of taxa is one of numerous distinctions between the contents and manner of filling of pits here and in the central area. An emphasis on day-to-day living is more apparent in many of the Stepleton pits (see 3.5.6). If this was so, it may be that activities such as food processing and artefact manufacture were the origin of the charred material. This interpretation would adequately explain the diversity of the assemblage. All of the taxa commonly represented are good fuel woods and/or have potentially useful functional properties for artefact manufacture. Significantly, none of the Stepleton pits contained the exotic artefacts recovered from the main causewayed enclosure pits. It seems likely, therefore, that the charcoal was deposited as fire debris, from burnt fuel and waste, reflecting disparate mundane activities.

The pit samples from the central area are less rich (eight taxa) than the ditch deposits (17 taxa). Pits in the central area contained only two taxa, *Pinus* and *Betula*, not identified from Stepleton pit samples. The esoteric functions proposed for this enclosure may be significant, but neither the composition of the charcoal assemblage from the pits as a whole, nor patterns in the composition of individual pit samples, stands out, unless, for reasons that are unclear, the restricted range of taxa represented is considered significant in itself, given the range of taxa that potentially could be present. Initially, therefore, it appears no claim can be convincingly made for the 'ritualised' symbolic deposition of charcoal, despite the nature of main causewayed enclosure pit deposits. Nonetheless, many taxa in the main causewayed enclosure pits have eclectic, and apparently ancient, symbolic associations, notably *Quercus* and *Fraxinus* (Frazer 1923). It is tempting to regard such associations as the primary reason for the presence of certain taxa in the main causewayed enclosure pits. We can only cautiously infer that special meaning may have been attributed in the past to some acts of deposition involving charcoal and, perhaps, specific taxa. Put in the context of the supposed functions of the enclosure, and persuasive evidence for the symbolic deposition of high-status objects, it seems a reasonable assumption to regard the charcoal in these pits as more than meaninglessly deposited waste.

Woodland management

It is often asserted that woodland management was practised in the Neolithic. Orme and Coles (1985), for example, document evidence of woodland management on the Somerset levels, while coppiced stools were found still rooted in the ditch of the Etton causewayed enclosure (Taylor 1998). Rackham (1977, 71) describes Neolithic coppicing as 'a surprisingly elaborate system', compared to modern and medieval practices, and suggests (Rackham 1979) that both the growing and use of wood were organised activities. There is no unequivocal evidence, direct or indirect, for woodland management at Hambledon Hill. Fragments were generally unsuitable for growth characteristic analysis or the determination of diameter when cut. *Corylus* fragments from structural deposits in the inner Stepleton outwork (see above) were composed of the innermost growth rings, and may have been roundwood. Nonetheless, none of the characteristics of the earliest rings indicating vigorous (re)growth associated with coppicing (Rackham 1977) were apparent in these fragments, or in others with innermost rings. The presence of posts and probability of wattle hurdles, associated with bank revetments, therefore, remains suggestive but is not evidence of management or systematic cropping.

Nonetheless, wood requirements for construction, fuel, and other purposes, must have necessitated ready supplies of suitable wood encouraging, perhaps, methodical resource management. Intermittent construction and the maintenance of existing structures could have had a significant impact on the structure and composition of the vegetation. Trees tend to develop a squat form when grown in open conditions, with retention of side branches, while dense, closed woodland favours the production of tall, straight boles (Desch and Dinwoodie 1981). At least during the earliest phases of the site, timbers suitable for substantial construction work may have been naturally available from existing closed woodland. More purposeful management of wood resources may have been implemented later, when reduced natural availability due to previous cropping and probable changes in woodland/vegetation structure threatened supplies. The principal taxa associated with structural features, *Quercus* and *Corylus*, respond extremely well to management (Edlin 1970). Coppicing (intended or incidental) of these, and other suitable taxa (eg *Fraxinus*, *Acer*), may have resulted if stools were not grubbed-up following felling. Subsequent regrowth would provide future potential supplies of wood and fodder (Rackham 1977).

6.1.4 Conclusion

This charcoal analysis suggests that the site was located in a temporary clearing at an ecotone, and functioned in a predominantly wooded mosaic of vegetation types throughout the Neolithic. Ongoing natural and anthropogenic disturbance probably contributed to the creation of open areas and a shifting patchwork of woodland types, of which secondary woodland was possibly a significant, and increasingly dominant, characteristic. Direct evidence of silviculture is lacking. Woodland is, however, likely to have been managed and, while management was probably not intensive, it may have affected the character of the vegetation in some areas. The occurrence of woodland regeneration suggests that woodland was a valued landscape feature, important perhaps not just as a source of wood and other potential resources, but also for more cultural/esoteric associations. A predominantly cattle-based pastoral economy, for example, such as that proposed for Hambledon during the Neolithic by Legge (Ch 8), may have encouraged the preservation of extensive wooded areas favourable for animal husbandry as well as for game. While clearance specifically for crops is a possibility, anthropogenic clearance may have been more a by-product of acquiring wood than a purposeful strategy for providing cleared land for other purposes.

A considerable range of wood-related resources were available locally. Others, such as *Vitis vinifera*, might have been imported as an exotic fruit from continental Europe or deliberately introduced and grown at the site. Intra-site variability in charcoal deposits is not distinctive. However, the charcoal assemblages from pits on the Stepleton spur and in the central area seem significantly different from each other and from those from ditch deposits, other than phase IV of the main enclosure on site G, and may partly reflect the different nature of activities carried out in these areas. Wood was possibly being exploited in both functional and non-functional capacities, and also perhaps featured in ceremonial activities in its own right and as part of larger symbolic concerns. The use of timber in the construction and maintenance of the earthworks would have had a continuing, if intermittent, impact on the surrounding woodland.

6.2 Evaluating the role of cereal cultivation in the Neolithic: charred plant remains from Hambledon Hill

Glynis Jones and A J Legge

6.2.1 Sampling and recovery

Charred plant remains were recovered from the central area, the Stepleton spur, the Hanford spur and Everley Water Meadow. Recovery methods included froth flotation (Jarman *et al* 1972), wet-sieving, dry-sieving and manual recovery. Flotation, using sieves of mesh size 1 mm and 300μ, was carried out by AJL at the main causewayed enclosure in 1974 and on the Stepleton spur in 1979 and 1981. In 1978 deposits from the Stepleton spur were wet-sieved using sieves of the same mesh sizes as those used for flotation.

Table 6.3 Charred plant remains. Recovery methods

Area	*No. of samples taken for:* Flotation	Wet-sieving	Dry-sieving	*Finds recovered manually*
Central area features 1974	>24			18
Central area features 1975				28
Central area features 1977			6	77
Main enclosure ditch	>11	13		106
Cross-dykes		1		37
Long barrow		1	*c* 11	14
Stepleton spur features 1978		60	1	40
Stepleton spur features 1979	45		6	17
Stepleton spur features 1980				40
Stepleton spur features 1981	184			291
Stepleton spur features 1982	3			52
Stepleton enclosure ditch	11			88
Stepleton outworks	6	3		115
Hanford spur		30	*c* 12	103
Everley Water Meadow		35		96

One-eighth of the large cereal deposit collected in 1982 from F39 outside the Stepleton enclosure was floated and wet-sieved in the laboratory, using sieves of mesh sizes 1 mm and 300 mm for the flot and 1 mm for the heavy residue. In other years and areas of the hill, charred plant remains were retrieved manually or by wet- or dry-sieving with a 0.25 inch mesh. Charred plant remains were also recovered from samples wet-sieved for molluscs in Everley Water Meadow (mesh size 0.5 mm) in 1983 and 1984. In all, *c* 1300 samples were taken (including *c* 450 samples for flotation or wet-sieving) either specifically for charred plant remains or for charcoal, molluscs etc. The breakdown of the different sample types taken from different areas is given in Table 6.3. Where samples were taken specifically for charred plant remains, these were chosen on the basis of visible charred remains. In the area of the Stepleton enclosure, pits were more intensively sampled than ditches (see Table 6.3).

The >1 mm fractions from flotation and wet-sieving were totally sorted for charred plant remains with one exception: the sample from ST82 F39 was subsampled after flotation/wet-sieving and one-eighth of the >1 mm flot, <1 mm flot and heavy residue were sorted (equivalent to 1/64 of the original sample). The <1 mm fractions for most of the other samples (and any heavy residues collected after flotation) were unavailable and were not sorted. Cereal and wild plant remains from these samples, as well as those from charcoal and mollusc samples etc, were identified by reference to modern comparative collections in the Department of Archaeology, University of Cambridge and the Department of Archaeology, University of Sheffield. Cereals were quantified by counting the embryo ends of grains, the bases of wheat glumes and the rachis internodes of barley and free-threshing wheat. Hazelnut shell was quantified by weight. The cereal identifications (with accompanying wild species) are presented in Tables 6.4–6.12, and the location of the samples is shown in Figures 3.70 and 3.132. The locations and size of hazelnut shell finds are shown in Figures 3.71 and 3.133.

The different recovery strategies are reflected in the quantity and quality of the charred plant remains recovered. Virtually all of the charred plant remains from the main causewayed enclosure were recovered in 1974 (Figs 3.70–71) and the few finds from other years, when recovery was mostly manual, were all of hazelnut shell. For the Stepleton spur, a contrast is apparent between the areas sampled for flotation or wet-sieving and those sampled manually. The only cereal find recovered from the areas sampled manually

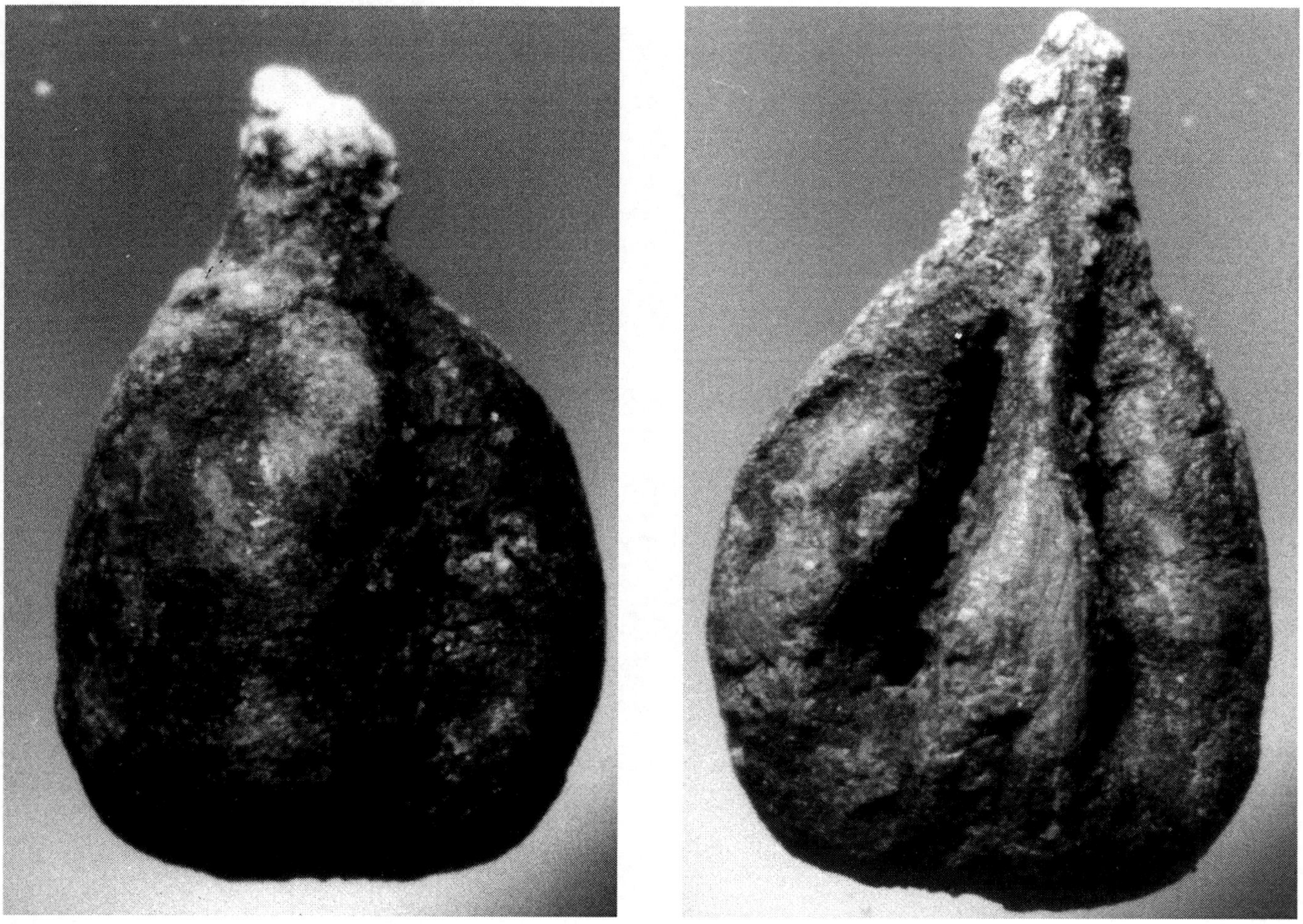

Fig 6.4 Two views of grape pip from 4B F53. Photos Glynis Jones

Table 6.4 Charred plant remains from Neolithic features in the central area 1974

+ = <10 g shell
gl = glume bases (everything else = seed)

Feature	*A F2*	*A F5*	*A F6*	*A F9*	*A F11*	*A F12*	*A F28*	*A F41A*	*A F41B*	*A F78*	*?*
Sample									*1, 2, 3 to 4, 3 to 6*		
Triticum dicoccum gl	0	0	0	0	0	0	0	1	1	0	0
Triticum dicoccum	2	2	0	0	2	3	3	70	82	4	1
T cf *dicoccum*	0	0	0	0	0	0	0	4	4	0	1
Triticum sp	2	0	0	0	0	2	3	60	39	0	2
Hordeum sp	0	0	0	0	1	0	0	0	6	0	0
cf *Hordeum* sp	0	0	0	0	0	0	0	0	4	0	1
indet cereal	3	0	1	1	0	0	0	23	26	2	0
Corylus avellana	+	0	+	0	0	0	0	+	+	0	+
indet fruit frags	0	0	0	0	0	0	0	0	0	0	0

(1980 and 1982) was the huge concentration found in 1982 and processed in the laboratory. In the wet-sieved area (1978), most of the cereal finds are large concentrations which may have been apparent to the naked eye (Fig 3.132). In the areas where flotation was also carried out (1979 and 1981), numerous smaller cereal finds are also well represented (Fig 3.132), reflecting a different sampling strategy not primarily directed towards visible concentrations of charred remains. On the Hanford spur (which was also wet-sieved), all the charred plant remains were recovered manually and all were of hazelnut shell. Throughout, cereal remains were recovered only by flotation or wet-sieving; manual recovery provided hazelnut shell only. This supports earlier observations at Neolithic sites (Moffett *et al* 1989).

6.2.2 Species represented

The predominant cereals, from the areas of both the main causewayed enclosure and the Stepleton enclosure, are *Triticum dicoccum* Schübl (emmer wheat) and *Hordeum* sp (barley). Most of the barley is unidentifiable either to species (two- or six-row) or as either hulled or naked, but six-row naked barley (*H vulgare* L var *nudum*) and one grain of hulled barley were identified from a Neolithic feature on the Stepleton spur. Two-row barley (*H distichum* L) was identified from a medieval (or later) sample from Everley Water Meadow. Several samples of Romano-British, medieval or later date also contained bread wheat (*T aestivum* L s l).

Hazelnut shell (*Corylus avellana* L) is common throughout the Neolithic site, and a single seed of grape (*Vitis vinifera* L), apparently of the cultivated variety, was found on the Stepleton spur (ST81 F53, Fig 6.4; Jones and Legge 1987). Finds of other wild species are sparse, with occasional finds of *Galium aparine* L (lady's bedstraw), *Vicia/Lathyrus* sp (vetch/vetchling) and *Bromus* sp (brome grass) as well as *Anthemis cotula* L (stinking mayweed) in one medieval (or later) sample from Everley Water Meadow.

Table 6.5 Charred plant remains from main causewayed enclosure ditch 1974

+ = <10 g shell

Segment	*2*	*3*	*3*
Feature		*1*	
Layer	*9*		*2*
Triticum sp	0	1	0
indet cereal	2	0	1
Corylus avellana	0	+	0
cf *Vicia/Lathyrus*	1	0	0

In all the Neolithic features (except ST82 F39 – see below), the cereals are apparently in a cleaned state with virtually no chaff remains (in the form of glume bases or rachis internodes) and with very few weed seeds. The absence of small-seeded weeds may be due to the fact that the <1 mm fractions have not been sorted but the paucity of weed seeds >1 mm cannot be attributed to this.

6.2.3 Spatial distribution

Most of the charred plant remains were recovered from within and around the Stepleton enclosure which may be partly a result of the more intensive sampling in this the smaller of the two enclosures. No cereal remains, and very little hazelnut shell, were found on the Hanford Spur despite wet-sieving.

Among the cereals, both emmer wheat and barley are represented at both enclosures. In the main enclosure, barley is represented by a few grains only (Tables 6.4–6.5) but this is true also of emmer except for one feature (HH74 F41) which yielded a concentration of emmer grains. Emmer predominated on the Stepleton spur (Tables 6.6–6.9), but some features also contained significant quantities of barley (notably 1A F110, where barley predominated). Given the small number of samples from the main enclosure, however, this difference may be fortuitous.

Table 6.6 Charred plant remains from Neolithic features on the Stepleton spur 1978

st = straight grains + = <10 g shell

Feature	*1A F7*	*1A F8*	*1A F57*	*1A F110*	*1A F205*	*1A F228*	*1A F229*	*1A F295*	*1A F350*
Sample(s)	*37, 39*	*80*	*18, 38, 67, 71, 79*	*17, 41–49, 61–53, 55, 84*	*82*	*76*	*93*	*85*	*86, 90, 106, 107, 111*
Triticum dicoccum	4	0	91	47	0	2	6	5	26
T cf *dicoccum*	3	0	35	5	0	0	6	2	14
Triticum sp	13	0	72	13	8	1	4	1	18
Hordeum, naked st	0	0	0	1	0	0	0	0	0
Hordeum, naked	0	0	0	5	0	0	0	0	0
Hordeum, hulled	0	1	0	0	0	0	0	0	0
Hordeum sp	1	1	16	285	0	1	1	1	17
cf *Hordeum* sp	0	0	5	0	0	0	1	2	1
indet cereal	0	1	22	77	5	0	11	3	12
Corylus avellana	+	0	+	+	+	0	+	+	+
Galium aparine	0	0	0	0	0	0	0	0	0

Hazelnut shell is unevenly distributed around the hill, even allowing for variations in sampling. In the area of the main enclosure, a very large concentration of nutshell was found in an upper level of one of the ditches of the south long barrow, and a smaller concentration (though it may have been larger before Desmond Bonney's 1959 excavation) in the slot of one of the south cross-dykes (Fig 3.71). On the Stepleton spur, larger quantities of hazelnut shell were found at the north end, both inside and outside the enclosure ditches (Fig 3.133). These concentrations are unlikely to be an artefact of the recovery programme, since the finds in the area of the main enclosure are so large that they would have been visible to the naked eye, and the variation across the Stepleton spur is apparent even though recovery methods were comparable across the site (especially when comparing the areas sampled for flotation in 1979 and 1981). Elsewhere on the hill small quantities of hazelnut shell are a common occurrence.

6.2.4 Contexts rich in charred plant remains

All of the contexts rich in cereal remains (ie with 50+ items) were pits of various types, except for one sample from the east butt of segment 12 of the Stepleton enclosure, which could nevertheless be the fill of a pit cut into the chalk rubble fills. Most of these were also rich in other finds (either hazelnut shell, charcoal, animal bone, struck flint or pottery, or a combination of these), but not invariably. Two of the pits in the Stepleton enclosure (1A F57 and 4B F137) were unique in containing fragments of infant skull (not complete inhumations). Emmer predominates in both, with small quantities of nutshell (and barley in F137). 1A F110 is unusual both in shape and in the complete absence of struck flint. Two fragments of iron were found in the pit but so were fragments of a small Neolithic cup, similar to the one from ST82 F39 (see below), and two of the barley grains from the pit have been dated to *3640–3490 cal BC (58% probability) or 3470–3370 cal BC (37% probability)* (4725±40 BP; OxA-7837) and *3630–3590 cal BC (7% probability) or 3530–3360 cal BC (88% probability)* (4670±40 BP; OxA-7838). This was also the only feature on the hill with a rich sample dominated by barley but it also contained significant quantities of emmer and nutshell.

ST82 F39 is unique, both in the quantity and nature of the cereal remains recovered. A large quantity of charred remains was apparently tipped into the pit at the north end (Fig 6.5). The sample consists almost entirely of emmer wheat with quantities of hazelnut shell and a few seeds of *Bromus* sp. A small Neolithic cup, other pottery and burnt flint were found among the grain, with burnt antler fragments above. Two of the emmer grains have been dated to *3650–3500 cal BC (75% probability) or 3440–3370 cal BC (20% probability)* (4750±40 BP; OxA-7839) and *3640–3490 cal BC (61% probability) or 3470–3370 cal BC (34% probability)* (4730±45 BP; OxA-7840). The state of the emmer is also unique in that numerous charred glume bases were found with the grain. Each spikelet of emmer usually consists of two grains surrounded by a pair of glumes and so a ratio of 1:1 for

Fig 6.5 Detail of charred grain in ST82 F39

Table 6.7 Charred plant remains from Neolithic features on the Stepleton spur 1979

+ = <10 g shell
st = straight grains, tw = twisted grains

Feature	*2A F7*	*2A F47*	*2A F48*	*2A F142*	*2A F159*	*2A F182*	*2A F184*	*2A F198*	*2A F201*	*2A F206*	*2A F217*	*2A F268*	*2A F321*	*2A F374*	*2A F 378*	*2A F409*	*2A F413*
Sample(s)	*T4*	*T2*	*T11*	*T32, T69*	*T34, T61, T66, –*					*T23, - -*		*T41, T42*	*T48*		*T51, –*		*T52*
Triticum dicoccum	0	1	1	1	12	8	1	4	0	24	4	0	135	0	0	22	0
T cf *dicoccum*	0	0	0	1	2	1	0	0	2	2	1	0	0	0	0	0	1
Triticum sp	0	0	0	0	4	5	1	1	0	11	12	2	0	2	2	1	0
H vulgare, naked tw	0	0	0	0	0	0	0	0	0	0	0	0	5	0	0	0	0
Hordeum, naked st	0	0	0	0	0	0	0	0	0	0	0	0	3	0	0	0	0
Hordeum, naked	0	0	0	0	0	0	0	0	0	0	0	0	11	0	0	0	0
Hordeum sp	0	0	0	0	2	1	0	0	0	0	0	0	18	0	0	0	0
cf *Hordeum* sp	1	0	0	0	0	0	0	0	1	0	0	1	0	0	0	0	1
indet cereal	0	1	2	0	5	8	3	3	4	13	6	2	5	5	3	0	0
Corylus avellana	+	+	0	0	0	0	0	0	+	0	0	0	0	0	0	+	0
cf *Vicia/Lathyrus*	0	0	0	0	0	0	0	0	1	0	0	0	0	0	0	0	0
Galium aparine	0	0	0	0	0	0	0	0	0	0	0	0	0	0	0	1	0

Table 6.8 Charred plant remains from Neolithic features on the Stepleton spur 1981

+ = <10 g shell

Feature	*4A F3*	*4A F3B*	*4B F47*	*4B F53*	*4B F60*	*4B F63*	*4B F64*	*4B F80*	*4B F82*	*4B F92*	*4B F129*	*4B F130*	*4B F137*	*4B F144*	*4B F153*	*4B F155*	*4B F164*	*4B F178*	*4B F198*	*4B F232*
Sample(s)	*T3, –*	*108*	*19*	*18*	*33*	*30*	*17*	*115*		*114*	*85*	*67*	*118*	*28*	*119*	*116, 122*	*103*	*120, 126*	*113, 121, 123*	*109*
Triticum dicoccum	0	0	0	13	0	1	1	3	3	2	13	17	23	1	2	5	0	19	18	0
T cf *dicoccum*	1	1	0	1	0	0	5	1	0	0	1	18	5	1	1	0	0	5	5	0
Triticum sp	1	0	0	15	0	2	3	1	0	1	3	9	12	0	0	1	0	4	5	0
Hordeum sp	0	0	0	1	0	0	1	0	0	1	1	3	0	0	1	0	0	17	5	0
cf *Hordeum* sp	0	0	0	8	0	0	0	0	0	1	1	0	0	0	1	0	0	0	0	0
indet cereal	2	1	1	23	1	0	2	0	1	4	7	30	15	1	1	6	1	25	11	1
Corylus avellana	+	0	0	0	0	0	0	0	0	0	0	+	+	0	0	0	0	0	0	0
Vitis vinifera	0	0	0	1	0	0	0	0	0	0	0	0	0	0	0	0	0	0	0	0

Table 6.9 Charred plant remains from 1/64 of fill of ST82 F39

1/8 sieved = 0.9 kg; 1/8 subsample sorted = 1/64 of total
gl = glume bases
+ = <10 g shell

	>1 mm flot	*<1 mm flot*	*heavy residue*	*totals*
Triticum dicoccum gl	640	132	77	849
Triticum dicoccum	1682	0	3	1685
cf *T dicoccum*	5	0	0	5
Corylus avellana	0	0	+	+
Bromus sp	3	0	0	3

grain to glume bases would be expected for spikelets which have not yet been dehusked. Glume bases survive charring less well than grain, however, so the 2:1 ratio of grains to glume bases in the subsample sorted is consistent with the deposition of whole spikelets, which disintegrate easily when charred (G Jones 1987). Indeed two or three pairs of grains, still attached to their glume bases, were found in the subsample. Glume wheats such as emmer are commonly stored in spikelet form and dehusked piecemeal as required (Hillman 1981a). This deposit therefore apparently represents emmer charred before dehusking, but it is not possible to determine whether the spikelets were deliberately burnt or accidentally charred, eg in storage or while parching prior to dehusking. The deposit of spikelets is certainly large compared to other Neolithic finds: the 1/64 subsample sorted is equivalent to 850 spikelets, making the total sample *c* 50,000 spikelets.

In the area of the main causewayed enclosure, the two largest concentrations of hazelnut shell were outside the enclosure, in the slot cut into in the south butt of the west ditch of the long barrow (dated to *3640–3370 cal BC* (4741±26 BP; UB-4270) and in the slot towards the W butt of the inner S cross-dyke (dated to *3520–3500 cal BC (2% probability) or 3470–3370 cal BC (93% probability)* (4714±33 BP; UB-4273). In the area of the Stepleton enclosure, the largest concentrations of hazelnut shell were again either outside the enclosure ditches (4B F129 and ST82 F4) or just inside (4B F198). Of the moderate concentrations, three were outside the ditches (4B F137 and F712 and ST82 F39), one was within the ditch (the east butt of segment 12), two were just inside the ditch (4B F155 and F178) and two were near the centre of the enclosure (1A F57 and 2A F268). 4B F712 contained a complete inhumation surrounded by flint nodules, stones, burnt chalk and clay, possibly related to the destruction of the innermost outwork rampart (see Ch 3.5.6). A fragment of nutshell from the pit was dated to *3640–3550 cal BC (23% probability) or 3540–3360 cal BC (72% probability)* (4700±45 BP; OxA-7843).

1A F227 and F239 have been tentatively interpreted as an almost ploughed out corn-drier, F227 being the oven and F239 the stokehole (Fig 3.116). Samples from both are dominated by emmer with some nutshell (and barley in the latter). Two of the emmer grains (from F227) have been dated to the Bronze Age: 1740–1490 cal BC (3315±45 BP; OxA-7841) and 1680–1430 cal BC (3255±40 BP; OxA-7842).

6.2.5 Discussion

In terms of the cereal species represented, Hambledon Hill holds no surprises: emmer wheat, naked and hulled barley (including six-row) all occur at other Neolithic sites (Moffett *et al* 1989; Jones and Rowley-Conwy 2007), including those in the region of Hambledon, eg Maiden Castle (Palmer and Jones 1991), Down Farm (M Jones 1991), Flagstones (Straker 1997) and Whitesheet Hill (Hinton 2004). Hazelnut shell is also a regular, and much commented upon, feature of Neolithic sites (eg Moffett *et al* 1989; J Thomas 1991; 1999; 2003; G Jones 2000; Robinson 2000). The occurrence on the Stepleton spur of a single grape pip, apparently of the cultivated variety and radiocarbon dated to *3640–3340 cal BC* (4660±80 BP; OxA-931; Jones and Legge 1987), is, however, unique. This find is complemented by one of *Vitis* charcoal from site G in the main causewayed enclosure (Austin *et al* this chapter), perhaps suggesting that vines were grown locally (though grapes could also have been transported on the vine). A picture of feasting accompanied by wine-drinking is conjured up but this is of course by no means proven by a single seed and a single fragment of charcoal.

Perhaps the most remarkable aspect of the Hambledon Hill plant assemblage is its sheer quantity (*c* 2,500 cereal grains plus a spikelet deposit with *c* 100,000 grains). Even without the spikelet deposit, this amounts to more cereal than that recovered from all other British Neolithic enclosures put together. In large part this can be attributed to the extent of the excavations and the scale of the sieving and flotation programme. In both enclosures, the charred remains consist of an uneven scatter of hazelnut shell and cereals (both emmer and barley).

The cereal remains, like those of many other Neolithic sites (eg Hillman 1981b; Legge 1981b; Moffett *et al* 1989; Fairweather and Ralston 1993, Jones and Rowley-Conwy 2007), consist almost entirely of cleaned grain, with very little surviving chaff or weed seeds, with the exception of the very large deposit of emmer spikelets to the north of the Stepleton enclosure. This find is comparable to the cereal remains from one of the timber buildings at Lismore Fields, Buxton, Derbyshire, where emmer spikelets may have been stored and dehusked (G Jones forthcoming; Jones and Rowley-Conwy 2007). The sample on the Stepleton spur had clearly been deposited after it became charred, but whether as refuse (from an accident in storage or during parching) or as a part of some ritual action is impossible to tell.

Table 6.10 Charred plant remains from Stepleton features of Bronze Age and uncertain date

+ = <10 g shell

Date	*BA*	*BA*	*?Neolithic*	*?Natural*	*?*	*?*	*?*	*?Neolithic*
Feature	*1A F227*	*1A F239*	*1A F278*	*2A F36*	*2A F41*	*2A F53*	*2A F80*	*2A F179*
Sample(s)	*63, 69, –*	*78, 81*	*75*	*T6*	*T10*	*T20*	*T16*	
Triticum dicoccum	63	63	0	0	1	0	9	7
T cf *dicoccum*	22	20	4	0	0	0	3	0
Triticum sp	54	81	8	1	0	0	1	1
Hordeum sp	0	15	4	0	0	0	0	1
cf *Hordeum* sp	1	10	2	0	3	1	2	2
indet cereal	25	49	0	0	0	0	0	0
Corylus avellana	+	+	+	0	0	0	+	0
Galium aparine	1	0	0	0	0	0	0	0

Table 6.11 Charred plant remains from the Stepleton enclosure and inner Stepleton outwork

	Stepleton enclosure					*Inner Stepleton outwork*			
Segment	*12*	*12*	*15*	*16*	*17*	*3*	*5*	*5*	*6*
Subdivision	*U5*	*U5*	*U9*	*U12*	*U14*	*U1*	*C10*	*C11*	*C1*
Layer	*6A*	*2A*	*3B*	*3D*	*3C*	*4C*	*5*	*2B*	*4A*
Triticum dicoccum	1	60	0	1	0	2	0	1	0
T cf *dicoccum*	1	14	0	0	0	1	0	0	0
Triticum sp	0	11	1	0	0	1	0	0	2
Hordeum sp	1	24	0	1	0	1	1	0	0
cf *Hordeum* sp	0	3	1	0	0	0	0	0	0
indet cereal	0	24	0	2	5	4	0	0	0
Galium aparine	0	8	0	0	0	0	0	0	0

Table 6.12 Charred plant remains from Everley Water Meadow mollusc samples

+ = <10 g shell
gl = glume bases, ra = rachis internodes

Date	*BA+*	*IA–Med*	*?*	*Med/PM*	*Med/PM*	*Med/PM*	*MBA*	*Post-med*	*RB+*	*RB+*	*Med?*	*Med/PM*	*recent*	*RB+*	*RB+*	*Med*
Area	*2X*	*2X*	*2X*	*2X*	*2X*	*2X*	*3*	*3*	*5*	*5*	*5*	*5*	*5*	*5*	*5*	*5*
Column	*2*	*2*	*2*	*2*	*2*	*2*		*spot #*	*3*	*3*	*3*	*3*	*3*	*spot #*	*spot #*	*spot #*
Sample	*4*	*5*	*7*	*8*	*9*	*10*		*14*	*19*	*20*	*21*	*22*	*23*	*24*	*25*	*26*
Triticum dicoccum gl	0	0	0	0	0	0	0	2	0	0	0	0	0	0	0	0
T cf *dicoccum*	0	0	0	0	0	0	0	2	0	0	0	0	0	0	0	0
T aestivum ra	0	0	0	0	0	0	0	20	0	1	0	0	5	0	1	0
T cf *aestivum*	0	0	0	5	2	3	0	18	7	19	15	0	3	24	9	2
Triticum sp	1	2	0	1	4	3	0	8	2	2	2	1	0	9	3	0
Hordeum distichum ra	0	0	0	0	0	0	0	1	0	0	0	0	0	0	0	0
Hordeum sp ra	0	0	0	0	0	0	0	1	0	0	0	0	0	0	0	0
Hordeum sp	1	1	3	0	0	0	2	4	0	0	1	0	0	0	4	0
cf *Hordeum* sp	0	0	0	1	0	0	0	2	0	0	0	0	0	0	0	0
indet cereal	3	0	0	0	7	0	0	13	0	3	2	0	0	5	3	0
Corylus avellana	0	0	0	0	0	+	0	0	0	0	0	0	0	0	0	0
Vicia/Lathyrus	0	0	0	1	0	0	1	2	0	0	0	0	0	1	0	0
Galium aparine	0	0	0	0	1	0	0	0	0	0	0	0	0	0	0	0
Bromus sp	0	0	0	0	0	0	0	7	2	0	0	0	0	0	0	0
Anthemis cotula	0	0	0	0	0	0	0	10	0	0	0	0	0	0	0	0

Indeed, for all the grain at Hambledon Hill, two possibilities exist: either they were burnt accidentally or deliberately, perhaps as part of some funeral rite. They are unlikely to represent the remains of feasting, as cereals are normally consumed either as bread or in the form of a gruel, neither of which is likely to yield quantities of whole, identifiable grains when subsequently burnt. Hazelnut shell, on the other hand, being a by-product of food preparation, could result from feasting or day-to-day consumption, the shells becoming burnt as waste or fuel.

The size of the Hambledon Hill plant assemblage provides an opportunity for re-evaluating the role of wild and cultivated plant foods. It has long been recognised that cereals tend to be under-represented in comparison with hazelnuts at unsieved sites (Moffett *et al* 1989; Legge 1989) and so Moffett *et al* (1989), in their review of plant remains at British Neolithic sites, considered only sites where deposits were sieved. They conclude, from the dearth of cereal remains, that there was 'considerable reliance on collected plant resources'. For most of the sites in their table (ibid, table 1), however, the number of samples taken was small, the largest number being from Hazelton (61 samples totalling 550 litres of deposit) where, in fact, quite a large number of cereal grains (283) was recovered. Indeed, the total volume of soil processed for this table amounts to *c* 3,000 litres (247 samples), less than the volume of the *c* 450 samples processed from Hambledon Hill. A larger number of Neolithic sites have since been sampled for charred plant remains, and the quantity of cereals is now much more impressive (Jones and Rowley-Conwy 2007).

There is also a fundamental difference between hazelnuts and cereals in that, for hazelnuts, the part of the plant most frequently recovered is the nutshell, which represents the waste product of consumption, whereas the waste products from cereal consumption are straw and chaff. All of these components may be used as fuel or kindling for fires but, whereas nutshell is robust and likely to survive burning in a charred form, cereal chaff is much more likely to be burnt to ash (Hillman 1981a; Boardman and Jones 1990). Cereal chaff and straw also have other uses, eg as fodder or temper, which do not apply to nutshell.

There is every reason therefore to think that cereal chaff and straw may be under-represented compared to hazelnut shell (G Jones 2000) and, in the case of cereal grain, there is no reason why it should be burnt at all other than by accident or by deliberate 'sacrifice'. In other words, in an economy where cereals provide the bulk of the diet but where hazelnuts (and other wild resources) are consumed in season, one might well expect the recoverable archaeological remains to be dominated by the more durable waste product of hazelnuts. Only when sampling is extensive, or when a house containing stored cereals is burnt down, might one reasonably expect to find the remains of the rare accidents which generate charred cereal grain. This, in fact, is exactly what one finds at Hambledon Hill (with extensive sampling) and in the timber buildings at Balbridie (Fairweather and Ralston 1993) and Lismore Fields (G Jones forthcoming). While this does not prove that the Neolithic diet was cereal-based, it is at least consistent with this hypothesis.

Using the conversion factor for hazelnut shell weight given by Hinton (2004), the largest concentration of nutshell at Hambledon Hill (in one of the long barrow ditches) is equivalent to *c* 350 nuts. As this represents about one-third of the hazelnut shell on the hill, it is not, in itself, evidence for hazelnut consumption on a grand scale. Similarly, the largest concentration of cereal remains (the spikelet deposit outside the Stepleton enclosure) amounts to *c* 7 litres. In both cases, the recovered charred remains probably represent a fraction, and for cereals a very small fraction, of the total plant food consumed. Any attempt to estimate the relative importance of each from a simple comparison of the quantities found is therefore meaningless.

6.2.6 Conclusions

It is clear that both cultivated cereals and collected wild plant foods contributed to the British Neolithic diet. There is debate, however, concerning the relative contribution of each (Moffett *et al* 1989; Entwistle and Grant 1989; Legge 1989; G Jones 2000; Rowley-Conwy 2000; Monk 2000), which has implications for our understanding of the type of communities in Britain at this time. It has been argued that a mobile economy based largely on wild plant foods would fit well with other evidence for mobility in the Neolithic, and the predominance of hazelnuts at Neolithic sites has been used as evidence to support this view (eg Moffett *et al* 1989; Entwistle and Grant 1989; J Thomas 1991; 1999). More recently, a case has been made for the ceremonial context of cereals which may reflect their use as a special-purpose food (J Thomas 1996; 1999; 2003). Others have argued that cereals were a staple food of the Neolithic, supplemented by wild plant foods when in season (eg Legge 1989; G Jones 2000; Rowley-Conwy 2000; Monk 2000, Jones and Rowley-Conwy 2007), and several reasons for the perceived scarcity of cereals in the British Neolithic have been suggested. These include the unsuitable recovery methods employed at many sites excavated before about 1980, the small scale of sampling at many sites, the predominance of excavated sites with a ritual purpose in southern Britain, and the biases inherent in the archaeological preservation of hazelnuts and cereals.

Where modern recovery techniques have been combined with large-scale sampling at Neolithic sites, as at Hambledon Hill, cereals are often found in quantity despite the biases against their preservation. While both wild and domesticated plants may have played a ceremonial role at causewayed enclosures, it is equally possible that they represent remains from the preparation of ordinary foods for consumption at the site, in which case, given the different taphonomic pathways involved, the quantity of grains relative to nutshells at Hambledon Hill (even without the spikelet deposit) is substantial, and may be indicative of their dietary contribution. Moreover, at Hambledon Hill, cereal grain (both emmer wheat and barley) was widely distributed in the interior pits of both the main and Stepleton enclosures, as was hazelnut shell. The largest concentrations of both plant foods were found near or just outside the enclosure ditches and, as both were deposited in similar contexts, it would be difficult to argue a special purpose for one and not the other.

7 Human remains and diet

7.1 The human remains

Jacqueline I McKinley

Incorporating parts of an earlier report by the late Robin Kenward

7.1.1 Introduction

History of analysis

The vast majority of the human remains from the excavations were originally examined by Mrs Robin Kenward (hereafter referred to as RK). The bone was received by her at intervals from 1974 to 1984, with some further material extracted from among the animal bone forwarded in 1985, the year in which she produced her report. In 1995, when the publication programme commenced, RK did not wish to continue her involvement with the project due to other pressures on her time and the osteological input passed to the writer.

Initially (in 1996), the writer compiled a report from RK's identifications, using parts of the original report submitted by her in 1985. Two skulls, excavated by Desmond Bonney from the east cross-dykes in 1960, were found to form part of the archive given to the Dorset County Museum by RCHME in 1996 and were incorporated in this report, following examination by the writer. Fragments of a human femur from the same excavation are recorded in Charles Higham's unpublished animal bone report, but have not been located. They are likely to be with the animal bone in the Cambridge University Museum. Human bone recovered from among the animal bone in two contexts was also forwarded to the writer in 1996.

In February and October 1997, as part of the selection procedure for human bone samples suitable for radiocarbon dating, the writer re-examined some of the bone from twenty finds. During this re-examination, it became apparent that there had been omissions in the original analysis; most significantly, there was no record of numerous cut-marks observed on some of the bone, which had clearly been made in antiquity. In view of the importance of the assemblage, particularly the potential significance of the cut-marks for understanding the treatment of the dead, a full re-scan of the assemblage was commissioned and was undertaken by the writer in the summer of 1998. The aims of the re-scan were specific and limited in scope, being essentially two-fold: to scan the bone for ancient modification, including cut-marks, gnawing and weathering, and to produce a comprehensive record of pathological lesions. The opportunity was also taken to make a consistent record of the number of bone fragments and precisely which parts of the bones were represented, an important taphonomic factor in an assemblage of this type. The re-scan was not intended to be a full re-evaluation of the bone; specifically there was no comprehensive checking of RK's suggested 'pairing' or 'joins' between bones and there was no provision for taking measurements additional to those taken by RK. Although not strictly part of the re-scan, the age and sex of individuals were re-evaluated, as, in some instances, was the number of individuals in specific finds. There was also a certain amount of reassessment of joins and pairing, but only that which came to light during the course of the re-scan.

The human remains

Human remains of Neolithic, Bronze Age, Iron Age and Anglo-Saxon date were recovered. Excluding the 12 Anglo-Saxon inhumation burials, which are referred to in this text by their grave numbers, the human remains are referred to here by their find numbers, of which 350 were allocated to human bone recovered from 16 main locations (Table 7.2). Finds were most abundant in the main causewayed enclosure ditch (39%) and the inner Stepleton outwork (10%).

Three basic types of deposit were represented among the prehistoric finds. The articulated skeletal remains of 13 individuals (including one dating to the Bronze Age and one to the Iron Age) were recovered from seven locations (Tables 7.1–2). Fifteen skulls, generally minus the mandible, were found in seven locations. The remaining 295 finds comprised more than 1,651 fragments of disarticulated bone.

7.1.2. Methods

The bone was washed and marked by RK, with some assistance from her extra-mural students. One of the aims of the analysis was to ascertain whether any bone fragments recovered from different localities would join together, which involved reconstruction undertaken by RK.

Numbers of individuals

The minimum number of individuals represented among the disarticulated, fragmentary bone was assessed from counts of the most frequently occurring skeletal element in all the finds (ie including articulated remains and skulls) within each of the 16 main locations (Table 7.1). That bone may have been dispersed

Table 7.1 Summary of human remains from prehistoric contexts

* in the Find column and *italics* elsewhere = bone unavailable for examination during re-scan, data taken from RK's identifications
% skel = % of articulated skeleton recovered
No. frags = number of fragments present
Skel elem = skeletal elements represented: sk = skull, a = axial skeleton, u = upper limb, l = lower limb, sk (m) = mandible only, without other parts of skull, s (t) = loose tooth or teeth only, without other parts of skull
Associations = associated finds of human bone
Type: artic = articulated remains, s = skull(s) with (+m) or without (–m) mandible, frag = disarticulated, fragmentary bone
Pathology: amtl = *ante mortem* tooth loss, pd = periodontal disease, oa = osteoarthritis, op = osteophytes, exo = exostoses, d l = destructive lesion, pnb = periostial new bone, ddd = degenerative disc disease, Sch = Schmorl's node, mv = morphological variation, C = cervical, T = thoracic, L = lumbar, S = sacral, bsm = body surface margins, man = mandibular, max = maxillary, a-c = acromio-clavicular, r/l = right/left, p/d = proximal/distal, IP = inter-phalangeal, ap = articular process, tp = transverse process
Wear/rm = wear/root (or fungal, or insect) marks, on a scale of 1 (low) to 5 (high)

Location	*Phase*	*Segment*	*Find*	*% skeleton*	*Type*	*No. frags*	*Skel elem*	*Associations*	*Age*	*Sex*	*Pathology*	*Condition*	*Wear/rm*
Central area													
Main enclosure	I	1	HH77 682		2 × sk-m		s	inc HH77 725, 848, 849, 852, 1037	1) young juvenile (6–7 yr) 2) older juvenile		1) calculus; mv – 'pegged' l max I2 2) mv – r max I2 'pegged'	1) cuts	/1–3
Main enclosure	I	4	HH74 HB 8		frag	1	l		adult				/1
Main enclosure	I	6.2	HH76 3030		frag	23	s(m) a u l	inc HH76 3034, 3036, 3038, 3040–43	older juvenile		pnb – innominate, femur shaft, visceral rib; hypoplasia; mv – retarded eruption man P2	?sooting	/<1
Main enclosure	I	7	HH76 2702		frag	1	s(t)		older juvenile/young subadult				1–2/1
Main enclosure	I	7	HH76 2833		frag	5	u		subadult/adult	??F			<1/<1
Main enclosure	I/II	18	HH76 1948	*c* 85%	artic				juvenile		calculus; *cribra orbitalia*; premature suture fusion		4–5/2
Main enclosure	II	1	HH77 621		frag	1	l		adult				/2–3
Main enclosure	II	1	HH77 911		frag	1	u		older subadult/adult				3/2–3
Main enclosure	II	2	HH74 AB 315		frag	4	a l	HH74 AB 346–7	juvenile				1/1
Main enclosure	II	3	HH74 HB 1a		sk-m				young juvenile (5–6 yr)		calculus; *cribra orbitalia*; endocranial new bone; mv – partial metopic suture		1/3
Main enclosure	II	3	HH74 1b		sk-m		s		mature adult (25–25 yr)	F	amtl; caries; abscess; calculus; mv – metopic suture		/2–3
Main enclosure	II	3	HH74 HB 6		sk-m		s	paired with HH74 HB 5	young subadult	?F			/1–2
Main enclosure	II	6.1	HH76 2032		frag	1	l	joins HH76 2044 (main enclosure III), ?=HH76 3030	older juvenile		pnb – femur shaft		
Main enclosure	II	6.1	HH76 2033		frag	1	a		adult			?sooting	
Main enclosure	II	6.1	HH76 2035		frag	5	l		adult	??M			
Main enclosure	II	6.1	HH76 2668		frag	1	u		subadult/adult			dry	<1/<1

Main enclosure	II	8	HH75 2101		frag	>25	s	?=HH 76 2183	subadult/adult	?F		cuts, charred	/2
Main enclosure	II	8	HH75 2109		frag	*c* 3	s		older infant/ young juvenile				1/3
Main enclosure	II	8	HH75 2115		frag	8	s		older infant/ young juvenile				/2
Main enclosure	II	8	HH75 2176		frag	1	a	?=HH75 2183	subadult				
Main enclosure	II	8	HH75 2177		frag	1	1		subadult/adult			dry	/3
Main enclosure	II	8	HH75 2183		frag	8	s (m) a 1	inc HH75 2136 (joins)	young subadult		calculus; hypoplasia		1–2/
Main enclosure	II	11	HH75 1848		frag	6	s (m)		older mature adult	??M	pd; calculus; abscess; hypoplasia; pnb – mandible; mv – man r M3 3-cusps		1/1
Main enclosure	II/III	6.1	HH76 *1868**		frag	1	1		*subadult/adult*				??
Main enclosure	II/III	6.1	HH76 2625	*c* 15%	artic		a 1		young/younger mature adult	M	exo – femur shafts; new bone – ischium; pitting — acetabula	cuts, canid gnawing, ?sooting	<1/1
Main enclosure	III	3	HH74 AB 346		frag	4	1	?=HH74 HB 2	juvenile			dry	
Main enclosure	III	4	HH74 HB 2		frag	6	s	?=HH74 AB 346	older juvenile (*c* 11yr)		calculus; mv – all man molars 5-cusp		<1/<1
Main enclosure	III	4	HH74 HB 3		frag	1	s		infant/juvenile				/<1
Main enclosure	III	4	HH74 HB 4		frag	>5	s		infant/juvenile				/<1
Main enclosure	III	4	HH74 HB 5		frag	5	s (m)	paired with HH74 HB 6	subadult	??F	mv – ?retarded development man r M2, paramolar cusp man l M2	dry	3/3
Main enclosure	III	4	HH74 AB 77		frag	3	1		juvenile			?canid gnawing	
Main enclosure	III	4	HH74 AB *300**		frag	1	1		*young adult*				??
Main enclosure	III	4	HH74 AB 301		frag	5	1	inc AB 308 (join) & 304 (paired)	adult		pnb – fibula shaft	?canid gnawing	4/1
Main enclosure	III	6.1	HH76 2029		frag	2	1	??= HH76 1870	subadult/adult			dry	/<1
Main enclosure	III	6.1	HH76 2044		frag	1	1	joins HH76 2032 (main enclosure II)	older juvenile			?sooting	
Main enclosure	III	8	HH75 337		frag	3	s		adult				
Main enclosure 3–4/3–4	III	8	HH75 2017		frag	1	1	?=HH75 2183	older juvenile/subadult				
Main enclosure	III	8	HH75 2023		frag		s	inc HH75 2138	infant (*c* 3 yr)		endocranial new bone – l & r sphenoid, r temporal	cuts	2/1–2
Main enclosure	III	8	HH75 2024		frag	>80	s	inc HH75 2025	infant				/2
Main enclosure	III	8	HH75 2135		frag	10	s		young infant (1.5–2yr)		*cribra orbitalia*		1–2/
Main enclosure	III	8	HH75 2137		frag	5	s (m)		young infant (1.5–2yr)				<1/1–2
Main enclosure	III	9	HH75 1179		sk-m & frags	*c* 43	s	inc HH75 1180 (join) & 1350 (paired)	1) young juvenile (6–7yr) 2) older infant/young juvenile		1) *cribra orbitalia*; hypervascularity	1) cuts	1)/<1 2) 3–4/ 3–4

Table 7.1 (*cont'd*)

Location	*Phase*	*Segment*	*Find*	*% skeleton*	*Type*	*No. frags*	*Skel elem*	*Associations*	*Age*	*Sex*	*Pathology*	*Condition*	*Wear/rm*
Main enclosure	III	11	HH75 1715		frag	3	a		older infant/juvenile				
Main enclosure	III	11	HH75 2128		frag	>8	s u/l?		juvenile			charred	/2
Main enclosure	III	14	HH76 2999		frag	10	1) s a u 2) l		1) older infant 2) adult				1/1
Main enclosure	III	19	HH76 2984		frag	3	s (t)	?=HH76 3052	older adult				
Main enclosure	IV	1	HH77 581		frag	2	l		adult				5/
Main enclosure	IV	1	HH77 610		frag	3	s (m)		older adult		amtl; pd; caries; oa – temporo-mandibular; mv – impaction l molars	cuts, ?sooting, dry	<1/<1
Main enclosure	IV	16	HH76 1598		frag	4	u	inc HH76 1929 (pair)	adult				3–4/3–4
Main enclosure	IV	17	HH76 2741		sk+m & frag	>30	s a	inc HH76 1158 & 2792 (join) & 2826 =	1) older juvenile 2) juvenile		calculus; hypoplasia; *cribra orbitalia*; mv – enamel pearl	dry	1–3/1–3
Main enclosure	IV	17	HH76 2796		frag	>6	s a		1) juvenile (*c* 9yr) 2) adult		1) calculus	dry	<1/<1
Main enclosure	IV	17	HH76 2923		frag	13	s		adult		mv — metopic suture	charred	/<1
Main enclosure	IV	18	HH76 2954		frag			Joins HH76 2956 from phase VI					
Main enclosure	IV	19	HH76 1621		frag	1	s (t)		older adult				/2–3
Main enclosure	IV	19	HH76 1823		sk+m		s a	inc HH76 1824 & 3052 (join), ?2984=	older adult	M	amtl; caries; hypercementosis; abscess; calculus; ddd – C; exo – patella; mv – enamel pearl; occipital bunning	cuts??	1–4/1–2
Main enclosure	IV	19	HH76 3053		frag	2	l		young/mature adult		mv – squatting facet		/<1
Main enclosure	V	3	HH74 AB 82		frag	1	l		subadult/adult				4–5/
Main enclosure	V	3	HH74 AB 260		frag	2	u		adult	??F			/<1
Main enclosure	V	3	HH74 AB 347		frag	1	l	?pair HH74 AB 346 (main enclosure III)	juvenile				
Main enclosure	V	7	HH76 1572		frag	12	s		older mature/older adult	??F		?sooting	4–5/
Main enclosure	VI	1	HH77 360		frag	>6	s		young subadult (13–15yr)		calculus		3–4/
Main enclosure	VI	1	HH77 590		frag	1	?l/		?human/?animal				4/4
Main enclosure	VI	3	HH74 AB 201		frag	5	u		adult	??M			3–4/<1
Main enclosure	VI	3	HH74 AB 211		frag	2	u		young/mature adult	F			1–2/

Main enclosure	VI	4	HH74 AB 357		frag	*c* 6	s	inc HH74 AB 358, 364, 382 & 384 (join)	young/mature adult	??M			5/5
Main enclosure	VI	5	HH76 1475		frag	10	s		subadult/young adult				1/1
Main enclosure	VI	5	HH76 1966		frag	1	l		subadult				
Main enclosure	VI	6.2	HH76 695		frag	*c* 15	s	??=HH76 1572	adult				
Main enclosure	VI	6.2	HH76 3009		frag	6	s	?=HH76 3011, ??=3012	subadult–mature adult		*cribra orbitalia*; ?trauma – depressed fracture?	?sooting/ ?charred	2–3/2–3
Main enclosure	VI	6.2	HH76 3011		frag	3	l	?=HH76 3009	subadult/adult	??F		dry	4/4
Main enclosure	VI	6.2	HH76 3012		frag	5	l	??=HH76 3009	1) subadult 2) adult			dry	1–2/
Main enclosure	VI	7	*HH76 1839**		frag	1	u	?=HH76 1870	*subadult*				??
Main enclosure	VI	7	HH76 1855		frag	2	l	inc HH76 1852 (pair)	subadult/adult			?charred	<1/
Main enclosure	VI	7	HH76 1856		frag	*c* 34	s	inc HH76 1870, 1908, 1912, 1928	older juvenile/young subadult (?×2)		mv – supernumerary tooth, 2 l max I shovelled, one with extra cusp		1–2/1
Main enclosure	VI	7	HH76 1911		frag	1	l		older subadult/adult	??F			3–4/3–4
Main enclosure	VI	7	*HH76 1915**		frag	*c* 3	a l		*subadult/adult*				??
Main enclosure	VI	8	HH75 238		frag	1	l		adult	??M			2–3/2–3
Main enclosure	VI	8	HH75 241		frag	1	l		adult	??F		cuts, dry	/1
Main enclosure	VI	8	HH75 1684		frag	1	u		subadult/adult				3/3
Main enclosure	VI	8	HH75 1753		frag	1	l		adult				4/1
Main enclosure	VI	9	HH75 598		frag	2	l	?pair HH75 653	older subadult/adult				2/1
Main enclosure	VI	9	HH75 607		frag	1	s	?=HH75 608	mature adult		?abscess		
Main enclosure	VI	9	HH75 608		frag	1	s	?=HH75 607	mature adult				<1/
Main enclosure	VI	9	HH75 653		frag	2	l	?pair HH75 598	adult		exo – femur shaft	??cuts	1/1
Main enclosure	VI	9	HH75 699		frag	13	s	inc HH75 700 (join)	young/mature adult			cut/nick	<1/<1
Main enclosure	VI	14	HH76 2193		frag	*c* 28	s	inc HH76 2206 & 2224 (join)	older mature/older adult			?sooting	3–5/
Main enclosure	VI	14	HH76 2799		frag	1	s (t)		older adult		calculus		
Main enclosure	VI	17	HH76 1071		frag	4	s (m)	inc HH76 1252 (join)	young adult	??M	calculus; caries; pnb – ramus; mv – large M3 5-cusp		3/3
Main enclosure	VI	17	HH76 1841		frag	1	l		adult				<1/1
Main enclosure	VI	18	HH76 1126		frag	1	s (t)		older adult		hypercementosis		1/
Main enclosure	VI	18	HH76 2956		frag	2	l	inc HH76 2954, ?=3053	adult			?cuts	1/1
Main enclosure	VI	19	HH76 988		frag	1	s		older mature adult				5/5
Main enclosure	VI	19	HH76 1177		frag	3	u	??=HH76 988	adult				3–4/3–4
Main enclosure	VI	19	*HH76 1183**		frag	1	s (t)		*adult*				??
Main enclosure	VII	17	HH76 3046	*c* 70%	artic				young juvenile		calculus; premature suture fusion		2–4/1
Main enclosure	VII/a	19	HH76 1101		frag	1	s (t)		older mature/older adult				4–5/4–5

Table 7.1 (*cont'd*)

Location	*Phase*	*Segment*	*Find*	*% skeleton*	*Type*	*No. frags*	*Skel elem*	*Associations*	*Age*	*Sex*	*Pathology*	*Condition*	*Wear/rm*
Main enclosure	VIII/a	3	*HH74 AB 79**		frag	1	s (t)		*young juvenile*				??
Main enclosure	VIII/a	5	HH76 2904		frag	1	l		adult			dry	3/1
Main enclosure	U/S	14	HH76 3014		frag	1	l		adult			?cut, dry, ?sooting	4–5/1–2
Inner E cross-dyke	I/II	4	HH60 (Bonney's trench L)		sk –m		s		mature adult	F	amtl; abscess; mv – bipartite P2 root		1/1
Inner E cross-dyke	III	5	HH75 1360		sk –m		s	? =HH75 1340	young adult	??M	*cribra orbitalia*	cuts, ?sooting	3/4
Inner E cross-dyke	V	5	HH75 1340		frag	5	s (m)	HH75 1775 from outer E cross-dyke (joins), =?1360	young/younger mature adult	??M			3/2–3
Inner E cross-dyke	VII/a	5	HH60 (Bonney's trench L)		frag	1	l		*?adult – missing*				??
Outer E cross-dyke	I/II	3	HH60 (Bonney's trench L)		sk –m		s		young/younger mature adult	F	abscess; mv – displacement tooth sockets		4/2–3
Outer E cross-dyke	III	3	HH75 441		frag	>1	s		juvenile/subadult				4/4
Outer E cross-dyke	V	3	HH75 1449		frag	1	l		subadult/adult				5/5
Outer E cross-dyke	VI	4	HH75 1949		frag	1	?l		adult		d l (?infection)		<1/
Outer E cross-dyke	VIII/a	5	HH75 1775		frag	1	s (t)	joins HH75 1340 from inner E cross-dyke	adult				3/2
Inner S cross-dyke	III	1	*HH77 572**		frag	1	l		*adult*				??
Inner S cross-dyke	III	1	*HH77 634**		frag	1	l		*adult*				??
Inner S cross-dyke	VIII/a	1	*HH77 75**		frag	1	u/l		*?*				??
Long barrow	I	1	HH77 1948		frag	1	?l		young adult				3–4/3–4
Long barrow	VI	3	HH77 700		frag	1	l	?pair to HH77 1677	subadult/adult				5/5
Long barrow	VI	3	HH77 916		frag	7	s (t)	inc HH77 94 & 142	1) subadult/young adult; 2) older mature/older adult		calculus; hypoplasia		

Long barrow	VIII	1	HH77 1677	frag	2	l	?pair to HH77 700	adult		exo – femur shaft		5/5
Long barrow	VIII	1	HH77 52	frag	3	s a u		adult			?sooting	<1/
Long barrow	VIII	1	HH77 57	frag	1	a		adult				<1/
Long barrow	VIII	1	HH77 59	frag	>17	a l	inc HH77 61 (join) & 78 (part joins), =77/99 (pair), ?=103	adult	?M			1/
Long barrow	VIII	1	HH77 69	frag	25	s (m) a u l	inc HH77 90 (joins)	adult (?parts of second)	M	mv – squatting facet	dry	1/1–2
Long barrow	VIII	1	HH77 77	frag	1	l	joins part HH77 99, pair to 59/61/ 78, ?=103	adult	?M		cuts, canid gnawing	<1/
Long barrow	VIII	1	HH77 78	frag	3	l	part joins HH77 59, rest different individual	adult				<1/
Long barrow	VIII	1	HH77 80	frag	40	s a u l	?inc HH77 2327, some ?=HH77 94	1) young/younger mature adult 2) ?adult	1) ?M		?sooting, dry	1–2/
Long barrow	VIII	1	HH77 82	frag	1	l	?=HH77 80	young/younger mature adult				2/
Long barrow	VIII	1	HH77 84	frag	1	s		immature >infant				4/
Long barrow	VIII	1	HH77 85	frag	4	a u l		young/mature adult				1/
Long barrow	VIII	1	HH77 88	frag	1	s		adult	?M	?depressed fracture/wound		
Long barrow	VIII	1	HH77 91	frag	7	a l	?=HH77 80	adult			dry	1/
Long barrow	VIII	1	HH77 94	frag	10	a u l	1) inc HH7 79 & 97 (join), joins 100	1) young/mature adult 2) adult	??M ??F	op – calcaneum	?sooting, dry	1–5/
Long barrow	VIII	1	HH77 95	frag	5	s a u l		mature adult			cuts, canid gnawing	1–2/
Long barrow	VIII	1	HH77 99	frag	*c* 30	a u l	part (?2) joins HH77 77, part (1) joins HH77 100	2 × young/younger mature adult	F ?M	1) op – rib, navicular; exo – femur shaft	dry	1–5/
Long barrow	VIII	1	HH77 100	frag	31	s a u l	joins HH77 94 & 99 (2 diff individuals)	1) young/mature adult 2) adult	M ?F		dry	1–3/
Long barrow	VIII	1	HH77 103	frag	27	s a u l	?=HH77 59 & 77	young/younger mature adult				1–2/
Long barrow	VIII	1	HH77 104	frag	>3	l		mature adult			?sooting	3/
Long barrow	VIII	1	*HH77 106**	frag	1	s (t)	?=HH77 80	*adult*				??
Long barrow	VIII	1	HH77 142	frag	2	s		adult				1/
Long barrow	VIII	1	HH77 143	frag	1	s		adult	??M			/<1
Long barrow	VIII	1	HH77 2327	frag	1	a		young/mature adult		op – rib facet		

Table 7.1 *(cont'd)*

Location	*Phase*	*Segment*	*Find*	*% skeleton*	*Type*	*No. frags*	*Skel elem*	*Associations*	*Age*	*Sex*	*Pathology*	*Condition*	*Wear/rm*
A F64			HH74 AB 433		frag	2	s (t)	inc 432	older infant/young juvenile				1/4
A F64			HH74 AB 440		frag	2	l		adult				4/
A F120			HH74 AB 484		frag	2	s, u		adult				2/2
B F14			HH75 611		frag	1	s		immature			charred	/1
B F1			HH75 432		frag	2	s		juvenile		*cribra orbitalia*		1/
B F1			HH75 701		frag	1	s(m)		young juvenile				1/1
N F11			HH77 604		frag	1	l		adult				2/
Shroton spur													
Shroton spur outwork	III	3	HH76 1604		frag	1	s (t)	?=HH76 1916	older adult				4–5/4–5
Shroton spur outwork	III	3	HH76 1606		frag	1	s (t)	fits HH76 1916	older adult		caries		
Shroton spur outwork	III	3	HH76 1916		frag	1	s (m)		older adult	F	pd; calculus	cuts	/<1
Shroton spur outwork	III	3	HH76 1917		frag	*c* 13	a l		young/mature adult	??M			<1/
Shroton spur outwork	III	3	HH76 1918		frag	>34	s (m) u l		adult		pnb – fibula		2–5+/ 2–5+
Shroton spur outwork	III	3	HH76 1919		frag	6	s (t)	?=HH76 1916	older adult				4–5+/
Shroton spur outwork	III	3	HH76 1920		frag	2	u /l ?		adult				/1–2
Shroton spur outwork	III	3	HH76 1958		frag	1	u		adult				/2–3
Shroton spur outwork	III	3	HH76 1959		frag	2	s (t)	?=HH76 1916	older adult				/5
Shroton spur outwork	III	3	HH76 1960		frag	2	u/l		>infant				4/4
Shroton spur outwork	III	3	HH76 1961		frag	12	u l	?=HH76 1968	adult		depression – cuneiform		/<1
Shroton spur outwork	III	3	HH76 1962		frag	1	l	??=HH76 1916	adult	??F			
Shroton spur outwork	III	3	HH76 1963		frag	10	u l		young/mature adult		oa – p radius; exo – radial tuberosity; pnb – fibula	?cuts	3–4/3–4
Shroton spur outwork	III	3	HH76 1967		frag	27	a		adult				/2–3
Shroton spur outwork	III	3	HH76 1968		frag	8	l	?=HH76 1961 & 1988	mature adult		oa – 1st proximal foot phalanx		1–3/

Shroton spur outwork	III	3	HH76 1988		frag	4	1		adult				
Shroton spur outwork	III	*3*	*HH76 1991**		frag	1	s (t)		*older infant/young juvenile*				??
Shroton spur outwork	III	3	HH76 1604		frag	1	s (t)	?=HH76 1916	older adult				5/5
Shroton spur outwork	VIII	33	HH76 2724		frag	1	s (t)	??=HH76 1916	older mature/older adult				3/
Shroton spur outwork	K F5	3	HH76 426		frag	1	1		adult				5/5
Stepleton spur													
Stepleton enclosure	IV	3	ST80 1310		frag	*c* 72	s		immature >infant				
Stepleton enclosure	III	4	ST80 647		frag	*c* 61	s u/l	inc ST80 648	older infant/young juvenile				2/3
Stepleton enclosure	III	7	ST81 1288		frag	3	1		adult				1/2
Stepleton enclosure	III	17	ST81 2107		frag	2	1		adult		exo – femur shaft		1/
Stepleton enclosure	III	12	ST81 1107		frag	1	1		adult	?M		dry	4/4
Stepleton enclosure	III	12	ST81 1296		frag	22	s		young infant			cuts	/2
Stepleton enclosure	IV	8	ST81 2399		frag	1	s		adult			?sooting	<1/<1
Stepleton enclosure	IV	10	ST81 3188	*c* 40%	artic			inc ST81 434, 766, 3187, 3189	mature adult	F	calculus; pd; op – C6–7, 1T, 2 l & 3 r ribs, r trapezoid, middle finger phalanx; oa – 1st ribs, d l – radius head; mv – man M3 5-cusp	dry, sooting, rodent gnawing	<1–3/1
Stepleton enclosure	VI	4	ST80 852		frag	7	1		adult				2/2
Stepleton enclosure	VI	8	ST81 874		frag	1	s	?=ST81 442	adult				1/
Stepleton enclosure	VI	7	ST81 875		frag	7	s		adult	?M	endocranial new bone	charred	2–3/
Stepleton enclosure	VIII/a	3	ST80 301		frag	1	s (t)		subadult		mv – shovelled max r I1		/2
Stepleton enclosure	VIII/a	3	ST80 2134		frag	1	s		adult				4–5/
Stepleton enclosure	VIII/a	4	ST80 258		frag	1	s (t)		older infant				2/2
Stepleton enclosure	VIII/a	6	ST80 383		frag	31	1		adult	??M			2/1

Table 7.1 *(cont'd)*

Location	*Phase*	*Segment*	*Find*	*% skeleton*	*Type*	*No. frags*	*Skel elem*	*Associations*	*Age*	*Sex*	*Pathology*	*Condition*	*Wear/rm*
Stepleton enclosure	VIII/a	8	ST81 442		frag	1	s	?ST81 874=	adult				1/1
Middle Stepleton outwork	III	6	ST79 2497	*c* 50%	frag	>106	s a u l	inc ST79 2187, 2202, 2511–8, 2520–7, 2673–5, 2678–89, 2691, 2693	young juvenile (*c* 6yr)		*cribra orbitalia*; new bone – r humerus shaft		2–3/ 2–3
Middle Stepleton outwork	VIII/a	3	ST78 1166		frag	1	s (t)		older subadult/young adult		calculus		
Inner Stepleton outwork	I	5	ST79 1354		frag	1	l		subadult/adult				/<1
Inner Stepleton outwork	I	5	ST79 1428		frag	8	s (m)		older adult	??M	calculus; pd		/1
Inner Stepleton outwork	I	5	ST79 1296		frag	4	l		immature				/1
Inner Stepleton outwork	I	6	ST79 1477		frag	2	l		adult				<1/1–2
Inner Stepleton outwork	I	7	ST78 2842		frag	>28	s		infant				/1–2
Inner Stepleton outwork	I	7	ST78 2944		frag	*c* 17	s		infant/juvenile				<1/
Inner Stepleton outwork	I	7	ST79 2726	*c* 95%	artic				older mature adult	M	calculus; *cribra orbitalia*; Sch – T12, L1–3; oa – 12th c-v; trauma – rib fracture, pitting – 3 rib facets; exo – l femur shaft, patella, calcaneum; op – T2 tp, L2 ap; mv – occipital bunning, vastus notch, partial sacralisation L5, calcaneum dual facets, squatting facets	cuts	2–3/ 2–4
Inner Stepleton outwork	I	9	ST78 2756	*c* 85%	artic				neonate (0–4 months)	??F	mv – metatarsals/carpals 3 centres ossification	?cut	
Inner Stepleton outwork	III	7	ST78 1101		frag	29	s		infant				/1–2
Inner Stepleton outwork	III	7	ST78 2755	*c* 98%	artic				older subadult/young adult (17–20yr)	M	calculus; d l – r 1st proximal phalanx; Sch – T5–10, T12, L1–3; pitting – C ap; mv – slight shovelling max I2, vastus notch, squatting facets, dual calcaneal facets	cuts, canid & rodent gnawing, ?sooting	/<1–2

Inner Stepleton outwork	III	7	ST78 2755a	frag	31	s a u		young infant (1.5–2yr)				
Inner Stepleton outwork	III	7	ST78 2795	frag	28	s		young/mature adult	??M			/<1
Inner Stepleton outwork	III	7	ST78 2845	frag	*c* 15	s a	?=ST78 2842	older infant				
Inner Stepleton outwork	III	9	ST78 1100	sk +m	>40	s a	inc ST78 2047	young/younger mature adult	F	calculus		4/1–4
Inner Stepleton outwork	III	9	ST78 1100a	frag	9	s		older infant (3–4 yr)		mv – max I2 shovelled		/2
Inner Stepleton outwork	III	9	ST78 1625	frag	1	s	?= ST78 2248	?immature				
Inner Stepleton outwork	III	9	ST78 2248	frag	>18	1) s a u/l 2) a		1) infant (*c* 3yr) 2) adult				1/<1
Inner Stepleton outwork	III	9	*ST78 2584**	frag	3/1	s u /s	1) ?=ST78 1100 2) ?=ST78 2756	*1) adult* *2) neonate/young infant*				??
Inner Stepleton outwork	III	9	ST78 2919a	frag	>11	s a u	inc ST 78 2870 & 2932	infant				/<1
Inner Stepleton outwork	III	9	ST78 2919b	frag	6	l	?=ST 78 1100	subadult/adult	F			<1
Inner Stepleton outwork	V/1	5	ST79 1112	frag	1	s		adult				2/4
Inner Stepleton outwork	V/2	6	*ST79 1751**	frag	1	u		*infant/juvenile*				??
Inner Stepleton outwork	V/2.	9	ST78 2871	frag	3	l	?=ST 78 1100	older subadult/adult	??F		dry	2–3/5
Inner Stepleton outwork	VIII/a	4	ST80 2115	frag	2	u		subadult/adult				3/2
Inner Stepleton outwork	VIII/a	5	ST80 1095	frag	1	l		adult				4/2
Inner Stepleton outwork	VIII/a	6	ST79 531	frag	>2	u l		juvenile/subadult				>5/>5
Inner Stepleton outwork	VIII/a	7	ST78 1185	frag	1	l		??immature >juvenile				>5/>5
Inner Stepleton outwork	VIII/a	7	ST79 1281	frag	1	l		?subadult				>5/>5
bank/topsoil	Inner outwork bank areas		ST78 69	frag	1	l		adult				<1
Outer Stepleton outwork	I	7	ST78 967	sk –m		+a	inc ST 78 968	older subadult	??F	*cribra orbitalia*; mv – atlas central groove		1/3

Table 7.1 (*cont'd*)

Location	*Phase*	*Segment*	*Find*	*% skeleton*	*Type*	*No. frags*	*Skel elem*	*Associations*	*Age*	*Sex*	*Pathology*	*Condition*	*Wear/rm*
Outer Stepleton outwork	I	3	ST80 1875	*c* 98%	artic				young adult	M	hypoplasia; calculus; pnb – l femur shaft; osteoid osteoma – l femur shaft; exo – calcaneum; mv – retention man deciduous m2, max I2 shovelled, wormian, squatting facet	cuts, rodent gnawing, arrowhead	1/
Outer Stepleton outwork	I	5	ST80 2069		frag	1	u		subadult/adult				1/3
1A F70			ST78 964	*c* 80%	artic			inc ST 78 710	older infant/young juvenile (*c* 5yr)		*cribra orbitalia*; mv – man M1 4-cusp	?sooting	3–4/3–4
1A F57			ST78 1235		frag	21	s		?young infant				2/1
2A F200			ST79 2025	*c* 40%	artic			inc ST 79 2386	older adult	??M	pd; calculus; abscess; oa – 1T, 1L; op – 5 proximal, 6 middle & 1 distal phalanx; exo – patella, r femur shaft	scorched	1/3
4B F137			ST81 2053		frag	12	s	inc ST 81 2036	infant/juvenile				<1/
4B F137			ST81 2172		frag	38	s	inc ST 81 2173	older infant/young juvenile		?sinus – parietal	?sooting	2–3/<1
4B F712			ST81 3181	*c* 98%	artic				young adult	M	calculus; op – 1 r & 1 l rib, auricular surfaces; oa – 1 r rib; mv – impaction man r M3, wormian, atlas dual facets, accessory transverse foramen C5–7, squatting facets		1–5/1–3
ST82 F16	BA		ST82 114	*c* 45%	artic		crtic	inc ST82 115, 117, 119–126, 130	mature/older adult	M	ddd – 2C; mv – man M1 4-cusps	dry, sooting, ?badly crushed	1–3/2
U/S			ST78 966		frag	1	s (t)		adult				2/
U/S			ST81 2576		frag	1	l		juvenile				1/2
Hanford spur													
Inner Hanford outwork	III	2	HN82 342		frag	3	s		infant/young juvenile				1/2
Inner Hanford outwork	III	2	HN82 344		frag	5	1.		subadult/adult				<1/1
Inner Hanford outwork	III	2	HN82 365		frag	4	s (m)		infant (*c* 3yr)				/<1
Inner Hanford outwork	V	2	HN82 334		frag	11	s (m)	?=HN82 236	older adult	?M	calculus; pd; abscess		1–2/1–2
Inner Hanford outwork	V	3	HN82 240		frag	3	s		older adult	??F			1–2/1–2
Inner Hanford outwork	V	3	HN82 270		frag	2	s		adult				>1/>1

Inner Hanford outwork	V	3	HN82 293	frag	1	u		adult				/>1
Inner Hanford outwork	V	3	HN82 403	frag	1	a		infant			canid gnawing, cut marks, dry	/1–2
Inner Hanford outwork	VII/a	3	HN82 236	sk –m			inc HN 82 257	mature/older adult	??M	osteomas		1–2/1
Inner Hanford outwork	VII/a	3	HN82 248	frag	8	l	inc HN 82 255 & 260 (join)	young/mature adult			rodent gnawing	/1
Inner Hanford outwork	VII/a	3	HN82 258	frag	*c* 4	a u l		adult	??F			
Inner Hanford outwork	VII/a	3	HN82 278	frag	3	l		young/mature adult		mv – squatting facet		/<1
Inner Hanford outwork	VII/a	3	HN82 339	frag	2	l		adult		hypervascularity – femur neck		2/2
Outer Hanford outwork	I	3	HN82 119	frag	5	l	?=HN82 200	adult				1–2/1–2
Outer Hanford outwork	I	3	HN82 200	sk –m				mature adult	F	mv – wormian		2–3/1–2
Outer Hanford outwork	I	3	HN82 221	frag	2	l	?=HN 82 200	adult				1–2
Outer Hanford outwork	III	1	HN82 416	frag	1	s (m)		older infant				
Outer Hanford outwork	V	2	HN78 2306	frag	1	s (m)		older mature/older adult	??M		abscess	/1
F854			HN82 721	frag	1	s (t)		older juvenile/young subadult				/2
'Flint mines'			HN82 572	frag	1	s		older mature/older adult				dry 2/
'Flint mines'			HN82 634	frag	1	s	?=HN82 572	adult				1/1
Hillfort												
Hillfort	IA		HH86 97	artic		r foot		mature/older adult		op – middle & proximal phalanges; exo – distal phalanx		<1/

within a limited area is demonstrated by joins or pairings (noted by RK) between fragments from different, though relatively closely spaced localities, for example the inner and outer east cross-dykes. Adult and immature bone was assessed separately, with a further breakdown into the different immature age categories; the age and sex attributed within the adult group was also considered. The most frequently occurring bone fragment in the adult skeletal assemblage was the femur shaft, the mandible being the most common element among the immature bone.

The checking of possible joins or pairing between bone fragments and skeletal elements was not one of the objectives of the re-scan and, therefore, was not systematically undertaken, nor was there a detailed study of possible links between different contexts or phases. Consequently, it was considered appropriate to include RK's estimates for the number of individuals (Table 7.2). RK appears to have estimated the minimum number of individuals represented by the disarticulated fragments of bone from obvious joins, between both broken bone fragments and articulating bones, pairing of bones, and correlation of age and sex, all with due consideration of the contextual data. However, some of RK's suggested 'pairings' and 'joins' were not substantiated in the re-scan and others had been overlooked. Two figures were generally arrived at by RK within each of the different site localities, a 'minimum' and a potential 'maximum' number. The 'minimum' figure was based on the probability that immediately adjacent or fairly closely spaced deposits of unduplicated skeletal elements, of similar age and sex but with no joins or pairing, might represent parts of the same individual. The 'maximum' figure was based on the assumption that all separately numbered bone fragments of similar age/sex where no pairing or joins were observed represented parts of different individuals. It should be noted that figures based on such premises will in all probability provide an over-estimate of numbers.

Age

In the re-scan, age was assessed from the stage of tooth development (van Beek 1983), epiphyseal bone fusion (Gray 1977; McMinn and Hutchings 1985), immature long bone dimensions (Bass 1987), degree of occlusal tooth wear (Brothwell 1972a), and the general degree of cranial suture fusion. The following age categories are employed:

Table 7.2 Original and revised estimates of numbers of individuals from Neolithic contexts

Artic = articulated skeletal remains, Skull = skull only
Totals include articulated remains, skulls and fragmentary remains, showing the minimum and potential maximum numbers of individuals (see 7.1.2)
* bone unavailable for examination during re-scan

	Original		***Revised***					
	Immature	*Adult*	*Immature Artic*	*Skull*	*Totals*	*Adult Artic*	*Skull*	*Totals*
Central area								
Main causewayed enclosure	24–44	21–36	2	6	19	1	2	11
Inner east cross-dyke		2–3					2	2
Outer east cross-dyke	1	4–5			1		1	2
Inner south cross-dyke	1	1			1			1*
Long barrow		4–7			1			4
Features	2–5	3–4			1			1
Totals	**26–49**	**35–56**	2	6	**23**	1	5	**21**
Shroton spur outwork	**1–3**	**3–4**			**1***			**2**
Stepleton spur								
Enclosure	3	11–13			3	1		2
Inner outwork	12–16	12–16	1		3	2	1	6
Middle outwork	2	1			1			1
Outer outwork	1	3		1	1	1		2
Features	4	3	1		1/?2	2		2
Totals	**23–29**	**33–40**	2	1	**9/?10**	6	1	**13**
Hanford spur								
Inner outwork	2–3	4–13			1		1	2
Outer outwork	1	2–4			1		1	1/?2
'Flint mines'	1	1–2						1
Totals	**4–5**	**7–19**			**2**		2	**4/?5**
Overall totals	**55–85**	**75–115**	4	7	**35/?36**	7	8	**40/?41**

foetus/neonate	<6 months
infant	6 months–4 years
juvenile	*c* 5–12 years
subadult	*c* 13–18 years
young adult	*c* 19–25 years
mature adult	*c* 26–45 years
older adult	*c* 45 years+

Where insufficient evidence was present for age assessment there may be overlaps between the assigned categories.

In the re-scan, sex was assessed from the sexually dimorphic traits of the skeleton (Bass 1987; Brothwell 1972a). The levels of reliability attributed reflect the quantity and quality of available traits on which the assessment was based; '??' denotes 'possible', '?' denotes 'probable'.

Skeletal indices

Stature was estimated using Trotter's and Gleser's regression equations (1952; 1958; Brothwell 1972a; 1981). Cranial index was calculated according to Brothwell (1972a; 1981). Platymeric and platycnemic indices were calculated according to Bass (1987).

Ancient modification

All bone fragments were visually scanned for indications of ancient cut-marks. All the cuts noted by the writer were described and marked prior to the bone being forwarded to A J Legge for verification. Owing largely to the condition of the bone, Legge attributed probability levels to each of the cuts or series of cuts.

Examination under a Scanning Electron Microscope (SEM) verified the character of the cuts first noted by the writer on the femur shaft during selection of bone for radiocarbon dating. A sample of nine bone fragments with cuts was subject to further SEM investigation and micrographs were produced by Malcolm Ward at the Ancient Monuments Laboratory. A series of 11 individual gold-coated casts (up to three being taken from two bone fragments with several groups of cuts) were made from a silicone-based precision-impressed dental material, Optosil P. The SEM was used in the backscatter mode with the anode at 15kV. Magnifications were between 10× and 100× and the image was inverted (black for white) to try to counteract the fact that 'hollows' appeared as 'hills' on the silicone impressions.

The condition of the bone, both general weathering and abrasion, and root/fungal/insect marks, was assessed on a scale of 1–5; 1 denoting slight wear or root (including fungal/insect) marking (cortical bone not quite 'fresh' in appearance), 5 denoting heavy wear or marking (cortical bone surface substantially eroded). Potential canid and rodent gnaw-marks were assessed with the advice of A J Legge and Peter Andrews.

The archive

Every bone fragment from prehistoric contexts was recorded on a numbered skeleton sheet showing, as near as possible, the precise area of bone represented (RK had completed skeleton sheets for only the 13 articulated skeletons from the prehistoric contexts together with five other general skeleton sheets). Where appropriate, dental record sheets show tooth wear patterns and the location of dental lesions. A number of measurements additional to those recorded by RK were taken where they were deemed of value, for example, for sexing or the calculation of indices. These did not form part of the re-scan, and were therefore small-scale and inconsistent. The archive includes detailed comments on morphology and descriptions of pathological lesions; the presence of any animal bone in an individual assemblage; location and form of cut-marks and gnawing with some additional descriptions by A J Legge; and the condition of the bone.

Skeleton sheets were not completed for the Anglo-Saxon burials, RK having already done so (for 10 of the 12 skeletons), but each burial has dental records sheets showing attrition and location of lesions and joint record sheets where appropriate.

RK's original report, including cranial/post-cranial measurement and skeleton sheets for the Saxon burials and some of the prehistoric bone, is also held in archive.

7.1.3 Results – Neolithic, Bronze Age and Iron Age

With the exception of a crushed but articulated Bronze Age individual from ST82 F16 on the Stepleton spur (ST82 114; Fig 3.117) and an articulated foot recovered from a feature in the bank area of the north cross rampart in the Iron Age hillfort (HH86 97; Fig 3.150), all other prehistoric human remains are of Neolithic date. It is probable that much, if not all of the material recovered from post-Neolithic contexts (most of it from phase VIII/a in the ditches) was reworked from earlier ones.

A summary of the results is presented in Table 7.1. To give an impression of the skeletal elements represented among the disarticulated fragments, four main skeletal categories are shown – skull, axial skeleton, upper limb and lower limb. It should be noted that one or more fragments from any of these categories may be all that is present (see key to Table 7.1). Thirteen bone finds (all disarticulated fragments) could not be located during the re-scan. These numbers are italicised in Table 7.1 and marked with an asterisk (*); the summary results given are taken from RK's records.

Condition of the bone and ancient modifications

Weathering and root-marks (Table 7.3)

In general terms the bone is in good condition, but varying degrees of weathering (surface wear/abrasion) and root-marking were observed throughout the

Table 7.3 Percentages of weathered and root-marked bone by deposit type. Heavily affected bone is scored 4 or 5 in Table 7.1

category	*% weathered*	*% root-marked*	*% heavily weathered*	*% heavily root marked*
skulls	80%	100%	18%	12%
articulated skeletal material	71%	71%	21%	14%
disarticulated fragments	49%	15%	47%	10%
overall rates	54%	60%	17%	11%

assemblage, and among bone fragments from individual finds. 'Root-marking' has been adopted as a general term, but may also cover surface marking produced as a result of fungal or insect activity (Armour-Chelu and Andrews 1996). It is often difficult to distinguish between such marks other than by microscopic examination, but it is probable that all three have been factors to some degree.

Among the articulated skeletons, the degree of weathering and root-marking was rarely uniform across a single skeleton; the condition of different skeletal elements sometimes varying considerably with scores from 0 to 5. There was no consistent pattern with respect to location or phase; bone recovered from pits and ditches showed similar variability, and bone from primary deposits displayed the same levels of wear and root-marks as those from tertiary deposits. Among the skulls, a single cranium was not always affected uniformly, for example only the right side of the vault of HH74 HB 6 was root-marked, and the right side of HH74 HB 1b was more heavily affected than the left. Among the disarticulated fragments weathering and root-marking were generally slight; bone from the Hanford spur was particularly lightly affected, with maximum scores of 3 for weathering and 2 for root-marks, while that from the Shroton spur was noticeably more heavily affected than the bone from elsewhere. Particularly heavy wear and root-marking were also noted in fragments from the phase VIII/a deposits in the inner Stepleton outwork; and root-marking increased in severity in the phase VI deposits in the main causewayed enclosure and in the upper levels of the east cross-dykes. Few of the fragments from the south long barrow were root-marked, but those that were affected generally scored 4–5.

There were numerous instances in which one end of a bone fragment was heavily worn or root-marked while the other end had a fresh appearance. This may have resulted from the position of the bone in the ground, experiments having shown preferential damage to the side of the bone facing up after burial due to the effects of percolating water (Armour-Chelu and Andrews 1996); alternatively, it may indicate that parts of the disarticulated bone fragments were left protruding above ground for some time after deposition, the rest of the fragment being buried.

A small proportion (7%) of the bone, all disarticulated fragments, had a distinctive form of fine longitudinal fissuring/cracking, characteristic of very dry bone. Such fissuring is characteristic of rapid drying (Wysocki 1998, 156), perhaps following soaking (?rain) followed by drying in intense sunlight. Small numbers of such fragments were found in all locations.

The patterns of weathering and root-marking noted in the human bone do not appear to be repeated in the animal bone. The animal bone from the deep deposits was generally fairly fresh in appearance, only that from the upper or disturbed levels showing indications of weathering (see Legge, Ch 8). The depth from which the bone was recovered does not appear to have been such a significant factor with regard to the condition of the human bone. Although there was an increase in the severity of root-marking in the later phases in some localities, and bone from the final phase on the Stepleton spur was more heavily worn than elsewhere, the condition of the bone from these phases was not uniform and heavy wear/root-marks also occurred in earlier phases. A similar variation in the degree of weathering was also noted between the (much smaller) human and animal bone assemblages from Etton, Cambridgeshire (Pryor 1998).

While there is some indication that location, and thereby possibly the burial micro-environment, was a factor in the condition of the bone, such variation may equally reflect different treatment of bone in the different localities. There is, for instance, some indication from the radiocarbon dates that human bone from the Shroton outwork had been subject to more re-working (?repeated redeposition or longer exposure prior to final burial) than bone from the Hanford outworks (Ch 4). It may be worth noting that the condition of the bone from the Anglo-Saxon graves on the Stepleton spur was considerably poorer than that of any from the Neolithic contexts, though this was almost certainly the result of plough-damage.

Of the three types of deposit, skulls were the most consistently worn and root-marked category. The articulated skeletal material was also substantially more frequently weathered and root-marked than the disarticulated bone fragments. The condition of the skulls indicates that they were subject to greater exposure to the elements than the rest of the assemblage, particularly since all, except some from the Hanford spur, were recovered from on or near the base of ditches. Most of the articulated skeletal remains were also recovered on or close to ditch bases, some were apparently deliberately covered, others not. The degree of weathering seen in this category suggests that at least some of the remains were exposed to the elements for some length of time. Skeleton ST78 2755 lay prone in a layer of chalk rubble in the inner Stepleton outwork and was believed to be associated with an attack on the Stepleton enclosure. Although the bone was slightly root-marked, there was no visual weathering, implying that this body was covered fairly rapidly. The highly variable condition of the disarticulated bone fragments seems to indicate that not all the material in this category was subject to the same taphonomic processes, or, if so, then for different lengths of time or for a different number of episodes. There were a number of instances in which non-adjacent fragments from different phases were found to match, for example HH74 HB 5 (mandible) and 6 (skull minus mandible) from different phases within adjoining segments of the main causewayed enclosure ditch – indicating re-working of material. Differential treatment of Neolithic remains deposited in different areas of the long cairn at Parc le Breos Cwm, Gower, has been suggested by Wysocki (1998), the remains from the chamber appearing far more weathered than those from the passage.

Fragmentation

Almost all (98.7%) of the disarticulated material consisted of bone fragments rather than complete bones. The only exceptions comprise a complete, but broken, radius from the Shroton spur (HH76 1963) and 20 hand or foot bones, half of which are from the south long barrow. In general, only the shafts of limb bones were recovered, a mere 1.7% of the assemblage comprising fragments of articular surface. Although breaks along the lengths of shafts were clearly either post-depositional (joining fragments) or of recent origin, the broken ends of long bones usually showed the same level of wear as the adjacent cortical surface. Since the bone was generally in fairly robust condition, the lack of spongy bone is not considered to have been a result of soil conditions adverse to bone survival, but is regarded chiefly as a consequence of its treatment prior to final deposition.

In addition to a large part of the assemblage clearly being deposited as 'dry' fragments, a certain amount of breakage probably occurred as the result of pressure from the burial environment. A large quantity of the human bone was recovered from fairly deep contexts and many of the fills comprised coarse chalk rubble. Over 40% of the disarticulated bone assemblage consisted of skull fragments – between one and 20 fragments in a single find – predominantly vault. The close proximity and distribution of many of these fragments, together with the joins between some, suggests that they were slightly less fragmentary at the time of deposition. Most of the 15 skulls deposited on or close to the ditch bases were shattered, some badly (>75 fragments), and several had been warped as a result of soil pressure. Some of the articulated skeletons were described as 'crushed' by RK, for example the older adult burial ST79 2025, the immature individual ST78 964 and the Bronze Age burial ST82 114, all from features on the Stepleton spur. The first may have suffered as a result of its position under the massive inner outwork bank or due to more recent agricultural activity. Although an articulated skeleton (ST78 2755) from the inner Stepleton outwork had apparently not been left exposed for long, the cranium was badly broken, with more than 283 very small fragments in addition to the 39 main fragments which could be joined.

The bulldozing of the mound of the south long barrow in the 1960s removed all the human remains contained within it from their original contexts, the nature of which must remain uncertain. The fragmentary human bone was found mostly within the south-west quadrant with some in the north-west, other fragments having been spread over the area between the long barrow and the south cross-dykes. With the exception of loose teeth and *c* 50% of the small bones of the hands and feet, the bones had been broken into small fragments by years of agricultural activity. The only human bone from the long barrow ditches was a fragment of long bone (HH77 1948) from the primary silts and five loose teeth found together in the phase VI slot cut into the south-east ditch. Much material was probably lost as a result of the recent disturbances, both through fragmentation and dispersal. One-hundred-and-seventy fragments were identifiable to a specific skeletal element, 58 fragments could only be described as long bone.

Gnawing

Since some of the animal bone recovered showed evidence of having been gnawed by carnivorous scavengers (a minimum of 2.7% of the animal bone fragments had been subject to dog gnawing, and 0.3% to rodent gnawing, see Legge, Ch 8), the human bone was examined for traces of similar activity. For reference, RK looked at recent collections of the remains of animals eaten by wolves and human bones from corpses dragged from shallow graves by hyænas. The latter provided useful information on which skeletal elements were most likely to show traces of gnawing, which included vertebral bodies, the iliac portion of the pelvic bones, the articular ends of long bones and the basal portion of the skull, leaving the cranial vault with characteristic bevelled edges. In other words, the more 'nutritious' spongy bones with their greater infiltration by cartilage and blood vessels, many functioning as a storehouse for marrow, were eaten, the more compact bone being left. The former skeletal elements would also have been physically easier to consume. In addition to the bevelled/crenellated edges produced when fresh bone breaks due to carnivore gnawing (often formed by conjoined punctures), puncture marks (which may appear as 'pock-marks' in the surface of compact bone) are created in the bone surface by the anterior teeth and grooves where the animal has gnawed across the grain of the bone. It has been observed, however, that carnivores can scavenge a corpse without leaving any visible marks on the bone (Haynes 1980; Horwitz and Smith 1988). The potential destructive power of carnivores is demonstrated by the mere 0.30–0.40 m length of long bone shaft which was all that remained of a reindeer eaten by wolves (RK). Dogs and foxes could consume a large proportion of the human skeleton (Legge, pers comm), as with the hyænas mentioned above, particularly the remains of young immature individuals.

A few fragments of human bone show clearly visible traces of gnawing, by both canids (dogs and/or foxes; seven finds, *c* 2%) and rodents (*c* 1%). There were no indications to suggest the activity of wolves, the presence of which in the vicinity of Hambledon during the Neolithic period would be highly unlikely (Legge, pers comm). It may be significant that four of the ten finds in which gnawed bone was positively noted were articulated skeletal material (canid and rodent gnawing), that is 33% of the articulated bone, compared with 2% of the fragmentary bone. Among the animal bone, gnawing was more frequent on the Stepleton spur than elsewhere (see Legge, Ch 8). Gnawed human remains were noted among the bone from three finds on the Stepleton spur (3%), three from the main causewayed enclosure (2%), three from the south long barrow (6%) and two from the Hanford spur (8%). The figures should, however, be treated with caution, since there is compelling indirect evidence that gnawing was far more widespread (see below).

Direct evidence for canid gnawing took the form of puncture marks, pock-marks on long bone shafts, crenellated broken edges to bone, and grooving. For example, bipolar puncture marks were recorded on either side of a fragment of immature ilium (HN82 403) from the inner Hanford outwork; two punctures are in the anterior side of the bone, one on the dorsal side (Figs 7.1–2).

Extensive gnawing was noted in the articulated remains of an adult male (HH76 2625), comprising just the lower axial skeleton and the femora, recovered from phase II/III of the main causewayed enclosure ditch (Figs 7.3–4). Here the iliac crests of the pelvic bones have crenellated edges and puncture marks in one side and there are two broad, diffuse grooves, 5 mm wide, *c* 4.3 mm apart in the anterior of the first sacral body. The proximal and distal ends of the left femur had partly been removed (the ball joints of the hips remaining intact) leaving crenellated edges, fractured puncture marks and pock-marks along the adjacent shafts (Figs 7.3–4). Pock-marks were also seen in the right femur proximal shaft concentrated over a 51 mm proximal–distal area, continuing – very dispersed – down the medial and dorsal sides. It is likely that the body was partly decomposed before removal to this position and that it was either dragged from a shallow grave or removed from an exposed position above ground. The probable weight of the body suggests that more than one animal was involved in its movement.

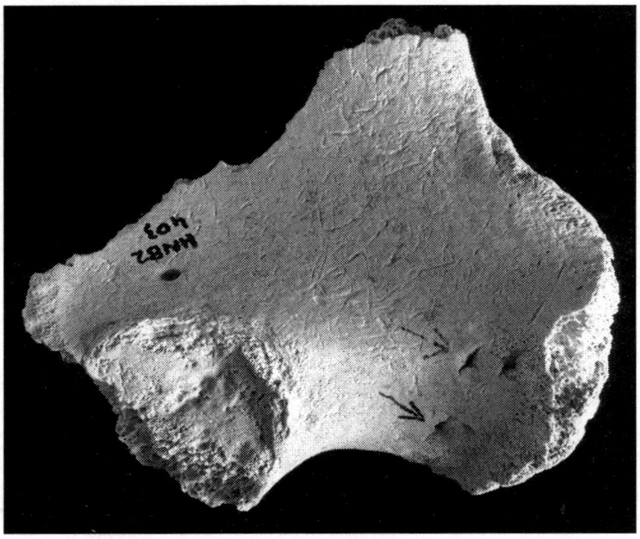

Fig 7.1 HN82 403 (infant); ventral view of left ilium (pelvic bone), showing puncture marks from canid gnawing. Photo Elaine Wakefield (Wessex Archaeology)

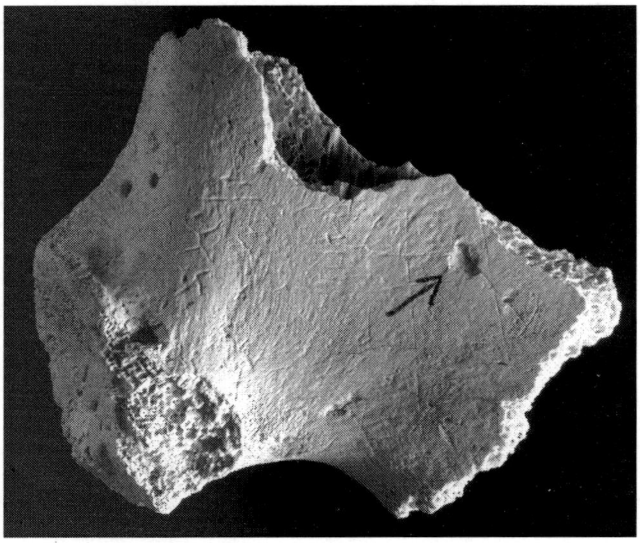

Fig 7.2 HN82 403; dorsal view of left ilium, showing puncture marks from canid gnawing (in opposition to those in Fig 7.1) and a series of cut-marks. Photo Elaine Wakefield (Wessex Archaeology)

Crenellated margins and puncture marks were also noted around the proximal end of a fragment of left femur from the south long barrow (HH77 77), with a series of four pock-marks in the anterior and posterior surfaces of the shaft (Fig 7.5). Several rib shaft fragments from the articulated skeleton ST 2755 from the Stepleton spur had puncture marks and crenellated areas on the upper or lower borders; in one right rib, a 9 mm area of rodent gnawing overlay a slightly larger area of canid gnawing (Fig 7.6).

Most of the punctures were in the region of 3.9–5 mm in diameter; the presence of some smaller ones, *c* 1.7 mm diameter, suggests either several species of scavenger, or both immature and adult individuals.

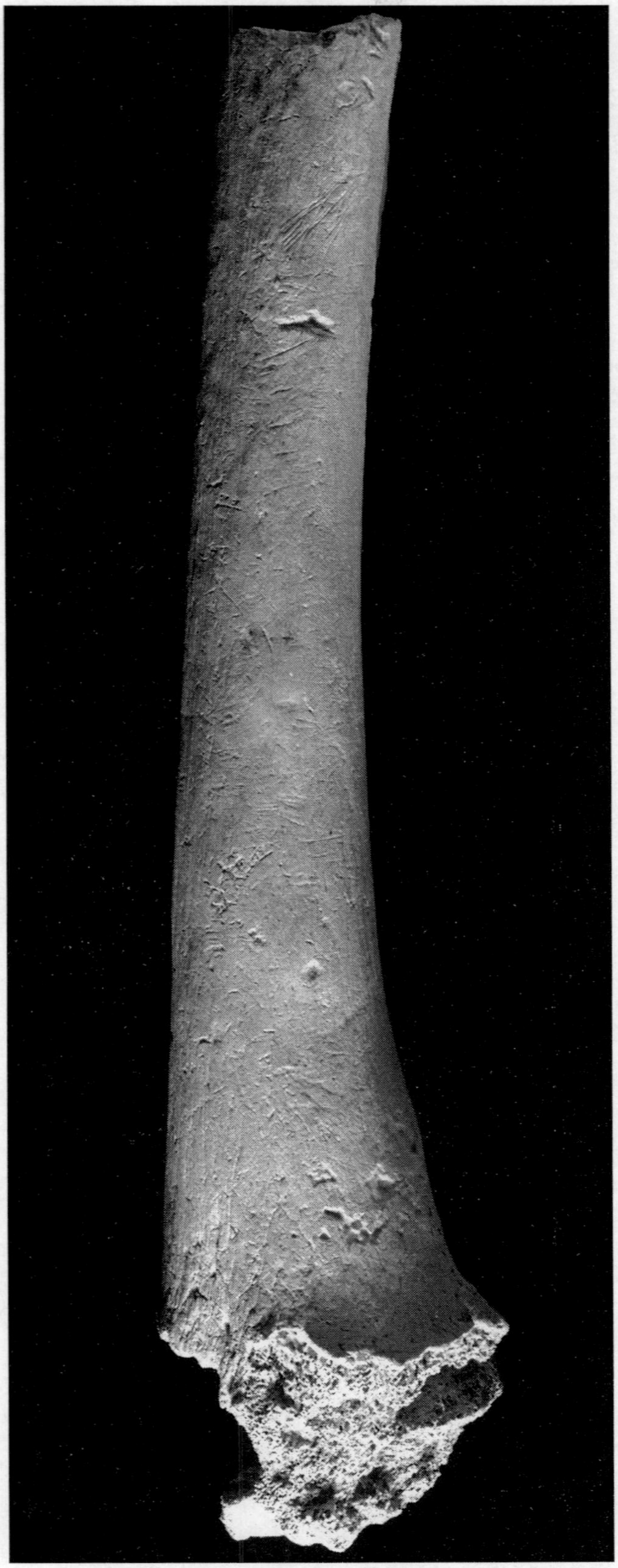

Fig 7.3 HH76 2625 (adult male 18–30 yr); anterior-lateral view of left mid-distal femur, showing several series of cut-marks and scrapes, canid gnawing to articular surface and pock-marks in the shaft, and changes due to various forms of weathering. Photo Elaine Wakefield (Wessex Archaeology)

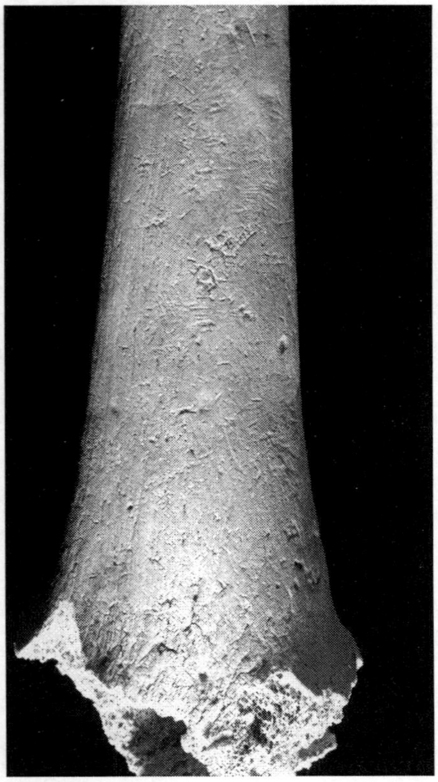

Fig 7.4 HH76 2625; anterior view of left distal femur showing several series of cut-marks and scrapes, canid gnawing to articular surface and pock-marks in the shaft, and changes due to various forms of weathering. Photo Elaine Wakefield (Wessex Archaeology)

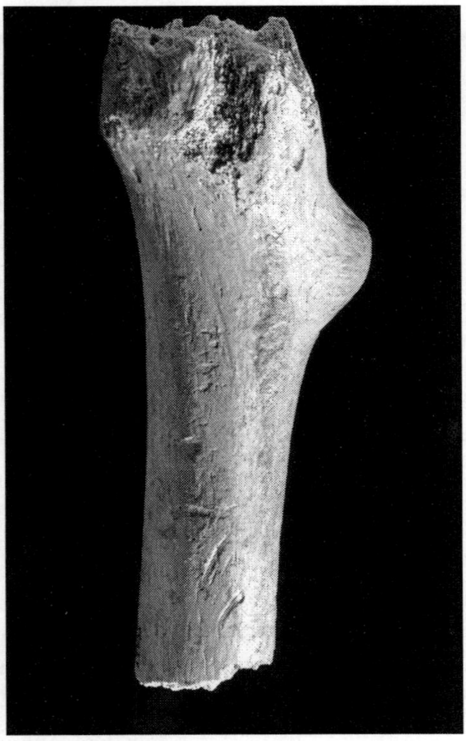

Fig 7.5 HH77 77 (adult ?male); lateral view of left proximal femur showing crenellations due to gnawing and puncture mark above lesser trochanter (to right). Photo Elaine Wakefield (Wessex Archaeology)

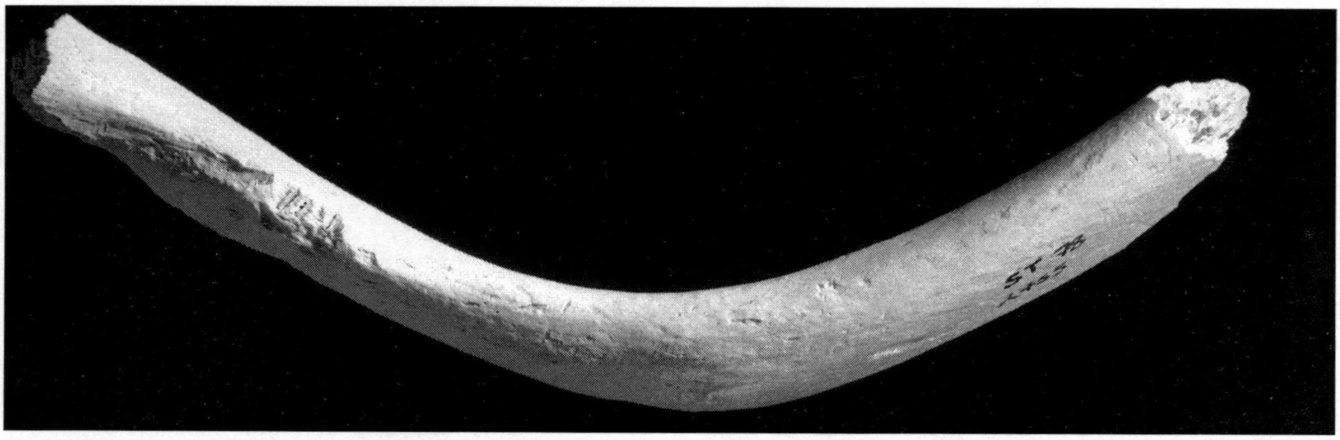

Fig 7.6 ST78 2755 (male, 17–20 yr); right rib showing area of rodent gnawing along superior border overlying canid gnawing and puncture in external surface of shaft (to left of number marked on bone). Photo Elaine Wakefield (Wessex Archaeology)

An extensive area – 56.6 × 37.0 mm – of rodent gnawing was noted along the sagittal suture of the skull of ST80 1875, extending through the exocranial surface and much of the diploë. Probable gnawing was also noted in other parts of the skull and on the margins of broken edges in the left scapula, right clavicle and left femur. The presence of rodent tooth marks need not necessarily suggest exposure of the body either in the open or in a shallow grave. In many places the ditch fills were vacuous and the possibility of access by rodents some time after final deposition should not be overlooked, though there are limits to the depth to which small rodents will burrow.

It is highly probable that these few examples of clearly evident gnawing represent a minimum number; subsequent weathering and abrasion obscuring the broken edges of bone fragments and rendering grooving difficult to distinguish from other surface marks. Indirect evidence suggests that the activity of scavengers was far more prevalent. There is a noticeable dearth among the disarticulated bone of fragments of vertebrae and pelvic bones (3.7%, most from the long barrow (0.8%) or from a single deposit made up of ST79 2497 and other finds in segment 6 of the middle Stepleton outwork (1.3%)), hand and foot bones (2.5%, most from the long barrow) and the articular surfaces of long bones (1.7%; 0.8% from the long barrow, 0.3% from the Hanford spur), ie the very parts of the skeleton most likely to be completely lost due to consumption by scavengers (Binford 1981, 171–73). The degree of weathering noted to the bone does not suggest that these skeletal elements or parts of bones have been lost owing to adverse soil conditions. While it may be that there were other taphonomic or cultural forces that may have affected the skeletal elements observed in analysis (see below), it is probable that a large proportion of this bone has been lost as a result of the activities of scavengers. Binford has discussed and illustrated the distinctive patterns in surviving long bone parts following canid gnawing, which includes the progressive removal of one or both ends of the long bone, the 'cylinder' – a segment of the central part of the long bone shaft – often comprising one of the last surviving parts (Binford 1981, 171–73, figs 4.56–57). His definition of animal gnawing as 'an attritional process resulting in the progressive deletion of certain parts from the assemblage' may be pertinent to the observed bone recovery in the human bone assemblage from Hambledon Hill. Similarly, the observation that 'Animals manipulate bones and carcasses by literally tearing them down structurally' may be seen to describe the dispersed distribution of partial cadavers.

It may be significant that a substantially higher percentage of the immature individuals in the assemblage were identified from the articulated remains and skulls (36%) as compared with the adults (15%), with a correspondingly lower percentage from among the disarticulated remains. Some infant and juvenile remains are likely to have been completely removed from the assemblage as a result of the activities of scavengers, particularly since it is known that wild animals tend to remove their food out of the open to a 'safe place' prior to consumption (Legge, pers comm).

There is no note of any gnawing, canid or rodent, to the human bone from the causewayed enclosure at Staines, Surrey (Robertson-MacKay 1987). However, Pryor (1998) reports that canid gnawing was recorded in half of the fifteen fragments of disarticulated human bone recovered from Etton. Here, as at Hambledon, the human bone differed from the animal bone in being more abraded, but, in apparent contrast, the human bone was more gnawed than the animal (4% of the 275 fragments of animal bone recovered were gnawed). About 50% of the human remains from the chambers at Parc le Breos Cwm had been gnawed (Wysocki 1998) and it was noted that long bones were most frequently represented by segments of shaft (no gnawing was noted to human bone from the passage). What could not be conclusively stated in the latter was how much of the gnawing had occurred prior to deposition in the cairn and how much subsequent to it, though Wysocki suggests that the former was principally the case. Lee (2006) observed no gnawing on the human bone from the long barrow at Haddenham, Cambridgeshire.

Charred bone and 'sooting'

Human bone in five finds showed positive evidence of charring (1.4%) giving a slightly higher figure than for the animal bone (0.7%). All were disarticulated fragments from both adult and immature individuals, and all except one came from the main causewayed enclosure.

Most of the charring was to fragments of skull vault. A fragment of immature vault from BF14 (HH75 611) is charred black. There is brown-black charring to the endocranial and exocranial surfaces of a right lateral frontal from segment 8 of the main enclosure (HH75 2101), crossing the broken edge of the fragment, and in the endocranium adjacent to the nasal sinus and left orbital vault; a few other fragments of vault were charred grey. The left lateral and right half of a frontal from segment 17 of the main enclosure (HH76 2923) is slightly charred (dark brown) in the exo- and endocranial surfaces (darker endo-). In ST81 875, from segment 7 of the Stepleton enclosure, there is brown and black charring to the frontal at the left medial supra-orbit and the left side of the glabella, where the bone is also broken (Fig 7.7). Two fragments of long bone from two other finds were very slightly charred (brown).

The condition of the bone (fragmentation and colour) indicates that it was burnt as dry, or close to dry, bone (McKinley 1994, 76–78), and probably when already fragmented. There is no evidence for cremated bone. Although a large proportion (*c* 41%) of the finds included fragments of vault, a similarly large proportion of long bone shaft fragments were also recovered. It appears significant, therefore, that most of the charred fragments were cranial.

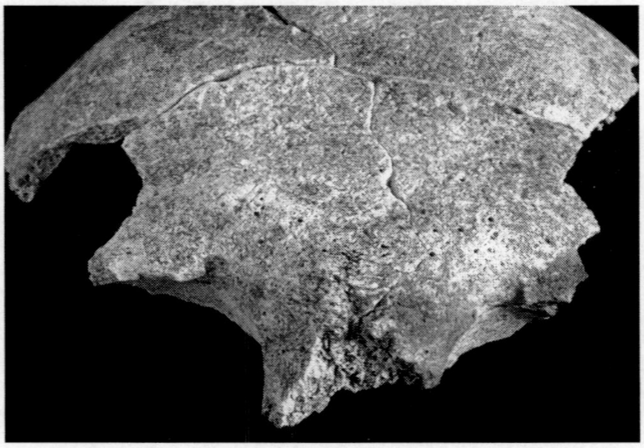

Fig 7.7 ST81 875 (adult ?male); frontal vault showing charring to left supra-orbit and glabella. Photo Elaine Wakefield (Wessex Archaeology)

There is no note of charring to the small amount of human bone recovered from the causewayed enclosures at Staines (Robertson-MacKay 1987) or Etton (Pryor 1998). Some bones from the Fussell's Lodge long barrow in Wiltshire were 'burnt and scorched' (Brothwell and Blake 1966, 40). Both cremated and dry burnt bone were recovered from the West Kennet long barrow in the same county (Wells 1962, 81; Piggott 1962, 24). A few fragments of charred and more thoroughly burnt bone occurred in undisturbed contexts at Hazleton, Gloucestershire (Saville 1990b, 104, 183 and 260), and 'charring' of uncertain nature was noted in several early long barrow excavations (Kinnes 1992, 101). The bone from Haddenham exhibits varying levels of oxidation (illustrated by the colour of the bone) which, together with the evidence for articulation, suggested that both green and dry bone may have been burnt *in situ* when the mortuary was fired (Lee 2006).

Clearly there are two separate types of activity reflected in these occurrences: cremation, as a mode of disposal of the dead, with subsequent interment of cremated bone in a similar vein to the deposition of the unburnt remains, and burning of already dry bone, the significance of which is debatable. The latter may have been deliberate and had some 'ritual' significance. Alternatively it may have been incidental, the distinction between human and animal bone or any other 'debris' no longer being maintained once the main mortuary ritual had been performed. The six contexts containing burnt human bone from Hambledon Hill also contained charcoal and animal bone, the latter showing some evidence of burning in two contexts. Fragments of disarticulated and fragmentary burnt human bone have also been found in numerous late Bronze Age/early Iron Age 'midden' deposits such as at Potterne, Wiltshire (McKinley 2000), and Iron Age 'structured' pit deposits such as those at Ham Hill, Somerset (McKinley 1999a), where the significance attached to the human remains is also believed to have altered from that attached to skeletal remains involved in a specific mortuary ritual.

Bone fragments from 23 finds (7%), including parts of two articulated skeletons, were noted to have a 'dirty' or dark-stained appearance, indicative of charcoal staining or 'sooting'. A small proportion (*c* 18%) of these finds were from charcoal-rich contexts and may have been stained during their final burial, though it should also be noted that many other fragments from charcoal-rich deposits were not stained. The remainder of the fragments were recovered from charcoal-free contexts, which suggests that they were stained or sooted prior to deposition.

Cut-marks

Cut-marks were recorded in bones from 23 of the finds (*c* 7%). Poor definition of possible cuts in eight of these, due to the erosive/masking effects of weathering/ root-marks and the shallow depth of incision into the bone, made conclusive identification impossible in some instances. The numbers involved included five articulated skeletons (36% of articulated material), three skulls (21% of skulls) and 15 disarticulated fragments (5% of this category).

Cuts were most commonly seen in the skull (43%) and femur (35%), two (9%) had cuts in parts of the pelvic bones (ischium and ilium) and there were single instances of cuts in the rib, radius, fibula and tibia (Table 7.4). Among the articulated skeletal material, cuts were most commonly seen in only one bone (three of five), though cuts were seen in both femora from one skeleton, and in the left radius and three ribs of another. Those affected include individuals across the age range (neonate to older adult) and of both sexes. Distribution covered all the main localities, including the south long barrow, with no significant concentration apparent within any particular area.

The sharp profile (sometimes diminished by weathering), apparent in visual inspection and confirmed by microscopic examination, demonstrated that the cuts were the result of human action. The profile was generally angled, having one side steeper than the other, with an acute base (Fig 7.8). The use of stone tools may be distinguished by longitudinal striations within the cut and 'feathering' towards the ends (Fig 7.9) created by the 'serrated' edge of the blade (P Andrews, pers comm).

The cut-marks were all of a similar form and type – short, shallow incisions, *c* 3.54–42 mm in length, commonly occurring as small groups of parallel or almost parallel lines, generally set at a transverse angle. Most of the marks were extremely shallow, though there were several slightly deeper incisions. In most instances, relatively few cuts (*c* 1–15) were evident in one skeletal element, however, in excess of 100 cuts were recorded along the length of the anterior shaft of the left femur of HH76 2625 (Figs 7.3–4, 7.8–9). Table 7.4 presents a description of the cuts and their location, and a guide to the associated muscle groups etc (these are not necessarily muscle insertions).

This type of cut is characteristically produced in the butchery of animals during 'filleting', ie defleshing. They are the 'shorter, more oblique cuts made to the underside of the exposed bone to free it from the mass of meat and/or sever muscle insertions' (Binford 1981, 129) and are characteristically 'very superficial, rarely deep' (Binford 1981, 131). Some of the marks may best be referred to as 'scrapes' rather than 'cuts', resulting from the action of scraping flesh off the bone as part of a cleaning process rather than the removal of any substantial quantity of soft tissue. This latter action, where undertaken by a highly skilled operative, may leave no marks on the bone at all (P Andrews, pers comm); conversely, it has been demonstrated that 'when the object of the activity was a cleaned bone, rather than meat, skeletal elements were expected to bear a relatively large number of cut-marks compared with skeletons defleshed for meat' (Russell 1987a; 1987b). While many of the marks noted are most likely to represent 'scrapes', some were slightly deeper and appear to have comprised the 'cuts' associated with defleshing rather than cleaning, eg one cut on the left femur of HH76 2625 (Fig 7.3) and those on the radius and ribs of ST78 2755 (Figs 7.10–11).

There was no indication of chop marks or of the specifically located (around the proximal and distal ends of long bones; eg Ubelaker 1984, 191, figs 101–2) cuts indicative of dismemberment (Binford 1981, 91–126), or of bone breakage to facilitate the

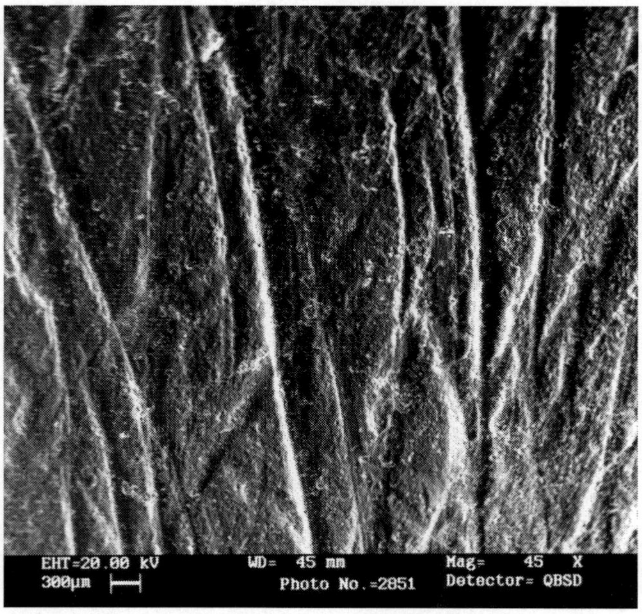

Fig 7.8 HH76 2625; SEM image of a cast of a group of cuts/scrapes (sharp profile) and ?abrasions/trampling (×45 magnification). Photo Malcolm Ward (English Heritage)

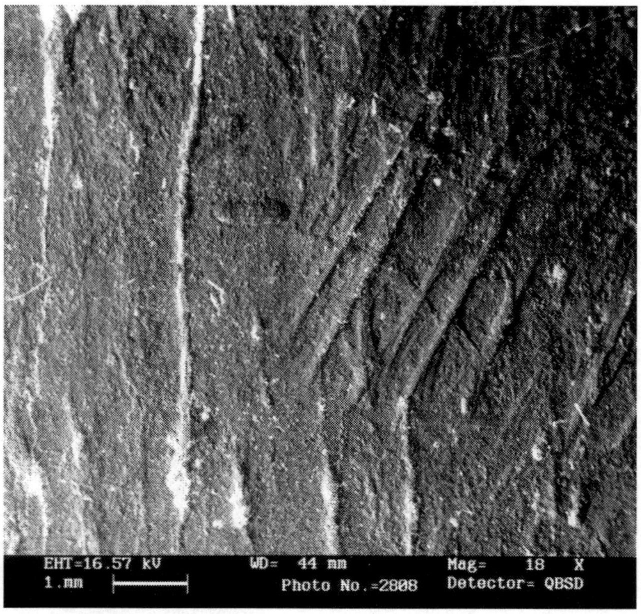

Fig 7.9 HH76 2625; SEM image of a cast of a group of scrapes and abrasions/trampling (×18 magnification). Photo Malcolm Ward (English Heritage)

extraction of marrow (ibid, 148–63). Comparison of the location and type of cuts seen in the human bone from Hambledon Hill with those observed in the animal bone, illustrates the difference in the processes of human manipulation of the two assemblages (see Legge, Ch 8).

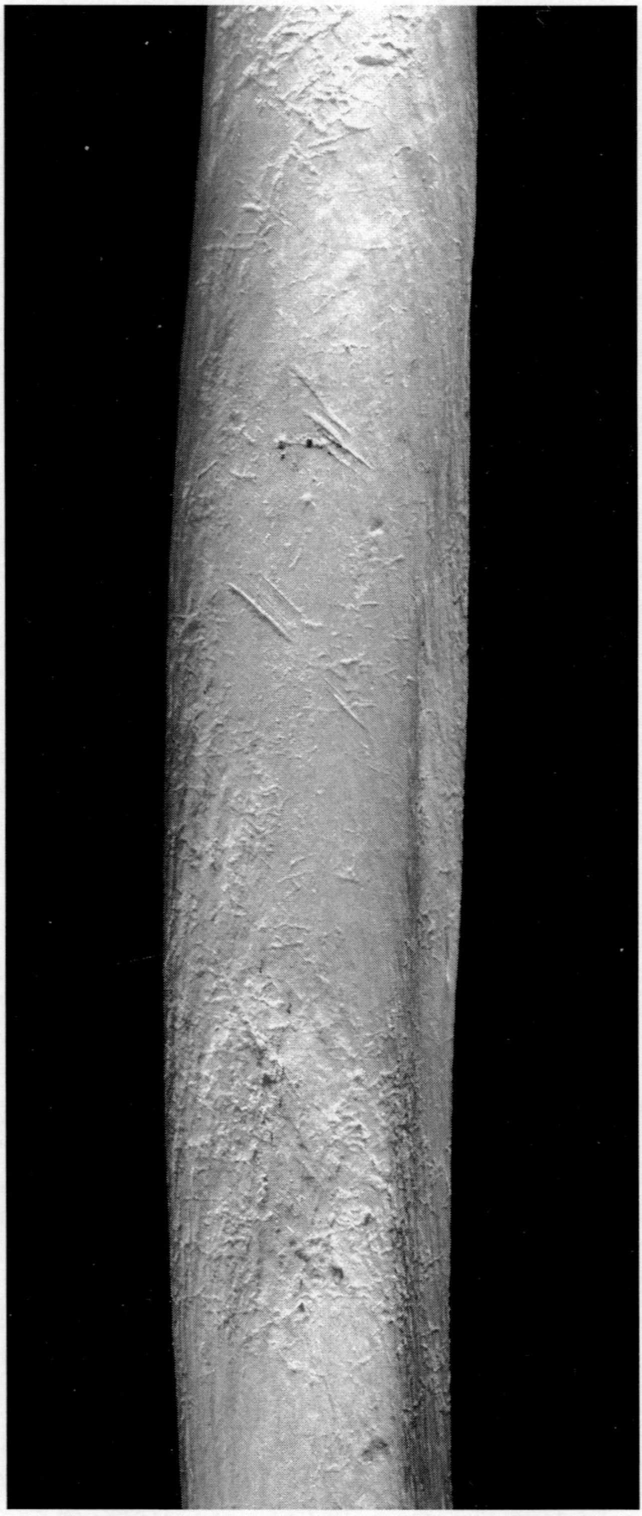

Fig 7.10 ST78 2755 (male 17–20 yr); dorso–lateral view of left proximal radius shaft showing three small groups of cut-marks. Photo Elaine Wakefield (Wessex Archaeology)

There were difficulties in distinguishing some of the cuts, due both to the nature of the incisions themselves and the condition of the bone. None of the cuts, by virtue of their nature, were very deep, only the very surface of the cortex being affected. Cuts of this type are likely to be completely erased from bone which has suffered moderate, possibly even relatively mild, weathering of the cortical surfaces; root-marking may both mask and mimic such cut-marks, making them difficult to distinguish, particularly where there is also erosion of the surface (see for example, Figs 7.1–4 and 7.10). Further potential difficulties were introduced by the burial environment, which often included quantities of flint, and undoubtedly there had been some post-depositional abrasion producing incidental scratches on the bone surface. In experiment, the latter has been noted to occur as the fill around the bone settles after deposition (Armour-Chelu and Andrews 1996). Pre-depositional abrasion due to trampling may create surface marks very similar to some of those seen in this assemblage (ibid), and with this assemblage it is known that bone lay exposed on the surface prior to burial. The effects of most of these factors are amply demonstrated in the femora of HH76 2625 (Figs 7.3–4).

It is highly probable that the cuts recorded here are a minimum, both within one deposit or find and the assemblage as a whole. This presents difficulties in interpretation with regard to both the treatment of the remains of individuals and what it may reflect of the mortuary rituals in general. The apparent exclusion (see below) of the Hanford spur from whatever general activity was occurring is probably genuine, given the relatively fresh condition of the bone from this locality (see above). In other areas, the activity was not confined to individuals of any particular age or sex.

In the majority of cases, the cuts can be linked with either the severing of specific muscle attachments (Table 7.4) and/or cleaning/stripping the bone of its soft tissues by repeated short scrapes, possibly accompanied by tugging away of the tissue. Although it is probable that some cuts will have been missed or effectively erased, the general impression is that the location of individual cuts or scrapes on the different bones do not follow a consistent pattern, and do not suggest systematic and complete defleshing of bodies and cleaning of the bones. Some of the cuts, to the visceral surfaces of ribs, lingual surface of mandible and the ischium for instance, would appear difficult to make other than to a body already partially defleshed and/or disarticulated.

One possible key to the interpretation of the rituals being practised is the inclusion of the articulated skeletal remains. Here, some clear, deep incisions were noted to either a single bone, or a few bones within the skeleton. It had previously appeared as though the articulated skeleton ST78 2755 from the Stepleton inner outwork ditch had rested undisturbed – though not exposed for long (see above) – in the position in

Table 7.4 Summary of cut-marked bone from Neolithic contexts, compiled in consultation with A J Legge (AJL)

Order follows that of Table 7.1

Find	*Age/Sex*	*Type*	*Description*
HH77 682	young juvenile	frag	Long, fine scratch mark, 41.5 mm, crossing medio-lateral right lateral parietal *c* 17.2 mm dorsal to coronal suture. ?2 parallel cuts mid-lateral right occipital, max 13.3 mm long, 1.3 mm apart, inferior-medial to superior-lateral at *c* 20°. *Temporoparietalis* or *temporalis* and *epicranius*
HH75 2101	subadult/adult ?female	frag	1) 2, closely spaced (*c* 0.02 mm apart), slightly curved, parallel lines, min. 34.7 mm long. Precise location unknown, area posterior-inferior of parietal. Sharply incised and angled, cut so deep that the fragment has partly broken, probably in excavation, along this line (Figs 7.15–16). 2) Centre frontal, 10.2 mm long, 26.5 mm superior to glabella at *c* 60°. 3) Possible 3 others – may be abrasion or trampling. *Temporoparietalis* or *temporalis*
HH76 2625	young/younger mature adult male	artic	1) Anterior ventral of left iliac surface, dorsal-ventral, horizontal to iliac border and *c* 20 mm superior to it, stopping short of inferior of public tubercle. Cut-mark, 20.7 mm long. Could have caught inferior anterior margin of *iliacus* but seems a little low. 2) Medial side left femur lesser trochanter, *c* 5 short – 3.7–8.9 mm cuts, medio-lateral in superior half. *Psoas major/?pectineus* 3) Extensive series small cuts, along length of left femur shaft from within 80 mm of distal end to with 42 mm of the broken proximal end. Mostly along anterior & anterior lateral shaft, with lesser numbers on anterior medial side (Figs 7.3–4, 7.8–9). Fine, short blade marks, occurring individually & in groups of up to 11, generally angled *c* 30–40°, inferior-lateral to superior-medial on medial side and inferior-medial to superior-lateral on lateral side. Left proximal shaft: several short – *c* 3.7 mm – cuts in proximal anterior margin, 1st *c* 56.8 mm inferior to greater trochanter, medio-lateral, then 4.4 mm lower group of three, then two more at a slight angle, over 17.6 mm length of bone. Next batch down, over 17 mm length of proximal lateral shaft, groups of 4, 1, 2, 1 & 1, cuts *c* 6.3 mm long at a slight angle. Next batch over *c* 8 mm length of shaft, 2 adjacent groups at different angles, cuts *c* 5.1 mm long. Distal half of shaft (from break – 193.6 mm length), covered in cuts, possible may not have recorded all proximal to distal: dense group of deep cuts over 20 mm length, at *c* 45° angle, lateral-medial shaft, 14 cuts, 15 mm long angle progressively more acute as go to lateral side, some cross each other. Fainter group above this, *c* 5, and numerous small cuts inferior and lateral, *c* 13.4 mm left to level of modern damage. Below this, dispersed collection faint and deep cuts all along anterior-lateral shaft over 77.2 mm length, generally at slight angle, *c* 22 cuts up to 9.5 mm long, some probably from trampling and/or abrasion. Distal *anterior* shaft, several small groups of 4–5 cuts, 3.8 mm long, down to second marker. 2 strong groups of cuts inferior to TL inferior marker, 93.4 mm from distal end, *c* 7 cuts in each group, short, one almost horizontal, other angled. Few below this but not many. *Vastus intermedius* 4) Right femur has a few cuts, but much less than left, anterior-lateral of shaft, two concentrations, 4 short (max 8.5 mm) cuts over 14.6 mm length, one groups horizontal other angled *c* 45°. In mid shaft, medial anterior group of 6 faint cuts, 4.5 mm area shaft, 4.5 mm long. TL (4), one cut over medial-lateral border, *c* 3.1 mm long. Possible other but very faint. All fine, short blade marks, not very deep, made into green bone. *Vastus intermedius* 5) Right femur lesser trochanter, area cuts on and around trochanter (TL) as in left. *Psoas major/?pectineus* and ilio-femoral ligament attachment.
HH75 1179	young juvenile	sk–m	Mostly medio-lateral across centre-right of frontal, 9–12 mm long, straight or slightly curved at one end. Series 5 cuts, 22 mm superior to orbital margin to within 10 mm coronal suture. Cranium has a large number of other scores and striae which may be due to human action, or trampling/abrasion. One medio-lateral cut in middle left parietal has possible *post-mortem* break along it – cut can just be seen running parallel to part of the break. *Epicranius*, *temporoparietalis* or *temporalis*
HH75 2023	infant	?frag/ ?sk–m	Right medio-distal parietal has series of *c* 6 cuts adjacent to sagittal & lambdoid sutures in groups of up to 3. One cut has a convincing oblique cross-section found when a flint tool is used at an angle. Others are eroded but have the appearance of multiple incisions at one point & along a similar line. Some cuts also noted in left parietal but bit less certain. Multiple scores & grooves, some probably result of trampling &/or abrasion, but good deal eroded, cannot be certain. ?*Epicranius* or removal of scalp?
HH76 1824	older adult male	sk+m	Left lateral occipital adjacent to lambdoid suture but not crossing it, three lines becoming progressively fainter superiorly, set at *c* 25–30° angle, max 12.4 mm long, similar orientation. 11.2 mm between inferior line & middle one, upper line 3.7 mm above the middle line, ?trampling/abrasion or human action?. Right distal parietal, anterior-posterior cut 20.5 mm long. ?*Epicranius*

Find	*Age/Sex*	*Type*	*Description*
HH77 610	older adult	frag	Medial side left condyle neck from posterior end of sigmoid, at 45 degree angle anterior and inferior, 7.5 mm long. *70%* probability *Pterygondeus lateralis*
HH75 241	adult ??female	frag	3 fine cuts across anterior surface of distal femur shaft *c* 23 mm *Articularis genus* or *vastus intermedius*
HH75 653	adult	frag	Small group 3–4 faint parallel marks (in max 5 mm area) + one other slightly higher up, across 6.8 mm area. Right proximal femur shaft, medial anterior surface. Bone surface eroded with numerous scores and striae, some of which go over rounded surfaces after the manner of cut marks – but too little definition to go beyond 'possible', some likely to be trampling/abrasion. *Vastus intermedius*
HH75 699	young/mature adult	frag	Small 'nick' in left superior-anterior parietal, 3.4 mm ?
HH76 2956	adult	frag	3 parallel cuts, 3.6 mm long, across posterior-medial of mid shaft femur over a 2.3 mm area. Ill-defined 60% probability. *Vastus intermedius* or *articularis genus*
HH76 3014	adult	frag	2, very faint parallel cuts, 1.5 mm apart on lateral side of proximal femur shaft, 6.8 mm long. May be others but bone very abraded. *Vastus intermedius*
HH75 1360	young adult male	sk–m	*c* 15.5 mm cut in left side occipital, crossing lambdoid suture to left parietal at *c* 80° angle, *c* 43 mm inferior to lambda. Margins of 'cuts' are rounded and eroded, causing loss of detail (85% probability). Many other striae and scores *Epicranius*
HH77 77	adult probable male	frag	2 short, 4.3 mm, roughly parallel cuts, angled across anterior lateral side femur shaft. *Vastus intermedius*
HH77 95	mature adult	frag	Pair of parallel lines in dorsal surface of inferior left ischium, surface adjacent to tuberosity, *c* 15.4 mm long, 2.1 mm apart, at angle *c* 180°, series of 8, shorter lines set at right angles, some crossing the longer two creating a box effect, some ceasing at margins of longer lines (Figs 7.13–14). *Obturator externus*
HH76 1916	older adult female	frag	2 vertical cuts on disto-buccal body of mandible at base of ramus, 19.4 mm long. *Pterygondeus medialis*
HH76 1963	young/mature adult	frag	2–3 parallel cuts, almost horizontally across one side of fibula shaft, *c* 1.6 mm apart. The whole shaft is covered by small marks crossing the shaft, but it is also heavily root marked & eroded so difficult to identify convincingly. One of five possible muscle attachments or interosseous membrane.
ST81 1296	young infant	frag	3 possible cut-marks on an undefined vault fragment, max 16.4 mm. Eroded with loss of definition (75% probability).
ST78 2756	neonate	artic	4 small, parallel marks angled across the anterior shaft towards broken end right femur (proximal half shaft). Over 7.16 mm length of shaft, each *c* 3.54 mm in length. Possible cuts? *Vastus intermedius*
ST79 2726	older mature adult male	artic	2 possible cuts to right lesser trochanter, 80° angle, superior-lateral to inferior-medial, max 10.7 mm long, 2 mm apart. *Psoas major.*
ST78 2755	older subadult/ young adult male	artic	Proximal end left radius, dorso-lateral side, *c* 77–110 mm from head, 3 small groups of cuts (2–5) max 4.6 mm long, all at similar (but not identical) 45° angle, superior-lateral to medio-inferior (Fig 7.10). Three right rib shafts have cut marks: 1) dorsal-lateral surface, 2, slightly curved parallel cuts *c* 8.8 mm long, almost vertical, cross inferior border, 2) in visceral surface, slightly angled 17.8 mm, 3) upper end of lateral surface, *c* 210 mm from head, angled front-rear and downwards, *c* six parallel cuts, spread over three small groups within 15 mm area, each a max of 5.3 mm long (Figs 7.11–12). *supinator* and *pronator teres* in radius
ST80 1875	young adult male	artic	Possible cuts in distal shaft right tibia, posterior-lateral surface, 3 short (max 3.8 mm), parallel cuts, one off-set between others, at 45° angle. 2.5 mm between adjacent cuts, off-set one (lateral) between these two. General appearance '= -' ?interosseous membrane.
HN82 403	infant	frag	Series of 4 cuts, maximum 22.6 mm long, in dorsal surface of left ilium, roughly parallel, between 3.5–8 mm apart, radiating out distally from superior margin (Fig 7.12). Several shorter cuts set at right-angles, one, *c* 12 mm long, crosses one longitudinal cut and terminates at the adjacent (most dorsal) one, series of *c* 7 short marks, *c* 2.2 mm, respect the anterior edge of the anterior-most of the longitudinal cuts. Covers *c* 16.9 × 27.6 mm area *gluteus minimus* and ?*gluteus medius*

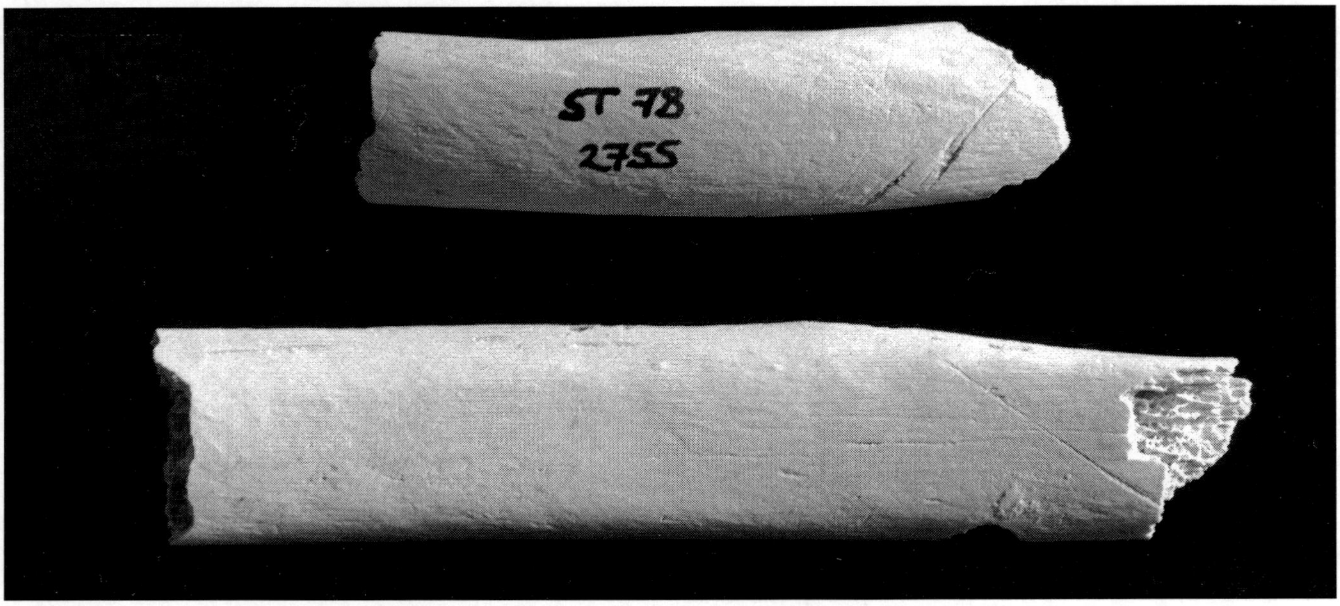

Fig 7.11 ST78 2755; view of dorsal (upper) and visceral (lower) surfaces of right rib shaft fragments with cut-marks. Photo Elaine Wakefield (Wessex Archaeology)

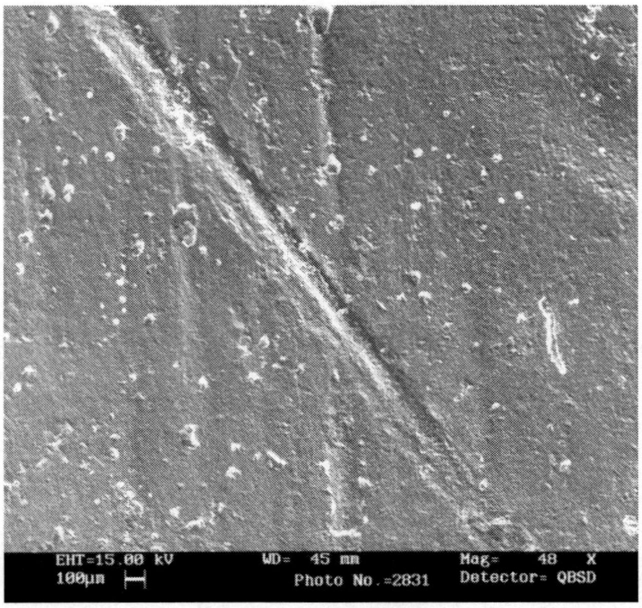

Fig 7.12 ST78 2755; SEM image of a cast of a cut-mark in visceral surface of right rib shaft. Photo Malcolm Ward (English Heritage)

which he fell, having been killed, probably during an attack on the enclosure (Figs 3.102–4). However, cuts to the left radius and three ribs (Figs 7.10–12) suggest this was not the case; some *post mortem* manipulation of the body appears to have occurred. The cuts to the radius are within the area of the supinator and pronator teres muscle attachments, the cuts in the ribs cross the dorso-lateral surface in two fragments, possibly extending to the attachments for the intercostal muscles and membranes, the cut in the third fragment crossing the area covered by the pleura. Cuts designed to sever individual muscle attachments to bone were obviously made to specific bones of this cadaver, but there was no apparent attempt at disarticulation. The corpse had also been subject to limited canid and rodent gnawing (see above). The myriad scrapes and cuts along the anterior shafts of the femora of HH76 2625, are mostly in the area covered by the vastus intermedius (Figs 7.3–4), and suggest both defleshing and cleaning of the bone; but why was activity limited to this anterior area and why did it appear to be concentrated on the left femur?

What the current evidence suggests is that cadavers were subject to partial removal or loosening of soft tissues and subsequent cleaning of the bones, possibly constituting part of an on-going process as the body reached various stages of decomposition, and representing components within a mortuary rite involving other modes of excarnation.

Odd exceptions, however, are provided by HH77 95 from the south long barrow and HN82 403 from the Hanford spur, each of which has a bizarre group of very shallow cuts on part of the pelvic bone (ischium and ilium respectively) forming a geometric pattern (Figs 7.2, 7.13–14). These cuts, although individually of a similar form to all the others, cannot be simply the products of defleshing or cleaning. The restricted distribution of this pattern of cuts to fragments of pelvic bone could be of significance, as may be the observation that HN82 403 is the only bone from the Hanford spur on which cut-marks were observed, while HH77 95 was one of only two from the long barrow. Several cattle bones from Etton had been 'firmly scored' with parallel diagonal or transverse lines which were apparently not associated with meat processing (Armour-Chelu 1998a). It was believed these may have comprised 'tally sticks'; did the odd marks on the pelvic bones from Hambledon serve some such similar purpose?

Fig 7.13 HH77 95 (mature adult); view of dorsal surface of ischium (pelvic bone) showing series of cut-marks creating 'boxed' effect and crenellated margins indicative of canid gnawing. Photo Elaine Wakefield (Wessex Archaeology)

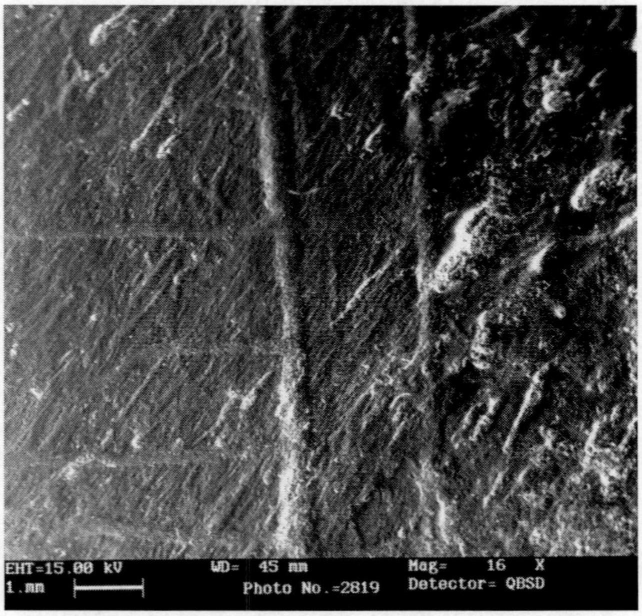

Fig 7.14 HH77 95; SEM image of a cast of cut-marks in the dorsal surface of the ischium. Photo Malcolm Ward (English Heritage)

One other point of note illustrated by the immature innominate HN82 403 is that the canid gnawing, at least in this instance, occurred after the cuts had been made to the bone (Fig 7.2). This does not, however, negate the possibility of earlier gnawing. The sequence of events was not clear in any other instance, there being no further overlaps between the two kinds of mark.

Similar cuts to those noted in the Hambledon Hill assemblage were observed on Neanderthal bones from Krapina in Croatia, though their distribution in the latter instance was far more consistent, demonstrating more systematic activity. Russell (1987a; 1987b) showed how the location and form of the cut-marks closely matched those on modern skeletons which had been defleshed with stone tools after partial decomposition in preparation for burial of the cleaned bones (see above – cleaning resulting in frequent marks).

Records of non-traumatic cut-marks to human bone from Neolithic contexts in Britain are very rare. The cut-marks noted in the human bones from the causewayed enclosure at Staines were either the result of traumatic injury or decapitation, and described as 'blows' rather than cuts. Harman and Evans (1991) noted one possible cut-mark to a fragment of humerus shaft from the Giants' Hills 2 long barrow in Lincolnshire, but describe neither the cut nor its location any further. A fragment of right distal humerus from the Haddenham long barrow had four groups (4–15 cuts) of short, parallel cut-marks in the anterior, medial and posterior surfaces in the areas of the brachialis and triceps attachments (Wakely 2006). The latter are of the same form and nature as those noted in the human bone from Hambledon Hill. One other cut was noted in this assemblage of almost 3,000 fragments (minimum seven individuals; Lee 2006), a *c* 5 mm long cut in a fragment of zygoma (Baxter, pers comm). Similar cut-marks were noted in two adult femora from the, probably Neolithic, assemblage excavated from Carsington Pasture Cave in Derbyshire (Chamberlain 1999); both femora were from the same individual, one of 20 identified. In this instance, however, the location of the cuts, around the distal end of the bones, is indicative of dismemberment rather than defleshing (Binford 1981, 91–126). A variety of non-pathological/traumatic cut-marks were recorded in human bone from the glacial period, at Gough's Cave in the Cheddar Gorge (Cook 1986). The nature of the manipulation in this instance was very different from that seen at Hambledon Hill, the remains apparently indicating scalping, beheading and butchery, including marrow extraction (Nuttall 1998). Wysocki and Whittle briefly mention 'evidence of corpse dismemberment with lithic implements' at Coldrum, Kent, and Eyford, Gloucestershire' (2000, 595), although they do not expand on the nature of that evidence.

Characteristics indicative of cannibalism have been discussed by Turner (1993) and are outlined by Roberts and Manchester (1997, 86); they include

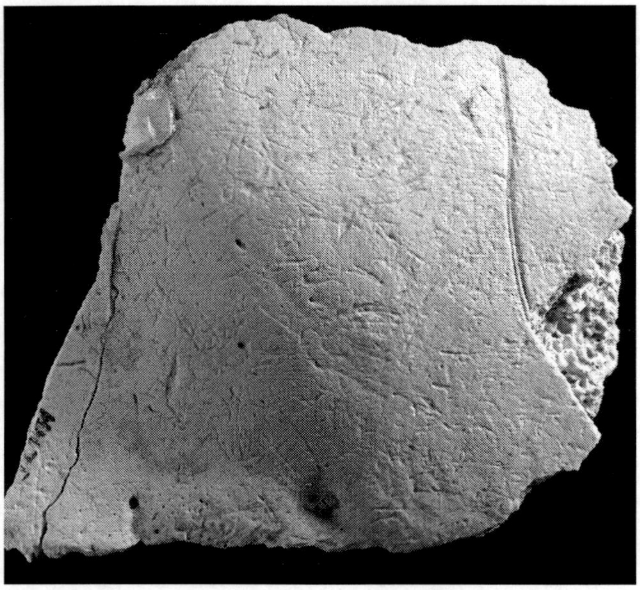

Fig 7.15 HH75 2101 (subadult/adult ?female); exocranial surface of a fragment of ?parietal vault, showing incised parallel lines. Photo Elaine Wakefield (Wessex Archaeology)

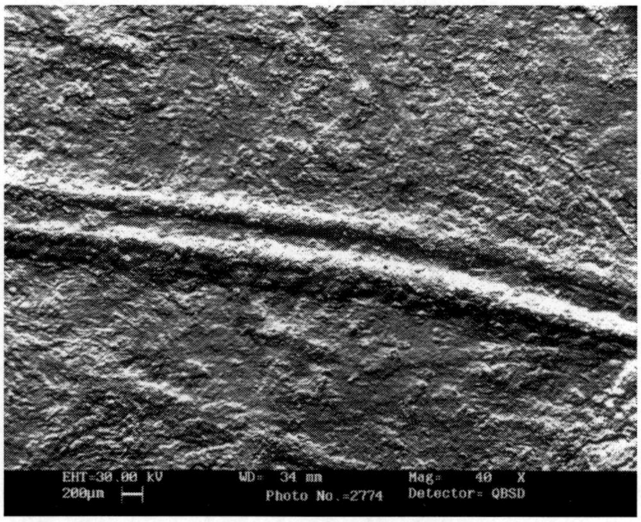

Fig 7.16 HH75 2101; SEM image of a cast of parallel lines in ?parietal vault. Photo Malcolm Ward (English Heritage)

numerous features which were not observed in the Hambledon Hill assemblage such as peri-mortem bone breaks, anvil-hammerstone abrasions and bone fragment end polishing. A case for Neolithic cannibalism was argued by Villa *et al* (1986) for the human remains from the cave at Fontbrégoua, near Salernes in southern France. Here, although there are some groups of short, shallow cuts similar to those seen in the Hambledon Hill bone, their distribution and frequency are quite different, and they are accompanied by much longer cuts of varied orientation and breakage of bone characteristic of marrow extraction and removal of the contents of the cranium (Bouville 1987). The authors also illustrate the similarities between the condition of the human and animal bone, indicating they were both subject to the same taphonomic processes (Villa *et al* 1986). Instances elsewhere in Neolithic Europe of cuts of a similar nature to those seen in the Hambledon Hill and Haddenham assemblages were discussed by Wakely (2006), from Furfooz in Belgium (de Laet 1958) and Ponte Paolina in Sicily (Fulchieri *et al* 1986).

That the cut-marks on the Hambledon Hill bone were overlooked in the original analysis raises a general cause for concern. By their nature these marks are relatively shallow, easily masked by the effects of weathering and root-marks, and more or less apparent depending on the light by which they are examined; they are also, it would seem, difficult to discern if the bone is not examined with the possibility of their existence in mind. Many of the Neolithic human bone assemblages from this country were assessed many years ago when human bone analysis was in its infancy and osteoarchaeology, as it is now practised, unknown. There is now, in the light of accumulating evidence, a case for re-assessment of at least the best-preserved of this previously excavated material, to ascertain the potential for cut-marks to the bone overlooked in the original examination.

Demography

Number of individuals (Table 7.2)

A minimum of four immature (under 18 yr) individuals and seven adults were identified from the articulated skeletal material. A further seven immature individuals and eight adults were represented by the skulls deposited on or near the bases of ditches. The minimum number estimates from the disarticulated, fragmentary material suggest that 24, possibly 25, immature individuals and 25, possibly 26, adults are represented. The overall minimum number obtained from the re-scan is therefore 75, possibly 77 individuals. As outlined above (7.1.1–2), RK employed a different methodology to estimate the number of individuals represented, calculating an overall minimum number of 132 individuals, with a potential overall maximum of 196; figures which included between 39 and 65 immature individuals and 64 and 102 adults from among the fragmentary, disarticulated bone. Even the minimum number of 75 individuals obtained from the re-scan would make this the largest known deposit of Neolithic human remains from England.

In the following discussion the figures and percentages presented are those estimated by the writer during the re-scan, including two skulls from Desmond Bonney's excavations which were not available to RK. RK's figures are given in *[italics]*. Table 7.2 presents the distribution of each type of deposit and number of individuals by location, and shows that the greatest number of individuals was identified from the main causewayed enclosure, 54% of immature individuals and 27% of adults *[44% and 27%]*, with 9% of immature individuals and 15% of adults *[22% and 15%]* from the inner Stepleton outwork.

Most of these remains were deposited between 3700 and 3300 cal BC, and direct dates for human remains, spanning this period, are available in 13 cases (Table 4.1). The stratigraphic phasing within the ditches summarised in Table 7.1 has limitations, arising from recuts and redeposition of material. For example, in the main causewayed enclosure, bone from phase IV contexts (the 'grey pits') may have been redeposited from phases I–III, and that in phase VI contexts (the slots) from phases I–V. Bone fragments from different phases within the same localities were found to join. In view of these difficulties it has been decided that any attempt at detailed discussion of phasing would produce results of limited value and integrity. On a broad scale however, it is clear that human bone, unlike artefacts, was being deposited predominantly in the early phases (Table 7.1, Figs 3.60–61, 3.124–5). In the main causewayed enclosure, of the estimated number of individuals, *c* 38% *[25%]* were in phase I–II deposits and *c* 31% *[18%]* in phase III deposits. Although a high percentage (*c* 21% *[31%]*) were recovered from phase VI contexts, they could include bone redeposited from phases I–V. Most deposits in the east cross-dykes were again early, and those in the inner outwork on the Stepleton spur were largely within the primary deposits *[c 43%]* or phase III *[c 30%]*. In contrast, most of the estimated number of individuals from the Stepleton enclosure were from the later and tertiary silts *[62%]*, as were most of those from the inner Hanford outwork *[64%]*. These figures may indicate a change in the focus of activity on the site over time.

Age (Table 7.5)

A high proportion of the estimated number of individuals identified were immature; 40% of those identified from articulated skeletal material or skulls and 45% of the total estimated number of individuals *[RK – 42%]*. It is probable that immature individuals, particularly neonates and young infants, are under-represented among the disarticulated material. In addition to the possible factors discussed above (see '*Gnawing*'), the fragile remains of such young individuals would be less likely to survive the various excarnation episodes to which this material was apparently subjected – which may explain the lower percentage of immature individuals represented among the fragmentary remains (65%) as compared with the adults (85%). The remains of a neonate in the inner Stepleton outwork ditch (ST78 2756) survived well because the individual had been placed in a crack in the chalk in the ditch side (Fig 3.92). In segment 8 of the main causewayed enclosure ditch, skull fragments from two young infants (HH75 2135 and 2137) were recovered from the phase III deposits (Fig 3.20). The mechanical destruction of the south long barrow, causing considerable damage to the bones buried there, may have been instrumental in the absence of immature remains in this locality.

The comparatively high death rate of infants and young juveniles (*c* 27% of the assemblage) accords with that expected in a 'normal population' (Brothwell 1972b). These are the years during which such young individuals are particularly prone to infectious diseases. High mortality among young and younger mature adults (*c* 15%) may be attributed to strenuous activity including work, warfare and childbearing. However, a relatively high proportion of adults, a minimum of *c* 6%, appear to have survived beyond *c* 45 years. This latter figure compares closely with that of 5.3% of adults >50 yr quoted by Brothwell for the English Neolithic (1972a, table 26).

The lack of completeness and questionable integrity of much of the Neolithic skeletal record has been highlighted by numerous writers (eg Saville 1990b; Kinnes 1992) and demands caution in attempting comparison between British Neolithic populations. Brothwell (1973, table 143) shows a 30% immature to 70% adult ratio for a Neolithic 'tomb' population and suggests that there may have been a bias against child burials in the chambered tombs (Brothwell 1971, 117). These figures are closely followed by Thorpe in his review of data from Wessex (1984, 48) where from an overall average of *c* 62% adult and 38% immature individuals, there is a clear distinction between long barrow populations (*c* 71% adult, 29% immature) and those from causewayed enclosures (*c* 37% adult, 63% immature). It should be noted, however, that the latter category includes data from Hambledon Hill which have subsequently been revised; if the figures used by Thorpe are the same as those quoted by Tilley (1994, 169) the 'Sixty per cent ...children' quoted is well above the 45% [*RK – 42%*] of the revised figures.

The figures from Hambledon Hill correspond closely with those from both the West Kennet long barrow (Piggott 1962) and Hazleton (Saville 1990b); from the former *c* 58% adult and 42% immature individuals were identified, from the latter *c* 52/64% and 36/43% respectively. This observation suggests that the previously held distinction between the long barrow and causewayed enclosure populations is not as consistent as has been implied, and that the data need to be reviewed with greater rigour and consideration of possible in-built biases with regard to survival, recovery and recognition of bone.

Sex (Table 7.6)

Of the minimum of 40, possibly 41 *[RK – 75]* adults identified, only 27 (*c* 66% *[RK – 36%]*) could be sexed, of which 10 (*c* 25% *[RK – 13%]*) were ascertained to be female (three subadults were also sexed as female) and 17 male (*c* 42% *[RK – 23%]*). Any significance which may be attached to this apparent disproportionately low number of females must be tempered by the fact that a high proportion of the estimated number of

Table 7.5 Estimated age at death of individuals from Neolithic contexts

All figures are from the re-scan except those marked *, which were missing
N/YI = neonate/young infant (0–2 yr), YI = young infant (6 mth–2 yr), I = infant (0–4 yr), OI = older infant (2–4 yr), OI/YJ = older infant/young juvenile (2–8 yr), YJ = young juvenile (*c* 5–8 yr), J = juvenile (*c* 5–12 yr), OJ = older juvenile (*c* 8–12 yr), J/S = juvenile/subadult (*c* 5–18 yr), YS = young subadult (*c* 13–15 yr), S = subadult (*c* 13–18 yr), OS = older subadult (*c* 15–18 yr), Ya = young adult (*c* 18–15 yr), Y/YMa = young/younger mature adult (*c* 18–30 yr), Ma = mature adult (*c* 25–45 yr), OMa = older mature adult (*c* 30–45 yr), OM/Oa = older mature/older adult (>30 yr), Oa = older adult (>45 yr), a = adult (>18 yr), S/a = subadult/adult (>13 yr)
A = articulated, S = skull, F = fragment(s)

	N/YI	*YI*	*I*	*OI*	*OI/YJ*	*YJ*	*J*	*OJ*	*J/S*	*YS*	*S*	*OS*	*OS/Ya*	*Ya*	*Y/YMa*	*Y/Ma*	*Ma*	*OMa*	*M/Oa*	*Oa*	*a*	*S/a*
Central area																						
Main causewayed enclosure	F2		?S1	F1	F2	A1 S3	A1	S2 F3		S1 F1	F1			F1	A1 F2		S1		F1	S1 F1	F3	
Inner E cross-dyke														S1			S1					
Outer E cross-dyke									F1							S1					F1	
Inner S cross-dyke										F1											*F1**	
Long barrow									F1					F1	F1	F1			F1			
Features						F1															F1	
Shroton spur outwork					*F1**												F1			F1		
Stepleton spur																						
Enclosure		F1		F1							F1						A1				F1	
Middle outwork						F1							F1									
Inner outwork	A1	F1	F1										A1 F1		S1	F1		A1				F1
Outer outwork												S1		A1								F1
Features					A1 F1									A1						A1		
Hanford spur																						
Inner outwork			F1															?F1	S1	F1		
Outer outwork				F1													S1 ?F1					
'Flint mines'																			F1			
Totals	A1 F2	F2	?S1 F2	F3	A1 F4	A1 S3 F2	A1	S2 F3	F2	S1 F2	F2	S1	A1 F2	A2 S1 F2	A1 S1 F2	S1 F2	A1 S3 F1/?2	A1 ?F1	S1 F3	A1 S1 F4	F7	F1

Table 7.6 Sexing of individuals from Neolithic contexts, re-scan figures

N/YI = neonate/young infant (0–2 yr), YI = young infant (6 mth–2 yr), I = infant (0–4 yr), OI = older infant (2–4 yr), OI/YJ = older infant/young juvenile (2–8 yr), YJ = young juvenile (*c* 5–8 yr), J = juvenile (*c* 5–12 yr), OJ = older juvenile (*c* 8–12 yr), J/S = juvenile/subadult (*c* 5–18 yr), YS = young subadult (*c* 13–15 yr), S = subadult (*c* 13–18 yr), OS = older subadult (*c* 15–18 yr), Ya = young adult (*c* 18–15 yr), Y/YMa = young/younger mature adult (*c* 18–30 yr), Ma = mature adult (*c* 25–45 yr), OMa = older mature adult (*c* 30–45 yr), OM/Oa = older mature/older adult (>30 yr), Oa = older adult (>45 yr), a = adult (>18 yr), S/a = subadult/adult (>13 yr)
?? = 'possible', ? = 'probable'
Confident identifications are included in 'total' column.

	Female			*Male*		
	??	*?*	*Totals*	*??*	*?*	*Totals*
Central area						
Main causewayed enclosure	1	1	3 (YS, S, Ma)	3		4 (Ya, Y/YMa, Y/Ma, Oa)
Outer east cross-dyke			2 (Y/YMa, Ma)	1		1 (Ya)
Long barrow			1 (Y/YMa)	1		2 (Ya, Y/Ma)
Shroton spur outwork			1 (Oa)			
Stepleton spur						
Stepleton enclosure			1 (Ma)			1 (a)
Inner outwork			2 (OS/Ya, Y/YMa)	2		4 (OS/Ya, Y/Ma, OMa, Oa)
Outer outwork	1		1 (OS)			1 (Ya)
Features				1		2 (Ya, Oa)
Hanford spur						
Inner outwork	1		1 (Oa)	2		2 (O/Ma, OMa)
Outer outwork			1 (Ma)			
Totals	3	1	13	10		17

adults was not sexed (33%), that is 64% of the estimated minimum total population. These unsexed individuals may include a greater proportion of females than males. The ease with which skeletal remains may be sexed is largely dependent on the level of skeletal recovery. That 75% of the articulated skeletal remains were male and only 12% female may indicate that the apparent bias within the sex ratio reflects more the type of deposit recovered than the general numbers of males and females within the population. Although it is possible that the apparent sexual imbalance in the Hambledon Hill population represents a true cultural bias, the writer would stress extreme caution against over-interpretation based on such incomplete data.

The median age range for the females was within the *c* 18–30 year range and that for the males in the *c* 18–45 year range, but, in general, there was little observable significant difference between the sexes. Though caution should be applied in view of the small numbers involved, the tendency for a preponderance of males in the slightly older adult age range has been noted elsewhere (Brothwell 1972b, table 25).

Brothwell has commented (1973, 284) that despite the incomplete nature of most Neolithic skeletons, rendering accurate sexing difficult, there is a marked preponderance of male Neolithic burials in comparison with those of females. This, he suggested, 'reflects the superimposition of a culturally determined sex bias on the true ratio'. It should be noted that Brothwell was referring to tomb populations, where it was apparently possible to attribute sex to a much greater proportion of the adults identified than in the Hambledon Hill assemblage. Of the 196 adults in Brothwell's table 143 (1973) only 18% were unsexed as compared with the much greater 44% from Hambledon Hill. Although in general terms there does appear to be a preponderance of males over females from the published tomb assemblages, this is not universally the case in individual barrows. Greater numbers of females than males were identified from both West Kennet (Piggott 1962) and Ascott-under-Wychwood (Chesterman 1977). Saville, for example (1990b, 261), rejects Brothwell's theory on the basis of the inherent difficulties of sexing disarticulated and fragmentary skeletal material (24–33% of the adults identified at Hazleton were unsexed) and the 'inclusion of suspect data from disarticulated samples'. The latter factor, alongside a temptation to over-interpret a limited database, will continue to bias our understanding of the true state of the 'cemetery' population in the British Neolithic.

Comment on population 'dynamics' is precluded partly by the nature of the deposits and partly by the time scale over which the deposition of human remains took place, which may have been up to 400 years. Viewed as a single assemblage, the population included individuals across a wide age range from neonate to older adult, in proportions not dissimilar to the 'normal', rural 'domestic' cemetery populations commonly seen in archaeological reports. Both sexes are represented across the adult age ranges. Other than the concentrations within the main causewayed enclosure and the inner Stepleton outwork discussed above, there is no apparent significance in the spatial distribution of individuals of either sex or within different age groups. Nor does there appear to be any age- or sex-based significance within the broad 'early' or 'late' groupings discussed above, with the exception of the main causewayed enclosure. Here, immature individuals were predominant in the early phases, I–III.

Physical anthropology

Stature estimation

Incomplete skeletal recovery precluded stature estimation in most cases. The long bones of only four individuals, all males, survived sufficiently intact to enable stature estimations to be made. The range was between 1.63 and 1.72 m (5' 4" and 5' 7¾"), with an average of 1.68 m. These figures compare closely with those given by Brothwell for Neolithic males (1973, table 149), with an identical mean of 1.68 m (5' 6").

Cranial indices

The cranial index was calculated from six complete skulls, two female, three male and one unsexed. Five were in the dolichocranial (long-headed) range, one (female) in the mesocranial, with indices between 66.68 and 76.5 and a mean of 71.2, SD 4.2. The male skulls were between 66.68 and 69.12, with a mean of 67.54 (SD 1.36); the two female skulls were 73.2 and 76.5. These figures fall within the peak-range of *c* 71–74 (dolichocranial) noted by Brothwell for British Neolithic skulls (1973, fig 65).

Asymmetry of long bone lengths

There were only four individuals whose upper and lower limb bones were complete enough to measure. There was no appreciable difference between left and right sides. The left femora from ST81 1875 (from the outer Stepleton outwork) and ST81 3181 (from pit 4B F712 outside the Stepleton enclosure) were very slightly longer than the right side (up to 5 mm) and the right femur of ST78 2755a (from the inner Stepleton outwork) was 4 mm longer than the left. The right humerus of ST81 3181 was 7 mm longer than the left and the deltoid tubercle of the clavicle was more prominent on the right side. The right humerus of ST81 1875 was 6 mm longer than the left. The significance of asymmetry in the length of the long bones of the upper limb has been considered by Steele and Mays (1995). They concluded that the asymmetry may be 'attributed to the effects of mechanical loading consequent to handedness bias'.

Platymeric and platycnemic indices

The degree of anterior-posterior flattening of the proximal femur (platymeric index) was calculated from five left and two right femora, from five adult males (re-scan). A range of 74.75 to 94.0 was recorded, with a mean of 81.4 and a SD of 6.1. Only the right femur from ST79 2726 (from the inner Stepleton outwork) was outside the platymeric range, the left femur from the same individual giving an 11.05 lower reading.

The platycnemic index (meso-lateral flattening of the tibia) was calculated from three male tibiae, giving a range of 63.71–66.16, a mean of 64.6 and a SD of 1.3 mm. Squatting facets were observed in all three tibiae, which may indicate a link between the condition and platycnemia as has been suggested elsewhere (Brothwell 1972a; Molleson 1993).

Dental attrition

There were a small number of cases where heavy wear to the anterior teeth was found in association with light wear on the molars, for example ST81 3188 (a mature adult female from the Stepleton enclosure), which RK believed could be due to use of the front teeth for some cultural activity similar to that of Eskimo women chewing hides, or to malocclusion of the molars. However, only 13 out of 32 teeth were recovered from 3188 and the right side of the maxilla was missing, hence it is possible that painful dental lesions in the absent dentition had affected the way in which this individual chewed her food. Malocclusion of the dentition in HH77 610 (an older adult from the phase VI slot in the main enclosure) is suggested by the labial angle of the left mandibular molars resulting in abnormal wear in the buccal surface of the teeth. A marked overbite was demonstrated in ST78 2755 by the uneven polish in the maxillary and mandibular incisors.

Pathology and morphological variations

The observed pathology among the Neolithic remains was undoubtedly affected by the pattern of bone survival, in itself a product of taphonomic and cultural processes (see above). The most frequently recovered skeletal elements were cranial and fragments of long bone shaft. Comparatively few vertebrae, articular surfaces, hand or foot bones were found; consequently there was particularly limited evidence of joint diseases.

Pathological lesions and/or morphological variations were noted in bone from 74 finds, including all the articulated skeletal remains (13 individuals) and all 15 skulls. The remains represent those of *c* 51 individuals. A summary of pathological lesions and morphological variations is presented in Table 7.1.

Dental disease

All or parts of a minimum of 29 erupted permanent dentitions were recorded, including a total of 439 erupted permanent teeth and 538 tooth positions (Table 7.7).

Ante mortem tooth loss was evident in five dentitions, two female, two male and one unsexed. A total of 9/538 teeth had been lost *ante mortem* (1.7%); 4/147 in the female dentitions (2.7%), 2/288 in the male dentitions (0.7%). Four of the lost teeth were molars, with three second incisors, one canine and one premolar.

Table 7.7 Numbers of mandibles and maxillae, erupted permanent teeth and socket positions

	mandibles		*maxillae*		*mandibular teeth*	*maxillary teeth*	*mandibular sockets*	*maxillary sockets*
	L	*R*	*L*	*R*				
female	4	4	7	6	35	65	54	93
male	13	12	10	7	140	91	179	109
unsexed	7	7	3	3	74	34	86	17
totals	24	23	20	16	249	190	319	219

Any comment on the apparent sex-based variation in prevalence would be inappropriate in view of the small number of dentitions involved. The general rate is very low, considerably less than the *c* 15% indicated by Brothwell (1972a, fig 56) for this period, and the 10.1% derived from figures recently compiled by Schulting (1998).

Tooth loss tends to increase with age and may be related to one or more factors, eg excess wear, diet and dental hygiene. Dental calculus (calcified plaque) harbours the bacteria which predisposes to periodontal disease (a gum infection) and the development of dental caries. Slight to moderate levels of calculus were noted in all permanent dentitions, including those of immature individuals, and some deciduous dentitions were also slightly affected. No severe cases were observed.

Slight periodontal disease was noted in nine permanent dentitions, always in association with calculus deposits. There was a general increase in severity with the age of the individual. Seven individuals also exhibited either dental caries, abscesses or *ante mortem* tooth loss, though there was no consistent link between the conditions, the latter also occurring in the absence of periodontal disease.

Carious lesions were noted in five permanent dentitions, with an overall rate of 7/439 (1.6%); 4/231 (1.7%) in the male dentitions, 1/100 (1%) in the female. No carious lesions were noted in the deciduous dentitions. Most of the affected teeth were molars (one canine), the majority of lesions being cervical in origin. With one exception – the canine, in which the crown was totally destroyed – all the lesions were slight. The overall rate is lower than the 5% given by Brothwell for Neolithic populations (1972a, figure 55) and the 2.5% calculated by Schulting in his review of 1748 teeth from early Neolithic sites in Britain (1998).

Infection from carious lesions may track down into the tooth sockets, resulting in the development of dental abscesses. Seven permanent dentitions (five male, two female) had abscesses in 9/538 (1.7%) of sockets; females 4/147 (2.7%) and males 5/288 (1.7%). The anterior teeth were chiefly affected including two incisors, two premolars and one canine. Only one of these dentitions had carious lesions, though this and two others had suffered *ante mortem* tooth loss which may have been affected by caries attack. In some cases, the associated tooth had been lost *post mortem* and potentially associated conditions within the tooth thereby lost. The high rate of lesions in the anterior teeth may have been related to excess occlusal wear or damage to the crowns, leading to exposure of the pulp cavity with subsequent infection. The low rates observed are consistent with other British Neolithic groups (Brothwell 1972a, 151), being slightly lower than the figure of 4.1% given by Schulting (1998).

Dental hypoplasia is a developmental defect in the tooth enamel formed in response to growth arrest in the immature individual. The predominant causes are believed to include periods of illness or nutritional stress (Hillson 1979). Slight enamel hypoplasia was noted in permanent dentitions recovered from one articulated skeleton, one skull and four fragmentary finds.

A harmless condition involving the excessive formation of secondary cementation, slight to mild hypercementosis was noted in two dentitions. The cause of the condition is not clear (Hillson 1990, 164), though possible factors may include age, periapical inflammation, mechanical stimulation or trauma.

The main factor affecting dental disease is diet (Hillson 1990, 283) and 'the interaction with the micro-organisms that live in the mouth', in which plaque deposits perform a major role. Different dietary intakes increase (carbohydrate, sugars) or decrease (proteins) the activity or presence of acid-producing bacteria. Hillson (1990) gives the presence of dental plaque (indicated by calculus in archaeological material) and carbohydrates in the diet as prerequisites for caries formation. The low rates of dental disease in the Hambledon Hill assemblage suggests a diet high in meat-based proteins (see also Richards, 7.2), inclusive of foods which would assist in the natural mechanical cleaning of the teeth, and relatively low in processed carbohydrates. The possible natural predisposition of the population to be more resistant to caries attack should not be overlooked (Hillson 1990, 287).

Deficiency disease

Cribra orbitalia, manifest as pitting in the roof of one or both orbits, is believed to be connected with childhood iron deficiency anaemia, although Molleson (1993) argues that vitamin C deficiency and intestinal parasites may also have played a contributory role. The condition was observed in 14/52 (27%) of orbital vaults, most lesions being porotic or cribotic (Robledo *et al* 1995). The rate is similar to that of 22.6% quoted for the British Neolithic by Brothwell (1973, table 156).

The vast majority of individuals affected were immature (infants and juveniles) where the rate was 50% (12/24), lesions being observed in only one adult male (1/13; 8%) and one unsexed adult. Higher rates among immature individuals may be expected given that they require greater amounts of iron as a consequence of growth requirements (Robledo *et al* 1995).

Trauma

Evidence for fractures to bone was noted in only one instance, in the right eleventh rib of ST79 2726 from the base of the inner Stepleton outwork (1/147, 0.06%), which had a well-healed vertical fracture at the dorsal angle. Such fractures most commonly result from a fall against a hard object (Adams 1987).

A smooth, concave depression, *c* 8.9 mm diameter and 2 mm deep was observed in the left lateral side of the frontal bone in HH76 3009 from the phase VI slot in the main enclosure (subadult/adult), 22 mm from the coronal suture. The depression may have resulted from a compression fracture in the skull, caused by a blunt instrument. An oval depression – 27.8 mm long, 7.1 mm wide and *c* 1 mm deep – was also observed in the left frontal of HH77 88, displaced from the long barrow (adult male), medial and parallel to the temporal line. This may also represent the well-healed remnants of a skull fracture.

Infections

Infection of the periosteal membrane covering bone may lead to the formation of periosteal new bone. Infection may be introduced directly to the bone as a result of trauma, develop in response to some adjacent soft tissue infection, or spread via the blood stream from foci elsewhere in the body (Roberts and Manchester 1997, 127–30). Lesions were noted in bone from one articulated skeleton and from seven fragmentary finds, and were most frequently seen in the femur and fibula shafts (five cases) with no associated lesions.

Lesions in the ventral surface of a rib shaft from HH76 3030 from the base of the main enclosure (older juvenile) may have been related to some form of pulmonary infection (Wakely *et al* 1991). The multiple involvement of other bones from this individual, including the ilium and femur, does not suggest the product of a secondary infective process (Roberts and Manchester 1997, 127) but what specific form of infection may have caused the lesions is unclear.

The small area of periosteal new bone bucco-distal to the third molar socket in HH75 1848 from the main enclosure (??male, 30–45 yr) may have been associated with some form of dental or soft tissue infection.

Extensive areas of endocranial new bone were noted in the skull bones of two immature individuals, HH75 2023 (*c* 3 yr) and HH74 HB 1a (5–6 yr), both from the main enclosure. The cerebral surfaces of the sphenoid greater wings were affected in both cases, with some extension into the squamous part of the temporal bones, and along the transverse sinus groove of the occipital in HH74 HB 1a. The area around the foramen ovale of the sphenoids was particularly affected. The lesions indicate an infection within the meningeal membrane (dura mater), the extensive nature of which is likely to have been at least a contributory factor in the death of these individuals.

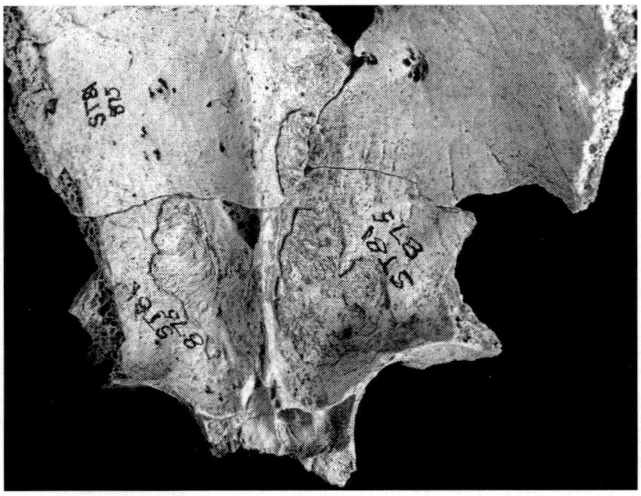

Fig 7.17 ST81 875 (adult ?male); endocranial surface of frontal vault showing plaque-like new bone. Photo Elaine Wakefield (Wessex Archaeology)

Plaque-like new bone was also observed in the endocranial surface of the frontal bone from ST81 875 (Fig 7.17) on either side of the frontal crest.

Tumours

Two large ivory osteomata, one in the right side of the frontal adjacent to the suture forming a smooth 'tumulus' (22.5 × 17.0 mm, 5.6 mm high) and the other in the left occipital adjacent to the bregma forming a 'button' (9.9 mm diameter, *c* 3 mm high), were recorded in the skull of HN82 236 from the inner Hanford outwork (??male over 25 yr). These benign tumours are unlikely to have had anything other than a 'cosmetic' effect on the individual (Roberts and Manchester 1997, 188). A similar lesion was noted in a male skull from Wayland's Smithy (Brothwell 1973, 296).

A smooth bony 'swelling' (*c* 39.43 mm long, 2.24 mm high) in the left femur distal shaft from ST80 1875 from the outer Stepleton outwork (male, 18–25 yr) has the morphological and radiographic characteristic of an osteoid osteoma (Roberts and Manchester 1997, 189). Although benign, they are reported to produce considerable persistent pain.

Joint disease

Osteoarthritis is manifest by eburnation of the joint surface and/or pitting in association with osteophytes on joint surface margins (Rogers *et al* 1987; Rogers and Waldron 1994). Lesions were observed in the remains of seven individuals, most over 30 yr and including a minimum of three males and one female.

With the exceptions of ST79 2025 (possible male, over 45 yr) and ST79 2726 (male *c* 30–45 yr), lesions were seen in only one joint.

Those affected included the vertebral articular process facets (2/251, *c* 0.6%), temporo-mandibular joint (1/26, 4.0%), a metatarsal-phalangeal joint (1/39, 2.6%), an elbow joint (radial articulation; 1/15, 6.6%), and the costo-vertebral joints (14/65, 21.5%), the latter including 12 affected facets from ST9 2726.

Only 97 adult vertebrae were recovered from the assemblage, among the remains from 10 individuals including five males and two females. Most (five) were from articulated remains, three represented cervical vertebrae found with skulls, only two complete vertebrae being recovered among the fragmentary finds.

Degenerative disc disease is characterised by pitting in the vertebral body surfaces often accompanied by osteophyte formation on the surface margins; they are most commonly found in the mid- and lower cervical, upper thoracic and lower lumbar regions of the spine (Rogers and Waldron 1994), and the prevalence of the disease increases with age. Lesions were noted in one spine, male over 25 yr, with lesions in cervical vertebrae (1/28 cervical).

Schmorl's nodes develop in response to a rupture in the intervertebral disc allowing the nucleus pulposus to protrude into the vertebral body. They most frequently occur in the vertebrae subject to greatest mechanical stress at points in the normal curvature of the spine (Manchester 1983). Lesions were noted in two male spines, both articulated skeletons from the inner Stepleton outwork. The younger male (15–25 yr) was most severely affected with lesions in 10 vertebrae, the 30–45 yr male having lesions in only four (all vertebra recovered from both). No vertebrae above T5 were affected, with lesions in 8/44 thoracic and 6/22 lumbar.

The distribution of other destructive lesions (including pitting) and new bone formation (osteophytes) associated with joints is shown in summary in Table 7.1. Osteophytes were seen in 1–12 joint surfaces in bones from *c* eight individuals (five articulated, three fragmentary) and pitting in up to three joint surfaces in three individuals (all articulated). Such lesions are often difficult to classify, but some may represent the early stages of osteoarthritis.

Miscellaneous conditions

Two crania showed the developmental defect of premature suture fusion, which can result in remodelling of the normal skull shape (Ortner and Putschar 1985). They were from articulated skeletons buried in adjacent segments of the main enclosure near the beginning and end of the Neolithic sequence, one (HH76 1948) on the base of segment 18, dated to *3660–3540 cal BC* (mean of OxA-7768 and -7769), the other (HH76 3046) in the upper fills of segment 17, dated to *3380–3320 cal BC* (mean of OxA-7039 and -7040). These skulls were examined by Dr M Briggs and Dr M Poole at the request of RK. With respect to the sagittal and partial fusion of the lambdoid sutures in HH76 1948 (juvenile), they observed that there was 'some asymmetry of the forehead and supra-orbital region, and the inside of the skull has excessive digital markings, and erosion of the posterior clinoids suggestive of raised intracranial pressure'. They concluded that such an individual may have been 'mentally retarded, suffered from epilepsy, possibly from visual loss as well', and that there would have been 'some visible deformity' of the frontal region and possibly the face. Although it was felt that the condition in itself would not have led to the death of the individual, the attendant dangers of possible epilepsy may have been a contributory factor. Premature fusion of the sagittal suture in HH76 3046 (young juvenile, *c* 5–8 yr) was believed unlikely to have led to any pathological problems secondary to the cosmetic one of the probable development of a scaphocranial skull shape. The occurrence of this relatively rare skeletal anomaly in two individuals whose remains were close to each other in space though not in time suggests that there was some genetic link between them.

Exostoses are bony growths which may develop at tendon and ligament insertions on the bone. Causative factors include advancing age, traumatic stress, or various diseases (Rogers and Waldron 1994, 24–25). It is not always possible to be conclusive with respect to the aetiology of particular lesions.

Very little conclusion with respect to lifestyle may be drawn from the pathological conditions observed. The recorded lesions can only represent a very small proportion of what must have existed, the nature of the assemblage severely curtailing the amount of retrievable data. The condition of the dentitions provides the most information, with indications of low rates of disease, even for the Neolithic, suggestive of a high meat-protein diet. The high rate of *cribra orbitalia* in the infants and juveniles may reflect other dietary inadequacies hampering the absorption of proteins and iron within the diet, or reflect the greater susceptibility of these young individuals to infection and parasitic disease (Robledo *et al* 1995).

Morphological variations

These are 'normal' variations in the skeletal morphology and may, with other predisposing factors, indicate genetic relationships within a 'population' (Berry and Berry 1967). Work by Finnegan (1978) has shown there may be some slight bias to one side in bilateral traits and a slight sex-based bias in the incidence of some variations, but neither appeared of great significance. Overall figures of incidence are not available for most of the variations. Twenty-two morphological variations were noted in the skeletal material from Hambledon Hill, a summary of which is presented in Table 7.1.

Shovel-shaped incisors were observed in five dentitions (*c* 17%), all except one from the Stepleton enclosure, with two from neighbouring deposits in the inner outwork. Two maxillary second incisors were 'pegged', both from individuals in the same find (HH77 682), whose skulls were built into a flint cairn on the base of the main causewayed enclosure ditch. The maxilla of HH76 1870 (9–15 yr) was examined by Professor A E W Miles at the request of RK. He noted the development of a molariform supernumerary tooth in the midline of the maxilla resulting in a slight distortion in the left first incisor, which had failed to erupt properly, and the displacement of the left second incisor. The midline of the maxillary incisor region is the most common place for supernumerary teeth to develop (Miles, pers comm to RK). Other dental variations include three 5-cusped mandibular third molars; two 4-cusped mandibular first molars, both from features on the Stepleton spur; two occurrences of enamel pearls, both from skulls deposited in phase IV within the main causewayed enclosure; and retention of deciduous mandibular molars with retarded or non-eruption of the premolars, eg ST80 1875 (male 18–25 yr) where a radiograph demonstrated the absence of the second premolar. Of the 29 appropriate areas of dentition available for study none showed absence of the third molars, a variation noted in 11% of British Neolithic dentitions by Brothwell (1973, 293).

Of the 27 crania in which the appropriate parts survived for examination, wormian bones were found in three of 27 recorded lambdoid sutures, that is 11% compared with the much higher 48% given by Brothwell for the British Neolithic (1973, table 152) and the 52% recorded from Hazleton by Rogers (1990, 198). A metopic suture was observed in three of the 35 (8.6%) frontal bones analysed, a similar figure to that of 7.5% quoted by Brothwell for British Neolithic communities (1973, abb 70) but higher than that of 5.5% noted by Rogers at Hazleton (1990, 198). Occipital bunning was noted in two of 27 (7.4%) occipital bones.

Dual facets in the superior articular surfaces were noted in two of seven atlas vertebrae. Small squatting facets were noted in the tibiae of seven of the nine individuals (mostly males) from which the distal tibia was recovered. Two of the eight individuals from which the patellae were recovered showed the presence of a vastus notch, both individuals being recovered from the inner Stepleton outwork.

The significance which may be attached to many of these variations is limited, and in some cases their status as 'natural' variations is open to question. There are arguments to suggest wormian bones develop in response to parturition trauma and 'squatting' facets' are often attributed as developmental defects in response to the adoption of prolonged periods spent in a squatting posture. While the suggestion of any 'genetic' links between individuals on the basis of any of these variations would be seriously open to question, it is of interest to note the frequency with which some occur within limited locations, occasionally in immediately adjacent skeletal material, while being absent from other parts of the assemblage.

The nature of the deposits

Articulated skeletal remains

These have not been classified as 'burials' since it is clear that not all the articulated skeletal remains could be described as such; formal 'burial' being characterised as deliberate deposition of the body (particularly within a grave) with subsequent coverage by earth or a stone cairn. Five of the eleven Neolithic deposits (ie excluding the Bronze Age burial ST82 114 and the Iron Age foot HH86 97) may have been the *in situ* remains of formal burials. Three individuals, ST79 2025 (??male, over 45 yr), ST78 964 (*c* 5 yr) and ST81 3181 (male, 18–25 yr), were buried in separate Neolithic pits on the Stepleton spur. At least one of these, ST81 3181, was associated with a rich deposit of charcoal, other burnt material, and artefacts. One immature individual (HH76 1948) was buried at the base of the main causewayed enclosure ditch under a flint cairn and a second (HH76 3046) was buried in a grave cut into the main enclosure, probably also under a flint cairn; both had grave goods (Fig 3.32). There also appeared to be a flattish spread of nodules over HH76 2625, the lower axial skeleton and femora discussed above, which may have been a deliberate covering (Fig 3.15).

Cadavers were deposited on the bases of ditches, including within recesses in the chalk, and higher up in the fills in the inner Stepleton inner outwork (ST79 2726; Figs 3.92, 3.100–4) and the outer outwork (ST 80 1875; Figs 3.105–6). Whether these bodies were covered in some way immediately after deposition is unknown, rendering their interpretation open to question. The complete, articulated skeleton HH78 2755 (male, 17–20 yr) may have been 'buried' in that he was covered with chalk rubble, apparently prior to full skeletalisation, but he does not seem to have been formally buried. The position (prone; Figs 3.102–3) and location (in chalk rubble at first interpreted as derived from a collapsed bank) of the skeleton, together with the recovery of a flint arrowhead from the thoracic region, originally led to the belief that the individual had been shot in the back while fleeing along the ditch during an attack on the enclosure and thereafter had laid undisturbed. There was no osteological evidence to support such a cause of death, though it is not implausible that an arrow may have passed between the ribs without damaging the bone. However, the presence of clear *post mortem* manipulation of the body (see *Cut-marks* and Table 7.4) and limited canid and rodent gnawing, together with the general evidence for excarnation practices (see above), leads one to speculate on a slightly different series of events. The position in which the body lay, slightly to the outside of centre towards the butt end of a ditch segment, over disarticulated bone fragments already deposited in the base of the ditch, may have been achieved by rolling the body into the ditch from the outside edge. While the individual may have been the victim of an arrow in the back, it is also possible that the arrowhead was contained within a 'pocket' attached to a belt or around the neck, and was unrelated to his cause of death.

An arrowhead in a similar position was recovered from HH80 1875 (male, 18–25 yr); this complete skeleton was laid flexed within a recess on the base of the outer Stepleton outwork, in one side of the butt end of a ditch segment. As with ST78 2755, there was no osteological evidence to support the inference that the individual had been shot, and there was possible evidence of *post mortem* manipulation of some of the bone (Table 7.4). Is it possible that these two individuals are illustrative of the earliest stages of the excarnation process?

A similarly positioned flint arrowhead was recovered from a broadly contemporary crouched inhumation burial in Wor Barrow (Pitt Rivers 1898, 63). Here again, the assumption, in the absence of associated osteological evidence, was that the individual (an adult male) had been shot. There are numerous other comparably located arrowheads without osteological evidence to support their interpretation as causes of death (Mercer 1999, 149). Two positive identifications have, however, been made: at Ascott-under-Wychwood, Oxfordshire, where a leaf arrowhead was found embedded in a lumbar vertebra, and at Pen-y-Wyrlod, Brecknock, where an arrowhead tip was lodged in a sternal rib fragment (Wysocki and Whittle 2000, 599–600).

The other articulated remains had been disturbed, leaving the precise nature of their deposition open to debate, but all were within ditch fills with no evidence of grave cuts, which suggests that they were of a similar nature to the cadavers placed on the ditch bases. At least one of these bodies (HH76 2625; male, 18–30 yr), from the main causewayed enclosure, had been subject to substantial gnawing by scavengers (Figs 7.3–4). Only the articulated lower axial skeleton and the femora survived (Figs 3.16–17), probably having been dragged from elsewhere or the rest of the body having been dragged away from this position (see '*Gnawing*'). In addition, the femora and part of the innominate had been substantially stripped of soft tissues by human action (see '*Cut-marks*' and Table 7.4). The implication is that the partly decomposed body was either removed from a shallow grave or an aboveground position, probably by animal action, preceded and/or followed by a deliberate process of defleshing and cleaning of bones. A similar scenario may be suggested for ST81 3188 from the Stepleton enclosure, where only the upper half of the articulated skeleton remained *in situ*, though in this instance no cut-marks were noted on the bone (see comment in '*Cut-marks*'). It appears that these latter remains are those of cadavers which had reached a later stage in the excarnation process.

A large proportion (six) of the articulated skeletal remains were those of adult males, mostly 18–25 yr, with one female and four immature individuals. Consequently, 35% of the males identified were from articulated remains, compared with only *c* 8% of the females and 12.5% of the immature individuals. What is unclear is whether this apparent imbalance is due to cultural, demographic or taphonomic factors (see '*Condition of the bone and ancient modifications*'). Also of note is the fact that eight (73%) of the finds in this category were from the Stepleton spur, with three from the main causewayed enclosure. The latter observation may reflect spatial variations in the treatment of cadavers.

Skulls

Of the 15 finds within this category, 12 (80%) were skulls minus the mandibles, though a cervical vertebra was recovered with one. The three skulls with mandibles all included between one and three cervical vertebrae, with none below the C4.

Eight of the skulls were placed directly on ditch floors, in the main causewayed enclosure (three), the east cross-dykes (two), the Stepleton outworks (two), and the Hanford outworks (one). Two from the main causewayed enclosure ditch, both juveniles, were placed on and in the same flint cairn. Three other skulls without mandibles were recovered from close to the ditch bases in the main causewayed enclosure ditch and the east cross-dykes. Another skull was from tertiary deposits in the Hanford ditches, with one from a disturbed context in the main causewayed enclosure ditch. In contrast to the articulated remains, the skulls were more widely distributed, with the majority (eight, *c* 67%) being recovered from the main causewayed enclosure ditch.

The largest proportion (seven) of the skulls were those of females (*c* 54% of identified females), with three male (*c* 18%) and five immature (*c* 16%). As was observed with regard to the articulated remains, it is unclear whether the apparent imbalance between the sexes is due to cultural, demographic or taphonomic factors (see '*Condition of the bone and ancient modifications*').

There was no osteological evidence for decapitation, although the inclusion of skulls with the mandible and some upper cervical vertebrae implies this may have occurred in the three cases observed. Vertebrae between the second cervical to the first thoracic have been noted as the point of severance in decapitation, with the mid-cervical (C3–4) forming the most common point (Harman *et al* 1981; Manchester 1983, 63; McKinley 1993). Had decapitation occurred it would be a matter for speculation whether it was *peri-* or *post-mortem*. The absence of the mandible in the majority of cases indicates the deposition of already disarticulated, probably dry bone.

Cut-marks were noted in three of the skulls without mandibles (two immature, one adult male). The cuts were of the same nature as those noted in the post-cranial skeletal elements and some could be associated with specific muscle attachments (Table 7.4). The location and orientation of the cuts are not characteristic of those seen in scalping (During and Nilsson 1991; Mays and Steele 1996), being more consistent with defleshing/cleaning as noted elsewhere.

Disarticulated bone fragments

Approximately 36% of finds in this category were fragments of skull alone, *c* 25% lower limb, *c* 5% fragments of upper limb bone only, and *c* 3% fragments of axial skeleton only. A mixture of skeletal areas was recovered from *c* 24% of the finds. Bone from the remaining finds was not identified to skeletal element (see Table 7.1). It should be noted that, although all the bone from the south long barrow falls into this category, it may largely do so as a result of the bulldozing of the mound in the 1960s. The original condition of the bone prior to this modern disturbance is not known, though there were a relatively substantial number of joins, pairing or matches between individual finds (Table 7.1) suggesting there had at least been *increased* fragmentation in the 1960s.

The parietal vault is the most frequently identified skull fragment (25 finds, 26 including the south long barrow). Fragments of occipital (15 finds) and frontal vault (16 finds, 18 including the long barrow), and mandible (16 finds, 18 including the long barrow) occur less frequently. Fragments of temporal vault (nine finds) are relatively rare.

Where lower limb bone was identified, the most commonly occurring fragment was the femur shaft (*c* 49%, 50% including the long barrow). This was the most frequently recovered fragment of adult bone among the disarticulated material (24 finds, 39 including the long barrow). There was no significant difference between recovery of left (13 finds, 17 including the long barrow) and right (15 finds, 20 including the long barrow) femora (all ages). Fragments of tibia (11 finds, 18 including the long barrow) and fibula shaft (19 finds, 24 including the long barrow) were commonly recovered, but foot bones were very rare. Only *c* 2% of finds in this category contained fragments of hand or foot bones, and it is probably significant that the majority were from the long barrow (see above, '*Condition of the bone and ancient modifications*', for taphonomic and cultural effects).

In several instances where bones from more than one skeletal area were recovered together, although clearly disarticulated, a large proportion of a single skeleton was recovered and certainly in one instance (ST79 2497) it appeared as though the skull at least had been largely intact at the time of deposition. The remains were found 'scattered' within a compact, *c* 1 m × 1 m area of chalk rubble fill in the middle Stepleton outwork (Fig 3.93). A similar deposit (HH76 3030) was found on the base of segment 6.2 of the main causewayed enclosure, where it was built into a flint cairn (Fig 3.18). In a third case, most of a skull, with cut-marks to the vault (HH75 2023), was found scattered across a restricted area of segment 8 of the main causewayed enclosure (Fig 3.20). All these cases involved the remains of immature individuals.

There is also evidence for movement of bone fragments derived from one skeleton both between phases and across parts of the site (see Table 7.1 for 'associations'); eg HH74 HB 5 and 6, a mandible and skull probably from the same subadult, were recovered from adjacent segments of the main causewayed enclosure ditch. What is unclear is whether this type of movement simply represents incidental redeposition of fragments during reworking of the ditch fills, redeposition of body parts due to animal activity (scavenging) or during manipulation as part of the excarnation process, or deliberate 'curation' of already 'dry' bone fragments. Nor can it be stated with any certainty over what distance across the hilltop such movement occurred – the main causewayed enclosure and that on the Stepleton spur were, for a large part of their existence, contemporary, and it is conceivable that body parts or dry bone fragments may have been exchanged between the two areas.

The condition of much of the bone in this category (see '*Condition of the bone and ancient modifications*') suggests that it represents material from the later stages of the excarnation process. Cut-marks were less frequently observed on material in this category than that in the other two (see cautionary note above), but there was a conspicuous absence of small bones, elements of the axial skeleton, and articular surfaces. An alternative suggestion may be that this bone represents the remains of more easily transportable material brought to the site from elsewhere.

7.1.4 Discussion – Neolithic

The vast majority of known Neolithic human remains in Britain have been recovered from 'tombs' (Brothwell 1973; Thorpe 1984, 48). Disarticulated human bone fragments and burials (predominantly of infants) have been found in ditches at other Neolithic enclosures, such as (in approximate chronological order) Windmill Hill, Wiltshire (Smith 1965, 136–40; Whittle *et al* 1999, 344–6, 361–2), Maiden Castle, Dorset (Sharples and Henderson 1991), Flagstones, Dorset (Healy 1997a, 37), Durrington Walls and Woodhenge, both in Wiltshire (Wainwright with Longworth 1971, 191), and Mount Pleasant, Dorset (Wainwright 1979a, 247–9), but the numbers of individuals identified from these locations are not on the scale seen at Hambledon Hill.

Formal 'burial', that is deliberate deposition of the body with subsequent coverage by earth or a stone cairn, of individual cadavers in the Neolithic at Hambledon Hill was rare, accounting for a maximum of *c* 7% of individuals. The only features which may be seen as nominal 'grave cuts' are the three pits on the Stepleton spur and one grave cut though the fill of the main causewayed enclosure ditch. Other depositions of articulated cadavers did not appear to involve a grave. Some bodies were apparently placed in position in the ditches where they may, or may not, have been covered in some way; certainly some of those on the ditch bases were covered with flint cairns. The cairns would, and obviously did, serve to keep off the scavengers which are known to have frequented the site, and this may have been their main purpose. Other, partially articulated skeletons, clearly arrived in their final position by way of non-human agencies.

The ditch burials from Windmill Hill were both of infants (Smith 1965, 136), although an adult male was buried under the outer bank (Whittle *et al* 1999, 79–82), and the only complete skeleton from the causewayed enclosure ditch at Maiden Castle was an infant (Sharples and Henderson 1991), as were both the ditch burials from Flagstones – excluding the one cremation burial – (Healy 1997a), and all the articulated skeletal remains ('burials') from the Mount Pleasant ditches (Wainwright 1979a). The possible cultural significance of this observation may be considered in the light of Brothwell's suggestion that there may have been a bias against child burials in the chambered tombs (1971, 117), a theory supported by the relatively low percentage of immature individuals identified from Neolithic tomb 'populations' (see *'Age'* above). That the distinction, if it existed, was not a simple one or universally adhered to is demonstrated by the fact that *c* 34% of the Hazleton tomb population was less than five years old (Rogers 1990, 183), as was *c* 30% of that from West Kennet (Wells 1962), while *c* 22% of the population from the cairn at Parc Le Breos Cwm, West Glamorgan, was <13 years old (Wysocki 1998). Of the immature individuals identified from Hambledon Hill, *c* 30% were represented among the articulated remains, 16% among the skulls, and *c* 54% among the disarticulated fragments. Also to be considered are the various factors which would seriously affect the survival of remains from such young individuals other than where protected by burial in a grave or under a cairn, for example destruction or removal by scavengers and preferential loss due to weathering (see '*Condition of the bone and ancient modifications*').

The recovery of fragments representative of all skeletal elements from the south long barrow, including the vast majority of the small hand and foot bones from among the disarticulated bone, strongly suggested that the remains of at least some complete skeletons, from cadavers which had not been subject to excarnation, were present prior to bulldozing in the 1960s. One can only speculate whether these would have comprised articulated 'burials' or if they were already disarticulated. However, cut-marks were noted on two fragments from the long barrow (including the 'geometric' marks on HH77 95) and two fragments showed clear evidence of canid gnawing, suggesting that a variety of deposition types may have been present.

Skulls will roll, particularly if pushed. It is, therefore, possible that at least some of the 13 skulls arrived in position by accident. However, the skulls recovered on or near the base of ditches do not have the appearance of accidental deposits (eg Figs 3.11–12); their placement, disarticulated and probably 'dry', appears deliberate. Two of the immature skulls were afforded the same treatment as two of the immature cadavers (and a collection of disarticulated immature bone fragments), being covered by or incorporated within flint cairns. The separation of dry, disarticulated skulls and long bones from each other and the rest of the skeletal elements has been observed in long barrows eg West Kennet, Wiltshire (Piggott 1962), Fussell's Lodge, Wiltshire (Ashbee 1966), and Hazleton, Gloucestershire (Saville 1990b). The significance of the skulls from Hambledon Hill appears to lie in their positioning, though the actual nature of the deposits is debatable. Head cults and the importance of the skull as an easily identifiable part of the human skeleton are common themes throughout prehistory, and the symbolic significance may be that the skull is seen as an easily recognisable token of the individual or the group and a clear marker of possession. The placing of these remains at Hambledon may, however, have served several purposes: they may have been totemic, or may have acted as a warning or as guardians. The predominance among them of females and of infants and children may seem incongruous here, but women and children are essential to the continuity of a community and form the hub of a family group, and, as such, would be ideal representations of a society, assuming, that is, that the choice was deliberate.

The predominance of skull fragments and fragments of long bone shaft among the disarticulated remains from Hambledon Hill echoes the skeletal elements recovered from other Neolithic enclosures. Bones from the ditches at Windmill Hill were nearly all parts of skulls and long bones (Smith 1965, 136–7), fragments of skull and long bones were recovered from Durrington Walls and Woodhenge (Wainwright with Longworth 1971), and adult skull fragments from Mount Pleasant (Wainwright 1979a). Thorpe (1984) compared the composition of the skeletal elements recovered from causewayed enclosures and from long barrows in Wessex. His graphs (ibid, figs 4.4 and 4.5) show considerable disparities between the two monument types. Skulls were much more frequent in causewayed enclosures than in long barrows, *c* 45 (44%) compared with *c* 21 (8%); and long bones rather less frequent, *c* 36 (35%) compared to *c* 109 (43%). A significant difference was in the third category, 'others', which comprised only 21% of skeletal elements from the causewayed enclosures compared to 49% from long barrows. Was this apparent selection due to natural causes or cultural ones?

There may be some significance in the observation that the skeletal elements most commonly recovered from the causewayed enclosures are the elements which have been noted as 'missing' from some long barrows. For example, Wells (1962) noted that both lower limb bones and skulls (minus mandible) had apparently been 'removed' from the assemblage at

West Kennet, and some of the long bones from Hazleton were observed to be absent (Saville 1990b). It is not uncommon for skeletal elements to be described as 'missing' from long barrow assemblages but there is no one exclusive pattern. Brothwell and Blake (1966, 62), having analysed the bone from Fussell's Lodge, commented that there was 'a relative lack of ribs, small bones of the hands and feet, patellae, clavicles, and scapulae', the most commonly occurring region being the skull. Chesterman (1977) noted that bones were missing from the Ascott-under-Wychwood assemblage in Oxfordshire, but specified no particular elements, and Whittle (1991) makes the same observation for Wayland's Smithy.

In their analysis of the bone from Fussell's Lodge, Brothwell and Blake (1966) concluded that '*burial* [present writers italics] initially took place elsewhere, and when the bones were partially or completely clear of soft tissue attachments major regions were removed for barrow burial'. This suggestion that the disarticulated remains from the long barrow were probably *exhumed* from elsewhere may be applied to the skulls and disarticulated remains recovered from Hambledon Hill and other similar sites. The articulated remains at Hambledon provide evidence for burial in shallow graves or under flint cairns, both of which would facilitate recovery after the required decomposition. The predominance of large bones, particularly skull and long bones, that is those easily identified with and easiest to physically recover, would all support this argument. An insight into excarnation of one individual is provided by a deep, eventually backfilled, grave sealed under the outer bank at Windmill Hill. On its floor was the essentially complete but rather displaced skeleton of an adult male, with several thousand amphibian bones and some small rodent bones, the most obvious interpretation being that the grave was left open, during which time the corpse decomposed and attracted rodents while frogs and toads fell into the almost vertical-sided open grave and could not get out. No gnawing or cut-marks were noted on the bone, suggesting that excarnation may in this case have been passive (Whittle *et al* 1999, 79–82, 344–6).

It has been demonstrated, however, that other forms of excarnation were (?also) being practised at Hambledon Hill. The cut-marks noted, though few (7% of finds), indicate that, at least, periodic defleshing and cleaning of individual cadavers was occurring, most probably as part of an ongoing process (see above). The effects of carnivorous scavengers on cadavers have been discussed in detail above ('*Gnawing*'). The skeletal elements recovered from among the disarticulated bone fragments at Hambledon Hill are precisely those one would expect to see had dogs or foxes had frequent access to exposed cadavers or those easily removed from shallow graves. There is some direct evidence (in the form of visible gnawing) for carnivorous scavengers at Hambledon Hill and compelling indirect evidence (from the skeletal elements and parts of bones recovered) that their activity was considerably more common. The location of much of the articulated skeletal material could also be interpreted as representing the remains of either exposed cadavers or those placed in shallow graves. It is likely that a complex process of excarnation, involving exhumation, exposure (with associated scavenging) and periodic defleshing and cleaning of bones was being practised at Hambledon Hill, either as individual rites or in combination. Nor would this exclude the possibility of further 'curation' of skeletalised remains. What may appear, to modern sensibilities, to represent a rather grotesque and unpleasant vision, would not necessarily have been viewed as such in a world where it constituted 'normal' behaviour.

The question which now arises is whether what was apparently occurring at Hambledon Hill was 'normal' practice. Evidence for defleshing is currently extremely scant, only Haddenham (Wakely 2006) having produced comparable evidence to date. The only gnaw marks noted on the skeletal material from Fussell's Lodge were those of rodents (Ashbee 1966). No gnaw marks were noted on the disarticulated bone recovered from the ditches at the other enclosure sites discussed above. However, Wysocki (1998) has reported extensive gnawing to the bone recovered from the chambers at Parc le Breos Cwm and argues for initial exposure of the cadavers with subsequent deposition of the skeletal remains in the cairn.

Possible links between long barrows and enclosure sites have been discussed by several authors. Such discussion generally centres around the absence of certain skeletal elements from long barrow assemblages – the varying degrees of articulation commonly seen in the tombs generally being attributed to re-arrangement of remains during subsequent burials (Saville 1990b, 263–5). The evidence from some barrows is for the removal of bone following decomposition, for example at West Kennet (Piggott 1962). Following the identification of a shortfall of skulls and long bones at West Kennet, Smith argued that the skulls and long bones from Windmill Hill could reflect the removal of bones from any or all of the four nearby chambered long barrows, perhaps as fetishes or mementos (1965, 137). Evidence from elsewhere has been used to support the view that bone was being brought into long barrows following a primary mortuary ritual elsewhere, for example at Fussell's Lodge (Brothwell and Blake 1966), Ascott-under-Wychwood (Chesterman 1977) and Parc le Breos Cwm (Wysocki 1998). Chesterman argued for exposure of cadavers prior to burial but not at any specified site (ibid), a similar argument being demonstrated convincingly by Wysocki (1998) for the remains deposited in the chamber (as distinct from the passage) at Parc le Breos Cwm. At Fussell's Lodge, Ashbee (1966) suggested the traffic may have been from enclosures to long barrows, or possibly both ways. For Wayland's Smithy, Whittle (1991) has cautiously, but probably realistically, opted for a mode of disposal which was not mutually exclusive of comings, goings or staying-put, without specifying any other potential associated locations.

In the light of these hypotheses it is perhaps an understatement to call 'unfortunate' the fact that the south long barrow at Hambledon Hill was bulldozed flat in the 1960s. A direct comparison between the two sets of data from such immediately adjacent deposits would have been of great value; currently it is only possible to suggest that the long barrow assemblage may also have represented a mix of deposition types.

There are indications that there were either slight temporal or locational shifts in the treatment of the human remains on the hill. The predominance of the Stepleton enclosure for the recovery of articulated remains and the main causewayed enclosure for the disarticulated fragments may simply reflect a variation in the scale of activity between the two areas, or a genuine variation in mortuary rite. Were bodies from Stepleton transferred to the main enclosure once the excarnation process had run its course? Was the treatment of corpses simply different in this location? Or was there a temporal shift in treatment which did not allow for the previously 'normal' practice to extend beyond the early stages? No articulated skeletal material was recovered from the Hanford spur, and both the skulls from there appear to have been deposited disarticulated and dry, and yet the majority of the bone from this location was less weathered than that recovered from other parts of the site, and the only set of cut-marks observed may not have been directly associated with defleshing or cleaning (Table 7.4). The latter observations may indicate that the bone from Hanford was subject to less 'curation' than that recovered from other parts of the hill.

Tilley (1994) has interpreted Hambledon Hill as 'death island' on the edge of the Cranborne Chase 'ocean' of barrows. Death is a transition, and the remains of the dead, in their different forms, most probably did acquire new roles. The 'circulation of ancestral bones' has previously been suggested as a theme in megalithic chambered tombs (Gresham 1972) and in itself is perfectly plausible. However, one major flaw in Tilley's argument is that he fails to consider the undoubted effect of scavengers on the taphonomy of the remains from the enclosure ditch, which the writer believes may be largely responsible for the skeletal elements represented. A further difficulty has to be the lack of reliable osteological analysis to link the skeletal material between the 'ocean' and the 'island', putting the theory to a practical test.

7.1.5 The Anglo-Saxon burials

Human remains were recovered from 11 of the 12 graves which formed a small cemetery located on and behind the Stepleton innermost outwork bank (3.5.7). A summary of the results is presented in Table 7.8.

Disturbance and condition

The majority of the graves, with one exception (grave 12, cutting Clay-with-Flints), were cut through the outwork bank into natural chalk, had been badly truncated by ploughing, and survived to depths of less than 0.20 m. Graves 1–11 formed a fairly regular row along a *c* 17 m north–south length of the outwork, Grave 12 being situated *c* 16 m to the south (Figs 3.116, 3.119–22). The outwork bank was badly ploughed-down and this, together with the very shallow remaining depth of the graves, makes the potential for loss of other burials fairly high. Further damage had been inflicted on the remains as a result of animal burrowing. Despite the level of post-depositional disturbance, skeletal recovery from the adult burials was relatively good, at between *c* 70% and *c* 98% (Table 7.8); the low levels of skeletal recovery from the immature graves was more the product of poor bone survival than disturbance.

Much of the bone was badly fragmented, presumably in consequence of the reduction in grave depth by ploughing. One of the skulls was badly warped (Grave 3). The bone was generally in poor condition, noticeably more so than the Neolithic remains, being eroded and root-marked, and sometimes dry and fissured; the neonatal bone was particularly badly eroded. Slight green staining was noted on the lateral border of the left scapula from Grave 1, suggestive of the possible one-time presence of copper-alloy in the grave, perhaps a cloak-pin or brooch. No items of copper-alloy were found in the grave, but artefacts may have been removed as a result of disturbance.

Bone from two of the skeletons – both recovered from the same outlying grave (12) – had dark staining, with the exception of the right arm bones from both. This suggests that the bodies may have been wrapped or covered in some form of organic material, from which the right arms protruded or were otherwise protected.

Demographic data

Twelve individuals were identified from the 11 graves, Grave 12 containing the remains of two adult females. Nine adults were identified, including five males and four females, with one (possibly male) older subadult and two neonates/young infants under 8 months (Table 7.8). There is no significant difference in the age of the adults dependent on sex, there being one female and one male of over 45 yr, and a similar distribution of sexes in the younger age ranges.

The cemetery population has the appearance of a small, 'extended family group'. The absence of more immature individuals, with only the two very young neonates/infants, is curious; however, in view of the very low skeletal recovery from the infant graves, it is possible that the remains of immature individuals have been preferentially lost due to truncation and detrimental soil conditions.

Table 7.8 Summary of Saxon inhumations

% skel = % of articulated skeleton recovered
No. frags = number of fragments present
amtl = *ante mortem* tooth loss, pd = periodontal disease, oa = osteoarthritis, op = osteophytes, exo = exostoses, dl = destructive lesion, pnb periostial new bone, ddd = degenerative disc disease, Sch = Schmorl's node, mv = morphological variation. C = cervical, T = thoracic, L = lumbar, S = sacral, bsm = body surface margins, man mandibular, max = maxillary, a-c = acromio-clavicular, r/l = right/left, p/d = proximal/distal, IP = inter-phalangeal, ap = articular process, tp = transverse process

Grave and find number	*% skel*	*Age*	*Sex*	*Pathology*
1 ST78 499	*c* 85%	adult *c* 25–30 yr	male	caries, calculus, hypoplasia, oa – bilateral sterno-clavicular, op – r pisiform, C1, T8 & L5 bsm, l rib, mv – overcrowding man teeth, C5 dual transverse forama, wormians, man M3 5 – cusp, premature fusion sagittal suture
2 ST78 890	*c* 93%	adult >25 yr	male	amtl, calculus, cribra orbitalia, Sch –T11, pitting – l a-c, r rib, op – l d ulna, 1st & 11th ribs, C1–-2, 5T bsm, oa – l c-v, mv – wormians (6), all man molars 5-cusp, impacted max M3
3 ST77 127	*c* 88%	adult >25 yr	male	calculus, trauma – ?r clavicle, ?r ulna, un-united fracture r radius, fractures l tibia & fibula, pnb – l tibia & fibula, dl – r d humerus, l acetabulum, r scapula, hyper-vascularity – r d humerus, r d radius, pitting – a-c, T10 rib, l 1st rib, cribra orbitalia, exo – p femur, op – l femur head, l patella, T5–6 & T8 bsm, L6-S1 bsm & ap, 2 r & 5 l rib, Sch – L1–2, mv – man l M3 6 – cusps + Carabelli cusp, max M3 root 'pegged', wormians, atlas central groove, sternal foramen, L6
4 ST77 133	*c* 96%	adult >30 yr	male	calculus, hypoplasia, abscess, op – r scapula, r d humerus, r sacro-iliac, 3 r & 1 l rib, C1–2, T5 & T9 ap, Sch – T8–11, L2–3, pitting – T3–4, T7, T9 & T11 (all ap), oa – l sacro-iliac, T3 ap, exo – p femora, mv – max gap-toothed, metopic suture, wormians (12), squatting facets, fusion middle & distal segments l 5th toe
5 ST77 132	*c* 97%	adult >45 yr	male	amtl, pd, calculus, abscess, ddd – C3–7, 3T, 3L, Sch – 2T, oa – r 1st IP joint, l hip, r sacro-iliac, r c-v, l 11/12th c-v, C3–4, C7, T1, 1L, exo – p femora, patellae, d fibulae, r p fibula, l calcaneum, iliac crests, r ischial tuberosity, ilia rectus femoris, op – l d femur, patellae, l calcaneum, r talus, l scapula, r acetabulum, l ankle, r talus, sesamoids, 3 r & 2 l ribs, C1–2, C5–7 ap, T1–5 & other 4T bsm, 3L bsm, pitting – r 3rd & 5th tarso-metatarsal joints, mclavicles, r tarsals, dl – r talus, r 1st & 5th proximal IP joint (LL), r 1st distal IP (LL), calcification costo-sternal cartilage, mv – max I2 'pegged', pseudo-facet l d fibula, calcaneal dual facets, atlas central groove, fusion 2L bodies
6 ST78 751, 1469	*c* 98%	adult *c* 25–30 yr	female	hypoplasia, calculus, dl – r 2/3rd proximal foot phalanx, l d humerus, ddd – S1, op – C1, T5-6 & T8 bsm, cribra orbitalia, mv – man l M^3 6-cusps & r 5-cusp with Carabelli, squatting facets, calcaneal dual facets, middle & distal segments both 5th toes fused, premature fusion sagittal suture
7 ST78 793	*c* 1%	neonate (0–4 mths)		
8 ST78 503	*c* 2%	neonate/ young infant (4–8 mths)		
9 ST78 1197	*c* 85%	adult >45 yr	female	amtl, abscess, calculus, endocranial new bone, osteoporosis – ass vertebral body collapse T12, L4–5, trauma – compression fracture T12, calcified rib cartilage, oa – r a-c, 3 r carpals, r hip, C2–5, T12 ap, T1 c-v, ddd – C3–7, T1–2, T8–9, L1–3, op – scapulae, l d humerus, p ulnae, patellae, knees, l d fibula, l talus, finger phalanges (1st proximal IP joints, 4 middle both IP, 5 distal IP), 3 l rib facet, C1, T3–7 & T10–11 bsm, L4–5 bsm, new bone – l d femur, exo – r d femur, l patella, pitting – r temporo-mandibular, 1st rib heads, L2 ap, mv – squatting facets, absence max M3
11 ST78 987	*c* 70%	subadult 15–18 yr	??male	caries, calculus, mv – overcrowding man teeth, man M3 5-cusp, man M1 6-cusp, 3 centre ossification 1st metacarpals, delayed ossification/calcification C1 & C2
12 ST78 2617	*c* 80%	adult *c* 18–25 yr	female	calculus, cribra orbitalia, op – C1, mv – metopic suture
12 ST78 2618	*c* 70%	adult *c* 30–45 yr	female	pd, calculus, caries, abscess, pitting – temporo-mandibular joints, l acetabulum, op – r p radius, l rib, Sch – 1L, modified l max canine (artefactual not pathological)

The evidence for a pre-seventh century Anglo-Saxon presence in Dorset is sparse, and the few – less than a dozen – early cemeteries, of which Hambledon Hill is one, often comprised small numbers of burials, possibly indicative of small, pioneering groups of settlers pushing westwards (Green 1984; Eagles 1994).

Physical anthropology

Stature estimation

It was possible to estimate the stature of seven of the adults. The height range for the males (four individuals) was between 1.71 and 1.74 m (5' 7¼"–5' 8½"), with an average of 1.72 m (5' 7¾"); for the females (three individuals) the range was 1.49 m (4' 11½") to 1.67 m (5' 5½"), with an average of 1.59 m (5' 2½"). The estimated heights of the females were significantly less than for the males. Other Anglo-Saxon groups show similar mean heights at, for example, 1.58 m for the females and 1.67 m for the males from Alton, Hampshire (Powers and Brothwell 1988). Further to the east, at Apple Down in Sussex (Harman 1990), the average estimated height for the males (38 individuals) was 1.74 m (5' 8½"), but a substantial proportion (16%) were 1.80 m (5' 10¾") and above. Contemporaneous, though culturally different, cemeteries in Dorset, comprising the indigenous population, also show similar mean heights – female 1.59 m and male 1.71 m at Ulwell (Waldron 1988) – or lower ones – female 1.56 m, males 1.89 m at Tolpuddle (McKinley 1999b).

The average height for the Anglo-Saxon males from Hambledon Hill was 40 mm greater than for the Neolithic males, the Anglo-Saxons having a much smaller range of heights and a maximum that was 20 mm higher than for the Neolithic males.

Cranial index

The cranial indices of six individuals (four male, two female) was calculated giving a range of 70–76.38. All except one fell into the dolichocranial range, that from Grave 5 (male) being in the mesocranial range. There was no significant variation within the group or between the Anglo-Saxon and Neolithic indices. The Saxon indices fall within the central area of the range of 66–81 recorded at Apple Down (Harman 1990), where the average was 74.4 and skulls were most commonly (48%) within the dolichocranial range. The tendency towards long-headedness corresponds with the general trend in the Anglo-Saxon period (Marlow 1992).

Pathological lesions and morphological variations

Some pathological lesions and morphological variations were noted in the remains of all the individuals identified except the two neonates (Table 7.8). The nature of some of the conditions is discussed in greater detail in the Neolithic section, to which the reader is referred.

Dental disease

Ten permanent dentitions were recorded; a total of 277 erupted permanent teeth were counted and 272 permanent tooth positions. Calculus deposits were noted in all the permanent dentitions, with heavy deposits in only one (Grave 5). Periodontal disease was observed in one male (Grave 5) and one female (Grave 12B) dentition, both exhibiting other dental lesions which may have been associated.

Ante mortem tooth loss was evident in three dentitions, one female and two male. In total, 30 out of the 272 teeth were lost (11%); 2% for the males, 24.6% for the females. The latter high rate is due to the older adult female (Grave 9) having lost almost all her teeth; there was a substantial reduction in the thickness of the mandibular body, which was only 7.3 mm wide and 6.4 mm deep, producing the characteristic 'slack jaw' which must have seriously restricted the type of food this individual was capable of consuming. In the two males, both molars and premolars had been lost (predominantly the latter). The overall rate is higher than that of 6.9% from Apple Down (Harman 1990), but slightly lower than that of *c* 14% shown by Brothwell (1972a) for Saxon populations.

Carious lesions were noted in three dentitions, two male and one female, with an overall rate of 2.5%. All the lesions were small, most were cervical in origin (71%), and molars were predominantly affected (86%). The rate is considerably lower than that of 10% from Apple Down (Harman 1990) and the 6% given by Brothwell for Saxon populations (1972a, fig 55). However, the significance of at least the former comparison should be measured against the higher *ante mortem* tooth loss rate from the Hambledon group, itself skewed by the condition of the older female dentition (Grave 9). Dental abscesses were observed in four dentitions, two male and two female, with an overall rate of 1.8%, 1.1% for the male, 3.3% for the females. The overall rate was again lower than that of 7.2% recorded at Apple Down (Harman 1990). With the exception of the higher rate of *ante mortem* tooth loss among the Saxons, there is little difference in the rates of various dental diseases between the two assemblages from Hambledon Hill, and it may be argued that the Saxon group had a similarly high-protein diet to that inferred for their Neolithic predecessors (see above). This may, in part, have been due to their 'settler' status; being, apparently, among the first Saxons to push westward in the seventh century, they may not have settled anywhere long enough to have established arable crops.

Deficiency disease

Cribra orbitalia was noted in four of the eight individuals where the orbital vaults survived, with a rate of 37%. Lesions were mostly mild porotic, with cribotic lesions in both orbits of the young adult female 12a. The rate is slightly higher than that noted among the Neolithic remains in general, significantly so in comparison with the low rate among the adults (8%). It is also slightly higher than the rates noted for the closely contemporary – though used by an indigenous group – cemetery at Tolpuddle (overall rate 28%), where the rate was far greater among the immature individuals than the adults (McKinley 1999b). The apparent discrepancy in the rates may be diet-related, reflecting the uncertain existence of this small group of early settlers.

Osteoporosis, rarefaction of the trabecular bone and thinning of the cortices, had led to the characteristic anterior collapse of the twelfth thoracic vertebra in the older adult female from Grave 9, with a healed compression fracture across the centre of the bone. This type of pathological fracture is not uncommon in association with senile osteoporosis (Adams 1986, 111; 1987, 102–3) and would have produced kyphosis (anglulation) of the spine. There was also lateral and posterior collapse of the fourth and fifth lumbar vertebral bodies respectively. The condition would have produced back pain, particularly in association with the fracture, and affected the breathing and mobility of this individual.

Trauma

A well-healed, but un-united fracture was observed in the distal half of the right radius from Grave 3 (Fig 7.18), which had resulted in shortening of the bone, and apparent rotation of the distal end. The X-radiograph indicated a spiral fracture, with well-healed margins and no indication of associated infectious changes. Fractures to the bones of the forearm, occurring as a result of direct force or a heavy fall onto the wrist (Adams 1987, 160), are prone to non-union as a consequence of either impaired blood supply or inadequate immobilisation with resultant rotational shearing movement between the broken fragments (the forearm being active in the pronation of the hand). Areas of hypervascularity (indicative of increased blood supply) in the right distal humerus and the distal radius shaft suggest there was a problem with the blood supply to the arm, but inadequate immobilisation is likely to have been a major factor in the non-union. Disruption to the contours of the right distal ulna and the medial shaft of the right clavicle are likely to have been associated with the same traumatic event. The strength and functioning of the forearm and hand must have been impaired in consequence of the injury.

The same individual, an adult male, had a well-healed, but misaligned spiral fracture in the left tibia and fibula, with medial displacement and shortening of the bones by *c* 15.3 mm (Fig 7.19). Fractures of this type are sustained by the exertion of a rotational force, such as may be inflicted in falling from some height. The X-radiograph of the tibia also showed what may have been a second spiral fracture, distal to the first, suggesting a compound fracture. The tibia and fibula shafts both have periosteal new bone on the medial surfaces, indicative of associated soft tissue infection. It is probable that both fractures were sustained in the same traumatic event.

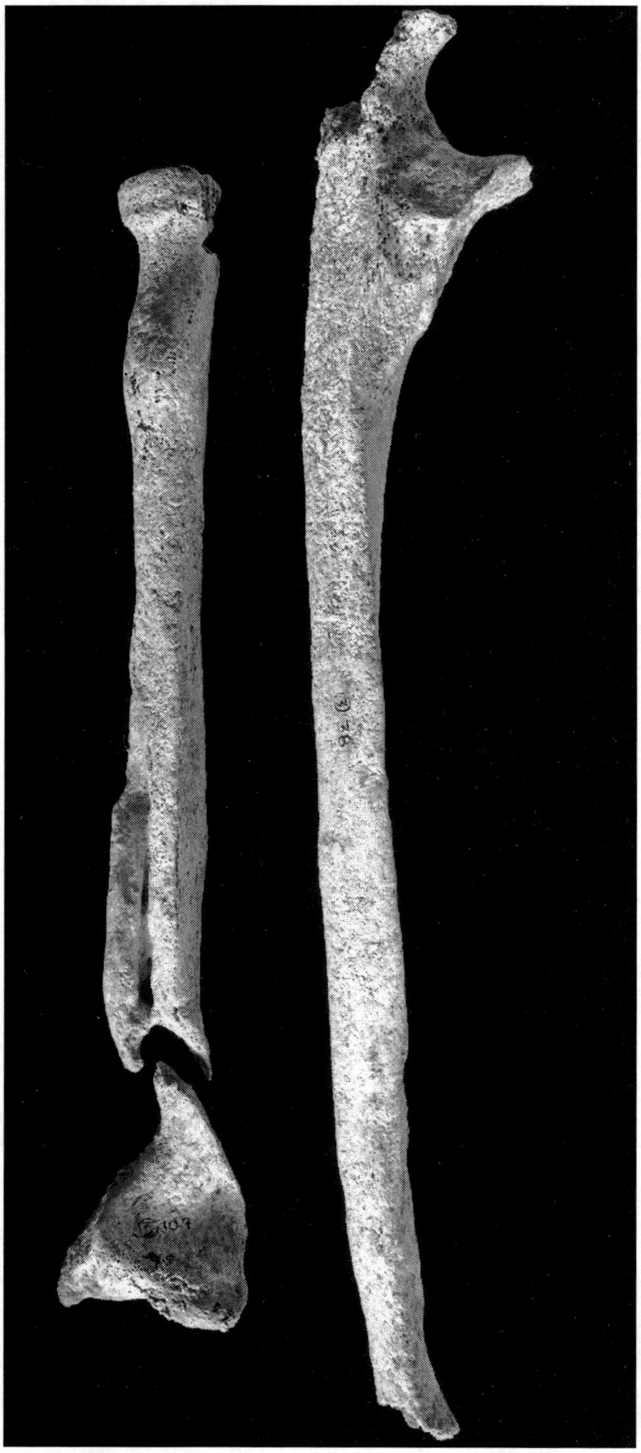

Fig 7.18 ST77 79/Saxon Grave 3 (male >25 yr); right radius (medial aspect) and ulna (lateral aspect) showing healed, un-fused fracture in distal radius and shortening of the bone. Photo Elaine Wakefield (Wessex Archaeology)

Joint disease

Lesions indicative of osteoarthritis were noted in the remains of five individuals, including four males and one female. Between one and eleven joints were affected in each individual, the number of joints involved increasing with age. The most commonly affected joints

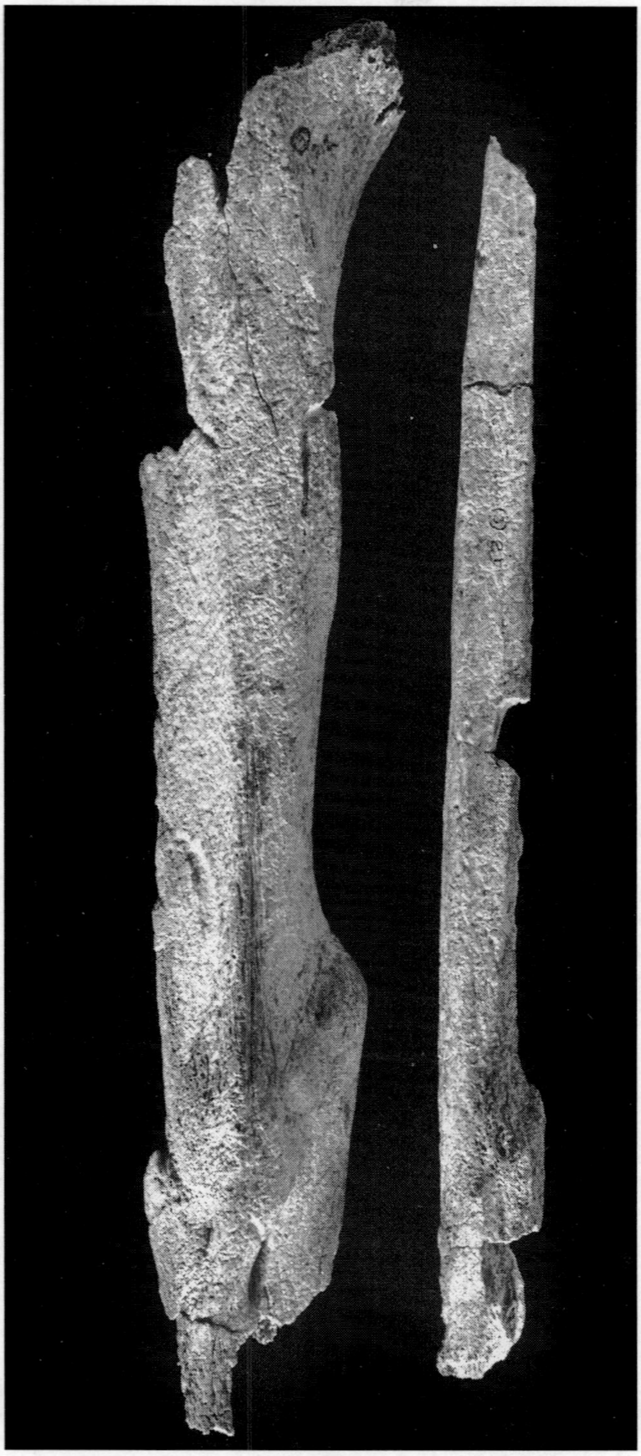

Fig 7.19 ST77 79/Saxon Grave 3; left tibia (lateral aspect) and fibula (medial aspect) showing a mis-aligned spiral fracture in the distal halves of the shafts, with shortening of the bone and associated pyogenic lesions. Photo Elaine Wakefield (Wessex Archaeology)

were the sterno-clavicular (22%), acromio-clavicular (12%) and cervical articular processes (12%). The numbers in each group were, however, small and no significant conclusions can be drawn from the figures.

Degenerative disc disease was noted in two of the female spines and one male, the scale of involvement apparently increasing with age in both sexes. All areas of the spine were involved, with higher prevalence in the upper and lower regions. Overall rates were cervical 18% (female 26%, male 12%), thoracic 7% (female 9%, male 4%), lumbar 14% (female 16%, male 11%) and first sacral 14% (female 33%).

Schmorl's nodes were observed in five spines, including four males and one female. Rates were highest in the lumbar spine at 12% (males 14%, females 7%), with 8% (males 10%) of thoracic vertebrae affected. No vertebrae above T8 were affected.

The distribution of other destructive lesions and osteophytes associated with joints is shown in Table 7.8. Osteophytes were seen in 1–34 joint surfaces in bones from all nine of the adults, with a marked increase in involvement in the two older adults (from Graves 5 and 9); lesions were more common in joints of the upper limbs in the female and the lower limbs in the male, both had frequent spinal lesions. Pitting was recorded in between two to six joints in six of the adults, most commonly in the older adult male (Grave 5).

Miscellaneous conditions

Exostoses and other new bone were noted at between one and eleven sites in four individuals, frequency again appearing to increase with age, the older adult male being most affected.

Morphological variations

A summary is presented in Table 7.8. Premature fusion and obliteration of the sagittal suture was observed in two younger mature adult crania from Graves 1 (male) and 6 (female). Wormian bones were present in the lambdoid sutures of four individuals (Graves 1–4, males), individuals from Graves 4 and 12a both having a metopic suture. Only four individuals share more than one trait; the adult male from Grave 1 and the subadult male from Grave 11 both have overcrowding of the anterior teeth and a five-cusped mandibular third molar, and the adult male from Grave 4 and adult female from Grave 6 both have fusion of the fifth middle and distal foot phalanges and squatting facets – though the latter is believed to be linked to behavioural formation rather than potentially genetic.

Evidence for an Anglo-Saxon presence in the west in the sixth century has been recovered from several Dorset hillforts and it has been suggested that this may be indicative of Saxon involvement in 'native struggles', with warriors bearing allegiance to some British leader (Eagles 1994, 27). The Anglo-Saxon assemblage from Hambledon Hill does not represent such a group, suggesting rather a shift to more peaceful attempts at settlement in the area to the west by a 'family-style' group, which comprised at least two elderly and infirm adults (a female and a male) who would have required a degree of care from the others within their small, possibly still mobile community.

7.2 Hambledon Hill stable isotope values

Michael P Richards

7.2.1 Introduction

This section presents bone collagen stable isotope values for Neolithic humans and fauna from Hambledon Hill. Stable isotope analysis provides us with direct evidence of the more general aspects of past human diets, which can then be related to the floral and faunal remains from the site. This assemblage is particularly interesting, as there are a wide range of ages of humans represented here, as well as large numbers of males and females, which has allowed some exploration of the links between gender, age and diet. This analysis addresses a number of questions. Firstly, what was the general diet at this site? Were marine foods part of the diet, suggesting movement between this site and the coast? And how much animal protein was in these people's diets? Secondly, were the diets similar for all these individuals, and therefore suggestive of the burial of a group of people with uniform subsistence? Thirdly, were there variations in the diets that could be linked to gender? And, finally, could the isotope values of the juveniles provide some insight into cultural practices such as weaning age?

Stable isotope analyses

Stable isotope analysis of human bone collagen can tell us about the protein sources in human diets of the last 5–15 years of life (depending on the bone element sampled; Schwarcz and Schoeninger 1991; Ambrose 1993). The carbon and nitrogen in that bone have come from foods eaten over a lifetime, and various foods have unique ratios of two isotopes of carbon (^{13}C and ^{12}C), and two isotopes of nitrogen (^{15}N and ^{14}N). These isotopes behave similarly chemically, but, as one is heavier than the other, fractionation can occur during various physiological reactions, such as photosynthesis. The ratios of the two carbon isotopes, the $\delta^{13}C$ value, and the ratios of nitrogen, the $\delta^{15}N$ value, are known for a wide range of foods. Therefore, if the $\delta^{13}C$ and $\delta^{15}N$ of human bone collagen are measured, then comparison of these values with the known food values makes it possible to infer what foods were eaten in the past.

Collagen is chosen for analyses as it is the best-preserved part of the bone, and is the same material extracted for radiocarbon dating of bone. It appears that, based on various feeding experiments (Ambrose and Norr 1993; Tieszen and Fagre 1993), collagen isotope values reflect the isotope values of dietary protein. And, as bone collagen is constantly being replaced ('bone turn-over'), the collagen $\delta^{13}C$ and $\delta^{15}N$ values are an average of the last 5–15 years of diet.

There is a great variation in $\delta^{13}C$ values between terrestrial and marine ecosystems. Therefore, a human who derives a predominant (>90%) amount of his or her protein from marine sources will have $\delta^{13}C$ values close to –12 ± 1‰. Those who have no marine protein in their diet will have $\delta^{13}C$ values closer to –20 ± 1‰. Individuals who derive 50% of their protein from marine, and 50% from terrestrial, sources will have $\delta^{13}C$ values between these two, *c* –16‰.

On the other hand, $\delta^{15}N$ values reflect the trophic level of an organism in a food chain. Generally, human collagen $\delta^{15}N$ values are 2–4‰ higher than the protein they consume. If we measure the $\delta^{15}N$ values of associated fauna, whose diets we have some idea about, we can compare these values to those of the humans in order to see whether humans behaved more like herbivores, with plant protein predominating, or carnivores, with animal protein being the most important. Usually, as humans are omnivores, their $\delta^{15}N$ values fit somewhere in between those of herbivores and carnivores. The $\delta^{15}N$ value then reflects the relative amounts of animal (meat or milk) *vs* plant protein in diets over the previous 5–15 years.

Table 7.9 Comparison of isotope values obtained from collagen extracted following the methods outlined by Richards (1998), 'MR' and collagen extracted as part of the radiocarbon dating process at the Oxford Radiocarbon Accelerator Unit, '^{14}C'. The measurement errors on each measurement are $\delta^{13}C$ ± 0.3 ‰, and $\delta^{15}N$±0.4 ‰

Sample	*Method*	*$\delta^{13}C$ (±0.3)*	*$\delta^{15}N$ (±0.4)*	*C:N*
ST81 3188	MR	–20.9	10.3	3.4
ST81 3188	^{14}C	–21.1	10.0	3.4
ST78 2755	MR	–20.5	7.8	3.4
ST78 2755	^{14}C	–20.6	7.9	3.0

7.2.2 The stable isotope results

Stable isotope analyses were undertaken of 51 Neolithic humans, mostly adults, from various areas of this site. The isotope values of an additional four humans and a large number of faunal remains were also measured as part of the radiocarbon dating process at the Oxford Radiocarbon Accelerator Unit, and these values are discussed below. For most samples, the collagen extraction procedure followed was standard, and is outlined by Richards and Hedges (1999). Radiocarbon samples are prepared in a similar manner, and the resulting isotope values between the two methods are, as expected, statistically identical (Table 7.9). All of the human isotope values are given in Table 7.10.

Fauna

The faunal isotope values from the site are plotted in Figure 7.20. The $\delta^{13}C$ values of all of the species are about –22 to –20‰, which is as expected for terrestrial animals. There is a single *Bos* sample that does stand

Table 7.10 Human stable isotope values

All results are for single measurements, except where indicated.
Age and sex identifications are from McKinley (this chapter): AD = adult, Y = young, M = mature, YM = younger mature, JUV = juvenile, O = older, INF = infant, NEO = neonate, SU = subadult
The bone elements sampled are: F = femur, C cranium, U = unidentifiable bone fragment, M = mandible, RA = radius, T= tibia, H = humerus, LB= long bone, P = parietal, O = occipital, RI = rib, V = various
The final sample, ST82 124, is later, dating to 1430–1130 cal BC (3050±45 BP; OxA-7849).

Sample	*Location*	*Sex*	*Age*	*Element*	*δ¹³C*	*δ¹⁵N*	*C:N*	*Method*	*No. of measurements*
HH74 HB 1b	Main enclosure	F	M AD	C	-1.1	10.0	3.4	MR	
HH74 AB 201	Main enclosure	??M	AD	H	-20.7	8.8	3.4	MR	
HH74 AB 260	Main enclosure	??F	AD	RA	-0.7	9.3	3.3	MR	
HH74 AB 304	Main enclosure	?	AD	T	-0.5	9.3	3.4	MR	
HH74 AB 315	Main enclosure	?	JUV	LB	-20.8	7.7	3.3	MR	
HH75 241	Main enclosure	??F	AD	F	-21.1	8.9	3.4	MR	
HH75 337	Main enclosure	?	AD	P	-21.3	9.2	3.4	MR	
HH76 695	Main enclosure	?	AD	P	-21.2	9.4	3.4	MR	
HH76 1177	Main enclosure	?	AD	H	-21.0	8.8	3.4	MR	
HH76 1948	Main enclosure	?	JUV	F	-21.4	8.9	3.4	14C	2
HH76 2206	Main enclosure	?	OM/O AD	O	-21.1	8.8	3.4	MR	
HH76 2625	Main enclosure	M	Y/YM AD	U	-20.7	8.4	3.2	MR	
HH76 3046	Main enclosure	?	Y JUV	U	-20.7	10.7	3.0	14C	4
HH76 3052	Main enclosure	M	O AD	U	-20.8	7.2	3.1	MR	
HH77 581	Main enclosure	?	AD	LB	-20.9	8.6	3.2	MR	
HH75 1360	Inner east cross-dyke	??M	Y AD	C	-20.5	9.4	3.3	MR	
HH77 59	Long barrow	?M	AD	?F	-20.2	8.8	3.2	MR	
HH77 69	Long barrow	M	AD	U	-20.5	9.8	3.3	MR	
HH77 80	Long barrow	?M	Y/YM AD	U	-20.9	9.6	3.3	MR	
HH77 85	Long barrow	?	Y/M AD	U	-20.7	9.9	3.4	MR	
HH77 91	Long barrow	?	AD	F	-20.8	9.1	3.3	MR	
HH77 94	Long barrow	?	Y/M AD	V	-20.6	9.7	3.3	MR	3
HH77 95	Long barrow	?	M AD	U	-20.3	10.2	3.2	MR	
HH74 AB 440	A F64	?	AD	F	-20.4	8.6	3.4	MR	
HH76 1963	Shroton spur	?	Y/M AD	RA	-20.3	10.1	3.3	MR	
HH76 1967	Shroton spur	?	AD	RI	-21.0	9.5	3.3	MR	
HH76 1968	Shroton spur		M AD		-20.4	10.2	2.9	14C	
ST80 383	Stepleton enclosure	??M	AD	T	-20.8	8.6	3.3	MR	
ST81 1288	Stepleton enclosure	?	AD	T	-20.8	9.3	3.4	MR	
ST81 3188	Stepleton enclosure	F	M AD	U	-21.0	10.2	3.4	MR/14C	3
ST79 2686	Middle Stepleton outwork	?	Y JUV	RI	-20.7	9.7	3.4	MR	
ST78 1100	Inner Stepleton outwork	F	Y/YM AD	U	-20.9	10.9	3.3	MR	
ST78 2755	Inner Stepleton outwork	M	O SU/AD	F	-20.5	7.8	3.1	MR/14C	2
ST 78 2755A	Inner Stepleton outwork	?	Y INF	U	-20.4	10.4	2.9	14C	2
ST78 2871	Inner Stepleton outwork	??F	O SU/AD	F	-20.9	9.3	3.3	MR	
ST78 2919	Inner Stepleton outwork	?	INF	?C/LB	-20.8	10.0	3.3	MR	2
ST 79 2756	Inner Stepleton outwork	?	NEO	U	-20.8	10.2	3.1	14C	2
ST79 2726	Inner Stepleton outwork	M	OM AD	U	-20.2	10.0	3.3	MR	
ST80 1095	Inner Stepleton outwork	?	AD	F	-21.8	9.3	3.7	MR	
ST78 967	Outer Stepleton outwork	??F	O SU	C	-20.2	8.1	3.3	MR	
ST80 1875	Outer Stepleton outwork	M	Y AD	F	-20.8	9.0	3.2	MR	
ST80 2069	Outer Stepleton outwork	?	SU/AD	RA	-21.3	8.2	3.4	MR	
ST78 1235	1A F57	?	?Y INF	C	-21.1	10.3	3.4	MR	
ST78 964	1A F70	?	O INF/Y JUV	F	-21.2	9.9	3.4	14C	
ST79 2025	2A F200	??M	O AD	F	-20.4	9.4	3.4	MR/14C	2
ST81 2173	4B F137	?	O INF	C	-21.1	10.3	3.4	MR	
ST81 3181	4B F712	M	Y AD	F	-20.3	9.7	3.3	MR	
HN82 236	Inner Hanford outwork	??M	M/O AD	C	-20.6	9.4	3.4	MR	
HN82 270	Inner Hanford outwork	?	AD	P	-21.2	9.3	3.4	MR	
HN82 278	Inner Hanford outwork	?	Y/M AD	T	-20.9	9.3	3.3	MR	
HN82 293	Inner Hanford outwork	?	AD	CL	-20.7	9.2	3.3	MR	
HN82 339	Inner Hanford outwork	?	AD	F	-21.0	9.7	3.3	MR	
HN82 344	Inner Hanford outwork	?	SU/AD	T	-20.9	8.8	3.3	MR	
HN82 200	Outer Hanford outwork	F	M AD	C	-20.9	9.3	3.3	MR	
HN82 221	Outer Hanford outwork	?	AD	T	-20.2	9.0	3.3	MR	
ST82 124	ST82 F16	M	M/O AD	F	-21.2	9.1	3.5	14C	

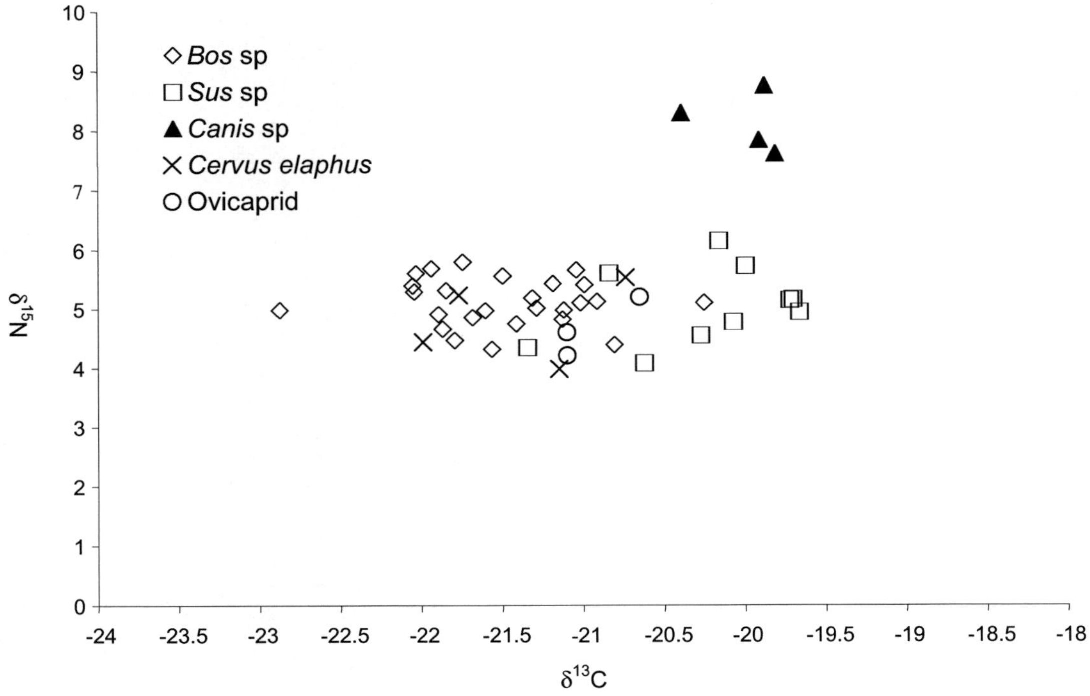

Fig 7.20 Animal bone collagen stable isotope values. These fauna come from many locations at the site, and date to the early/middle Neolithic.

out though, with a $\delta^{13}C$ value of –22.8 ‰ (HH77 2123 from beneath the inner south cross-dyke bank). There are indications that forest vegetation may be more negative in $\delta^{13}C$ than plants grown in the open (van der Merwe and Medina 1991), and this vegetation $\delta^{13}C$ difference will be reflected in the bone collagen $\delta^{13}C$ values of animals that live in the two different ecosystems. Could this *Bos* sample with the more negative $\delta^{13}C$ value be a forest dweller, and therefore be from a wild, rather than domesticated, cattle? The dog values are more positive than the herbivores/omnivores. It is most likely that what is observed here is the approximately 1‰ shift in $\delta^{13}C$ values that have been observed by others for carnivores (Bocherens *et al* 1995).

The $\delta^{15}N$ values are more variable than the $\delta^{13}C$ values, and nicely show the differences in $\delta^{15}N$ related to the source of dietary protein. The herbivores (cattle and red deer) are at about 5‰, which is the same value observed for other areas in Europe in the Holocene (Bocherens *et al* 1991; Katzenberg and Weber 1999; Richards 2000). The dog values are about 3‰ higher, indicating that their dietary protein has come entirely from herbivores, although we cannot, unfortunately, narrow down the species consumed. The values obtained for pigs are interesting. Wild pigs, as omnivores, might be expected to have $\delta^{15}N$ values between those of herbivores and carnivores, in the region of 6 or 7‰. Pig bone from the site does not, however. It has values indicative of a purely plant protein diet, which may suggest that they are domestic animals whose diets are being controlled by humans, or may simply indicate that wild pigs had a largely herbivorous diet.

Adult human isotope values

All of the human adult isotope values are plotted together with the average faunal values in Figure 7.21. The $\delta^{13}C$ values cluster around –21‰, indicating that the dietary protein was entirely from terrestrial sources, with no significant input of marine foods. The $\delta^{13}C$ values are actually quite similar, and only range over about 1‰. As discussed above with the dog $\delta^{13}C$ values, some of this variation might relate to differing amounts of animal protein in the diet.

There is a wider range of $\delta^{15}N$ values, here definitely indicating different sources of dietary protein, particularly in the amounts of animal *vs* plant protein in the diet. Most of the individuals have $\delta^{15}N$ values between 9 and 10‰, which, when compared with the faunal values, indicate a diet with most of the protein coming from animal, rather than plant, sources (herbivores at 5–6‰, plus the $\delta^{15}N$ enrichment of 2–4‰, would equal 'carnivore' $\delta^{15}N$ human values of up to 10‰). Individuals with lower $\delta^{15}N$ values obtained their dietary protein from both plant and animal sources.

The differences in diets evidenced by the wide range of $\delta^{15}N$ values leads one to question whether they may be reflecting cultural differences in diet. To see if the diet varied between male and female, values were plotted from adult samples whose sex could be identified fairly confidently using McKinley's criteria. She has four categories for sex: unidentifiable, possible male or female (denoted by ??), probable male or female (?) and likely male or female. Values are plotted in Figure 7.22 only for samples that were in the last

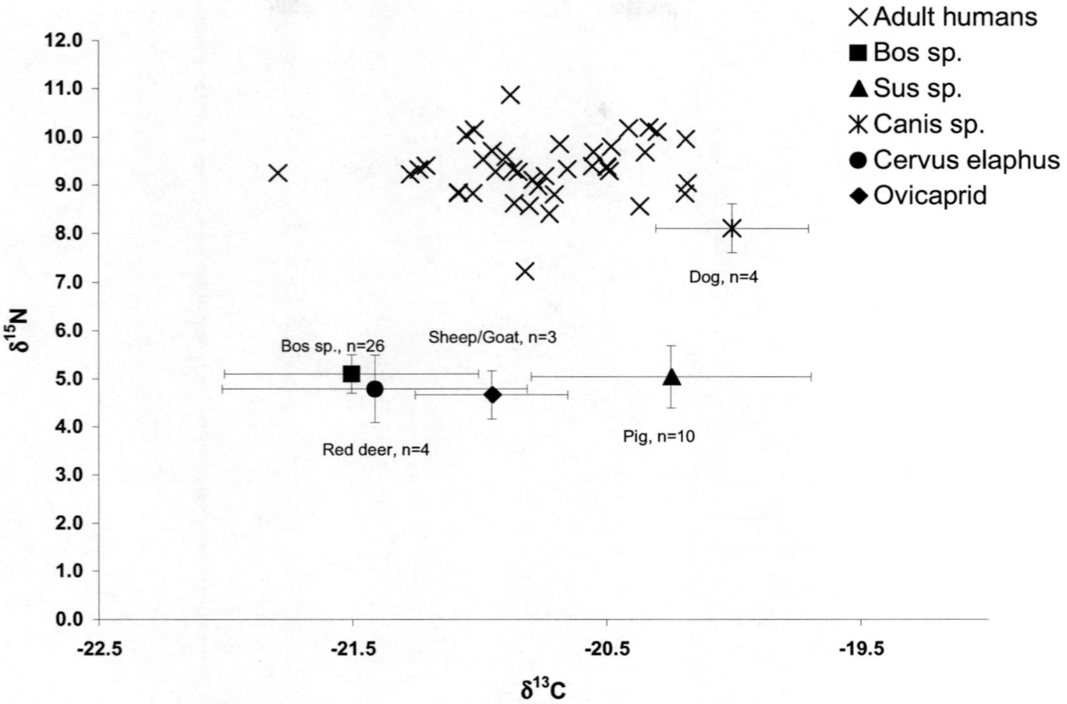

Fig 7.21 Adult human stable isotope values. These values are plotted with the average faunal isotope values for comparison.

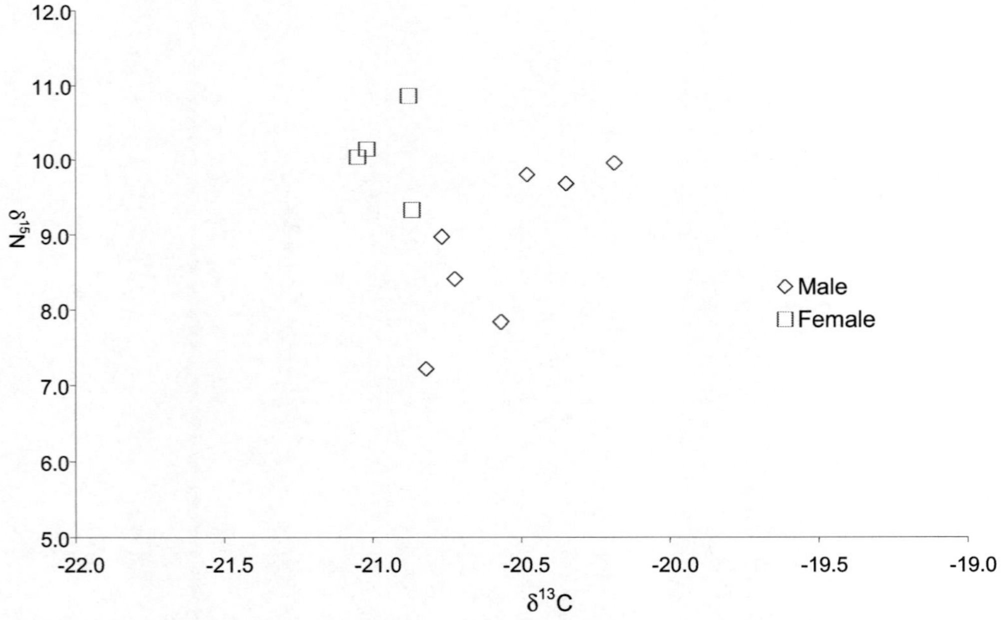

Fig 7.22 Adult human isotope values plotted by sex, as determined by McKinley (7.1).

category. The numbers of samples are small (too small to draw any real conclusions), but it does seem that there are more males with lower $\delta^{15}N$ values.

To see if there was any correlation between the location of the samples and the isotope values, the adult values from the main causewayed enclosure, Stepleton enclosure, south long barrow, Shroton outwork and the Hanford spur are plotted in Figure 7.23. There are no obvious patterns, as the data seem to vary regardless of location. There is, however, one exception, as the long barrow values are very similar to each other. Based on the sex identification and elements sampled, at least three different individuals should have been measured, so the similar values are not due to multiple measurements on the same individual.

Juvenile human isotope values

No isotope values of children are plotted in Figures 7.21–23 because of the possible complications of the 'weaning effect'. This occurs in children who are breastfeeding, as they have elevated $\delta^{15}N$ values, as,

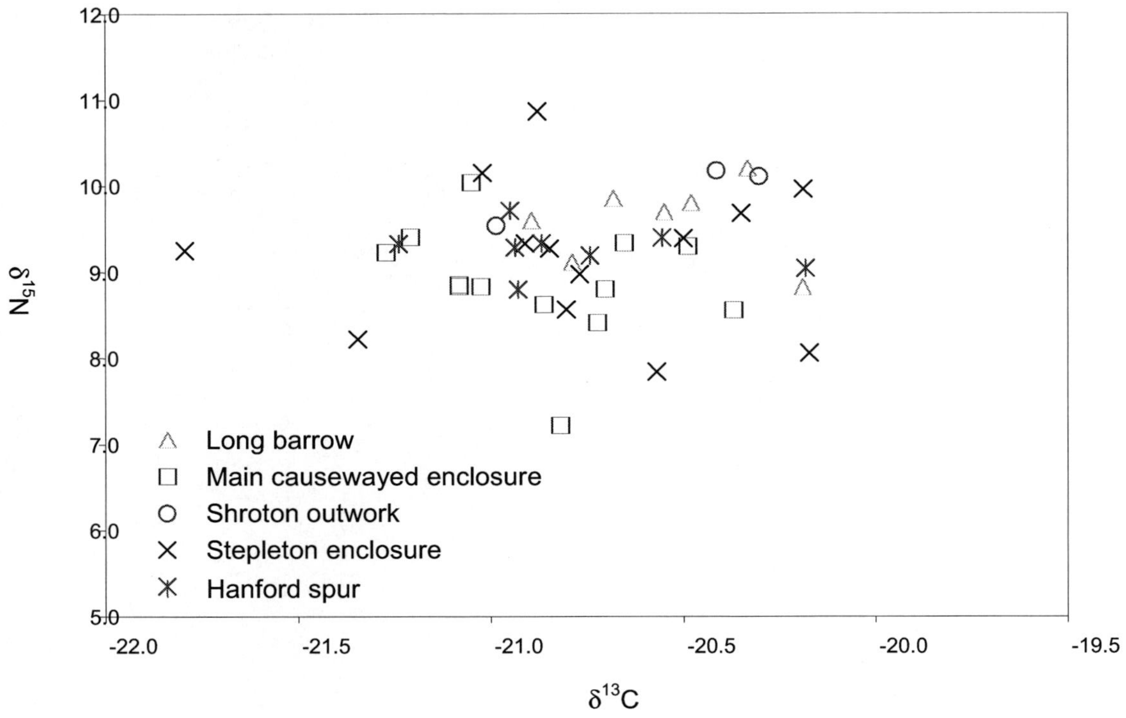

Fig 7.23 Adult human isotope values, plotted according to the location from which they were recovered at the site.

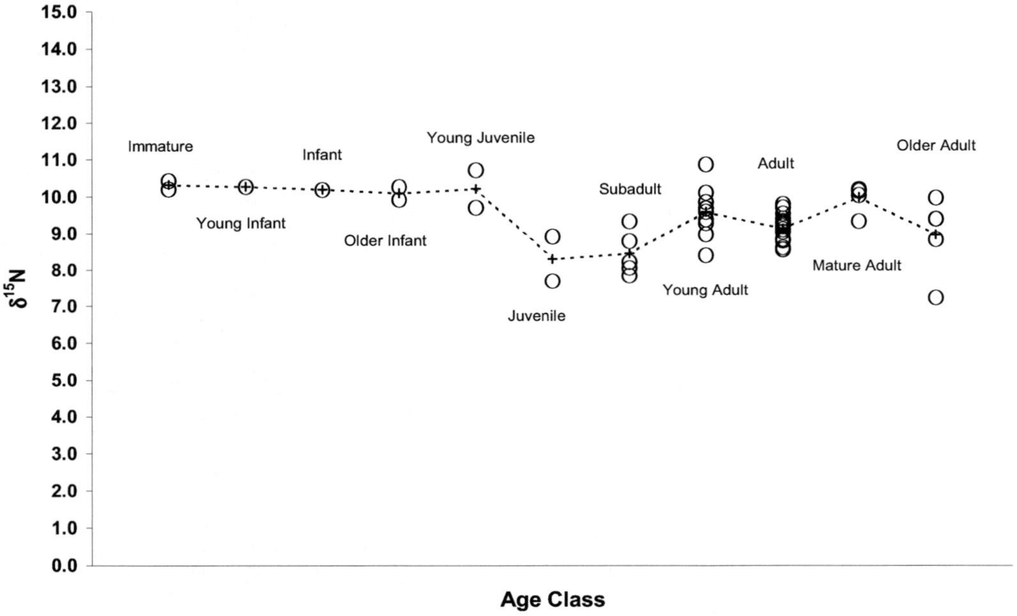

Fig 7.24 All of the Hambledon Hill humans, including juveniles, plotted using the age categories given by McKinley (7.1).

essentially, they are 'feeding' off their mothers. This means that bone collagen laid down while the child is breastfeeding will have $\delta^{15}N$ values 2–4‰ higher than their mothers (due to the trophic level increase; Katzenberg and Pfeiffer 1995; Herring *et al* 1998; Richards *et al* 2002). Therefore the children's $\delta^{15}N$ values were not plotted with the adults, as some of their bone collagen may have been elevated, reflecting their breast milk diet rather than their $\delta^{15}N$ values derived from other foods. Instead, the $\delta^{15}N$ values of all individuals are plotted with their associated age categories assigned by McKinley in Figure 7.24. As predicted, most of the children do have high bone collagen $\delta^{15}N$ values. With more data, and finer age categories, it is possible to see the point where weaning actually occurred in a population, as we would then see a drop in children's $\delta^{15}N$ values. There is another interesting feature of this plot, as it appears that there is a dip in $\delta^{15}N$ values in the older juveniles. This $\delta^{15}N$ 'dip' has been predicted for children that are in a growth period, such as puberty. Again, with better data from children, it might be possible to determine the age at which this event occurs in a prehistoric population, which would in turn reflect the general health and nutrition of that population.

7.2.3 Conclusions

Stable isotope analysis here has shown that there was a wide range of diets represented in the human burials at Hambledon Hill. It is clear from the $\delta^{13}C$ values that marine foods were not an important part of the diet, and the $\delta^{15}N$ values showed there was a wide range of diets reflecting different amounts of animal (meat or milk) and plant protein. However, most of the adults obtained their protein from animal (meat or milk) sources. Interestingly, from some preliminary data given here, it did look as if women had more animal protein than men, but much larger sample sizes are needed before definite conclusions can be reached.

7.3 Organic residue analysis of pottery vessels: determination of vessel use and radiocarbon dates

Mark Copley, Robert Berstan, Andrew Stott and Richard Evershed

7.3.1 Introduction

During the processing of organic materials in unglazed pottery vessels lipids can be absorbed into the vessel wall, due to the porous nature of the ceramic fabric. Organic compounds such as animal fats, plant oils and plant waxes are known to survive burial in this state for several thousand years (Evershed *et al* 1999). Once these lipids are extracted, quantification and identification is accomplished through the use of modern analytical techniques, primarily via high temperature-gas chromatography (HT-GC) and HT-GC/mass spectrometry (HT-GC/MS; Evershed *et al* 1990). Characterisation of lipid extracts to commodity type has only been possible through detailed knowledge of diagnostic compounds and their associated degradation products that are likely to be produced during vessel use (eg during cooking) and/or burial. For example, triacylglycerols (TAGs) are found in abundance in fresh animal fats; however, they are degraded to diacylglycerols (DAGs), monoacylglycerols (MAGs) and free fatty acids during burial/vessel use, and in archaeological pottery it is the free fatty acids that tend to predominate (Evershed 1993). Furthermore, this has been shown through laboratory degradation experiments (eg Charters *et al* 1997; Dudd *et al* 1998). As such it has been possible to detect the processing of animal fats (eg Evershed *et al* 1992), leafy vegetables (Evershed *et al* 1991; Evershed *et al* 1994), specific plant oils (Evershed *et al* 1999), palm fruit (Copley *et al* 2001) and beeswax (Evershed *et al* 1997b). The chemical structures of some commonly detected lipids from archaeological pottery are shown in Figure 7.25.

Recent work has shown that compound-specific stable carbon isotope measurements provide a further criterion for assigning the origins of organic residues preserved in archaeological ceramics. To this end we use a GC-combustion-isotope ratio mass spectrometer (GC-C-IRMS), which allows the carbon stable isotope ($\delta^{13}C$) values of individual compounds within complex mixtures to be determined. We have found that the $\delta^{13}C$ values for the principal fatty acids ($C_{16:0}$ and $C_{18:0}$) are crucial in distinguishing between different animal fats, eg ruminant and non-ruminant adipose fats and dairy fats (Evershed *et al* 1997a; Dudd and Evershed 1998; Mottram *et al* 1999), as well as in the identification of the mixing of commodities (Evershed *et al* 1999; Copley *et al* 2001). For an overview of the use of compound-specific stable isotopes in archaeology, see (Evershed *et al* 1999).

A new aspect of the application of preserved lipids to archaeological research developed in this laboratory is the radiocarbon dating of specific compounds present in the lipid extracts of potsherds (Stott *et al* 2001). The major advantages of this approach are that dates are derived from compounds that can be directly linked to the use of the vessels; thus potential problems of contamination are minimised, ensuring that exogenous carbon from contaminants (principally plasticisers from plastic storage bags, etc) do not compromise the measured radiocarbon date.

As part of a wider study into vessel use in southern Britain in prehistory, we have analysed over 900 pottery samples from 13 sites, ranging from the early Neolithic to late Iron Age (Copley *et al* 2003). Although we have been largely focusing on the question of the extent of dairying in southern Britain, it has also been possible to determine the relative importance of the processing of ruminant and non-ruminant animal products, as well as plant and bee products (eg beeswax), and thus build up a more complete picture of vessel use in prehistory. The organic residue analysis of pottery vessels from Hambledon Hill constitutes an important component of this wider study.

7.3.2 Materials and methods

Lipid analyses were performed using our established protocols that are described in detail in earlier publications (eg Evershed *et al* 1990; Evershed *et al* 1999). Briefly, analyses proceeded as follows.

Samples

The pottery vessels were held at the Dorset County Museum, and a total of 72 sherds were submitted for organic residue analysis (Table 7.11). These sherds were selected from excavations on both the central area and the Stepleton spur. Sherds originating from different parts of the same vessel are identified in Table 7.11. Their illustration numbers, find numbers and contexts are listed in Table 7.12.

Table 7.11 Lipid components of the potsherds from Hambledon Hill and their assignments to commodity origin

FFa = free fatty acids; MAG = monoacylglycerols; DAG = diacylglycerols; TAG = triacylglycerols; ALK = *n*-alkanes; ALC = *n*-alcohols; WE = wax esters; K = ketones; n/d = not detected; tr = trace concentrations
* = samples submitted for GC-C-IRMS analysis; † = samples submitted for compound-specific ^{14}C analysis.

Sample number	*Same vessel as*	*Lipid concentration (mg g^{-1})*	*Lipid components detected*	*Assignment based on TAG distributions*	*Assignment based on δ^{13}C values*	*Assignment based on ($\delta^{13}C_{18:0}$–$\delta^{13}C_{16:0}$) values*
HH1		tr	n/d	n/d		
HH2		tr	n/d	n/d		
HH3*		0.23	FFa	n/d	dairy fat?	dairy fat
HH4		tr	FFa (tr)	n/d		
HH5*		0.05	FFa; MAG	n/d	ruminant fat?	dairy fat??
HH6*		0.63	FFa; MAG (tr);	ruminant fat?	dairy fat	dairy fat
HH7*	HH61	0.02	FFa (tr) DAG (tr); TAG	n/d	mixed dairy/ruminant fat?	dairy fat??
HH8*		0.03	FFa; MAG	n/d	dairy fat	dairy fat
HH9*		0.04	FFa; K	n/d	dairy fat	dairy fat
HH10*		0.04	FFa	n/d	mixed animal fats	mixed animal fats
HH11		tr	FFa (tr)	n/d		
HH12		0.03	FFa (tr)	n/d		
HH13	HH64	tr		n/d		
HH14*		0.24	TAG; K	ruminant fat (tr)	mixed animal fats	mixed animal fats
HH15		tr	n/d	n/d		
HH16		0.07	FFa (tr); K	n/d		
HH17*		0.11	FFa; MAG; DAG; TAG	ruminant fat?	dairy fat?	dairy fat
HH18*		0.50	FFa; K	n/d	dairy fat	dairy fat
HH19		tr	n/d	n/d		
HH20		tr	FFa (tr)	n/d		
HH21		tr	n/d	n/d		
HH22*		0.17	FFa; MAG	n/d	dairy fat?	dairy fat
HH23		tr	n/d	n/d		
HH24		tr	n/d	n/d		
HH25		tr	n/d	n/d		
HH26		0.03	FFa (tr); K	n/d		
HH27*		0.78	FFa; MAG; DAG; TAG; K	mixed animal fats	dairy fat	dairy fat
HH28*		0.68	FFa; MAG (tr)	n/d	mixed animal fat	mixed animal fat
HH29		tr	n/d	n/d		
HH30		0.09	FFa (tr)	n/d		
HH31*		0.06	FFa; MAG; DAG; TAG; ALK (tr); ALC (tr); WE (tr)	ruminant fat	mixed animal fat	mixed animal fat
HH32	HH69	tr	n/d	n/d		
HH33*		0.14	FFa; MAG; DAG; K; ALK (tr); ALC (tr); WE (tr)	n/d	ruminant fat	ruminant fat
HH34*		0.89	FFa; K	n/d	dairy fat	dairy fat
HH35		tr	n/d	n/d		
HH36		0.08	FFa (tr)	n/d		
HH37		0.11	FFa (tr); MAG; K	n/d		
HH38		tr	n/d	n/d		
HH39*		0.14	FFa; MAG (tr); DAG; TAG	ruminant fat?	dairy fat	dairy fat
HH40		tr	n/d	n/d		
HH41		tr	n/d	n/d		
HH42*		0.18	FFa	n/d	mixed animal fat	mixed animal fat
HH43		tr	n/d	n/d		
HH44	HH72	0.08	FFa (tr); MAG (tr)	n/d		
HH45	HH71	tr	n/d	n/d		
HH46		0.06	FFa (tr); MAG; ALK (tr); ALC (tr)	n/d		

Sample number	*Same vessel as*	*Lipid concentration (mg g^{-1})*	*Lipid components detected*	*Assignment based on TAG distributions*	*Assignment based on $\delta^{13}C$ values*	*Assignment based on ($\delta^{13}C_{18:0}$–$\delta^{13}C_{16:0}$) values*
HH47*	HH59	0.09	FFa; ALK (tr); ALC (tr); WE (tr)	n/d	dairy fat?	dairy fat
HH48		0.01	K	n/d		
HH49		tr	n/d	n/d		
HH50		0.08	FFa (tr)	n/d		
HH51*		0.08	FFa; MAG; DAG (tr); TAG	mixed animal fat	ruminant fat??	ruminant fat
HH52*		0.11	FFa; MAG; DAG; TAG	mixed animal fat	ruminant fat??	ruminant fat
HH53*	HH56	0.80	FFa; MAG; DAG; TAG	mixed animal fat	ruminant fat?	ruminant fat
HH54*†		0.08	FFa	n/d	mixed ruminant/dairy fat	dairy fat??
HH55*		0.09	FFa; MAG; DAG; TAG	ruminant fat	ruminant fat?	ruminant fat
HH56*†	HH53	0.13	FFa; MAG; DAG; TAG; K	mixed animal fat	ruminant fat	ruminant fat
HH57	HH25, HH58	tr	n/d	n/d		
HH58	HH 25, HH57	tr	n/d	n/d		
HH59	HH47	0.06	FFa (tr)	n/d		
HH60*		0.11	FFa; MAG; DAG; TAG; ALK (tr); ALC (tr)	mixed animal fat?	mixed ruminant/dairy fat	dairy fat??
HH61	HH7	tr	n/d	n/d		
HH62*		0.50	FFa; TAG; K	mixed animal fat?	dairy fat?	dairy fat
HH63		0.27	FFa; TAG (tr)	n/d		
HH64	HH13	tr	n/d	n/d		
HH65	HH66–67	tr	n/d	n/d		
HH66	HH65, HH67	tr	n/d	n/d		
HH67	HH65–66	tr	n/d	n/d		
HH68		tr	n/d	n/d		
HH69	HH32	tr	n/d	n/d		
HH70		tr	n/d	n/d		
HH71	HH45	0.04	FFa; MAG; DAG; TAG	ruminant fat		
HH72†	HH44	0.20	FFa; MAG; DAG; TAG	ruminant fat (tr)		

Solvent extraction of lipid residues

Approximately 2 g samples were taken and their surfaces cleaned using a modelling drill to remove any exogenous surface lipids (eg soil or finger lipids due to handling). The samples were then ground to a fine powder, accurately weighed and a known amount (20 µg) of internal standard (*n*-tetratriacontane) added. The lipids were extracted with a mixture of chloroform and methanol (2:1 v/v). Following separation from the ground potsherd, the solvent was evaporated under a gentle stream of nitrogen to obtain the total lipid extract (TLE). Portions (generally one-fifth aliquots) of the extracts were then trimethylsilylated and submitted directly to analysis by GC. Where necessary, combined GC/MS analyses were also performed on trimethylsilylated aliquots of the lipid extracts enabling the elucidation of structures of components not identifiable on the basis of GC retention time alone.

Preparation of trimethylsilyl derivatives

Portions of the total lipid extracts were derivatised using N,*O*-bis(trimethylsilyl) trifluoroacetamide (20 µl; 70°C; 20 min; Sigma-Aldrich Company Ltd, Gillingham, UK) and analysed by GC and GC/MS.

Saponification of total lipid extracts

Methanolic sodium hydroxide (5% v/v) was added to the TLE and heated at 70°C for 1 h. Following neutralisation, lipids were extracted into hexane and the solvent evaporated under a gentle stream of nitrogen.

Preparation of fatty acid methyl ester (FAME) derivatives

FAMEs were prepared by reaction with BF_3-methanol (14% w/v; 2 ml; Sigma-Aldrich, Gillingham, UK) at

Table 7.12 Contexts of the analysed potsherds from Hambledon Hill

Sample no.	*Illustration no.*	*Site code*	*Find no.*	*Context*
HH1	P2	HH75		Central area, pit B F14, L3
HH2	P1	HH75		Central area, pit B F14, L3
HH3	P12	HH74	992	Main causewayed enclosure, segment 4, L4, phase V
HH4	P18	HH74	1209	Long Barrow, W ditch (segment 1), LB3 SII, phase III
HH5	P3	HH77	22	Main causewayed enclosure, site P1 bank area, L2 (topsoil)
HH6	P21	ST80	1269	Stepleton enclosure, segment 4, U8, L2A, phase IV
HH7	P13	ST79	2223	Stepleton spur pit 2A F134
HH8	P14	HH75	2120	Main causewayed enclosure, segment 8, L7A, phase II
HH9	P16	ST82	98	Stepleton spur, pit ST82 F39
HH10	P20	ST79	2585	Inner Stepleton outwork, segment 5, C4, L5A, phase III/a
HH11	P82	HH75	902	Main causewayed enclosure, segment 9, L6, L7, phases III, VI
HH12	P54	ST81	2393	Stepleton spur pit 4B F80
HH13	P77	ST79	2001	Stepleton spur pit 2A F268
HH14	P114	HH74	580	Main causewayed enclosure, segment 3, L5, phase VI
HH15	P23	ST78	703	Stepleton spur, pit 1A F57, L2
HH16	P31	HH76	2003	Main causewayed enclosure, segment 17, L8 phase VI
HH17	P37	HH75	1846	Main causewayed enclosure, segment 8, L6/7, phase III
HH18	P34	ST80	52	Stepleton spur pit 3A F94
HH19	P32	ST80	1896	Stepleton enclosure, segment 6, L4, phase III
HH20	P36	ST81	870	Stepleton enclosure, segment 7, L2, phase VI
HH21	P33	ST81	2369	Stepleton enclosure, segment 16, L3D, phase III
HH22	P38	HH77	1591	Long Barrow, W ditch (segment 1), LB2 SII, L22, phase VI
HH23	P42	ST81	962	Stepleton enclosure, segment 14, L2, phase VI
HH24	P61	ST79	2564	Stepleton spur pit 2A F201
HH25	P57	HH75	852	Main causewayed enclosure, segment 9, L7, phase III
HH26	P98	HH74	721	Main causewayed enclosure, segment 4, L5, phase VI
HH27	P107	ST81	607	Stepleton enclosure, segment 11, L2, phase VI
HH28	P108	HH76	1468	Main causewayed enclosure, segment 16, L9, phase V
HH29	P118	ST78	719	Stepleton spur pit 1A F57, L2
HH30	P41	HH77	853	Main causewayed enclosure, segment 1, F7, phase VI
HH31	P63	HH77	2089	Central area, pit N F42, L3/4
HH32	P144	ST81	518	Stepleton enclosure, segment 14, L2, phase VI
HH33	P48	ST81	1265	Stepleton enclosure, segment 8, U3, L2A, phase IV
HH34	P47	ST80	1480	Inner Stepleton outwork, segment, 4.2, L4A, phase I
HH35	P113	HH76	1099	Main causewayed enclosure, segment 18, L10, phase III
HH36	P103	ST81	1240	Stepleton enclosure, segment 8, U3 L2A, phase IV
HH37	P121	HH75	1461	Main causewayed enclosure, segment 11, L6, phaseVI
HH38	P85	ST79	1684	Stepleton spur, pit 4B F137
HH39	P109	ST81	365	Stepleton enclosure, segment 7, L2, phase VI
HH40	P102	ST80	119	Stepleton enclosure, segment 5, L1, phase VIII/a
HH41	P110	HH74	1119	Central area, pit A F64
HH42	P55	HH74	751	Main causewayed enclosure, segment 3, L5, phase VI
HH43	P51	HH77	2295	Long barrow, W ditch (segment 1), LB3 L34, phase I
HH44	P79	HH77	1924	Long barrow, E ditch (segment 3), LB5 L17, phase I
HH45	P71	HN82	310/370	Inner Hanford outwork, segment 3, L4/L3C, phase III
HH46	P68	ST79	1018	Inner Stepleton outwork, segment 6, C3, in base of L4, perhaps already in place when rubble entered ditch, phase I/phase III interface
HH47	P74	ST79	1659	Stepleton spur pit 2A F159, L1
HH48	P147	ST80	1071	Stepleton enclosure, segment 4, U8 L2A, phase IV
HH49	P150	ST80	506	Stepleton enclosure, segment 2, L1, phase VIII/a
HH50	P24	ST78	721	Stepleton spur, pit 1A F57, L2 (base)
HH51		ST81	179	Stepleton enclosure, segment 15, L1, phase VIII/a
HH52		ST81	735	Stepleton enclosure, segment 15, L3B, phase III
HH53		ST81	257	Stepleton enclosure, segment 15, L3B, phase III
HH54		ST81	938	Stepleton enclosure, segment 14, L3B, phase III
HH55		ST81	2241	Stepleton enclosure, segment 17, L3B, phase III
HH56		ST81	96	Stepleton enclosure, segment 15, L3B, phase III
HH57	P57	HH75	900	Main causewayed enclosure, segment 9, L9, phase I
HH58	P57	HH75	1169	Main causewayed enclosure, segment 9, L7, phase III
HH59	P74	ST79	1659	Stepleton spur pit 2A F159, L1
HH60	P61	ST79	2564	Stepleton spur pit 2A F201
HH61	P13	ST79	2223	Stepleton spur pit 2A F134

Sample no.	*Illustration no.*	*Site code*	*Find no.*	*Context*
HH62		ST80	1137	Inner Stepleton outwork, segment 4.2, U4, L4A, phase I
HH63	P21	ST80	1269	Stepleton enclosure, segment 4, U8, L2A, phase IV
HH64	P77	ST79	2035	Stepleton spur pit 2A F268
HH65	P46	WOWK82	121	Inner south cross-dyke, segment 2, L7, phase VI
HH66	P46	WOWK82	115	Inner south cross-dyke, segment 2, L7, phase VI
HH67	P46	WOWK82	29	Inner south cross-dyke, segment 2, L7, phase VI
HH68	P11	HH77	2184	Central area, pit N F82, L3
HH69	P144	ST81	518	Stepleton enclosure, segment 14, L2, phase VI
HH70		HH77	564	Inner south cross-dyke, segment 1, L8, phase VI
HH71	P71	HH82	369	Inner Hanford outwork, segment 3, L3C, phase III
HH72	P79	HH77	1924	Long barrow, E ditch (segment 3), LB5 L17, phase I

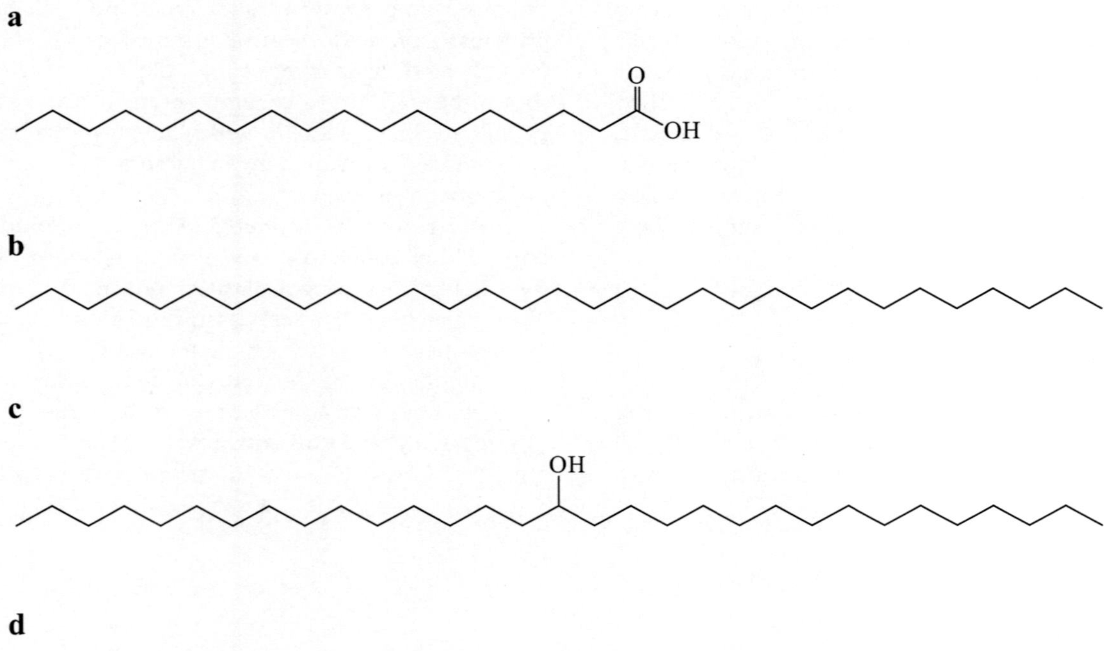

Fig 7.25 Some commonly occurring lipids: a) n-octadecanoic acid ($C_{18:0}$ fatty acid), b) n-untriacosane (C_{31} alkane), c) n-)untriacosan-16-ol (C_{31} alcohol), d) n-untriacosan-16-one (C_{31} ketone), e) tripalmitin (C_{48} triacylglycerol), and f) triacosanyl palmitate (C_{46} palmitic wax ester).

70°C for 1 h. The methyl ester derivatives were extracted with chloroform and the solvent removed under nitrogen. FAMEs were re-dissolved into hexane for analysis by GC and GC-C-IRMS.

Preparation of FAME derivatives for compound-specific radiocarbon dating

The FAMEs were prepared as described by Stott *et al* (2001). The individual fatty acids were isolated via preparative capillary gas chromatography (PCGC) comprising a Hewlett Packard 7673 autosampler coupled to a Hewlett Packard 5890 Series II GC interfaced to a Gerstal preparative fraction collector. Separations were achieved using a 'megabore' fused silica capillary column (30 m × 0.53 mm i.d.) coated with a dimethyl polysiloxane stationary phase (DB-1, 0.5 mm film thickness). Typically *c* 100 preparative 'runs' were required to isolate sufficient (>200 μg per compound) of each component for accelerator mass spectrometry (AMS) at the Oxford Radiocarbon Accelerator.

7.3.3 Results

The GC and GC/MS analyses served to quantify and identify compounds in the lipid extract, such that it is possible to determine the presence of: (i) an animal fat or plant oil, (ii) plant epicuticular waxes, (iii) beeswax or other sealants, and/or (iv) mid-chain ketones that indicate that the vessel has been subjected to heating to >300°C (Evershed *et al* 1995; Raven *et al* 1997). Furthermore, GC-C-IRMS analyses can distinguish between ruminant and non-ruminant adipose fats and dairy fats by determining the $\delta^{13}C_{16:0}$, $\delta^{13}C_{18:0}$ and ($\delta^{13}C_{18:0}$–$\delta^{13}C_{16:0}$) values.

GC analyses were performed on the solvent extracts of a sub-sample of each potsherd. The results of screening by GC are summarised in Table 7.11 on a sample-by-sample basis, giving the total lipid concentration per gram of powdered sherd, and a brief description of the compounds detected. Where sufficient concentrations of lipid were present in the extracts, $\delta^{13}C$ values of the principal fatty acids were determined by GC-C-IRMS (as indicated by an asterisk in Table 7.11). Figure 7.26 shows the partial gas chromatogram of the total lipid extract of sherd HH17, which displays the range of compounds that were detected amongst the extracts of potsherds investigated.

Forty-two of the 72 sherds (58%) from Hambledon Hill yielded concentrations of lipid residues of up to 0.89 mg g^{-1} dry weight of sherd (mean 0.11 mg g^{-1}). The majority of extracts comprised degraded animal fat residues which are characterised by (a) relatively high abundances of $C_{18:0}$ fatty acid, (b) monoacylglycerols with acyl carbon number in the range of C_{32} to C_{34}, (c) diacylglycerols with acyl carbon number in the region of C_{32} to C_{36} and (d) triacylglycerols with acyl

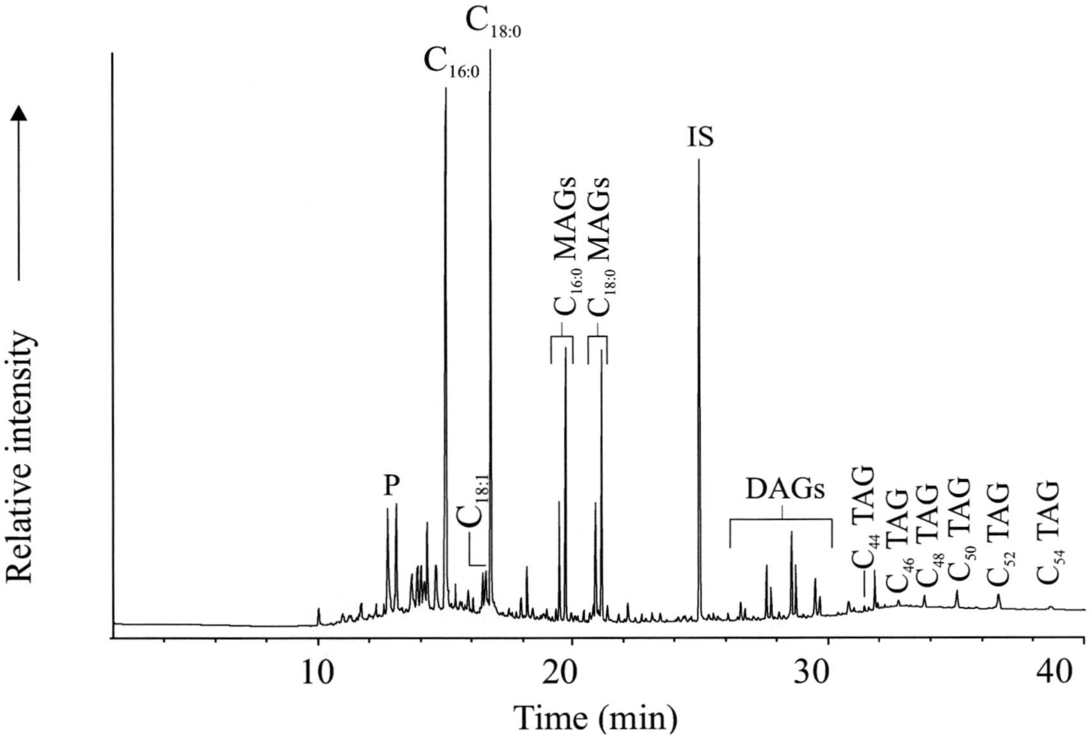

Fig 7.26 Partial HTGC profile of the trimethylsilylated total lipid extract from sample HH17, containing lipid components characteristic of a degraded animal fat. Key: FAx:y are free fatty acids of carbon length x, and degree of unsaturation y. $C_{X:0}$ MAGs are monoacylglycerols of carbon length x, DAGs are diacylglycerols, and C_x TAG are triacylglycerols of carbon length x. IS is the internal standard (C^{34} n-alkane). P is a plasticiser probably originating from the plastic bags in which the sherds were originally stored in the museum.

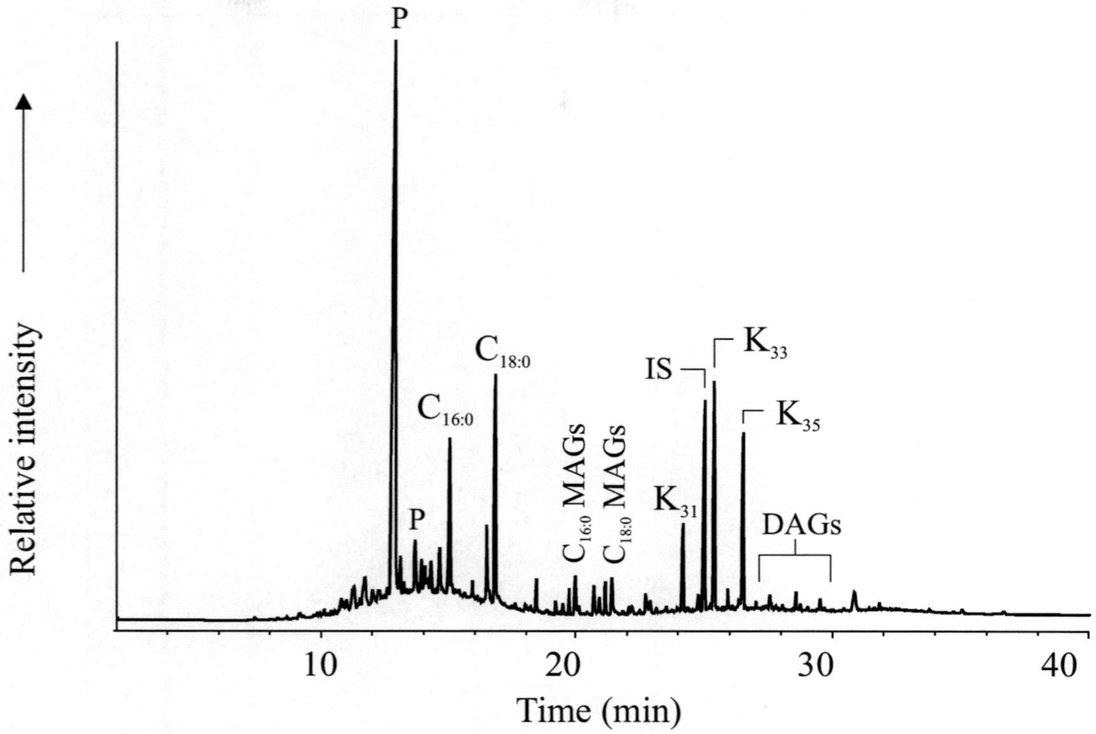

Fig 7.27 Partial HTGC profile of the trimethylsilylated total lipid extract from sample HH14, containing lipid components characteristic of a degraded animal fat. Key: FAx:y are free fatty acids of carbon length x, and degree of unsaturation y. $C_{X:0}$ MAGs are monoacylglycerols of carbon length x, DAGs are diacylglycerols, and K_x are mid-chain ketones of carbon length x. IS is the internal standard (C_{34} n-alkane). P is a plasticiser probably originating from the plastic bags in which the sherds were originally stored in the museum.

$$CH_3(CH_2)_nCO_2H + CH_3(CH_2)_mCO_2H \xrightarrow[-CO_2,\ -H_2O]{\Delta,\ >300^{\circ}C} CH_3(CH_2)_nC(=O)(CH_2)_mCH_3$$

Fig 7.28 The ketonic decarboxylation of free fatty acids which leads to the formation of ketones by condensation of the fatty acids. The reaction is catalysed by metal oxides and proceeds at temperatures in excess of 300°C. The subscripts n and m correspond to alkyl chain lengths in the range 13–16 (Evershed et al *1995; Raven* et al *1997).*

carbon number in the range of C_{46} to C_{54} with C_{48} to C_{52} predominating (eg Fig 7.26). The TAG distributions seen in fresh milk fat contrast to those detected in adipose fats in that they are characteristically wide, owing to the inclusion of lower molecular weight (minor) TAGs (C_{40} to C_{44}). During vessel use/burial, these lower molecular weight TAGs are preferentially lost (Dudd and Evershed 1998), resulting in a degraded TAG distribution that resembles that of a ruminant adipose fat. Indeed, neither these lower molecular weight TAGs, nor the short chain fatty acids derived from them, were detected in any of the sherds.

Direct evidence for the heating of the vessels to high temperatures was observed in 12 (17%) of the vessels, in the form of mid-chain ketones (eg the sherd shown in Fig 7.27). Ketones are formed through the heating of free fatty acids in the presence of clay minerals at temperatures in excess of 300°C (Evershed *et al* 1995; Raven *et al* 1997), this reaction is shown in Figure 7.28.

The primary lipid constituents of epicuticular leaf waxes are *n*-alkanes, primary alcohols and wax esters. *n*-Alkanes and alcohols were detected in five of the sherds, three of which also contained wax esters, thereby indicating the processing of plants in these vessels (see Table 7.11).

Figure 7.29 shows a graph of the $\delta^{13}C_{18:0}$ versus $\delta^{13}C_{16:0}$ values for the 27 extracts that contained significant concentrations of these fatty acids. Values obtained for modern reference animal fats from the major domesticated animals exploited in British prehistory are grouped within ellipses. Onto this, values for the archaeological sherds have been overlaid. The $\delta^{13}C$ values for the $C_{18:0}$ fatty acid are more depleted in milk fats than in ruminant adipose fats, thus enabling distinctions to be drawn between milk and adipose fats from ruminant animals (Dudd and Evershed 1998). This is witnessed in the 2.3‰ shift between the centroids of the reference ruminant adipose fat and ruminant dairy

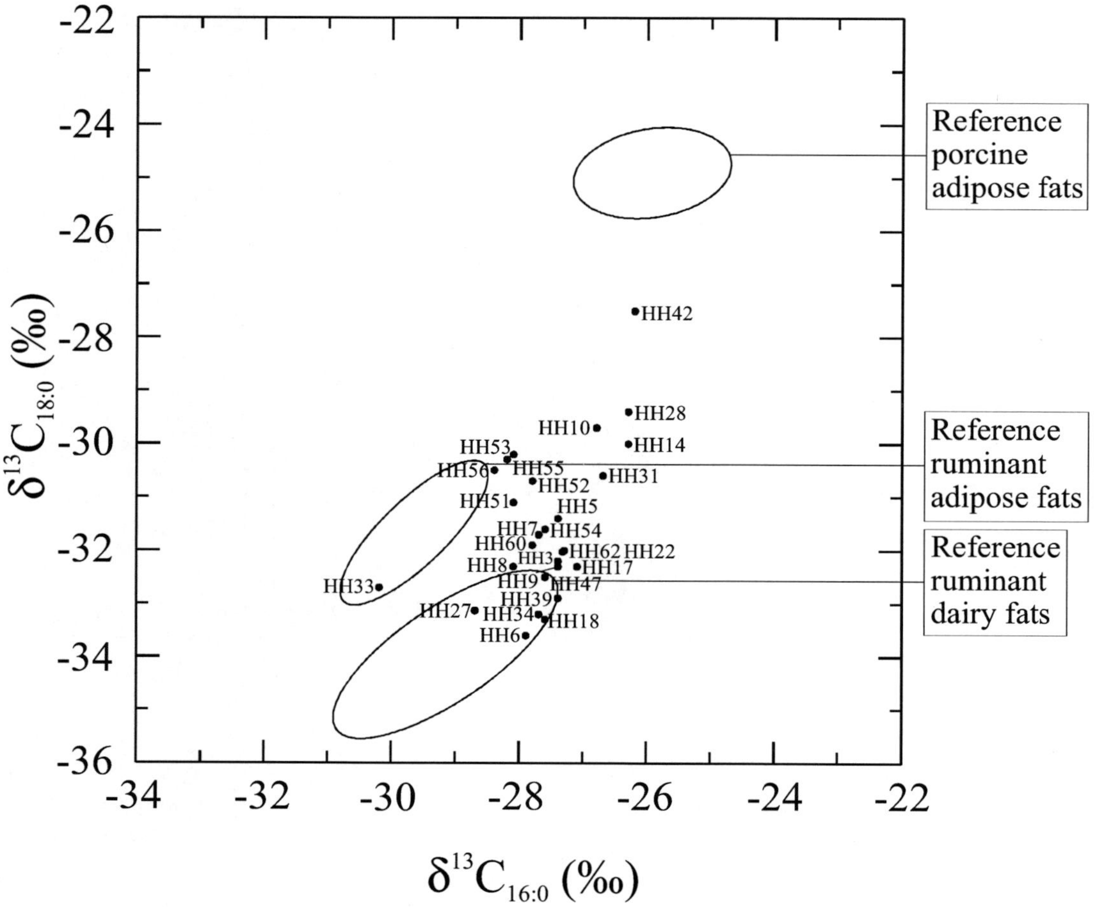

*Fig 7.29 Plot of the $\delta^{13}C$ values of the fatty acid methyl esters prepared from lipid extracts from the Hambledon Hill assemblage. The reference fats are represented by confidence ellipses (1 standard deviation). Sherds that plot in between the ruminant and non-ruminant reference fats are indicative of the mixing of these two fats in the pottery vessel. The carbon stable isotope values have been corrected for the contribution of carbon from the derivatising methyl group and expressed as being relative to the v-PDB standard (*Bellemnitella americana*), $\delta^{13}C = 1000[(R_{sample}-R_{standard})/R_{standard}]$, where R is $^{13}C/^{12}C$ in per mil (‰). All the animals were raised on C_3 diets. The $\delta^{13}C$ values for the fatty acids have been adjusted for post-Industrial Revolution effects of fossil fuel burning, which has led to more depleted atmospheric $\delta^{13}CO_2$ values, and has been calculated to be 1.2‰ (Friedli* et al *1986). Instrumental precision is ±0.3‰.*

fat ellipses. The less depleted $\delta^{13}C$ values seen for the fatty acids in non-ruminant fats compared to those in ruminant fats, are believed to be due to differences in diet and in the metabolic and biochemical processes involved in the formation of body fats in ruminant and non-ruminant animals.

Seven of the sherds plot within the dairy fat field, and a further nine plot just outside of the ellipse (but still have $\delta^{13}C_{18:0}$–$\delta^{13}C_{16:0}$ values in the range of –4.1‰ to –5.5‰, which is characteristic of dairy fats). Two of the sherds plot within/close to the ruminant adipose fat ellipse. A further two sherds plot along the axis of the ruminant adipose reference fat ellipse, and are likely to be indicative of predominantly bovine/ovine adipose fats, as determined by their $\delta^{13}C_{18:0}$–$\delta^{13}C_{16:0}$ values. None of the sherds plot within the porcine adipose fat field; however, seven sherds plot in the area of the graph associated with mixed ruminant and non-ruminant adipose fats. This mixing may have occurred either contemporaneously or through re-use of the vessels in antiquity.

Three of the sherds were selected for compound-specific ^{14}C dating (samples HH54, HH56 and HH72; labelled † in Table 7.11) since these were those yielding the highest abundances of free fatty acids and/or fatty acyl lipids. The $C_{16:0}$ and $C_{18:0}$ fatty acid components were isolated (as their methyl ester derivatives) and submitted for compound-specific AMS dating. The radiocarbon dates obtained (corrected for the derivatising methanol) are given in Table 7.13.

7.3.4 Discussion

The lipids contained in the pottery from Hambledon Hill are reasonably well preserved compared to other prehistoric sites we have investigated. It is noteworthy that TAGs are still detectable in significant abundances in 15 out of 72 (21%) of the sherds. Some of the sherds analysed herein originated from the same vessel (as shown in Table 7.11) and it is reassuring that similar results were obtained for these replicate analyses

Table 7.13 Compound-specific radiocarbon dates of absorbed lipid residues in pottery vessels

*Corrected for contribution from the derivatisation reagent

Sample	*Target fatty acid*	*Date±error BP**	*Calibrated date (2σ) BC**	*OxA-X sample codes*	*Context*
HH54	$C_{16:0}$	4280±60	3090–2670	806-10	Stepleton enclosure, segment 14, L3B, phase III
	$C_{18:0}$	4550±90	3550–2900	806-11	
HH56	$C_{16:0}$	4780±80	3700–3370	807-12	Stepleton enclosure, segment 15, L3B, phase III
	$C_{18:0}$	4840±60	3770–3380	807-13	
HH72	$C_{18:0}$	4540±80	3550–2900	849-10	South long barrow, E ditch (segment 3), LB5, L17, phase I

although, not unexpectedly, the lipid concentrations were found to differ, probably as a result of either the physical behaviour of lipid during vessel use, ie lipid concentrations have been shown to vary significantly down the profile of specific vessel forms (Charters *et al* 1993; Charters *et al* 1995), and/or localised differences in the burial environment which affect preservation. However, it should be noted that we generally attempt to minimise variations related to use by only sampling rim/upper body sherds.

The $\delta^{13}C$ values of the fatty acids extracted from the sherds are indicative of a mixed economy, and are consistent with the mixing of both non-ruminant (porcine) and ruminant fats, as well as ruminant adipose and dairy fats. Seven (26%) of the sherds contain fatty acids with $\delta^{13}C$ values indicative of dairy fats, and a further nine probably also contain fatty acids of predominantly a dairy fat origin (based on their $\delta^{13}C_{18:0}$–$\delta^{13}C_{16:0}$ values). Unlike the fatty acyl lipid distributions (ratios of fatty and acid abundances and TAG distributions) the $\delta^{13}C$ values provide a robust chemical signal unaffected by decay, thus, providing direct evidence for the presence of dairy fats in these latter sherds.

Fifteen per cent of the sherds contained predominantly ruminant adipose fats, but none of the sherds contained fatty acids with $\delta^{13}C$ values indicative of purely a non-ruminant (eg porcine) fat. However, out of the 27 sherds that contained sufficient concentrations of fatty acids for GC-C-IRMS analysis, seven (26%) contained fatty acids that were characteristic of the mixing of ruminant and non-ruminant fats. This is in accordance with the faunal evidence, which indicates a predominance of cattle bone at the site, although in some contexts large quantities of pig bones have been detected (Legge 1981a; see Legge Ch 8). Lipids characteristic of higher plants were detected in five of the sherds, thereby indicating the mixing of animal products (both dairy and adipose fats) and plant lipids through vessel use and/or re-use in antiquity.

The compound-specific ^{14}C dates obtained for the three sherds (Table 7.13) are in accordance with the early Neolithic date of the site. It should be emphasised that these are among the first compound-specific dates reported for archaeological pottery and were recorded during research aimed at developing this as a new approach to dating archaeological pottery. This development work is still in progress and improvements in precision are anticipated.

In summary, 42 out of 72 (58%) of the sherds contained significant lipid concentrations, of which 27 exhibited free/bound fatty acids in sufficiently high abundances for isotopic analysis. Of these, 26% (7 out of 27) contained predominantly dairy fats, 7% (2/27) contained ruminant adipose fats, and 67% (18 out of 27) contained mixtures of non-ruminant and ruminant (adipose and dairy) fats. The presence of dairy fats in at least 26% of the vessels suggests that dairying was a very important element of animal husbandry at Hambledon Hill. Similar results have also been obtained from other early Neolithic British sites such as Windmill Hill, where 54% of the sherds that contained fatty acid residues were found to have been used in the processing of dairy products, and from Eton Rowing Lake where 78% of the sherds that contained fatty acid residues were found to have been used in the processing of dairy products (Copley *et al* 2003). These results confirm that the processing of dairy products in vessels, such as those analysed herein, was widespread from the early Neolithic in southern Britain.

8 Livestock and Neolithic society at Hambledon Hill

A J Legge

8.1 The Neolithic ditches and pits

8.1.1 Introduction

The animal bones come from the two Neolithic causewayed enclosures with their associated features and a Neolithic long barrow. The Neolithic enclosure ditches are made up of many separate segments and the stratification in these is complex as a result of frequent recutting in Neolithic times, as is described elsewhere in this volume. Thus, although the bone sample is large, there are relatively few instances in which a single layer from any one feature presented a sufficient number of bones for numerical analysis to have much meaning at that level. In consequence much of the numerical analysis in part 1 of this report (8.1.2) is based upon combined samples, for example treating all bones from one phase in an entire ditch circuit as a single sample. Part 2 of the report (8.1.3) considers bone representation in smaller units of the stratigraphy and, where possible, at the level of single features. The stratigraphic analysis shows that some proportion of the bone will have been disturbed and redeposited and, while in almost all cases the Neolithic association is secure, there are relatively few deposits which are the result of a discrete period of human activity.

Method of recording the sample

All identifiable bones were recorded by their stratigraphic provenance and then according to the species identified, the bone element or part element, the side of the body, fusion state, and other conditions such as gnawing, burning, cut or chop marks and pathology. Where the term 'referred' is used below, this indicates that some poorly preserved bones are attributed to the species concerned, but with less than the usual level of confidence. All records were made in simple numerical codes that were counted and sorted using a commercially available database package. During the excavation it was recognised that some groups of bones were in articulation and these were carefully excavated and recorded and were bagged together. In other instances groups of bones were identified during the bench analysis for which, by the closeness of fit between complex joint surfaces, a record of 'probable articulation' could be made with some degree of confidence. This record is of obvious importance in the interpretation of the site. Subsequently, the use of bones for radiocarbon dating selected from articulated – and thus undisturbed – bone groups has resolved certain problems raised in the dating of charcoal samples from the site (Ch 4).

The total identified bone sample from the Neolithic sites is 6340 post-cranial bone fragments and 1522 part tooth rows and loose teeth. The mandibles show different degrees of fragmentation from one context to another, but the samples were sufficiently intact for age determinations to be made with confidence. On the other hand, crania and maxillary tooth rows were heavily fragmented, and most upper teeth were found loose, as is common in prehistoric bone samples from southern Britain and elsewhere. The tooth counts in the tables below are therefore based upon complete or partially complete mandibular tooth rows which contain the lower third deciduous (dp_4) and/or permanent lower third molars (M_3). Loose specimens of these same teeth are also incorporated in the mandibular counts, with due allowance for the short period of overlap when both teeth are present in the mandible.

Preservation of the bone sample

The bone sample from the hilltop is generally well preserved and it was skilfully excavated under good stratigraphic control. The best preservation is found in the deeper ditch segments and in the pits where the bone was close to, or in contact with, the basal chalk. In such cases the bone preservation is almost perfect and surface modifications such as cut-marks or gnawing by carnivores and other mammals can readily be identified. In more superficial deposits and in some rather loose chalk rubble ditch fills there has been some degree of erosion of the bone surface by percolating water and other agencies. In these specimens, cut-marks are likely to be obscured and the presence of dog gnawing cannot be identified with confidence so that the recorded frequency of these activities must be regarded as a minimum statement.

Figure 8.1 shows the observed frequency of dog gnawing on pig, cattle and caprine bones from the ditches and from the pits at each site, in each case as a proportion of the identified post-cranial bones of the identified species. The overall frequency of gnawing is low. The Stepleton enclosure and inner outwork show the highest incidence, which is significantly greater there than elsewhere in the complex. In the Stepleton ditches, 8% of pig bones, 6% of cattle bones and 3% of caprine bones are gnawed whereas at the other sites only cattle bones show about 2.5–3% incidence of gnawing and other species show little or none.

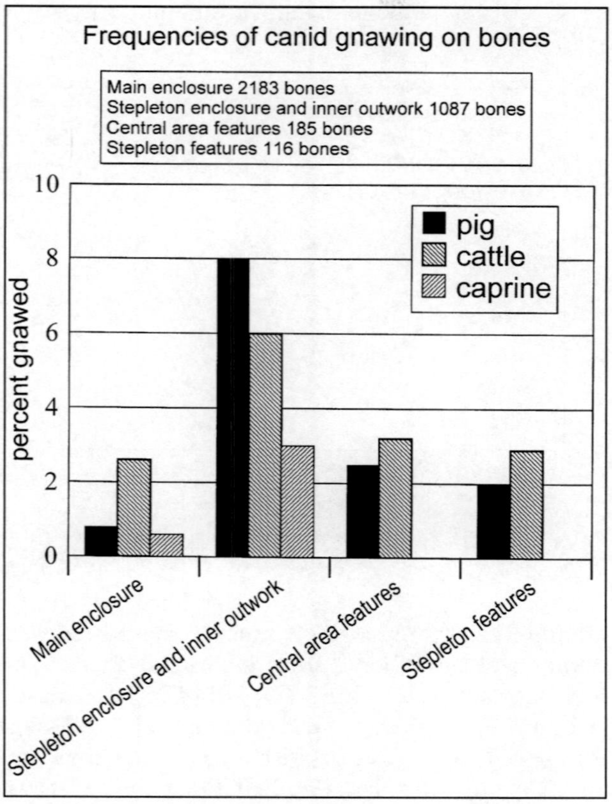

Fig 8.1 Frequencies of canid gnawing on the bones of three species.

The nature of the site was such that some bones appear to have been exposed on the ground surface for some time before being buried, while other bones were directly deposited in ditch segments or pits and rapidly buried. Significantly higher levels of dog gnawing were noted on the small early Iron Age assemblage excavated from the hillfort (8.3), where 18% of pig bones, 15% of cattle bones and 9% of caprine bones were gnawed. Although the variable state of preservation of the Hambledon bone assemblage places inevitable limitations on the observation of dog gnawing, it would appear that dogs were not a major agency in the destruction of bone at the site. However, the animal bone, as is the case with the human bone at the site, was doubtless dispersed in part by the activities of dogs.

8.1.2 Results part 1. The species found

At the gross level, the fauna of both areas is heavily dominated by large cattle, which make up 60–70% of the identified bones and jaws in most contexts. The pig is second in abundance at about 20–30% of the identified bones and caprines form 15–20%. The red deer is present in a small proportion, though the bones are more abundant on the Stepleton spur than in the central area. Antlers of red deer were commonly found but these were clearly imported for use as artefacts and are separately treated below. The proportions of the common species vary considerably in particular contexts and in a few of these pig bones are more common than those of cattle. The small number of bones identified from the Bronze Age site of Everley Water Meadow does not allow conclusions to be made about the faunal composition at that time. The bones from the early Iron Age house excavated at the hill fort are heavily dominated by caprines and pig.

Domestic mammals

The predominant species in the entire Neolithic fauna, though not in every context, is that of domestic cattle, *Bos taurus*. The bones of domestic pigs (*Sus scrofa*) are also common and from the counts of both post-cranial bones and from the mandibles, these are second in numerical abundance when averaged across the entirety of each site. However, an important point should be noted here. At both enclosures cattle form the largest proportion of the faunas from the numbers of identified post-cranial bones but are rather less well represented by identified mandibles. Pigs, on the other hand, are better represented by the counts of identified mandibles and on this basis even exceed cattle on the Stepleton spur (Fig 8.2). In general, both caprines and pigs have higher representations from mandible counts than from post-cranial bones, which suggests a higher

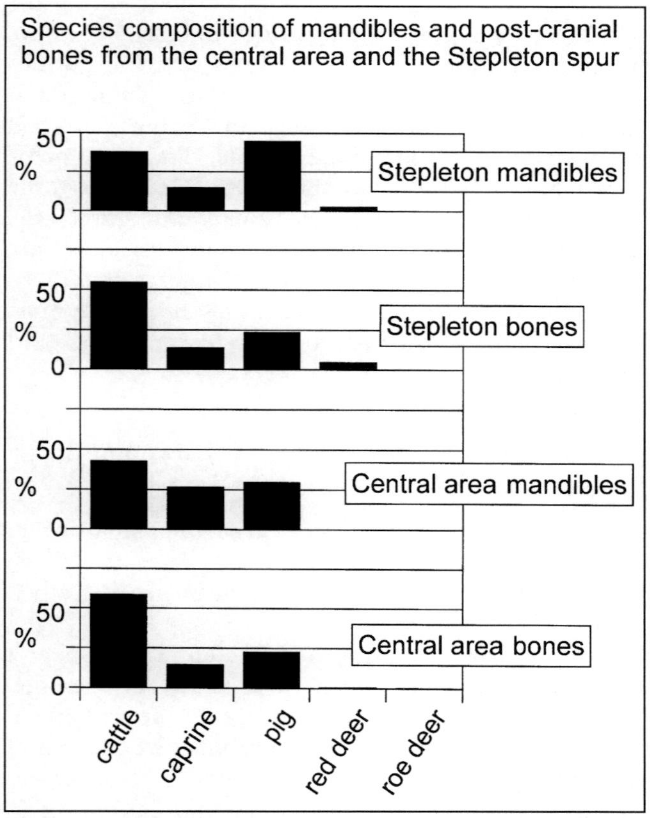

Fig 8.2 Species composition as expressed by frequencies of identified mandibles and post-cranial bones from the central area and the Stepleton spur.

level of attrition working on the smaller bones, especially in the main causewayed enclosure ditch fills. The larger and more robust cattle bones show a better survival in relation to the mandibles, and, especially where the pig is concerned, this is related to the very young ages at which these were killed. Most pigs were infantile or juvenile at death and thus with skeletons that were largely unfused. The attrition of the bone sample, both by dogs and by adverse burial conditions, was high under such circumstances. This aspect of the bone remains is further considered below.

Domestic sheep and goat are grouped below as 'caprines,' and in almost all contexts these are the least abundant of the three domestic food species. Sheep (*Ovis aries*) form more than 98% of those caprine bones that can be reliably identified to the species level. The goat (*Capra hircus*) is certainly present in the Neolithic fauna, though the species was rather uncommon. The bones of domestic dogs, *Canis lupus familiaris*, were found widely among the sites at Hambledon, though their bones were not found in all contexts. The presence of cut-marks on the dog bones at points not likely to be associated with skinning alone is suggestive that these too were eaten, though this cannot be proven.

Wild mammals

A small proportion of the cattle bones are those of the wild ancestral species *Bos primigenius* and, of the pig bones, a few bones were identified as wild pig on the basis of large size. The bones of red deer (*Cervus elaphus*) and roe deer (*Capreolus capreolus*) were found at most sites within the Neolithic complex but as a small proportion of the identified sample. There are occasional finds of bones from the beaver (*Castor fiber*), the badger (*Meles meles*), the otter (*Lutra lutra*) and the fox (*Vulpes vulpes*). Bones from the smaller mammals are limited to occasional specimens from the hare (*Lepus europaeus*), voles (mostly *Arvicola terrestris*), the mole (*Talpa europaea)*, the pine marten (*Martes martes*) and the red squirrel (*Sciurus vulgaris*).

Cattle: bone measurements, body size and the proportion of sexes in the cull

All bone measurements were taken in mm, using in part the measurements designated by Dreisch (1976). Other measurements that were taken are described here.

It has long been known that adult cattle show a marked sexual dimorphism, in contrast, for example, to sheep, which do not. Because of this, the sex ratio in the adult cattle cull can be determined by the use of the appropriate bone measurements. The measurements taken from the bones of male cattle are, in almost all instances, significantly larger than those of female cattle. When these measurements are plotted as a scatter diagram of two measurements or even as a histogram using only a single measurement, the measurements of cattle bones show a bimodal distribution when both sexes are found (Degerbøl 1970; Grigson 1982, 1999; Higham 1968; Higham and Message 1969; Jewell 1963a; Legge 1981b; 1992). Where a proportion of the wild, large-bodied *Bos primigenius* was also killed, the situation is more complex and the resulting scatter is more difficult to interpret. Where a single measurement is plotted, for example the articular width of the distal metacarpal or distal humerus, against the numbers of specimens in defined size classes, the diagram is likely to show three peaks of abundance. This is because the females of the wild form and the males of the domestic form show similar widths so that the three groups are (a) smallest – domestic females, (b) intermediate – domestic males and wild females, and (c) largest – wild males.

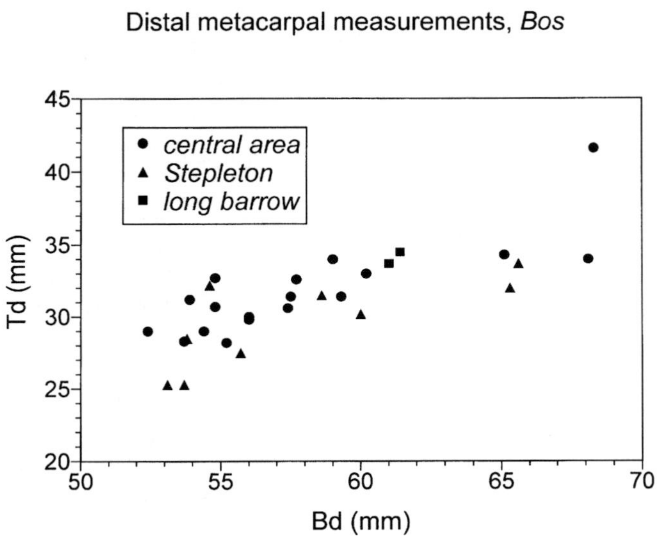

Fig 8.3 Measurements of distal metacarpals of cattle, Bos.

Figure 8.3 shows the scatter of the distal metacarpal measurements, and the interpretation of the diagram is relatively straightforward. Twenty-four distal metacarpals have Bd measurements below 63 mm, and Td measurements below 35 mm (fifteen central area, seven Stepleton and two long barrow). These are interpreted as being the females of domestic cattle, those killed after the age of 30 months or so when the distal metacarpal undergoes bone fusion. In addition to these, there are two further specimens, not shown on the diagram, which have Bd measurements of about 53 mm but on which damage prevented the Td measurement being taken. These obviously also belong to the female group. To the right of the female group are the metacarpals of four larger cattle (two from the central area and two from Stepleton) and these are interpreted as being from adult males. A single large metacarpal, with an Td measurement of more than 40 mm, falls outside these groups, with measurements within the range of known *Bos primigenius* females. The diagram thus shows 24 female domestic cattle to 4 male, a ratio of 6 female cattle to each male.

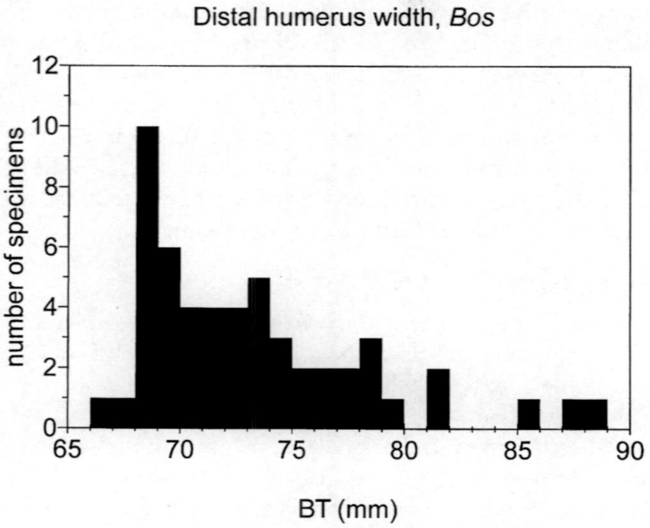

Fig 8.4 The distal humerus widths of Bos.

The measurements of the distal humerus offer a larger sample of both domestic and wild cattle. It may be noted that this bone is not ideal for this type of analysis, as it fuses early in the animal's life and it is very probably subject to some degree of post-fusion bone growth. As many of the cattle were killed when young, a significant proportion of the distal humeri would have been recently fused, and thus subject to further growth. In consequence of this, the width measurement, when taken alone, is problematic to interpret. This is illustrated in Figure 8.4, where the BT measurement is plotted in 2 mm size classes against the number of specimens falling in each size class. The histogram shows a bias towards the smaller animals, and those with BT measurements below 78 mm or so are the putative domestic cows. The larger animals, with measurements of 78 mm and upwards, are comparatively few and these will be both domestic males and an uncertain proportion of wild *Bos primigenius*.

These data can be better interpreted by the means of a scatter diagram, as is shown in Figure 8.5. Here the same width measurement, BT, is plotted against a second measurement, designated as HT, using the same sample of *Bos* distal humeri. This measurement is not featured in Dreisch (1976), but is taken on the medial margin of the distal humerus, the line of the measurement being parallel to the long axis of the bone. Two groups can be discerned on the basis of their measurements. The specimens which have an HT measurement of *less* than 46 mm are interpreted as being those from domestic cattle. This group can be further subdivided. Those having a BT measurement of less than 75 mm are interpreted as coming from the females, while those being larger than this dimension (but still with an HT measurement of less than 46 mm) are interpreted as the domestic males. It is not claimed here that this division is absolute, especially remembering the problems of possible post-fusion growth shown by the distal humerus as outlined above, and the sex of specimens with a BT measurement of a few millimetres above or below 75 mm is, of course, uncertain. However, as with the metacarpal measurements, the scatter shows a marked bias towards the smaller females. There is then a group of larger animals, in which specimens have an HT measurement of 48 mm and above, and these are interpreted as being examples of wild cattle, *Bos primigenius*. These fall within the known size range of Danish *Bos primigenius* as were published by Degerbøl (1970). As he noted, there is a significant difference in the form of the distal humerus

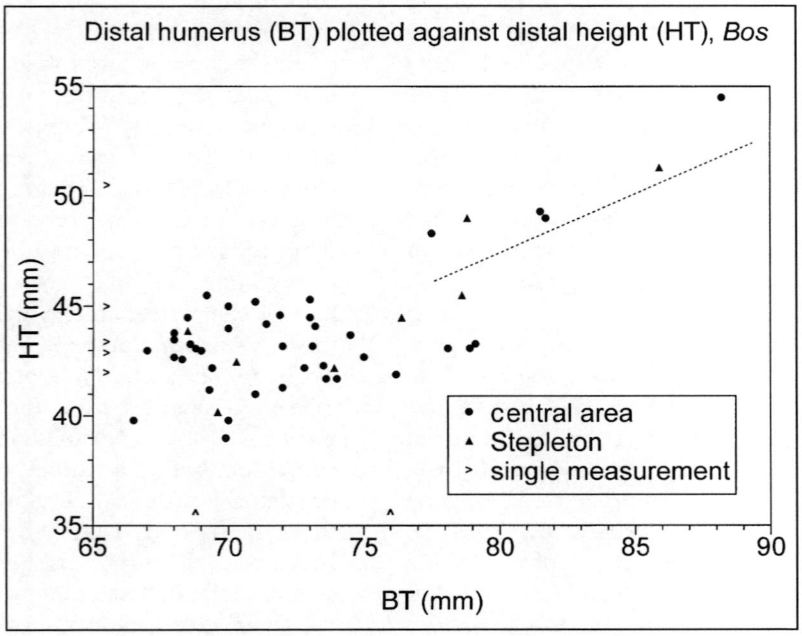

Fig 8.5 Distal humerus width plotted against height, Bos. *The six specimens falling above the broken line are interpreted as being from* Bos primigenius.

articulation between male domestic cattle and female *Bos primigenius*. Significantly, Neolithic male domestic cattle usually show a similar range of articular *width* (BT) to female wild cattle, but the *thickness* (HT) measurement is proportionately greater in both males and females of the wild form of cattle. This method has been used to discriminate between the distal humeri of wild and domestic cattle from the Neolithic site of Selevac in Serbia (Legge 1990), and the same method is applied here to the data from Hambledon Hill. The six specimens showing the more robust HT measurements of 48 mm or greater (four central area, two Stepleton) are interpreted as being both males and females of *Bos primigenius*.

There are some additional specimens included in the diagram from which only one measurement was possible. These are shown as open symbols at the axis for which that measurement was taken. The HT measurement shows an additional four female domestic cattle and one of *Bos primigenius*, while the BT measurement adds a further two female domestic cattle. The distal humerus measurements are thus interpreted as being from 49 domestic cattle, of which 42 or so were female and five to seven were male, a female:male ratio again of 6:1 or 7:1. The seven large cattle (including one specimen with an HT measurement of 50.5 mm) are interpreted as *Bos primigenius*, with both sexes being about equally represented.

Figures 8.3–5 thus show that the domestic cattle were killed in a female:male ratio of about 6:1. Other Neolithic causewayed enclosures and henge monuments have also been found to have a predominance of female cattle in the cull population, as was shown by Grigson (1965; 1982; 1999).

The reasons that underlie the predominance of female cattle bones at Hambledon and other sites are of obvious interest in the interpretation of the earlier Neolithic economy. In the demonstrations of the sex ratio from cattle limb bones shown above, only fully fused specimens were measured; that is, those where the diaphysis (shaft) and epiphysis (the joint surface) are fused together and the cartilaginous junction at this point in the immature mammal is wholly eliminated. Ideally the measurements will be taken from those bones which fuse later in the animal's life, when growth is largely, though not necessarily entirely, complete. A further caution is necessary. The survival of bones in archaeological assemblages is greatly increased after fusion, when the bone attains its full hardness and density. Before this event the more weakly ossified end parts of the bone are readily destroyed, as any large pet dog will willingly demonstrate for its owner. Gnawed bones, from a well-preserved sample, can easily be recognised by their scored and channelled surface. However, while the ideal approach would combine these facts and measure only a well-preserved and numerous sample of late-fusing bones, this is seldom possible. Post-fusion growth in early-fusing bones means that their measurements will give less clear-cut patterns than those based upon data from later-fusing bones, yet the nature of bone survival is such that seldom are there sufficient measurable (undamaged) late-fusing bones to provide a sufficient sample. In spite of these limitations, it is clear that the distal humerus measurements are sufficiently dimorphic that the adult sex ratio can be determined from these and that most of the cull cattle at Hambledon were female.

The age structure of the cull

The attribution of an age at death to the mandibles of domestic mammals in archaeological samples has been the subject of much debate in recent decades. Silver (1969) published tabulations of the ages attributed to tooth eruption events in cattle, caprines and pig, which were derived from recent and earlier veterinary publications. These data appeared to show that tooth eruption in domestic mammals was observed to be significantly slower in the eighteenth and nineteenth centuries than is found in the same species in more recent times. He further suggested that these 'long' ages should be applied to domestic mammal bones of archaeological origin, suggesting that the advantages of modern breeding and feeding would not then have been apparent, and bodily development consequently slower. In spite of the assumptions contained in this belief, it was for some time accepted that the 'long' tooth eruption ages should be applied to archaeological samples. Not until the 1980s was this assumption questioned.

New data on tooth eruption ages were gathered with specific archaeological approaches in mind (Bull and Payne 1982; Deniz and Payne 1982; Beasley *et al* 1984). Further, detailed reviews of the early literature on which Silver's paper was based showed that some of these sources were highly doubtful and were usually copied without acknowledgement from yet earlier sources (Legge 1992, 18–20). A close review of the relevant literature showed that the only reliable and original source for tooth eruption events in early nineteenth-century domestic mammals was that of Simonds (1854). Even this work was republished by Brown (1902) with scant acknowledgement to the original. In his comprehensive study, Simonds gave tooth eruption ages, based on the direct observation of a very large sample of known-age cattle from the first half of the nineteenth century, that are the same as those found in domestic cattle now. Further, recent work on the development of cattle dentition from well-preserved samples from the Bronze Age middens at Grime's Graves, Norfolk, involving both X-ray and cementum banding studies, showed that teeth in these prehistoric cattle had developed at the same time as do those in modern cattle (Beasley *et al* forthcoming). From this, the ages attributed here to tooth eruption events in the domestic mammals found at Hambledon are those given by Simonds (1854). While objection may be raised that tooth *wear* rates could have differed between sites, the use of these attributed ages is defended on the grounds that (a) much of the discussion below concerns tooth *eruption* and not tooth wear, and (b) even the attribution of age-related wear stages gives a more realistic slaughter pattern than does the use of arbitrary wear stages of unequal and unknown duration.

The complexity of the Hambledon sites means that the sample, though large, is divided between many different contexts. Few of these have sufficient cattle mandibles and teeth to provide a sample with numerical meaning. Inevitably some samples must be grouped by phase or type of feature to provide a background against which subsamples from more limited areas or phases can be tested. As shown above, cattle were the predominant species found in the excavations when considered in terms of identified bone numbers. Obviously the large size of Neolithic cattle means that, in terms of biomass, this species was by far of the greatest importance at the site. The age structure of the population is therefore of particular interest in reflecting the economic and social strategy that underlay the slaughter policy.

Mandible fragments which contain several teeth can be quite closely aged. Many of the Hambledon mandibles were found to be fragmented and, in consequence, large numbers of loose teeth were also identified. The eruption and wear patterns shown by the more intact specimens were used to attribute ages to the more fragmented molars and the isolated teeth, in particular the lower third deciduous (milk) molars and lower third permanent molars, respectively noted here below as dp_4 and M_3. Care was taken to exclude any dp_4 which showed the root damage that is caused by the eruption of the fourth permanent premolar (P_4) which replaces it; such teeth were likely to have fallen from the mouths of living animals. The cattle mandibles and teeth were placed into one of nine age classes which span from birth to senescence (Legge 1992, 20–25), where the ages attributed to certain events are set out in some detail.

The cattle from all sites at Hambledon Hill show a restricted age distribution and were found to be predominantly from their early adult years (Fig 8.5). The most common wear state found for the M_3 was characteristic of an age of 18–36 months, shown by the erupting or erupted but unworn tooth (*c* 24 months of age) through to the same tooth showing early wear on the third cusp (*c* 30–36 months; Simonds 1854, figs 30, 31). By these criteria, some 55–60% of the cattle were killed between 18 and 36 months of age. Few cattle were killed below six months of age and, as an average figure, only about 20% were killed below one year of age. Cattle in older age classes are again rather uncommon with about 18% of the cattle mandibles coming from animals aged between three and six years. Only rarely were cattle killed at ages greater than six years. Figure 8.6 shows the population structure derived from the cattle mandibles grouped for three main ditch fills; those of the two enclosures and the inner

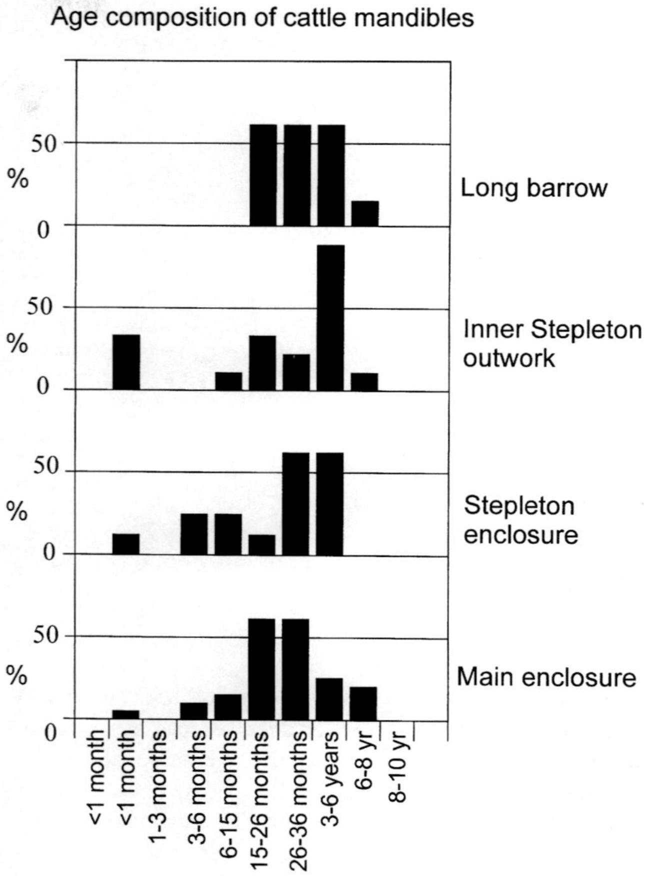

Fig 8.6 Distribution of age classes in cattle mandibles from four areas.

Stepleton outwork. The curves are essentially very similar, with low proportions of subadult cattle, but with the cull rising sharply between one-and-a-half and four years of age. Only 10% of the cattle were killed after that time, so that very few older cows can be represented. The data from a large sample of Bronze Age cattle mandibles excavated at Grime's Graves, and aged by the same method, are added for comparative purposes (Legge 1992). The sample from the south long barrow at Hambledon is very similar, with the exception that no infantile cattle mandibles were found. The inner Stepleton outwork has a rather higher proportion of cattle less than one year of age (about 28%) and none likely to be of more than five or six years of age (Fig 8.7).

The limited bone recovery practised in some earlier excavations at Neolithic sites means that few samples are sufficient for detailed comparison. A modest quantity of bone was reported from the 'pre-enclosure' and 'enclosure' phases of settlement at Windmill Hill, including a few mandibles and some loose teeth of cattle, and more has been reported from recent excavations. The cattle horncores found at Windmill Hill were nearly all from mature and older females of five years old and above (Grigson 1965; 1982; 1999; Jope 1965). However, while the horncores reflect the predominance of female domestic cattle at the site,

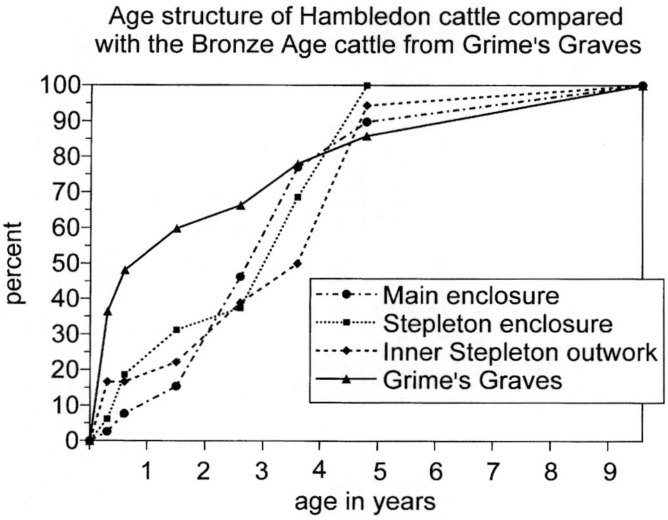

Fig 8.7 Slaughter pattern (age at death) in cattle mandibles from three areas compared with those from Bronze Age Grime's Graves.

Grigson has suggested that those from older cattle survive better due to their higher density, so that this finding may not accurately reflect the age structure of the cattle population (Grigson 1982, 33). A more accurate system of ageing is possible from the teeth, though the samples from Windmill Hill are of only moderate numbers. The wear states shown by the teeth were placed into four classes, of unworn, slight wear, medium wear and strong wear (Grigson 1982). Table 8.1 shows the proportions given in these wear classes.

The dp_4 with slight wear or no wear obviously belong to small calves. The dp_4 with 'strong' wear must be from an animal of two years or more in age, as this tooth is not replaced until 30 months. The undifferentiated M_1 and M_2 with 'medium' wear are likely to be from animals of between 12 months (M_1 medium wear) and 24 months (M_2 medium wear). An age cannot be attributed to the M_1 and M_2 which show 'strong wear' as the M_1 can show quite heavy wear by 36 months of age. The M_3 with slight and medium wear would fall in the 24–36 month age class and only those with 'strong' wear would be older than this, though by how much is impossible to determine. The side of the

Table 8.1 Wear classes of mandibular teeth from Windmill Hill, from Grigson (1982)

* = part mandible; only the 'oldest' tooth from each mandible is counted in the table

Tooth wear states as given	dp_4	M_1 or M_2	M_1*	M_2*	M_3
unworn	2	1	1	1	
slight wear	1	5			4
medium wear		11			2
strong wear	1	7		2	2

jaw from which the mandible fragment or tooth is derived is not given. In spite of the uncertainties of these data, the three unworn or lightly worn dp_4 come from animals of less than six months of age. Four M_3 are from young adults and two are a little more mature. Only two teeth come from older animals. The combined M_1/M_2 sample does not contradict this, with most teeth falling into the medium wear category characteristic of young adult cattle. More recently it has been shown that of seven lower third permanent molars, four were in early stages of wear and three were in full wear (Grigson 1999, 220).

The Windmill Hill cattle are also aged on the basis of the frequency of fused and unfused bones (Grigson 1999, table 147, 219). The problems of defining slaughter policy from the proportions of unfused and fused bones are too well known to be discussed fully here; not the least of these is that the forces that work against the survival of unfused bones ensure that this part of the assemblage is grossly understated in most instances. This is further explored below and elsewhere (Legge 1992). Grigson shows the proportions in which the different bones at Windmill Hill were found either unfused or fused (Grigson 1999, 147, 219). She concludes from these data that half the cattle '... survived until the age of 3½–4 years'. Of the group of bones which fuse latest (42–48 months), 17 were found unfused and 26 fused (39% unfused) when the 1988 and Keiller/Smith excavation totals are combined.

On the other hand, the larger mandible sample from Hambledon does allow a fairly detailed reconstruction of the age structure of the cull (Figs 8.5–7). From the slaughter pattern shown in Figure 8.6, about half of the cattle were over 36 months when killed but only 20% were older than 48 months. These figures can be used to cross-check the quality of post-cranial bone survival (see below for discussion of this). At the Hambledon complex this indicates that some 85–90% of the fused bones do survive of the number that can be predicted as discarded when fused, but that only 5–25% of the bones survive that were predicted as discarded unfused. If this example can be extended to the data from Windmill Hill, then the number of unfused bones would have to be multiplied by 3 or 4 times to compare with those found in the fused state. It would therefore appear likely that subadult and young adult cattle were killed rather more often, and perhaps in a narrower band of age classes, at Windmill Hill than Grigson allows in her conclusions that '... clearly old and moderately old cattle predominated in the life of the inhabitants of Windmill Hill' (Grigson 1999, 220).

At the Etton causewayed enclosure near Peterborough, Armour-Chelu (1992; 1998a) has reported a small sample of cattle mandibles from phase I of the enclosure ditch, and seven dp_4 and 11 M_3 from the buried soil. Using Grant's (1982) system of recording cattle tooth eruption and wear, the complete

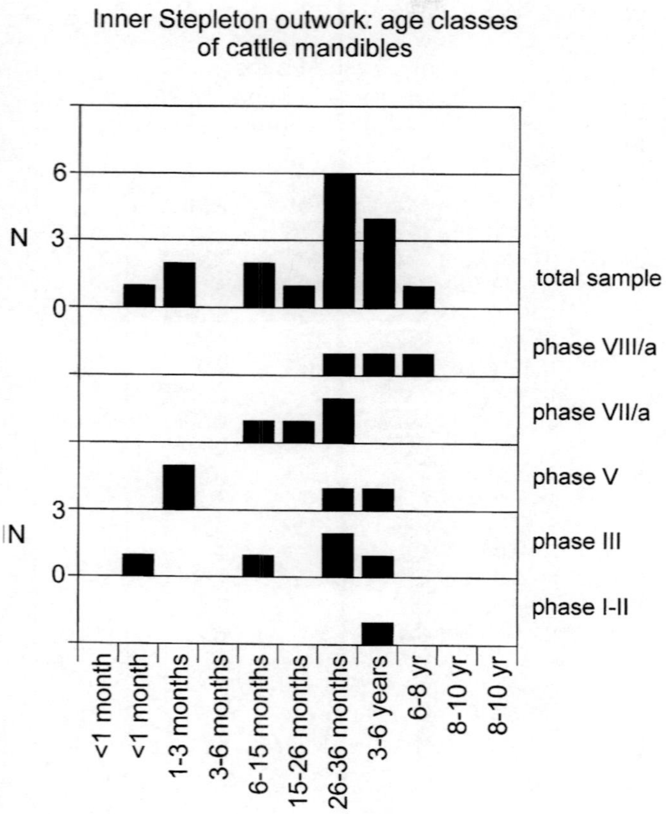

Fig 8.8 Distribution of age classes in cattle mandibles from five phases of the inner Stepleton outwork.

mandibles from phase I were judged to be 'fully mature' at the time of death. From the range of 'mean wear stages' as given, most of the mandibles would be from young adults, as were seven of the eleven loose M_3. Seven loose dp_4 were from cattle of under six months in age. The Etton sample is thus quite similar to the population age structure found at Hambledon Hill. Unfortunately other published causewayed enclosure excavations have too little bone for additional comparisons.

Interpretation of the cattle cull

The cattle age structure found at Hambledon, and possibly also at some other causewayed enclosures, cannot be characteristic of the cull from an entire breeding herd, as few mature, breeding age females are represented. On the contrary, the young cull ages mean that few of the cows that were killed at Hambledon could have reproduced themselves; indeed, this may even have been the reason why these were chosen in the predominant age classes. The slaughter pattern at Hambledon is thus in marked contrast to those reported from the few earlier prehistoric sites which have been interpreted as being of a domestic character. Yet at middle Bronze Age Grime's Graves (Legge 1981a; 1992) the cull of adult cattle was also found to be about 6:1 in favour of cows, though the age profile of the cull cattle showed that large numbers of calves were killed, often at very early ages, while the adult female cattle survived well into maturity and even up to ten years old. This slaughter pattern has been interpreted as that derived from the purposeful cull, with occasional natural death, of cattle from the age profile found within a breeding herd, in this case with a specific leaning towards maximising dairy outputs. It is a simple inference, from the adult sex ratio, that the cull calves – those of only a few weeks or months of age – would mostly have been male, killed in this case at ages before the earliest bone fusion.

At Hambledon the greater part of the cattle killed were female, and most of these were of subadult or young adult ages. The age structure of the cattle cull makes it unlikely that this was derived from a resident herd. On the other hand, the narrow age range of the majority leads to the conclusion that it may reasonably be regarded as the product of deliberate selection. This may have been because cows in this age class were the most commonly available surplus animals, or for some other reason that is less readily deduced. It has been shown that most fused cattle bones at Grime's Graves were also those of females and this, combined with the high incidence of infantile slaughter, suggested that animal husbandry was based upon the conservation of adult, productive livestock by means of milk production. It is well known that this system of food production provides the highest return, especially where the grazing area is constrained, though the human labour inputs to the system are high. Milk production has the further advantage that a highly palatable food is produced on a daily basis, and that this is easily processed by volume reduction into equally palatable forms that may also be stored in the medium to long term, as was tentatively suggested in Legge 1981a and 1989). On the basis of this model it is possible to identify a source of the cull cattle at Hambledon. At Grime's Graves, few males were carried much beyond infancy, and it would seem that only sufficient males survived into adult life to secure the reproduction of the herd. On the other hand, most females were probably retained to that point where the husbandman makes the final selection of the young cows to keep for breeding and those for cull. This was perhaps on the basis of body conformation, or on reproductive success. For instance, experience might encourage the retention of those cows which conceived early, while those which failed to conceive were selected for cull. Such a model would explain both the predominance both of cows and of the young age classes found at the site.

The alternative view might consider that cattle in the Neolithic period were important only as meat supplies. This raises an important question about the size of the consuming Neolithic community, when a single beast of near adult size would have provided some 300 kg of meat, offal and fat – a considerable investment both in the killing and in the consumption. If the cattle killed at Hambledon were *not* from a resident breeding herd, then it is plausible that selected animals were taken there from a wider physical and social catchment.

Hambledon Hill could thus be viewed as a gathering place within a wide social catchment, at which the slaughter of cattle were events of conspicuous consumption. If so, it would seem that young cows were rather more acceptable as slaughter, or possibly were simply more available, than were young steers. Whatever the manner or motive of the slaughter events, the fact remains that few young males were culled at Hambledon, which implies that few such animals were raised. It is possible that young cows were selected for reasons of belief, ritual or social preference, or possibly these were the surplus adults from a husbandry system in which cattle were exploited on a day-to-day basis for outputs other than meat. Only the discovery and proper excavation of a domestic bone sample within the putative social catchment of Hambledon Hill can resolve these questions.

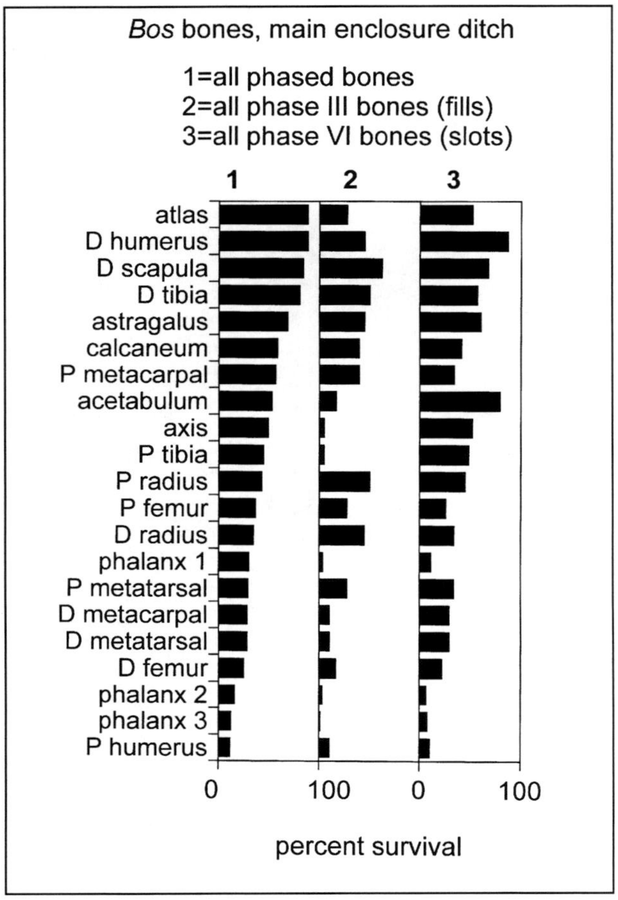

Fig 8.9 Cattle bone survival in (a) the combined sample from the main enclosure ditch and (b) two subsamples from phases III and IV.

Cattle: bone survival and bone representation at Hambledon Hill

A consideration of the pattern of bone survival at Hambledon is of obvious concern in the further interpretation of the sample. For instance, it is possible that the cattle bones arrived only as parts of animals, being transported in joints of meat, or that entire animals were driven to the site for slaughter. The abundance of mandibles argues for the latter as most probable, though this interpretation needs to be supported by a consideration of the pattern of bone representation. It is also possible that bones were differentially deposited within the site according to a system of human belief or of behaviour; this is further considered in the second part of this report. Attractive as such conclusions may be, it is first necessary to examine the pattern of bone survival for more mundane influences.

The discussion that follows is based on the cattle bones, as these are both the most numerous and form the most robust species that was found. The different cattle bones, as with all mammals, fuse in a known sequence and at about the same age in all individuals within a population, subject to the normal variation found in living organisms. It has been emphasised that when bones pass through the fusion process, the likelihood of their survival is greatly enhanced. This pattern can be discerned in bone assemblages from all periods and recovered from widely different places. Those bones which fuse early in the animal's life, such as the distal humerus and proximal scapula, are usually well preserved in bone assemblages, while late-fusing bones (for example the proximal humerus, proximal tibia, and both proximal and distal femur) are much less commonly found. Destruction of the less dense, unfused bones is easily accomplished by dogs, a process subsequently magnified under rather harsh burial conditions. This pattern of bone survival is wholly typical of the assemblages from Hambledon Hill and the point is strikingly illustrated in Figure 8.9, which shows the bone survival for the main enclosure ditch for three different groups of bone. The diagram is set out in the conventional manner, by simply depicting the relative abundance of each bone, in declining frequency, making due allowance for paired and axial bones. It is necessary to use combined samples in these diagrams, as single layers in ditch segments, or the bones from a single feature, are usually too few. It can be seen that bones which fuse early, such as the distal humerus, scapula, distal tibia are well represented, as are bones with no fusion point like the astragalus or proximal metacarpal. This suggests that fusion age has indeed had a marked effect upon bone survival. This can be seen even more clearly for those bones which have a fusion point, and for which approximate fusion ages are known. Figure 8.10 shows the relationship between fusion age (based upon the data given by Silver 1969) and bone survival for the sample from phase VI of the main enclosure ditch, and Figure 8.11 displays the data from the Stepleton enclosure ditch. In both diagrams, the relationship between fusion age and bone survival is strikingly evident, with the early-fusing bones being common and the bones then progressively less common with increased fusion age. The relationship which emerges is remarkably

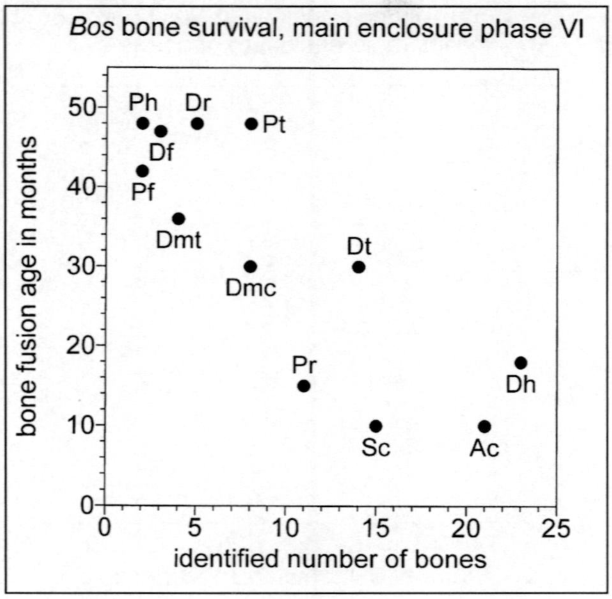

Fig 8.10 Cattle bone survival from phase VI of the main enclosure ditch. P=proximal end D=distal end; Sc=scapula; h=humerus; r=radius; mc=metacarpal; Ac=acetabulum of pelvis; f=femur; t=tibia; mt=metatarsal.

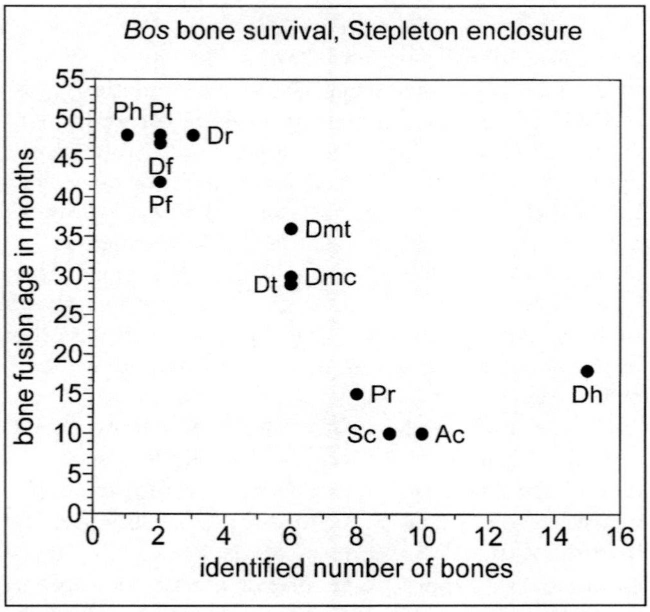

Fig 8.11 Cattle bone survival from the Stepleton enclosure ditch. Key as Figure 8.10.

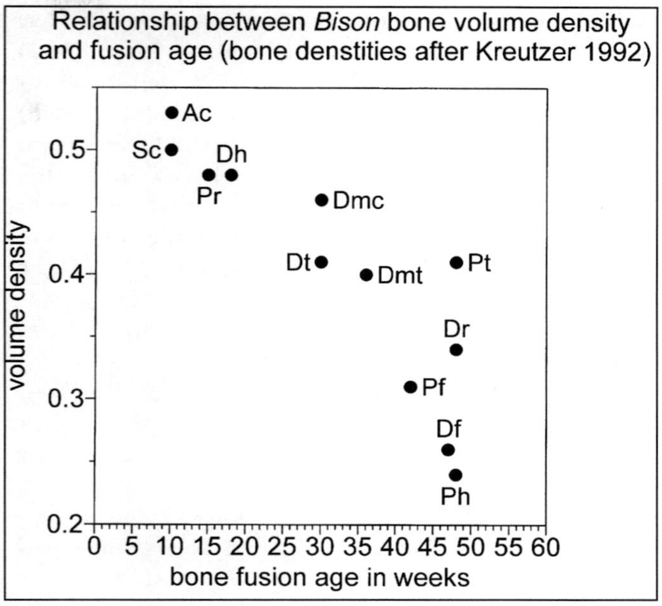

Fig 8.12 Relationship between bone density and the survival of cattle bone. Values for volume density after Kreutzer 1992. Key as Figure 8.10.

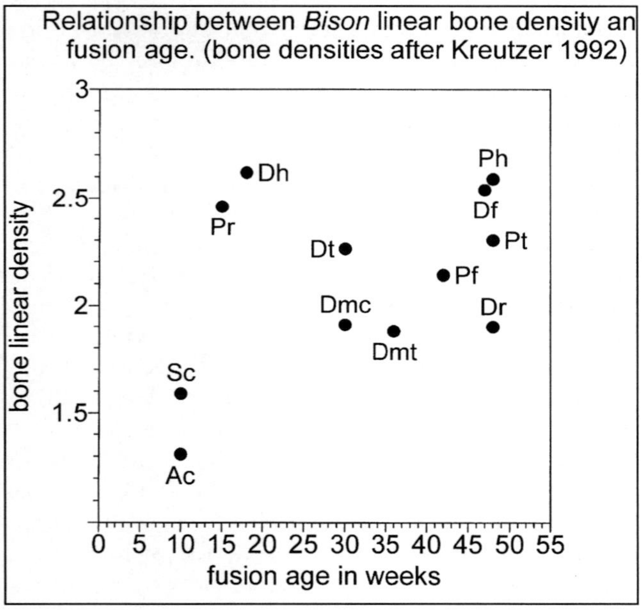

Fig 8.13 Relationship between bone density and the survival of cattle bone. Values for linear bone density after Kreutzer 1992. Key as Figure 8.10.

constant for an archaeological sample. The early-fusing bones (in particular the acetabulum, distal humerus, distal radius and scapula glenoid, designated Ac, Dh, Sc, Pr), are particularly common in the archaeological sample while at the other extreme, the late-fusing bones (proximal humerus, Ph, distal radius, Dr, proximal and distal femur, Pf and Df, proximal tibia, Pt) were found to be much less common. Bones with fusion ages which are intermediate between the earliest and latest fusion ages also show a constant relationship.

The relationships between bone density and bone survival has been a major interest in faunal studies of recent times, though on occasions with insufficient regard for the age profile of the cull population from which the bone sample was derived (Legge 1992. The relevant sources for the measurement of bone density and the effects of this on bone survival are too numerous to list here, but these were comprehensively reviewed by Lyman (1998). Bone density values were originally calculated by simple displacement in water (Brain 1969), though more recently by a variety of other methods. Recently photon densitometry has been applied to these measurements (Lyman 1984) and also by Kreutzer (1992), who has used the technique to measure bone density in 12 adult (fused) skeletons of the American bison, *Bison occidentalis.* Kreutzer initially measured 'linear density' across the bison bones, and then modified these density measurements in relation to the volume of the bone at the scan site, thus producing 'volume densities' (and see Kreutzer 1992 for a discussion of the limitations of linear density measurements by this technique). The American bison is a closely related bovid species of a size near enough to large Neolithic cattle for the density measurements to be borrowed for comparative purposes and, at the time of writing, Kreutzer's measurements provide the best available comparison for bone density in European *Bos taurus*. The pattern seen in Figure 8.12 suggests that this borrowing is reasonably valid. Here, Kreutzer's calculated values for bone 'volume density' from *Bison occidentalis* are set against the familiar bone fusion ages for the epiphyses of cattle limb bones. Figure 8.13 shows her 'linear densities' used in the same way, and it can be seen that any relationship between the two values is at best highly variable. In Figure 8.12 the relationship between bone fusion age and volume density is reasonably constant, with the early-fusing bones having the highest post-fusion densities and, as the time of bone fusion proceeds though the animal's life, the density of the fused bone falls progressively in a notably consistent relationship, especially bearing in mind the uncertainties of the published bone fusion ages for cattle and other species (Silver 1969) and the borrowing between species in this exercise.

The relationship shown above, in which bone fusion age and bone density are so closely linked, has obviously been the significant factor in the formation of the Hambledon cattle bone assemblages. Figure 8.14 shows the survival of cattle bone from the main enclosure, where the number of identified specimens of each bone is plotted against Kreutzer's volume density measurements. The relationship between the bone volume density and the survival of the different bones is marked; as volume density rises, so too does the number of identified bones in a constant relationship.

Using Kreutzer's figures, it has been shown that the early-fusing cattle bones have high volume densities and that the late-fusing bones have low volume densities and that these conditions are closely related to the survival of cattle bones at the Hambledon sites. This effect is also particularly marked on the cattle bone assemblage because of the age structure of the cattle cull. It has been shown above that about 60% of the cattle were selected for cull at between 18 and 36 months of age, the very period during which the different bones of the cattle skeleton undergo their sequential fusion. This means that most cattle were killed at an age when their *early*-fusing bones had passed through this process, while the *late*-fusing bones had not.

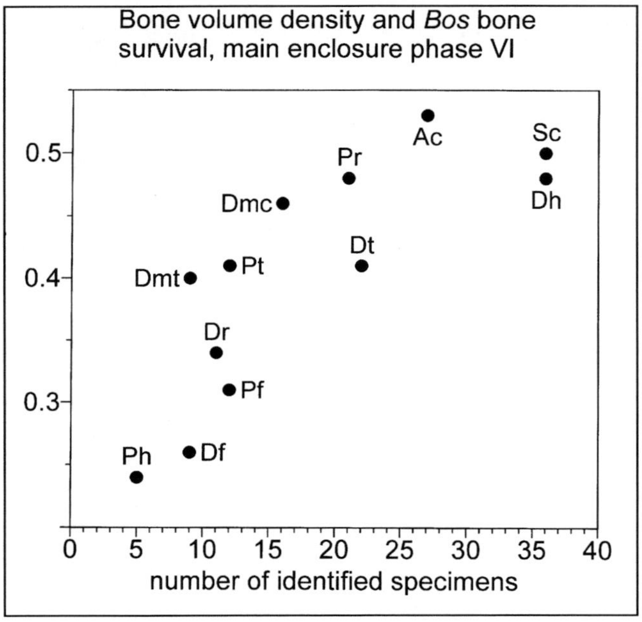

Fig 8.14 Relationship between bone density and the survival of cattle bone in the main enclosure phase VI. Values for volume density after Kreutzer 1992. Key as Figure 8.10.

The pattern of bone representation at Hambledon Hill is thus density-dependent and also closely related to the particular age structure of the population. It is possible to examine the pattern of bone survival in yet more detail, in particular in relation to the proportions in which unfused and fused bones have survived. From the slaughter pattern (Fig 8.6) it is possible to measure the percentage of cattle that were killed at the time when each limb bone will have become fused. These percentages will then show the proportion of each different limb bone that were discarded in the unfused and the fused state, as predicted by the age profile of the surviving jaws. The fills of the main enclosure ditch contained mandibles which indicate a minimum number of 23 cattle. The limb bones discarded after slaughter and butchery would obviously be twice this number (NISp=46). The number of identified, fused specimens of each bone is then expressed as a percentage of the predicted number that were discarded in that state. The same may then be calculated for the unfused bones that were identified in the assemblage. It is recognised that this method contains certain assumptions, not the least in that the bone fusion ages used here may be inaccurate, as has been found for tooth eruption data derived from veterinary sources. However, in spite of such limitations, it appears reasonable to attempt such investigations rather than to simply assume that all bones were equally likely to survive regardless of their fusion state or, even more seriously, to assume that the proportions in which mammal bones survive in archaeological assemblages have any meaning when separated from the age profile of the cull population.

Table 8.2 Main enclosure. Numbers of identified cattle bones, their fusion ages and the predicted number that were discarded related to the numbers of identified bones

Bone	*Fusion age (months)*	*Percentage slaughtered above this age*	*Predicted number discarded fused*	*Identified number of bones*	*Per cent survival of predicted number*
Scapula	10	90%	41	36	88%
P humerus	48	25%	12	6	50%
D humerus	18	83%	38	38	100%
P radius	15	85%	39	21	54%
D radius	48	25%	12	11	92%
Acetabulum	10	88%	40	27	68%
P femur	42	35%	16	12	75%
D femur	48	25%	12	9	75%
P tibia	48	25%	12	12	100%
D tibia	30	60%	28	22	79%
D metacarpal	30	60%	28	16	57%
D metatarsal	36	55%	25	10	40%

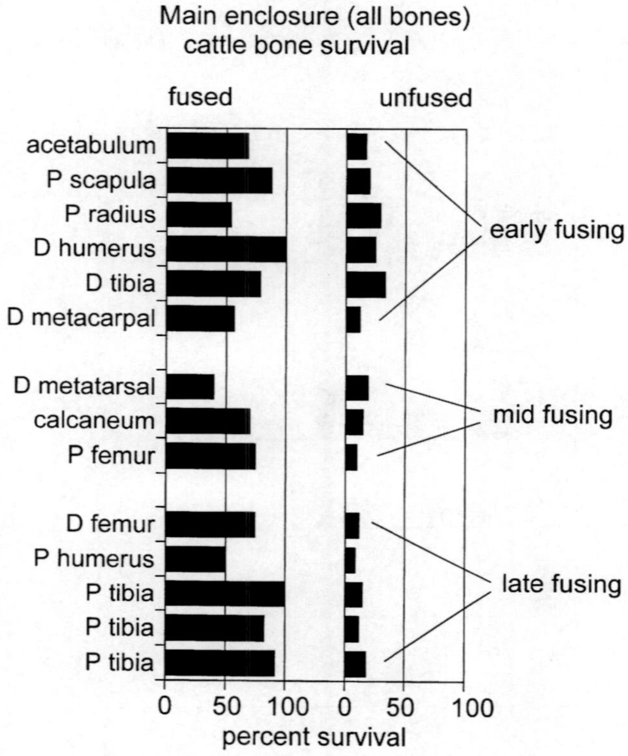

Fig 8.15 Survival of the fused and unfused bones of cattle in the main enclosure ditch, whole sample.

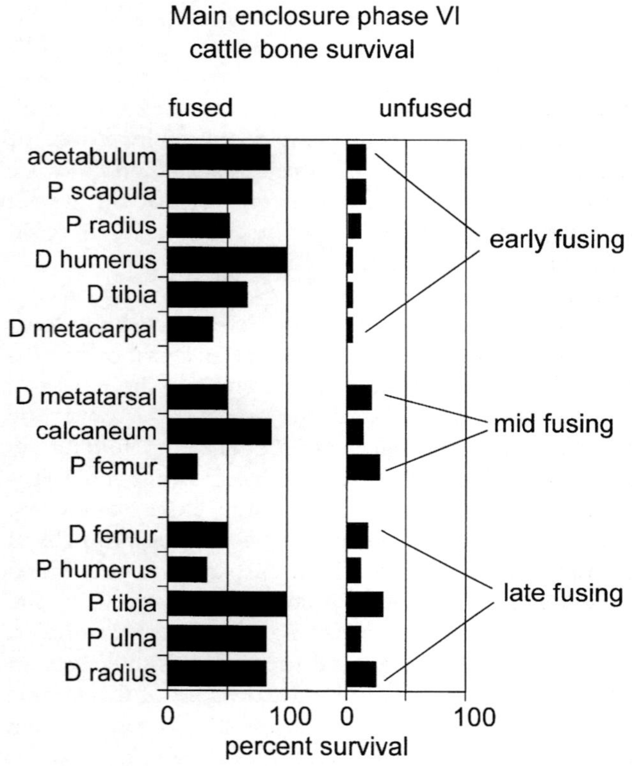

Fig 8.16 Survival of the fused and unfused bones of cattle in phase VI of the main enclosure ditch.

For example:

1. Fusion in the cattle scapula occurs at 10 months of age
2. Percentage of cattle killed beyond 10 months of age at Hambledon Hill = 90%
3. From this, the number of scapulae predicted as discarded older than 10 months = 90% of 46 = 41 (to the nearest whole number)
4. Number of fused scapulae that were identified in the sample = 36
5. The proportion of fused scapulae surviving is 36 of the 41 specimens predicted as discarded when fused = 88% survival.

The numbers of identified bones, their fusion ages and the predicted number that were discarded are given in Table 8.2. The result of this calculation is shown in Figures 8.15–16, which show the survival of fused and unfused cattle bones calculated in the same way, for the whole sample from the main enclosure ditch, and then only for phase VI of that ditch fill. This method of calculation produces the striking result that some of the late-fusing bones actually survive to a large proportion of those predicted as discarded when fused. Conversely, it is evident that the survival of most unfused limb bones is very much worse, in the range 5% to 25% of the predicted number that were discarded.

The bone representation for *fused limb* bones is thus much more constant than the crude unadjusted figures would appear to show, with most fused limb bones surviving at 70–100% of the predicted number that were discarded. Most notably, this method redresses the bias that is inherent against the survival of late-fusing bones.

From this, it may be argued that the observed pattern of cattle bone representation at Hambledon Hill is strongly conditioned by density-related conditions, closely connected to bone fusion and the age profile of the cull population. The bone representation is the product of post-discard attrition due to the large numbers of unfused bones that were discarded. The relative completeness of the representation of adult cattle bones supports the interpretation that living cattle were brought to the site, there to be slaughtered and the meat consumed close by.

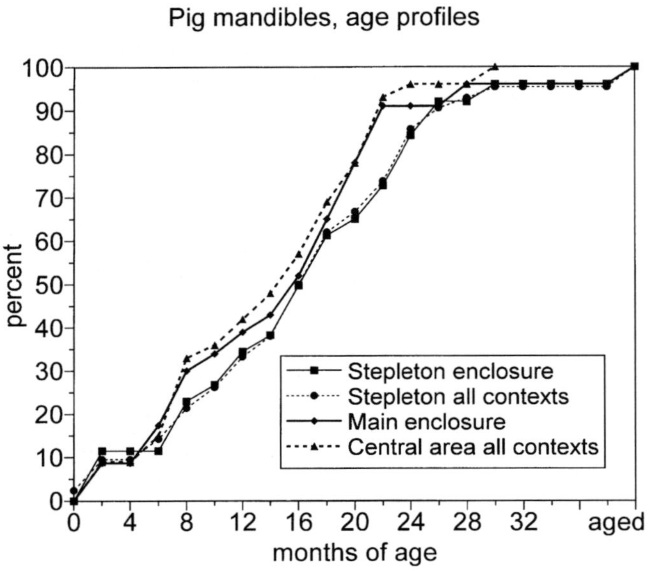

Fig 8.17 Slaughter patterns (age at death) in pig mandibles from four areas.

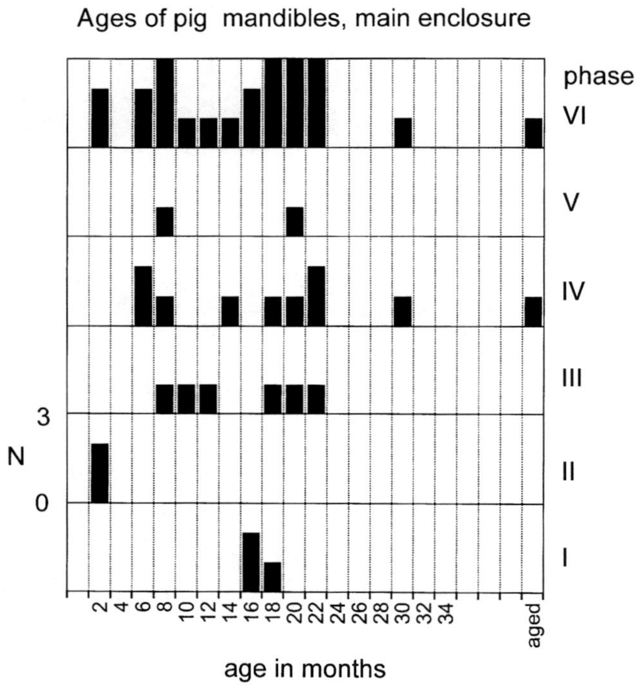

Fig 8.18 The distribution of age classes in pig mandibles from 6 phases from the main enclosure.

Age structure of the pig cull

The pig is the second most abundant mammal at all sites and in some contexts pig mandibles equal or exceed those of cattle in number. The pig mandibles are generally very fragmented and complete tooth rows are rare. The dentition of pigs can be closely aged up to 30 months or so, by which time the dentition shows considerable wear and age estimates become less certain. This is because the pig has low crowned (bunodont) teeth and, once the enamel of the occlusal surface is worn away, few age-related changes can be observed apart from a general wearing away of the tooth. Pig teeth lack the internal enamel pillars and folding (in particular the infundibulum), which change more visibly in cattle, deer and caprines into older age classes. However, this does not present a serious problem at Hambledon, as almost all of the pigs that were killed were young, aged below 24 months at death. The total sample consisted of 125 mandibles and part mandibles.

The age profiles for the various sites are given in Figures 8.17–18. Inevitably the division of the sample between many ditch segments and phases within them results in some very small samples, so the age profiles given here are also combined into larger units. For example Figure 8.17 shows the cull pattern for all pig mandibles from each of the two enclosure ditches, and also for the entire sample from each area, including the pits. Data are also presented as histograms of age classes for the larger sample from the different phases of the main enclosure ditch (Fig 8.18) and for the various ditches and features on the Stepleton spur (Fig 8.19).

From Figure 8.17 two important facts emerge. Firstly, it is notable that the pigs were not selected for cull in any particular age class, beyond the fact that the greater majority were below 24 months of age. In both areas, pigs were killed in all age classes up to that point, and only a very small proportion of the mandibles were found to come from pigs older than this (given collectively as 'aged' in Figures 8.17 and 8.18). Secondly, the age profiles found from the main enclosure ditch, the Stepleton enclosure ditch and the total samples from both sites, are remarkably similar (Fig 8.17). The mean age at death is closely similar in both samples: 13.4 months in the main enclosure ditch and 14.4 months in the Stepleton enclosure ditch. Only one site differs significantly from this general pattern, that of the enigmatic third millennium cal BC 'flint mines' on the Hanford Spur, where rather more pigs were found to have been killed below six months of age. This sample is further discussed below.

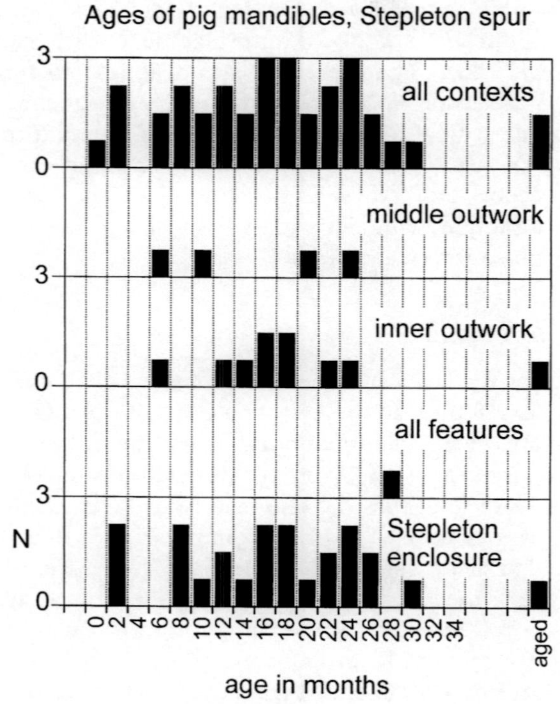

Fig 8.19 The distribution of age classes in pig mandibles from four areas and a combined sample.

The age structure of the pigs is therefore rather predictable. Animals of all ages below two years were killed at the site, a familiar and preferred age for human consumption. Indeed, because of the nature of reproduction in the pig, with multiple rather than single births, all pig populations, even in the wild, are predominantly made up of subadult individuals. The consistent age patterns found across the sites do argue that the greater part of the pigs were also taken to the site having been selected from domestic herds, and that wild pig bones at the site were few. The selection was for young animals but, as has been noted, this is an almost invariable human practice in a wide variety of circumstances.

Pig bones and the body size

Although the pig is second in abundance in most of the contexts excavated at Hambledon, it is shown above that most were juvenile and in consequence few bones could be measured. Only 12 specimens of even the early-fusing distal humerus were sufficiently intact. Little comparative data are available for this species. Harcourt (1971) gave the 'distal width' measurement of some pig humeri and it is highly likely that this is the same as the BT measurement used here. Comparison of the BT measurements from 11 pig humeri published from the later Neolithic site of Durrington Walls can be compared with 12 distal humeri from the main and Stepleton enclosures, with a BT measurement of 29–40 mm. Harcourt (1971, 339) gives a range of 27–35 mm for a further 122 distal fragments specimens. Harcourt (1979) further gives the range of 29–35 mm for the BT measurement of 17 specimens excavated at Mount Pleasant. There is little scope for detailed comparison, owing to the small number of specimens and the paucity of comparative data. It is probable that some of the larger specimens from Hambledon were wild pigs, though most appear to fall within the range of known Neolithic domestic pigs.

Age structure of the caprine cull

The mandibles of caprines at Hambledon were identified as being all from sheep. In common with the post-cranial bones, the mandibles are highly fragmented. This causes inevitable uncertainties in attributing ages to some specimens. For example, the largest sample comes from the main enclosure ditch; of 20 specimens that have been placed into one of nine age classes following the method of Payne (1973), only four are teeth that have remained rooted in the bone; the remainder are isolated dp_4 and M_3. As discussed above, these teeth are both carried for a short while as the deciduous molars are replaced shortly after the eruption of the M_3 (Simonds 1854, figs 40, 42, 91–95). Consequently, with fragmented material, there is the possibility of counting a specimen twice when these teeth are separately aged, even with due allowance for the short period when both teeth may be found in the jaw. Two heavily worn specimens of dp_4 and 2 unworn or lightly worn M_3 in one sample were treated as coming from two broken mandibles.

Only three sites have samples of more than ten specimens to which ages can be attributed (Fig 8.20). The two largest samples, from the main enclosure and the Stepleton enclosure, are further plotted on a cumulative graph and compared there with a large sample

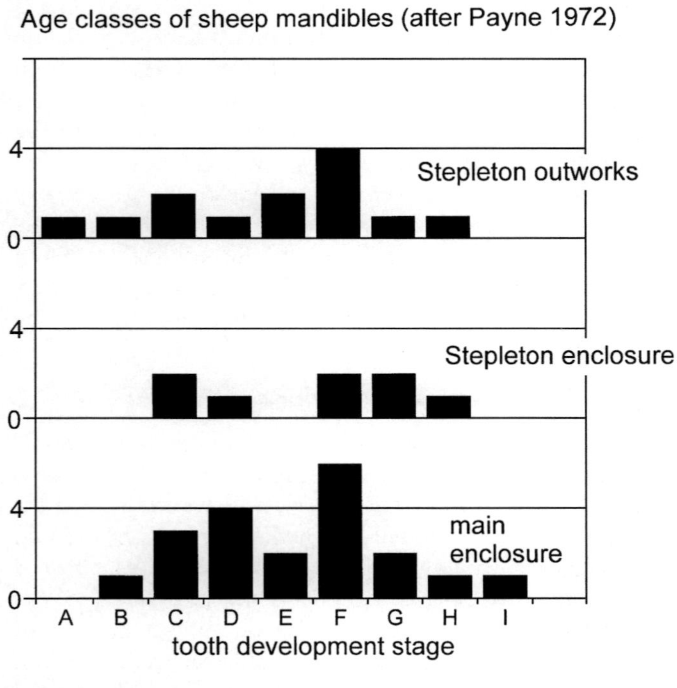

Fig 8.20 Age classes in sheep mandibles from three areas.

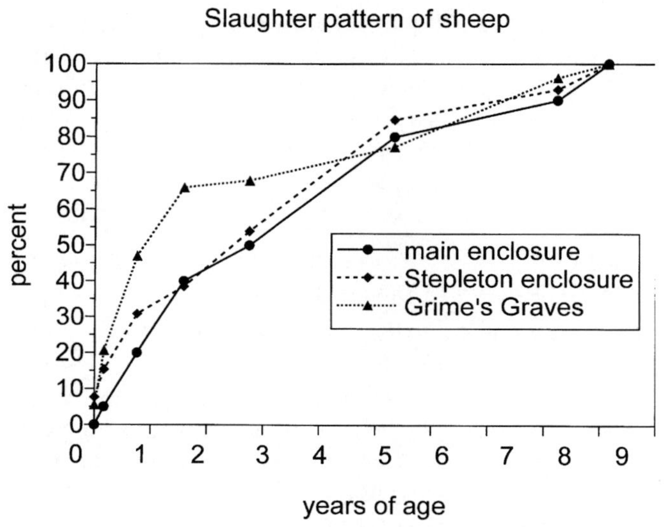

Fig 8.21 Slaughter patterns (age at death) in sheep mandibles from two areas compared with Grime's Graves.

from a domestic settlement from the Bronze Age at Grime's Graves (Legge 1992; Fig 8.21). As is shown in that report, the large samples of mandibles from two excavations at that site give very similar slaughter patterns and these conform to that generally found in sheep husbandry. The Grime's Graves samples show that the major part of the cull fell between ten months and two years of age (stages C and D after Payne 1973), with a slower rate thereafter as the older breeding animals were culled (or would die) towards the latter part of their lives. The pattern at Hambledon is somewhat different, as far as can be determined from the small and fragmented samples. The cull has few animals of one year or below and few of the oldest age classes G to H. The majority were culled between one year and about five or six years of age. This pattern is not readily susceptible to interpretation. It seems quite probable that, with evidence of heavy fragmentation, more mandibles would have been destroyed from the youngest specimens, though the oldest would be expected to have better survival. It is evident, however, that the sheep were not selected for cull in a relatively narrow age band, as has been found with the cattle mandibles, but appear to reflect the full age spectrum that was available in the Neolithic breeding herds, perhaps with fewer aged specimens than might usually be found.

Caprine bones and their body size

Most of the caprine bones from all sites were heavily fragmented and in consequence few could be measured. Goat bones were rare, with few certain identifications, which included fragments of horncore and one distal metacarpal. More than 98% of the caprine bones were identified as being those of sheep. Because of the few measurements little can be said about the size of the sheep at Hambledon. The BT measurements of four distal humeri, identified as those of sheep, fall within the range given for eight specimens from Durrington Walls of 24–28 mm (Harcourt 1971, table XXXVI, 343). The Neolithic sheep appear to have been a little more robust than adult male specimens of the modern feral Soay sheep (Legge and Payne forthcoming); three of the four distal humeri from Hambledon Hill are slightly larger than the largest from a sample of modern male Soay sheep that were raised in southern England.

Red deer bones

Bones of red deer are a small proportion of the large mammals found at the two enclosures, and average about 2% of the identified bones from the central area enclosure and 5–7% from the Stepleton spur. Few bones were found in any one feature or layer, so that the representation of red deer bones can only be considered at the gross level. Figure 8.22 shows the relative abundance of red deer bones in the central area and on the Stepleton spur, comparing both with the gross (uncorrected) proportions of identified cattle bones from the main enclosure ditch. The bones of red deer are mostly those which fuse early and are of high density, again showing an assemblage that has undergone a high rate of attrition. Only a few animals need be represented at each site. The bones in the larger sample, from Stepleton, need come from no more than five animals (five proximal left metatarsals, five right calcanea) and those from the central area from no more than three. This is at best only a measure of relative abundance as, from few bones so widely dispersed, the minimum number of individuals is even more uncertain than is usual with such calculations.

Figure 8.22 shows that there is a marked representation of the distal limb at both sites (metapodials, navicular-cuboid and the calcaneum at Stepleton) and certain upper limb bones which show early fusion with the consequent high survival in most bone assemblages (distal scapula, distal humerus, distal tibia). Bones of higher meat utility, (other than the scapula and humerus) such as the pelvic bones, femur, and proximal tibia are scarce. The red deer would have been hunted, and those from the Neolithic period were large, even as big as those from the Mesolithic site of Star Carr (Fig 8.23). The overall bone representation pattern appears to have been influenced by their large size. Firstly, the head parts of the red deer are hardly represented with the exception of the abundant antler, which was found in almost all context groups. However, it must be stressed that it is improbable that more than a very small proportion of this antler was derived from animals killed while the site was occupied. Most of the antler is 'shed', that is, naturally cast in the annual cycle of replacement and growth of that organ. Even when the specimen comes from a deer killed while carrying antlers, it is probable that the time and place of its death were remote from the activity on the hilltop (and see below, 8.2). Apart from the antlers,

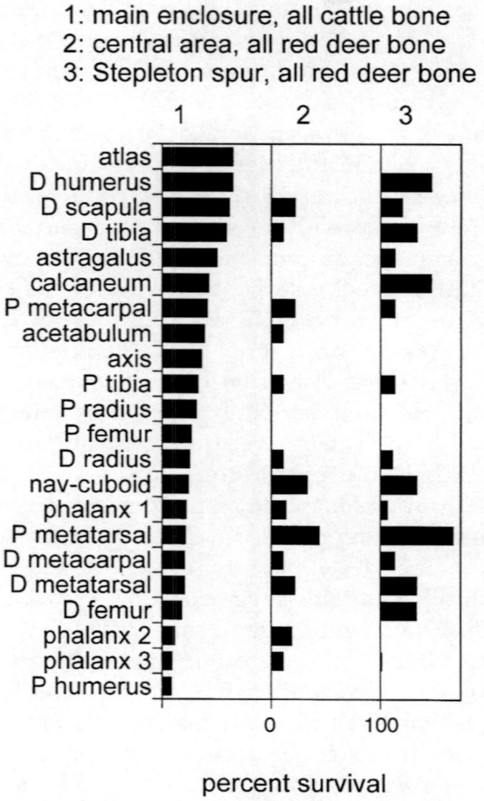

Fig 8.22 Survival of red deer bones from two areas compared with the gross survival of cattle bones from the main enclosure.

other cranial parts were very seldom found. Two fragmentary red deer mandibles and a small number of loose maxillary teeth come from the inner Stepleton outwork and a few maxillary teeth from the outer outwork. In the main enclosure, a left mandible came from layer 9 (phase VI) in segment 14 of the inner ditch. All of the jaws and loose teeth come from young adult red deer.

The low proportion of cranial parts suggests that the deer were hunted remotely from the hill, and that limb segments were carried to the site from killing points elsewhere, while the heads were abandoned. The large red deer of Neolithic times would weigh 100–150 kg (Whitehead 1964) and, when killed, the carcass would obviously need to be segmented for transportation. It is a familiar concept that certain parts, notably the head, are more likely to be consumed at the point of kill than removed to a distance. This appears to be the case with the Hambledon red deer. The low proportion of late-fusing, higher meat utility bones can be explained by the processes of attrition that had worked on all bones at the site. The small sample of red deer – as with the cattle – come from animals in which the later-fusing bones may still have been unfused and would thus be more attractive to dogs when discarded. It is probable that the red deer arrived at the sites as parts of carcasses. Even if deer were abundant in the immediate locality, it may be that the people had preoccupations other than that of hunting.

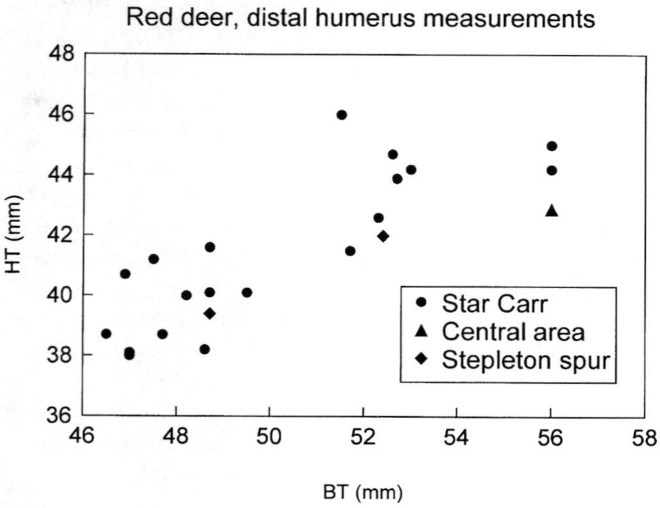

Fig 8.23 Measurements of distal humeri of red deer from two areas compared with those from the Mesolithic site of Star Carr.

The large red deer from Hambledon are indicative of good environmental conditions for this species, which prefers a habitat of open woodland for much of the year. Figure 8.23 shows the three measurable distal humeri from Hambledon compared with measurements of the same bone taken from the Mesolithic red deer at Star Carr, which are known to be of large body size compared to modern populations of the same animal in Britain (Legge and Rowley-Conwy 1988, fig 25). This measurement needs to be used with caution as it is known that this increases significantly after bone fusion (ibid, fig 23). The specimens from Hambledon would appear to be from fully mature specimens, as one from the main enclosure is as large as any from Star Carr and two from the Stepleton spur fall well within the same population. Besides these, an astragalus, a distal metatarsal and a metacarpal all have measurements that fall within those taken from the equivalent bones from Star Carr.

The preferred habitat of red deer is one of fairly open woodland, with a diet which, especially in winter, is dependant upon a good deal of browsing of young twigs from woody plants (Mitchell *et al* 1977; Ahlen 1965). However, the low proportion of red deer from the Hambledon Neolithic complex is unlikely to be a close reflection of the prevailing landscape, as it would appear that the human population had preoccupations other than hunting when at Hambledon Hill. The scarcity of red deer in British Neolithic sites contrasts sharply with some Neolithic and even Bronze Age sites from mainland Europe where the proportion of red deer in site faunas can be large, even exceeding in abundance the proportion of any one domestic species (Higham 1968; Legge 1990; 1994).

The roe deer bones

The roe deer is an uncommon component of the fauna at Hambledon Hill. This small deer has a retiring habit and prefers low and thick cover in which it seeks concealment. Although it appears to have been locally abundant in Neolithic Britain (Maltby 1990), it was little hunted around Hambledon Hill, and was seldom taken to the site. The bones that survive are mainly those of the distal limb extremities, while cranial fragments are few. However, the few measurements that were possible also suggest that the animals came from a habitat that was satisfactory for this species. Three distal humeri from Hambledon have BT measurements of 27.2 mm, 25.3 mm and 24.6 mm. The largest of these exceeds any of the eight specimens from Star Carr, and the two others fall in the upper part of the Star Carr range, as does a single distal metatarsal.

Besides the post-cranial bones, some roe deer antlers have been found among the digging implements discarded in the ditch fills, although most are from juvenile animals (see below, 8.2).

Evidence for the season of use at Hambledon

The manner in which causewayed enclosures were used has been the subject of speculation since the time of their first recognition. The interrupted banks and ditches led to the suggestion that such sites were gathering places rather than defensive enclosures, and they were often thought to be associated with large-scale cattle herding. The Neolithic farming economy was considered (albeit from virtually no evidence) as largely mobile or, at best, semi-sedentary, although, somewhat oddly, such speculations did not encourage the systematic collection of data to test these beliefs. Scant regard was given to the systematic collection of bones in earlier excavations and even less to the recovery of charred plant remains. Though there is now some improvement in data recovery, few sites have yet been excavated to an acceptable standard.

One important development in animal bone studies has been testing for occasional, seasonal, or year-round use of archaeological sites. Certain time-dependent changes in mammalian hard tissues can be related to the seasons of death. Obvious examples are the development of the dentition of wild mammals in the early months after birth and the annual growth and shedding cycle of deer antlers.

Clark (1954) used the presence of both shed and unshed antlers of red deer and elk to argue that Star Carr was occupied principally in the late winter and spring seasons. Later work on the faunal remains of this site has questioned this reasoning on several grounds (Caulfield 1978; Legge and Rowley-Conwy 1988. Firstly, almost all of the red deer antlers were worked in some way, and could better be regarded, like the flint nodules at the site, as a raw material subject to transportation and storage. Secondly, the small roe deer antlers are not worked, and their fully developed state, as found at Star Carr, is characteristic of summer deaths, and not of those occurring in the winter season. This interpretation is further supported by the presence of infantile mandibles from roe deer (*Capreolus capreolus*), red deer (*Cervus elaphus*) and elk (*Alces alces*) and of immature mandibles of the same species that show stages of tooth development that are also typical of early summer deaths.

Hambledon has also yielded large quantities of antler, and in prehistoric times this was an important material for the excavation of the ditches and other features. However, as with the case of Star Carr or with the abundant antlers found at Neolithic flint mining sites (Clutton-Brock 1984; Legge 1981a), the season at which an antler was collected needs bear little relation to the season in which it was finally used and discarded. Antler was clearly an important raw material during the Neolithic period and would have been the subject of long-distance trade and probably of long-term accumulation against future needs.

More exact tests are possible from the developing mandibles of young mammals. These have the advantage that the developmental stage of the young mandible allows a fairly precise age to be attributed to its death. In mammals a deciduous (milk) set of teeth – present from birth or soon after – is gradually replaced as the animal develops towards maturity. Wild mammals living in temperate climates usually show a birth season that is closely related to the prevailing climatic regime which, in this northerly latitude, is usually in the spring, a time which ensures good nutrition for the mother and her new offspring. Where the season of birth is known (usually drawn from modern studies of the same species) the degree of eruption and wear on the juvenile teeth can determine the time of year in which the mammal was killed within reasonably close limits. However, it has been shown above that the proportion of red and roe deer among the mammal remains at Hambledon is low, and consequently their mandibles are few. Most of the mandibles recovered at Hambledon come from the domestic species of cattle, sheep and pig. Of these, the sheep are the most likely to have shown a marked birth season.

The development of sheep mandibles

In the latitude of southern Britain domestic sheep exhibit a highly seasonal reproductive cycle (Hafez 1968). Oestrus in the female is stimulated by the shortening autumn day length and, given free access for the rams, the greater part of the births will occur in the following spring. This has obvious survival advantages for the offspring, as they are born when grass growth is good and the summer season allows an extended growth period before the young face the winter season. It should be noted that, under simple systems of husbandry, there is little opportunity to modify this natural pattern. Births may be delayed by restricting access of the rams to the females, so that conception occurs at the next oestrus cycle some 20 days later, and births can be spread out by such means. However, this presents the danger that returns may be diminished as each subsequent oestrus cycle shows reduced levels of fertility. Furthermore, delaying birth too much will

Table 8.3 The development of juvenile sheep mandibles

'Early to moderate wear' represents the states of wear in which only the tips of the cusps are worn (early wear) through to a stage where dentine is exposed, but the infundibulae are still 'open' (moderate wear)
* = inferred from modern comparative material. The Soay sheep data are from a collection of modern skeletons (Holmes, Legge, and Payne in prep)

site	*sample*	*age*	*dp_4*	*M_1*
Harlow temple (IA)	12	6–8 mo	early to moderate wear	eruption to early wear
Harlow temple (Roman)	60	6–8 mo	early to moderate wear	eruption to early wear
Grime's Graves (BA)	23	6–8 mo	early to moderate wear	eruption to early wear
Chesterford temple (Roman)	118	<3 mo	early to moderate wear	not erupted
Chesterford temple (Roman)	227	6 mo	early to moderate wear	eruption to early wear
Modern Soay*	6	5–8 mo	early to moderate wear	eruption to early wear

result in summer births and the risk that lambs may be too small at the end of summer to survive the following winter successfully.

The question of birth season in prehistoric and Roman sheep was investigated in some detail at two temple sites; Harlow temple (Legge and Dorrington 1987) and Chesterford temple (Legge *et al* 1991; 1999). At both sites large numbers of lambs were sacrificed, but only in highly restricted age classes. At Harlow, lambs were killed at one of two discrete ages, at six months or about 18 months old. This pattern was found both in the Iron Age levels at the temple site and in the succeeding Roman temple. Various possibilities were considered to explain these findings though the preferred interpretation was that lambs then, as now, were born in spring and sacrifice took place in the autumn season, with the offering either of a 6-month or 18-month lamb, depending upon the affluence or need of the person giving sacrifice.

The pattern found at the Chesterford temple was somewhat different. Here lambs were again killed in one of only two age classes, but either as infantiles (under two months old) or as juveniles of six to eight months old. Again, the two age classes as defined by tooth eruption and wear were very narrow and were clearly separate; no jaws were found in intermediate stages of development. Together, the evidence from these temple sites shows that ritual events were closely defined by the season of the year and further supports the interpretation that both the Iron Age and Roman sheep gave birth in spring, under a natural seasonal regime, as indeed, with few exceptions, the species does now. Conversely, at residential sites with evidence for a full range of domestic activities and the residues of a farming economy, sheep mandibles will be found in *all* developmental stages from infancy to senescence, as was shown at Down Farm (Legge 1991) or Grime's Graves (Legge 1992).

In the same way the sheep mandibles and one from a roe deer provide some information about the use of Hambledon. The charred plant remains suggest that food was taken to the settlement in a partly prepared state; in other words, the site does not appear to be concerned with primary cereal production (see Jones and Legge, Ch 6). The same also applies to the sheep, in which the population structure shows a very low percentage of immature animals, lower than would be expected at a site concerned with the husbandry of this species. It would seem that, here too, selected animals were taken to the site and that the full range of age classes found in a breeding flock were not represented in the cull. In consequence, the number of subadult teeth is low and many are isolated from the jaws. Ageing has been done mainly from the deciduous third molar (dp_4), from both upper and lower jaws.

Evidence for the development of juvenile sheep mandibles is available from several sites and this can be supported both by modern comparative samples and certain other published sources (Table 8.3). Fourteen caprine dp_4 come from various Neolithic contexts across the hill. These are set out in ascending order of age in Table 8.4 using the alphabetic designations of tooth wear stage as illustrated by Grant (1982).

The small sample of caprine teeth does not point to an unequivocal, single season of use for the Hambledon enclosure. Four specimens come from caprines that were newborn or aged only a few weeks at the time of death. One specimen with erupting M_1 can be closely aged to a little less than three months and a further specimen is perhaps a month or so older still (Simonds 1854, fig 35, 84). One part mandible and six isolated dp_4 show the same wear state, equivalent to Grant's stage g or h, and these can be aged to 6–9 months. A single left mandible of the roe deer, found in the Stepleton enclosure, has moderate wear on the dp_4 and light wear on the M_1 and can be aged to about six months (Legge and Rowley-Conwy 1988). The caprine jaws aged from one year and upwards are not included in the table.

It was argued that the data from the Harlow Roman temple showed that sheep gave birth in spring in both Iron Age and Roman times, as they do now. Spring births of lambs are necessary to allow time for growth so as to ensure their best survival in the first winter. It seems probable that this was also the pattern in Neolithic times. If this is correct, the lambs of less than three months of age are evidence of a human presence during the spring at Hambledon Hill and the 6–9 month lambs would have been killed in the late summer

Table 8.4 Caprine dp_4 from Neolithic contexts, set out in ascending order of age using alphabetic designations of tooth wear stage illustrated by Grant (1982)

site	*find*	dp_4	M_1	M_2	*comment*
Shroton spur phase III	HH76 1904	b	–	–	almost unworn; newborn
Main enclosure phase VI	HH76 623	c	–	–	slight wear; less than 1 month of age
Inner Stepleton outwork phase V	ST79 1395	d	–	–	slight wear, less than 2 months of age
Outer Stepleton outwork phase III	ST80 2335	d	–	–	slight wear, less than 2 months of age.
Stepleton enclosure phase III	ST81 1107	f	c	–	slight wear on M_1, about 3 months of age.
Inner Stepleton outwork phase VII/a	ST78 2707	f	c	–	slight wear on M_1, about 3 months of age
Main enclosure phase VI	HH75 1837	f	d	V	moderate wear on M_1, about 3 months of age
Inner Hanford outwork phase III	HN82 344	g	f	–	6–9 months of age
Main enclosure phase VI	HH76 421	g	–	–	6–9 months of age
Stepleton enclosure phase III	ST81 437	g	–	–	6–9 months of age
B F2	HH75 215	g	–	–	6–9 months of age
Main enclosure phase IV	HH74 420	g	–	–	6–9 months of age
Stepleton enclosure phase VI	ST81 3187	g	–	–	6–9 months of age
Inner E cross-dyke phase I–II	HH75 1981	h	–	–	6–9 months age
Inner E cross-dyke phase VI	HH75 1473	h	d	b	Slight wear on M_2, 6–9 months of age

and autumn. Although the specimens are few, Table 8.4 shows that these two age groups appear to be separate and that no specimens fall between them. This implies – but certainly does not prove – a summer gap in the caprine slaughter. It would seem that the site was visited in the spring and late summer/early autumn, possibly with little or no use during the mid-summer and with no evidence for use in winter. An alternative possibility is that the few lambs of less than 3 months of age were summer births, and were killed at the same time as those aged at 6–8 months, all as autumn culls. This would have the effect of suggesting a more restricted human presence, only in the autumn.

In the light of the evidence for the prevalence of spring births in prehistoric and other early sheep, the first interpretation is preferred, in which the site was mainly used in the spring and late summer but with no evidence for winter use. However, with the small sample, and consequently limited data available, this point cannot be settled with certainty.

Conclusions

The sites on Hambledon Hill have together provided one of the larger bone samples from the British Neolithic. The bones come from a large number of different contexts and the sample has been analysed with regard to the complexity of the stratification. However, many of the resulting samples are of low numbers and not all samples from the excavated area are sufficiently large to have any numerical meaning alone. Consequently samples have been examined both from discrete contexts and 'lumped' by area, layer and/or phase. In some instances dense bone accumulations can be identified as the product of single or short-term events, and this is further explored in Part 2 (8.1.3 below).

The predominance of cattle in the fauna, and the general composition of the fauna, agree well with what is known of other causewayed enclosure sites. At Windmill Hill, Grigson (1999, table 145.3, 212) has reported that cattle form more than 63% to 71% of the three samples excavated from that site during the twentieth century. The cattle remains from Hambledon show some notable features, especially in relation to both the age profiles and to the sex ratio, both of were highly selected. The age profile is not that of a typical herd structure, which itself would be unsustainable with so few mature cows. This allows some further interpretation. These were animals that were *selected* for slaughter, but from a herd which is otherwise not represented at the site, and which must therefore have been housed elsewhere. This is a powerful argument that the cattle thus selected were taken from their living place, where the breeding herd was housed, to the site where they were killed.

A second point is also relevant to this discussion. It has been shown that the cattle were mainly killed as young adults, at ages where some, but not all, of the bones of the body would have been fused. While it is recognised that considerable post-fusion growth does take place in bones, sufficient work has been done on modern comparative samples to show that discrimination between the sexes is possible from these bones. Measurements of the earlier-fusing bones are indicative of a population that was predominantly female. The possible objections to this deduction have been set out above, but it is argued here that the findings relating to limb bone measurements from this and other sites and from the cattle horncores found at Durrington Walls does show that Neolithic cattle herds were largely made up of adult females.

The low numbers of wild animals are also characteristic of the known Neolithic sites in Britain, most of which are apparently of a ceremonial or ritual kind, in particular causewayed enclosures, henges, or often enigmatic pit fills. It would be reasonable to anticipate that domestic sites from the earlier Neolithic in Britain would be marked by high frequencies of wild mammals, both large and small, especially those that are fur-bearing, though this is not the case. An exception to this is the appropriately named Coneybury 'anomaly', an early Neolithic pit excavated near the Coneybury Henge in Wiltshire (Maltby 1990). The fill contained a substantial number of bones, apparently the remains of one butchery event, in which about eight cattle were slaughtered. Most of the cattle were young, and six were selected for cull in the same age group of 15–26 months which predominates at Hambledon Hill. Maltby identified the cattle as domestic, which is apparent from the selected age structure of the cull.

The Coneybury pit fauna is exceptional in that the primary fills of the pit contained 450 cattle bones, and also 304 roe deer bones, a proportion that Maltby described as '... unparalleled in Britain' for the early Neolithic period (ibid, 60). The high proportion of roe deer can be partly attributed to the more complete skeletal representation: for the roe deer, most bones of the body were identified while the cattle remains were mostly distal limbs. Even so, the frequency of roe deer is striking. At the same time, this abundance is in sharp contrast to the rather low proportion of red deer bones. This would suggest that the Neolithic hunters had access to areas of woodland with rather low, dense cover, which is preferred by the small, shy roe deer while the larger red deer prefers a more open woodland habitat. It is also possible that the roe deer were taken by collaborative drives using nets or traps, as was common for this species in later times (Whitehead 1964, 214–19).

It is unlikely that the Coneybury fauna was derived from a domestic settlement. Whatever the circumstance of its deposition, however, it emphasises the nature of the Hambledon Hill fauna, lacking as it does the degree of diversity that would be anticipated in settlements of the earlier Neolithic period.

It has often been assumed that the contents of such Neolithic pits are unstructured dumps of domestic rubbish, even in the absence of direct evidence to that end. Yet the evidence of deliberate arrangement of some such pit fills also needs to be considered (Barrett *et al* 1991; Legge 1991) and the bones from the Coneybury pit are evidently related to a brief and sumptuous slaughter event. However such sites are interpreted, and as much as recent archaeological theory interweaves the 'domestic' and the 'ritual', in the writer's view the Neolithic sites as yet excavated in southern Britain do not reflect the full range of daily maintenance activities and, in consequence, show only certain aspects of the Neolithic food-producing economy. The absence of a full range of anticipated debris and wastes of domestic food processing has been used to argue for a form of 'gathering' economy within the Neolithic, apparently of a form whereby domestic animals are commonplace, wild animals are rare, and the charred remains of both wild and domestic plants are also rare. As is shown elsewhere in this volume, at least where the charred plant remains are concerned, the apparent absence of evidence is more a reflection of minuscule sampling strategies in earlier excavations. Again, the cereals at Hambledon appear to have arrived in a semi-processed state; where, therefore, were the sites at which the processing was done? It is from these sites that bone remains may say something of the actual usage of the landscape and something of its form.

The nature of the activity at Hambledon, with several phases of recutting of ditches, has resulted in most of the bone samples being fragmented and dispersed. Only locally do articulated bones survive and, in some instances, substantial parts of entire carcasses are found. This suggests that butchery involved the stripping of meat from the bones and the partial processing of bones for fat extraction at one point. How cooking was accomplished in the Neolithic remains an open question, as roasting before a fire does not necessarily result in charring to the bones. In the writer's experience with cooking sheep, pigs and cattle in this manner, by the stage that any protruding bones are burnt, the meat has been rendered inedible by charring. It seems more likely that meat was cooked off the bone, by boiling or roasting. Whether the meals were prepared and eaten communally or in smaller groups remains an open question.

The number of cattle killed at Hambledon can be approximately calculated from the surviving teeth and bones (Table 8.5). The numbers of right and left mandibular teeth agree quite well in both instances, though the post-cranial bones give rather lower figures. In the central area the post-cranial bones suggest cattle numbers at about 52–80% of those indicated by the jaws while on the Stepleton spur, where the bones evidently underwent more harsh attrition, the bones suggest 30–60% of the number of cattle indicated by the jaws. Neither site was fully excavated. In the central area only about 20% of the enclosure ditch was excavated, and a smaller proportion of the interior and the

Table 8.5 Minimum number of cattle killed at Hambledon from the identified teeth and bones

	mandible	*proximal scapula*	*distal tibia*	*astragalus*
Central area ditches and features	36 right 38 left	26 right 30 left	27 right 23 left	25 right 20 left
Stepleton spur enclosure ditches and features	24 right 25 left	17 right 15 left	5 right 7 left	9 right 10 left

other ditches. At Stepleton a larger proportion of the enclosure ditch was excavated, amounting to about 70% of the ditch fills, together with almost all of the interior and varying proportions of the outworks. Taking the higher figures of cattle numbers as indicated by the mandibular teeth, it may be suggested that about 100 individual cattle were killed in the central area, while for Stepleton the figure is lower at perhaps 35–40. There are many factors, both known and unknown, that have worked against the survival of bones at these sites. Even so, the relative abundance of cattle bones and the number of beasts indicated do give some idea of the relative activity at the two sites.

8.1.3 Results part 2. Patterns of distribution at the Hambledon sites: species and bones

There is some evidence that the bone assemblages from the Hambledon sites were the product of substantial social gatherings. This raises the question as to the extent to which the distribution of bones within the site can throw any light on the nature of these events. The bone assemblage was clearly altered by dogs and, in some cases, probably by surface weathering before burial. The pattern of survival of cattle bones has been examined in detail as the most numerous and the most robust species found at the site.

Much effort is now expended in animal bone studies on understanding the processes that were involved in the dispersal and burial of animal bones, and it has long been recognised that the density of particular bones has a marked influence on their survival. Some of these problems have been discussed in Part 1 above. This part considers the distribution of the species and bones as these were found rather than a predicted pattern of discard based upon the cull ages.

Variation between sites in the Hambledon Neolithic complex

The nature of the site and its complex stratigraphy and phasing require that the composition of the fauna is considered at a local level where this is numerically possible. However, an overall view of the assemblage in the two main enclosure ditches – the main enclosure ditch and the Stepleton enclosure ditch – will serve as a background against which local deviations from this average can be seen.

The main enclosure ditch

The segmented main enclosure ditch produced a gross sample of 2307 identified bones and 366 jaws and loose teeth. Eighteen segments of the enclosure ditch have been excavated, and the Neolithic stratigraphy has been grouped into six phases (I–VI). The bone sample is firstly considered at this level. The tabulation of the proportions of species below are based upon limb bones (1988 specimens), as vertebrae, ribs and skulls were very fragmentary and had sometimes suffered further damage in excavation, with the attendant problems of quantification (Table 8.6). The proportions of the species show some degree of variation, although it should be noted that sample numbers differ greatly between the phases. Cattle predominate in all, though the proportion of these is lowest in phases IV and V. However, the final phase VI of the ditch fill, the upper 'slots', with their dense bone concentrations,

Table 8.6 Main enclosure ditch. Post-cranial bones (per cent)

	all ditch	*phases I+II*	*phase III*	*phase IV*	*phase V*	*phase VI*
cattle	59.4	66.3	71.9	49.0	55.8	60.9
caprines	15.4	13.8	12.3	18.8	15.9	16.0
pig	22.6	15.1	12.6	29.0	27.4	20.5
red deer	1.2	0	0.8	2.2	0.9	1.0
roe deer	0.7	0	0.5	0.6	0	0.8
dog	0.7	0	1.6	0.3	0	0.8
samples (no. of specimens)	2283	86	373	357	113	1059

Table 8.7 Main enclosure ditch. Mandibles (per cent)

	all ditch	*phases I+II*	*phase III*	*phase IV*	*phase V*	*phase VI*
cattle	43.3	18.2	73.7	34.8	33.3	45.0
caprines	26.9	36.3	21.0	39.1	33.3	17.5
pig	29.8	45.5	5.3	26.1	33.3	35.0
red deer	0		0			2.5
roe deer	0		0			0
dog			0			0
samples (no. of specimens)	104	11	20	23	6	40

shows a high proportion of cattle consistent within the earlier phases of the ditch fill, suggesting that the proportions in which the species were killed remained broadly consistent throughout the construction and sedimentation of the main enclosure ditch.

In tabulating the proportions of species from dentition (Table 8.7), loose teeth have not been included in the counts except in the cases of isolated dp_4 and M_3. With this method there is a small possibility that an animal might be counted twice as, during the development of the dentition, these two teeth are both present in the jaw for a short while until the dp_4 is shed. When this tooth falls, the roots show evidence of considerable resorbtion caused by pressure from the erupting P_4 from below. Where this root damage was present on a dp_4 it was not included in the counts. Samples with very few mandibles are not separately listed in the table. The mandible counts are much more variable between the phases of the enclosure ditch. Although cattle again are the major part of the fauna from the entire sample, caprines and pig make up a larger proportion of the fauna and the latter species is the most abundant mammal in phases I+II and phase VI. It must be remembered that both mandibles and maxillae are usually highly fragmented and, in the light of other evidence that some of the bone samples were disturbed subsequent to redeposition, it seems likely that the 'entire' sample is the more accurate reflection of the overall killing pattern at the site. The relatively small samples from some phases mean that variation may be more strongly influenced by local killing events. There is also some evidence for the differential deposition of head parts. In the 'entire' sample from each phase the mandible counts indicate a higher number of individuals than do the post-cranial bones, while the reverse is found in some ditch segments. Accordingly, the bones in each ditch segment have been examined for local evidence of variation. The following discussion concentrates mainly on the bones of cattle as these are, in most instances, numerically superior and because the robust skeleton of this species has better withstood the processes of attrition that work upon the bones.

Figure 8.24 shows the cattle bone survival for three of the largest samples which come from a single layer within a ditch segment, compared with the gross sample of identified bones from the main enclosure. The subsamples come from the denser bone accumulations in the 'slots' cut into the upper ditch fills. The basal sediments, and the ditch fills, have small samples which by their nature are highly variable. Sample 1 consists of the cattle bones from the 'phased' sample, ordered in decreasing abundance. The atlas vertebra shows the highest level of survival, closely followed by the distal humerus, distal scapula and distal tibia, all of which fuse early during the skeletal maturation. Later-fusing bones such as the proximal and distal femur, proximal tibia and distal metapodials have much lower rates of survival, as has been considered elsewhere.

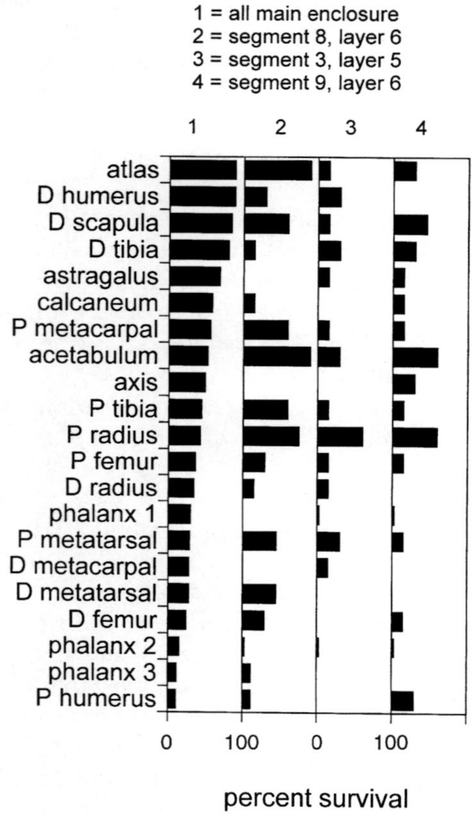

Fig 8.24 Survival of cattle bones from the three largest single-context samples compared with the gross sample from the main enclosure.

The whole sample from the enclosure ditches provides a broad pattern against which the bone representation in more local deposits can be considered. However, it must be remembered that the pattern of bone representation will reflect a wider range of events than human activity alone, as was shown in part 1 of this report.

Three of the larger cattle bone samples are compared with this pattern, each from one layer in one ditch segment. The sample from layer 6 in segment 8 is 103 bones. Some articulated bones of pig (left metacarpals III and IV) and caprine (phalanx 1–3) in this layer suggest that it was not disturbed after deposition. The cattle limb bones indicate a minimum of three animals in this layer, based on three atlas vertebrae, three right proximal tibia (one left), three right proximal metatarsals (no left), and three right proximal radius (two left). The mandibles in the same layer come from two infant cattle (dp_4 in early wear) and two adult cattle (two right and one left mandibles), giving a rather higher MNI count than do the bones. Some bones in the layer clearly come from infant cattle, though only a small proportion of these survive due to their fragility. Certain bones show significantly higher survival than is seen in the 'average' sample; in particular, the acetabulum of the pelvis, the proximal radius, proximal tibia and proximal metapodials.

Sample 3, from layer 5 in segment 3, consists of 54 identified cattle bones. It contains the bones of two, possibly three, cattle (three right proximal scapula, two each of right and left proximal radius, two left distal tibiae, two right acetabula). In this instance both the maxillary tooth rows and the mandibles also come from two adult cattle.

Sample 4 is from layer 6 in segment 9, based upon 45 identified cattle bones. The right proximal radius, left distal tibia and right acetabulum all suggest a minimum of two animals, though there are three right scapula articulations. The fragmentary mandibles also represent two animals.

The fills of the 'slots' thus appear to contain the bones of a small number of cattle, which it seems likely were killed and butchered in discrete events. The representation of skeletal parts is comparatively uniform between the samples, but with the later-fusing bones strongly represented due in particular to the age structure of the cattle cull at Hambledon.

A more detailed comparison is possible only if the samples are combined. Figure 8.24 shows the cattle bone representation in the three most prolific slots compared with the remaining parts of the fills from the ditch segments. The number of individuals (MInd) represented by jaws and by bones in these combined samples is shown in Table 8.8. Survival percentage is thus calculated upon a MInd count of 12 cattle for the 'slots' sample and 8 for the ditch fill sample. It is evident that the 'slots' sample has a better bone representation than that from the ditch fills, having as it does higher counts of the late-fusing bones, such as the axis and atlas vertebrae, and the acetabulum, proximal tibia, distal femur and distal metapodials. This supports the interpretation that the bones were accumulated as deliberate deposits in the 'slots' and were relatively little disturbed thereafter, while the bone accumulations in the fills had undergone a longer process of accumulation.

There is one bird bone from the main enclosure, the left radius of a small species of goose, from layer 8A (phase III) in segment 9. The specimen is somewhat smaller than that of the Greylag Goose, *Anser anser*. This suggests, on the basis of modern distributions, either the White-fronted Goose *Anser albifrons* or the Pink-footed Goose, *Anser brachyrhynchus*.

The inner east cross-dyke

This contained a sample of 222 identified bones, although most were from phase VI, in which cattle and pig bones were equal in number (Table 8.9). The larger sample, from phase VI, the 'slots' cut into the fill, has several examples of bones in articulation. In layer 6c in segment 4 was an articulated joint from the distal hind limb of pig, consisting of the astragalus, calcaneum and metatarsals III and IV. The distal metatarsals were fused. Paired pig metacarpals were also found in segment layer 6 of the same segment.

A large group of associated *Bos* bones in the upper fill of segment 1 appear to be from a relatively undisturbed deposit from a single event of consumption, which occurred in the early third millennium, on the evidence of a date of 2920–2700 cal BC (4255±50 BP; OxA-8893) for two articulated cattle vertebrae. The bones of two adult cattle were found, representing most elements of the skeleton. Some bones were found either as proximal or distal ends and these had been broken through the mid shaft for marrow extraction, while others were discarded whole, indicating that not all of the bones were processed in a manner to extract all available food. None of the bones were observed to show dog gnawing or burning. Only an unfused lumbar vertebra showed a single cut-mark. With these were further infantile cattle bones, and some bones of pigs and caprines. Two articulated caprine cervical vertebrae formed part of the same deposit (see below).

Table 8.8 Main enclosure. Minimum numbers of cattle in phase VI 'slots' and other ditch fills

cattle bones, phase VI 'slots'		*cattle bone, other ditch fills*	
mandibles	*post-cranial bones*	*mandibles*	*post-cranial bones*
9 right and 12 left	axis – 14	6 right and 7 left	axis – 8
	distal humerus –12		distal humerus – 8
	acetabulum – 11		scapula – 8

Table 8.9 Inner East cross-dyke

	phase I/II	*phase II*	*phase III*	*phase V*	*phase VI*	*phase VII*
cattle	2		3	9	31	46
caprine	2		5	3	24	13
pig	1		3	6	68	6
red deer					2	
roe deer						
dog		1				
totals	5	1	11	18	125	65

The cattle bones were:
Cranium: Fragmented skull and horncore. The mandible fragments come from at least three animals; 1 right M_3 is from an animal of about 30 months of age, and 2 right dp_4 come from animals of about 3 months and 24 months of age. Two left M_3 are from young adult cattle.

The axial skeleton:
Two cervical vertebrae, one fused, one unfused
5 thoracic vertebrae, all unfused
2 lumbar vertebra, unfused, one infantile
sacrum, with the centrum in process of fusion
1 right ischium of the pelvis.

The limb bones:
2 left scapulae, fused
1 complete left humerus, fused, and 1 right and 1 left proximal humeri, fused
1 complete left radius, 1 right and 1 left proximal radius, 1 right distal radius, all fused
2 right ulnae, fused
1 left distal femur, fused, and right shaft fragments
1 complete right tibia, 1 right proximal tibia, and right and left distal tibia, all fused
2 right proximal and one right distal metacarpals, fused
1 right proximal, and one right and three left distal metatarsals, fused. One infantile right metatarsal shaft and part of unfused distal articulation
1 right and 1 left astragalus
1 right navicular-cuboid
1 phalanx 1

A group of caprine bones was found in the same context and these are thought to be from one individual. These did not include head parts, but were all fused. These were: left distal humerus, right proximal radius, left proximal femur, left ischium, right proximal metacarpal and fragments, left calcaneum, 2 phalanx 1. Two associated caprine cervical vertebra were recorded as probably articulating.

The cattle post-cranial bones probably represent two animals which appear to have been deposited in a single brief event. If this was so, a prodigious quantity of meat would have been consumed, suggesting a gathering of some size. The large cattle of the Neolithic period would each have weighed 400–500 kg, so that the two cows together would be some 800 kg deadweight. About 500 kg of this would be immediately edible as meat and offal, suggesting that some hundreds of people would be present as consumers.

The bone representation, which includes much fragmented bone but also some complete limb bones, suggests that much of this was processed – and possibly consumed – in the immediate vicinity of the site. Almost all limb bones come from two animals, with only the femur and pelvic bones being under represented. Possibly these high-value joints were carried away from the kill site, though it must be remembered that these cattle were killed as young adults, as were most in the earlier episodes of activity at Hambledon, and thus before fusion of the femur and proximal tibia. This markedly reduces the likelihood of the survival of these bones owing to their lower density and a careful selection shown by dogs in taking such bones. It would seem that the site retained some social purpose, even into the later Neolithic.

The outer east cross-dyke

This ditch has a relatively small number of bones, and only in phase VI are these in any quantity (Table 8.10). The red deer bone in phase V is a right distal radius with the articulation in process of fusion. Most of the teeth in these levels were found loose. Phase I has fragments of a right caprine mandible, including an M_3 in full wear. Phase III has right and left M^3 from a young adult pig. Phase VI, with a larger sample, has two right mandible fragments of 20 months or so in age, and three left mandible fragments of cattle (two animals) again of young adults.

In phase VI, the 'slots' cut in the upper ditch fills, a good deal of the bone was deposited either in articulation or as discrete events. There is an unusual concentration of goat bones, probably of one individual. Several articulated limb segments were present in layer 4 of segment 4 (Table 8.11). Skull and rib fragments were also recorded from this context, and two adult caprine mandibles with M_3 in early wear to cusp 3,

Table 8.10 The outer east cross dyke

	phase I	*phase III*	*phase V*	*phase VI*
cattle	4	8	8	27
caprines		3	3	34
pig	1		7	12
red deer			1	
totals	5	11	19	73

Table 8.11 Outer east cross-dyke. Caprine bones in phase VI in segment 4

	recorded as goat	*recorded as caprine*
axial skeleton:	atlas, axis, 2 cervical and 1 thoracic vertebrae	
scapula		fragments only
humerus	1 right	fragments of left
radius/ulna		1 right
metacarpal	1 right	
femur		shaft fragments only
tibia	1 right	shaft fragments only
astragalus	1 right, 1 left	
calcaneum	1 right	
metatarsal	1 left	
phalanges	3 first, 1 second, 1 third	2 first
vertebrae		fragments of 2 cervical

though these were recovered only as complete sets of loose teeth. In Table 8.11 the fused, distal right metacarpal, two phalanx 1 and one phalanx 2 were recorded as an articulated group. A further sample from layer 4A, the fill of a second slot, which cut layer 4, comprised a fused right distal tibia, right astragalus and calcaneum. These too were recorded as an articulated sample. Layer 4 also contained a cattle acetabulum, ilium and pubis, which though not joined, were from the same specimen.

The inner south cross-dyke

A small sample of 63 identified post-cranial bones came from the phased Neolithic levels and bank deposits (Table 8.12). The small sample is of interest again because of the evidence for articulated segments of limbs that were deposited in the bank area and in the 'slots' cut into the upper ditch fill. In layer 2B beneath the bank was an articulated joint from a lower left hind limb of *Bos*, consisting of the distal tibia, astragalus, calcaneum, navicular-cuboid, the lateral and small cuneiform bones. There is also part of a proximal left metacarpal and right calcaneum. Parts of the vertebral column of *Bos* were found articulated in layer 9 of the ditch (phase VI/a): an axis vertebra and a cervical vertebra were articulated, as were two thoracic vertebrae and three lumbar vertebrae with a sacrum. It would appear that segments of the vertebral column were deposited while still joined by soft tissues. Jaws were highly fragmented and most teeth were loose premolars and molars, but with no third permanent molars. A group of isolated caprine teeth were probably from a right mandible, with an unerupted M_3, giving an age of 15–18 months.

Table 8.12 Inner south cross dyke. Identified bones by phase

	phase I	*phase III*	*phase VI*
cattle	6	7	27
caprines		4	3
pig	3	1	2
red deer			1
totals	9	12	33

The outer south cross-dyke

This ditch has a very small bone sample from the Neolithic levels, with only fragments of a goat skull from phase I, identified from the cross section of the horncore base. Phase II has fragments of infantile pig scapula (R), humerus (L) and radius (R), and left calcaneum, while cattle is represented by a fragmented right ilium and part ischium. The same phase has a part worn cattle M_3, again from a young adult. The possible Iron Age recut has the following numbers of identified bones: ten cattle, seven pig, two caprine and one roe deer. The composition of this group has the appearance of being derived from disturbed Neolithic fills.

The western outwork

This ditch produced only a small bone sample of 20 identified bones, 19 of which were from phase III, the chalk rubble fills. Of these, 17 are from cattle and two from pig. The bones were not disturbed after burial as in two instances conjoining fragments were found; the unfused proximal articulation and shaft of a right tibia in area 4 and lumbar vertebrae 4 and 5 in area 1. Together the two samples contain the following bones of *Bos*, some of which had been gnawed by dogs (indicated by * in the following list). The fragments were: one scapula, one humerus, two radii, one ulna, one ilium, four femora (one*), two tibia (one*), one metatarsal, one calcaneum*, and three vertebrae. The bones of more than one *Bos* are represented. For instance, an unfused articulation from a metacarpal cannot be from the same animal as a fused distal radius; proximal tibiae are present both fused and unfused, and the femur fragments were recorded as infantile. The few bones therefore represent parts of three individuals; one infantile, one of less than four years and one greater than that age. No mandibles or teeth were found in the basal silts or fills.

The south long barrow

The long barrow stratigraphy is divided into eight phases and the stratification requires that the bones are firstly considered by phases, as subdivision beyond this level results in very small samples in each context (Table 8.13). The largest samples come from phases III (chalk rubble ditch fills), VI (ditch 'slots') and VIII (tertiary fills and disturbance). The jaws are somewhat less fragmented than is found at most sites within the Neolithic complex, and 19 of 25 'countable' specimens have teeth remaining in their sockets (Table 8.14). The exception is the 'slots', where the pig mandibles are relatively intact but the cattle teeth were found loose.

The small sample of cattle bones in the basal silts does not present any particular feature; three fragments of right scapula, two distal right fused metacarpals, one phalanx 1 and two vertebra fragments were found. The largest sample is from the phase III ditch fills. In these, certain groups of bones were probably deposited in association. Segment 3 layer 13 has 25 cattle bones, of an unusual character. These include the following vertebrae: two atlas, two axis, three thoracic, one sacrum and two vertebral fragments. The vertebrae were all fully adult apart from one infantile thoracic vertebra. The low survival of vertebrae at the site in general makes the chance conjunction of these specimens very unlikely. Four fused distal metatarsals, two right and two left, were also found in the same segment and layer, with two phalanx 1, two phalanx 2 and one phalanx 3. The remaining bones are fragments of femur, ischium, pubis and a navicular-cuboid. This context also produced fragments of a radius and tibia of roe deer, both left side. In layer 19 of segment 1 two complete, right-hand-side

Table 8.13 Long barrow. Identified bones by phase

	phases I and II	*phase III*	*phase IV*	*phase V*	*phase VI*	*VI/I and II*	*phase VII*	*phase VIII*	*totals*
cattle	8	67	14	15	62	7	4	32	209
caprine		16	1	2	15	3	2	7	46
pig	2	13	4	4	7		4	13	47
red deer		2			2			1	5
roe deer		2							2
dog			1						1
totals	10	100	20	21	86	10	10	53	310

Table 8.14 Long barrow: identified mandibles by phase

	phase I	*phase III*	*phase IV*	*phase V*	*phase VI*	*inter slot silts*	*Phase VII*	*VIII –*	*totals*
cattle		3	1	1	5		1		11
caprine		2							2
pig		2	1		3				6
red deer									
roe deer									
dog									
totals		7	2	1	8		1		19

metacarpals were found together (HH771199). The measurements of these show that they were derived from large cows (see above).

The small bone sample from the phase IV deposit in the butt of the south-west ditch included 14 cattle bones, of which five were vertebrae, plus fragments of femur, metacarpal, rib, two mandibular hinges and two phalanges. Cattle bone in the 'slow silts' included a large proximal right metacarpal and a metatarsal, both identified as *Bos primigenius*. Further fragmentary *Bos primigenius* bones were identified from the 'slots'. The articulation of a left scapula, and a right distal humerus, though unfused, were identified as wild cattle and fragments of femur and tibia shaft were referred to that species. The slots in both ditches again have unusual quantities of associated vertebrae. Layer 18 in section IV in the north-west of segment 1 contained one cervical vertebra, one thoracic, three lumbar and fragments of possibly eight further vertebrae, as well as a right and a left fused acetabulum with ilium and pubis fragments, two left proximal radius and one scapula, two fused right distal tibia, an infantile right humerus shaft fragment and two phalanx 2. The same layer in section VI had one thoracic vertebra and eleven fragments of thoracic vertebra with right and left scapula, right and left proximal radius, left acetabulum and ischium, a right fused proximal femur, a left proximal metatarsal and skull and rib fragments. In the phase III fills, one pig and three cattle bones were gnawed by dogs, while this was not seen on any bones from the 'slots'. Two bones were charred; one bone from the grey pit and one from the slots.

Certain contexts and features of the long barrow present unusual associations of bones. These are often paired or in multiples of the same bone and significant numbers of vertebrae were also identified. It is probable that better preservation of the fragmentary specimens would have shown these to have been deposited in articulation. Other bones besides the vertebrae, such as the pelvis and the femur, also have very high meat values and it might be inferred that such joints were being preferentially deposited. However, this does not appear to have been the case. Figure 8.25 shows the bone representation for the cattle bones in phases III (chalk rubble fills) and VI (slots), compared with the whole barrow sample and that from the main enclosure ditch. As is shown above, bone representation in the main enclosure declines in relation to a complex interaction of bone density and bone fusion age, with the latter having a profound effect upon bone survival due to the particular age classes selected for slaughter at the site. Phases III and VI of the long barrow obviously have a less complete pattern of bone representation, largely due to the small sample sizes. It is also evident that certain bones are well represented in phases II and VI, in particular the scapula articulation, distal humerus, acetabulum, distal tibia, distal metacarpal and distal metatarsal, and in phase VI the proximal radius. These are all bones that fuse early, and would have been fused in most of the cattle killed at Hambledon. It would appear that the same processes of attrition had worked upon the bones deposited at the barrow as in most of the remaining areas of the site.

Features in the central area

The features were mainly rather shallow pits, truncated by modern ploughing. Ninety-three identified bones and 44 jaws and loose teeth come from 26 features, among which cattle bones predominate (Fig

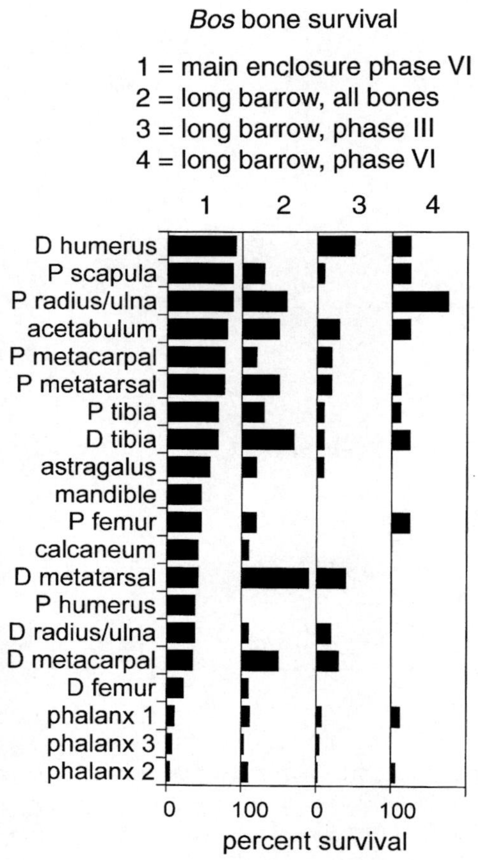

Fig 8.25 Survival of cattle bones from the entire south long barrow sample and phases III and VI of the barrow compared with those of phase VI (the slots) from the main enclosure.

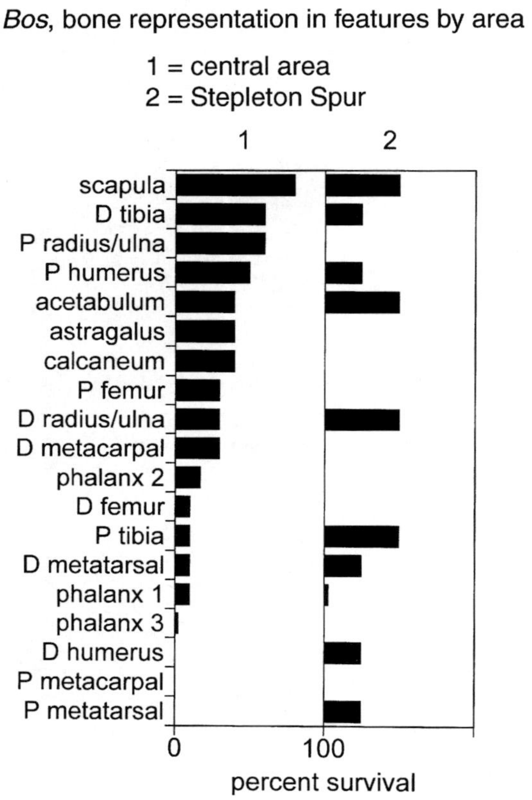

Fig 8.26 Cattle bone survival in the discrete features of the central area and Stepleton spur.

8.26). Skulls and mandibles are very fragmented and most identifications of cranial parts are of loose teeth. These need represent no more than four pig, three cattle and two caprines. Most of the features have few bones:

P2 F14 Of the 13 identified bones from this feature, seven are fragments of distal limb (cattle five and caprine two).

N F 1 contained 11 identified bones, five of which are fragments from at least three cattle ribs.

N F 7i/ii contained only a single pig incisor, and the mandibular ramus of a dog. A more diverse fauna is represented by the post-cranial bones. Pig bones were mainly shaft fragments of scapula (right and left), right radius and ulna, and the right ilium and ischium of the pelvis. A right radius fragment was referred to red deer. Cattle bones are again mainly from the hind limb; right ilium and left ischium, right distal fused femur, right distal fused tibia and shaft fragments (both right and left), and a part axis vertebra, one thoracic vertebra, a complete sacrum and five rib fragments. A fragment of left humerus shaft was identified as caprine.

N F11, layer 3. This feature contained three right M_3 of pig. Two of these were loose and in early wear on the first cusp and one was erupting through the bone of a mandible fragment. These represent three young adult animals, aged about 16–18 months. Only an isolated cattle molar represented any other species.

Limb bones of pigs comprised a distal fused tibia and two fragmentary vertebrae in process of fusion. Cattle bones were relatively more common, and comprise parts of two cattle hind limbs and some fragments of forelimb. A right innominate (ilium and ischium) was found in process of fusion, together with two unfused proximal femoral articulations, shaft fragments of tibia, two left astragali, a navicular-cuboid, two phalanx 1 and fragments of lumbar and other vertebrae. The front limb was represented by a very fragmented right scapula, right humerus, and right ulna. A left immature cattle radius was also present. Only three caprine bones were found; a fused left distal tibia, right astragalus and a fused lumbar vertebra.

Figure 8.27 shows the cattle bone representation in features N F11, layer 3 and N F7i/ii, layer 3, compared with the bone representation in all features that were excavated in the central area. In both features the front limb is represented by scapula and radius-ulna, though the humerus is absent from N F11 L3. There are, though, few metacarpal bones. The axial skeleton is quite well represented by pelvic bones, recorded here as 'acetabulum' and the hind limb by the proximal

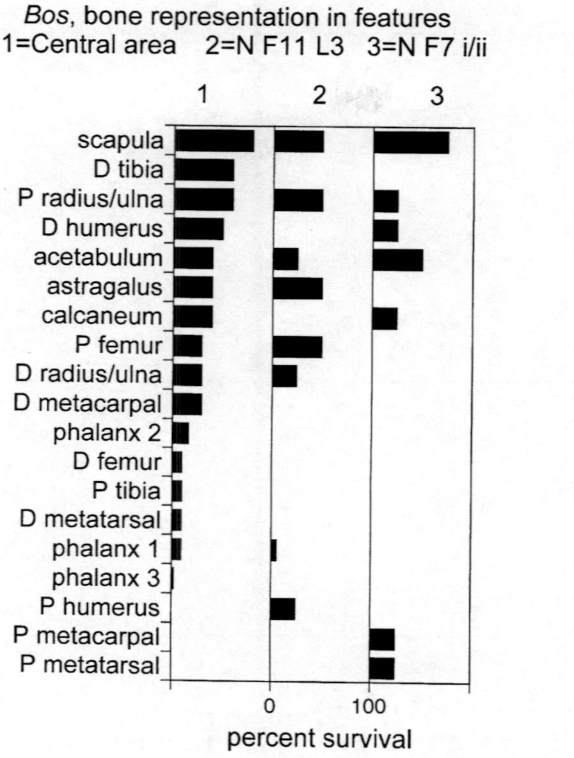

Fig 8.27 Cattle bone survival in a combined sample from all features in the central area compared with the two largest samples from features there.

Table 8.15 Selected central area features. Totals of cattle limb and pelvic bones and totals of pelvis fragments among them

feature	*no. of identified cattle limb and pelvic bones*	*no. of* Bos *pelvic fragments*
B F2	3	1
N F1 layer 3	3	1
N F6 layer 3	4	0
N F7i/ii layer 3	14	2
N F7iii layer 3	12	4
N F10 layer 3	3	2
N F11 layer 3	19	4
N F25	11	4

femur in N F11 L3. Pelvic bones are highly prone to fragmentation but, bearing this in mind, there are substantial fragments, and these form a rather high proportion of the identified bones (Table 8.15). This tabulation excludes ribs and vertebrae which, because of their fragmented state, are problematic to quantify. Of 71 identified cattle limb and pelvic bones, nearly one-third – 18 fragments – are from the pelvis. The pelvis is of high meat value and, although the associated femur is less common, the narrow age range of slaughter for the cattle would mean that most of these were discarded unfused with a consequent low probability of survival. The presence of the femur in N F11, and the general scatter of the somewhat denser pelvic bones does suggest that discrete events of consumption may be represented by the larger pit fills. On the other hand, 15 of the pits have less than 10 identified bones in each and some contain a large proportion of limb extremities. While such body parts are of obvious utility, there is no pattern common to all pits.

The Shroton spur outwork

There is a sample of only 143 identified post-cranial bones, 100 of which come from the phased Neolithic levels (Table 8.16). The basal silts of segment 1 contained the partial skeleton of a dog (HH76 2864), consisting of the skull and mandible, with bones of the left forelimb, consisting of humerus, scapula, radius and ulna, carpals, with metacarpals I–IV. A few bones from the right forelimb were found, consisting of one metacarpal IV and three of the carpal bones. Beside the dog were the bones of two distal sheep limbs, presumably deposited at one time: right and left proximal metacarpals, right and left distal metacarpals, one complete left metatarsal, one phalanx 1, two phalanx 2 and two phalanx 3. The phase III fills of segment 2 had associated pig bones – an immature radius and ulna, found together, and phase II in the same segment 2, layer 8, had pig metacarpals IV and V, also found in association. A second articulated dog (HH76 1608) was exposed in a phase III deposit in the south face of the excavation. Only some vertebrae and ribs were recovered.

Teeth and jaws:
Phase I in segment 1: a left mandible from the semi-complete dog, with adult teeth P_2 to M_2 with little wear.
Phase III in segment 3: pig dp_4 with heavy wear, about 10–12 months of age. Cattle: left M_3 with slight wear, aged about 26 months, right mandible, aged about 28 months, and right mandible aged about 3–5 years. Caprine: right dp_4 infantile, and, in segment 2, left M^3, about 24 months.

The Stepleton enclosure ditch

The Stepleton enclosure ditch has produced a sample of 598 identifiable bones from the phased Neolithic deposits and 37 mandibles and loose teeth. The proportions of the species are shown in Table 8.17. Table 8.18 shows the composition of mandibles alone. Besides those listed in the table, there were an immature dog mandible found in phase I, an adult right dog mandible in phase III and the fragmentary cranium of an immature dog in phase IV.

The most striking feature of the faunal assemblage is that the different tabulations, based firstly upon the identified post-cranial bones and then on the number of jaws, show certain divergences. The proportions of species show a good deal of variation from one site to another, with cattle forming a smaller proportion of the bones than is found in the various phases of the

Table 8.16 Shroton spur. Identified bones by phase

		phase I+II	*phase III*	*phase V*	*phase VIII/a*	*totals*
cattle	3	4	30 (44.8%)	2	23 (53.5%)	62
caprine		15	11 (16.4%)	1	8 (18.6%)	35
pig		1	22 (32.8%)	2	9 (20.9%)	34
red deer					3 (7.0%)	3
dog			4 (6.0%)			4
totals	3	20	67	5	43	

Table 8.17 Stepleton enclosure ditch 1: post-cranial bones (per cent)

	all ditch	*phase III*	*phase IV*	*phase V*	*phase VI*	*phase VIII/a*
cattle	54.7	50.4	67.4	46.3	56.3	53.2
caprines	14.4	23.6	12.2	4.9	11.3	14.6
pig	24.1	19.3	14.3	43.9	26.3	24.4
red deer	4.8	6.7	4.1	4.9	1.9	6.7
roe deer	1.0	0	2.0	0	1.4	0.6
dog	1.0	0	0	0	2.8	0
sample	598	119	49	41	213	164

Table 8.18 Stepleton enclosure. Mandibles (per cent)

* = isolated upper tooth only

	all ditch	*phase VI*	*phase VIII/a*
cattle	35.1	50.0	36.4
caprines	13.5	10.0	18.2
pig	40.5	30.0	27.3
red deer	2.7	0	9.0
roe deer	*	0	0
dog	8.1	0	9.0
sample	37	10	11

Table 8.19 Middle Stepleton outwork. Bone by phase

phase	*pig*	*roe deer*	*red deer*	*cattle*	*caprine*	*totals*
I	1	0	1	6	3	**11**
II	2	0	0	5	2	**9**
III	7	1	2	13	9	**32**
V	3	1	0	8	3	**15**
Misc and unstratified	1	0	0	0	0	**1**
totals	14	2	3	32	17	

main enclosure ditch, while pig bones are significantly more common. Caprine bones are variable from phase to phase. Red deer make up 6.7% of the identified bones in the ditch fills, the highest proportion found in the Neolithic complex. Even so, no more than one animal needs be represented. All bones in which this state could be determined were fused; right and left scapulae, left proximal and left distal metatarsals, fragments of left tibia shaft, a left navicular-cuboid and right calcaneum (the latter having the appearance of being from an aged animal), sacrum and a single phalanx 1. Interestingly, the right scapula is pierced, apparently by a projectile.

Few articulated bones were found. In the phase III fills a left distal tibia and astragalus of *Bos* appeared to articulate well (segment 15, U10, layer 3B), and in the 'midden like' phase VI deposits (segment 3, U9D, layer 2) conjoining parts of a right innominate, and a tibia and patella probably came from a dog, most of which remained in articulation at the interface of the phase III and phase VI fills. In the supposed old ploughsoils a right distal cattle tibia and right astragalus articulate well (segment 2, U16B, layer 1).

The middle Stepleton outwork (Ditch 3)

This provided a small sample of identified bones, teeth and jaws (Table 8.19). In spite of the small sample, several groups of bones were found in articulation. In the basal silts of the ditch a *Bos* right astragalus and calcaneum were found in a group of bone at the interface of the phase II and phase III silts (segment 5, layer 4A, phase I) and a *Bos* phalanx 1 and phalanx 2 in the phase I–II silts (segment 11 layer 5). The phase III fills contained part of an immature caprine (segment 5 layer 3A) consisting of a scapula, humerus and radius. Also in phase III (segment 6 layer 4), several *Bos* vertebrae were found in articulation, including two well-preserved and five fragmentary cervical and lumbar vertebrae (ST79 2152). One of these, identified as C5, was heavily diseased.

The dentition from the ditch is again very fragmentary. Phase II has two left maxillary dp^4 from pigs aged

Table 8.20 Inner Stepleton outwork. Bone by phase

phase	*cattle*	*caprine*	*pig*	*red deer*	*roe deer*	***totals***
I	5		3			8
II	4	2	1			7
III	74 (55.2)	16 (11.9)	30 (22.5)	12 (8.9)	2 (1.5)	134
V	55 (43.3)	27 (21.2)	33 (26.0)	7 (5.5)	5 (4.0)	127
VII	53 (45.7)	22 (19.0)	27 (23.2)	8 (6.9)	6 (5.2)	116
VIII/a	53 (45.7)	28 (24.1)	23 (19.8)	9 (7.8)	3 (2.6)	116
Totals	244	95	117	36	16	

Table 8.21 Inner Stepleton outwork. Mandibles

phase	*pig*	*roe deer*	*red deer*	*cattle*	*caprine*	*totals*
II	1			1		2
III	2	1	0	3	1	7
V	2	1	0	3	2	8
VII	2	1	1 tooth	3	2	8
VIII/a	2	0	1 tooth	3	2	7
totals	9	3		13	7	

Table 8.22 Inner Stepleton outwork. Survival of bones in relation to jaws and loose teeth, based on that part of the sample summarised in Tables 8.39–40

	bones	*jaws*	*ratio bones:jaws*
cattle	244	13	23.5:1
caprine	95	7	13.6:1
pig	117	9	13.0:1
roe deer	16	3	5.3:1

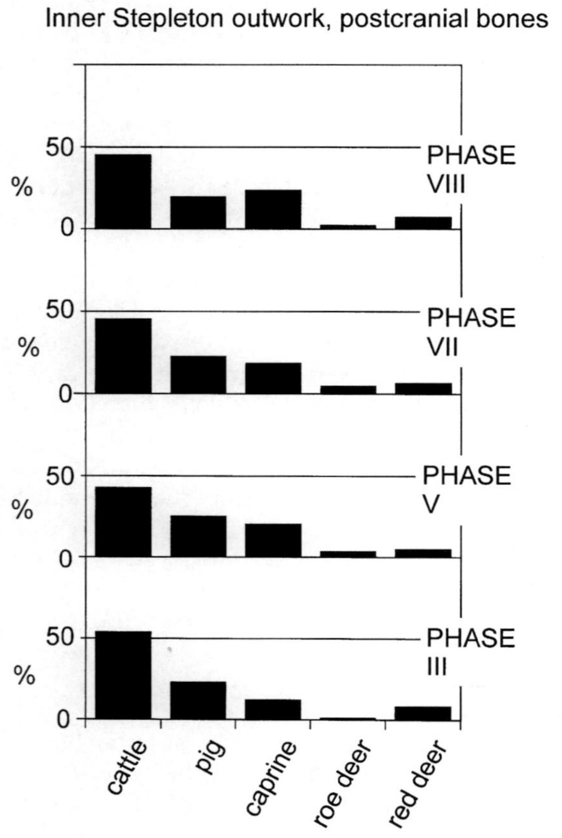

Fig 8.28 Species composition from post-cranial bones only from the inner Stepleton outwork.

a few weeks, and a left M^3 from a young adult. Phase III has two left dp^4, again from pigs aged only a few weeks, and the left mandibular dp_4 from a young lamb. Phase V has a left mandibular tooth row (M_1–M_3) of a pig, with unworn M_3, aged about 18 months. The same phase has a mandibular tooth row (M_2 and M_3) of *Bos*, aged 24–30 months.

The inner Stepleton outwork (Ditch 2)

The ditch provided a sample of 508 identified post-cranial bones from six phases (Table 8.20). Only four of these have more than 100 post-cranial bones. The distribution of the five most common species, based only on the numbers of identified specimens, is quite uniform (Fig 8.28). The mandibles from all phases are highly fragmented, and most teeth are found loose. Consequently the calculation of the number each species represented is based upon upper or lower teeth, both loose and in jaws, by counting third deciduous and third permanent molars (Table 8.21). The survival of bones in relation to jaws and loose teeth is shown in Table 8.22. This shows that the bones and jaws have undergone a good deal of attrition, and that the bones are more fragmented and preservation is generally poorer here than in the central area. The best survival of bones is from the cattle, as the most robust species, with caprines and pigs showing a much lower ratio. The low survival of roe deer bones might in part result from differential transportation. The low number of pig bones surviving relative to the jaws is related to the early ages at which most pigs were killed so that a large proportion of the pig bones were discarded as infantile bones or in the unfused state.

In spite of the evidence of a high level of attrition shown by the ratios of identified bones to mandibles, several groups of articulated bones were found in the following contexts:

Phase III, segment 6, C2, layer 4

Several cattle vertebrae, found in articulation (ST 79 601)

Phase V (segment 5, C11, layer 3B)

A concentration of bones suggests that the post-cranial bones of two sheep and some articulated beaver bones were deposited at the same time. The sheep bones consist of: one left scapula, two right and two left distal humerus (all fused), two right and 1 left proximal radius, one right and one left proximal ulna, two right femur shaft, two left distal tibia (both fused), left patella, left proximal metacarpal, five fragmentary vertebrae, and rib fragments. In this same context was part of the right hind limb of a beaver, comprising the innominate, femur shaft, tibia shaft (unfused proximal) a metatarsal IV, and astragalus and calcaneum. No cranial parts of the sheep were found, but a single upper beaver tooth was recorded from the same context.

Phase V (segment 8, layer 3)

Right and left fused distal humeri of roe deer, found together and recorded as a probable pair from the same animal. The right scapula, right proximal radius and a part metatarsal shaft were also present in the same layer of the same segment. In segment 6 there was a part right femur shaft of roe deer. The proximity of the specimens, and the general rarity of roe deer at the site, suggests that these may all be parts of the same individual.

Phase VIII/a (segment 3, layer 3)

A concentration of foot bones from pig were found, consisting of right and left metatarsals III, metacarpal IV and phalanx 1 and phalanx 2.

Phase VII/a

This phase was recorded in excavation as having the character of a midden. However, the bones present no particular features other than being highly fragmented. None were recorded as articulating.

Other species from the Inner Stepleton outwork

Dog: a left tibia shaft, phase III and a right tibia shaft, phase V

Fox: an axis vertebra, phase III, and a right ulna, phase V

Frog: a partial skeleton in phase III

Bird: two bird bones were found together in layer 6 in cutting 5 (both ST79 1027):

1. Proximal right coracoid, articular surface damaged. Due to this damage, on both form and size this fits well with the Carrion Crow *Corvus corone corone* or possibly the Rook *Corvus frugilegus.*
2. Shaft fragment of proximal left humerus, articulation missing. This resembles that of the Great Crested Grebe *Podiceps cristatus* though the identification is tentative.

Rabbit: bones were found in phases V (one bone), VII (seven bones), VII/a (one bone and most of one skeleton). These bones are regarded as intrusive.

The proportions of the larger mammals found in the inner Stepleton outwork do not differ from the rest of the site with the exception that red and roe deer are rather more common. The age profile of the cattle shows a rather greater spread in the age classes and increased younger animals in the cull. Of 17 part mandibles and loose teeth that can be placed into age classes, six are from very young calves, six come from 6–26 month animals, and five are older than 36 months.

The outer Stepleton outwork (ditch 4)

This ditch produced only a small sample of 50 identified bones (Table 8.23). Three cattle bones showed significant dog gnawing (two in phase III, one in phase VII/a) and a cow horncore in phase III showed rodent gnawing. The caprine bones in phase I (segment 7, layer 4) were a left and right distal tibia, with a right astragalus and navicular cuboid. The right-hand bones appeared to have been deposited in articulation.

The rabbit bones in phase VIII/a (Site 1B, segment 7, layer 2) were found as a partial skeleton and are regarded as intrusive.

Few mandibles were recovered from this ditch. A *Bos* left M^3 in phase VIII/a is from a young adult and in superficial contexts an M_3 came from an animal of 8 years or more in age. In phase I and phase VIII/a isolated dp_4 were from pigs of a few weeks of age. In phase I was a right maxilla with the dentition P^4– M_3 is from a pig aged between 24 and 30 months. Caprines and red deer are represented only by isolated teeth.

Table 8.23 The outer Stepleton outwork. Bone by phase

phase	*pig*	*roe deer*	*red deer*	*cattle*	*caprine*	*totals*
II	0	0	0	1	6	7
III	2	0	1	23	3	29
VII/a	0	0	0	2	0	2
VIII/a	0	0	1	0	2	1
Misc and unstratified	1	0	1	1	0	3
totals	3	0	3	27	11	

Stepleton features

Skulls and mandibles are also very fragmented in these features, mainly represented by loose teeth. Reduced to a minimum number, there would be no more than two pigs, two cattle and one caprine. A single roe deer upper molar was identified. The 118 identified bones were predominantly those of pig. The identified specimens are distributed among 25 features, with most from 4B F137 (four pig, nine cattle, nine caprine) and 4B F178 (24 pig, 6 cattle, 12 caprine). The remaining features have five or less identified bones in each. One bone each of red deer (metatarsal fragment, 2A F182) and roe deer (metatarsal, 4B F130) were identified. ST82 F39, which contained a large amount of charred grain, produced only an unfused pig metatarsal and a proximal fused tibia of *Bos*. The largest sample of any one species – the 24 pig bones from feature 4B F178 – are predominantly foot bones, plus four fragments of pelvis and five from bones of the font limb.

Inner Hanford outwork

A sample of only 141 post-cranial bones was found in this ditch (Table 8.24). The cattle bones in the basal silts (phase I) were fragments of radius and ulna, two right distal metacarpals, one fused and one unfused, a right innominate, an axis vertebra, lumbar vertebra and sacrum, and horncore and rib fragments. No articulated groups of bone were identified.

Teeth and jaws:
phase I: *Bos* – left maxilla of young adult
phase III: sheep – right mandible of adult and left mandible of immature
phase III: pig – right mandible, 24 month old.
phase VII/1: pig – right dp^4, a few months old
phase VII/a: pig – a left maxilla, about 6 months old.

Outer Hanford outwork

This ditch has a small sample of bones and jaws, though with some large segments of articulated or associated *Bos* skeleton (Table 8.25).

Very few jaws and teeth were found. Phase I had two right mandibles of pig, one aged about 4 months and the second 12 months. In phase VII/1 was the left mandible of a pig of about 24 months.

In the phase I (segment 3, U1, layer 5, find HN82 153) were seven cattle lumbar vertebrae and a sacrum, which were discarded in articulation. A further group of associated bones from the same context (find HN82 154) consisted of a complete right innominate and fragments of the left, with a complete left tibia. All bones were fully fused. It is very probable that both groups of bones were derived from the butchery of the same animal. From the same segment but in layer 5A and from farther north, were two thoracic and two lumbar *Bos* vertebrae, probably originally articulated. The two lumbar vertebrae were fused together by pathological exostoses. In the basal silts of segment 2 (phase I, U7, layer 5C) was part of an articulated hind limb of pig, comprising the astragalus, calcaneum, the navicular and the cuboid.

'Flint mines'

The bone sample from these features is unusual in two respects. Firstly, the fauna has greater diversity than is found elsewhere on the site and, secondly, the majority of the bones and jaws from the larger mammals, with the exception of the cattle, are infantile and juvenile (Table 8.26). It is probable that at least some of the immature animals were deposited as whole carcasses. Some of the bones are scattered and fragmented but piglet bones in layer 2 of F644 come from two newborn individuals that were deposited entire. An infantile mandible and other pig bones in layer 3 of F601 may also represent one individual, as may caprine bones in layer 2 of F644. Evidence for dog gnawing on the caprine tibia suggests that a whole or part carcass may have been partially destroyed. A fused right distal humerus in layer 2 of F618, though slightly eroded and the measurement consequently estimated, is from a male of *Bos primigenius*. Badger bones in layer 1 of F601 come from a right forelimb (humerus and radius/ulna), with also a fused, left distal tibia. Roe deer bones in layer 2 of F644 are mainly those of the distal hind limb, right and left metatarsal fragments and phalanges. Red deer are represented by right and left metatarsals and a right metacarpal plus metacarpal

Table 8.24 Inner Hanford outwork. Bone by phase

	phase I	*phase III*	*phase VII/1*	*phase VII/a–b*
cattle	18	36	13	31
caprine	2	10	2	3
pig	1	14	8	5
red deer		1		1
roe deer				1
dog		1		
totals	21	62	23	41

Table 8.25 Outer Hanford outwork. Bone by phase

	phase I	*phase III*	*phase VII/1*	*phase VII/a*	*totals*
cattle	24	6	13	3	46
caprine	4	1	3		8
pig	14	4	2	1	21
red deer			1		1
roe deer			1		1
totals	42	11	20	4	

Table 8.26 'Flint mines'. Identified post-cranial bones

* infantile individuals

species	*post-cranial bones*
dog	14
pig	16 + 2 individuals*, ?3rd individual*
roe deer	16
red deer	6
cattle (domestic)	42
caprines	26 + ?1 individual*
badger	10
fox	9
otter	1
hare	3
squirrel	1
rabbit	2
mole	6

fragment in layer 2 of F618, and, in layer 3 of F601, by a fused distal metacarpal and metatarsal fragment. In layer 2 of F644 was the proximal left ulna of a medium-sized duck, with the articulation damaged. This specimen is possibly from the Mallard *Anas platyrhynchos* or the Widgeon, *Anas penelope*.

The tooth rows are also largely those of immature and even neonatal animals:

Pig
Two left mandibles, newborn. Right mandible, aged 6 months. Three isolated milk teeth are probably derived from these specimens. The mandibles with two skeletons of piglets, the mandibles showing these to be newborn. Left mandible, newborn. Right mandible, about three months of age. Loose upper and lower deciduous teeth probably come from these specimens.

Cattle
Four upper permanent premolars and one M^1 are fully adult. Two loose upper and lower molars, adult. Upper left maxilla, from an aged specimen with permanent molars in heavy wear.

Caprines
A right mandible aged 3–4 months. Left maxilla, about 3–4 months of age and unfused shaft of left ulna, left femur, right tibia (gnawed distal), left metacarpal and metapodial fragments, phalanges 1 and 2. In addition, fragmentary right and left maxillae, about 18 months of age. Right and left mandibles, probably paired, aged 2–3 months.

Dog
Left mandible with unworn milk dentition.

Fox
Right and left mandibles and a fragmentary right maxilla. All infantile. Skull and mandible fragments, adult. A fragmentary skull, with adult but unworn dentition.

Roe deer
A left mandible with slightly worn premolars; about one year of age. Right and left maxilla fragments, with lightly worn dp^4; aged a few weeks only.

In addition to the above, the fills of these features contained large numbers of amphibian bones, both of frogs (*Rana* sp) and toad (*Bufo* sp). It is probable that these derive from entire skeletons as most of the bones were unbroken and were found in local concentrations. Consequently these are regarded as bone accumulations from deaths during hibernation. Smith (1954) records that toads often hibernate in places far removed from their spawning places, and frequently use the burrows of other mammals as places of concealment. A toad had apparently (and unsuccessfully) hibernated in the post-orbital fossa of a cow skull from a Neolithic pit at Down Farm in Dorset (Legge 1991). The frog prefers to hibernate in or near water, though Smith (1954) reports that the hibernation sites may on occasions be at some distance from water.

Modern skeletons of the common toad *Bufo bufo* and the common frog *Rana temporaria* were used for comparison and, from the similarity of the comparative and prehistoric specimens, it is probable that these species were the common forms found in the prehistoric levels. The bones were, in most cases, unbroken, showing that these species were not food items derived from the fox or badger. They amounted to at least 59 individuals, mainly of *Bufo*.

The bones of at least some of the smaller animals are thus likely to be intrusive, and this may also explain the presence of the fox and badger bones, mammals also likely to have burrowed into the sediments. The hare and squirrel do not burrow and the otter would be unlikely to live in the hilltop setting. However, a modern fox skeleton in the author's reference collection was a stray find during archaeological excavations in Cambridgeshire, the animal having died in its burrow. Careful retrieval showed the stomach contents to have been five hare feet. Possibly the few bones of the hare, beaver and squirrel were food remains carried by foxes or other meat-eating mammals. Rabbit bones have been found in many of the superficial sediments at Hambledon Hill and there is little evidence that the species was present in Britain in prehistoric times. The pit contents are likely therefore to be a mixture of adventitious and discarded bones, and not the product only of human intent, especially as the pits seem to have been backfilled. Possibly the loose fill proved attractive for borrowing mammals, which occasionally died there. The infantile pig and caprine specimens might be regarded as scavenged carcasses, carried to den areas by the carnivorous mammals, though the infrequent evidence for gnawing argues against this. The original purpose of pits can seldom be inferred from the contents, which are usually secondary to the primary purpose. This seems to be the case here, where an unusual diversity of species arose from a combination of circumstances.

8.1.4 Conclusions

The fills of ditches and features at Hambledon present a variety of conditions for both deposition and preservation of the bones. The bones have been examined in detail in relation to the complex stratification of the site. Although the bone sample is large, division into the many segments and phases of the ditch fills means that some samples are of low numbers. For example, the main enclosure ditch has 18 excavated segments and six main phases of sedimentation within these. A sample of 2283 identified bones, divided between 108 contexts, gives samples that show a high degree of variation in the species found. As has been shown, the combined sample – whether from the entire Neolithic ditch fill, or from the different phases into which this has been subdivided – shows that cattle predominate in the fauna. When examined at the level of individual contexts, pig bones often equal or exceed those of cattle. This is commonly found in the analysis of archaeological samples where variability can be closely related to sample size. In the case of the main enclosure ditch fills, the variability may well be real and a reflection of the periodic human activities there, though in most instances the bone samples show variable degrees of attrition, which has been further clouded by the multiple recutting and the inevitable incorporation of reworked bones back into the sediments.

The samples from the Stepleton ditches are smaller than those from the main enclosure, though the comparison of the whole samples from both ditches suggests that the faunas were very similar. It is striking that at both sites the post-cranial bones show a predominance of cattle at 55–60% and pig bones at 23–24%, while comparison of the mandibles shows pigs to have been rather more common than cattle on the Stepleton spur, at 40.5% in the Stepleton enclosure ditch against 30% in the main enclosure ditch. It is quite possible that the mandibles give a better reflection than the post-cranial bones of the proportions in which the species were killed. A large proportion of pigs were killed when very young, and almost all were under two years of age. It has been shown that bone survival in this species, in relation to the mandible count, is little more than half that found for the cattle bones. However, although more pigs may have been killed than cattle at certain times and places at the site, it must be remembered that these were mostly small animals while the cattle were large and in early maturity. A further difference which appears to be genuine is the consistently higher proportion of red deer bones at the Stepleton enclosure.

The uppermost ditch recuts in the central area, designated as the 'slots', do reveal discrete events of slaughter and consumption, often with evidence that several cattle were killed at one time. In these features the bone representation tends to be more complete and the bones are commonly in larger fragments and found in articulation. Many of these bone deposits suggest that the meat was removed from the bones by stripping away the muscle groups and the bones then discarded with relatively little further processing. This, combined with the evidence for the highly selected ages of the cull cattle, supports the interpretation that events of a particular character were associated with the use of the site, and that part of these activities was the consumption of meat in large quantities.

Given that the bird bones are so few in number, little can be said about their significance. The specimens of duck and goose were likely to have been eaten, but also would have provided feathers for the flights of arrows, among other purposes. The evident abundance of carrion at the site – as both human and non-human remains – would have provided considerable encouragement to both rooks and crows to visit. Both species were used as food in the past, even, if rarely, into recent times. The gathering of young rooks was the more favoured due to the colony nesting habit of the species. However, the meat is regarded as '... dry and coarse' (Davidson 1999).

8.1.5 Appendix: measurements

Dog

The dog bones from Hambledon Hill are, in the main, scattered and fragmentary. The measurements that could be taken show that the dogs were of the comparatively uniform Neolithic type as described by Harcourt (1974). The factors used by Harcourt to calculate shoulder height from limb bone length in dogs are used here (ibid, 154).

The dog skeleton from segment 3 of the Stepleton enclosure has complete humerus and radius from both sides and a complete left tibia. It seems very probable that Harcourt's 'total length' measurement for these bones is the same as the measurement GL after Dreisch (1976). Using Harcourt's factors for these bones, the stature of this dog is calculated from the humerus at 0.46 m and at 0.45 m from both the radius and tibia. Another complete humerus, found with a few cranial and vertebral fragments, is from a slightly smaller dog and in this instance the shoulder height is calculated as 0.41 m. These fall within, or close, to the size range calculated from long bone measurements given by Harcourt (1974, 157, table 1, and multiplication factors, 154).

Cranial measurements from Hambledon Hill are few, but those available again agree closely with Harcourt's data. One complete maxillary tooth row (P^2 to M^2) has a length measurement of 59.9 mm. This is equivalent to Harcourt's measurement XI, for which he lists five Neolithic specimens from southern England as 58 mm and 65 mm (Windmill Hill), 61 and 64 mm (Maiden Castle) and 60 mm (Easton Down). Harcourt gives the 'mandibular cheek tooth row length' for these same specimens, which is evidently the same as measurement 13 of Dreisch (1976, fig 23a) as 64 mm and 71 mm (Windmill Hill), 68 mm and 69 mm (Maiden Castle) and 67 mm (Easton Down). The mandible from the Hambledon dog skeleton has a length of 65.6 mm for this measurement and a second specimen from the Shroton outwork is 63.0 mm on this dimension. The skull and mandible measurements from Hambledon Hill thus fall within the range of contemporary dogs from the locality.

The measured bones

ST81 1156. Stepleton enclosure, segment 3, interface of layers 3B and 2, phase IV. The complete skeleton of a dog. All bones are fused, including the vertebrae, and the mandibular teeth have significant wear, showing that the dog was fully adult. The cranium, ribs and some other bones were fragmented to the point where measurements could not be taken. The measurements are listed below, following the designations of Dreisch (1976).

Mandible, left side:
4=102.0 5=99.0 6=103.4 7=67.3 8=65.6 9=62.0
10=31.6 11=35.0 12=27.0 13=18.2 14=17.8 18=57.0
19=19.9

Atlas vertebra:
GL=33.4 LAd=12.3

Axis vertebra:
H=35.4 LAPa=45.0 LCDe=40.9

Scapula:
right: SLC=20.4 GLP=25.3 LG=23.0 BG=14.6
left: SLC=21.0 GLP=25.0 LG=23.0 BG=14.5

Humerus:
right: GL=142.0 GLC=137.4 DP=34.2 BD=25.0
left: GL=141.2 GLC=137.6 DP=33.8 BD=25.8

Radius:
right: GL=136.0 SD=9.8 BP=14.8 BD=20.0
left: GL=136.5 SD=9.8 BP=15.0 BD=20.0

Ulna:
right: SDO=18.0 DPA=20.0

Femur
right: SD=11.4 BD=25.3 left: BP=30.4 DC=16.0

Tibia:
left: GL=152.0 BP=29.8 SD=10.0 BD=18.0

Astragalus:
right: GL=21.2

Calcaneum:
right: GL=36.6 GB=14.6
left: GL=36.7 GB=14.6

HH76 2864. Shroton spur outwork, site K/L, layer 8, phase I. Canis, fragmented skull, axis, five cervical vertebrae, the fragmentary bones of the left fore limb and seven rib articulations.

right maxilla, with teeth P^4–M^2

16=15.8 P^4 L=16.5 GB=8.9 M^1 L=12.0 M^1 B=14.0 M^2 L=7.4

M^2 B=9.4
left maxilla, complete tooth row (P^1 and P^2 alveolus only)

15=59.9 16=16.2 17=45.3 P^4 L=16.3 GB=8.9 M^1 L=12.0

M^1 B=13.8 M^2 L=7.0 M^2 B=9.3

HH76 2226.Main enclosure, segment 14, layer 9, phase VI. Dog, left metatarsal IV. GL=58.0.

HH76 2835. Main enclosure, segment 14, cutting k, layer 11, phase VI. Adult left mandible: 8=63.0.
HH76 2099. Main enclosure, segment 14, cutting k, layer 7, phase VI. Canis, fragmentary right humerus and ulna, probably originally articulated.
humerus: Bd=25.9 SD=10.5
radius: SDO=17.2 DPA=19.6

Table 8.27 *Bos* distal humerus measurements

Certain measurements, where the bone had suffered slight damage, were estimated and these specimens are designated by the letter 'E' in this and all similar tables

code	*find*	*R/L*	*BT (mm)*	*HT (mm)*	*group*
HH74	100	R	76.2	41.9	7
HH74	124	L	74.0E	41.7	7
HH74	126	L	71.0	45.2	7
HH74	144	L	–	42.0	7
HH74	144	L	68.8	43.1	7
HH74	145	L	71.0	41.0	7
HH74	192	R	69.0	43.0	7
HH74	193	L	70.0	45.0	7
HH74	216	R	69.9	39.0	7
HH74	259	R	73.1	43.2	4
HH77	918	L	77.5	48.3	3
HH75	342	L	88.2	54.5	10
HH75	382	R	69.2	45.3	1
HH75	588	R	81.5	49.3	7
HH75	636	L	70.0	44.0	7
HH75	652	R	68.0	43.8	7
HH75	812	R	70.0	39.8	4
HH75	911	R	74.5	43.7	4
HH75	1078	R	73.2	44.1	4
HH75	1527	L	68.5	44.5	
HH75	1708	L	87.4	55.2	7
HH75	2121	L	72.0	43.2	22
HH76	278	R	78.9	43.1	52
HH76	476	R	73.6	41.7	10
HH76	825	R	69.3	41.2	15
HH76	1230	R	68.3	42.6	5
HH76	1376	R	–	42.9	7
HH76	1473	R	69.4	42.2	7
HH76	1808	L	72.0	41.3	5
HH76	1965	R	66.5	39.8	3
HH76	2089	L	68.8	–	7.1
HH76	2172	L	68.0	42.7	52
HH76	2175	R	73.0	44.5	49
HH76	2176	R	68.0	43.5	49
HH76	2204	R	71.4	41.6	7
HH76	2227	R	81.7	49.0E	7
HH76	2252	R	67.0	43.0	7
HH76	2808	L	75.0	42.7	4
HH76	2882	L	78.1	43.1	6
HH76	2926	L	72.8	42.2	3
HH76	2970	L	79.1	43.3	4
HH77	316	R	71.9	44.6	33
HH77	323	R	73.2	42.3	33
HH77	1403	L	–	45.0	37.2
HH77	2089	L	73.0	45.3	
HH77	2209	L	68.6	43.3	38
ST79	994	L	76.0E	–	65
ST80	341	R	73.9	42.2	60
ST80	908	L	78.6E	45.5	60
ST80	1415	R	76.4	44.5	72
ST81	48	R	72.3	44.2	
ST81	73	R	–	43.5	60
ST81	346	R	69.6	40.2	60
ST81	2	R	–	50.5	
ST81	2370	L	68.5E	43.9	53
ST81	2095	L	78.8	49.0	57
ST81	3189	L	70.3E	42.5	59
ST81	3189	R	85.9	51.3	59
HN82			86.0	50.2	

Table 8.28 *Bos* distal metacarpal measurements

code	find	R/L	Bd (mm)	Td (mm)	group
HH74	57	L	56.0	30.0	7
HH74	78	R	52.4	29.0	3
HH74	140	L	68.1	34.0E	7
HH75	316	R	59.0	34.0	15
HH75	438	L	54.8	30.7	19
HH75	773	R	57.5	31.4	4
HH75	1236	R	60.2	33.0E	7
HH75	1786	L	53.9	31.2	9
HH76	582	R	54.4	29.0	3
HH76	1594	L	65.1	34.2	5
HH76	1935	L	68.3	41.6	
HH76	2091	L	56.0	29.8	7.1
HH76	2095	R	57.7	32.6	7.1
HH76	2750	L	53.7	28.3	5
HH76	2892	L	59.3	31.4	7
HH76	2970	L	57.4	30.6	4
HH77	560	R	55.2	28.2	28
HH77	1199	R	61.4	34.5E	37
HH77	1199	R	61.0	33.7	37
HN82	283	R	53.1	–	89
HN82	288	L	55.7	27.5E	92.1
HN82	469	R	50.9	30.6	85
ST78	985	R	53.7	–	72
ST80	541	R	65.6	33.7	68
ST80	864	R	54.6	32.2	60
ST80	1469	L	58.6	31.5	60
ST81	2	R	53.8	28.5	
ST81	341	R	60.0	30.2	59
ST81	1322	R	65.3	31.0E	58
			65.3E	32.0E	

Table 8.29 *Bos* proximal metacarpal measurements

code	find	R/L	Bp (mm)	Dp (mm)	group
HH74	136	R	54.8	32.7	7
ST78	2700	R	56.7	33.7	65
HH76	678	R	56.7	35.2	16.1

Table 8.31 *Bos* proximal metatarsal measurements

code	find	R/L	Bp (mm)	Dp (mm)	group
HH74	250	R	43.0	46.0	7
HH75	564	L	48.0	49.4	7
HH75	592	R	50.9	55.0	7
HH76	1895	R	44.0	47.8	5
HH77	78	R	51.8	–	65?
HN82	336	L	43.4	44.4	88.2
ST78	2919	R	–	41.7	64

Table 8.32 *Bos* astragalus measurements

code	find no.	R/L	GLI (mm)	Bd (mm)	group
HH75	2062	R	71.5	48.2	4
HH76	1256	L	60.8	–	7
HH76	1738	R	60.9	43.7	5
HH76	1929	R	61.5	-	5
HH76	2869	L	67.0	47.0	7
HH76	2970	L	64.9	43.8	4
HH77	514	R	73.0	47.1	7
HH77	1464	L	66.2	–	1
HH77	1946	L	68.4	–	1
HH77	2123	L	64.2	44.7	25
ST78	2045	L	70.2	–	64
ST78	2915	L	64.2	–	64
ST81	1991	L	67.0	41.3	53

HH76 2216. Main enclosure, segment 14, cutting k, layer 9, phase VI. A complete, fused humerus. The same context produced one dog tooth and four vertebral fragments.
left humerus: GL=128.5 GLC=124.0 Bd=25.0 SD=10.3

ST79 1806. Inner Stepleton outwork, segment 6, cutting 9, layer 3, phase VII/a. The canid bones from this context were largely fragmentary and were: right and left ulna, right femur, atlas, four vertebra fragments, one metacarpal V and two phalanx 1.
left ulna: DPA=31.9
left metacarpal V: GL=72.2
phalanx 1: GL=30.4 Bp=9.7

HN82 802. F606, layer 1, 'flint mines'. A right canid ulna, fused proximal end.
SDO=27.8 DPA=32.6

Cattle, pig, deer and caprines

The data in Tables 8.27–45 are in part based on the conventions of Dreisch (1976). In that work rather few measurements are designated for the articular ends of limb bones. There are other differences that should be noted. In Dreisch's figure 44h the designation Bd is used for the maximum *articular* width of the distal metacarpal, while the same designation refers to the maximum *epiphyseal* width of the distal metatarsal, taken above the articular surface. In the tables published here, the measurement Bd is taken at the maximum width of the *articular* surface of both the metacarpal and metatarsal. Certain measurements, where the bone had suffered slight damage, were estimated and these specimens are designated by the letter 'E'. All measurements are expressed in mm. Where possible, the final column of each table attributes the find to one of the context groups defined in Table 3.1. This makes it possible to distinguish specimens from securely Neolithic contexts (the vast majority) from the remainder.

Table 8.33 Pig – *Sus scrofa*, distal humerus measurements

code	*find no.*	*R/L*	*BT (mm)*	*HT (mm)*	*group*
HH74	149	L	30.4E	27.2	7
HH75	565	R	36.2	30.1	7
HH75	2162	R	34.2	–	21
HH76	1231	R	–	30.0	5
HH76	1880	R	32.3	30.5	5
HH76	1898	R	29.1	27.9	5
HH76	2815	L	40.4	30.4	7
HN82	323	R	–	34.0	91
ST78	2764	L	33.4	30.8	64
ST79	1775	R	36.0	31.0	67
ST80	279	L	34.4	28.5	60
ST80	829	L	34.2	28.5	60
ST80	1476	R	33.5	30.7	59
ST81	3187	L	37.5	29.1	58.1

Table 8.34 Pig – *Sus scrofa*, astragalus measurements

code	*find*	*R/L*	*GLC (mm)*	*group*
HH76	1220	L	45.1	49
HH76	1929	L	37.5	5
ST78	1470	L	45.0	63
ST79	2027	L	43.8	65
ST79	2038	R	41.2	78

Table 8.35 Roe deer – *Capreolus capreolus*, distal humerus measurements

code	*find*	*R/L*	*BT (mm)*	*HT (mm)*	*group*
HH76	1839	L	25.3	19.9	7
ST78	1063	R	24.6	22.3	65
ST80	694	L	27.2	21.8	74

Table 8.36 Red deer – *Cervus elaphus*, distal humerus measurements

code	*find*	*R/L*	*BT (mm)*	*HT (mm)*	*group*
HH75	235	R	56.0	42.9	7
ST79	991	R	52.5	42.0	64
ST79	333	L	–	41.6	67
ST79	1215	R	48.7	39.4	64

Table 8.37 Red deer – *Cervus elaphus*, proximal metacarpal measurements

code	*find*	*R/L*	*Bp (mm)*	*Dp (mm)*	*group*
ST80	2114	L	39.3	28.1	80

Table 8.38 Red deer – *Cervus elaphus*, proximal metatarsal measurements

code	*find*	*R/L*	*Bp (mm)*	*Dp (mm)*	*group*
ST79	979	L	37.8	35.1	68
ST80	939	L	37.5	34.2	56

Table 8.39 Red deer – *Cervus elaphus*, distal metatarsal

code	*find*	*R/L*	*Bd (mm)*	*Td (mm)*	*group*
ST80	1089	R	40.2	27.8	72

Table 8.40 Red deer – *Cervus elaphus*, distal tibia measurements

code	*find*	*R/L*	*Bd (mm)*	*Td (mm)*	*group*
ST80	738	R	45.6E	43.5	83

Table 8.41 Red deer – *Cervus elaphus*, astragalus measurements

code	*find*	*R/L*	*GLl (mm)*	*Bd (mm)*	*group*
ST79	2039	R	54.3	35.1	68

Table 8.42 Sheep – *Ovis aries*, distal humerus measurements

code	*find*	*R/L*	*BT (mm)*	*HT (mm)*	*group*
HH76	2129	L	27.3	–	7
HH77	1734	R	27.9	16.0	1
ST79	1098	L	24.0	14.9	65
ST79	459	R	27.9	18.1	65

Table 8.43 Sheep – *Ovis aries*, distal metacarpal measurements

code	*find*	*R/L*	*Bd (mm)*	*Td (mm)*	*group*
HH75	1949	R	27.1	16.3	22

Table 8.44 Sheep – *Ovis aries*, distal metatarsal measurements

code	*find*	*R/L*	*Bd (mm)*	*Td (mm)*	*group*
HH76	2864	L	23.7	15.2	48

Table 8.45 Goat – *Capra hircus*, horncore base measurement

code	*find*	*R/L*	*41*	*42*	*group*
HH77	552	R	31.5	22.5	7
HH76	1905	L	28.5	19.6	5

8.2 The antlers and implements made of antler

As with the bones of mammals from the site, the preservation of antler is variable. That which was most deeply buried is generally well preserved, but within the more superficial sediments the antler shows more variable preservation and some is quite severely eroded. Most of the antler found is from the red deer (*Cervus elaphus*) and a few antlers were found from the roe deer (*Capreolus capreolus*), some of which show traces of working or of possible utilisation.

The antler of red deer provides the surviving evidence for the manner in which the ditches and other features were excavated into the chalk bedrock. Antler is tough and resilient and was the strongest organic material that was available within the Neolithic period (MacGregor 1985). It has been shown above that red deer bones were only a small proportion of those identified from the complex. Consequently the red deer that were killed at or near the sites cannot have provided very much of the antler that was used. There is also some evidence that the site was utilised only on occasions, probably in periods during the late summer months. This is the time when red deer stags would be in the process of growing new antlers, which are fully mature only by the autumn season, usually by mid- to late September. Most of the antler was utilised in a 'cast' or 'shed' condition, that state when the antler naturally detaches from the skull of the stag. Such shed antler would have been encountered as a stray find within the deer range, especially during the spring and early summer. Sixty-three antler picks have the base of the antler preserved, and, of these, 76% were made on shed antlers and only 24% came from deer that had been killed or found dead with antlers held on the skull. Obviously most of the antler would have been stored and then transported to the site from considerable distances, whether from animals killed or from stray finds. Only a small part would have been obtained from animals killed at or near the site.

The naming of the various parts of the red deer antler and the manner in which the lower tines (named the brow, bez and trez tines) were cut away to make the familiar antler 'picks' is illustrated by Legge (1981a). At the extremity of the antler, the termination develops two or more tines as the deer matures; where three tines develop to form a cup shape; this is known in deer parlance as the 'crown'. The term 'crown' is used below for all such antler terminals of two or more tines. As was noted by Sandars (1910) the detached crown was also often utilised as an implement that he termed a 'rake', and that term is used below.

The manner in which the antler picks were used is still open to question. In constructing the Overton Down experimental earthwork, the diggers found that the antler picks were effective when swung in the manner of a modern metal pick, though their experimental models were made from very much larger deer than those found at Hambledon Hill (Jewell 1963b). Earlier investigations suggested that other methods of digging may have been used. The results of early experimental trials were published in 1875 by Lane-Fox, who found that the most effective means was to detach the antler tines and then use these as wedges, driving them into the fissured chalk by means of blows from the back of the beam. The 'pick' was thus used both as a mallet to drive in the wedges and as a lever to prise up the loosened blocks. W G Clarke (1915) showed that this results in some battering to the backs of the antler beams, but only a stone hammer used on the beam produced severe battering like that found on the Grime's Graves antler picks. It is possible that percussion caused by using the back of the beam to dress flint blanks would result in similar damage. The tests by Lane-Fox resulted in the removal of 0.48 cu m of chalk per hour of work (given as 1.5 man hours per cubic yard), while the Overton experiment attained 5.9 hours per cubic metre (4.5 hours per cubic yard). However, the manufacture and use of antler implements in excavating the ditches appears to have been of much less standard form at Hambledon Hill than was found at Grime's Graves. None of the detached antler tines showed evidence for having been hammered into the chalk, and of the antler beams, only 44% showed evidence of battering on the burr or on the back of the beam in the 55 specimens where this part was well preserved (Table 8.46). This contrasts markedly with the picks found in one sample at Grime's Graves where 93% were battered (Legge 1981a) or the 91% in another sample from the same site and 68% for Durrington Walls (Clutton-Brock 1984).

8.2.1 The development cycle of antler

Red deer stags grow and cast their antlers in an annual cycle that begins with new antler growth in the early summer. Immature deer develop only small and unbranched antlers, beginning just as a spike. As the animal matures the new antlers will grow larger each year, attaining their full mature size at 6–8 years, by which time many develop a double brow tine. As the deer become more aged the antlers again become smaller in each year. Antler size is very much related to the quality of feeding for the deer; those in parkland and deciduous woodland in southern Britain usually develop the largest 'heads' (sets of antlers), while those in less fertile regions are smaller. Through the summer the growing antlers have a highly vascular skin and by autumn the antlers have grown to their final form. The vascular skin dies and peels away, and the antlers are rubbed clean by the deer in time for the late autumn breeding combat (the 'rut'). Through the winter and into the spring the fully developed antler is carried on the head and antlers designated as 'unshed' below are from animals killed (or found dead) during that time. The deer cause a good deal of abrasion to the antlers during the time that they are carried ('burnishing' in deer jargon). The new antlers are cleaned by rubbing against trees and other vegetation which may cause abrasion to the surface of the beam. During the rut the antlers may also be used to dig into the ground and there is further damage from direct conflict with other stags. Occasionally antlers are broken during this activity. An examination of antlers from recently culled deer will show that, by late winter, the degree of wear to the tips of the tines may be considerable. In an ancient specimen this could easily be taken as the result of human use and this was considered in determining the degree of human modification made to the antlers in the manufacture of the picks and in their usage.

In the spring a natural process causes the attachment of the antler, a little above the skull, to weaken so that the worn antler is cast and, shortly after this, new antler growth begins. The shed antler will soon be chewed by the deer and other mammals, both wild and domestic, to recover the calcium that it contains, especially in areas of acidic soil conditions, but less so where the ground water and soils are highly calcareous. In the study of the specimens listed below a careful search was made for gnawing by deer and other mammals.

Much of the antler had been fashioned into antler 'picks' – a familiar name used here without implication as to the manner of usage. To make these implements the crown of the antler was usually (but not always) cut away and sometimes other tines were also removed. Antler possesses a hard outer skin, 4 mm or so in thickness with the interior filled with a more spongy, fibrous tissue. The antler was worked by sawing and cutting through the outer skin until it could be snapped through the exposed fibrous core. Where the beam or unwanted tines were removed in this way the antler surface was cut around in a ring until it could be broken. The exposed surfaces were then sometimes smoothed by light charring in a fire, as was commonly found too among specimens from Grime's Graves. However, it must be emphasised that the pattern of manufacture at Hambledon was highly variable and, in general, the individual implements are less carefully fashioned, and to a less standard form, than has been found at flint-mining sites (Legge 1981a). Mining tools were generally fashioned to have the beam cut to 0.30–0.60 m, often with the crown separated at or near the trez tine, which along with the second brow (or bez) tine, where this had developed, was also cut away. The standard form of the flint miners' picks would have been influenced by the need to work in narrow underground galleries, while those made for use at Hambledon were used in the open air.

Forty-three antlers can be identified as formed into the typical 'picks', though a larger number were probably originally made into this form, as evidenced by the frequency of battering on antler beams as shown in Table 8.46. It is easy to determine whether an antler was cast or not where the burr (the base of the antler) remains in fair condition (Table 8.46).

Other specimens were too fragmentary to determine the degree of working or the form of the implement that may have been made, although the burr area was found. Probably most were originally made as picks, or they are fragments of picks that were broken in use. In most cases the side could not be determined. In this category there were a further 17 shed antler burrs and four were unshed. Interestingly, among the latter, two specimens from the Stepleton enclosure (one from phase IV and one from phase VIII/a) were in the early stages of being shed, with evidence of resorbtion of the bone across the base of the pedicel. This shows that the antlers were collected from a deer killed or dying in the spring, though this bears little relation to the season of activity at the site.

It is perhaps remarkable that the antlers from both the central area and the Stepleton spur were mostly rather small (Fig 8.29). Precise measurements from antler are rather problematic through the lack of clearly definable measurement points. The burr area is highly variable in shape so that measurements taken there have an uncertain relationship to antler size. Consequently the measurement most often taken was the circumference of the beam above the brow, or brow/bez, tines, at that point where the antler again becomes roughly cylindrical. This measurement at least has the advantage of comparability of the ancient

Table 8.46 Incidence of battered antler bases at Hambledon Hill

site	*slight?*	*slight*	*medium*	*heavy*	*none*
Main enclosure.	1	0	2	1	5
Cross-dykes	0	0	0	0	0
Central area features	0	2	0	0	2
Shroton spur	0	0	0	0	1
Stepleton enclosure	2	2	3	1	10
Middle Stepleton outwork	0	0	0	3	1
Inner Stepleton outwork	1	0	3	1	6
Outer Stepleton outwork		0	0	0	0
Stepleton spur features	1	0	0	0	2
Hanford spur	0	0	0	1	4
totals	5 (9%)	4 (7.2%)	8 (14.5%)	7 (12.7%)	31 (56.6%)

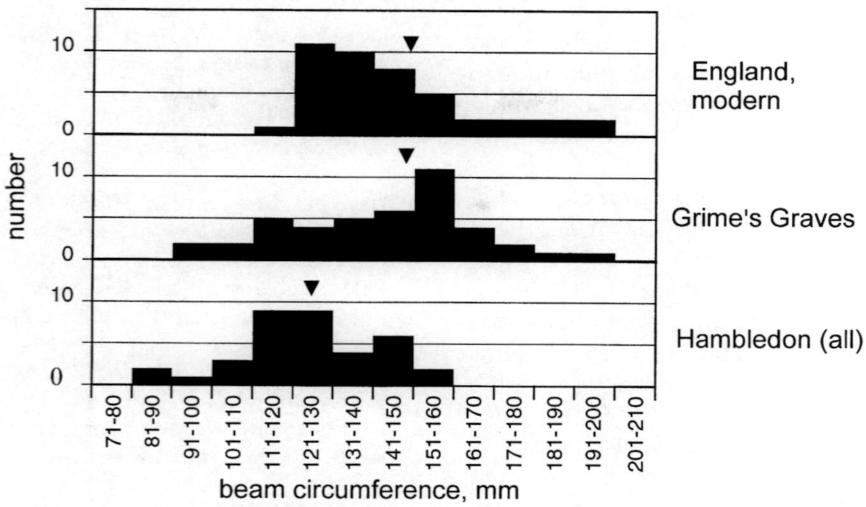

Fig 8.29 Beam circumference in the Hambledon red deer antlers compared with the late Neolithic antler picks from Grime's Graves and a modern sample of trophy specimens. The mean for each sample is indicated by a downward-pointing arrow.

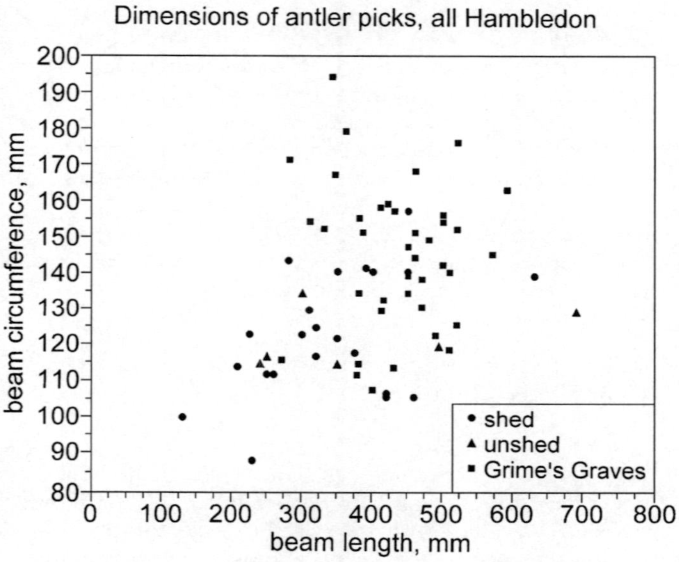

Fig 8.30 Relationship between the length of beam and beam circumference for the antler picks from Hambledon and Grime's Graves.

population with a corpus of modern data. Figure 8.30 shows the range of distribution of the antler beam sizes as circumference in 10 mm size classes. The Hambledon sample is compared with the later Neolithic antler picks from Grime's Graves (Legge 1981a, fig 56) and measurements from modern trophy heads published by Ward (1929). The arrow above each distribution shows the mean dimension. The Grime's Graves antlers are large, and the mean circumference (147.2 mm) is only slightly smaller than that of modern trophy animals (149.5 mm). However, the sample clearly contains more large antlers than could be obtained even by modern rifle hunting. The Hambledon sample has a notably smaller beam circumference (125.0 mm), which is 22 mm less than that found in the deer from Grime's Graves, and smaller even than a sample of modern Scottish red deer that lived in an environment not wholly suited to the development of large antlers (Legge 1981a, fig 56). Clutton-Brock (1984, 25) also found that a sample of Grime's Graves antlers had been carefully selected and that there were few of small size. Further, the Grime's Graves sample was significantly larger than that recovered from Durrington Walls. It would seem that the professional miners were more selective in their raw materials, or possibly could obtain the best materials in exchange for their flint blanks. On the other hand, the people who constructed causewayed enclosures were perhaps less familiar with cutting chalk with antler tools and also utilised smaller antlers that were prepared in a less standardised manner.

The length of the picks used was also less at Hambledon than found at Grime's Graves. Figure 8.30 shows the length of the Hambledon picks, plotted against the beam circumference. This shows a tendency, with a good deal of variation, for the more robust antlers to be made into longer picks. Obviously the larger antlers offered a longer beam segment that was formed as the pick handle. The mean length of the Hambledon antler picks was 319 mm (sample of 36 measurable), while from Grime's Graves the mean length was 434 mm (Legge 1981a, sample of 41) and 437 mm (Clutton-Brock 1984, sample of 244).

Obviously the small size of the Hambledon deer antlers could be explained in a number of ways. Possibly the red deer within the vicinity of the site were poorly nourished. This seems improbable, in that the few bone measurements given above were from deer of large body size. Further, the area is now well suited to both pastoral husbandry and to forest growth and in most of the area chalk is found just below the ground surface. It seems more likely that the red deer antlers found at Hambledon were derived mainly from younger animals, in which antler development had yet to reach its full potential. This would occur in an area where sustained deer hunting resulted in a population structure with relatively few older adult animals. On the other hand, large antlers from older animals would occasionally be found in such a circumstance, and these are quite absent at Hambledon. The third possibility is that antler was so prized as a raw material that much was taken away from the site after it had been utilised for digging. This is shown by the four specimens that have evidence for the 'groove and splinter' technique of antler working, by which strips have been removed, possibly for the manufacture of small points and needles. It is likely that the larger specimens, even when the tines were broken while being used for digging, would nonetheless have provided large sections of robust beam as a valuable raw material, later carried away from the site rather than abandoned there.

8.2.2 Working on the antler implements

Many of the antler implements show obvious traces of working, both from manufacture and use. These are described below. 'Length' is measured along the axis of the beam from the burr to the extremity and is given where the original length of the implement can be determined.

8.2.3 Catalogue of antler implements

Main enclosure ditch

'Picks'

Segment 9 L7 phase III. HH75 830. An antler pick, made from a left shed antler. Length = 320 mm. The crown was detached by an ancient (?)snap. The brow tine is broken at about its mid-point, probably anciently, but with some recent damage. The short bez tine remains, with the tip worn flat from use. An area on the back of the beam 80 mm long and from the burr upwards is battered from use. Further battering is evident on the medial face of the beam, between the bez and trez tines.

Segment 4 L10 phase III. HH74 401. An antler pick, made from a right unshed antler. Length = 350 mm. The antler had been cut from the skull through the pedicel, and the cut surface of this was heavily battered during use. The crown had been detached above the trez tine probably by ring cutting and a snap, though damage obscures the detail of this. The trez tine and double brow tines were all anciently broken from the beam.

Table 8.47 Incidence of right- and left-side antlers

right side		*left side*		*side not determined*	
shed	*unshed*	*shed*	*unshed*	*shed*	*unshed*
12	5	17	6	2	0

Rakes

Segment 4 L9 phase III. HH74 261. A three-point crown, probably right side, broken from the antler. Length = 323 mm. The tips of the tines are worn flat, with each facet having a different plane showing that use was not consistently in one single direction. A 'rake' following Sandars (1910).

Segment 9 L8 phase III. HH75 1178. A four-point crown, anciently snapped from the beam but with some recent damage at the break. Length = 405 mm. Three tines show tip wear, with flattened points, abrasion and scratching. The tip of the fourth tine had been broken in excavation.

Segment 9 L6 phase VI/b. HH75 582. A three-point crown, possibly cut from the beam by chopping. Length = 325 mm. Two tines show heavy tip wear with abrasion, pitting and cut marks. The third tine was anciently snapped off.

Roe deer antlers

Segment 1 L7 Phase II. HH77 771. A complete, right, unshed roe deer antler, with three small terminal tines the tips of which were broken in excavation. Not worked and apparently not utilised.

Segment 8 D1 L7a Phase III. HH75 312. A left, shed roe deer antler. The burr area shows wear. At the termination of the antler, the small forward tine is broken off, possibly recently. The terminal tine is worn and rounded rather more than would be caused while carried by the deer. A cut is visible on the antler surface at the bifurcation of the terminal tines.

Segment 9 L8 phase III. HH75 1080. A ?left shed roe antler; small, probably juvenile, with a recent break which has removed the distal tines. Possibly some use wear to the very small anterior tine.

Central area features

'Picks'

N F1 L4 HH77 1944. A probable antler pick, made from the upper beam and trez tine, from a left antler. The beam was snapped below the crown and again below the trez tine, leaving this tine with a short length of beam. The broken distal end is smoothed by wear. The tip of the trez tine shows wear that is probably greater than would be caused while carried by the deer. This is a familiar implement from the Hambledon complex and appears to be a second form of pick, made from the upper antler rather than the base and brow tine or tines.

Rakes

N F6 L4 HH77 2042. A right antler crown of four tines. Length = 350 mm. The beam was anciently snapped above the trez tine. The four tines all show wear, an unlikely state to be caused while carried by the deer. Two tines have broken tips, the damage probably ancient. One has a distinct cut mark.

N F6 L4 HH77 2043/2. A left crown of three tines. Length = 160 mm. The crown was broken from the beam above the trez tine. One tine had been broken off, probably anciently. The two remaining tine tips show heavy wear from use.

N F6 L4 HH77 2043/3. A left crown of three tines, showing an ancient greenstick break to the beam above the trez tine.

Length = 160 mm. The three tines all show tip wear. This specimen is similar to HH77 2043/2 above, but the crowns are of very different form and size, indicating that these are not right and left from the same deer.

The same feature and layer produced other fragments of antler: HH77 2043/1 is a segment of antler beam showing ancient breaks with slight charring on the distal end. HH77 2043/4 is a detached brow or bez tine, recently broken, and showing heavy tip wear. HH77 2043/5 is another tine, probably a brow tine, showing tip wear and abrasion for 50–60 mm from the tip.

N F7v HH77 2307. A shed left antler. Length = 195 mm. The brow and bez tines show moderate tip wear. The beam above these is anciently snapped, but with some recent damage. The burr shows some battering damage on its back.

N F22 L6 HH77 1826/1. From the same pit as the specimen described below, a two-point crown anciently broken from the beam. Both tines show heavy wear. After this use two deep, parallel, 'V' shaped burin grooves were cut on the back of the antler though the resulting splint between them was not detached. The cuts extend onto the worn surface of the distal terminal tip, and beyond the ancient break through the proximal part of the beam, showing that this was broken after the burin work.

N F22 L6 HH77 1826/2. A short (100 mm) segment of a slender antler beam with a short tine. The beam is cut above the tine by ring cutting and apparently sawing to give a flat surface. Slight charring and smoothing can be seen on the break below the tine.

B F57 L1 HH75 1330. An almost intact, shed left antler, but with evidence for human use. Length = 420 mm. The brow and bez tines were broken off, probably anciently. The remaining trez tine shows tip wear and damage. The crown is of four tines, all of which show wear, heavy on the tips of three. Two of these pointed to the rear in the deer's life and this presents an unlikely site for 'natural' wear. The burr shows anterior battering and damage.

B F57 L1 HH75 579. From the same pit as that above; a small crown of two tines and one vestigial tine. One tine was broken recently, the other anciently. The crown shows a greenstick break from the beam. The small vestigial tine near the one anciently broken shows heavy wear and battering.

N F7iii L3 surface. HH77 1945. The unshed base of a left antler. The brow and bez tines are broken, the age of which cannot be determined. Some battering is evident on the burr.

Stepleton enclosure

'Picks'

Segment 1 (2B F1) L4A phase II. ST79 2615. A pick made from a large unshed antler, right side. The burr of the antler is heavily worn by battering in use. The double brow tines were broken anciently, presumably in use. The beam is broken through a little above the brow tine and associated beam fragments suggest that this was post-depositional damage.

Segment 1 (2B F1) L4 phase III. ST79 2149. A pick made on the upper beam of a ?right antler. The beam is snapped below the trez tine with slight charring evident, and chopped through below the crown tines, the cut clearly showing multiple chops, presumably from a stone axe. The trez tine shows tip wear extending 100 mm or so along the tine, but much or all of this may be of natural occurrence. An implement, but probably unused or little used.

Segment 1 (2B F1) L4 phase III. ST79 2150 (Fig 8.31). A pick made on the base of a large, unshed left antler, detached from the cranium by snapping through the pedicel. Length = 320 mm. The beam was snapped through above the bez tine. There is damage to the burr and posterior beam, predominantly from gnawing, the nature of which is characteristic of gnawing by a red deer, as was done to recover the calcium during the growth of new antler. From the positioning of the gnawing this probably occurred after the implement was discarded, probably by a domestic caprine. The brow and bez tines are slightly worn, but no more than might be encountered from natural causes. A very small second brow tine has been broken away recently.

Segment 3 U9A L4 phase III ST80 1473. A pick made on the base of a small shed antler. The burr is heavily abraded, probably from use. The single brow tine was broken anciently at the beam, which is broken a little above that tine.

Segment 3 U9A L4 phase III. ST80 1125. The broken base of a pick made on a small, shed left antler, with a heavily battered brow tine. Not well preserved, but the break suggests that the implement was broken while being used for levering.

Segment 3 U9B L1 phase VIII/a. ST80 2250. The base of a probable pick made on a large, but now poorly preserved, unshed antler, the base and beam fragments of which survive. The pedicel shows the early stages of the process of shedding.

Segment 3 U9D L1 phase VIII/a. ST80 1351. A pick made on a shed right antler. Length = 220 mm. The base is undamaged; slight damage to the burr was probably caused post-deposition. The beam is snapped through below the trez tine, with some evidence of ancient percussion at the break. The brow and bez tines are broken away, probably during use.

Segment 3 U11 L6 phase I. ST80 2013. An antler pick, made from the mid beam, probably right side. Length = 240 mm. The beam is snapped through below and above the trez tine, with this forming the working part of the implement. The distal beak – above the trez tine – shows slight charring. The tip of the tine is worn rather more than is usually seen inflicted by the deer.

Segment 3 U10/11 L6 phase I. ST80 1972. An almost entire left, shed antler of six points with a double brow tine, but small for this state of development. The three small crown tines were snapped off anciently. The tips of the brow and bez tines are missing, the brow certainly anciently and the bez possibly so. The tip of the trez tine shows wear and slight scratches, probably inflicted by the deer.

Segment 3 U13A L6 phase I. ST80 1882. A shed left antler, almost intact. Length = 630 mm. The shed base and burr have some damage, probably recent, and are not battered. The brow tine was anciently snapped away. The tip of the bez tine is worn and flattened, probably from human use. The trez tine, a fourth tine and the crown tines all show slight wear, probably from human use supplementing the natural wear.

Segment 3 U13B L6 phase I. ST80 1880. A complete, unshed right antler. Length from burr to tip = 690 mm. Part of the frontal bone remains attached to the pedicel and this shows slight charring, which extends up to the posterior aspect of the burr. The tips of the brow and bez tines are missing from ancient breaks, but wear is evident on the remaining part. The trez tine is unworn. Of the three crown tines, two were broken anciently by percussion. The remaining forward tine is worn and chipped. The undamaged state of this specimen is a fine example of skilled excavation.

Segment 3 U13B L6 phase I. ST80 1879. An antler with the burr area anciently broken away below the brow tine; possibly, therefore, an unshed specimen. Broken through the beam below the crown and with slight charring at the break. The tips of the brow and bez tines are broken away, probably anciently. The trez tine shows slight tip wear, but no more than may occur by natural causes.

Segment 3 U13A L6 phase I. ST80 1886. The terminal part of an antler, fashioned as a pick by snapping below the small trez tine, which was broken away anciently, probably in use. The break to the beam shows smoothing and charring, possibly being ring cut before breaking. Length = 610 mm. The two crown terminals show tip damage, scratching and slight charring on the rear tine.

Segment 4 U6 L2 phase VI. ST80 1132. The base of a small, ?right shed antler. Length = 130 mm. The beam shows fine, longitudinal burin grooves at the break, though without evidence of splinters being detached. The beam is broken across these grooves, having been partially cut to facilitate the break. The small brow tine was snapped anciently, but use damage is apparent on the remaining part.

Segment 4 U7 L6 phase I. ST80 799 (2). A pick formed from a right shed antler. Length = 270 mm. The beam was anciently snapped below the trez tine. The base and the burr are not battered. The brow tine shows slight wear and chipping, probably for human use. The bez tine above is snapped anciently and the broken surface shows slight charring.

Segment 4 U8 L2A phase IV. ST80 1459. The unshed base of a right antler, the beam broken though below the brow tine. The pedicel shows the early stages of the development of shedding. The attached frontal bone has 8–10 fine cuts on the lateral margin, indicative of skinning (for other similar examples, see Binford 1981, 102, fig 4.11a).

Segment 5 U4 L5 phase II. ST80 1081. A pick made on a shed left antler. Length = 225 mm. The shed base and burr are undamaged. The tips of the brow and bez tines are slightly flattened by wear and show scratching and abrasion. The beam was snapped below the burr and the break shows slight charring.

Segment 5 U4 L5 phase II. ST80 1082. A pick made on a shed right antler. Length = 260 mm. The lateral margin of the burr has some damage, probably ancient and there is abrasion at the base of the brow tine on the lateral face. The bez tine was broken away, probably recently. The beam was snapped through at the base of the trez tine.

Segment 5 U4 L5 phase II. ST80 1083. A pick made on a right shed antler. The base is damaged, but probably not from battering. The tips of the brow and bez tines are flattened by wear and abraded. There is slight rodent gnawing on the surface of the brow tine. The beam was snapped through below the trez tine, and the broken end was charred.

Segment 5 U4 L4B phase III. ST80 800 (Fig 8.31) An antler pick made on a right shed antler. The brow tine was broken recently. The bez tine is flattened and abraded at the tip by use. The trez tine was broken away, possibly recently. The beam was ring cut and snapped above the trez tine. There is ancient damage, probably from blows, on the anterior beam between the bez and trez tines.

Segment 10 U1/2 L2 phase VI. ST81 3189/1. A pick made from a left shed antler, now broken. The brow and bez tines are broken, possibly recently. One associated tine fragment shows a moderate degree of tip wear.

Segment 10 U1/2 L2 phase VI. ST81 3189/2. Fragments of a pick, made on a shed antler, but poorly preserved.

Segment 12 U4 L5 phase II. ST81 1259 (Fig 8.31). A pick made from a shed antler. Length = 320 mm. The base of the antler and the burr are heavily battered for *c* 50 mm along the beam. The tip of the brow tine is flattened and abraded by use. The bez and trez tines were snapped away anciently. The beam was ring cut and snapped above the trez tine. Subsequent to this, five grooves were gouged into the back of the beam, parallel to its axis, in the manner of the groove and splinter method of antler working, but the splinters were not removed.

Segment 12 U4 L5 phase II. ST81 1261. A pick made from the upper beam of a right antler. Length = 520 mm. Snapped through the beam below the trez tine with smoothing and slight charring on the break. The tip of the trez tine is scored and worn from use. The two terminal tines show use, one being abraded and worn, the other having tip damage with abrasion and wear on the broken surface.

Segment 12 U4 L4 phase III. ST81 1095. A pick made from a shed left antler. Length = 350 mm. The base and burr are undamaged. The tip of the brow tine is worn flat and is scratched and abraded for 100 mm from the tip. The bez and trez tines were broken anciently and the broken ends were smoothed, probably during use.

Segment 12 U5 L5 phase II. ST81 1342. A probable antler pick, made from a ?left shed antler. Length = 155 mm. The shed base and burr are undamaged. The brow tine shows tip wear and abrasion, probably from human use. The bez tine was broken away, probably anciently. The beam was broken above the bez tine, making a short pick, and with the surface of the break smoothed.

Segment 15 U10 L3A phase III. ST81 357. The base of an antler pick, made on a shed right antler. The burr shows some battering. The brow and bez tines and the beam were broken in excavation.

Segment 15 U9 interface of L4 and L3B phase III. ST81 1318 (L3B) and 1428 (L4). Two fragments of a pick made on a small, shed antler. The base and burr show damage, which may be recent. The tip of the brow tine is worn. The implement has a good deal of surface erosion.

Segment 17 U4 L4 phase III. ST81 2324/5 and 2324/6. A pick made on a shed right antler. The base and burr are heavily

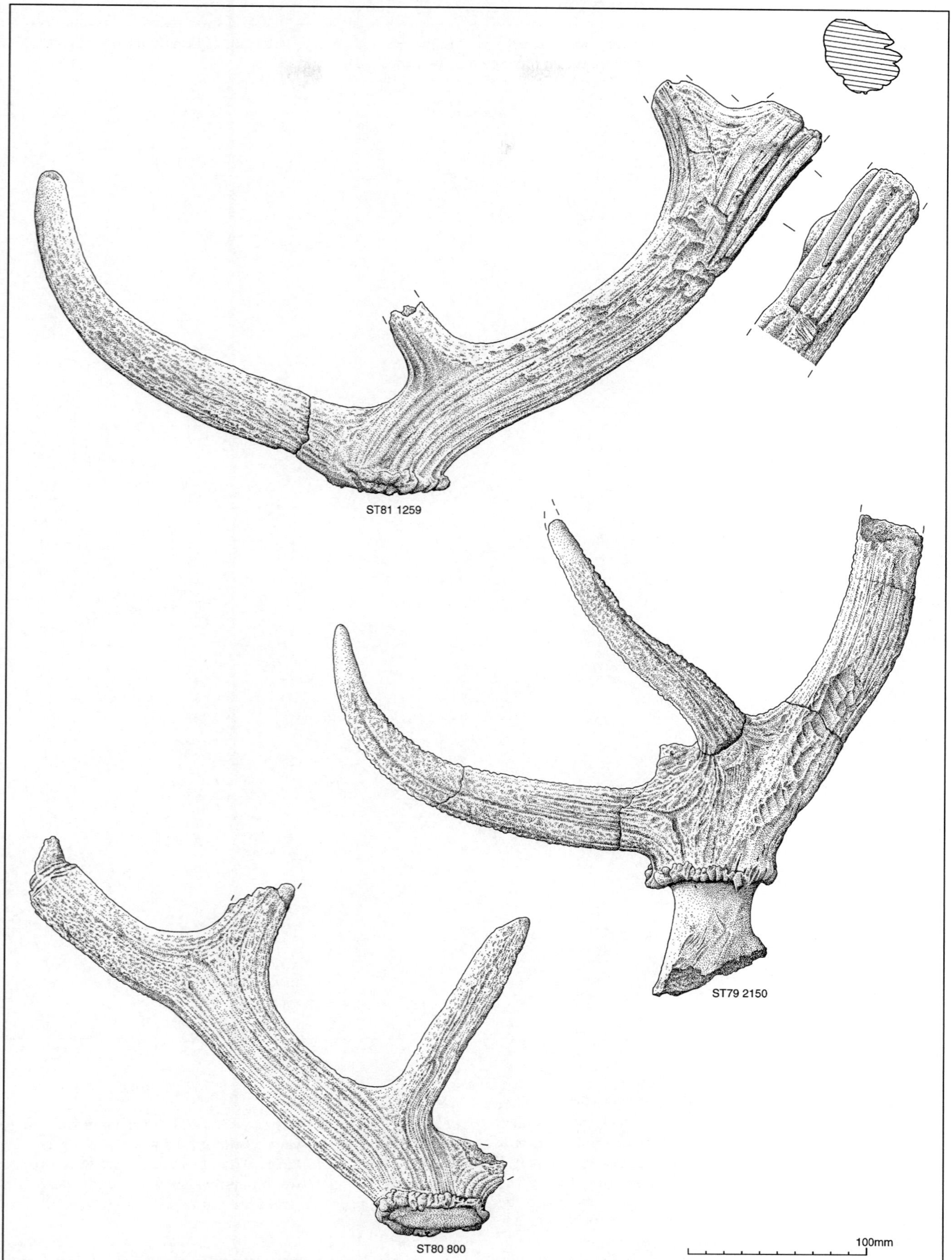

Fig 8.31 Modified and used antlers. Particulars in catalogue.

Table 8.48 Summary of antler distribution

All specimens in the tables are red deer antlers unless otherwise designated. The figures with a query mark are thought to be picks, but due to damage or fragmentation the precise form cannot be exactly determined.
See also Figures 3.62 and 3.126.

site	*phase*	*picks*	*beam frags*	*crowns*	*tines*	*other*
Main enclosure	I					
	II	1+1?		1		1 roe
	III	4		3		1 roe
	IV					
	V	1+1?		1	1	1 roe
	VI	1		2		
	VII					
	VIII					
	totals	6+2?		7	1	
Inner cross-dykes	I			1		
	VI	1	1	1		
	totals	1	1	2		
Outer cross-dykes	I	1?		1		
Long barrow	I				2	
	II					
	III	1?	2			1 unworked
	V				1	
	VI				1	
	?			1	3	
	totals	1	2	1	7	
Central area features	5+1?	2	5	8		
Shroton outwork	I	4			1	
Stepleton enclosure	I–II	12		6	8	
	III	11	4	3	12	
	V		1		2	
	IV		2		2	
	VI	4+1?	2		4	1 roe
	VIII/a	1	1		3	
	Totals	27+1?	9	8	29	
Middle Stepleton outwork	I		1		2	1
	III	3+1?	3	1	2	
	V		3		5	
	VIII/a	1?			5	
	Totals	2+3?	7	1	9	
Inner Stepleton outwork	I	2+1?	2		3	
	III	2+1?	4		6	
	V	4+1?				1 roe
	VII	5	2	1	1	
	VIII/a	1+1?	3		1	
	Totals	14+4?	12	2	13	
Outer Stepleton outwork	III		1		4	
Stepleton features	4	2		1	1 pedicel	
Hanford spur	5+2?	11	2	9		

battered on the posterior surface. The brow and bez tines are heavily worn from use, with rounded tips showing scratches and abrasion. The beam was broken through the base of trez tine, with many fragments suggesting that this was damaged in excavation. With this specimen is a crown of three tines, with tips worn and scored, again with recent damage to the broken beam. One tine has a flake removed from the surface at the tip, probably by a blow, with abrasion and wear spreading over the break. Probably worn from human use; the two parts are likely to be from the same antler.

Rakes

Segment 13 U6 L6 phase I. ST81 1260. A crown of four tines, with the beam showing a smooth or worn surface on the break. Length = 440 mm. The tips of two tines were broken anciently and the two remaining show signs of wear and scratching, probably from human use.

Segment 13 U6 L6 phase I. ST81261. A crown of three tines, the beam broken anciently by snapping at the trez tine. Length = 535 mm. The middle tine of the terminal shows an ancient break and has its tip missing. The two tines remaining show moderate flat wear, of a form associated with human use.

Segment 3 U13B L6 phase I. ST80 1881. A crown of four points, broken anciently from the beam, with the break surface smoothed. The two forward pointing tines are worn and scratched at their tips. Of the two rear and topmost tines, one shows scratching and abrasion, the second has tip damage.

Segment 14 U7 L5 phase II. ST81 1258. An unshed left antler, with parts of the cranium (frontal, parietal and temporal bones) joined. Length = 495 mm. There are clear skinning cuts around the base of the antler pedicel and on the occipital bone (and see specimen ST80 1459 segment 4 U8 L2A above). The brow tine is heavily worn at the tip, exposing the spongy inner tissues. The bez and trez tines were broken away anciently. The two tines of the terminal crown show damage and wear.

Segment 3 U11 L6 phase I. ST80 1350. A crown of three tines, charred where broken from the beam. The lower tine has a broken tip, but with wear and chipping. The middle tine has a scratched and worn tip and the terminal tine has its tip missing but is worn on the broken surface, showing scraping and abrasion marks.

Segment 3 U13B L6 phase I. ST80 1878. An unusually shaped crown of three points, having very splayed tines. Length = 350 mm. The beam is anciently snapped through above the trez tine. The tip of the forward tine is missing from recent damage, but all show smooth wear. Although consistent in form with a 'rake', a natural origin for the wear cannot be eliminated.

Single tines

Segment 3 U11 L6 phase I. ST80 2181. A tine of oddly sinuous form, the result of damage or injury during growth. Length = 185 mm. Apparent chop marks on the surface are judged to be recent trowel damage. The point of the tine has been enhanced by grinding or smoothing to a finer point than is natural. The point shows slight chipping from use.

Segment 11 U3 L6 phase I. ST81 1134. A single tine, showing flat tip wear with chipping. An area on the anterior surface of the tine is smoothed by wear, possibly from human use as a fulcrum point while levering.

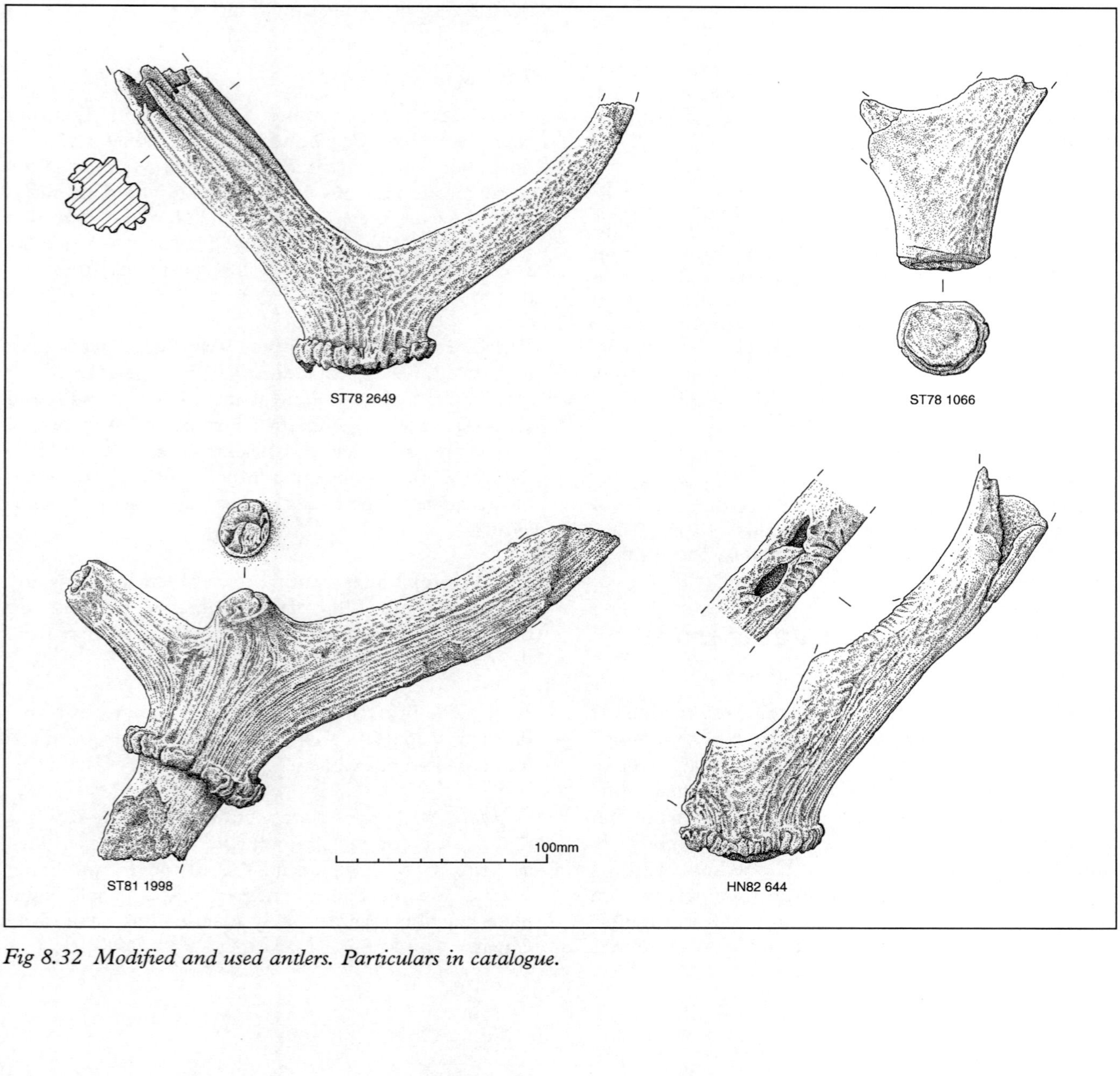

Fig 8.32 Modified and used antlers. Particulars in catalogue.

Miscellaneous illustrated antler

4B F178 ST81 1998 (Fig 8.32). The base of an unshed antler, which was detached from the skull by breaking through the pedicel. The specimen is from a mature deer with two brow tines. The beam was snapped through about 150 mm above the upper tine. The lower brow tine is missing and the cut or broken surface is worn. The base of the upper brow tine clearly shows that ring cutting or sawing was used to allow the tine to be snapped off.

Inner Stepleton outwork, segment 8 SCT7 L3 phase V. ST78 2649 (Fig 8.32). The base of a left shed antler. The tip of the single brow tine was anciently broken off. The beam was cut or broken through about 150 mm above the brow tine. The beam was then cut by grooving around its whole circumference, with 14 or 15 separate grooves. The profile of these suggests that different flint tools were used to groove the antler. The technique was again similar to the familiar Mesolithic 'groove and splinter' method of antler working, where the burin cuts follow the natural 'gutters' (the imprints of blood vessels made during antler growth). In this instance the splints do not appear to have been removed. The implement is thus of unusual form for the period. Length = 200 mm.

Hanford 'flint mines' F618 L2. HN82 644 (Fig 8.32). The beam of a shed antler. The brow and bez tines are missing, and the beam was apparently snapped through. The point where the bez tine was removed has been extensively gnawed, either by deer or possibly by a domestic sheep. Length = 235 mm.

Middle Stepleton outwork segment 10, L6. Phase I. ST78 1066 (Fig 8.32). A section of antler from the mid beam, from the point where the upper (bez) tine branches off. Both the upper beam and the bez tine were broken, while the lower beam shows how the antler was purposefully cut. This was accomplished by sawing with a suitable flint tool, the cut surface showing that the saw was applied in a number of places around the circumference of the beam. The saw cuts were made through the hard outer skin of the antler to a depth of 5–6 mm, and down to the porous core, thus allowing the beam to be snapped at the chosen point.

Roe deer antler

Stepleton enclosure segment 3 U12/13 L2 Phase VI. ST80 2179. A small, right, shed antler, in which the brow tine is undeveloped; probably of the first year. Length = 140 mm. There is evidence of tip wear and slight splintering, possibly from use.

8.3 The mammal remains from the hillfort

Most of the mammal bone excavated from the hillfort comes from an early Iron Age house, with a small number of specimens of earlier or uncertain age. In total, 755 post-cranial bones could be identified to the level of species and element, but very few mandibles and loose teeth were found. Most bones were from cattle, caprines, pig and dog, with rare horse and fox bones (Table 8.49). Red and roe deer are absent from the Iron Age sample. The number of identifiable mandibles is exceptionally low in relation to the sample of bones (Table 8.50). For example, from the main Neolithic enclosure ditch, there are about 12 identified caprine bones for each identified caprine mandible, and about 16 pig bones for each identified mandible. From the Iron Age house, there is only one identified caprine mandible and four loose lower teeth could come from, at most, another three mandibles, giving a minimum of 77 bones for each mandible. Three pig mandibles were identified and the two loose teeth probably represent a fourth, giving about 46 bones for each identified mandible.

The numbers of identified post-cranial bones in relation to identified mandibles is unusually high. At Neolithic and Bronze Age sites the ratio of identified caprine bones to identified jaws can be as low as 2:1 (bones:jaws) in harsh conditions of preservation and as high as 30:1 where preservation is excellent (Legge 1992, 40), while for pig bones in good preservation conditions the ratio varies from 13:1 to 36:1. It is thus very probable that the high ratio of post-cranial bones to mandibles in the Iron Age house is due to the domestic nature of the refuse, and the organisation of the place of slaughter and butchery.

The species

Besides the more common bones of cattle, pig and caprines, eleven dog bones, two fox bones and four horse bones were identified. The fragmentation of the bone meant that few measurements could be taken from the Iron Age sample, although it was evident that the bones of cattle, caprines and pig were of small body size as may be anticipated for specimens from this period.

Dog. The dog bones identified were fragments of right and left humerus, left radius, left fibula, right and left metapodial fragments, one phalanx 1, two carpals, and an atlas vertebra. The atlas vertebra showed several fine cut-marks which were orientated at right angles to the axis of the spine, apparently from the decapitation of the carcass. The bones probably represent one individual.

Fox. The fox bones were a proximal left humerus and a left tibia shaft. While possibly intrusive, the bone was not regarded as showing different preservation from the rest of the sample.

Horse. The horse bones were two fragments of proximal left scapula, a shaft fragment of the right distal humerus and one phalanx 3.

Caprines. 307 bones were identified as being caprine, that is, sheep or goat and a further 113 were identified as being from sheep using the customary published criteria for these distinctions. Only a single complete left tibia was definitely identified as being from a goat.

Table 8.49 Hillfort. Most common species

	cattle		*caprines*		*pig*		*dog*	
	N	%	*N*	%	*N*	%	*N*	%
mandibles	0	–	1	–	3	–	0	–
maxillae	0	–	0	–	3	–	0	–
loose teeth	0	–	6	–	2	–	0	–
bones	134	17.7	307	55.8	185	24.5	11	1.5

Table 8.50 Hillfort. Identified mandibles in relation to post-cranial bones

	caprines			*pig*		
site	*identified mandibles*	*identified bones*	*ratio*	*identified mandibles*	*identified bones*	*ratio*
IA house	4	307	77:1	4	185	46:1
Main enclosure ditch (Neolithic)	28	352	13:1	31	516	17:1

Burning, gnawing and cut-marks

Only twelve bones showed traces of burning: one horse bone, one pig bone and eight caprine bones and two unidentified bone fragments. Canine gnawing is more evident, with 18% of the pig bones, 15% of the cattle bones and 9% of the caprine bone showing this. As is usual in domestic assemblages, it is the high density bones with good survival, such as the proximal radius/ulna and distal tibia, which show the highest frequency. The cut-marks observed were those characteristic of carcass butchery and disarticulation. Cuts were most common on the cattle bones (11 were noted), and these include a thoracic and a lumbar vertebra, two scapulae and two distal humeri. Pig bones showed cut-marks on an axis and a thoracic vertebra and a sacrum and some pelvic fragments. Caprine bones had few cut-marks which were observed on a proximal and a distal humerus, an astragalus and a rib fragment. The dog atlas vertebrae, as noted above, had lateral cut-marks indicative of decapitation, though whether this species was eaten cannot be established from the few bones that were present.

The fauna

The fauna of the hill fort occupation is consistent with other assemblages from the region which are dated to the earlier Iron Age. In contrast with the Neolithic fauna in which cattle predominate, this species is now comparatively uncommon and caprine bones make up 56% of those identified, and pig almost 25% (Table 8.50). However, in assemblages that have undergone high levels of attrition by dogs, it is probable that the post-cranial bones alone provide at best an uncertain view of the original faunal composition. The very low mandible counts at the site mean that there is no comparison for the proportions of species derived from the post-cranial bones.

8.4 Everley Water Meadow

Small samples of bones were recovered from a number of contexts.

The middle Bronze Age 'burnt mound'

The old land surface below the mound yielded no identifiable bone fragments and the mound itself produced only a cattle first phalanx and a left caprine navicular-cuboid. A rather larger sample of 27 identifiable bones and five teeth came from gravels derived from the mound, although these incorporated post-Bronze Age artefacts. Of these, five were from pig, thirteen were cattle, and nine were caprine. The body of a cattle navicular-cuboid had the small tarsal fused to it by bone growth. The few associated teeth were loose and fragmentary, but included a right canid P^4, from its size likely to be that of a dog and a right upper molar of a horse, a species that is known more widely in the Bronze Age. Two teeth were from cattle and one from a caprine.

A channel of Iron Age or later date (SMX layer 8) contained the partly charred proximal left coracoid of a corvid (SM82 108). The specimen might be that from the Carrion Crow *Corvus corone corone* or the Rook *Corvus frugilegus.*

Samples post-dating alluviation

Area 2 F5 and Area 3–4 F7/1A. This feature, a channel of the post-medieval water meadow, produced 42 bones, three part tooth rows and four loose teeth.

Horse was represented by an unfused left proximal femur and a single left central carpal. The six pig bones were fragments of the femur, tibia and a first phalanx and of an immature right femur and tibia, while six cattle bones were part of a left ulna, a distal right femur, a fragment of immature femur, and skull and rib fragments. The 22 caprine bones were probably from one animal as most parts of the body were represented. The identified bones included right and left radius, ulna, innominate, metacarpal and metatarsal, the form of which show that this was a sheep; there were further fragments of right caprine humerus and radius. A left tibiotarsus and a right tarso-metatarsus were identified as the goose *Anser anser*. A left ulna, right coracoid and a left femur were identified as the domestic chicken, *Gallus gallus*.

The mandibles and teeth from this sample included the left M_3 of a horse, an immature left pig mandible, a left cattle M_3, a right cattle mandibular ramus, and a mature left sheep mandible, besides other loose caprine teeth, both upper and lower.

The sample from the possible sluice within F7 consisted of six identifiable caprine limb bone fragments and a distal right bird femur, again identified as the domestic chicken, *Gallus gallus*.

Area 4, F3. This feature contained a bone assemblage which included canid and a number of bird bones. Three bones, consisting of two fragments of right scapula and a right tibia, were identified as dog, while a small and fragmentary metatarsal was identified as the fox, *Vulpes vulpes*. Of the bird bones, a fragmentary proximal metatarsal was referred to *Anser anser*, the greylag goose which, by the medieval period, is likely to have been present as a domestic animal. In addition, one complete left and one broken right femur were identified as from the domestic chicken, *Gallus gallus*. A small left femur was probably from the blackbird, *Turdus merula*. Apart from the dog bones, other domestic mammals were represented only by a fragmentary left caprine innominate. There were no specimens of mammalian dentition.

Unstratified bones

A further sample of identified bones, tooth rows and loose teeth were from unstratified sediments. The identified bones consisted of one from dog, eleven horse, six pig, twenty cattle, nineteen caprine and one red deer – a complete right metatarsal. Of the bird bones, one was identified as goose, three as chicken and one as the mallard duck, *Anas platyrhynchos*. The mandibles and loose teeth were identified as from dog (one), horse (one), pig (one), cattle (nine), and caprine (eleven).

8.5 Bone artefacts

Tools of bone and antler – apart from the 'picks' formed from red deer antlers (8.2) – are few from the Neolithic levels at Hambledon. This points to the somewhat specialised nature of the settlement there. In a wholly domestic setting the frequency of bone tools would probably be higher.

Main enclosure

Segment 7 L10 phase I. HH76 289. (Fig 8.33). Two specimens:

1. An implement made on the shaft of a metatarsal, probably sheep. The shaft was ground to a point at one end and the surface shows striations from scraping and abrasion. Both ends are broken. Surviving length = 76 mm
2. A metatarsal shaft, probably sheep. The bone was grooved by the use of a burin or similar implement, preparatory to its splitting. The bone is broken at both ends and the task was abandoned. This was probably intended as a point similar to HH77 2134 described below

Segment 18, with child burial HH76 1948, phase I or II HH76 2004 (Fig 3.34). Three worked bones from this context appear to be simple beads, either complete or in process of working.

1. A tubular bead, cut from a large bird bone. The surface is polished and smoothed. The specimen agrees well in size and form with the distal tibia of the mute swan, *Cygnus olor*. Length = 39 mm
2. A small segment cut from a large bird limb bone. The surface appears to have been smoothed, but the surface condition of the specimen is now poor. L = 14.7 mm. Numbered TN 36 on the original plan
3. A segment, probably of a mammalian bone, with evidence of ring-sawing as a stage in the preparation of a bead. The specimen agrees well with the mid shaft of a sheep first phalanx. L = 16.0 mm. Numbered TN 37 on the original plan

The south long barrow

Segment 1, LB3 SIII, L21 phase III HH77 2134 (Fig 8.33). The distal, medial condyle of a sheep metatarsal. This is from a bone that was divided lengthways by means of burin cuts on the anterior and posterior surfaces of the bone. After the shaft was thus divided, it was ground to a point, retaining the condyle as a terminal. This is a familiar implement type from prehistoric sites in Britain (see for example Legge 1992, figs 25, 63: A45–A47). The tip of the implement is missing. Remaining length = 50 mm.

Pit in the central area

N F7iii/vii L3 HH77 2150 (Fig 8.33). A complete bone point, made on the metacarpal of a sheep. Although made on the fore limb bone rather than that of the hind, otherwise identical to HH77 2134 above. The bone was divided lengthways by saw cuts and the shaft ground and polished, retaining the distal condyle as a terminal. The specimen has lost only 3–5 mm of the tip broken. Surviving length = 75.0 mm.

Stepleton enclosure

Segment 4 L2 phase VI ST80 900 (Fig 8.33). A bone point made by grinding the tip of an irregular splinter from a robust limb bone. The splinter shows saw or burin cuts at the broader end.

Segment 10 L2 phase VI ST81 395 (Fig 8.33). The distal, medial condyle of the left metacarpal from a roe deer, *Capreolus capreolus*. The shaft has been split lengthways, following grooving by means of a burin on the anterior and posterior shaft

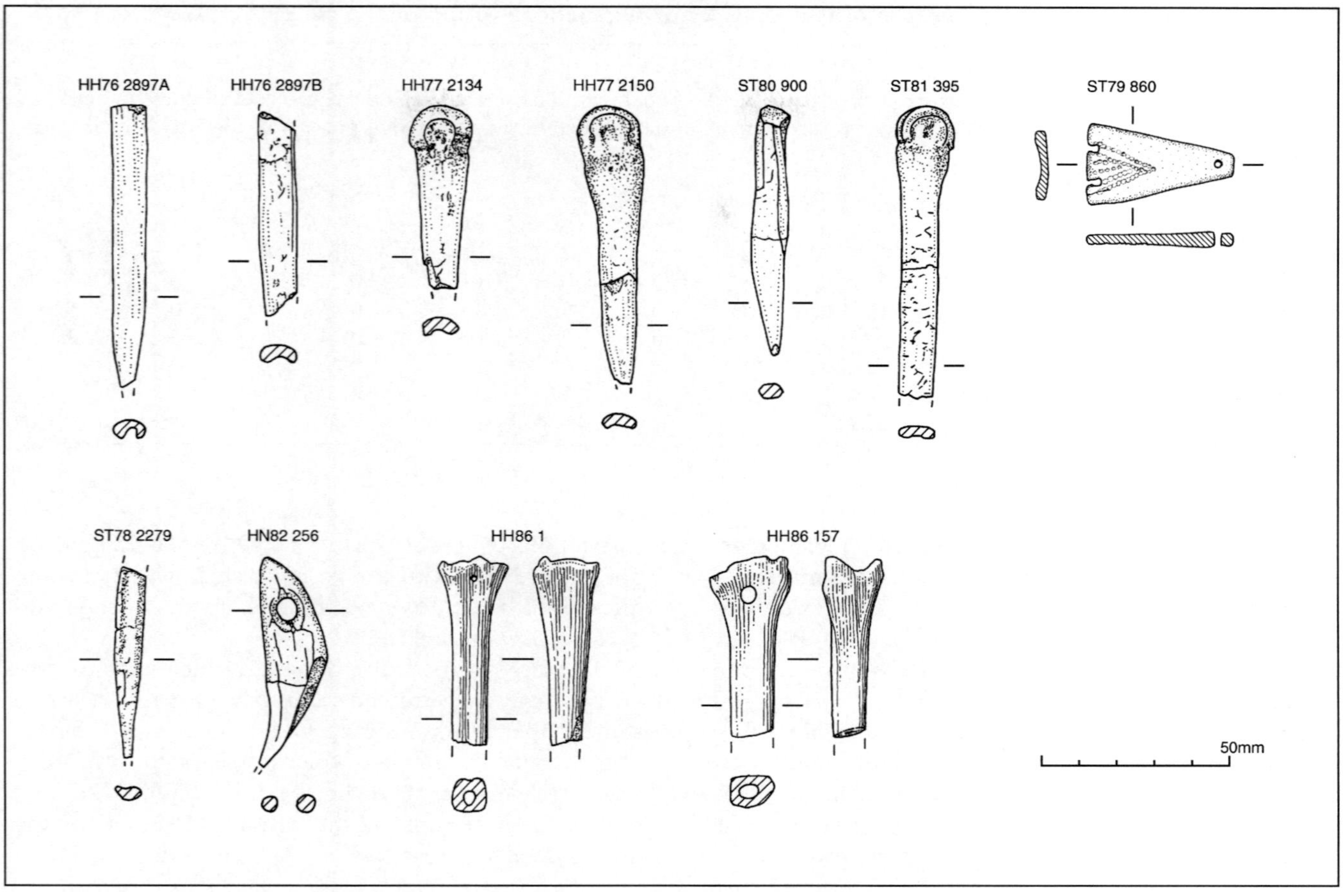

Fig 8.33 Bone artefacts. Particulars in catalogue.

surfaces, in the same manner as specimen 2134 and other specimens described above. In the roe deer, the metacarpal has deep natural grooves on the anterior and posterior surfaces which assist in guiding the burin. The divided shaft was ground and polished to a point. 10–15 mm are missing from the tip of the implement. Surviving length = 78.0 mm.

Inner Stepleton outwork

Segment 6 L2B phase VII/a ST79 860 (Fig 8.33). A small bone (or possibly antler) pendant or bead of triangular form, with dot decoration made by shallow pits drilled in the surface by means of a rotary drill. At the narrow end, a drilled hole of 2.0 mm diameter was for suspension or attachment. Two holes drilled at the wider end appear to have been broken through the margin of the piece, presumably during use. Length = 37.5 mm, width = 21.2 mm.

Features on the Stepleton spur

1A F6 = Saxon grave 12 ST78 2279 (Fig 8.33). Tip of a small bone point, broken in use. Poorly preserved, possibly derived from Neolithic pit 1A F278, which was cut by the grave.

Inner Hanford outwork

Segment 3 L2D Phase VII/a HN82 256 (Fig 8.33). Perforated lower left canine of a canid. The root is pierced by a double V-perforation, made by drilling from each side, and 5.5 mm at its narrowest. The interior of the perforation is highly polished from suspension on a thread or thong, as evidence of long use. The anterior crown enamel of the tooth is chipped away, presumably by accident in wearing. The large size of the tooth, which is greater than that usually found in Neolithic dogs from this or other English sites, suggests that the tooth may be from a wolf, *Canis lupus*. Length = 56.5 mm.

The hillfort

Clearance of hut surface layer HH86 1 (Fig 8.33). The proximal left metatarsal of a sheep. The posterior surface has been pierced by a small hole, about 1.5 mm in diameter.

Trench Extension L2 HH86 157 (Fig 8.33). The distal tibia of a caprine, probably sheep. The shaft has been snapped through. The distal articulation has been pierced by a cylindrical hole, about 4 mm in diameter.

8.6 Marine mollusc shell

Elizabeth Somerville

8.6.1 Method

Samples from the 1979 excavations in segments 5 and 6 of the inner Stepleton outwork were received by the writer. Shell was initially identified to species (Fish and Fish 1989), and weighed. Bivalves were counted as complete right/left valves, right/left and unsidable umbos or as fragments.

Table 8.51 Composition of marine mollusc shell from segments 5 and 6 of the inner Stepleton outwork

u/s = unsided

Only the *Pecten maximus* (scallop) fragments are from a Neolithic context. The phase VIII/a ploughsoils in the tops of both segments contained Roman pottery, and the single fragments of oyster shell in the underlying phase VII fills are likely to have been intrusive from them.

segment	*phase*	*species*	*weight (g)*	*fragments*	*umbos*			*valves*			*MNI*
					u/s	*right*	*left*	*u/s*	*right*	*left*	
5	III	*Pecten maximus*	7.3	4	0	0	0	0	0	0	1
5	VII	*Ostrea edulis*	7.5	1	0	0	0	0	0	0	1
5	VIII/a	*Ostrea edulis*	146	4	1	3	1	0	2	0	5
6	VII	*Ostrea edulis*	0.5	1	0	0	0	0	0	0	1
6	VIII/a	*Mytilus edulis*	5.7	11	2	0	0	0	0	0	2
Unspecified	VIII/a	*Ostrea edulis*	106.8	8	1	1	1	0	1	0	2
		total	273.8	–	–	–	–	–	–	–	–

The maximum length (from umbo to opposite margin) and width (orthogonal to length) were measured for whole oysters. Whole oyster shells were examined for a number of other characteristics, including age and whether the surface bore the marks of infestation by the polychaete worms *Polydora ciliata*, *P hoplura* and the burrowing sponge *Cliona celata*. The shell surface was also examined for calcareous tubes, sandtubes, bryozoans and barnacles, any damage to the shell by predatory molluscs (drillholes) or evidence of the reuse of the shell by people. Because so few whole valves were recovered, the presence/absence of these species and marks were also noted for the right and left umbos. A spreadsheet recording a full description of all identified shell forms part of the project archive.

8.6.2 Results

Shell of three marine molluscs was present – the majority being *Ostrea edulis*, with a small amount of *Mytilus edulis* and fragments from both the left and right valve of *Pecten maximus*. Table 8.51 summarises the quantitative data on the shell by phase. This is a very small assemblage, although the domination by *Ostrea edulis* is clear. However, measurement of shell length was only possible for three *O edulis* right valves (58 mm, 85 mm and 93 mm). A minimum age could be obtained for nine of the eleven umbos and valves and this ranged from three to nine years with a mode at five years. Inspection of the surface of the larger fragments, umbos and valves of the *O edulis* shell revealed some infestation by *Polydora ciliata* on six pieces of shell and by *P hoplura* on one shell.

The largest right valve had been glued back together, although not entirely accurately, and this revealed some evidence for working in the form of a lozenge-shaped hole through it, which appears to have been made by working from the exterior of the shell. The maximum dimensions of the hole are 15 mm along the line of breakage ×10 mm orthogonal to this.

8.6.3 Discussion

The small size of the assemblage precludes any detailed interpretation. The *Ostrea edulis* shell is of a fairly modest size and its morphology is consistent with an uncrowded bed. However, the modal age is older than would be expected for a harvest of a farmed population (Walne 1974), assuming growth conditions similar to the present. The dominance of *P ciliata* as the infesting polychaete indicates the exploitation of a population living in shallow water (Cole 1956; P S Smith 1987; Winder 1992). *Mytilus edulis* is also found in shallow water, and on rocks. *Pecten maximus*, however, is a sublittoral species and would not normally be taken live under the same conditions as the other species, but the dead shell may be found along the channel coast.

9 Pottery and fired clay

9.1 The pottery from the hilltop excavations of 1974–82

The late Isobel Smith

9.1.1 Earlier Neolithic

A. The total assemblage and its relationships

In total, 850 vessels have been identified, principally by 710 rims; the remaining 140 are represented by body sherds with distinguishing attributes (curvature of cups, necks/carinations of bipartite bowls, decoration) and by detached lugs and cordons (Table 9.1). No vessels were complete.

The two major sub-assemblages comprise 439 vessels from the central area (Table 9.5) and 361 from the Stepleton enclosure, pits and inner outwork (Table 9.6). The remaining 50 come from the middle and outer Stepleton outworks (12), the Shroton outwork (5), the western outwork (6), the Hanford outworks (20); and pits on the Hanford spur (7).

A concordance of pottery illustrations, find numbers, contexts and fabrics concludes this report.

Fabrics

Forty-three sherds chosen to represent the range of fabrics were examined in thin section by T C Darvill; his report on the petrology (9.2) defines eight fabric groups on the basis of raw materials – clays, natural inclusions and additives – and describes his survey of potential sources.

As shown in Table 9.1, three of the groups (7, 6, and 2 in descending order of frequency) account for nearly 90% of the assemblage. The clay matrix of group 7 (47.9%) is closely matched by Kimmeridge clay some 2.5 km west of Hambledon Hill. The flint temper varies widely in particle size and density. The general effect is that of well-shaped vessels with fairly smooth surfaces; also present are a few exceptionally fine and some extremely rough examples.

Fabric group 6 (25.5%) is characterised by numerous small red (iron-rich clay) pellets which, together with a somewhat silty texture, may suggest a riverine origin, possibly in the near vicinity of Hambledon Hill, although Fiona Roe suggests a source area in south-east Dorset (10.1.2). The common temper is flint, but five other additives were occasionally used (9.2). Surface treatment seems usually to have been confined to a perfunctory hand-smoothing, with little attempt to reduce irregularities. Some bowls are markedly asymmetrical and clumsy, and the standard appears low in comparison with products attributed to other fabric groups.

Fabric group 2 (19.0%) comprises six subgroups which probably originate from at least three localities along the Jurassic limestone outcrops to the west and north-west of Hambledon Hill. The subgroups can be distinguished by macroscopic inspection, but the discovery that adjacent coils in a single sherd represent two distinct subgroups (Fig 9.14) shows that raw materials from separate sources were sometimes used together. For present purposes, therefore, all the Jurassic fabrics are treated as one. Calcareous inclusions (ooliths, fossil shell, limestone) have been lost from sherds exposed to weathering. Among the best-preserved pieces are some with unconcealed inclusions, but the overall impression is that these vessels were probably superior in appearance to much of the other pottery.

Fabric 1, gabbroic ware (1.2%) is the smallest of the five minor groups and the most interesting because of its origin on the Lizard Head in south-west Cornwall and distribution eastward as far as north Wiltshire (Peacock 1969; 1988). All the gabbroic feature sherds from Hambledon Hill are illustrated (P1–P10). Even weathered or refired pieces clearly represent pottery of a standard rarely achieved in Wessex and correspond to the 'fine' or 'medium' quality observed in the entirely gabbroic assemblage from Carn Brea (Smith 1981, 162). The best-preserved parts of the two large bowls, P1 and P2, retain burnished red surfaces; P5 and P9 display the smooth black coating present on some of the pottery from Carn Brea (ibid, 170).

Fabric group 8 (4.1%) contains only quartz sand in varying quantities and probably comes, like fabric 7, from the Kimmeridge clay. The sources of the three remaining groups are as yet unlocated: fabric 3 (1.4%), calcite-tempered, usually well-smoothed, occasionally burnished; fabric 4 (1.4%), organic-tempered; and fabric 5 (2.5%), filled with fresh shell and flint that is often coarse and protruding. Cleal has suggested a source in Purbeck for calcite-tempered Neolithic fabrics from Maiden Castle which are similar to fabric 3 (1991a, 173).

The clay on Hambledon Hill itself was apparently not used for pottery, but a sample from a fissure in the Chalk inside the Stepleton spur provides a close match for burnt clay from that site (see 9.2).

Table 9.1 Vessel form:fabric correlations in total assemblage

Figures in *italics* denote decorated vessels

	Fabric groups 1	*2*	*3*	*4*	*5*	*6*	*7*	*8*	*subtotals*	*totals*	*% decorated*
Cups	–	14	2	7	1	52	36	14	126		
	–	–	–	–	–	*2*	*6*	*3*	*11*	137	8.0
Carinated cups	–	–	–	–	–	2	1	1	4		
	–	–	–	–	–	–	*1*	–	*1*	5	20.0
Necked cups	–	–	–	–	–	1	1	–	2	2	
Carinated bowls	–	8	1	–	–	1	18	–	28		
	–	*1*	–	–	–	–	*2*	–	*3*	31	9.6
Necked bowls	–	2	–	–	–	1	2	–	5		
	–	–	–	–	–	*2*	*1*	–	*3*	8	37.5
Open bowls	4	6	4	1	–	2	25	–	42		
	–	–	–	–	*1*	–	–	–	*1*	43	2.3
Other bowls:											
rims	5	86	4	3	15	122	250	8	493		
	–	*5*	*1*	–	–	*3*	*14*	–	*23*	516	4.6
decorated body sherds	–	–	–	–	–	*9*	*11*	*1*	*21*	21	100
detached lugs	1	13	–	1	4	18	35	8	80		
	–	–	–	–	–	–	*1*	–	*1*	81	1.2
detached cordons	–	1	–	–	–	2	3	–	6	6	
Totals	10	136	12	12	21	217	407	35		850	
% of assemblage	1.2	16.0	1.4	1.4	2.5	25.5	47.9	4.1		100.0	
% decorated	–	4.4	8.3	–	4.8	7.4	8.8	11.4		7.5	

Vessel forms

All vessels appear to have been round-based. Forms are defined by size and shape. Correlations with fabric groups are given in Table 9.1.

Cups, up to 120 mm in diameter, account for 19.1% of the assemblage. Shapes are generally open (P75) or neutral (P60), occasionally closed (P69). Rims are simple; several cups carry small lugs (see below). Within this size range are also five *carinated cups* (0.6%; P42, P39 with lugs on the shoulder) and two *necked cups* (0.2%; P43, P45).

Carinated bowls (3.6% of the assemblage) display a range of profiles, from sharp carinations and concave necks (P36) to slack, nearly straight-necked examples (P33). Forms are generally neutral; a few are slightly open (P38) or closed (P34). Rims are simple (P38), rolled over (P34) or externally extended (P32, P37). Several bowls carry solid or perforated lugs on the carinations (P31, P34, P37, P38).

Necked bowls (0.9% of the assemblage) are best exemplified by P41 and P57, where the cylindrical necks and rounded bodies are clearly differentiated. The profiles of the other six (P61, P63, P98, P107, P108, P118) are weakly defined.

Open bowls (4.9% of the assemblage) range in shape from conical (P1) to hemispherical (P2). Incurved rims (P2, P12, P18) and trumpet lugs (P2, P3) seem to be specific but not invariable attributes.

Other bowls are represented mainly by 517 rims too fragmentary to indicate vessel shapes. The 63 that are better preserved include a few that may be described as closed (P47, P48); the rest are divided more or less equally between forms that are straight-sided or neutral (P46, P51) and those with slightly contracted rims (P68, P79).

Table 9.1 indicates several disparities in the representation of vessel forms across the three main fabric groups: the high proportion of cups made of fabric 6; the rarity of fabric 6 among the carinated and open bowls; the absolute dominance of fabrics 2 and 7 among the carinated bowls and of fabric 7 among the open bowls.

Rim forms

The morphology and fabric attributions of the 710 rims are set out in Table 9.2. Forms defined are:

Simple, 75.5% of the total, comprising four variants: rounded (eg P55), 33.9%; squared, often with sharp edges (eg P54), 22.6%; pointed (eg P61, P80), 13.1%; irregular, 5.9%.
Rolled over, 11.4% of the total (eg P33, P53).
Incurved, 4.9% of the total, confined to open bowls; rounded exterior drawn inwards to join interior as a thin vertical (eg P2) or slightly overhanging (eg P16) lip.
Externally extended, 3.5% of the total, horizontal (eg P102) or tilted inwards (eg P83).
Enlarged, 2.1% of the total, bulbous (eg P96) or thickened internally (eg P89).

Table 9.2 Rim form:fabric correlations in total assemblage

Figures in *italics* denote decorated vessels

	Fabric groups 1	2	3	4	5	6	7	8	*subtotals*	*totals*	*% decorated*
Simple											
rounded	3	42	3	3	3	53	122	6	235		
	–	–	–	–	–	–	*4*	*2*	*6*	241	2.6
squared	1	26	3	2	5	48	71	2	158		
	–	–	–	–	*1*	*1*	*1*	–	*3*	161	1.8
pointed	1	7	–	4	–	22	43	13	90		
	–	–	–	–	–	*1*	*2*	–	*3*	93	3.1
irregular	–	2	2	–	1	27	9	1	42	42	
Rolled-over	1	15	1	2	2	15	42	1	79		
	–	–	–	–	–	–	*2*	–	*2*	81	2.4
Incurved	3	4	2	–	–	1	25	–	35	35	
Externally extended	–	5			1	2	11	–	19		
	–	*2*	–	–	–	–	*4*	–	*6*	25	24.0
Enlarged	–	4	–	–	4	1	2	–	11		
	–	–	–	–	–	*1*	*3*	–	*4*	15	26.6
Internally extended	–	–	–	–	–	7	1	–	8		
	–	–	–	–	–	*1*	–	–	*1*	9	11.0
T-shaped	–	4	–	–	–	–	3	–	7		
	–	*1*	–	–	–	–	–	–	*1*	8	12.5
Totals	9	112	11	11	17	180	345	25		710	
% of 710 rims	1.3	15.8	1.5	1.5	2.4	25.4	48.6	3.5		100.0	
% decorated	–	2.0	–	–	5.8	2.2	4.6	8.0		3.6	

Internally extended, 1.3% of the total (eg P86).
T-shaped, 1.1% of the total (eg P87, P91).

Rims of fabric 6, the second largest fabric group, are proportionately over-represented in the 'irregular' subgroup of the 'simple' form and in the 'internally extended' form, and under-represented in the 'incurved' form.

Lugs and cordons

There are 129 classifiable lugs; all surviving pairs are counted as single units. Eleven trumpet lugs comprise: six perforated horizontally and made of fabric 1 (P2, P3, P5 and remnant on P4), fabric 2 (P25), and fabric 7 (not illustrated); one perforated vertically and made of fabric 5 (P105); and four imperforate, made of fabric 6 (P13, P27) and fabric 7 (P26, P28). A single tubular lug with unexpanded ends (not illustrated) is made of fabric 2.

Ten bilobate (or divided) lugs include eight that are imperforate and made of fabric 3 (P11), fabric 6 (P29, P64), and fabric 7 (P30, P97, plus three not illustrated); one perforated horizontally, made of fabric 2 (P19); and one of fabric 7, pierced vertically (not illustrated).

Less distinctive lugs, represented in all fabrics except 1 and 3, include a narrow ring-handle set on a shoulder (P120) and eight of oblong shape perforated horizontally, two of them set on cordons (eg P79, P81). Two of the eleven with vertical perforations are set on shoulders (P34, P37). A further six are too fragmentary to show the direction of perforation. The 81 unpierced lugs are generally oval in shape (eg P65, P66). Variants include round knobs (eg P118) and elongated forms (eg P31, P55, P101). A rectangular version with broad horizontal depression (eg P99) occurs twice.

Lugs were attached by tenons set into holes in the walls (eg P29, P48, P74, P97) and by luting. The pit on the body of P120 may be an unused mortise for the adjacent ring-handle rather than a decorative feature. Reduced versions of round, oval and bilobate lugs were attached to cups (P62, P64, P65, P67, P138). A miniature trumpet lug, only 20 mm across (P28), will also have come from a cup.

Eight bowls (fabrics 2, 6 and 7) carried cordons, on P79–P80 set high on the body. The lugs on P79 and P81 were noted above.

Decoration

Decoration appears on and/or beneath 5.6% of the 710 rims and on 7.5% of the total assemblage if rimless fragments are included (Table 9.1). It was applied sparely to simple and rolled rims, proportionately most often to the forms with expanded surfaces (Table 9.2), and is absent only from vessels of fabrics 1 and 4, necked cups, incurved and irregular simple rims. All decorated pieces are illustrated except one cup and nine body sherds.

Techniques comprise impressions made with points, fingernails and twisted cord, and incisions made with sharp or blunt tools; only two vessels show impressions and incisions in combination (P116, P127). Pattern-burnishing was not observed.

Seven bowls of medium to large sizes carry a line of round pits (eg P117, P121) or pre-firing perforations (eg P118, P119) beneath simple rims. A variant combines pinpricks with irregular impressions (P113). Round pricks or, rarely, stabs (eg P133) occur on eight vessels, once above a carination (P126) and otherwise on cups or small bowls, where they were usually aligned horizontally (eg P127–P129). The fragments of a carinated cup (P124) show a horizontal row inside the rim and vertical rows on the neck. On two examples the impressions seem randomly disposed (eg P123).

Fingernail impressions occur on 13 vessels: on the tops of rims (eg P102, P104, P105) or on the body, where they stand in rows (P140–P142), form part of a curved motif (P146) or are apparently placed at random (P147, P153). Fingertip impressions were applied to two rims (P108, P110) and a body sherd (P152).

Twisted cord impressions are confined to three externally extended rims (P111, P112, P115).

The incised decoration on 20 vessels was made with sharp tools, perhaps flint flakes (eg P114), and with blunt points (eg P103). Transverse or oblique incisions decorate the tops or inner surfaces of rims (P109, P116, P132) and extend vertically over the neck of one carinated bowl (P103). Diagonal incisions on body sherds may have been arranged in zones (as on P150–P151); a single lug carries vertical incisions (P154).

'Thumb-grooves' and allied features

The external hollow beneath the rim of P139 represents the defining characteristic of a 'thumb-groove bowl', a special category in Cleal's (1992) classification of earlier Neolithic ceramic forms. P148, although less typical, may also fall within this category. Six sherds have internal grooves: P145 has a groove close to the rim and a slight external swelling; P144, a deep groove inside a straight wall and pronounced external ridge; on P143 and three others the profiles are incomplete but appear to have been similar to P144. (For comparanda see '*Connections*', below.) The shallow grooves and ridges on the rim sherd P149 appear to have been decorative in intent.

A presence/absence chart (Table 9.3) illustrates the spread of individual decorative techniques and of 'thumb-grooves' across vessels of all fabric groups except the entirely plain 1 and 4.

Black coating

Traces similar to those already noted on two fabric 1 sherds (P5, P9) remain on a few non-gabbroic pieces. They are best preserved on the fragment from a fabric 7 open bowl (P14), where both surfaces are covered.

Repair holes

The secondary holes present on 19 vessels probably represent devices for binding cracks; only one complete pair has survived. The hole on P57 had been started from both faces and abandoned before completion. Drilled holes on four cups (eg P65, P72) show that even these small and easily made containers were worth repairing.

Table 9.3 Presence/absence of individual decorative techniques and of 'thumb-grooves' across vessels of all fabric groups, except the entirely plain 1 and 4

	Fabric groups					
Techniques	*2*	*3*	*5*	*6*	*7*	*8*
Incisions	+	–	–	+	+	+
Fingernail impressions	+	–	+	+	+	+
Fingertip impressions	–	–	–	+	+	–
Irregular impressions	–	–	–	–	+	–
Round/oblique pin pricks	+	–	–	+	+	+
Line of pits/perforations under rim	+	–	–	+	+	–
Twisted cord impressions	+	–	–	–	+	–
Combination of techniques	+	–	–	–	+	–
'Thumb-grooves'	–	+	–	+	+	–

Vessel sizes

The external diameters of the 156 rims that afford reasonably accurate measurements are set out in Table 9.4. Cups, 60–120 mm, are represented in all fabrics except fabric 1 and account for 37% of the total, a much higher proportion than the *c* 5% to 13% recorded in other large assemblages for which equivalent information is available (Abingdon, Avery 1982, table 6; Maiden Castle, Cleal 1991a, table 58; Carn Brea, Smith 1981, 166; Windmill Hill, Smith 1965, 49; Broome Heath, Wainwright 1972, 24). An alternative calculation, based on the figures given in Table 9.1, suggests that cups (including carinated and necked forms) constitute *c* 17% of the assemblage. The three largest bowls, with diameters exceeding 300 mm, comprise P117 (fabric 2), probably from the vicinity of the Jurassic limestone outcrop west or north-west of Hambledon Hill, together with P1 and P2 (fabric 1) from south-west Cornwall.

Connections

The burnished red and black fabric 1 bowls, some of impressive size (P1, P2), attest to direct or indirect transactions with the potters exploiting the gabbroic clay on the Lizard peninsula in south-west Cornwall (area shown by Peacock 1969, fig 1). A charred twig of Cornish heath from the same location (see Austin *et al*, 6.1) is a plausible residue of packing that had protected such vessels in transit and may imply direct deliveries to Hambledon Hill. West Country connections seem deliberately emphasised by the burial of a complete stone axe of Cornish origin beneath the remains of P1 and P2 in a pit inside the main causewayed enclosure (Figs 3.54–55). The significance attached to the imported bowls at this site is also apparent from the

Table 9.4 External rim diameters of 156 vessels in total assemblage

	Fabric groups									
Diameters (mm)	*1*	*2*	*3*	*4*	*5*	*6*	*7*	*8*	*totals*	*%*
60–120	–	3	2	4	–	27	15	7	58	37.2
120–180	–	4	–	2	1	5	18	–	30	19.2
180–240	–	14	3	–	1	7	23	–	48	30.8
240–300	–	2	–	–	1	5	9	–	17	10.9
310	1	1	–	–	–	–	–	–	2	1.3
400	1	–	–	–	–	–	–	–	1	0.6
Totals	2	24	5	6	3	44	65	7	156	

concentration of their fragments in the enclosure's internal pits where they constitute 7% of the countable vessels. The proportion is comparable with the *c* 6% of gabbroic ware in the assemblages from the two nearest enclosures – Maiden Castle, Dorset (Cleal 1991a, 171) and Whitesheet Hill, Wiltshire (Cleal 2004). But Cleal has noted at each of those sites a different mode of disposal of this pottery – burial of large pieces deep in the enclosure ditches.

Together with the imports, the greater part of the locally made pottery used at Hambledon Hill adheres to the conventions of the South-western regional style, distributed from Cornwall to north Wiltshire (Whittle 1977, 77–82). The vessel characteristic of this style, consistently found in all but the smallest assemblages, is the plain uncarinated open bowl with simple or incurved rim and horizontally perforated trumpet lugs. At Hambledon Hill half of the gabbroic feature sherds (P1–P5) conform to this specification. The small rim sherds (P6–P10) may come from gabbroic forms less frequently carried to Wessex such as a neutral bowl with trumpet lug from Whitesheet Hill (Cleal 2004), carinated bowls from Maiden Castle (Cleal 1991a, 177–8), or a closed bowl from Windmill Hill, Wiltshire (Smith 1965, 46).

The open bowls made of the local fabrics 2–7 are noticeably smaller than the imports, and several of the trumpet lugs are imperforate, in this respect resembling some gabbroic specimens from Cornwall – at Carn Brea (Smith 1981) and from the Lizard itself (Smith and Harris 1982; G H Smith 1987). There is one departure from the South-western tradition: the expanded ends of the lug on P105 mimic the trumpet form, but it is pierced vertically and set low on the only decorated open bowl in the assemblage. A comparable breach is recorded from Whitesheet Hill: a classic trumpet lug applied to the neck of a locally made closed carinated bowl (Cleal 2004).

The bilobate (divided, double, or notched) lug is also found on open, or occasionally neutral, bowls and may be derived from the trumpet form (cf a compressed lug from Hazard Hill (Houlder 1963, fig 6: 26). Peacock has identified (1969, 146) a possible gabbroic example from Hembury, Devon (Liddell 1935, P332). Other specimens are made of local materials: two from Hembury (Liddell 1931, P84; 1932, P304), one from Maiden Castle (Cleal 1991a, 179), one from Hampshire (Piggott 1937, fig 3: 7), four from Windmill Hill (Smith 1965, P111–P114), and ten (fabrics 2, 3, 6, 7) from Hambledon Hill (eg P11, P19).

Another typical South-western device is the girth-cordon, sometimes surmounted by lugs, on large utilitarian vessels of neutral or closed form. In Cornwall, the only gabbroic examples are from Carn Brea (Smith 1981, 168–70). At Helman Tor, in the east of the county, the combination recurs in a local fabric (Smith 1997). In Devon cordons are reported on similar vessels from Haldon (Willock 1936), Hazard Hill (Houlder 1963) and Hembury (Liddell 1931; 1932; 1935). The lug and cordon combination reappears in Dorset at Maiden Castle (Wheeler 1943, fig 37: 139), and at Hambledon Hill (P79, P81). Farther east, at Windmill Hill and Staines, Surrey, cordons are found on single fragments of neutral jars, more frequently on smaller closed bowls (Smith 1965; Robertson-Mackay 1987); they are absent from other assemblages of the Decorated and Eastern styles.

The burnished black or dark finish added to some South-western pottery is a less durable attribute, vulnerable to weathering or re-firing. At Hambledon Hill it is preserved only on the gabbroic sherds P5 and P9, on the fabric 7 sherd P14 and in small patches on a few other local products. It survives on around a quarter of the all-gabbroic pottery from Carn Brea (Smith 1981, 170–72) and on a sixth of the mixed assemblage from Helman Tor, composed of gabbroic and three local fabrics (Smith 1997). In Devon and Wessex black-surfaced gabbroic bowls are recorded from Hembury (personal observation), Maiden Castle (Cleal 1991a, 181), Whitesheet Hill (Cleal 2004), Robin Hood's Ball (Thomas 1964, 18, pl II: 2, fig 4: 17) and Windmill Hill (Smith 1965, 46, pl XVIIa, top right). A notable series of fine carinated bowls, made of local clays, their surface finishes well preserved in peat, demonstrates that the technique was known to potters in the south-west before the tree-ring date of 3807/3806 BC, when they were discarded along the Sweet Track in the Somerset Levels (Coles and Coles 1990, 218; Smith 1976; Kinnes 1979).

The numerically significant indicators of south-western connections are high proportions of undecorated vessels, here 93%, and of simple rims, 75% – quantities comparable with those calculated by Cleal (1991a, 175) for Maiden Castle and Carn Brea. The 'intrusive' elements of the Decorated style (Whittle 1977, 85) – developed rims, 8%, and ornamented vessels, 7% – were made in all fabrics except 1 and 4. There are no exclusive links between individual fabrics and specific rim forms or methods of decoration. Decorated vessels were evenly spread between the central area and the Stepleton spur (Tables 9.8 and 9.9) and stratification in their ditches indicates that developed rims were present when the earliest surviving deposits were made (section C, below).

This fraction of the assemblage seems to reflect contacts with potters producing the Decorated wares found in the causewayed enclosures on Windmill Hill in north Wiltshire, at Abingdon and Staines in the Thames valley, and at Whitehawk in Sussex. Cord-impressed ornament appears to have been confined to the first three sites – five examples from Windmill Hill (Smith 1965, P223–P227), 23 from Abingdon (Avery 1982, table 7), one from Staines (Robertson-Mackay 1987, P146) – and one more from the West Kennet long barrow near Windmill Hill (Piggott 1962, fig 10: W1). The rims conform closely to a uniform specification: the twisted cord almost always wrapped diagonally across enlarged rounded surfaces. The transverse impressions on P111 and P115 and the short diagonals on P112 have been applied to the broad flat horizontal or tilted surfaces of externally extended rims. This rim form is represented at Hambledon Hill by 22 further examples (eg P37, P83, P102) and rarely elsewhere except at Abingdon where, under the classification 'angular, outturned', 53 examples are recorded (Avery 1982, table 3, fig 14: 2 for the horizontal variant; Leeds 1927, fig 6: 2–3 for the tilted variant). The other 32 developed rims from Hambledon Hill – enlarged, internally extended, T-shaped – are less specific to any single assemblage and can be matched at Windmill Hill (Smith 1965, fig 11) as well as at Abingdon or Staines (Robertson-Mackay 1987, fig 37).

Windmill Hill provides the geographically nearest source of comparanda (Smith 1965, figs 25–27) for the incised and tool-impressed decoration like that of P103, P106, P121, P124, P129. The line of pits and/or pre-firing perforations, not always continuous, beneath rims that are usually simple and undecorated is a minor but recurrent motif in assemblages across southern England from Norfolk (Healy 1988a) to Cornwall (Smith 1997). Two small perforated sherds from a sealed deposit of South-western pottery in a pit known as the Coneybury 'anomaly' indicate a presence in Wiltshire by 4050–3640 cal BC (5050±100 BP; OxA-1402; Cleal 1990, 53; Richards 1990, table 137). As the motif is sparingly represented in most contexts, the presence of seven examples at Hambledon Hill, eg P117–P119, with P113 as an inventive variant, suggests familiarity with the potters who supplied the major concentration of 37 at Windmill Hill (Smith 1965, 52, fig 25). But fingernail and fingertip impressions are rare at that site (ibid, fig 13) and, although reported as the most frequent type of impressed decoration at Staines (Robertson-Mackay 1987, 88), were used there to different effect. The fingernail-impressed pattern on P142 is a close match for that on a bowl from Whitehawk (Ross Williamson 1930, pl IV: 2), where, as described below, a further, more significant, connection involving the use of this technique is also to be found.

'Thumb-groove' bowls like P139 are widely distributed but usually limited to one or two examples in individual assemblages. Seventeen bowls like P139 are known from Windmill Hill, as well as several with lightly drawn internal grooves (Smith 1965, 50, fig 18); the other significant concentration, at Staines (Robertson-Mackay 1987, 74), is differentiated only by flattening of the rims. The sources of the unusual fragments P143 and P144 – their internal grooves drawn within straight walls and raising external ridges – are revealed by a more complete bowl from Staines (ibid, P141) where the external feature, *c* 30 mm beneath the rim, is accompanied by conventional shoulder-zone decoration. The technique seems to have been an alternative to the more usual method(s) of creating bipartite bowls. P145, with groove and raised band close beneath the rim, also has a counterpart at Staines (ibid, P149). Other examples of this technique, all with prominent external ridges, are known from Runnymede Bridge, 1 km south of the Staines enclosure (Longworth and Varndell 1996, NP 69) and from Whitehawk (Ross Williamson 1930, pl XI: 55–56).

Finally, shared peculiarities of form and decoration suggest connections between Hambledon Hill and the nearest enclosures. The only known counterpart to the two necked cups, P43 and P45, comes from Maiden Castle; and one of the few decorated vessels from that site is a cup displaying parallel rows of round impressions like those on P124 (Wheeler 1943, fig 29: 59, fig 28: 34; Cleal 1991a, 179, 181). The curving line of fingernail impressions on P146 is reminiscent of a similar motif on the inner surface of the single decorated bowl from Whitesheet Hill and is, in turn, comparable to ornament on a small carinated bowl from Remenham, Berkshire (Cleal 2004; Holgate and Start 1983–5) and also to the curving lines of oval impressions on the neck of a carinated bowl from Whitehawk (Piggott 1936a, 80, fig 2).

B. Analyses of the sub-assemblages from the two enclosures

The substantial quantities of sherds recovered from pits and ditches in and around each enclosure provide a basis for analysis of variations in modes of disposal and in distributions of vessel forms and fabrics (Tables 9.5 and 9.6). But the loss of unknown proportions of

Table 9.5 Distribution of vessel forms in the central area

Figures in *italics* denote decorated vessels

	Pits	*Main enclosure ditch*	*Inner cross-dykes*	*Outer cross-dykes*	*Long barrow*	*subtotals*	*totals*
Cups	20	39	2	1	6	68	
	5	*3*	–	–	*1*	*9*	77
Carinated cups	–	1	–	–	–	1	
	–	*1*	–	–	–	*1*	2
Carinated bowls	2	8	1	–	1	12	
	–	*1*	–	–	–	*1*	13
Necked bowls	1	3	–	–	–	4	
	–	*1*	–	–	–	*1*	*5*
Open bowls	11	13	–	–	4	28	
	–	–	–	–	*1*	*1*	*29*
Other bowls:							
rims	60	139	11	7	25	242	
	3	*9*	*1*	–	*1*	*14*	256
decorated body sherds	*2*	*5*	–	–	*1*	*8*	8
detached lugs	10	29	3	2	4		48
detached cordon	–	–	1	–	–		1
Totals	114	252	19	10	44		439
% decorated	8.8	7.9	5.3	–	9.0		7.9

Table 9.6 Distribution of vessel forms in the Stepleton pits, enclosure and inner outwork

Figures in *italics* denote decorated vessels

	Pits	*Enclosure ditch*	*Inner outwork*	*subtotals*	*totals*
Cups	22	24	6	52	
	1	*1*	–	*2*	54
Carinated cups	–	3			3
Necked cups	–	1	–		1
Carinated bowls	2	11	–	13	
	1	*1*	–	*2*	15
Necked bowls	2	–	–	2	
	–	*1*	–	*1*	3
Open bowls	6	4	2		12
Other bowls:					
rims	62	121	35	218	
	2	*5*	*3*	*10*	228
decorated body sherds	*4*	9	–	*13*	13
detached lugs	4	16	6	26	
	–	*1*	–	*1*	27
detached cordons	1	4	–		5
Totals	107	202	52		361
% decorated	7.5	8.9	5.7		8.0

the original contents of the pits in both enclosures must be kept in mind when considering the figures in these tables.

Modes of disposal

Pottery was found in 73 pit bases within the central area, but only 38 contained feature sherds, representing in all 108 vessels (the total of 114 given in Tables 9.5, 9.7 and 9.10 includes six feature sherds assumed to have been ploughed out from pits). The highest number of vessels represented in a single pit is eight, and 27 pits yielded only one to three. Weathered or refired sherds frequently occurred together with those that appear to be in fresh condition, and mixtures of vessel and fabric types are the rule when any quantity of pottery is present. Fragments are generally small and few joins were identified. Diameters can be estimated for only eight bowls and three cups. Parts of the same vessel were in no instance recognised in more than one pit. The circumstances may suggest that the sherds, or some of them, had lain in exposed deposits before transference to the pits. Excavations of the Neolithic midden sealed beneath the Hazleton North long cairn in Gloucestershire (Saville 1990b) and the Bronze Age midden at Potterne, Wiltshire (Lawson 2000) have demonstrated similar fragmentation, dispersal and mixtures of fresh, weathered and refired sherds.

The contents of one pit (B F14) are exceptional in quantity, condition and variety. Impacted on the surface of the basal fill (layer 4) were a substantial portion (about two-thirds) of a roughly finished fabric 7 cup (P58) and an entire axe of Cornish greenstone (Figs 3.54–55). Within the overlying and distinct layer 3 were parts of two restorable gabbroic (fabric 1) open bowls: P1, represented by about one-third of the rim, and P2, with half of the rim surviving as well as a trumpet lug and the full profile. Eroded areas on both bowls suggest partial exposure to weathering, and abrupt colour changes show that some of the conjoining fragments had been refired after the bowls were broken. Layer 3 also contained small feature sherds from five fabric 7 vessels, including the decorated cup P138, and a charred, immature human skull fragment came from an unknown context in the pit.

Three further pits (A F64, A F120, N F11) and one natural feature (B F1) also contained fragmentary human bones as well as pottery. Neither character nor condition distinguishes the sherds from those in other pits.

Pottery was recovered from 71 of the pit bases within and adjacent to the Stepleton enclosure: 41 produced feature sherds representing 97 vessels (the total of 107 given in Tables 9.6, 9.7 and 9.10 includes ten assumed to have been ploughed out from pits). Again, numbers of vessels represented by feature sherds were small: 29 pits yielded one to three and the highest number from a single pit was six. The condition of the material from the majority of pits is similar to that described from the pits within the main causewayed enclosure and suggests that here, too, some of it had been taken from surface deposits.

Conjunctions of human remains and pottery occurred in four features. There was a single sherd in the fill of one grave (1A F70), and the ceramic content of a second grave (4B F712) is identified below as part of the post-conflagration debris used as grave-filling. Two pits contained fragmentary human bones: the pottery from 4B F137 consists of a quantity of mostly very small sherds, some of them weathered; sherds from Feature 1A F57 are nearly all in fresh condition and comprise fairly large parts of five vessels: P17, a fabric 2 bowl; P23 and P24, open bowls of fabrics 7 and 6 respectively; and P118, a fabric 7 necked bowl with a row of perforations beneath the rim and high-set lug(s). In no instance does it seem that any particular significance was attached to the pottery in these features.

The contents of six other pits stand apart because, as in feature 1A F57, the pottery had been freshly broken when deposited; in these pits, however, the sherds represent only one or two vessels. There are also two examples of simultaneous deposition in contiguous pits. Sherds of the bowl P77 had been distributed equally in each of Features 2A F268 and F269. Features 1A F228, F229+F295 and F350 were linked by the presence of sherds from two distinctive vessels, represented by the decorated body sherd P152 and another distinguished by minor peculiarities of fabric, among other fresh and weathered pottery and burnt clay. A slightly higher proportion of relatively large fragments in the Stepleton pits, as compared with those at the main causewayed enclosure, has allowed diameter measurements for twelve bowls and four cups.

At both enclosures the general practice governing disposal of pottery in pits seems to have involved the redeposition of fragments that had accumulated in the open. The occasional associations with human remains appear to have been coincidental. At Stepleton the contents of a few pits deviated from the norm in containing freshly broken pottery.

As discussed in Section C, fragmentation or weathering of pottery in enclosure ditches could reflect disruptions of silt formation rather than the nature of the immediate sources outside the ditches. The recurrence of refired sherds in deposits of all phases in the ditches of the two enclosures, in each instance constituting about 8% of all feature sherds, can be taken as evidence that some of the pottery had been derived, but vessels that may have been freshly broken when deposited are also present. In neither enclosure were parts of the same vessel found to link pits with ditches or one ditch segment with another (except on two occasions among sherds from the upper fills of adjoining segments). Within the limited confines of the south long barrow, however, parts of four individual vessels had been distributed in both ditches, and here nearly 14% of the feature sherds had been refired, including those from three vessels to which unaltered sherds could also be attributed.

The distribution of pottery in ditches seems to be unrelated to the presence or absence of human remains; feature sherds were, for example, rare in the phase I–II 'primary' deposits and in the phase IV 'grey pits' in the ditch of the main causewayed enclosure. On the other hand, the ditches of the south long barrow, not themselves used as places of interment, contained parts of over 40 vessels. Concentrations of feature sherds in individual ditch segments are not entirely explicable in terms of size of segment or the proportion excavated. In the ditches of the south long barrow, 66% of all feature sherds from the phase VI slots came from the south end of the west ditch. In the ditch of the main causewayed enclosure, 22% of feature sherds from Phase VI slots came from segment 3 and 23% from segment 14. In the Stepleton enclosure ditch, 25% of the feature sherds from the phase III and IV fills were in segment 12, as were 18% of those from phase VI. Other phase VI concentrations were 16%

from segment 7 and 26% from segment 8. If segment 8 had originally been a terminal at the side of an entrance to the enclosure, comparison might be made with the high density of pottery in segment VII of the Inner Ditch at Windmill Hill, also on the south side of a putative entrance in the north-west sector (Smith 1965, 5, plan, fig 3).

Observations on a further aspect of disposal in ditches will be found in Section C.

Distributions of vessel forms

Tables 9.5 and 9.6 set out the numbers of vessels, classified by form, from separate context groups within the central area (the pits, enclosure ditch, cross-dykes and south long barrow) and the Stepleton spur (pits, Stepleton enclosure and inner Stepleton outwork). The proportional representations of vessel forms from the three most prolific contexts at each enclosure are summarised in Table 9.7.

Inter-site differences in the relative frequencies of individual vessel types are slight. At the main causewayed enclosure there are 2.5% more cups and 3.1% more open bowls than at Stepleton, where there are 4.3% more unclassified bowls. Distributions of rim forms in the two sub-assemblages do not deviate significantly from the proportions established for the total assemblage (Table 9.2), and the percentages of decorated vessels are virtually identical. Specialised types of lug are, however, noticeably more numerous in the central area, where there were six more or less well-made trumpet lugs and seven bilobate lugs, as against only two of each type from Stepleton. The higher numbers of these (mainly detached) lugs in the central area is probably correlated with the higher frequency there of open bowls. Nine vessels with repair-holes came from the central area and ten from the Stepleton spur; it would seem that damaged vessels were not excluded from use in either context.

The figures given in Table 9.7, showing proportional representations of vessel types in separate contexts, seem to suggest rather surprising conformities of *intra-site* distributions in the pits and in the ditches of the two enclosures. At each site higher percentages of cups and of open bowls came from pits, while carinated bowls were relatively more numerous in ditches. The data may suggest common patterns of selective deposition, but the small numbers of vessels in some categories inhibit confident interpretation. The proportions of decorated vessels from pits and from enclosure ditches provide no evidence for selection (Tables 9.5 and 9.6). Figures for the south long barrow and for the inner Stepleton outwork are included in Table 9.7 for the sake of completeness but the quantities of pottery from these contexts are too limited to support interpretation.

Distributions of fabrics

Tables 9.8 and 9.9 present analyses of vessel form:fabric relationships in the sub-assemblages from the two enclosures. Fabric groups 3–5 and 8, represented at each site by small numbers of vessels, will not be considered here. As described in Section A (above), the remaining four fabric groups can be ranked in descending order of refinement with fabric 1 (gabbroic ware) at the head of the list, followed by the Jurassic wares (grouped together as fabric 2) and the two wares of more local origin – fabric 7, of variable quality, and the relatively crude products made of fabric 6. The following comments on distribution relate to feature sherds – countable vessels – only. Total sherd counts for the relevant fabrics and contexts will be found in Tables 9.12–13.

Inter-site variations in the distributions show a strong bias in favour of fabrics 1, 2, and 7 in the central area. All of the recorded fabric 1 feature sherds (P1–P10) were concentrated there; only a few small body fragments came from Stepleton. Fabric 2 constitutes 20% of the sub-assemblage from the central area and 10% of that from Stepleton. With fabric 7 the discrepancy is greater still: 55% and 37%. Conversely, fabric 6 is dominant at Stepleton, with 44%, but represents only 12% in the central area. Such contrasts may reflect the predominantly ceremonial nature of activities in and around the main enclosure and the perhaps more secular aspect of those at Stepleton.

Table 9.7 Proportional representation of vessel forms in the six most prolific contexts at the two causewayed enclosures

	Central area			*Stepleton spur*		
	Pits	*Enclosure ditch*	*Long barrow*	*Pits*	*Enclosure ditch*	*Inner outwork*
Vessel numbers	114	252	44	107	202	52
Cups	21.9%	16.7%	15.9%	21.5%	12.4%	11.3%
Carinated cups	–	0.8%	–	–	1.4%	–
Necked cups	–	–	–	–	0.5%	–
Carinated bowls	1.7%	3.5%	2.2%	2.8%	6.0%	–
Necked bowls	0.8%	1.5%	–	1.8%	0.5%	–
Open bowls	9.6%	5.2%	11.3%	5.6%	2.0%	3.7%
Other bowls	65.7%	72.2%	70.4%	69.1%	76.7%	84.9%

Table 9.8 Vessel form:fabric correlations in the sub-assemblage from the central area

Figures in *italics* denote decorated vessels

	Fabric groups									
	1	*2*	*3*	*4*	*5*	*6*	*7*	*8*	*subtotals*	*totals*
Cups	–	9	–	2	1	21	26	9	68	
	–	–	–	–	–	*1*	*6*	*2*	*9*	77
Carinated cups	–	–	–	–	–	–	–	1	1	
	–	–	–	–	–	–	*1*	–	*1*	2
Carinated bowls	–	5	–	–	–	–	7		12	
	–	*1*	–	–	–	–	–	–	*1*	13
Necked bowls	–	2	–	–	–	–	2	–	4	
	–	–	–	–	–	*1*	–	–	*1*	5
Open bowls	4	5	3	–	–	–	16	–	28	
	–	–	–	–	*1*	–	–	–	*1*	29
Other bowls:										
rims	5	52	1	2	10	26	141	5	242	
	–	*5*	–	–	–	–	*9*	–	*14*	256
decorated body sherds	–	–	–	–	–	–	*7*	*1*	*8*	8
detached lugs	1	9	–	–	3	2	27	6		48
detached cordon	–	–	–	–	–	–	1	–		1
Totals	10	88	4	4	15	51	243	24		439
% of sub-assemblage	2.3	20.0	0.9	0.9	3.4	11.6	55.4	5.5		
% decorated	–	6.8	–	6.7	3.9	9.5	12.5			7.9

Table 9.9 Vessel form:fabric correlations in the sub-assemblage from the Stepleton spur

Figures in *italics* denote decorated vessels

	Fabric groups									
	1	*2*	*3*	*4*	*5*	*6*	*7*	*8*	*subtotals*	*totals*
Cups	–	4	2	5	–	27	10	4	52	
	–	–	–	–	–	*1*	–	*1*	*2*	54
Carinated cups	–	–	–	–	–	2	1	–		3
Necked cups	–	–	–	–	–	2	1	–		1
Carinated bowls	–	2	1	–	–	1	9	–	13	
	–	–	–	–	–	–	*2*	–	*2*	15
Necked bowls	–	–	–	–	–	–	1	–	1	
	–	–	–	–	–	*1*	*1*	–	*2*	3
Open bowls	–	1	1	1	–	2	7	–		12
Other bowls:										
rims	–	27	3	1	5	93	87	3	219	
	–	–	*1*	–	–	*3*	*5*	–	*9*	228
decorated body sherds	–	–	–	–	–	*9*	*4*	–	*13*	13
detached lugs	–	1	–	1	1	16	5	2	26	
	–	–	–	–	–	–	*1*	–	*1*	27
detached cordons	–	1	–	–	–	2	2	–		5
Totals	–	36	8	8	6	159	134	10		361
% of sub-assemblage	–	10.0	2.2	2.2	1.7	44.2	36.6	2.8		
% decorated	–	–	12.5	–	–	8.8	9.7	10.0		8.0

Patterns of *intra-site* deposition (Table 9.10) show a further anomaly in the distribution of fabric 1 vessels: they constitute 7.0% of all feature sherds from pits within the main enclosure (including here P10, found in ploughsoil in the interior, presumed to derive from a pit) and less than 1% of those from the enclosure ditch (for details see catalogue, P1–P10). The restricted distribution implies that gabbroic bowls were reserved almost exclusively for use within the main enclosure and that disposal of their fragments was deliberately confined to the internal pits. P5 from the phase VI slot is the only feature sherd securely stratified in the ditch; P3, from the topsoil of the bank area on site P1, was unstratified.

C. Stratification and relative chronology

The known series of systematic disruptions of the fill in the ditch of the main causewayed enclosure – virtually complete removal of the initial silts, leaving only a remnant; the digging of the phase IV 'grey pits' into the phase III silts; the cutting of the phase VI slots to varying depths – affected the integrity of all but, if not including, the earliest deposits. A list of recognised displacements of parts of individual vessels offers a sample of the many that must have gone undetected:

P57, necked bowl (4 sherds): segment 9, phases I, III
P12, open bowl (2 sherds): segment 4, phases III, V
P31, carinated bowl (3 sherds): segment 17, phases III, V, VI
P82, bowl with lugs (13 sherds): segment 9, phases III, VI
P19, open bowl (3 sherds): segment 16, phases IV, VI
P114, decorated bowl (6 sherds): segment 3, phases V, VI, VIII/a

This evidence from widely separated parts of the ditch (segments 3, 4, 9, 16 and 17) suggests that during each disturbance the spoil, with contained artefacts, was systematically placed alongside the segment from which it had been removed. Some sherds, possibly further broken and/or weathered, drifted back to be incorporated in subsequent silts. As mentioned above, no instances of inter-segment displacement were noted except two involving sherds from the phase VI slots in adjoining segments. This pattern of confined redistribution may support Mercer's speculation (1980, 36) that the divisions in the enclosure ditch could represent family or clan divisions. It clearly diverges from those observed at Abingdon (Avery 1982, 30–2) and at Windmill Hill (Smith 1965, 14) where sherds of individual vessels had been widely dispersed both horizontally and vertically.

Two instances of vertical distribution were also recorded from the ditches of the Long Barrow:

P38, carinated bowl (4 sherds): W ditch (quadrant LB2), phases I, IV
P51, large bowl (10 sherds): W ditch (quadrant LB3), phases I, III, IV, VI

In these ditches the only recorded disturbances are the phase VI recuts. The circumstances mentioned above, that four vessels are represented in both east and west ditches, may relate to this monument's status as a tomb under unitary control.

On the Stepleton spur, where the fills had accumulated with less disturbance, a case of partial displacement had occurred when the south end of segment 23 of the enclosure was replaced by segment 9 of the inner outwork. One of the two sherds of the distinctive rim P96 had remained *in situ* in the phase III fill in the enclosure; the other was found in the phase VIII/a cultivation horizon in segment 8 of the inner outwork. One sherd of P107 was found in phase VI in segment 11 of the enclosure, and two in phase VIII/a of segment 8. There were also instances of vertical displacement.

Enclosure ditch

P33, carinated bowl (8 sherds): segment 16, in two separate layers within phase III
P69, cup (at least 3 sherds): segment 12, phases III, IV

Outer Stepleton outwork

P95, bowl (3 sherds): segment 4, phases III, VII/a

The few sherds that may be presumed to derive from any pre-construction context in the central area are those retrieved from features beneath the bank of the main enclosure on site P1 and, less certainly, from the truncated soils in which those features were cut, in which intrusive material is more likely to have been present. Treethrow hole P1 F24+F24A contained body sherds in fabrics 2, 6, 7 and 8. Layer 4, the surrounding soil, contained more abundant sherds in the same fabrics, including two simple rims, an expanded rim and a fragment with an applied cordon. F25 and F29, postholes probably contemporary with the construction of the enclosure, contained sherds in fabric groups 2 and 7, including a rolled-over rim.

Pottery recovered from the earliest surviving deposits in the ditches of the south long barrow and the main enclosure includes representatives of both the Decorated and the South-western styles. The stratigraphically earliest ornamented sherds in the ditches of the long barrow (part of P105) are probably from primary contexts (see 3.3.6). In the ditch of the main enclosure, the 16 feature sherds from the remnants of initial silts (phase I) and the 11 from the 'primary' deposits (phase II) include two plain but developed rims characteristic of the Decorated style: an enlarged form similar to P96 and an externally extended form like P37. Actual ornament is first recorded in this ditch on P113, a bowl from phase III. In the inner east crossdyke, the first decorated sherd (P117) is also from phase III. The only feature sherd among the small amount of pottery from the remnants of initial silts (phase I) in the Stepleton enclosure was an in-turned rim fragment, heavier rims (including P96) appearing among the more abundant material from phase III, and occurring with decoration in phase IV, from which comes P111, the most flamboyant Decorated rim in the entire assemblage – with wide external extension and transverse cord impressions. (Its near counterparts, P112 and P115, came from phase VIII/a.)

Pottery from the ditch of the main enclosure and from the Stepleton enclosure seems to show temporal change in the form of increasing numbers of decorated vessels (Table 9.11). In assessing the evidence, account must be taken of the circumstances of deposition in the late phases of each ditch. Formal deposition in both seems to have ceased with the last placements of phase

Table 9.10 Proportional representation of fabrics in the six most prolific contexts at the two enclosures

	Central area			*Stepleton spur*		
	Pits	*Enclosure ditch*	*Long barrow*	*Pits*	*Enclosure ditch*	*Inner outwork*
Vessel numbers	114	252	44	107	202	52
Fabric group 1	7.0%	0.8%	–	–	–	–
Fabric group 2	14.0%	20.1%	26.7%	7.5%	12.4%	7.7%
Fabric group 3	3.5%	–	–	0.9%	1.9%	3.8%
Fabric group 4	0.8%	1.2%	2.2%	2.8%	1.9%	–
Fabric group 5	4.3%	3.3%	2.2%	–	1.5%	5.8%
Fabric group 6	11.4%	10.5%	26.7%	49.5%	41.8%	32.7%
Fabric group 7	51.7%	57.1%	40.0%	38.3%	37.3%	46.2%
Fabric group 8	7.0%	6.7%	2.2%	0.9%	2.9%	3.8%

Table 9.11 Phased distribution of decorated vessels in the ditch of the main enclosure and the Stepleton enclosure ditches

Main enclosure				*Stepleton enclosure*			
Phases	*All vessels*	*No. decorated*	*Per cent decorated*	*Phases*	*All vessels*	*No. decorated*	*Per cent decorated*
I–II	27	0	0	I–II	3	0	0
III–V	96	5	5	III–V	61	4	6
VI	90	10	11	VI	101	13	13
VIII	25	3	12	VIII	35	3	9

VI, which, although different in character, followed periods of natural silting and stabilisation during which few artefacts entered either ditch, so that some interval will have separated them from the phase I–IV deposits. Earlier Neolithic feature sherds from phase VIII/a presumably comprise material swept into the top of the ditches by natural agencies and/or ploughing. The sherds in question were derived or residual but may, in the circumstances, be taken as representative of the pottery current during the latter stages of earlier Neolithic activity in the vicinity of these ditches.

The material from the outworks is relatively sparse. The replacement of the eastern and southern parts of the Stepleton enclosure by the inner outwork must suggest that some of the pottery recovered from the latter had been derived from the former. The single identified example is provided by the two sherds from the rim P96, one found *in situ* in the enclosure, the other in the top of the outwork, as described above. A total of 52 feature sherds came from the inner outwork (Tables 9.6 and 9.10). Several, all plain, were in place when the burning rampart collapsed, including P60 (fabric 6), P68 (fabric 7) and P85 (fabric 7), which is partly covered with scorched clay (and see description of pottery from pit 4B F712, below). In the east butt of segment 4.2, others, including P47 (fabric 5), would have entered the ditch immediately afterwards. These were represented by relatively large, freshly broken fragments, as were P15 from the rubble fills (fabric 3), and P20 from the phase III/a recut (fabric 7). The remaining feature sherds, including three decorated sherds (P115, P125, P145), came from the chalky silt above the rubble and from post-Neolithic levels. In this ditch no decorated sherd is demonstrably from a primary deposit and fabric 7 feature sherds outnumber those made of fabric 6, a reversal of the relationship in the enclosure (Table 9.10).

Pottery from the time of the destruction of the inner outwork was also found in a grave, Feature 4B F712, where it seems to have been introduced with the material packed around the body. Some of the 35 sherds and crumbs, together with a quern fragment, flints and animal bones, had been exposed to fire and subsequently gathered up with scorched chalk rubble from the inner outwork after the collapse of the rampart. The pottery, all plain, included a small piece from a fabric 2 bowl and a few conjoining sherds from two bowls with simple rims, made of fabrics 6 and 7.

There are only 49 feature sherds from the fills of the middle and inner Stepleton outworks (12), the western and the Shroton outworks (5 and 5), the Hanford outworks (20) and the Hanford pits (7). At these sites contamination from residual material seems improbable except in the Stepleton outworks, where ceramic debris could have been lying about in the vicinity of the enclosure. In these contexts fabrics 3, 4, and 5 are represented by body sherds; among the feature sherds fabrics 2, 6, 7 and 8 account for 24%, 14%, 60%, and 2% respectively. The descending orders of frequency of the three major fabrics – 7, 2, 6 – correspond with those in the ditch of the main enclosure (Table 9.10). The vessels, all plain, include six cups, one necked cup (P43), three

Table 9.12 Summary of pottery from the central area, the Shroton spur, the Stepleton spur and the Hanford spur

Recorded by Rachael Seager Smith. Pottery from Desmond Bonney's excavations of 1958–60 is included in italics, but is not incorporated in Dr Isobel Smith's report

	Neolithic Bowl		*Peterborough Ware*		*Beaker*		*Early/middle Bronze Age*		*Late Bronze/ early Iron Age*		*Mid to late Iron Age*		*Roman*		*Other*	
	No.	*Wt (g)*	*No.*	*Wt (g)*	*No.*	*Wt (g)*	*No.*	*Wt (g)*	*No*	*Wt (g)*	*No.*	*Wt (g)*	*No.*	*Wt (g)*	*No.*	*Wt (g)*
Main enclosure	6004	26202			583	1320	5	29	11	100			3	6	43	74
	80	*507*	*1?*	*26*	*9*	*22*										
Inner east cross-dyke	355	1237			518	638										
	6	*96*			*121*	*418*	*11*	*52*								
Outer east cross-dyke	176	918			9	30							5	8		
	10	*23*			*1*	*1*	*2*	*19*					*1*	*4*		
Inner south cross-dyke	593	2260			5	9	4	113					1	4		
	119	*1526*			*3*	*8*	*3*	*19*	*1*	*12*			*1*	*2*	*4*	*3*
Outer south cross-dyke	15	46														
	8	*81*											*1*	*1*	*3*	*2*
Long barrow	1721	7056			28	42	1	12					10	11	17	32
Western outwork	49	302														
Central area Neolithic pits	3822	10957			2	12							1	4	14	41
Central area misc	889	2029	1	3	25	98									17	38
	14	*96*														
Shroton spur	114	395			24	99	10	48							71	140
	10	*63*											*1*	*2*		
Stepleton enclosure	5442	21235	1	14	59	134	16	99	135	891			16	36	17	23
Middle Stepleton outwork	130	321	41	59	62	115	22	50							5	12
Inner Stepleton outwork	1289	5642	1	8	54	178	241	1560	64	212	13	44	783	2649	99	223
Outer Stepleton outwork	187	626			83	513	13	81					10	49	15	23
Stepleton Neolithic pits	3525	10885			1	1	2	2	4	14	1	3	4	53	14	23
Stepleton spur misc	241	609			4	12	28	62	2	28	6	14	17	127	3	5
Inner Hanford outwork	851	2754			6	14	1	3								
Outer Hanford outwork	170	474			18	18	1	10								
Hanford Neolithic pits	130	209														
Hanford 'flint mines'	75	226														
Hanford misc	7	10													9	7
Totals	26032	96785	44	110	1615	3682	360	2159	217	1257	20	61	854	2956	331	646

Table 9.13 Summary of earlier Neolithic pottery fabric groups from the central area, the Shroton spur, the Stepleton spur and the Hanford spur

Recorded by Rachael Seager Smith. Pottery from Desmond Bonney's excavations of 1958–60 is included in italics, but is not incorporated in Dr Isobel Smith's report.
1 = Gabbroic, 2 = Jurassic, 3 = calcite, 4 = organic, 5 = fresh shell and flint, 6 = red pellets, 7 = flint, 8 = sand

Fabric group	*1*		*2*		*3*		*4*		*5*		*6*		*7*		*8*		*other*		*Totals*	
	No.	*Wt (g)*	*No.*	*Wt (g)*	*No.*	*Wt (g)*	*No.*	*Wt (g)*	*No.*	*Wt (g)*	*No.*	*Wt (g)*	*No.*	*Wt (g)*	*No.*	*Wt (g)*	*No.*	*Wt (g)*	*No.*	*Wt(g)*
Main enclosure	9	174	1556	7315	44	263	178	436	50	117	144	574	3546	15654	457	1607	20	62	6004	26202
			17	*108*									*63*	*399*					*80*	*507*
Inner east cross-dyke			36	227			1	4			2	2	283	806	33	198			355	1237
													6	*96*					*6*	*96*
Outer east cross-dyke			119	659			2	4					49	210	6	45			176	918
													10	*23*					*10*	*23*
Inner south cross-dyke			103	303	2	4					4	20	464	1877	20	56			593	2260
			13	*72*									*106*	*1454*					*119*	*1526*
Outer south cross-dyke			1	3							3	15	11	28					15	46
													8	*81*					*8*	*81*
Long barrow	1	17	103	805	1	1	7	12	49	242	253	1606	1178	4211	28	130	21	32	1721	7056
Western outwork			7	103			1	16			1	3	40	180					49	302
Central area Neolithic pits	154	1218	955	2213	178	762	93	117	66	105	145	416	1782	5118	379	815	70	193	3822	10957
Central area misc	17	83	206	406	7	24	15	57			52	155	397	1051	195	253			889	2029
			1	*8*									*13*	*88*					*14*	*96*
Shroton spur			11	62			2	4					67	246	34	83			114	395
													10	*63*					*10*	*63*
Stepleton enclosure	7	39	473	1673	19	71	137	590	117	521	1979	8164	2517	9540	179	572	14	65	5442	21235
Middle Stepleton outwork			13	45			7	20	3	3	3	6	99	239	5	8			130	321
Inner Stepleton outwork	4	18	80	429	18	90	7	36	2	11	274	1003	864	3900	38	147	2	8	1289	5642
Outer Stepleton outwork	3	7	40	163	5	25	6	12					104	283	28	116	1	20	187	626
Stepleton Neolithic pits	2	15	216	442	1	4	22	68			1199	3629	2003	6576	67	111	15	40	3525	10885
Stepleton spur misc	1	2	4	20							44	94	192	493					241	609
Inner Hanford outwork			35	275	4	36			6	24	4	26	801	2391	1	2			851	2754
Outer Hanford outwork			16	46	8	20	1	2	12	27	9	9	113	340	11	30			170	474
Hanford Neolithic pits			1	2			31	59			22	31	53	102	23	15			130	209
Hanford 'flint mines'			3	7			1	1			6	44	59	172	6	2			75	226
Hanford misc													7	10					7	10
Totals	198	1573	4089	15386	287	1300	511	1438	305	1050	4144	15797	14845	55631	1510	4190	143	420	26032	96785

carinated bowls (eg P40), two open bowls, and less specialised forms (eg P49, P52, P71). There is one T-shaped rim (P88). Lugs include a minute imperforate example of the trumpet form (P28) and one that is bilobate (P97).

And perhaps one decorative technique, distinctive of the Hambledon Hill assemblage, survived to be incorporated in the pottery of a subsequent generation. The next known event in the ceramic history of the site was the deposition, near the top of the phase III fills in the middle outwork at Stepleton, of a substantial portion of the Mortlake bowl P159. The zones of thumb-nail impressions around the lower part of its body are strongly reminiscent of the decoration on the bodies of P116, P142 and P146, all from phase VI slots in the ditch of the main enclosure, and, less specifically, of P147 and P153 from, respectively, phases IV and VIII/a of the Stepleton enclosure. The suggestion finds support in Frances Healy's discussion (1995, 175) of evidence for a comparable transference, involving several attributes, in East Anglia.

9.1.2 Other pottery

Peterborough ware

The remains of five bowls attest sporadic visits by the users of this pottery after the end of the main period of activity. The only restorable and *in situ* bowl (P156) came from the chalky silt of the upper phase III fills of segment 6 of the middle outwork at Stepleton. It is of Mortlake type, with rows of small complex impressions on the rim, neck and upper body, and irregular rows of oblique thumb-nail impressions above the round base. The other four bowls are represented by single small sherds from superficial and widely separated contexts: P157 and a body sherd with whipped cord impressions (not illustrated) from the interior of the main causewayed enclosure; P158 and P159, the latter belonging to a Fengate-style vessel with collar, from the Stepleton spur.

Beakers

Despite the extremely fragmentary condition of most of this pottery, it can be seen to belong essentially to Clarke's (1970) Developed, Late and Final Southern British Beaker groups, S2–S4, and to fall within Steps 6 and 7 of the Lanting and van der Waals (1972) scheme for Wessex. Most of the informative sherds are illustrated as P160–P168. The distribution pattern and the relatively small numbers of sherds from the contexts listed below may suggest a single, probably brief, period of activity on Hambledon Hill. The 1974–82 material thus contrasts with a stylistically early assemblage from segment 4 of the inner east cross-dyke, most of which was excavated by Desmond Bonney in 1960 (see 3.3.3).

In the central area there were a few sherds from the ploughsoil in the interior and from the tops of two or three pits. Ten sherds, apparently from one Beaker, came from shallow pits cut in to the top fill of the east ditch of the south long barrow. All the rest were recovered from ditches on the east side of the site. Segment 8 of the enclosure ditch yielded 60 sherds, including P161, P163–P165, P168, and numerous minute fragments; segment 10 yielded 12 sherds, including P162. Segment 1 of the inner east cross-dyke held 60 small sherds from one unreconstructable Beaker, perhaps similar to P168; 30 sherds came from segment 4, the residue of the assemblage excavated by Bonney, and a few scraps from segment 5. Three sherds came from segment 3 of the outer east cross-dyke.

At Stepleton there was again a very thin scatter from ploughsoil and from the tops of two pits. Some 40 sherds, including P160, P166 and P167, were sparsely distributed in the superficial contexts in the ditch tops.

More interest attaches to three concentrations of pottery. In feature 511, a phase VII/a recut through the first cultivated horizon in segment 2 of the outer outwork, two complete bases of Beakers were found *in situ*, one of them placed in an upright position. Each had been truncated at about 30 mm above the base; the lower wall of one is plain, the other carries part of a typical S2–S3 decorative motif. Also present was part of a third base and an undecorated outbent rim, possibly from a biconical S4 Beaker like one from Wiltshire (Clarke 1970, fig 1036). None of the wall sherds has survived. In segment 5 of the same ditch some 40 sherds represent at least eight Beakers; six display S2–S3 motifs, one is finger-pinched, and one may have been decorated with an all-over herringbone motif impressed with a plain spatula. This group of sherds was stratified partly in a possible recut and partly in overlying phase VIII/a cultivation horizon. In the third instance, 12 sherds seem to have been lying in a recut in segment 9 of the Stepleton enclosure. At least three Beakers are represented: one with an S2–S5 motif, one with finger-pinched decoration and a cordon, and one that may have been plain.

Small and weathered Beaker sherds also came from the ditches of the Shroton and Hanford outworks, three and 24 respectively.

Bronze Age

Biconical Urn

Five weathered sherds, including one from a rim with traces of horizontal twisted cord impressions and three from a flat base, came from phase VIII/a of the main causewayed enclosure ditch. This form may also be represented at Stepleton (see below).

Deverel-Rimbury

Two Globular Urns of Calkin's (1957) type IIa, with furrowed necks, are represented by rim sherds from superficial contexts in segment 1 of the Shroton outwork ditch (P169) and segment 8 of the inner Stepleton outwork (P170). Eighteen small sherds from the phase VIII/a fills in the same segment carry type IIb decoration, with motifs including concentric arcs, swags, multiple horizontal lines and stab-marks (P171–P174). One sherd (not illustrated) retains part of a lug. Lids, now recognised as components of Deverel-Rimbury assemblages (Tomalin 1982, 235), are represented on the Shroton (P176) and Stepleton spurs (P175) by fragments from the ditch segments that contained the urn sherds. Parts of three similar lids were recovered from other contexts on the Stepleton spur. A coarse ware, distributed over segments 5–8 of the inner Stepleton outwork, consists mainly of featureless fragments. A single sherd from a markedly biconical vessel may suggest a pre-Deverel-Rimbury element, but Bucket Urns may also be represented. The five small rim sherds lack distinctive attributes; base sherds include one that gives a diameter of 160 mm; there are three detached knobs or bosses, all imperforate.

Later Bronze Age

A concentration of some 60 sherds in the phase VIII/a ploughsoils of segments 2 and 3 of the Stepleton enclosure seems to represent a 'plain ware' tradition. The more compact texture and smoother finish distinguish this pottery from the coarse ware discussed above. The rims (P177, P178, P180) may be compared with some of the representative 'plain ware' forms illustrated by Barrett (1980, fig 5: 6 and 8).

A furrowed haematite-coated bowl, surviving as 21 tiny fragments from the rim, shoulder and body, came from a butt of segment 5 in the inner Stepleton outwork.

Romano-British

Apart from sparse surface and ditch-top finds, especially on the Stepleton spur, this pottery was concentrated in Coombe Bottom and Stepleton Lynchet. The small, abraded sherds, consisting largely of Black Burnished ware, are apparently datable to the first century BC–fourth century AD.

9.1.3 Catalogue of illustrated pottery

Entries are arranged thus: drawing number, prefixed with 'P'. Find number(s). Site, context(s), phase(s). Fabric group

In addition to the fabric groups defined in the text, additional ones are employed for the later pottery. These are 9 (grog-tempered) and 12 (grog- and flint-tempered).

Part 1. Earlier Neolithic

P1. HH75 400, 401, 557. Central area, pit B F14, L3. Fabric group 1.

P2. HH75 402–406, 499, 500, 609, 624. Central area, pit B F14, L3. Fabric group 1.

P3. HH77 22. Main causewayed enclosure, site P1 bank area, L2 (topsoil). Fabric group 1.

P4. HH77 1845. Central area, pit N F42, L3. Fabric group 1.

P5. HH76 2914. Main causewayed enclosure, segment 17, L6, phase VI. Fabric group 1.

P6. HH75 250. Central area, solution hollow B F12. Fabric group 1.

P7. HH75 334. Central area, solution hollow B F12, L2. Fabric group 1.

P8. HH75 276. Central area, pit C F3, L1. Fabric group 1.

P9. HH75 273. Central area, pit C F3, L1. Fabric group 1.

P10. HH74 235. Central area, interior, surface. Fabric group 1.

P11. HH77 2184, 2247. Central area, pit N F82, L3–4. Fabric group 3.

P12. HH74 854, 992. Main causewayed enclosure, segment 4, L9, L4, phases III, V. Fabric group 7.

P13. ST79 2223. Stepleton spur pit 2A F134. Fabric group 6.

P14. HH75 2120. Main causewayed enclosure, segment 8, L7A, phase II. Fabric group 7.

P15. ST79 2699. Inner Stepleton outwork, segment 5, C13, L4, phase III. Fabric group 3.

P16. ST82 69, 82, 98, 101. Stepleton spur, pit ST82 F39. Fabric group 7.

P17. ST78 735–6. Stepleton spur, pit 1A F57, L2–3. Fabric group 2.

P18. HH77 1207, 1209, 1626, 1648. Long Barrow, W ditch (segment 1), LB3 SII, L17, L18, L19, phases III, IV, VI. Fabric group 2.

P19. HH76 560, 1726, 2112. Main causewayed enclosure, segment 16, L9A, L6, phases IV and VI. Fabric group 2.

P20. ST79 2585. Inner Stepleton outwork, segment 5, C4, L5A, phase III/a. Fabric group 7.

P21. ST80 1269. Stepleton enclosure, segment 4, U8, L2A, phase IV. Fabric group 7.

P22. HH77 1423, 1560. Central area, pit N F7(i), L3. Fabric group 3.

P23. ST78 703. Stepleton spur, pit 1A F57, L2. Fabric group 7.

P24. ST78 721. Stepleton spur, pit 1A F57, L2 (base). Fabric group 6.

P25. HH77 826, 1424. Central area, pit N F23, L2–3. Fabric group 6.

P26. HH76 1115. Main causewayed enclosure, segment 19, L5, phase VII/a. Fabric group 7.

P27. ST81 1234. Stepleton enclosure, segment 8, L2, phase VI. Fabric group 6.

P28. HN82 698. Hanford spur, pit F854, L2. Fabric group 7.

P29. ST81 966. Stepleton enclosure, segment 14, L2, phase VI. Fabric group 6.

P30. HH76 1311. Main causewayed enclosure, segment 5, L5, phase VI. Fabric group 7.

P31. HH76 2003, 2883, 3000. Main causewayed enclosure, segment 17, L8, L9, L10, phases III, V, VI. Fabric group 2.

P32. ST80 1896. Stepleton enclosure, segment 6, L4, phase III. Fabric group 7.

P33. ST81 2200, 2569. Stepleton enclosure, segment 16, L3B, L3D, phase III. Fabric group 7.

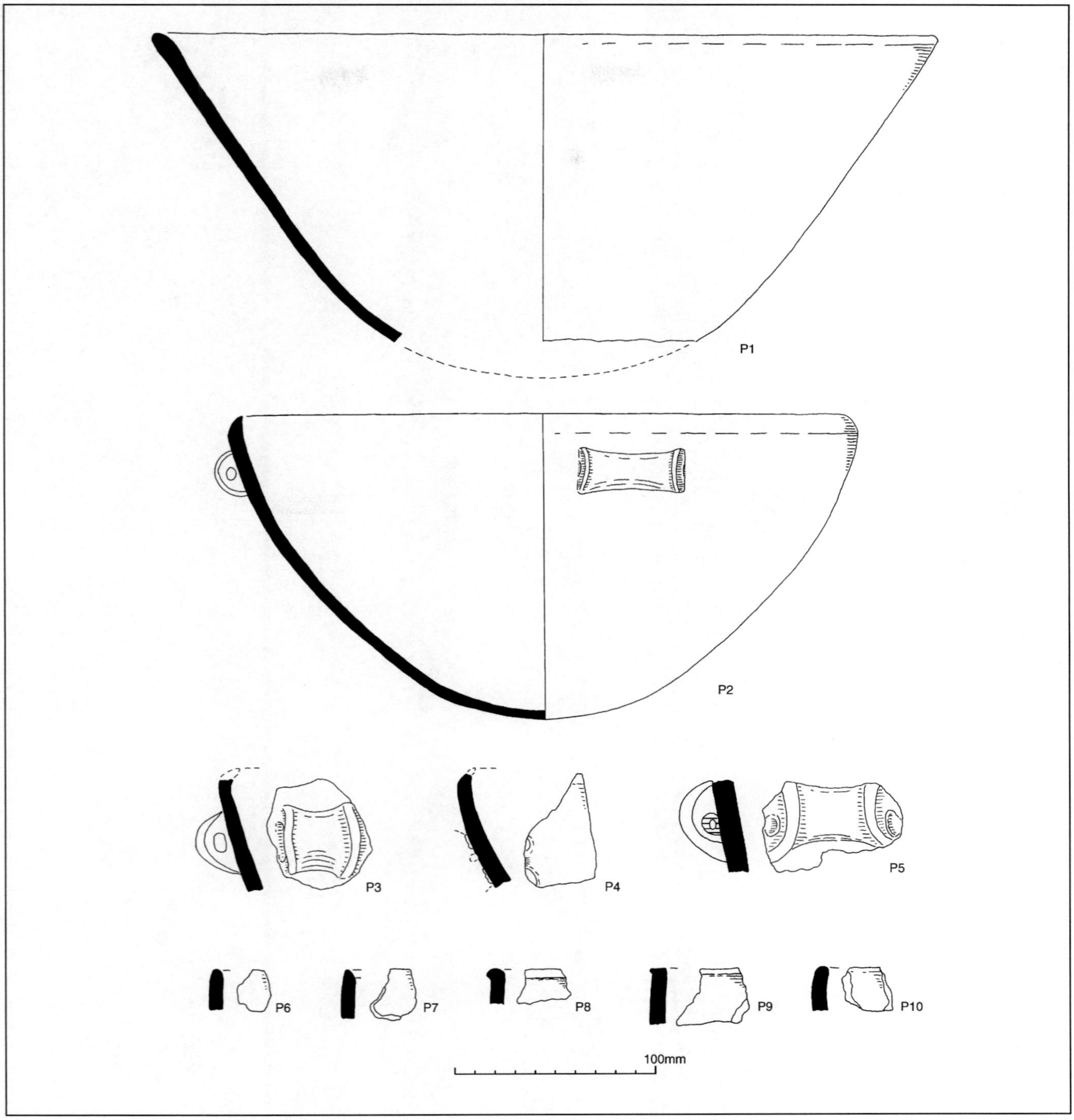

Fig 9.1 Gabbroic vessels and sherds. Particulars in catalogue.

P34. ST80 52, 57. Stepleton spur pit 3A F94. Fabric group 6.

P35. ST81 1851, 2193. Stepleton enclosure, segment 16, L3, phase V. Fabric group 7.

P36. ST81 349, 375, 692, 763, 795, 870. Stepleton enclosure, segment 7, L2, phase VI. Fabric group 7.

P37. HH75 1846, 2013. Main causewayed enclosure, segment 8, L6/7, L7, phase III. Fabric group 7.

P38. HH77 1588, 1591, 1594, 2303. Long Barrow, W ditch (segment 1), LB2 SII, SV, L22, L26, L27, phases I, VI. Fabric group 7.

P39. HH74 1154. Main causewayed enclosure, segment 4, L9, phase III. Fabric group 8.

P40. HN82 299. Inner Hanford outwork, segment 3, L4, phase III. Fabric group 7.

P41. HH77 508, 853. Main causewayed enclosure, segment 1, F7, phase VI. Fabric group 2.

P42. ST81 962, 964–5, 981. Stepleton enclosure, segment 14, L2, phase VI. Fabric group 7.

P43. HN82 45, 113–4, 139. Outer Hanford outwork, segment 2, L3, L3C, L5C, phases I, III, VII. Fabric group 7.

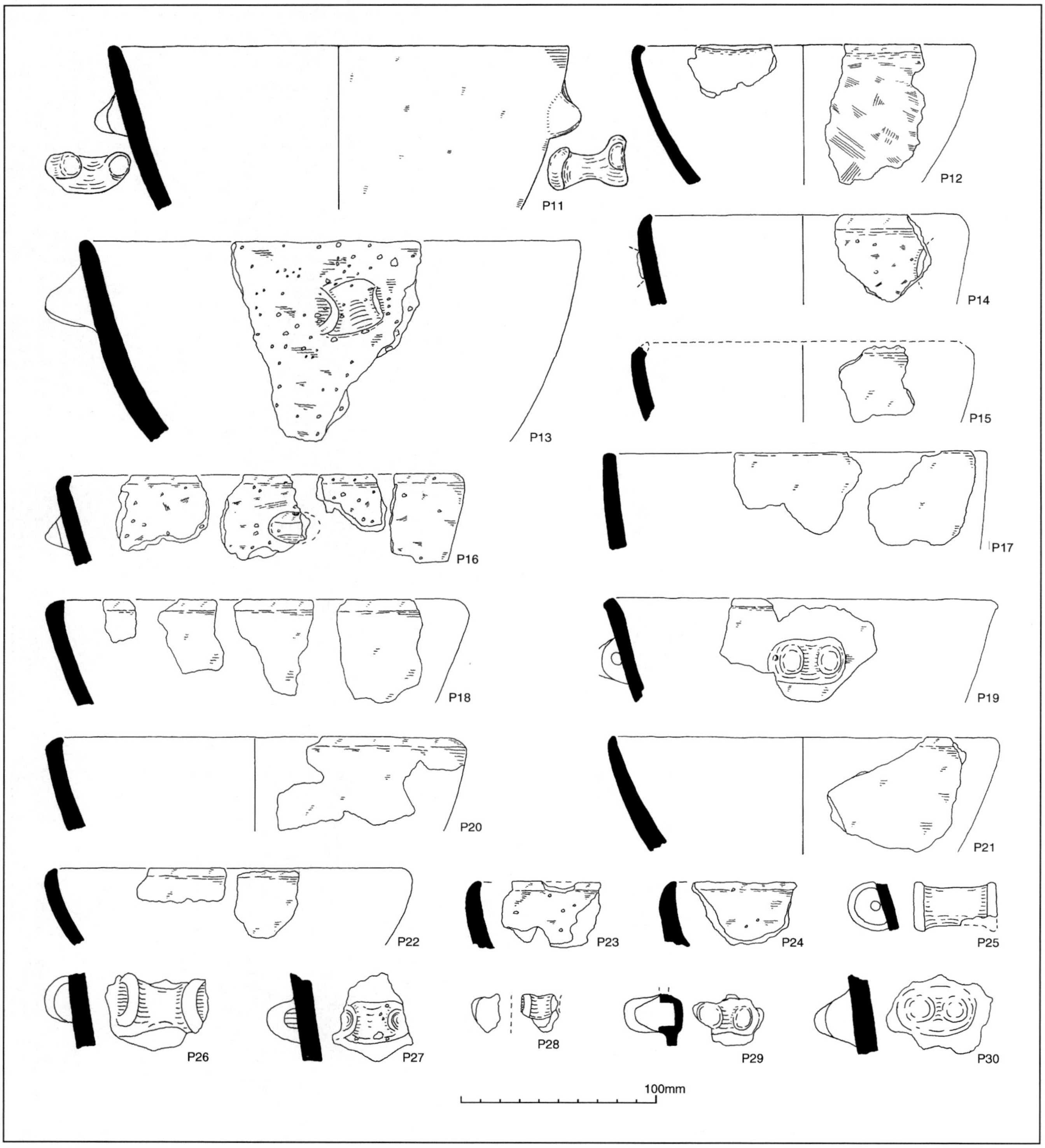

Fig 9.2 Neolithic Bowl pottery. Particulars in catalogue.

P44. ST81 678. Stepleton enclosure, segment 12, L3A, phase III. Fabric group 6.

P45. ST81 193. Stepleton enclosure, segment 10, L2, phase VI. Fabric group 6.

P46. W0WK82 29, 115, 121. Inner south cross-dyke, segment 2, L7, phase VI. Fabric group 7.

P47. ST80 1322, 1337. Inner Stepleton outwork, segment, 4. 2, L4A, phase I. Fabric group 5.

P48. ST81 1265, 1273. Stepleton enclosure, segment 8, U3, L2A, phase IV. Fabric group 4.

P49. ST78 2953. Middle Stepleton outwork. segment 10, L5+L6, phases I–II. Fabric group 7.

P50. ST80 1007. Stepleton enclosure, segment 4, L1, phase VIII/a. Fabric group 6.

P51. HH77 1527, 1922, 2083, 2206, 2208, 2271, 2274, 2292, 2295, 2297. Long barrow, W ditch (segment 1), LB3 L17, L19, L34, L35, L41, phases I, III, IV, VI. Fabric group 6.

P52. HN82 685. Hanford spur, 'flint mines' F618, L2. Fabric group 7.

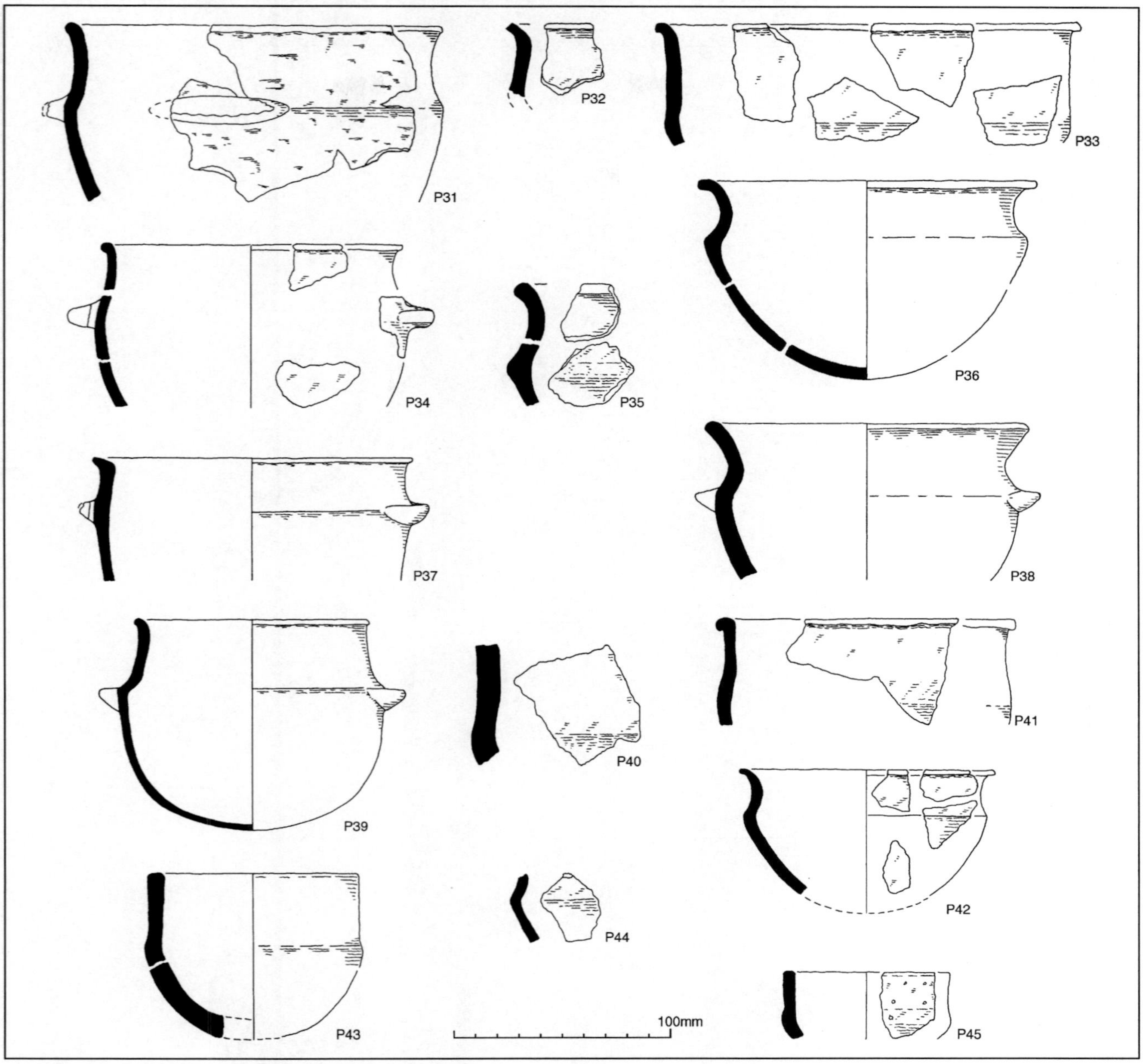

Fig 9.3 Neolithic Bowl pottery. Particulars in catalogue.

P53. ST81 2244, 2249. Stepleton enclosure, segment 17, L3C, phase III. Fabric group 2.

P54. ST81 2393. Stepleton spur pit 4B F80. Fabric group 7.

P55. HH74 751. Main causewayed enclosure, segment 3, L7, phase VI. Fabric group 7.

P56. HH74 569. Main causewayed enclosure, segment 2, L3, phase VIII/a. Fabric group 4.

P57. HH75 852–3, 900, 1169. Main causewayed enclosure, segment 9, L9, L7, phases I, III. Fabric group 7.

P58. HH75 551, 610. Central area, pit B F14, L3–4. Fabric group 7.

P59. ST82 96. Stepleton spur pit ST82 F39. Fabric group 7.

P60. ST79 1015, 1016, 1018, 1019. Inner Stepleton outwork, segment 6, C3, L6 and overlying part of base of L4, phase I/phase III interface. Fabric group 6.

P61. ST79 2564, 2612. Stepleton spur pit 2A F201. Fabric group 6.

P62. ST78 1157, 1189, 1192, 1193. Stepleton spur pit 1A F110 L2. Fabric group 6.

P63. HH77 2089. Central area, pit N F42, L3–4. Fabric group 7.

P64. ST81 279. Stepleton enclosure, segment 8, L1, phase VIII/a. Fabric group 6.

P65. HH76 2995, 2997. Main causewayed enclosure, segment 18, L8, phase VI. Fabric group 6.

P66. HH74 648, 763. Main causewayed enclosure, segments 3 and 4, L5, phase VI. Fabric group 2.

P67. ST81 871. Stepleton spur pit 4A F3. Fabric group 6.

P68. ST79 1016, 1017. Inner Stepleton outwork, segment 6, C3, in base of L4 with some sherds of P60, perhaps already in place when rubble entered ditch, phase I/phase III interface. Fabric group 7.

P69. ST81 1069, 1072, 1073. Stepleton enclosure, segment 12, L3A, L2A, phases III, IV. Fabric group 4.

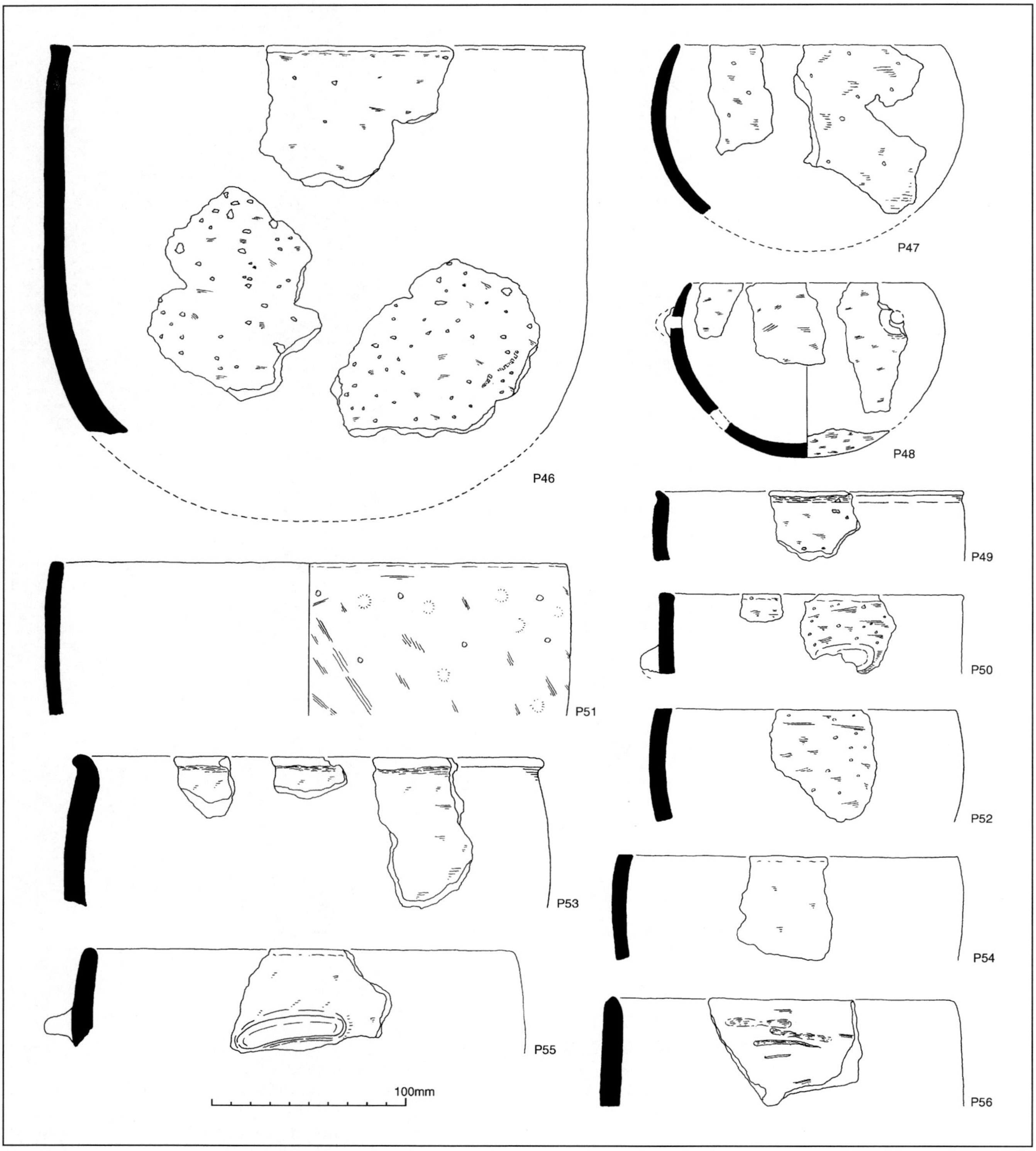

Fig 9.4 Neolithic Bowl pottery. Particulars in catalogue.

P70. ST81 1061. Stepleton enclosure, segment 14, L2, phase VI. Fabric group 3.

P71. HN82 310, 369, 370, 393. Inner Hanford outwork, segment 3, L4, L3C, phase III. Fabric group 7.

P72. HH74 1215. Central area, pit A F120. Fabric group 7.

P73. HH77 2053, 2207. Long barrow, W ditch (segment 1), LB3 SIII L34, phase I. Fabric group 6.

P74. ST79 1659, 2066. Stepleton spur pit 2A F159, L1. Fabric group 7.

P75. HH75 605. Central area, pit B F57A, L1. Fabric group 6.

P76. ST81 646. Stepleton enclosure, segment 12, L2, phase VI. Fabric group 6.

P77. ST79 2001, 2015, 2035, 2509. Stepleton spur pits 2A F268, F269. Fabric group 7.

P78. ST80 954. Stepleton enclosure, segment 5, L1, phase VIII/a. Fabric group 8.

P79. HH77 1924. Long barrow, E ditch (segment 3), LB5 L17, phase I. Fabric group 7.

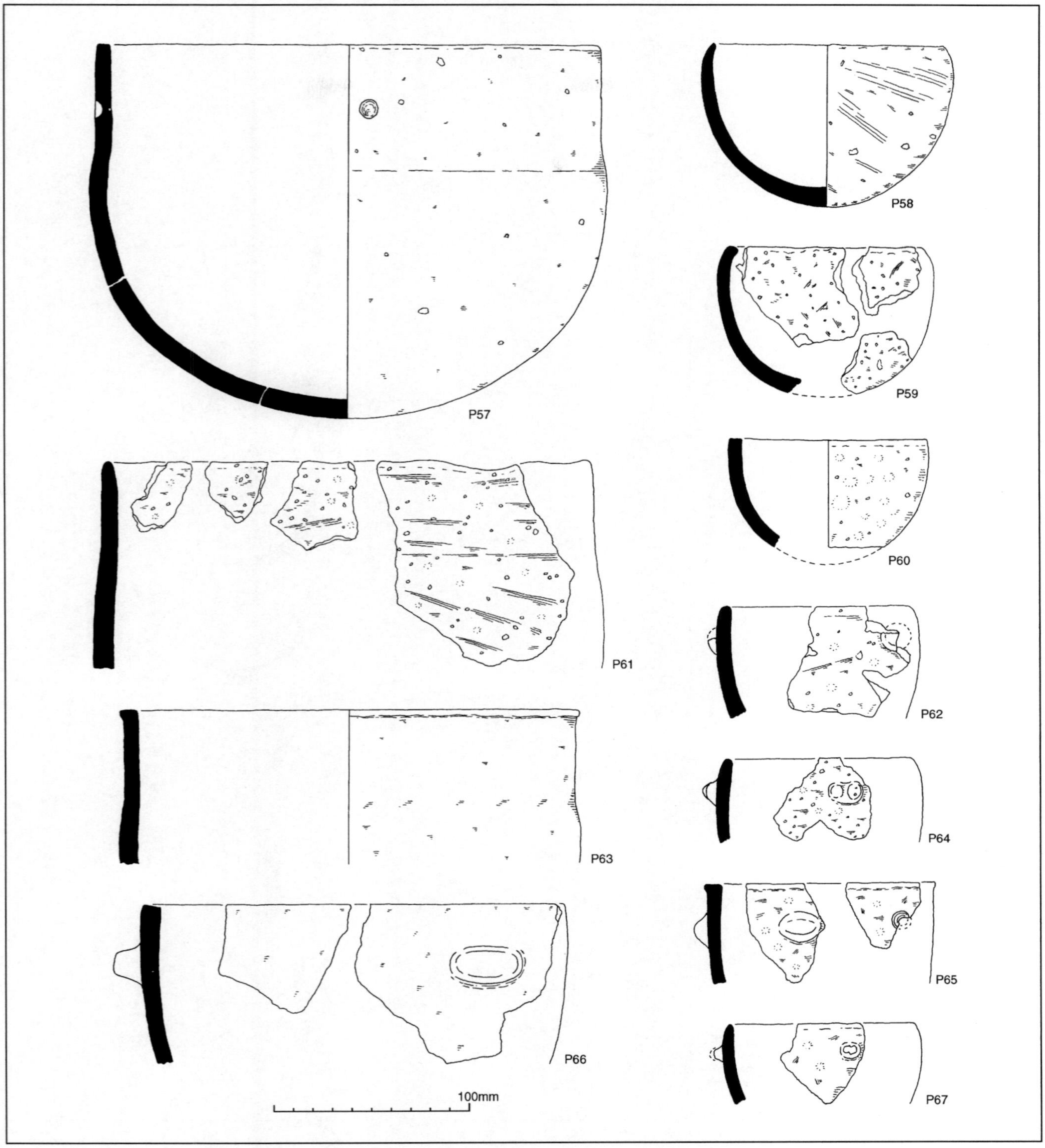

Fig 9.5 Neolithic Bowl pottery. Particulars in catalogue.

P80. HH76 1937. Main causewayed enclosure, segment 9. 1, L7, phase III. Fabric group 7.

P81. ST81 1102. Stepleton enclosure, segment 11, L3B, phase III. Fabric group 2.

P82. HH75 657, 720, 723, 726–9, 734, 755, 789, 902, 903, 905. Main causewayed enclosure, segment 9, L6, L7, phases III, VI. Fabric group 7.

P83. HH75 416, 418, 419. Main causewayed enclosure, segment 9, L3, phase VIII/a. Fabric group 2.

P84. HH75 681. Central area, pit C F3, L2. Fabric group 7.

P85. ST79 1567, 1684, 1685. Inner Stepleton outwork, segment 6, C1, L4A, phase I; pit 4B F137. Fabric group 7.

P86. ST81 880. Stepleton enclosure, segment 14, L3, phase V. Fabric group 6.

P87. HH77 468. Main causewayed enclosure, segment 1, F5, phase VI. Fabric group 2.

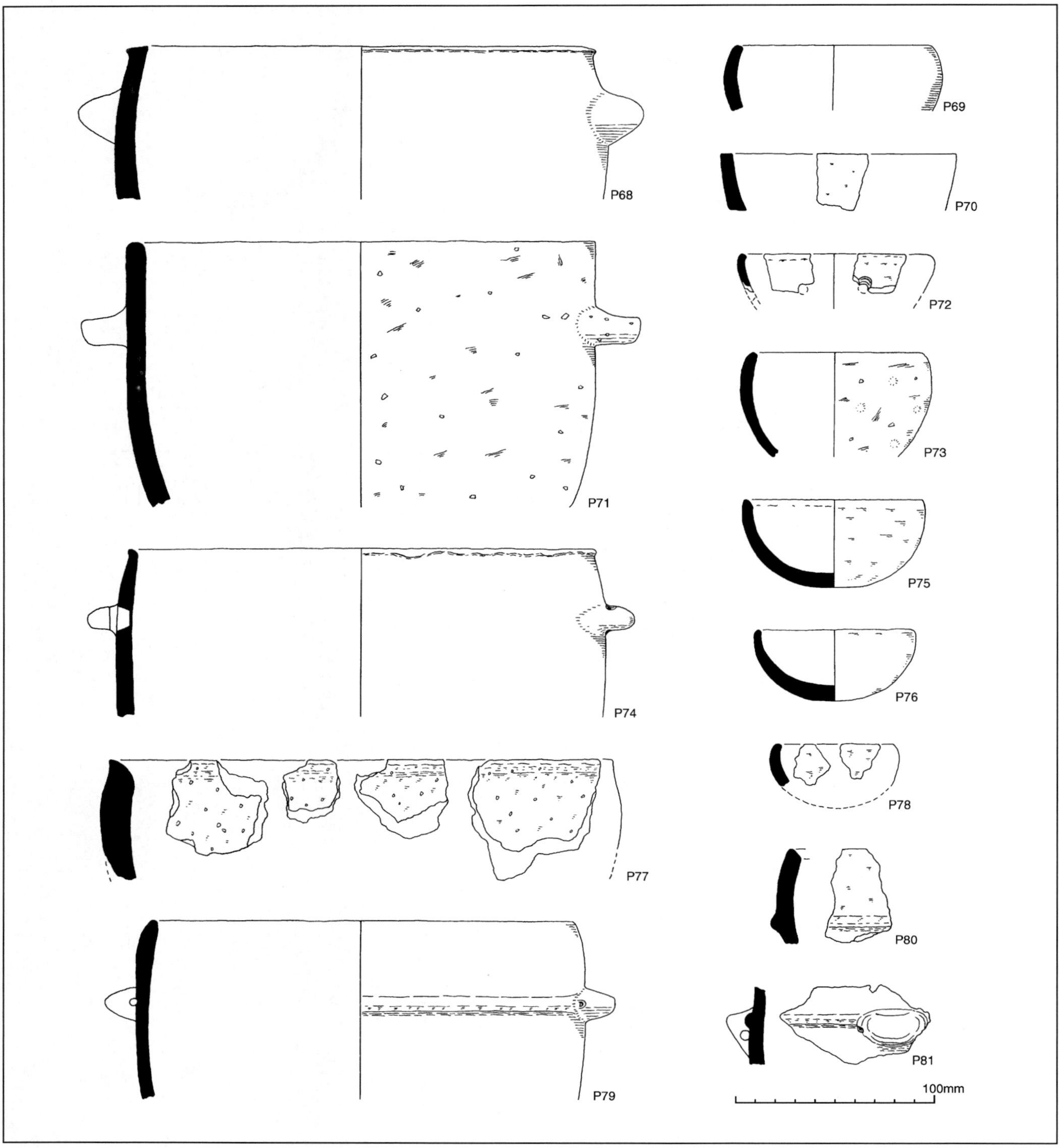

Fig 9.6 Neolithic Bowl pottery. Particulars in catalogue.

P88. HN82 300. Inner Hanford outwork, segment 3, L3C, Phase III. Fabric group 2.

P89. ST81 361. Stepleton enclosure, segment 8, L2, phase VI. Fabric group 5.

P90. HH74 736. Central area, pit A F6. Fabric group 5.

P91. HH77 1490. Central area, pit N F7(i), L3. Fabric group 2.

P92. HH77 1621, 1683. Long barrow, W ditch (segment 1), LB3 SII L17, phase IV. Fabric group 7.

P93. HH76 1397. Main causewayed enclosure, segment 16, L8A, phase VI. Fabric group 7.

P94. HH76 2914. Main causewayed enclosure, segment 17, L6, phase VI. Fabric group 2.

P95. ST80 1610, 1799, 1821. Outer Stepleton outwork, segment 4, L3A, L2A, phases III, VII/a. Fabric group 2.

P96. ST78 2928, ST78 782. Stepleton enclosure, segment 23, phase III, inner Stepleton outwork, segment 8, L2, phase VIII/a. Fabric group 7.

P97. HN82 378. Inner Hanford outwork, segment 3, L3C, phase III. Fabric group 7.

P98. HH74 721. Main causewayed enclosure, segment 4, L5, phase VI. Fabric group 2.

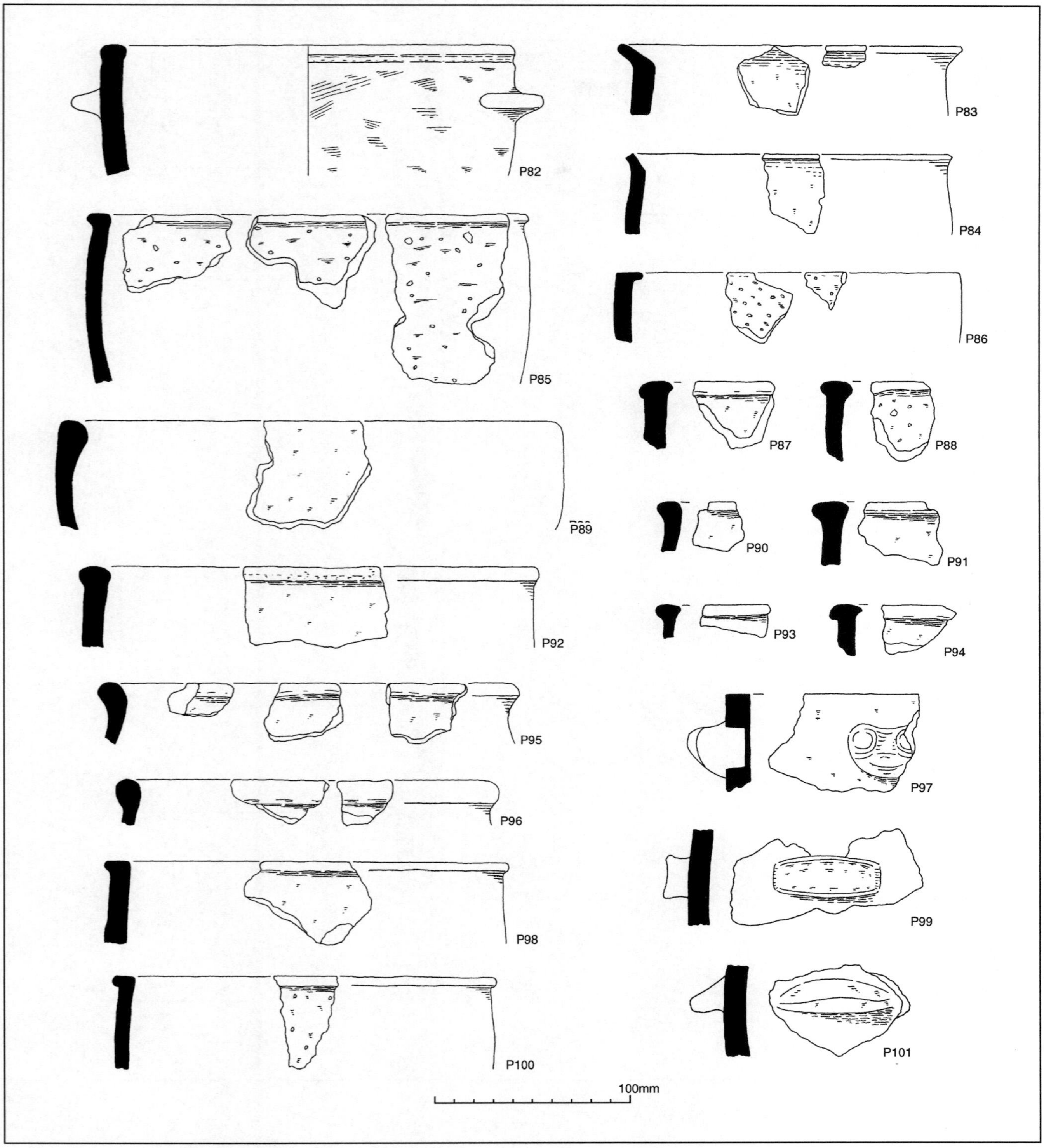

Fig 9.7 Neolithic Bowl pottery. Particulars in catalogue.

P99. HH77 1030, 2274. Long barrow, W ditch (segment 1), LB3, SIV, L19; E ditch (segment 3), LB5 F5, phases III, VII/a. Fabric group 6.

P100. ST81 1173. Stepleton enclosure, segment 7, L2, phase VI. Fabric group 6.

P101. HH77 1015. Long barrow, W ditch (segment 1), LB3 L19, phase III. Fabric group 7.

P102. ST80 119, 569, 946, 1214. Stepleton enclosure, segment 5, L1, phase VIII/a. Fabric group 7.

P103. ST81 1240. Stepleton enclosure, segment 8, U3 L2A, phase IV. Fabric group 7.

P104. HH74 756. Main causewayed enclosure, segment 2, L4, phase VI. Fabric group 2.

P105. HH77 905, 2076, 2158. Long barrow, W ditch (segment 1), LB2, SV, SVII L26; E ditch (segment 3), LB4, F4, phase I in SW ditch, phase VI in NW. Fabric group 5.

P106. HH76 568, 1957, 2221, 2236. Main causewayed

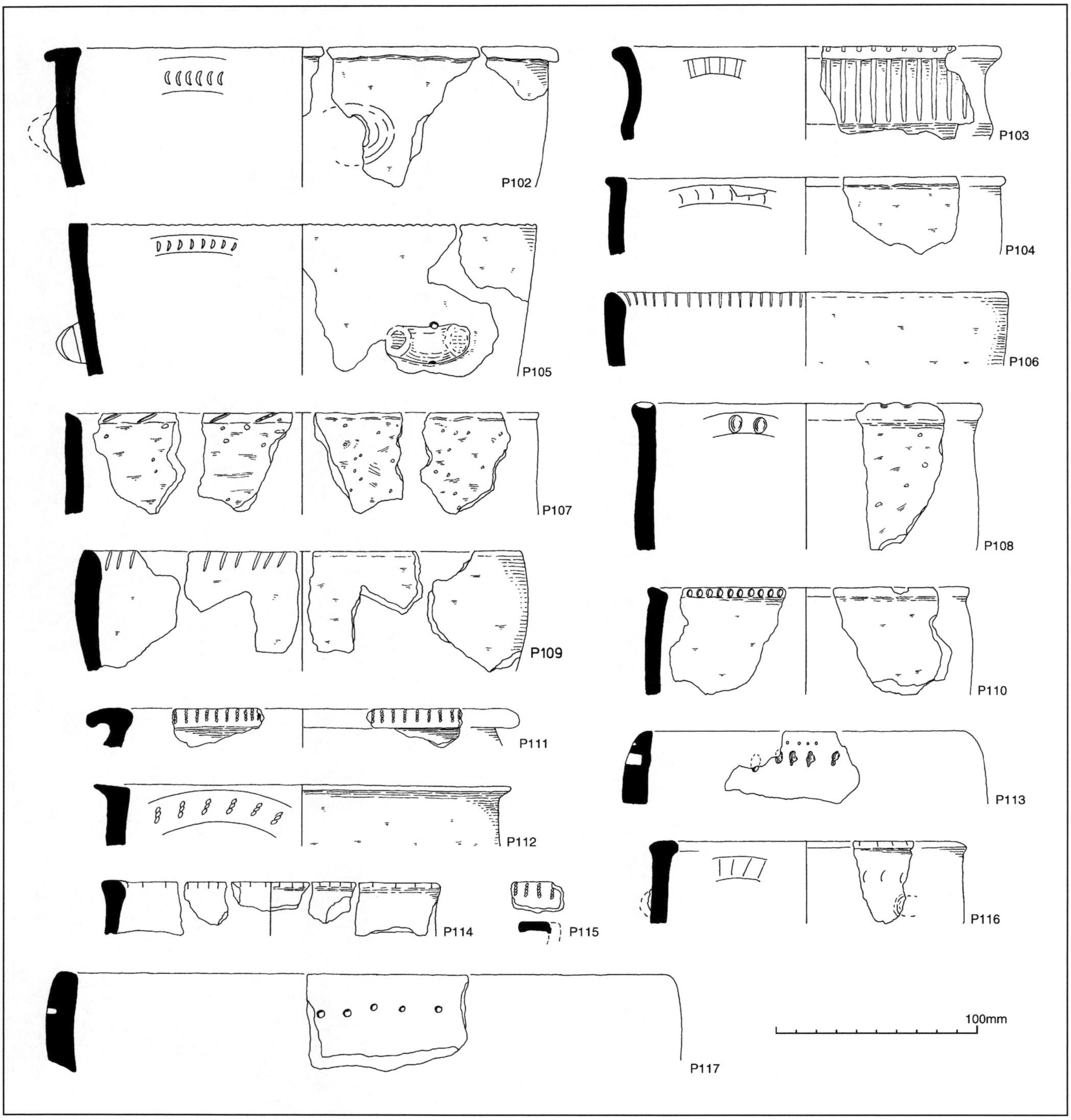

Fig 9.8 Neolithic Bowl pottery. Particulars in catalogue.

enclosure, segment 13, L5, segment 14, L6, L9, phase VI. Fabric group 7.

P107. ST81 142, 160, 607. Stepleton enclosure, segment 8, L1, L2; segment 11, L2, phases VI, VIII/a. Fabric group 6.

P108. HH76 1468. Main causewayed enclosure, segment 16, L9, phase V. Fabric group 6.

P109. ST81 51, 221, 365. Stepleton enclosure, segment 7, L1, L2, phases VI, VIII/a. Fabric group 7.

P110. HH74 1119. Central area, pit A F64. Fabric group 7.

P111. ST80 1210. Stepleton enclosure, segment 2, L3C, phase IV. Fabric group 7.

P112. HH75 421, 424. Main causewayed enclosure, segment 9, L3, phase VIII/a. Fabric group 2.

P113. HH76 1099. Main causewayed enclosure, segment 18, L10, phase III. Fabric group 7.

P114. HH74 187, 481, 528, 580, 610, 613. Main causewayed enclosure, segment 3, L3, L4, L5, phases V, VI, VIII/a. Fabric group 7.

P115. ST79 2305. Inner Stepleton outwork, L2, phase VIII/a. Fabric group 7.

P116. HH74 1049. Main causewayed enclosure, segment 4, L5, phase VI. Fabric group 2.

P117. HH75 2043. Inner east cross-dyke, segment 4, L7,

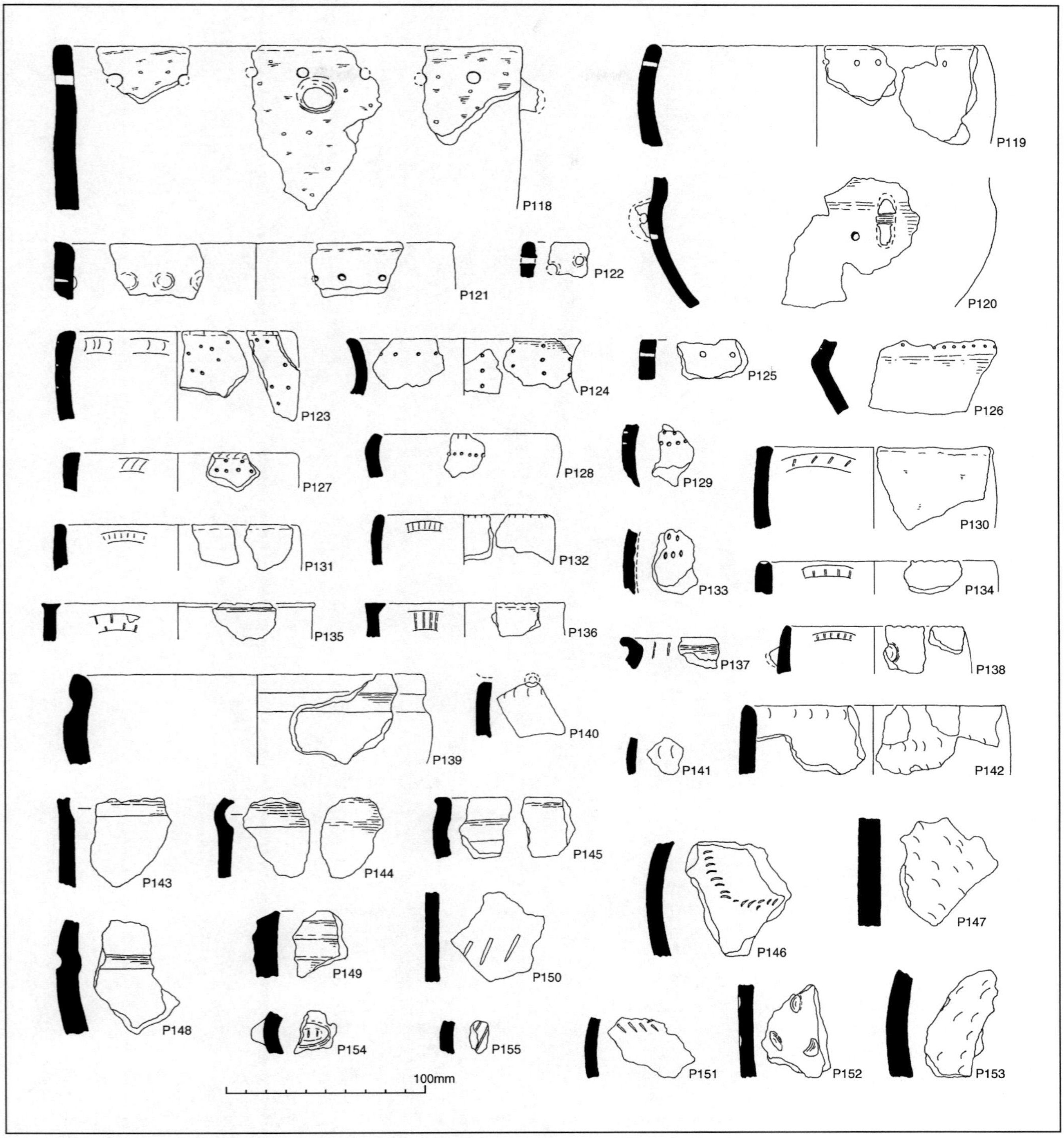

Fig 9.9 Neolithic Bowl pottery. Particulars in catalogue.

phase V. Fabric group 2.

P118. ST78 719, 734, 996. Stepleton spur pit 1A F57, L1, L2. Fabric group 7.

P119. HH77 2101. Long barrow, W ditch (segment 1), SIII, L18, phase VI. Fabric group 2.

P120. ST81 2272. Stepleton spur pit 4B F198. Fabric group 7.

P121. HH75 1461. Main causewayed enclosure, segment 11, L6, phaseVI. Fabric group 7.

P122. HH74 928. Central area, pit A F41. Fabric group 7.

P123. HH74 746. Main causewayed enclosure, segment 3, L5, phaseVI. Fabric group 7.

P124. HH76 990. Main causewayed enclosure, segment 19, L3B, phaseVI. Fabric group 7.

P125. ST79 869. Inner Stepleton outwork, segment 5, C6, L2B, phase VII/a. Fabric group 6.

P126. HH76 2877. Main causewayed enclosure, segment 17, L9A, phase IV. Fabric group 2.

P127. HH74 1167. Central area, pit A F78. Fabric group 7.

P128. HH75 363. Central area, pit B F57, L1. Fabric group 7.

P129. ST79 2456. Stepleton spur pit 2A F24 (upper fill). Fabric group 6.

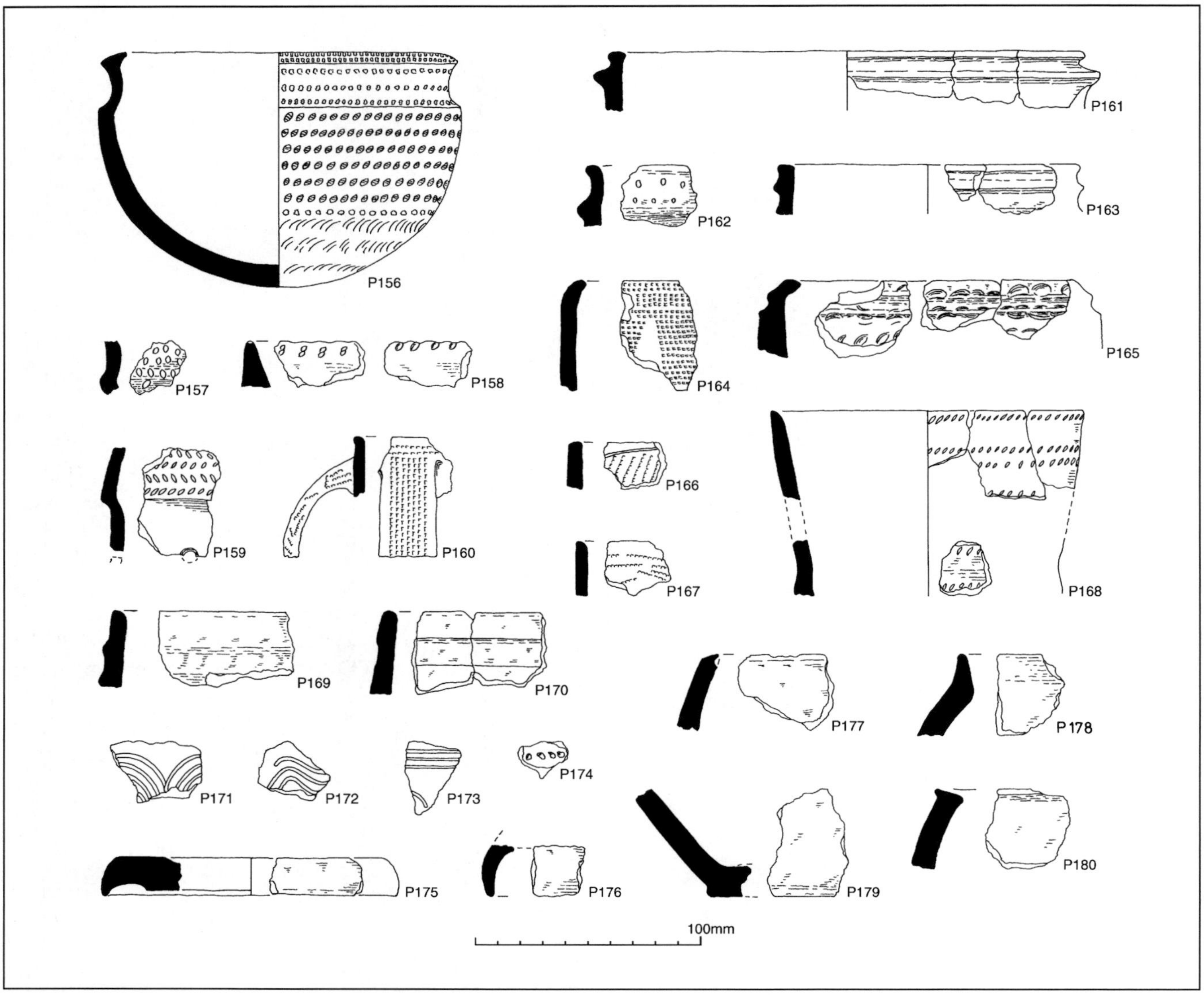

Fig 9.10 Peterborough Ware, Beaker and Bronze Age pottery. Particulars in catalogue.

P130. HH77 975, 1111. Long barrow, W ditch (segment 1), LB3 SI L20, L21, phases III, V. Fabric group 8.

P131. HH75 504. Central area, solution hollow B F12, L2. Fabric group 7.

P132. ST81 1056, 1089. Stepleton enclosure, segment 12, U5, L2A, phase IV. Fabric group 8.

P133. HH74 695. Main causewayed enclosure, segment 4, L7, phase VI. Fabric group 8.

P134. HH75 1232. Central area, recent quarry B F1C, L2. Fabric group 7.

P135. ST81 753. Stepleton enclosure, segment 12, L2, phase VI. Fabric group 6.

P136. ST81 2423. Stepleton spur pit 4B F80. Fabric group 6.

P137. HH75 213. Central area, pit B F2. Fabric group 7.

P138. HH75 557. Central area, pit B F14, L3. Fabric group 7.

P139. HH74 714. Main causewayed enclosure, segment 3, L5, phase VI. Fabric group 7.

P140. HH77 1465. Central area, pit N F6, L3. Fabric group 7.

P141. HH75 416. Main causewayed enclosure, segment 9, L3, phase VIII/a. Fabric group 8.

P142. HH74 969. Main causewayed enclosure, segment 3, L4, phase VI. Fabric group 7.

P143. HH76 2980. Main causewayed enclosure, segment 14, L9, phase VI. Fabric group 7.

P144. ST81 518. Stepleton enclosure, segment 14, L2, phase VI. Fabric group 6.

P145. ST81 2463. Inner Stepleton outwork, segment 4. 1, U2, L3, phase VIII/a. Fabric group 3.

P146 HH75 1697. Main causewayed enclosure, segment 8, L6, phase VI. Fabric group 7.

P147. ST80 1071. Stepleton enclosure, segment 4, U8 L2A, phase IV. Fabric group 6.

P148. HH74 1215. Central area, pit A F120. Fabric group 7.

P149. ST81 1151. Stepleton enclosure, segment 7, L2, phase VI. Fabric group 6.

P150. ST80 506. Stepleton enclosure, segment 2, L1, phase VIII/a. Fabric group 6.

P151 HH77 781. Long barrow, W ditch (segment 3), LB4 F1, phase VI. Fabric group 7.

P152. ST78 1645. Stepleton spur pit 1A F229, L2. Fabric group 6.
P153. ST81 188. Stepleton enclosure, segment 15, U10, L1, phase VIII/a. Fabric group 6.
P154. ST81 711. Stepleton enclosure, segment 8, L2, phase VI. Fabric group 7.
P155. ST81 235. Stepleton enclosure, segment 10, L2, phase VI. Fabric group 7.

Part 2. Peterborough Ware, Beaker and Bronze Age.

P156. ST79 2051. Middle Stepleton outwork, segment 6, C1 L3A, phase III. Fabric group 7.
P157. HH74 551. Central area, interior, surface. Fabric group 7.
P158. ST79 326. Inner Stepleton outwork, segment 6, L1A, phase VIII/a. Fabric group 7.
P159. ST81 746. Stepleton enclosure, segment 7, L2, phase VI. Fabric group 7.
P160. ST78 906. Middle Stepleton outwork, segment 10, L2, phase VIII/a. Fabric group 9.
P161. HH75 1371. Main causewayed enclosure, segment 8, L3, phase VIII/a. Fabric group 9.
P162. HH75 1660. Main causewayed enclosure, segment 10, L6, phase VII/a. Fabric group 9.
P163. HH75 100, 159. Main causewayed enclosure, segment 8, L3, phase VIII/a. Fabric group 9.
P164. HH75 1564. Main causewayed enclosure, segment 8, L6, phase VII/a. Fabric group 9.
P165. HH75 1341, 1356, 1668, 1750. Main causewayed enclosure, segment 8, L3, L3A, phases VII/a, VIII/a. Fabric group 9.
P166. ST79 690. Inner Stepleton outwork, segment 5, C5, L2B, phase VII/a. Fabric group 9.
P167. ST79 2665. Middle Stepleton outwork, segment 8, C3 L1A, phase VIII/a. Fabric group 9.
P168. HH75 1310, 1521, 1570, 1665, 1675, 1676, 1802, 1860. Main causewayed enclosure, segment 8, L3A, L6, phase VII/a. Fabric group 9.
P169. HH76 483. Shroton spur outwork site M (segment 1), L4, phase VIII/a. Fabric group 7.
P170. ST77 136, ST78 171. Inner Stepleton outwork, segment 8, unstratified. Fabric group 9.
P171. ST78 585. Inner Stepleton outwork, segment 8, L2, phase VIII/a. Fabric group 9
P172. ST78 779. Inner Stepleton outwork, segment 8, L2, phase VIII/a. Fabric group 9.
P173. ST 78 781. Inner Stepleton outwork, segment 8, L2, phase VIII/a. Fabric group 9.
P174. ST78 592. Inner Stepleton outwork, segment 8, L2, phase VIII/a. Fabric group 9.
P175. ST78 584. Inner Stepleton outwork, segment 8, L2, phase VIII/a. Fabric group 9.
P176. HH76 91. Shroton spur outwork, site M (segments 1–2), L2, phase VIII/a. Fabric group 9.
P177. ST80 194. Stepleton enclosure, segment 3, L1, phase VIII/a. Fabric group 12.
P178. ST80 495. Stepleton enclosure, segment 2, L1, phase VIII/a. Fabric group 12.
P179. ST80 499, 511. Stepleton enclosure, segment 3, L1, phase VIII/a. Fabric group 12.
P180. ST80 118. Stepleton enclosure, segment 2/3, L1, phase VIII/a. Fabric group 12.

9.2 A petrological analysis of the ceramic fabrics represented among the Neolithic pottery from Hambledon Hill, Dorset

Timothy Darvill

9.2.1 Introduction

A series of 43 sample sherds from the early Neolithic pottery assemblage was studied in thin section with a view to defining fabric groups, identifying likely fabric sources, and assessing the techniques of pottery production. The sample was selected by Dr I F Smith as representative of the range of fabrics distinguished on the basis of preliminary macroscopic inspection. Table 9.14 lists the sherd numbers of the samples studied.

The usual methods of thin section preparation (Tite 1972, 215) were modified to take account of the relatively friable nature of the pottery (Darvill 1983a, 552–62). The samples were sorted into fabric groups on the basis of the nature and the size of the clastic inclusions, and on the mineralogy and texture of the clay matrix. In all, eight groups were defined, some of them divisible into a number of subgroups (see Table 9.14). For convenience, fabric groups are identified in this report by the most diagnostic characteristic used for their definition. The relative abundance of fabric groups across the excavated sites, and through the recorded phases of occupation is discussed above by Dr Smith (9.1).

Six types of clay outcrop within 10 kilometres of Hambledon Hill (Fig 9.11). Five of these were sampled for comparison with the Neolithic fabrics (Figure 9.11 shows the position of four sample points, the fifth, on the Oxford Clay, lies just off the map to the west).

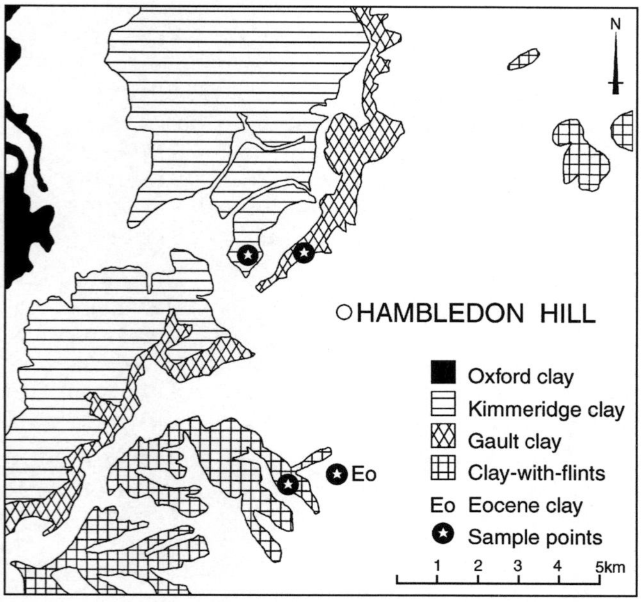

Fig 9.11 The extent of the clay outcrops around Hambledon Hill, and the origin of clay samples used in the analysis.

Table 9.14 Fabric groupings and sample details

The 'thin section no.' column records catalogue numbers in the thin section library of the Department of Archaeology, University of Southampton

Fabric no.	*Principal inclusions*	*Sherds sampled*	*Thin section no.*	*Context*
1	Gabbroic rock fragments	HH74 104	N257	Main causewayed enclosure, segment 4, L1, topsoil
		HH77 1167	N258	Central area, pit N F5, L3
		ST79 2622	N385	Stepleton spur, pit 2A F181
2.i	Ooliths	HH74 427	N221	Main causewayed enclosure, segment 3 or 4, AII L2/3, upper levels
		HH74 581	N259	Main causewayed enclosure, segment 3, AII L4, phase II
		ST79 3242	N375	Stepleton spur, site unstratified
2.ii	Ooliths, fossil shell and calcite	HH74 271	N223	Main causewayed enclosure, segment 4, AIII L5, phase III
		HH74 667	N260	Main causewayed enclosure, segment 2, L4, phase VI
2.iii	Ooliths and flint	HH74 710	N222	Main causewayed enclosure, segment 3, L5, phase VI
		HH74 232	N261	Main causewayed enclosure, segment 3, L4 phase VI
2.iv	Fossil shell and recrystalised ooliths	HH77 595	N263	Main causewayed enclosure, segment 1, F5, phase VI
2.v	Fossil shell and flint	HH74 492	N264	Main causewayed enclosure, segment 3, AI L7, phase V
		ST79 1096	N377	Stepleton enclosure, segment 1, L4
2.vi	Fossil shell and limestone	HH74 533	N274	Main causewayed enclosure, segment 3, AII L3, phase VIII/a
		ST79 1580	N376	Inner Stepleton outwork, segment 7, C15 L4, phase III
		ST79 557	N378	Inner Stepleton outwork, segment 6, C1 L3A, phase V
		ST79 1969	N379	Inner Stepleton outwork, segment 5, C7 L5A, phase III
3	Calcite	HH74 190	N265	Main causewayed enclosure, segment 3, AI L3, phase VIII/a
		HH77 1842	N266	Central area, pit N F22, L3
		ST79 2143	N383	Inner Stepleton outwork, segment 5, C14 L3A, phase V
4	Organic material (chaff or dung?)	HH74 355	N267	Central area, site A, topsoil
		ST79 130	N384	Outer Stepleton outwork, segment 5, L2, phase VIII/a
5	Fresh shell and flint	HH74 270	N262	Main causewayed enclosure, segment 4, AIII L7, phase VI
6	Red pellets (and flint)	ST79 637	N386	Inner Stepleton outwork, segment 6, C1 L1D, phase III
	Red pellets (and snail shell and chalk)	ST79 1963	N387	Inner Stepleton outwork, segment 6, C1 L1F phase III
	Red pellets (and sandstone and flint)	ST79 760	N388	Inner Stepleton outwork, segment 6, C1 L1D, phase III
	Red pellets (and quartz/quartzite)	ST79 1576	N389	Inner Stepleton outwork, segment 6 C3 L2B, phase VII/a
	Red pellets (and flint)	ST79 119	N390	Inner Stepleton outwork bank area, unstratified
	Red pellets (and fresh shell)	ST79 905	N391	Inner Stepleton outwork, segment 5, C4 L3B, phase V
	Red pellets (and flint)	ST79 907	N392	Inner Stepleton outwork, segment 5, C11 L3B, phase V
	Red pellets (and flint)	ST79 1498	N393	Inner Stepleton outwork, segment 6, C3 L3, phase VII/a
	Red pellets (and flint)	ST79 2539	N394	Stepleton spur, pit 2A F189
	Red pellets (and sandstone)	ST79 869	N395	Inner Stepleton outwork, segment 5, C4 L3B, phase V
7	Flint	HH74 1063	N268	Central area, pit A F62
		HH74 603	N269	Central area, pit A F5
		HH74 101	N270	Main causewayed enclosure, segment 2 or 3, L1, topsoil
		HH74 928	N271	Central area, pit A F41
		ST79 2064	N380	Middle Stepleton outwork, segment 6, C1 L4, phase III
		ST79 2655	N381	Inner Stepleton outwork, segment 5, C17 L6, phase I
8	Sand	HH74 973	N272	Main causewayed enclosure, segment 2 or 3, L1, topsoil
		HH74 490	N273	Main causewayed enclosure, segment 3, AI L9, phase III
		ST79 761	N382	Inner Stepleton outwork, segment 6, C1 L1A, phase VIII/a
Burnt clay		ST79 554	N396	Inner Stepleton outwork, segment 6, C1 L1D, phase III

The riverine clay in the valley of the Stour was not sampled, since its present composition is unlikely to be the same as in Neolithic times because of erosion and down-cutting into new deposits. Clay from a fissure within the Stepleton enclosure was also collected and studied. Each clay sample was wedged, made into a brickette, dried and then fired at a temperature of 900–1000°C for three hours.

A thin section was then prepared from each brickette. No simulation of mixed clays was attempted. All the sampled clays, with the exception of the Stepleton fissure type, were used individually for brick-making in recent times (Osborne White 1923, 94). At present, there is no reason to suspect that in Neolithic pottery traditions clays were extensively altered by mixing.

Throughout this report individual thin sections are referred to by their accession number (eg N257) in the thin section library of the Department of Archaeology, University of Southampton.

9.2.2 The fabrics

Fabric group 1 – Gabbroic

This fabric group falls within the general class of gabbroic wares defined by Peacock (1969). Macroscopically it is characterised by a liberal scatter of angular rock fragments. In thin section large angular grains of feldspar, amphibole and quartz can be seen in an optically anisotropic fired clay groundmass. The feldspars are turbid and intensely altered, although some fresh grains of plagioclase are visible (Fig 9.12: A). The amphiboles are green or colourless varieties.

The sample from the Stepleton enclosure (N385) is very similar to those from the Hambledon enclosure, but the rock fragments in the latter tend to be smaller, presumably more completely crushed during manufacture to produce a finer-textured clay. Gabbroic ware vessels in the same fabric occur at Maiden Castle (eg N3) and at Hembury (eg N8), but the gabbroic wares known to the author from Carn Brea, Cornwall (eg N4 and N5), are rather different, having a much coarser fabric. The source of the Hambledon Hill gabbroic ware is probably on the Lizard in Cornwall (Peacock 1969; 1988; Harrad 2004), some 240 km or so away to the south-west.

Fabric group 2 – Oolitic and shelly limestone-tempered wares

This is a large and complex group of fabrics in which six subdivisions can be recognised. All are linked by the presence of Jurassic limestone detritus as the predominant tempering agent.

2.i Oolitic wares

The tempering agents in this fabric are almost exclusively ooliths, with only very occasional admixed fragments of shell. In thin section the ooliths dominate the field of view and display well-defined concentric layering (Fig 9.12: B). About 50% show central nuclei of rounded quartz grains. Most of the ooliths measure less than 0.4 mm across, but a few are up to 0.66 mm. Almost all are single and isolated; only slide N221 contained a rock fragment composed of several ooliths. The ooliths are set within a fine-grained groundmass containing small, subangular to rounded quartz grains up to 0.24 mm across, and a few flecks of muscovite mica up to 0.01 mm long, but these are rare.

An identical fabric has been identified at West Kennet long barrow, Wiltshire (N35 and N36), and at several other sites in central southern England. It is not present among the material known to the author from Maiden Castle, Dorset, to the south, or from Neolithic sites in Gloucestershire to the north. The source of the Oolitic wares probably lies somewhere along the Jurassic outcrops in west Dorset or west Wiltshire.

2.ii Ooliths, shell- and calcite-tempered wares

Although broadly similar to fabric 2.i under the microscope, this fabric contains a wider range of inclusions. In addition to the ooliths there is a light scatter of fossil shell and occasional calcite crystals. The shell is well crushed; fragments rarely exceed 0.75 mm across. The calcite shows well-marked cleavage planes, and occurs as angular crystals up to 3.0 mm across.

A comparable fabric is recorded at Robin Hood's Ball, Wiltshire (N62), and at Windmill Hill, Wiltshire (Smith 1965, pl xvi: e). The source of this fabric, like that of fabric 2.i, probably lies along the Jurassic outcrops west or north-west of Hambledon Hill, although not necessarily as far north as the Bath–Frome area as suggested by Cornwall and Hodges (1964) or indeed the Bradenstoke area (Darvill 1983b, 97).

2.iii Ooliths and flint-tempered wares

This fabric is macroscopically similar to fabric 2.i, the main difference being that along with ooliths there is also a light scatter of flint fragments. These flints are not common, and in a sherd of about 10 mm³ only four pieces were found. All were over 1 mm long, but none occurred in the thin section plane. Under the microscope this fabric is very similar to both 2.i and 2.ii, and simply represents a variation in the range of Oolitic wares.

A sample from Robin Hood's Ball (N77) provides a good match for the Hambledon Hill fabric, and somewhat similar wares undoubtedly occur elsewhere in the area. Sofranoff (1976, 56–60) undertook a heavy mineral analysis of sherd HH74 710, and found that the mineral suite was not unlike that of the Bridport–Yeovil–Midford sands which occur extensively along the length of the Jurassic ridge (Boswell 1924). The presence of fragments of flint within the fabric need not alter the proposed source of the Oolitic wares among the Jurassic outcrops since such fragments would have been common wherever flint was worked.

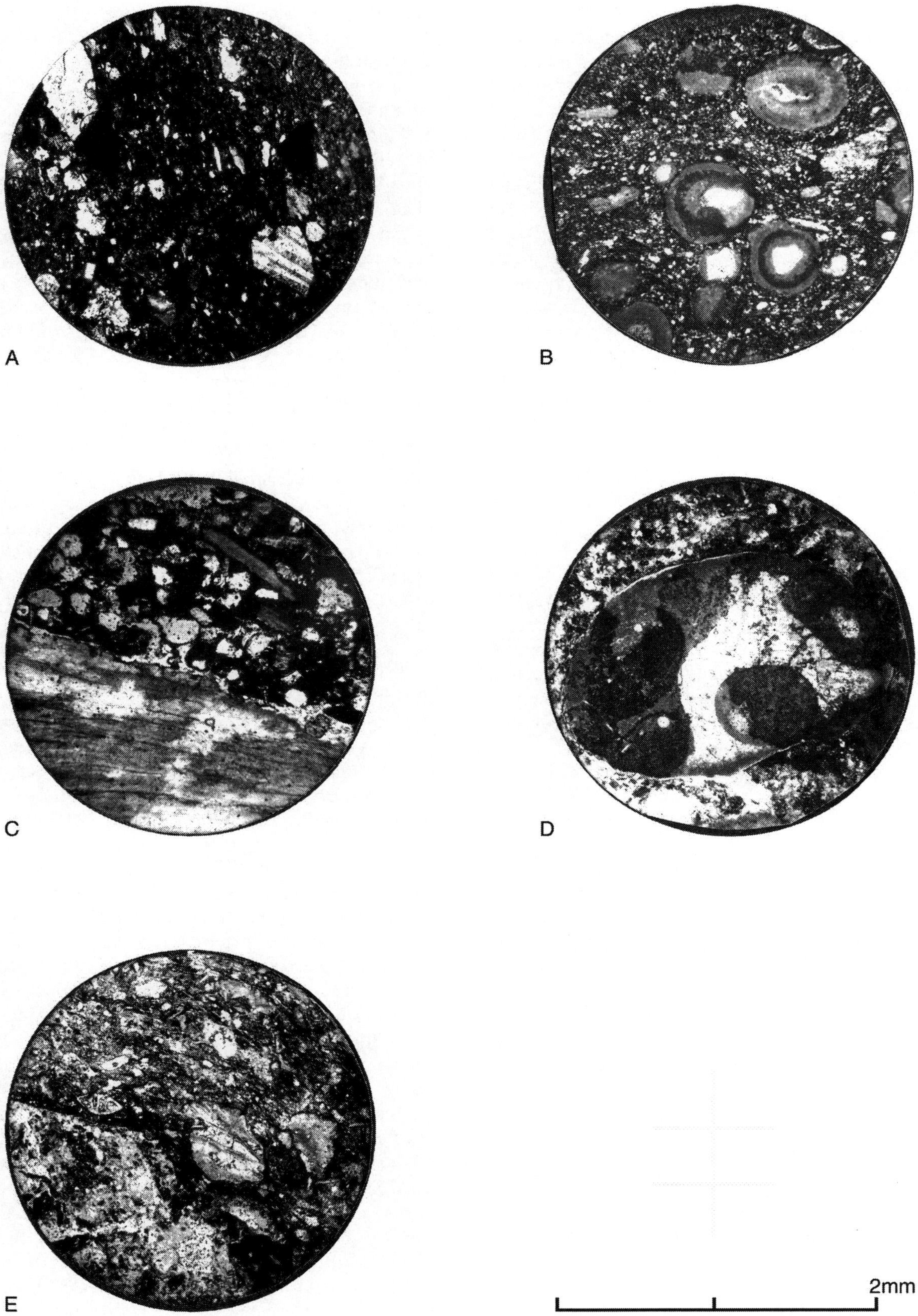

Fig 9.12 A photomicrograph of fabric 1, B photomicrograph of fabric 2.ii, C photomicrograph of fabric 5, D photomicrograph of fabric 2.iv, E photomicrograph of fabric 2.v.

2.iv Fossil shell and re-crystallised oolith-tempered wares

Abundant tempering is visible in the hand specimen, and microscopic examination shows it to consist of a mixture of small shell fragments and rounded pieces of rock containing re-crystallised ooliths. One small chip of flint was noted in the hand specimen, but no pieces were present in the thin section. The shell is well crushed, most pieces being less than 1 mm long. The rock fragments containing re-crystallised ooliths are, in contrast, rounded and up to 3 mm across (see Fig 9.12: D). The calcitic cement in which the ooliths are set is thick and evenly distributed. In addition, a few small pieces of siltstone were observed in the fabric, and one, which was prized out of the surface of the sample sherd, resembled a tiny pebble about 2.0 mm across. The groundmass in which these clasts are set is fine-grained and slightly micaceous. There is a light scatter of quartz fragments, mostly under 0.06 mm across, and a few dried clay pellets not fully mixed into the clay during wedging.

No parallels can be cited at present. A source in the same general area as fabric 2.i–iii is likely, but it is improbable that exactly the same clay and rock outcrops are involved.

2.v Fossil shell and flint-tempered wares

In the hand, specimen fragments of fossil shell and flint can easily be seen with the naked eye. Under the microscope, shell is the dominant element, and occurs in pieces up to 2 mm long, although much of it is rather smaller. Some shell fragments are cemented together, and there is no doubt that this is fossil shell. Flint fragments are not common, and fall within the size range 1.0–1.5 mm across. The groundmass is anisotropic and is practically barren except for the clasts already mentioned and occasional pieces of quartz up to 0.1 mm across (Fig 9.12: E).

No directly comparable fabrics can at present be cited, although many samples from sites in central southern England are broadly similar. Again, a source along the Jurassic outcrops is most likely, although the clay used differs from that in any of the other fabrics in group 2.

2.vi Fossil shell and limestone-tempered wares

This fabric is broadly similar to fabric 2.v in the hand specimen, but does not contain flint. In thin section it can be seen to represent a distinct fabric. The clay matrix is fine-grained and contains a light scatter of angular quartz grains and flecks of muscovite mica. The principal clasts are shell fragments, often fused together with calcitic cement. Foraminifera fossils are also present (Fig 9.13: F). Slight variations in the texture of clasts was noted among the samples studied.

Comparable fabrics have been recorded from Maiden Castle, Dorset (N84), and from fabric group 5 at Cherhill, Wiltshire (Darvill 1983b, 95). It is interesting to note that sherd HH74 667 cross-cut a junction between two coils of clay used in making the pot (see 9.2.3 below). The lower coil was of fabric 2.vi, the upper of fabric 2.ii (Fig 9.14). Thus both fabrics were presumably available in the same place at the same time.

This vivid example of the connections identifiable between fabric groups serves to emphasise the need for further research into the Jurassic-tempered wares. All the fabrics classed here as group 2 probably derive from somewhere along the Jurassic outcrops, but at least three separate sources are probably involved, some perhaps near to Hambledon Hill, others perhaps rather further away. Without more work greater precision is impossible.

Oolith-tempered wares are widely believed to originate from somewhere along the Jurassic Ridge (Cornwall and Hodges 1964). If they did, then the heavy minerals should resemble those of the Bridport–Yeovil–Midford Sands, which stretch from southern Dorset to the Cotswolds. Boswell (1924) analysed these minerals from over 80 samples. He found that the sands were remarkably homogeneous, but that the quantity and variety of minerals increased from north to south. His findings resemble the Hambledon Hill material but more detailed comparisons between the sands and the sherds are necessary before anything definite can be said. If the resemblance to these sands is close enough to assume they are the source of the Hambledon Hill heavy minerals, it would still be possible to include most of the Jurassic Ridge in this category, since the sands are homogeneous. The only indication as to specific source is the inclusion of flint in the clay of the sherd. The point at which oolite, sand and flint outcrop closest to each other is in the Bridport area of southern Dorset. At all other points along the Jurassic Ridge the flint outcrops are further away from the oolite and sands. This sherd does not come from the Kimmeridge Clay or the Portland Sand, as they all contain abundant tourmaline (Boswell 1924).

Fabric group 3 – Calcite-tempered wares

The presence of large angular fragments of calcite up to 4 mm across is a distinctive feature of this fabric in the hand specimen. In thin section the slightly rectilinear crystal form and clear cleavage planes of the calcite fragments can easily be seen. The groundmass is fine-grained, slightly micaceous, and contains angular fragments of quartz up to 0.4 mm across, together with occasional pieces of non-translucent iron ore (Fig 9.13: G). A perfect cube of iron pyrites about 1.1 mm^3 was found in the break of sherd HH74 1842, and a small chip of flint was noted in HH74 190 during macroscopic examination.

Calcite-tempered Neolithic wares comparable to those from Hambledon Hill form a discrete group in Dorset (Sofranoff 1976, fig 16), and accordingly it might be suggested that the Jurassic outcrops provide

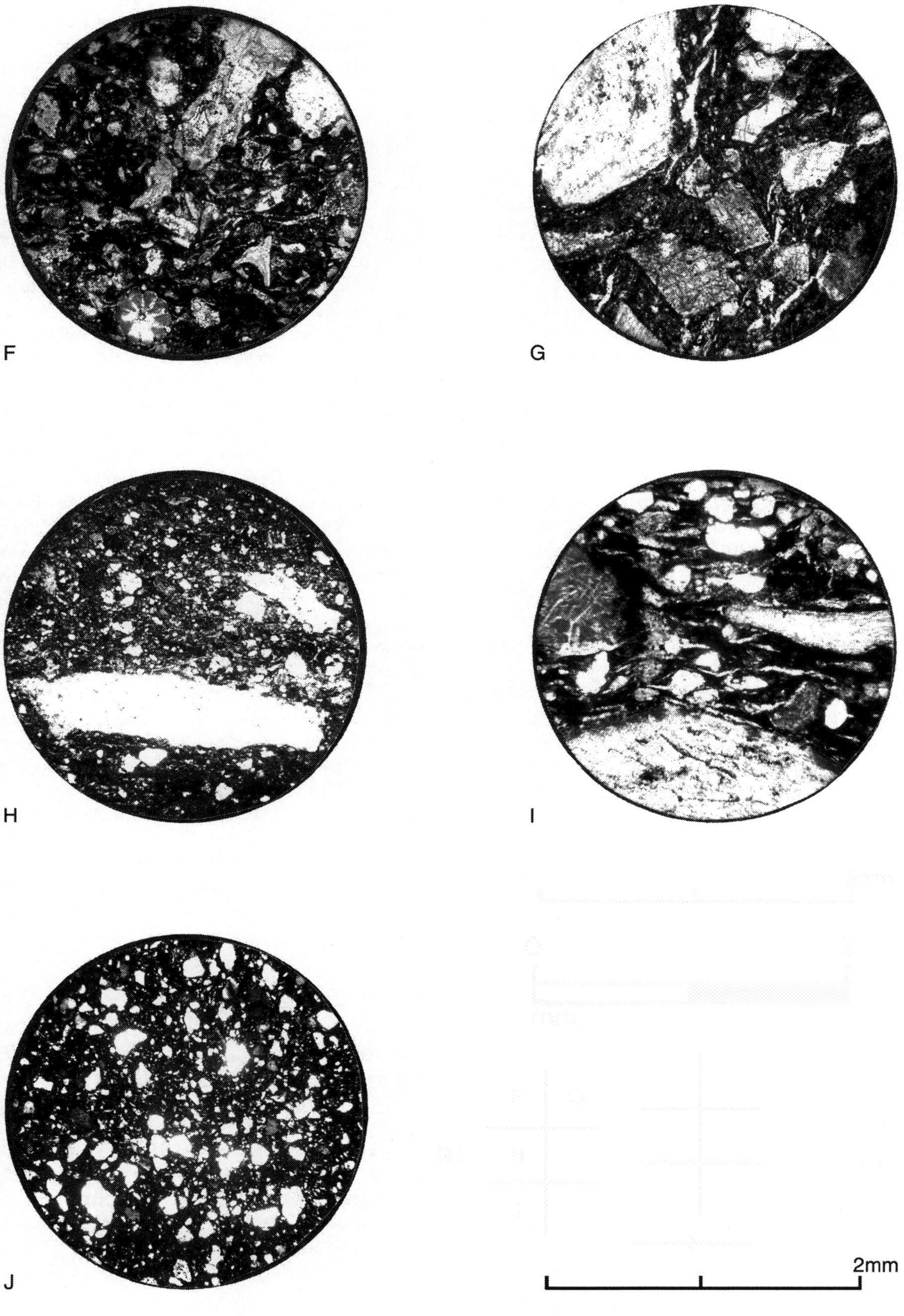

Fig 9.13 F photomicrograph of fabric 2.vi, G photomicrograph of fabric 3, H photomicrograph of fabric 4, I photomicrograph of fabric 7, J photomicrograph of Kimmeridge clay sample.

the most likely source area. However, crystalline calcite outcrops widely in numerous sedimentary formations, and other source areas are equally possible. In support of a Dorset origin for this particular group of calcite-tempered wares is the fact that calcite tempering is not common in Wiltshire (cf Smith 1965, 46), and that, although calcite was heavily used as a tempering agent in many Cotswold potting traditions, the clays are quite different (Smith and Darvill 1990). None of the clays sampled from the vicinity of Hambledon Hill match those used in the manufacture of fabric group 3 vessels. A source in Purbeck has subsequently been suggested for similar Neolithic fabrics from Maiden Castle (Cleal 1991a, 173).

Fabric group 4 – Organic-tempered wares

In the hand specimen this fabric is slightly vesicular with a granular feel. A close examination of the voids showed that many contained carbon residues and this, coupled with the fact that slight striations could be detected on the walls of the voids, led to the conclusion that organic matter had been used as a tempering agent. Latex casts of the voids were made by Mr Francis Green of Southampton University in an effort to identify the material used. Although the resolution of detail on the casts was low, and the voids small, enough could be seen to lead Mr Green to the conclusion that chaff or dung had once filled the voids.

In thin section the angular voids can be clearly seen, surrounded by an anisotropic groundmass (Fig 9.13: H). Within the groundmass is a light scatter of rounded quartz grains up to 0.3 mm across, and a few flecks of muscovite mica.

No exact match for this fabric is known to the author. However, the use of organic tempering agents is widespread in Britain and has been reported from a number of sites including Windmill Hill, Wiltshire (Smith 1965, 46) and Fengate, Cambridgeshire (Pryor 1974, 8). At Gwernvale, Powys, organic-tempered wares represented 76% of the pre-cairn (early Neolithic) assemblage (Darvill 1984, 112). Organic-tempered pottery was also a feature of several British and European Neolithic potting traditions (Darvill 2004; Hulthén 1977, 49).

The source of the clays used for fabric group 4 is not known.

Fabric group 5 – Fresh shell and flint-tempered wares

Macroscopically the dominant component of this fabric is the fresh-looking crushed shell, which ranges in size from 0.75 mm up to 4.5 mm long. Occasional pieces of flint can be seen in the fabric. In thin section the pieces of shell show clear laminar structure and clean edges (Fig 9.12: C). A thorough examination revealed no traces of cement residues on the shell and it must be concluded that it is fresh rather than fossil shell. Intermixed with the shell are fragments of white calcined flint up to, but not exceeding, 0.5 mm across. The groundmass in which these clasts are set is heavily iron-stained and contained numerous angular and sometimes crazed quartz and quartzite grains. These were mostly up to 0.38 mm across, but occasionally over 2.0 mm. Quartz grains dominate the groundmass visible under the microscope (Fig 9.12: C), probably covering 25% (Shvetsov 1955) of the area not covered by the shell.

No fabric match is known to the author, and none of the local clays sampled is in any way similar to this fabric.

Fabric group 6 – red pellet wares

This fabric can easily be recognised in the hand specimen by the presence of small, roughly spherical, red-coloured pellets. A considerable variety of clastic inclusions have been noted in association with this fabric, including flint (samples N386, N390, N392, N393, N394), crushed land mollusc shell and chalk (N387), sandstone and flint (N388), crushed quartz or quartzite (N389), fresh shell (N391) and sandstone (N395). In all cases these inclusions are set within a fine-grained slightly micaceous clay matrix with a light scatter of well-sorted subangular quartz grains up to 0.25 mm across. The red pellets can be seen to be iron-rich clay pellets under the microscope, and iron staining is widespread within the matrix as a whole. Dried clay pellets up to 1.0 mm across betray the fact that the clay was not especially well wedged before use.

No fabric matches can be cited. Although none of the clay samples from the vicinity of Hambledon Hill match that used in this fabric a fairly local source cannot be ruled out; the mineralogy and texture of the matrix hints at a riverine clay source. The eclectic range of inclusions could all have derived from natural deposits or broken-up tools such as would be present among settlement debris. Roe suggests a source area for broadly similar heathstones, red clays, and sandstones in south-east Dorset (see 10.1.2).

Fabric group 7 – Flint-tempered wares

Characterised in the hand specimen by the presence of flint fragments, this fabric group covers a wide range of wares with varying amounts of flint additives. In thin section the density of flint ranges from 7% to 25% of the field of view (Shvetsov 1955), and the fragments themselves range in size from under 0.5 mm across up to 4.0 mm across. Characteristically they are thick and angular. Samples N269 and N271 contain smaller, splinter-like fragments of flint. The clay matrix is anisotropic and contains abundant quartz grains which range in size from 0.08 mm up to 0.25 mm across. There is much iron staining in the fabric resulting from ferrous material in the clay (Fig 9.13: I). Air pockets and a slightly laminar structure betray poor clay preparation.

Many sites in central–southern England have broadly comparable fabrics, although no identical matches could be located among the samples available for study. The specimen of Kimmeridge Clay from about 2.5 km west of Hambledon Hill (Fig 9.11) provides a very close match for the clays used in fabric group 7 (cf Fig 9.13: I and J).

Fabric group 8 – Sandy wares

Of all the fabric groups present, this one is probably the most variable. The clay matrix is anisotropic with a certain amount of iron staining present. It is impossible to determine how much of the quartz present is naturally in the clay and how much has been added. The density of quartz varies greatly between samples; N272 is almost barren of quartz while in N382 the density reaches perhaps 15% (Shevtsov 1955).

In view of such variety in the amount of quartz present, it is difficult to find parallels for this fabric group. There are, however, many similarities with the flint-tempered wares of fabric group 7, and it is very likely that Kimmeridge Clays were also used for making fabric group 8 wares.

Burnt clay

A single sample of burnt clay from the inner Stepleton outwork was examined. The fabric was fine-grained and sandy. In thin section the anisotropic groundmass contained much fine quartz, occasionally in fragments up to 0.9 mm across, and iron specks. There were also occasional rounded pieces of calcareous material, ?chalk. The fabric does not match any of the pottery examined, but is very similar to the clay derived from the fissure on the Stepleton spur, and there can be little doubt that the daub derived from such superficial clay deposits somewhere on the hilltop.

9.2.3 Technology and production

Something of the great range in vessel quality will be evident from the descriptions of individual vessels given above (9.1). Variety also exists in the technology of production exhibited within the assemblage. In general, the clays selected for use were well prepared and thoroughly wedged, but there are exceptions, and the dried clay pellets and laminar structure of several samples designated fabric groups 6 and 7 show that for some classes of ware preparation was less thorough.

Insights into the way pots were made are given by the coil junction in sherd HH74 667 (Fig 9.14). In coil-pot construction long cylindrical ‘worms’ of clay are rolled out and then set one on top of another to build up the walls of the vessel. As each coil is added the joint is smoothed over with a wet hand or a smooth pebble (Hodges 1964, 26). The use of slightly different clays in the two adjacent coils represented in sherd HH74 667 has been described above, and provides a useful insight into the range of clays available to an

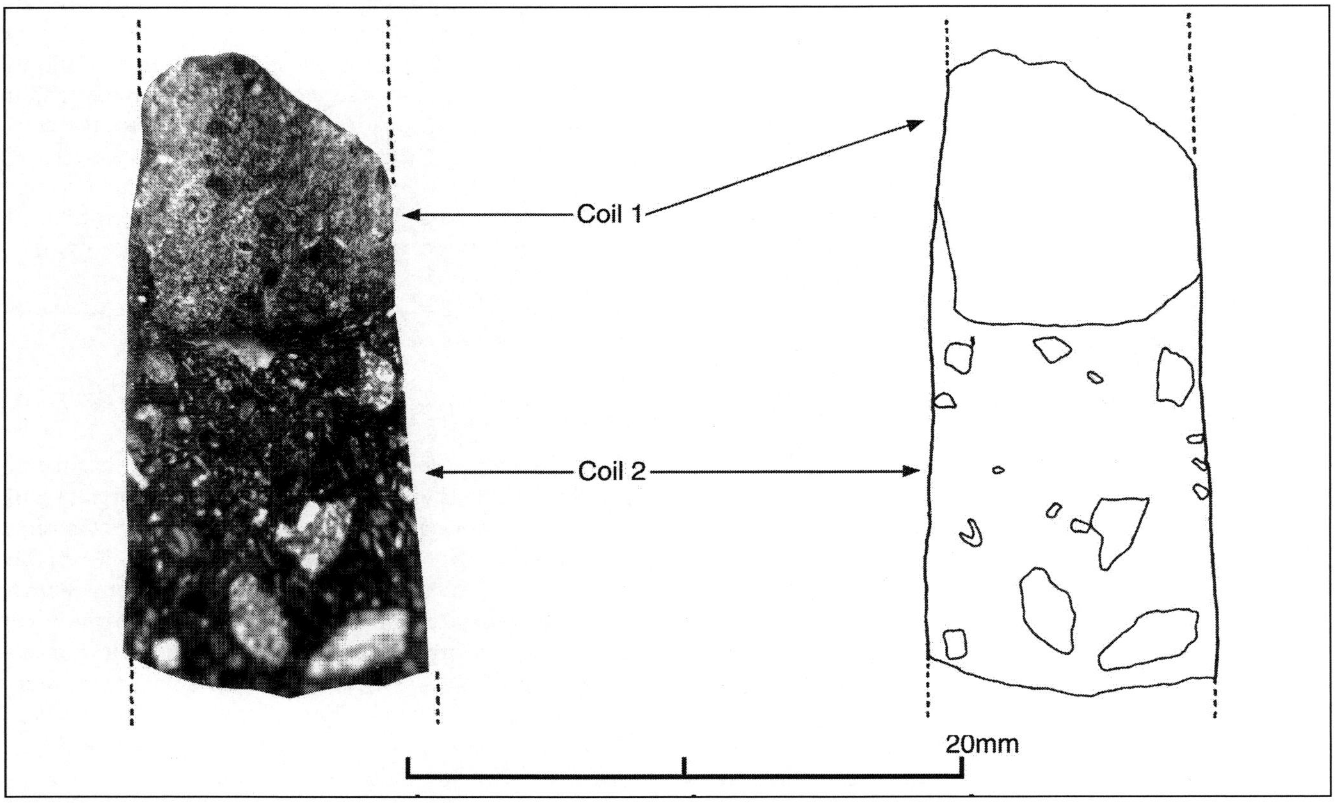

Fig 9.14 Photomicrograph and interpretative drawing of the polished face of sherd HH74 667 showing a coil junction and the contrasting fabrics used for each coil.

individual potter. The technique of coil-building has been observed in other studies of Neolithic pottery (eg Smith 1965, 47; Lynch 1975, 24), and it seems to have been the usual method adopted by Neolithic potters.

Assessing firing temperature is always difficult with prehistoric pottery, and can really only be gauged by the condition of the minerals and clasts in the fabric. Many of the fabrics discussed here retain calcareous inclusions, and this would suggest that temperatures in excess of *c* 750° C were not achieved. Firing atmosphere varied not only between fabrics, but also between vessels of a single fabric group and, sometimes, even over the surface of individual vessels. Only the gabbroic wares (fabric group 1) show consistent firing. Some sherds have reduced inner faces and oxidised outer surfaces, indicating that the pots were either inverted or stacked one inside another during firing. Other sherds are fired the same on both faces, indicating widespread atmospheric conditions during firing. A bonfire or simple clamp kiln, which would leave no trace in the archaeological record, was probably used for firing the vessels represented in the Hambledon Hill assemblage.

9.2.4 Discussion

The fabric composition of the ceramic assemblage from Hambledon Hill is clearly extremely complex. Its overall characteristics accrued over a long period of time, and undoubtedly result from a wide range of activities. Analysis is made difficult by the problems of assigning precise origins to sedimentary rock and clay outcrops, thus making full appraisal of the sources exploited almost impossible. Notwithstanding these difficulties, a number of general points about the assemblage can be made.

A considerable number of separate sources provided clay or vessels for use on Hambledon Hill. The gabbroic wares represent the most clear-cut examples of imported wares, but at least some of the fabrics containing Jurassic limestone inclusions probably travelled a considerable distance to the site. In contrast, fabric groups 7 and 8 almost certainly derive from clays available within a few kilometres of the hilltop and other fabrics may also represent local sources. Almost all the pottery is from areas to the west of Hambledon Hill.

Early and middle Neolithic pottery assemblages frequently display a wide range of fabrics, as at Windmill Hill, Wiltshire (Smith 1965) or the Peak, Gloucestershire (Darvill in prep), but the Hambledon Hill assemblage is the first such group where it is possible to examine intra-site variation. The distribution of fabric groups is described above (Smith, 9.1). There is little evidence for correlations between form and fabric which might imply functional partitioning of the assemblage, although the types of tempering used may have constrained the use of some fabrics. Cooking pots, for example, require resistance to thermal shock and the ability to withstand rapid changes in temperature, whereas containers intended for cooling liquids would need just the right degree of porosity to allow slow evaporation through the vessel walls.

Likewise, there is only limited correlation between fabric and the quality of product. At the fine-ware end of the scale lie the gabbroic wares, while at the opposite extreme lie fabric group 6 wares, which tend to be roughly finished and irregular in shape. In between lie vessels of all qualities made in all fabrics. Cups (diameter 60–120 mm) are found in fabric groups 2–8; open bowls in fabric groups 2–4 and 6–7; carinated bowls in fabric groups 2–3 and 6–7; and less clearly differentiated forms in all fabrics. It is noticeable that half of the fabric group 4 and fabric group 8 vessels are cups. Decoration was applied indifferently to both finely and roughly finished vessels of all sizes, and the same range of decorative techniques is found on vessels of fabric groups 2–3 and 5–8. No heavy-duty storage category vessels can be isolated on the criteria of size, shape or distinctive fabric. Overall, the assemblage comprises small- to medium-sized vessels, and most fabrics are used for the manufacture of the entire range of vessel forms and sizes

Only two fabric groups from Hambledon Hill can be matched by wares from other middle Neolithic sites in Wessex and the south-west of England. These are the gabbroic wares (fabric group 1) and the Jurassic rock-tempered wares (fabric group 2). Together these wares account for over 22% of the pottery from the main enclosure but only about 10% from the Stepleton enclosure. It is possible that the production and distribution of these two classes of pottery was governed by mechanisms distinct from those determining the circulation of other wares. Establishing exactly what processes were involved, however, is a matter for future research.

9.3 Later prehistoric pottery from the hillfort

Lisa Brown

A total of 3217 sherds deriving from 22 contexts was examined and sorted by fabric type (Table 9.15). Examination was undertaken with the aid of a 10× hand lens with the occasional aid of a 20× binocular microscope. A notable feature of this assemblage was the small sherd size and the high degree of abrasion exhibited by the majority of sherds. For this reason, specific identification of vessel forms was often impossible, although rim, basal and decorated sherds were individually quantified.

The following fabric categories were identified:

A. Fine/medium sand

Fine/medium quartz common to abundant up to 0.5 mm, usually well sorted. May have rare inclusions of powdery reddish haematite.

Table 9.15 The hillfort: fabric quantification

Fabric	*A*	*B*	*C*	*D*	*E*	*F*	*G*
Sherds	639	112	1131	891	193	146	105
% total	19.9	3.5	35.2	27.7	6.0	4.5	3.3

B. Large sand

Dominant temper is coarse quartz sand, grains ranging in size from 0.5–1.0 mm. May also contain rare additional inclusions of flint, limestone, quartzite. Category includes Wareham–Poole Harbour fabrics.

C. Flint

C(1) Finely sanded clay containing rare to common quantities of grey and white flint, often calcined, usually below 2.0 mm. Surfaces or whole sherd often oxidised.
C(2) Smooth or lightly sanded clay containing common to abundant ill-assorted fragments of white, grey or reddish non-calcined flint pieces up to 3.0–4.0 mm. May contain additional rare inclusions of haematite and small rounded pellets (unidentified) below 2.0 mm. A much more coarsely tempered and finished fabric than C(1).

D. Oolitic Limestone

Smooth clay or finely sanded paste containing oolites and occasional plates of limestone in sparse to abundant quantities. Other inclusions rare.

E. Shell/fossil shell/limestone/calcite

Smooth or lightly sanded clay containing all or some of the tempers listed above, generally in rare to moderate quantities. The grade of the temper is often fairly coarse and the finish of the vessels is crude.

F. Coarse sand and grit

A coarse textured fabric containing a combination of quartz grains 0.5–1.0 mm and smooth, perhaps water rolled, non-quartz particles 1.0 mm+ in size.

G. Organic temper (briquetage?)

Soapy or finely sanded vesicular fabric. Vesicules indicate original temper of grass, straw or chaff. It is likely most examples are briquetage but the sherds are too fragmentary and abraded for secure identification.

The fabric range was wide, the most common fabric types being flint-tempered and oolitic limestone-tempered wares. Most of the fabrics were likely to have a relatively local source. Calcareous fabric groups D and E probably derived from the Jurassic Ridge and resemble varieties recovered from Maiden Castle (L Brown 1991). The flint-tempered fabrics may have had their source in the Clay-with-Flints capping of the chalk downlands of the region. The sand-tempered wares were more difficult to source, and may have derived from a small variety of local and perhaps non-local sources. Considering the condition of the assemblage and the difficulties of linking fabric to vessel typology, no petrological analysis was undertaken. Among the sand-tempered group, however, 18 sherds were recognised as clear examples of Wareham–Poole Harbour ware. All examples were recovered from contexts relating to the occupation of the hut and all are heavily abraded and of unidentifiable form. Considering the character of the associated ceramics, it is likely that the Poole Harbour ware fragments represent vessels of early Iron Age date rather than later Durotrigian wares. The exploitation of this clay/sand source in the early Iron Age has been demonstrated at Hengistbury Head – fabric H19 (Brown 1987), Rope Lake Hole (Davies 1986) and Maiden Castle. A single sherd from layer 1 of the 'extension' (ie the topsoil) does, however, resemble the post-conquest Black Burnished Ware I type and may indicate a limited Roman presence on the site.

The majority of sherds were classifiable by fabric type only, but rim, basal and decorated sherds were individually recorded. These constituted only a small proportion of the total with rim sherds numbering 240 (7.5% of the assemblage) and basal sherds numbering 119 (3.7%). Most of these could not be assigned to a specific vessel form owing to their small size and poor condition. Complete profiles were absent within the assemblage, and even the occurrence of shoulder regions extant with rims is uncommon. Despite this shortcoming, the combined evidence allows the proposal of a typology and chronology which is reasonably clear and is consistent with several other assemblages within the general region.

Most classifiable sherds belonged to flared-rim tripartite bowls and situlate jars with upright rims. Surviving shoulder profiles of the bowls appeared to be rounded rather than sharply angled and jars were, on the whole, slack-shouldered. Five lug or handle fragments were identified, one in oolitic ware and four in flint-tempered ware. Decoration of any type was uncommon, although a few sherds exhibited a fingertip/nail-impressed design on rim tops and shoulders or, less commonly, slash marks. The occupation layer associated with the hut floor produced a possible fragment of a furrowed bowl (P190) and the double groove below the neck of P188 resembles the decoration on a vessel from an early Iron Age group from Corfe Mullen (Calkin 1965). Thirty-five red-finished sherds were identified, including a small number which preserved traces of genuine haematite slip. More commonly, the red finish had been achieved by the use of burnishing and firing techniques which bring to the surface of the vessel traces of haematite present within the fabric. All red-finished vessels from Hambledon were flared-rim bowls.

The Hambledon Hill assemblage incorporates characteristics of a number of other ceramic groups from the western sector of the Wessex area.

Hambledon Hill's near neighbour, Hod Hill, clearly contained an early Iron Age component within its ceramic assemblage, but most relevant sherds are ill-provenanced within an area of excavation designed primarily to assess the Roman occupation of the site (Richmond 1968). Contexts assigned to period I at Gussage All Saints (Wainwright 1979b) produced a similar range of vessel forms, including a single furrowed bowl, with an equally diverse fabric range. In contrast to Hambledon Hill, however, oolitic limestone-tempered ware was represented by a mere four sherds at Gussage, despite the relative proximity of the two sites. The bipartite bowl form which is characteristic of the period 1 assemblage from Rope Lake Hole on Purbeck, Kimmeridge II (Davies 1936), and is a minor component of the Hengistbury Head assemblage (Cunliffe 1987) is apparently absent at Hambledon, indicating that a date in the earliest Iron Age (eighth–seventh century) is not appropriate for this assemblage. The Hambledon assemblage correlates best with period II at Eldon's Seat (Cunliffe and Phillipson 1968), period 2 at Rope Lake Hole (when flared-rim tripartite bowls become common) and site D at Chalbury Camp (Whitley 1943). The 1985–6 excavations at Maiden Castle produced little pottery for the corresponding period, phase 5, but this small group, taken together with the much larger early Iron Age assemblage from Wheeler's excavations (Wheeler 1943) compares well with the Hambledon assemblage, particularly in the incidence of slack-shouldered jars and the relatively high proportion of oolite-tempered ware.

No middle or late Iron Age pottery was positively identified within the assemblage and, despite the limited scope of the Hambledon Hill excavation, the early Iron Age character of the ceramic assemblage seems consistent with a sixth–fifth-century date, at least for the occupation layer associated with the hut and the features cut into the adjacent chalk bank, the deposits from which the majority of sherds were recovered. The date of 770–400 cal BC (2450±35 BP; OxA-7776) for a bone fragment from the ditch underlying the hut terrace (see Ch 4) combines with the stratigraphy (Fig 3.152) to suggest that the ditch may have been allowed to infill relatively quickly.

Catalogue of illustrated sherds

P181. Flared-rim bowl with haematite slip. Fabric C. Context: Extension to cutting – Layer 1 HH86 115.

P182. Flared-rim bowl, surface heavily abraded. Fabric D. Context: Turf – Layer 1. HH86 9.

P183. Flared-rim bowl, roughly smoothed surface. Fabric C1. Context: Turf – Layer 1. HH86 9.

P184. Flared-rim bowl, roughly smoothed surface. Fabric C1. Context: occupation layer (extension). HH86 218.

P185. Flared-rim bowl, partial burnish. Fabric D. Red-finish. Context: occupation layer (extension). HH86 218.

P186. Flared-rim tripartite bowl, partial burnish. Fabric D. Context: occupation layer, layer 3 (central baulk). HH86 68.

P187. Bowl fragment with burnished chevron decoration on shoulder. Burnished surface. Fabric C1. Context: occupation layer, layer 3 (central baulk). HH86 68.

P188. Bowl with double groove below neck. Fabric C1. High burnish and oxidised but not red finished. Context: occupation layer, south sector. HH86 53.

P189. Bowl fragment with traces of red haematite slip. Fabric E. Context: occupation layer, south sector. HH86 53.

P190. Fragment of a furrowed ?bowl with highly burnished, oxidised surface. Fabric C1. Context: occupation layer, south sector. HH86 31.

P191. Small jar or bowl, roughly finished. Fabric C2. Context: occupation layer, south sector. HH86 31.

P192. Small jar, coarse surface. Fabric C2 with traces of powdery red slip or coat. Context: occupation layer, south sector. HH86 31.

P193. Small jar, coarse finish. Fabric C2. Context: occupation layer, south sector. HH86 53.

P194. Small jar, roughly smoothed surface. Fabric B. Context: hut surface (clearing). HH86 44.

P195. Jar rim, unfinished surface. Fabric A. Context: hut surface (clearing). HH86 44.

P196. Jar rim, roughly smoothed surface. Fabric D. Context: extension overlying second occupation layer. HH86 213.

P197. Large jar rim, roughly smoothed surface. Fabric D. Context: extension to cutting – Layer 1. HH86 115.

P198. Jar rim, roughly smoothed surface. Fabric D. Context: occupation layer, north side. HH86 60.

P199. Jar rim, roughly smoothed surface. Fabric C2. Context: occupation layer (extension). HH86 218. HH86 60.

P200. Jar rim bearing trace of red haematite paste or slip. Smoothed interior. Fabric D. Context: hut surface (clearing). HH86 44.

P201. Jar rim, roughly smoothed surface. Fabric A. Context: occupation layer, south sector. HH86 53.

P202. Straight-sided jar (proto-saucepan pot form), roughly smoothed surface. Fabric C1. Context: hut surface (clearing). HH86 44.

P203. Shoulder fragment with fingernail-impressed decoration, roughly smoothed surface. Fabric E. Context: occupation layer (extension). HH86 218.

P204. Base of small jar, unfinished surface. Fabric F. Context: hut surface (clearing). HH86 44.

P205. Base of large jar, unfinished surface. Fabric C2. Context: occupation layer, layer 3 (central baulk. HH86 68.

P206. Flared-rim bowl, abraded surface. Fabric D. Context: East strip, layer 2. HH86 111.

P207. Flared-rim bowl with smoothed, oxidised surface, but not red finished. Fabric C1. Context: trench extension, layer 2. HH86 160.

P208. Flared-rim bowl, unfinished surface. Fabric C2. Context: trench extension, layer 2. HH86 160.

P209. Small jar with upright rim. Abraded, coarsely finished surface. Fabric D. Context: trench extension, layer 2. HH86 160.

P210. Basal sherd with three perforations produced as modifications to fired vessel. Roughly smoothed surface. Fabric C2. Context: trench extension, layer2. HH86 160.

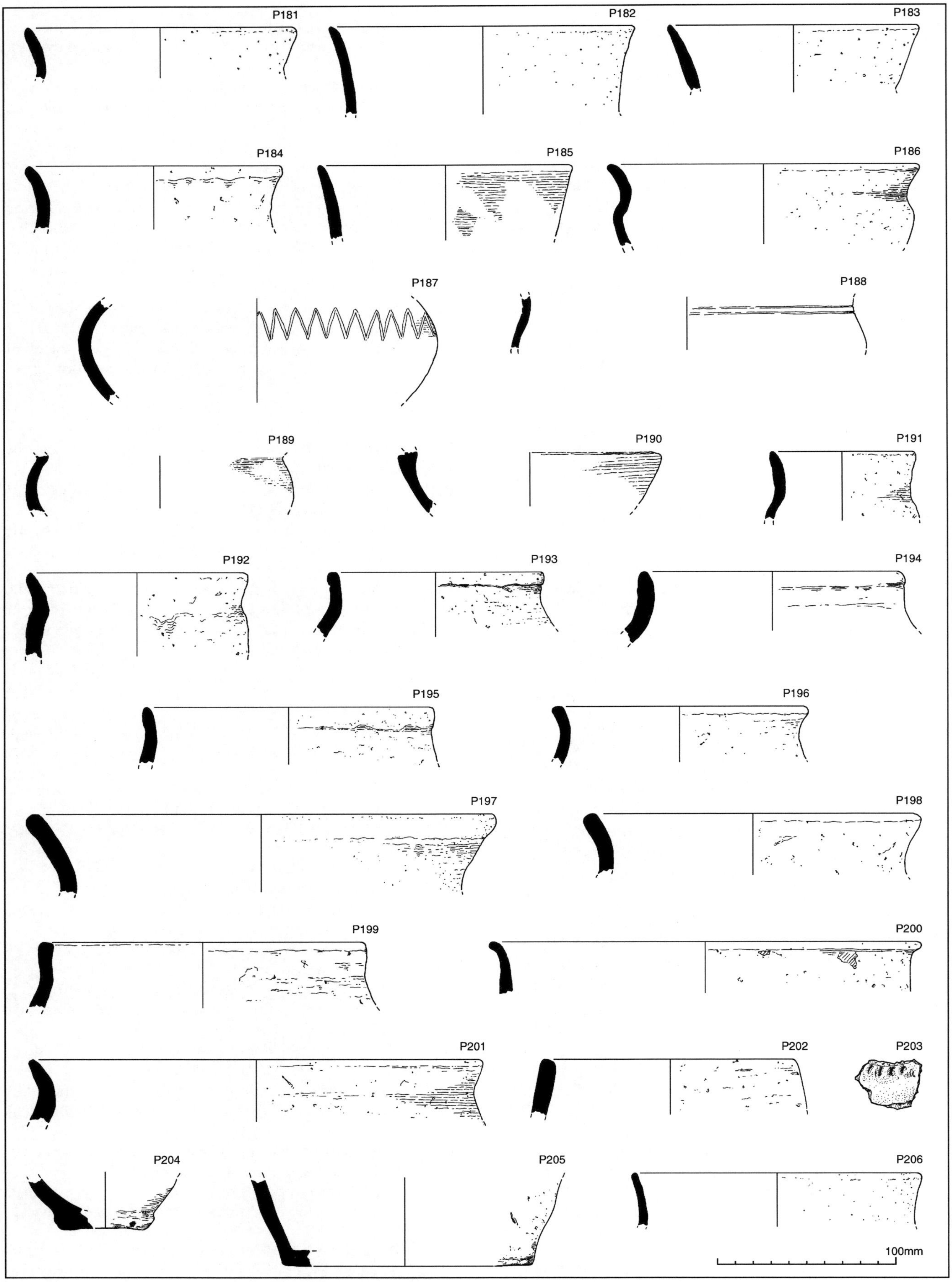

Fig 9.15 Iron Age pottery from the hillfort. Scale 1:3

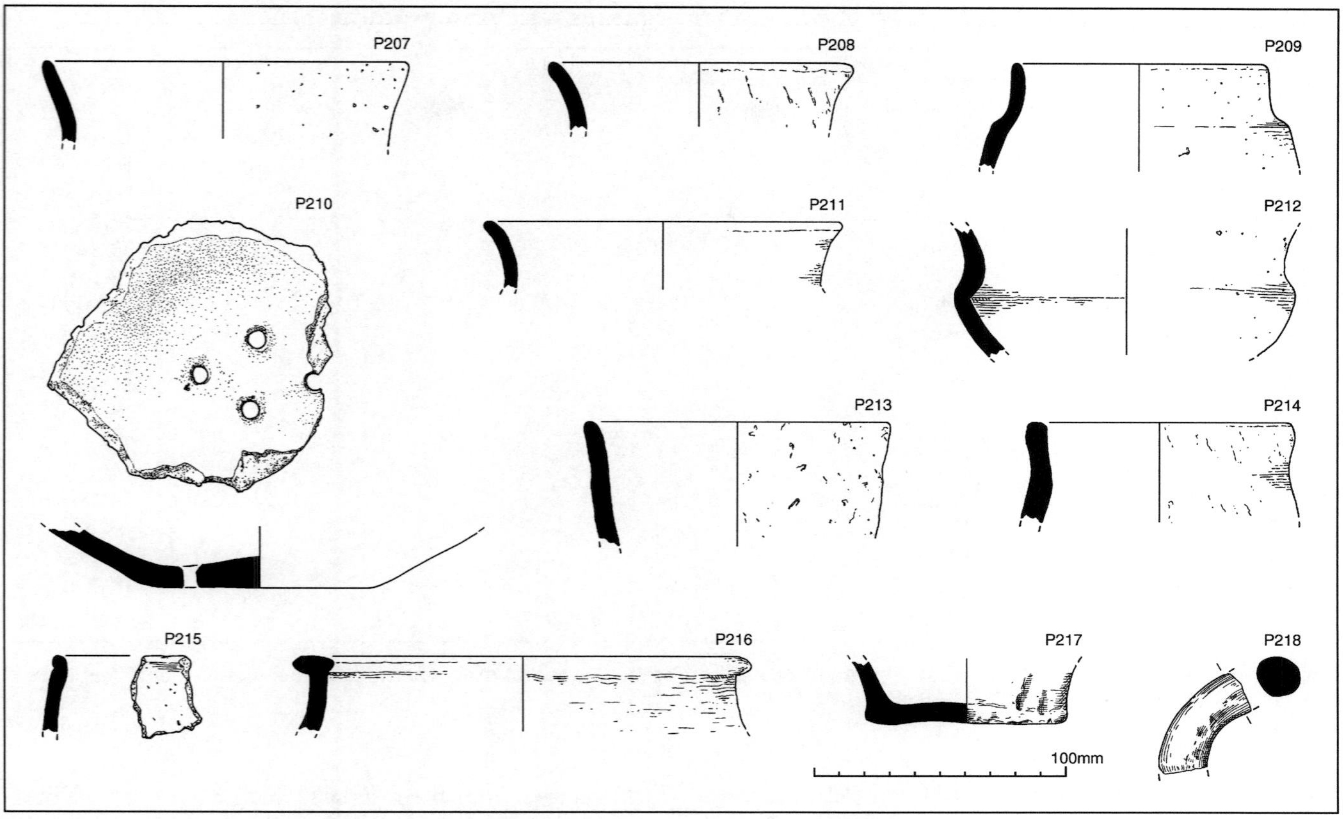

Fig 9.16 Iron Age pottery from the hillfort. Scale 1:3

P211. Flared-rim bowl, smoothed surface with red haematite slip. Fabric D. Context: trench extension, layer 3. HH86 260.

P212. Tripartite bowl fragment, partially burnished, with traces of red haematite slip. Fabric C2. Context: trench extension, layer 3. HH86 260.

P213. Straight-sided ?jar, coarse fabric and finish. Fabric A. Context: trench extension, layer 3. HH86 260.

P214. Small jar with upright rim, streaky, discontinuous burnish. Fabric A. Context: trench extension, layer 3. HH86 260.

P215. Straight-sided ?jar, smoothed surface. Fabric C1. Context: trench extension, layer 3. HH86 260.

P216. Jar with expanded rim, partial burnish. Fabric D. Context: trench extension, layer 3. HH86 260.

P217. Basal fragment of small jar, very coarse finish. Fabric C2. Context: trench extension, layer 3. HH86 260.

P218. Round section handle fragment, abraded surface, oxidised. Fabric C1. Context: trench extension, layer 3. HH86 260.

9.4 Fired clay

Alistair Barclay

9.4.1 Introduction

The assemblage consists of 564 fragments (4641 g) of fired clay. It includes structural clay, loomweights, a crucible fragment and a cup-shaped object. Most of the structural clay has been fired and is thought to derive from the collapsed Neolithic rampart, while the crucible and loomweight fragments belong to the later Iron Age occupation. Fired clay is a good indicator of domestic occupation and a wide range of activities. The loomweights provide direct evidence for textile production and the structural clay provides indirect evidence for ovens built from wattle and clay, and for burnt daub walls, no doubt derived from demolished structures.

Methodology

A quantification of fragments by number and weight is given in Table 9.16. Five fabrics were identified and are listed below. The fired clay was examined for evidence of wattle or other impressions, possible objects and structural pieces.

Fabrics

1 Natural clay with no added inclusions. Rare (<1%) angular flint.

2 Natural clay which is slightly sandy in texture with no added inclusions.

3 Hard fabric with sparse (<7%) medium (1–3 mm) angular flint inclusions.

4 Soft fabric with common (<15%) voids from burnt-out organic matter and sparse (<7%) coarse (over 3 mm) flint inclusions.

5 Clay with coarse burnt-out organic matter (stems).

Table 9.16 Quantification of all fired clay (number of pieces/weight in grammes)

Context group	*Amorphous clay fragments*	*Potting clay*	*Structural clay*	*Objects*			*Totals*
				Misc	*Crucible*	*Loomweight*	
Main causewayed enclosure	1/2 g						1/2 g
Inner east cross dyke				1/2 g			1/2 g
Discrete features in central area	1/3 g	3/32 g					4/35 g
Shroton spur outwork	31/170 g		32/113 g				63/283 g
Stepleton enclosure ditch	9/11 g						8/11 g
Inner Stepleton outwork	94/152 g		168/3427 g	1/2 g	1/2 g		263/3564 g
Discrete features on Stepleton spur	114/208 g		12/22 g				126/ 230 g
Stepleton spur miscellaneous and unstratified	43/59 g						43/59 g
Outer Hanford outwork	2/3 g						2/3 g
Hanford spur, pit F864	9/3 g						9/3 g
Hillfort	2/23 g			*		32/366 g	34/389 g
Coombe Bottom	2/4 g						2/4 g
Stepleton Lynchet	6/13 g						6/13 g
Everley Water Meadow	1/24 g						1/24 g
Totals	314/675 g	3/32 g	212/3562 g	2/4 g	1/2 g	32/366 g	564/4641 g

* A fragmentary spindle whorl and what appears to be a fired clay bead were missing when this report was written. There are photographs of both

Most structural clay is in fabrics 1 and 2. Fabric 1 may be a less sandy version of fabric 2 and both may derive from the same source. A sample of fabric 2 was thin-sectioned and compared with a sample taken from the fissure outcrop on the Stepleton spur by Timothy Darvill, who concluded that the sample derived from this or a similar deposit of superficial clay (9.2). Fabrics 3 and 4 both contain angular flint inclusions, and it is suggested that they may represent potting clay. The organic-tempered fabric 5 is rare and may not be of Neolithic date.

9.4.2 Description

Amorphous clay fragments including potting clay

Most of the fired clay examined can be described as amorphous, with no visible surfaces or diagnostic features. The majority of this material consists of oxidised reddish-brown lumps. It may, however, derive from a variety of sources, including burnt daub and hearths, and as such is an indirect indicator of domestic occupation. Nearly all of this material was in fabrics 1–2 with the exception of a small number of fragments in the flint-tempered fabrics 2–3. These pieces were in some cases too large to be considered as very worn pottery sherds and it is suggested that they represent potting clay of Neolithic date.

Structural clay

Most of the structural clay was recorded from the 1979 excavations on the Stepleton spur, and the majority of this comes from the rampart which had collapsed into segment 6 of the inner outwork ditch (Tables 9.17–18).

A few fragments with wattle impressions were noted from various contexts and these are listed in Table 9.18. One fragment (HH76 1414) has both vertical sail and horizontal rod impressions, while a number of fragments (HH76 1509, ST78 244, ST79 297 and 1490, ST81 980) have less diagnostic wattle impressions. HH76 1414 was the only piece to have both vertical sail and horizontal rod impressions and came from a superficial layer over the protected chalk of the Shroton outwork. The impressions on HH76 1509 were more ambiguous, and they could represent finger-moulding rather than actual wattle impressions. The early Neolithic pit 1A F228 contained 12 fragments (ST78 1305) of fired clay in fabric 1, including one with a concave surface possibly made by a wattle. In addition three fragments (ST78 244) one of which had a single wattle impression, were recovered from a shallow depression (1A F5, possibly a pit base) in the same area. A single fragment (ST81 980) in fabric 2 had two wattle impressions. It was recovered from phase VI deposits in segment 14 of the Stepleton enclosure which also contained much Bowl pottery. A further fragment (ST79 297) was recovered from tertiary fills of the inner outwork that contained a range of pottery, including Romano-British.

The highest concentration of fired clay was in segment 6 of the inner Stepleton outwork, where the ditch cut through a localised natural outcrop of Clay-with-Flints. Here the rampart was thought to have been constructed out of clay dug from the ditch, and much of the fired clay is assumed to have derived from the collapse of the bank (Fig 3.99, Pls VIII–IX). Over 3.3 kg of fired,

Table 9.17 Fired clay from the inner Stepleton outwork by segment and phase (number of pieces/weight in grammes)

Phase		*Segment* *4.2*	*5*	*6*	*8*	*5 or 6*
I	Amorphous clay fragments			29/391 g		
	Structural clay			115/2946 g		
III	Amorphous clay fragments			46/107 g		
V	Amorphous clay fragments			3/8 g		
VII/a	Amorphous clay fragments		1/1 g	14/22 g		
VIII/a	Amorphous clay fragments	2/12 g	1/1 g	55/78 g	4/14 g	6/14 g
	Structural clay			1/19 g		
	Crucible		1/2 g			
	Miscellaneous object		1/2 g			
Upper levels and unstratified	Amorphous clay fragments					9/24 g

Table 9.18 Structural clay (number of pieces/weight in grammes)

Context	*Find*	*Number/ weight*	*Fabric*	*Comment*
Main causewayed enclosure, segment 17, L9A, phase IV	HH76 1509	6/24 g	1	Impressions probably from wattles but could be from finger-moulding
Shroton outwork, site M, bank area, L2	HH76 1414	32/113 g	1	With sail and rod impressions
Stepleton enclosure, segment 14, U7, L2, phase VI	ST81 980	1/24 g	2	Has two wattle impressions
Inner Stepleton outwork segment 6, cutting 1, L4A (phase I)	ST79 1557	27/495 g	1	As above. One fragment has an impression from a split oak timber
Inner Stepleton outwork segment 6, cutting 1, L4A (phase I)	ST79 1585	28/390 g	1	Some fragments have one lumpy surface
Inner Stepleton outwork segment 6, cutting 1, L4A (phase I)	ST79 1609	64/1060 g	1	Some fragments have one lumpy surface. There is a single ?wood impressions, but this is less convincing than ST79 1557
Inner Stepleton outwork segment 6, cutting 1, L4A (phase I)	ST79 1896	24/1391 g	1	Some fragments have one lumpy surface. Some fragments are baked rather than fired, while others (some with surfaces) are unfired
Inner Stepleton outwork segment 5, cutting 11, L2 (phase VIII/a)	ST79 297	1/2 g	1	This fragment has either a wattle impression or a broken perforation
Inner Stepleton outwork segment 6, cutting 1, L1A (phase VIII/a)	ST79 1490	1/19 g	1	Impression possibly made from the end of a wattle
Possible feature 1A F5	ST78 244	3/8 g	2	Includes one fragment with wattle impression
Early Neolithic pit 1A F288	ST78 1305	12/22 g	1	Possible fired daub fragment with one concave edge

baked and unfired clay were recovered from this segment. No fragments with wattle marks were identified, although a number of pieces retained their original surfaces and two had impressions made from split timber (ST79 1557 and 1609). The fragment from ST79 1557, although small in size, has fresh breaks indicating that it was once part of a larger fragment. One impression can be clearly identified as that of a radially split piece of oak (Dr Mark Robinson, pers comm; Fig 9.17). Such an impression could have been made if the plastic clay was pressed against a split oak timber.

Cup-like disc

A small and incomplete disc of clay (HH75 1075) in fabric 1 has been pinched into a cup and fired. This object was recovered from a layer of the inner east cross-dyke that contained much Beaker pottery. The disc is similar in manufacture to the bowl end of some earlier Neolithic clay spoons, but much smaller in size (Anon 1934, 423). Piggott notes that the spoons from Glenluce and the Sun Hole, Mendip, were found alongside Beaker material (1954, 75).

Fig 9.17 Impression of radially split oak on fired clay fragment ST79 1557 from the inner Stepleton outwork. Scale in centimetres

Crucible fragment

The phase VIII/a fill of segment 5 of the inner Stepleton outwork contained a single crucible fragment (ST79 500) weighing 2 g. The same deposit contained pottery of mixed date that included Romano-British. The sherd contains no readily identifiable inclusions, is 9 mm thick and has a vitrified black glassy interior surface. It is probably no earlier than late Iron Age in date (Dr Peter Northover, pers comm).

Loomweight fragments

Two contexts in the hillfort excavations contained small fragments (HH86 188 and 266) of probably triangular loomweights of Iron Age date. The largest fragment is from the corner of a triangular loomweight with a broken perforation.

Spindle whorl

A fragmentary clay spindle whorl (HH86 25) was found during the hillfort excavations. It is missing (2003) and known only from a photograph.

Bead?

A small perforated clay object, perhaps a bead (HH86 158), also from the hillfort excavation, is similarly missing.

9.4.3 The distribution of fired clay across the site

The main causewayed enclosure ditch

Segments 3 and 17 of the main causewayed enclosure ditch produced single finds of fired clay. The fragment (HH74 712) from a phase VI deposit in segment 3 was small and amorphous, while the six fragments (HH76 1509) from a phase IV deposit in segment 17 carried impressions made either by wattles or by finger moulding.

The inner east cross dyke

The only find of fired clay from the inner east cross dyke was a cup-like disc (HH75 1075).

Features in the central area

Four features within the main causewayed enclosure contained fired clay. Small quantities of probable potting clay were recovered from pits B F56 and B F57, while pit N F11 contained one or two tiny fragments of amorphous fired clay, as did probably recent quarry B F1A, which cut a treethrow hole containing Neolithic and Beaker material.

The Shroton spur outwork

Seventy-three fragments (168 g) of fired clay were recovered, almost all from site M, where nine tiny crumbs (4 g) were recovered from the fill of posthole 7, part of the gate structure (Fig 3.75). A further 128 fragments came from superficial contexts in the bank area, including a fragment of daub with sail and rod impressions. The remaining 16 fragments came from the phase VIII/a fills of the ditch.

The Stepleton enclosure

Phase VI produced two fragments of fired clay, one of which is an amorphous crumb (ST 81 252). The other (ST81 980) is a fragment of structural clay with two wattle impressions. Phase VIII/a, the tertiary fills, produced only small amorphous fragments of fired clay (ST80 142, 228, 247).

The inner Stepleton outwork

Almost all the fired clay came from cutting 1 in segment 6 (Table 9.17). The burnt layers on and near the base of the ditch contained 146 fragments (*c* 3.4 kg) of burnt and unburnt clay in fabric 1. A number of these fragments have lumpy surfaces, while a further two fragments have impressions of split oak timbers. The phase VIII/a fills in segment 5 contained a crucible fragment of probable late Iron Age date.

Discrete features on the Stepleton spur

Most of the fired clay (154 pieces/251 g) comprised amorphous fragments. Notable concentrations occurred in pits 1A F206, F228 and F350, all on the clay-filled fissure. Probable daub fragments were recorded from early Neolithic pit 1A F228 and from possibly early Neolithic pit 1A F5.

The Hillfort

Loomweight fragments and two fragments of amorphous fired clay were recovered from the area of Iron Age occupation excavated in 1986. The loomweight fragments are relatively small and include pieces with one or more flat surfaces, corners and at least one perforation.

9.4.4 Discussion

Little structural clay has been recorded from earlier Neolithic sites, and it is notably absent from other causewayed enclosures (Bradley 1994, appendix 2). It is difficult to judge whether this general absence really indicates a lack of the use of clay for daub walls and other less substantial structures or, in fact, whether it reflects the general absence of domestic structures. Certainly the presence of fired clay on sites of later prehistoric date (eg hillforts) often reflects the scale, range and nature of domestic settlement. At Hambledon the presence of at least a small quantity of fired clay in Neolithic contexts other than the collapsed, burnt inner Stepleton outwork bank, may be taken as an indicator of structures and more permanent occupation. Bamford notes possible potting clay of earlier Neolithic date from the Briar Hill causewayed enclosure, and a single fragment of structural clay, albeit from a Mortlake Ware-associated pit deposit (Bamford 1985, 118). At Hazleton North, Gloucestershire, a single piece of fired clay daub with a wattle impression was recorded from the pre-cairn midden deposit (Saville 1990c, 181). At Padholme Road, Fengate, Cambridgeshire, 143 g of burnt daub was recorded from the wall slots of a probable Neolithic house (Pryor 1974, 8).

10 Lithics

10.1 Stone

10.1.1 Stone axes

The late Isobel Smith

Petrological information about the stone axes and axe fragments, numbered Sl–S21 for the purpose of this report, is based on the results of microscopic examination of thin sections removed from each specimen. The individual identifications, provided by the Implement Petrology Survey of the South-West, the corresponding county survey numbers, and site contexts will be found in the catalogue below and are summarised in Table 10.2. R V Davis was responsible for 17 identifications; the other four were undertaken by W Campbell Smith (S3), Hilary Howard (S20, S21) and Fiona Roe (S19).

The assemblage consists of six relatively complete implements (five axes, one adze; Fig 10.1) and 15 fragments, representing altogether 17 tools made of 14 varieties of rock. Eight varieties are represented by single items attributable to three petrological groups (IV, VI, VIII) and to five ungrouped rocks: nephrite (S3), jadeite (S11), amphibolite (S21), banded tuff, and siltstone. Two implements are made of greenstone 'similar to' and 'near' Group XVII (S6, S19). One axe, complete when found (S1), and a fragment from a second, belong to Group XVI. Parts of two axes made of rocks not recorded elsewhere on Hambledon Hill come from the south-west ditch of the long barrow. One is represented by two fragments of altered gabbro, S15 from phase I and S16 from phase III. The two pieces of group I rock come respectively from phase I (S14) and from the recent turf and topsoil preserved under bulldozed mound material (S17). The three parts of an axe of altered amphibolite (S4, S5, S10), another rock with a restricted distribution on the site, were found in phase III deposits in the opposed ends of segments 8 and 9 of the main enclosure ditch and in the phase V silts at the north end of segment 10. The two flakes of undifferentiated greenstone, one from a probable treethrow hole in the central area (S2), the other from the Stepleton spur (S20), are presumed to derive from two axes. Representation of axes within the two main sites is uneven: 14 from the central area, three from the Stepleton spur.

Among the axes ascribed to recognised petrological groups, five are of Cornish origin – Group I, Mount's Bay area, near Penzance (S14, S17); Group IV, Balstone Down, Callington (S8); and Group XVI, Camborne area (S1, S7). A further two are 'similar to' or 'near' the Group XVII rock from sources at St Austell and St Erth (S6, S19). One flake (S12) derives from a Group VI axe of Lake District origin and another (S13) is of Group VIII rock from south-west Wales (David and Williams 1995). A fragment made of banded tuff (S9) could have belonged to an axe carried from Wales or from the Charnwood Forest area of Leicestershire.

Hambledon Hill stands at the eastern limit of the effective distribution of axes of Groups IV and XVI (Clough and Cummins 1988, maps 5, 15), and at the south-western limit of the effective distribution of axes of Group VI (ibid, map 6). Group VIII axes are more thinly dispersed (ibid, map 8). The representation of the four groups on this site is therefore unremarkable. But the site also stands within the area of southern England in which Group I axes constitute the largest individual group (ibid, map 2), and it is here that, for the first time outside Cornwall, an axe of this group has been found stratified in an earlier Neolithic context (S14 from the primary silt in the west ditch of the long barrow).

The two axes of continental origin, S3 (nephrite) and S11 (jadeite), were recovered from ploughsoil, but there is no reason to dissociate them from the main period of Neolithic activity. In the list of eight nephrite axes from the British Isles compiled by Jones *et al* (1977, 293) S3 is the sole example found in a significant context. S11 also adds to the small number of jadeite axes with useful associations; these include an unstratified fragment from the earlier Neolithic site at High Peak, Sidmouth, Devon, loosely associated with the radiocarbon date of 4000–3100 cal BC (4810±150 BP; BM-214), and the splendid ceremonial axe found beside the Sweet Track in the Somerset Levels (Coles *et al* 1974), now with a tree-ring date of 3807–3806 BC (Coles and Coles 1990).

S11 was analysed in September 2007 as part of Projet Jade, an international research project focusing on Neolithic axeheads of jadeitite and other Alpine rocks. Non-destructive mineralogical analysis using spectroradiometry, undertaken by Dr Michel Errera, confirmed that the rock is indeed likely to have originated in the Italian Alps. Its precise composition differs slightly from the jadeitites used for numerous Neolithic axeheads, although it compares with a few artefacts from Italy. Its main constituent is probably jadeite and the rock may be a jadeitite from an unknown occurrence or an altered jadeite.

Catalogue of stone axes (Fig 10.1)

Note. Each entry includes the petrological survey county number (eg DO 133) and the find number (eg HH75 550), except for casual finds S3 and S21.

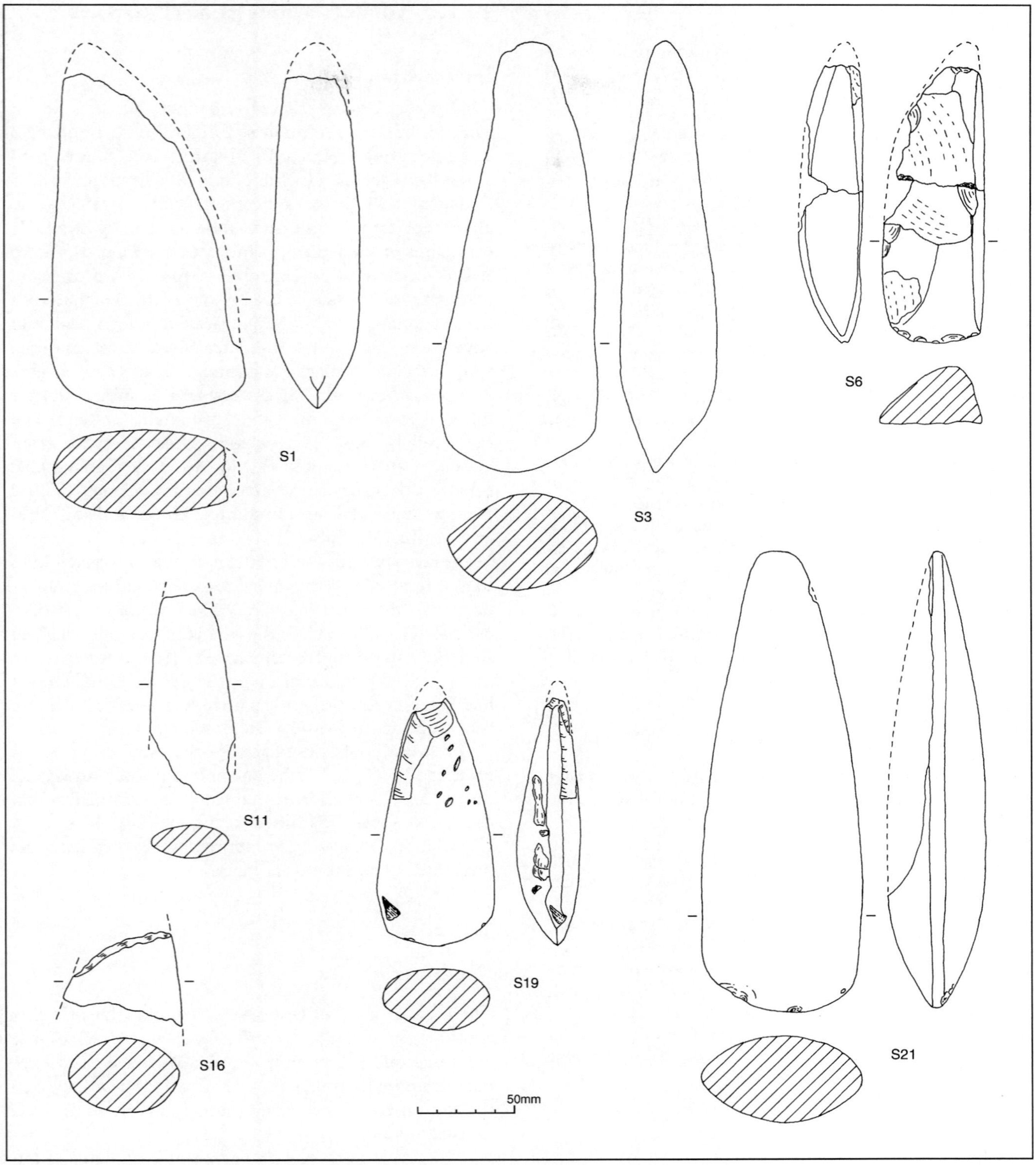

Fig 10.1 Stone axes. SI, Group XVI. S3, nephrite. S6, greenstone, similar to Group XVII. S11, jadeite. S16, altered gabbro. S19, greenstone, near Group XVII. S21, amphibolite. Particulars in catalogue. Scale 1:3

Main causewayed enclosure

S1. Axe: Group XVI. DO 133. HH75 550. Intact when uncovered (Figs 3.54–5), now partly disintegrated. Pit B F14, on surface of layer 4 together with the larger part of plain cup P58. Two gabbroic ware bowls (P1, P2) in layer 3, together with fragments of other vessels, including a decorated cup (P138).

S2. Small flake: Greenstone. DO 126. HH74 597. Top of A F2 (probably a treethrow hole, containing Neolithic pottery and struck flint and cut by Neolithic pit A F5)

S3. Axe: nephrite. DO 93. Ploughsoil, 1963, 'about 50 yards within the main enclosure ditch at SE'. Found and owned by Mr L E A Burd of Shroton. Drawing based on sketch on implement petrology record card.

Campbell Smith 1965, 31: no. 12b; Evens *et al* 1972, 270; Jones *et al* 1977, 293: no. 2.

S4. Disintegrating pieces, probably from butt of axe: altered amphibolite. DO 137. HH75 307. Main enclosure ditch, segment 8, layer 7, phase III. Probably from same axe as S5 and S10.

S5. Disintegrating fragments, possibly from a butt: altered amphibolite. DO 138. HH75 815. Main enclosure ditch, segment 9, layer 8, phase III. Probably from same axe as S4 and S10.

S6. Adze: greenstone, similar to Group XVII. DO 134. HH75 1440 + 1677. Main enclosure ditch, segment 10, layer 6B, phase VI. The two conjoining pieces were found *c* 0.50 m apart; all damage is due to impact. Butt and large portion of upper face missing.

S7. Fragment from cutting edge of large axe: Group XVI. DO 124. HH74 442. Main enclosure ditch, segment 3, layer 4, phase VI.

S8. Flake from face of large axe: Group IV. DO 125. HH74 1050. Main enclosure ditch, segment 4, layer 5, phase VI.

S9. Weathered fragment from middle of axe with rounded side: banded tuff. DO 143. HH76 923. Main enclosure ditch, segment 7, layer 4, phase VI.

S10. Fragment from middle of large axe: altered amphibolite. DO 136. HH75 2165. Main enclosure ditch, segment 10, layer 4, phase V. Probably from same axe as S4 and S5.

S11. Incomplete axe, severely weathered: jadeite. DO 135. HH75 950. Main enclosure ditch, segment 8, ploughsoil, phase VIII/g. Jones *et al* 1977, 290, 292: no. 104; pl 22.

East cross-dykes

S12. Small flake: Group VI. DO 140. HH75 1008. Inner east cross-dyke, segment 4, cutting IV, layer 2, phase VIII/d.

S13. Small flake: Group VIII. DO 139. HH75 1995. Outer east cross-dyke, segment 5, layer 4, phase VI.

Long Barrow

S14. Small fragment: Group I. DO 147. HH77 2228. LB3, SIII, layer 26, phase I. Probably from same axe as S17.

S15. Small flake: altered gabbro. DO 145. HH77 1984. LB3, SIII, layer 40, phase I. Probably from same axe as S16.

S16. Fragment from middle of axe with oval cross-section: altered gabbro. DO 144. HH77 2035. LB3, SIII, layer 21, phase III. Probably from same axe as S15.

S17. Small fragment from side of axe: Group I. DO 146. HH77 699. LB3, SII, layer 7, phase VIII/d. Probably from same axe as S14.

S18. Small flake: siltstone. DO 148. HH77 829. LB4, unstratified.

Stepleton Spur

S19. Axe: greenstone, near Group XVII. DO 162. ST78 2545. Stepleton enclosue, segment 23, ST1, at interface of layers 2 and 3, 'hard onto chalk at ditch edge', probably phase V. Intact except for small part of butt; some original flake scars unobliterated.

S20. Flake: greenstone. DO 149. ST79 1720. Inner outwork segment 5, C8S, layer 2B, phase VII/a.

S21. Axe: amphibolite. DO 160. Found 1981 in ploughsoil 30 m south-west of Stepleton enclosure. Property of Sturminster Newton High School. Cutting edge blunt and chipped, large flake missing from one face.

10.1.2 Worked stone other than axes

Fiona Roe

Introduction

This report describes over 400 finds, made from 12 varieties of stone, summarised in Tables 10.1 and 10.3 and selectively illustrated in Figure 10.2. The worked stone from secure Neolithic contexts amounts to 196 finds, of which 65 are recognisable artefacts, an altogether larger collection than is usually available from sites of the period. It includes 46 fragments from saddle querns or grain rubbers that retain signs of working, as well as 86 fragments of quern materials that no longer show working traces, although all would have been imported to the site. Most of the material from later and superficial contexts in the central area and on the Shroton, Stepleton, and Hanford spurs is likely to be of Neolithic date, a probability enhanced by the similar range and balance of stone types from Neolithic and other contexts in each area (Table 10.3). Small collections came from mainly Iron Age and Roman contexts on the hillfort spur and on sites around the hill (Table 10.1).

An unexpected result of the work was the recognition that at least two of the quern materials had been transported to the site from some distance, and were concentrated in different parts of the complex. Mendip Old Red Sandstone had been brought from some 40 km away and occurred mainly in the central area; Dorset heathstone came from a distance of at least 20 km and was found mainly on the Stepleton spur.

Four materials were used for the Neolithic querns: greensand, sarsen, heathstone and Old Red Sandstone. Since these are all reasonably coarse-grained rocks, they have been examined using a hand lens only. Calculations can only be approximate, owing to the fragmentary nature of the material.

Materials

Upper Greensand

The local greensand was extensively used for grinding equipment, accounting for around one-third of the Neolithic quern materials (Fig 10.3). It seems to have been marginally preferred over Old Red Sandstone in the central area, where it amounts to about 40% of the utilised stone.

The excavated greensand always contains glauconite, but is otherwise varied in character, reflecting the variations in lithology found in the district (Bristow *et al* 1995, 98). None of the upper greensand found on Hambledon Hill need have been transported further than 13 km or so, as useable stone outcrops in a band between Hambledon Hill itself and Shaftesbury (Bristow *et al* 1995, fig 2). The nearest occurrence of greensand is in fact just north of the hillfort (Bristow *et al* 1995, 105), where there are several pits at ST 844 134. Some of the greensand here is sandy and friable, and so was probably little used, though one Neolithic rubber (HH74 1166, from A F78) is made from this variety of stone. A hard, gritty greensand, containing a scattering of larger quartz grains, but only rare fossil shells, was often used, and this could have been obtained from the same area on the edge of Child Okeford, or from Shaftesbury, where similar greensand was seen in the Wilderness quarry at ST 866 225 (Osborne White 1923, 51). A harder and more cherty greensand containing fossil sponge spicules was used for a number of querns and rubbers, and similar stone was seen in a quarry south-west of Melbury at ST 875 201 (Bristow *et al* 1995, 102). This cherty greensand is probably the stone used for quern or rubber fragments excavated in 1960 in Bonney's trench L, described as glauconitic quartzite (Evens *et al* 1972, 273). One (DO 106) was in a phase VII/a pit in the inner east cross-dyke with Early-style Beaker pottery; several fragments, one of which was identified (DO 107), lay together at the tail of the inner east cross-dyke bank. A pebble-hammer of similar stone is also recorded as a surface find from the hill (DO 57, Evens *et al* 1972, 266).

Upper Greensand was used almost exclusively for querns and rubbers (eg S24). It was also found suitable for making a few smaller items, such as two stone balls (S30 and HH76 2872) from the phase VI slot in segment 2 of the inner east cross dyke and from N F82, a small cylindrical object (HH76 1395) from a phase V layer in segment 16 of the main enclosure, and a point sharpener (HH77 1857) from N F90. An incompletely perforated object, possibly a spindlewhorl (HH76 139), from a hollow on site G, is of uncertain date.

Sarsen

Sarsen was the least exploited of the four quern materials, although it was well suited to use for saddle querns. It amounts to only about 15% of the worked stone from Neolithic contexts. At other sites, in areas where sarsen was available, it was much utilised from the Neolithic onwards. There were concentrations of 'grey wethers' in particular in north Wiltshire and south-west Dorset (Bowen and Smith 1977, 188, fig 1). It may be that only small quantities of sarsen were to be found in the area around Hambledon Hill, although elsewhere in Dorset it could have been obtained quite readily. It occurs, for instance, in the area of the Deverel barrow (Bowen and Smith 1977, 189) only some 13 km away. Surviving areas of sarsen boulders are also known around Broadmayne (Arkell 1947, 241) at a distance of 28 km, and in the Valley of the Stones, Littlebredy (Nash *et al* 1998, 241) some 35 km from Hambledon.

Two main varieties of sarsen were utilised. Most of the fragments have a medium-grained, saccharoidal texture, consisting of almost pure quartz grains, this being the most typical form in which sarsen occurs. A finer-grained saccharoidal variety was used for an axe-polisher (S26). There is also a more cherty variety of sarsen (Arkell 1947, 241), and this was utilised for one (HH77 2180) of two quern fragments from the primary silts of the south-west long barrow ditch. Sarsen was also used for a hollowed object, perhaps a small mortar (S28), which may have formed part of the packing of a vestigial posthole in the Shroton spur outwork bank (Fig 3.78), although the ploughed-down state of the earthwork makes the date of its introduction uncertain.

Heathstone

Heathstone accounts for 20% of the Neolithic quern materials, rising to more than 40% on the Stepleton spur (Fig 10.3, Table 10.1), although the attraction of this gritty and friable ironstone is not immediately apparent. Heathstone is a Tertiary sandstone, and was collected from quite different areas from those that might have supplied the other quern materials. There are Tertiary Bagshot Beds in south-east Dorset, between Wareham and Poole Harbour, and here a dark red to purple, iron-rich, variable sandstone can be found, occurring typically on today's heathlands (Arkell 1947, 355). It contains angular quartz grains together with clasts of other rocks, notably flint. The nearest locality to Hambledon Hill where stone could be obtained is probably at Sturminster Marshall, some 20 km to the south-east, down the river Stour. This river could have provided an easy passage for quern material right up to the base of the hill. However, the best quality stone may have been found nearer to the coast.

This sandstone has not survived well, and there are only two identifiable quern fragments, one (HH77 2314) from the phase VI slot in the west ditch of the long barrow, and one (ST81 794) from the phase VI deposits in the Stepleton enclosure ditch, the remainder consisting of small fragments without grinding surfaces.

Old Red Sandstone

Old Red Sandstone from the Mendips was used almost exclusively to make saddle querns and rubbers and accounts for some 25% of the Neolithic quern materials, rising to 40% in the central area (Fig 10.3, Table 10.1), where it may have been even more abundant, since several sandstone fragments, some from Neolithic contexts, were discarded during the 1974–7 excavations. The only other artefact is a small cylindrical object resembling a weight (S27). The quern fragments, unlike those made from heathstone, have survived relatively well (eg S22, S23, S25).

The Old Red Sandstone found at Hambledon Hill is a hard feldspathic sandstone, slightly micaceous and buff to light pink in colour, having been somewhat bleached by weathering. It outcrops in four separate areas of the Mendips (Green and Welch 1965, 10), so that it is not possible to pinpoint any particular source, but a minimum journey of around 40 km would have been needed to reach an outcrop.

Other utilised stone

Chalk artefacts include a possible spindlewhorl fragment (S33), from a lens of charcoal and ash interleaved with the phase III chalk rubble fills of the Shroton spur outwork; a ball (S31) from the phase III fills of segment 9 of the main enclosure, a puddled chalk object (S32) from the same segment, another ball (HN82 801) scattered in three pieces with two echinoids in a deposit that had probably underlain the inner Hanford outwork bank, and two grooved, bun-shaped objects behind the head of a child burial inserted into segment 17 of the main enclosure (HH76 3046, Fig 3.34). Further finds from Hanford consist of two perforated fragments (S34a and b) from the primary silts of segment 2 of the outer Hanford outwork and a striated fragment (HN82 800) from 'flint mine' F848. Another ball, this time of chert from the Upper Greensand, was found in the phase VI slot in segment 5 of the outer east cross-dyke (HH75 2026).

Quartzite and flint pebbles are most prominent in the early Iron Age assemblage from the hillfort spur, where 122 flint beach pebbles and four quartzite ones seem to have served as slingstones, and were probably brought from Chesil Beach, some 40 km to the south-west, where the pebbles are mainly of flint. The pebbles on Chesil Beach are graded in size from west to east, ranging from ones the size of peas at Bridport to large cobbles at Chesilton (Arkell 1947, 338). It would therefore have been a simple matter to visit the section of the beach where pebbles of the right size for slingstones could be collected.

Both also occurred in Neolithic contexts, sometimes utilised, sometimes unmodified. Quartzite pebbles make good hammerstones, and there are 12 of these from the central area, with a further one from the Shroton spur. Nine, including two of the three from Neolithic contexts, may have come from Chesil Beach. Flint beach pebbles, both unmodified and used as hammerstones, were also found in the central area (Fig 3.69; see Saville, 10.2), eleven of them in Neolithic contexts. A quartzite polisher, with one smoothly worn side, came from the primary silts of the west ditch of the long barrow (HH77 2248). The only other quartzite artefact is a possible small rubber or weight, which was a surface find (HH76 2686).

There is only one unmodified quartzite pebble from the Stepleton spur, where there were no utilised ones and no flint beach pebbles. Where non-beach pebbles are concerned, the discrepancy may reflect immediate availability. Unmodified pebbles, whether retained or discarded (the latter largely unidentified), amounted to around 20 on the Stepleton spur in contrast to over 300 in the central area, where they came predominantly from natural or superficial contexts, which suggests that they were naturally present there, although not on such a scale as to be readily visible in the present ploughsoil. One source could be the Clay-with-Flints, although it contains only up to 10% pebbles of varied materials (Bristow *et al* 1995, 140) and is also present on the Stepleton spur. Another possible source could be shallow Palaeogene or other deposits now incorporated in topsoil (Ch 1).

Shale or jet from Neolithic contexts was confined to a bead, now missing (2003), found near the base of the phase VI slot in segment 3 of the outer east cross-dyke. The nearest and most likely source is the Kimmeridge shale beds of Purbeck, some 30 km to the south. Shale finds from later contexts comprised armlet fragments from Everley Water Meadow (S37) and Stepleton Lynchet (S36) and unworked scraps from Everley Water Meadow (SM82 23) and the phase VIII/a ploughsoils in the top of segment 10 of the main enclosure (HH75 1307).

Limestone fragments were few, unworked, and generally unstratified. Neolithic finds are confined to a shelly Jurassic limestone pebble from a phase II deposit in segment 11 of the main enclosure (HH75 1969), two small fragments of indeterminate limestone from pit N F7i (HH77 1978), and another from the slow silts of the Stepleton enclosure (ST80 408). A fragment from a possible smoother of Jurassic limestone was found in early Iron Age deposits on the hillfort spur (HH86 219).

Three further varieties of stone, all imported, relate only to post-Neolithic activity. A late Bronze Age axe mould fragment of syenite from Wales or the south-west is described and discussed by Stuart Needham below (10.1.4). A whetstone fragment of Kentish Rag (S35) from the relict ploughsoils in the top of the inner outwork ditch on the Stepleton spur may date as late as the Roman pottery which is the most abundant in these deposits. A Roman date also seems likely for weathered fragments of Niedermendig lava from the south area in Everley Water Meadow, where they were found in gravels containing nails, brick, and samian pottery (EWM83 98, 204 and 310).

Artefacts

Querns and quern materials

The querns are nearly all very fragmentary, the largest Neolithic piece, made from Old Red Sandstone, being only about one-quarter complete (S22). Grinding equipment from Neolithic contexts amounts to 12 finds of saddle quern fragments, identified by concave grinding surfaces, seven probable rubbers, with convex grinding surfaces (eg S23, S25), 30 finds of quern or rubber fragments, and 79 finds of quern materials without grinding surfaces. From other contexts there are eight finds of quern fragments, five of rubbers or rubber fragments (eg S24), 33 of quern or rubber fragments, and 70 of quern materials. Useable querns were not left on the site. Exceptionally, 14 small matching pieces of Old Red Sandstone from segment 6 of the inner outwork on the Stepleton spur appear to have come from the same artefact; the earliest came from a Neolithic level, most from relict post-Neolithic plough-soils. Quern materials were sometimes burnt as well as fragmented: numerous burnt sarsen fragments from N F23, one retaining a grinding surface, may derive from a single artefact.

The Neolithic saddle querns were probably all relatively small, with correspondingly small rubbers. Iron Age querns seem sometimes to have been a good deal larger, as for instance at Allard's Quarry, Marnhull, Dorset, where the saddle querns measured up to 0.53 by 0.25 m (Williams 1950, 61), and at Gussage All Saints, Dorset, where a rotary quern of Old Red Sandstone weighed over 25 kg (Buckley 1979, 91). The largest surviving Neolithic fragment at Hambledon (S22) measured at most 0.35 m by 0.33 m when complete. The fact that this quern had to be brought from the Mendips may well have influenced the size of the slab that was selected. There is a saddle quern of comparable size built into the long cairn at Burn Ground, Hampnett, Gloucestershire (Grimes 1960, 75), which would originally have measured about 0.37 × 0.19 m, and was made from stone that had been transported a similar distance, in this case of May Hill sandstone, from May Hill itself (Roe 1999, 416). Further earlier Neolithic querns of modest size are known from Gwernvale, Powys (Britnell and Savory 1984, 134). By contrast, the sarsen saddle querns from Windmill Hill, Wiltshire, are a good deal thicker (Smith 1965, fig 52), and weigh 9.80 kg or more, although not necessarily greater in surface area. These substantial querns reflect the availability of quantities of sarsen only about 1.5 km from the site (Smith 1965, 120). Saddle querns may have remained small until wheeled transport was available in the late Bronze Age or the Iron Age.

The quern materials from Hambledon Hill demonstrate that varieties of good grinding stone were identified early on. Once recognised, the same varieties of stone continued to be used first for saddle querns and then for rotary querns, and even sometimes millstones, into the Roman period and beyond. At the time of writing (1999), the use of Mendip Old Red Sandstone at other Neolithic sites in Dorset remains unconfirmed, although there was a small Old Red Sandstone saddle quern in a pit with earlier Neolithic pottery at Camerton, Somerset (Wedlake 1958, 19, 244; Saunders 1998, 207). Greensand was used for middle Bronze Age saddle querns from Cranborne Chase, both from the bottom of the Angle Ditch, and from South Lodge (Pitt Rivers 1898, 37, pl 242: 10, 108, pl 263: 5), and for another of the same date from Rowden, Winterbourne Steepleton (Cox 1991, 95). There is also some Hembury Ware from the Angle Ditch (Cleal 1991b, 134), so there is a possibility that this quern is in fact earlier.

Two complete saddle querns probably of heathstone have been recorded from a cluster of early Neolithic pits at Pamphill, Dorset, although one came from a pit without other finds and the other from a pit which contained a possibly intrusive Bronze Age sherd as well as better preserved fragments from a single Neolithic Bowl (Addison 1989, 18–27). Another, probably of middle Bronze Age date, was found at Bestwall Quarry, Wareham (Ladle 1996, 144). Sarsen saddle querns are attested in the causewayed enclosure ditch at Maiden Castle, Dorset (Laws 1991, 230; Wheeler 1943, 322) and in internal features at Whitesheet Hill, Wiltshire (Rawlings *et al* 2004).

At Hambledon, the early Iron Age quern fragments from the hillfort are mainly of local Upper Greensand with some Old Red Sandstone, both materials, as can now be seen, that had already been in use for querns for almost 3,000 years, as had heathstone. Dorset examples include greensand and heathstone querns from Hog Cliff Hill, Maiden Newton (Ellison and Rahtz 1987, 247) and from Gussage All Saints, where there were also a few Mendip Old Red Sandstone rotary querns (Buckley 1979, 89–90). Further greensand examples from the early Iron Age include saddle quern fragments at Heron Grove, Sturminster Marshall (Valentin 1993, 68), and Allard's Quarry, Marnhull (Williams 1950, 61). There were also numerous greensand quern fragments from Hod Hill (Ellis 1968, 135), where they must date either to later in the Iron Age or to the Roman period. Mendip Old Red Sandstone was extensively used for querns at South Cadbury (Roe 2000, 263).

Weathered fragments of Niedermendig lava from Everley Water Meadow can perhaps be interpreted as the last surviving traces of a water-mill on the river Iwerne, which could have served the Roman fort on Hod Hill or the Roman site at Iwerne (Hawkes 1947). Niedermendig lava querns and millstones are widespread, although the greatest concentrations are probably in south-east England (Black 1987, 117), while there is a good number of finds from eastern England and the Thames Valley (Peacock 1980, 50). Further finds have nevertheless been recorded in Dorset from Poundbury (Green 1987, 105), and some even reached Exeter (Bell and Bradshaw 1983).

Spindlewhorl?

Spindlewhorls are not, as a rule, recorded from Neolithic sites, and yet a broken, perforated, chalk fragment from a phase III deposit in the Shroton spur outwork (S33) would be seen as a spindlewhorl of disc type if found in an Iron Age or Roman context. The most certain evidence for weaving in Neolithic Britain comes in the form of textile impressions on earlier Neolithic pottery found at Rowden (Crowfoot 1991, 99). A fired clay fragment retaining part of a perforation, from a posthole of the southern circle at Durrington Walls, has been reconstructed as a spindlewhorl (Wainwright and Longworth 1971, 188, fig 82).

Table 10.1 Summary of stone finds by area, artefact class, and rock type

	Axeheads and flakes	*Querns and rubbers*	*Perforated objects*	*Cylindrical objects*	*Balls*	*Axe polisher*	*Hammerstones*	*Miscellaneous*	*Total artefacts*	*Unworked*	*Totals*
CENTRAL AREA											
Igneous and metamorphic rocks	14								14		14
Upper Greensand		13	1	1	2			point sharpener?	18	32	50
Sarsen		8				1			9	10	19
Heathstone		3							3	7	10
Old Red Sandstone		24[1]		1					25	23	48
Chalk					1			2 grooved objects at head of child burial HH76 3046 subcylindrical object, apparently modelled from puddled chalk	4	many	4
Quartzite				1			11	polisher	13	many	13
Chert					1				1	some	1
Sandstone								rubber or smoother	1	some	1
Limestone										3	3
Kimmeridge shale								bead	1	1	2
Central area totals	*14*	*48*	*1*	*3*	*4*	*1*	*11*	*7*	*89*	*>76*	*>165*
SHROTON SPUR											
Upper Greensand										1	1
Sarsen								mortar?	1		1
Heathstone		1							1	1	2
Old Red Sandstone		1							1	2	3
Chalk			1						1	some	1
Quartzite							1		1		1
Shroton spur totals		*2*	*1*				*1*	*1*	*5*	*4*	*9*
STEPLETON SPUR											
Igneous and metamorphic rocks	3								3		3
Upper Greensand		3							3	22	25
Sarsen		2							2	4	6
Heathstone		12							12	35	47
Old Red Sandstone		9[2]							9[2]	7[3]	16
Kentish Rag								whetstone fragment	1		1
Limestone										2	2
Stepleton spur totals	*3*	*26*						*1*	*30*	*70*	*100*

HANFORD SPUR											
Sarsen		1							1	1	2
Heathstone										1	1
Old Red Sandstone		1							1	1	2
Chalk			2		1			striated piece	4		4
Hanford spur totals		*2*	*2*		*1*			*1*	*6*	*3*	*9*
HILLFORT SPUR											
Upper Greensand		8							8	22	30
Old Red Sandstone		4							4	2	6
Quartzite										4 (slingstones)	4
Flint beach pebbles									122 (slingstones)		122
Hillfort spur totals		*12*							*12*	*150*	*162*
STEPLETON LYNCHET											
Upper Greensand										1	1
Limestone										4	4
Kimmeridge shale								armlet fragment	1		1
Stepleton Lynchet totals								*1*	*1*	*5*	*6*
EVERLEY WATER MEADOW											
Upper Greensand								worked fragment	1	3	4
Heathstone										1	1
Niedermendig lava										3	3
Kimmeridge shale								armlet fragment	1	2	3
Limestone										1	1
Syenite								axe mould fragment	1		1
Everley Water Meadow totals								*3*	*3*	*10*	*13*
COOMBE BOTTOM											
Oolitic limestone										1	1
ROLF'S WOOD											
Heathstone										1	1
Overall totals	*17*	*90*	*4*	*3*	*5*	*1*	*12*	*14*	*146*	*>320*	*>466*

1 Two joining fragments of Old Red Sandstone rubber from L10 and L5 in segment 4 of the main enclosure (S25) are counted as one

2 Eight fragments of Old Red Sandstone quern from L3 and L1A in cutting 1 of segment 6 of the inner Stepleton outwork apparently belong to the same piece of stone and have been counted as one

3 Two fragments of Old Red Sandstone from L1A in cutting 1 of segment 6 of the inner Stepleton outwork apparently belong to the same piece of stone and have been counted as one

Evidence for Neolithic textile manufacture in Britain remains slight. Remains of flax are rare before the Bronze Age (Vanessa Straker, pers comm), but seed impressions are in fact known from Windmill Hill (Helbaek 1952, 197), and it is also known from the Neolithic in Holland (Jessen and Helbaek 1944, 57), and from waterlogged deposits of the Cortaillod culture in Switzerland, where quite sophisticated weaving techniques were being employed (Vogt 1937).

Cylindrical objects

There are three small cylindrical objects with diameters of about 50 mm, all from the central area, made of greensand (HH76 1395), Old Red Sandstone (S27) and quartzite (HH76 2686). On an Iron Age site these might be identified as small weights, as at South Cadbury (Roe 2000). Similar artefacts of sarsen are also known from Windmill Hill (Smith 1965, 123, fig 52: S22, S23).

Balls

The presence of greensand and chert balls as well as chalk ones is exceptional. At other sites where similar balls have been found, they have almost invariably been made of chalk, although there is an unstratified sandstone example from Stonehenge, as well as chalk ones from primary and later levels (Cleal *et al* 1995, 394–402, figs 216, 219, 221). The tradition seems to have been a long-lasting one, with finds both from causewayed enclosures and henge monuments. Thirty chalk balls were found at Windmill Hill, in all levels (Smith 1965, 132). In the Dorchester area, at the Flagstones enclosure, a chalk ball came from the primary chalk rubble fill of one of the segments, dated to the late fourth millennium cal BC (Smith *et al* 1997, 129), and third millennium examples came from Mount Pleasant and Maumbury Rings (Wainwright 1979a, 167; Bradley 1976, 25, fig 7; Bradley and Thomas 1984).

Axe-polisher

The axe-polisher (S26) is made from a finer-grained variety of sarsen than that used for querns. Both faces have been worn hollow, with distinctive, highly polished surfaces. Two other pieces may have had similar uses. One (HH77 2248) from the primary silt of the long barrow is a quartzite pebble with one side worn to a glossy surface, the other (HH75 450) from phase III deposits in segment 8 of the main enclosure is a worn pebble of grey sandstone, classed as a rubber in Table 10.1.

Portable axe-polishers from causewayed enclosures include examples from the Trundle, Sussex, Etton, Cambridgeshire (Edmonds 1998, 266), and Briar Hill, Northampton (Bamford 1985, 93, fig 48). A highly polished fragment of sarsen from the ditch of the round barrow at Windmill Hill may have been of Neolithic origin (Smith 1965, 124). Sarsen seems to have been well suited to this particular use. A sarsen axe-polisher somewhat similar to S21 formed part of the pavement of the mortuary structure under the primary mound at Wayland's Smithy, Berkshire (Whittle 1991, 70, 87, fig 11:9), and a massive, fixed, sarsen axe-polisher was incorporated in the chamber of the West Kennet Long Barrow (Piggott 1962, 16). A large portable axe-polisher with similar wear to S21 was built into the Gwernvale long cairn, Powys (Britnell and Savory 1984, 132 and fig 60).

Slingstones

The Chesil Beach pebbles from early Iron Age contexts on the hillfort spur correspond to the large numbers of the pebbles taken to Iron Age hillforts in the region, such as South Cadbury (Roe 2000), Maiden Castle (Laws 1991, 232) and Ham Hill (Adkins and Adkins 1991, 93). Some of the apparently imported beach pebbles from Neolithic contexts at Hambledon may also have been used as slingstones (10.1.3). Their transport inland is echoed in Cranborne Chase, where Pitt Rivers reported 'seashore pebbles' from Neolithic and Bronze Age sites such as Handley Hill, Wor Barrow and Martin Down (1898, 50, 67, 200).

Whetstone

Whetstones of Kentish Rag, like the fragment from the Stepleton spur (S35) are frequent on Roman sites, including further finds in the West Country (Roe 2001). It is likely to relate to the contemporary cultivation of the spur.

Miscellaneous

A missing shale or jet bead from the inner east cross-dyke (HH75 1358) is remembered as grey and dull in colour, disc-shaped, approximately 25 mm in diameter and less than 5 mm thick, with a central hourglass perforation. Proximity to Purbeck makes it likely to have been of shale. Several earlier Neolithic shale beads are known, including examples from causewayed enclosures (Piggott 1962, 51). They tend, however, to be larger than this example and are often elongated. The least dissimilar forms may be the longitudinally perforated discoidal beads from burials in the Severn–Cotswold tombs at Eyford and Notgrove, both in Gloucestershire (Clarke *et al* 1985, illus 7.2, 7.3) and some of the smaller beads among those from the rather later blocking of the West Kennet Long Barrow, Wiltshire (Piggott 1962, fig 18; Clarke *et al* 1985, illus 2.9).

The objects behind the head of child burial 3046 (Fig 3.32) are likely, from their size and position, to have had hair wound around them in a bun, a possibility supported by their smoothed, worn state. They are difficult to parallel, even among the diverse Neolithic chalk objects reviewed by Varndell (1991, 105–6).

Catalogue of illustrated stone artefacts other than axeheads

S22. Part of saddle quern: Old Red Sandstone. ST81 3140. Stepleton spur, 4B F712, layer 2, overlying inhumation

S23. Rubber: Old Red Sandstone. HH74 1114. Central area, Pit A F64

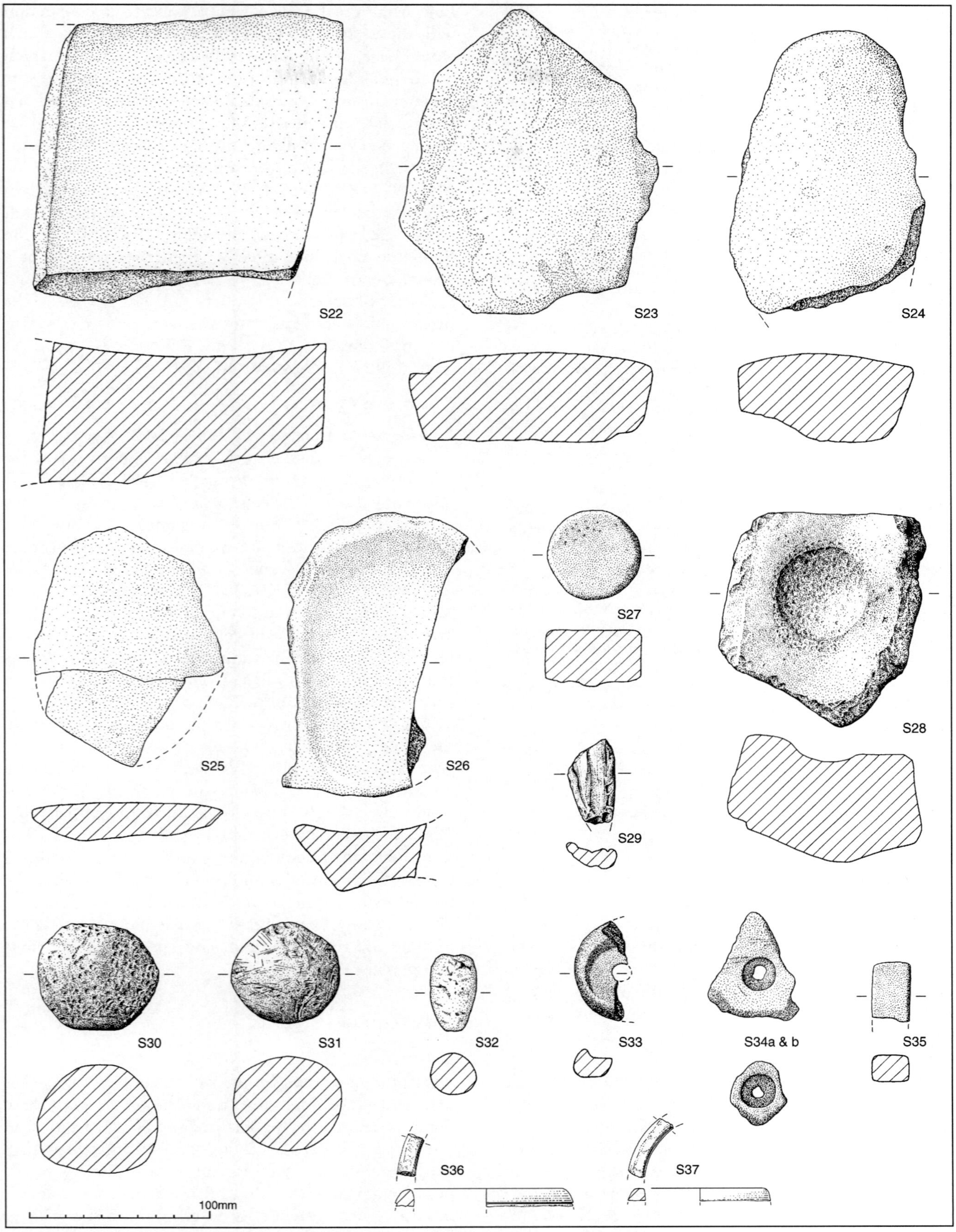

Fig 10.2 Stone artefacts. S22, quern fragment. S23–S25, grain rubbers. S26, axe-polisher. S27, cylindrical object. S28, mortar. S29, point-sharpener. S30–S31, balls. S32, puddled chalk object. S33. ?Spindlewhorl. S34a, S34b, perforated plaques. S35 ?hone. S36–S37, armlet fragments. Particulars in catalogue. Scale 1:3

S24. Part of rubber: Greensand. HH76 2016. Central area, surface, within main causewayed enclosure.
S25. Rubber: Old Red Sandstone. HH74 1043+1057. Central area, main enclosure ditch, segment 4, 1057 layer 10, phase III; 1043 layer 5, phase VI.
S26. Axe-polisher: fine-grained sarsen. HH74 735. Central area, A F6
S27. Cylindrical object: Old Red Sandstone. HH75 1479. Central area, inner east cross-dyke, segment 5, layer 6, phase VI.
S28. Mortar: sarsen. HH76 2992. Shroton spur, K F4, layer 2
S29. Point-sharpener? Upper Greensand. HH77 1857. Central area, N F90, layer 3
S30. Ball: Greensand. HH77 2178. Central area, N F82, layer 3
S31. Ball: Chalk. HH75 775. Central area, main enclosure ditch, segment 9, layer 7, phase III
S32. Subcylindrical object. Puddled chalk. Apparently complete, with smoothed surface and base, HH75 867. Central area, main enclosure ditch, segment 9, layer 8, phase III.
S33. Spindlewhorl?: Chalk. HH76 1042. Shroton spur outwork, site K, layer 6, phase III. Found while sieving sample from area of charcoal and ash.
S34a, S34b. Perforated plaques: Chalk. HN82 101. Outer Hanford outwork, segment 2, U9, layer 5, horizon HN2/6. Found together.
S35. Hone: Kentish Rag. ST79 316. Stepleton spur, inner outwork, segment 5, C11/12, layer 2, horizon ST2/22
S36. Armlet fragment. Shale. SL82 89. Stepleton Lynchet. Probably lathe-turned, internal diameter 100 mm, 7% surviving, broken horizontally, perhaps below median groove
S37. Armlet fragment. Shale. EWM83 temporary number 15/9/83 26. Everley Water meadow area 1, section 1, layer 1, spit 2. Armlet fragment, probably lathe-turned, internal diameter 80 mm, 15% surviving, broken horizontally

10.1.3 Chronology and distribution

The late Isobel Smith, Fiona Roe and Frances Healy

Chronology

Individual artefacts

Table 10.4 lists radiocarbon determinations on samples from contexts containing stone axeheads. Given the durability of the artefacts, the relation to them of even the most satisfactory dates remains uncertain, although the certainly early date of Group I and ungrouped altered dolerite axe fragments from the primary silts of the long barrow is noteworthy. The finds most convincingly associated with radiocarbon dates are from burials. The illustrated Old Red Sandstone quern fragment (S22) was placed in a pit with a young male, the two dates on whose skeleton have a mean of *3630–3580 cal BC (22%) or 3535–3495 cal BC (20%) or 3460–3375 cal BC (53%)* (4711±19 BP; UB-4311, OxA-7818), in agreement with another of *3640–3550 cal BC (23%) or 3540–3360 cal BC (72%)* (4700±45 BP; OxA-7843) made on one of the charred hazelnut shells spread over the skeleton. Burnt clay, chalk and flint from the burial strongly indicate a connection with the destruction of the inner outwork bank, which would have rapidly followed its construction, for which a date of *3620–3520 cal BC* is estimated (Ch 4). In the main enclosure, two chalk objects behind the head of a young juvenile burial in the upper fills (Fig 3.32) should be close in age to the skeleton itself, the measurements for which have a mean of *3380–3320 cal BC* (4557±42 BP; OxA-7039, -7040). On less certain ground, the salvage of the upper skeleton of an adult female from just below the phase VI deposits in the Stepleton enclosure ditch entailed the recovery of a sarsen quern fragment, a heathstone fragment, and Old Red Sandstone fragments (all ST81 3184). The juxtaposition suggests association, although this cannot be demonstrated. The skeleton is dated to *3530–3390 cal BC* (4680±30 BP (OxA-7814).

The overall pattern

Phasing is summarised in Tables 10.2–3, and Figure 10.3 shows the incidence of axe and quern materials. The only axe materials from the lower (phase I–III) fills of any ditch in the central area were Group I (S14), altered amphibolite (S4, S5) and altered gabbro (S15, S16), all from the south-west. In the upper (phase V–VI) fills there were also implements of Groups IV (S8), VIII (S13) and XVI (S7), a rock similar to Group XVII (S6), and an ungrouped banded tuff. These include rocks from sources outside the south-west, Group VIII from Wales and the banded tuff perhaps from the midlands. A flake (S12) from a Group VI axe was from a post-Neolithic context.

Stratified stone was most abundant in pits and in the upper ditch fills, the single most prolific context groups being the phase VI slots of the central area ditches and the Stepleton enclosure, as with other cultural material. The bias towards pits and upper ditch fills is particularly marked in the central area (Fig 10.3) where it corresponds to the packing of slots and pit-tops with flint nodules and other rocks. This raises the possibility that some or all of the artefacts in these contexts may have been already present and were gathered up with the rest of the flint and stone when the slots and pits were filled.

Distribution

Central area

Distributions do not, on the whole, suggest any particular patterns of disposal, except for a preponderance of finds in the pits in the north of site N, where most of the sarsen occurred. This is more circumscribed than the generally larger quantities of cultural material in pits near the crown of the hill, which, where other materials are concerned, extends to pit group I on site B (Figs 3.62–66, 3.68). There is, however, one unusually dense concentration within the relatively confined space of sections SII and SIII in the south-west ditch of the long barrow, where a large quantity of pottery and other

Table 10.2 Stone axeheads and fragments by material and context
Fragments of a single artefact are counted as one

	Phase	*Jadeite/ nephrite*	*I*	*IV*	*VI*	*VIII*	*XVI*	*cf XVII*	*Greenstone*	*Amphibolite*	*Altered amphibolite*	*Altered gabbro*	*Banded tuff*	*Siltstone*	*Totals*
CENTRAL AREA															
Main enclosure	III										2 (S4, S5)[1]				1
	V										1 (S10)[1]				
	VI			1 (S8)			1 (S7)	1 (S6)					1 (S9)		4
Outer E cross-dyke	VI					1 (S13)									1
Long barrow	I		1 (S14)[2]									1 (S15)[3]			2
	III											1 (S16)[3]			
Neolithic pits							1 (S1)								1
Unstratified and miscellaneous		2 (S3, S11)	1 (S17)[2]		1 (S12)				1 (S2)					1 (S18)	5
Central area totals		*2*	*1*	*1*	*1*	*1*	*2*	*1*	*1*		*1*	*1*	*1*	*1*	*14*
STEPLETON SPUR															
Stepleton enclosure	V?							1 (S19)							1
	VII/a								1 (S20)						1
Unstratified and miscellaneous										1 (S21)					1
Stepleton spur totals								*1*	*1*	*1*					*3*

1 probably fragments of one implement
2 probably fragments of one implement
3 probably fragments of one implement

Table 10.3 Summary of stone finds other than axes and axe fragments from the central area, Shroton spur, Stepleton spur and Hanford spur by rock type, context group and phase

	Phase	*Upper Greensand*	*Sarsen*	*Heathstone*	*Old Red Sandstone*	*Chalk*	*Quartzite*	*Flint beach pebbles*	*Chert*	*Sandstone*	*Limestone*	*Kentish Rag*	*Kimmeridge shale*	*Totals*
CENTRAL AREA														
Main enclosure	I/II				2						1			3
	III	2			2	2		2		1				9
	IV	1												1
	V	3			3									6
	VI & ?post-VI	13	2	2	4	2	2							25
Inner E cross-dyke	V	1			1			1						3
	VI				2									2
Outer E cross-dyke	VI	1	1						1				1	4
Long barrow	I		2				1							3
	III			1										1
	V				1									1
	VI			1										1
Western outwork	I						1							1
Neolithic pits		12	13	1	13						1			40
	Central area Neolithic totals	*33*	*18*	*5*	*28*	*4*	*4*	*3*	*1*	*1*	*2*		*1*	*100*
Beaker/EBA (VII/a)		1		1	3									5
Relict ploughsoils (VIII/a)		5		2	5		3	1					1	17
Unstratified & miscellaneous		11	1	2	12		9	3			1			39
	Central area remaining contexts totals	*17*	*1*	*5*	*20*		*12*	*4*			*1*		*1*	*61*
SHROTON SPUR														
Outwork ditch	III					1								1
	Shroton spur Neolithic totals					*1*								*1*
Relict ploughsoils (VIII/a)		1		1	2									4
Unstratified & miscellaneous			1	1	1		1							4
	Shroton spur remaining contexts totals	*1*	*1*	*2*	*3*		*1*							*8*

STEPLETON SPUR														
Stepleton enclosure	Chalk rubble and related fills (phase III)	3	1	1										5
	Upper Neolithic levels (phases IV, V, VI)	3	1	9	6						1			20
Middle outwork	Chalk rubble fills (phase III)	1												1
Inner outwork	Chalk rubble and related fills (phase III)	1		1										2
	Slow silts (phase V)	2												2
Neolithic pits		5	2	9	1									17
	Stepleton spur Neolithic totals	*15*	*4*	*20*	*7*						*1*			*47*
All Stepleton ditches	Beaker/EBA (phase VII/a)	2		1	3						1			7
	Relict post-Neolithic plough-soils (phase VIII/a)	6	2	19	3							1		31
Unstratified & miscellaneou		2		7	3									12
	Stepleton spur remaining contexts totals	*10*	*2*	*27*	*9*						*1*	*1*		*50*
HANFORD SPUR														
Outer Hanford outwork	Basal silts (phases I–II)					2								2
Neolithic pits				1		1								2
	Hanford spur Neolithic totals			*1*		*3*								*4*
'Flint mines'						1								1
All Hanford ditches	Beaker/EBA (phase VII/a)				1									1
	Relict post-Neolithic plough-soils (phase VIII/a)		1		1									2
Unstratified & miscellaneous			1											1
	Hanford spur remaining contexts totals		*2*		*2*	*1*								*5*

Table 10.4 Radiocarbon determinations associated with stone axeheads

In the case of the long barrow, the estimated date is the estimated construction date for the monument. Further information is to be found in Chapter 4

Rock type	*Drawing*	*Sample*	*BP*	*Cal BC (95% confidence)*	*Estimated date (Ch 4)*	*Comment*
Group I and altered gabbro	S14, S15	Cattle metatarsal from primary silt of W ditch of long barrow	4950±55 BP (OxA-7848)	3940–3640	*3680–3640 cal BC*	Estimated date for construction of barrow
		Cattle scapula fragments from primary silt of W ditch of long barrow	4875±40 BP (OxA-8846)	3710–3540	as above	as above
		Cattle phalanx from primary silt of W ditch of long barrow	4835±45 BP (OxA-8847)	3710–3520	as above	as above
		Indeterminate animal bone fragment from primary silt of W ditch of long barrow	4760±50 (OxA-8848)	3650–3370	as above	as above
		Red deer antler crown with two terminal tines embedded in natural chalk in base of E ditch of long barrow	4870±35 BP (OxA-8845)	3710–3540	as above	as above
Group XVI	S1	Oak, hazel & hawthorn-type charcoal, not twiggy, from same pit as S1	4830±80 BP (HAR-9167)	3780–3370	*3780–3490 cal BC (84%) or 3460–3370 cal BC (11%)*	Presence of oak charcoal means that measurement may pre-date context
cf Group XVII	S6	Articulated cattle tibia & astragalus from same layer as S6	4810±50 BP (OxA-8850)	3700–3380	*3670–3510 cal BC (90%) or 3420–3380 cal BC (5%)*	Sample likely to be close in age to context and to deposition of S6
Altered Amphibolite	S4, S5	Articulating dog metacarpals and phalanx from same layer as S4	4865±33 BP (mean of OxA-7097–8)	3710–3540	*3710–3630 cal BC (88%) or 3560–3530 cal BC (7%)*	Sample may have been redeposited
		Articulated cattle radius-ulna and carpals from silty chalk rubble (L8A) grading laterally into chalk and flint rubble (L8) containing S4	4712±42 BP (mean of OxA-7015–6)	3640–3370	*3460–3360 cal BC*	Sample likely to be close in age to context and deposition of S4

artefacts had also been deposited (Fig 3.50). Here were four fragments (S14–S17) from probably two stone axes, as well as fragments from sarsen and heathstone querns, an Old Red Sandstone fragment, a quartzite polisher, a flint beach pebble hammerstone and a quartzite pebble fragment. It is important to note that these items were not all deposited at one time; they represent a gradual accumulation, spread throughout the entire sequence of fills from phase I upwards. This would appear to attest a deliberate practice, maintained over a considerable period of time. It may relate to an entrance to the main enclosure to the west of segment 1, the use of which would have entailed walking along the side of the west ditch of the long barrow, on the way to and from the Stepleton spur (3.5.2, 3.5.6).

Another possible entrance, between segments 8 and 9 in the east of the main enclosure, also showed a distinctive pattern of stone finds. Fragments from the same altered amphibolite axe (S4, S5) occurred in each of the opposed butts in phase III, during which a greensand quern or rubber fragment and a sandstone rubber or smoother were deposited in the north butt of segment 8, together with two flint Chesil Beach pebbles, one of them used as a hammerstone; there was no stone from the rest of the segment in this phase. Phase III in segment 9 saw the deposition of a chalk ball (S31), a puddled chalk object (S32) and two Old Red Sandstone fragments, as well as three flint Chesil beach pebbles, two of them used as hammerstones. The two finds that were precisely located (the puddled chalk object and one hammerstone), came from the south butt, like the axe fragment. In subsequent levels, stone finds accumulated along the whole length of segment 8, together with two further flint beach pebble hammerstones. The jadeite axe (S11) came from the ploughsoil over segment 8. Stone finds were less abundant in segment 9, but included a quartzite hammerstone, while a further flint beach pebble came from the ploughsoil of site D, overlying segment 9 and the north butt of segment 8.

Seven of the 17 flint beach pebbles from the site were found in the immediate area of this possible entrance, as were two hammerstones of nodular flint and two quartzite hammerstones. The coincidence of entrance, beach pebbles, and hammerstones may reflect their use as missiles, perhaps slingstones, in the fourth millennium. A further possible entrance, between segments 13 and 14, corresponds to a slighter concentration of stone finds, this time starting in phase V. Here there were two flint beach pebbles, one used as a hammerstone (HH76 1045) and one unutilised (HH76 693), as well as a discarded beach pebble of unspecified material, two sandstone pebbles, and at least 12 further pebbles discarded at the time of excavation.

More speculatively, the naturally spherical pebbles may have been seen as analogous to the artificially spherical chalk ball. The elongated puddled chalk object (S32), unique on the site, may have been phallic, given the presence of chalk balls and phalli in some

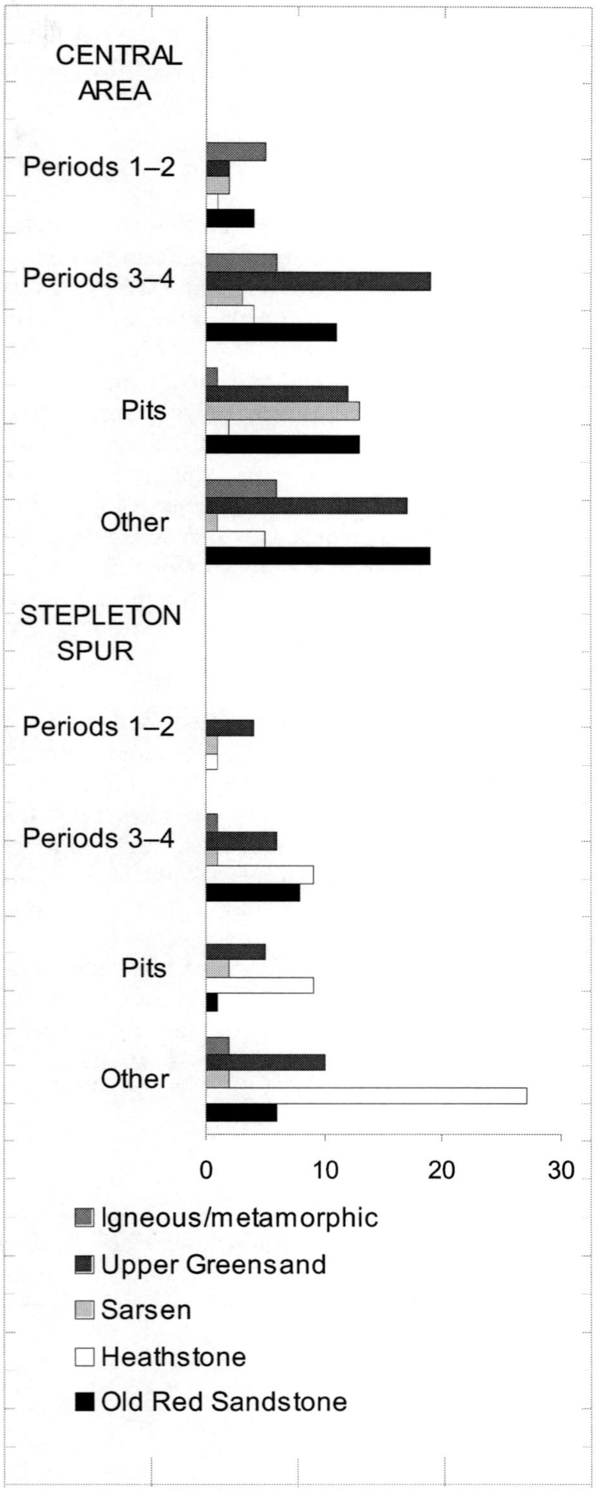

Fig 10.3 Principal stone types from earlier and later ditch fills and other contexts in the central area and on the Stepleton spur. Ditch fills included in periods 1–2 are south long barrow phases I–III, main enclosure phases I–III, Stepleton enclosure phases I–III middle Stepleton outwork phases I–III, and inner Stepleton outwork phases I–III. Ditch fills included in periods 3–4 are main enclosure phase IV, western outwork phase I, main enclosure, south long barrow and cross-dykes phases V and VI, Stepleton enclosure phases IV–VI, inner Stepleton outwork phases V–VII.

causewayed enclosures (Smith 1965, 132, fig 57; Varndell 1991, 105), and of what may be a fired clay phallus from the same context as a fired clay ball at Etton (Kinnes and Pryor 1998, fig 241). If so, S32 is distinctly unnaturalistic.

Stepleton spur

Most stratified stone came from the Stepleton enclosure ditch itself, rather than from the substantial excavated length of the inner outwork (Table 10.1). It was concentrated in the west and north of the circuit, with no finds at all in segments 16 to 23. The high proportion of stone from unstratified and miscellaneous contexts on the spur (Fig 10.3) may reflect more intense Bronze Age and later activity than in the central area. It certainly reflects the large size of the inner outwork ditch, the top of which provided a bigger trap for later ploughsoils and the artefacts they contained than did the other ditch-tops. The scarcity of stone finds in its Neolithic levels suggests that those in the relict ploughsoils were derived from the interior.

Contrasts between the two main areas

The subassemblages of stone implements and imported stone from the central area and the Stepleton spur differ substantially (Tables 10.1–10.3, Fig 10.3). There are only one-third as many stone artefacts from the Stepleton spur as from the central area, despite a more equal balance of total stone finds (Table 10.5). This may reflect the poor preservation of the heathstone which was frequent on the Stepleton spur and which occurred mainly as fragments which had lost any modified surfaces (Roe, 10.1.2). Differential preservation of quern material may also partly account for the very narrow range of stone artefact types from the spur, where (disregarding a post-Neolithic hone) there are only axeheads and quern or rubber fragments. In the central area these were augmented by a variety of other objects (Table 10.3). Many of the types lacking from Stepleton are, however, made of quern materials, notably a sarsen axe-polisher (S26), cylindrical objects of greensand and Old Red Sandstone (eg S27), a greensand point-sharpener (S29), and greensand balls (eg S30, S31). If equivalent forms had been made of heathstone they might no longer be recognisable. This consideration cannot, however, account for the complete absence from Stepleton of worked chalk, especially as examples were recovered in far less extensive excavations on the Shroton and Hanford spurs (eg S33, S34).

Striking variations in the numbers of both stone axes and quartzite hammerstones are reduced when flint examples are also taken into consideration, although axeheads remain more prevalent in the central area (Table 10.5). The contrast in materials remains, emphasised by the fact that some of the flint hammerstones from the central area are beach pebbles which must have been imported. This dichotomy mirrors that between the quern materials preferred in the two areas (Fig 10.3), as well as differences in pottery fabrics.

It is difficult not to see implications of territory, or at least of catchment, in these patterns. The Cornish greenstones, Old Red Sandstone, Chesil Beach pebbles and occasional limestone fragments of the central area combine with pottery from a range of Jurassic sources and with small quantities of gabbroic ware (see Smith, 9.1; Darvill, 9.2) to point to a resource base lying in a south-west to north-west arc. The heathstone prevalent on the Stepleton spur derived from the south-east, where red clays interbedded with the sandstones (Bristow *et al* 1991, 23–32) may have provided the raw material for pottery of fabric group 6 (see Darvill, 9.2), also prevalent on the spur. The overall

Table 10.5 The relative frequency of stone finds and other materials in the central area and on the Stepleton spur

	Central area	*Stepleton spur*	*Ratio*
Total stone finds	165	100	1.7:1
Total stone artefacts	89	30	2.9:1
Number of Neolithic stone artefact types	14	2	7:1
Stone axeheads and fragments	14	3	5.3:1
Flint axeheads and flakes (including four from 1958–60 excavations)	20	14	1.4:1
All axeheads and flakes/fragments	*34*	*17*	*2:1*
Quartzite hammerstones	12	–	–
Flint hammerstones	15 (some beach pebbles)	25 (no beach pebbles)	0.6:1
All hammerstones	*27*	*25*	*1.1:1*
For comparison:			
Neolithic Bowl pottery	13,870 sherds/53.35 kg	10, 814 sherds/39.32 kg	1.3:1
Struck flint (excluding hammerstones and unclassified burnt flint)	23,895	40,055	0.6:1
Fully identified animal bone specimens (excluding teeth)	3347	1520	2.2:1

scarcity of sarsen, which could have been obtained at no greater distance than heathstone, may be a negative image of territory.

The stone materials also differ in quality. Stone axe materials from remote sources were, like gabbroic clays, used to produce expertly made and finished artefacts of some rarity in their final environment and, to a modern eye, of some aesthetic appeal. Old Red Sandstone made durable, hard-wearing grinding equipment (Roe, 10.1.2), and pots from Jurassic sources were well made and well finished (see Smith, 9.1). Heathstone was of lower quality than Old Red Sandstone, and vessels of fabric group 6, possibly from the same area, were roughly made and summarily finished (see Smith, 9.1). There are connotations of function and status as well as of catchment.

10.1.4 The Everley Water Meadow stone mould

Stuart Needham
with contributions by H Howard and M Cowell

A fragment of stone mould valve (SM82 132; Fig 10.4) was excavated from SMX L15, gravels laid down in the Roman period at the earliest, since they contained nails, brick and pottery recorded as samian, as well as one sherd in an early or middle Bronze Age fabric and three in late Bronze Age or early Iron Age fabrics (see 5.3.3).

The mould has the characteristic neat shaping of most stone moulds of final early Bronze Age (Arreton) date onwards. The bottom end would have been D-shaped when complete, the maximum breadth being 34 mm. Just over half survives, retaining a V-carved transverse groove perpendicular to the flat contact face and approximately central to the end. Such grooves are commonly found on stone moulds and are regarded as registration aids (eg Needham 1981, 28). The length of the fragment is 68 mm and the extant side is gently bowed. The corner of a matrix 57 mm long is cut into the flat face of the block. The matrix is evidently for an axe blade, which tapers in profile to a small bevelled step at the bottom and has a fairly crisp body angle in cross-section.

For material identification the mould was examined and core-sampled by Hilary Howard for the South-Western Implement Petrology Committee (DO 161). On macroscopic inspection Howard described 'a pinkish-brown coarse-grained rock with pinkish felspar crystals clearly visible'. Under the microscope it appeared as 'a coarsely crystalline rock composed in the main of plagioclase and potash felspar. Grains of the latter show partial alteration to sericite. Mafic minerals have all been altered to chloritic substances. Brown mica is present. Acicular apatite is common'. Howard identified the rock as syenite, which is a coarse-grained variety within the keratophyre petrological suite known to have been used for other Bronze Age moulds (Needham 1981, 26–7). The origin of this material is likely to be in south Wales or the south-west peninsula.

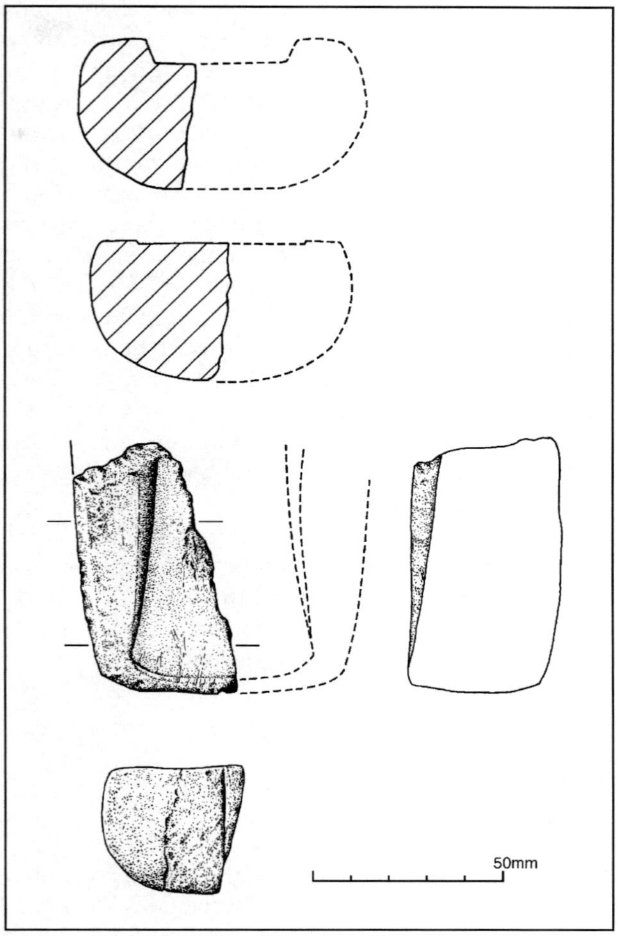

Fig 10.4 The stone axe-blade mould (SM82 132). The possible reconstruction of the full width is based on assumed symmetry about an axial line through the basal groove. Scale 1:2

The mould was also examined by X-ray fluorescence (non-destructive) by Mike Cowell of the British Museum's Department of Conservation, Documentation and Science, to look for metal traces. The matrix surface, where evidence of casting material might be expected, was analysed, but also a broken edge as background control. Elements normally associated with stone such as iron, calcium, silicon, titanium, potassium, strontium and zirconium were detected in both areas. However, the face of the mould alone also contained substantial amounts of lead. Although sought, copper and tin were not detected. The survival of lead alone does not necessarily imply the casting of a lead object in the mould, since experimental work by Barnes (1984) and other analytical results (Needham and Hook 1988) suggest that alloy constituents may be differentially preserved on matrix surfaces. It does, however, suggest that leaded bronze was cast into the mould, which is consistent with a late Bronze Age date.

There is little in the surviving fragment to characterise the type of bronze axe cast. Assuming that the basal groove is roughly central and that the slightly curved base was perpendicular to the original long axis, a fairly gently expanding blade is suggested: about 45 mm wide at the cutting edge and 42 mm wide at the upper break. This shape is more consistent with certain socketed axe blades than with any other form of axe. This deduction, in conjunction with petrology and location, suggests that the mould is likely to belong to the Bulford–Helsbury group, of which three previous examples, from Wessex and the Thames Valley, have similar petrological identifications. The predicted blade shape of the Everley matrix certainly falls within the range known for the Stogursey axe type produced in Bulford–Helsbury moulds. It should be noted, however, that although keratophyre is only known in association with the Bulford–Helsbury group, a few other late Bronze Age stone moulds from southern Britain remain to be identified.

Stogursey axes, otherwise known as South Welsh axes, probably span much of the Late Bronze Age, perhaps from the 11th to the 9th centuries BC. Their production appears to have been widespread across southern England and south-east Wales.

10.2 The flint and chert artefacts

Alan Saville

10.2.1 Introduction

The excavations at Hambledon Hill produced a collection of over 89,000 struck lithic artefacts (weighing over 900 kg), almost entirely of flint (Table 10.6). Surprisingly, these artefacts exhibit little obvious sign of cultural, typo-chronological admixture. There are virtually no flint artefacts of pre-Neolithic character from the hilltop (except one core – ST79 2120 from Neolithic pit 2A F142 – which is almost certainly Mesolithic, and another core – HH76 2210 from phase VIII/a deposits in segment 12 of the main enclosure – which might be), and the only diagnostic indicators of any later Neolithic or Bronze Age activity on the hill are an oblique arrowhead (Fig 10.15: 142) and a tanged arrowhead (Fig 10.15: 143). Even from the hillfort cutting, nothing other than the burnt flints was considered likely to be post-Neolithic. A possible gunflint (RW82 15) from Rolf's Wood (Table 10.60) is the only hint of post-prehistoric flint use.

Table 10.6 Basic composition of the total collection of struck lithic artefacts from the hilltop

Category	*Number*	*%*	*Weight (g)*	*%*
Unretouched flakes	65111	94	617115	72
Core pieces	1108	2	193148	22
Retouched pieces	2766	4	53107	6
Subtotal	68985	100	863370	100
Unretouched flakes	65111	73	617115	68
Core pieces	1108	1	193148	21
Retouched pieces	2766	3	53107	6
Unclassified burnt pieces	20302	23	46722	5
Grand total	89287	100	910092	100

In essence, therefore, the hilltop collection can be regarded as belonging, on diagnostic typological grounds, to the early/middle Neolithic period, representing tools and knapping debris produced during the main period or periods of the construction and occupation of the hilltop enclosure complex in the fourth millennium cal BC. (There are some instances of artefacts with two-phase cortication, showing the reworking of material struck long enough previous for the retouch to have a different state of cortication to that of the blank, but these are relatively rare and not usually from well-stratified contexts.)

In this report the lithic artefact collection is discussed within the framework of the major subdivisions of the site. This is followed by a consideration of the typology involved, an account of the refitting exercise, and then a final discussion of the overall implications. Artefacts collected during excavations on the hillfort and off the hilltop, and during the surface survey of the fields around Hambledon Hill, are considered in sections 10.2.9–10. The artefacts from Neolithic pits in the central area and on the Stepleton spur are respectively in the feature catalogues in sections 3.3.7 and 3.5.6. These provide the data for assessment of the lithic artefacts most closely linked to the life of the two enclosures in terms of presumed internal activities during and after construction during the Neolithic. Detailed data on the lithic artefacts from all other contexts, beyond the level of the tables accompanying this report, will be found in the site archive.

It will be clear from the accounts of the excavations and the other finds, especially the pottery, that the chronological range of activity on the hilltop extends beyond the early/middle Neolithic and that some of the context groups relate wholly to late Neolithic and Bronze Age activity. While the flint assemblage does not appear to reflect this typologically, these later contexts do frequently contain large amounts of flint. This is an inevitable consequence of the virtual indestructibility of flint and its propensity to occur as a residual element in all contexts subsequent to its initial deposition (Saville 2002). This is especially so since the production and discard of struck flint on the hilltop in the earlier phases had been so intense and widespread. The ramifications of this, and the possibility that post-middle Neolithic indicators might be present but smothered, will be considered in the discussion.

This report follows convention in the application of typological analysis to British later prehistoric flint assemblages, as exemplified initially by Clark *et al* (1960) and Smith (1965). The terminology used is well established, the designations of artefact and implement types being self-explanatory or adequately described in previous literature (see especially Saville 1981a and 1981b). Any subdivisions of particular types or classes are described when they are analysed, and the meaning of the symbols used in the artefact illustrations is explained in Figure 10.5.

Unclassified burnt pieces in this collection are only rarely of 'pot-boiler' type. The burnt fragments appear for the most part to be the product of fortuitous burning, comprising the remains of former artefacts, which are no longer identifiable as such, probably as well as some wholly unstruck flint shattered by heat. They are usually present in relatively small numbers, but an exception is provided by the flint assemblage from the Stepleton spur, with a massive number of burnt pieces, including 'pot-boiler' flints, from the southern part of the excavated area, especially in the post-Neolithic upper fills of the inner outwork, which evidence an extraordinarily high concentration (Table 10.18).

The designation 'flaked lumps' is used here as a convenient term for pieces or nodules of flint which show evidence of some human modification or testing, but where this is limited usually to just a few removals from one or more irregular platforms. These pieces show insufficient overall regularity and usage to be classed as cores. In the case of one subassemblage, from the Romano-British hollow way through the gateway of the inner Stepleton outwork, it was necessary to introduce the additional designation 'abraded lump', to describe relatively small pieces of flint which had been modified radically by a non-knapping process, probably wear underfoot by humans and animals (there were 51 of these abraded lumps, weighing in total 670.5 g; they are not otherwise included in the lists and totals).

The methodology of the post-excavation analysis is simply described. Following preliminary sorting (and washing and marking where feasible) and the discarding of all 'natural', unstruck flint, an initial inspection was made of the whole collection. At this stage every artefact was classified, counted, and weighed (unretouched flakes with the same find number were usually weighed in groups, not individually), to produce a basic catalogue of the collection, organised by excavation season and subsite (eg HH74, site A). Selected artefact types (eg scrapers) and groups of artefacts (eg from the internal features of the main enclosure) were then studied in more detail.

Trial re-analysis of selected groups has suggested that the initial rapid analysis will have failed to identify a proportion of the implements, especially such types as fragmentary serrated-edge flakes, unretouched flakes with edge-gloss, and flakes from polished axeheads on which the remaining polished area is small. Re-analysis also indicated a likelihood of some incorrect classification, especially in the case of serrated-edge flakes and unretouched flakes incorrectly catalogued as edge-trimmed flakes. Confirmation of the identification or otherwise of these types often required examination beneath a 10× binocular microscope, which was not used to study every piece during the initial analysis. It is impossible to offer any kind of correction factor for the whole collection to allow for this likely under-identification of implements, but it needs to be emphasised that the figures quoted will accordingly never be exact, though the writer is confident that any errors will not materially affect the general trends and proportions reported. Refitting was not a normal part of the analysis, and was systematically undertaken only in the case of two groups of artefacts from the Stepleton ditches, which the preliminary analysis suggested would be particularly susceptible to this technique. Use-wear analyses were not attempted, but would almost certainly have been impracticable in view of the condition of most of the flints in the collection (see below). The location of flint artefacts on site was generally recorded only by area and context, not by coordinates, so that no detailed reconstruction or plotting of flint artefact distributions is normally possible. The exception concerns certain ditch fill contexts on the Stepleton spur, for which some large-scale drawings of flint artefact-rich deposits were made.

The excavated flint artefacts vary considerably in condition depending on context. Flints from superficial horizons are heavily corticated (Shepherd 1972, 115) and dense white or cream in colour, sometimes with crusty, vesicular surfaces, and can often be extensively abraded and iron-stained. Flint artefacts from protected horizons in the fills of pits or ditches are far less corticated, commonly having a light grey/grey-white or blue-grey/white discolouration, while from some lower ditch fills, particularly where a ditch cut a Clay-with-Flints patch, the artefacts can be totally uncorticated and not discoloured. The stratified flints are in a relatively sharp and unabraded condition, though calcium carbonate encrustation on flints from the lower ditch fills is a common phenomenon.

The condition of the artefacts from the superficial horizons is such as to hamper their analysis considerably. Damage and breakage caused by ploughing have probably inflated the number of miscellaneous retouched pieces, while edge-modified flake-tools like serrated-edge flakes and edge-gloss flakes from superficial contexts are particularly susceptible to damage, which obscures their typology, rendering them unclassifiable as implements. In fact, however, the normal method of initial excavation, involving mechanical stripping of the topsoil, has meant that many of the flint artefacts from superficial deposits have been discarded, only a small proportion (inevitably biased towards larger specimens), being retained. Thus estimates of the true densities of struck flint distribution on the hilltop would be difficult to ascertain, and it must be remembered that the present total assemblage is only a sample.

As a general rule, all flint recovery during excavation depended on immediate visual observation on the part of individual workers, with sieving rarely undertaken. From small hand-excavated features the recovery of most or all of the extant flint artefacts during excavation was probably the norm, though this was not specifically tested for, while from the ditch fills it is clear that a bias did exist against the recovery of smaller flint artefacts and that, although the quality of recovery inevitably varied, total recovery from the larger ditch contexts was never achieved.

Some post-excavation analysis of the flint collection was carried out in the 1970s, each season's finds being deposited with the writer, who was then based at Cheltenham Art Gallery and Museum. However, the bulk of the primary analysis, cataloguing, and refitting on which this report is founded was undertaken in the year 1983–84, when the writer was seconded to the Hambledon Hill Project for this purpose. The illustrations of the lithic artefacts were completed by Joanna Richards in 1984–86, and sporadic further work towards compilation of this report took place until 1989, when the writer moved to Edinburgh. A brief interim report giving a perspective on the Hambledon flint assemblage as it seemed in 1987 was published at this time (Saville 1990a). Arrangements for the housing of the substantial flint collection were concluded in 1994, with its removal from Cheltenham to the Dorset County Museum at Dorchester. The final stage of work on the flint report, including a complete reworking of the previous phasing, began in 1997 and continued intermittently until 2000, when the report was completed.

The objective from the beginning was a formal characterisation of the complete assemblage. It was regarded as important to examine, catalogue, and quantify everything recovered, since, on the one hand, the assemblage was likely to be the biggest and best indicator available of lithic production and use at British Neolithic sites of this category, and, on the other, it was realised that, despite its size, the assemblage would still only be a partial sample of the struck flint from the hill.

An essentially 'broad-brush' approach seemed the appropriate one for analysis to match site circumstances and excavation strategy. It must be appreciated that the Hambledon collection as a whole cannot be compared to high-integrity assemblages recovered from knapping-floors on earlier prehistoric sites (Pettitt 1997), where there is potential for interpretation in terms of the output of individual knappers or actual activity events. The Hambledon flints are likely to have been jumbled in various ways before (and perhaps after) final deposition in their Neolithic contexts. Cultural meaning cannot be extracted from them (except in rare instances of refitting) at the level of the individual producer or user or the event, only at a broader, more generalised technological level. The collection will not necessarily reflect the totality of activities involving flint manufacture and use on the hilltop, but it is likely to reflect the most common of these, and inferences about the implications of the flint assemblage will be made on this basis.

10.2.2 Raw material

Hambledon Hill is an outlier of the Upper Chalk, which extends over its highest, central parts, with the underlying Middle Chalk exposed on the lower slopes, including almost all of the excavated part of the Stepleton spur (Fig 1.2). Flint is present on the hilltop in the Upper Chalk and on its weathered surface, and in extensive pockets of Clay-with-Flints. Indeed, until the ploughing of the main enclosure in 1960, that part of the hilltop was pock-marked with depressions resulting from the grubbing-up of flint for building/roadstone during recent centuries (Fig 2.3; Mercer 1980, 18–19). Some of the hilltop flint nodules, particularly those from the Clay-with-Flints, were suitable for knapping, and were almost certainly the source of some of the raw material used during the Neolithic period. The flint used at Hambledon Hill is all of good quality and was undoubtedly in a fresh condition when knapped. It would seem probable that many nodules were unearthed in the course of the extensive ditch-digging which the Neolithic occupants undertook across the hilltop. The intensification of knapping debris in precisely those areas of the hilltop where ditch-digging coincided with patches of Clay-with-Flints points to ready exploitation of this local resource.

The flint nodules and natural flint debris present in the topsoil and uppermost horizons of the chalk are today largely 'rotten' and quite unsuitable for knapping or for any kind of exploitation, other than the *ad hoc* use of a naturally sharp edge or point. While superficially occurring flint may have been marginally less 'rotten' in the Neolithic period, prior to the intervening millennia of cultivation and erosion, it is unlikely that this ever represented a significant resource for knapping. This is equally the case with the *in situ* bands of tabular flint within the upper few metres of the chalk, as exposed in the edges of the large irregular pits on the Hanford spur (3.6.3). This tabular flint is very distinctive in general character and would be easy to recognise had it been used for knapping, because the cores would be equally distinctive. No such cores are present. The only observed instance of used tabular flint from the hilltop was a hammerstone (ST81 1160) from a phase III context in the Stepleton enclosure ditch.

The question of how much flint was imported to Hambledon Hill in the form of raw material is difficult to resolve. The illustrations of refitted flint nodules (Figs 10.21, 10.23, 10.26, 10.29–34, 10.37, 10.40–41) give a clear picture of the kind of raw material involved. Some of these nodules have wholly cortex-covered exteriors, others have part of their surfaces exposed by thermal action. The nature of some of these nodules, particularly those with more 'chalky' cortex and/or relatively fragile prominent projections which remain intact, raises questions about where exactly on the hilltop they could have originated. There are also a few artefacts recorded during analysis as having a thicker, unabraded cortex than the majority (eg core ST78 1574 from a phase III context in the inner Stepleton outwork ditch) and these must have been imported. Similarly, a very few instances of smooth, presumably water-worn, cortex were noted. One of these pieces,

Table 10.7 Incidence of chert artefacts, typology and location

Context group	*Artefact type*	*Location*	*Weight in grams*
2	Unretouched flake	Main enclosure bank area, posthole P1 F29	0.2
5	Misc retouched piece	Main enclosure ditch, segment 17 L9A phase IV	42.1
6	Edge-trimmed flake	Main enclosure ditch, segment 7 L5 phase V	4.5
7	Unretouched flake	Main enclosure ditch, segment 2 AI L4 phase VI	0.5
11	Unretouched flake	Main enclosure ditch, segment 4 L1 – recent ploughsoil	3.0
11	Unretouched flake	Main enclosure ditch, segment 8 L1 – recent ploughsoil	2.5
11	Unretouched flake	Main enclosure ditch, segment 8 L1 – recent ploughsoil	0.5
11	Unretouched flake	Main enclosure ditch, segment 8 L1 – recent ploughsoil	2.0
14	Unretouched flake	Inner east cross-dyke ditch, segment 5, L5 phase V	1.0
18	Misc retouched piece	Inner east cross-dyke ditch, segment 5 L2 — recent turfline	2.6
22	Unretouched flake	Outer east cross-dyke ditch, segment 5, L4 phase VI	15.0
23	Unretouched flake	Outer east cross-dyke ditch, segment 4, L3 phase VIII/a	0.5
25	Unretouched flake	Pit P2 F14	0.1
25	Unretouched flake	Pit P2 F14	0.3
25	Unretouched flake	Pit P2 F14	0.3
25	Leaf-shaped arrowhead	Pit P2 F14	0.6
25	Leaf-shaped arrowhead	Pit P2 F14	0.2
25	Leaf-shaped arrowhead	Pit P2 F14	0.7
41	Unretouched flake	Long barrow ditch LB5 L1 – recent turf and topsoil	2.5
1	Unretouched flake	Pit A F64	0.5
1	Unretouched flake	Pit or treethrow hole E2 F1 L1	0.5
1	Unretouched flake	Pit or treethrow hole E2 F1 L1	0.5
1	Unretouched flake	Pit N F6	0.5
1	Unretouched flake	Pit N F7i	1.5
1	Unretouched flake	Pit N F7v	4.0
1	Unretouched flake	Pit N F23	0.5
1	Edge-trimmed flake	Pit N F7iii	29.6
1	Edge-trimmed flake	Pit N F17	4.9
1	Leaf-shaped arrowhead	Pit A F41	0.5
1	Leaf-shaped arrowhead	Pit N F42	2.4
46	Unretouched flake	Site E2 – recent ploughsoil	0.5
46	Unretouched flake	Site N – recent ploughsoil	6.0
46	Unretouched flake	Site B – recent ploughsoil	1.0
46	Leaf-shaped arrowhead	Site A – recent ploughsoil	2.0
46	Misc retouched piece	Natural hollow N F12	5.4
65	Unretouched flake	Inner Stepleton outwork, segment 7 L3A phase V	3.0
65	Unretouched flake	Inner Stepleton outwork, segment 7 L3A phase V	4.0
67	Unretouched flake	Inner Stepleton outwork, segment 6 L3 phase VII/a	1.0
67	Unretouched flake	Inner Stepleton outwork, segment 6 L3 phase VII/a	23.0
	Total		170.4

from the main enclosure ditch, was a primary flake (HH76 1045, from phase VI), suggesting the import of a cobble for knapping (or use as a hammerstone). Other probable beach pebbles without clear signs of use or used only as hammerstones were noticed (eg HH77 1386 from a superficial context on site N; HH77 807, from phase VI in the south long barrow). Fiona Roe (10.1.2) has identified several of the flint hammerstones as being Chesil Beach pebbles (eg HH77 2286 from Neolithic pit N F7iv and HH75 294 from phase III in the main enclosure ditch).

Almost all the artefacts were made on flint, the exception being 39 chert artefacts, mostly comprising unretouched flakes (Table 10.7). Chert does not occur naturally at Hambledon, nor in any quantity in the immediate vicinity. The chert was almost all of matt appearance, except for one flake of 'quartzy' type, resembling greensand chert, and an arrowhead of crystalline character and grey-brown colour. The colours of the 37 pieces of matt chert were recorded as follows: grey/blue (1); medium grey (7); medium/dark grey (6); dark grey (15); grey/black (6); black (2). All of these matt pieces can be matched within the variability of 'Portland' chert, and an ultimate source from the Dorset coast in the Portland Bill area is possible, though they could perhaps have been acquired as Portland 'erratics' from other locations within a wider surrounding zone (cf Sharples 1991, 254).

There are no chert cores from the site, and most of the flakes are small or fragmentary, though one of the unretouched flakes (HH77 1519 from the topsoil on site N), a complete example, 33 mm long, does raise the possibility of the knapping of this raw material on site. Otherwise, the importation of prepared implements and/or blanks is more probable. This must especially be the case with the chert leaf-shaped arrowheads. That six of the 42 leaf-shaped arrowheads from Hambledon should be of chert (Table 10.51), together with the fact that one of the leaf-shaped arrowheads (HH76 683 from phase VIII/a in segment 7 of the main enclosure) is of an unusual, and presumably non-local, variegated (red/white) flint, suggests, in view of their overall low numbers at Hambledon, that these implements were primarily 'exotic', and not made on site.

However, this does not appear to be the case with the flint axeheads. These are made of a raw material which cannot be distinguished from that of the general run of artefacts on the site, and therefore they cannot necessarily be seen as imported implements. Since the chert artefacts constitute an insignificant percentage of the collection, it would appear that, apart perhaps from the arrowheads, there was no attempt to organise its importation. This would further imply, since chert would not have been difficult to obtain, that this raw material was perhaps not in general seen to have any practical or symbolic advantage.

On the other hand, the distribution of chert artefacts is strongly weighted towards the central area, with only four chert flakes from Stepleton and none from Hanford. There is a 'concentration' in the fills of Neolithic features of the central area but, given the overall low presence of chert artefacts, it is difficult to attach any specific importance to this other than perhaps in the case of the arrowheads.

Table 10.8 Incidence of flint hammerstones and hammerstone fragments

Note: this table includes flint hammerstones identified by Fiona Roe, for which weights are not available
For the central area see also Figure 3.69

Context group	*Find*	*Location*	*Burnt*	*Weight in grams*
4	HH75 294	Main enclosure ditch, segment 8 L7 phase III		
4	HH75 851	Main enclosure ditch, segment 9 L7 phase III		
4	HH75 1004	Main enclosure ditch, segment 9 L8 phase III		
5	HH76 2746	Main enclosure ditch, segment 17 L9A phase IV	yes	60.4
7	HH75 204	Main enclosure ditch, segment 8 L6 phase VI		272.4
7	HH75 1601	Main enclosure ditch, segment 8 L6 phase VI		
9	HH75 1366	Main enclosure ditch, segment 8 L3A phase VII/a		
9	HH75 1705	Main enclosure ditch, segment 8 L3A phase VII/a		
28	HH77 1397	Inner south cross-dyke ditch, segment 1 L9 phase VI	yes	33.6
29	HH77 273	Inner south cross-dyke ditch, segment 1 L5 phase VII/a		115.0
37	HH77 967	Long barrow ditch, LB4 L13 phase III		182.5
37	HH77 1151	Long barrow ditch, LB5 L13 phase III		326.3
38	HH77 679	Long barrow ditch, LB4 L9 phase VI		180.0
1	HH77 2286	Pit N F7iv		
46	HH74 29	Central area, unstratified		171.2
53	ST80 1938	Pit 3A F66		400.0
53	ST81 1660	Pit 4B F130		250.0
53	ST81 1963	Pit 4B F153		445.0
53	ST81 2408	Pit 4B F198		225.0
55	ST80 1160	Stepleton enclosure, segment 2 L5B phase II		220.0
55	ST80 1160	Stepleton enclosure, segment 2 L5B phase II		310.0
55	ST80 1992	Stepleton enclosure, segment 3 L6 phase I		117.0
56	ST80 2468	Stepleton enclosure, segment 3 L4C phase III		580.0
56	ST80 2468	Stepleton enclosure, segment 3 L4C phase III		600.0
56	ST81 386	Stepleton enclosure, segment 15 L4B phase III		470.0
56	ST81 818	Stepleton enclosure, segment 15 L3A phase III		208.5
56	ST81 824	Stepleton enclosure, segment 12 L3B phase III		400.0
56	ST81 1160	Stepleton enclosure, segment 7 L3A phase III		290.0
56	ST81 1292	Stepleton enclosure, segment 12 L3A phase III		197.0
60	ST79 871	Stepleton enclosure, segment 1 L2A phase VIII/a	yes	189.7
60	ST81 412	Stepleton enclosure, segment 14 L1, phase VIII/a	yes	162.6
71	ST78 1087	Middle Stepleton outwork, segment 10 L6 phase I		370.0
62	ST78 2902	Inner Stepleton outwork, bank area, posthole 1B F11		275.0
62	ST80 2442	Inner Stepleton outwork bank area, pit 3B F435	yes	275.0
64	ST78 2772	Inner Stepleton outwork, segment 7 L4 phase III		194.0
64	ST81 2573	Inner Stepleton outwork, segment 4 L3B phase V		222.4
68	ST78 380	Inner Stepleton outwork, segment 8 L2 phase VIII/a		280.0
68	ST78 1354	Inner Stepleton outwork, segment 7 L2 phase VIII/a		510.0
68	ST79 1035	Inner Stepleton outwork, segment 5 L2 phase VIII/a		360.0
85	HN82 387	Inner Hanford outwork, segment 3 L5 phase I		226.6

10.2.3 Technology

Direct information on knapping methods and procedures comes from two sources, the flint artefacts themselves and the recovery of hammerstones. In the former category, by far the most significant information comes from the refitting exercise undertaken on some of the Stepleton material (10.2.6) and to a lesser extent from analyses of the cores and the unretouched flakes, which are also relevant to the observation of reduction strategies (10.2.3).

From the examination of artefacts throughout the collection, it was concluded, albeit impressionistically, that hard-hammer flaking was far more prevalent than soft-hammer flaking, but it also has to be admitted that the smaller debitage from finer retouching has not generally been recovered, introducing a significant bias into this conclusion.

Hard hammers of flint were present in the numbers shown in Table 10.8. These were mainly spherical or subspherical pieces of flint (or parts thereof) with abraded, crush-marked surface areas of various extents. Cores reused as hammers were counted as hammerstones somewhat arbitrarily on the basis of the extent of the crushing, so that some cores exhibiting only minor traces of hammering, with the core class still obvious, were classified as cores rather than as hammers. However, this only applies to about ten cores in the whole collection.

The total of 40 hammerstones seems fairly substantial given that these tools are generally regarded as highly curatable personal gear (Saville 1990b, 176). If the fragmentary, damaged, and perfunctorily used examples are excluded, however, only a few 'classic' spherical flint hammers are present (eg ST79 871; ST80 1938; ST81 824). To these, however, must be added the quartzitic cobble hammerstones discussed by Fiona Roe (see 10.1.2).

The distribution of the flint hammerstones does not correlate especially well with concentrations of knapping debris. For example, one might expect more hammers from the phase VIII/a fills of the inner Stepleton outwork, to equate with the mass of cores and flakes found there (Fig 3.131); or from segments 12–14 of the main enclosure rather than the less flint-rich segments 8 and 9 (Figs 3.68–69). This lack of correlation may reinforce the interpretation of hammerstones as curated items.

10.2.4 Distribution

The main enclosure ditch

(context groups 3–11; Tables 10.9–11)

The complex stratigraphy of the ditch infills not only made precise allocation of finds to contexts difficult during excavation, but the recutting episodes, natural weathering and silting, and any backfilling or bioturbation, have all combined to ensure the probability of a high degree of residuality and mixture among the ditch assemblages, especially the upper ones. Only the basal silts and the primary chalk rubble (Table 10.11) can be relied on to provide a relatively uncontaminated sample of early/middle Neolithic activity, and these, unfortunately for the flint analysis, are among the least flintiferous horizons. Other horizons, though chronologically subsequent in formation, will inevitably contain residual earlier flints as well (potentially) as artefacts contemporary with their formation. The pottery evidence makes this clear (see Smith, 9.1), but whereas it is relatively easy to distinguish potsherds chronologically by means of form, fabric, and style, this is not the case with the lithic artefacts, save in rare diagnostic cases. The masses of flint artefacts in the upper horizons must be regarded as a completely mixed bag, of little interest other than in gross terms of quantity and typological representation.

The phase I–II basal silts (context group 3) were fairly vestigial contexts and unsurprisingly contained little flint. This assemblage is of some interest in that the presence of the serrated-edge flakes and the axehead fragment confirms the primary context of these two types. However, the assemblage is too small for the absence of other types, such as leaf-shaped arrowheads and 'laurel-leaf' bifacials, to be used as negative evidence. One refit was noted, between an unretouched secondary flake and a core fragment, both from segment 13.

Implements from the phase III chalk rubble fills (context group 4) are slightly more numerous than from the basal silts, but they serve only to confirm the nature of that assemblage, adding no new types apart from the piercer. Primary knapping debris of unretouched flakes and cores dominates this material, the cores alone representing a significant part of the whole assemblage (25% by weight).

The phase IV 'grey pits' (context group 5) produced a small assemblage which sees the first occurrences in the ditch infills of a leaf-shaped arrowhead, a chert artefact, and an unclassified bifacial piece. It also contains the only implement classified as a splintered piece from the hilltop. This is a flake (HH76 1460) from segment 16 with bifacial retouch at the base and removals across the ventral surface at the distal end, presumably as a result of use. The arrowhead (HH76 1934), also from segment 16, is a broken tip only.

The phase V silts (context group 6) have proportionally fewer core pieces and more retouched items than group 4, and in particular a high representation of serrated-edge flakes, predominantly from segment 7, which had 13 examples. Segment 13 contained three distinctive flakes obviously struck from the same nodule, but they did not refit.

The phase VI 'slots' (context group 7) are very flint-rich deposits, containing almost as many pieces as all the underlying horizons together. The trend is continued from group 6 towards fewer core pieces and increased numbers of implements. One refit was noted between an unretouched tertiary blade and a core, both from segment 12.

Table 10.9 Central area. Summary of struck lithic artefacts

b = burnt. Weights are in grams, rounded to the nearest gram

		Main enclosure					*Inner E cross-dyke*				*Outer E cross-dyke*				*Inner S cross-dyke*			*Outer S cross-dyke*		*Western outwork*				*Long barrow*							
		Phases I–III	*Phase IV*	*Phase V*	*Phase VI*	*Phases VII–VIII*	*Phases I–III*	*Phase V*	*Phase VI*	*Phases VII–VIII*	*Phases I–III*	*Phase V*	*Phase VI*	*Phases VII–VIII*	*Phases I–III*	*Phase VI*	*Phases VII–VIII*	*Phases I–III*	*Phases R & VIII*	*Phases I–III*	*Phase V*	*Phase VI*	*Phase VIII*	*Phases I–III*	*Phase IV*	*Phase V*	*Phase IV*	*Phases VII–VIII*	*Pits*	*Remainder*	*Totals*
Unretouched flakes	no.	1720	193	1025	2558	4462	120	41	71	186	11	113	156	102	45	36	64	13	51	1	11	141	33	770	22	202	880	2020	2858	3756	21661
	wt	*18673*	*836*	*8063*	*19822*	*35088*	*718*	*273*	*567*	*1627*	*169*	*930*	*735*	*797*	*412*	*265*	*755*	*89*	*666*	*15*	*141*	*257*	*459*	*8861*	*111*	*2212*	*9426*	*17934*	*13320*	*22196*	*165417*
Unretouched flakes, chert	no.				1	4		1					1	1														1	7	7	23
	wt				*1*	*8*		*1*					*15*	*1*														*3*	*8*	*9*	*46*
Unretouched flakes, burnt	no.	2	8	4	5	23		1					1	2		1								2	13	1	3		82	34	182
	wt	*14*	*29*	*15*	*27*	*108*		*7*					*2*	*4*		*16*								*6*	*45*	*5*	*17*		*316*	*151*	*762*
Cores	no.	31		3	28	32	2	2		2			3		1							2		13		1	31	6	25	13	195
	wt	*7308*		*469*	*3529*	*3003*	*211*	*194*		*150*			*243*		*113*							*178*		*2760*		*41*	*6271*	*435*	*1836*	*1224*	*27965*
Core fragments	no.	9		1	6	6				1														4			4		6	5	42
	wt	*1290*		*118*	*535*	*436*				*170*														*321*			*577*		*441*	*330*	*4218*
Flaked lumps	no.	13		3	5	3		1																3			15	3	3	1	50
	wt	*3719*		*375*	*459*	*354*		*70*																*542*			*2779*	*363*	*152*	*83*	*8896*
Serrated-edged flakes	no.	10	9	20	55	23	3	3	5	5	1	2	3	1										4			3	1	160	35	343
	wt	*73*	*73*	*142*	*473*	*138*	*42*	*30*	*27*	*41*	*8*	*10*	*18*	*6*										*35*			*28*	*5*	*1073*	*233*	*2455*
Unretouched flakes with edge-gloss	no.			1	1																								5	1	8
	wt			*6*	*14*																								*25*	*10*	*55*
Edge-trimmed flakes (class A)	no.	2			9	10							1				1		1							2	1	1	22	12	62
	wt	*22*			*184*	*130*							*30*				*7*		*7*							*20*	*15*	*5*	*237*	*107*	*764*
Edge-trimmed flakes	no.	22	7	15	55	64		2	7	3	1	3	10	2	1	1								4	1		7	3	81	59	348
	wt	*195*	*116*	*151*	*529*	*640*		*34*	*90*	*22*	*7*	*37*	*99*	*4*	*23*	*12*								*88*	*24*		*96*	*29*	*741*	*620*	*3557*
Edge-trimmed flakes, chert	no.																												2		2
	wt																												*35*		*35*
Scrapers	no.	16		9	49	72		1	4	16	1	3	3	3	2	7							2	7		4	15	20	43	72	349
	wt	*444*		*260*	*1524*	*1757*		*18*	*112*	*285*	*49*	*119*	*47*	*35*	*66*	*152*							*81*	*225*		*99*	*447*	*445*	*1038*	*1664*	*8867*
Piercers	no.	2	1	3	7	21			3	3			2											2			2	5	12	21	84
	wt	*32*	*9*	*33*	*81*	*257*			*70*	*18*			*18*											*19*			*17*	*89*	*140*	*267*	*1050*
Leaf-shaped arrowheads	no.		1	1	4	3			2	1			1																5	5	23
	wt		*1*	*1*	*6*	*5*			*5*	*3*			*1*																*8*	*7*	*37*
Leaf-shaped arrowheads, chert	no.																												2	4	6
	wt																												*3*	*4*	*7*
Oblique arrowhead	no.					1																									1
	wt					*2*																									*2*

		Main enclosure					Inner E cross-dyke				Outer E cross-dyke				Inner S cross-dyke			Outer S cross-dyke		Western outwork				Long barrow							
		Phases I–III	*Phase IV*	*Phase V*	*Phase VI*	*Phases VII–VIII*	*Phases I–III*	*Phase V*	*Phase VI*	*Phases VII–VIII*	*Phases I–III*	*Phase V*	*Phase VI*	*Phases VII–VIII*	*Phases I–III*	*Phase VI*	*Phases VII–VIII*	*Phases I–III*	*Phases R & VIII*	*Phases I–III*	*Phase V*	*Phase VI*	*Phase VIII*	*Phases I–III*	*Phase IV*	*Phase V*	*Phase IV*	*Phases VII–VIII*	*Pits*	*Remainder*	*Totals*
'Laurel leaf'	no.					2																							1		3
bifacial pieces	*wt*					*33*																							*14*		*47*
Polished axeheads	no.	1			2									1															2		6
& fragments	*wt*	*36*			*191*									*112*															*223*		*562*
Flakes from	no.	1	1		1																			1					3	3	10
polished axeheads	*wt*	*36*	*7*		*2*																			*5*					*31*	*14*	*95*
Knives	no.				1	5																								1	7
	wt				*18*	*100*																								*10*	*128*
Picks/roughouts	no.				1	1							1																		3
	wt				*117*	*146*							*57*																		*320*
Unclassified	no.		1[b]	1	1	3				2			1																	2	11
bifacial pieces	*wt*		*25*	*16*	*37*	*70*				*12*			*50*																	*41*	*251*
Rods	no.					1							1		1													1		1	5
	wt					*36*							*17*		*91*													*40*		*13*	*197*
'Fabricators'	no.					2																									2
	wt					*48*																									*48*
Saw	no.																													1	1
	wt																													*10*	*10*
Splintered piece	no.		1																												1
	wt		*14*																												*14*
Miscellaneous	no.	23	4	14	34	111	1	1	6	12		5	8	3		1					2		1	7		3	10	27	53	112	438
retouched pieces	*wt*	*758*	*142*	*334*	*1051*	*2171*	*53*	*14*	*60*	*129*		*78*	*147*	*79*		*7*					*42*		*14*	*241*		*47*	*210*	*495*	*840*	*1465*	*8377*
Misc retouched	no.																													1	1
piece, chert	*wt*																													*5*	*5*
Unclassified burnt	no.	6	57		56	71							5	1		2							1	2	234	1	3	4	597	147	1187
pieces	*wt*	*83*	*91*		*105*	*375*							*21*	*1*		*44*							*14*	*3*	*400*	*4*	*66*	*97*	*2991*	*794*	*5089*
Totals	no.	1858	283	1100	2879	4920	126	53	98	231	14	126	197	116	50	48	65	13	52	1	13	143	37	819	270	214	974	2092	3969	4293	25054
	wt	*32683*	*1343*	*9983*	*28705*	*44905*	*1024*	*641*	*931*	*2457*	*233*	*1174*	*1500*	*1039*	*705*	*496*	*762*	*89*	*673*	*15*	*183*	*435*	*568*	*13106*	*580*	*2428*	*19949*	*19940*	*23472*	*29257*	*239276*

The bulk of the flints in the phase VII/a 'Beaker' deposits (context group 9) derives from two segments: segment 8 with 65 pieces, and segment 10 with 184 pieces. The oblique arrowhead (Fig 10.15: 142), which is from segment 10, is a late Neolithic type, but otherwise the assemblage appears residual from the main activity, with no other obvious clues of admixture and certainly no flints which are transparently 'Beaker' period.

The extensive upper fills of the ditches (context groups 10–11) predictably contain a mass of flint artefacts. These add nothing to the enclosure inventory apart from the three knives from segment 8 (see below) and the 'fabricator' (HH74 113) from segment 4, an atypical flat-flake example (cf Saville 1973, 15), which is perhaps most likely to post-date the main activity, but could post-date it very considerably, since it is not necessarily prehistoric.

Table 10.10 gives a breakdown of the whole ditch assemblage of 11,040 artefacts by segment and context grouping. These figures are of course biased by the size of each segment and the extent of excavation in each. Even so, the facts that 48% derives from segment 13, and that segments 12–15 together produced over 69% of the whole ditch assemblage, are noteworthy. A plausible explanation for this concentration is provided by the location of these segments in a zone of Clay-with-Flints. It seems highly probable that the flint nodules derived from the excavation of the ditch in this area were used in the immediate vicinity for knapping, the debris remaining local and becoming incorporated through different episodes as indicated by the context groupings. This seems to be supported by the character of the material from these segments, which comprises 74% of all unretouched flakes and 69% of all cores from the ditches, but only 23% of the scrapers and 20% of the serrated-edge flakes. Thus this material has a predominantly industrial character, much more so than that from the other excavated ditch areas of the main Hambledon enclosure.

This was investigated further by looking more selectively at the stratigraphic make-up of the assemblages from the ditch segments. Phases I–III were taken together as an indicator of the material most closely related to spatially patterned activities associated with the early period of enclosure construction and use (Table 10.11). From these phases, 82% of the artefacts derive from segments 12–13, which includes most

Table 10.10 Main enclosure ditch: numbers of lithic artefacts by phase and segment

Segment X – artefacts in this row could be allocated to specific phases, but not to segments

Ditch segment	*Phases I–II*	*Phase III*	*Phase IV*	*Phase V*	*Phase VI*	*Phase VII*	*Phase VII/a*	*Phase VIII/a*	*Miscellaneous and unstratified*	*Total no.*	*Totals %*
1	18		63	4	75	76		14	40	290	2.6
2	10	5			51			35	3	104	0.9
3	2	3		30	65			29	101	230	2.1
4	3	29	1	19	89			47	231	419	3.8
5	5			1	14			2		22	0.2
6		1	1		18					20	0.2
7	3	2		73	56			20		154	1.4
8	8	31		16	80		65	99	178	477	4.3
9	26	36		16	1			30		109	1.0
10					50		184	18	13	265	2.4
11	12	8		2	26		3	11	71	133	1.2
12		289		62	231			60	292	934	8.5
13	82	1145		702	1263			1878	226	5296	48.0
14	8	36			627			106	83	860	7.8
15	2	67			2			1	9	81	0.7
16		7	137	126	13		1	20	10	314	2.9
17		2	77	25	62			15		181	1.6
18		2	3	1	47		2	21	21	97	0.9
19	10	1			92		2	99		204	1.8
X		5	1	23	17			3	801	850	7.7
Total no.	189	1669	283	1100	2879	76	257	2508	2079	11040	
Total %	1.7	15.1	2.6	10.0	26.1	0.7	2.3	22.7	18.8		

Table 10.11 Main enclosure ditch. Lithic artefact types from phases I–III combined, subdivided by ditch segment

X – artefacts in this column could be allocated to specific phases, but not to segments
No artefacts from segment 10 were attributed to these phases

	Segment 1	2	3	4	5	6	7	8	9	11	12	13	14	15	16	17	18	19	X	*Total no.*	*Total %*
Unretouched flakes	16	10	5	26	5	1	4	24	39	19	273	1182	40	57	5	1	2	8	5	1722	92.7
Cores							1		2		7	17	1	1				2		31	1.7
Core frags.											1	7	1							9	0.5
Flaked lumps											4	9								13	0.7
Serrated		1						3	1		1		1	1	1			1		10	0.5
Edge-trimmed				3				3	3		1	5	1	7		1				24	1.3
Scrapers	2			3				3	6					1	1					16	0.9
Piercers									1			1								2	0.1
Axe/pick										1										1	0.1
Axe flake									1											1	0.1
Misc ret.								5	9		2	5		2						23	1.2
Uncl burnt		4						1				1								6	0.3
Total no.	18	15	5	32	5	1	5	39	62	20	289	1227	44	69	7	2	2	11	5	1858	
Total %	1	1		2				2	3	1	16	66	2	4				1			

of the cores and all the core fragments and flaked lumps. By contrast, only 19% of the retouched pieces from these phases come from these segments.

The east cross-dykes

The excavated inner east cross-dyke ditch segments (context groups 12–18; Table 10.9) produced about half the total number of artefacts as the adjacent Hambledon enclosure ditch segments on Sites J1, D1, and E1 (ie 508 compared to 1180). However, they share the same assemblage profile, with a relatively high proportion of retouched pieces. Two of the leaf-shaped arrowheads are illustrated (Fig 10.15: 129–30).

The outer east cross-dyke ditch fills (context groups 19–24; Table 10.9) contained slightly fewer artefacts than the inner east cross-dyke ditch in total, though this varies between segments, with more from the outer than the inner on Site E2. A far smaller percentage is derived from the primary fills, however, suggesting little flint production or use in this area in the initial stages. The assemblage profile is similar, but with proportionally fewer retouched pieces.

The south cross-dykes

Of the total of 925 artefacts from the inner south cross-dyke bank area (context group 25), 347 come from general contexts, the rest from features. The three features with struck flints were: P2 F8 (25 artefacts); F9+F12 (35 artefacts); and F14 (518 artefacts). The last, dug into the surface under the inner south cross-dyke bank, contained an interesting sealed assemblage (Table 10.12), with three chert unretouched flakes and three fragmentary chert leaf-shaped arrowheads.

Table 10.12 Lithic artefacts from the fill of pit P2 F14 in the area of the bank of the inner south cross-dyke

	Number	*Weight in grams*
Unretouched flakes	431	648.7
Unretouched flakes, chert	3	0.7
Unretouched flakes, burnt	5	9.5
Cores	2	481.5
Flaked lump	1	83.1
Edge-trimmed flake	1	6.4
Scraper	1	32.4
Leaf-shaped arrowheads, fragmentary, chert	3	1.5
Flake from a polished flint axehead	1	10.0
Miscellaneous retouched piece	1	24.8
Unclassified burnt pieces	69	154.5
Total	518	1453.1

The assemblage from the inner south cross-dyke, ditch fills (context groups 26–31; Table 10.9) is a small one, with the artefacts fairly evenly spread between the phases. Most of them derive from the cross-dyke ditch on Site P2, with only 25 artefacts from the ditch terminal sampled in 1982 on the WOWK4 area, from context groups 28 and 31. This terminal was where Desmond Bonney found three polished flint axeheads in a primary context (3.3.4). These implements were described as '3 chipped & polished flint axes within a few inches of one other', but are apparently now lost.

Only a minimal scatter was present through the fills of the outer south cross-dyke ditch (context groups 32.2–35; Table 10.9), composed almost exclusively of unretouched flakes, as was the material from the adjacent bank area.

The western outwork (Table 10.9)

Very little struck flint was recorded from the ditch. The basal silts and the chalk rubble fills together contained only a single flint flake. This is a small assemblage with virtually no implements of note, apart from a tiny flake from a polished flint axehead from the topsoil of the bank area in WOWK 2.

The south long barrow

Overall the ditches of the long barrow (context groups 36–41; Table 10.9) produced a sizable but restricted assemblage of a largely industrial nature corresponding to the local presence of Clay-with-Flints. The paucity of serrated-edge flakes from this area is noticeable, but seems to reflect a pattern on this part of the hilltop. Only the phase IV 'grey pit' deposit (LB3 L17) is anomalous in containing so many unclassifiable burnt pieces (and burnt unretouched flakes). These dominate the burnt categories from the long barrow ditches, giving a somewhat skewed picture when the overall figures are considered.

The major part of the concentration of cores, core fragments, and flaked lumps in phase VI derives from a single context, LB4–5 F4, a pit cut into the north butt of the east ditch. The raw material represented is local to the hilltop and it seems probable that it was derived from the long barrow ditches when originally dug. The flint was probably exploited on the spot, then the residues incorporated into the long barrow mound, to eventually erode back into the ditch.

Material from the phase VII/a pits cut into the silted east ditch (context group 39.1) is dominated by unretouched flakes and contains no implements that are in any way distinctive. The flint is likely to be entirely residual rather than contemporary with the more recent pottery from these contexts.

Discrete early/middle Neolithic features in the central area (context group 1) (Tables 10.9, 10.13–16)

A collection of 3969 artefacts was recovered from these features, and this represents one of the most significant subassemblages, in terms of lithic implement use assumed to be contemporary with the main phase of activity at the main enclosure. Table 10.13 gives the typological detail of this collection, while the contents of each feature are listed in the catalogue which concludes section 3.7 of Chapter 3. The overall typological and structural characteristics of the collection will be considered in the subsequent discussion, since these elements derive significance from comparison with the collections from other context groups and other sites. Some points can be made on occurrence and distribution, however.

Table 10.13 Struck flint from Neolithic features in the central area (context group 1) and on the Stepleton spur (context group 53)

	Central area				*Stepleton spur*			
	No.	*No. %*	*Weight in grams*	*Wt %*	*No.*	*No. %*	*Weight in grams*	*Wt %*
Unretouched flakes	**2858**	72	13320.4	57	**2159**	72	11554.5	55
Unretouched flakes, chert	**7**		8.0					
Unretouched flakes, burnt	**82**	2	315.5	1	**155**	5	612.9	3
Cores	**25**		1835.9	8	**20**	1	3666.4	17
Core fragments	**6**		440.9	2	**3**		187.5	1
Flaked lumps	**3**		152.0		**4**		478.0	2
Serrated-edge flakes	**160**	4	1073.1	5	**62**	2	499.7	2
Unretouched flakes with edge-gloss	**5**		25.0		**7**		28.7	
Edge-trimmed flakes (class A)	**22**		237.4	1	**5**		65.7	
Edge-trimmed flakes	**81**	2	740.9	3	**44**[1]	2	824.0	4
Edge-trimmed flakes, chert	**2**		34.5					
Scrapers	**43**	1	1038.2	4	**24**	1	601.6	3
Piercers	**12**		140.2		**3**		42.9	
Leaf-shaped arrowheads	**5**		7.6					
Leaf-shaped arrowheads, chert	**2**		2.9					
Polished flint axeheads & fragments	**2**		223.0	1	**2**[2]		134.6	1
Flakes from polished flint axeheads	**3**		31.3		**3**		10.4	
'Laurel-leaf' bifacial piece	**1**		13.5		**1**		13.0	
Rod, burnt					**1**		71.6	
Miscellaneous retouched pieces	**53**	1	840.4	4	**22**[3]	1	778.7	4
Unclassified burnt pieces	**597**	15	2991.1	13	**468**	16	1630.6	8
Totals	**3969**		23471.8		**2983**		21200.8	

1 2 of these, weighing 8.3 g, are burnt
2 1 of these, weighing 5.1g, is burnt
3 1 of these, weighing 4.5g, is burnt

Table 10.14 Quantification of lithic artefacts (including unclassified burnt pieces) from features in the central area (context group 1) and the Stepleton spur (context group 53), expressed in ranges of total numbers per feature

	1–10 artefacts per pit	*11–50 artefacts per pit*	*51–100 artefacts per pit*	*>100 artefacts per pit*	*Total number of pits*
Central area	18	29	14	10	71
Stepleton spur	48	31	5	9	93
Totals	66	60	19	19	164

Table 10.15 Central area Neolithic pits (context group 1) containing more than 100 lithic artefacts

Flakes etc = all unretouched flakes, including chert and burnt; cores etc = all core pieces, including fragments and flaked lumps; serrated flakes = all serrated-edge flakes including unretouched flakes with edge-gloss; edge-trimmed = all edge-trimmed flakes, including class A; others = all other specific implement categories; misc ret pieces = all miscellaneous retouched pieces; uncl burnt pieces = all unclassified burnt pieces

Feature		*Flakes etc*	*Cores etc*	*Serrated flakes*	*Edge-trimmed*	*Scrapers*	*Piercers*	*Others*	*Misc ret pieces*	*Uncl burnt pieces*	*Totals*
A F 41	no.	200	2	3	1	2	4	3	4	321	540
	%	37		1			1	1	1	59	
A F 64	no.	101	1		1	6	1			21	131
	%	77	1			4	1			16	
B F2	no.	137	1	8	4	1	1		3		155
	%	88	1	5	2	1	1		2		
N F6	no.	124		7						23	154
	%	81		4						15	
N F7i/ii	no.	255	13	11	7	3		1	2	15	307
	%	83	4	4	2	1			1	5	
N F 11	no.	109		4				1	4	14	132
	%	83		3				1	3	11	
N F 22	no.	127		7	4				1	18	157
	%	81		4	2				1	12	
N F 23	no.	149		18	5		2		1	17	192
	%	78		9	3		1			9	
N F 25	no.	144		7	10	2	1		2	9	175
	%	83		4	6	1			1	5	
N F 90	no.	92	2	2	7					13	116
	%	79	2	2	6					11	
All features	no.	1438	19	67	39	14	9	5	17	451	2059
above no.	%	70	1	3	2	1			1	22	
Total group 1	no.	2947	34	165	105	43	12	13	53	597	3969
	%	74	1	4	3	1			1	15	

A total of 71 features, which for convenience can all be regarded as pits, contained struck lithic material within their fills. The numerical range, which varied between a minimum of one item and a maximum of 540 pieces, is summarised in Table 10.14 This shows that the majority of pits have less than 50 artefacts and that few pits have more than 100 artefacts. Potential lithic content is obviously linked to the actual size of each pit and, if this is taken into account, there would appear to be no especially significant concentrations or clusters of lithic finds in features within the excavated areas. Searching for patterning in this way would anyway be problematic, since it cannot be known which features are precisely contemporary with each other. No conjoins were noted between lithic artefacts from different features during analysis, though this was not rigorously tested. The contents of the ten most prolific pits have been listed together and shown in percentage terms (Table 10.15) to examine for any divergence from the overall norm.

In general there is a recurrent pattern of the contents being dominated by unretouched flakes, with low numbers of core pieces and relatively high numbers of implements, especially serrated-edge flakes. Nevertheless, some feature contents stand out as unusual. The most obvious is A F41, which contained the highest total of lithic artefacts, 59% of which were unclassified burnt pieces. Site records indicate that a further 'bucket of burnt flint' came from this feature, but was not kept. For the collection from the 71 features as a whole, the representation of burnt flints is 15% or, expressed another way, feature A F41 contained more than 53% of all the unclassified burnt pieces from this context group. Adjacent features A F27 and N F90 do not share a predominance of burnt pieces, so there has been some specificity about the accumulation of the assemblage in A F41.

Another unusual collection comes from pit cluster II, on site N, near the centre of the enclosure, in that it contains the largest proportion of cores. On the other hand these are relatively large features, which altogether contain 489 artefacts or 12% of the whole collection from context group 1 (17% by weight). If the figures for this cluster are combined with those from the adjacent features N F5, F6, F10, and F11, then the totals are 899 artefacts representing 23% of context group 1 (24.5% by weight). This concentration near the centre of the enclosure is of potential interest, especially in view of the almost total absence of features with struck flint from the adjacent excavated areas (Fig 3.68).

Pit N F23 has an unusual assemblage in terms of the relatively large number of serrated-edge flakes, proportionally twice as numerous as in the combined totals for context group 1. This feature and the adjacent N F22 have 15% of all serrated-edge flakes from the group, which may hint at a particular focus in this part of the enclosure.

A central question in considering the pits in the central area is whether the lithic assemblages within them have any specific meaning, either in themselves, or in relation to the features in which they occur. The writer has no information to suggest that any patterned placement of lithic items in the features was observed during excavation. Thus analysis is reliant on the typology itself, and on any patterning within the typological data, for any clues which might indicate non-randomness. This does not seem to be the case.

One of the largest assemblages from a single feature (N F7i) was examined in detail to investigate any potential for refitting within a single feature, since in this instance both cores and flakes were present (Table 10.16) There were no refits, and the varied cortex on the secondary flakes and cores indicated derivation from many different nodules, probably from different sources. The flakes also had a varied range of cortication and discolouration, which strongly suggests they did not all arrive in the feature in a fresh condition or at the same time. The conclusion is that the assemblage from this pit represented mixed, general debris and not the product of a nearby knapping event or a cache.

It can be noted that small numbers of unclassified burnt pieces and burnt artefacts occur in most features, pointing to a general spread of burnt material across the area of the enclosure, also seen in the widespread presence of charcoal. These burnt pieces are always in association with unburnt artefacts, which clearly suggests the lithic contents of the features do not derive directly from a single source, in which flints would either be burnt or unburnt. The formation processes from which the contents of each pit derive are unknowable, but they probably varied and are regarded here as unlikely to reflect purposeful deposition. If it is accepted that the contents of each feature do not reflect single acts of deposition, then the individual feature assemblages are of little import.

Table 10.16 Lithic artefacts from the fill of pit N F7i (context group 1) in the central area

	Number	*Weight in grams*
Unretouched flakes, primary	10	61.3
Unretouched flakes, secondary	162	1138.6
Unretouched flakes, tertiary	73	205.7
Unretouched flake, chert	1	1.5
Unretouched flakes, burnt	5	32.0
Cores	7	484.6
Core fragments	3	119.5
Flaked lumps	3	152.0
Serrated-edge flakes	11	93.9
Edge-trimmed flakes	7	70.8
Scrapers	3	80.2
Flake from polished flint axehead	1	6.3
Miscellaneous retouched piece	1	17.0
Unclassified burnt fragments	15	35.0
Total	302	2498.4

The only complete flint axehead (Fig 10.17: 152) from any of these features (A F71) is not an implement in pristine condition and is unlikely to have been cached for future use or ritually buried. It is damaged through use at the cutting edge and probably has been discarded. It could, theoretically, have been rechipped and/or reground, but the morphology suggests this may have already been the case and that, in view of the size and asymmetric profile, further exploitation may not have been cost-effective. The other axehead (HH74 980) from an internal feature (A F41) is a medial fragment, disfigured by burning. The seven arrowheads are all fragmentary or damaged (the most complete are illustrated: Fig 10.15: 128, 134, 136, 138, and 141). Only the well-preserved 'laurel-leaf' bifacial (Fig 10.16: 145), from pit N F5, could perhaps be used to argue a case for pre-discard condition, but loss is just as probable.

Miscellaneous and unstratified finds from the central area

Struck flint from natural features and from superficial or otherwise unstratified recoveries comprises a substantial collection of over 3000 pieces of knapping debris and implements which complements and bulks up the assemblages from the central area features and the ditches. Although this collection does not add to

Table 10.17 Shroton spur. Summary of struck lithic artefacts

Weights are in grams, rounded to the nearest gram

		Bank area	*Phases I–II*	*Phase III*	*Phase V*	*Phase VIII/a*	*Remainder*	*Total no.*	*Total wt*
Unretouched flakes	no.	12	3	63	23	119	97	317	
	Wt	*180*	*26*	*718*	*292*	*1032*	*1014*		*3262*
Cores	no.					1	1	2	
	Wt					*160*	*121*		*281*
Serrated-edged flakes	no.	1					3	4	
	Wt	*12*					*17*		*29*
Edge-trimmed flake	no.						1	1	
(class A)	*Wt*						*2*		*2*
Edge-trimmed flakes	no.	1		3			2	6	
	Wt	*13*		*62*			*14*		*89*
Scrapers	no.			2	1	1	3	7	
	Wt			*76*	*42*	*15*	*80*		*213*
Piercers	no.					1	2	3	
	Wt					*14*	*21*		*35*
Leaf-shaped arrowheads	no.			2		1	1	4	
	Wt			*3*		*4*	*1*		*8*
Polished flint axeheads	no.	1					1	2	
and fragments	*Wt*	*252*					*580*		*832*
Flakes from polished	no.					5		5	
flint axeheads	*Wt*					*21*			*21*
Miscellaneous retouched	no.			1	2	6	2	11	
pieces	*Wt*			*26*	*16*	*81*	*35*		*158*
Unclassified burnt pieces	no.			2		12	7	21	
	Wt			*26*		*50*	*38*		*114*
Totals	no.	15	3	73	26	146	120	383	
	Wt	*457*	*26*	*911*	*350*	*1377*	*1923*		*5044*

the repertoire already defined, it is of interest in reinforcing the strong association of certain types, especially serrated-edge flakes and leaf-shaped arrowheads, with the enclosure.

The Shroton spur

The assemblage is small in total (context groups 47–52; Table 10.17), but of some interest because of the relatively high number of implements, which include two axeheads and four leaf-shaped arrowheads. The implements were in general not concentrated, coming almost equally from the ditch segments on sites K/L and M, and mostly from different horizons. All the leaf-shaped arrowheads, however, came from the ditch on site K/L, two from the phase III infill (HH76 745, HH76 975), one (HH76 299) from the phase VIII/a fill, and the other (HH76 588) from a superficial horizon. One of the axeheads (HH76 2975, a surface find from site K/L) is complete, with some rechipping subsequent to grinding. The other example (HH76 81, from posthole M F1 in the bank area – Fig 3.76), is the pointed butt end of a completely polished flint axehead, which is burnt and shattered, and has been reconstructed to its present form by the refitting of nine flakes and chips to the butt stub. Five further polished axehead flakes found with it are almost certainly from the same axehead, moreover ten unclassified burnt fragments probably also come from this axehead, but none can be refitted.

The Stepleton enclosure ditch

(context groups 55–61; Tables 10.18–20)

As with the main enclosure ditch assemblage, the struck flint from the Stepleton enclosure is presented in tables which give the overall breakdowns by type and context group, by context group and ditch segment, and by type and ditch segment for the material from the lower ditch infills.

The most flint-rich segments were numbers 2, 3, and 8. Unusually, the most productive horizon was the chalky phase III infill, particularly in segments 3 and 8. In artefact terms, there is a contrast between these segments, in that segment 3, like segments 2 and 22, has a significant number of core pieces, whereas segment 8 is wholly dominated by unretouched flakes. One aspect which is striking about the fills of this ditch is the scarcity of burnt lithic material.

The number of core pieces is significant for the phase I and II silts (context group 55). In fact many of the pieces (257) derive from a single segment (segment 2, where most of them formed a compact deposit on the surface of the primary silt in one butt – Fig 3.84: L5B).

Table 10.18 Stepleton spur. Summary of struck lithic artefacts

Weights are in grams, rounded to the nearest gram

		Stepleton enclosure					*Middle outwork*			*Inner outwork*			*Outer outwork*				
		Phases I–III	*Phase IV*	*Phase V*	*Phase VI*	*Phases VII–VIII*	*Phases I–III*	*Phase V*	*Phase VIII*	*Phases I–III*	*Phase V*	*Phases VII–VIII*	*Phases I–III*	*Phases VII–VIII*	*Pits*	*Remainder*	*Totals*
Unretouched flakes	no.	2627	571	297	974	1238	1058	248	354	3995	1986	18193	2277	1140	2159	3952	41069
	wt	*29708*	*5367*	*2727*	*10164*	*15592*	*11402*	*4837*	*4578*	*42962*	*25479*	*190652*	*23357*	*11086*	*11555*	*45284*	*434750*
Unretouched flakes, chert	no.										2	2					4
	wt										*7*	*24*					*31*
Unretouched flakes, burnt	no.	10	80	2	10	6				11	1	33		1	155	23	332
	wt	*83*	*78*	*10*	*47*	*42*				*136*	*8*	*270*		*2*	*613*	*85*	*1374*
Cores	no.	50	3	2	5	6	13	10	1	62	29	279[1]	22	7	20	54	563
	wt	*17403*	*659*	*197*	*455*	*1014*	*4232*	*2619*	*113*	*10357*	*4085*	*41831*	*4977*	*1434*	*3666*	*6063*	*99105*
Core fragments	no.	3	1	1			3	2		3	1	35[2]			3	5	57
	wt	*1090*	*27*	*92*			*415*	*337*		*670*	*58*	*2987*			*188*	*555*	*6419*
Flaked lumps	no.	33	1	1				2		10	3	95	9	7	4	16	181
	wt	*16480*	*480*	*190*				*860*		*2616*	*350*	*12885*	*4716*	*899*	*478*	*1573*	*41527*
Serrated-edged flakes	no.	8[3]	20	1	22	10				2	2	4			62	15	146
	wt	*70*	*117*	*13*	*179*	*72*				*15*	*8*	*62*			*500*	*164*	*1200*
Unretouched flakes with edge-gloss	no.		2	2	6	1			1			1			7	5	25
	wt		*11*	*24*	*54*	*5*			*1*			*3*			*29*	*64*	*191*
Edge-trimmed flakes, class A	no.						1			2		1			5	1	10
	wt						*24*			*19*		*12*			*66*	*15*	*136*
Edge-trimmed flakes	no.	14	14	3	15	23	2	2	1	7	3	12	1	2	44[4]	31	174
	wt	*172*	*196*	*25*	*336*	*400*	*47*	*37*	*13*	*104*	*48*	*148*	*11*	*57*	*824*	*363*	*2781*
Scrapers	no.	9	5	2	13	14	2		2	8	7	115		6	24	33	240
	wt	*311*	*99*	*69*	*469*	*414*	*118*		*117*	*272*	*307*	*2799*		*81*	*602*	*938*	*6596*
Piercers	no.	1			4	1			1	1		25		3	3	10	49
	wt	*41*			*30*	*38*			*61*	*92*		*606*		*51*	*43*	*232*	*1194*
Leaf-shaped arrowheads	no.	1	1			1	1			1		2	1			1	9
	wt	*2*	*1*			*1*	*2*			*2*		*2*	*2*			*1*	*13*
Tanged arrowhead	no.															1	1
	wt															*2*	*2*
'Laurel leaf' bifacials	no.										2				1		3
	wt										*31*				*13*		*44*
Polished axeheads & fragments	no.			1		1				1		1			2[5]	1[6]	7
	wt			*113*		*101*				*156*		*156*			*135*	*120*	*781*

Flakes from polished axeheads	no.	1		1											3	1	6
	wt	*9*		*2*											*10*	*3*	*24*
Knives	no.											4					4
	wt											*152*					*152*
Pick/roughout	no.	1										1					2
	wt	*123*										*135*					*258*
Unclassified bifacial pieces	no.											3				1	4
	wt											*69*				*29*	*98*
Rods	no.													1	1	2	4
	wt													*42*	*72*	*126*	*240*
'Fabricators'	no.											1				1	2
	wt											*26*				*21*	*47*
Backed flake	no.										1						1
	wt										*13*						*13*
Miscellaneous retouched pieces	no.	6	2	1	5	14	3	3	6	16	4	151	5	6	22[7]	42	286
	wt	*371*	*135*	*2*	*178*	*246*	*53*	*124*	*219*	*638*	*84*	*5738*	*199*	*211*	*779*	*1251*	*10228*
Unclassified burnt pieces	no.	20	31	14	38	11		1	26	1772	103	16054	2	14	468	535	19089
	wt	*272*	*67*	*1512*	*451*	*573*		*30*	*275*	*5845*	*2264*	*24388*	*367*	*292*	*1631*	*3512*	*41479*
Totals	no.	2784	731	328	1092	1326	1083	268	392	5891	2144	35012	2317	1187	2983	4730	62268
	wt	*66135*	*7237*	*4976*	*12363*	*18498*	*16293*	*8844*	*5377*	*63884*	*32742*	*282945*	*33629*	*14155*	*21204*	*60401*	*648683*

1 includes 2 burnt cores, weighing 420 g and 69 g
2 includes 2 burnt fragments, weighing 203 g
3 1 of these, weighing 11 g, is burnt
4 2 of these, weighing 8.3 g, are burnt
5 1 of these, weighing 5.1 g, is burnt
6 burnt
7 1 of these, weighing 4.5 g, is burnt

Table 10.19 Stepleton enclosure: numbers of lithic artefacts by phase and segment

Ditch segment	*Phases I–II*	*Phase III*	*Phase IV*	*Phase V*	*Phase VI*	*Phase VIII/a*	*Miscellaneous and unstratified*	*Totals no.*	*Totals %*
1		218				27		245	3.9
2	257	95	123	4	151	135	24	789	12.6
3	59	403	25		124	249	2	862	13.8
4	5	17	12		40	138		212	3.4
5	48	208			33	217		506	8.1
6	46	47		9	115	154		371	5.9
7	44	124	102	27	171	14		482	7.7
8	26	723	195	2	142	94		1182	18.9
9	19	5		23	5			52	0.8
10					14			14	0.2
11	2	25	26		4	5		62	1.0
12	6	37	213	3	244	11		514	8.2
13		1		5	4			10	0.2
14		2		9	14	1		26	0.4
15		19		1	10	8		38	0.6
16	5	87		60	11			163	2.6
17	2	8	24	37				71	1.1
18		1		20				21	0.3
20	4	11		15				30	0.5
21	4	1		64				69	1.1
22	50	135	11	31				227	3.6
23		40		18			77	135	2.2
X*					10	170		180	2.9
Total no.	577	2207	731	328	1092	1223	103	6261	
Total %	9	35	12	5	17	20	2		

* artefacts listed in this row could be allocated to specific phases, but there was uncertainty over the segment from which they derived.
There were no artefacts from Segment 19.

The phase III assemblage (context group 56), the most prolific from the enclosure, continues the trend of phases I–II, with an emphasis on core pieces and waste flakes rather than implements. Segment 2 (95 artefacts) is no longer the most productive, however, since segments 1 (218), 3 (403), 5 (208), and especially 8 (723) have far more artefacts. These figures may nevertheless indicate complementarity rather than contrast, assuming there could have been some difficulty in the classification of finds as coming from either the lower chalk rubble or the basal silts. Segment 3 contained numerous refitting pieces (Figs 10.21–25).

The combined figures for phases I–III make clear that, on the basis of the core pieces, there is an industrial element, which is focused on segments 2, 3, and 22. Segment 3 is the largest segment, but since the largest assemblage comes from segment 8, which is much smaller, the concentration of core pieces in segment 3 still seems of significance. The phase V silts (context group 57) are the least productive of all the fills of this ditch except the most superficial, although the assemblage includes a polished flint axehead fragment from segment 16 (Fig 10.17: 154).

Surprisingly, perhaps, there are more serrated-edge flakes from the phase IV recuts (context group 58) than from earlier contexts. This results from an anomalous concentration in segment 12, where 15 serrated-edge flakes and eight edge-trimmed flakes are present within a total assemblage of 213 pieces. There is a leaf-shaped arrowhead from segment 2 (Fig 10.15: 131).

A relatively high presence again in the upper fills, including the phase VI deposits (context group 59), of serrated-edge, edge-trimmed, and edge-gloss implements reflects a more equitable distribution between segments than with group 58. However, minor peaks occur in segment 8 (6 serrated; 2 edge-trimmed) and segment 12 (7 serrated; 4 edge-trimmed; 2 edge-gloss), the latter suggesting some overlap between contexts with context group 58, thus reinforcing the anomalous character of the segment 12 fill.

The middle Stepleton outwork
(context groups 71–75; Tables 10.18, 10.21)

The normal pattern of occurrence is apparently reversed in this ditch fill, since the basal silts (context group 71) contained the largest assemblage of all the horizons, with significant core presence and a leaf-shaped arrowhead from segment 5 (Fig 10.15: 140). As Table 10.21 shows, however, this is entirely due to the situation in a single segment (10), where 36% of the whole middle outwork assemblage was contained

Table 10.20 Stepleton enclosure. Lithic artefact types from Phases I–III combined, subdivided by ditch segment

	Segment 1	2	3	4	5	6	7	8	9	11	12	13	14	15	16	17	18	20	21	22	23	*total no.*	*total %*
Unretouched flakes	208	322	427	19	254	89	161	739	24	27	34		2	17	75	8		14	5	168	34	2627	94.4
Unretouched flakes, burnt		3		1								1			5							10	0.4
Cores	1	11	17			1	3	3												10	4	50	1.8
Core fragments			1		1															1		3	0.1
Flaked lumps	1	12	13					2							1					4		33	1.2
Serrated-edge flakes			1								3			1	2	1						8	0.3
Edge-trimmed flakes	1	1			1	1	1	1			5			1	1						1	14	0.5
Scrapers	1	1		1			2				1				1			1		1		9	0.3
Piercers								1														1	
Leaf-shaped arrowhead																					1	1	
Axe/pick				1																		1	
Flake from polished axehead								1														1	
Miscellaneous retouched pieces		2	2													1	1					6	0.2
Unclassified burnt pieces	6		1			2	1	2							7					1		20	0.7
Total no.	218	352	462	22	256	93	168	749	24	27	43	1	2	19	92	10	1	15	5	185	40	2784	
Total %	8	13	17	1	9	3	6	27	1	1	2			1	3					7	1		

Table 10.21 Middle Stepleton outwork: Lithic artefact types from phases I–III combined, subdivided by ditch segment

	Segment 3	4	5	6	8	10	11	*total no.*	*total %*
Unretouched flakes	7	152	126	33	115	620	5	1058	97.7
Cores					1	12		13	1.2
Core fragments					1	2		3	0.3
Edge-trimmed flakes, class A		1						1	0.1
Edge-trimmed flakes			1			1		2	0.2
Scrapers			1			1		2	0.2
Leaf-shaped arrowhead			1					1	0.1
Misc retouched pieces		2	1					3	0.3
Total no.	7	155	130	33	117	636	5	1083	
Total %	0.7	14.3	12.0	3.1	10.8	58.7	0.5		

Table 10.22 Inner Stepleton outwork. Lithic artefact types from phases I–III combined, subdivided by ditch segment

	Segment 3	4	5	6	7	8	9	*totals no.*	*totals %*
Unretouched flakes	70	239	2163	875	345	66	237	3995	67.8
Unretouched flakes, burnt		1	3	3	6			13	0.2
Cores	3	1	32	6	6		14	62	1.1
Core fragments			2		1			3	0.1
Flaked lumps			9				1	10	0.2
Serrated-edge flakes	1				1			2	
Edge-trimmed, class A				1			1	2	
Edge-trimmed flakes			4		1		2	7	0.1
Scrapers	1	1	2	2	1		1	8	0.1
Piercers		1						1	
Leaf-shaped arrowhead					1			1	
Axe/pick			1					1	
Misc retouched pieces		5	2	7	1		1	16	0.3
Unclassified burnt pieces		12	105	1642	10		1	1770	30.1
Total no.	75	260	2323	2536	373	66	258	5891	
Total %	1.3	4.4	39.4	43.1	6.3	1.1	4.4		

in the basal silt (Fig 3.131). There is no obvious explanation for this, although segment 10 was extensively excavated and therefore the amount of basal silt sampled was proportionately greater than in many other segments. The secondary and tertiary ditch fills are by contrast impoverished, which is particularly noteworthy since the adjacent inner outwork fills were so rich in flint. Thus the richness of segments 5 and 6 of the inner outwork does not find an echo in 6 and 8 of the middle outwork, although it should be noted that the latter ditch segments were subject to limited excavation only.

The inner Stepleton outwork

(context groups 63–69; Tables 10.18, 10.22)

A high proportion of the sizable collection from the inner outwork bank area derives from the features (mainly postholes) allocated to context group 62. A total of 61 features contained flints: 45 contained between one and ten pieces; 14 between 11 and 50 pieces; one contained 59 pieces; and one contained 240 pieces. Thus most features contained just a few flints, among which the burnt pieces were well dispersed. The most prolific feature (1B F12, possibly a posthole) produced a balanced sample quite in character with the early/middle Neolithic pattern.

The inner outwork ditch is by far the single most productive part of the whole Hambledon Hill lithic assemblage in terms of numbers of pieces, even taking into account the distortion produced by the huge number of unclassified burnt pieces in phase VIII/a.

The phase I–II silts (context group 63) contained predominantly unretouched flakes, the majority found in two adjacent segments (5 and 6). From the phase III fills (context group 64) a large assemblage is dominated by unretouched flakes and unclassified burnt pieces, with a significant presence of core pieces. Each of these categories was clustered. Segment 5 had an assemblage with 1576 unretouched flakes, 32 cores,

Table 10.23 Outer Stepleton outwork. Lithic artefact types from phases I–III combined, subdivided by ditch segment

	Segment 2	*3*	*4*	*5*	*7*	*8*	*9*	*total no.*	*total %*
Unretouched flakes	4	202	1888	14	78	72	19	2277	98.3
Cores			19		1	2		22	1.0
Flaked lumps			9					9	0.4
Edge-trimmed flake	1							1	
Leaf arrowhead			1					1	
Misc retouched pieces		1	3			1		5	0.2
Unclass burnt pieces			1		1			2	0.1
Total no.	5	203	1921	14	80	75	19	2317	
Total %	0.2	8.8	82.9	0.6	3.5	3.2	0.8		

one core fragment, and eight flaked lumps, but this was easily the most substantial of the segments in terms of size and proportion excavated. The adjacent segment 6 had 1642 of the unclassified burnt pieces. A further 14 cores were in segment 9. The implements include a leaf-shaped arrowhead from segment 7 (Fig 10.15: 139).

The phase V silts (context group 65) contain a significant presence of core pieces, which derive exclusively from the adjacent segments 5 (15 cores, 2 flaked lumps), 6 (8 cores, 1 core fragment, 1 flaked lump), and 7 (6 cores). Both 'laurel leaf' bifacials are from this group in segment 7 (one is illustrated: Fig 10.16: 147).

Similarly in the phase VII/a fills (context group 66), the bulk of the assemblage and especially the core pieces come from segments 5 (11 cores), 6 (14 cores, 5 flaked lumps), and 7 (4 cores, 1 core fragment, 1 flaked lump). The 'midden' (context group 67) is only present in segment 5 and the adjacent terminal of segment 6. It is the tertiary and superficial fills (context groups 68–69) which produced an absolutely massive assemblage, inflated by the remarkable number of unclassified burnt pieces, most of which, at least some 14,739, are from segment 5. The number of unretouched flakes and cores represents a very substantial assemblage in its own right. Implements include a leaf-shaped arrowhead (Fig 10.15: 133), a flint axehead (Fig 10.18: 157), a 'fabricator' (Fig 10.20: 163), three knives from segment 7, a pick, two unclassified bifacial pieces and a 'fabricator'. On the other hand serrated-edge flakes, edge-gloss and edge-trimmed flakes are present in only very small numbers.

Segment 5 is both the largest and the deepest of the inner outwork segments, so the fact that it contains 50% of all the flints from the ditch is perhaps not surprising. This makes it all the more interesting that, when only the lower infill horizons are considered, the much smaller segment 6 contains slightly more flints than segment 5. This is entirely because of the amount of burnt material in segment 6, whereas it is segment 5 and, to a lesser extent, segment 9 that have the core pieces.

The outer Stepleton outwork
(context groups 77–81; Tables 10.18, 10.23)

The outer outwork fills were far more productive of lithic artefacts than those of middle outwork, though the pattern of occurrence is more normal, in that it is the secondary fills rather than the basal silts which contain the most flints. Again, however, this is because of a single prolific segment (4), which produced over 60% of the assemblage from the ditch and is the segment that produced the most extensive sequences of refitting from anywhere on Hambledon Hill (Figs 10.29–40). The outer outwork assemblage, like that from the middle outwork, includes a leaf-shaped arrowhead from the basal silts (segment 3; Fig 10.15: 132) and, also like the middle outwork, contained hardly any burnt flints. This contrasts so dramatically with the situation in the inner outwork as to emphasise a very divergent history for the formation processes of their respective fills.

Discrete Neolithic features on the Stepleton spur
(context group 53; Tables 10.13–14, 10.18, 10.24)

In total, 2983 artefacts were recovered from 93 features, the contents of which are itemised individually in the catalogue which concludes section 3.5.6. These artefacts, deriving as they do from Neolithic pits, form an assemblage directly comparable with that from the pits at the main enclosure (context group 1) and for that reason are listed in the same table. Despite the larger number of pits and the near-complete excavation of the enclosure, the Stepleton assemblage is considerably smaller in number (if not in weight). However, the character of the assemblages is quite remarkably similar in some respects in terms of artefact categories and their proportional presence. The Stepleton assemblage could be characterised as more 'industrial', in that cores are twice as common and serrated-edge flakes only half as common, but otherwise the main differences are the absence of any leaf-shaped arrowheads or chert from the Stepleton pits.

Table 10.24 Stepleton spur features (Context Group 53) containing more than 100 struck lithic artefacts

Flakes etc = all unretouched flakes, including chert and burnt; cores etc = all core pieces, including fragments and flaked lumps; serrated flakes = all serrated-edge flakes including unretouched flakes with edge-gloss; edge-trimmed = all edge-trimmed flakes, including class A; others = all other specific implement categories; misc ret pieces = all miscellaneous retouched pieces; uncl burnt pieces = all unclassified burnt pieces

Feature	*Flakes etc*	*Cores etc*	*Serrated*	*Trimmed*	*Scrapers*	*Piercers*	*Others*	*Misc ret*	*Uncl burnt*	*Total*
ST78 1A F228 no.	181	2	10	8	2		1	1	3	208
%	87	1	5	4	1		0.5	0.5	1	
ST78 1A F229 no	133	6	1	1	2			1		144
%	92	4	1	1	1			1		
ST78 1A F295 no.	97	1	2	2	1				1	104
%	93	1	2	2	1				1	
ST78 1A F350 no.	376	6	12	16	14	1		5	66	496
%	76	1	2	3	3			1	13	
ST79 2A F154 no.	104			2			1		1	108
%	96			2			1		1	
ST79 2A F159 no.	176		9	1				3	76	265
%	66		3					1	29	
ST81 4B F129 no.	73			1			2		41	117
%	62			1			2		35	
ST81 4B F130 no.	145		2				1			148
%	98		1				1			
ST81 4B F137 no.	50		2						70	122
%	41		2						57	
All features above no.	1335	15	38	31	19	1	5	10	258	1712
%	78	1	2	2	1			1	15	
Total group 53 no.	2314	27	69	49	24	3	7	22	468	2983
%	77	1	2	2	1			1	16	

The numerical range of artefacts per pit is shown in Table 10.14, the maximum in any feature being 376 and the minimum one. Proportionately more pits from the Stepleton enclosure contain only a few flints, but it is also the case that the Stepleton features are, on average, smaller in size than those at the main enclosure (Fig 3.52). None of the Stepleton feature contents can be described as particularly unusual or irregular. They are characterised by repetitious waste material more than anything else. Included, however, are a 'laurel-leaf' bifacial from 2A F154 (Fig 10.16: 150), a polished flint axehead from 1A F228 (Fig 10.18: 156), and a rod-type implement from 4B F712 (Fig 10.20: 162).

The contents of the most productive features are listed in Table 10.24 and may be compared with Table 10.15 for the data from the central area pits. The composition of these pit contents is recurrent, the only significant fluctuation, in both areas, being caused by the amount of unclassified burnt material present.

Miscellaneous and unstratified finds from the Stepleton spur (context group 82)

This random collection of artefacts encompasses all the struck flint from natural features and from superficial or otherwise unstratified recoveries. As with the comparable context group 46 material from the central area, it represents a substantial collection of knapping debris and implements, which in general matches the stratified assemblages in character. This includes the presence of a leaf-shaped arrowhead, a type not actually present in any of the Stepleton features, serrated-edge and other edge-modified flakes and surprisingly low numbers of scrapers and miscellaneous retouched pieces. However, this group does include the only tanged arrowhead from the hilltop (Fig 10.15: 143), one of the few rods (Fig 10.19: 161), a 'fabricator', and one of the unclassified bifacial pieces (Fig 10.16: 146).

The Hanford spur
(context groups 83–93; Table 10.25)

The total assemblage from the excavations in this area is small and of no particular note. The implement categories match those from elsewhere on the hilltop and suggest that the area is simply receiving a relatively small sample of the general early–middle Neolithic flint discard. As mentioned elsewhere, a significant point is that the flint from the tabular seam dug through in the 'flint-mines' was not used for the artefacts found here, which utilise the same raw material as elsewhere on the hilltop.

Table 10.25 Hanford spur. Summary of struck lithic artefacts

Weights are in grams, rounded to the nearest gram

		Inner outwork				*Outer outwork*								
		Phases I–II	*Phase III*	*Phase V*	*Phases VII–VIII*	*Phases I–II*	*Phase III*	*Phase V*	*Phases VII–VIII*	*Neolithic pits*	*'Flint mines'*	*Remainder*	*Total no.*	*Total wt*
Unretouched flakes	no.	71	79	26	33	1091	17	63	72	6	13	54	1525	
	wt	*779*	*797*	*368*	*258*	*6704*	*197*	*763*	*932*	*14*	*60*	*680*		*11552*
Unretouched flakes, burnt	no.									1	1		2	
	wt									*8*	*10*			*18*
Cores	no.	1	1		2	6		1				2	13	
	wt	*99*	*99*		*497*	*1541*		*330*				*184*		*2750*
Core fragment	no.	1											1	
	wt	*101*												*101*
Flaked lumps	no.				1	1						2	4	
	wt				*1500*	*240*						*146*		*1886*
Serrated-edged flakes	no.		4		1					1			6	
	wt		*42*		*22*					*5*				*69*
Unretouched flakes with edge-gloss	no.							1			1		2	
	wt							*5*			*2*			*7*
Edge-trimmed flakes	no.								2			2	4	
	wt								*35*			*48*		*83*
Scrapers	no.								5			5	10	
	wt								*188*			*130*		*318*
Flakes from polished axeheads	no.	1			1								2	
	wt	*21*			*3*									*24*
Miscellaneous retouched pieces	no.		1					2			1	5	9	
	wt		*31*					*95*			*34*	*173*		*333*
Unclassified burnt pieces	no.				1					3		1	5	
	wt				*23*					*13*		*4*		*40*
Totals	no.	74	85	26	39	1098	17	67	79	11	16	71	1583	
	wt	*1000*	*969*	*368*	*2303*	*8485*	*197*	*1193*	*1155*	*40*	*106*	*1365*		*17181*

10.2.5 Typology

Assemblage composition (Table 10.6)

The overall composition of the lithic collections is conventional insofar as it is dominated by unretouched (waste) flakes, which numerically are overwhelmingly significant, though proportionally less so when considered by weight, since, as expected, this aspect highlights the importance of the core pieces. The unclassified burnt pieces are listed separately since they constitute such a large part (over 20% numerically) of the overall collection, but in fact, as previously commented, most of the burnt pieces are almost certainly unretouched flakes. If this assumption is made and the burnt pieces are added to the total of unretouched flakes, this would increase their numerical percentage within the whole collection to 96% and the percentage by weight to 73%.

The divergences from these means have been shown by the analyses of the subassemblages, and can be characterised crudely as more 'industrial' or more 'domestic' depending on the proportions of the components shown in Table 10.6. The divergence is most marked in the case of the assemblages from features (groups 1 and 53) which have a 'domestic' character, with higher values for retouched pieces and lower for core pieces, whereas the ditch assemblages tend to reverse this.

In the following sections the typology of the individual components of the major assemblage subdivisions are examined.

Unretouched flakes

As with the cores, these were primarily recovered from the enclosure peripheries and ditches, creating the impression that most knapping took place there. This may be somewhat misleading because of the erosion affecting other contexts, the removal by machine during excavation of flints from superficial horizons within the enclosures, and the absence of very many, or any very large, internal features. Nevertheless, it is clear from those internal features that were excavated that they do not contain the remains of complete knapping episodes.

Table 10.26 Composition of samples of complete unretouched flakes from selected internal features

Flake type	*N/F7i* *No.*	*%*	*Wt*	*Mean wt*	*1A/F350* *No.*	*%*	*Wt.*	*Mean wt*
Primary	8	6	52.3g	6.5g	5	4	58.2g	11.6g
Secondary	91	65	767.6g	8.4g	95	66	918.9g	9.7g
Tertiary	40	29	150.7g	3.8g	43	30	115.8g	2.7g
Totals	139		970.6g	7.0g	143		1092.9g	7.6g

Table 10.27 Length ranges of complete unretouched flakes from the fill of features N F7i and 1A F350

Length in mm ranges	*N F7i* *Primary and secondary*	*Tertiary*	*Total no.*	*Total %*	*1A F350* *Primary and secondary*	*Tertiary*	*Total no.*	*Total %*
0–9.9		1	1	0.7				
10–19.9	17	11	28	20.1	7	11	18	12.6
20–29.9	28	13	41	29.5	20	13	33	23.1
30–39.9	30	8	38	27.3	34	17	51	35.6
40–49.9	13	6	19	13.7	22	2	24	16.8
50–59.9	6		6	4.3	13		13	9.1
60–69.9	4		4	2.9	2		2	1.4
70–79.9	1	1	2	1.4	2		2	1.4
Totals	99	40	139		100	43	143	

Table 10.28 Maximum thickness ranges of all complete flakes longer and/or broader than 20 mm from the fill of features N F7i and 1A F350

Thickness in mm ranges	*N F7i* *Primary and secondary*	*Tertiary*	*Total no.*	*Total %*	*1A F350* *Primary and secondary*	*Tertiary*	*Total no.*	*Total %*
0–4.9	25	11	36	30	16	14	30	23
5–9.9	41	18	59	49	45	14	59	46
10–14.9	13	2	15	12	23	5	28	22
15–19.9	8		8	7	10		10	8
20–24.9	1		1	1				
25>	1		1	1	1		1	1
Totals	89	31	120		95	33	128	

Table 10.29 Length/breadth index values of all complete flakes longer and/or broader than 20 mm from the fills of features N F7i and 1A F350

L/B index	*N F7i* *Primary and secondary*	*Tertiary*	*Total no.*	*Total %*	*1A F350* *Primary and secondary*	*Tertiary*	*Total no.*	*Total %*	*Shape*
0.0–0.5	3	1	4	3.3		1	1	0.8	Very broad
0.6–1.0	32	12	44	36.7	24	6	30	23.4	Broad
1.1–1.5	31	10	41	34.2	47	16	63	49.2	Medium/broad
1.6–2.0	15	6	21	17.5	17	7	24	18.8	Medium/narrow
2.1–2.5	7	1	8	6.7	4	1	5	3.9	Narrow
2.6>	1	1	2	1.7	3	2	5	3.9	Very narrow
Totals	89	31	120		95	33	128		

Table 10.30 Composition of samples of complete unretouched flakes from selected horizons within the fill of segment 13 of the main enclosure ditch

Flake type	*Phase III* *No.*	*%*	*Wt*	*Mean wt*	*Phase V* *No.*	*%*	*Wt*	*Ave wt*	*Phase VI* *No.*	*%*	*Wt*	*Mean wt*
Primary	123	24	2149.9g	17.5g	41	20	429.8g	10.5g	60	22	766.5g	12.8g
Secondary	296	58	3488.3g	11.8g	117	56	1205.6g	10.3g	167	60	1465.8g	8.8g
Tertiary	90	18	345.3g	3.8g	50	24	188.5g	3.8g	49	18	218.4g	4.5g
Totals	509		5983.5g	11.8g	208		1823.9g	8.8g	276		2450.7g	8.9g

Table 10.31 Length ranges of all complete unretouched flakes from phases III, V and VI in segment 13 of the main enclosure ditch

	Length in mm ranges	*Primary*	*Secondary*	*Tertiary*	*Total number*	*Total %*
Phase III	10–19.9	1	9	10	20	4
	20–29.9	8	52	39	99	19
	30–39.9	31	101	25	157	31
	40–49.9	39	67	12	118	23
	50–59.9	18	40	4	62	12
	60–69.9	20	19		39	8
	70–79.9	4	5		9	2
	80–89.9	2	2		4	1
	90–99.9		1		1	
	Totals	123	296	90	509	
Phase V	10–19.9	2	4	10	16	8
	20–29.9	8	30	20	58	28
	30–39.9	7	50	14	71	34
	40–49.9	17	16	5	38	18
	50–59.9	3	9	1	13	6
	60–69.9	3	5		8	4
	70–79.9	1	2		3	1
	80–89.9					
	90–99.9		1		1	
	Totals	41	117	50	208	
Phase VI	10–19.9	1	14	6	21	8
	20–29.9	13	44	19	76	28
	30–39.9	26	47	13	86	31
	40–49.9	13	31	9	53	19
	50–59.9	5	24		29	11
	60–69.9		3	1	4	1
	70–79.9	1	3	1	5	2
	80–89.9	1	1		2	
	90–99.9					
	Totals	60	167	49	276	

In other words, it does not appear that knapping took place next to open pits/holes into which the waste flakes were collected directly. The occurrence of unretouched flakes in the internal features is apparently a much more fortuitous affair, and it is not to be expected that these contexts will be very informative about reduction strategies and preferences.

As a test, two collections of unretouched flakes from internal features were studied in detail. The first consisted of 249 flint flakes from the fill of N F7(i) within the main enclosure (3.3.7). Of the 249 flakes, 139 were complete. The second sample comprised the 344 flint flakes from the fill of 1A F350 (3.5.6) within the Stepleton enclosure. All levels of the feature fills were considered together in order to obtain a sufficient sample of 143 complete flakes. The composition of the two samples, which both had overall average flake weights of approximately 7 g, was essentially similar (Table 10.26). All the flakes from both samples had plain, pronounced and unlipped striking-platforms, except one faceted-butt tertiary flake from 1A F350, and are probably hard-hammer products. Two flakes in each sample were core rejuvenation flakes.

The samples were examined further in terms of flake size and shape by analysing length, thickness, and length/breadth index (Tables 10.27–29) The figures in these tables characterise the samples as lacking many very small flakes or chips, as dominated by flakes in the 20–40 mm length ranges and 5–10 mm thickness ranges, and as predominantly broad in shape. The absence of small flakes or chips, from contexts where recovery will have been good, indicates that this material is not the product of individual knapping events or sequences. This is confirmed by the condition of the flakes in the sample, since they exhibit a range of cortication-related discolouration effects. In the case of the F350 assemblage, however, the appearance of the flakes suggests that about half the overall total of 344 could have derived from a single nodule or flaking event. Even so, no refitting could be achieved, suggesting that only a partial sample of the residue from the knapping event (and minus the chips and spalls) found its way into the feature fill. The flakes from both features are essentially the product of general nodule preparation and core reduction and include few, if any, flakes which are suitable blanks for implement production. As with

Table 10.32 Maximum thickness ranges of all complete unretouched flakes longer and/or broader than 20 mm from phases III, V and VI in segment 13 of the main enclosure ditch

	Thickness in mm ranges	*Primary*	*Secondary*	*Tertiary*	*Total number*	*Total %*
Phase III	0–4.9	3	42	40	85	17
	5–9.9	47	129	31	207	42
	10–14.9	41	95	9	145	29
	15–19.9	23	20	1	44	9
	20–24.9	7	6		13	2.5
	25>	2	1		3	0.5
	Totals	123	293	81	497	
Phase V	0–4.9	7	19	21	47	23
	5–9.9	17	66	20	103	51
	10–14.9	14	22	3	39	19
	15–19.9	3	5		8	4
	20–24.9		5		5	3
	25>					
	Totals	41	117	44	202	
Phase VI	0–4.9	2	31	21	54	21
	5–9.9	28	80	20	128	49
	10–14.9	24	31	3	58	22
	15–19.9	3	11	1	15	6
	20–24.9	1	3		4	2
	25>	1			1	
	Totals	59	156	45	260	

Table 10.33 Length/breadth index values of all complete unretouched flakes longer and/or broader than 20 mm from phases III. V and VI in segment 13 of the main enclosure ditch

	L/B index	*Primary*	*Secondary*	*Tertiary*	*Total number*	*Total %*	*Shape*
Phase III	0.0–0.5		1		1		Very broad
	0.6–1.0	28	63	25	116	23	Broad
	1.1–1.5	61	148	26	235	47	Medium/broad
	1.6–2.0	24	58	15	97	20	Medium/narrow
	2.1–2.5	6	15	9	30	6	Narrow
	2.6>	4	8	6	18	4	Very narrow
	Totals	123	293	81	497		
Phase V	0.0–0.5			1	1		Very broad
	0.6–1.0	7	31	15	53	26	Broad
	1.1–1.5	19	56	19	94	47	Medium/broad
	1.6–2.0	11	22	6	39	19	Medium/narrow
	2.1–2.5	2	8	1	11	5	Narrow
	2.6>	2		2	4	2	Very narrow
	Totals	41	117	44	202		
Phase VI	0.0–0.5						Very broad
	0.6–1.0	16	31	9	56	22	Broad
	1.1–1.5	32	75	23	130	50	Medium/broad
	1.6–2.0	8	37	8	53	20	Medium/narrow
	2.1–2.5	2	9	2	13	5	Narrow
	2.6>	1	4	3	8	3	Very narrow
	Totals	59	156	45	260		

the flint contents of all the feature fills, the impression gained is that the flakes represent haphazard, arbitrary accumulations.

As a comparison for these flake samples from internal features, analyses were made of the prolific material from the fill of segment 13 of the main enclosure ditch, which included a total of some 5156 unretouched flakes from phase I upwards (context groups 3–11). The lowest stratified sample of any size was from phase III, the chalk rubble fills, which comprised a total of 1106 flakes. Other numerically significant samples comprised 688 flakes from phase V (context

Table 10.34 Mean weights of unretouched flakes in different context groups (chert and burnt flakes are excluded from these totals)

Context group	*Number*	*Weight (g)*	*Mean weight*
Main enclosure ditch	9958	82482	8.3
Inner east cross-dyke ditch	418	3185	7.6
Outer east cross-dyke ditch	382	2631	6.9
Inner south cross-dyke ditch	205	2090	10.2
Western outwork ditch	186	872	4.7
Long barrow ditches	3894	38544	9.9
Neolithic pits in the central area	2858	13320	4.7
Miscellaneous contexts in the central area	3756	22196	5.9
Shroton spur	317	3262	10.3
Stepleton enclosure ditch	5707	63558	11.1
Middle Stepleton outwork ditch	1660	20817	12.5
Inner Stepleton outwork ditch	24174	259093	10.7
Outer Stepleton outwork ditch	3417	34443	10.1
Neolithic pits on the Stepleton spur	2159	11555	5.4
Miscellaneous contexts on the Stepleton spur	3952	45284	11.5
Hanford spur	1525	11552	7.6
Totals	64568	614884	9.5

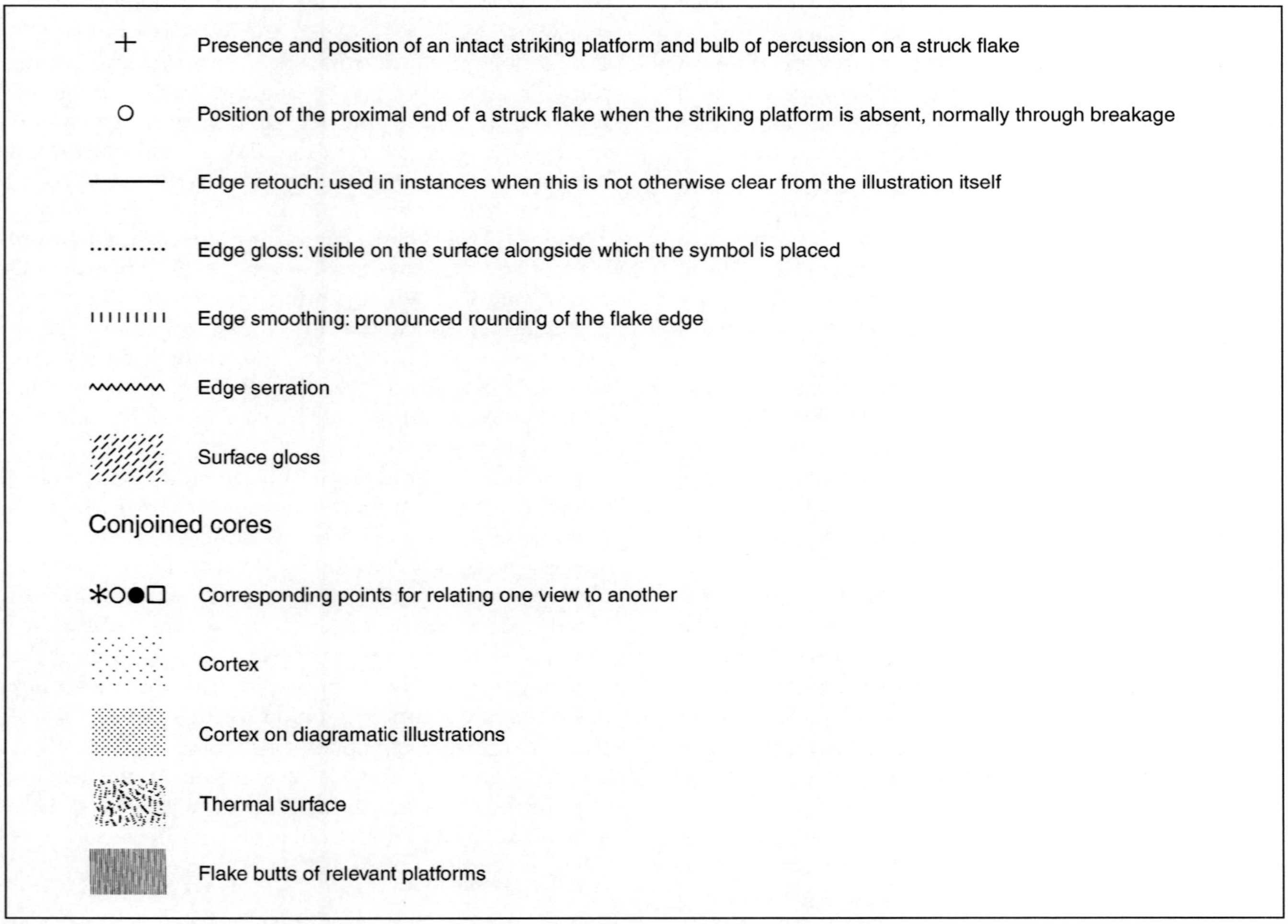

Fig 10.5 Key to the symbol and shading conventions used in the flint artefact illustrations. Note that 'American projection' (Martingell and Saville 1988, 4) is not used consistently in the following figures, so that the juxtaposition of different views or profiles of the same artefact may vary in each case.

group 6) and 1227 from phase VI (context group 7). The composition of the decreasing proportions of complete flakes from these contexts is shown in Table 10.30, and the contrast with the two pit samples (Table 10.26) is striking, because of the prevalence in the ditch of heavy, primary flakes. The contrast is further demonstrated by considering the lengths, thicknesses, and length/breadth indices of the flakes (Tables 10.31–33).

This 'industrial' nature of the assemblages from segment 13 and adjacent segments where the ditch cuts through Clay-with-Flints has already been noted. This is confirmed by the unretouched flake data, which show a predominance of heavy, cortical flakes, the number of primary flakes indicating the importance of initial nodule reduction. Only one flake (secondary) from phase III had a faceted striking platform, two flakes (one secondary, one tertiary) from phase V, and none from phase VI. Two of the phase III flakes were from core rejuvenation, three from phase VI and none from phase V.

The samples are notable for the low numbers of tertiary flakes and the high proportion of primary ones, and for the lack of tiny flakes (only 20 flakes, 3.9% of the total, were shorter than 20 mm). Inevitably, there are always more small flakes among tertiary ones than among cortical flakes, hence the low representations of tertiary flakes and small flakes are interrelated. This absence of small flakes may reflect an excavation bias against the recovery of small flakes from ditch contexts, and gravitational selection may to a certain extent have favoured the deposition of larger flakes in the fill. The knapping strategies in this area may also have had some influence, since it is clear that a lot of the flakes do reflect primary trimming of nodules and core preparation, and that this was the most significant element in the creation of the debris. Nevertheless, it is the case that all flaking inevitably produces small flakes and chips. The ditch samples show a remarkable consistency between the phases although, given the residuality effect, there may be little or no chronological difference between the flakes in these horizons.

An overview of the average weight of unretouched flakes from different context groups (Table 10.34) emphasises the distinction between the flakes from features and other contexts, especially the Stepleton ditches. This overview is inevitably 'broad-brush', not least because it takes no account of the proportion of incomplete flakes in each sample, but it probably does provide statistics which reflect the greater number of primary and cortical waste flakes in the context groups with higher average weights.

While it is clear that non-cortical or partially cortical flakes were the most significant product used for the common tools (Figs 10.7–14), a few primary and many extensively cortical flakes were used as blanks for scrapers. It is equally clear that the choice of flake blanks for implements was highly selective. The abandoned flakes involved in the conjoin groups (Figs 10.21–41) include many examples which are superficially very similar to those used on site for edge-trimmed and serrated flakes, scrapers and piercers, yet which were not actually selected for use at all.

Cores (Fig 10.6)

The cores from the interiors of both enclosures were analysed in terms of their type (Clark *et al* 1960), maximum dimension, and weight, and the maximum length of surviving flake scars, and compared on this basis with those from other selected context groups, six of them 'early' context groups (1, 53, 71, 4, 37, and 64) and four of them 'later', more potentially mixed, context groups (7, 38, 10/11, and 68; Tables 10.35–38). Although not especially marked, there is perhaps an overall contrast in that cores from the lower ditch fills are larger and heavier and have longer surviving flake scar lengths. This could correlate in relevant areas with less intensive use of nodules when first obtained from the digging of the ditch segments – the cores then becoming 'lost' by incorporation in the lower ditch fills – and the more intensive use of nodules away from the ditches.

Allowing for relatively low numbers in the groups analysed, the core types are similar throughout, with the simple A2 (Fig 10.6: 10) and B2 classes of single- and double-platform cores predominant, and multi-platform cores (Fig 10.6: 12) surprisingly infrequent. It should be noted, however, that many of the class A and B cores retained truncated flake scars indicative of previous flaking from other platforms (Fig 10.6: 10), and that their present forms tend to be residual ones. The only class E cores came from the main enclosure interior and the inner Stepleton outwork, while class D cores (Fig 10.6: 11), again few in number, were more widely dispersed. An overall contrast is that those cores from the internal features and upper ditch fills tend to be smaller and lighter, but the numbers available from each context group are admittedly rather low for this kind of comparison.

The refitting study (see 10.2.6 below) throws considerably more light on the cores and their methods of reduction. The normal pattern is for the nodule to be opened by using a convenient projection or flat surface for the initial blow(s), leading to rapid establishment of a platform. Further reduction utilises the flaking face of the core as the next platform, and so on until the core is either exhausted or abandoned. Such alternate flaking involves simple rotation of the core as successive core faces become platforms and vice-versa. While there is some trimming and abrasion of the leading edge of the platforms to facilitate flake removals, there is no structured preparation of the platform as such.

Implements

Some 2766 artefacts were identified during analysis as having obvious modification consistent with their classification as implements (Table 10.39). This modification can be the result of use, as with the edge-gloss

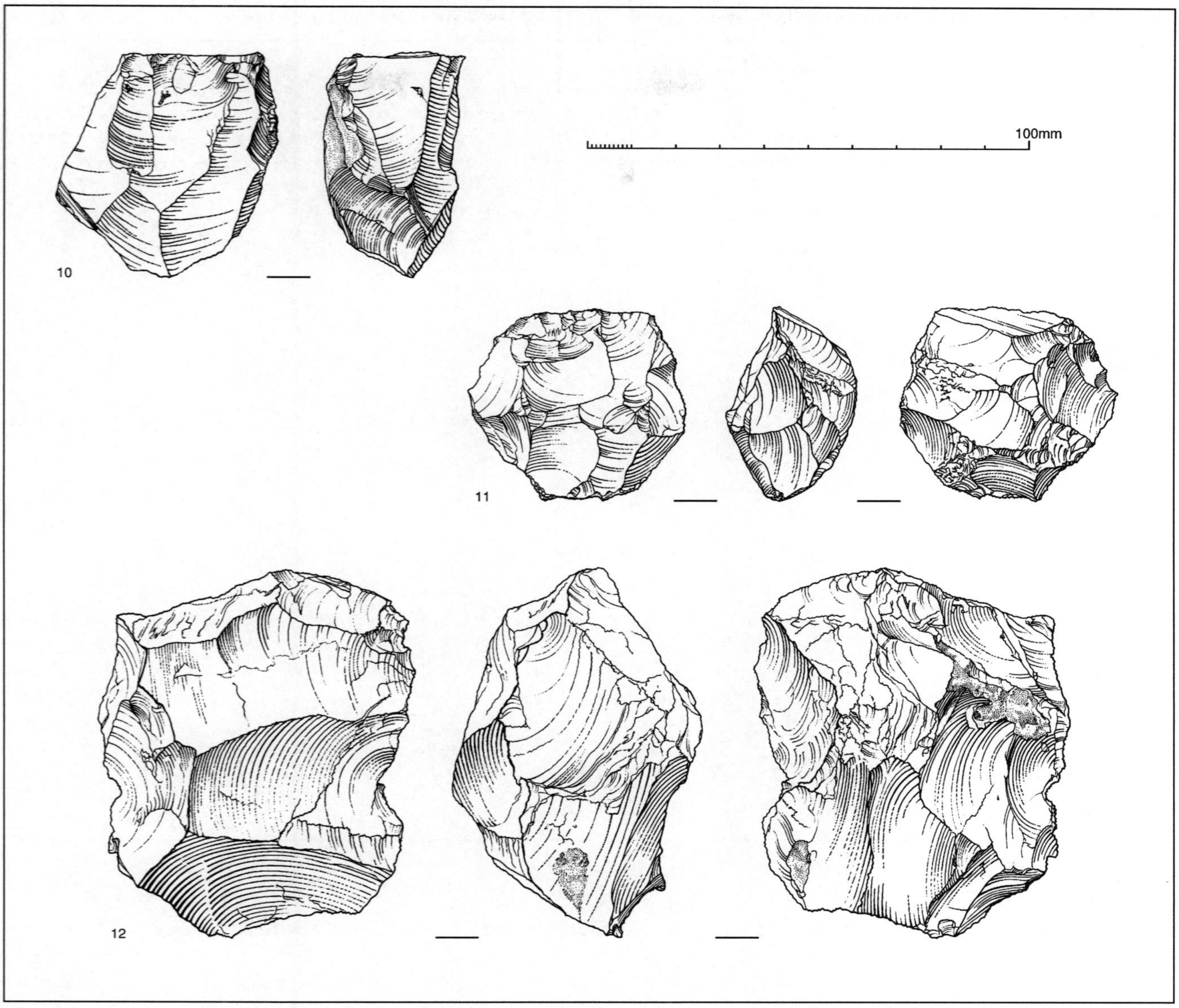

Fig 10.6 Cores, all from the main enclosure ditch on site H. Particulars in catalogue.

flakes and some of the edge-trimmed flakes, but in the main it arises from deliberate retouch which has resulted in recurrent, typologically recognisable tool-forms. Most of these artefacts can be categorised into a restricted range of formal types (eg scrapers) well known from the British Neolithic (Piggott 1954, 75–80), even if, as with the 'laurel-leaf' bifacials for example, their role and function remain obscure. The implements are dominated by scrapers, piercers, and edge-modified flakes, which comprise 68% by number (or 90% if the miscellaneous retouched pieces are excluded from the calculation), and 56% (or 87%) by weight.

The distribution across the hilltop is summarised by context group for the major implement categories in Table 10.40. The concentrations of implements correlate on the whole with the distribution of the total collection from the hilltop, but there is a certain amount of variability within the implement distribution itself. This is best exemplified by the percentage comparison between the implements from the internal features and elsewhere (Table 10.41). The only context groups containing sufficient implements for this comparison are either superficial ones or ones with relatively low numbers of implements, but, insofar as it goes, the contrast is quite marked and recurrent. The pits (context groups 1 and 53) produce much higher values for edge-modified flakes and lower values for scrapers, piercers, and miscellaneous retouched pieces.

Taken as a whole, edge-modified flakes are by far the most common tool-type in the assemblage and in reality were probably originally more common. This is because of the problems of identification. On the one hand the modified edges are very susceptible to damage and will frequently escape identification for that reason, and on the other hand the nature of the modification, such as short zones of serration, often requires examination under magnification to be detected.

Table 10.35 Core types from selected 'early' and 'later' context groups

The following information applies to Tables 10.35–10.38
'Early' context groups: 1 Neolithic features in the central area; 53 Neolithic features on the Stepleton spur; 71 middle Stepleton outwork, phases I–II; 4 main causewayed enclosure phase III; 37 long barrow phase III; 64 inner Stepleton outwork, phase III
'Later' context groups: 7 main causewayed enclosure phase VI; 38 long barrow phase VI; 10/11 main causewayed enclosure phase VIII/a and superficial levels; 68 inner Stepleton outwork phase VIII/a. The last two groups are liable to be of mixed chronological origin
Note: the group 64 and 71 totals are from the 1978 excavation season only

'Early' groups	*Core type*	*Group 1*	*Group 53*	*Group 71*	*Group 4*	*Group 37*	*Group 64*	*Total no.*	*Total %*
	A1	1			1			2	1.8
	A2	9	11	5	9	6	13	53	46.9
	B1						1	1	0.9
	B2	9	4	5	7	3	3	31	27.4
	B3	1		1	1			3	2.7
	C(3)	2	4	1	6	3	2	18	15.9
	C(4)				1			1	0.9
	D	1			1			2	1.8
	E	2						2	1.8
	Total	25	19	12	26	12	19	113	
'Later' groups		*Group 7*	*Group 38*	*Groups 10/11*	*Group 68*				
	A1	2		1				3	1.5
	A2	11	16	10	57			94	48.2
	B1			1				1	0.5
	B2	7	10	10	34			61	31.3
	B3		1	1	4			6	3.1
	C(3)	6	4	2	9			21	10.8
	C(4)	1			1			2	1.0
	D	1		3	2			6	3.1
	E				1			1	0.5
	Total	28	31	28	108			195	

Table 10.36 Maximum dimensions of cores from selected 'early' and 'later' context groups

'Early' groups	*Range i n mm*	*Group 1*	*Group 53*	*Group 71*	*Group 4*	*Group 37*	*Group 64*	*Total no.*	*Total %*
	30–39.9	1						1	1
	40–49.9	7	4		2			13	12
	50–59.9	7	1	2	3	1	1	15	13
	60–69.9	6	3	1	2	2	4	18	16
	70–79.9	3	5	1	6	4	6	25	22
	80–89.9	1	2	1	7	4	7	22	20
	90–99.9		2	2	2		1	7	6
	100–109.9			1	3			4	4
	110–119.9		2	3	-	1	-	6	5
	120 >			1	1			2	2
	Total	25	19	12	26	12	19	113	
'Later' groups		*Group 7*	*Group 38*	*Groups 10/11*	*Group 68*				
	30–39.9			2				2	1
	40–49.9	1		6	3			10	5
	50–59.9	8	5	7	16			36	18
	60–69.9	9	8	2	38			57	29
	70–79.9	6	6	7	20			39	20
	80–89.9	3	5	2	21			31	16
	90–99.9		3	1	6			10	5
	100–109.9	1	3	1	4			9	5
	110–119.9		1					1	1
	Total	28	31	28	108			195	

Table 10.37 Maximum surviving flake scar lengths on cores from selected 'early' and 'later' context groups

'Early' groups	*Length range in mm*	*Group 1*	*Group 53*	*Group 71*	*Group 4*	*Group 37*	*Group 64*	*Total no.*	*Total %*
	10–19.9	3	1				1	5	4
	20–29.9	6	3		3	2	1	15	13
	30–39.9	12	5	2	8	3	6	36	32
	40–49.9	2	5	4	5	2	5	23	20
	50–59.9	2	3	5	6	5	4	25	22
	60–69.9		2	1	4		1	8	7
	70>						1	1	1
	Total	25	19	12	26	12	19	113	
'Later' groups		*Group 7*	*Group 38*	*Groups 10/11*	*Group 68*				
	10–19.9			2				2	1
	20–29.9	10	2	10	16			38	20
	30–39.9	11	16	7	43			77	40
	40–49.9	5	6	6	28			45	23
	50–59.9	2	5	3	18			28	14
	60–69.9		2		2			4	2
	70>				1			1	1
	Total	28	31	28	108			195	

Table 10.38 Weights of cores from selected 'early' and 'later' context groups

'Early' groups	*Weight range in grams*	*Group 1*	*Group 53*	*Group 71*	*Group 4*	*Group 37*	*Group 64*	*Total no.*	*Total %*
	0–49.9	9	3		2		1	15	13
	50–99.9	8	3	2	3	1	3	20	18
	100–149.9	8	6		5	6	2	27	24
	150–199.9		3	1	3	1	8	16	14
	200–299.9		1	3	5	2	5	16	14
	300–399.9			1	4			5	4
	400–499.9		1	1	1	1		4	4
	500–999.9		2	4	2	1		9	8
	1000>				1			1	1
	Total	25	19	12	26	12	19	113	
'Later' groups		*Group 7*	*Group 38*	*Groups 10/11*	*Group 68*				
	0–49.9	3		8	10			21	11
	50–99.9	9	6	9	29			53	27
	100–149.9	8	8	5	31			52	27
	150–199.9	5	7	4	14			30	15
	200–299.9	1	4	2	21			28	14
	300–399.9	2	4		1			7	4
	400–499.9		1		2			3	2
	500–999.9		1					1	1
	Total	28	31	28	108			195	

Table 10.39 Total collection of retouched artefacts from the hilltop

	Number	*No. %*	*Weight in grams*	*Wt %*
Serrated-edge flakes	499	18	3747.0	7
Unretouched flakes with edge gloss	35	1	253.4	1
Edge-trimmed flakes (class A)	72	3	892.0	2
Edge-trimmed flakes	534	19	6542.3	12
Scrapers	608	22	16048.2	30
Piercers	138	5	2285.7	4
Leaf-shaped arrowheads	42	2	64.4	
Other arrowheads	2		3.1	
Laurel-leaf bifacials	6		90.9	
Polished flint axeheads (& fragments)	15	1	2174.1	4
Flakes from polished flint axeheads	23	1	164.3	
Knives	11		279.0	1
Picks/roughouts	5		577.6	1
Unclassified bifacial pieces	15	1	349.0	1
Rods	9		436.6	1
Fabricators	4		94.8	
Splintered piece	1		13.8	
Saw	1		10.3	
Backed flake	1		12.6	
Miscellaneous retouched pieces	745	27	19067.6	36
Total	2766		53106.7	

Thus the number of these flakes in the assemblage is probably an underestimate, in contrast to the next most prolific type, the scraper, which has distinctive traits which make non-identification less likely. The edge-modified flakes are divided into three major categories: serrated-edge flakes (Figs 10.7–9), edge-trimmed flakes (Figs 10.9–11), and unretouched flakes with edge-gloss.

Serrated-edge flakes

These flakes, sometimes known as microdenticulates (Bocquet 1980), have one or more zones of fine denticulation, the number of near-microscopic serrations per 10 mm varying within the same ranges recorded on other English Neolithic sites (Healey and Robertson-Mackay 1983, 5; Smith 1965, 91). As the illustrations show, there is considerable flexibility in the length and positioning of the serrated zones in relation to the available edges on the flakes selected, and in whether the serrated zone is convex, concave, straight, or a mixture. For more detailed analysis, the wholly complete examples were selected from four subsamples, comprising the pits in the central area (context group 1), the main enclosure ditch fills (context groups 3–11), the pits on the Stepleton spur (context group 53), and the Stepleton enclosure ditch fills (context groups 55–60) (Table 10.42).

The length, thickness, and length/breadth data for the 260 complete serrated-edge flakes are presented in Tables 10.43–45. Of the total 260, 198 (76%) are secondary flakes with some cortex. Only 5 flakes (2%) have faceted platforms. The figures indicate that flakes between 40–60 mm in length and 5–10 mm in thickness were preferred, with a distinct bias towards the selection of narrower, more blade-like shapes.

Looked at from the dorsal surface with the platform at the base, 127 flakes have the serrations on the right edge, 96 on the left edge, 14 on both edges, and one broad flake has serrations on its distal edge (Fig 10.7: 22). Overall, 161 flakes (62%) have clear signs of edge gloss in addition to the serrations.

The position of gloss was only recorded for the flakes in the samples from context groups 53 and 55–60. Of the 82 complete flakes, 50 have edge gloss. Forty-two of these have a single serrated edge with the gloss on the serrated area; seven are flakes with two serrated edges, and in four cases the gloss is only on one edge and in three cases on both (total = 49; details of one of the 50 were not recorded).

Ancillary retouch or serration is rarely found in combination with another tool form. There is one case of serrations and edge gloss on the right-hand edge of a flake, which is also an end scraper (HH76 820 from a phase VI deposit in the main enclosure); another with serrations and edge gloss on the left-hand edge of a flake which also supported a distal, bilaterally formed piercer (HH76 531 from a phase VIII/a deposit in the main enclosure). Three flakes which are serrated on the left-hand edge have blunting retouch down the opposite edge (HH76 1510 from a phase V context in the main enclosure); HH77 1844 and 2167 from pits in the central area), and one serrated-edge flake is on a flake from a polished flint implement, presumably an axehead (HH76 873 from a phase VI context in the main enclosure). Only one of the serrated-edge flakes from the measured sample is burnt.

Unretouched flakes with edge-gloss

The only modification observable on the 35 flakes in this category is the presence of pronounced gloss (Jensen 1994, 50–68; Saville 1981a, 126–32) on one or, in three instances, both edges. In four cases it was noted that there are possible traces of former serrations, now worn and/or damaged to the extent that they could not be positively identified. It seems probable that many of the flakes in this category are actually serrated-edge flakes on which the serrations have been damaged or otherwise obscured. Others, if not originally serrated, are likely to be related to the serrated-edge flakes in terms of function. Some 23 of these flakes, weighing 197 g, are complete, and analysis of their dimensions and shape shows them to be closely comparable to the serrated-edge flakes. More subjectively, they include some flakes of striking appearance, including some very elongated blades, and general appearance may have been a factor in being able to

Table 10.40 Occurrence of implements by major area subdivisions

Implement type	*Central area pits*		*Stepleton pits*		*Main enclosure ditch*		*Stepleton ditches*		*Long barrow ditches*		*Unstratified and miscellaneous*		*Remainder*		*Total*	
	No.	*%*	*No.*	*%*	*No.*	*%*	*No.*	*%*	*No.*	*%*	*No.*	*%*	*No.*	*%*	*No.*	*%*
Serrated-edge flakes	160	41	62	36	117	17	69	11	8	6	38	9	45	15	499	18
Unretouched flakes with edge-gloss	5	1	7	4	2		13	2			4	1	4	1	35	1
Edge-trimmed flakes (class A)	22	6	5	3	21	3	4	1	4	3	11	3	5	2	72	3
Edge-trimmed flakes	83	21	44	25	163	23	99	15	15	11	76	19	54	18	534	19
Scrapers	43	11	24	14	146	21	183	28	46	35	94	23	72	24	608	22
Piercers	12	3	3	2	34	5	36	6	9	7	27	7	17	6	138	5
Leaf-shaped arrowheads	7	2			9	1	8	1			6	2	12	4	42	2
Other arrowheads					1						1				2	
'Laurel-leaf' bifacials	1		1		2		2								6	
Polished flint axeheads	2	1	2	1	3		4				1		3	1	15	1
Flakes from polished axeheads	3	1	3	2	3		2		1	1	2		9	3	23	1
Knives					6	1	4	1			1				11	
Picks					2		2						1		5	
Unclassified bifacial pieces					6	1	3				3	1	3	1	15	1
Rods			1		1		1		1	1	2		3	1	9	
'Fabricators'					2		1				1				4	
Splintered piece					1										1	
Saw													1		1	
Backed piece							1								1	
Misc retouched pieces	53	14	22	13	186	26	223	34	48	36	141	35	72	24	745	27
Total	391		174		705		655		132		408		301		2766	

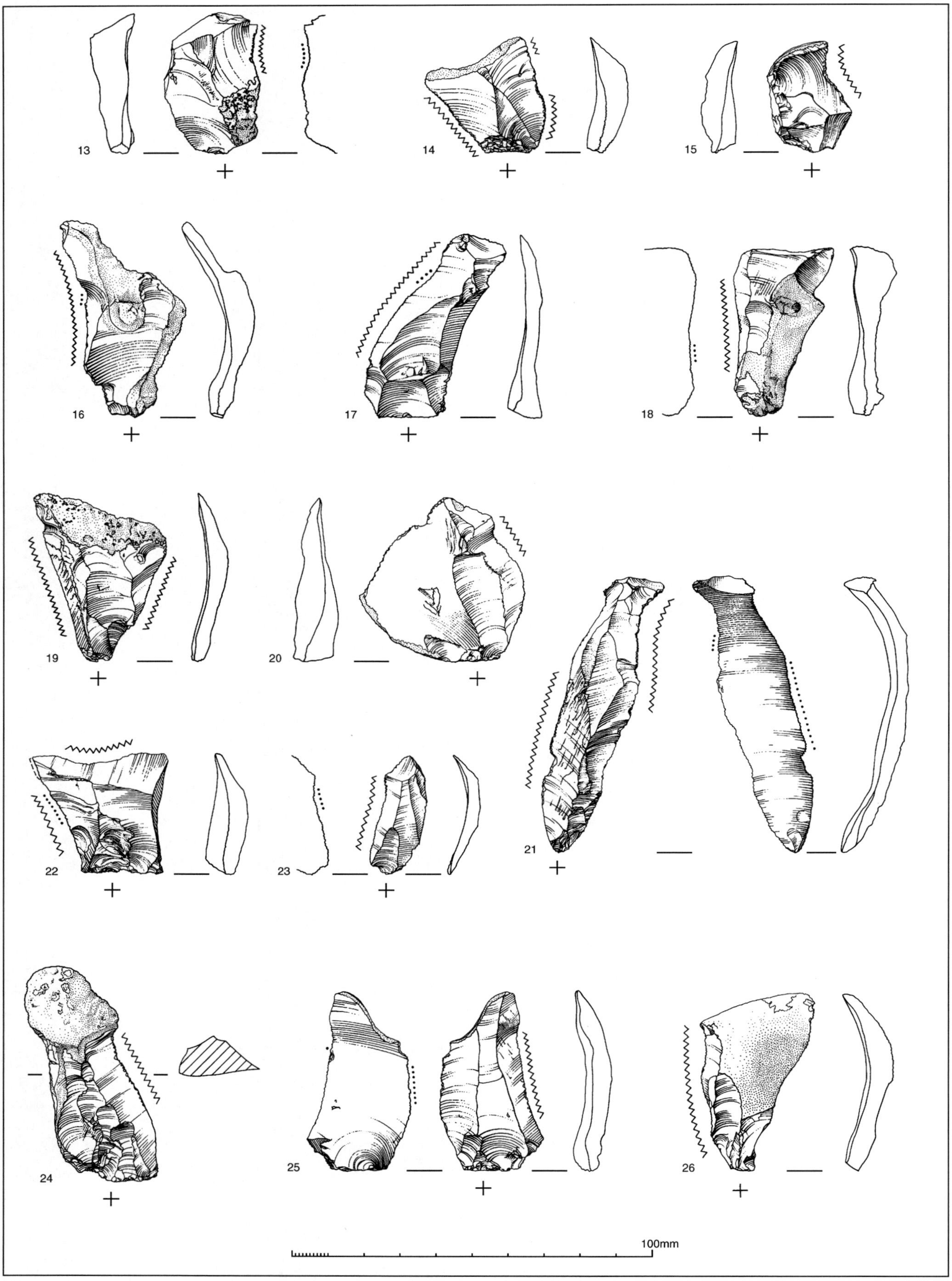

Fig 10.7 Serrated-edge flakes. All the illustrated examples are from Neolithic features on site N. The symbols on the illustrations (keyed in Fig 10.5) show the presence and position of edge gloss as well as the serrations; the symbols for gloss are placed against the dorsal or ventral surface as appropriate. Particulars in catalogue.

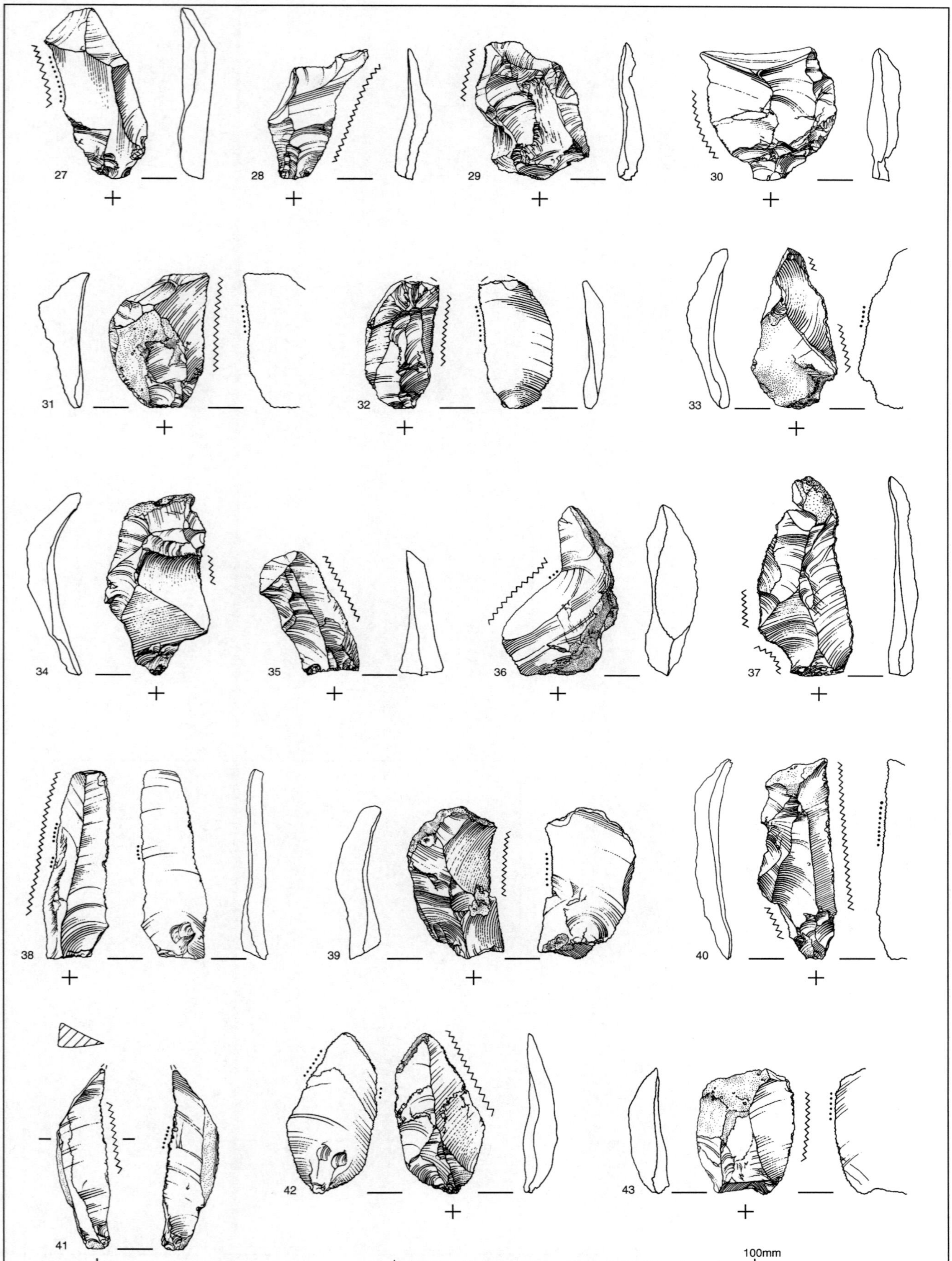

Fig 10.8 Serrated-edge flakes. All the illustrated examples are from Neolithic features on site N. The symbols on the illustrations (keyed in Fig 10.5) show the presence and position of edge gloss as well as the serrations; the symbols for gloss are placed against the dorsal or ventral surface as appropriate. Particulars in catalogue.

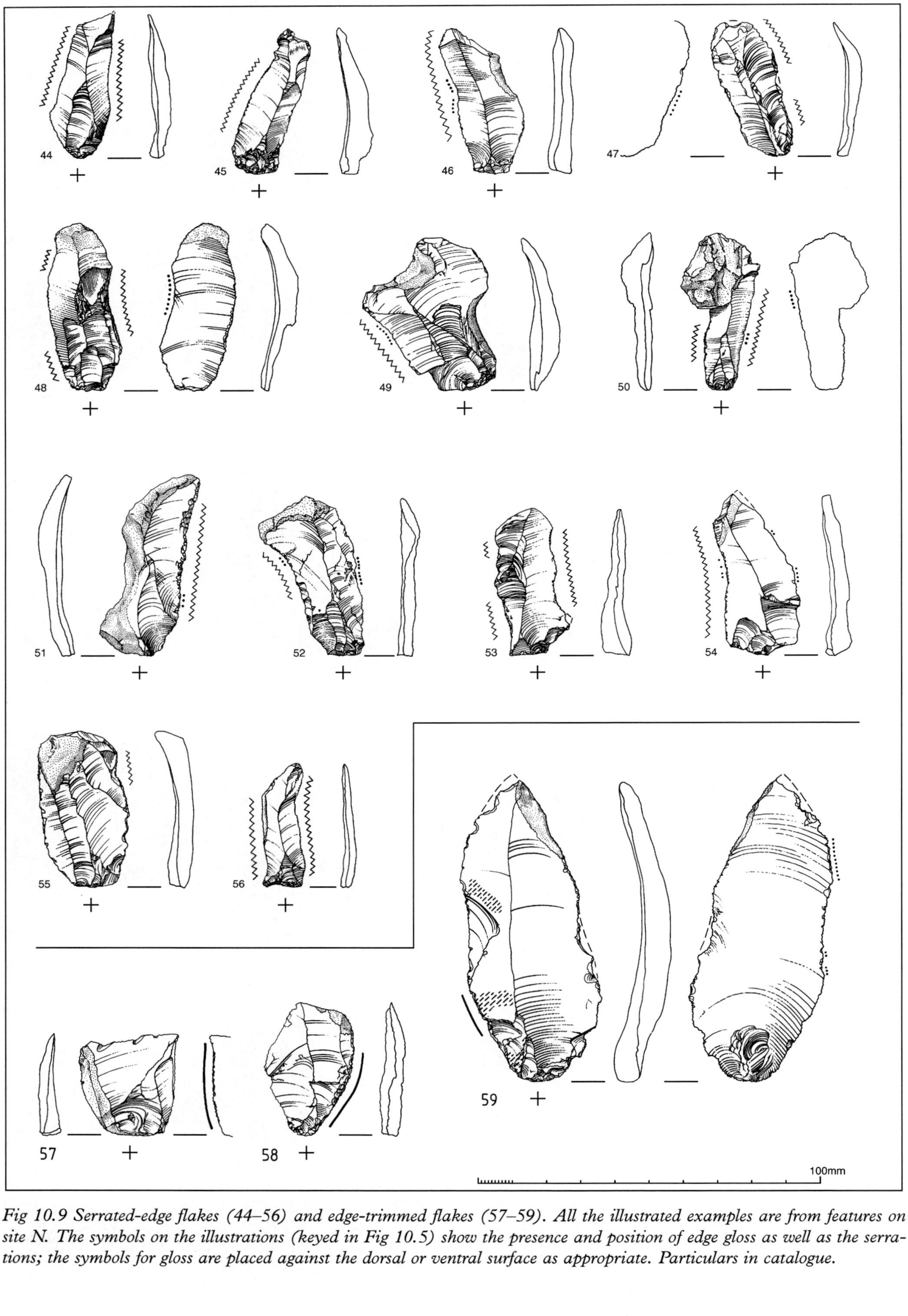

Fig 10.9 Serrated-edge flakes (44–56) and edge-trimmed flakes (57–59). All the illustrated examples are from features on site N. The symbols on the illustrations (keyed in Fig 10.5) show the presence and position of edge gloss as well as the serrations; the symbols for gloss are placed against the dorsal or ventral surface as appropriate. Particulars in catalogue.

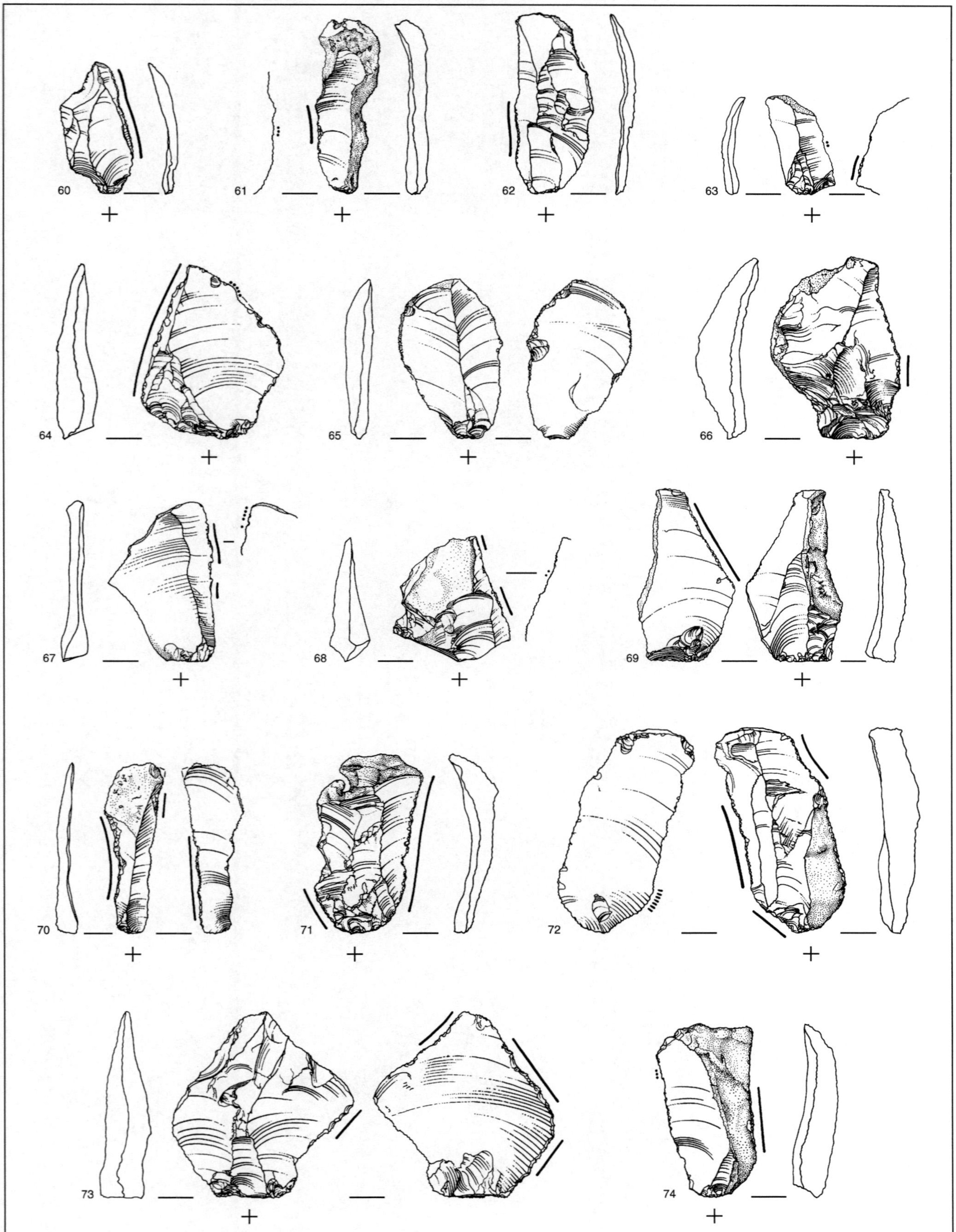

Fig 10.10 Edge-trimmed flakes. All the illustrated examples are from features on site N. Particulars in catalogue.

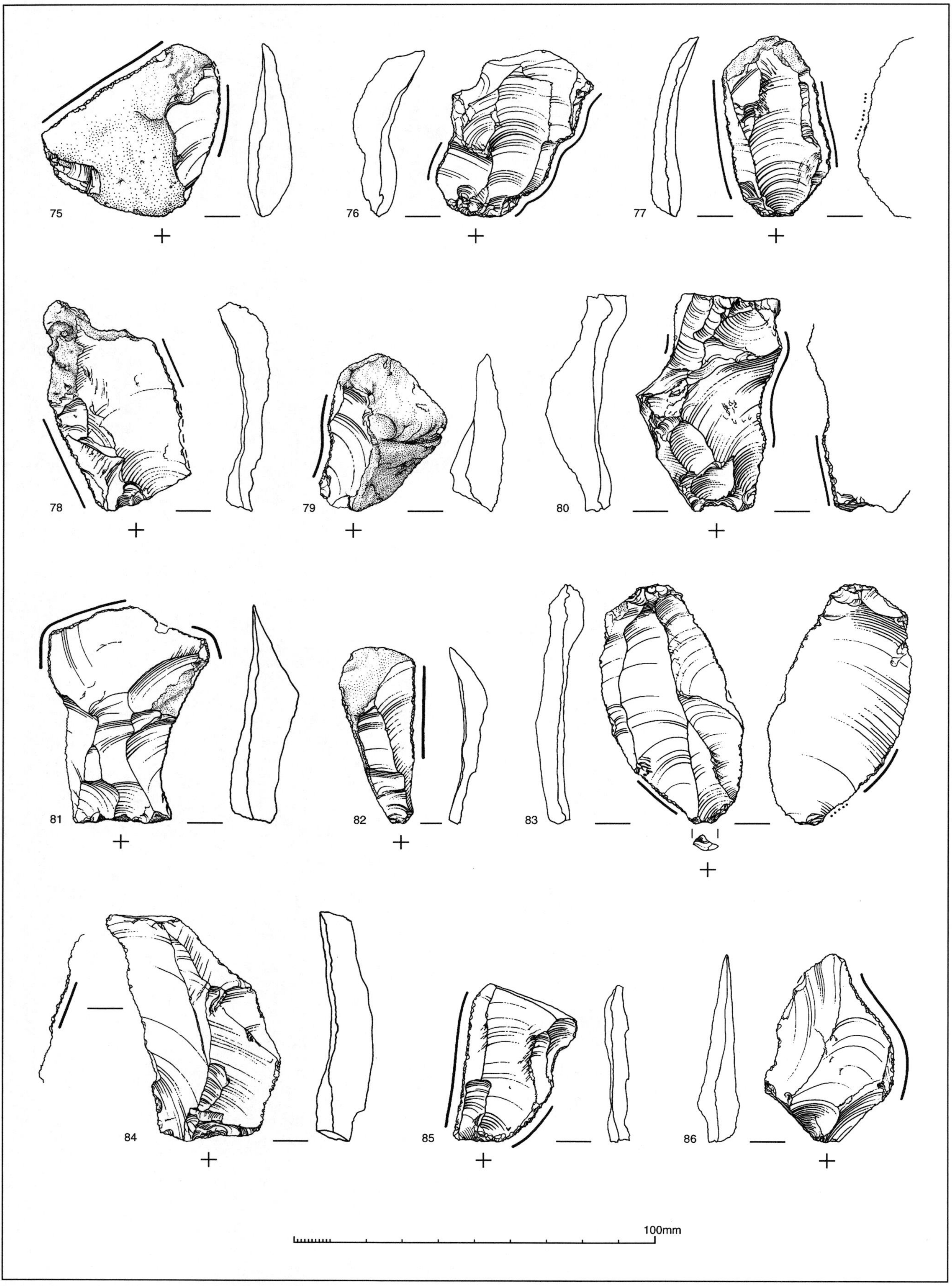

Fig 10.11 Edge-trimmed flakes. All the illustrated examples are from features on site N. Particulars in catalogue.

Table 10.41 Comparison by percentages of the major implement categories in those context groups with sixty or more artefacts in these categories

Group	*Serrated-edge and edge gloss*	*Edge-trimmed*	*Scrapers*	*Piercers*	*Misc retouched*	*Total number*
1. Central area features	44%	28%	11%	3%	14%	378
4. Main enclosure phase III	13%	33%	18%	3%	32%	60
6. Main enclosures phase V	34%	23%	15%	5%	23%	62
7. Main enclosure phase VI	27%	31%	23%	3%	16%	210
10. Main enclosure phase VIII/a	11%	31%	17%	7%	35%	101
11. Main enclosure unstratified and miscellaneous	5%	21%	27%	8%	39%	168
46. Central area unstratified and miscellaneous	11%	22%	24%	6%	37%	288
53 Stepleton spur features	41%	29%	14%	2%	13%	167
59. Stepleton enclosure phase VI	43%	23%	20%	6%	8%	65
60. Stepleton enclosure phase VIII/a	18%	38%	21%	2%	21%	61
68. Inner Stepleton outwork phase VIII/a	2%	4%	40%	8%	46%	250
82. Stepleton spur unstratified and miscellaneous	11%	22%	25%	8%	34%	103
Mean	22%	24%	22%	5%	27%	

Table 10.42 Serrated-edge and edge-trimmed flakes from selected context groups and the sample sizes of wholly complete examples (weights in grams)

Group 1 Neolithic features in central area, groups 3–11, main enclosure ditch; group 53 Neolithic features on Stepleton spur, groups 55–60 Stepleton enclosure ditch

	Serrated-edge flakes				*Edge-trimmed flakes*			
	Total no.	*Total weight*	*Complete no.*	*Complete weight*	*Total no.*	*Total weight*	*Complete no.*	*Complete weight*
Group 1	160	1073	100	775	103	978	52	589
Groups 3–11	119	921	78	700	184	1965	106	1328
Group 53	62	500	39	363	49	890	33	689
Groups 55–60	63	450	43	376	69	1129	44	876
Total	404	2944	260	2214	405	4962	235	3482

distinguish these pieces during analysis from the mass of unmodified flakes. Such bias is a standard analytical problem and need not be over-emphasised here, except that this is a difficult tool category to identify and the bias may have operated variably through the sorting process and influenced the apparently unusual distributional pattern. The fact that more of the flakes in this category come from contexts outwith the main enclosure may be because these contexts were analysed at a later stage of the post-excavation process when greater familiarity with the assemblage was achieved.

Edge-trimmed flakes

These are flakes which exhibit distinct edge-modification to a lesser or greater extent, ranging from regular edge-retouch (normally non-invasive) to edge-damage assumed to be consistent with use. A fuller definition has been given elsewhere (Saville 1981a, 126) but some further discussion is necessary in view of the unavoidably subjective element of the definition. Those with experience of lithic analysis will appreciate the difficulties. Irrespective of the fact that the Hambledon Hill flints are not in a condition to respond to microwear studies, it would not be practical to undertake such detailed examination of the 608 artefacts in this grouping. The typological approach is here being used as a compromise, which attempts to deal with the observation that so many flakes exhibit edge modification and that this recurrent trait has meaning in terms of the production and use of flakes at Hambledon Hill.

A proportion of the flakes in this category have quite regular, semi-blunting trimming (eg Fig 10.9: 58; Fig 10.10: 60, 69, 71; Fig 10.11: 75–80, 82, 85), equating them with what have previously been described as 'class A utilised' flakes (Smith 1965, fig 39). These 72 pieces are listed separately in most of the tables and in all the archive records, but there is no hard and fast subdivision between them and the other edge-trimmed flakes and they should not be regarded as a distinct type so much as at one end of a spectrum.

The same context groups as for the serrated-flakes were used to obtain subsamples of the edge-trimmed flakes (Table 10.42). The length, thickness, and

Table 10.43 Length ranges of complete serrated-edge and edge-trimmed flakes from selected context groups

Group 1 Neolithic features in central area, groups 3–11, main enclosure ditch; group 53 Neolithic features on Stepleton spur, groups 55–60 Stepleton enclosure ditch

	Serrated-edge flakes						*Edge-trimmed flakes*					
Length in mm ranges	*Group 1*	*Groups 3–11*	*Group 53*	*Groups 55–60*	*Total no.*	*Total %*	*Group 1*	*Groups 3–11*	*Group 53*	*Groups 55–60*	*Total no.*	*Total %*
20–29.9	2			1	3	1	5	1	1		7	3
30–39.9	26	8	2	6	42	16	7	17	3	3	30	13
40–49.9	42	36	14	17	109	42	19	37	7	9	72	30
50–59.9	23	23	18	11	75	29	16	31	15	14	76	32
60–69.9	6	6	2	6	20	8	4	17	4	10	35	15
70–79.9		5	3	2	10	4	1	1		2	4	2
80–89.9	1				1				2	5	7	3
90–99.9								2	1	1	4	2
Total	100	78	39	43	260		52	106	33	44	235	

Table 10.44 Thickness ranges of complete serrated-edge flakes and edge-trimmed flakes from selected context groups

Group 1 Neolithic features in central area, groups 3–11 main enclosure ditch; group 53 Neolithic features on Stepleton spur, groups 55–60 Stepleton enclosure ditch

	Serrated-edge flakes						*Edge-trimmed flakes*					
Thickness in mm ranges	*Group 1*	*Groups 3–11*	*Group 53*	*Groups 55–60*	*Total no.*	*Total %*	*Group 1*	*Groups 3–11*	*Group 53*	*Groups 55–60*	*Total no.*	*Total %*
00–4.9	12	11	4	3	30	12	8	9	4	2	23	10
05–9.9	70	52	27	30	179	69	31	62	16	25	134	57
10–14.9	15	13	8	9	45	17	12	31	7	12	62	26
15–19.9	3	2	–	1	6	2	–	2	3	4	9	4
20–24.9							1	2	3	1	7	3
Total	100	78	39	43	260		52	106	33	44	235	

Table 10.45 Length/breadth index values of complete serrated-edge flakes and edge-trimmed flakes from selected context groups

Group 1 Neolithic features in central area, groups 3–11 main enclosure ditch; group 53 Neolithic features on Stepleton spur, groups 55–60 Stepleton enclosure ditch

	Serrated-edge flakes						*Edge-trimmed flakes*						
L/B index	*Group 1*	*Groups 3–11*	*Group 53*	*Groups 55–60*	*Total no.*	*Total %*	*Group 1*	*Groups 3–11*	*Group 53*	*Groups 55–60*	*Total no.*	*Total %*	*Shape*
0.6–1.0	6	3	1	4	14	5	3	10	3	2	18	8	Broad
1.1–1.5	27	14	14	6	61	23	23	38	17	19	97	41	Medium/ broad
1.6–2.0	45	33	13	17	108	42	18	41	10	16	85	36	Medium/ narrow
2.1–2.5	15	20	9	10	54	21	6	14	3	3	26	11	Narrow
2.6>	7	8	2	6	23	9	2	3		4	9	4	Very narrow
Total	100	78	39	43	260		52	106	33	44	235		

length/breadth data for the 235 complete flakes are presented in Tables 10.43–45. Of the total 235, 177 (75%) are secondary flakes with some cortex. Only ten flakes (4%) have faceted platforms. The figures indicate that flakes between 40–60 mm in length and 5–10 mm in maximum thickness were preferred, with shapes predominantly in the medium/broad, medium/narrow ranges.

The positioning of the edge-trimming was only consistently recorded for flakes from Neolithic pits on the Stepleton spur and from the Stepleton enclosure ditch, comprising 77 cases: 23 have trimming on the right edge; 26 on the left edge; 21 on both lateral edges; one on a broad distal edge; two on the right edge and the distal edge; two on the left edge and the distal edge; and two on both lateral edges and the distal edge. Overall, 49 flakes (21%) have clear signs of edge gloss in addition to the trimming.

The edge-trimmed flakes present some contrasts with the serrated-edge flakes. The average weights for the complete examples of 14.8 g for edge-trimmed, 8.5 g for serrated-edge, and 8.6 g for edge-gloss, indicate that, in general, larger and/or chunkier flakes are used for the edge-trimmed. Twenty-two per cent of the edge-trimmed flakes are longer than 60 mm, as opposed to only 12% of the serrated flakes and 33% have a maximum thickness greater than 10 mm, as opposed to only 19% in the case of the serrated-edge flakes. The proportion of true blades used as blanks for the serrated flakes (30%) is double that for the edge-trimmed ones (15%). The blanks used for these edge-modified flakes may also be compared to the samples of unretouched flakes analysed in the previous section, from which it is clear, as might be expected, that on the whole it was larger and narrower flakes which were selected for modification.

The illustrated edge-trimmed flakes (Figs 10.9–11) are all from the central area, mostly from the fill of Neolithic features.

Scrapers

In total 608 scrapers are present in the whole assemblage, with a fairly even distribution, relatively speaking, throughout the context groups (Tables 10.40–41). Any apparent accumulation of scrapers in miscellaneous and superficial contexts is probably to some degree a factor of the relative indestructibility and ease of recognition of this tool type.

For analysis a subset of 386 scrapers was selected using context groups shown in Table 10.46. Typologically, this category is dominated by simple end scrapers with a convex scraping edge at the distal end of a bulbar flake. Blanks are normally plain apart from the scraping edge, but occasional ancillary retouch does occur (Fig 10.12: 92). Extended-end scrapers are variants where, largely as a result of the morphology of the flake blank, the retouch of the scraping edge extends down one or both lateral edges to a lesser or greater extent. End-and-side scrapers (Fig 10.13: 104) are similar, but have a more pronounced angle between the distal and lateral retouch, while remaining basically end scrapers rather than side scrapers.

Table 10.46 Scrapers from selected context groups and the sample sizes of wholly complete, measured examples (only complete scrapers on bulbar flakes with intact platforms were measured); weights are in grams

Group 1 Neolithic features in central area, groups 3–11 main enclosure ditch; group 53 Neolithic features on Stepleton spur, groups 55–61 Stepleton enclosure ditch, groups 63–69 inner Stepleton outwork ditch

	Type	*Group1*	*Groups 3–11*	*Group 53*	*Groups 55–61*	*Groups 63–69*	*Total no.*	*Total %*	*Total wt*	*Mean wt*
Total scrapers	End	33	100	18	22	62	235	61		
	Extended end	2	23	4	18	41	88	23		
	Double end	1	1			1	3	1		
	End & side(s)	3	6		1	4	14	4		
	Double end & side					1	1			
	Side	2	9		2	12	25	6		
	Side & base		1				1			
	Disc		1			2	3	1		
	Unclassified	2	5	2		7	16	4		
	Total	43	146	24	43	130	386			
Complete scrapers	End	19	80	15	18	42	174	61	4588	26
	Extended end	2	20	3	17	33	75	26	2112	28
	End & side	2	4		1	2	9	3	300	33
	Side	1	8		1	10	20	7	545	27
	Disc					1	1		4	
	Unclassified		3	1		2	6	2	170	28
	Total number	24	115	19	37	90	285			
	Total weight	494	3111	523	1201	2390			7719	27

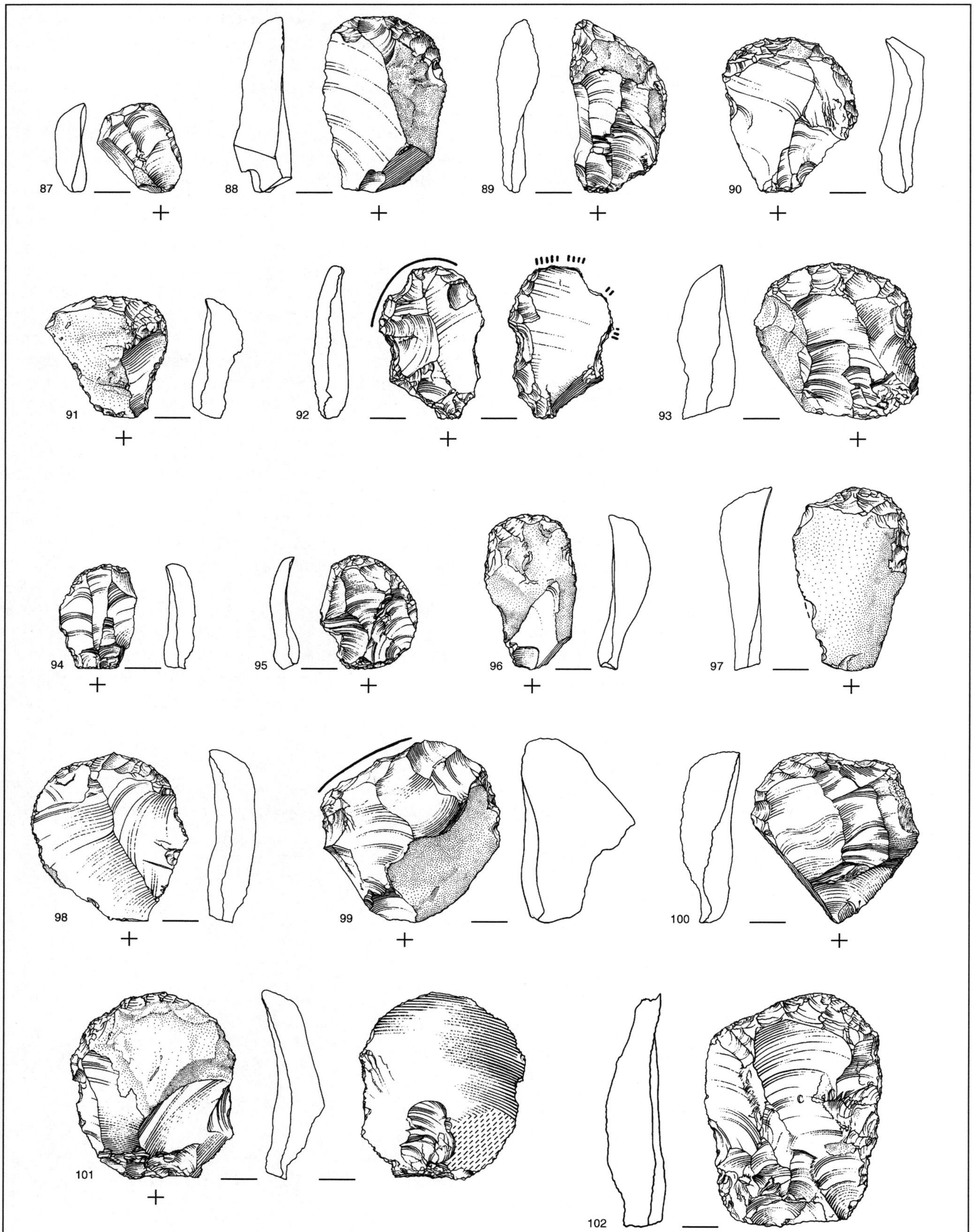

Fig 10.12 Scrapers. All the illustrated examples are from features on site A. Particulars in catalogue.

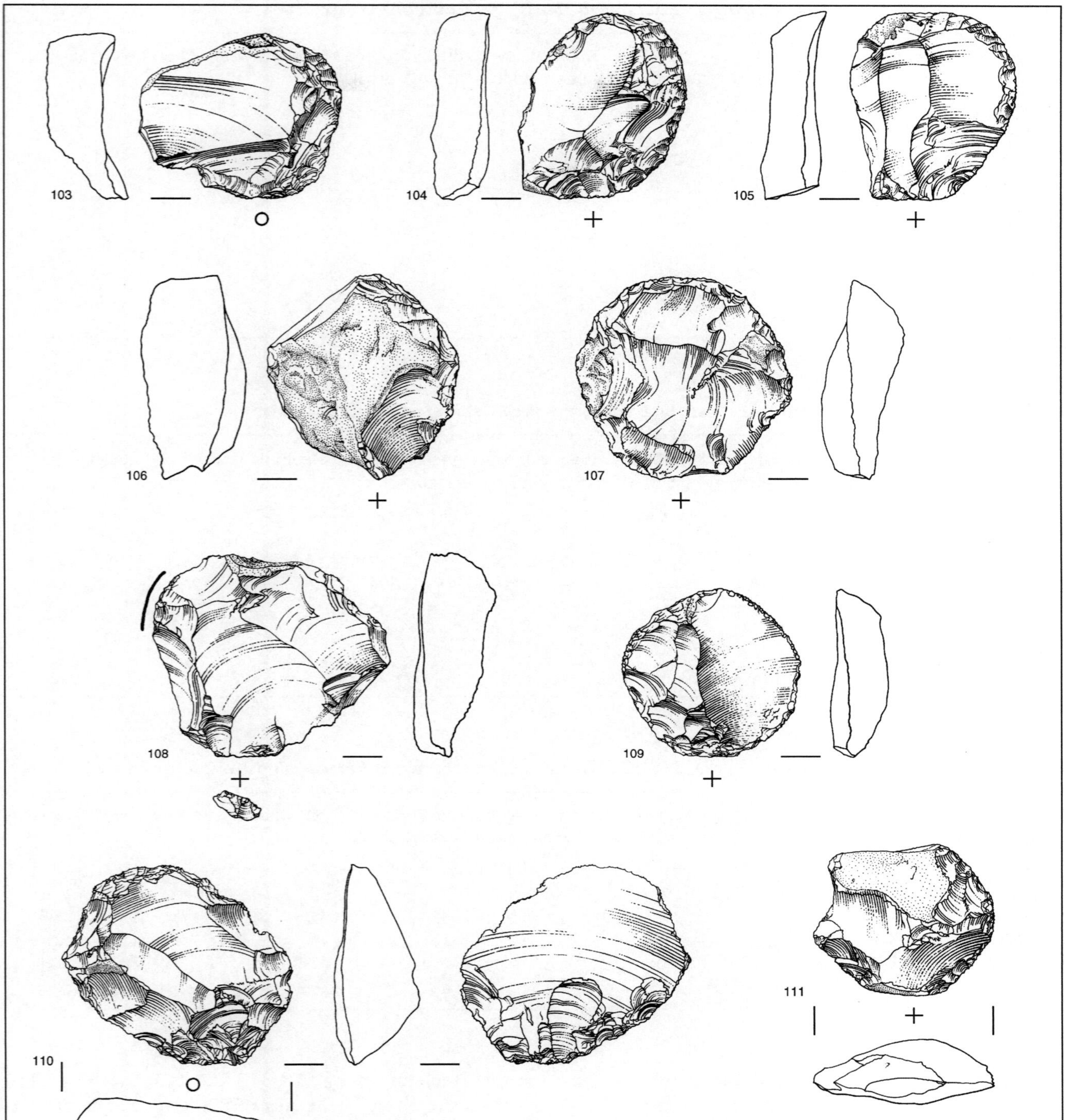

Fig 10.13 Scrapers. 104, 107 and 103 are from features on site A, the remainder are from the main enclosure ditch. Particulars in catalogue.

Table 10.47 Length ranges of complete scrapers from selected context groups

Group 1 Neolithic features in central area, groups 3–11 main enclosure ditch; group 53 Neolithic features on Stepleton spur, groups 55–61 Stepleton enclosure ditch, groups 63–69 inner Stepleton outwork ditch

Length in mm ranges	*Group 1*	*Groups 3–11*	*Group 53*	*Groups 55–61*	*Groups 63–69*	*Total no.*	*Total %*
20–29.9	2	3			5	10	4
30–39.9	2	12	2	3	16	35	12
40–49.9	13	48	8	11	29	109	38
50–59.9	6	34	5	17	26	88	31
60–69.9	1	14	2	1	10	28	10
70–79.9		4	2	1	2	9	3
80–89.9				4	2	6	2
Totals	24	115	19	37	90	285	

Table 10.48 Thickness ranges of complete scrapers from selected context groups

Group 1 Neolithic features in central area, groups 3–11 main enclosure ditch; group 53 Neolithic features on Stepleton spur, groups 55–61 Stepleton enclosure ditch, groups 63–69 inner Stepleton outwork ditch

Thickness in mm ranges	*Group 1*	*Groups 3–11*	*Group 53*	*Groups 55–61*	*Groups 63–69*	*Total no.*	*Total %*
05–9.9	7	32	4	4	28	75	26
10–14.9	11	50	8	19	41	129	45
15–19.9	6	22	5	11	10	54	19
20–24.9		9	2	2	9	22	8
25>		2		1	2	5	2
Total no.	24	115	19	37	90	285	

Table 10.49 Length/breadth index values of complete scrapers from selected context groups

Group 1 Neolithic features in central area, groups 3–11 main enclosure ditch; group 53 Neolithic features on Stepleton spur, groups 55–61 Stepleton enclosure ditch, groups 63–69 inner Stepleton outwork ditch

L/B index	*Group 1*	*Groups 3–11*	*Group 53*	*Groups 55–61*	*Groups 63–69*	*Total no..*	*Total %*	*Shape*
0.6–1.0	4	35	4	10	25	78	27	Broad
1.1–1.5	14	59	10	23	53	159	56	Medium/broad
1.6–2.0	5	21	4	4	12	46	16	Medium/narrow
2.1–2.5	1		1			2	1	Narrow
Total	24	115	19	37	90	285		

Double-end scrapers are a further variant with a convex scraping edge at the proximal as well as the distal end. Taking all these categories together, they represent 88% of all the scrapers in the subset.

Other types are side (Fig 10.13: 106, 108 and 111) and rare disc scrapers, and those scrapers which are otherwise atypical or unclassifiable. The latter include an incomplete scraper on a flake from a polished flint axehead (ST81 3004 from the phase III fills of the inner Stepleton outwork) and five scrapers on what appear to be thermal rather than struck flakes, but which are otherwise conventional convex-edge types. Scrapers with denticulated edges, ie basically convex end scrapers but with pronounced undulation between flake scars (Saville 1981b, 9), are rare and are included in the atypical category: ST78 2633 from a pit on the Stepleton and ST78 372 and 621 and ST79 410 from the phase VIII/a fills of the inner Stepleton outwork. Other oddities include a side-and-base scraper (Fig 10.13: 103), a scraper with a straight and pointed edge (HH74 461 from the phase VIII/a fills of the main enclosure) and what appears to be a scraper with a slightly concave edge (ST78 134 from the phase VIII/a fills of the inner Stepleton outwork). Apart from the pointed scraper just mentioned, only three have retouched edges which are straight rather than convex, and these are all catalogued as end scrapers rather than truncated flakes, because of the invasive rather than blunting nature of the retouch.

Twelve scrapers have prepared bases, in the sense of post-flake modification to flatten the bulb or otherwise thin the flake at the butt end. These comprise an

Table 10.50 Scraping-edge angles of all scrapers with complete scraping edges from selected context groups

Group 1 Neolithic features in central area, groups 3–11 main enclosure ditch; group 53 Neolithic features on Stepleton spur, groups 55–61 Stepleton enclosure ditch, groups 63–69 inner Stepleton outwork ditch

Angle range in degrees	*Group 1*	*Groups 3–11*	*Group 53*	*Groups 55–61*	*Groups 63–69*	*Total no.*	*Total %*
20–40°					1	1	
20–50°		1				1	
30–40°		2	1		4	7	2
30–50°		6		1	3	10	3
30–60°		1				1	
30–90°		1				1	
40–50°	3	10	4	7	9	33	10
40–60°	4	15	6	5	22	52	16
40–70°	1	7			2	10	3
40–80°		5			1	6	2
50–60°	4	17		5	16	42	13
50–70°	7	19	3	8	25	62	19
50–80°	2	11		1	5	19	6
50–90°		4				4	1
60–70°	1	5	2	3	3	14	4
60–80°	7	10	3	7	12	39	12
60–90°	4	5			1	10	3
70–80°		3			1	4	1
70–90°	2	2				4	1
Total	35	124	19	37	105	320	

end-and-side scraper (HH75 616 from a pit in the central area; one end scraper (Fig 10.13: 110) from phase III in the main enclosure ditch and one side scraper (HH76 871) from a superficial context in the same ditch, extended-end (ST81 1304), one end-and-side (ST81 779, and one side scraper (ST81 2440) from phases IV, VI and III in the Stepleton enclosure ditch, and, from the inner Stepleton outwork, an end scraper (ST79 845) from phase V, another (ST79 2111) from phase VIII/a), two extended-end scrapers (ST79 2033, ST78 1613) from phases V and VIII/a, one side scraper (ST78 914) from phase VII/a , and one atypical scraper or denticulate (ST79 410) from phase VIII/a. On the last of these the 'prepared base' flaking is through the original cortication.

The extended-end scrapers include five which could be classed size-wise as 'thumb' scrapers, short stumpy scrapers with extensive lateral retouch, all of which come from the phase VIII/a fills of the inner Stepleton outwork (ST78 784, 785, 2527, 2529 – all segment 8 – and ST78 1136 – segment 6), though quite small, short, end scrapers could occur in most contexts (eg Fig 10.12: 87 and 94). None of these small scrapers has the regular, shallow, invasive retouch typical of classic 'Beaker' scrapers (Clark 1933, 272; Smith 1965, 107), although the five 'thumb' scrapers are on relatively thin flakes and do have comparatively shallow angles. There are also two scrapers which have two-phase cortication, that is the scraper-edge retouch considerably post-dates the production of the flake blank, from a superficial context in the main enclosure (HH76 861) and phase VIII/a in the inner Stepleton outwork (ST78 1613).

For metrical purposes all the complete scrapers on bulbar flakes with intact platforms were isolated as in Table 10.46. One of the disc scrapers is included in this group of 285 because the retouch was, unusually, all inverse, and so only affected the dorsal surface of the butt, leaving the bulb and platform otherwise intact. Tables 10.47–49 show the preferred length for the scrapers as 40–60 mm, the preferred thickness as 10–15 mm, and the preferred shape as medium/broad.

From the selected sample of 386 complete scrapers a total of 330 have intact striking platforms, only seven of which (2%) are faceted. Four of the 386 scrapers are burnt, and five are on thermal rather than struck flakes. Of the measured sample of 285 scrapers, 227 (80%) are on flakes retaining some cortex.

320 of the scrapers have a scraping edge intact enough for a calculation of the scraping-edge angle (Table 10.50), using a series of overlapping angle-ranges (Saville 1981b, 9). These data demonstrate a broad spread of scraping-edge angles without any dominant preference, although scrapers with basically low angles (50° or less) are rather few (*c* 15%), while scrapers with steeper angles (50° or more) are much more common (*c* 60%). The contexts of the 52 low-angled scrapers were investigated and found to belong to the following context groups (numbers of scrapers in brackets): Neolithic pits in the central area (3);

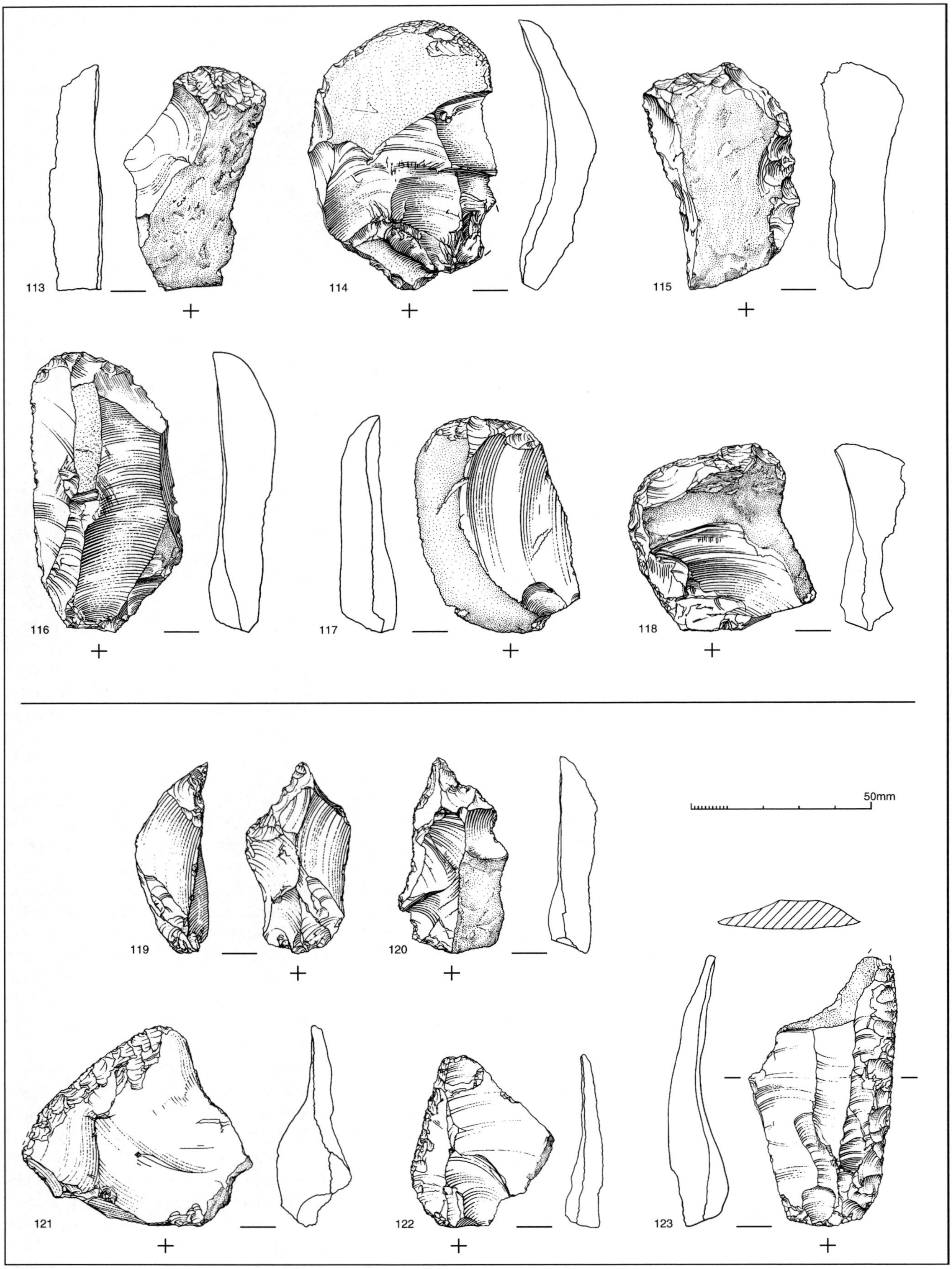

Fig 10.14 Scrapers. 115 and 118 are from features on site A, the remainder are from the main enclosure ditch. Piercers (119–20) and knives (121–3). Particulars in catalogue.

phases I–II in the main enclosure ditch (1); phase III in the main enclosure ditch (2); phase V in the main enclosure ditch (1); phase VI in the main enclosure ditch (7); phase VII/a in the main enclosure ditch (3); phase VIII/a in the main enclosure ditch (2); superficial contexts in the main enclosure ditch (3); Neolithic features on the Stepleton spur (5); phase V in the Stepleton enclosure (1); phase IV in the Stepleton enclosure (2); phase VI in the Stepleton enclosure (3); phase VIII/a in the Stepleton enclosure (2); phase V in the inner Stepleton outwork (1); phase VII/a in the inner Stepleton outwork (3); and phase VIII/a in the same outwork (13). Thus at Hambledon it appears unlikely that this trait can be correlated in any straightforward fashion with any trend towards lowering of scraper-edge angles through time.

The illustrated scrapers (Figs 10.12–14) are all from the central area, either from the Neolithic features or from the main enclosure ditch fills (mainly phase VI).

Piercers

These are implements with one or more pointed projections formed by deliberate modification. They are normally on flake blanks. In many cases the modification by trimming or by more pronounced retouch enhances a natural projection on the blank. The very nature of the tool makes it vulnerable to damage and hence potential non-recognition. The total of 136 piercers may therefore under-represent the importance of this tool-type, with other examples hidden within the miscellaneous retouched pieces or the incomplete unretouched flakes. Normally there is little sign of obvious wear, but three piercers have points which were worn smooth or more noticeably abraded (HH76 509 from phase VI in the main enclosure; HH77 864 from a natural feature in the central area; and ST78 1616 from a Neolithic feature on the Stepleton spur).

The Hambledon piercers are overwhelmingly of the simple, distally pointed type, with the point formed by unilateral or bilateral retouch on the dorsal face. The two illustrated examples (Fig 10.14: 119–120) are both distal piercers with bilaterally retouched points. These two have quite pronounced retouch on relatively thick flakes, producing robust points. Other examples may have much more restricted retouch and thinner points. A few examples have additional inverse retouch at the point and several have ancillary trimming elsewhere on the blank. One of the distally pointed piercers has the point formed by the oblique truncation of a blade (HH75 309 from phase VI in the inner east cross-dyke) and another has a double-pointed distal end (HH74 997 from a Neolithic feature in the central area).

Apart from the simple, distal piercers, there are occasional examples with a point formed on a lateral flake edge (HH74 979 from a Neolithic pit in the central area; HH75 1107 from phase VII/a in the main enclosure; HH77 1661 from the topsoil over the long barrow); or at the proximal end of a flake (ST79 929 from phase VIII/a in the inner Stepleton outwork).

There are six instances of true borers, with alternate retouch at the distal point (HH76 34 from phase VIII/a in the main enclosure; HH76 234 from a recent quarry in the central area; HH76 947 from a superficial context in the main enclosure; ST78 804 from the topsoil on the Stepleton spur; ST79 1035 from phase VIII/a in the inner Stepleton outwork and ST79 2328 from the bank area of the inner Stepleton outwork). One piercer has a triangular-sectioned point worked on all three faces (ST81 2619, unstratified on the Stepleton spur). There are five instances of 'spurred' piercer types (Smith 1965, 105), with a short, pointed projection from a zone of scraper-like retouch (ST78 1707 and ST79 12 from phase VIII/a in the inner Stepleton outwork; ST80 300 from phase VIII/a in the Stepleton enclosure; ST80 476 from a superficial context in the inner Stepleton outwork; and ST80 2119 from phase VI in the Stepleton enclosure ditch).

A small group of seven piercers, almost all from Stepleton, resemble or approach the classic late Neolithic/Bronze Age forms (Saville 1978 and 1981b, 9), with elongated, thick points (HH76 2017 from phase III in the main enclosure; ST78 372, ST79 63, ST79 480 and ST79 929 all from phase VIII/a in the inner Stepleton outwork; ST78 1277 from Saxon grave 12; and ST79 1518 from phase VII/a in the inner Stepleton outwork).

One piercer is formed on a core (ST78 609 from phase VIII/a in the inner Stepleton outwork); one on a flaked lump (ST79 480 from the same context group); one on a thermal lump (ST79 1727 from phase VIII/a in the outer Stepleton outwork); three on thermal flakes (HH75 890 from a superficial context in segment 8 of the main enclosure; HH77 493 from phase VII/a in the same segment; ST80 635 from phase VIII/a in the inner Stepleton outwork); and two on flakes from polished flint axeheads (HH76 5 from a superficial context on site G; ST80 300 from phase VIII/a in the Stepleton enclosure. Two piercers are formed on large, heavy flakes, and almost verge on the pick category, including one which is bifacially retouched (HH77 864 from a natural hollow on site N).

Finally, three piercers have the retouch forming the points struck through the surface discolouration of flakes which were being reused at a much later date (HH74 460 from phase VIII/a in the main enclosure; ST78 64 unstratified, and ST78 188 from phase VIII/a in the inner Stepleton outwork).

Leaf-shaped arrowheads

Only 42 of these distinctive projectile points were found (Table 10.51). Few are wholly complete and several are represented only by small segments. No conjoining segments were noted among those recovered, but in many cases the missing broken fragments would have been too small for recovery without sieving.

The eleven most intact examples (Table 10.51) have relatively minor edge damage or slight breaks at the distal and/or proximal tips so that the existing

Table 10.51 Provenance of all leaf-shaped arrowheads (weights in grams), with dimensions (in mm) of those complete enough for measurement

Arrowhead class after Clark *et al.* (1960, 220) and Smith (1965, 100); arrowhead type after H S Green (1984, 21). Illustration number refers to Figure 10.15

Find	*Group*	*Location*	*Material*	*Wt*	*Illus no.*	*L*	*B*	*Th*	*Class*	*L×B*	*L÷B*	*Type*
HH74 978	1	Pit A F41	Chert	0.5								
HH74 1221	1	Pit A F113	Flint	0.9								
HH77 1253	1	Pit N F11	Flint	1.7	134							
HH77 1539	1	Pit N F42	Chert	2.4	141							
HH77 1586	1	Pit N F1	Flint	1.4	138	38.5	18.5	3.0	B	712	2.1	3B
HH77 1587	1	Pit N F1	Flint	2.6	128	45	18	3.0	B	810	2.5	3C
HH76 1934	5	Main enclosure, segment 16 L9A phase IV	Flint	0.8								
HH76 1401	6	Main enclosure, segment 16 L8 phase V	Flint	1.0								
HH76 668	7	Main enclosure, segment 13 L5 phase VI	Flint	2.5								
HH76 811	7	Main enclosure, segment 17, L6 phase VI	Flint	1.0	124	35	17	2.5	A	595	2.1	3B
HH77 534	7	Main enclosure, segment 7, L4A phase VI	Flint	1.5								
HH77 2622	7	Main enclosure, segment 6, 1 L5A phase VI	Flint	1.2	126							
HH74 570	10	Main enclosure, segment 2, L3 phase VIII/a	Flint	1.0								
HH76 434	10	Main enclosure, segment 17, L3 phase VIII/a	Flint	2.6	125	49	22	3.0	A	1078	2.23	2B
HH77 683	10	Main enclosure, segment 7, L3B phase VIII/a	Flint	1.5								
HH75 1124	15	Inner east cross-dyke segment 4, L6 phase VI	Flint	2.5	129	39	17.5	3.5	B	683	2.23	3B
HH77 606	15	Inner east cross-dyke segment 1, L5A phase VI	Flint	2.6								
HH75 1290	17	Inner east cross-dyke segment 5, L3 phase VIII/a	Flint	3.0	130	37	19.5	4.0	B	722	1.9	3B
HH75 1711	22	Outer east cross-dyke segment 5, L4 phase VI	Flint	0.7								
HH77 558	25	Inner south cross-dyke bank area L4	Flint	1.2								
HH77 1988	25	Pit P2 F14	Chert	0.2								
HH77 2164	25	Pit P2 F14	Chert	0.6								
HH77 2333	25	Pit P2 F14	Chert	0.7								
HH75 6	46	Site C, unstratified	Flint	0.5	127							
HH74 596	46	Site A, unstratified	Chert	2.0								
HH76 117	46	Site H, unstratified	Flint	1.6								
HH77 1498	46	Recent pit N F44	Flint	1.0	136							
HH77 532	46	Site N, unstratified	Flint	0.9	135	28	15	3.0	A	420	1.9	4B
HH77 803	46	Central area, unstratified	Flint	2.6	137							
HH76 745	49	Shroton outwork, segment 3, L6 phase III	Flint	1.1								
HH76 975	49	Shroton outwork, segment 3, L6 phase III	Flint	1.8								
HH76 299	51	Shroton outwork, segment 3, L3, phase VIII/a	Flint	3.5								
HH76 588	52	Shroton outwork, segment 3, superficial feature A	Flint	1.3								
ST78 2834	56	Stepleton enclosure, segment 23, L4 phase III	Flint	1.7		34	15	4.0	A	510	2.27	3C
ST80 1234	58	Stepleton enclosure segment 2 L5A phase IV	Flint	1.2	131	27	16	4.0	B	432	1.69	4A
ST80 398	60	Stepleton enclosure, segment 6 L1 phase VIII/a	Flint	0.8								
ST78 2730	64	Inner Stepleton outwork, segment 7 L4 phase III	Flint	2.1	139							
ST79 1570	66	Inner Stepleton outwork, segment 7 L3 phase VII/a	Flint	1.2								
ST79 1867	68	Inner Stepleton outwork, segment 5 L2 or L2B, phase VII/a or VIII/a	Flint	1.3	133	31	16	2.5	A	496	1.94	3B
ST80 1425	71	Middle Stepleton outwork, segment 5, L6 phase I	Flint	2.3	140							
ST80 1877	77	Outer Stepleton outwork, segment 3, phase I	Flint	2.1	132	43	15.5	3.0	B	666.5	2.77	3C
ST78 2710	82	Site 1A, Clay-with-Flints	Flint	1.3								

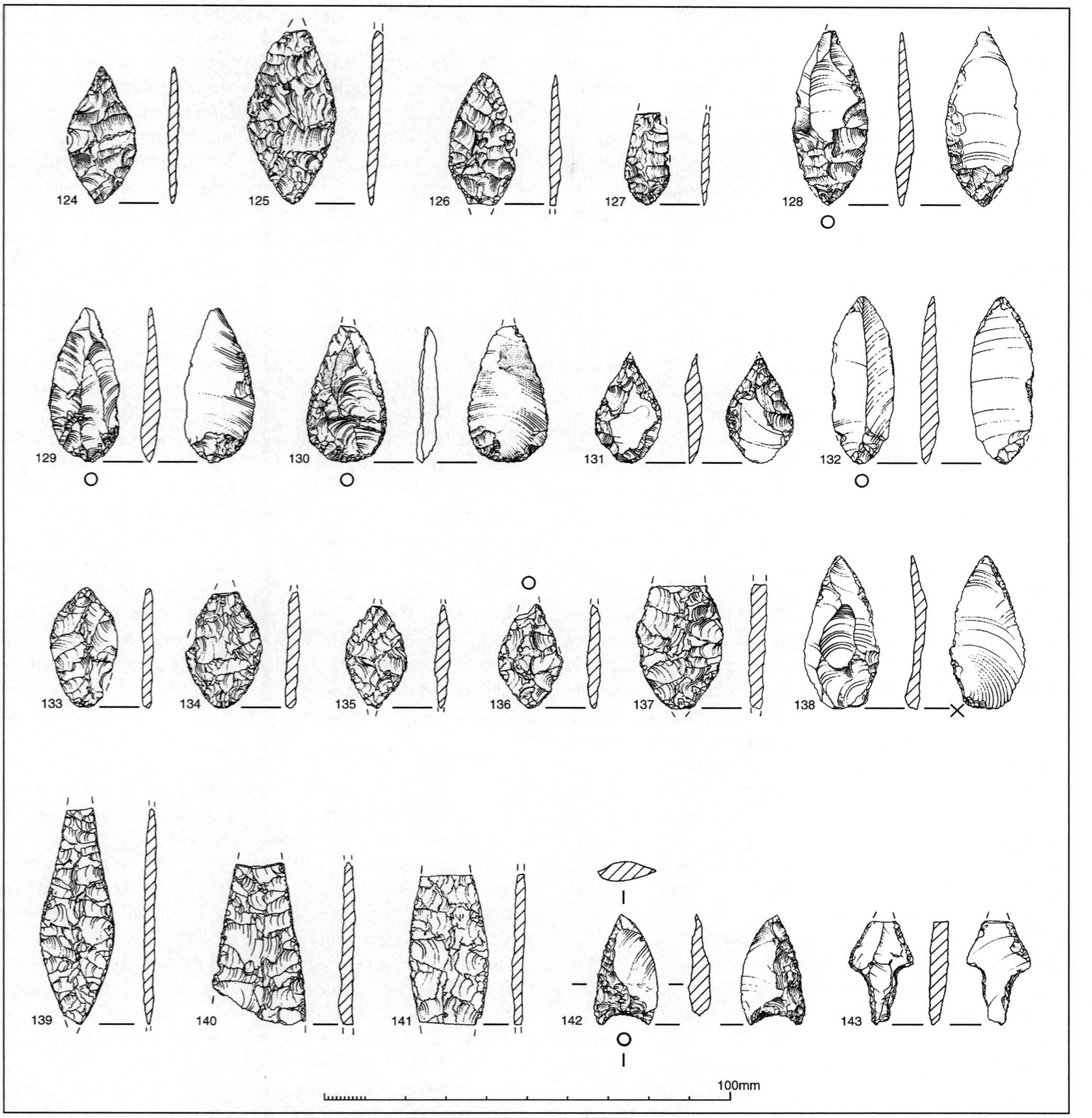

Fig 10.15 Leaf-shaped arrowheads (124–41), oblique arrowhead (142) and tanged arrowhead (143). Particulars in catalogue.

dimensions can be taken as representative of the original size and shape. Medium types (ie type 3B in Green's (1984) terminology) are the most common, but there are also one large (type 2B), three slender (type 3C), and two small (type 4A/B) examples. Two have an ogival character (Fig 10.15: 124 and 131), but they are both cases of 'attenuated points' rather than being ogivals proper (cf Green 1984, 21). One example (ST78 2834 from phase III in the Stepleton enclosure) is the distal fragment of a larger arrowhead, which has been retouched at the base after breakage to form the present arrowhead, and another example may have been modified at the tip after breakage in a similar way (Fig 10.15: 133).

That these intact examples do not encompass the variability of the arrowheads from Hambledon is clear from the fragments, such as those illustrated (Fig 10.15: 127, 139–141). One extreme is shown by the basal segment of a small, slender type (127), another by an unusually elongated ogival arrowhead (139), which is broken at both ends but is still, at 54 mm, longer than any other arrowhead in this collection.

The maximum thickness of this arrowhead is only two millimetres, making it a wafer-thin and quite exceptional piece of prehistoric craftwork. Because of the almost uniform thickness throughout this arrowhead, it is not clear which is the tip and which the base.

While the majority of the arrowheads are of class A, with complete bifacial pressure-flaking, a relatively high proportion (11 examples) are of class B. The latter range from those with partial bifacial pressure-flaking (Fig 10.15: 128 and 131) to those with only peripheral trimming (129–130), which can sometimes be minimal (132 and 138). The flake origin of some of the arrowheads is obvious (128, 129, 130, 132) and in one case part of the original faceted platform of the parent flake remains (138). Examples like these (especially 129, 130, 138) are sometimes regarded as typologically borderline arrowheads (Green 1984, 20).

Six of the arrowheads are of chert (Table 10.51), and one fragmentary example (HH76 683 from phase VIII/a in the main enclosure ditch) is of unusual red and white particoloured flint. This significant use of 'exotic' raw material is exclusive to this category of artefact at Hambledon Hill, and is restricted to the vicinity of the main enclosure. Two of the chert arrowheads come from features (A F41 and N F42) within the enclosure, three are from a feature (P2 F14) on the inner south cross-dyke bank area, and the sixth is a surface find. The group of three chert arrowheads from P2 F14, which was almost certainly under the inner south cross-dyke bank, is noteworthy; they are all fragmentary but from separate implements.

In all there are seven leaf-shaped arrowheads from features within the main enclosure, two from the same feature, and nine from various segments of the main enclosure ditch. Three segments – 7, 16, and 17 – produced two arrowheads each, but all from different horizons of the fill.

Four arrowheads are from the Shroton spur outwork and eight from various ditch segments of the Stepleton enclosure, though none of these 12 examples is of obviously exotic raw material. Those from the Shroton spur comprise three class B and one class A. The latter (HH76 975) is a fragment of a very fine specimen, which must have been of exceptional size (current dimensions: L >46 mm × B >19 mm × Th 2.5 mm). All four are from segment 3 (site K/L), but only two are from the same infill horizon (phase III) and were not found close together.

Two arrowheads, both from the Stepleton enclosure ditch, were found in direct association with human skeletons. One (Fig 10.15: 132) is a minimally retouched class B type from among the ribs of a young male in segment 3 of the outer outwork (Fig 3.105), the other is the elongated ogival example (Fig 10.15: 139) from segment 7 of the inner outwork. The latter was found in the rib-cage of a complete young male skeleton (Figs 3.102 and 3.104). It is of interest to note Green's comments (1980, 87) on similar examples, especially their apparent high frequency in funerary contexts. Green suggests that the two elongated examples from the Shoscombe I, Somerset, burial chamber could be special funerary items, but the evidence from the Stepleton ditch could be more consistent with the arrowheads being the cause of death rather than being grave-goods. It is not possible to be certain about this, however, especially since the bones of the two skeletons do not show any damage by projectile point nor do they retain any broken tips of arrowheads. Another possibility would be that the persons involved had the arrowheads with them, as personal possessions, at the time of death.

Other arrowheads

Two arrowheads not of leaf-shaped type were recovered during the excavation. One is an oblique arrowhead (Fig 10.15: 142) of later Neolithic type (Class F; Clark 1934) from a phase VII/a horizon in segment 10 of the main enclosure ditch. The other is a tanged arrowhead (Fig 10.15: 143 from the topsoil on the Stepleton spur) formed by blunting retouch throughout, except for a small area of invasive scalar trimming on the ventral surface of the blade. Its form resembles Bronze Age arrowhead types, but the retouch is more in character with Mesolithic flintwork, so as a type it is somewhat enigmatic. A somewhat similar example was found in a middle Neolithic ditch context at Etton causewayed enclosure, Cambridgeshire (Middleton 1998, 234 and fig 228: 134).

'Laurel-leaf' bifacial pieces

Six of these bifacially retouched points (Clark *et al* 1960, 223) are present. In many respects reminiscent of leaf-shaped arrowheads, they are distinguished by their greater size and weight. They have a near-symmetrical shape in plan, lenticular cross-section, pointed terminals, a slender and regular profile, and usually complete bifacial surface flaking. Their function remains unproven, but one possibility is they are for hafting as spear- or lance-tips. It can be the case, however, that the terminals lack sharpness, which makes an alternative explanation as elaborate knives rather than projectile points more plausible. One of the present group is relevant here (Fig 10.16: 148) since, although now damaged and shattered at several places along one edge and at the terminals, and presumably a discard after use, it also has a naturally blunted area (at the upper RHS of the left planview in the illustration). This has been used as a platform for retouch but not thinned, and it would have impeded any use of the piece as a projectile point.

The illustrations (Fig 10.16: 144–145, 147–148, 150) and the dimensions given in Table 10.52 give an indication of the appearance, size, and weight of these implements. One (Fig 10.16: 150), which has only peripheral ventral retouch, gives an insight into the type of blank selected, in this case clearly a very broad flake, on which the implement is formed transverse-fashion. This may be unusual, however, since another

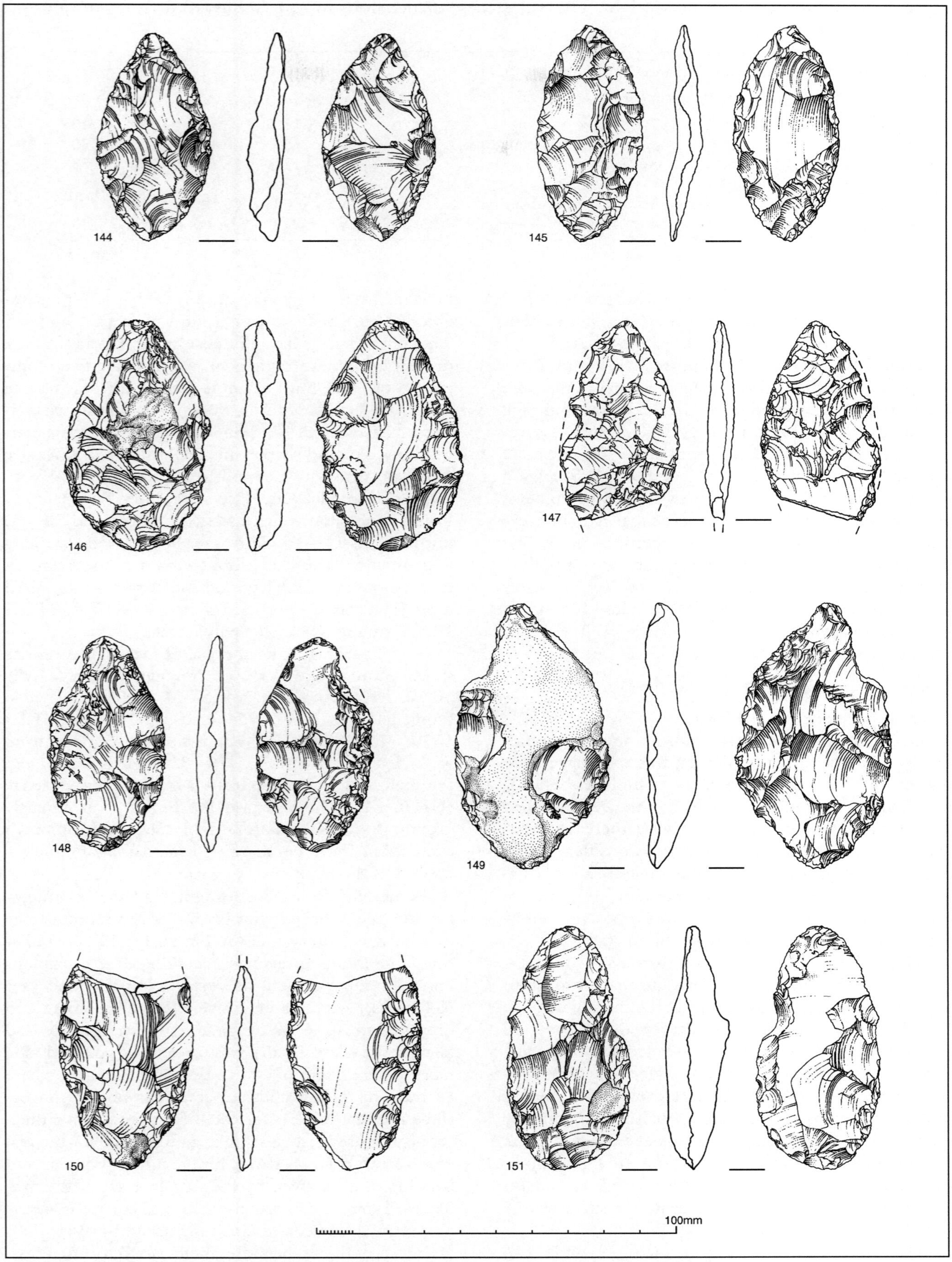

Fig 10.16 Laurel-leaf bifacial pieces (144–5, 147–8, 150) and unclassified bifacial pieces (146, 149, 151). Particulars in catalogue.

Table 10.52 Provenance of 'laurel-leaf' bifacial pieces (dimensions in mm are given for the complete and near complete examples)

Note: illustration numbers refer to Figure 10.16

Find	*Group*	*Location (and dimensions)*	*Weight in grams*	*Illus no.*	*L*	*B*	*Th*
HH77 1517	1	Pit N F5	13.5	145	65	29	7
HH76 26	11	Main enclosure, segment 13, L1, ploughsoil	15.9	144	60	32	9
HH76 1335	11	Main enclosure, site G, unstratified	17.5	148	62	33	8
ST79 1973	53	Pit 2A F154	13.0	150			
ST79 1569	65	Inner Stepleton outwork, S butt of segment 7, L3A, phase V	10.0	147			
ST79 1571	65	Inner Stepleton outwork, S butt of segment 7, L3A, phase V	21.0	Not illus	76	40	8

example with only peripheral ventral trimming (ST79 1571 from phase V in the inner Stepleton outwork) is formed longitudinally to the flake's bulbar axis.

Two of the 'laurel-leaf' bifacials were found in the fills of Neolithic pits, one within the main enclosure (Fig 10.16: 145), the other on the Stepleton spur (Fig 10.16: 150), two came from post-Neolithic levels in the main enclosure, and two from phase V contexts in the south-west butt of segment 7 of the inner Stepleton outwork. Given the rarity of this implement type at Hambledon Hill this is a significant association at the macro-level, but the excavation records indicate that they were found 3.20 m apart horizontally and 0.30 m apart vertically, so they cannot be described as closely associated at the micro-level. One of these has extensive edge-damage (Fig 10.16: 147), as well as being broken, so was most probably a discard.

Polished flint axeheads (Table 10.53)

There is only one polished axehead (Fig 10.17: 152) which is essentially complete with no obvious modification by reflaking, though even this may have been reground. Then there are three complete axeheads with polished cutting-edges, which have been modified on the body by reflaking. Otherwise there are fragments of polished axeheads and numerous flakes from polished flint axeheads, which demonstrate a more significant presence for this tool type than the complete examples would indicate, and also support the interpretation of their use and reworking on site.

The axehead (Fig 10.17: 152) from an internal feature of the main enclosure is complete apart from chips and flake-scar damage from use at the cutting edge. It is polished all over but deeper scars remain visible on the butt. The lateral edges are bevelled and only truly flat-faceted at the butt on one side. The profile is asymmetric due to heavier, more prolonged grinding of the cutting-edge on one face, effected subsequently to the polish of the cutting edge on the opposite face. It is impossible to be certain, but this could well indicate regrinding of the cutting-edge after previous damage or even, given its present relatively small size, a significant break.

The three axeheads with reflaking include two rather similar examples (Fig 10.17: 155 and Fig 10.18: 156), where only the original cutting-edge end of a polished axehead remains after reflaking the (presumably broken) body to give a kind of tanged support. The reflaked areas have not been ground at all. In their present form these implements are assumed to be complete tools. The third example (HH76 2975, a surface find from the Shroton outwork) is a substantial polished axehead, still 172 mm long, which retains a conventional axehead shape and profile after less extensive reflaking through the polished surface down both edges and at the butt. This is the only flint axehead from Hambledon which has the kind of mass (580 g) normally associated with the heavy wood-working implements of this class, though many of the fragmentary examples could have derived from similar-sized tools. The complete or near complete examples (Table 10.53) are otherwise all small in size.

The other fragments of polished axeheads comprise three cutting-edge ends or fragments thereof (Fig 10.17: 153; and ST79 794; ST79 2349), five medial segments (Fig 10.17: 154; and HH74 980; HH75 1870; ST79 1036; ST80 72), two small segments from at or close to the butt (HH75 1824; ST79 2582), and the major part of an axehead lacking its cutting-edge (HH76 81). There is also the butt-end of a partly ground flint axehead found in Desmond Bonney's excavation, from the phase III chalk rubble fill of segment 8 of the main enclosure ditch (3.3.2).

Some of these axehead fragments have been comprehensively reflaked after breakage, but more usually in a fairly desultory way (eg Fig 10.17: 153–4) rather than attempting to recreate a working edge or exploiting their full potential as cores, except in one case (ST80 72), which is extensively flaked as a core and only recognisable as originating from an axehead because of a small surviving area of a polished side facet. There could of course be other instances where all trace of former polished areas has been removed, since the raw material selected for axehead manufacture is not obviously dissimilar to that used for the rest of the assemblage. A strong hint that local nodular flint is being used is given by the fact that six of the axeheads (Table 10.53) retain patches of cortex, in several cases with the cortex area fully ground-over.

Seven of the axehead fragments are burnt to a lesser or greater extent (Table 10.53). In one case (HH76 81) a substantial polished axehead fragment, minus its

Table 10.53 Provenance of all polished flint axeheads, axehead fragments, and flakes from polished flint axeheads

Dimensions in mm are given for the complete or near complete axeheads
Illustration numbers refer to Figures 10.17–18

Group	*Find*	*Class*	*Location*	*Weight in grams*	*Illus no.*	*L*	*B*	*Th*	*Cortex*	*Burnt*
1	HH74 980	Axehead fragment	Pit A F41	60					yes	yes
1	HH74 1147	Axehead	Pit A F71	163	152	104	51.5	26	yes	
1	HH74 1016	Flake	Pit A F41	12.7						
1	HH74 1213	Flake	Pit A F114	12.3						
1	HH77 1462	Flake	Pit N F7i	6.3						
3	HH75 1824	Axehead fragment	Main enclosure, segment 11, L11 phase II	36.2						yes
4	HH75 1081	Flake	Main enclosure, segment 9, L7 phase III	35.6						
5	HH77 580	Flake	Main enclosure, segment 1, F9, phase IV	6.5						
7	HH75 1870	Axehead fragment	Main enclosure, segment 10, L6 phase VI	109.1					yes	yes
7	HH77 505	Axehead	Main enclosure, segment 1, F5 phase VI	82.3	155	79	47	27		
7	HH76 757	Flake	Main enclosure, segment 13, L5 phase VI	1.8						
22.1	HH75 151	Axehead fragment	Outer east cross-dyke segment 2, L4 phase VII/a	111.9	153				yes	
25	HH77 2333	Flake	Inner south cross-dyke bank, pit P2 F14	10						
37	HH77 1553	Flake	W long barrow ditch, LB3 L35 phase III	5						
42	WOWK 82 17	Flake	Western outwork bank area WOWK2 L1 – topsoil	2.1						
46	HH75 517	Flake	?treethrow hole C F26	2.3						
47	HH76 81	Axehead fragment and 5 flakes	Shroton outwork bank area, posthole M F1	272.8						yes
52	HH76 2975	Axehead	Shroton Spur surface	580		172	74	37		
53	ST80 1300	Axehead	Pit 1A F228	129.5	156	89	51	31		
53	ST79 2349	Axehead fragment	Pit 2A F321	5.1						yes
53	ST81 1880	Flake	Pit 4B F129	2.2						yes
53	ST81 2111	Flake	Pit 4B F129	2.4						yes
53	ST81 1514	Flake	Pit 4B F130	5.8						
56	ST81 2431	Flake	Stepleton enclosure, segment 8, L3A phase III	8.8						
57	ST81 1859	Axehead fragment	Stepleton enclosure, segment 16, L3 phase V	113.1	154					
57	ST81 125	Flake	Stepleton enclosure, segment 15, L3 phase V	2.1						
60	ST80 72	Axehead fragment	Stepleton enclosure, segment 2, L1 phase VIII/a	100.7						
64	ST79 2582	Axehead fragment	Inner Stepleton outwork, segment 5, L5A phase III/a	156.1					yes	
68	ST79 1036	Axehead fragment	Inner Stepleton outwork, segment 5, L2 phase VIII/a	155.5						yes
82	ST79 794	Axehead fragment	Area 2B L1 – ploughsoil	119.8					yes	yes
82	ST78 1005	Flake	Area 1A – Clay-with-Flints	3.3						
85	HN82 388	Flake	Inner Hanford outwork, segment 3 L5 phase I	20.9						
88	HN82 161	Flake	Inner Hanford outwork, segment 3, L2C phase VII/a	3.2						

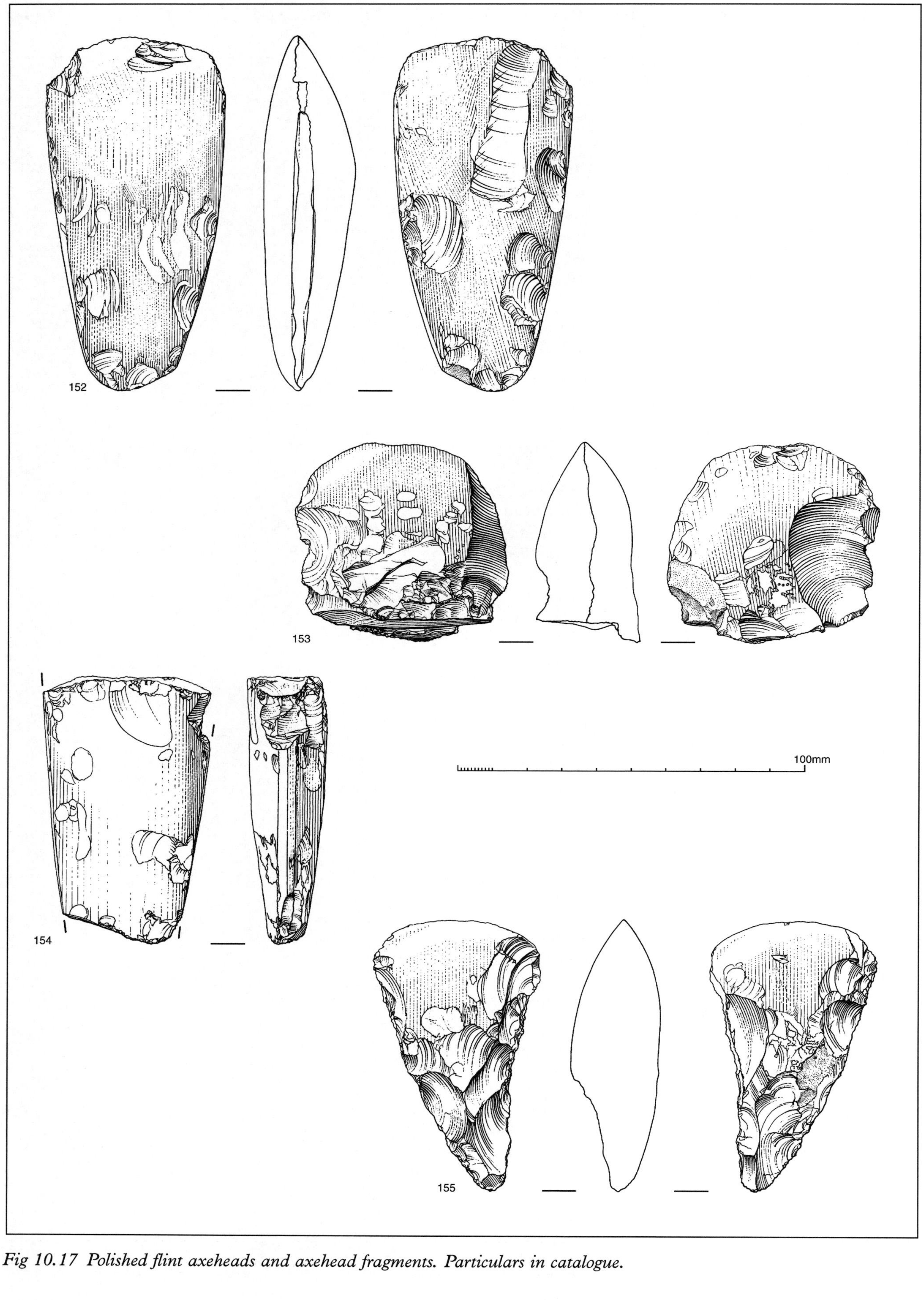

Fig 10.17 Polished flint axeheads and axehead fragments. Particulars in catalogue.

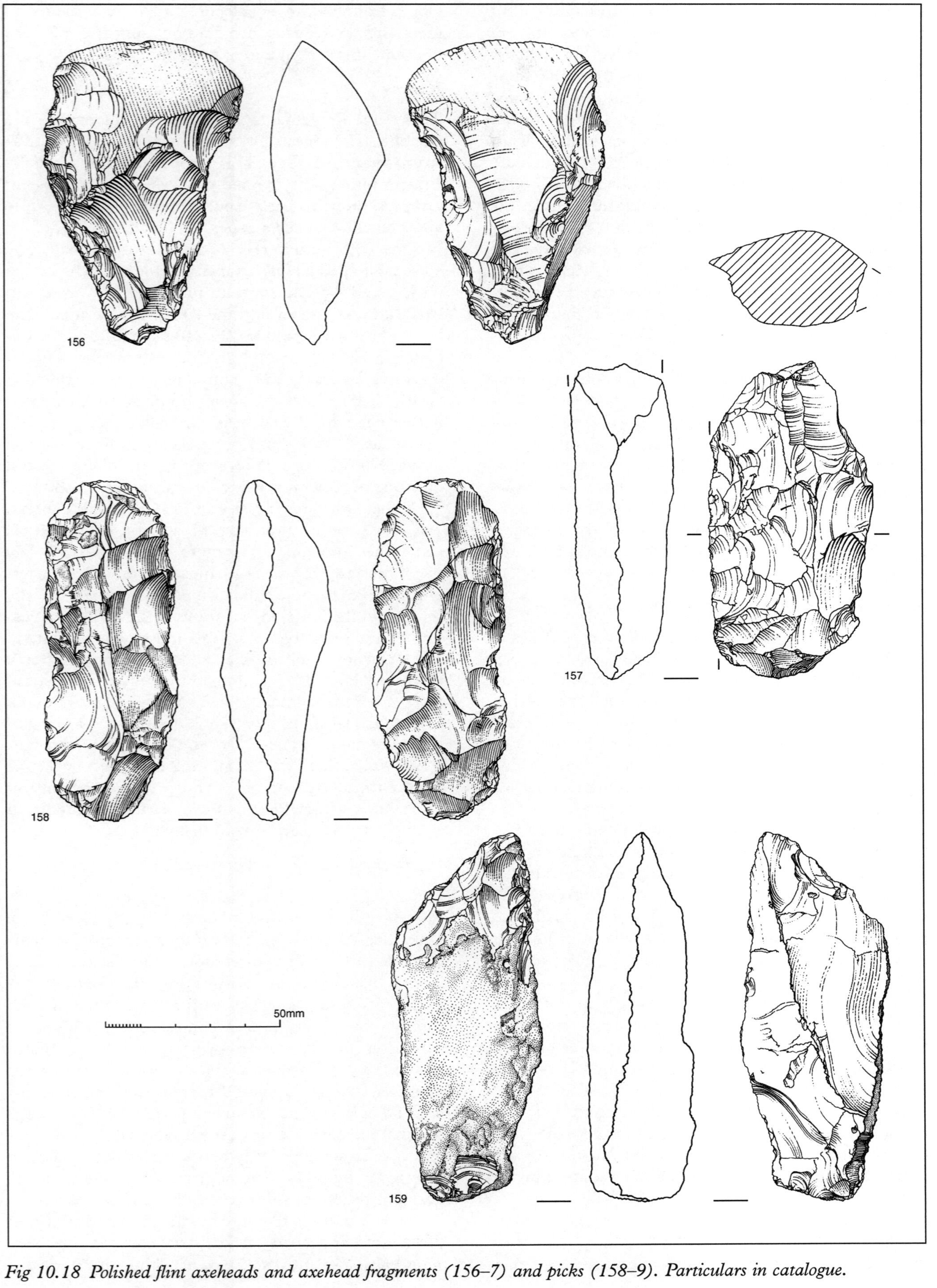

Fig 10.18 Polished flint axeheads and axehead fragments (156–7) and picks (158–9). Particulars in catalogue.

cutting edge, was extensively burnt and nine burnt fragments found with it could be refitted to it (and are included in the weight of 252 g). Five burnt flakes (weight 21 g) retaining polish came from the same posthole and, although they do not refit, they almost certainly came from the same axehead, as did a further ten small unclassified burnt fragments (weight 9 g). Two fragments (HH75 1870 and HH75 1824) that are only slightly burnt share some traits, which, although they do not refit, suggest they could derive from the same axehead, despite coming from different contexts in adjacent ditch segments of the main enclosure. The smallest axehead fragment (ST79 2349), which is part of a cutting edge, is extensively burnt and is probably a thermally produced fragment, rather than being burnt after breakage, something which in most cases is impossible to assess.

Contextually (Table 10.53), four of the axeheads are from the fills of Neolithic pits (two at each enclosure) and one from the primary fill of the main enclosure ditch. It should also be mentioned that the '3 chipped & polished flint axes within a few inches of one other', found during Desmond Bonney's excavation (3.3.4) were in the basal fill of the inner south cross-dyke ditch, an area otherwise devoid of axehead finds apart from a flake from a polished axehead from the bank area.

Flakes from polished flint axeheads

The presence of a polished surface allowed 23 flakes to be identified as originating from polished flint axeheads (Table 10.53), even though they are uninformative about the kind of axehead from which they derive. Apart from the five flakes (HH76 81) already mentioned, it was not possible to link these flakes to any of the identified axehead fragments, though one (ST81 1514) has a very similar character, on both its polished and unpolished surfaces, to one of the axeheads (Fig 10.18: 156). Both it and the axehead come from features on the Stepleton spur, and it is just possible that the flake could be one of the early reshaping flakes, which does not now conjoin. Two of the flakes (ST81 1880 and 2111) are small thermal 'pot-lid' spalls that conjoin and represent successive spalls from an axehead surface, but apart from these the other polished axehead flakes are unburnt.

The largest polished piece in this group is a broad flake (HH75 1081) with some non-specific retouch. It might have functioned as a crude scraper. Other polished flakes which have been converted into classifiable tools are incorporated in their respective sections, and comprise a scraper (ST81 3004 from phase VIII/a in the inner Stepleton outwork), a serrated-edge flake (HH76 873 from phase VI in the main enclosure), and a piercer (HH76 2 from a superficial context in the main enclosure).

The contexts of the flakes from axeheads echo those of the polished axeheads in including three each from the main enclosure and Stepleton enclosure pit fills. One is from the same enclosure pit as one of the burnt fragmentary axeheads, but does not appear to be from the same implement and is itself unburnt.

Knives

These 11 implements are defined chiefly by the attribute of at least one sharp, shallow-angled, invasively retouched edge. This retouched edge is usually straight rather than markedly convex, as in the case of scrapers, though a precise cut-off point between a knife and a shallow-angled scraper can be difficult to define.

One of this group (HH76 2212) was originally listed separately as a knife/scraper and the retouched areas on it may have had separate functions, the distal end being an end scraper and the lateral edge a knife. The three illustrated examples (Fig 10.14: 121–3) are complete or virtually complete, and exhibit the kind of extensive, invasive, and continuous retouch, which so clearly distinguishes the knives from the edge-trimmed flakes. The retouched edge is normally a lateral one, but in one case (ST79 756) a broad flake has the retouch on its wide distal edge. The supports are mainly flakes, only one of the knives being on a blade (HH76 30).

None of the knives is from a firm Neolithic context, and the precise chronological horizon of this type, sometimes thought of as more relevant to the late Neolithic/early Bronze Age, must be somewhat uncertain for Hambledon Hill. In one case (HH76 30) the retouch of the knife-edge is through the earlier cortication of the blade blank, so this must be a 'late' item, but it is from an unstratified superficial context. Some clear distributional grouping of the knives is apparent: three are from segment 8 of the main enclosure ditch, where there was a concentration of Beaker pottery; and three are from segment 7 of the inner Stepleton outwork, where there was plain, grog-tempered Beaker or early Bronze Age pottery. The precise proximity of these finds within their contexts is not recorded, but such clustering is unlikely to be by chance.

Picks (and ?axehead roughouts)

Five tools are grouped together under this category, though only two are complete and wholly classifiable. One (Fig 10.18: 158) is an elaborate, quadrangular-sectioned core-tool with complete bifacial retouch. It lacks a distinct cutting- or working-edge, but one terminal (at the top as illustrated) is abraded as though through use. This implement resembles Mesolithic core-tools but its appearance and condition, which match the other artefacts from the same and adjacent contexts, indicate it should be regarded as Neolithic. The other complete pick (Fig 10.18: 159) is a large thermal flake with a cortical exterior, retouched bilaterally, but asymmetrically and essential unifacially, to form a strong point. The opposite, butt end has some abrasion marks, possibly caused by hammer-blows.

The other three tools are fragmentary and are either picks or unpolished, flaked axeheads, or axehead roughouts. The most substantial of these is the medial segment of a bifacially flaked core-tool (Fig 10.18: 157), which has had some reflaking after breakage. Another (ST80 1841), also bifacially flaked, is the pointed butt-end of a core-tool. The third tool (HH75 1577) is on a flake, possibly thermal, and is complete except for damage at the tip, around which there are also signs of smoothing from wear.

None of the specimens in this category are burnt.

Unclassified bifacial pieces

The 15 items included here are a total mixture of types, grouped for convenience by the common trait of bifacial retouch and separated by this from artefacts in the miscellaneous retouched category.

In a few cases these pieces resemble the 'laurel-leaf' bifacials, but are either too fragmentary (HH75 154; HH76 2014) or too irregular and/or chunky to be classified as such. In the latter category, Fig 10.16: 146 is one of the most symmetric and most extensively retouched, but is very thick, lacks pointed terminals, and is irregularly edged. Another (Fig 10.16: 149) is perhaps closer to a 'laurel-leaf' bifacial, despite the minimal flaking across the cortical dorsal surface, and it does have pointed terminals, but it is otherwise heavy, thick, and asymmetric.

Four pieces are quite small and somewhat arrowhead-like. Two resemble transverse arrowheads, though one (HH75 1267) is too fragmentary for certainty and the other (HH75 16), which is complete, seems too thick (8 mm) and too heavy (6.6 g). Two resemble leaf-shaped arrowheads but in both cases (HH75 1379; ST78 2361), at 8.2 and 8.6 g respectively, they seem too heavy.

A further example is an elaborately retouched tool, similar in dimensions and planform to the 'laurel-leaf' bifacials, but thick and relatively heavy (Fig 10.16: 151). It is more reminiscent of a small axehead/pick type of implement, though it is unclear which terminal would have formed a working edge. Two other bifacial tools are somewhat axehead- or pick-like in character. One (HH75 1577) is fashioned on a (possibly thermal) flake, with a wedge-shaped cross-section. The thick lateral edge is bifacially retouched and the thin lateral edge unmodified, while the distal terminal is pointed. The other (HH76 2100) is a short chunky piece, with extensive flaking but without an obvious working-edge terminal.

In terms of provenance none of these are from Neolithic features and most are from superficial horizons. The only example from an early context (HH76 2911) is burnt and fragmentary and typologically inexplicit, and the latter also applies to the piece (ST79 2643) from the phase VII/a deposit in the inner Stepleton outwork.

Rods

There are nine examples of these robust, normally prismatic, tools with steep unilateral or bilateral retouch (Saville 1981b, 10). At least two of them are on thermal flakes (HH75 754; HH77 1095). The three illustrated examples are on bulbar flakes and demonstrate some of the variability within this classification. Figure 10.19: 160 has a naturally blunted, cortical lower left-hand edge and steep blunting retouch on the lower right. The distal tip is pointed and the lateral retouch becomes more invasive as the flake thins distally. Figure 10.19: 161 has steep bilateral blunting retouch, with some bulbar thinning, and a broad distal edge, which has some modification by damage but no deliberate retouch. Figure 10.20: 162 has only one steep, blunted edge, the opposite edge being sharp. Another example (HH77 569) has steep lateral retouch combined with a convex, scraper-like, retouched distal edge.

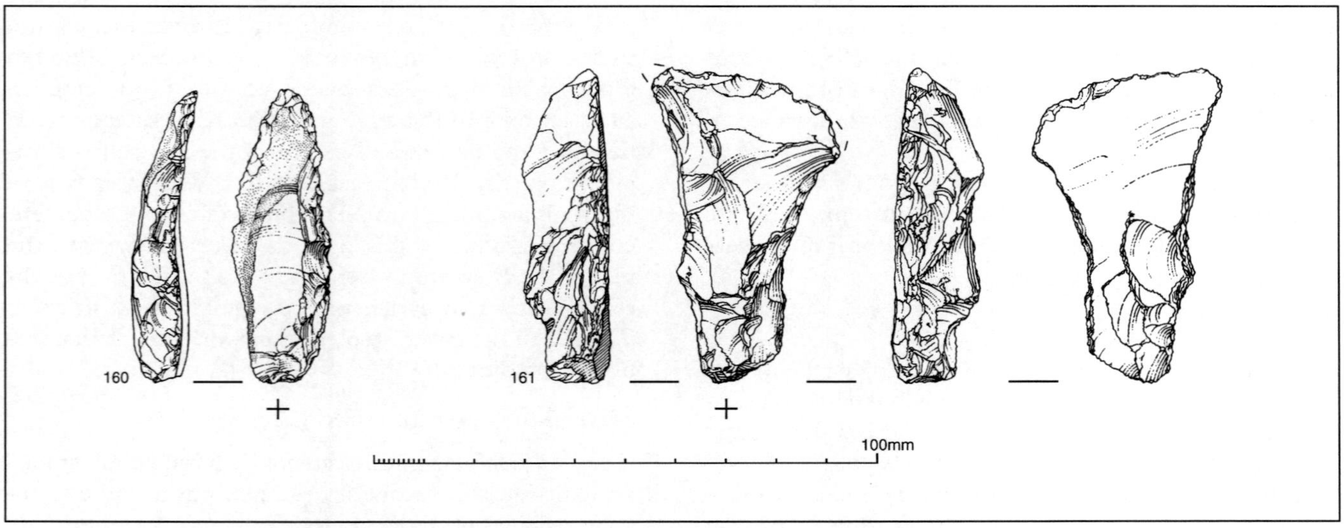

Fig 10.19 Rods. Particulars in catalogue.

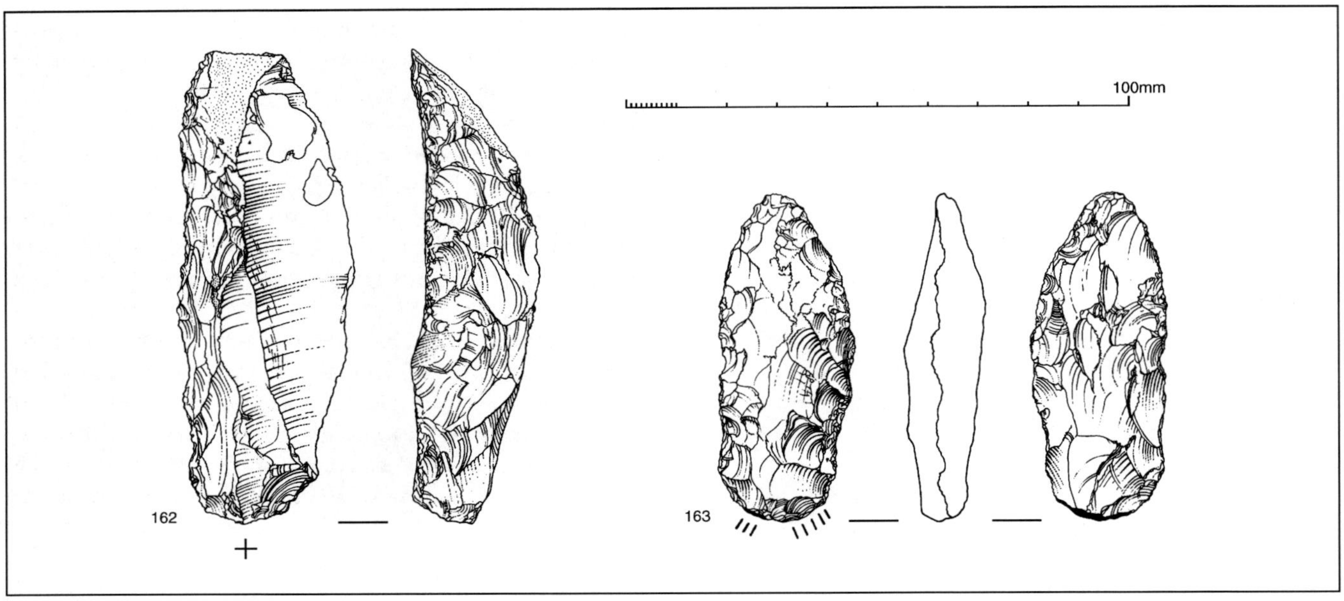

Fig 10.20 Rod (162) and 'Fabricator' (163). Particulars in catalogue.

Figure 10.20: 162, which is the only burnt example, is also the only rod from a firm Neolithic context, being within the fill of grave 4B F712 at the Stepleton enclosure. Otherwise, apart from HH77 569 from the chalk rubble fill of the inner south cross-dyke, the rest are from more superficial horizons.

There has been some debate about the chronological position of this tool form at its *locus classicus* of Grimes Graves, Norfolk (Herne 1991; Saville 1991), but using the kind of broad definition of the type as here, it would seem to be an implement with a range from early Neolithic to middle Bronze Age.

'Fabricators'

'Fabricators' often share with rods a prismatic form, but their distinguishing feature is pronounced wear, manifest by abrasion, smoothing, and/or rounding at one or more terminals. This is the case with Fig 10.20: 163, which has the wear at the proximal terminal of a completely bifacially flaked blank. Two of the other examples are prismatic, while the third (HH74 113) is a flat flake, with abrasion along the edges of the blank as well as at the base, where some parts are worn completely smooth.

Since none of the 'fabricators' is from a well-stratified context, and since as a type they occur elsewhere in contexts of diverse periods, it is unclear if they relate to the Neolithic use of the site.

Splintered piece

A leaf-shaped flake (HH76 1460 from phase IV in segment 16 of the main enclosure) has bifacial modification at its base and some removals across the ventral surface at the distal tip, accompanied by traces of abrasion but no smoothing. The splintered effect seems to result from use, rather than as a by-product of bipolar anvil flaking, and may be secondary to the blank, since the modified areas are slightly differently discoloured. Apart from one other artefact (HH75 19 from the topsoil in the main enclosure) with less pronounced modification of this type, which is included in the miscellaneous retouched category, this is a one-off and not specifically attributable to the Neolithic activity.

Saw

A broad flake with coarse but regular denticulation on the transverse distal edge was classified as a saw (HH77 1899) with the indentations more deeply notched and more widely spaced than on the serrated-edge flakes. It is from a layer in the bank area of the inner south cross-dyke which contained Beaker or early Bronze Age sherds as well as Neolithic ones.

Backed flake

This is a bulbar flake, damaged at the tip, with blunting retouch down the whole of the left-hand edge (ST79 653). The right-hand edge is unretouched and sharp, but with no obvious signs of use. Although blunting retouch does occur on other implements, such as some in the edge-modified flake categories, in this case the nature and extent of the retouch is sufficient to justify discrete classification. While this type of blunting is unusual on Neolithic implements, the general appearance of this piece is in character with the rest of the Stepleton assemblage, and it is not thought residual from an earlier period, though its position in phase V of the inner Stepleton outwork means that it is not well stratified.

Miscellaneous retouched pieces

The 743 artefacts in this category exhibit some, apparently deliberate, secondary retouch but are unclassifiable to formal tool types. Over half of them are fragmentary and undoubtedly include many broken tools, particularly scrapers and piercers, which do not retain sufficient of the retouched edge to be fully diagnostic. In other cases there must remain some uncertainty as to the intentional nature of the retouch, particularly with examples from superficial contexts where the retouch is differentially discoloured from the blank on which it is located (eg HH74 8, HH75 1929, HH76 1432 from Neolithic features in the central area; HH75 6, HH76 308, HH77 886 unstratified in the central area; ST77 6, ST78 137 from phase VIII/a in the inner Stepleton outwork). This is also the case with pieces with areas of irregular denticulate-type retouch, which tend to be disproportionately from superficial contexts and could in some cases result from plough damage, though there are occasional instances from Neolithic features and lower ditch fills (eg HH75 335 from phase III in the main enclosure ditch, HH77 603 from pit N F11).

This category is intentionally broad and inclusive and therefore can have little analytical potential, other than to provide an indication that the numbers of implements included in the formal tool groups are not finite. It is unlikely, however, that the miscellaneous retouched pieces represent a residue which would markedly distort the relative proportions of the formal tool categories.

As Table 10.41 shows, while miscellaneous retouched pieces are present in Neolithic contexts, it is in the superficial and unstratified context groups that they come to dominate. This is such a consistent pattern, however, that it could reflect either a chronological or a taphonomic factor, or perhaps a combination of the two.

10.2.6 Refitting

During excavations on the Stepleton spur, several groups or concentrations of struck lithic debris within ditch infills were noted and recorded in detail as likely to represent discrete deposits. These included the south butts of segments 2 and 3 of the enclosure and the west butt and the centre of segment 4 of the outer outwork. The flints from segment 2 were on the surface of the phase II silts (Fig 3.84), the others were from phase III deposits – the chalk rubble secondary silts. Two of these groups when examined during post-excavation had obvious potential for refitting and considerable time was devoted to the isolation of conjoinable sequences from them, with the results described below.

Stepleton enclosure, segment 3

The south-east butt end of this segment, referred to during excavation as unit 13, contained a concentration of knapping debris within the secondary chalk rubble infill (context group 56). This concentration (recorded as layer 4C), covered a horizontal area *c* 2.10 by 0.90 m, aligned along the longitudinal axis of the segment (Fig 3.85). Within the overall concentration were denser clusters, mainly towards the south end, and the maximum vertical differential between the flints was approximately 200 mm. The concentration did not appear to continue northwards into the baulk left across the ditch during excavation.

The flints from this horizon, listed in Table 10.54 suggest a very 'industrial' deposit, with a substantial core component and large, mainly cortical flakes, with an above-average mean weight (17.5 g). This concentration also contained several unretouched flint nodules (not recorded here but the nodules are retained in the archive) and an antler tine.

The refitting analysis of this material isolated three main conjoin groups, and these are described individually below. In addition there were: three cores with single conjoining secondary flakes; one core with two conjoining secondary flakes; a further core with one tertiary and two secondary flakes conjoining; a group of three conjoining secondary flakes; three groups of two conjoining secondary flakes; and one group of two conjoining tertiary flakes. Two separate flakes which had split longitudinally by Siret fracture could be reassembled.

This scatter within the chalky rubble was plotted in detail on three successive drawings as excavation proceeded and flints were uplifted. The positions of all the elements of conjoin group 1 were recorded, showing them to be contained within a small area approximately 0.35 m east–west by 0.2 m north–south. Of conjoin group 2 the position of nine of the ten flakes are known, but not that of the core itself. The nine flakes lay close together in an area 0.3 m north-west/south-east by 0.15 m north-east/south-west. All the elements of conjoin group 3 were plotted, mostly forming a

Table 10.54 Main components of the artefact clusters from which the refitting groups derive

	*Stepleton enclosure segment 3**		*Outer Stepleton outwork segment 4*	
Type	*Number*	*Weight in grams*	*Number*	*Weight in grams*
Unretouched flakes	288	5040	509	9204
Cores	14	7270	17	4450
Flaked lumps	12	8305	7	3811
Total	314	20615	533	17465

* This cluster also included two flint hammerstones, weighing together 1180 grams

compact scatter some 0.25 m north–south by 0.2 m east–west, except for one flake detached from this group some 0.3 m to the east. Conjoin groups 2 and 3 were in exactly the same location at the same horizon, as though deposited or infilled together, comprising most of the content of the scatter at the north end. Group 1 on the other hand was at the epicentre of the whole scatter, which, apart from the lesser conjoins already mentioned, contained no other long refitting sequences.

Considering all the evidence for refitting, there remain six cores to which no flakes could be conjoined, and 237 flakes which could not be refitted to other flakes or to cores. Assuming both recovery in the field and the refitting analysis to have been thorough, then this deposit is clearly a rather incomplete sample of a knapping episode (or series of episodes).

As an introduction to the series of illustrations by Joanna Richards of the refitted cores (Figs 10.21–39), it is necessary to explain that two separate techniques were used. With conjoin groups 1, 2, and 4, in addition to drawings of the reassembled cores or nodules, there are exploded views to show how the flakes refit and separate outline drawings of all the flakes. The purpose of the latter was to illustrate a good sample of the kind of unretouched flakes being produced to provide a comparison with the flake blanks used for the implements shown in the other illustrations. The exploded views demonstrate the sequence and 'nesting' of the flakes, but are only feasible for the relatively simple reduction sequences. The technique used for the other conjoin groups has been to show the core at each of its major platform stages. As an aid to following a core through its reduction sequence, symbols – dots, asterisks, squares – have been placed at appropriate points. These points are constant within each sequence and thus should assist comparison and orientation through the stages. Various types of tone have been used to indicate cortex, thermal fracture surfaces, and the striking platforms of flakes.

Conjoin group 1 (Figs 10.21–22)

This simple single platform (A2) core (ST80 2468/41) has a maximum dimension of 105 mm, a maximum surviving flake scar length of 65 mm, weighs 490 g, and has a 'chalky', unweathered cortex. There are 12 flakes and two chips which conjoin, creating a still incomplete nodule in the form of a larger A2 core with a maximum dimension of 122 mm and weighing 754 g. One of the projecting knobs of the nodule has been battered, but not in any obvious attempt to create another striking platform. The original nodule was of knobbly shape, with one face formed by a thermal fracture, giving a matt black surface rather than cortex in this area.

The initial large primary flake detached from the nodule to create a platform is absent, as are at least two primary or near primary flakes and several chips from the flaking face. Thereafter, flaking proceeded in successive, unidirectional removals from a single platform down one face of the core to a point at which the core was abandoned. The final three removals, flakes 1o, 1n, and 1m (Fig 10.22) have all hinged out and the core would have required rejuvenation, but in fact relatively little depth remained.

At the very end of the reduction sequence there are the negative scars on the core face of several short, hinged-out flakes, less than 40 mm in length, which are absent. Otherwise, the only major absence from the flake sequence occurs between flakes 1j/k and 1l, and would have been a blade-like flake some 70 mm long and 30 mm broad.

Conjoin group 2 (Figs 10.23–25)

Another simple single platform (A2) core (ST80 2468/95) with a maximum dimension of 112 mm, maximum surviving flake scar length of 72 mm, and weighing 920 g. The internal flint is distinctively mottled or speckled and the unworn external cortex is less 'chalky' than core 1, with some brown staining. Ten flakes refit to the core to produce a near complete, roughly spherical nodule with several knobbed projections and a circular hollow 30 mm across and 50 mm deep. Maximum dimension of the reconstructed nodule is 132 mm and the weight 1320 g.

Initial preparation involved removal of a primary flake (2a) by a blow against a broken projection on the nodule surface. This created a temporary platform from which near-primary flake 2d was detached, in turn creating the platform for the detachment of flake 2b in the same direction and plane as the first flake (2a). This removal created a working platform for all the subsequent detachments, starting with 2c and 2e (hinged). The next two removals (2f and 2g) are small flakes with vestigial platforms and may have been detached at the same time as flake 2c. Several small flakes and chips, none larger than flake 2e, are absent at this point, before the three final removals – flakes 2h, 2i, and 2j – at which point the core was abandoned. None of the final three flakes is hinged. There are no significant flakes missing from the reduction sequence, the largest absent flake being 27 mm long.

Conjoin group 3 (not illustrated)

Another single platform (A2) core (ST80 2468/87), which has a maximum dimension of 114 mm, a maximum surviving flake scar length of 48 mm, and weighs 670 g. It has eight refitting flakes and chips, which conjoin to form an almost intact nodule – maximum dimension 139 mm and weight 838 g – of knobbly form and with an unweathered 'chalky' cortex.

One projecting knob of the nodule has two flakes removed (not present) and may have been an attempt to initiate a platform but was not followed through. The actual reduction sequence began with blows against another projecting knob, detaching impact chips (not present) which provided a percussion point for the removal of the first main, near-primary flake, which created a small platform. From this were struck a near-primary flake and a chip, creating a platform from which the remaining flakes were removed unidirectionally from one face of the nodule and the core was then abandoned. The final flake from the core face is absent, but was a stubby hinged-out tertiary flake 36 mm long and 30 mm broad. Otherwise, apart from various chips and spalls, the only absent flakes were three small internal tertiary flakes of maximum lengths 16, 32, and 35 mm respectively.

Outer Stepleton outwork, segment 4

The west butt end of this segment (unit 2), contained a concentration of knapping debris within a horizon of the secondary, phase III, chalk rubble, ditch infill (recorded as layer 3B). This concentration was contained within an area 1.65 m east–west by 1 m north–south in plan, the longer axis being aligned with the longitudinal axis of the segment (Fig 3.105). There is a strong probability that this scatter continued eastwards into the baulk left across the segment during excavation, perhaps even linking with the scatters recorded in units 3 and 4 of the segment. The vertical thickness of this deposit was not recorded but can be inferred to have been less than 200 mm.

The flints from this concentration (Table 10.54), as with those from segment 3 of the enclosure, have an 'industrial' character, lacking any implements, and the flakes have an equally higher than average mean weight (18 g). It is not recorded if there were any unretouched nodules associated with this scatter.

The refitting analysis demonstrated a large number of significant conjoin groups (described below), mostly involving cores but also some nests of flakes without cores. The scatter was plotted on two successive drawings, but only 185 of the total 533 artefacts from the concentration have their locations recorded. This has the result that too few from each conjoin group are plotted to permit any definitive conclusions about patterning within the concentration. What can be said derives from the conjoin groups with the most flakes plotted, which were as follows:

Conjoin group 5: core and eight flakes plotted – maximum area *c* 0.6 m east–west, 0.4 m north–south
Conjoin group 7: core and ten flakes plotted – maximum area *c* 0.6 m east–west, 0.5 m north–south
Conjoin group 9: core and fourteen flakes plotted – maximum area *c* 0.85 m east–west, 0.7 m north–south
Conjoin group 10: core and six flakes plotted – maximum area *c* 0.6 m east–west, 0.3 m north–south
Conjoin group 14: core and eight flakes plotted – maximum area *c* 0.6 m east–west, 0.3 m north–south
Conjoin group 15: ten flakes plotted – maximum area *c* 1.0 m east–west, 0.5 m north–south
Conjoin group 17: eleven flakes plotted – maximum area *c* 0.35 m east–west, 0.35 m north–south

The most compact cluster on the basis of these data is group 17, the most dispersed groups 9 and 15, though there can be no guarantee that the unplotted elements of any of these conjoin groups lay within the same confines. Even so, the plotted artefacts are all within the main part of the concentration and jumbled, without any suggestion of placement in discrete heaps. After all the refits had been obtained, there remained only four cores, seven flaked lumps, and 46 unretouched flakes which could not be conjoined to or with anything else. This very high level of refitting among the flakes and cores gives a strong indication of immediacy about the deposit and its origin in perhaps a single session of knapping. However, there is no hard evidence on the question of precise superimposition of artefacts or the interleaving of chalk rubble within the scatter and therefore it is difficult to come to any conclusion about the probable formation process of the deposit(s).

Conjoin group 4 (Figs 10.26–28)

A single platform (A2) core (ST80 2415/156) of maximum dimension 105 mm, maximum surviving flake scar length 33 mm, and weight 298 g, with 25 refitting flakes which conjoin to form a complete nodule. The nodule, of maximum dimension 139 mm and weighing 515 g, is of irregular shape with projections and has a mixed exterior surface. This is part cortex, somewhat weathered and stained brown, and part thermally fractured surface, of matt black appearance with some orange staining.

The reduction process has been simple in two main stages. Firstly, using the partly flat and partly curved surface provided by the thermal fracture as the initial platform, flakes 4a–k have been successively removed across the top of the nodule. There are only a few chips and spalls missing from this sequence of removals, which has been of a preparatory nature. The negative scar surface left by these removals has provided the platform for the second stage of knapping, perpendicular to the first, without any additional preparation whatsoever.

This second sequence of removals produced the flakes 4l–y. This sequence is almost intact save for chips and spalls and the butt ends of flakes 4n, 4p, and 4q. There is only one substantial absent flake, a tertiary example, immediately subsequent to flakes 4r and 4s, approximately 40 mm long by 40 broad and with a slightly hinged-out termination.

After the final removals this core is essentially residual with no real potential for further exploitation.

Conjoin group 5 (not illustrated)

A single platform (A2) core (ST80 2399/211) of maximum dimension 76 mm, maximum surviving flake scar length 43 mm, and weight 195 g has 25 refitting flakes through four reduction stages to form a partially intact nodule, from which preliminary removals in three directions are absent. The nodule is irregular

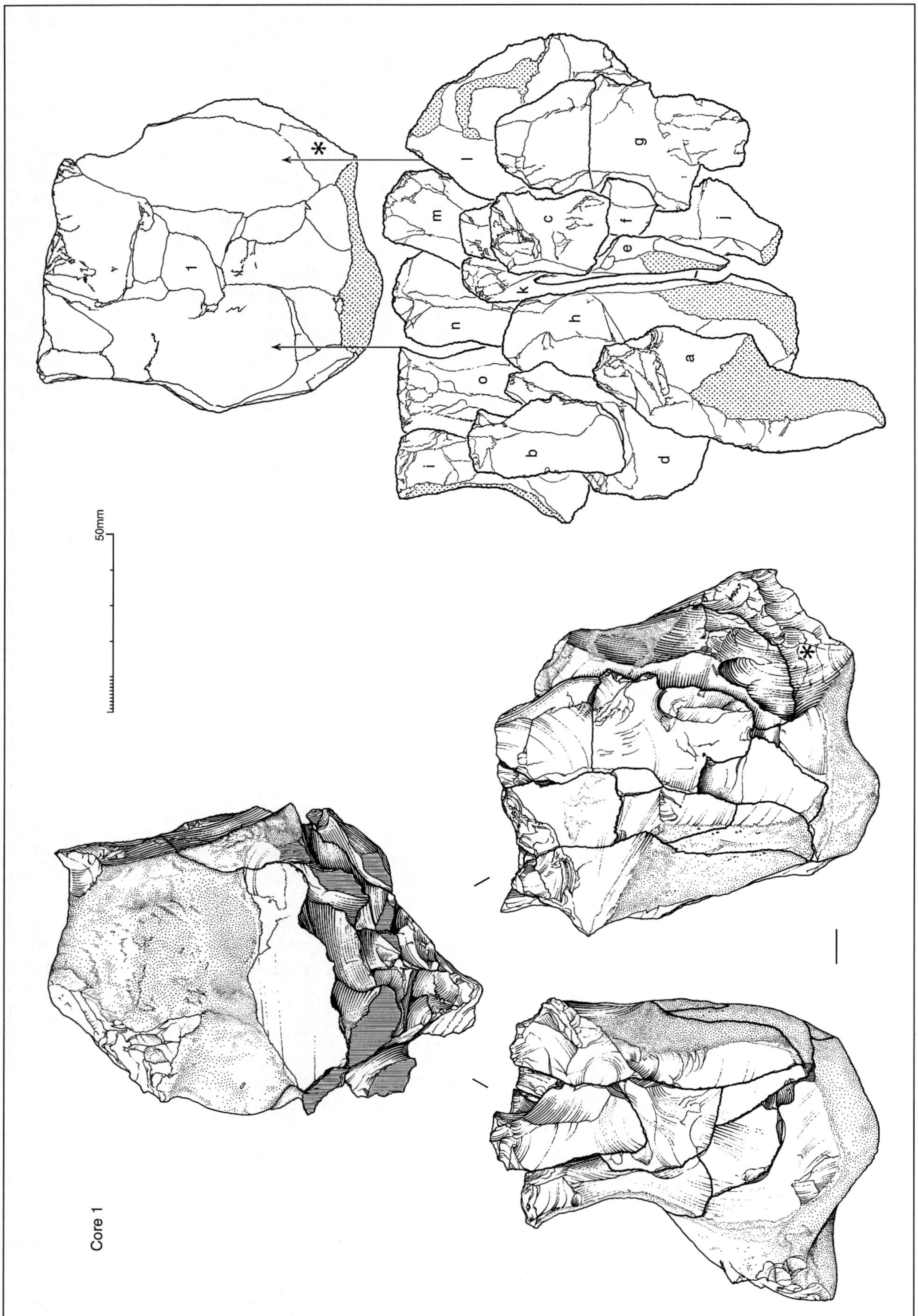

Fig 10.21 Core/flake conjoin 1 (context group 56 – Stepleton enclosure, segment 3, Unit 13A/B, Layer 4c, phase III; find nos: ST80 2099, 2406, 2414 and 2468). Left: three views of the core with all conjoining flakes refitted; right: schematic exploded view of core and refitting flakes.

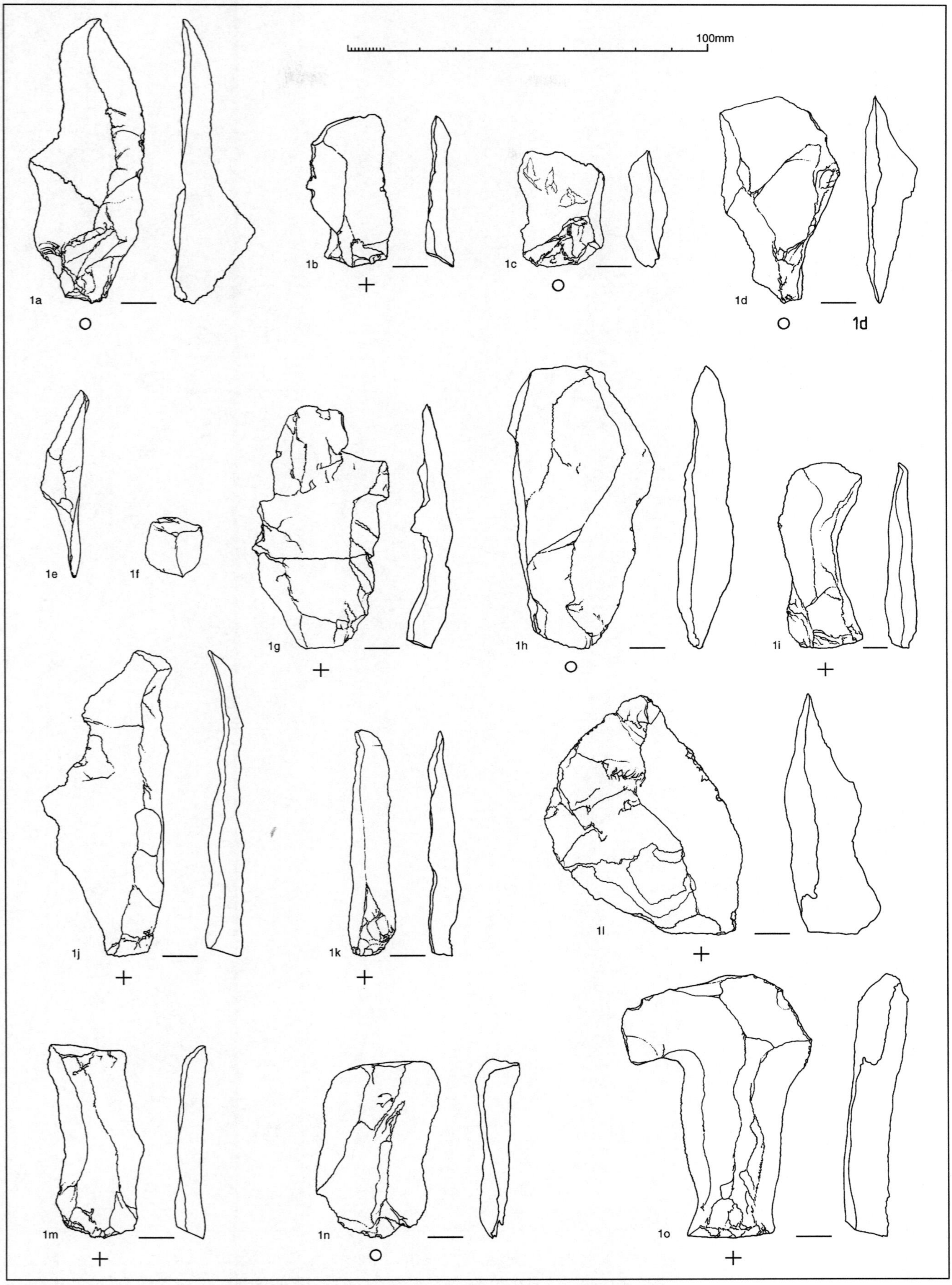

Fig 10.22 Core/flake conjoin 1: outline drawings of all the refitting flakes (see Fig 10.21).

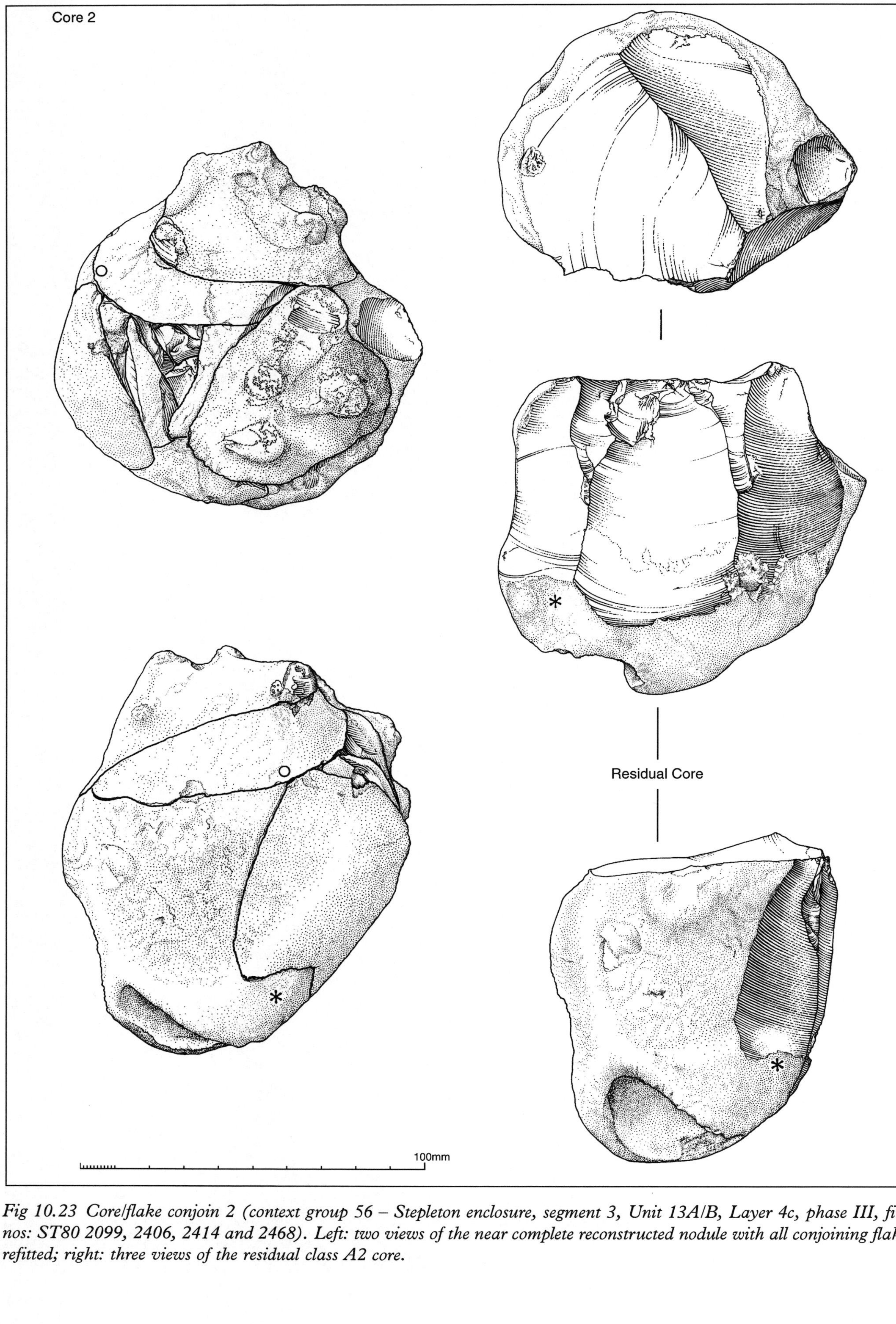

Fig 10.23 Core/flake conjoin 2 (context group 56 – Stepleton enclosure, segment 3, Unit 13A/B, Layer 4c, phase III, find nos: ST80 2099, 2406, 2414 and 2468). Left: two views of the near complete reconstructed nodule with all conjoining flakes refitted; right: three views of the residual class A2 core.

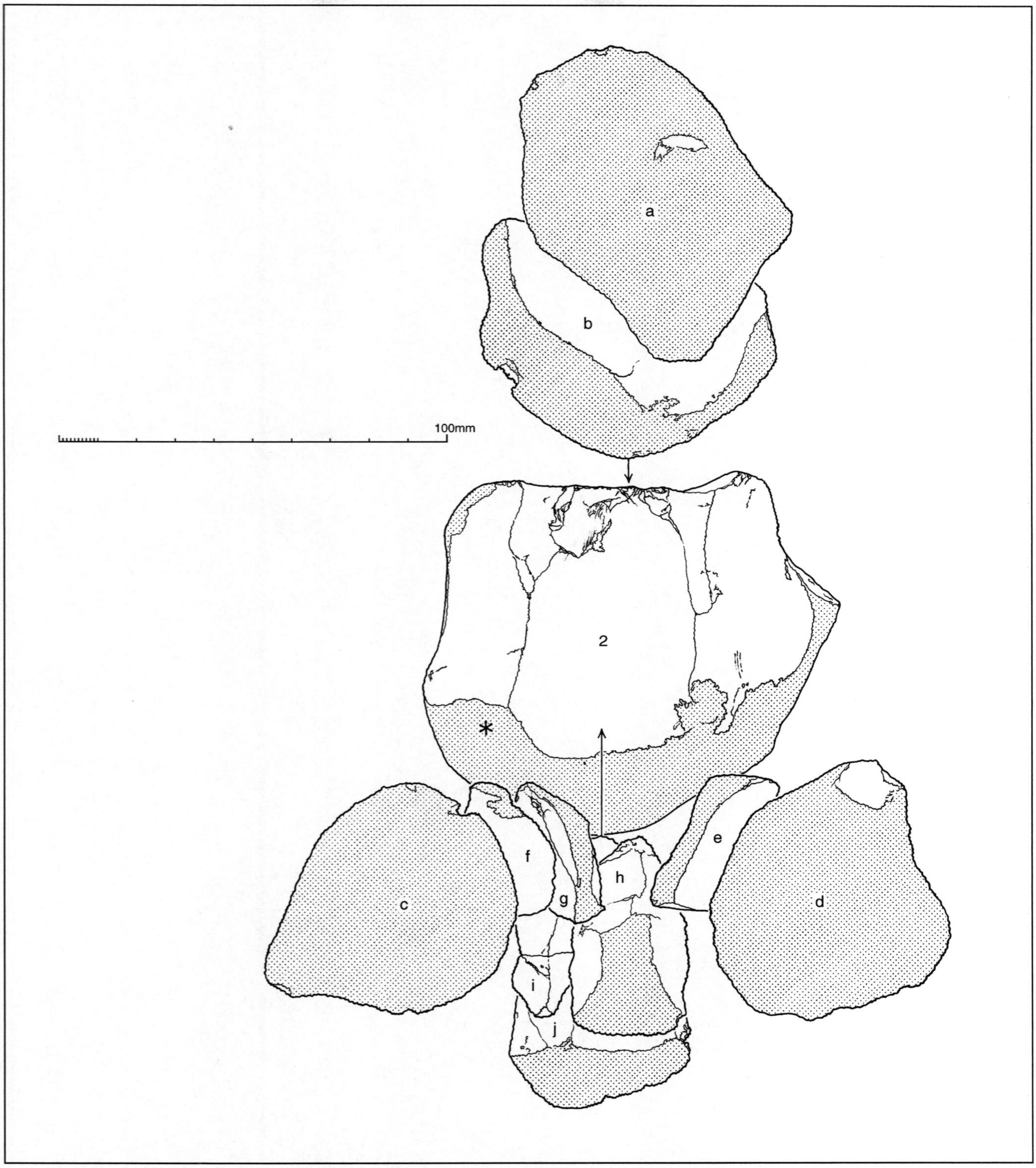

Fig 10.24 Core/flake conjoin 2: schematic exploded view of core and refitting flakes (see Fig 10.23).

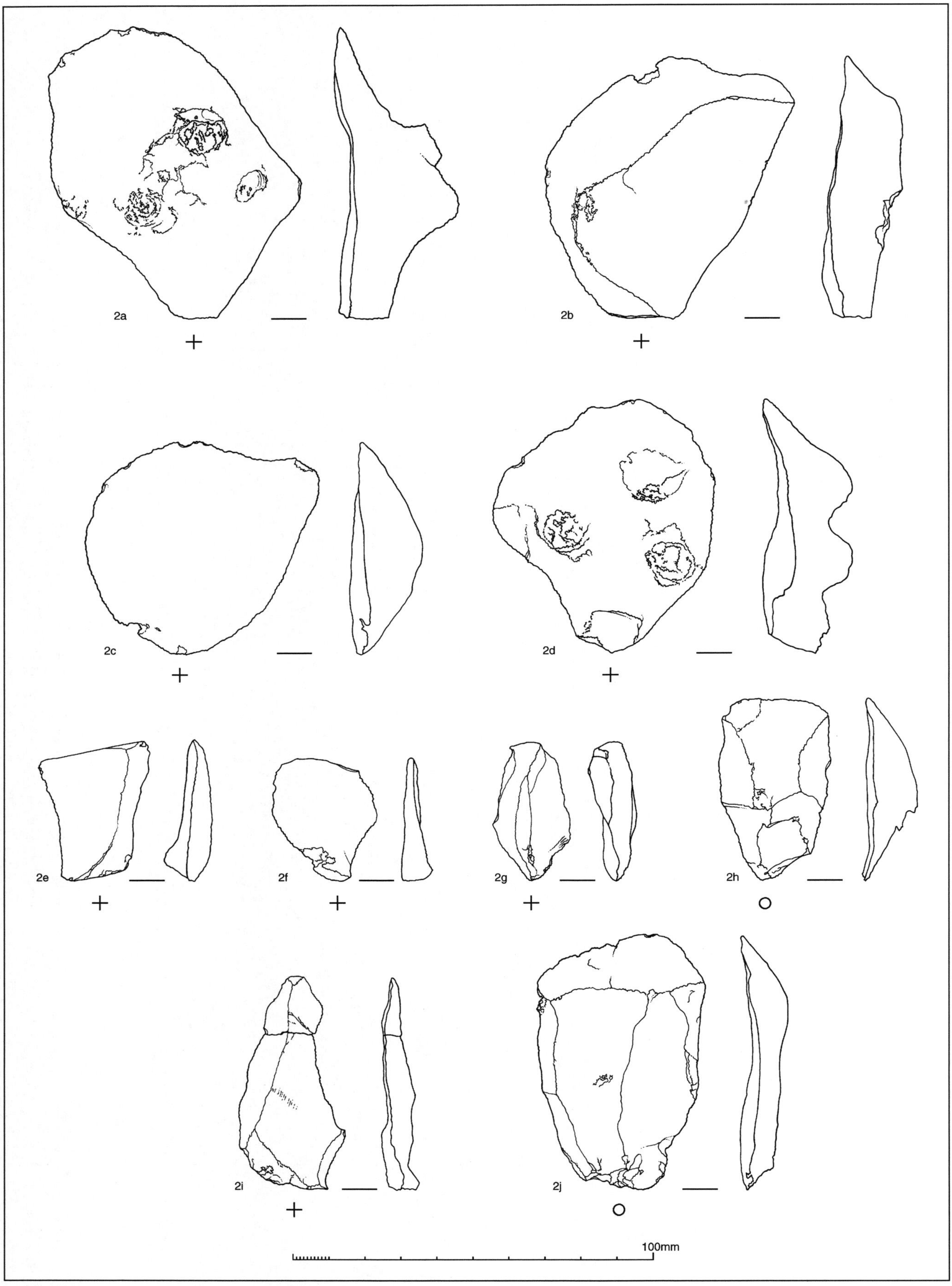

Fig 10.25 Core/flake conjoin 2: outline drawings of all the refitting flakes (see Figs 10.23–4).

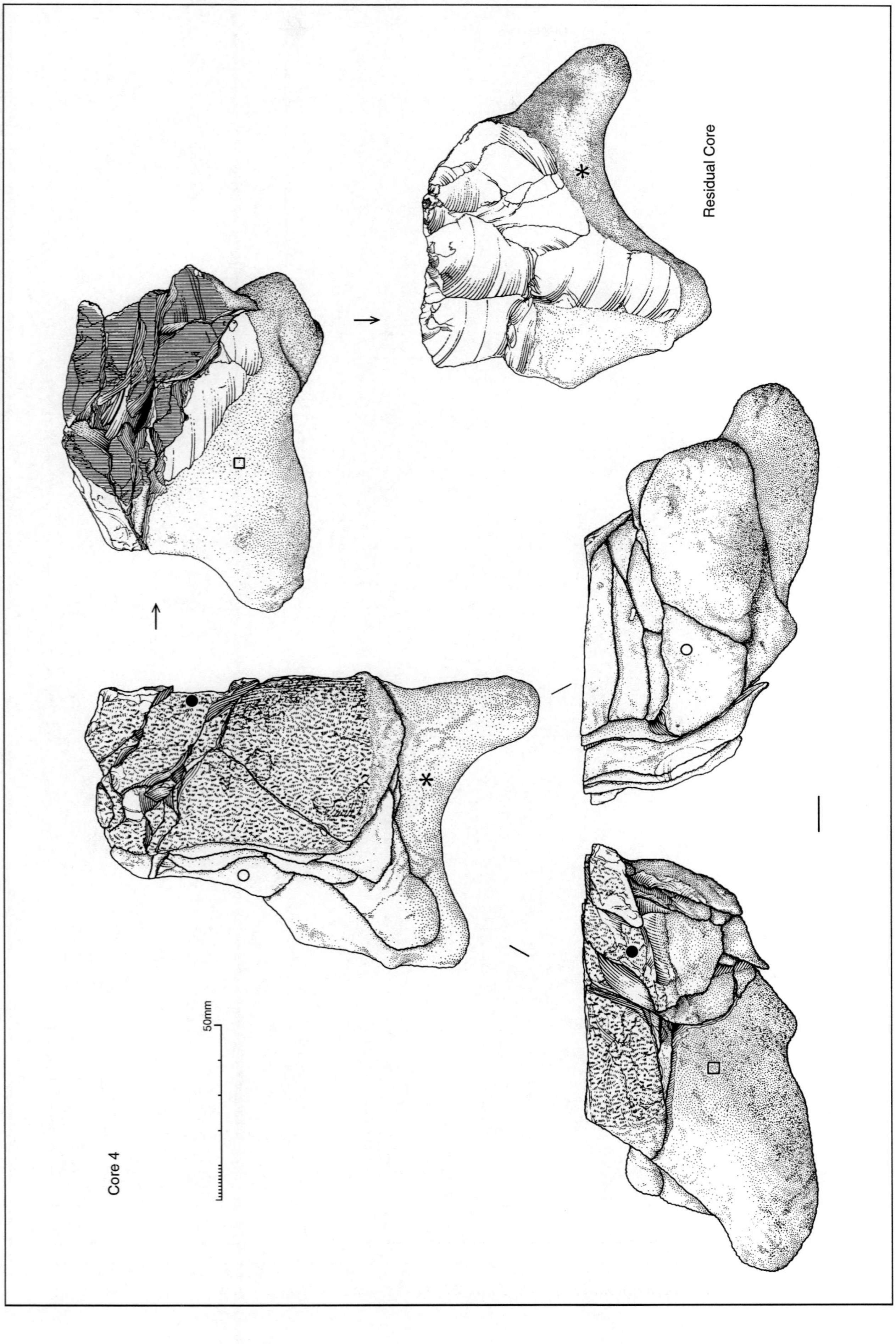

Fig 10.26 Core/flake conjoin 4 (context group 78 – outer Stepleton outwork, segment 4, Unit 2, Layer 3b, phase III; find nos: ST80 2395, 2415 and 2467). Left: three views of the near complete nodule with all conjoining flakes refitted; upper right: main platform viewed from above with covering flakes omitted; lower right: residual class A2 core.

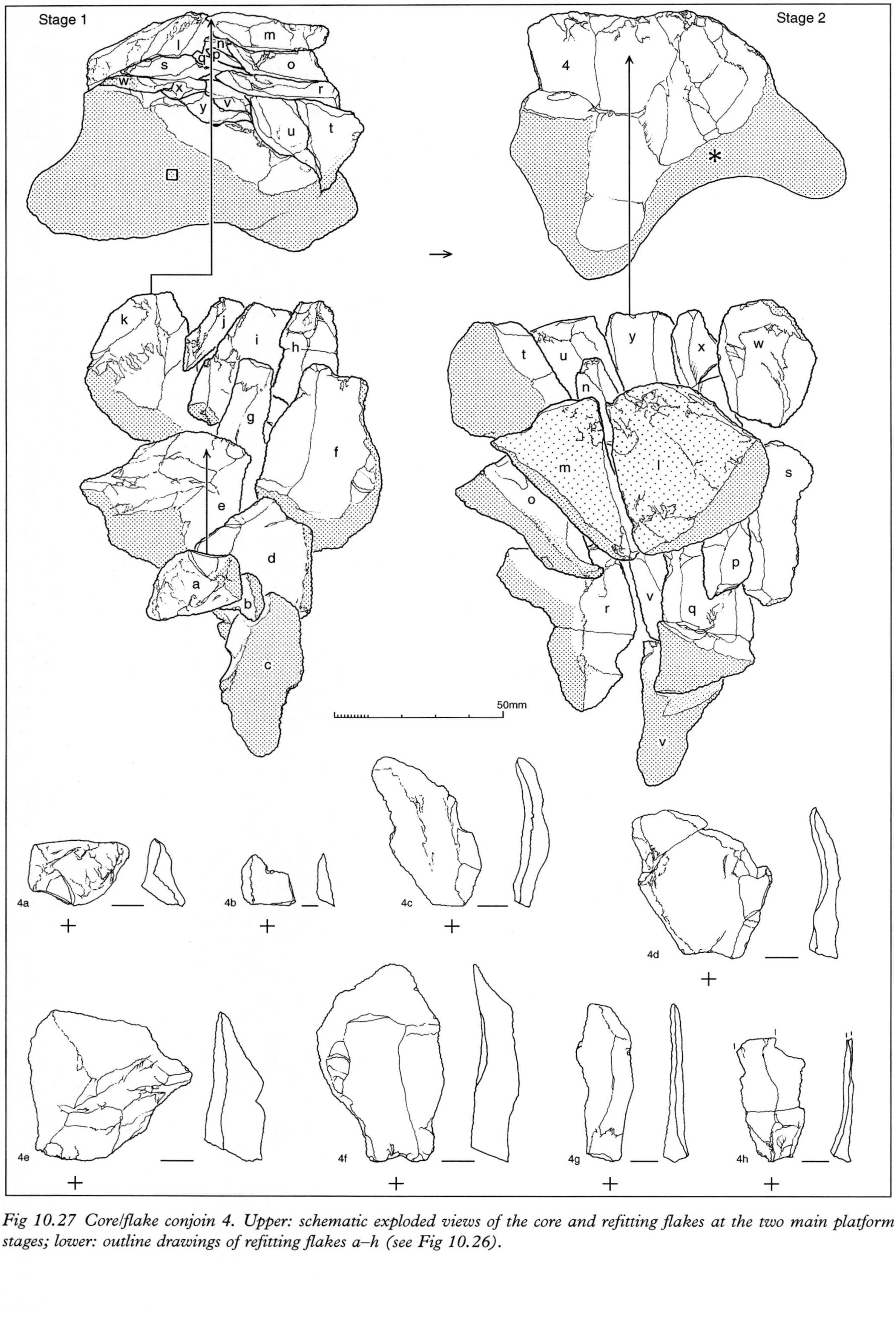

Fig 10.27 Core/flake conjoin 4. Upper: schematic exploded views of the core and refitting flakes at the two main platform stages; lower: outline drawings of refitting flakes a–h (see Fig 10.26).

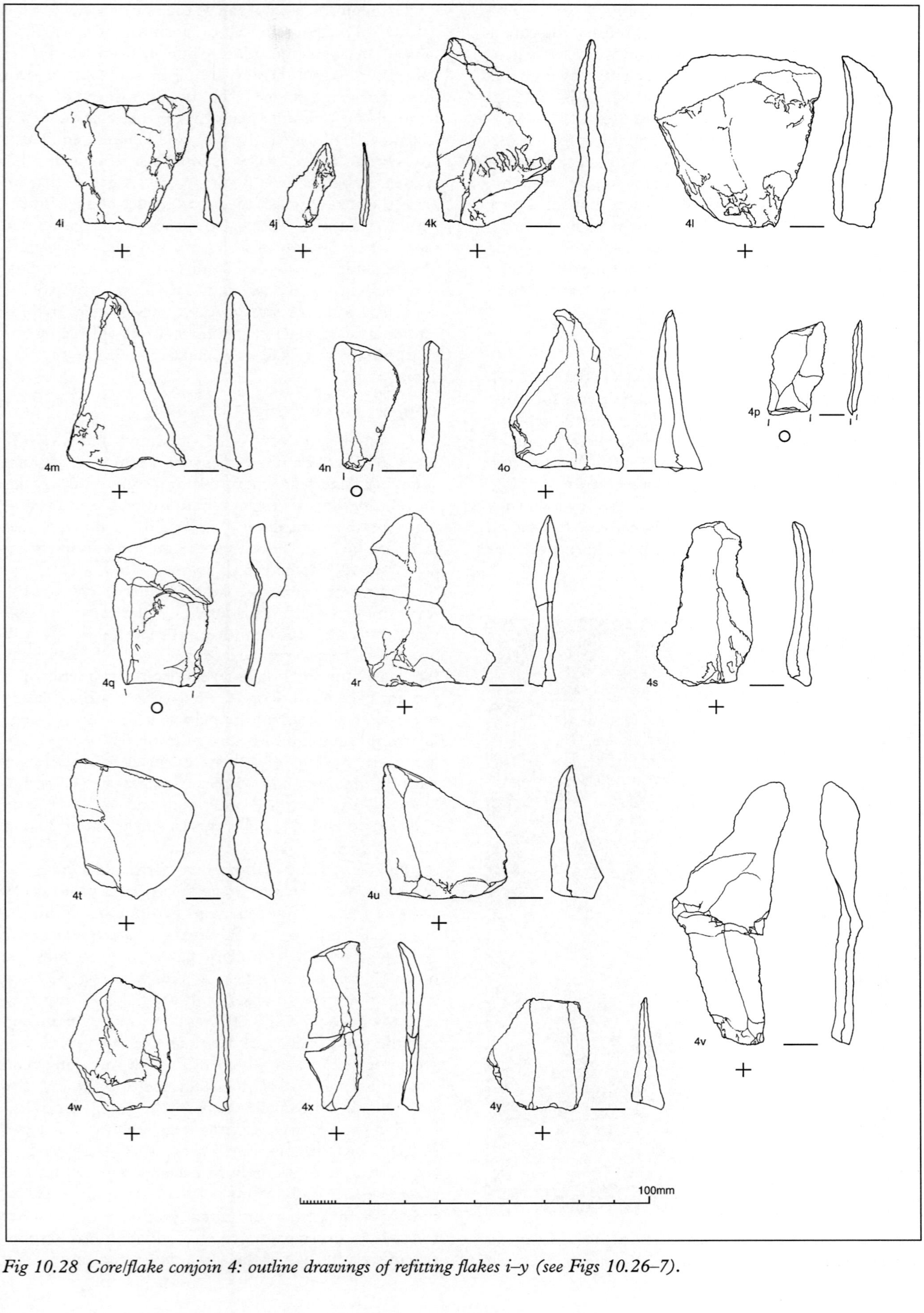

Fig 10.28 Core/flake conjoin 4: outline drawings of refitting flakes i–y (see Figs 10.26–7).

with knobs, and has a largely unabraded cortex with some brown staining. With all flakes refitted the core is 124 mm in maximum dimension and weighs 734 g.

The first stage of reduction represented by the refits involves a single very chunky flake which is the final removal in a sequence not otherwise present. The negative scar of this flake provides the platform for the second stage removal of 12 flakes, from the middle of which sequence a single secondary flake, 50 mm long, is absent. After this the third stage comprises a very substantial rejuvenation flake struck from the side, wholly removing the previous platform and creating the final stage platform. This final stage has 11 refitting flakes with only one substantial missing tertiary flake some 52 mm long.

Conjoin group 6 (Fig 10.29)

A residual single platform (A2) core (ST80 2399/234), maximum dimension 88 mm, maximum surviving flake scar length 31 mm, weight 207 g, has 28 refitting flakes conjoining to produce an incomplete nodule of 134 mm maximum dimension and a weight of 606 g. The cortex is unabraded with some brown staining, and one terminal of the nodule is formed by a thermal fracture surface. This naturally flat surface has served as the platform for one major removal (absent) but was not continued with.

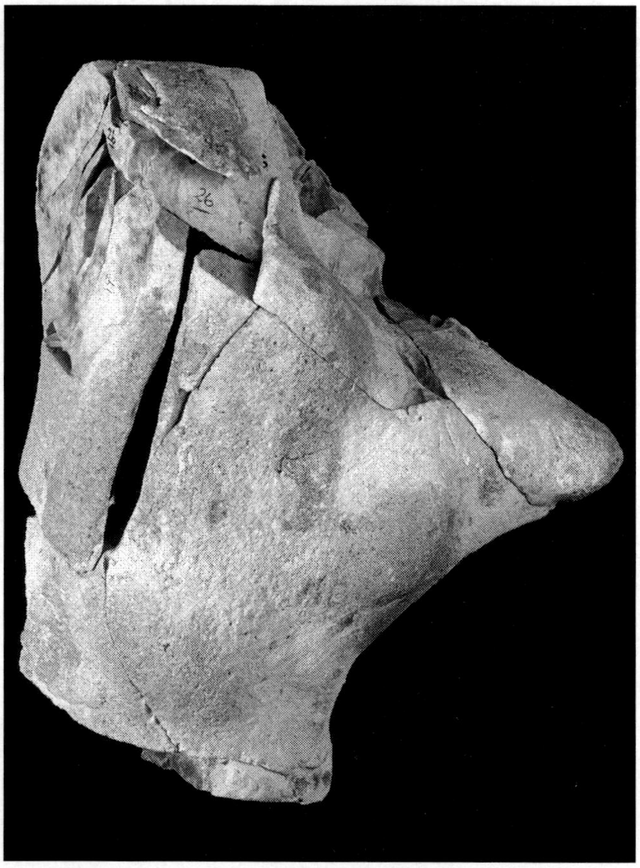

Fig 10.29 Conjoin group 6: the refitted nodule. Maximum dimension 134 mm. Photo: National Museums of Scotland

The major flaking began at the opposite pole of the nodule with the removal of a single primary flake (absent) to create an initial platform from which four flakes were struck. These are all present but three of them are fragmentary. The negative scars of these removals provided the platform for the main sequence of removals, of which 21 flakes could be refitted. There are several minor flakes and spalls absent in this sequence and at one point several larger flakes are absent, which obscures the precise order of detachment within this series. Altogether there are at least three major flakes absent, of which the longest was 58 mm. The penultimate removal from this platform is a massive plunging flake, which has effectively ruined the core. An attempt was made to rejuvenate by two removals to create a final platform, from which only one short hinged-out flake was detached and then the core abandoned.

Conjoin group 7 (Figs 10.30–32)

This single platform (A2) residual core (ST80 2399/212), maximum dimension 78 mm, maximum surviving flake scar length 69 mm, weight 201 g, has 42 refitting flakes which conjoin to form a near complete nodule, maximum dimension 148 mm and weighing 665 g. The compact nodule has an unabraded cortex with some brown staining.

The single primary flake struck from one pole to form the first platform is absent. From this first stage platform were struck the five refitting flakes a, aa, b, bb, and c. This sequence lacks several spalls, one small flake, and the final flake struck from this platform, a tertiary flake 33 mm long. The flake scar surface left by these removals formed the platform for the next stage involving the removal of five refitting flakes cc, d, dd, e, and ee. Absent from this sequence are a secondary flake 30 mm long and 25 mm wide between cc and d, a secondary flake 74 mm long and 45 mm wide between dd and e, and a secondary flake about 20 mm long between e and ee.

The third stage platform was formed by the negative scars of the second stage flakes, and from this 16 refitting flakes – f to mm (and two not visible on the stage 3 illustration) – were struck in a sequence with several gaps: two secondary flakes, one 30 mm the other 15 mm long are missing after g and gg; between k and l there are an absent tertiary flake 25 mm long and a secondary flake 50 mm long; between m and mm there is a major absence of one or more tertiary or secondary flakes, of which one is 76 mm long; and from the final face of this stage there is the negative scar of an absent small tertiary flake 17 mm long.

The penultimate, fourth stage platform is again formed by the negative scars from the previous sequence. There are only two main removals, nn and o, which are both chunky, broad, secondary flakes, designed to create the final platform. The other removal at this stage, n, is a chip which probably spontaneously detached at the same time as nn or o.

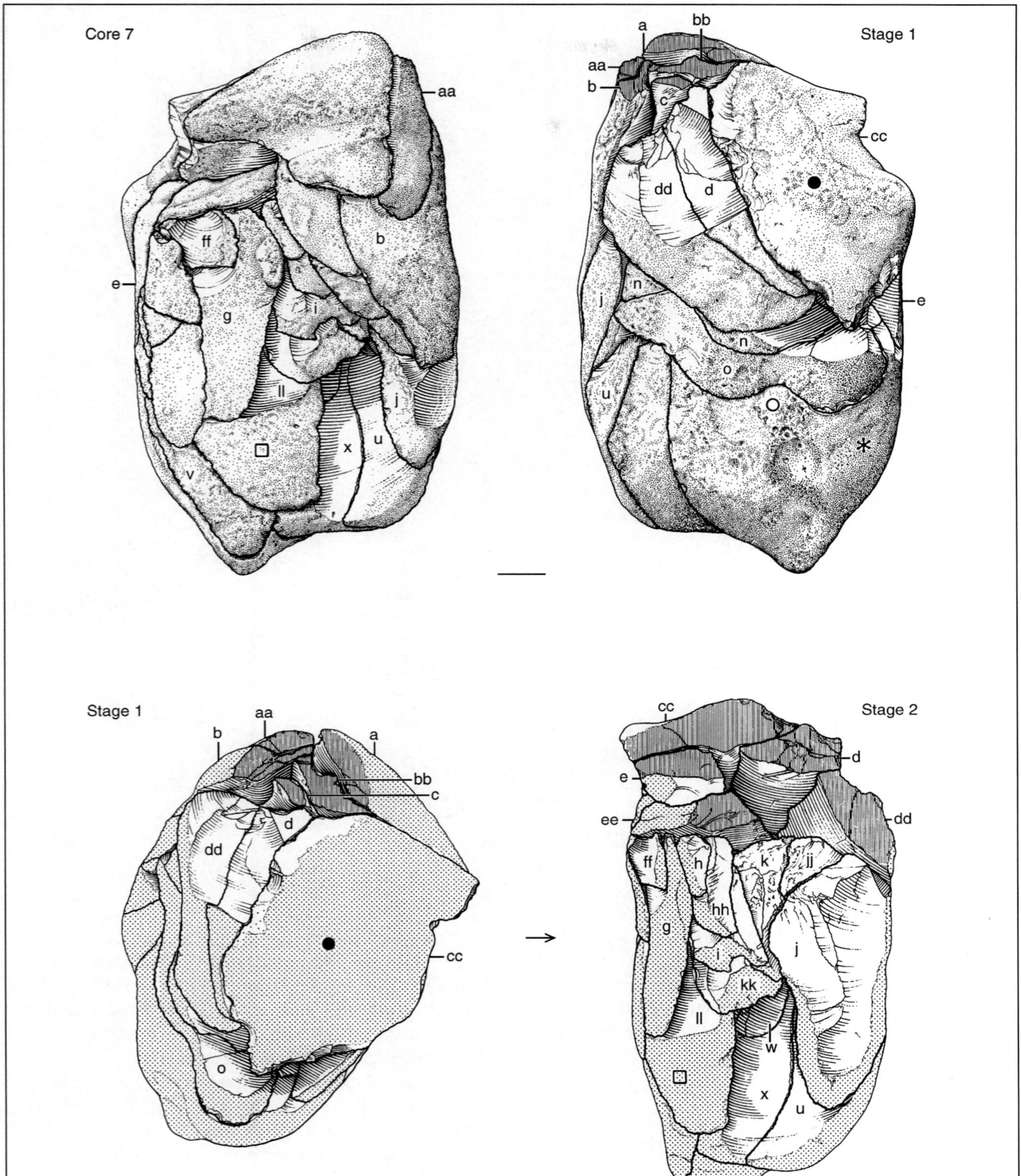

Fig 10.30 Core/flake conjoin 7 (context group 78 – outer Stepleton outwork, segment 4, Unit 2, Layer 3b, phase III; find nos: ST80 2395, 2399 and 2467). Upper: two views of the near complete nodule with all conjoining flakes refitted; lower: first and second stages of the reduction sequence.

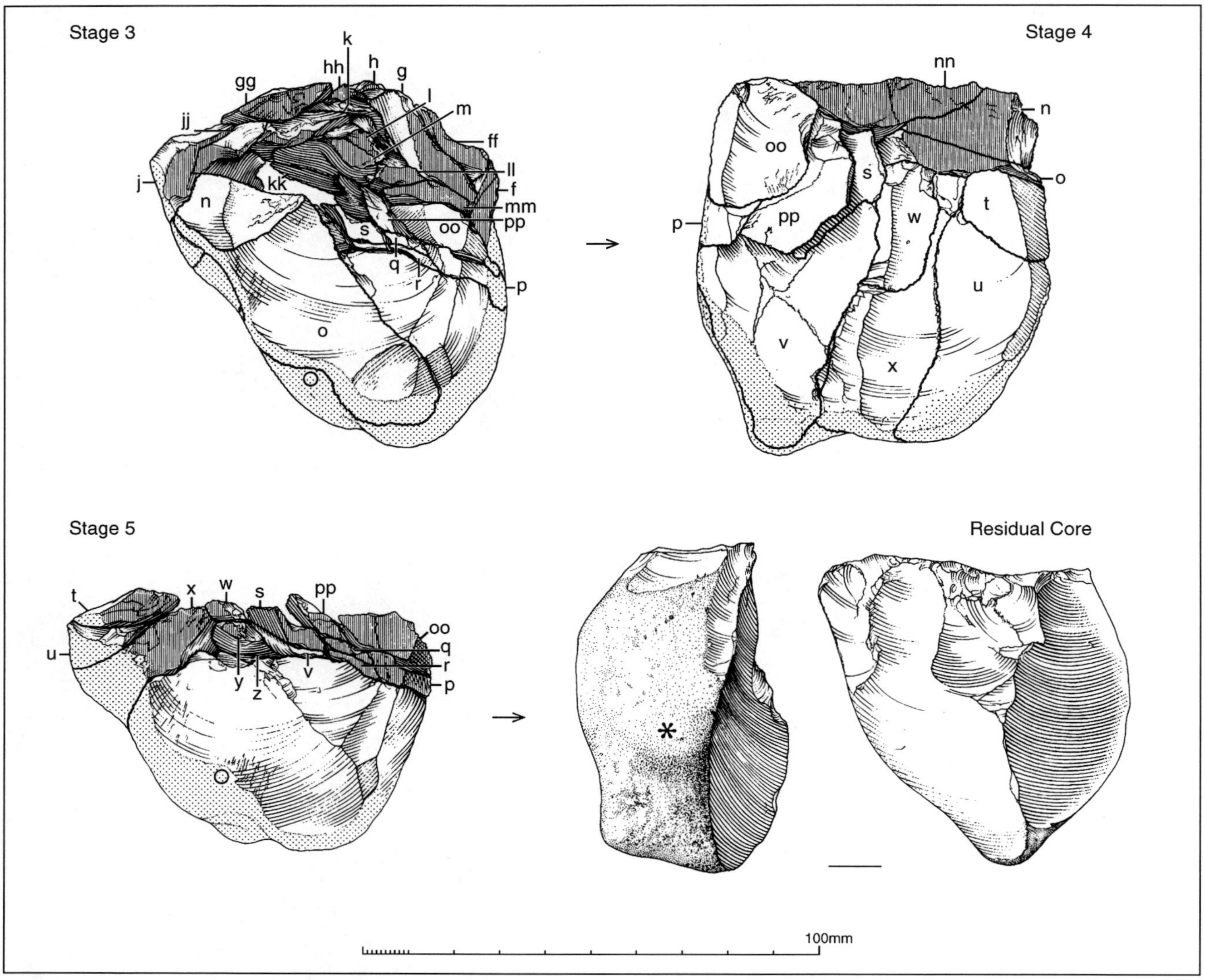

Fig 10.31 Core/flake conjoin 7: third, fourth, and fifth stages of the reduction sequence, with two views of the residual class A2 core (see Fig 10.30).

The final platform, back in the same plane as the third stage platform, has thirteen refitting flakes, oo to z. The only significant absences from this sequence occur between pp and q, where a tertiary blade 55 mm long by 15 mm broad and a small tertiary flake are missing, and right at the end where the tertiary flakes which created the scars in the middle of the face of the residual core are absent.

Conjoin group 8 (Figs 10.33–36)

A residual (type D) core (ST80 2399/231) with a bifacial platform along a keeled edge, maximum dimension 79 mm, maximum surviving flake scar length of 54 mm, and weight 160 g, has 69 refitting flakes, which conjoin to form a near complete nodule of maximum dimension 178 mm and weight 930 g. The nodule is of elongated, waisted form, with several knobbed projections and two areas of early truncation where the exterior surface is a matt thermal one rather than cortical. The cortex is largely unabraded with large areas of brown staining.

The lengthy reduction sequence begins with a few small spalls struck from one of the thermally exposed poles, followed by the nodule being opened by a single primary flake (a) which removed the flat thermal surface at this end from the side. A second flake (aa) is then removed in the same plane but from a different side to create at this third stage the first proper platform. From the reduction of this platform thirteen refitting flakes aaa–eee are present, without any significant absences in the sequence, though the proximal ends of flakes aaa, bb, and eee are missing.

The negative surface from the removal of flake eee forms the fourth stage platform, from which there are eight refitting flakes f–hh. The only major absence in this reduction sequence is at the end, where the flaked face has the scar of a missing tertiary flake 50 mm long.

The fifth stage platform also uses the previous negative surface and has twelve refitting flakes hhh–ll. Within this sequence of removals there are numerous gaps: between hhh and jj are several absences, including

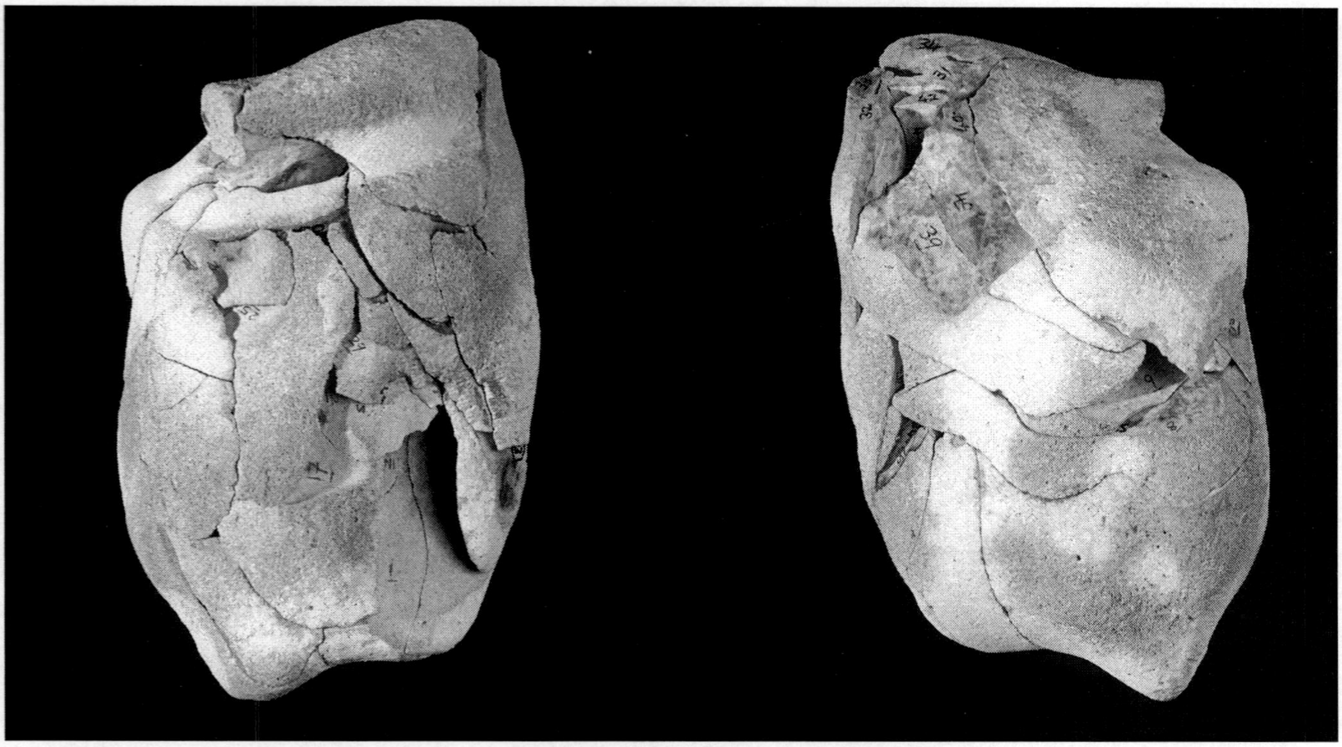

Fig 10.32 Conjoin group 7: two views of the refitted nodule. Maximum dimension 148 mm. See Figs 10.30–31. Photo: National Museums of Scotland

a secondary flake up to 60 mm in length; between jj and kkk a tertiary flake 54 mm long is absent; between iii and kkk a tertiary flake 21 mm long is absent; and between kkk and ll a secondary flake 71 mm long and a tertiary blade 65 mm long by 25 broad are absent.

The sixth stage again has a platform at right-angles to the previous, struck direct from the negative flake scars, and has six refitting flakes lll–nn. Only three are the result of separate blows, the other three resulting from breaks during detachment. There is an initial flake before mm absent from this sequence, and three or more small flakes missing from the end of this sequence after mm, n, and nn with a maximum length of 30 mm.

The seventh stage platform at right-angles to the sixth and in the same plane as the fifth, has just four refitting flakes nnn–ooo, with no significant absences. One of these flakes is large (oo – weight 65 g) and this represents a substantial rejuvenation stage.

At right-angles to the previous flaking direction, the eighth stage platform has two removals p–pp, with flake p a large example in three separate pieces, weighing together 53 g. Flake pp has hinged out and the core was subsequently turned again for the ninth platform stage. There are six refitting flakes ppp–rr, with no absences of significance.

The tenth, eleventh, and twelfth stages are all part of the sequential exploitation of a keeled edge in the final stages of the core reduction. Stage 10 has six refitting flakes s–uu with some small flakes absent between s and t; two tertiary flakes, one only 13 mm long, the other 33 mm long, absent between u and uu; and a tertiary flake 28 mm long absent between uu and the final flaking face. Stage 11 has just the two refitting flakes v–vv, while the final stage 12 has eight refitting flakes w–zz, with among the sequence about four missing flakes, of lengths 13, 17, 21, and 50 mm respectively. The latter was a blade 15 mm broad.

Conjoin group 9 (Figs 10.37–39)

A residual single platform (A2) core (ST80 2399/169), maximum dimension 95 mm, maximum flake scar length 79 mm, and weight 165 g, has 42 refitting flakes which conjoin to form a near complete nodule. The residual core was initially classified as a flake, because the surface subsequently seen to be a thermal exterior was regarded as a flake surface. This confusion arose because there are two kinds of thermal fracture surface present on this nodule. One type, forming the flat base of the core as positioned in Figure 10.37, is the conventional one resulting from early fragmentation, probably in geological context, where the surface has a matt character and has resisted cortication. The other type, which may result from a more recent fragmentation, has acquired a mainly grey-white discolouration only marginally different to that of the surfaces of the refitting flakes and the negative scars on the residual core. Without refitting, this differential character of the original nodule would not have been apparent. It is the thermal breakage which gives the nodule its distinctive angular form. The remaining cortex is stained brown in places, and is somewhat weathered.

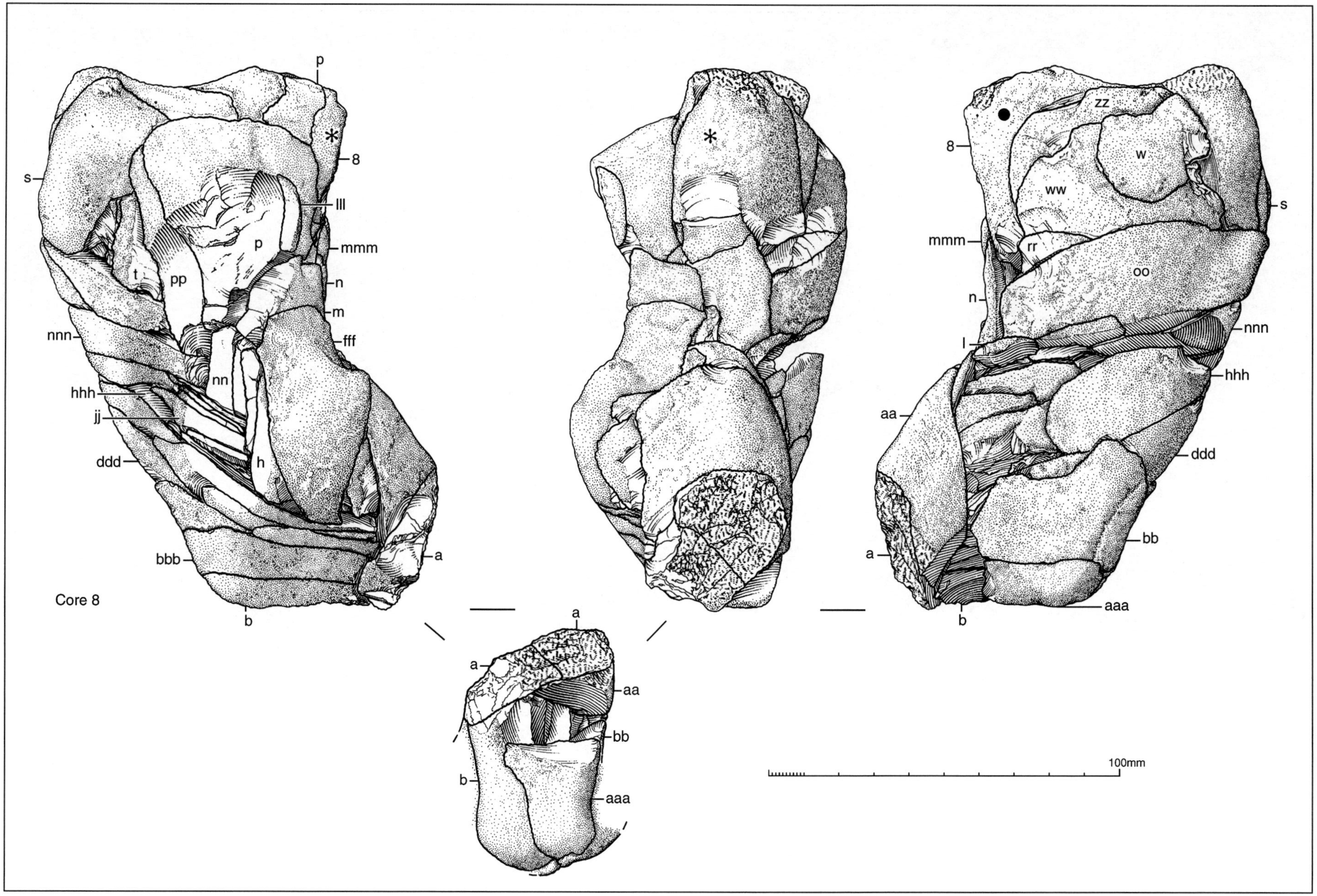

Fig 10.33 Core/flake conjoin 8 (context group 78 – outer Stepleton outwork, segment 4, Unit 2, Layer 3b, phase III; find nos ST80 2395, 2399 and 2467). Three views (and inset detail) of the near complete nodule with all conjoining flakes refitted.

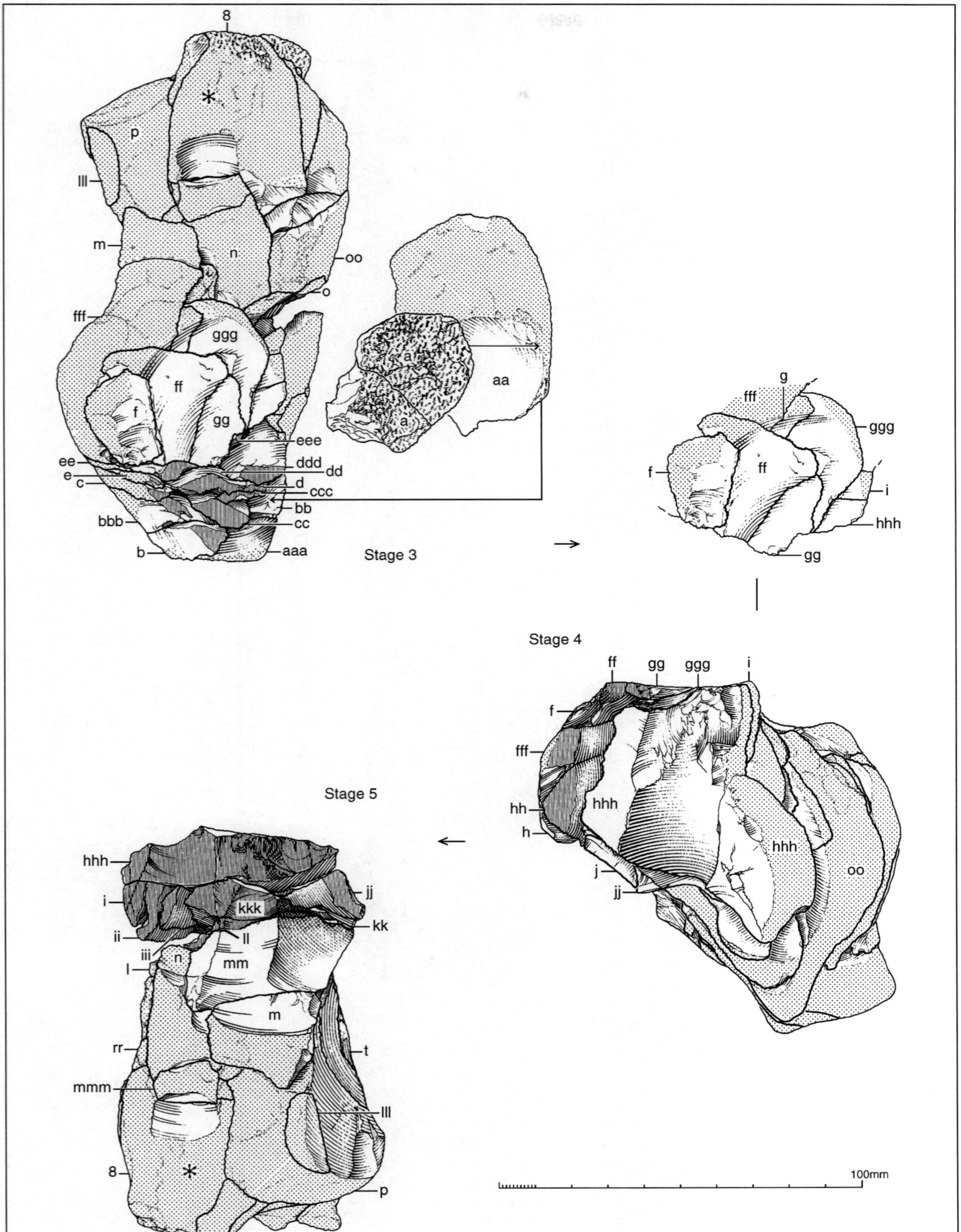

Fig 10.34 Core/flake conjoin 8: third, fourth, and fifth stages of the reduction sequence, with the single removals of the first and second stages shown adjacent to the third stage and an inset detail between the third and fourth stages (see Fig 10.33).

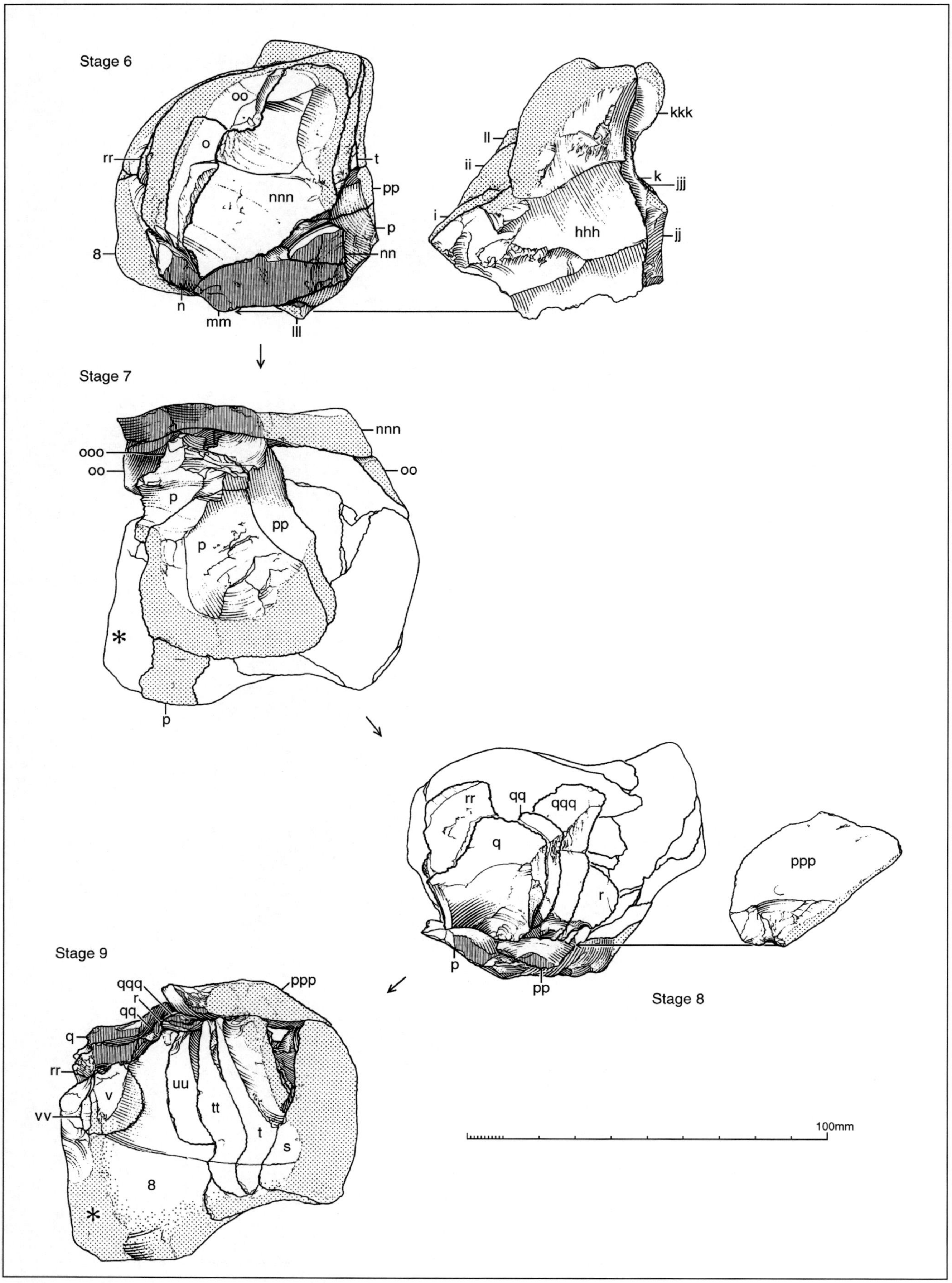

Fig 10.35 Core/flake conjoin 8: sixth, seventh, eighth, and ninth stages of the reduction sequence (see Figs 10.33–4).

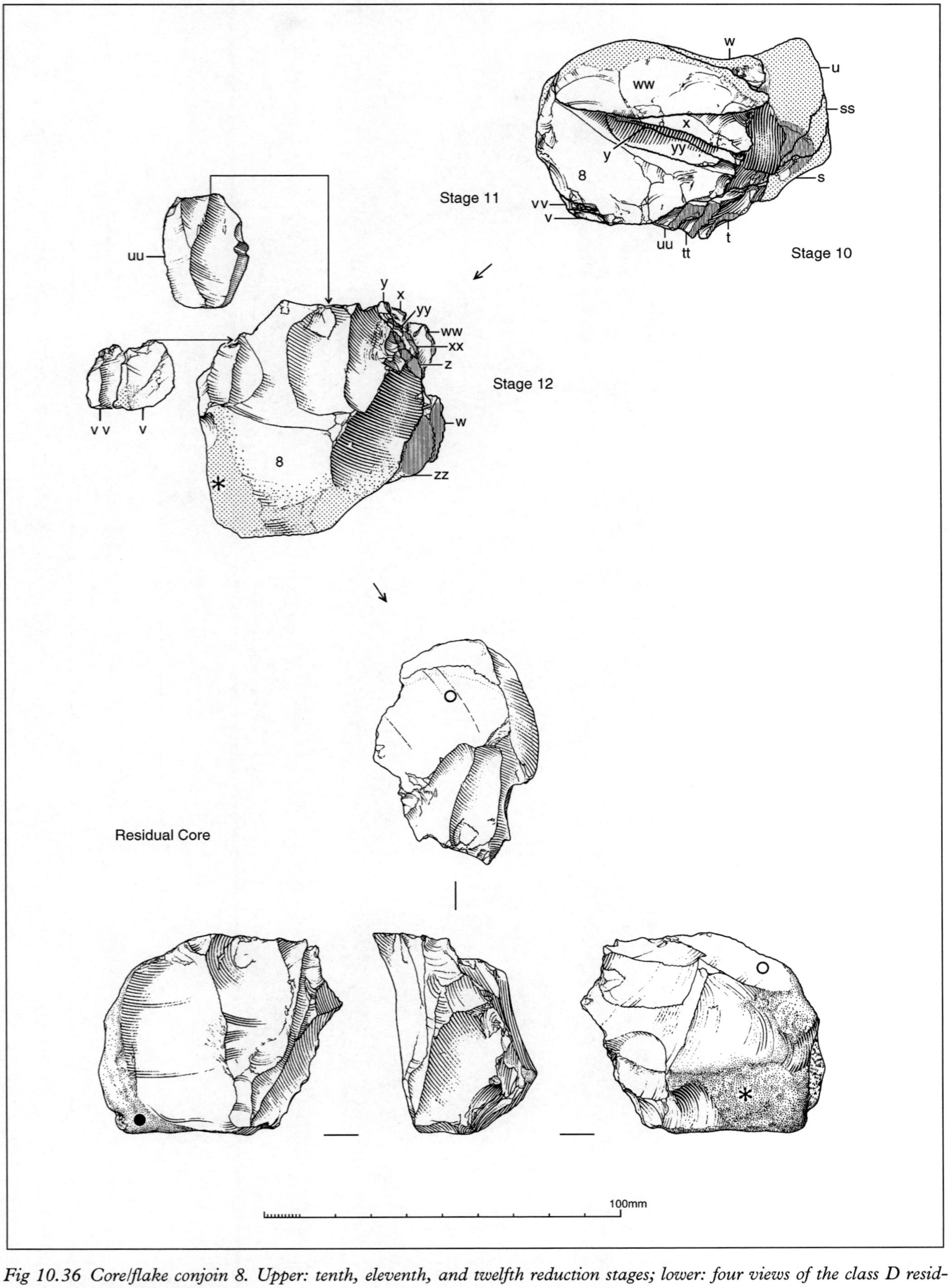

Fig 10.36 Core/flake conjoin 8. Upper: tenth, eleventh, and twelfth reduction stages; lower: four views of the class D residual core (see Figs 10.33–5).

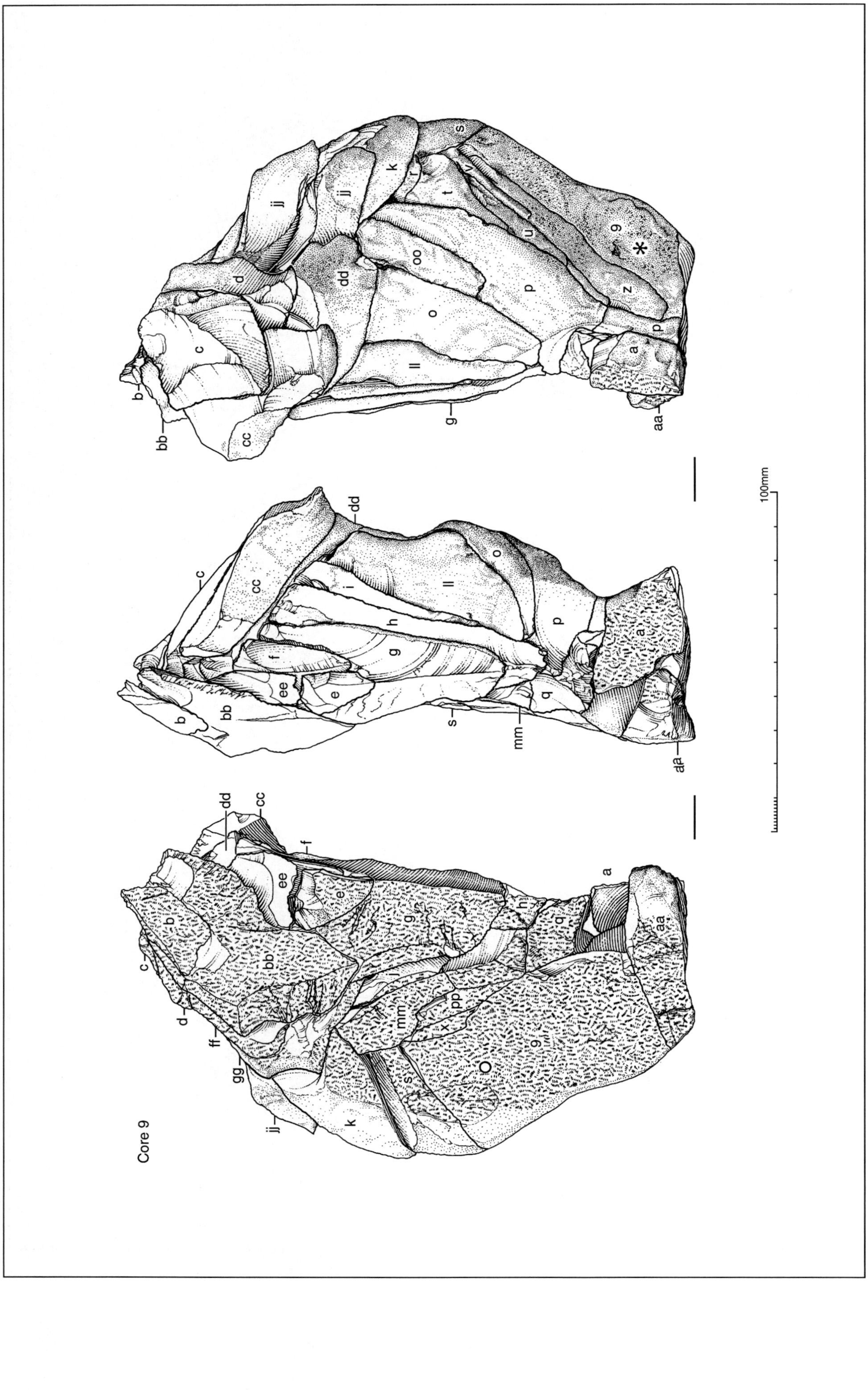

Fig 10.37 Core/flake conjoin 9 (context group 78 – outer Stepleton outwork, segment 4, Unit 2, Layer 3b, phase III; find nos: ST80 2395, 2399, 2415 and 2467). Three views of the near-complete nodule with all conjoining flakes refitted.

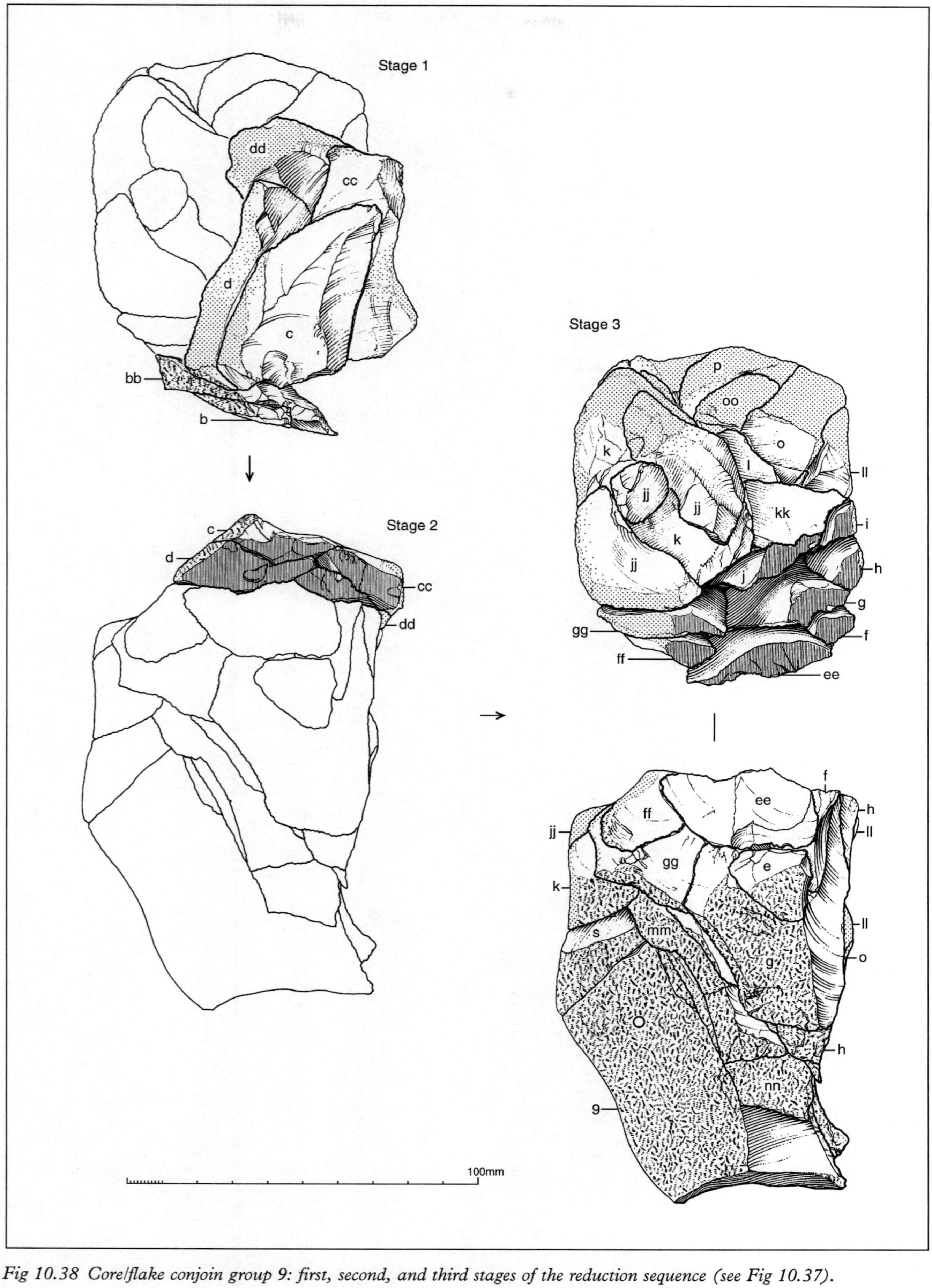

Fig 10.38 Core/flake conjoin group 9: first, second, and third stages of the reduction sequence (see Fig 10.37).

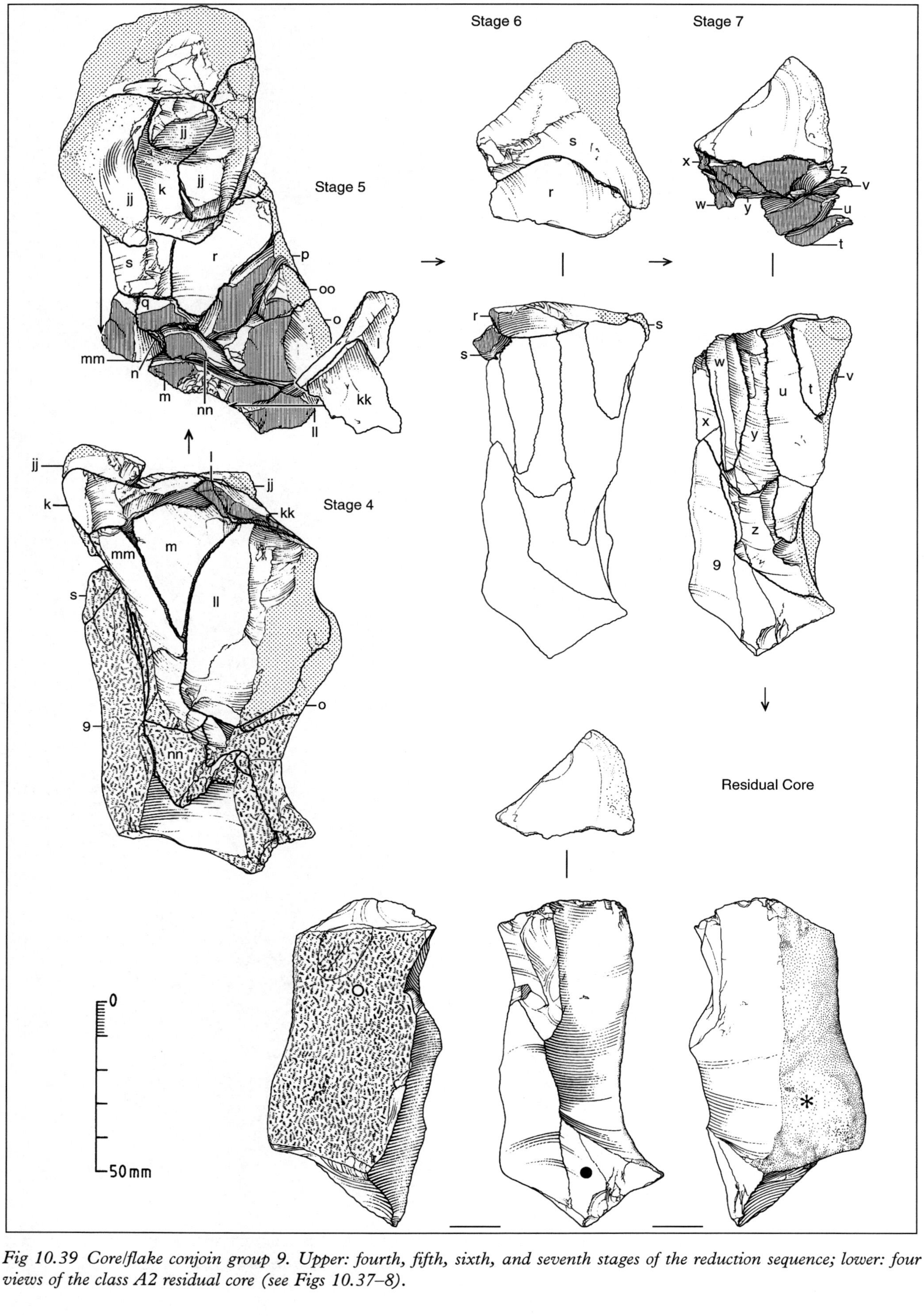

Fig 10.39 Core/flake conjoin group 9. Upper: fourth, fifth, sixth, and seventh stages of the reduction sequence; lower: four views of the class A2 residual core (see Figs 10.37–8).

The initial opening of the nodule in stage one is by the removal of two flakes b–bb. Parts of the proximal and distal portions of flake b are absent. The middle view of Figure 10.37 shows clearly how the more substantial flake bb creates the platform for the second stage removals. One flake about 30 mm long is absent after bb. The four refitting flakes c–dd from the second stage lack the initial flake or flakes to fit the negative dorsal scar on flake c, and a flake 57 mm long is absent between cc and d.

The third stage platform uses the negative flake scars of the previous flaking. The eleven refitting flakes e–j from this stage include a fragmented flake (e/ee) and two flakes (hh and ii) which lack their proximal ends. The sequence has a gap between flakes h–hh, where one or more flakes up to 55 mm in length are absent.

Stage four is in the same plane as the second stage and is a rejuvenation of the third stage platform. The four refitting flakes jj–l include one (jj) in three incomplete segments and a small secondary flake is absent after kk.

The fifth stage platform has ten refitting flakes ll–q, of which pp lacks its proximal end. There are several minor absences in this sequence, the largest being a secondary flake about 23 mm long.

Stage six is again a rejuvenation, continuing the same sequence of planes, with two refitting flakes r–s. An absent flake precedes these two, but they provide the surface for the seventh and final stage platform, to which there are seven refitting flakes t–z. Between flakes u and v/w there is an absent flake 60 mm long.

At some stage prior to the detachment of flake q, which lacks its distal terminal, two flakes a–aa were detached at right-angles to each other from the base of the core as shown in Fig 10.37, but no further flaking was undertaken from that end of the nodule.

Conjoin group 10 (Fig 10.40)

A two platform (type B2) core (ST80 2415/132), maximum dimension 108 mm, maximum flake scar length 61 mm, and weighing 400 g, has 39 refitting flakes which conjoin to create a near complete nodule, of maximum dimension 164 mm and weight 1120 g. There is also a further small flake which could be positively identified as from this nodule, but which did not refit.

The flaking at one end of the core, involving removal of a primary cortical flake to create a platform, from which two main flakes and some spalls have been struck, has proceeded no further, and none of the flakes are present. This abandoned platform could relate to knapping simply to facilitate handling of the nodule or perhaps to a previous, exploratory knapping episode.

The nodule itself is thermally split, probably in original geological context, and has a broad non-cortical thermal external surface, discoloured to a matt grey-cream. The cortical part of the nodule has three projecting knobs, each truncated in geological time.

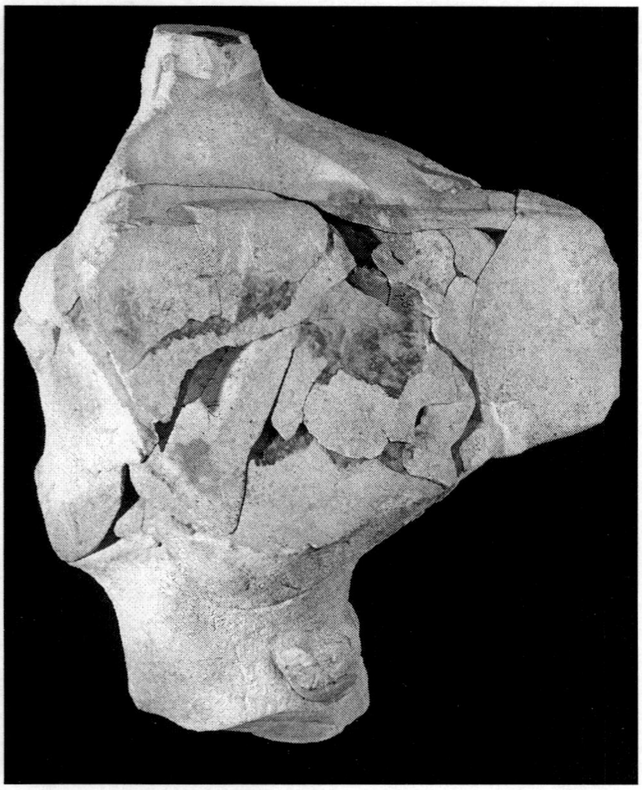

Fig 10.40 Conjoin group 10: the refitted nodule. Maximum dimension 164 mm. Photo: National Museums of Scotland

The cortex has some brown staining and calcareous accretion and some signs of weathering. A prominent fossil remains on the cortical part of the residual core.

Creation of the initial platform involved the removal of a single large flake (112 g) struck from the flat thermal external surface. The second stage has four refitting flakes, one of which has the proximal end missing. The only absent flake from this sequence is a secondary flake 55 mm long. The third stage reverts to flaking from the original thermal exterior surface, from which eight refitting flakes and chips are present. There are only minor absences of small flakes and spalls from this sequence. The fourth and final platform utilises the negative flake surface left by the previous removals. Twenty-five refitting flakes belong to this stage, in a sequence which has some small flakes missing from outer face, then only minor absences apart from three flakes, respectively 40 mm, 50 mm, and 60 mm in length.

Conjoin group 11 (not illustrated)

A single platform (A2) core (ST80 2415/158), maximum dimension 97 mm, maximum flake scar length 64 mm, weight 275 g, which has three refitting flakes that conjoin to make a complete nodule of maximum dimension 111 mm and weight 392 g. The complete nodule is actually just one fragment of a larger nodule, split in geological context so that it has a large, flat, thermal, non-cortical, matt grey-white facet. The rest of the exterior is very irregular, with three intact projecting knobs and one truncated one. There is some brown staining and some abrasion of the cortex.

This has not been a successful or productive core. There is only one platform, formed by the thermal external surface, knapped to remove two flakes on one side, and one flake on the other. There are no absent flakes.

Conjoin group 12 (not illustrated)

A two-platform (B2) core (ST80 2415/157), maximum dimension 124 mm, maximum flake scar length 73 mm, weight 750 g, with seven refitting flakes which conjoin to form a nodule with two areas where cortical primary flakes are absent. The nodule has fractured thermally on two faces, one thermal surface having a matt grey-white discolouration, the other a matt mixture of grey-white and the original black. The latter area has served as the platform for the removal of seven or more flakes, none of which are present, so this may represent an entirely previous episode of flaking. The cortex area has some brown staining and calcareous accretion.

Flaking in the sequence to which the refitting flakes belong appears to have begun on part of the nodule exterior marked by a depression formed by fossil inclusion. Flakes from at least two preliminary stages are absent, before the first refitting flake (weight 131 g) – and a non-bulbar spall – have been detached to create what is perhaps the fourth stage platform. This again has only a single large removal (weight 87 g), which is similarly preparatory of a further platform. This final platform has four refitting flakes, with just one absent flake about 70 mm long.

The residual core is still a substantial chunk of flint.

Conjoin group 13 (not illustrated)

This is a refitting nest of 24 flakes (weight 392 g), lacking the small residual core to which they would conjoin. The nest allows the form of the original nodule to be reconstructed. It is one end of a larger nodule, split off by thermal fracture leaving a flat thermal surface with a matt grey-white discolouration and some iron staining. The cortex areas have some orange-brown staining and some limited abrasion.

The initial stage of flaking uses the thermal external surface as the platform. There are 12 refitting flakes from this stage, from which no substantial but several minor flakes are missing, as is the distal segment of one of the larger primary flakes. Subsequent to these removals the next stage is a single massive rejuvenation flake (weight 220 g), which removes over half of the remaining core. The scar bed of this flake provides the platform for the final stage of removals, in the same plane as the first, and from this sequence eleven refitting flakes are present. Two of these lack their proximal ends, and another lacks its distal end, and there are an unknown number of flakes absent altogether.

Conjoin group 14 (not illustrated)

A two-platform (B2) core (ST80 2415/127), maximum dimension 81 mm, maximum flake scar length 73 mm, weight 210 g, has 18 refitting flakes, which conjoin to form an incomplete nodule portion with three thermal surfaces, of maximum dimension 140 mm and weight 616 g. The cortex has brown staining and two knobbed projections.

The initial reduction phases are obscure, but there is the distal portion of one primary flake which truncates one of the matt thermal surfaces and which might have been removed at an early stage. The first identifiable stage for which there are refits involves use of one of the flat thermal surfaces as a platform, from which there are four refitting flakes and several absent small flakes. The second stage is the removal of a large chunk at right-angles to the previous platform, which is a partially successful rejuvenation. This leads to the third stage with ten refitting flakes. In this sequence at least one large flake and one blade are absent. The final platform is on the opposite site of the remaining core, to which two substantial secondary blades refit, though one is incomplete.

Conjoin group 15 (not illustrated)

A single platform (A2) core (ST80 2467), maximum dimension 79 mm, maximum flake scar length 54 mm, weight 131 g, with 33 refitting flakes, which conjoin to form a near complete nodule portion, of maximum dimension 127 mm and weight 472 g. The portion is an almost tabular segment of a nodule which has thermal surfaces on both faces and cortex around the intervening periphery.

The first stage flaking is represented only by the final flake of the sequence, the negative scar surface of which provided the second stage platform. Three refitting flakes are present from the reduction of this platform, with one 33 mm long flake and a small spall absent. The third stage is another single removal following the same plane as the initial stage, simply rejuvenating the second stage platform for the fourth stage, which has a single refitting flake, and an absent flake and several absent spalls.

The fifth stage of reduction moves to a separate part of the nodule, with two refitting flakes struck from the naturally flat platform provided by one of the thermal surfaces. Only a couple of small flakes are missing from this sequence. The sixth stage returns to the previously worked side of the core and involves the removal of a single large rejuvenation flake (weight 69 g), to form the final seventh stage platform from which 22 refitting flakes were struck. Apart from spalls, there would seem to be only one large tertiary flake missing from this sequence.

In addition to the flakes itemised, there are two refitting spalls from the exterior surface which probably detached spontaneously during knapping.

Conjoin group 16 (not illustrated)

A single platform (A2) core (ST80 2395/52), maximum dimension 111 mm, maximum flake scar length 70 mm, weighing 330 g, with 13 refitting flakes that conjoin to form a part nodule, of maximum dimension 112 mm and weight 443 g. The residual core has some abrasion at one pole, probably from casual use as a hammerstone, which must post-date the final stage of flaking. The part nodule is the elongated and knobbed end of a nodule, with unweathered brown-stained cortex, and has split from the rest of the nodule thermally. The flat surface from this split provides the platform for the first stage flaking at two points. In one place a single refitting flake has been removed without further development, in another there are three refitting flakes, the initial one of which has a Siret fracture and only one half is present. The latter removals have provided the platform for the second stage flaking, from which there are three refitting flakes and an absent blade 60 mm long. The third stage flaking is rejuvenation in the same plane as the first stage, and only one of the two flakes from this stage is present. The fourth stage flaking, in the same plane as the second, has the main removals, all five flakes of which are present. A final fifth stage of rejuvenation flaking has no refitting flakes and has not led to any further removals.

Conjoin group 17 (not illustrated)

A group of 28 flakes (in two nests of 12 and 16 flakes; total weight 445g), which conjoin to form an almost complete nodule, lacking the residual core, which must have been small, in the region of 70 mm in maximum dimension. The nodule has an unabraded, 'chalky' cortex with one sharply pointed knobbed protrusion and one anciently broken projection, the break surface of which is discoloured dense white.

The primary flake struck to form the second stage platform is absent. From this platform there are 12 flakes which refit in a sequence lacking numerous small flakes and spalls but no substantial flakes are absent. The negative flake bed of these removals becomes the third stage platform with flakes removed in a plane at right-angles to the previous one. Fifteen flakes refit in a sequence from which several minor flakes and spalls and two tertiary flakes about 50 mm long are missing. Another small refitting flake on this nest, from the exterior of the nodule, is probably a spontaneous product during knapping.

Conjoin group 18/19 (Fig 10.41)

A group of 21 flakes (in two nests of 10 and 11 flakes; total weight 225 g), which conjoin to form a partial nodule with an absent core. The nodule has a cortex which is partly white and partly brown-stained.

The first nest of eleven flakes lacks any of the flakes from the first stage (or stages) of opening the nodule. The negative flake beds from this flaking form the platform for the second stage removal of a single refitting flake, thus rejuvenating the previous platform, from which seven refitting flakes are present. One of these third stage flakes is a distal tip only, two others lack their distal tips, and some small flakes/spalls are absent. The fourth stage is a repeat rejuvenation with a single refitting flake in the same plane as the second stage. This creates the fifth stage platform which has two refitting flakes, which in fact are also by way of rejuvenation of the core since it is the broad bed of the

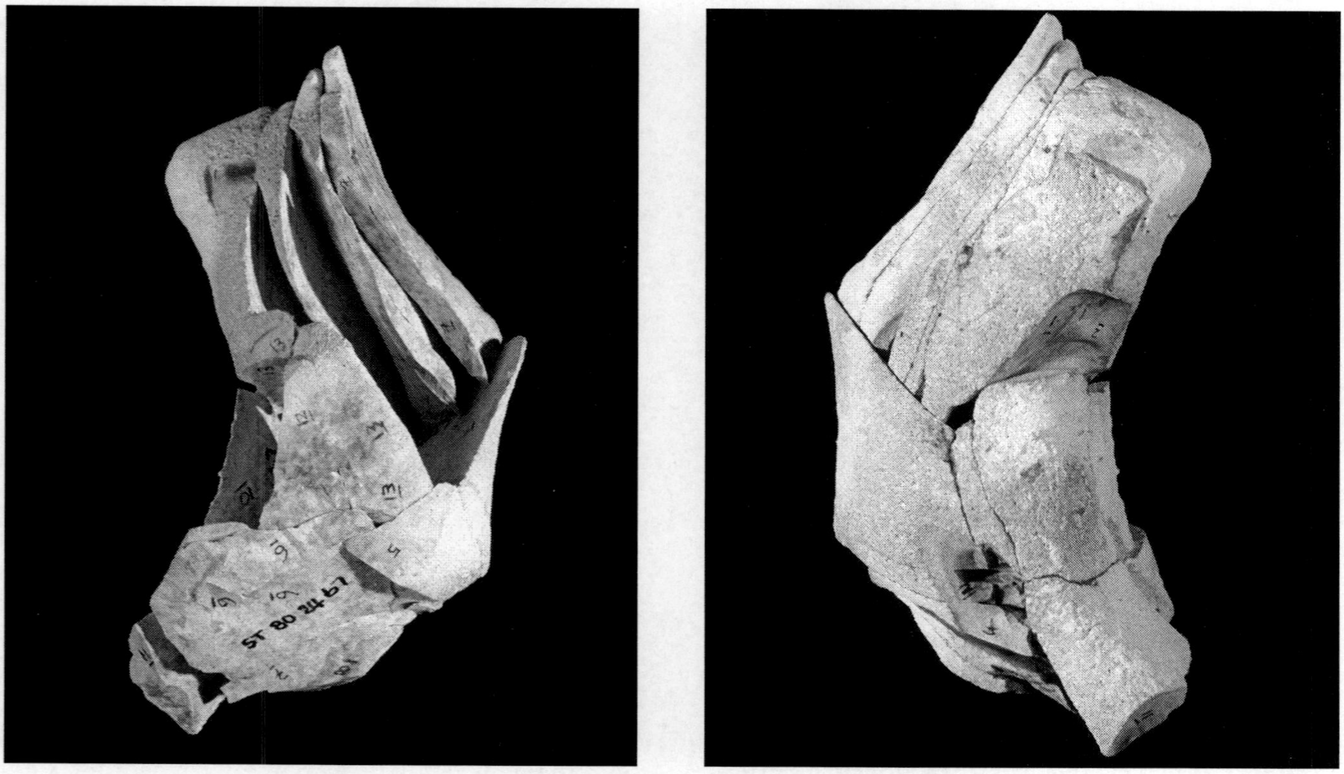

Fig 10.41 Conjoin group 18/19: two views of the refitted flake clusters. Maximum dimension 115 mm. Photo: National Museums of Scotland

final of these two which provides the platform for the sixth and last stage of removals, involving the second nest of ten refitting flakes. This is a very partial sequence with flakes from one side of the flaking face of the core entirely absent.

Only four of the flakes from this conjoin group appear on the plans of the scatter in the west butt of the segment. These lie a maximum of 0.30 m apart and are towards the east edge of the scatter, so the missing flakes could well be within the unexcavated baulk (Fig 3.105).

Conjoin group 20 (not illustrated)

A nest of 13 refitting flakes (weight 56 g) all struck from a single platform, which conjoin to form part of the exterior of what would have been an almost cylindrical nodule (or portion of one). The cortex is largely stained brown and closely resembles in character the cortex on conjoin group 18/19. Only one of the flakes from this group was plotted, but it lies immediately adjacent to one of the plotted flakes from group 18/19. While the two groups do not quite refit, they do obviously derive from the same core and the relative positioning on the original nodule is apparent. It is of some interest to note that this nodule would have been quite small, slender, and in part cylindrical, and not an obvious choice for knapping. There are no substantial flakes missing from the sequence, though some of those present lack either their distal or proximal ends.

Conjoin group 21 (not illustrated)

A nest of 11 refitting flakes (weight 182 g) from the early stages of core reduction, the core itself being absent. The flakes conjoin to form one end of a nodule with a very 'chalky' cortex and some iron staining. The pole of the nodule has an ancient thermal break, giving a flat surface with matt grey discolouration. This surface is used as the first platform for removing an initial primary flake, which is present, as is a second primary flake removed at right-angles to it. The bed of this flake has provided the platform for the third and final stage of flaking, to which the remaining nine refitting flakes belong. There is one flake 40 mm long absent from this sequence.

Conjoin group 22 (not illustrated)

A single platform (A2) core (ST80 2415/131), maximum dimension 98 mm, maximum flake scar length 62 mm, and weight 330 g, with 17 refitting flakes, which refit to form a larger A2 core, of maximum dimension 143 mm and weighing 640 g. The refitted core comprises the main part of a knobbly nodule with cortex partially stained brown. The first stage (or stages) of removals are entirely absent, as are the initial removals of the second stage at right-angles to the first. Sixteen of the refitting flakes are from this second stage, the 17th flake being a spall from the cortical exterior removed during this sequence but from a different direction. Within the main sequence of removals, apart from small flakes and spalls, at least two substantial secondary blades are absent, one 88 mm long the other 96 mm.

Conjoin group 23 (not illustrated)

A set of four refitting flakes (weight 253 g) from the exterior of a nodule, reflecting the preparatory trimming of the nodule prior to any productive flaking. The core is absent. The parent nodule has brown staining of the white cortex. The first primary flake is struck direct against the side of a projecting cortical knob on the nodule exterior. This provides the platform for the next removal, a chunky flake which is dorsally entirely cortical, and the negative scar of this flake forms the platform for the third stage to which two similarly dorsally cortical flakes refit.

Discussion of the refitting results

The evidence from the conjoining groups indicates the employment of very simple, straightforward reduction strategies. These principally involve a single, continuous knapping sequence per nodule, rather than complex sequences starting from different parts of the same nodule. Platforms tend to alternate at approximate right-angles to each other, following a simple turn of the nodule in the knapper's hand. Flaking is by hard hammer and is without preparation, the unmodified negative flake scars of the previous removals providing the platform beds. The recurrently absent spalls from the proximal dorsal edges of flakes probably indicate that platform edges were regularly refreshed before each flake was struck, but this is not the same as extensive pre-trimming.

While the reduction strategies may be simple, they are certainly not without skill. The knappers have carefully studied the available nodules and then exploited them in a remarkably successful fashion, especially given the unprepossessing shape of many of the nodules. This statement judges success in terms of the ability to reduce a nodule through a continuous series of stages down to a small residual core.

Assessment of whether the reduction was successful in the provision of useful blanks is harder to judge. The absent flakes from each conjoin group have been noted above, but it is impossible to say whether they are absent because they have been removed for (potential) use, whether they were present somewhere in the ditch deposits but not recovered archaeologically, or whether they were not recognised during the refitting process. The latter is regarded as rather unlikely and the explanation probably involves both of the former. Potential use would apply most particularly to absent flakes longer than 40 mm, which analyses have shown (Tables 10.43 and 10.45) to be the preferred size for implements. That so few of these flakes are absent from the reduction sequences need not occasion surprise. Superficially, knapping is by nature a very wasteful process, and knappers tend to be highly selective about their products, especially if the supply of raw material is not an overriding concern. Comparison of the illustrated flakes left behind from the reduction sequences (Figs 10.22, 10.25, 10.27, 10.28) with those used for flake tools (Figs 10.7–14) shows that they include examples of precisely the same general nature.

The refitting analyses have also shown the routes by which residual single platform cores – characteristic of the Hambledon Hill assemblages and of the early/middle Neolithic period in general (Healy 1988a, 46) – are created. The technology in evidence here is comparable to that shown by the refitting sequences from the phase 1 early Neolithic causewayed ditch of the Amesbury 42 long barrow, Wiltshire (Harding 1990, figs 68–9), by at least one of the refitting groups from the early Neolithic site at Rowden, Dorset (Harding 1991, fig 41), and by the refitted nodule from the late Neolithic ring ditch in Firtree Field, Down Farm, Dorset (A G Brown 1991, fig 6.1). In the case of Firtree Field, it was concluded that the refitting scatter in the ditch represented symbolic, non-utilitarian deposition (Brown 1991, 106), whereas the knapping at Amesbury 42 and Rowden is implicitly accepted as utilitarian.

At Amesbury 42 long barrow the disposition of the refitting scatter over an area *c* 0.4 m by 0.3 m in the butt of a ditch segment is in many ways analogous to the situation of those in the Stepleton ditches. Harding (1990, 104) concluded these resulted from *in situ* knapping in the shelter of the ditch and not from dumping or silting, because: the refitting groups were probably superimposed; there were similar spatial relationships between types of individual pieces within each group; there was near total presence; and a complete range of small flakes and chips. The Stepleton data are insufficient to allow comparison on all these points, so it remains uncertain whether the refitting deposits could represent *in situ* knapping or dumped deposition from knapping elsewhere. However, the incomplete nature of the refitting sequences from segment 3 of the enclosure argues more strongly for dumping (or even erosion into the ditch), while the near complete sequences from segment 4 of the outer outwork could be suggested to be more compatible with *in situ* knapping.

10.2.7 Discussion

Table 10.6 (p 648) indicates the fundamental character of the assemblage. Manufacture has taken place on site, leaving behind a substantial residue of cores, core fragments, tested nodules, and unretouched flakes. The distribution of this material across the hilltop appears universal, insofar as it is reflected by the ditches and other features which have acted as catchments for it. Concentrations within these catchments occur, and a parsimonious explanation has been sought, which relates the concentrations to the patterning of raw material availability, in particular as produced by the patches of Clay-with-Flints. Patterning which may be rather more cultural than this can perhaps be seen in the relative proportions of the major assemblage elements from the internal features of the enclosures and the lower fills of the encompassing ditches (Table 10.55). This is a crude measure, but it suggests that retouched pieces are a more significant part of the feature fills than the ditches, and that cores – more so at Stepleton than the main enclosure – are characteristically part of the ditch fills. There are various ways in which this might be interpreted, but two factors that may well have influenced the pattern could be preferential use (and discard) of implements within the enclosure and preferential knapping and/or waste disposal towards the edges. This could be characterised as a more 'domestic' aspect to the material from the enclosure interiors and a more 'industrial' aspect to that from their perimeters.

It can be hypothesised that, in the normal course of events, most of the waste debris from knapping would be kept clear of other activities, either by accumulation in flint waste-heaps or general middens, or put in convenient exposures, such as ditches. In the latter case it does not necessarily follow that creation of the waste had to occur close to a ditch. However, the evidence of the refits from two of the Stepleton ditches where these were clustered, indicated that, at least in these two instances, knapping did take place close by, otherwise the individual reduction sequences would have become more widely scattered.

The distribution of burnt material is perhaps one of the most patterned elements of this data-set. Comparison of Table 10.6 with Table 10.18 indicates

Table 10.55 Struck lithic artefacts from pits and lower ditch fills of the main and Stepleton enclosures, expressed by number and percentage

Type	*Central area pits no.*	*Central area pits %*	*Main ditch no.*	*Main ditch %*	*Stepleton pits no.*	*Stepleton pits %*	*Stepleton ditches no.*	*Stepleton ditches %*
Unretouched flakes	2944	87	1722	93	2314	92	6643	97
Cores etc	34	1	53	3	27	1	161	2
All retouched	391	12	77	4	174	7	79	1
Total	3369		1852		2515		6883	

that 88% of all unclassified burnt pieces come from the inner Stepleton outwork, mostly from the upper infill and mostly from segment 5. A similar, far less marked, but nevertheless locally significant circumstance is the concentration of unclassified burnt pieces in one of the features inside the main enclosure (A F41). In both cases this patterning must represent unusual events or situations, but presumably not ones which are specifically relevant to the production and use of stone tools. Otherwise there is a slight but persistent presence of burnt pieces in most of the context groups.

The content of individual features has been analysed for both enclosures (Table 10.14) and it is clear that in most cases the number of struck lithic artefacts per pit is small – 40% have ten or fewer artefacts; 77% have 50 or fewer artefacts. The largest pit groups (Tables 10.15, 10.24) do not have a composition which diverges significantly from the overall norm for the pit groups, other than the large number of unclassified burnt pieces from pit A F41. The two pit assemblages examined in more detail (Tables 10.12, 10.16) confirmed the overall impression that these assemblages were mixed in origin and probably in time, since they contained the products of different nodules, they contained artefacts in different conditions, they had both burnt and unburnt artefacts, and they did not have any refitting reduction sequences.

It can be argued that the collections from Neolithic pits in the central area and on the Stepleton spur do have some distinctive characteristics, but that these are distinctive mainly in relation to the ditch collections, and relate to the overall way in which lithic material was produced and used within and around the enclosure. The pits have preserved samples of the lithic material produced and/or used in association with the activities taking place, but only after the artefacts have been discarded, abandoned, or lost. The pits thus acted as traps for the essentially random accumulation of these samples and there is little to suggest any specific intentionality about this.

On the assumption that the pits groups with low numbers of artefacts could perhaps be more indicative of specific deposition or placement, the composition of all pits with ten or fewer artefacts was analysed (Table 10.56). Of the 66 pits involved, 34 contained only unretouched flake(s), one contained two serrated-edge flakes, one contained a single scraper, and another had only an unclassified burnt fragment. It is noteworthy that so many of the Stepleton pits contained only unretouched flakes, but this probably relates to the far higher proportion of Stepleton pits with less than ten artefacts. The remaining 29 pits had unretouched flake(s) in combination with one or more common unretouched artefact types or implements. These combinations in each pit reflect the general distribution of artefact types within the pits (Tables 10.15, 10.24) and offer no obvious indications of structured deposition or placement. It is also the case that presence within the same feature does not necessarily imply precise contemporaneity. In the absence of refits, this would apply even if there were detailed information about the disposition and relationship of the artefacts within each pit.

It is the overall, repetitious content of the pit assemblages which is perhaps the most significant aspect. By far the most common items, as from all other contexts, are unretouched flakes and burnt fragments. This is waste material *par excellence* and of an entirely unremarkable nature. It is extremely improbable that the

Table 10.56 Frequency of occurrence of types of struck lithic artefacts from the fills of features containing ten or fewer artefacts

Artefact type(s)	*Central area pits*	*Stepleton spur pits*	*Total*
Unretouched flake(s) only	7	27	34
Serrated-edge flakes only		1	1
Scraper only	1		1
Unclassified burnt piece only		1	1
Unretouched flakes & core		1	1
Unretouched flakes & flaked lump		1	1
Unretouched flake(s) & unclass burnt piece(s)	1	6	7
Unretouched flake(s) & unretouched flake(s) burnt & unclass burnt piece(s)		2	2
Unretouched flake(s) & serrated-edge flake	2	4	6
Unretouched flakes & serrated-edge flake & cores		1	1
Unretouched flakes & serrated-edge flake & unclass burnt piece	1		1
Unretouched flakes & edge-trim flake		1	1
Unretouched flakes & edge-trim flake & scraper	1		1
Unretouched flakes & edge-trim flake & leaf arrowhead & unclass burnt piece	1		1
Unretouched flakes & edge-trim flake & misc retouched piece		1	1
Unretouched flake burnt & edge-trim flake & unclass burnt pieces	1		1
Unretouched flake & unretouched flake burnt & scraper	1		1
Unretouched flake(s) & misc retouched piece	2	2	4
Total pits with ten or fewer artefacts	18	48	66

presence of this material in the features reflects any special intentionality. Serendipity is the most likely explanation for the presence of the unretouched flakes and, by extension, all the other items as well.

Looking at the overall representation of implements within the whole Hambledon Hill assemblage (Table 10.39), it can be argued that the pattern is very much what might be expected from any early/middle Neolithic site in southern England. This pattern does not vary much across the hilltop (Table 10.40), the main contrasts being in actual numbers and density of implements in different locations rather than any contrast in assemblage character. Attention could be drawn to presence/absences, such as the lack of flint axeheads from the south long barrow ditches, or to relative presence, such as the lower number of leaf-shaped arrowheads from the Stepleton spur, but it is hard to avoid the conclusion that the overall profile of implements throughout is essentially similar.

Where there is contrast, as Table 10.40 makes clear, is between the pit assemblages from both enclosures and all other contexts. The contrast lies essentially in the higher proportions of serrated-edge flakes (and to a lesser extent other edge-trimmed flakes) from the pits, and the correspondingly lower proportions of scrapers, piercers, and miscellaneous retouched pieces. It is tempting to link this to the functional 'domestic'/'industrial' distinction drawn between the enclosure interior and the periphery on the basis of the non-retouched component. The contrast probably cannot be explained wholly in terms of the better preservation of the delicate serrated-edge forms in the interior features, though this may be a significant factor in their low representation from superficial contexts.

A crucial question to be addressed at this point is whether the assemblage is, in reality, all early/middle Neolithic or not? A definitive conclusion on this would require greater chronological precision over typological assessment than current data can bear, but one approach is to look at the occurrence of those implement types which are conventionally early/middle Neolithic and those which could be later Neolithic/ Bronze Age. The distribution within context groups is shown for the major implement categories in Table 10.41.

The generally accepted criteria for early/middle Neolithic implement assemblages (eg Healy 1988a, 46; Richards 1990, 18) would be a restricted range of implements to include leaf-shaped arrowheads, scrapers (not normally scale-flaked), serrated-edge flakes, piercers (not normally elongated), and polished flint axeheads, of which scrapers and serrated-edge flakes would be the most numerous. 'Laurel-leaf' bifacials of regular form are also a classic earlier Neolithic type (Clark *et al* 1960, 226; Smith 1965, 100). Later Neolithic/early Bronze Age collections would include a wider range of retouched forms, including transverse and barbed-and-tanged arrowheads, more extensively retouched and scale-flaked scrapers, scale-flaked knives (including plano-convex types), more elongated piercers, saws, and rods, with serrated-edge flakes less common and 'fabricators' more common (Healy 1988a, 46; Richards 1990, 18). Also later Neolithic/ early Bronze Age are ground-edge knives of various shapes, a whole variety of 'rough, heavy artefacts' (Gardiner 1991c, 62) including picks, Y-shaped implements, and other core tools. More subjectively, heavier utilisation indicated by abrasion and by use-polish on scrapers and piercers, are sometimes cited as later Neolithic traits (Gardiner 1991c, 64).

These criteria reinforce the identification of the collections from the pits as the most representative 'early' assemblages from Hambledon Hill. 'Early' types like serrated-edge flakes, leaf-shaped arrowheads, and 'laurel-leaf' bifacials do predominantly occur in 'early' contexts, but they also occur in 'later' ones in which they could be residual. Perhaps the strongest correlation occurs in the case of the potentially 'later' types: picks, rods, 'fabricators', and knives. Apart from one rod (Fig 10.20: 162) from a grave on the Stepleton spur, none of these types occur in the 'early' contexts represented by pit fills and lower ditch silts. On typological grounds a case could be made for most of the rods being 'later' types, especially one of the unstratified examples (Fig 10.19: 161). Similarly with the scale-flaked knives (Fig 10.14: 121–3), which occur only in 'later' or unstratified contexts. These types occur in very small numbers, however, so their occurrence could be misleading, as with the saw (another potentially 'later' type), of which there is only one example. On the other hand, the clustering of the knives – three from 'late' horizons in segment 8 of the main enclosure ditch where there was a concentration of Beaker pottery, and three from a 'late' horizon in segment 7 of the inner Stepleton outwork, where there was Bronze Age pottery – argues for a non-random pattern which could be compatible with later deposition.

Typo-chronological assessment of the more common implement types other than the serrated-edge flakes is difficult, but subjective judgement would suggest that few 'later' types occur among the piercers and scrapers. Certainly there are only a few which can be compared with the archetypal later kinds of elongated and robust piercers (Saville 1981b, 61), and these are from late or unstratified contexts. As for scrapers, the present author (Saville 1981b, 59) suggested some time ago that, other than in the case of small 'Beaker' scrapers, metrical data are unlikely to produce meaningful distinctions irrespective of the raw material exploited. More recently the notion that scraper thickness decreased through the Neolithic, and therefore could provide a chronometric indicator has been revived by Riley (1990; cf Bradley 1970, 357). Table 10.57 gives the mean thicknesses for intact flake scrapers from selected context groups. There seems little evidence here to suggest trends in any direction and one must conclude again, as recently has Pollard (1999, 335), that it is really only the 'thumbnail' scrapers,

Table 10.57 Mean thickness values for complete scrapers on struck flakes from selected context groups

Group 1 Neolithic features in central area, groups 3–4 main enclosure ditch phases I–III, groups 6–9 main enclosure ditch phases V–VII/a, groups 10–11 main enclosure ditch phase VIII/a and superficial levels, group 53 Neolithic features on Stepleton spur, groups 55–56 Stepleton enclosure ditch phases I–III, groups 57–59 Stepleton enclosure ditch IV–VI, groups 60–61 Stepleton enclosure ditch phase VIII/a and superficial levels, groups 63–64 inner Stepleton outwork ditch phases I–III, groups 65–67 inner Stepleton outwork ditch phases V–VII, groups 68–69 inner Stepleton outwork ditch phase VIII/a and superficial levels

Groups	*Total no. in sample*	*Total thickness value in mm*	*Mean thickness in mm*
1	24	282.0	11.8
3–4	14	167.5	12.0
6–9	56	757.5	13.5
10–11	45	552.5	12.3
53	19	250.5	13.2
55–56	8	125.0	15.6
57–59	18	240.0	13.3
60–61	11	137.0	12.5
63–64	6	98.0	16.3
65–67	10	140.0	14.0
68–69	74	888.0	12.0
Samples combined	285	3638.0	12.8

small and with shallow invasive flaking, that are chronologically and culturally diagnostic. The fact that this type of scraper is absent from Hambledon Hill is in itself of course a pointer to the non-existence there of any 'Beaker' flint industry as such, as is the lack of transverse arrowheads to the absence of any significant late Neolithic presence. Similarly, the only scraper type with a convincing Bronze Age pedigree when common, the denticulate scraper (Harding 1991, 85; Saville 1981b, 58), is also virtually absent at Hambledon Hill.

It might be objected that the miscellaneous retouched pieces are being overlooked. These pieces certainly do have a much higher profile in 'later' or unstratified contexts than the regular tool forms and could conceivably be regarded as a product of some 'later' activity which was less concerned with formal implements. However, many of these miscellaneous pieces appear to be broken examples of regular tools, which are disproportionately common in superficial contexts because those contexts are the ones most likely to contain broken tools. Also there may be other taphonomic factors involved in this pattern, such as the probable higher incidence of miscellaneous pieces created by plough-damage or other natural processes in the 'later' and superficial contexts. Explanations along these lines are more satisfactory than the notion of a 'later' phase of activity on Hambledon Hill being dominated by the use of irregular and otherwise unclassifiable retouched pieces. Since a significant element of the miscellaneous retouched pieces must be residual from the 'early' contexts (13–14% even in the pit fills), their proportions in the 'later' contexts in no way approach the levels observed in some middle/late Bronze Age assemblages (Harding 1991, 85).

This is perhaps rather inconclusive, but the general impression gained is that, while there may be some indicators of 'later' implement types, any such 'later' presence was not significant in terms of implement discard and the composition of the implement assemblage as a whole. The entire Hambledon Hill assemblage stands out in this regard in comparison to those from other causewayed enclosures, in particular from Windmill Hill, Wiltshire, where late Neolithic/early Bronze Age activity on that hilltop left a clearly recognisable implement component of small scale-flaked scrapers, flake tools with polished edges, elongated piercers, and transverse and barbed-and-tanged arrowheads (Smith 1965, 103–9).

If the implement component does not support much chronological differentiation, what about the waste material? In terms of core types in southern England, while simple single and double platform cares are omnipresent, there does appear to be a trend during the Neolithic and into the Bronze Age for multi-platform, discoidal, and keeled cores to increase proportionately, and for platform preparation to be applied more frequently (Saville 1981b, 47–48). At Hambledon Hill simple single and double platform cores dominate throughout and multiplatform cores, always small in number, are if anything more common in the 'early' contexts (Table 10.35). Platform preparation is virtually absent and no other potentially chronological trends emerged from analysis. Near-identical reduction sequences to those of the refitted cores at Stepleton, using alternate flaking without other platform preparation, have been published by Harding (1990, fig 69; 1991, fig 41) and by A G Brown (1991, fig 6.1). These are early–middle Neolithic except in the case of the refitted nodule from the late Neolithic Firtree Field ring-ditch, Down Farm, Dorset (A G Brown 1991).

Collections of unretouched flakes have been shown to exhibit a general trend from predominantly narrow, more blade-like characteristics towards broader flake

Table 10.58 Breadth:length ratio values for complete unretouched flakes 20 mm or more in length and/or breadth from selected contexts

Range	*Main enclosure, fill of pit N F7i* No.	%	*Stepleton enclosure, fill of pit 1A F350* No.	%	*Main enclosure ditch, segment 13 phase III* No.	%	*Main enclosure ditch, segment 13 phase V* No.	%	*Main enclosure ditch, segment 13 phase VI* No.	%
1:5–2:5	2	2	6	5	20	4	4	2	9	4
2:5–3:5	26	22	19	15	80	16	40	20	40	15
3:5–4:5	22	18	50	39	172	35	60	30	102	39
4:5–5:5	29	24	30	23	140	28	58	29	67	26
5:5–6:5	23	19	18	14	55	11	24	12	26	10
>6:5	18	15	5	4	30	6	16	8	16	6
Total nos	120		128		497		202		260	

types during the course of the Neolithic and Bronze Age (Ford 1987; Pitts and Jacobi 1979; Saville 1981b). This trend has been seen to have some reality and applicability, even given all the problems of isolating truly comparable samples and the use of different analytical methodologies. A problem at Hambledon Hill, given the lack of sealed stratified samples and the omnipresent residuality, is that there is little scope for looking at potential change through time. The only relevant samples for which metrical data have been recorded are those from segment 13 of the main enclosure ditch. Comparison of the length/breadth index values (Table 10.33) shows very little difference in flake shape between the lower and higher fills of the ditch. Even the higher percentage of primary flakes in the lower ditch fills cannot be shown to bias the figures unduly and the conclusion must be that there is no trend here to which any chronological interpretation could be attached. Some subassemblages which were not investigated metrically, but which have good later ceramic associations (such as the upper levels of segments 8 and 10 of the main enclosure or of segment 1 of the Shroton spur outwork), might provide data for investigating chronological aspects of flake-shape trends further.

It is of interest, however, to contrast the shape of flakes from Hambledon Hill with those from other sites to investigate any abnormalities. Length/breadth index values as used in this report are preferable as a measure (Saville 1980; 1981a, 147) but since most previous analysts have relied on breadth:length ratios it is convenient by way of comparison to give these for the Hambledon Hill samples as well (Table 10.58). Each of the Hambledon Hill samples exhibits a comparable range between 19 and 24 per cent of flakes narrower than 3:5, and between 41 and 58 per cent broader than 4:5. Although blades are obviously present, these statistics show that the Hambledon Hill samples lack blades as an especially significant element and in theory this situates them chronologically with the later Neolithic (Saville 1981b, 43–44). The most relevant and most striking contrasts are provided by Windmill Hill, Wiltshire, where from the primary levels 41% of waste flakes are 3:5 or narrower, and only 35% broader than 4:5 (Smith 1965) and Maiden Castle, Dorset, where from the Neolithic enclosure ditches 58% are narrower than 3:5 and only 20% broader than 4:5 (Edmonds and Bellamy 1991, 217). The proportions from the Staines enclosure, Surrey (Healey and Robertson-Mackay 1983), fall mid-way between the two, while those from Etton (Middleton 1998, fig 218) appear rather closer to Hambledon Hill. In retrospect one would wish for different and larger measured flake samples from Hambledon Hill. However, Ford (1987) has drawn attention to the overlap in shape ranges between earlier and later Neolithic flake populations and it is clear that the trend towards broader flakes during the Neolithic period cannot be treated quite as simplistically as has previously been the case using this statistic (Saville 1981b).

Table 10.39 gives the overall representation of implements within the hilltop collection, and all the expected types for a Neolithic assemblage are present. This is a consistent picture for assemblages from causewayed enclosures in England (Table 10.59) and in itself need occasion no surprises. Indeed, there is a case for saying this picture is completely standard and that the differences apparent in this table are more likely to reflect inconsistencies in compilation of the data rather than in the data themselves.

I have discussed elsewhere what can be deduced from the presence of different lithic implement types at causewayed enclosures (Saville 2002) and here it is only appropriate to mention a few aspects. A crucial point is the predominance of serrated-edge and other edge-modified flakes. Much attention has been paid to serrated-edge flakes, which have long been recognised as quintessential accompaniments of causewayed enclosures (Curwen 1937, 87). They are also found at Neolithic enclosures throughout Europe, but they are not a phenomenon exclusive to causewayed enclosures so much as a commonplace tool of the early/middle Neolithic (Saville 2002). The work of Jensen (1988a; 1988b; 1994) in particular has shown conclusively that serrated-edge flakes were not harvesting tools, but rather were used in some manufacturing or maintenance process involving silicious plant material, perhaps vegetable fibres.

Table 10.59 Total numbers of selected flint implement types from Hambledon Hill and other causewayed enclosures in England

Numbers are derived from the following sources: Etton from Middleton (1998), Windmill Hill from Smith (1965), Briar Hill from Bamford (1985), Staines from Healey and Robertson-Mackay (1983; 1987), Abingdon from Avery (1982), Maiden Castle from Edmonds and Bellamy (1991) and Wheeler (1943)

Type	*Hambledon Central area*	*Stepleton*	*Etton*	*Windmill Hill*	*Briar Hill*	*Staines*	*Abingdon*	*Maiden Castle*
Scrapers	351	240	253	1399	181	377	166	421
Edge-trimmed flakes	411	184	410	457	x	x	370	x
Serrated-edge flakes	343	146	219	627+	83	195+	272	188
Piercers	86	49	58	68	34	160	5	17
Leaf arrowheads	29	9	29	132	18	34	17	28
Axeheads, etc	19	15	18	90	3+	21	11	49
'Laurel-leaf' bifacials	3	3	5	25	1	66(?)	5	2
Knives	7	4	1	84+	11	104(?)	10	12
'Fabricators'/rods	7	6	9	2+	2	12	2	4

Leaf-shaped arrowheads are significant for their relative scarcity at causewayed enclosures. Finds of leaf-shaped arrowheads embedded in human bones (H S Green 1984, 35) make it clear that the bow-and-arrow was a practical anti-personnel weapon, whether or not it was also used in hunting. The evidence from two Neolithic enclosures, Crickley Hill, Gloucestershire (Dixon 1988), and Carn Brea, Cornwall (Mercer 1981a), where extremely high numbers of leaf-shaped arrowheads were found – at Crickley Hill in highly significant association with the enclosure entrances – demonstrates the reality of armed conflict at this period.

Thus the low frequency of such arrowheads at Hambledon Hill and other causewayed enclosures indicates that attack and defence were not a regular part of their history or rationale. Even at Windmill Hill, which has one of the largest numbers of arrowheads of all the causewayed enclosures, the absolute total is insignificant in proportion both to their presence at Crickley Hill and Carn Brea and to the huge size of the overall Windmill Hill assemblage. In fact the only causewayed enclosure where the proportion of leaf-shaped arrowheads does seem very high is Hembury, Devon, where excavations in the 1930s produced over 140 examples (Liddell 1935, 162). The precise significance of arrowheads at Hembury is difficult to assess because of limited documentation of the rest of the assemblage, but it is perhaps too soon to dismiss warfare at this enclosure altogether as Brown (1989) has done. Caution is required since the total of 140-plus leaf-shaped arrowheads from Hembury is clearly of a different order of magnitude to the 42 at Hambledon Hill, which is a much larger site and assemblage, especially given the recovery and analytical procedures at Hembury, which can be expected to have resulted in an under-representation of broken arrowheads. Absence of information about the precise sequence of activity at Hembury allows for the possibility that, as at Crickley Hill, the arrowheads may belong to a post-causewayed enclosure phase of the site's history.

At Hambledon Hill, the close association of arrowheads with two skeletons does of course raise the strong possibility of individual acts of aggression; these could be isolated events with no necessary implication for the overall character of the two enclosures or they could, bearing in mind the earlier burning of one and probably two outworks, point to a more overtly bellicose context.

Axeheads, with justification, are seen as implements with the potential for special symbolic significance in Neolithic society (Bradley and Edmonds 1993), but they can also be workaday tools and there seems little doubt that much of the axehead evidence from causewayed enclosures points to the latter. This is particularly so in the way they exhibit evidence for use and reuse, a circumstance repeated at most Neolithic enclosures (Fouéré 1990, fig 20; Smith 1965, 103) and not something necessarily with chronological overtones (Gardiner 1991c, 62–64).

Evidence for structured deposition of axeheads at Hambledon Hill is restricted principally to the lost group of three axeheads found in the west terminal of the inner south cross-dyke ditch. However, this group, and the other cases of axehead 'hoards' known from Combe Hill, Sussex (Drewett 1994, figs 11–12), and Maiden Castle, Dorset (Wheeler 1943, fig 39, 8–9), could be explained as unrecovered caches rather than ritual placements. There might be better grounds for suggesting special treatment in the way that axeheads appear to become preferentially burnt, which could involve a ritual process of some kind (Larsson 2000). Seven of the fifteen axeheads at Hambledon Hill are burnt, which is a higher proportion than for any other tool category and thus unlikely to have arisen naturally.

Ritual practice, however, is not something normally discernible with any ease from collections of lithic artefacts. Indeed, the presence of lithic waste alongside other artefacts deemed in some way special may counteract such an interpretation. For example, a pit from the main enclosure at Hambledon Hill, which has a complete stone axehead, a plain ceramic cup, and large parts of two gabbroic bowls, also has 66 struck lithic artefacts (56 unretouched flakes, 1 burnt unretouched flake, 5 serrated-edge flakes, 3 edge-trimmed flakes, and 1 unclassified burnt piece). It is not easy to see why in such a case the pit should be regarded as ritual just because it has some whole artefacts (*pace* Andersen 1997, 321). Patterns of selection and placement, which are then interpreted as evidence of ritual and ceremonial structured deposition (Pryor 1998, 362), cannot be said to be revealed by the lithic artefact data at Hambledon Hill or elsewhere in any obvious fashion. Such interpretations are inevitably an intellectual imposition (A G Brown 1989, 49) and in a sense abuse the potential of the lithic artefact evidence.

10.2.8 Conclusion

As explained in the introduction, this report has been a long time in gestation and it is inevitably in some ways a victim of the passage of time. Writing the discussion in 2000, using data amassed largely by 1984, one is bound to have some regrets about aspects of what have, and what have not, been included in the analysis. The report has, however, made its antecedents clear and its quantifications and analyses are relevant within the conventions of the study of lithic artefact collections from comparable sites in the second half of the twentieth century. Thus, at least within the canon of reports on lithic artefacts from causewayed enclosures – from Windmill Hill (Smith 1965) to Etton (Middleton 1998) – it will be intelligible in those terms.

That the framework of my own research on lithic artefacts here and elsewhere involves a 'processual economic imperative' (Brown 1995, 29) may to a certain extent be true, but whether that in itself constitutes a useful criticism of lithic studies is open to debate. In fact my own position has shifted somewhat, in part in reaction to the particular emphasis on context of post-processual writers such as A G Brown (1991), by becoming ever more cautious about the level of interpretation which the lithic artefact evidence will support. My advocacy in this report of a 'broad-brush' approach reflects a concern that the complexities of taphonomy and the formation process at Neolithic enclosures have not been, and perhaps cannot be, fully appreciated. This applies to all material culture residues, but especially to those of flint and stone because of their durability and hence inevitable propensity for residuality.

I have considered the question of residuality and other biasing factors more fully elsewhere (Saville 2002). Taken together, these considerations dictate caution in view of the limited potential which lithic artefact assemblages can have for answering specific questions about the meaning and significance of causewayed enclosures. For example, this report has shown that the Hambledon assemblages, like those from other enclosures, do not exhibit the specialised production or higher craft skill which might suggest these sites were centres of social power (Olausson 1997). The lithic artefacts do carry signatures relevant to function, but these are difficult to decipher and anyway relate mostly to the kind of maintenance activities embedded in Neolithic life irrespective of site type (Jensen 1994, 166).

That the lithic artefact evidence can contribute to interpretation is obvious in the case of the third millennium BC Hanford 'flint-mines'. The fact that the tabular flint from this location was not present at all in the flaked artefact assemblage showed that, whatever the function of the quarrying was, it was not to obtain flint for knapping on site. Similarly, unless the view is taken that significant data have been lost with the ploughsoil, the excavated assemblages indicate that any later use of the hilltop did not involve the production, use and discard of flaked lithic artefacts to anything like the same extent as during the early/middle Neolithic period.

The parameters of this production, use and discard associated with the Hambledon Hill enclosures remain frustratingly indefinite, but as this report has shown, I am not persuaded that any of this activity can responsibly be explained in terms of ritual and structured deposition. Even if it were suggested that artefacts from the Neolithic pits and lower ditch fills were in some way ritually deposited, these artefacts are qualitatively no different from those forming the vast bulk of the hilltop collection, which is without primary context. One would have to imagine a great number of archaeologically unrecoverable contexts to accommodate the original deposition of these artefacts in a structured fashion.

Moreover, the flaked lithic assemblages from causewayed enclosures are at base not qualitatively different from those from other contemporary sites. In terms of cultural explanation they are signifying the importance and relevance of the mundane and diurnal. Therefore, my own interpretation of the lithic residues from Hambledon Hill – both the waste and the implements – is that they are the natural concomitant of reasonably intensive normal technological and social activity in association with the construction and use of the enclosures. Had these residues not been present then there would be justification in seeking an interpretation involving the exclusion of everyday activities; as it is, the opposite must be the case.

Such an interpretation, that the residues are essentially the outcome of 'domestic' occupation, has of course been advanced by many excavators of causewayed enclosures (eg Avery 1982, 40; Bamford 1985, 134; Sharples 1991, 253–7), and does not by itself stand in contradiction to the concept of ritual deposition. So my final point would be to emphasise that the inclusion of flaked lithic residues within a cosmological construct of the ritualisation of all depositional activities at causewayed enclosures (Whittle and Pollard 1999) is not, and cannot be, validated as such by the artefacts described here from Hambledon Hill.

10.2.9 Minor assemblages from excavations away from the main Neolithic areas

The hillfort spur

The hillfort trench produced a small assemblage of 192 pieces of flint (Table 10.60) which is dominated by unclassified burnt pieces. These are mostly of 'potboiler' type and derive in the main from contexts directly associated with the Iron Age occupation. Only one of the pieces from other categories, an unretouched flake (HH86 162), was burnt.

The struck flint, irrespective of context, appears largely uniform in character and condition with that from the adjacent Neolithic enclosure, though there are no individually diagnostic pieces in the absence of any classifiable implements. One of the miscellaneous retouched pieces (HH86 171) could be regarded as a denticulate-type scraper, another example of which (HH77 1524), came from a superficial context adjacent to the main causewayed enclosure.

The relatively high weight of the miscellaneous pieces is due to the inclusion of a single large flake (HH86 64; weight 199 g), which has a 'bruised', bifacially spalled edge, of the type often associated with chopping bone or antler (Barton 1986). This piece was from an Iron Age occupation context and, in the absence of any parallels from the Hambledon or Stepleton enclosures, could perhaps indicate some later prehistoric *ad hoc* usage.

Everley Water Meadow

The typology of the 332 struck lithic pieces recovered from this location is given in Table 10.60. These pieces are subdivided into those from the south area, the north area, and from fieldwalking in the 1982 season. The only significant contexts, both of middle Bronze Age date, are F10 in the south area and the burnt mound and its underlying soil in the north area. Neither of these contexts is prolific in terms of struck lithic artefacts nor do they provide any diagnostic implement types. All the pieces are of flint except one chert scraper (SM82 155).

The most distinctive find is the chisel arrowhead (EWM83 351; from trench 1, layer 16), of approximate late Neolithic date (Green 1984). The arrowhead (Fig 10.42: 164) is in sharp condition, uncorticated, and

Table 10.60 Lithic artefacts from the hillfort spur, Rolf's Wood, Coombe Bottom, Stepleton Lynchet, and Everley Water Meadow

Weights are in grams, rounded to the nearest gram

						Everley Water Meadow					
		Hillfort	*Rolf's Wood*	*Coombe Bottom*	*Stepleton lynchet*	*South area F10*	*North area burnt mound*	*South area general*	*North area general*	*Field-walking*	*Total*
Unretouched flakes	No.	72	1	28	2	3	22	42	53	12	132
	Wt	*581*	*12*	*249*	*24*	*8*	*262*	*431*	*409*	*202*	*1312*
Cores	No.		1	1			1	3		3	7
	Wt		*78*	*54*			*39*	*134*		*238*	*411*
Core fragment	No.	1					1				1
	Wt	*45*					*35*				*35*
Flaked lumps	No.								1	1	2
	Wt								*84*	*68*	*152*
Edge-trimmed flakes	No.			2			1				1
	Wt			*30*			*11*				*11*
Scrapers	No.						3	4*	2		9
	Wt						*47*	*91*	*64*		*202*
Piercers	No.			3		1		1		1	3
	Wt			*15*		*14*		*9*		*43*	*66*
Chisel arrowhead	No.							1			1
	Wt							*4*			*4*
Flake from pol. axehead	No.								1		1
	Wt								*9*		*9*
?Gunflint	No.		1								
	Wt		*9*								
Misc retouched	No.	5	3	2			4	14	7	3	28
	Wt	*302*	*33*	*92*			*20*	*211*	*134*	*29*	*394*
Unclass burnt	No.	114	43		1	25	24	90	5	3	147
	Wt	*1339*	*1385*		*27*	*256*	*208*	*1391*	*32*	*106*	*1993*
Total	No.	192	49	36	3	29	56	155	69	23	332
	Wt	*2267*	*1517*	*440*	*51*	*278*	*622*	*2271*	*732*	*686*	*4589*

* one of these scrapers is of chert

Note: Total refers to Everley Water Meadow only

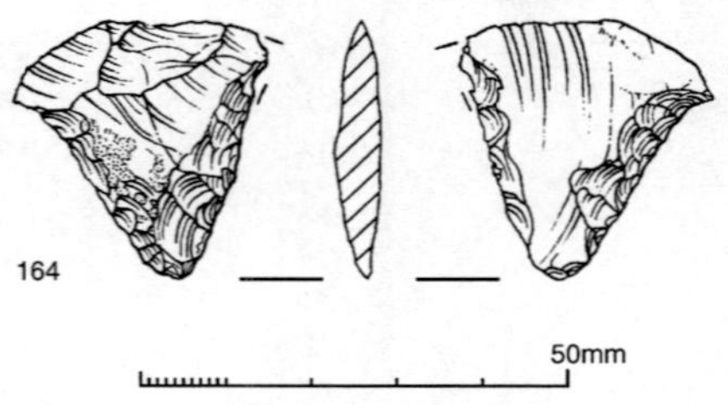

Fig 10.42 Chisel arrowhead (EWM83 353, Everley Water Meadow, Trench 1, layer 16).

intact, save for damage at one upper corner, possibly the result of impact spalling. Isolated arrowheads are particularly liable to be chance finds and there is nothing else in this assemblage to which it need obviously relate. The only parallel from the whole of the Hambledon Hill flint collection is the oblique arrowhead from the main enclosure ditch (Fig 10.15: 142), also likely to be of late Neolithic date and also a possible casual loss during hunting, not necessarily related to settlement or other activity in the immediate vicinity.

The nine scrapers include at least one example (EWM84 229), a large end scraper on a cortical flake from the north area, which would comfortably fit the hilltop assemblage. Two of the scrapers have interesting features. One, an end scraper on a blade (EWM83 400), from beneath the burnt mound, has elaborate trimming on both lateral edges; the other, a broad end scraper (EWM83 394), from the burnt mound, has notching either side of the base, removing the platform and creating a stubby tang.

The small flake from a polished flint axehead (EWM84 18) is abraded, with secondary edge damage, and is clearly residual. One of the miscellaneous retouched pieces (EWM84 254), from the north area, is a possible gunflint, though not regular enough for positive identification.

At least one implement, a scraper (SM82 51) from the south area, has its retouch through a corticated flake surface and there are other signs of the exploitation of previously struck flint. Another of the scrapers (EWM84 317), from the burnt mound and itself burnt, and one of the miscellaneous retouched pieces (SM82 49), from the south area, are on natural, thermally produced flakes. There is also some use of 'gravel'-type raw material, as well as of irregular nodules, such as the cylindrical nodule used for one of the cores (EWM83 384) from the south area.

In addition to the flints described here, over 180 kg of burnt flint was recorded from the burnt mound but not kept. This is likely to have comprised unclassified burnt material of 'potboiler' type. Despite this apparent abundance of burnt flint, of the struck material only a relatively few pieces showed signs of burning (five unretouched flakes; one scraper; and one miscellaneous retouched piece).

This assemblage is, on the basis of typology and condition, likely to be of mixed chronology and is anyway, if the unclassified burnt pieces are excluded, so restricted that it could not be a helpful indicator of activity or site function. The small number of core pieces suggests that knapping was not especially significant at or near the areas excavated. Of the artefacts which are in any way distinctive, apart from the arrowhead, some could relate to the same time frame as the Neolithic hilltop activity. There is no specific element of the assemblage, other perhaps than the (largely unretained) burnt flint, which is readily assignable to the middle Bronze Age in association with the pottery from this location. On the other hand there is almost certainly a post-Neolithic representation within the struck flint, and it is entirely possible that some of the less heavily corticated flakes could belong to the same phase as the pottery.

10.2.10 Flint artefacts recovered from surface survey

Surface surveys were undertaken around Hambledon Hill between 1976 and 1982 (most intensively in 1976–77) as part of a study of the local prehistoric settlement patterns. All available ploughed fields within an approximate radius of 4 km around Hambledon Hill were surveyed. The survey involved linear traverses at 20 m intervals, with total recovery of surface artefacts within a scan-range of about 1 m to each side of the traverse, thus producing an approximate ten per cent sample (Ch 2).

This surface recovery produced a collection of over 7000 flints (weighing over 171 kg), of which virtually all, except for two post-medieval gunflints, were indicative of prehistoric activity (Table 10.61).Three major concentrations were located, and the typological breakdown in Table 10.61 isolates these from the remainder. Several caveats need to be entered about the typology, because of the often rather poor condition of these surface flints. For example, it is surprising that even one serrated-edge flake could be identified, since this kind of delicate retouch is highly vulnerable once the implement is incorporated in ploughsoil. The same applies to edge-trimmed flakes in general, which are unlikely to survive in easily identifiable form as surface finds. Scrapers on the other hand are highly resilient in the sense of remaining identifiable, because of their compact, robust morphology. The normal criteria for identification of miscellaneous retouched pieces cannot be applied to this material because of the prevalence of removals which could be either retouch or damage. Only those pieces on which the removals appear regular and relatively continuous are classified as retouched. The implement illustrated in Fig 10.43: 165 demonstrates some of these problems: the outline drawings show the extent of obvious modern damage on this very robust tool. Implements with thinner, sharper edges would obviously be even more vulnerable.

Table 10.61 Hambledon environs survey: flint artefact totals and major concentrations

Type	*Shroton Spur*	*Boyne's Lane*	*Smuggler's Lane*	*Remainder*	*Total*
Unretouched flakes	1070	1705	944	2244	5963
Cores	49	47	24	71	191
Core fragments	4	8	2	6	20
Flaked lumps	8	29	2	23	62
Abraded lumps				2	2
Hammerstones				2	2
Serrated-edge flake				1	1
Scrapers	41	77	61	169	348
Piercers	3	52	11	22	88
Transverse arrowheads		2	1	1	4
Barbed-and-tanged arrowheads		1	1		2
Flake from polished flint axehead			1		1
Knives				2	2
Pick		1			1
Unclassified bifacial pieces	1	1			2
Rods		1		1	2
Combination tool			1		1
Gunflints				2	2
Miscellaneous retouched pieces	18	180	42	156	396
Unclassified burnt pieces				25	25
Total	1194	2104	1090	2727	7115

The Shroton spur concentration contained material which in terms of typology, technology, and raw material is indistinguishable from the excavated Hambledon assemblages, and points to a continuation of the Neolithic activity on this area of the hilltop. In so doing it also reinforces the picture of virtually exclusive Neolithic flint production and use on the hilltop, without obvious contamination from artefacts of earlier or later periods. As might be expected, the surface flints from the area of the Hambledon hilltop extending between the Hanford and Stepleton spurs, which comprised a collection of 772 artefacts, also matched the excavated assemblages very closely.

The two other concentrations occurred in the east of Iwerne Stepleton parish at Boyne's Lane (ST 891 125) and Smuggler's Lane (ST 880 116), where they probably formed part of what was in reality a single extensive settlement or industrial area, exploiting the local deposits of Clay-with-Flints (Fig 2.2). The collections from these areas are in marked contrast to the hilltop assemblage and on typological grounds can be classed as mainly late Neolithic/early Bronze Age. They are characterised by a predominance of scrapers, piercers, and miscellaneous retouched pieces, as well as by the presence of more culturally diagnostic forms such as the three transverse and two barbed-and-tanged arrowheads. The pick and the elaborate rod (Fig 10.43: 165) perhaps also relate to this time-frame, though the latter is more heavily discoloured than most of the assemblage. The scatter is given greater archaeological significance by the presence within it of a ploughed-out round barrow at ST 887 119 and a cropmark enclosure system centred on ST 891 126. Clearly this location around Everley Hill Farm could be of considerable importance for the study of later prehistoric settlement in the Hambledon area. This location may also possibly have been the source of the late Neolithic 'heavy flint' industry from Stourpaine parish mentioned by Piggott (1954, 280–3), although this cannot now be ascertained with certainty (F Healy, pers comm.).

Other distinctive assemblages among the surface collections were rare. An exception was a group of 66 flints centred on ST 890 133, which, although comprising only knapping debris without any diagnostic implements, could be regarded as Mesolithic in character and may well correlate with the Iwerne Minster Mesolithic site identified by Summers (1941). Otherwise the collections of flints from individual areas were too small, too mixed, or too characterless for any typo-chronological assessment, other than to say that indications of earlier Neolithic flintworking resembling the excavated assemblages were not visible away from the hilltop. This situation requires archaeological explanation, but there are at least two potentially biasing factors to be considered. Firstly, the survey was rather too restricted in area for its results to be conclusive. The dictation of the study areas by the availability of ploughed fields introduced a non-random bias which could have weighed against the discovery of preferred foci of earlier Neolithic settlement or activity. Secondly, post-depositional factors such as colluviation could bias the relative visibility of earlier Neolithic as opposed to later scatters. In this regard the propensity for surface-recovered flintwork to reflect predominantly later activity on sites where excavation has shown both earlier and later activity to be present, should be considered (Healy 1983; 1987; 1988a).

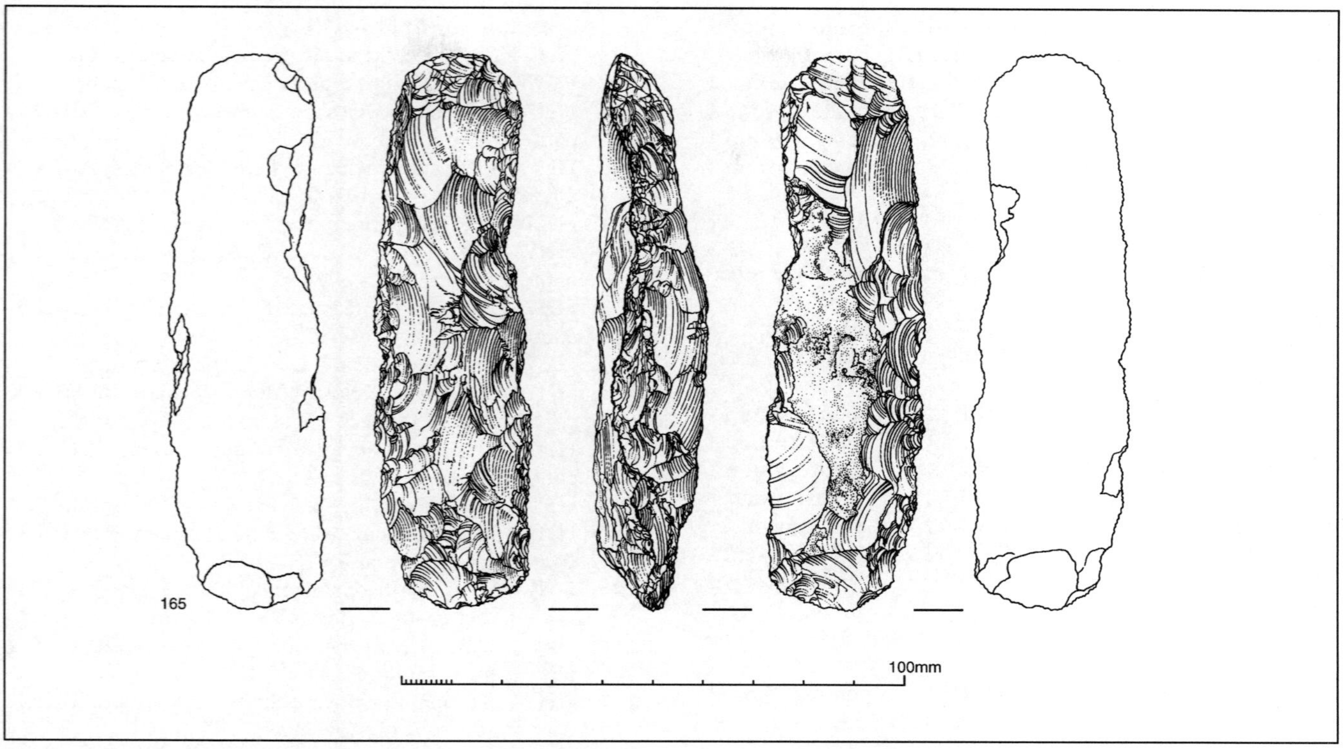

Fig 10.43 Rod (HHS 76, Hambledon survey, surface find from NGR ST 891 125). The outline drawings show the extent of the modern damage affecting this piece.

Alternatively, the survey results could be taken at face value to suggest the existence of intensive early/middle Neolithic settlement and lithic exploitation only on the Hambledon hilltop, with later settlement and exploitation primarily away from the hilltop. Such a hypothesis, of mutually exclusive zones through time, could be of general importance in assessing the socio-economic dimension to prehistoric settlement in the area, and might confirm the existence of particular historical conditions for the apparently unusual use of the highest ground during the earlier Neolithic. Whatever the conclusion, it is of considerable interest that the overall pattern of lithic material produced from this survey matches that obtained in a wider survey of Cranborne Chase (Barrett *et al* 1991).

10.2.11 Catalogue of illustrated struck lithic artefacts

Cores

10 HH76 2110, class A2, main enclosure, segment 14, L11, context group 7, phase VI
11 HH76 2166, class D, main enclosure, segment 15, L7, context group 4, phase III
12 HH76 2613, class C3, main enclosure, segment 12, L11, context group 4, phase III

Serrated-edge flakes

13 HH77 1770, Neolithic pit N F7i, L3, context group 1
14 HH77 1974, Neolithic pit N F10, L3, context group 1
15 HH77 1489, Neolithic pit N F42, L3, context group 1
16 HH77 1562, Neolithic pit N F6, L4, context group 1
17 HH77 1879, Neolithic pit N F25, L3, context group 1
18 HH77 2133, Neolithic pit N F7iii, L3, context group 1
19 HH77 1974, Neolithic pit N F10, L3, context group 1
20 HH77 1762, Neolithic pit N F7i, L3, context group 1
21 HH77 1819, Neolithic pit N F7i, L3, context group 1
22 HH77 2133, Neolithic pit N F7iii, L3, context group 1
23 HH77 1921, Neolithic pit N F7iii, L3, context group 1
24 HH77 1745, Neolithic pit N F25, L4, context group 1
25 HH77 1929, Neolithic pit N F6, L5, context group 1
26 HH77 1493, Neolithic pit N F7i, L3, context group 1
27 HH77 2133, Neolithic pit N F7iii, L3, context group 1
28 HH77 2132, Neolithic pit N F10, L3, context group 1
29 HH77 2024, Neolithic pit N F82, L4, context group 1
30 HH77 2133, Neolithic pit N F7iii, L3, context group 1
31 HH77 2133, Neolithic pit N F7iii, L3, context group 1
32 HH77 1729, Neolithic pit N F82, L3, context group 1
33 HH77 1605, Neolithic pit N F22, L3, context group 1
34 HH77 1879, Neolithic pit N F25, L3, context group 1
35 HH77 1493, Neolithic pit N F7i, L3, context group 1
36 HH77 1486, Neolithic pit N F7i, L3, context group 1
37 HH77 1844, Neolithic pit N F22, L3, context group 1
38 HH77 2217, Neolithic pit N F7iii, L4, context group 1
39 HH77 2037, Neolithic pit N F7i, context group 1
40 HH77 1970, Neolithic pit N F22, L4, context group 1
41 HH77 2265, Neolithic pit N F7iii, L3, context group 1
42 HH77 1438, Neolithic pit N F10, L3, context group 1
43 HH77 2265, Neolithic pit N F7iii, L3, context group 1
44 HH77 2133, Neolithic pit N F7iii, L3, context group 1
45 HH77 2265, Neolithic pit N F7iii, L3, context group 1
46 HH77 1562, Neolithic pit N F6, L4, context group 1
47 HH77 1672, Neolithic pit N F42, L3, context group 1
48 HH77 1462, Neolithic pit N F7i, L3, context group 1
49 HH77 1754, Neolithic pit N F42, L3, context group 1
50 HH77 2265, Neolithic pit N F7iii, L3, context group 1

51 HH77 1605, Neolithic pit N F22, L3, context group 1
52 HH77 1389, Neolithic pit N F6, L3, context group 1
53 HH77 1489, Neolithic pit N F42, L3, context group 1
54 HH77 2265, Neolithic pit N F7iii, L3, context group 1
55 HH77 1489, Neolithic pit N F42, L3, context group 1
56 HH77 2107, Neolithic pit N F25, L4, context group 1

Edge-trimmed flakes

57 HH77 2301, Neolithic pit N F7iv, L3, context group 1
58 Class A HH77 1879, Neolithic pit N F25, L3, context group 1
59 HH77 2283, Neolithic pit N F93, context group 1
60 Class A HH77 2296, Neolithic pit N F7vi, L3, context group 1
61 HH77 1605, Neolithic pit N F22, L3, context group 1
62 HH77 1605, Neolithic pit N F22, L3, context group 1
63 HH77 1484, Neolithic pit N F22, L3, context group 1
64 HH77 1462, Neolithic pit N F7i, L3, context group 1
65 HH77 2283, Neolithic pit N F93, context group 1
66 HH77 2265, Neolithic pit N F7iii, L3, context group 1
67 HH77 2201, Neolithic pit N F7v, L3, context group 1
68 HH77 1762, Neolithic pit N F7i, L3, context group 1
69 Class A HH77 1879, Neolithic pit N F25, L3, context group 1
70 HH77 1729, Neolithic pit N F82, L3, context group 1
71 Class A HH77 1879, Neolithic pit N F25, L3, context group 1
72 HH77 1958, Neolithic pit N F25, L3, context group 1
73 HH77 1974, Neolithic pit N F10, L4, context group 1
74 HH77 2296, Neolithic pit N F7vi, L3, context group 1
75 Class A HH77 1438, Neolithic pit N F10, L3, context group 1
76 Class A HH77 1970, Neolithic pit N F22, L4, context group 1
77 Class A HH77 1904, Neolithic pit N F90, L3, context group 1
78 Class A HH77 2301, Neolithic pit N F7iv, L3, context group 1
79 Class A HH77 1891, Neolithic pit N F42, L3, context group 1
80 Class A HH77 1730, Neolithic pit N F90, L5, context group 1
81 HH77 1614, Neolithic pit N F19, layer 3, context group 1
82 Class A HH77 1974, Neolithic pit N F10, L3, context group 1
83 HH77 1729, Neolithic pit N F82, L3, context group 1
84 Chert HH77 2265, Neolithic pit N F7iii, L3, context group 1
86 HH77 2245, Neolithic pit N F90, L4, context group 1
85 Class A HH77 1983, hollow N F7, context group 46

Scrapers

87 HH74 1143, Neolithic pit A F64, context group 1
88 HH74 1111, Neolithic pit A F64, context group 1
89 HH74 1123, Neolithic pit A F57, context group 1
90 HH74 1184, Neolithic pit A F116, context group 1
91 HH74 1165, Neolithic pit A F78, context group 1
92 HH74 1214a, Neolithic pit A F120, context group 1
93 HH74 1059, main enclosure ditch, segment 4, AII L6, context group 7, phase VI
94 HH74 307, main enclosure ditch, segment 4, AIII L8, context group 7, phase VI
95 HH74 342, main enclosure ditch, segment 4, AIII L9, context group 4, phase III
96 HH74 653, main enclosure ditch, segment 4, AII L5, context group 7, phase VI
97 HH74 1149, Neolithic pit A F74, context group 1
98 HH74 1131, Neolithic pit A F64, context group 1
99 HH74 895, main enclosure ditch, segment 4, AIII L7, context group 7, phase VI
100 HH74 896, main enclosure ditch, segment 4, AIII L7, context group 7, phase VI
101 HH74 1071, Neolithic pit A F62, context group 1
102 HH74 652, main enclosure ditch, segment 4, AII L5, context group 7, phase VI
103 HH74 574, main enclosure ditch, segment 4, AII L5, context group 7, phase VI
104 HH74 951, Neolithic pit A F45, context group 1
105 HH74 659, main enclosure ditch, segment 3, AII L5, context group 7, phase VI
106 HH74 1048, main enclosure ditch, segment 4, AII L5, context group 7, phase VI
107 HH74 1207, Neolithic pit A F105, context group 1
108 HH74 608, main enclosure ditch, segment 3, AII L5, context group 7, phase VI
109 HH74 1026, main enclosure ditch, , segment 4, AII L5, context group 7, phase VI
110 HH74 1081, main enclosure ditch, segment 4, AII L10, context group 4, phase III
111 HH74 898, main enclosure ditch, segment 4, AIII L7, context group 7, phase VI
112 HH74 586, main enclosure ditch, segment 3 or 4, AII L4, context group 6, phase V
113 HH74 899, main enclosure ditch, segment 4, AIII L7, context group 7, phase VI
114 HH74 770, main enclosure ditch, segment 4, AIII L9, context group 4, phase III
115 HH74 1213, Neolithic pit A F114, context group 1
116 HH74 666, main enclosure ditch, segment 2, AI L4, context group 7, phase VI
117 HH74 605, main enclosure ditch, segment 4, AII L5, context group 7, phase VI
118 HH74 1214, Neolithic pit A F120, context group 1

Piercers

119 HH77 925, site N, ploughsoil context group 46
120 HH77 1788, Neolithic pit N F25, L4, context group 1

Knives

121 HH75 1438, main enclosure ditch, segment 8, L1, context group 11, phase VIII/g
122 HH75 1749, main enclosure ditch, segment 8, site F L3, context group 10, phase VIII/a
123 HH74 454, main enclosure ditch, segment 4, L2, context group 11, phase VIII/b-g

Leaf-shaped arrowheads

124 HH76 811, main enclosure ditch, segment 17, L6, context group 7, phase VI
125 HH76 434, main enclosure ditch, segment 17, L3, context group 10, phase VIII/a
126 HH76 2622, main enclosure ditch, segment 6.1, L5A, context group 7, phase VI
127 HH75 6, Site C, ploughsoil, context group 46
128 HH77 1587, Neolithic pit N F1, L3 context group 1
129 HH75 1124, inner east cross-dyke ditch, segment 4, L6, context group 15, phase VI
130 HH75 1290, inner east cross-dyke ditch, segment 5, L3, context group 17, phase VIII/a
131 ST80 1234, Stepleton enclosure, segment 2, L5A, context group 58, phase IV

132 ST80 1877, outer Stepleton outwork, segment 3, L5, context group 77, among ribs of young adult male skeleton
133 ST79 1867, inner Stepleton outwork, segment 5, cutting 7, L2, context group 68, phase VIII/a
134 HH77 1253, Neolithic pit N F11, L3, context group 1
135 HH77 532, site N, ploughsoil, context group 46
136 HH77 1498, recent pit N F44, L3, context group 46
137 HH77 803, site N, ploughsoil, context group 46
138 HH77 1586, Neolithic pit N F1, L3, context group 1
139 ST78 2730, Inner Stepleton outwork, segment 7, quadrant 4, L4, context group 64, phase III
140 ST80 1425, Middle Stepleton outwork, segment 5, unit 5, L6, context group 71, phase I
141 chert, HH77 1539, Neolithic pit N F42, L3, context group 1

Oblique arrowhead

142 HH75 1233, main enclosure ditch, segment 10, L6, context group 9, phase VII/a

Tanged arrowhead

143 ST78 1, Stepleton spur, ploughsoil, context group 82

Laurel-leaf bifacial pieces

144 HH76 26, main enclosure ditch, segment 13, L1, context group 11, phase VIII/g
145 HH77 1517, Neolithic pit N F5, L5, context group 1
147 ST79 1569, inner Stepleton outwork, segment 7, cutting 15, L3A, context group 65, phase V
148 HH76 1335, area of main enclosure ditch, site G, unstratified, context group 11
150 ST79 1973, Neolithic pit 2A F154, context group 53

Unclassified bifacial pieces

146 ST81 2760, Stepleton spur, Area 4E, unstratified, context group 82
149 HH76 516, main enclosure ditch, Site H, context group 10, phase VIII, segment 13, L2
151 HH77 862, Site N, ploughsoil, context group 46

Polished flint axeheads and axehead fragments

152 HH74 1147, Neolithic pit A F71 context group 1
153 HH75 151, outer east cross-dyke ditch, segment 2, L4, context group 22.1, phase VII/a
154 ST81 1859, Stepleton enclosure, segment 16, unit 12, L3, context group 57, phase V
155 HH77 505, main enclosure ditch, segment 1, F5, context group 7, phase VI
156 ST78 1300, Neolithic pit 1A F228, L2, context group 53
157 ST77 25, Inner Stepleton outwork, context group 68, segment 8, L2.

Picks

158 HH75 2029, main enclosure ditch, segment 8, site F L6, context group 7, phase VI
159 HH76 1977, main enclosure ditch, segment 14, L3, context group 10, phase VIII/a

Rods

160 HH74 1104, Hambledon enclosure, Site N, hollow N F7, L3, context group 46
161 ST78 18, area 1A, ploughsoil, context group 82
162 ST81 3023, grave 4B F712, L1

'Fabricator'

163 ST78 1137, inner Stepleton outwork segment 6, L2, context group 68, phase VIII/a

Chisel arrowhead

164 EWM83 351, Everley Water Meadow, trench 1, L16.

Rod

165 HHS76, Hambledon survey, surface find from NGR ST 891 125. The outline drawings show the extent of the modern damage affecting this piece.

11 In conclusion ...

It now remains to draw together the various strands of information, interpretation, and reconstruction that have emerged from the different archaeological and other analytical processes that have been directed at the massive accrual of data resulting from the twelve seasons of excavation (very largely funded by English Heritage or its predecessor bodies) at Hambledon Hill between 1974 and 1986. During that time some 102 weeks of excavations were conducted seasonally in July–September, employing many hundreds of (often, but by no means always) young excavators under a dedicated, but necessarily changing, team of supervisors. The cost of the excavation programme is difficult to express in terms that mean very much to a financial view operating in the year 2006. Every effort was made to limit costs and much help in kind was received locally, from the School of Signals, Blandford, and from Edinburgh University. Put into 2006 money terms, each full season cost in the order of £50,000 (1974–82) with 1983–84 and 1986 costing a fraction of that sum. Added to this was a research associate post from 1975–1986 to secure the excavation record and to manage post-excavation demands (in 2006 terms *c* £15,000 pa). In 1996 English Heritage agreed to fund a publication/further analysis programme totalling some £200,000. The timescale that brings an excavation to publication some thirty years after it was commenced and nearly twenty after its completion is a matter of embarrassment, but it can honestly be said that work has never ceased upon the project, that much of that work has been achieved at very low cost and, most importantly, that this prolonged maturation has led to the exploitation of a number of routes of enquiry that would have been unimaginable in 1974 (or indeed 1986). It is a matter of considerable relief, and some shared pride, that at no stage has the excavation record been found inadequate to those unforeseen demands made upon it.

The aim and objectives of the excavation as undertaken in 1974 and elaborated thenceforward have been set out in section 1.7 of Chapter 1. It now remains to draw together the evidence accrued from all sources towards a conclusion.

11.1 The nature of Neolithic enclosure construction at Hambledon Hill

Roger Mercer

It is the intention of this section to examine, first of all, the nature of the enclosive works at Hambledon – what form did they take? – and having reached, hopefully, some persuasive conclusions upon that point, to discuss how they were constructed and something of the ergonomics of that task. This is undertaken in the face of considerable difficulties posed by the extremely damaged nature of this site and the virtual absence of evidence for earthwork construction other than the secondary evidence of the filling of the quarry ditches, whence the material for the construction of the earthworks was extracted.

The evidence that there were earthworks at all takes two forms. First and almost universally the phenomenon termed during the excavation 'protected chalk' – a term retained in this publication. This comprised a band, usually very clearly discernible and easily traced and measured, that almost universally ran behind the excavated causewayed ditches, usually with a berm of 'non-protected' highly eroded chalk in between, as in Figure 3.9. This band of protected chalk, often scored by recent ploughing, was homogeneous, usually solid, in contrast to the 'compacted rubble' effect of natural chalk elsewhere on the site, and often of a far purer whiteness than the brown-stained broken chalk surface surrounding it. Usually the surface of this band of 'protected chalk' was elevated by up to 0.20 m over the corrupted chalk surface around it and this 'hump' was reflected in the surface profile of the turf prior to excavation. This visible 'hump' constantly provoked the hope that structural bank material might survive *in situ*, but there are no certain instances where this proved to be the case. In rare instances where such material *might* have survived it was so disturbed by root, animal, and agricultural action as to be evidentially uninformative, as on site P (3.3.2, 3.3.4). It seems to be the only reasonable conclusion that this consistently located band of protected chalk was the 'shadow' or 'footprint' of the bank construction, whatever form that took, within the interior of the quarry-source causewayed ditches. The questions of course remain: how did this 'footprint' come about and to what degree does this 'footprint' represent the actual extent of the original bank?

To answer the first of these questions is very difficult, and some suggestions are all that can be made. Upon those suggestions will depend the answer to the second question. The band of protected chalk will not, presumably, be so obliging as to represent the precise or nearly precise outline of the original bank erected within, and with material obtained from, the ditch.

This obstacle will have eroded and decayed relatively early in its life, spreading its contained bulk, both inwards towards the interior and outwards towards the quarry ditch. It is in this rapidly arrived at, decayed, state that it will have settled down to create the 'footprint' which we have recognised – a process involving many centuries, even millennia, of probably complex and ill-understood interactions. The decayed earthwork would still have presented a considerable obstacle to agricultural and other human activity, if not to the less dramatic forces of solution and decomposition. However, a cuspal point will have been reached when erosive forces began to eat back into the protective cladding of the collapsed obstacle – thus slowly diminishing the extent of the protected chalk surface. It is likely, however, that this invasive process began quite (in relative terms) recently. Furthermore, judging by the damage inflicted on this band of hard chalk by a very recent episode of punitive ploughing, this diminishing effect will have been very slow. It is therefore the *opinion* of this close observer of the site that, if anything, this protected band will generally retain a width somewhat greater than the original, constructed width of the obstacle (or bank). This view is supported by the fact that, in those very few instances over the site as a whole where the groundfast remains of external cladding for such an obstacle survived, they were almost always located *within* the protected chalk band. If we accept that the protected chalk, where it survives in coherent masses on the site, represents something slightly greater than the width of the original, now vanished, earthwork obstacle then, if the assumption is made that all of the material dug from the ditch was incorporated to construct this obstacle, certain conclusions follow. Figure 11.1 shows, to scale, a typical ditch cross-section, located beside the requisite width of

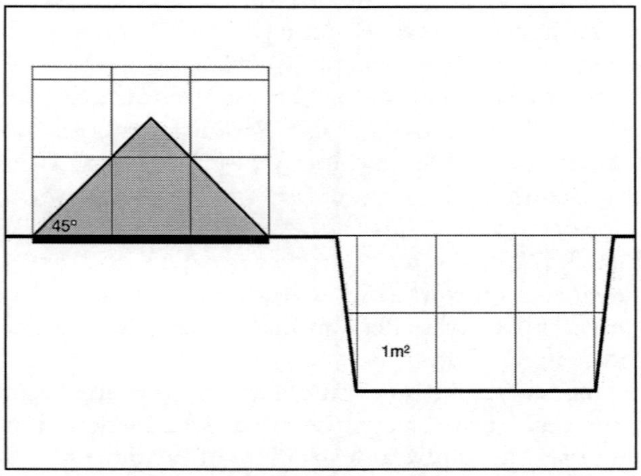

Fig 11.1 Diagram to show a ditch with a volume of 6.5 cu m per linear metre with reconstructions of a 'dump' rampart (at a 45° angle of rest) and a box frame rampart, both set over a 3 m-wide band of protected chalk. The illustration shows that a vertical frame is necessary if 6.5 cu m are to be piled onto the 3 m-wide base.

protected chalk 'platform'. There is drawn, conventionally, as much of the content of the ditch as would fit onto the 'platform' at the maximum angle of stability for chalk rubble, 45° (McConnell, 1919, 93). It should be noted at this stage that the Overton Down experimental earthwork (to which we shall return) was piled at 30°, although the maximum angle of repose was found to be 37.5° (Jewell 1963b, 37) – the comparison is made all the more telling by the construction of the obstacle at Hambledon on a varying but consistently present slope.

In this diagrammatic representation no account has been taken of the expansion factor brought about by the conversion of solid chalk bedrock to rubble by the process of digging. The reason for this is the difficulty of establishing a figure. During the Overton Down experiment the expansion factor on digging and dumping was ascertained to be 1:1.42 or 42%. McConnell, without much explanation, suggests (1919, 93) that 15 units of dug solid chalk will furnish 16 rubble units in embankment, an expansion factor of only 7% – although there is a hint in the text that this may reflect ramming of material. In sum, it will be seen that this exercise was conducted using the maximum conceivable angle of rest and with no allowance for an uncertain but inevitable expansion factor. These elements, which will, of course, tend to underestimate the volume of the bank, will be, to some extent, mitigated by the existence of un-dug causeways – themselves possibly reflecting the lack of necessity for further dug material to furnish a bank of the required stature.

Comparing volume extracted against the width of protected chalk as a two-dimensional exercise, it is apparent that a bank built 'dump' fashion from the entire contents of the ditch would oversail the available width. If the interpretation of the 'protected chalk' as a relict reflection of bank width is accepted, this observation would appear to the writer to reflect an uncomfortable superfluity of dug material for the available bank space – if dump construction obtained. In the same figure a reconstructed 'box-rampart' configuration is set out, again two-dimensionally, reflecting the maximally efficient profile of such a structure, near-square in section. Such a reconstructed structure will sit comfortably within the width of the protected chalk at all points, allowing some space for initial lateral dilapidation, as discussed above. This exercise would suggest a 'wall' 1.5–4 m wide and 1.5–3 m high.

The difficulty in pressing this model of obstacle construction lies, of course, in the general, but not total, lack of evidence for the earthfast, chalk-cut postholes that would be the *sine qua non* of such a structure. Yet this is, perhaps, an objection that can be overcome. Colluvial erosion, agricultural destruction and dissolution of the chalk surface have been massive at Hambledon. The truncated fillings of features in the interior of the main causewayed enclosure suggest the loss of up to 0.50 m of bedrock surface (see 1.3). It is likely that such a degree of erosion would eliminate, or,

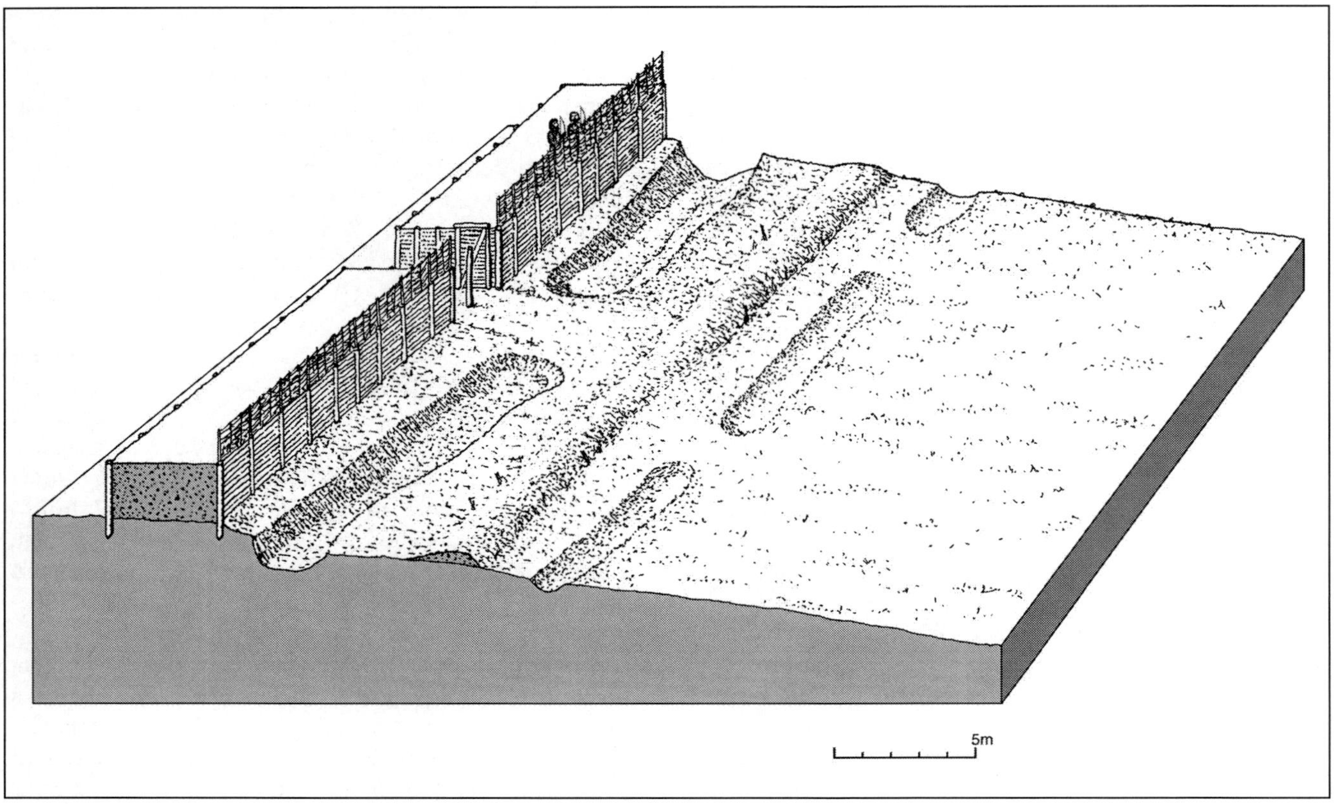

Fig 11.2 Reconstruction of the gateway in the inner Stepleton outwork.

at least, render unrecognisable the sockets of such posts. That such structures did exist on the site is not in doubt. The inner Stepleton outwork is in every way the most massive construction on the site. It seems likely that surviving remnants of its structure are due to this enhanced stature and to its partial protection beneath the head lynchet of a later prehistoric field system. Set within (by a margin of about 1 metre both at rearward and forward edges) the band of protected chalk would appear to be two constructional phases of a box-frame rampart. The earlier was a substantial construction 4 m wide. The later (which may have pertained only to this gateway area) was the slighter of the two, somewhat, less than 3 m in width. The position of the surviving sockets would suggest that the preferred interval was about 1.5 m centre-to-centre at both front and rear of the 'wall' (Fig 3.111). Reconstruction of this length of earthwork (Fig 11.2) would indicate that, from the known scale of the ditch at this point and the known width of the rampart, the height of the obstacle would be approximately 3 m. Those familiar with the 'ten foot wall' on assault courses will need no convincing of how daunting an obstacle this can be. This height may, of course, have been augmented by some form of breastwork.

Further indication of the nature of this particular structure emerged some 80 m to the east in segment 6, where a bank deposit occurred in the bottom of the ditch that would appear to represent elements of timber framework predominantly executed in hazel (Fig 3.99, Pls VIII–IX). At this point only one or two post-sockets survived within the protected chalk – the slightest of evidence for any wall structure. This deposit is, however, more easily interpreted as some sort of hurdling panel that, set between timber uprights, would have performed the necessary retentive function for the rubble wall-filling and may, of course, have been carried on upwards as a breastwork structure. A similar structure is evidenced in the more limited investigations of the Shroton spur outwork (see 3.4; Figs 3.75–6, 3.78, Pl IV). Vestigial postholes furthermore survive in the less well-preserved areas of protected chalk flanking some of the other earthworks: the main enclosure (Fig 3.6), the inner east cross-dyke (Figs 3.37–8), the inner south cross-dyke (Fig 3.42), the western outwork (Fig 3.45), the middle and outer Stepleton outworks (Fig 3.81), and both Hanford outworks (Fig 3.136).

One further line of enquiry remains to us in pursuit of the evanescent bank structure at Hambledon. This comprises the nature and structure of the ditch fillings which may tell a story about how this structure collapsed. If we compare these fillings with those accumulating within the ditch of the Overton Down experimental earthwork, ie from a dump earthwork set behind a ditch of similar scale, their structure is very different. It must immediately be pointed out that four factors preclude direct comparison between the two:

1. At Overton the earthwork was constructed on, to all intents and purposes, level ground while at Hambledon an element, more or less, of slope must enter into the equation.
2. At Overton the ditch was left to silt without intervention, while at Hambledon consistent disturbance of ditch fillings was the rule, not the exception.
3. At Overton a particularly wide berm was deliberately left, to ensure that the silting of the ditch could be observed without 'interference' from the bank. It is impossible to determine the original width of the berms at Hambledon. They may, however, have been significantly narrower than the Overton one.
4. At Overton, the ditch was proportionately wide, dug with a depth:width ratio in the chalk (excluding the topsoil) of 1:1.6 (Jewell and Dimbleby 1966, fig 1), which had weathered to 1:3.4 over 32 years (Bell *et al* 1996, fig 7.6). Many of the Hambledon ditches were narrower. The equivalent ratios for the extensively excavated ones, where large numbers of sections should provide representative proportions, ranged from 1:1.7 for the Stepleton enclosure to 1:3.1 for the outer Stepleton outwork, with a mean of 1:2.4. If the Hambledon ditches were proportionately narrower after more than five millennia than the Overton Down one was after 32 years, then their proportions would have been even narrower than Overton's when they were first dug. In consequence, the erosion of their sides will have filled the lower parts of the ditches more rapidly than the same process has at Overton.

This is evident from the extent to which the chalk rubble filling is symmetrically derived from both sides, a feature most marked in the ditch of the Stepleton enclosure, corresponding to its narrow proportions and the relatively gentle slope of the ground on which it lay (Figs 3.84–5, 3.88, 3.90–2). Any excess over symmetry at the inner edge must be derived from the banks, accelerated by slope, in a manner precluded at Overton by the width of the berm and the level ground. This is most marked in some of the sections through the inner Stepleton outwork (Figs 3.92, 3.94–102). In some parts of this ditch, the lower fills show a similar pattern to that observed at Overton Down, modified by the greater bulk and the asymmetry discussed above: varying amounts of chalk rubble become progressively smaller, less angular and more concreted from bottom to top and are frequently interleaved with finer silts, suggesting that the sides and bank weathered gradually into the ditch (eg all the sections except KK–KK' in Fig 3.94, Fig 3.95, Fig 3.96: section TT–TT'). Some idea of the timescale of this process is provided in segment 7 by dates for an articulated skeleton underneath the chalk rubble fills and another near the top of those fills, of, respectively, *3600–3490 cal BC (80%)* or *3440–3380 cal BC (15%)* (4738±28 BP; UB-4242) and *3500–3420 cal BC (31%)* or *3390–3320 cal BC (64%)* (mean of 4598±40 BP for OxA-7044 and -7045; Figs 3.100–4; Fig 4.6: *UB-4242, R_Combine ST78 2755A*). In other parts of the same ditch, however, the vast bulk of the fill had arrived quite quickly from the interior as clean, unweathered chalk rubble. The most striking instance of this is on the east side of the gateway, in the west butt of segment 5 (Fig 3.96: section RR–RR'). Others can be seen elsewhere (eg Fig 3.92, Fig 3.94: section KK–KK', Fig 3.96: section VV–VV', Fig 3.98). Such massive fresh rubble collapse would appear to the writer to witness a fundamentally unstable 'bank' structure which is only answered by the structural diagnosis arrived at early by volumetric calculation and indeed, by archaeological witness albeit only in isolated locations on the site.

Thus the writer, despite the problems posed by the very antiquity of the site and the degree of erosion to which it has been subject, is confident that the causewayed ditch quarrying on the site took place to furnish sufficient (and no more) material for the filling of a box-frame construction wall. He is certain that this wall varied in stature at various points to reflect its differing functions – simply enclosive in the main and Stepleton enclosures; systematically definitive in the cross-dykes and the western and Hanford outworks; and designedly defensive in the Stepleton and Shroton outworks. Even within these broad categories it is likely, indeed it is probably in evidence, that gateway areas were enhanced in otherwise slighter constructional elements in order to reinforce likely points of attack or indeed simply to add greater impact on the eye to those parts of the enclosive complex that were most likely to be seen.

It is therefore suggested that all parts of the Hambledon Hill complex were defined by a causewayed quarry ditch behind which stood a timber- and hurdling-reinforced, chalk rubble-filled wall. It is suggested that this wall varied in scale between *c* 2 m and 4 m in width and 2 m and 3 m in height (plus the height of any breastwork). These suggestions are based upon the evidence of:

a existing archaeological evidence on the site.
b The volumetric calculation of chalk rubble production and its standing *vis à vis* the phenomenon of 'protected chalk' still surviving to a more or less damaged extent on the inner side of the quarry ditches.
c The uneven and massive fresh rubble content of some of the ditch fillings.

11.1.1 The material required

Having thus established a model for enclosure construction at Hambledon Hill which satisfies all the requirements of the evidence, it now remains to examine the material requirements of such a model and then to examine its ergonomic implications. It will be apparent that one of the essential components of box-frame construction is that its strength resides in lateral as well as vertical members and in their joining. It is evident from the limited evidence available that uprights at about 1.50 m centre-to-centre were a preferred basis for this system. This frame will not, of course, retain the rubble infill – it simply supplies the strength for that retention by screens. In the Neolithic construction such screens were probably not only applied along the front and rear of the construction but also *through* the body of the wall to induce lateral as well as frontal stability, like hurdles in the South Street and Beckhampton Road long barrows, in Wiltshire (Ashbee *et al* 1979), and the long mound at Raunds, Northamptonshire (Harding and Healy forthcoming), or like stone-built partitions in the Hazleton long cairn, Gloucestershire (Saville 1990b, figs 46–58) and within the walls of the outer enclosure at Carn Brea in Cornwall (Mercer 1981a, 63). For a truly effective box structure the front and rear uprights must be linked by at least two jointed cross members 2–4 m in length. In turn each such 'frame' will require to be limited laterally by at least two members of 1.5 m (but actually preferably 3 m) to the neighbouring frame(s). This is the minimum requirement to induce a stable structure. Hurdling screens will, of necessity, have to be applied to the whole rear and front length of the frame, and it has been suggested on parallel evidence from other sites of the period across the system from time to time. It will immediately be apparent that a box-frame of the required degree of stability will actually need relatively little in the way of groundfast support, which simply provides anchorage. Hence the relatively shallow postholes that, after five millennia, have proved so elusive at Hambledon.

11.1.2 The ergonomic requirement

It will immediately be seen that the calculation of any ergonomic input to the process of construction of such an obstacle is both complex and, consequently, uncertain. It nevertheless seems appropriate to attempt such a calculation, not to be conducted in any sense of precision, but only to give some impression of the impact of the effort to construct such a site as Hambledon Hill, over the period it was constructed, upon the subsistence farming communities that engendered it. To this end no precise figures will be used, quite deliberately, lest their use be seen as offering some spurious accuracy to the outcome. The objective is, quite simply, to offer an 'order of magnitude' to the problem. It may well be that, when placed against the great longevity of the site in its total conception that these figures will not be so very surprising for the reader.

It is proposed to examine each element of the construction of the enclosure complex in terms of its ergonomic implications on the basis of the information given above. While it is clear that earthwork construction was episodic, and the scale and date of some elements are well defined, others come less clearly into focus, while yet others remain speculative (Chs 2–4). The exercise follows the provisional periodisation of Table 4.4 and Figure 1.9. The calculations are quite deliberately maintained at a minimum likely level (2 m width and 2 m–3 m height of wall – while evidence might suggest greater dimensions, at least in places. The intention is to provide, based upon the argued nature of these earthworks, some estimate of the timber and other organic requirements likely to be required in their construction. This will, at the least, enable a readily appreciable comparison between the requirement of different components of the site and may also serve to illustrate in a simplistic, and probably minimalist, way, the actual requirements of site construction. It must be remembered that the stages listed below took place over a period of some 400 years. Nevertheless, for those who like numbers the following calculations have been made.

Timber and hurdling

Calculations have been made as follows, taking the inner Stepleton outwork as an example, and employing the figures set out in Table 11.1.

The earthwork displays a length of at least 300 m, and possibly much more (3.5.1). The minimum length would have called for:

(300÷1.5) × 6 timbers 2–3 m long = 1200 timbers = 2400–3600 linear metres
and
(300÷1.5) × 2 screens of hurdling = *c* 400 screens of 3m^2 each = *c* 1200 m^2 of hurdling

Iversen points out (1956) that, during an experiment mounted in young oak forest in Jutland, Denmark, in which flint axes were used to fell oaks of less than 35 centimetres, each tree was felled in *c* 30 minutes, and 500 m^2 of oak forest cleared by three men in four hours. On this basis, assuming 25 trees per 500 m^2, one man could clear 0.2 ha in a week. Iversen further states that in Upper Canada in the eighteenth century, *c* 0.4 ha could be cleared by one man in a week using steel axes. In another experiment Semenov

Table 11.1 Minimum material requirements for the construction of a 1.50 m length of a box-framed wall

Material	*Approximate dimensions*
2 uprights	*c* 2 m–3 m
2 cross members	*c* 2 m–4 m
2 lateral members	*c* 1.5 m (or possibly 2 m × 3 m every other length of 1.50 m)
2 hurdling screens	2 m–3 m × 1.50 m
1 hurdling screen	2 m–4 m × 2 m–3 m

(1964, 130) suggested that a pine tree *c* 0.25 m in diameter could be chopped down in *c* 20 minutes with polished axes of nephrite.

N D James in *The Forester's Companion* states (1966, 201) that oak weighs 45 lb per cubic foot (= 720 kg per m^3). The evidence available from post sockets at Hambledon Hill suggests that large poles 0.10–0.20 m in diameter were in evidence (see 3.5.4). If the length above ground is 2–3 m (say 2.5 m), then it is argued (Mercer 1981b, 149–51) that a ratio (average) of 1:3.5 for post length below and above ground is indicated on the basis of excavated timber postholes where a ramp-approach for raising the timber is in evidence. Thus for a 2.5 m length the probable socket depth would be 0.55 m and for a 3 m length 0.66 m. This information may help to suggest the loss of at least 0.3 m of subsoil surface around postholes relating to this outwork: 0.55 m was in fact the maximum depth to which any postholes survived, their mean depth being only 0.17 m. This series of calculations, of course, takes no account of the time spent in managing oak forest in a manner that allowed the creation of the poles, probably over a period of 40–50 years.

The volume of each pole @ 3 m × 0.20 m diameter = $\pi r^2 h = \pi(0.1 \times 0.1) \times 3 = 0.09$ cu m (= 3.18 cubic feet). At 45 lb per cubic foot (=720 kg per m^3), each timber would weigh 64 kg (141 lb).

An approximate total of four hours of labour per timber length might be made up of half an hour to fell, half an hour to prepare, an hour to hitch and drag to site, another hour to dig the earthfast socket and a final hour to erect and joint the timber.

To these considerations must be added the time taken for hurdling/scantling preparation. Observation of modern hurdle makers by Coles and Darrah (1977, 32–8) indicates that to make a hurdle 2.9 m long × 1.1 m high with 60–70 rods and 5–6 sails would take two craftsmen 10 hours. Experiment by the same authors in the production of a hurdle modelled on a Neolithic example from Walton Heath in the Somerset Levels produced an altogether faster production rate, again for a team of two, of approximately two hours, including cutting and cleaning the poles. This was for a hurdle 2.9 m long and 1.1 m high, weighing 30 kg. Allowing an additional 30 minutes for transport to site and fixing, it is therefore taken that 3.5 m^2 of hurdling could be produced in 2.5 hours × 2 =5 worker hours.

Ditch-digging

In order to estimate the volume of excavated material for each ditched structure, it is necessary to calculate the proportion of ditch to causeway on the basis of the (sometimes minimally known) sample excavated. Then it is necessary to suggest on impressionistic but informed grounds the average ditch depth and width. This suggestion must be tempered by an understanding that the depth of ditches will have been reduced and their width increased by weathering. In the absence of any relevant information, however imprecise, it has been assumed that for the purposes of this exercise these factors broadly cancel each other out. The accepted loss of *c* 0.50 m of subsoil surface (1.3) and the reconstruction of original ditch form on the basis of basal profile suggest that this may well have been (approximately) the case.

To calculate the implication of ditch digging we may use the following figures, drawn from McConnell (1919):

15 cubic ft (0.4247m^3) = 1 ton (1.016 tonnes) of grey chalk would be quarried by a team of three diggers, one filler, one wheeler (barrow) in a day's work of 10 hours (ibid, 92).
3 cubic yards (2.5 m^3) in the quarry amount to about 4 cubic yards (3 m^3) in rubble (ibid, 92).
4 cubic yards (3 m^3) of 'soft stone easily parted' could be quarried in a day's work (ibid, 91).
'A man accustomed to the work will build 7 cubic yards (5.25 m^3) of dry rubble wall in a day' (ibid, 94).

The above are, of course, twentieth-century figures with an array of post-Neolithic provisions attached to them, including the use of modern technology (steel tools, the wheel) and twentieth-century concepts of 'work'.

We also have the Overton Down experimental earthwork work study (Jewell 1963, 50–8). While the McConnell figures are clearly exaggerated in terms of prehistoric work capacity, it is also clear that the workforce at Overton was not particularly experienced, and, while this writer admires their work and achievement, he suspects that in the event of a play-off between the Overton Delvers (late second millennium AD) and Hambledon Howkers (early fourth millennium BC) there might have been a certain amount of 'ragging' by the latter in the pavilion both before and after the event.

The Overton figures are nevertheless full of interest – based upon an optimum working team of three (picker, shoveller and basketer) and the premise that 1 cubic foot of chalk (0.02832 m^3) = 1 cwt (50.8 kg).

A day-long rate of 15 cwt (762 kg) per person per hour was judged appropriate for modern workers – that is digging, carrying, and dumping on the angle-of-rest bank designed at Overton – with modern tools. With ancient tools the 'Stakhanovite' shift managed to work for a relatively short period (40 minutes) at a rate of 8.3 cwt (422 kg) per hour (dug, transported and dumped), ie in Overton terms 8+ cubic feet (*c* 400 kg). A more typical average for the exercise was *c* 4.5–5 cwt (229–254 kg) per hour.

The chalk at Hambledon Hill is, and almost certainly in the Neolithic was, more rotten, fissured, and corrupted than that at Overton. Given this fact, this writer is prepared to estimate a rate of 10 cwt (508 kg) or 10 cubic feet (0.2832 m^3) per hour for a prehistoric

Table 11.2 Elements of the complex for which material and ergonomic requirements have been estimated

Period (s)	*Earthwork*	*Considerations*	*Notes*
1A	Main enclosure		
1A	Long barrow		No estimate made for timber or hurdles
?1A	Hillfort long barrow	Considered an early element by analogy with the excavated long barrow and other long barrows	No estimate made for timber or hurdles. Width of ditches and lengths of segments and causeways taken from earthwork survey of E ditch, where they are fairly clear (Fig 2.14). Depth taken from S ditch of South Street long barrow (the deeper of the two; Evans 1979a, fig 24)
1A, 3, ?3, 4, ?4	Cross-dykes	Built progressively on the evidence of radiocarbon dates for east cross-dykes and inner south cross-dyke. Others undated. North cross-dykes inferred from topography and symmetry. A vestige of them may be visible emerging beneath the SW gateway annexe of the hillfort (2.4.2, Fig 2.8)	Lengths of segments and causeways for S and N cross-dykes taken from E cross-dykes. Width and depth of inner S cross-dyke are based on only two sections and may not be representative. Widths and depths of N cross dykes are used for outer S cross dyke, the original form of which was destroyed by a probably Iron Age recut, and for the inferred N cross-dykes
1B	Stepleton enclosure		
1B	Shroton outwork	The possibility of a second, outer earthwork here remains open (3.4)	Lengths of segments and causeways taken from earthwork survey (Fig 3.73)
1B	Middle Stepleton outwork	Taken provisionally to be one of two earthworks running from the Stepleton enclosure to a point roughly 200 m W of it, where a change of course may mark new construction (2.4.2, 3.5.1)	
2	Inner Stepleton outwork	Taken conservatively to end approximately 150 m W of the Stepleton enclosure, between sites 4G and 4F, but may extend much farther (2.4.2, 3.5.1)	Lower sectional area than for Shroton spur outwork reflects disparity between massive segments in E and centre of excavated area and slighter ones in W
3	Outer Stepleton outwork	Taken provisionally to be one of two earthworks running from the Stepleton enclosure to a point roughly 200 m W of it, where a change of course may mark new construction (2.4.2, 3.5.1)	
?3	Inner and outer Hanford spur works	May have been built before more extensive earthworks linked them to the Stepleton spur (2.4.2, 3.6, 4.7.7). Respectively equivalent to segments 1–3 of the inner Hanford outwork and 1–2 of the outer	
4	Western outwork	Remains little known. Much of its length obscured by Iron Age hillfort	Extent of earthwork employed here corresponds to that shown in Figure 1.9. Segment and causeway lengths taken from earthwork survey (Fig 2.9). Width and depth known from only two sections, which may not be representative
?4	Inner and outer Stepleton–Hanford outworks	Apparently linking Stepleton outworks and Hanford spurworks. Respectively equivalent to segment 3 of the inner Hanford outwork and segment 4 of the outer	Lengths of segment and causeways taken from outer Stepleton outwork. Mean width and depth for inner outwork taken from outer because the only excavated part of the inner was an expanded butt which is unlikely to be representative

'specialist' population, bearing in mind McConnell's estimate of 15 cwt. This estimate for digging, transport and dumping may have been constrained somewhat by the additional effort required of tipping appropriately within a box-frame. Nevertheless, if only for the purpose of suitable approximation, we will use the figure of 10 cubic ft (0.2832 m^3) – taken as 0.28 m^3 per hour for a team of three.

It now remains to calculate the volume of chalk removed from the various components of the Hambledon complex. This is not, of course, a simple task. We are not dealing with ditches of even form – nor, even, are we dealing with continuous digging. Complex volumetric calculations would be possible which would only serve to furnish exactitude where it does not exist. The calculations have been made as follows, again using the inner Stepleton outwork as an example. The sectional area of each ditch has been taken as the product of the mean surviving depth and width on the grounds that (1) decrease in the former is likely to be balanced out by increase in the latter, as discussed above, and (2) the ditches are likely to have been flat-bottomed and steep-sided, on the evidence of the surviving, unweathered bases of their profiles:

Total ditch length (excavated and unexcavated): at least 300 m.
Total known length of excavated or exposed segments: 200.10 m.
Total known length of excavated or exposed causeways: 37.20 m.
Known length of segments as % of known length = (200.10 × 100) ÷ (200.10+37.20) = 84.32%.
Estimated total segment length (excavated and unexcavated) = 84.32% of 300 = 252.97.
Mean depth of excavated sections: 1.50 m.
Mean width of excavated sections: 3.75 m.
Estimated total volume = 1.50 × 3.75 × 252.97 = 1422.96 cu m (3350.5 tonnes).
Estimated total hours of work for a team of three = 1422.96 ÷ 0.28 = 5082.
Estimated total worker days = (5082 ÷10) × 3 = 1524.6.

The estimates achieved by this means and assembled in Table 11.3 and Figure 11.3 are based on varying levels of supposition as to the dimensions, extent and chronology of the earthworks. Those for the two enclosures, the inner east and south cross-dykes and the Shroton spur outwork are the most surely founded in all three respects. The extent of all the Stepleton outworks remains problematic (see 2.4.2, 3.5.1) and conservative, minimum lengths are employed here. Both the dates and dimensions of the hillfort long barrow, the north cross-dykes and the outer south cross-dyke are inferred from other earthworks (Table 11.2). The western outwork is the greatest enigma. It was built late in the sequence, and, on the evidence of field survey, extended along the entire west side of the hillfort spur. It is impossible to judge whether it extended farther than this or, indeed, whether it was built in a single operation.

The picture that emerges from these notional calculations is, naturally, an uncertain one. If 100 people were set to the task of creating the main enclosure between mid-September, after harvest, and the end of November, when conditions might become difficult, they would have 80 working days. The monument could have been created in under two years, and the Stepleton enclosure in another month. The cross-dykes, progressively constructed works of definition, could each have been built in three weeks or less. The defensive outworks, at the minimum extents used in these calculations and given the same number of people working over the same period, would, with one exception, each require a single two-month 'off season'. The exception is a signal one. The western outwork would have had the highest resource budget of all, calling for more input than the main enclosure, although still falling within the 'two season' limit of feasibility.

Our chronological information would suggest that the early Neolithic use of the hill took place over a period of 300–400 years, with the construction of the main enclosure modelled at *3680–3630 cal BC* and that of the western outwork at *3510–3360 cal BC* (Table 4.2). The reader will immediately appreciate the range of possibilities that lies before us. A total of 41,760 worker days spread over 400 years could, for example, amount to 20 days of work by five people each year or one of the 80-day periods of work by 100 people proposed above every 80 years. The writer believes in the notion of critical mass as a determinator of any human project. He does not believe that anyone, ever, would attempt the task of building Hambledon Hill with five people. He is convinced that the building of Hambledon Hill was, anyway, an expression of the social and economic command of the hierarchy that conceived and put together the project. The writer therefore prefers the '100 person' model. With 200 (or 500) people then it is clear that all phases of the 'Neolithic' Hambledon project' could have been completed within an 'off season' of one or two years of well-organised labour (the writer has allowed 10% time for this 'well organised' as part of the suggested social commitment), not a major undertaking for a population of 1000 (100 families) who thought that it was important enough.

In sum, the initial construction of the main enclosure may, on a very reasonable basis, have taken two years, and most subsequent episodes one year. The western outwork, even in its imperfectly known state, seems to have been on a different scale from the rest. It was also of different construction, since its segments are much shorter than those of the other outworks, with a mean length of only *c* 9 m in contrast to 11 m for the Shroton spur outwork and 25 m for the completely exposed segments of all three Stepleton outworks; the excavated segments on the Hanford spur

Table 11.3 Estimated material and ergonomic requirements for the construction of the elements of the complex

Commissariat is estimated as 10% of worker days, a day is estimated as 10 hours. Totals are rounded.

Period	*Earthwork*	*Earthwork length (m)*	*Estimated total segment length (m)*	*Average sectional area (sq m)*	*Volume (cu m)*	*Excavation (worker days)*	*Hurdles*	*Hurdling (worker days)*	*2–3 m timbers (no.)*	*Timber (worker days)*	*Subtotal worker days*	*Commissariat (worker days)*	*Total worker days*
1A	Main enclosure	1000	870	4.4	3830	4105	1335	670	4000	1600	6375	640	7015
1A	Inner E cross-dyke	280	265	1.6	425	455	375	190	1120	450	1095	110	1205
1A	Long barrow	57	55	3.35	185	200				0	200	20	220
?1A	Hillfort long barrow	140	115	8.75	1010	1080				0	1080	110	1190
1B	Shroton outwork	290	200	8.3	1660	1780	390	195	1160	465	2440	245	2685
1B	Stepleton enclosure	375	290	2.5	725	780	500	250	1500	600	1630	165	1795
1B	Middle Stepleton outwork	500	445	2.3	1025	1100	670	335	2000	800	2235	225	2460
2	Inner Stepleton outwork	300	250	5.65	1415	1520	400	200	1200	480	2200	220	2420
3	Inner S cross-dyke	170	160	3.7	590	630	225	110	680	270	1010	100	1110
3	Outer Stepleton outwork	500	435	3.2	1390	1490	670	335	2000	800	2625	260	2885
?3	Inner N cross-dyke	140	130	1.67	220	235	190	95	560	225	555	55	610
?3	Inner Hanford spur work	160	115	2.93	340	365	215	110	640	255	730	75	805
?3	Outer Hanford spur work	140	110	2.42	270	290	190	95	560	225	610	60	670
4	Outer E cross-dyke	280	250	2.09	525	560	375	190	1120	450	1200	120	1320
4	Western outwork	1650	995	3.75	3730	4000	2200	1100	6600	2640	7740	775	8515
4	Outer Stepleton–Hanford outwork	500	430	2.58	1110	1190	665	335	2000	800	2325	230	2555
?4	Outer S cross-dyke	170	150	3.75	560	600	225	115	680	270	985	100	1085
?4	Outer N cross-dyke	140	125	2.09	260	280	185	95	560	225	600	60	660
?4	Inner Stepleton–Hanford outwork	500	430	2.58	1110	1190	665	335	2000	800	2325	230	2555
	Totals	7292	5820		20,380	21,850	9475	4755	28,380	11,355	37,960	3800	41,760

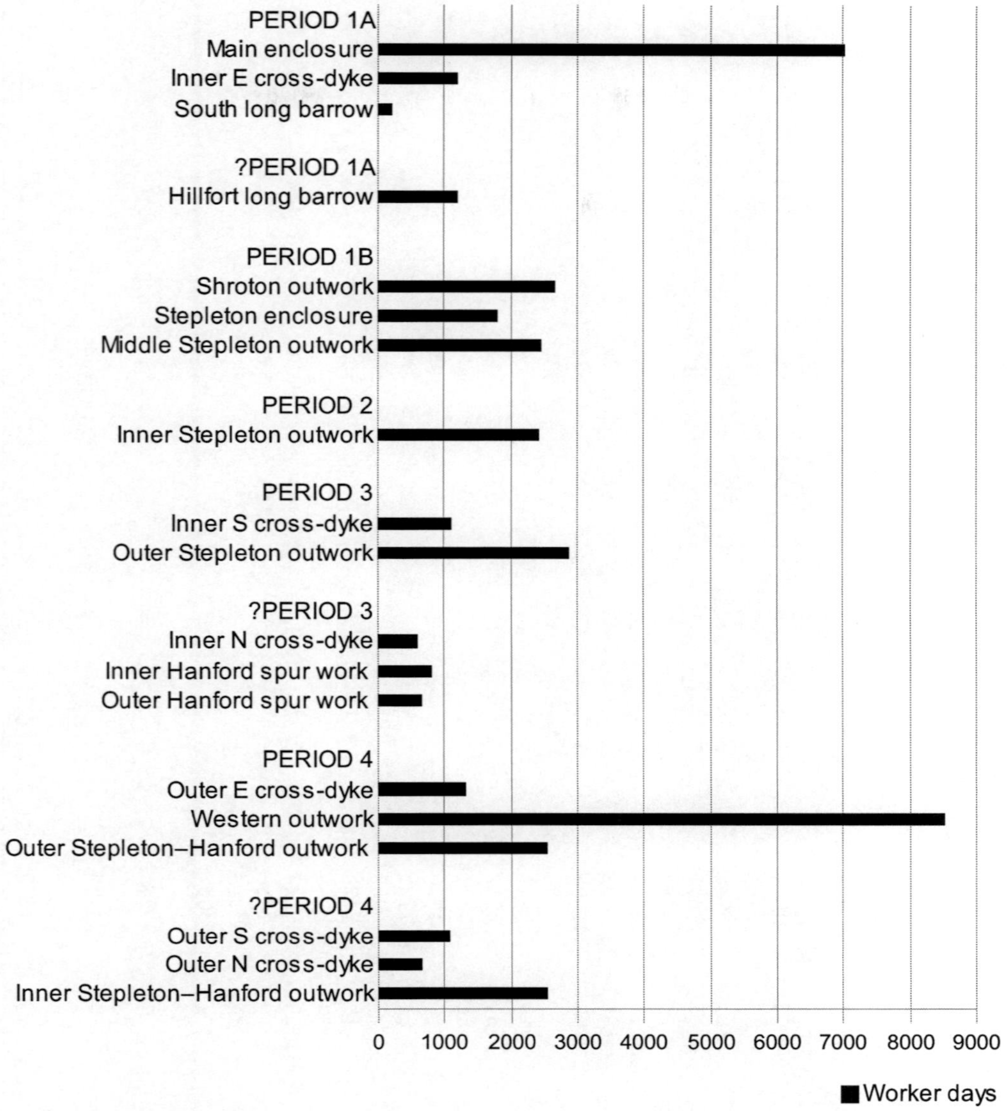

Fig 11.3 Estimates of the material and ergonomic requirement for the construction of the Hambledon earthworks.

were also clearly longer, although none was fully exposed (compare Figure 2.9 with Figures 3.73, 3.81 and 3.134). Could shorter segments reflect the simultaneous participation of larger numbers of kin groups in this large-scale construction than in smaller ones, as well as a lower 'wall'?

11.2 The Neolithic uses of the complex

11.2.1 How many and who?

The whole hilltop was encompassed by Neolithic activity as well as by Neolithic earthworks. Not only was there a massive long barrow on the hillfort spur, the relatively small quantity of struck flint found during the excavation of a section across the first millennium north cross-rampart within the hillfort was overwhelmingly early Neolithic in character (see Saville, 10.2.9), and sherds of Neolithic Bowl pottery have been found in a rabbit scrape in the hillfort (RCHME 1996, 95–96). On the Stepleton spur, artefacts and food remains were often at least as abundant in fills entering the ditches from the exterior as from the interior, and some charcoal-rich fills in the middle and inner outworks derived from the exterior (Tables 3.10–11), as did some particularly rich deposits, notably the fill of a recut in the east butt of segment 5 of the inner outwork, and refitting knapping debris in phase III of segment 4 of the outer outwork (3.5.8). There were pits outside the Stepleton enclosure, between the cross-dykes surrounding the main enclosure, and on the Hanford spur away from both enclosures. There were early Neolithic flint scatters north-west of the Stepleton enclosure, and east of the Shroton spur outwork (Figs 2.2, 3.73; see Saville, 10.2.10). All this suggests that those visiting the complex may have lived, however temporarily, outside the earthworks, although not ubiquitously: features outside the Stepleton enclosure were concentrated in the north

Table 11.4 Estimated total assemblage, spread over time

Totals for the north cross-dykes are based on those for the south cross-dykes and totals for the hillfort long barrow are based on those for the excavated long barrow, adjusted for different lengths. Unworked burnt flint is not included.

	% excavated	*Bowl pottery sherds*		*Struck flint and chert*		*People (minimum numbers)*		*Identified post-cranial animal bones*		*Cattle (minimum numbers)*	
		Actual	*Estimated*	*Actual*	*Estimated*	*Actual*	*Estimated*	*Actual*	*Estimated*	*Actual*	*Estimated*
Main enclosure	18	6084	34149	10850	60900	30	168	4271	23973		
Inner E cross-dyke	14	361	2552	507	3585	1	7	225	1591		
Long barrow	90	1721	1908	4125	4574	5	6	310	344		
Hillfort long barrow			3990		9564		12		719		
Shroton outwork	12	124	1051	383	3246	3	25	138	1169		
Stepleton enclosure	45	5442	12121	6147	13691	5	11	164	365		
Middle Stepleton outwork	13	130	1029	1716	13588	2	16	68	538		
Inner Stepleton outwork	48	1289	2697	25118	52548	9	19	507	1061		
Inner S cross-dyke	5	712	15189	161	3435	2	43	54	1152		
Outer Stepleton outwork	9	187	2199	3488	41008	3	35	54	635		
Inner N cross-dyke			12341		2791		35		936		
Inner Hanford spurwork	9	851	9787	206	2369	1	12	145	1668		
Outer Hanford spurwork	17	170	1005	161	952	3	18	58	343		
Outer E cross-dyke	12	186	1566	448	3771	2	17	108	909		
Western outwork	1	49	9751	180	35820			20	3980		
Outer S cross-dyke	4	23	575	69	1725			29	725		
Outer N cross-dyke			288		863				363		
Inner Stepleton–Hanford outwork	1			19	2476			6	782		
Outer Stepleton–Hanford outwork	4	2	53	1089	28906			20	531		
Central area, features, etc	15	4725	31500	7518	50120	2	13	93	620		
Stepleton spur, features, etc	90	3766	4184	6710	7456	3	3	118	131		
Hanford spur, features, etc	100	212	212	23	23	1	1	283	283		
Unexcavated areas excluding ditches and enclosure interiors (20% of sum of other estimated totals)			29630		68682		88		8563		
Actual totals		26034		68918		72		6671		63	
Estimated totals			177777		412090		528		51380		522
Per annum over 400 yr (rounded)			**440**		**1030**		**1**		**130**		**1**
Per annum over 300 yr (rounded)			**600**		**1370**		**2**		**170**		**2**

and north-west, and the Stepleton and Shroton flint scatters were localised. Similar practice may be reflected by an earlier Neolithic element in a flint scatter outside the Abingdon causewayed enclosure, Oxfordshire (Bradley 1999), in an extensive scatter on the southern slope of Windmill Hill, below the enclosure, where earlier Neolithic pits were also found (Whittle *et al* 2000), in an earlier Neolithic flint scatter and pit cluster outside Robin Hood's Ball, Wiltshire (Richards 1990, 61–65), and in numerous pits outside the Etton causewayed enclosure in Cambridgeshire (Evans and Hodder 2006).

Hambledon's episodic history of construction and recutting over three to four hundred years reinforces Chris Evans' contention that building and reworking were an inherent part of the use of causewayed enclosures (1988). Numerous strands of evidence combine to indicate that use, as well as construction, was intermittent. To the end of the Neolithic use of the site, mollusc samples from the hill reflect the vicinity of mature shady habitats in an environment dominated by varying degrees of woodland (see Bell *et al*, 5.2). This is not the vegetation that would be expected in an area habitually used by people and livestock, and contrasts with the development of more open conditions by this time in some areas of Cranborne Chase (11.5.2). There are similar contrasts between the fourth millennium vegetation of the Maiden Castle causewayed enclosure (Evans and Rouse 1991b), and the Dorchester area to the north (Allen 1997a) and between the fourth millennium vegetation of Windmill Hill and the nearby long barrows (Fishpool 1999). It seems that, at least on the southern chalk, causewayed enclosures were built at the edges of more habitually used areas, and visited only occasionally (Evans *et al* 1988), while the successor monuments were built in occupied areas.

An intermittent human presence is also reflected in the interplay between natural silting and human intervention in the ditch fills. The pottery shows a prevalence of small bowls and cups, suitable for cooking and eating, and a scarcity of larger vessels suitable for storage (see Smith, 9.1.1, Table 9.4). The cattle butchered on the hill were predominantly females between one and a half and four years of age (ie subadults and young adults), with notably lower proportions of younger and older animals and of males. This does not reflect the complete cull of a sustainable herd, which, whether reared primarily for dairy products or for meat, would include more calves and more mature, breeding-age females. The animals killed at Hambledon were thus selected from their herds for a combination of cultural preferences and practical considerations and brought there to be consumed (see Legge, 8.1). With the exception of a single large deposit of charred emmer spikelets, the charred cereal consists almost entirely of cleaned grain, with very little chaff or weed seeds, and was probably brought to the hill already processed (see Jones and Legge, 6.2).

If people visited the complex occasionally, in what numbers did they do so? The scale is to some extent defined by the labour requirements calculated above, which would have a workforce of a hundred working on the construction of the main enclosure hill for two months in late summer/early autumn. Episodes of consumption may have involved larger numbers. One of the young cows that dominate the faunal remains would have provided some 300 kg of meat, offal and fat, yet some of the phase VI recuts in the central area, which seem to have been cut and filled in single events, contained the remains of two or three such animals (see Legge, 8.1). This points to gatherings of hundreds – many hundreds if several such consumption events took place simultaneously. The events in question may have included the building of some of the later earthworks. But the recutting of a ditch segment or the digging and filling of a pit could have been the work of a handful, and visits to the hill may have been made by groups of every size, in circumstances of many kinds. The seasons in which Hambledon was visited remain elusive. A hint comes from a small sample of immature caprine mandibles, which fall into two groups, one of less than three months of age and another of 6–9 months of age. Assuming spring-time birth, this could reflect a human presence in early summer and in autumn (see Legge, 8.1).

The intervals at which the hill was frequented are equally elusive. A human presence, even a substantial one, need not have left any material trace, and the extent to which such traces were left may have varied over time, as discussed below. With these severe limitations the surviving material *could* be compatible with distinctly infrequent use. Projecting the density of the excavated assemblage onto the totality of the uninvestigated Neolithic archaeology is beset with problems. While it is possible to guess the total content of detectable ditches and of enclosure interiors where areas of pits have been excavated, it is impossible to guess how many pits and artefact scatters exist on the rest of the hill. For this reason the estimated totals for ditches and enclosure interiors have been increased by an arbitrary 20% (Table 11.4). If the notional totals so arrived at are spread over the 300–400 years for which the complex was in use, the numbers per year become low, of the order of some bones from one or two people, 440–600 pot sherds, 1030–1370 pieces of struck flint, and the remains of one or two cows. The abiding impression is that the site was little used, and that, when it was used, it was for occupation for short periods, at specific seasons, for short-term *ad hoc* activities involving feasting and building. Enclosure creation appears to be an end quite as important as enclosure use. In their analysis of the Haddenham enclosure, in Cambridgeshire, Evans and Hodder (2006) conclude from a total assemblage even more thinly spread than that at Hambledon that there may have been no large gatherings other than those relating to construction. This remains a possibility for Hambledon too.

11.2.2 Actions, artefacts and food remains

Isobel Smith was among the first to recognise that deposits in causewayed enclosure ditches may have had 'a special, even sacramental, significance', that there was '... no doubt whatever that the mass of this material was deliberately thrown or placed in the hollows' (1965, 7, 20). Pattern is everywhere at Hambledon. At a gross level, the two enclosures and the areas around them were used in myriad different ways, some of which are summarised in Table 11.5. The unexcavated areas of the hill, including the ditches of the hillfort long barrow, could have equally distinctive signatures. But there are also variations between ditches and, on a more intimate scale, between individual pits and ditch segments. In the central area the frequency of ditch recutting and, generally, the density of cultural material were at their highest in the main enclosure, lower in the cross-dykes, and at their lowest in the western outwork. The ditches of the south long barrow were also recut and rich in cultural material, and its location at an entrance to the main enclosure is reflected in preferential deposition in the west ditch, the side along which those walking between the two enclosures would have passed (Fig 3.5). This provides a hint of the extent to which movement about the complex may have been channelled and directed, a practice vividly evidenced by the fenced and metalled paths within the Crickley Hill enclosure (Dixon 1988), by screens, a central fence and changing gateway arrangements at Etton (Pryor 1998, 98–109, 366–69, figs 102–3, 115), the entrance structure at Orsett (Hedges and Buckley 1978, fig 6), and lengths of probably Neolithic palisade in the interior of the Staines enclosure (Robertson-Mackay 1987, fig 12).

The introduction to the site of non-local objects and materials, including pottery and querns as well as axeheads from remote sources, was long-lived. The south long barrow was one of the earliest elements of the complex (Figs 1.9, 4.25), and the artefacts from the primary silts of its ditches included a fragment from a Group I axehead from the south-west peninsula, a sherd of gabbroic ware from the same region, others of clays characterised by iron-rich red pellets, possibly originating in south-east Dorset, and still others of clays containing fossil shell from the limestone to the west and north-west, more of which was in the primary silts of the main enclosure and in a treethrow hole under its bank.

What changed was the frequency with which all kinds of cultural material were placed in the ditches. At both Hambledon enclosures, by far the largest assemblages came from the upper ditch fills. In the central area these were shallow phase VI 'slots' cut, sometimes repeatedly, into the largely silted ditches of the main enclosure, its cross-dykes, and the south long barrow, like the stone-packed finds-rich recuts retrospectively recognised at Hembury (Smith 1971, fig 15), the 'black triangles' in the inner circuits at the Trundle and Whitehawk, in Sussex (Curwen 1929; 1931; 1936; Ross Williamson 1930), the 'midden' in the inner ditch at Abingdon, Oxfordshire (Avery 1982, 16–17), or the phase 1C recuts at Etton (Pryor 1998, 13–51). In the Stepleton enclosure there were less structured but equally rich phase VI deposits, rarely in recuts, and comparable with successive 'midden' layers in the inner ditch at Maiden Castle (Sharples 1991, 50–51), or with the concentration of artefacts and animal bone in spit 3 of the inner ditch at Windmill Hill (Smith 1965, 9, 12, fig 6); Whittle *et al* 1999, 105–10). While these deposits may have accompanied the construction of the later outworks, they are unlikely to reflect the gathering of more people than before, since at least equally large numbers must have been needed for the initial episodes of construction (11.1), when little was deposited. It must reflect a change in practice, and one which extended, at least in some regards, from East Anglia to the south-west peninsula.

At Hambledon, this change in practice followed a lull in the use of both enclosures, during which relatively finds-poor silts accumulated. The phase VI deposits give the impression of increased standardisation. Until then individual segments, even adjacent ones, had had very different depositional histories, histories of the kind which prompted Pryor to see each segment of the Etton enclosure as the preserve of a single kin group, encapsulating its needs, rites and beliefs (1998, 367). But with slot-cutting and midden-deposition all the segments were treated in much the same way, repeatedly so in the case of slot-cutting. The artefacts and food remains in the phase VI deposits at Hambledon seem to have been freshly introduced rather than reworked from earlier contexts. Decoration and heavier rims are more frequent there than in the underlying layers (see Smith, 9.1.1), as are the main non-local pottery fabrics (Figs 3.67, 3.130). In the central area these deposits often included articulated animal bone. Indeed, the numerous unworked flint nodules and fragments which characterise these deposits may have protected them against predators – canid gnawing was more frequent on animal bone on the Stepleton spur, where flint was not piled among and over the phase VI deposits (Fig 8.1).

Some usages, however, remained constant across time. On a large scale, many of the numerous differences between the deposits in the ditches of the two enclosures persisted throughout their use (Table 11.5). These are discussed in greater detail below. In essence, formal – arguably ceremonial – deposits, recutting, and objects – some of them fine and rare – from remote sources were all far more frequent in the main enclosure than in the Stepleton enclosure. On a more intimate scale, there are suggestions that the uses of particular segments were remembered, as Whittle *et al* suggest for recurrent deposits in single segments at Windmill Hill (1999, 368). The south butt of the west ditch of the long barrow at Hambledon contained a

Table 11.5 Some of the distinctions between the Neolithic uses of the central area and the Stepleton spur

Main enclosure and central area	*Stepleton enclosure and spur*
Recutting frequent and complex, with a measure of regularity around enclosure, many pits also recut	Recutting of ditch less frequent and less regular, pits rarely recut at all
Upper, linear recuts ('slots') in enclosure and cross-dyke ditches, and recuts in pits both often packed with unworked flint nodules and fragments	Only one flint-packed recut in an enclosure segment, close to entrance giving onto route to main enclosure
Human remains placed in ditches from first	Human remains placed in ditches only after some fill had accumulated
Deer bone (as distinct from antler) rare	Deer bone (as distinct from antler) less rare
Articulated animal bone most abundant in final linear recuts ('slots') made in almost fully silted ditch, which were the ditch contexts richest in bone and other cultural material	Articulated animal bone rarer than in main enclosure and virtually absent from final midden-like deposits made in almost fully silted ditch, although these were the ditch contexts richest in bone
Material in 'slots' often placed in discrete piles	Little obvious placement of material in midden-like upper deposits
Antler implements concentrated in pits in interior	Antler implements concentrated in enclosure ditch throughout sequence
Almost no refitting knapping debris	Clusters of refitting knapping debris on ditch floors and higher up sequence
Almost all of the 39 chert artefacts from the site, including 6 leaf arrowheads; also 1 leaf arrowhead of variegated red/white flint	Almost none of the 39 chert artefacts from the site; no chert or coloured flint arrowheads
Hammerstones include beach pebbles	No beach pebbles
Many axeheads and fragments of rocks from remote sources	Almost all axeheads, and fragments, of flint
Most frequent non-local quern material Old Red Sandstone from Mendips	Most frequent non-local quern material heathstone from between Wareham and Poole, in south-east Dorset
Gabbroic vessels from south-west peninsula concentrated in pits in interior	Gabbroic ware extremely rare
Most abundant non-local pottery well made and finished and derived from limestone ridge to north-west and west	Most abundant non-local pottery roughly made and finished and possibly derived from same area as heathstone

number of fragmentary stone artefacts, and 'It is important to note that these items were not all deposited at one time; they represent a gradual accumulation, spread throughout the entire sequence of fills from phase I upwards. This would appear to attest a deliberate practice, maintained over a considerable period of time' (Smith *et al* 10.1.3; Fig 3.49). It would have been a practice that marked arrival at or departure from the main enclosure, the south entrance to which was along this side of the barrow (3.3.4). Its eastern counterpart, the probable entrance giving onto the Stepleton spur between segments 8 and 9 of the main enclosure, was also marked by a concentration of stone objects, this time from phase III upwards rather than phase I, and with a higher proportion of hammerstones and unworked beach pebbles (see Smith *et al* 10.1.3; Fig 3.69). Despite the later start, this too must result from a pattern of behaviour spanning generations. In the north-west of the main enclosure, articulated animal bone, especially feet, was recurrently deposited in segments 16–18 from phase III to phase VI. The most striking recurrence occurs in this same part of the circuit: the only two articulated child burials in the central area lay in adjacent segments, one at the beginning of the sequence and one at the end (Figs 3.27, 3.29–30, 3.32–5; Fig 4.12: *R_Combine HH76 1948*, *R_Combine HH76 3046*). Both children were accompanied by personal accoutrements (Fig 3.34) and both suffered from premature fusion of some of the sutures of the skull, which would probably have affected their appearance (see McKinley, 7.1). It was not simply thought appropriate to bury children at this location, on two occasions 200–300 years apart, it was thought appropriate to bury children with the same abnormality, who, if this was hereditary, may have come from the same kin group.

The overall incidence of the main pottery fabrics more or less corresponds to that documented for Neolithic Bowl pottery in Wessex by Cleal (1995), with potentially local flint- or flint- and sand-tempered wares accounting for just over half the total, and shell and other calcareous tempers for a substantial proportion of the rest. But the distribution of fabric groups is far from even across the hill (see Smith, 9.1.1), whether between the two main excavated areas (Fig 3.72) or between the components of each (Figs 3.67, 3.130).

There seems to have been a sense for what kinds of vessel should be deposited where (Healy 2006). Flint or flint- and sand-tempered fabrics were most frequent in cross-dykes and outworks, rising to almost 90%, and least frequent, at 40–50%, in the two enclosures, their associated pits, and the south long barrow. Non-local wares varied according to location. Gabbroic wares, a tiny minority of the total, were concentrated in pits in the interior of the main enclosure (Fig 3.64). Most of the non-local wares in the central area were of fabric group 2, tempered with a range of Jurassic material, generally including fossil shell. On the Stepleton spur, the Jurassic inclusions were equally diverse, but more often included ooliths, while the wares containing them were out-numbered by fabrics containing the red clay pellets described above. The ditches of the south long barrow, outside the main enclosure and on the way to and from the Stepleton spur, are the only features in the central area to contain a substantial proportion of this fabric group (Fig 3.66).

Apparently utilitarian distributions appear less so on closer inspection (*pace* Saville, 10.2.7). In the central area, knapping debris is concentrated in areas with deposits of Clay-with-Flints, which provides flint superior to the degraded material from the Upper Chalk of the hill, which was not used in the Neolithic (see Saville, 10.2.2). But the distribution of hammerstones bears little relation to this, concentrating instead around what was almost certainly an entrance in the east side of the main enclosure, where other stone artefacts were clustered (Figs 3.68–69). This brings into focus the notion of a hammerstone as a curated, personal item (see Saville, 10.2), perhaps to be deposited on entering or leaving the circuit. This view of hammerstones as personal equipment accords with the burial of a quartzite example near the left hand of an articulated male skeleton also accompanied by a flint core at Hazleton, Gloucestershire (Saville 1990b, 103–4, fig 115).

The Middle Chalk of the Stepleton spur contains no flint, and Clay-with-Flints there is confined to a single fissure, with no indication in the composition of the feature fills of formerly more extensive coverage. Yet here there are numerous clusters of refitting knapping debris, sometimes including hammers of both flint and antler. Most were well removed from the Clay-with-Flints (Fig 3.131), and all of them were originally sizeable nodules of good quality, although not pristine, chalk flint (see Saville, 10.2; Figs 10.29, 10.32, 10.40–1). They could not have been extracted during the excavation of the ditch segments in which the results of their reduction were deposited. They must have been brought to these locations, probably from at least a few kilometres away. Just as causewayed enclosures may have been foci for the exchange of stone implements, so they may have been foci for the exchange of flint (Smith 1971, 105). The extent to which flint from the chalk was transported westwards has been explored many times, with some disagreement as to the scale of this activity, but none as to its reality (Saville 1982; Healy 1988b; Tingle 1998, 89–98). It may have been moved in greater bulk than any other material in the fourth millennium. It occurs in Neolithic assemblages throughout the south-west, including the Mendips (Bond 2004) and the Somerset Levels where it is present from the early fourth millennium onwards, notably at the Sweet Track (Coles *et al* 1973, 289–90, pl XXXIX; Coles and Orme 1979, fig 40). Hambledon's location at the interface of the chalk and the non-flint-bearing geology of the south-west, and the probability that some (many?) of those who came to the hill came from the west, argue for a role for the complex in flint exchange. Paradoxically, the burial of some of this material and of some stone axeheads at the site may emphasise its significance in the dissemination of both.

The distribution of antler at Hambledon is uneven. While antler implements were probably used to excavate all of the ditches, they were found regularly in only some of them. In the central area, antler was concentrated in pits near the centre of the main enclosure, and was found only occasionally in the ditches, mainly those segments of the main enclosure and the inner east cross-dyke which flanked the eastern entrance. There was something of a concentration of antler fragments, but not implements, in the west ditch of the long barrow. Where antler implements did occur in ditches, they were often in upper fills with no direct relation to ditch-digging or recutting (Fig 3.62). If they are to be related to episodes of excavation, they may have entered the ditches after some time on the surface, or have been used in the excavation of later earthworks or pits. In the Shroton spur outwork there were four antler picks on the base of the only substantially excavated segment (3.4). On the Stepleton spur, antler implements were scarce in primary and subsequent levels in outwork ditches and in pits. They were instead concentrated in the segments of the enclosure, where they were far more frequent than in the larger outwork ditches. Here, many were indeed on the ditch floor, often carefully placed in pairs or larger groups. But they were spread very unevenly among the segments, with marked concentrations in the north and south-west of the circuit and none in many of the segments to the west. Here too, many were in the upper fills with no direct relation to ditch-digging or recutting (Fig 3.126). At least three implements had not been abandoned immediately after use, since they had undergone groove-and-splinter working (see Legge, 8.2). The deposition of antler implements was a matter of choice, rather than the routine abandonment of worn or damaged implements at the end of a task. It may be that it was appropriate to leave the implements used to dig some segments of some ditches *in situ*. Given, however, that antlers were much used both as digging implements and as raw material for smaller artefacts, they are likely to have been exchanged and curated (Smith 1965, 20). As well as being brought to the site, many may have been carried away from it, a scenario frequently entertained for other kinds of artefact and raw material at enclosures.

11.2.3 Mortuary practice

The question of who frequented the complex may perhaps be entertained through the imperfect proxy of those whose largely disarticulated remains were deposited there. These seem to have been drawn from an entire population. They were demographically balanced, unlike the livestock, the excavated sample comprising a minimum of 35–36 children and 40–41 adults of whom only 10 females and 17 males could be sexed (see McKinley, 7.1). They furthermore ranged from those who may have obtained almost all of their dietary protein from animal sources to those whose diet had included both animal and plant protein (see Richards, 7.2; Richards 2000). This last observation might reflect variations in status (especially as those from the south long barrow had all consumed comparably high levels of animal protein) or the deposition of the remains of members of several communities, with different dietary habits.

Alternating frequentation and abandonment would have had a particular impact on the condition of the human and animal bone at the site. Both were exposed to canids and rodents, and the former may have been largely responsible for the under-representation of the less robust bones of all species. Human remains, however, tend to be more severely weathered and otherwise degraded than those of animals (see McKinley, 7.1; Evans 2000), as they do at Etton (Armour-Chelu 1998b), suggesting that the process of excarnation, which almost all had undergone, had entailed prolonged exposure. Bones normally entered ditches or pits after total excarnation and disarticulation, as when femurs from two individuals were placed crossed over each other in a ditch butt beside an entrance to the main enclosure (Fig 3.21). In these cases the bones could have been brought from elsewhere. Evidence for intermediate stages in the process, however, shows that at least some excarnation took place on the hill. It is possible to envisage corpses left in the open, their bones buried at a later date in enclosures, pits, cross-dykes and outworks. Instances include *c* 50% of the disarticulated bones of a juvenile placed together in segment 6 of the middle Stepleton outwork ditch; and *c* 40% of the bones of an older juvenile built into a flint cairn on the base of segment 6.2 of the main enclosure ditch, in both cases as if they had been gathered up while still undispersed. Excarnation on the hill is even more probable for the two still-articulated half skeletons, one of them in segment 6.1 of the main enclosure (Figs 3.15–17), the other in segment 10 of the Stepleton enclosure (Fig 3.88).

Excarnation was not, however, left entirely to time, carnivores and the elements. Cut marks have been identified on the remains of 23 individuals and, given the weathered condition of the bone and the faintness of the cuts, this is likely to be a minimum. The cuts contrast with the butchery practised on the animal bone from the site and seem to have resulted from not-very-systematic excarnation. They range from over a hundred more-or-less transverse cuts on the anterior surface of one femur to two parallel cuts on a mandible. Some had been made with a scraping rather than a cutting motion. They were found on articulated skeletons as well as on disarticulated bone (see McKinley, 7.1; Evans 2000). Comparable cuts have been noted on the human remains from the West Tump long barrow, Gloucestershire (Smith and Brickley 2004), and the Haddenham long barrow, Cambridgeshire (Evans and Hodder 2006). As at Hambledon, these marks are compatible with defleshing rather than butchery, leaving the possibility of contemporary cannibalism a remote but not totally excluded one. There are also so far unspecified traces of dismemberment with lithic implements at the chambered tombs of Coldrum in Kent and Eyford in Gloucestershire (Wysocki and Whittle 2000). Manipulation of the fleshed human corpse, as well as of defleshed bones, may have been far more prevalent than it has so far appeared.

Once disarticulated, human bone could have been retained among the living or moved from one burial context to another (Smith 1965, 137). Burial contexts can, to some extent, be identified, most obviously in pits and long barrows on the Wessex Chalk and in long barrows and caves in the Mendips. Indeed, the marking of otherwise inconspicuous burials with posts may, among other functions, have facilitated future exhumation, although this did not always take place. On Crichel Down in Cranborne Chase two successive posts were set at the feet of an articulated adult (Piggott and Piggott 1944, 51–52, fig 22, pl XIII); and on Handley Hill, not far from Wor Barrow, a feature reinterpreted by Piggott as a large posthole of early Neolithic date contained human remains perhaps not long out of articulation, since the pelvis remained complete, although the accompanying skull and mandible were separated, as were the humerus and ulna (Pitt Rivers 1898, 49–50, 54–56, pl 245; Piggott 1936b). Similar practice may be echoed at Hambledon by two vestigial postholes at the head and feet of a crouched child burial at the centre of the Stepleton enclosure (Fig 3.113: 1A F70). In the main enclosure, the insertion of a stake into at least one pit and its subsequent removal before the pit was recut (3.3.7, Fig 3.59: N F10) may perhaps have related to the temporary burial of human remains.

But above-ground contexts may have figured significantly. Diverse histories for the disarticulated remains on Hambledon are evidenced by small numbers of fragments (mainly skull) which were charred when already dry; others which, though not charred, showed dark staining not always attributable to their final burial environment; and others marked by a distinctive pattern of fissuring, characteristic of rapid drying, perhaps in intense sunlight following soaking (see McKinley, 7.1). Foot and toe bones found in apparent articulation in the rubble fills of the Shroton spur outwork ditch (Fig 4.9: *OxA-7102*) were older than antler picks and an articulated dog which lay beneath them on the base of the same segment (Fig 4.9: *R_Combine HH76 2864*, *UB-4148*, *UB-4149*, *UB-4150*). This may apply to all of the larger group of jumbled human remains (from at least two individuals) of which the dated bones formed a part, and in which a radius and a fibula had been placed side-by-side, giving the impression of a complete forearm (Fig 3.79). It would be no surprise if the defleshed skulls placed on the bases of several of the ditches were already old when deposited. None has yet been dated, because the dating programme focused on articulated samples likely to be coeval with their contexts. Skulls, however, tend to be particularly weathered and worn, and McKinley concludes that most of them were subject to greater exposure to the elements than the rest of the human remains (7.1).

Hambledon confirms that a minority of individuals were buried fully articulated in the earlier fourth millennium. Three were in single graves. The earliest (Fig 4.6: *OxA-7835*) was a possible male of 45 or more, very tightly contracted in a small pit in the protected chalk of the ploughed-down inner Stepleton outwork bank (Fig 3.113: 2A F200). The burial had taken place before the construction of the outwork bank. The location and the maturity of the subject, although not other aspects of the burial, recall the interment of an adult male beneath the outer bank of Windmill Hill (Whittle *et al* 1999, 79–81, 344–6). An almost equally early child burial, on or near the base of the main enclosure ditch (Fig 4.12: *R_Combine HH76 1948*), includes personal accoutrements, in the form of three bone beads in the head area (Fig 3.34). There were distinctions even among the few who were singled out for this exceptional treatment, notably between two men who may both have died when the inner Stepleton outwork burnt down, one of whom was buried in a pit some way away and the other of whom was placed, or left, in the ditch (Figs 3.100–1, 3.113: 4B F712). Barring cremation, the gamut of earlier fourth millennium funerary practice is represented on the hill. The treatment of human remains was at least as diverse as the roles which individuals may have filled in life. This and the varying sources of dietary protein may point to the existence of hierarchy in what has often been seen as an egalitarian society.

11.2.4 Fire and arrows

Although the Hambledon outworks were built sequentially (Fig 1.9), they appear to accumulate to form a systematic defensive design, as if a plan were brought slowly, when feasible, to fruition. The most obviously defensive is the most massive of them, the inner Stepleton outwork with its timber reinforcement and massive gateway (Fig 3.111). This outwork showed signs of hasty construction and of abandonment in an incomplete state. The ditch was the most irregular on the hill, and was cut in such a way as to maximise speed and minimise effort. Unlike the more regular pre-existing middle outwork, which ran outside the Stepleton enclosure, part of the inner outwork followed the enclosure ditch, where the existing bank could be incorporated in the larger new one and the ditch fills would have been easier and quicker to excavate than solid chalk. Where the outwork was cut in solid chalk, some of the irregularity seems to have been due to the use of natural fissures as starting points for excavation. On the north-east side of the enclosure, its surviving depth dropped abruptly from 1.20 m to less than 0.20 m, its line continuing as a slight depression outside the enclosure ditch for a further 60 m, suggesting that this part was never finished (Figs 3.91–2). To the west of the enclosure, depth and width diminished, although not to the same extent (Figs 3.94–5), and there is a 22 m-wide causeway less than 50 m west of the timber-lined gateway where the ditch was at its widest and deepest (Fig 3.81). If it was intended as a defensive work, it has an unfinished aspect. It is as if the outwork's construction was begun in response to a perceived threat and abruptly abandoned when that threat materialised. After primary silt had accumulated and, in some segments, been cleaned out, the earthwork was burnt for 200 m (Pls V–IX), in an episode that probably entailed the deaths of two men. While the stratigraphic position of the burnt deposits indicates that destruction followed soon after construction, some of the charcoal from on or close to the ditch base and from postholes in the bank shows signs of decay, interpreted as showing that the rampart had stood for some time (see Austin *et al*, 6.1). The contradiction can be resolved by adopting those authors' second option: that poles and posts might have been stockpiled, or even reused. This would be compatible with the hasty construction suggested above and with a degree of prefabrication that would in any case be likely.

Charcoal from the postholes of the inner outwork bank was almost exclusively oak, and, where charcoal from burnt deposits on or near the ditch bottoms has been identified, it is predominantly of oak and hazel, with small quantities of other species – some of it altered in such a way as to suggest that it was burnt at temperatures over 700°C (see Austin *et al*, 6.1). The predominance of oak and hazel accords with the oak in the postholes of the rampart structure and with the criss-cross pattern of the charred timbers at one point in the ditch (Fig 3.99, Pl VIII), which suggests that the screening of the rampart was made of hurdling, for which hazel has been the material of choice from at least the early Neolithic (Coles *et al* 1988; Coles and Darrah 1977) to the present day. It contrasts with the more diverse composition of the charcoal from most other Neolithic contexts on the hill, whether ditches or pits.

The only other place where the charcoal is so dominated by oak and hazel is the Shroton spur outwork, where there was also a massive gateway (Figs 3.75–6). Excavation here was more restricted than on the Stepleton spur, but the combined results from work in 1976 and from trenches cut by Desmond Bonney in 1960 indicate that there were posts, some of them burnt, in the bank area, and that charcoal and other burnt material entered the ditch from the inner edge along a distance, if the process was continuous, of 140 m. Burnt material was densest on the surface of the primary silt, although it also occurred at higher levels (3.4). Here too, a rampart may have burnt shortly after its construction, and here too there is a hint of rebuilding in a posthole in the probable gateway, oak charcoal from which is considerably younger than the earthwork (Fig 4.9: *HAR-2368*). It is surely pertinent that the Shroton and Stepleton spurs provide the easiest approaches to the hill (Fig 1.4, Pl I). In the light of this observation, the burning of oak timbers in a slot forming part of a gateway on the Hanford spur, which afforded relatively easy access to the hill from the west, may also reflect assault, but here there is no comparable input of burnt material into the ditches (see 3.6).

The destruction of the inner Stepleton outwork was, however, far from the end of activity on the spur. Shortly afterwards, a setting of sherds and animal bone was placed on the surface of the burnt material in the ditch base at one side of the gateway (Fig 3.95); the overlying fills of the outwork ditch contained newly deposited artefacts, including compact clusters of knapping debris, and animal bone, some of it articulated; a recut which removed the burnt material from the butt of one segment contained a particularly rich deposit of artefacts and animal bone; and the richest deposits in the enclosure ditch were yet to be made. The gateway seems to have been rebuilt, on the evidence of the replacement of at least one burnt post with an unburnt one (Fig 3.112: F601). This may have occurred at the same time as the construction of the third and final outwork on the spur. This too coincided with a violent event: the body of a young man with a leaf arrowhead among his ribs was placed in a natural cavity in the butt of one segment as soon as it was excavated (Figs 3.105–6). It is impossible to tell if his death formed part of larger-scale hostilities, but it could have coincided with that of a second young man with an arrowhead in his rib cage, found prone in the fill of the partly silted inner outwork (Figs 3.102–4; Fig 4.6: *UB-4243*, *R_Combine ST78 2755A*). These deaths by arrowshot are not unique in the area. There was a leaf arrowhead among the ribs of the Crichel Down 13 burial mentioned above (Piggott and Piggott 1944, 51, 75, fig 23: 3), and another among those of an individual buried in the Wor Barrow ditch (Pitt Rivers 1898, 63). The wider evidence for the use of arrows with leaf-shaped tips against human targets is summarised by Green (1980).

Whatever the nature of these events at Hambledon, they were different from other apparently hostile encounters of the period, reconstructed on the basis of the evidence excavated at Crickley Hill, Gloucestershire, and Carn Brea, Cornwall, where hundreds of flint-tipped arrows were shot (Dixon 1988; Mercer 1981a; Saville 2002, 96–98). Arrowheads were scarce at Hambledon, totalling 42 out of a flint and chert assemblage of 89,287, and they were thinly spread in time and space (see Saville 10.2, Tables 10.40, 10.51). It is also worth remembering that non-defensive early Neolithic structures were burnt, apparently in the course of ceremony rather than of conflict, although the practice was rare in the south of England, where the firing of the forecourt structure of the Nutbane long barrow on the Hampshire chalk (Morgan 1959) echoes events more frequent in the north and east (Kinnes 1992, 93).

The addition of defensive elements to an originally ceremonial focus began early in the history of the complex, the middle Stepleton outwork and the Shroton spur outwork being built at most a century after the main enclosure and probably less (Fig 4.25). It is possible to speculate as to the reasons for this transformation. The gathering of otherwise scattered populations could provide opportunities for hostilities on a scale otherwise impossible, and could prompt the construction of defences. The scale of the Hambledon complex and, by implication, its importance and the numbers of people associated with it, could have made its users particularly conspicuous and vulnerable. The ecotonal – even frontier – location of the site may have made it more of a theatre for conflict than many other enclosures. Furthermore, the construction of defensive works continued intermittently for another three hundred years. Within that period, the two burnt ramparts at Hambledon probably reflect two episodes of conflict and two deaths by arrowshot may reflect one or two more. The attendant deaths and destruction would not only have deprived the community of some of its members but undone the work of many more. Yet these would have been three or four violent events in as many centuries. However great their impact, defence was only one function of a complex which encapsulated multifarious aspects of contemporary life of which conflict, on whatever scale, was one.

11.2.5 How did the complex function?

It is argued above that people came to the hill for short periods, sometimes in early summer or autumn, sometimes up to a few hundred at a time, sometimes in smaller numbers. They came from distances of up to 45 km away to the south, and perhaps as much as 80 km away to the north-west. They brought with them already disarticulated human remains, wheat, barley, hazelnuts, red deer antler, occasionally venison, grinding equipment and pots from the areas where they lived, a few pots and axeheads exchanged from farther to the south-west, and livestock on the hoof, especially cattle. These last may have done double duty as beasts of burden and as meat for consumption. While on the hill, people carried on the everyday activities of life, but also did everything that a scattered population would do when gathered together. There is tangible evidence of feasting – of meat-consumption on a level clearly not usual for at least some of the population. Some gatherings equally tangibly included construction of new earthworks and maintenance of existing ones; a few were occasions of attack; and carefully placed deposits were made in both pits and ditches, some of them reopened for the purpose. The rest can only be guessed at: exchange not only of artefacts but of knowledge, skills, marriage partners; sacrifice; ceremony; dance; song ... As Isobel Smith wrote of Windmill Hill (1965, 19):

> '... the enclosure may be seen to have served as a centre or rallying-point for the population of a fairly wide area.
>
> Such rallying-points play an essential role in the lives of some contemporary communities living in a comparable stage of economic and technological development ... Assembly of the scattered families of tribal units takes place at one or more intervals during the year, at the slack periods in the agricultural and/or stock-tending cycle, and affords opportunities for the transaction of the necessary business of tribal life. In addition to those matters which may come within the political field in its broadest sense, such other matters can be attended to as the holding of initiation ceremonies, match-makings and weddings, the exchange of stock and seed corn and perhaps of more durable goods. Rites and ceremonies are performed to ensure the fertility of the flocks and herds and the growing of the corn, and finally to celebrate the harvest. Communal feasts are an inevitable accompaniment of such occasions, and some industrial activities may be undertaken, either because they are less tedious when performed to the accompaniment of a lively exchange of news and gossip, or because there is insufficient time at other seasons.'

This picture is instantly recognisable in interpretations of more recently excavated enclosures like Etton in Cambridgeshire (Pryor 1998), in the reworking of the Windmill Hill record by Whittle *et al* (1999), and in the vivid semi-fictional narrative of Edmonds (1999, 106–8, 130–2), because it continues to fit an expanding body of evidence.

At first sight, the numerous differences between the two enclosures and their related features might suggest the expression of the identities of two principal social groups, in terms of their practices, the areas from which they came, and the extent of their access to goods from remote sources (Table 11.5). It is even arguable that the composition of pottery fabrics and the way in which pits were left to silt on the Hanford spur, where a gateway provided access to those approaching the complex from the west, ally it more to the central area than to the Stepleton spur (3.6.4). But the picture is more complex. There are pointers to movement between the two enclosures at either end of the route between them: in the high frequency in the south long barrow ditches of fabric group 6, the main non-local ceramic of the Stepleton spur (Figs 3.66–7), and in the location of the only flint-packed slot in the Stepleton enclosure in segment 8, at its north-west entrance (Fig 3.88). The source areas of the materials deposited in the two parts of the complex do not fall into two groups, but overlap and interweave (Table 11.5). The most abundant non-local quern materials from the Stepleton spur came from south Dorset, near the coast, and the most abundant non-local ceramics may have done the same, as may a couple of scallop shells. Yet beach pebbles are confined to the central area, which also has most of the 'Portland' chert, from the same general zone whether obtained from Portland itself or from the Carstens series soils of the Dorchester area (Woodward and Bellamy 1991, 31). Gabbroic pottery and stone axeheads from the south-west peninsula are strongly concentrated in the central area. But charred fragments of Cornish Heath (*Erica vagans*), now native in Britain only on the Lizard peninsula and in the north-west of Ireland, came from a pit on the Stepleton spur. Another pit on the Stepleton spur yielded a grape pip dated to the mid-fourth millennium (see Jones and Legge, 6.2; Jones and Legge 1987). Yet the only charred grape vine fragment so far identified is from the main enclosure (see Austin *et al*, 6.1).

Etton in fact provides a model for the interpretation of the differences between the two enclosures at Hambledon. There, in a single circuit much the size of the Stepleton enclosure, there were contrasts of a comparable order but different nature between the east and west sides. Pryor's view of this dichotomy as reflecting spheres in which different kinds and scales of ceremony were enacted and different kinds of deposit were made (1998, 363–8) would fit the Hambledon record. It is even possible to envisage individuals or crowds proceeding from one to the other. The topography ensures that, for most of the gentle ascent from the Stepleton spur to the central dome of the hill, the main enclosure and the surrounding earthworks remain out of sight, bursting into view quite suddenly at a late stage of the approach. This effect would have been heightened by the largely wooded conditions inferred from the molluscs. Its impact on those who knew the significance of the earthworks and at least the general nature of what was to take place inside them can only be guessed at. Expressions of group, even individual, identity are perhaps more likely to lie in the distinctions between deposits in ditch segments, pit groups, or individual pits.

The evidence from Hambledon is similar to that from other causewayed enclosures, not only in outline, but in the minute details of ditch recutting and of the assembly of deposits, irrespective of location or topography. This bespeaks beliefs and traditions shared over a large tract of territory, as Pryor emphasises (1998, 374–7). Furthermore, usage in north-west Europe seems to draw on the same common pool of practice: repeated recutting, carefully placed deposits in ditches and pits, emphasis on axeheads, emphasis on the skull and on cattle, intermingling of human and animal (especially cattle) remains, are all to be found in the Sarup enclosures on Fünen, and in the other enclosures reviewed by Andersen in the same volume (1997). The Hambledon complex stands out by its so far unparalleled scale. The proximity of other enclosures (Whitesheet Hill at 22 km, Maiden Castle at 30) raises the question of the relationships between populations and monuments. The recurrent clustering of causewayed enclosures (Oswald *et al* 2001, fig 1.1) suggests significant areas in which several communities each maintained a ceremonial focus, and that there may have been a hierarchy among those foci. Such a hierarchy may even be reflected in the apparent catchments of different enclosures.

11.3 The Neolithic subsistence base

Hambledon provides a wealth of evidence for contemporary subsistence, although this must be interpreted in the light of its undoubtedly special functions. The starting point must be Richards' demonstration (7.2) that dietary protein was terrestrial and that, while most adults derived most of their protein from meat and/or milk rather than plant sources, the proportions derived from animal and plant sources varied from person to person. McKinley correspondingly notes (7.1) that low levels of dental disease suggest a diet high in animal protein, and that there is little dental hypoplasia, an indicator of nutritional stress. Meat consumption is directly evidenced on the hill, and Legge's preferred interpretation of the cattle slaughtered there as the surplus adults from dairy herds (8.1) is reinforced by the frequency of milk lipids in a sample of sherds from the site (see Copley *et al*, 7.3; Copley *et al* 2003). Milk or its derivatives may have been the normal day-to-day source of animal protein, with the kind of meat-eating which took place at enclosures reserved for special gatherings. More than a quarter of orbital vaults, however, show signs of *cribra orbitalia*, which is generally thought to result from childhood iron deficiency anaemia, although other factors may be involved (see 7.1).

Two sources of plant protein are directly represented: grain (especially wheat) and hazelnuts. Some 50,000 emmer spikelets in a pit outside the Stepleton enclosure are so far the largest deposit of charred grain from the period in Britain, and small quantities of grain were retrieved wherever flotation was practiced on pit fills (see Jones and Legge, 6.2). These authors argue persuasively that the apparent scarcity of Neolithic cereals in Britain is the compound result of the recovery methods previously practised and of the destructibility of straw and chaff, which are likely to burn to ash and may be used as animal fodder, in contrast to nutshells which are far more robust and durable and likely to survive recognisably in the charred state.

The exploitation of hazelnuts certainly does not imply a significant reliance on wild plant foods. They were an economic resource in Cranborne Chase in the market economy of historical times, as recounted by John Aubrey in the seventeenth century (Britton 1847, 56):

> 'the nutts of the Chase are of great note, and are sold yearly beyond sea. They sell them at Woodbery Hill faire &C.; and the price of them is the price of a buscell of wheate'.

This trade long remained important, as recorded by Chafin (1818, 62–3):

> 'The Woods consist chiefly of hazel, which produce nuts in great profusion, to the relief and benefit of all the hamlets and villages for miles around it [the Chase]. It is their second harvest; for when all the corn hath been got in, and the leasing in the fields at an end, the inhabitants betake themselves to the woods; whole families from distant places flock to the Chase ... and make their abode there for whole weeks at a time if the weather will permit ... The neighbouring towns, particularly the seaports, are a sure and ready market for their wares, and the price is generally on a par with wheat.'

This harvest was from stands of coppiced hazel, which provided poles for various local industries and fodder for livestock (ibid, 64–9), while also affording the relatively light, open conditions which favour nut-production. Coppicing may have been practised more frequently in the fourth millennium than before, in line with increased use of hurdles and other structural elements, and this may in turn have promoted nut production and consumption (cf Gale 2004; Hinton 2004).

The presence of a fragment of grape vine charcoal as well as a charred grape pip indicates that grapes were growing nearby in the fourth millennium, and are likely to have been a Neolithic introduction. The innovations of the fourth millennium probably included mind-altering substances as well as food crops, monuments and artefacts. The identification of opium poppy seeds in a waterlogged sample from near the base of an early fourth millennium long barrow ditch at Raunds, Northamptonshire (Campbell and Robinson forthcoming), is now echoed by a further identification in a previously unanalysed sample from the Etton causewayed enclosure (Robinson in prep).

11.4 The local context

11.4.1 Hambledon Hill's place in the landscape

Any discussion of Hambledon Hill and its sequence of function and activity must focus upon its location both in terms of its immediate surroundings and of its wider context in south-west England, revisiting topics briefly introduced in Chapter 1. In every aspect of this consideration will be found paradox as unsatisfying to the modern geographically and spatially conditioned scholar as it may have been profoundly necessary to early farming people with their necessarily completely different understanding and perception of 'the landscape' (that which you can see at once) and 'the world' (that which you know of).

From a close perspective, from all but one direction Hambledon is not a striking eminence. It squats as a three-spurred hummock separated from Cranborne Chase only by the deeply incised valley of the river Iwerne. Because of the gentle convexity of the Chase and similarity in general height, Hambledon does not become visible to eyes directed from the east, south-east or north-east until those eyes are situated well onto the forward (western) slope of the Chase, within a distance of 2 to 4 km. To eyes approaching from the south-east along the valley of the river Stour, the hill is effectively concealed behind Hod Hill and, turning into the Iwerne valley, one could proceed several kilometres north before realising that Hambledon was even there, and then only from the north. As from Cranborne Chase, so to the south-west the gentle convexity of the downs and the similarity of height again lead to a lack of any consciousness of the mass of Hambledon until the eyes are situated well onto the forward slope, at a distance of no more than, again, 2 to 4 km. From three cardinal points Hambledon is a well-kept secret in terms of its visibility over distances greater than 2 to 4 km and, even when it is visible, its form and structure are scarcely apparent.

If the eyes, however, approach from an arc from the north-west around to the north the impression is very different. In this direction, across what are now the meadows of the Vale of Blackmoor, the broad floodplain of the river Stour and its sluggish tributaries, Hambledon is visible to more-or-less its whole extent from distances in excess of 15 to 20 km. The hill proclaims itself as the dominant feature on the skyline with its form readily apparent. Not a secret place, therefore, but three-quarters of a secret place. Hambledon Hill may have been something of an island, partly secluded but partly of a high profile, an Avalon among its local populations in the fifth and fourth millennia BC.

Yet, once access was gained to the hill, the extension of the 'world', as opposed to the 'landscape' was enormous. 'On a good day' (but how, in memory, seldom!), the eyes of an observer standing on Hambledon and looking to the south-east would skim across the summit of Hod Hill to a clear view of the Isle of Wight and Ryde harbour. To the north-west, again with good visibility, those eyes would perceive the Mendip Hills – a vast swathe of south-west England. This is a paradox indeed; a secret place and an isolated place from which one could perceive the 'world'. Yet an obvious and notable place in terms of its own stature and its perception from one cardinal direction.

11.4.2 Before the Hambledon complex was built

There is an abundance of Mesolithic lithics in Cranborne Chase, some dating back to the early Holocene, and all, regardless of period, concentrated on the Clay-with-Flints, which caps the higher ground and provided the best locally available flint for artefact manufacture (Barrett *et al* 1991, 29–30; Arnold *et al* 1988; Green 2000, 20–28). On Hambledon Hill, on the other hand, an excavated collection of some 89,000 pieces of struck flint includes one, possibly two, Mesolithic artefacts (see Saville, 10.2). Yet pine charcoal from two posthole-like features on the hill is dated to the eighth millennium cal BC (see 3.2). Given the lack of contemporary lithics, the hill seems to have been a vantage point rather than a living, or even a hunting, place. Both features were in break-of-slope positions, where posts set in them or fires lit close to them would have been conspicuous, especially if the surrounding landscape included areas of calcareous grassland, as pollen analysis in the Allen valley in the occupied chalkland of Cranborne Chase, suggests (Scaife 2003). They would not, however, have been visible from this direction, since both were on the west side of the hill (Fig 3.2). They would instead have commanded and been visible from the open vista to the north-west. Those who generated the eighth millennium pine charcoal on the hill seem to have looked to this region, where contemporary activity is evidenced not in the adjacent Blackmoor Vale, but beyond it on the Mendips and Quantocks and in the Somerset Levels (Jacobi 1982).

In the later Flandrian period, Simmons (1996) has argued, on the basis of locations where peat has survived in sufficient depth to be a source of evidence, that a consistent pattern can be observed throughout the British Isles for the alteration of the forest environment by hunting communities using fire as an instrument of intentional clearance. In so doing they created conditions that favoured the successful hunting of ungulates by encouraging the development of a limited and defined forest grazing environment. He suggests that, in terms of the locations where such activity can be studied today, the most likely situations for such activity would appear to be near lakes, in the zone between hilltops and the spring line, and near to the spring line, especially just above it (Simmons 1996, 107). The area around Hambledon Hill, on the junction of Chalk and Greensand and at the confluence of two rivers, would have been an ideal situation in which to encourage the density of ungulate populations further and would also have furnished abundant and diverse small game (including beaver), fish, and plant foods. In all likelihood it saw relatively intensive exploitation. Such exploitation may have included the managed running of ungulate herds in a forest margin environment exploiting clearings and areas of natural meadow in the river valleys. Relatively open conditions would have favoured the flowering and fruiting of hazel trees.

Mesolithic activity in Cranborne Chase continued up to the adoption of Neolithic traditions. The principal evidence for this comes from the remarkable sequence of dated deposits preserved in a natural swallow-hole, the Fir Tree Field shaft, in Gussage St Michael parish, some 15 km east of Hambledon Hill (Allen and Green 1998; Allen 2000a; Allen 2002). The excavated deposits went back to the Boreal (the period of the possible postholes on Hambledon Hill), but had mainly accumulated during the late fifth and early fourth millennia cal BC. The deposits had two main components: rapidly accumulated rubble fills, but including the skeletons of two roe deer, overlain by soil fills which had silted into the weathering cone at the top of the shaft. Hazel charcoal from the topmost rubble fill is dated to 4330–4040 cal BC (5355±45 BP; OxA-8011). Above this layer, in the lowest soil fills, were seven microliths in fresh condition, clustered as if they had formed part of a spearhead or other composite implement, as well as other Mesolithic lithics and bones of red deer and ?aurochs, dated to the late fifth or earliest fourth millennium. The molluscs from the sequence indicate closed but light forest in the early fifth millennium, giving way to denser woodland, which was the subject of a short-lived clearance at the time the microliths were deposited, only to regenerate thereafter (Allen 2000a, 42).

Stratified above these layers was a hearth associated with Neolithic Bowl pottery. Ash wood charcoal from it is dated to 4050–3790 cal BC (5150±45 BP; OxA-8010) and charred clematis roots from nearby to 3960–3710 cal BC (5045±45 BP; OxA-8009). The sequence is most readily interpreted as reflecting a fairly rapid transition from one tradition to the next, with only a short period of co-existence. Its chronology is furthermore compatible with the dendrochronologically precise construction dates of 3807/3806 BC for the Sweet Track and of 3838 BC for its predecessor, the Post Track, in the Somerset Levels (Coles and Coles 1990, 218), which make it clear that Neolithic artefacts (pottery, single-piece arrowheads, and a jadeite axehead brought from the Alps) were already current at the beginning of the fourth millennium, and that the surrounding woodland was managed and, to some extent, cleared, grazed and cultivated (Coles and Coles 1986; Caseldine 1984). Elsewhere in Britain the possibility of a rapid transition is reinforced. Dates reliably associated with Mesolithic artefacts extend into the early fourth millennium (eg Spikins 2002, 43); and some Neolithic monuments, including long barrows and cairns, were being built from *c* 3800 cal BC on the evidence of radiocarbon measurements on the contained human remains, including some of those listed by Richards and Hedges (1999). Dietary change at this time seems to have been abrupt (Richards 2003). The potential for the adoption of Neolithic lifeways within a couple of generations becomes a real one, with connotations of the persuasive power of new beliefs as well as new practices (Richards 2003; Thomas 2003; Mercer 2004; Harding and Healy forthcoming).

11.4.3 During Hambledon's *floruit*

The evidence for fourth millennium activity in the surrounding areas is uneven and diverse. To the east, despite the extent of excavation and surface collection in Cranborne Chase, the sum of early Neolithic artefacts recovered is small. The total collection of Neolithic Bowl pottery is outnumbered many times over by that from Hambledon (Table 11.6). The lithics reflect a similar picture. They are scarce, and some are from monumental or funerary rather than settlement contexts (Gardiner 1991b). The only apparent living sites, both exiguous and almost certainly short-lived, lie on the surface beneath the Thickthorn Down long barrow and by the hearth in the Fir Tree Field shaft. Lithics collected in the course of the Hambledon Hill Survey similarly give the impression that early Neolithic activity was confined to the hill (see Saville, 10.2.10). Yet people and their animals seem to have had more of an impact on the vegetation here than on Hambledon Hill where their artefacts and food remains are so abundant. Hambledon remained at least partly wooded throughout its Neolithic use (see Bell *et al*, Ch 5); while there were local clearances around the early fourth millennium hearth in the Fir Tree Field shaft (Allen in prep) and the perhaps rather later Handley Down mortuary enclosure (Allen 2000a, 43–4). Established open grassland, on the other hand, already obtained in the areas of the Thickthorn Down long barrow and another long barrow on Gussage Cow Down by the time they were built (French *et al* 2003, 229). Expanding clearance in the Chase is suggested by the large tract of grassland which surrounded the Monkton-up-Wimborne 'temple', built during the second half of the fourth millennium, and by the mosaic of scrub and lightly grazed grassland through which the Dorset cursus was built in the same period (Allen 2002, 61–63). The Chase was indeed occupied, but not intensively.

Evidence for earlier Neolithic settlement is markedly more abundant on the coastal plain to the south and south-east than in Cranborne Chase. Hambledon and the Chase are linked to this area by the rivers Stour and Avon and, on the lower reaches of both, where they approach Christchurch harbour, there is a long record of finds of early Neolithic lithics and pottery, often from pits, with only one apparently contemporary monument. This raises the possibility of a less sparsely occupied coastal zone for which Hambledon and the Chase together formed a ceremonial focus and possibly a boundary zone (Barrett *et al* 1991, 31–4).

Table 11.6 Summary of Neolithic and Beaker pottery from Cranborne Chase and Hambledon Hill

The numbers given for Cranborne Chase in the first row for each tradition are taken from the quantification of Cleal (1991b). They are followed in the second row by notes of subsequent finds.

	Cranborne Chase totals	*Hambledon Hill totals*
Neolithic Bowl	>56 sherds – minimum 13 vessels	26,032 sherds – minimum 850 vessels
	Plus 1 sherd from Handley Hill mortuary enclosure (Green 2000, 55) and a few sherds from the Fir Tree Field shaft (Allen 2000a, 41)	
Peterborough Ware	324 sherds – minimum 59 vessels	44 sherds – minimum 5 vessels
	Plus sherds from Monkton-up-Wimborne 'temple' (Green 2000, 78) and Fir Tree Field shaft (Allen 2000a, 40), scraps from Wyke Down henge 2 (Green 2000, 87)	
Grooved Ware	>507 sherds – minimum 36 vessels	–
	Plus substantial assemblages, including semi-complete vessels, from subsequently excavated pits and structures (Green 2000, 71–6) and Wyke Down henge 2 (ibid, 86–9)	
Beaker	>540 sherds and 3 complete vessels – minimum 132 vessels	1615 sherds – minimum no. of vessels not calculated
	Plus substantial settlement assemblage from over and around the Fir Tree Field shaft (Green 2000, 100–1) and sherds from Monkton-up-Wimborne 'temple' (ibid, 101)	

The Neolithic, indeed the prehistoric, record of the Blackmoor Vale is virtually null. Along the Jurassic ridge beyond it, however, there is a scatter of early Neolithic sites and finds, including plausible settlement traces in the form of pottery, struck flint including leaf arrowheads, animal bone, and charcoal, some in pits, at Cadbury Castle, just 25 km from Hambledon across the Vale (Alcock 1980, 665; Barrett *et al* 2000, 53–4, 86–8). Beyond this again lie the prodigiously and innovatively explored Somerset Levels, crossed as the period progressed by more and more wooden tracks linking uplands and islands (Coles and Coles 1986), flanked by the Mendips and the Quantocks, the first of these, especially, rich in multi-period flint scatters, and caves, some occupied or used for burial in this period, as well as long barrows and long cairns (Minnitt 1982; Bond 2004).

The earliest elements of the Hambledon complex, the main enclosure, the south long barrow and the inner east cross-dyke, are estimated to have been built in *3690–3620 cal BC (95% probability*; Table 4.2; Fig 1.9*)*. They seem quite deliberately to turn away from the 'grand vista' to the north and north-west. The main enclosure with the partial outer circuit formed by the cross-dyke is eccentrically sited on the summit of the hill, and slightly 'tipped' to the south-east (Fig 1.4), so as not (and only just not) to be visible from the Vale of Blackmoor. Here in these initial stages we may see the affirmation of the 'secret place' aspect of this chosen site. The subsequently built earthworks, the Shroton spur outwork, the Stepleton enclosure, the middle Stepleton outwork and its successor the inner Stepleton outwork, all emphasised this original orientation (Fig 1.9), the Stepleton enclosure sited on the crown of the spur overlooking low-lying ground to the south and east. The only possible exception here is the massive, undated hillfort long barrow (Fig 2.14). If this too was one of the earlier elements, as its form might suggest, its skyline position, on a narrow ridge forming one of the highest parts of the hill, would make it eminently conspicuous from all directions.

Many causewayed enclosures are located across the contours rather than on hilltops, and most seem designed to face in a particular direction, as Isobel Smith long ago pointed out (1971, 92). This observation has been persuasively elaborated by Oswald *et al* (2001, 91–106), who propose connections between enclosures and the areas to which they are 'tilted' and with which they are often intervisible. In the case of Hambledon Hill, the relationship is ambiguous, since intervisibility with the Chase is slight, but there is a quite intimate morphological relationship between the south long barrow on Hambledon and those to the east. Many of the long barrows in Cranborne Chase, especially those close to the Dorset cursus, have long been recognised as a distinctive form, relatively short and surrounded either by a continuous ditch or by a U-plan ditch, sometimes with slight causeways (Barrett *et al* 1991, 36–49). The south Hambledon long barrow conforms to this local tradition, even down to the detail of a posthole in a causeway in the ditch at the south end (Fig 3.47: LB5 F6), which echoes the three equally non-structural postholes at the east end of the Thickthorn Down long barrow (Drew and Piggott 1936, 82–3). It is possible to imagine the posts that occupied these sockets as markers used in the course of ceremonies, and/or as supports on which significant objects were displayed.

The only one of these barrows to have been excavated in addition to the Hambledon and Thickthorn Down examples is Wor Barrow, investigated by General Pitt Rivers (1898). Each had a very different structural and depositional history (Barrett *et al* 1991,

36–43), the starkest contrast being between the absence of primary burials from the Thickthorn Down long barrow and the presence of both articulated and disarticulated human remains beneath Wor Barrow. The available dates do not preclude contemporaneity but do little to demonstrate it. The construction date of the Hambledon barrow is estimated as *3680–3640 cal BC (95% confidence*; Table 4.2). For that of the Thickthorn Down barrow, however, there is only a *terminus post quem*, provided by a measurement of 4050–3800 cal BC (5160±45 BP; BM-2355) on animal bone from the old land surface beneath the mound, a sample the apparent age of which may have been increased by the application of PVA (Barrett and Bradley 1991, 10). At Wor Barrow the standard deviations of measurements on antler picks from the ditch base and the primary silts are so large that their probability distributions span most of the fourth millennium and all of the Neolithic use of Hambledon Hill: 3800–3100 cal BC (4740±130 BP; BM-2284R) and 3700–3000 cal BC (4660±130 BP; BM-2283R). The strongest argument for the broad contemporaneity of all three barrows is similarity of their final forms and the presence in them of Neolithic Bowl pottery and early Neolithic lithics in primary contexts. The distinctive morphology alone suggests that the south Hambledon long barrow and the long barrows in the Chase were built by people with common traditions.

Nevertheless, the Cranborne Chase barrows as a group appear to 'turn their back' on the highest ground of the north-west-facing façade of Cranborne Chase that overlooks the area dominated by Hambledon Hill. Their distribution is striking by its intimate relationship with the headwaters of a series of rivers that all run south-eastwards to the occupied coastal plain. Hambledon and the barrows seem to focus upon altogether different components of the landscape, perhaps with a *cordon sanitaire* of unexploited land between them. Projected backwards in time, this would accord with the very different level of Mesolithic presence in each. If this distinction is recognised, the crucial importance of Hambledon Hill's position becomes manifest. It commands the principal corridor of contact between areas of high Neolithic impact on the coastal plain of south-east Dorset and those on the uplands and in the levels of north-west Dorset and Somerset.

The evidence of artefacts and materials is significant here. If the more abundant kinds of quern material and non-local ceramics found at Hambledon are regarded as domestic equipment (Smith 1965, 42), in contrast to rare objects from more remote locations that may have been exchanged over long distances, then they may be a rough index of the overall territory from which people gathered on the hill. The sources in question form an arc running from the south-east Dorset coast through the Jurassic ridge to the Mendips, in other words the area visible from the hill (11.4.1). Some of them correspond to the apparent concentration of early Neolithic settlement on the coastal plain to the south and south-east of Hambledon and the Chase: beach pebbles of both flint and quartzite, some of them used as hammerstones (see Roe, 10.1.2; Saville, 10.2); scallop shells (see Somerville, 8.6); heathstone from between Wareham and Poole (see Roe, 10.1.2); pottery made from clays characterised by iron-rich red pellets (see Darvill, 9.2), possibly originating in the same area as the heathstone (see Roe, 10.1.2); and a small amount of pottery tempered with fresh, as distinct from fossil, shell (see Darvill, 9.2). Their source area overlaps with the concentration of early Neolithic finds mapped by Barrett *et al* (1991, fig 2.5) and extends to the west of it, especially if Roe is correct in attributing the beach pebbles to the Chesil Beach. That concentration itself, however, may reflect an acceleration of discovery in the course of gravel quarrying around the Bournemouth conurbation and of construction within it. The import of these materials to Hambledon accords with the use of the complex by people who lived towards the coast, 30–45 km away.

Other objects and materials were brought from the west and north-west, from the land rising beyond the Blackmoor Vale. These were pottery of clays from a range of locations along the limestone ridge, 25–60 km away (see Darvill 9.2), and Old Red Sandstone from the Mendips, 40–80 km away (see Roe 10.1.2). The catchment of the complex may well have extended this far, at most a couple or three days' walk. Travel by individuals over distances of this order is made all the more plausible by the history of a woman buried in the Monkton-up-Wimborne 'temple' towards or after the end of the use of the Hambledon complex. The level of lead in her bones was such that the nearest area in which she could have lived a substantial part of her life could only be the Mendips (Green 2000, 77–84). The terrain visible from the hill encompasses the source areas of the more abundant non-local materials brought to it, and they were brought to it from the start of the sequence (Figs 3.64–6, 3.128–9; Tables 10.2–3). What if this is the territory to which the complex was most closely related? A scarcity of sarsen, often the main quern material on chalkland sites, may also be significant here, as may a low frequency and under-elaboration of carved chalk, compared with what is found in enclosures in Sussex and the rest of Wessex. Hambledon looked both ways, but many of those who frequented it came from the west and south, and the first of the earthworks which they built were designed to make a statement to those living to the east.

Earthwork building started relatively late on the west side of the hill (Fig 1.9), where the first stage may have been double ditches and banks with an imposing gateway (Fig 3.136), across the Hanford spur, which provides the easiest approach to the hill for those approaching from the west (Fig 1.4). It was only in the later part of Hambledon's Neolithic use, in the third quarter of the fourth millennium, that the inward-looking, 'secretive' approach to earthwork design was fully rejected, with the construction of the western outwork and perhaps the linkage of the outworks on the Stepleton and Hanford spurs (Fig 1.9), forming an almost continuous line of defence along the west of the hill, sited so as to be clearly visible to the north and north-west, while slopes that were no steeper were left undefended on the east (Cranborne Chase) side. Here would seem to be a reversal of approaches to the use of the hill, now displaying its *strength* in a sky-line position, not, as formerly, displaying itself to the east, but dominating the basin of the Vale of Blackmoor to the west and north-west. Requirements had clearly changed 'politically'. Formerly the need had been for a 'statement' of physical presence (a statement constantly renewed by ditch recutting-episodes 'celebrated' by the deposit of feasting debris) and a statement of the *extent* of the enclosed area, designed to be inclusive in a geopolitical relationship focused towards the east and Cranborne Chase. Latterly the desire seems to be to impress and exclude, with these intentions focused towards the west and the Vale of Blackmoor.

The proposed southerly and westerly orientation may be exaggerated by the recognisability of materials from these areas. The flint-tempered pottery and flint nodules of the Wessex chalk cannot be pinned down with even this level of imprecision, and it is, after all, local materials that dominate the assemblages from the hill. The location of Hambledon Hill between Cranborne Chase and the Vale of Blackmoor recalls Barker's and Webley's observation (1978) that upland enclosures, and at least some of their lowland counterparts, sit at junctions within the terrestrial environment between areas of different geology and pedology and, thereby, the different vegetations and faunas that these support. In the case of Hambledon the geological junction is between the Chalk and the Greensand (Fig 1.2), as it is at Whitesheet, Knap Hill, Rybury, and Windmill Hill. It may be no coincidence that Whitesheet provides the only apparent comparison for the Hambledon complex: only the causewayed enclosure there is dated, but it is accompanied by further possibly Neolithic earthworks in the form of a second, smaller, ovoid enclosure, possibly a third enclosure underlying the hillfort, and perhaps cross-dykes, although a Neolithic date is now arguable only for the most northerly cross-dyke of the three, since sectioning of the other two has suggested that they are respectively Romano-British and Bronze Age (Rawlings *et al* 2004). This highly visible boundary between two provinces, the Wessex chalk and the physically and culturally distinct south-west, may have had particular meaning.

11.4.4 As Hambledon declined

The *floruit* of Hambledon Hill ended in the late fourth millennium (Table 4.4). Peterborough Ware, current *c* 3400–2500 cal BC (Gibson and Kinnes 1997), is confined to one semi-complete vessel and a few scattered sherds, all from the Stepleton spur. There are no chisel arrowheads from the hill and only a single oblique one. The initial use of other causewayed enclosures ended at about the same time – as is vividly exemplified at Maiden Castle by the construction of the Long Mound across the silted enclosure ditches (Sharples 1991, 54–7). But the use of Hambledon seems to have fallen off particularly abruptly. It is difficult not to link this to events to the east. The ideological, perhaps cosmological, transformations of the late fourth millennium reached their apogee in the building of the Dorset cursus in *3360–3030 cal BC (91% probability;* Barclay and Bayliss 1999, 22–3), when Hambledon was going out of use. One major monumental focus may have directly replaced another. Like Hambledon, the Dorset cursus is the largest known monument of its kind in Britain. With its construction, the monumental and ceremonial focus was shifted from the largely unoccupied boundary of the Chalk and the land to the south-west into the heart of the chalk downland of Cranborne Chase, where numerous smaller monuments were built in the late fourth and the early third millennium, and where middle and late Neolithic pottery and lithics abound (Barrett *et al* 1991, 59–108; Green 2000, 64–90; Saville 10.2.10). The late fourth millennium date of the Dorset cursus reduces the plausibility of Tilley's suggestion that movement along it played a part in the circulation of human remains to and from Hambledon Hill (1994, 200), although the cursus may have formalised, even closed off, an older route, as Johnston (1999) suggests, a route marked by long barrows.

The Dorset cursus has, clearly, two axes: a north-west/south-east axis of *linearity*, aligned on a number of the long barrows mentioned above, but also, as Bradley (1993) and Tilley (1994) have pointed out, a north-east/south-west axis of *partition*. Here its very construction, differentially as a deep barrier on its south-east side as opposed to a less assertive boundary on its north-west side (Barrett *et al* 1991, 43–6) might suggest a boundary function with, as Harding points out (1999, 32), the densest areas of Neolithic settlement set 5 km to the north-west of the monument (Barrett *et al* 1991, figs 2.4, 3.2).

Peterborough Ware, far more abundant in the Chase than early Neolithic pottery (Table 11.6; Barrett *et al* 1991, fig 4.4), was deposited in the upper levels of the already silted cursus ditch and in newly built monuments like Handley barrows 26 and 27 near Wor Barrow, and the Monkton-up-Wimborne 'temple' (Barrett *et al* 1991, 51, 70–3, 84–7; Green 2000, 77–80). It was also placed in much older sites, not only on Hambledon Hill, but in the upper fills of the Fir Tree Field shaft, and the ditches of Wor Barrow and the Thickthorn Down long barrow (Cleal 1991b; Allen 2000a, 40). Grooved Ware, current *c* 2900–2100 cal BC in southern Britain (Garwood 1999), is totally absent from Hambledon and from the older monuments in the Chase. Instead, it has been found in quantity in pits and in newly built monuments like both Wyke Down henges (Barrett *et al* 1991, 59–108; Green 2000, 54–90). The focus around the cursus was maintained, but by the construction of new monuments rather than the continued use of old ones, and a new, lower-lying, focus was developed further down the river Allen at Knowlton where major henge monuments were built (Green 2000, 85–90). It is as if the disjunctures of the later fourth millennium grew from existing beliefs and practices, just as Peterborough Ware developed from Neolithic Bowl, while those of the early third millennium were a more abrupt break with the past, just as Grooved Ware appeared in new forms and fabrics and with new decorative motifs.

Despite the absence of Grooved Ware from Hambledon, one of the largest animal bone deposits there, a compact heap in the top of the inner east cross-dyke ditch including the remains of two adult cattle, one caprine and some bones of infantile cattle and of pig, is dated to 2920–2700 cal BC (Table 4.1: OxA-8893), firmly within the currency of Grooved Ware. The results of this slaughter could have fed hundreds of people – a feast by any standards (see Legge, 8.1), but it took place in a period when, on all the other available evidence, the hill was disused. The absence of artefacts clearly does not mean the absence of activity, but it strongly suggests that activity was confined to specific events.

On Hambledon Hill, the earth was again turned, and artefacts were again deposited, after Beaker pottery, current *c* 2500–1700 cal BC (Needham 2005), had come into use. Recuts were made in some of the ditches, and 'flint mines' were excavated on the Hanford spur (3.6.3) in a far more open environment than had prevailed in the fourth millennium (see Bell *et al*, 5.2). Round barrows, of admittedly uncertain date, were built on the hill (see Palmer and Oswald, Ch 2), This too is part of a wider development. Disparate distributions for Grooved Ware and Beaker are widespread, although the character of the disparity varies from region to region. One recurrent feature is that Beaker pottery tends to occur in the same Neolithic monuments, and sometimes in the same distinct areas, as Peterborough Ware, with which it was almost certainly not contemporary, more than it does at monuments and in areas associated with Grooved Ware, with which it was contemporary, probably for some centuries. This holds true in Cranborne Chase (Barrett *et al* 1991, 111–16) and, for example, on Salisbury Plain (Cleal *et al* 1995, 477; Thomas 1999, 174–83; Allen 1997c, pls 3–5), in the area around Dorchester, Dorset (Healy 1997b, 285–7), in the upper Thames catchment (Thomas 1999, 188–97; Barclay 1999), in the Nene valley (Harding and Healy forthcoming), and in Yorkshire (Thorpe and Richards 1984, 70–73; Manby 1988, figs 4.7, 4.15, 4.16).

It is as if sectors of society other than those allied with henge monuments, and all that went with them, had progressively become more powerful, and had severed themselves from the existing regime by adopting new, ultimately continental, technologies, artefact styles and modes of burial, at the same time emphasising customs which had a pedigree more ancient than prevailing beliefs. In a climate of validation by affiliation with an ancient past, use of old monuments would have had a rationale (Harding and Healy forthcoming). This may be the context of the late third/early second millennium use of Hambledon Hill, as well as of Beaker burials inserted into the Thickthorn Down long barrow (Drew and Piggott 1936, 80), Beaker sherds in the ditch of Wor Barrow and the Dorset cursus (Cleal 1991b) and in the upper fills of the central pit at Monkton-up-Wimborne (Green 2000, 100–1).

Hamilton (1999) has argued that use of causewayed enclosures in this period is indistinguishable from the contemporary settlement and funerary remains which extend across the landscape, and may thus form part of that pattern rather than reflect any conscious recognition of the pre-existing monuments. At Hambledon, this may apply to the round barrows, which are part of an extensive spread across the Chase, including major cemeteries (Barrett *et al* 1991, fig 4.6). It is also a reasonable characterisation of the Beaker assemblages themselves, which include fragments of both fine and rusticated vessels, sometimes in association with animal bone, struck flint, charcoal and other burnt material. It does not, however, take account of the relationship of the assemblages to what would at that time have been clearly visible earthworks. In the central area, Beaker material was concentrated at the two identified entrances. In the south, on the route to and from the Stepleton spur, shallow pits packed with flint and chalk sometimes with a few plain and rusticated Beaker sherds (and in one case with more than 400 pieces of struck flint), were cut into the two butts of the silted east ditch of the Long Barrow (3.3.6). The two densest concentrations of Beaker settlement material, both of very limited extent, were on either side of the entrance giving onto the Shroton spur, and were typologically distinct, suggesting two separate episodes (3.3.8). The more abundant of the two, in segment 4 of the inner east cross-dyke, was in a pit cut through the Neolithic ditch fills. Similar pit-like recuts, far poorer in artefacts, occurred at the same stratigraphic horizon elsewhere in the same segment, in segment 2 of the outer east cross-dyke and segments 10 and 11 of the main enclosure (3.3.2–3). These are unlikely to have been part of a wider scatter of pits, since the excavation of *c* 15% of the interior of the main enclosure revealed many Neolithic pits but no Beaker ones. There was, indeed, very little Beaker or early Bronze Age pottery in the interior at all, the largest assemblage consisting of a mere 16 sherds/86 g from a treethrow hole and recent features cutting it on site B (Table 3.6).

On the Stepleton spur, an emphasis on entrances similarly accompanied a dearth of Beaker material in the almost completely excavated interior. The only recut of this date in the Stepleton enclosure was in segment 9, at the putative entrance giving onto the obvious route to the main enclosure (3.5.2). In the inner outwork, a possible south-east entrance between segments 5 and 6 was marked by midden-like deposits in the opposed butts of both (3.5.4), containing pottery (among which early Bronze Age wares out-numbered Beaker ones), lithics, animal bone, charcoal, 'pot-boilers', a copper alloy awl and a bone ornament which seems to be a replica of a jet or amber spacer bead (Fig 8.33: ST79 860). The deposit extended for some 27 m, occupying most of the length of segment 5, and was sometimes clearly in a recut (Figs 3.96–7: L2B). Its presence in the butt, and only the butt, of segment 6, where the bone bead was found (Fig 3.98), suggests that there was an intention to mark the causeway. Typology aside, the assemblage is of similar character to those from the phase VI Neolithic deposits. It may, indeed, also have resulted from the deposition of the residue of an episode of gathering, eating and drinking. In the outer outwork there was probably a localised recut containing Beaker pottery in one butt of segment 5, and a recut of unknown extent was sectioned in segment 2 (3.5.5). This recut is exceptional. It was the only one to contain a pottery assemblage which could scarcely be described as domestic (there were three bases and a rim fragment without other sherds, and at least one base was found upright and was hence, perhaps, an originally intact pot truncated by ploughing). It was also the only recut of this date on the Stepleton spur or in the central area to be made *after* ploughsoils had begun to accumulate in the ditch top. All the recuts described so far were made in gradually accumulated silts and were truncated together with them by subsequent ploughing. Bearing in mind that this segment was well away from the Stepleton enclosure; this suggests that ploughing started sooner outside the enclosure than inside it and immediately around it, reinforcing the impression that the enclosure continued to be recognised and used into the second millennium BC. The same sequence was recorded more extensively on the Hanford spur, where narrow, shallow, linear recuts were made along the outer edge of almost the entire excavated length of both outwork ditches after ploughing had taken place over them (3.6.2, Figs 3.137–40). The recut in segment 3 of the inner outwork contained a small amount of Beaker and early Bronze Age pottery, and, in the south butt, human bone disturbed from underlying layers seemed to have been rearranged. The same butt, next to a Neolithic entrance, was subsequently the site of a localised, pit-like recut (Fig 3.138).

The Hanford record thus reinforces the impression that ploughing may have started outside the Stepleton enclosure while the enclosure itself was still used and frequented to some extent and that, after this, both Hanford outworks were redefined, over a distance of at least 100 m. It is even possible that this redefinition extended for as much as 700 m, from the Hanford spur to the Stepleton spur. The extent of the recut in segment 2 of the outer Stepleton outwork is unknown: it spanned the 4 m wide section in which it was recorded and, within those 4 m, appeared trench-like rather than pit-like. It could have been linear. Segment 1, to the west of it (Fig 3.81), was planned but not excavated, so that it is not known whether it too was recut. There may have been an extensive, though exiguous, redefinition of the outworks on the south-west side of the hill after their line had been blurred by ploughing. The redefinition of the Hanford outworks may relate to another event, the excavation of what were at first thought to be flint mines on the Hanford spur. These features defy interpretation. They were of later third millennium date (see Bayliss *et al*, 4.7.15); they were pits, interlinked in some instances by short 'galleries' or 'port-holes', sunk to a seam of low-quality tabular flint which does not figure in the industries of the site (see Saville, 10.2); they contained an exceptional, often wild fauna (see Legge, 8.1); both the flint and chalk removed from them were deployed elsewhere, the pits being backfilled with soil (3.6.3); and there are surface indications of other similar features (see Palmer and Oswald, Ch 2; Fig 2.7). The date would accord with the Beaker pottery in the ditch recuts. Was material from the quarries piled onto the banks? A comparable event may be represented by a small bank built between the inner and outer ditches of the Maiden Castle causewayed enclosure after an episode of cultivation. It post-dated the enclosure, on the evidence of *termini post quos* in the form of an animal bone dated to the later fourth millennium and a Mortlake-ware sherd. Its coincidence with a concentration of Beaker pottery in the enclosure ditch enhances the possibility of a late third/early second millennium date (Sharples 1991, 57, 103, 113, 256).

The Neolithic earthworks at Hambledon were recognised as significant more than a thousand years after their construction. That significance is unlikely to have born any relation to the beliefs and practices of those who built and originally used the complex, but the disposition of the cultural material of this period reflects conscious use of the earthworks rather than settlement fortuitously located on them.

Eventual disregard of the earthworks is evidenced by a vestigial, undated field system on the saddle between the main enclosure and the Stepleton spur, which runs obliquely to the Stepleton–Hanford outworks, laid out as if they did not exist (see Palmer and Oswald, Ch 2; Fig 2.7). It is possible to disentangle the much degraded elements of a middle to late Bronze Age settlement from the excavated record of the Stepleton spur (3.5.7), and this may well have been coeval with the nearby field system and, indeed, with other fields on the hillfort spur, which pre-dated at least some of the Iron Age earthworks (see Palmer and Oswald, Ch 2; 3.7; Fig 3.148), as well as with the burnt mound in Everley Water Meadow (5.3.3). At this stage, the hill seems to have become part of the landscape of increasingly visible settlements and increasingly partitioned farmland which extended over the Chase

(Barrett *et al* 1991, 223–6) and much of the downland of southern England. The small, perhaps lineage-scale, cemeteries and isolated burials, often juxtaposed to settlements, find an echo in a late second millennium inhumation burial just outside the Stepleton enclosure (3.5.7). The continuation of ceremony on a larger scale is, exceptionally, evidenced on Ogden Down, close to the cursus, by the construction of a post-lined avenue linking two pre-existing round barrows, one of which was at the same time surrounded by multiple post circles (Green 2000, 113–17, pl 20).

This extensive, enclosive mode of settlement ended early in the first millennium. Cranborne Chase is devoid of late Bronze Age settlement or pottery, despite the presence of some metalwork of the period (Barrett *et al* 1991, 228; O'Connor 1991). This suggests that settlement became more nucleated, and is of low visibility because that nucleation took place on the sites of the hillforts that surround the Chase and/or on those of the later first millennium settlements within it (Barrett *et al* 1991, figs 6.1–2). Low levels of investigation of both kinds of site leave ample scope for speculation. In this context, small quantities of late Bronze Age pottery from Hambledon Hill have some interest, especially given their location. There is a handful from the north-west of the main enclosure, close to the hillfort spur (3.3.2), and rather more from the south and west of the excavated part of the Stepleton spur (see Smith, 9.1.2), close to Hod Hill. Also close to Hod Hill is Everley Water Meadow, where a couple of late Bronze Age sherds and fragment of a stone mould for a type of socketed axe perhaps current from the eleventh to the ninth centuries BC (see Needham, 10.1.4) were found in the gravels of the south area, downstream from the burnt mound (5.3.3). A late Bronze Age socketed gouge has also been found on Hod Hill itself (Pearce 1983, pl 110: 444). These finds hint, and only hint, that settlement on the sites of both hillforts may have begun early in the first millennium, although it may have preceded fortification, since the earliest rampart on the hillfort spur, the north cross-dyke, is likely to have been built between the late eighth and the late sixth century BC (3.7.3).

The limited evidence tends to favour the hillforts. No vast late second/early first millennium midden accumulations like Potterne (Lawson 2000) or Chisenbury (McOmish 1996), both in Wiltshire, themselves bespeaking aggregation, have been identified in the area. The unexcavated settlement enclosures of Cranborne Chase are morphologically of late Iron Age/early Romano-British type, and, of the ten or so excavated first millennium BC settlements, only two, Gussage all Saints (Wainwright 1979b) and Pimperne (Harding *et al* 1993) go back to the early Iron Age, let alone the late Bronze Age (Barrett *et al* 1991, 229), although there are two or three surface finds of early Iron Age pottery (ibid, 233, 236). First millennium metalwork finds from the area are overwhelmingly late Iron Age (ibid, table 6.1). Hambledon was occupied, on the evidence of numerous hut-platforms (Figs 2.13, 3.148); the one excavated example was early Iron Age and others could be earlier (3.7.4). Hod Hill was equally obviously occupied, but none of the numerous hut platforms within it (Crawford and Keiller 1928, pl I) has been dated to the early Iron Age, despite an early Iron Age component among the pottery from the site (see Brown, 9.3).

The proximity of these two hillforts, which are little more than 1.5 km apart, inevitably raises the question of their relationship. The Hambledon sequence, as far as it is known, seems to have been punctuated by periodic lulls, suggesting that the focus of power and activity may have pulsed between them. The cleanliness of the naturally accumulated silts of the north cross rampart ditch (excavated in 1986) suggests an interval of abandonment between its construction and the establishment over it of a house platform. If the 'tiers' and the scarps on which multivallate ramparts were built in the east-centre of the fort were indeed cultivation terraces that post-dated the south cross rampart as well as the north, as argued above (3.7.3), then an interval long enough for them to form (one of decades, if not of centuries) would have elapsed between the construction of the south cross rampart and that of the multivallation. The final swing of the pendulum seems to have been towards Hod Hill, since the late Iron Age presence is far more marked there – as far as we know – than on Hambledon, and was certainly a reality at the time of Vespasian's campaign. In terms of the location and physical characteristics of the sites, this may have been a move from a refuge to a political centre (Giles 1993).

It thus appears that, in the, early first millennium, there may have been a nucleation of the population in the hillforts around the Chase, followed only much later by the development of numerous settlements within it accompanied by elaborate, multi-ditched boundaries (marking much older divisions including that first signalled by the cursus) and focused on an oppidum-like complex of enclosures and high-status finds on Gussage Hill (Green 2000, 126–9), the whole reaching its maximum development in the century before the Roman conquest. This picture is made all the more plausible by the record of the Dorchester area, where, despite extensive excavation, late Bronze Age and early to middle Iron Age settlement remains scarce outside the local hillforts, and widespread settlement of the areas around and between them seems a development of the late Iron Age (Sharples 1991, 257–64; Healy 1997c, 298–9; R J C Smith 1997, 299–300). Sharples sees the initial nucleation into defended sites as reflecting aggressive competition for control of agricultural land among communities who could no longer compete for status through control of copper, tin and objects made from them, the most successful and long-lived hillforts being those located at the interface of complementary terrains, like Maiden Castle, Hod Hill, and Hambledon Hill. Towards the end of the second century BC he sees Maiden Castle, South Cadbury in Somerset, Hod Hill and – by association – Hambledon Hill as coalescing into a single area of influence, defined by the Maiden Castle/Marnhull pottery style, a development which diminished the need for defences and furthered the proliferation of unfortified settlements (1991, 260–3).

11.5 Hambledon among other causewayed enclosures

Roger Mercer

This section will attempt to avoid repetition of material already published by this writer (Mercer 1988; 1990; 2003).

11.5.1 The act of enclosure

Enclosures in all their variety, over six millennia of European prehistory, offer an unfading attraction to the archaeologist. By their very nature they exhibit an 'internal' and 'external' logic in their seeming synchronic unity, or diachronic complexity, that encourages, indeed demands, a degree of classification and order that is, apparently, denied to less obviously 'organised' structures. Such classification and ordering may, however, offer only illusory security to the scholar who may be led quite unconsciously, or at least semi-consciously, into functionalist and cultural assumptions, often ethnocentric, and usually unjustified. One of the most common of such assumptions relates to 'defence' and what constitutes defensive and non-defensive enclosure, a discussion more often than not conducted in accord with notions associated with artillery warfare and relatively modern ideas of military discipline and conduct.

Such classifications are indeed imperilled if it is postulated that the nature of the enclosure may *not* be 'enclosive' as 'an event', but a cumulative statement over a period of many months or seasons, monumental in its ultimate outcome and perhaps intention, and, perhaps, 'enclosive' as only an ultimate stage of its development –where the accomplishment of the outcome is more important than the outcome itself. Such cumulicity may well be deniable either on the basis of 'Occam's razor', or on the basis of 'unity of conception' in later enclosures, but for those of the early farming period with their distinctive 'causewayed' or 'interrupted ditch' construction it is usually, if not always, impossible to *demonstrate* with certainty any unity of execution of the project. Indeed the waywardness of the alignment of the segments of causewayed ditch, whether in Denmark, Britain or Central Europe, and the quite individual filling patterns of contiguous segments that is frequently in evidence, might support the notion of individual events in a long, but by no means continuous, process.

Yet, where evidence survives for the banks, ramparts or walls of these enclosures, as at Hambledon Hill (11.1); Crickley Hill, Gloucestershire, Carn Brea, Cornwall, or Orsett, Essex, they display an internal logic which suggests that, whether on the grounds of the inter-relationship of timber ground-fast supports, or on the basis of the existence of evanescent or relict traces of the substance of a bank, that these obstacles were continuous and do not reflect directly the discontinuous appearance of the ditch segments. Yet how certain can we be of the unity of a linear earthwork without total excavation over a substantial distance – an investigation that has seldom taken place?

Furthermore the nature of these inner linear barriers appears, where it is susceptible to interpretation, to be extremely variable. It needs to be understood that relatively few excavations have taken place in Britain, or indeed Europe, that allow any complete understanding of the nature of the barrier that existed behind the ditch. Indeed the more such excavations that take place the greater the degree of variety that appears to be witnessed.

11.5.2 The nature of enclosure

In Britain, at the seminal site of Windmill Hill, the inner barriers of all three circuits of ditch have been argued on the basis of both relict traces and of the filling of the ditches by both Smith (1965) and Whittle *et al* (1999) to have been continuous, 'dump-style' banks of piled white chalk, with the site itself carefully offset on the low summit of the hill to promote intervisibility with lower areas set to the north and north-west. A similar situation is postulated on the basis of the extensive excavations at Briar Hill, Northamptonshire (Bamford 1985) where, on the basis of the asymmetry of the ditch filling, once again the excavator reconstructed a simple dump-style bank – but in this instance of rust-red Northampton Sand with Ironstone. Also, the issues associated with the inter-visibility of the nature of enclosure with its hinterland have been briefly explored by Oswald *et al* (2001), who classify this enclosure along with a series of others in having a valley side, and therefore 'tilted', location that offered prospects to and from the valley hinterland. The nature of the ditch-fillings at Briar Hill also made abundantly clear that which had been suspected on the less archaeologically transparent blocky fillings of the chalk-based sites, that multiple and complex phases of deliberate re-cutting of the ditch fills had taken place with the selective placement of debris within the declivities so created. To this widespread (although *not* universal) feature of early enclosure use we shall return.

The focus to the west

The combination, as at Hambledon, of inclusive/celebrative and exclusive/impressive roles is witnessed elsewhere in Britain. Two such sites are about equidistant from Hambledon in the southern English context. Hembury, in Devon, was one of the earliest causewayed enclosure sites to be investigated (Liddell 1930; 1931; 1932; 1935), and excavated extremely well by the standards of the time, by Dorothy Liddell, sister-in-law of Alexander Keiller, the prime force behind the excavations at Windmill Hill. Hembury is a promontory site set on a Greensand geological base overlooking the lowlands of south Devon, in very much a similar circumstance to that of Hambledon Hill dominating the flatlands of Blackmoor. It was recognised archaeologically by virtue of the late first millennium ramparts prominent upon the site, and only Liddell's excavations revealed the relatively minimal Neolithic earthworks lying beneath. Our understanding of this earthwork is limited, as a result of the severely constrained excavation possible within Liddell's resources, but it is probably a single causewayed ditch with, set on its inner edge, a continuous rampart that appears to have been vertically faced and revetted with timber. This obstacle appears to have been subjected to firing in an episode that led to burning timbers collapsing into the ditch where their remains were located in direct association with a large number (*c* 80) of leaf-shaped arrowheads, many of which exhibited traces of calcining through heat. Such was the heat generated by the burning timber that the greensand rock was widely oxidised to a deep red wine colour. At Hembury this 1 ha promontory enclosure appears to have enclosed, again on the evidence of very limited excavation, an area subject to intensive structural and pit-digging activity, producing very large quantities of cultural debris – and subject also, apparently, to extensive burning.

The 1 ha enclosure at Hembury forms the focus of an altogether larger enclosure system, one element of which was located by Liddell, which may indicate an enclosure of as much as 3 ha in extent. This outer earthwork, comprising a 2 m-deep flat-bottomed ditch, also betrayed traces of burning, and the apparent disruption of the bank-obstacle built on its interior side with additional traces of a possible timber-built counterscarp feature as well. Hembury bears ready comparison with a further group of Neolithic enclosures to the south-west in Devon and, particularly, Cornwall. The direct comparisons are facilitated by a common suite of raw materials and fixed-origin artefacts passing along exchange-lines that clearly link the sites, and by common factors involving large outer enclosures and the presence of evident archery-accompanied attacks (Mercer 2003).

The second enclosure complex to which the writer would refer in this context is set on the very edge of the Cotswold scarp near Cheltenham, Gloucestershire. Like Hembury the site was excavated (in this case by Dr Philip Dixon) because of the visible traces of an early first millennium BC fortification, the remains of which were apparent from surface examination. It was only after several seasons of work on the site that the earlier, Neolithic, causewayed enclosure was found (there are a number of examples of this sequence of events – Wheeler's excavations at Maiden Castle, Dorset, being another). The sequence of events at Crickley Hill is, however, of particular interest in the context of Hambledon Hill as, unlike the absent 'sequence' at Hembury (largely a product of limited excavation, one suspects), at Crickley Hill (once again with a massive vista over a flatland area, in this case the Severn floodplain) the excavation was on a very large scale and sequence is an issue that has been well addressed (Dixon 1988 and pers comm).

It is not yet tied to the outcome of any available radiocarbon dating programme, but, at its earliest stratigraphic point, the only apparent structures on this promontory site, in Dixon's phase 1a, were a cluster of small, oval post-built structures, and a small, insignificant almost, oval barrow with no archaeological trace of any burial.

The structures were succeeded in Dixon's phase 1bi by an initial circuit of causewayed ditch enclosing about 1 ha (which was to become the outer ditch as the nature of the site developed). The ditch was broad, shallow and flat-bottomed with at least three, possibly five, entrances aligned so as to focus on the centre of the enclosed element of the promontory. The obstacle/bank of the enclosure set on the interior side of the ditch was interpreted as broad and low at the inner side of which, further from the bank, were the post-sockets of a palisade that, to judge by the depth of the sockets, was of no great height. It would seem at least possible that this first stage of enclosure was subject to attack (or at least targeting) by archers.

This circuit was recut and augmented in Dixon's phase 1bii by the digging, some 22 m within the lbi ditch, of a parallel set of pits which were somewhat deeper and separated by a larger number of 'causeways', many of them too small to be considered as access points. Three, and probably four, causeways were, however, matched by gate furniture all of which were aligned on the gates previously established within the lbi circuit. The inner obstacle/bank that lay within this circuit would appear, also, to have been similar in design to that of phase lbi. The phase 1a barrow was levelled (and its barrow's flanking ditches infilled) in order to allow the construction of this inner enclosure. The emphatic change with this second enclosure phase resides in the fact that at this time the interior of the double enclosure appears to have been furnished with a large number of integral post-supported rectangular structures interpreted as houses.

It is this double obstacle (lbii) enclosure with 'houses' set in the interior (houses, the posthole patterns of which survived owing to the unique circumstances at Crickley Hill where *no* cultivation has taken place) that is subject to what appears to be the first full-scale targeting by archers on the site, after which the two ditches appear to have been deliberately infilled with burning brushwood thrown into the ditch and promptly buried, with heat of sufficient intensity generated to slake the surrounding limestone. Into this backfilling, over a considerable period, five phases (Dixon's lci–v) of recutting associated with deliberate deposits of animal bone and pottery were made.

After this interval, currently of unknown length, the promontory is once again isolated by a single 'uninterrupted' continuous ditch with two causeways marking well-defined gateways in the internal obstacle (Dixon's phase ld). The ditch is, relatively speaking, massive, well over 2 m in depth, and curiously, where, in the process of its digging, breakthroughs have been made into the earlier phase lbii ditch, careful and illogical processes of blocking were undertaken which, far from taking advantage of the apparently accidentally discovered 'vein' of easy digging, chose to shut it off and to continue to dig native bedrock instead. This act of 'memorialisation' is paralleled by the fact that with this new barrier the two new causeways still focus on the earlier disposition of two causeways on the site – that would appear to represent a cultural continuum. The internal obstacle constructed from the product of this ditch digging was also, apparently, closely related to earlier concepts on the site in producing a broad, low bank 0.50 m in height by some 10 m in breath with a palisade on its innermost edge. The gateways of the obstacle lie flanked by the inner and outer 'barbicans' of timber-lined roadways that lead into the interior where aligned house-type rectilinear structures, ranging from 2 × 5 m to 10 × 5 m in size, are aligned upon them. This was apparently a settlement, but other issues supervene, however, as the occupation component is more-or-less confined to the eastern sector of the enclosure (nearest the ditches) while the western component seems to have been reserved for a most complex series of ceremonial activities associated with a range of platform-type structures, where the immensely careful excavational approaches of Dr Dixon have informed an extraordinarily detailed account of Neolithic conduct on and around them.

Once again Dixon phase ld appears to have been brought to a violent end by a second attack of focused and intensive archery, that, rather like Hembury, appears to be directed closely upon the entrances and where the palisade at the inner face of the 'bank' appears to have stopped many missiles (Dixon 1988). After this, apparently ultimate, phase of destruction, the site of Crickley Hill was deserted for many centuries.

Evidence of intense burning was also recovered by Sharples (1991, 51) at Maiden Castle, Dorset. When Wheeler (1943) excavated this site in the mid-1930s he was anxious to prioritise the exploration of the Iron Age aspects of the site and did not accord the filling of these unexpected Neolithic ditches the degree of recording and comment that he committed elsewhere. He did, however, record an entrance through the causewayed ditches some 6 m wide, with the ditches surviving to 1.50 m in depth and enclosing an area of about 4 ha. Of the two ditches Wheeler cleared about 70 m aggregate length, and the inner of them was by far the richer in terms of the deposition of cultural debris. Wheeler found at least ten leaf arrowheads in this ditch, mostly in the immediate locality of the eastern entrance. A further five were located in the make up of the long mound – presumably incorporated from the immediate locale during the construction of this monument after the Neolithic enclosure had gone out of use. Sharples records (1991, 51) that, in his trench, he located 'midden' debris (see 1991, 253) the deposits beneath which are, however, described as follows. 'At the base of the ditch were the chalk silts ... These were probably deposited by rainwater almost immediately after the ditch had been created. On top of these silts, and intermingled with silt layers were the much thicker and relatively unconsolidated layers of chalk rubble. ... The rubble contained considerable quantities of charcoal, largely mature oak, which was at least partially created by a fire which had scorched many of the chalk blocks.' This sounds (and looks in the published figures) very like the evidence retrieved from Hambledon Hill which, there, is interpreted as massive bank collapse induced by the burning of a timber casing. This interpretation is consistent with Rowena Gale's Maiden Castle charcoal identifications. While most samples recovered from the inner ditch in Sharples' Trenches I and II include charcoal of various deciduous taxa, those from the rubble layers in his trench I consist almost entirely of oak and hazel, like the remains of the inner Stepleton outwork (Gale 1991, microfiche M6:C10–C12). Furthermore, Paul Martin's examination of the leaf arrowheads from the site (2001) has shown that (1) most of the leaf arrowheads surviving from the Wheeler excavations had indeed been hafted, on the evidence of microscopic traces of organic residues, which could be from adhesives such as birch bark tar; (2) if, following the results of experiments by others, both proximal and distal breakage to an arrowhead can result from impact, then the frequency of both at Maiden Castle (Wheeler 1943, figs 42–43; Edmonds and Bellamy 1991, fig 178) could reflect their use as weapons; and (3) 13 of the 24 leaf arrowheads which could be located with any precision were concentrated in the area of the scorched rubble and charcoal. Against the possibility of defence and attack was the vertical distribution of the arrowheads in this area, some of which came from the inner ditch and others from the turfline beneath the long mound, suggesting that they had accumulated over a period of time. It is, however, possible that most of them might derive from a single episode, some progressively entering the ditch from the surrounding surface. Given the limited extent of excavation in the area, the boundaries of the concentration remain to be defined.

Further to the south-west, the characteristic format of causewayed ditch enclosed sites continues to its known extent with the site at Raddon Hill, Devon. Here the 2 ha main enclosure, sited squarely on the hill summit (Oswald *et al* 2001, fig 5.2), is accompanied by a further causewayed component, probably of Neolithic date, which offers enclosed *space* outside the main enclosure (Gent and Quinnell 1999, figs 2, 3, 11) – as at Hambledon and Hembury, although on a lesser scale. This pattern is continued into the furthest part of the Cornish peninsula. However, in this, generally hard-rock, region, the constructional format of the enclosures changes, with boulder walls creating inner enclosures of roughly 1 ha extent. In two known instances, Carn Brea (Mercer 1981a) and Helman Tor (Mercer 1997), both in Cornwall, there are known to be outer enclosures, boulder-built, but in the case of Carn Brea, clearly defensive and constructed, it would seem, at least partly, upon an internal 'stone-box' system that offered *enclosed space* outside the inner enclosure. Certainly the site at Carn Brea exhibits extensive burning and has produced vast numbers (over 800) of leaf arrowheads which, both in terms of their condition and circumstances, would appear to represent a site subject to massive archery attack.

The sites at Carn Brea, Helman Tor, Hembury, Maiden Castle and Hambledon, as well as other less major interspersed sites not mentioned here (but see Mercer 2003), are linked by a common distributional pattern of artefacts and raw materials apparently being circulated by whatever mechanism over very considerable distances. Materials are moving both eastward and westward – pottery, flint, other quarried stone – and, while these materials do pass beyond Hambledon further into Wessex, those of westerly origin begin to fall off sharply in frequency of retrieved deposition.

Thus in the south-west of England we appear to have a series of enclosures linked by common, although not universally common, links of situation, design, multiple function, disposition to disturbance by violence and common exchange patterns. This commonality of links, seems, currently, to break down gradually beyond the 'boundary zone' of the chalk massif of central Wessex. Does this pattern reinforce the 'frontier' position of Hambledon Hill itself? Does the 'reversal' of role and focus of Hambledon from eastward to westward and from display/ceremonial in focus to defensive/dominant focus reflect that 'frontier' position and its possible reversal by communities that we know are in an energetic state of development on Cranborne Chase (Barrett *et al* 1991) and further to the north-east by the mid and later fourth millennium BC?

The focus to the east

Certainly, further to the east, causewayed enclosures exhibit broadly similar overall enclosive design but perhaps rather different layout, little evidence of violence, less apparent functional variety, and different exchange linkages. Let us examine these briefly.

It was Palmer (1976a) who first suggested the division of causewayed enclosures into four regional groups centred on Sussex, the Thames valley, the East Midlands and the South West of England which he recognised upon the grounds of morphological analysis in which he saw, broadly, greater complexity of layout in the Midlands and Thames than further to the south and west. It is interesting to compare this analysis with another, based upon an approach by Colin Renfrew (1973) founded upon a purely spatial-proximity analysis using the Theissen polygonal method that sought to develop an understanding of 'territories as revealed by the location of causewayed enclosures in Wessex' (an area that by and large has *not* seen a massive increase in their numbers) as compared with the cluster of long-barrows that surround them (or appear to), a linkage that has been lent added intimacy as a result of the work at Hambledon Hill itself. This study sees a complex of territories which are, however, all shut off by polygons isolating the south-west, from Poole Harbour to the Cotswolds, from the rest of Southern England – the very hinterland overviewed and bounded by Hambledon Hill.

All of this is purely retrospective construct. Let us review briefly what happens to the east of that quite 'imaginary line'. To this point we have seen an aspect of early Neolithic enclosure function in Britain which, whether at Crickley Hill, Hambledon Hill, Hembury, or enclosures of a rather different character further to the south-west has an apparent unity of conception, interlinkage and developing functionality that is quite impressive. When we turn eastwards from Hambledon Hill the degree of unity seems to change quite sharply.

The foundation of causewayed enclosure studies is the work conducted by Alexander Keiller at Windmill Hill, Wiltshire (Smith 1965). This site seems to be positioned in a manner familiar at all upland sites across southern Britain (including Hambledon, Maiden Castle, Whitesheet, Crickley Hill and most of the Sussex upland enclosures (Oswald *et al* 2001). The favoured location is a spur or ridge with extensive views in one principal direction. In most instances the enclosure is positioned in slightly 'off-set' tilted posture, so that it lies slightly off-summit in the direction on the view commanded – thus presumably promoting the intervisibility from each to the other. At Windmill Hill this focus is to the north and all three, inner, middle and site circuits, are tilted in this way. But at Windmill Hill, unlike any enclosure to the west, the enclosure ditches are not 'grouped' in order to be mutually reinforcing, whether psychologically or physically, nor are they 'focused' at particular approaches to the eminence upon which they are placed (as at Whitesheet, Hambledon, Hembury and Maiden Castle). At Windmill Hill a more or less 'neutral', 'concentric' pattern is adopted with, however, the earthworks increasing in stature towards the outermost.

Once we come to examine the archaeology of the use of the Windmill Hill enclosure, however, we observe a close accord with aspects of activity, although not the discontinuity, seen in the south-west. Smith's (1965) account of the excavation by Keiller, as well as Whittle's smaller scale investigations (Whittle *et al* 1999), indicates that feasting and the disposal of that feasting debris, as well as the disposal of human remains was a consistent process mediated archaeologically by the repeated recutting of ditch deposits and the placement of components of this debris within those recuts. Under archaeological examination these deposits may seem rich but, as at Hambledon, when taken in the context of the likely chronological longevity of the site they may reflect only a very few episodes of celebration every few years (11.3.1). It is probably dangerous to embark further on this course of enquiry with sites less adequately sampled, dated or documented, but, impressionistically, we can observe that such very exiguous assemblages, per chronological range, apply widely elsewhere with an emphasis that increases as one moves further to the east (see below).

Another issue that relates to change as we move not only from west to east, but from chalk upland enclosures to the less elevated enclosures of eastern river valleys, is their relationship with the contemporary landscape. Usually on the basis of molluscan evidence, the upland enclosures at Offham, Sussex (Drewett 1977), Windmill Hill, Hambledon Hill, and Maiden Castle are understood to have existed in landscapes that fostered the prevalent presence of shade-loving species. It would appear that these enclosures were set in marginal woodland of greater or lesser density, certainly not an environment created by the ruminant animals that form the principal traces of meat consumption on these sites. Again the impression gained from the whole ambit of the evidence would suggest periodic visiting by small groups to sites of prestigious status set in marginal, indeed, perhaps territorially peripheral contexts – visits during which food and objects brought from a distance were consumed and/or deposited. The circumstances of the excavation at Hambledon Hill have suggested a very strong link between these periodic (perhaps in this instance seasonal) visits and the delivery to the site (and perhaps the removal from it) of human cadaveric and skeletal remains.

The site at Etton, Cambridgeshire, is held by its excavator (Pryor 1998) to parallel closely the activities reflected at Hambledon, characterised by periodic visits with special deposition episodes. Yet as we move into the valleys of eastern England, we encounter sites apparently far less dramatically sited, yet still in 'locally' marginal locations, as at Etton; Staines, Surrey (Robertson-Mackay 1987), possibly Orsett, Essex (Hedges and Buckley 1978), and Haddenham Cambridgeshire (Evans and Hodder 2006 and pers comm). Yet these sites are still the focus of some long-distance contact (in terms of much worked down Group VI and VII axe fragments from Etton) although there is relatively little evidence of the widespread ceramic contacts witnessed at Hambledon and Windmill Hill. Etton would appear to have been set at the margin of a landscape already substantially cleared of trees.

If the eastern river valley enclosures are more locally focused, commanding recognition among smaller, less distantly derived, communities, then there is also evidence that activity in their immediate vicinity was less intensive. To examine this issue this writer has interrogated the presence of worked flint and flint implements upon those sites where the sample was felt, upon inspection, sound enough to be recovered and recorded, and large enough to be indicative. The same exercise could be undertaken with other materials but only flint, it was felt, had the taphonomic resilience to allow comparison between widely varying sites. The question remains, of course, of the local availability of flint, which is difficult to assess, but in no instance is any site at considerably more than one day's walk from a good flint source – except, of course, those in Cornwall which, in themselves, furnish an interesting object lesson in this regard. There is no doubt that measuring excavated areas on plan and counting finds lists may often lead to error, and the writer has no doubt that error may have occurred here, but not such error as could seriously impact upon the order of magnitude of differences encountered. It can be suggested that rather than calculating 'area excavated', one ought perhaps to calculate volume of archaeological deposit excavated' (ie take into account the depth and length of archaeological features – ditches and pits – uncovered), but this exercise only builds in its own biases and uncertainty. The result is as set out in Table 11.7. Its plausibility is enhanced by the fact that a comparable one has been reached by Evans *et al* (2006), employing a different method of calculation and applying it only to material from enclosure ditches.

The outcome of this exercise shows very clear distinctions between the lithic assemblages and their intensity on the examined sites. Those sites that, in the far south-west of England, are interpreted (by this writer) as settlement sites, enclosed and lived in for extended periods, despite their situation far from bedrock deposits of flint, produce 16–20 fragments of worked flint per m^2. This order of magnitude begins to parallel that of European Neolithic settlement sites, and indeed those recognised elsewhere in Britain. Hembury, Devon, is clearly closely related.

Hambledon Hill, well within the flint-rich zone, stands at 2.0–6.6 items per m^2. Then we are faced with the completely exceptional nature of the Windmill Hill assemblage related, presumably, to the massive flint-working activity that has been known since the 1920s on the southern slope of the hill. The results of the most recent excavations there suggest that much of this mass of lithics may post-date the enclosure and have no relation to this discussion: irrespective of ditch circuit, high flint densities occur only at a late stage in each section and consistently coincide with the first occurrence in that section of later Neolithic pottery (Whittle *et al* 1999, tables 155–61, 173–9). Staines and Abingdon in the Thames valley compare closely to Hambledon, whereas Offham, Sussex, at 1.4 items per m^2 lies at approximately half the Hambledon rate, yet, surely, in an area of equivalent flint availability.

When we reach the east of England we find, by comparison tiny amounts of flint – a third to a tenth that of Hambledon. Rog Palmer (1976a) indicates, as

Table 11.7 Density per m² excavated of worked flint and flint implements at a selection of Neolithic enclosures and other sites in southern England

Site	*Area excavated m² (approx)*	*Total struck flint (as published)*	*Total implements (as published)*	*Implements per m²*	*Struck flint per m²*	*Source(s)*
Staines, Surrey	6675	23,355	1,344	0.2	3.5	Robertson-Mackay (1987)
Abingdon, Oxfordshire	1280	5137	842	0.6	4.0	Avery (1982); Leeds (1927; 1928)
Orsett, Essex	1725	1637	64	0.03	0.9	Hedges and Buckley (1978)
Briar Hill, Northants	14,196	2815	868	0.06	0.2	Bamford (1985)
Etton, Cambridgeshire	14,000	7,152	746	0.05	0.5	Pryor (1998)
Haddenham, Cambridgeshire	8878	2,245	*c* 220	*c* 0.025	0.25	Evans and Hodder (2006)
Offham, Sussex	4780	6,830	23	0.005	1.42	Drewett (1977)
Windmill Hill, Wiltshire	3233	98,273	4078	1.26	30.4	Smith (1965)
Hambledon Hill, Dorset (main enclosure)	10,000	36,146	1227	0.13	3.6	This volume
Hambledon Hill, Dorset (Stepleton enclosure)	16,000	36,094	828	0.05	2.25	This volume
Hembury, Devon	2295	32,000	1171	0.51	13.9	Liddell (1930; 1931; 1932; 1935)
Helman Tor, Cornwall	72	1371	233	3.24	19.0	Saville (1997)
Carn Brea, Cornwall	1631	26,382	3611	2.20	16.2	Saville (1981a)
Hurst Fen, Suffolk	1858	14,500	1298	0.7	7.8	Clark *et al* (1960)

we have seen, on the basis of the evidence of the aerial photographic recording of causewayed enclosures, by virtue of which the vast majority have been discovered, that four morphological and territorial groups exist. That grouping has been supported in a more recent review of the evidence (Oswald *et al* 2001). From the point of view of the excavator of Hambledon Hill, that four-fold division is indeed powerful and suggests that Hambledon itself was very much on a frontier – a frontier that continued in time, although quite differently marked by the complex of earthworks centring upon the Dorset cursus on Cranborne Chase – a frontier to be recognisable into the Iron Age. West of that frontier, complex events led to quasi-political unity over long distances and equally quasi-political prominence for some sites as 'symbolic' of the social solidarity that they had come to represent. A recognisable approximation to what we, today, call defence arose from this. These influences created a complexity of sequence for sites in this western area (including Crickley Hill, Hambledon, Maiden Castle, Hembury and sites further west) that is reflected in the variability of their archaeological expression. Across the boundary to the east this complexity seems never to have materialised during the earlier Neolithic. In Wessex and Sussex similar isolated sites never took on the 'career' of western sites. Further to the east such central places were also created but more locally focused, still marginally located within their local communities, and still the centre of only occasional attention. Currently there is no reliable evidence for chronological priority one way or the other. Nor is there very much evidence as to the contexts to which these clearly locally focused sites related. Our appreciation of their role now relies upon further exploration of the hinterlands of which they were clearly only a part and upon the process of inter- and intra-site chronological refinement, which is only now becoming a feasible prospect.

11.6 Questions, answered and unanswered

The research aims

Most of the questions posed at various stages in the project's history (see 1.7) have been substantially answered. Those formulated for the final post-excavation project are reviewed here.

1. What were the complete form and extent of the complex? How many hitherto undated or undiscovered elements formed part of it? Was there a third Neolithic enclosure on the northern, hillfort, spur?

The demonstrated scale of the complex, let alone its potential scale, makes it unique among earthworks of the earlier fourth millennium BC in Britain. Neolithic outworks extend around the steeper parts of every spur of the hill, such that the massive long barrow on the hillfort spur is within the enclosive earthworks rather than beyond them. What had appeared to be a third Neolithic enclosure on that spur, however, has proved to date from the earlier first millennium BC.

2. What was the chronology of its construction and use?

The chronology of the complex has achieved a resolution which affects the entire interpretation of the site and of other causewayed enclosures: episodic construction and continued use of the existing earthworks spanned 300–400 years. 'Flint mines' on the Hanford spur have proved to date from the third millennium BC, after the complex had gone out of use.

This timescale provides perspective for a superficially vast assemblage. Spread over time, this seems to reflect only an intermittent presence at the complex, although at least sometimes – on the evidence of cattle slaughter – of large numbers of people

3. How did its components articulate in function and layout? Could the cross-dykes have been defensive, as their location suggested? How much diversity of use was there between the various components?

The uses of the complex embraced almost every aspect of contemporary life. Distinct, complementary practices at the two enclosures are detectable from the first and persisted over the centuries during which the hill remained a focal aggregation site for the people of a catchment which extended at least to the Mendips and the Dorset coast. Each enclosure filled different functions, and saw different styles of deposition of food remains and of artefacts from different sources, the distinctions persisting as the practices changed over time. The cross-dykes now appear to have functioned as additional circuits of the enclosure, their limited extent a response to the immediate topography. Outworks, however, were demonstrably defensive and were the sites of rather different depositional practices from the enclosure ditches. The Shroton spur outwork and the inner Stepleton outwork were both burnt, almost certainly in the course of hostilities, which are evidenced at a later date by two deaths by arrowshot. Inter-group conflict, and its anticipation, are emphatically demonstrated.

Although outworks were built progressively from an early stage in the sequence, their location and character changed over time. The outworks of periods 1–3 were sited on the relatively gentle slopes which provide the easiest access to the hill and incorporated gateways, on the Shroton, Stepleton and Hanford spurs. The main outworks of period 4 – the Western outwork with the outer, and perhaps the inner, Stepleton–Hanford outwork – were of a different kind: they were built along extended lengths of hillside, steep as well as gently sloping (Fig 1.9), and they entailed a greater input of labour than any previous constructions (Fig 11.3). Furthermore, while the early outworks had presented a series of imposing walls to those approaching from the east, these, for the first time, presented an even more imposing façade to those approaching from the west. This shifting location bespeaks a shift in the visible (and socio-political?) orientation of the complex. It may reflect a denial of the westerly links evident through most of the history of the complex and absorption into the developing ritual focus in Cranborne Chase to the east.

4. How was the complex built and what were its implications for contemporary resources, demography and social organisation?

The ergonomic requirements of the successive episodes of construction have been estimated, based on the inferred original form of the earthworks. They indicate a minimum workforce for each successive episode of construction which is surprisingly low in relation to the size of the complex – of the order of 100 people in a couple of annual episodes in late summer and autumn. Cumulative rather than simultaneous construction reduces the scale of the society which built the complex, and, given the extent of the potential catchment, could suggest a thinly scattered population.

It should be remembered, however, that the minimum workforce called for in practical terms may have borne no relation to the number of people who chose, or needed, to participate. It is pertinent that, more than two thousand years later, the construction of a modest timber monument subsequently known as Seahenge, less than 7 m in diameter and made up of 55 posts and a central tree trunk, entailed the use of 51 different axes, the marks of which survived on the timbers. The excavators interpret this as reflecting the participation not only of 51 axe-wielders, but of many more people, on the grounds that each of the 15–20 trees used to build the monument would have been felled, dressed and transported by a team of three or four, with others involved in construction (Brennand and Taylor 2003, 24–30, 62).

Relationships between members of that workforce can only be guessed at. It is possible to envisage scattered groups, or fractions of them, from a catchment perhaps extending to the Mendips and the Dorset coast, converging on the hill to work, united, more or less closely, by lineage, allegiance, belief, or all three. Some measure of co-ordinating authority, as distinct from common interest and common will, is implicit in the construction methods and their end results, and varying levels of meat consumption among those whose remains were buried there hint at social hierarchy, especially given consistently high meat consumption by those buried in the south long barrow (see Richards, 7.2). The importance of the coastal plain, as a relatively close focus of population (11.4.3) may be considerable here.

5. What were the genesis and nature of the numerous deposits of largely disarticulated human bone? What processes had brought them to their final state? How did these remains relate to the far more restricted burial environments of the two long barrows? How far could the intermingling of funerary and other ceremony with the debris of everyday life be interpreted?

The dead and their remains were intimately bound up with the preoccupations and practices of the living. Excarnation followed by disarticulation and the inhumation of complete, fleshed corpses were both practised from the first, the former sometimes on the hill itself. The condition and composition of the excavated human remains were the result of, among other factors, weathering, gnawing by dogs, and human selection. Excarnation was active as well as passive, with flesh deliberately cut away from the bones, even to 'token' extent from those of articulated skeletons. The purposes for which small quantities of human flesh were removed can only be guessed at. Among a people who selected, retained, transported and manipulated human bones, practices pertaining to the flesh as well would be unsurprising.

6. How could the collection of artefacts and food remains from the site be best interpreted to create a picture of the socio-economic base of the period?

Meat consumption at Hambledon may hold up a distorting mirror to everyday diet. The frequency with which dairy products and cereals were consumed is brought home by several converging strands of evidence: indirectly by the kill-off patterns of the cattle, which suggest the cull of surplus animals from dairy herds, and by the presence of numerous querns and rubbers; directly by dairy fat residues in pottery, by the significant role which vegetable proteins played in the diets of some of the population, by the extensive recovery of charred cereal grains, and by the discovery of a single pit containing many litres of charred wheat. Jones' and Legge's argument for the inherent under-representation of cereals in the archaeological record of this period is a telling one.

7. What was the local context of the complex, in terms of contemporary settlement and of human impact on the natural environment? What light could valley-bottom deposits at the foot of the hill shed on these questions?

Molluscan evidence for woodland cover on the hill during the earlier fourth millennium highlights the probability of occasional rather than frequent use, as at other chalkland causewayed enclosures. This complements evidence for patchily more open conditions in Cranborne Chase to the east. Local early Neolithic settlement retains a low visibility, except on the coastal plain to the south, whence, on artefactual evidence, some of those who built and used Hambledon came.

Valley bottom deposits of this period did not survive, having been scoured out, perhaps because of the extensive agricultural landuse of the second millennium BC.

8. What were the subsequent human uses of the complex? Was Everley Water Meadow, in the Iwerne valley below the hill, a Bronze Age metalworking site?

Uses of the hill and of Cranborne Chase to the east continued to complement each other, in an extended cycle of dispersal and aggregation, extending into the first millennium BC. The middle Bronze Age burnt mound in Everley Water Meadow can now be linked to the development of second-millennium fields and settlement on the hill above, part of the widespread contemporary enclosure of the downland. It pre-dates the late Bronze Age axe mould from the same excavation, which has proved to come, with a few contemporary sherds, from gravels reworked in Roman times. It nonetheless provides evidence for late Bronze Age metalworking in the vicinity, at a time when a high-status enclosure, in the form of the hillfort on the northern spur, may have been established, and settlement probably began to nucleate in the nascent hillforts of the area.

The future

The acquisition of so much information has inevitably raised further questions, many of which could be practically addressed.

- What was the nature and extent of earlier Neolithic activity over the unexcavated parts of the hill, especially outside and between the enclosures?
- Was there a further, outer outwork on the Shroton spur (3.4)?
- Can the relation between the Stepleton and Hanford earthworks be better defined?

Investigation in and either side of the area where the outworks swing across the contours could clarify this point.

- What was the extent of Neolithic earthworks on the hillfort spur?

The Iron Age ramparts may conceal even more extensive Neolithic earthworks than have been identified. The location of Neolithic entrances on the gentle slopes of the Shroton, Stepleton and Hanford spurs suggests that there may be another at the south-east angle of the hillfort spur.

- Can environmental evidence from the hill itself be enhanced, at least to match advances in Cranborne Chase?

If the technical difficulties could be overcome, a section at a location where a Neolithic earthwork is known to underlie Iron Age ones could yield sealed soils of both dates, as well as the potential for taking stratified sequences of mollusc samples through ditch fills of both dates.

- Can the character, landuse history, and chronology of the apparent concentration of Neolithic settlement on the coastal plain to the south be elucidated?

Targeted fieldwork is an obvious tool here. There is also the still-untapped potential of the unpublished excavation of numerous pits, some with Bowl pottery in the south-western style, at Moortown, on the lower Stour (Horsey and Jarvis 1984).

- Can the prehistory of the Blackmoor Vale be elucidated?

The area remains an archaeological and palaeoenvironmental blank, and with that blank persistent, understanding of the local human presence is one-sided. Its fluviatile deposits could provide a history of its human use, and might encapsulate stratified archaeological material.

These thoughts must form an *envoi* to those willing to explore further the archaeological potential of this 'frontier zone' – where different aspects and expressions of Britain's early Neolithic meet. It is precisely in this context where inter-relationships, and by the means of these, greater clarity in interpretation, are to be anticipated. To this end, and on an entirely culturally inappropriate (and currently, perhaps, unfashionable) note – Good hunting!

Plate I The Shroton spur and the central dome of the hill (left) and the hillfort (right), viewed from the east side of the Iwerne valley. Photo Rog Palmer

Plate II View to the west from the Hanford spur during the 1982 excavations.

Plate III The yew wood on the west side of the hill from the floodplain of the river Stour.

Plate IV Shroton spur outwork, site L. South-east face of excavation, showing charcoal-rich silt (L9) entering ditch from interior. Equivalent to Figure 3.78: section A–A'.

Plate V Inner Stepleton outwork. The east butt of segment 4.2, flanking the gateway, showing ashy silt with charcoal and chalk lumps (L4A) on base of ditch. Equivalent to Figure 3.95: section QQ–QQ'.

Plate VI Inner Stepleton outwork. The west face of unit 2, in the west butt of segment 5, close to the gateway, showing reddening of the ditch bottom (in which there is a natural fissure) and of the fills that progressively entered it.

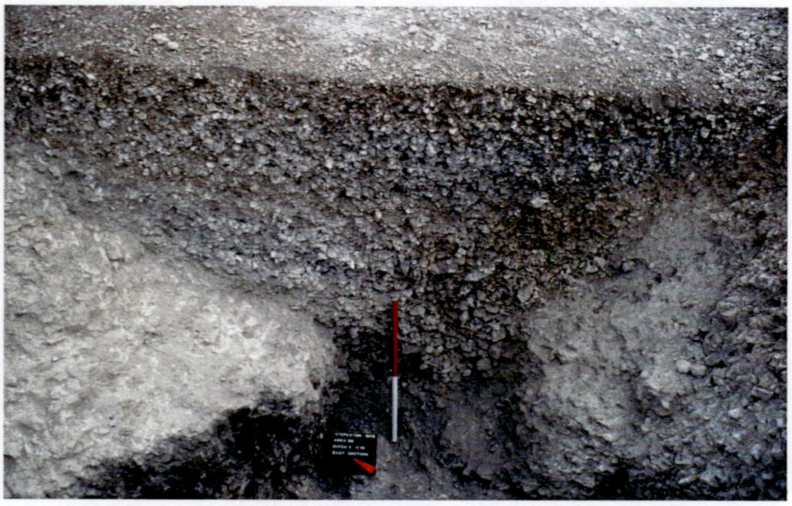

Plate VII Inner Stepleton outwork. The east face of cutting 13, roughly mid-way along segment 5, showing discoloured red-grey fills. There is a natural fissure in the base of the ditch.

Plate VIII Inner Stepleton outwork. Burnt clay and wood in L4A in cutting 1 in the centre of segment 6, where the ditch was cut through Clay-with-Flints. From north-east. Includes the area of Figure 3.99.

Plate IX Inner Stepleton outwork. Detail of burnt deposit shown in Plate VIII, including some of the sherds of P85 (ST79 1567).

Bibliography

Abbreviations

BM British Museum
DCM Dorset County Museum
RCHME Royal Commission on the Historical Monuments of England

Adams, J C, 1986 *Outline of orthopaedics*, London: Churchill Livingstone

—, 1987 *Outline of fractures*, London: Churchill Livingstone

Addison, P, 1989 Excavation of Neolithic and Bronze Age pits and a section of Roman road on a pipeline near Lodge Farm, Pamphill, Dorset, *Proc Dorset Natur Hist Archaeol Soc* **111**, 15–29

Adkins, L, and Adkins, R, 1991 Excavations at Ham Hill 1991, *Proc Somerset Archaeol Natur Hist Soc* **135**, 89–94

Ahlen, I, 1965 Studies on the red deer *Cervus elaphus* L in Scandinavia III; ecological investigations, *Viltrevy* **3**, 177–376.

Alcock, L, 1980 The Cadbury Castle sequence in the first millennium BC, *Bull Board Celtic Stud* **28**, 656–718

Allen, M J, 1992 Products of erosion and the prehistoric land use of the Wessex Chalk, in *Past and present soil erosion* (eds M G Bell and J Boardman), 37–92, Oxford: Oxbow Books

—, 1995a Ditch and feature fills, in Cleal *et al* 1995, 4–6

—, 1995b Before Stonehenge, in Cleal *et al* 1995, 41–46

—, 1995c Geographical and topographical setting, in Cleal *et al* 1995, 34

—, 1997a Landscape, land-use and farming, in Smith *et al* 1997, 277–83

—, 1997b Land-use history: land molluscan evidence, in Smith *et al* 1997, 166–83, 260–7

—, 1997c Environment and land-use; the economic development of the communities who built Stonehenge; an economy to support the stones, in *Science and Stonehenge* (eds B Cunliffe, and C Renfrew), Proc Brit Acad **92**, 115–44, Oxford: Oxford University Press

—, 1998 A note on reconstructing the prehistoric landscape environment in Cranborne Chase; the Allen Valley, *Proc Dorset Natur Hist Archaeol Soc* **120**, 39–44

—, 1999 Land snail evidence, in *A35 Tolpuddle to Puddletown Bypass, DBFO, Dorset, 1996-8* (C M Hearne and V Birbeck), Wessex Archaeol Rep **15**, 173–87. Salisbury: Trust for Wessex Archaeology

—, 2000a Soils, pollen and lots of snails, in Green 2000, 36–49

—, 2000b High resolution mapping of Neolithic and Bronze Age landscapes and land-use; the combination of multiple palaeo-environmental analysis and topographic modelling, in *Plants in Neolithic Britain and beyond. Landscape and environment, economy and society* (ed A S Fairburn), Neolithic Studies Group Seminar Pap **5**, 9–26, Oxford: Oxbow Books

—, 2002 The chalkland landscape of Cranborne Chase: a prehistoric human ecology, *Landscapes* **13**, 55–69

—, 2004 Land snails, in Investigation of the Whitesheet Down environs 1989–90: Neolithic causewayed enclosure and Iron Age settlement (M Rawlings, M J Allen, and F Healy), *Wiltshire Studies* **97**, 171–4

—, 2005a Considering prehistoric environmental change on the Marlborough Downs, in *The Avebury landscape; aspects of the field archaeology of the Marlborough Downs* (eds G Brown, D Field and D McOmish), 77–86. Oxford: Oxbow Books

—, 2005b Beaker settlement and environment on the chalk downs of southern England, *Proc Prehist Soc* **71**, 219–245

Allen, M J, and Gardiner J, 2002 A sense of time – cultural markers in the Mesolithic of southern England?, in *Inscribed landscapes. Marking and making place* (eds B David and M Wilson), 139–53, Honolulu: University of Hawai'i Press

Allen, M J, and Green, M, 1998 The Fir Tree Field shaft; the date and archaeological and palaeo-environmental potential of a chalk swallowhole feature, *Proc Dorset Natur Hist Archaeol Soc* **120**, 25–37

Allen, M J, and Scaife, R G, 1991 The exploitation of the flora and fauna and its impact on the natural and derived landscape, in *Redeemed from the heath: the archaeology of the Wytch Farm oilfield (1987–90)* (P W Cox and C M Hearne), Dorset Natur Hist Archaeol Soc Mono **9**, 216–20. Dorchester: Dorset Natural History and Archaeology Society

Allen, M J, Entwistle, R, and Richards, J C, 1990 Molluscan studies, in Richards 1990, 253–6

Ambers, J, Bowman, S, Garwood, P, Hedges, R, and Housley, R, 1999 Appendix 1: radiocarbon dating, in Barclay and Halpin 1999, 330–7

Ambrose, S H, 1993 Isotopic analysis of paleodiets: Methodological and interpretive considerations, in *Investigations of ancient human tissue: chemical analyses in anthropology* (ed M K Sandford), 59–130, Langhorne Pennsylvania: Gordon and Breach Science Publishers

Ambrose, S H, and Norr, L, 1993 Experimental evidence for the relationship of the carbon isotope ratios of whole diet and dietary protein to those of bone collagen and carbonate, in *Prehistoric human bone: archaeology at the molecular level* (eds J Lambert and G Grupe), 1–37, Berlin and London: Springer-Verlag

Andersen, N H, 1997 *Sarup vol 1: the Sarup enclosures.* Moesgaard: Jutland Archaeological Society

Anon 1934 The Hassocks Neolithic spoons, *Antiq J* **14(4)**, 422–3

Arkell, W J, 1947 *The geology of the country around Weymouth, Swanage, Corfe and Lulworth. Memoir for sheets 341, 343, with small portions of sheets 327, 328, 329.* London: HMSO

Armour-Chelu, M, 1992 Vertebrate resource exploitation, ecology and taphonomy in Neolithic Britain, with special reference to the sites of the Links of Noltland, Etton and Maiden Castle, unpubl PhD thesis, Institute of Archaeology, University of London

—, 1998a The animal bone, in Pryor1998, 273–88

—, 1998b The human bone, in Pryor 1998, 271–2

Armour-Chelu, M, and Andrews, P, 1996 Surface modification of bone, in Bell *et al* 1996, 178–95

Arnold, J, Green, M, Lewis, B, and Bradley, R, 1988 The Mesolithic of Cranborne Chase, *Proc Dorset Natur Hist Archaeol Soc* **110**, 117–25

Ashbee, P, 1966 The Fussell's Lodge long barrow excavations 1957, *Archaeologia* **100**, 1–80

Ashbee, P, Smith, I F, and Evans, J G, 1979 Excavation of three long barrows near Avebury, Wiltshire, *Proc Prehist Soc* **45**, 207–300

Ashmore, P, 1999 Radiocarbon dating: avoiding errors by avoiding mixed samples, *Antiquity* **73**, 124–30

Atkinson, R J C, 1957 Worms and weathering, *Antiquity* **31**, 219–33

Aubrey, J, *Monumenta Britannica or a Miscellanie of British Antiquities* (edition of 1980; eds R Legg, W Hoade, R J Briggs and J Fowles). Sherborne, Dorset Publishing Company

Austin, P J, 1995 An analysis and interpretation of the wood charcoal remains from Neolithic pit contexts at the Stepleton Enclosure, Hambledon Hill, Dorset, England, unpubl BSc dissertation, Institute of Archaeology, University College, London

Avery, M, 1982 The Neolithic causewayed enclosure, Abingdon, in *Settlement patterns in the Oxford region: excavations at the Abingdon causewayed enclosure and other sites* (eds H J Case and A W R.Whittle, Counc Brit Archaeol Res Rep **44**, 10–50. London: Council for British Archaeology

Avery, M, Sutton, J E G, and Banks, J W, 1967 Rainsborough, Northants, England: excavation 1961–65, *Proc Prehist Soc* **33**, 207–306

Bamford, H M, 1985 *Briar Hill. Excavation 1974–1978*, Northampton Development Corporation Archaeol Mono **3**. Northampton: Northampton Development Corporation

Barber, K, Zolitschka, B, Tarasov, P, and Cotter, A F 2004 Atlantic to Urals – the Holocene climatic record of mid-latitiude Europe, in *Past climate variability through Europe and Africa* (eds R W Battarbee, F Gasse and C E Stickley), 417–42. Dordrecht: Springer

Barber, M, Field, D, and Topping, P, 1999 *Neolithic flint mines in England*. Swindon: English Heritage/RCHME

Barclay, A 1999 Grooved Ware from the Upper Thames region, in *Grooved Ware in Britain and Ireland* (eds R Cleal and A MacSween, Neolithic Studies Group Seminar Papers **3**, 19–22. Oxford and Oakville: Oxbow Books

Barclay, A and Bayliss, A, 1999 Cursus monuments and the radiocarbon problem, in *Pathways and ceremonies: the cursus monuments of Britain and Ireland* (eds A Barclay and J Harding), 11–29, Oxbow Mono. Oxford and Oakville: Oxbow Books

Barclay, A, and Halpin, C, 1999 *Excavations at Barrow Hills, Radley, Oxfordshire. Volume I. The Neolithic and Bronze Age monument complex*, Thames Valley Landscapes **11.** Oxford: Oxford Archaeological Unit

Barker, G, and Webley, D, 1978 Causewayed camps and early Neolithic economies in central south England, *Proc Prehist Soc* **44**, 161–86

Barnes, I, 1984 The analysis and re-creation of bronze and brass mould residues, in *The laboratories of the National Museum of Antiquities of Scotland* **2** (eds T Bryce and J Tate), 40–46. Edinburgh: National Museum of Antiquities of Scotland

Barrett, J C, 1980 The pottery of the later Bronze Age in lowland England, *Proc Prehist Soc* **46**, 297–320

Barrett, J, and Bradley, R, 1991 The Cranborne Chase project and its publication, in *Papers on the prehistoric archaeology of Cranborne Chase* (eds J Barrett, R Bradley and M Hall), Oxbow Mono **11**, 1–10, Oxford: Oxbow Books

Barrett, J C, Bradley, R, and Green, M, 1991 *Landscape, monuments and society. The prehistory of Cranborne Chase.* Cambridge, Cambridge University Press

Barrett, J C, Freeman, P W M, and Woodward, A, 2000 *Cadbury Castle, Somerset: the later prehistoric and early historic archaeology*, English Heritage Archaeol Rep **20.** London: English Heritage

Barton, R N E, 1986 Experiments with long blades from Sproughton, near Ipswich, Suffolk, in *Studies in the Upper Palaeolithic of Britain and Northwest Europe* (ed D A Roe), Brit Archaeol Rep Internat Ser **296**, 129–41, Oxford: British Archaeological Reports

Bass, W M, 1987 *Human osteology*, Columbia: Missouri Archaeological Society

Batten, R, Gillespie, R, Gowlett, J A J, and Hedges, R E M, 1986 The AMS dating of separate fractions in archaeology, *Radiocarbon* **28**, 698–701

Bayliss, A, 1998 Some thoughts on using scientific dating in English archaeology and buildings analysis for the next decade, in *Science in archaeology: an agenda for the future* (ed J Bayley), 95–108. London: English Heritage

Bayliss, A, and Bronk Ramsey, C, forthcoming Bayesian sensitivity analyses and the dating of Hambledon Hill, *Radiocarbon*

Bayliss, A, Bronk Ramsey, C, and McCormac, F G, 1997 Dating Stonehenge, *Proc Brit Acad* **92**, 39–59

Beasley, M, Brown, B A B, and Legge, A J, 1987 Ageing cattle by their teeth, *Ark, J Rare Breeds Survival Trust* **14(1)**, 22–24

Bell, M, 1981a Valley sediments and environmental change, in *The environment of man: the Iron Age to the Anglo-Saxon period* (eds M Jones and G W Dimbleby), Brit Archaeol Rep Brit Ser **87**, 75–91, Oxford; British Archaeological Reports

—, 1981b Valley sediments as evidence of prehistoric land-use: a study based on dry valleys in south-east England, unpubl PhD thesis, Institute of Archaeology, University of London

—, 1983 Valley sediments as evidence of prehistoric land-use on the South Downs, *Proc Prehist Soc* **49**, 119–50

—, 1986 Archaeological evidence for the date, cause and extent of soil erosion on the chalk, *SEESOIL* **3**, 72–83

—, 1990 Sedimentation rates in the primary fills of chalk-cut features, in *Experimentation and reconstruction in environmental archaeology* (ed D E Robinson), 237–48, Oxford: Oxbow Books

—, 1992 The prehistory of soil erosion, in *Past and present soil erosion* (eds M G Bell and J Boardman), 21–3, Oxford: Oxbow Books

Bell, M, and Allen, M J, 1985 Valley sediments and molluscs from around Hambledon Hill, Dorset, unpubl report for Hambledon Hill project

Bell, M, and Bradshaw, R, 1983 Roman lava querns from Exeter, *Proc Devon Archaeol Soc* **41**, 128–30

Bell, M, and Johnson, J, 1996 Land molluscs, in Bell *et al* 1996, 140–42

Bell, M, and Walker, M J C, 1992 *Late Quaternary environmental change: physical and human perspectives*, Harlow: Longman

Bell, M, Fowler, P J, and Hillson, S W (eds), 1996 *The experimental earthwork project, 1960–1992*, Counc Brit Archaeol Res Rep **100.** York: Council for British Archaeology

Bellamy, P 1997 Flaked stone assemblages, in Smith *et al* 1997, 136–54

Berrie, A and Wright, J, 1984 The Winterbourne stream, in *Ecology of European rivers* (ed B A Whitton), 176–206, Oxford: Blackwell

Berry, A C and Berry, R J, 1967 Epigenetic variation in the human cranium, *J Anatomy* **101(2)**, 261–379

Binford, L R, 1981 *Bones: ancient men and modern myths*, New York, London, Sydney, Toronto and San Francisco: Academic Press

Birks, H J B, Deacon, J, and Peglar, S, 1975 Pollen maps for the British Isles 5000 years ago, *Proc Roy Soc London B* **189**, 87–105

Black, E W, 1987 *The Roman villas of south-east England*, Brit Archaeol Rep Brit Ser **177**. Oxford: British Archaeological Reports

Boardman, J, 1992 Current erosion on the South Downs: implications for the past, in *Past and present soil erosion* (eds M G Bell and J Boardman), 9–20, Oxford: Oxbow Books

Boardman, S, and Jones, G, 1990 Experiments on the effects of charring on cereal plant components, *J Archaeol Sci* **17**, 1–11

Bocherens, H, Fizet, M, Mariotti, A, Lange-Badre, B, Vandermeersch, B, Borel, J P, and Bellon, G, 1991 Isotopic biogeochemistry (^{13}C, ^{15}N) of fossil vertebrate collagen: application to the study of a past food web including Neanderthal man, *J Human Evolution* **20**, 481–92

Bocherens, H, Fogel, M, Tuross, N, and Zeder, M 1995 Trophic structure and climatic information from isotopic signatures in Pleistocene cave fauna of southern England, *J Archaeol Sci* **22**, 327–40

Bocquet, A, 1980 Le microdenticulé, un outil mal connu: essai de typologie, *Bulletin de la Société Préhistorique Française* **77(3)**, 76–85

Böhner, K, 1958 *Die Frankischen Altertümer des Trierer Landes*, Berlin, Germanische Denkmäler der Völkerwanderungszeit, Ser B; Band **1**

Bond, C J, 2004 The supply of raw materials for later prehistoric stone tool assemblages and the maintenance of memorable places in central Somerset, in *Lithics in action. Papers from the conference Lithic Studies in the Year 2000* (eds E A Walker, F Wenban-Smith and F Healy), Oxford: Oxbow Books, 124–39

Bonney, D, 1966 Pagan Saxon burials and boundaries in Wiltshire, *Wiltshire Archaeol Natur Hist Mag* **61**, 25–30

Boswell, P G H, 1924 The petrography of the sands of the Upper Lias and Lower Inferior Oolite of the west of England, *Geol Mag* **61**, 246–64

Bouville, C 1987 Les restes humains de la Baume Fontbrégoua à Salernes (Var), in *Premières communautés paysannes en Méditerraneée occidentale. Actes du colloque international du CNRS*, 501–5, Paris: Centre National de la Recherche Scientifique

Bowden, M, 1984 *General Pitt Rivers: the father of scientific archaeology*. Salisbury: Salisbury and South Wiltshire Museum

Bowen H C, 1978 'Celtic' fields and 'ranch' boundaries in Wessex, in *The Effect of man on the landscape: the lowland zone* (eds S Limbrey and J G Evans), Counc British Archaeol Res Rep **21**, 115–25. London: Council for British Archaeology

Bowen, H C, and Smith, I F, 1977 Sarsen stones in Wessex: the Society's first investigations in the evolution of the landscape project, *Antiq J* **57**, 185–96

Bowman, S, 1990 *Radiocarbon Dating*, London, British Museum Publications

Boyd, W E, 1988 Methodological problems in the analysis of fossil non-artifactual wood assemblages from archaeological sites, *J Archaeol Sci* **15**, 603–19

Bradley, P, 1994 Assemblage variation and spatial patterning of artefacts in the earlier Neolithic of southern England with special reference to causewayed enclosures, unpubl M Phil thesis, Univ of Sheffield

Bradley, P, 1999 Results [of the fieldwalking survey], in Barclay and Halpin 1999, 14–16

Bradley, R, 1970 The excavation of a Beaker settlement at Belle Tout, East Sussex, England, *Proc Prehist Soc* **36**, 312–79

—, 1976 Maumbury Rings, Dorchester: the excavations of 1908–1913, *Archaeologia* **105**, 1–97

—, 1978 *The prehistoric settlement of Britain*, London: Routledge and Keagan Paul

—, 1984a The bank barrows and related monuments of Dorset in the light of recent fieldwork, *Proc Dorset Natur Hist Archaeol Soc* **105**, 15–20

—, 1984b *The social foundations of prehistoric Britain. Themes and variations on the archaeology of power*. London and New York: Longman

—, 1993 *Altering the earth. The origins of monuments in Britain and continental Europe*, Soc Antiq Scotland, Mono **32**. Edinburgh: Society of Antiquaries of Scotland

Bradley, R, and Edmonds, M, 1993 *Interpreting the axe trade: production and exchange in Neolithic Britain*, Cambridge: Cambridge University Press

Bradley, R, and Thomas, J, 1984 Some new information on the henge monument at Maumbury Rings, Dorchester, *Proc Dorset Natur Hist Archaeol Soc* **106**, 132–4

Bradley, R, Entwistle, R and Raymond, F, 1994 *Prehistoric land divisions on Salisbury Plain*, English Heritage Archaeol Rep **2**. London: English Heritage

Brain, C K, 1969 The contribution of Namib desert Hottentots to the understanding of Australopithecine bone accumulations, *Scientific Pap Namib Desert Research Station* **39**, 13–22

Brennand, M, and Taylor, M, 2003 The survey and excavation of a Bronze Age timber circle at Holme-next-the-Sea, Norfolk 1998–9, *Proc Prehist Soc* **69**, 1–84

Bristow, C R, Freshney, E C, and Penn, I E, 1991 *Geology of the country around Bournemouth. British Geological Survey, memoir for sheet 329*, London: HMSO

Bristow, C R, Barton, C M, Freshney, E C, Wood, C J, Evans, D J, Cox, D M, Ivimey-Cook, H C, and Taylor, R T, 1995 *Geology of the country around Shaftesbury. British Geological Survey, memoir for sheet 313*, London: HMSO

Britnell, W J, and Savory, H N, 1984 *Gwernvale and Penwyrlod: two Neolithic long cairns in the Black Mountains of Brecknock*. Cambrian Mono 2: Cardiff: Cambrian Archaeological Association

Britton, J (ed), 1847 *The natural history of Wiltshire by John Aubrey FRS (written between 1656 and 1691)*, Salisbury: Wiltshire Topographical Society. Reprinted by David & Charles, Newton Abbot, 1969

Bronk Ramsey, C, 1994 Oxcal (v2.0): A radiocarbon calibration and analysis program, Oxford: Oxford Radiocarbon Accelerator Unit

—, 1995 Radiocarbon calibration and analysis of stratigraphy, *Radiocarbon* **36**, 425–30

—, 1998 Probability and dating, *Radiocarbon* **40**, 461–74

Bronk Ramsey, C, and Hedges, R E M, 1997 Hybrid ion sources: radiocarbon measurements from microgram to milligram, *Nuclear Instruments and Methods in Physics Research B* **123**, 539–45

Bronk Ramsey, C, Pettitt, P B, Hedges, R E M, Hodgins, G W L and Owen, D C 2000 Radiocarbon dates from the Oxford AMS system: *Archaeometry* datelist 29'. *Archaeometry* **42**, 243–54

Brothwell, D R, 1971 Palaeodemography, in *Biological aspects of demography* (ed W Bass), 11–127, London

—, 1972a *Digging up bones*. London: British Museum (Natural History)

—, 1972b Palaeodemography and earlier British populations, *World Archaeol* **4:1**, 75–87

—, 1973 The human biology of the Neolithic population of Britain, in *Die Anfänge des Neolithikums vom Orient bis*

Nordeuropa. Teil VIIIa. Anthropologie. 1 Teil (ed I Schwidetzky), Fundamenta Reihe B, Band **3**, 280–99, Cologne and Vienna: Böhlau Verlag

—, D R, 1981 *Digging up bones*, London: British Museum (Natural History)

—, 1999 Human remains, in Whittle *et al* 1999, 344–6

Brothwell, D R, and Blake, M L, 1966 The human remains from the Fussell's Lodge long barrow: their morphology, discontinuous traits and pathology, in Ashbee 1966, 48–62

Brown, A G, 1989 The social life of flint at Neolithic Hembury, *Lithics* **10**, 46–9

—, 1991 Structured deposition and technological change among the flaked stone artefacts from Cranborne Chase, in *Papers on the Prehistoric Archaeology of Cranborne Chase* (eds J Barrett, R Bradley and M Hall), Oxbow Mono **11**, 101–33, Oxford: Oxbow Books

—, 1995 Beyond Stone Age economics: a strategy for a contextual lithic analysis, in *Lithics in context* (ed A J Schofield), 27–36. London: Lithic Studies Society

Brown, G, 1902 *Dentition as indicative of the age of the animals of the farm* (revised edition), London: Royal Agricultural Society

Brown, L, 1987 The late prehistoric pottery, in *Hengistbury Head, Dorset. Vol 1: prehistoric and Roman settlement, 3500 BC–AD 500* (B W Cunliffe), OUCA Mono **13**, 207–303. Oxford: Oxford University Committee for Archaeology

—, 1991 Later prehistoric pottery, in Sharples 1991, 185–205

Brown, N, 1997 Re-defining native woodland, *Forestry* **70(3)**, 191–8

Brown, T, 1997 Clearances and clearings: deforestation in Mesolithic/Neolithic Britain. *Oxford J Archaeol* **16(2)**, 133–46

Buck, C E, Kenworthy, J B, Litton, C D, and Smith, A F M, 1991 Combining archaeological and radiocarbon information: a Bayesian approach to calibration, *Antiquity* **65**, 808–21

Buck, C E, Litton, C D, and Smith, A F M, 1992 Calibration of radiocarbon results pertaining to related archaeological events, *J Archaeol Sci* **19**, 497–512

Buck, C E, Christen, J A, Kenworthy, J B, and Litton, C D, 1994 Estimating the duration of archaeological activity using ^{14}C determinations, *Oxford J Archaeol* **13**, 229–40

Buck, C E, Litton, C D, and Scott, E M, 1994 Making the most of radiocarbon dating: some statistical considerations, *Antiquity* **68**, 252–63

Buckley, D G, 1979 The stone, in *Gussage All Saints: an Iron Age settlement in Dorset* (G J Wainwright), Department of the Environment Archaeol Rep **10**, 89–97. London: HMSO

Bull, G, and Payne, S, 1982 Tooth eruption and epiphyseal fusion in pigs and wild boar, in *Ageing and sexing animal bones from archaeological sites* (eds B Wilson, C Grigson and S Payne), Brit Archaeol Rep Brit Ser **109**, 55–71. Oxford: British Archaeological Reports

Butcher, S, 1982 The brooches, in *Excavations at Catsgore 1970–1973* (R Leech), Western Archaeol Trust Excav Mono **2**, 105–10. Cheltenham: Western Archaeological Trust

Calkin, J B, 1957 Barrels, buckets and globulars, *Proc Dorset Natur Hist Archaeol Soc* **79**, 104–5

—, 1965 Some early Iron Age sites in the Bournemouth area, *Proc Dorset Natur Hist Archaeol Soc* **86**, 120–30

Callow, W J, Baker, M J, and Pritchard, D H, 1963 National Physical Laboratory Radiocarbon Measurements I, *Radiocarbon* **5**, 34–8

Callow, W J, Baker, M J, and Hassall, G I, 1965 National Physical Laboratory Radiocarbon Measurements III, *Radiocarbon* **7**, 156–61

Campbell, G, and Robinson, M, forthcoming Environment and land use in the valley bottom, in *Raunds area project. The Neolithic and Bronze Age landscapes of West Cotton, Stanwick and Irthlingborough, Northamptonshire* (J Harding and F Healy), English Heritage Archaeol Rep. Swindon: English Heritage

Campbell Smith, W, 1965 The distribution of jade axes from sites in Europe with a supplement to the catalogue of those from the British Isles, *Proc Prehist Soc* **51**, 25–55

Carruthers, W J, and Thomas, R, 1991 The charcoal identifications, in Woodward 1991, 111–14

Cartwright, C R, 1976 Appendix III: charcoal and other environmental evidence from on site flotation, in The excavation of a Neolithic causewayed enclosure on Offham Hill, East Sussex (P Drewett), *Proc Prehist Soc* **43**, 232–34

—, 1997 The wood charcoal, in Whittle 1997b, 129–34

Caseldine, A E, 1984 Palaeobotanical investigations at the Sweet Track, *Somerset Levels Pap* **10**, 65–78

Casey, H and Ladle, M, 1976 Chemistry and biology of the South Winterbourne, Dorset, England, *Freshwater Biology* **6**, 1–12

Catherall P D, Barnett, M, and McClean, H, 1984 *The Southern Feeder: the archaeology of a gas pipeline*, London

Caulfield, S, 1978 Star Carr – an alternative view, *Irish Archaeol Res Forum* **5**, 15–22

Chafin, W 1818 *Anecdotes respecting Cranbourn Chase with a very concise account of it; together with the rural amusements it afforded our ancestors in the days of yore*, London: J Nichols, Son, and Bentley

Chamberlain, A T, 1999 Carsington Pasture Cave, Brassington, Derbyshire: a prehistoric burial site. *Capra* **1**, http://www.shef.ac.uk/~capra/1/carsing.html

Charters, S, Evershed, R P, Goad, L J, Heron, C, and Blinkhorn, P, 1993 Identification of an adhesive used to repair a Roman jar, *Archaeometry* **35**, 91–101

Charters, S, Evershed, R P, Blinkhorn, P W, and Denham, V, 1995 Evidence for the mixing of fats and waxes in archaeological ceramics, *Archaeometry* **37**, 113–27

Charters, S, Evershed, R P, Quye, A, Blinkhorn, P W, and Reeves, V, 1997 Simulation experiments for determining the use of ancient pottery vessels: the behaviour of epicuticular leaf wax during boiling of a leafy vegetable, *J Archaeol Sci* **24**, 1–7

Chatwin, C P, 1960 *British regional geology. The Hampshire Basin and adjoining areas. Third edition*, London: Natural Environment Research Council, Institute of Geological Sciences, Geological Survey and Museum. London: HMSO

Chesterman, J T, 1977 Burial rites in a Cotswold long barrow, *Man* **12**; 22–32

Chisham, C, 1994 A charcoal analysis of the Neolithic causewayed enclosure of Hambledon Hill, upubl MSc thesis, Institute of Archaeology, University College, London

Clark, J G D, 1933 Report on an early Bronze Age site in the south-eastern Fens, *Antiq J* **13**, 266–96

Clark, J G D, 1934 Derivative forms of the *petit tranchet* in Britain, *Archaeol J* **91**, 32–58

—, 1954 *Star Carr*, Cambridge: Cambridge University Press

Clark, J G D, Higgs, E S, and Longworth, I H, 1960 Excavations at the Neolithic site at Hurst Fen, Mildenhall,

Suffolk (1954, 1957 and 1958), *Proc Prehist Soc* **26**, 202–45

Clarke, D L, 1970 *Beaker pottery of Great Britain and Ireland*, Cambridge: Cambridge University Press

Clarke, D V, Cowie, T G, and Foxon, A, 1985 *Symbols of power at the time of Stonehenge*, Edinburgh: National Museum of Antiquities of Scotland

Clarke, W G, 1915 The antler picks, in *Report on the excavations at Grime's Graves, Weeting, Norfolk, March–May 1914* (ed W G Clarke), 142–46, Prehistoric Society of East Anglia, London: H K Lewis

Cleal, R M J, 1990 The prehistoric pottery [from the Coneybury 'Anomaly'], in Richards 1990, 45–57

—, 1991a The earlier prehistoric pottery, in Sharples 1991, 171–85

—, 1991b Cranborne Chase – the earlier prehistoric pottery, in *Papers on the prehistoric archaeology of Cranborne Chase* (eds J Barrett, R Bradley and M Hall), Oxbow Mono **11**, 134–200, Oxford: Oxbow Books

—, 1992 Significant form: ceramic styles in the earlier Neolithic of southern England, in *Vessels for the ancestors* (eds N Sharples and A Sheridan), 286–304, Edinburgh: Edinburgh University Press

—, 1995 Pottery fabrics in Wessex in the fourth to second millennia BC, in *'Unbaked urns of rudely shape'. Essays on British and Irish pottery for Ian Longworth* (eds I Kinnes and G Varndell), 185–94, Oxbow Monograph **55**, Oxford: Oxbow Books

—, 2004 Pottery, in Investigation of the Whitesheet Down environs 1989–90: Neolithic causewayed enclosure and Iron Age settlement (M Rawlings, M J Allen and F Healy), *Wiltshire Studies* **97**, 155–60

Cleal, R M J, and Allen, M J, 1995 Stonehenge in its landscape, in Cleal *et al* 1995, 464–94

Cleal, R M J, Walker, K E, and Montague, R, 1995 *Stonehenge in its landscape. Twentieth-century excavations*, London: English Heritage Archaeol Rep **10**. London: English Heritage

Clough, T H McK, and Cummins, W A (eds), 1988 *Stone axe studies volume 2. The petrology of prehistoric stone implements from the British Isles*, Counc Brit Archaeol Res Rep **67**. London: Council for British Archaeology

Clutton-Brock, J, 1984 *Neolithic antler picks from Grimes Graves, Norfolk and Durrington Walls, Wiltshire: a biometrical analysis*, Excavations at Grimes Graves 1972–76 Fasicule 1, London: British Museum Publications

Coker, J 1732 *A survey of Dorsetshire containing the antiquities and natural history of that county, and a copious genealogical account of three hundred of the principal families, to which is prefixed a map of the county. Published from an original manuscript of Mr Coker*, London: J Wilcox (facsimile edition 1980, with an afterword by R Legg, Sherborne: Dorset Publishing Company)

Colborne, G J N, Cope, D W, Harrod, T R, Hogan, D V, and Staines, S J, 1983 *1:250,000 soil map of England and Wales, sheet 5*, Southampton: Soil Survey of England and Wales

Cole, H A, 1956 *Oyster cultivation in Britain*, London: HMSO

Coles, B, and Coles, J, 1986 *Sweet Track to Glastonbury*, London: Thames and Hudson

Coles, J M, and Coles, B J, 1990 Part II: the Sweet Track date, in Dendrochronology of the English Neolithic (J Hillam, C M Groves, D M Brown, M G L Baillie, J M Coles, and B J Coles), *Antiquity* **64**, 216–20

Coles, J M, and Darrah, R, 1977 Experimental investigations in hurdle making, *Somerset Levels Pap* **3**, 32–8

Coles, J M, and Orme, B J, 1979 The Sweet Track: drove site, *Somerset Levels Pap* **5**, 43–64

Coles, J M, Hibbert, F A, and Orme, B J, 1973 Prehistoric roads and tracks in Somerset, England: 3. The Sweet Track, *Proc Prehist Soc* **39**, 256–93

Coles, J, Orme, B, Bishop, A C, and Woolley, A R, 1974 A jade axe from the Somerset Levels, *Antiquity* **48**, 216–20

Coles, J M, Caseldine, A E, and Morgan, R A, 1988 A Neolithic hurdle on Franks' Ground, 1984, *Somerset Levels Pap* **14**, 44–9

Connah, G, 1965 Excavations at Knap Hill, Alton Priors, 1961, *Wiltshire Archaeol Natur Hist Mag* **60**, 1–23

Cook, H F, 1994 Field-scale water management in southern England to AD 1900, *Landscape History* **16**, 53–66

Cook, J, 1986 Marked human bones from Gough's cave, Somerset, *Proc Univ Bristol Spelaeol Soc* **17(3)**, 275–85

Copley, M S, Rose, P J, Clapham, A, Edwards, D N, Horton, M C, and Evershed, R P, 2001 Processing palm fruits in the Nile Valley – biomolecular evidence from Qasr Ibrim, *Antiquity* **75**, 538–42

Copley, M S, Berstan, R, Dudd, S N, Docherty, G, Mukherjee, A J, Straker, V, Payne, S, and Evershed, R P, 2003 Direct chemical evidence for widespread dairying in prehistoric Britain, *Proc National Acad Sci* **100(4)**, 1524–9

Cornwall, I, and Hodges, H, 1964 Thin sections of British Neolithic pottery, *Bull Inst Archaeol London* **4**, 29–33

Cowan, M 1982 *Floated water meadows in the Salisbury area*, South Wiltshire Industrial Archaeol Soc Hist Mono **9.** Salisbury: South Wiltshire Industrial Archaeology Society

Cox, P W, 1991 Portable stone objects, in Woodward 1991, 95

Crawford, O G S, and Keiller, A, 1928 *Wessex from the air*, Oxford: Clarendon Press

Crowfoot, E, 1991 Textile impressions on two early Neolithic pottery sherds, in Woodward 1991, 99

Cunliffe, B W, 1987 *Hengistbury Head, Dorset. Vol 1: prehistoric and Roman settlement, 3500 BC–AD 500*, OUCA Mono **13**, Oxford: Oxford University Committee for Archaeology

Cunliffe, B W, and Phillipson, D W, 1968 Excavations at Eldon's Seat, Encombe, Dorset, *Proc Prehist Soc* **34**, 191–237

Cunnington, M E, 1895 Hambledon Hill, Dorset, *Proc Dorset Nat Hist and Antiquarian Fld Club* **16**, 156–8

—, 1923 *An early Iron Age inhabited site at All Canning Cross Farm*, Devizes

Curwen, E C, 1929 Excavations in The Trundle, Goodwood, 1928, *Sussex Archaeol Collect* **70**, 33–85

—, 1931 Excavations in the Trundle, Goodwood (second season) 1930, *Sussex Archaeol Collect* **72**, 100–49

—, 1936 Excavations in Whitehawk Camp, Brighton, third season, 1935, *Sussex Archaeol Collect* **77**, 60–92

—, 1937 *The archaeology of Sussex*, London: Methuen

Darvill, T C, 1983a The Neolithic of Wales and the mid-west of England: a systemic analysis of social change through the application of action theory. Unpubl PhD thesis, Univ of Southampton.

—, 1983b The petrology of the Neolithic pottery from Cherhill, in Excavations at Cherhill, north Wiltshire, 1967 (J G Evans and I F Smith), *Proc Prehist Soc* **49**, 92–8

—, 1984 A study of the Neolithic pottery fabrics from Gwernvale, in *Gwernvale and Pen y wyrlod: two Neolithic long cairns in the Black Mountains of Brecknock* (W J Britnell and H N Savory), 110–13, Cardiff: Cambrian Archaeol Assoc

—, 2004 Soft rock and organic tempering in British Neolithic pottery, in *Monuments and material culture. Papers in honour of an Avebury archaeologist: Isobel Smith* (eds R Cleal and J Pollard), 193–206, East Knoyle: Hobnob Press

David, A, and Williams, G, 1995 Stone axe-head manufacture: new evidence from the Presceli hills, west Wales, *Proc Prehist Soc* **61**, 433–60

Davidson, A, 1999 *The Oxford companion to food*, Oxford: Oxford University Press

Davies, D, 1988 The evocative symbolism of trees, in *The iconography of landscapes* (eds D Cosgrove and S Daniels), 32–42, Cambridge: Cambridge University Press

Davies, H, 1936 The shale industries at Kimmeridge, Dorset, *Archaeol J* **93**, 200–19

Davies, P, 1998 Numerical analysis of subfossil wet-ground molluscan taxocenes from overbank alluvium at Kingsmead Bridge, Wiltshire, *J Archaeol Sci* **25**, 39–52

—, 1999 Molluscan total assemblages across a woodland-grassland boundary and their palaeoecological relevance, *Environmental Archaeol* **4**, 57–65

Davies, P, Gale, C H, and Lees, M, 1996 Quantitative studies of modern wet-ground molluscan faunas from Bossington, Hampshire, *J Biogeography* **23**, 371–77

Davies, S M, 1986 The coarse pottery [from Rope Lake Hole], in *Romano-British industries in Purbeck* (eds N Sunter and P J Woodward), Dorset Natur Hist Archaeol Soc Mono **6**, 150–7. Dorchester: Dorset Natural History and Archaeological Society

de Laet, S J, 1958 *The Low Countries*, London: Thames and Hudson

Degerbøl, M, 1970 The Urus (*Bos primigenius* Boj) and Neolithic domesticated cattle (*Bos taurus domesticus* Linne) in Denmark, *Det Kongelige Danske Vildenskabernes Selskab, Biologiske Skrifter* **17(1)**, 1–177

Dehling, H, and van der Plicht, J, 1993 Statistical problems in calibrating radiocarbon dates, *Radiocarbon* **35**, 239–44

Delcourt, H R, Delcourt, P A, and Webb III, T, 1983 Dynamic plant ecology: the spectrum of vegetational change in space and time, *Quaternary Sci Review* **1**, 153–75

Deniz, E, and Payne, S, 1982 Eruption and wear in the mandibular dentition as an aid to ageing Turkish Angora goats, in *Ageing and sexing animal bones from archaeological sites* (eds B Wilson, C Grigson and S Payne), Brit Archaeol Rep Brit Ser **109**, 155–206. Oxford: British Archaeological Reports

Desch, H E, and Dinwoodie, J M, 1981 *Timber, its structure, properties and utilization* (6th edition), London: Macmillan

Dimbleby, G W, Keef, P A M, and Wymer, J J, 1965 A Mesolithic site on Iping Common, Sussex, England, *Proc Prehist Soc* **6**, 85–92

Dixon, P, 1988 The Neolithic settlements on Crickley Hill, in *Enclosures and defences in the Neolithic of Western Europe* (eds C Burgess, P Topping, C Mordant and M Maddison), Brit Archaeol Rep Internat Ser **403(i)**, 75–87. Oxford: British Archaeological Reports

Doherty, J, 1985 Water over the meadows, *Natural World* **12**, 17–19

Drake, C M, 1999 A review of the status, distribution and habitat requirements of *Vertigo moulinsiana* in England, *J Conchology* **36(6)**, 63–79

Dreisch, A von den, 1976 *A guide to the measurement of animal bones from archaeological sites*, Harvard: Peabody Museum

Drew, C D and Piggott, S, 1936 The excavation of long barrow 163a on Thickthorn Down, Dorset, *Proc Prehist Soc* **2**, 77–96

Drewett, P L, 1977 The excavation of a Neolithic causewayed enclosure on Offham Hill, East Sussex, 1976, *Proc Prehist Soc* **43**, 201–42

—, 1994 Dr V Seton Williams' excavations at Combe Hill, 1962, and the role of Neolithic causewayed enclosures in Sussex, *Sussex Archaeol Collect* **132**, 7–24

Dudd, S N, and Evershed, R P, 1998 Direct demonstration of milk as an element of archaeological economies, *Science* **282**, 1478–81

Dudd, S N, Regert, M, and Evershed, R P, 1998 Assessing microbial lipid contributions during laboratory degradations of fats and oils and pure triacylglycerols absorbed in ceramic potsherds, *Organic Geochemistry* **29**, 1345–54

During, E M, and Nilsson, L, 1991 Mechanical surface analysis of bone: a case study of cut marks and enamel hypoplasia on a Neolithic cranium from Sweden' *Amer J Phys Anthropol* **84**, 113–25

Eagles, B, 1994 The archaeological evidence for settlement in the fifth to seventh centuries AD, in *The medieval landscape of Wessex* (eds M Aston and C Lewis), Oxbow Mono **46**, 13–32, Oxford: Oxbow Books

Edlin, H L, 1949 *British woodland trees* (3rd edition), London: Batsford

—, 1970 *Trees, woods and man* (3rd edition), London: Collins

Edmonds, M, 1993 Interpreting causewayed enclosures in the past and present, in *Interpretative Archaeology* (ed C Tilley), 99–142, Oxford: Berg

—, 1998 Polished stone axes and associated artefacts, in Pryor 1998, 260–8

—, 1999 *Ancestral geographies of the Neolithic. Landscapes, monuments and memory*, London and New York: Routledge

Edmonds, M, and Bellamy, P, 1991 The flaked stone, in Sharples 1991, 214–29

Ellenberg, H, 1988 *Vegetation ecology of central Europe* (fourth edition), Cambridge: Cambrige University Press

Ellis, S E, 1968 Notes on the stones, in *Hod Hill volume 2. Excavations carried out between 1951 and 1958 for the Trustees of the British Museum* (I Richmond), 135–7, London: Trustees of the British Museum

Ellison, A, and Rahtz, P, 1987 Excavations at Hog Cliff Hill, Maiden Newton, Dorset, *Proc Prehist Soc* **53**, 223–69

English Nature 1987 *Hambledon Hill: national nature reserve* (visitors' leaflet), Wareham: English Nature

Entwistle, R, 1990 Statistical appraisal, in Richards 1990, 254

Entwistle, R, and Bowden, M, 1991 Cranborne Chase: the molluscan evidence, in *Papers on the prehistoric archaeology of Cranborne Chase* (eds J Barrett, R Bradley and M Hall), Oxbow Mono **11**, 20–48. Oxford: Oxbow Books

Entwistle, R, and Grant, A, 1989 The evidence for cereal cultivation and animal husbandry in the southern British Neolithic and Bronze Age, in *The beginnings of agriculture* (eds A Milles, D Williams, and N. Gardner), Brit Archaeol Rep Internat Ser S496, 203–15. Oxford: British Archaeological Reports

Evans, C, 1988 Acts of enclosure: a consideration of concentrically-organised causewayed enclosures, in *The archaeology of context in the Neolithic and Bronze Age: recent trends* (eds J C Barrett and I Kinnes), Recent Trends Series **3**, 85–96, Sheffield: Department of Archaeology and Prehistory

Evans, C, and Hodder, I, 2006 *A woodland archaeology. Neolithic Sites at Haddenham. The Haddenham project: volume 1.* Cambridge: MacDonald Institute for

Archaeological Research. Cambridge: MacDonald Institute

Evans, C, Pollard, J, and Knight, M, 1999 Life in woods: tree-throws, 'settlement' and forest cognition, *Oxford J Archaeol* **18(3)**, 241–54.

Evans, C, Edmonds, M, and Boreham, S, 2006 'Total archaeology' and model landscapes: excavation of the Great Wilbraham causewayed enclosure, Cambrideshire, 1975–76, *Proc Prehist Soc* **72**, 113–62

Evans, D M, 1983 Magnetometer survey at the Neolithic to Iron Age site at Hambledon Hill, Dorset, in *Geophysical surveys 1982* (ed J A Pocock), University of Bradford Department of Archaeological Sciences Occas Pap **3**, 97–116. Bradford: University of Bradford Department of Archaeological Sciences

Evans, E-J, 2000 Neolithic burial practices at Hambledon Hill, unpubl dissertation submitted in partial fulfilment of the requirements of MA Osteoarcheology by instructional course, University of Southampton

Evans, J G, 1971 Durrington Walls: the pre-henge environment, in Wainwright with Longworth 1971, 329–37

—, 1972 *Land snails in archaeology*, London: Seminar Press

—, 1979a The South Street long barrow, in Excavation of three long barrows near Avebury, Wiltshire (P Ashbee, I F Smith and J G Evans), *Proc Prehist Soc* **45**, 250–75

—, 1979b The environment, in Excavation of three long barrows near Avebury, Wiltshire (P Ashbee, I F Smith and J G Evans), *Proc Prehist Soc* **45**, 275–98

—, 1980 Molluscan analysis, in *Runnymede Bridge 1976: Excavations on the site of a late Bronze Age settlement* (D Longley and S Needham, Surrey Archaeol Soc Res Vol **6**, 80–3, Guildford: Surrey Archaeological Society

—, 1983 Molluscan analysis, in Excavation at Cherhill, north Wiltshire, 1967 (J G Evans and I F Smith), *Proc Prehist Soc* **49**, 101–5

—, 1991 The environment, in Sharples 1991, 250–3

—, 1993 The influence of human communities on the English chalklands from the Mesolithic to the Iron Age: the molluscan evidence, in *Climatic change and human impact on the landscape* (ed F M Chambers), 147–56, London: Chapman and Hall

Evans, J G, and Jones, H, 1973 Subfossil and modern land-snail faunas from rock-rubble habitats, *J Conchology* **28**, 103–29

Evans, J G, and Jones, H, 1979 The land Mollusca, in Wainwright 1979a, 190–213

Evans, J G, and O'Connor, T, 1998 *Environmental archaeology: principles and methods*, Stroud: Sutton

Evans, J G, and Rouse, A, 1991a The river valleys of the South Winterbourne and Frome, in Sharples 1991, 15–17

—, 1991b The land Mollusca, in Sharples 1991, 118–25

Evans J G, and Smith, I F, 1983 Excavations at Cherhill, North Wiltshire 1967, *Proc Prehist Soc* **49**, 101–9

Evans, J G, Rouse, A, and Sharples, N, 1988 The landscape setting of causewayed camps: recent work on the Maiden Castle enclosure, in *The archaeology of context in the Neolithic and Bronze Age: recent trends* (eds J C Barrett and I Kinnes), Recent Trends Series **3**, 73–8, Sheffield: Department of Archaeology and Prehistory

Evans, J G, Davies, P, Mount, R, and Williams, D, 1992 Molluscan taxocenes from Holocene overbank alluvium in central southern England, in *Alluvial archaeology in Britain* (eds S Needham and M G Macklin), Oxbow Mono **27**, 65–74, Oxford: Oxbow Books

Evans, J G, Limbrey, S, Maté, I, and Mount, R, 1993 An environmental history of the upper Kennet valley, Wiltshire, for the last 10,000 years, *Proc Prehist Soc* **59**, 139–95

Evans, R, 1990 Erosion in England and Wales – the present, the key to the past, in *Past and present soil erosion* (eds M G Bell and J Boardman), 53–66, Oxford: Oxbow Books

Evens, E D, Smith, I F, and Wallis, F S, 1972 The petrological identification of stone implements from south-western England, *Proc Prehist Soc* **58**, 255–75

Evershed, R P, 1993 Biomolecular archaeology and lipids, *World Archaeol* **25**, 74–93

Evershed, R P, Heron, C, and Goad, L J, 1990 Analysis of organic residues of archaeological origin by high-temperature gas-chromatography and gas-chromatography mass-spectrometry, *Analyst* **115**, 1339–42

—, 1991 Epicuticular wax components preserved in potsherds as chemical indicators of leafy vegetables in ancient diets, *Antiquity* **65**, 540–44

Evershed, R P, Heron, C, Charters, S, and Goad, L J, 1992 The survival of food residues: new methods of analysis, interpretation and application, in *New developments in archaeological science* (ed AM Pollard), 187–208, Oxford: Oxford University Press

Evershed, R P, Arnot, K I, Collister, J, Eglinton, G, and Charters, S, 1994 Application of isotope ratio monitoring gas-chromatography mass-spectrometry to the analysis of organic residues of archaeological origin, *Analyst* **119**, 909–14

Evershed, R P, Stott, A W, Raven, A, Dudd, S N, Charters, S, and Leyden, A, 1995 Formation of long-chain ketones in ancient pottery vessels by pyrolysis of acyl lipids, *Tetrahedron Letters* **36**, 8875–8

Evershed, R P, Mottram, H R, Dudd, S N, Charters, S, Stott, A W, Lawrence, G J, Gibson, A M, Conner, A, Blinkhorn, P W, and Reeves, V, 1997a New criteria for the identification of animal fats preserved in archaeological pottery, *Naturwissenschaften* **84**, 402–6

Evershed, R P, Vaughan, S J, Dudd, S N, and Soles, J S, 1997b Fuel for thought? Beeswax in lamps and conical cups from the late Minoan Crete, *Antiquity* **71**, 979–85

Evershed, R P, Dudd, S N, Charters, S, Mottram, H, Stott, A W, Raven, A, van Bergen, P F, and Bland, H A, 1999 Lipids as carriers of anthropogenic signals from prehistory, *Phil Trans Royal Soc London B* **354**, 19–31

Evison, V I, 1968 The Anglo-Saxon finds from Hardown Hill, *Proc Dorset Natur Hist Archaeol Soc* **90**, 232–40

Fairweather, A D, and Ralston, I B M, 1993 The Neolithic timber hall at Balbridie, Grampian region, Scotland: the building, the date, the plant macrofossils, *Antiquity* **67**, 313–23

Farrar, R A H, 1951 Archaeological fieldwork in Dorset in 1951, *Proc Dorset Natur Hist Archaeol Soc* **73**, 85–115

Findlay, D C, Colborne, G J N, Cope, D W, Harrod, T R, Hogan, D V, and Staines, S J, 1984 *Soils and their use in south-west England*, Soil Survey of England and Wales Bulletin **14**, Harpenden: Soil Survey of England and Wales

Finnegan, M, 1978 Non-metric variations of the infracranial skeleton, *J Anatomy* **125(1)**, 23–37

Fish, J D, and Fish, S, 1989 *A student's guide to the seashore*, London: Unwin

Fisher, P F, 1991 The physical environment of Cranborne Chase, in *Papers on the prehistoric archaeology of Cranborne Chase* (eds J Barrett, R Bradley and M Hall), Oxbow Mono **11**, 11–19, Oxford: Oxbow Books

Fishpool, M, 1999 Land Mollusca, in Whittle *et al* 1999, 127–38

Ford, S, 1987 Chronological and functional aspects of flint assemblages, in *Lithic analysis and later British prehistory* (eds A G Brown and M R Edmonds), Brit Archaeol Rep Brit Ser **162**, 67–85. Oxford: British Archaeological Reports

Fouéré, P, 1990 L'industrie lithique du camp néolithique de Réjolles à Biron, *Bulletin de la Société Préhistorique Française* **87**, 378–86

Frazer, J, 1923 *The golden bough. A study in magic and religion* (1993 facsimile edition), Ware: Wordsworth editions

French, C A I, Lewis, H, Allen, M J, and Scaife, R, 2000 Palaeoenvironmental and archaeological investigations on Wyke Down and in the upper Allen Valley, Cranborne Chase, *Proc Dorset, Natur Hist Archaeol Soc* **122**, 53–71

French, C, Lewis, H, Allen, M J, Scaife, R G, and Green, M, 2003 Archaeological and palaeo-environmental investigations of the upper Allen valley, Cranborne Chase, Dorset (1998–2000): a new model of earlier Holocene landscape development, *Proc Prehist Soc* **69**, 201–34

French, C, Lewis, H, Allen, M J, Scaife, R G, and Gardiner, J, 2007. *Prehistoric landscape development and human impact in the Upper Allen Valley, Cranborne Chase, Dorset*, Cambridge: McDonald Institute

Friedli, H, Lotscher, H, Oeschger, H, Siegenthaler, U, and Stauffer, B, 1986 Ice core record of the $^{13}C/^{12}C$ ratio of atmospheric CO_2 in the past two centuries, *Nature* **324**, 237–8

Fulchieri, E, Rabino Massa, E, and Doro Garetto, T, 1986 Differential diagnosis between palaeopathological and non-pathological *post mortem* environmental factors in ancient human remains, *J Human Evolution* **15**, 71–5

Gale, R, 1990 Charcoals, in Richards 1990, 252–3

—, 1991 Charred wood, in Sharples 1991, 125–9

—, 2004 Charcoal, in Investigation of the Whitesheet Down environs 1989–90: Neolithic causewayed enclosure and Iron Age settlement (M Rawlings, M J Allen and F Healy), *Wiltshire Studies* **97**, 174–5

Gardiner, J P, 1991a Flint procurement and axe production during the Neolithic on the South Downs: a re-assessment, *Oxford J Archaeol* **9**, 119–40

—, 1991b The [earlier Neolithic] flint industries in the study area, in *Landscape, monuments and society. The prehistory of Cranborne Chase* (J C Barrett, R Bradley and M Green), 31, Cambridge: Cambridge University Press

—, 1991c The [later Neolithic] flint industries of the study area, in *Landscape, monuments and society. The prehistory of Cranborne Chase* (J C Barrett, R Bradley and M Green), 59–69, Cambridge, Cambridge University Press

Gardner, E, 1928 Hambledon Hill, in *Wessex from the air* (O G S Crawford and A Keiller), 44–55, Oxford: Clarendon Press

Garwood, P, 1999 Grooved Ware in southern Britain: chronology and interpretation, in *Grooved Ware in Britain and Ireland* (eds R Cleal and A MacSween), Neolithic Studies Group Seminar Papers 3, 145–76, Oxford and Oakville: Oxbow Books

Gent, T H, and Quinnell, H, 1999 Excavation of a causewayed enclosure and hillfort on Raddon Hill, Stockleigh Pomeroy, *Proc Devon Archaeol Soc* **57**, 1–75

Gelfand, A E, and Smith, A F M, 1990 Sampling approaches to calculating marginal densities, *J Amer Stat Assoc* **85**, 398–409

Gibson, A, and Kinnes, I, 1997 On the urns of a dilemna; radiocarbon and the Peterborough problem, *Oxford J Archaeol* **16(1)**, 65–72

Giles, M 1993 A study of Iron Age settlement in Dorset, unpubl BA dissertation, University of Sheffield

Gilks, W R, Richardson, S, and Spiegelhalther, D J, 1996 *Markov chain Monte Carlo in practice*, London: Chapman and Hall

Gillespie, R, 1989 Fundamentals of bone degradation chemistry: collagen is not 'the way', *Radiocarbon* **31**, 239–46

Godwin, H, 1975 *History of the British flora. A factual basis for phytogeography*, Cambridge: Cambridge University Press

Godwin, H, and Tansley, A, 1941 Prehistoric charcoals as evidence of former vegetation, soil and climate, *J Ecology* **29**, 117–25

Grant, A, 1982 The use of tooth wear as a guide to the age of domestic ungulates, in *Ageing and sexing animal bones from archaeological sites* (eds B Wilson, C Grigson and S Payne), Brit Archaeol Rep Brit Ser **109**, 91–108. Oxford: British Archaeological Reports

Gray, H, 1977 *Anatomy*, New York: Bounty Books

Green, C S, 1984 Early Anglo-Saxon burials at the *Trumpet Major* public house, Alington Avenue, Dorchester, *Proc Dorset Natur Hist Archaeol Soc* **106**, 149–52

—, 1987 *Excavations at Poundbury, Dorchester, Dorset 1966–82. Vol 1: the settlements*, Dorset Natur Hist Archaeol Soc Mono **7**

Green, C, Lynch, F and White, H, 1982 The excavation of two round barrows on Launceston Down, Dorset (Long Crichel 5 and 7). Appendix II. The Saxon secondary burials by A M Cook, *Proc Dorset Natur Hist Archaeol Soc* **104**, 39–59

Green, G W, and Welch, F B A, 1965 *Geology of the country around Wells and Cheddar. Institute of Geological Sciences, memoir for sheet 280*, London: HMSO

Green, H S, 1980 *The flint arrowheads of the British Isles*, Brit Archaeol Rep Brit Ser **75**. Oxford: British Archaeological Reports

—, 1984 Flint arrowheads: typology and interpretation, *Lithics* **5**, 19–39

Green, M, 2000 *A landscape revealed: 10,000 years on a chalkland farm*, Stroud: Tempus

Green, M, and Allen, M, 1997 An early prehistoric shaft on Cranborne Chase, *Oxford J Archaeol* **16(2)**, 121–31

Greenlee, D M, 1992 Effects of recovery techniques and postdepositional environment on archaeological wood charcoal assemblages, in *Deciphering a shell midden* (ed J K Stein), 261–82, New York: Academic Press

Grieve, M, 1976 *A modern herbal*, Harmondsworth: Penguin

Gresham, C A, 1972 Burials in megalithic chambered tombs, in *Prehistoric man in Wales and the west* (eds F Lynch and C Burgess), 65–6, Bath: Adams and Dart

Grigson, C, 1965 Measurements of bones, horncores, antlers and teeth, in I F Smith 1965, 145–67

—, 1982 Sexing Neolithic cattle skulls and horn cores, in *Ageing and sexing animal bones from archaeological sites* (eds B Wilson, C Grigson and S Payne), Brit Archaeol Rep Brit Ser **109**, 25–36. Oxford: British Archaeological Reports

—, 1999 The mammalian remains, in *The Harmony of symbols: the Windmill Hill causewayed enclosure, Wiltshire* (A Whittle, J Pollard, and C Grigson), Cardiff Studies in Archaeology, 164–252, Oxford: Oxbow Books

Grimes, W F, 1960 *Excavations on defence sites 1939–1945. Mainly Neolithic–Bronze Age*. London: HMSO

Grinsell, L V, 1959 *Dorset barrows*, Dorchester: Dorset Natural History and Archaeology Society

Guido, M, 1978 *The glass beads of the prehistoric and Roman periods in Britain and Ireland.* Rep Res Comm Soc Antiq London **35**. London: Society of Antiquaries of London

Hadfield, M, 1974 The oak and its legends, in *The British oak: its history and natural history* (eds M G Morris and F H Perring), BSBI Conference Rep **14**, 123–9, Faringdon: E W Classey

Hafez, E S E, 1968 *Adaptation in domestic mammals*, Philadelphia: Lea and Febiger

Hamilton, M, 1999 Secondary use of causewayed enclosures in the region and beyond: Peterborough Ware, Beaker pottery and round barrows, in Whittle *et al* 1999, 373–5

Harcourt, R A, 1971 Animal bones from Durrington Walls, in Wainwright with Longworth 1971, 338–50

—, 1974 The dog in prehistoric and early historic Britain, *J Archaeol Sci* **1(2)**, 151–76

—, 1979 The animal bones, in Wainwright 1979a, 214–23

Harding, D W, Blake, I M, and Reynolds, P J, 1993 *An Iron Age settlement in Dorset. Excavation and reconstruction*, University of Edinburgh Department of Archaeology Mono **1**, Edinburgh: University of Edinburgh Department of Archaeology

Harding, J, 1999 Pathways to new realms: cursus monuments and symbolic territories, in *Pathways and ceremonies. The cursus monuments of Britain and Ireland* (eds A Barclay and J Harding), 30–8, Neolithic Studies Group Seminar Papers **4**, Oxford and Oakville: Oxbow Books

Harding, J and Healy, F forthcoming *The Raunds Area Project. A Neolithic and Bronze Age Landscape in Northamptonshire*, English Heritage Archaeol Rep Swindon: English Heritage

Harding, P, 1990 The analysis of a sealed knapping deposit from the phase 1 ditch, in Richards 1990, 99–104

—, 1991 The worked stone, in Woodward 1991, 73–87

Harman, M, 1990 The human remains, in *Chichester excavations VII: Apple Down and the Mardens* (A Down and M Welch), 183–94, Chichester: Chichester District Council

Harman, M, and Evans, J G, 1991 The burial deposit, in Giants' Hills 2 long barrow, Skendleby, Lincolnshire (J G Evans and D D A Simpson), *Archaeologia* **109**, 14–17

Harman, M, Molleson, T I, and Price, J L, 1981 Burials, bodies and beheadings in Romano-British and Anglo-Saxon cemeteries, *Bull Brit Mus NaturHist (Geol)* **35(3)**; 145–88

Harrad, L 2004 Gabbroic clay sources in Cornwall: a petrological study of prehistoric pottery and clay samples, *Oxford J Archaeol* **23(3)**, 271–86

Harris, D R, 1987 The impact on archaeology of radiocarbon dating by accelerator mass spectrometry, *Phil Trans R Soc Lond* **323**, Ser A, 23–43

Harris, L, 1983 Taphonomy of Mollusca in an Alpine river, *Quaternary Newsletter* **41**, 37

Hastorf, C A, and Johannessen, S, 1991 Understanding changing people/plant relationships in the Prehispanic Andes, in *Processual and post-processual archaeologies: multiple ways of knowing the past* (ed R W Preucel), 140–55, Southern Illinois University Occas Pap **10.** Carbondale: Southern Illinois University

Hawkes, C F C, 1947 Iwerne, *Archaeol J* **104**, 48–62

Haynes, G, 1980 Prey bones and predators: potential ecological information from analysis of bone sites, *Ossa* **7**, 75–97

Healey, E, and Robertson-Mackay, R, 1983 The lithic industries from Staines causewayed enclosure and their relationship to other earlier Neolithic industries in southern Britain, *Lithics* **4**, 1–27

Healey, E, and Robertson-Mackay, R, 1987 The flint industry, in The Neolithic causewayed enclosure at Staines, Surrey: excavations 1961–63 (R Robertson-Mackay), *Proc Prehist Soc* **53**, 95–118

Healy, F, 1983 Are first impressions only topsoil-deep? The evidence from Tattershall Thorpe, Lincolnshire, *Lithics* **4**, 28–33

—, Prediction or prejudice? The relationship between field survey and excavation, in *Lithic analysis and later British prehistory* (eds A G Brown and M R Edmonds), Brit Archaeol Rep Brit Ser **162**, 9–17.Oxford: British Archaeological Reports

—, 1988a *The Anglo-Saxon cemetery at Spong Hill, North Elmham. Part VI: occupation during the seventh to second millennia BC*, E Anglian Archaeol **39.** Gressenhall: Norfolk Archaeological Unit

—, Reports on prehistoric pottery and lithic material, in A barrow cemetery on Davidstow Moor, Cornwall. Wartime excavations by C K Croft Andrew (P M Christie), *Cornish Archaeol* **27**, 27–169

—, 1995 Pots, pits and peat: ceramics and settlement in East Anglia, in *'Unbaked urns of rudely shape': essays on British and Irish pottery for Ian Longworth* (eds I Kinnes and G Varndell), Oxbow Mono **55**, 173–84, Oxford: Oxbow Books

—, 1997a Site 3. Flagstones, in Smith *et al* 1997, 27–48

—, 1997b Communal monuments and burials. Neolithic and Bronze Age, in Smith *et al* 1997, 283–91

—, 1997c Settlement. Neolithic and Bronze Age, Smith *et al* 1997, 295–99

—, 2006 Pottery deposition at Hambledon Hill, in *Prehistoric pottery: some recent research* (ed A. Gibson), Brit Archaeol Rep Internat Ser **1509**, 11–37. Oxford: British Archaeological Reports

Hedges, J, and Buckley, D G, 1978 Excavations at a Neolithic Causewayed enclosure, Orsett, Essex, 1975, *Proc Prehist Soc* **44**, 219–308

Hedges, R E M, and Law, I, 1989 The radiocarbon dating of bone, *Applied Geochemistry* **4**, 249–54

Hedges, R E M, and van Klinken, G J, 1992 A review of current approaches in the pretreatment of bone for radiocarbon dating by AMS, *Radiocarbon* **34**, 279–91

Hedges, R E M, Bronk, C R, and Housley, R A, 1989 The Oxford Accelerator Mass Spectrometry facility: technical developments in routine dating, *Archaeometry* **31**, 99–113

Heizer, R F, 1963 Domestic fuel in primitive society, *J Roy Anthrop Inst Great Britain Ireland* **93(2)**, 186–94

Helbaek, H, 1952 Early crops in southern England, *Proc Prehist Soc* **18**, 194–233

Herne, A, 1991 The flint assemblage, in *Excavations at Grimes Graves, Norfolk 1972–1976. Fascicule 3, Shaft X: Bronze Age flint, chalk and metal working* (I Longworth, A Herne, G Varndell and S Needham), 21–93, London: British Museum

Herring, D A, Saunders, S R, and Katzenberg, M A, 1998 Investigating the weaning process in past populations, *Amer J Physical Anthropol* 105, 425–39

Heywood Sumner 1913 *The ancient earthworks of Cranborne Chase*, London: Chiswick Press

Hicken, N E, 1975 *The insect factor in wood decay an account of wood boring insects with particular reference to timber indoors*, London: Associated Business Programmes

Higham, C F W, 1968 Patterns of prehistoric economic exploitation on the Alpine Foreland, *Vierteljahrsschrift der Naturforshenden Gesellschaft in Zurich* **113(1)**, 41–92

Higham, C F W, and Message, M, 1969 An assessment of a prehistoric technique of bovine husbandry, in *Science in archaeology* (eds D Brothwell and E Higgs; second edition), 315–30, London: Thames and Hudson

Hillman, G, 1981a Reconstructing crop husbandry practices from charred remains of crops, in *Farming practice in British prehistory* (ed R Mercer), 123–62, Edinburgh: Edinburgh University Press

Hillman, G C, 1981b Crop husbandry: evidence from macroscopic remains, in *The environment in British prehistory* (eds I Simmons and M Tooley), 183–91, London: Duckworth

Hillson, S W, 1979 Diet and dental disease, *World Archaeol* **2(2)**, 147–62

—, 1990 *Teeth* (Cambridge Manuals in Archaeology), Cambridge: Cambridge University Press

Hinton, P, 2004 Plant remains in Investigation of the Whitesheet Down environs 1989–90: Neolithic causewayed enclosure and Iron Age settlement (M Rawlings, M J Allen and F Healy), *Wiltshire Studies* **97**, 177–9

Hodges, H 1964 *Artefacts*, London: John Baker

Holden, E, 1963 Excavations at the deserted medieval village of Hangleton, Part 1, *Sussex Archaeol Collect* **101**, 54–181

Holgate, R, and Start, D, 1983–5 A Neolithic pit at Remenham, near Henley-on-Thames, Berkshire, *Berkshire Archaeol J* **72**, 1–7

Horsey, I, and Jarvis, K, 1984 The Stour valley gravels project, *Proc Dorset Natur Hist Archaeol Soc* **106**, 114

Horwitz, L K, and Smith, P, 1988 The effects of striped hyæna activity on human remains, *J Archaeol Sci* **15**, 471–84

Houlder, C H, 1963 A Neolithic settlement on Hazard Hill, Totnes, *Trans Devon Archaeol Explor Soc* **21**, 2–31

Hulthén, B, 1977 *On ceramic technology during the Scanian Neolithic and Bronze Age*, Theses and Papers in North European Archaeology **6**, Stockholm

IAWA Committee, 1989 IAWA list of microscopic features for hardwood identification, *IAWA Bulletin* **10(3)**, 219–332

Ingold, T, 1993 The temporality of landscape, *World Archaeol* **25(2)**, 152–74

Iversen, J, 1956 Forest clearance in the Stone Age, *Scientific American* **194**, 36–41

Jacobi, R 1982 Mesolithic hunter-gatherers 9000–4000 BC, in *The Archaeology of Somerset. A review to 1500 AD* (eds M Aston and I Burrow), 11–21. Taunton: Somerset County Council

James, N D G, 1966 *The forester's companion*, Oxford: Basil Blackwell

Jarman, H N, Legge, A J, and Charles, J A, 1972 Retrieval of plant remains from archaeological sites by froth flotation, in *Papers in economic prehistory* (ed E S Higgs), 39–48, Cambridge: Cambridge University Press

Jensen, H J, 1988a Microdenticulates in the Danish Stone Age: a functional puzzle, in *Industries lithiques, tracéologie et technologie. Volume 1: aspects archéologiques* (ed S Beyries), Brit Archaeol Rep Internat Ser **411(i)**, 231–52. Oxford: British Archaeological Reports

—, 1988b Plant harvesting and processing with flint implements in the Danish Stone Age, *Acta Archaeologica* **59**, 131–42

—, 1994 *Flint tools and plant working*, Aarhus: Aarhus University Press

Jessen, K, and Helbaek, H, 1944 Cereals in Great Britain and Ireland in pre- and early historic times, *Det Kongelige Danske Videnskabernes Selskab Biologiske Skrifter* Bind **III (2)**

Jewell, P A, 1963a Cattle from British archaeological sites, in *Man and cattle* (eds A E Mourant and F E Zeuner), Royal Anthropological Institute Occas Pap **18**, 80–91. London: Royal Anthropological Institute

— (ed), 1963b *The experimental earthwork on Overton Down, Wiltshire, 1960*. London: British Association for the Advancement of Science

Jewell, P A, and Dimbleby, G W (eds), 1966 The experimental earthwork on Overton Down, Wiltshire, England: the first four years, *Proc Prehist Soc* **32**, 313–42

Johnston, R, 1999 An empty path? Processions, memories and the Dorset cursus, in *Pathways and ceremonies. The cursus monuments of Britain and Ireland* (eds A Barclay and J Harding), Neolithic Studies Group Seminar Papers 4, 39–48, Oxford and Oakville: Oxbow Books

Jones, G, 1987 Agricultural practice in Greek prehistory, *Annual Brit School Athens* **82**, 115–23

—, 2000 Evaluating the importance of cultivation and collecting in Neolithic Britain, in *Plants in Neolithic Britain and beyond* (ed A Fairbairn), Neolithic Studies Group Seminar Papers 5, 79–84, Oxford: Oxbow Books

—, forthcoming Charred plant remains from the Neolithic settlement at Lismore Fields, Buxton, in The excavation of a Mesolithic and Neolithic settlement area at Lismore Fields, Buxton, Derbyshire (D Garton)

Jones, G, and Legge, A, 1987 The grape (*Vitis vinifera* L) in the Neolithic of Britain, *Antiquity* **61**, 452–5

Jones, G, and Rowley-Conwy, P, 2007 On the importance of cereal cultivation in the British Neolithic, in *The origin and spread of domestic plants in Southwest Asia and Europe* (eds S Colledge and J Conolly), 391–419. Walnut Creek, California: Left Coast Press

Jones, M, 1991 Down Farm, Woodcutts: the carbonised plant remains, in *Papers on the prehistoric archaeology of Cranborne Chase* (eds J Barrett, R Bradley and M Hall), Oxbow Mono **11**, 49–53, Oxford: Oxbow Books

Jones, V, Bishop, A C, and Woolley, A R, 1977 Third supplement to the catalogue of jade axes from sites in the British Isles, *Proc Prehist Soc* **45**, 287–95

Jope, M, 1965 Faunal remains; the frequency and age of the species, in I F Smith 1965, 142–5

Katzenberg, M A, and Pfeiffer, S, 1995 Nitrogen isotope evidence for weaning age in a nineteenth century Canadian skeletal sample, in *Bodies of evidence: reconstructing history through skeletal analysis* (ed A L Grauer), 221–35, New York: Wiley-Liss

Katzenberg, M A, and Weber, A, 1999 Stable isotope ecology and palaeodiet in the Lake Baikal Region of Siberia. *J Archaeol Sci* **26**, 651–59

Keepax, C, 1988 Charcoal analysis with particular reference to archaeological sites in Britain, unpubl PhD thesis, University of London.

Kerney, M P, 1963 Late-glacial deposits on the Chalk of south-east England, *Phil Trans Roy Soc London* B **246**, 203–54

—, 1977 A proposed zonation scheme for Late-glacial and Postglacial deposits using land Mollusca, *J Archaeol Sci* **4**, 387–90

—, 1999 *Atlas of the land and freshwater molluscs of Britain and Ireland*, Colchester: Harley Books

Kerney, M P, and Cameron, R A D, 1979 *A field guide to the land snails of Britain and north-west Europe*, London: Collins

Kerney, M P, Brown, E H, and Chandler, T J, 1964 The Late-Glacial and Post- Glacial history of the chalk escarpment near Brook, Kent, *Phil Trans Roy Soc London* B **248**, 135–204

Kinnes, I A, 1979 Description of the Neolithic bowl, in The Sweet Track: drove site (J M Coles and B J Orme), *Somerset Levels Papers* **5**, 43–64

—, 1992 *Non-megalithic long barrows and allied structures in the British Neolithic* (Brit Mus Occas Pap **52**), London: British Museum

Kinnes, I, and Pryor, F, 1998 Fired clay, in Pryor 1998, 269–70

Kreutzer, L A, 1992 Bison and deer bone mineral densities: comparisons and implications for the interpretations of archaeological faunas, *J Archaeol Sci* **19**, 271–94

Ladle, L, 1996 Excavations: Bestwall quarry archaeological project: interim report 1996, *Proc Dorset Natur Hist Archaeol Soc* **118**, 144

Ladle, M, and Bass, J A B, 1981 The ecology of a small chalk stream and its responses to drying during drought condition, *Archive für Hydrobiologie* **90(4)**, 448–66

Lane-Fox, A H, 1875 Excavations at Cissbury Camp, Sussex, *J Anthropol Inst* **5**, 357–90

Lanting, J N, and van der Waals, J D, 1972 British beakers as seen from the Continent, *Helinium* **12**, 20–46

Larsson, L, 2000 The passage of axes: fire transformation of flint objects in the Neolithic of southern Sweden, *Antiquity* **74(285)**, 602–10

Law, I A, and Hedges, R E M, 1989 A semi-automated pretreatment system and the pretreatment of older and contaminated samples, *Radiocarbon* **31**, 247–53

Laws, K, 1991 The foreign stone, in Sharples 1991, 229–33

Lawson, A J , 2000 *Potterne 1982–5 animal husbandry in later prehistoric Wessex*, Wessex Archaeol Rep **17**, Salisbury: Wessex Archaeology

Lee, F, 2006 Human skeletal remains, in *A woodland archaeology. Neolithic Sites at Haddenham. The Haddenham project: volume 1*, 140–53 (C Evans and I Hodder), Cambridge: MacDonald Institute for Archaeological Research

Leeds, E T, 1927 A Neolithic site at Abingdon, Berks, *Antiq J* 7, 438–64

—, 1928 A Neolithic site at Abingdon, Berkshire (second report), *Antiq J* **8**, 461–77

Legge, A J, 1981a The agricultural economy, in *Grimes Graves, Norfolk: excavations 1971–72: Volume I* (R J Mercer), Department of the Environment Archaeol Rep **11**, 79–103, London: HMSO

—, 1981b Aspects of cattle husbandry, in *Farming practice in British prehistory* (ed R Mercer), 169–81, Edinburgh: Edinburgh University Press

—, 1989 Milking the evidence; a reply to Entwhistle and Grant, in *The beginnings of agriculture* (eds A Milles, D Williams, and N. Gardner), Brit Archaeol Rep Internat Ser **496**, 217–42. Oxford: British Archaeological Reports

—, 1990 Animals, environment and economy at Selevac, in *Selevac; a Neolithic village in Serbia* (Ruth Tringham and Dusan Krstic), Monumenta Archaeologia **15**; 215–42, University of California, Institute of Archaeology

—, 1991 Animal remains from six sites at Down Farm, Woodcuts, in *Papers on the archaeology of Cranborne Chase* (eds J Barrett, R Bradley, and M Hall), Oxbow Mono **11**, 54–100, Oxford: Oxbow Books

—, 1992 *Excavations at Grimes Graves, Norfolk 1972–76*, Fascicule 4: *Animals, environment and the Bronze Age economy*, London: British Museum Press

—, 1994 The animal remains and their interpretation, in *Moncín: un Poblado de la Edad del Bronce (Borja, Zaragoza)* (R J Harrison, G Moreno-López and A J Legge), Colección Arqueología **16**, Gobierno de Aragón, 453–82, Zaragoza: Cometa

Legge, A J, and Dorrington, E, 1987 Harlow temple: the animal bones, in *The Romano-British temple at Harlow, Essex* (N E France and M Gobel; eds F R Clark and I K Jones), 122–34, Harlow: West Essex Archaeological Group

Legge, A J, and Rowley-Conwy, P A, 1988 *Star Carr revisited: a re-analysis of the large mammals*, London: University of London, Birkbeck College, Centre for Extra-Mural Studies

Legge, A J, Williams, J, and Williams, P, 1991 The determination of season of death from the mandibles and bones of the domestic sheep (*Ovis aries*), in *Archeologia della pastorizia nell'Europa meridionale* (eds R.Maggi, R Nesbit, and G Barker), Revista di Studi Liguri A **57(1–4)**, 49–65

Legge, A J, Williams, J, and Williams, P, 1999 Lambs to the slaughter, in *Animal bones, human societies* (ed P A Rowley-Conwy), 152–7, Oxford: Oxbow

Legge, A J, Payne, S, and Holmes, J, in prep Tooth eruption and bone fusion in the Soay sheep raised under farm conditions

Leney, L, and Casteel, R W, 1975 Simplified procedure for examining charcoal specimens for identification, *J Archaeol Sci* **2**, 153–9

Liddell, D 1930 Report on the excavations of Hembury Fort, Devon, 1930, *Proc Devon Archaeol Explor Soc* **1**, 39–63

—, 1931 Report of the excavations at Hembury Fort, Devon: second season, 1931, *Proc Devon Archaeol Explor Soc* **1**, 90–119

—, 1932 Report on the excavations at Hembury Fort, Devon: third season, 1932, *Proc Devon Archaeol Explor Soc* 1, 162–90

—, 1935 Report on the excavations at Hembury Fort, Devon: fourth and fifth seasons, 1934 and 1935, *Proc Devon Archaeol Explor Soc* 2, 135–75

Limbrey, S, 1975 *Soil science and archaeology*, London: Academic Press

—, 1983 Archaeology and palaeohydrology, in *Introduction to palaeohydrology* (ed K J Gregory), 189–212, Chichester: John Wiley

Limbrey, S, and Robinson, S, 1988 Dry land to wetland: soil resources in the Upper Thames valley, in *The exploitation of wetlands* (eds P Murphy and C French), Brit Archaeol Rep Brit Ser **186**, 129–44. Oxford: British Archaeological Reports

Lockwood, J G, 1983 Modelling climatic change, in *Introduction to palaeohydrology* (ed K J Gregory), 25–50, Chichester: John Wiley

Longin, R, 1971 New method of collagen extraction for radiocarbon dating, *Nature* **230**, 241–2

Longworth, I, and Varndell, G, 1996 The Neolithic pottery, in *Refuse and disposal at area 16 east, Runnymede* (S Needham and T Spence), Runnymede Bridge Research Excavations **2**, 100–5, London: British Museum Press

Lopinot, N H, 1984 Archaeobotanical formation processes and late middle archaic human-plant interrelationships in the midcontinental USA, unpubl PhD thesis, Southern Illinois University at Carbondale

Lyman, R L, 1984 Bone densities and the differential survival of fossil classes, *J Anthropo Archaeo* **3**, 259–99

Lyman, R L, 1998 *Taphonomy*, Cambridge: Cambridge University Press

Lynch, F M, 1975 Excavations at Carreg Samson megalithic tomb, Mathry, Pembrokeshire, *Archaeologia Cambrensis* **124**, 15–35

Mabey, R, 1996 *Flora Britannica*, London: Sinclair-Stevenson

McClintock, D, 1989 The heathers of Europe and adjacent areas, *Botanical J Linnean Soc* **101**, 279–89

McConnell, P, 1919 *Note-book of agricultural facts and figures for farmers and farm students*, ninth edition, revised and enlarged, London: Crosby Lockwood & Son

McCormac, F G, 1992 Liquid scintillation counter characterisation, optimisation, and benzene purity correction, *Radiocarbon* **34**, 37–45

McCormac, F G, and Housley, R, 1995 Radiocarbon analysis, in Cleal *et al* 1995, 515–16

McCormac, F G, Kalin, R M, and Long, A, 1993 Radiocarbon dating beyond 50,000 years by liquid scintillation counting, in *Liquid scintillation spectrometry* (eds J E Noakes, F Shonhofer, and H A Polach), 125–33

McCormac, F G, Hogg, A G, Higham, T F G, Baillie, M G L, Palmer, J G, Limin Xiong, Pilcher, J R, Brown, D, and Hoper, S T, 1998 Variations of radiocarbon in tree-rings: southern hemisphere offset preliminary results, *Radiocarbon* **40**, 1153–9

MacGregor, A, 1985 *Bone, ivory, antler and horn: the technology of skeletal material since the Roman period*, London: Croom Helm

McKinley, J I, 1993 A decapitation from the Romano-British cemetery at Baldock, Hertfordshire, *Internat J Osteoarchaeology* **3**, 41–4

—, 1994 *The Anglo-Saxon cemetery at Spong Hill, North Elmham. Part VIII: the cremations.* East Anglian Archaeol **69**, Gressenhall: Field Archaeology Division, Norfolk Museums Service

—, 1999a Excavations at Ham Hill, Montacute, Somerset 1994 and 1998, *Somerset Archaeol Natur Hist* **142**, 77–137

—, 1999b Human bone from Tolpuddle Ball, in *A35 Tolpuddle to Puddletown Bypass DBFO, Dorset, 1996–8* (C M Hearne and V Birbeck), Wessex Archaeol Rep **15,** 150–61, Salisbury: Trust for Wessex Archaeology

—, 2000 Human bone, in *Potterne 1982–5 animal husbandry in later prehistoric Wessex* (A J Lawson), Wessex Archaeol Rep **17**, 95–101, Salisbury: Trust for Wessex Archaeology

McMinn, R M H, and Hutchings, R T, 1985 *A colour atlas of human anatomy*, London: Wolfe Medical Publications

McOmish, D, 1996 East Chisenbury: ritual and rubbish at the British Bronze Age-Iron Age transition, *Antiquity* **70(267)**, 68–76

Macphail, R I, 1991 The archaeological soils and sediments, in Sharples 1991, 106–18

Maltby, M, 1990 Animal bones, in Richards 1990, 57–61

Manby, T G, 1988 The Neolithic period in eastern Yorkshire, in *Archaeology in Eastern Yorkshire. Essays in Honour of T C M Brewster* (ed T G Manby), 35–88, Sheffield: Department of Archaeology and Prehistory

Manchester, K, 1983 *The archaeology of disease*, Bradford: University of Bradford Press

Manning, W H, 1985 *Catalogue of the Romano-British iron tools, fittings and weapons in the British Museum*, London: British Museum Publications

Mant, A K, 1987 Knowledge acquired from post-war exhumations, in *Death, decay, and reconstruction* (eds A Boddington, A N Garland, and R C Janaway), 65–80

March, R J, 1992 L'utilisation du bois dans les foyers préhistoriques: une approche expérimentale, *Bulletin de la Société Botanique de France* **139**, 245–53, Actualité Botanique

Marlow, M, 1992 The population, in *An Anglo-Saxon cemetery at Norton, Cleveland* (S J Sherlock and M G Welch), Counc Brit Archaeol Res Rep **82,** 107–18. York: Council for British Archaeology

Marrs, R H, and Proctor, J, 1978 Chemical and ecological studies of heath plants and soils of the Lizard peninsula, Cornwall, *J Ecology* **66**, 417–32

Martin, P, 2001 *Was Maiden Castle defended in the Neolithic?* Unpublished dissertation submitted in part requirement for the BSc degree, University of Bournemouth

Martingell, H, and Saville, A, 1988 *The illustration of lithic artefacts: a guide to drawing stone tools for specialist reports.* Lithic Studies Society Occas Pap **3** and Association of Archaeological Illustrators and Surveyors Tech Pap **9.** Northampton: Lithic Studies Society and Association of Archaeological Illustrators and Surveyors

Mays, S, and Steele, J, 1996 A mutilated human skull from Roman St Albans, Hertfordshire, England, *Antiquity* **70(267)**, 155–61

Meaney, A L, 1964 *A gazetteer of early Anglo-Saxon burial sites*, London

Mellars, P, 1976 Fire ecology, animal populations and man: a study of some ecological relationships in prehistory, *Proc Prehist Soc* **42**, 15–45

Mercer, R, 1980 *Hambledon Hill. A Neolithic landscape.* Edinburgh: Edinburgh University Press

Mercer, R J, 1981a Excavations at Carn Brea, Illogan, Cornwall, 1970–1973: a Neolithic fortified complex of the third millennium bc, *Cornish Archaeol* **20**

—, 1981b The excavation of a late Neolithic henge-type enclosure at Balfarg, Markinch, Fife, Scotland, 1977–78, *Proc Soc Antiq Scot* **111**, 63–171

—, 1983 Everley Water Meadow, in 29th Annual Report of Department of Archaeology, University of Edinburgh, 13–14

—, 1984a Everley Water Meadow, Iwerne Stepleton, Dorset, *Proc Dorset Natur Hist Archaeol Soc* **106**, 110–11

—, 1984b Everley Water Meadow, in 30th Annual Report of Department of Archaeology, University of Edinburgh

—, 1985 A Neolithic fortress and funeral center, *Scientific American*, **252(3)**, 94–101

—, 1986 *Hambledon Hill fieldwork and excavation project. The hillfort spur: 1986 interim report.* Informally circulated interim report

—, 1987 A flint quarry in the Hambledon Hill Neolithic enclosure complex, in *The human uses of flint and chert: papers from the fourth international flint symposium* (eds G de G Sieveking and M H Newcomer), 160–3, Cambridge: Cambridge University Press

—, 1988 Hambledon Hill, Dorset, England, in *Enclosures and defences in the Neolithic of western Europe* (eds C Burgess, P Topping, C Mordant and M Maddison), Brit Archaeol Rep Int Ser **403**, 89–106. Oxford: British Archaeological Reports

—, 1990 *Causewayed enclosures*, Princes Risborough: Shire Publications

—, 1997 The excavation of a Neolithic enclosure complex at Helman Tor, Lostwithiel, Cornwall, *Cornish Archaeol* **36**, 5–61

—, 1999 The origins of warfare in the British Isles, in *Ancient warfare* (eds J Carman and A Harding), 143–56, Stroud: Sutton Publishing Ltd

—, 2003 The early farming settlement of south western England in the Neolithic, in *Neolithic settlement in Ireland and western Britain* (eds I Armit, E Murphy, E Nelis, and D Simpson), Oxford: Oxbow Books, 56–70

—, 2004 Enclosures and monumentality and the Mesolithic-Neolithic continuum, in *Monuments and material culture.*

Papers in honour of an Avebury archaeologist: Isobel Smith (eds R M J Cleal and J Pollard), East Knoyle: Hobnob Press, 39–46

Middleton, H R, 1998 Flint and chert artefacts, in Pryor 1998, 215–50

Millgate, M (ed), 1984 *The life and work of Thomas Hardy* by Thomas Hardy, London and Basingstoke: The Macmillan Press Ltd

Minnitt, S 1982 Farmers and field monuments 4000–2000 BC, in *The Archaeology of Somerset. A review to 1500 AD* (eds M Aston and I Burrow), 23–28. Taunton: Somerset County Council

Mitchell, B, Staines, B W, and Welch, D, 1977 *Ecology of red deer*, Cambridge: Institute of Terrestrial Ecology

Moffett, L, Robinson, M A, and Straker, V, 1989 Cereals, fruit and nuts: charred plant remains from Neolithic sites in England and Wales and the Neolithic economy, in *The beginnings of agriculture* (eds A Milles, D Williams and N Gardner), Brit Archaeol Rep Internat Ser **S196**, 243–61. Oxford: British Archaeological Reports

Molleson, T I, 1993 The human remains, in *Poundbury volume 2: the cemeteries* (D E Farwell and T I Molleson), Dorset Natur Hist Archaeol Soc Mono **11**, 142–214, Dorchester

Monk, M, 2000 Seeds and soils of discontent: an environmental archaeological contribution to the nature of the early Neolithic, in *New agendas in Irish prehistory: papers presented in memory of Liz Anderson* (eds A Desmond, G Johnson, M McCarthy, J Sheehan, and E Shee Twohig), 67–87, Wicklow: Wordwell

Mook, W G, 1984 Archaeological and geological interest in applying ^{14}C AMS to small samples, *Nuclear Instruments and Methods in Physics Research B* **5**, 297–302

—, 1986 Business meeting: recommendations/resolutions adopted by the twelfth international radiocarbon conference, *Radiocarbon* **28**, 799

Moore, J, and Jennings, D, 1992 *Reading Business Park. A Bronze Age landscape*, Thames Valley Landscapes: the Kennet Valley **1**, Oxford: Oxford Archaeological Unit

Moore, N W, 1962 The heaths of Dorset and their conservation, *J Ecology* **50**, 369–91

Morgan, F de M, 1959 The excavation of a long barrow at Nutbane, Hants, *Proc Prehist Soc* **25**, 15–51

Mottram, H R, Dudd, S N, Lawrence, G J, Stott, A W, and Evershed, R P, 1999 New chromatographic, mass spectrometric and stable isotope approaches to the classification of degraded animal fats preserved in archaeological pottery, *J Chromatography A* **833**, 209–21

Nash, D J, Shaw, P A, and Ullyot, J S, 1998 Drainage-line silcretes of the middle Kalahari: An analogue for Cenozoic sarsen trains?, *Proc Geol Assoc* **109**, 241–54

Needham, S P, 1981 *The Bulford–Helsbury manufacturing tradition: the production of Stogursey socketed axes during the later Bronze Age in southern Britain*, British Museum Occas Pap **13**, London: British Museum Publications

—, 1996 Chronology and periodisation in the British Bronze Age, *Acta Archaeologica* **67**, 121–40

—, 2005 Transforming Beaker culture in north-west Europe; processes of fusion and fission, *Proc Prehist Soc* **71**, 171–217

Needham, S P, and Hook, D R, 1988 Lead and lead alloys in the Bronze Age: recent finds from Runnymede Bridge, in *Science and Archaeology, Glasgow, 1987* (eds E A Slater and J Tate), Brit Archaeol Rep Brit Ser **196**, 259–74. Oxford: British Archaeological Reports

Needham, S, Bronk Ramsey, C, Coombs, D, Cartwright, C, and Pettitt, P, 1997 An independent chronology for British Bronze Age metalwork: the results of the Oxford radiocarbon accelerator programme, *Archaeol J* **154**, 55–107

Noakes, J E, Kim, S M, and Stipp, J J, 1965 Chemical and counting advances in liquid scintillation age dating, in *Proceedings of the 6th international conference on radiocarbon and tritium dating* (eds E A Olsson and R M Chatters), 68–92

Nuttall, N, 1998 Having people for dinner has always been popular, *The Times* 12.3.1998

O'Connor, B, 1991 Bronze Age metalwork from Cranborne Chase: a catalogue, in *Papers on the prehistoric archaeology of Cranborne Chase* (eds J Barrett, R Bradley and M Hall), Oxbow Mono **11**, 134–200, Oxford: Oxbow Books

O'Connor, T P, 1977 Land Mollusca from the settlement, in Excavations at Bishopstone (M Bell), *Sussex Archaeol Collect* **115**, 267–73

Olausson, D, 1997 Craft specialization as an agent of social power in the south Scandinavian Neolithic, in *Man and flint* (eds R Schild and Z Sulgostowska), 269–77, Warsaw: Institute of Archaeology and Ethnology, Polish Academy of Sciences

Orme, B J, and Coles, J M, 1985 Prehistoric woodworking from the Somerset Levels: 2. species selection and prehistoric woodlands, *Somerset Levels Pap* **11**, 7–25

Ortner, D J, and Putschar, W G J, 1985 *Identification of pathological conditions in human skeletal remains*, Washington: Smithsonian Institute

Osborne White, H J, 1923 *The geology of the country south and west of Shaftsbury. Geol Survey of Great Britain, memoir for sheet 313.* London: HMSO

Oswald, A, Dyer, C, and Barber, M, 2001 *The creation of monuments. Neolithic causewayed enclosures in the British Isles*, Swindon: English Heritage

Otlet, R L, 1977 Harwell radiocarbon measurements II, *Radiocarbon* **19**, 400–23

—, 1979 An assessment of laboratory errors in liquid scintillation methods of ^{14}C dating, in *Proceedings of the ninth international radiocarbon conference* (eds R Berger and H E Suess), 256–67, Univ California Press

Otlet, R L, and Warchal, R M, 1978 Liquid scintillation counting of low-level ^{14}C dating, *Liquid Scintillation Counting* **5**, 210–18

Otlet, R L, Walker, A J, Hewson, A D, and Burleigh, R, 1980 ^{14}C interlaboratory comparison in the UK: experiment design, preparation, and preliminary results, *Radiocarbon* **22**, 936–46

Otlet, R L, Huxtable, G, Evans, G V, Humphreys, D G, Short, T D, and Conchie, S J, 1983 Development and operation of the Harwell small counter facility for the measurement of ^{14}C in very small samples, *Radiocarbon* **25**, 565–75

Otlet, R L, Huxtable, G, and Sanderson, D C W, 1986 The development of practical systems for ^{14}C measurement in small samples using miniature counters, *Radiocarbon* **28**, 603–14

Packham, J R, Harding, D J M, Hilton, G M, and Stuttard, R A, 1992 *Functional ecology of woodlands and forests*, London: Chapman & Hall

Palmer, C, and Jones, M, 1991 Plant resources, in Sharples 1991, 129–39

Palmer, R, 1976a Interrupted ditch enclosures in Britain: the use of aerial photography for comparative studies, *Proc Prehist Soc* **42**, 161–86

—, 1976b A method of transcribing archaeological sites from oblique aerial photographs, *J Archaeol Sci* **3**, 391–94

Palmer, S, 1977 *Mesolithic cultures of Britain*, Poole: Dolphin

Payne, S, 1973 Kill-off patterns in sheep and goats: the mandibles from Asvan Kale, *Anatolian Studies*, **23**, 281–303

Peacock, D P S, 1969 Neolithic pottery production in Cornwall. *Antiquity* **43**, 145–9

—, 1980 The Roman millstone trade: a petrological sketch, *World Archaeol* **12(1)**, 43–53

—, 1988 The gabbroic pottery of Cornwall, *Antiquity* **62**, 302–4

Pearce, S M, 1983 *The Bronze Age metalwork of south western Britain*, Brit Archaeol Rep Brit Ser **120.** Oxford: British Archaeological Reports

Pearson, G W, 1984 The development of high-precision ^{14}C measurement and its application to archaeological time-scale problems, unpubl PhD thesis, Queens Univ Belfast

Pearson, G W, and Stuiver, M, 1986 High-precision calibration of the radiocarbon time scale, 500–2500 BC, *Radiocarbon* **28**, 839–62

Peterken, G, 1993 *Woodland conservation and management* (second edition), London: Chapman and Hall

—, 1996 *Natural woodlands*, Cambridge: Cambridge University Press

Pettitt, P B, 1997 High resolution Neanderthals? Interpreting Middle Palaeolithic intrasite spatial data, *World Archaeol* **29(2)**, 208–24

Piggott, S, 1936a The pottery, in Excavations in Whitehawk Camp, Brighton: third season, 1935 (E C Curwen), *Sussex Archaeol Collect* 77, 60–92

—, 1936b Handley Hill, Dorset – a Neolithic bowl and the date of the entrenchment, *Proc Prehist Soc* **2**, 229–30

—, 1937 The excavation of a long barrow in Holdenhurst parish, near Christchurch, Hants (no. 183 of Neolithic Wessex Map), *Proc Prehist Soc* **3**, 1–14

—, 1954 *Neolithic cultures of the British Isles*, Cambridge: Cambridge University Press

—, 1962 *The West Kennet Long Barrow excavations 1955–56*, Ministry of Works Archaeol Rep **4**, London: HMSO

Piggott, S, and Piggott, C M, 1944 Excavation of barrows on Crichel and Launceston Downs, Dorset, *Archaeologia* **90**, 47–80

Pitt Rivers, A H L-F, 1887 *Excavations in Cranborne Chase near Rushmore, on the borders of Dorset and Wilts*, Vol **I.** Privately printed

—, 1898 *Excavations in Cranborne Chase near Rushmore, on the borders of Dorset and Wiltshire 1893–1896*, Vol **IV.** Privately printed

Pitts, M W, and Jacobi, R M, 1979 Some aspects of change in flaked stone industries of the Mesolithic and Neolithic in southern Britain, *J Archaeol Sci* **6**, 163–77

Pollard, J, 1999 Flint, in *The harmony of symbols: the Windmill Hill causewayed enclosure, Wiltshire* (A Whittle, J Pollard and C Grigson), 318–37, Oxford: Oxbow Books

Polunin, O, and Walters, M, 1985 *A guide to the vegetation of Britain and Europe*, Oxford: Oxford University Press

Popper, V S, 1988 Selecting qualitative measurements in palaeoethnobotany, in *Current palaeoethnobotany* (C A Hastorf and V S Popper), Chicago and London: University of Chicago, 53–71

Porteous, A, 1928 *Forest folklore, mythology, and romance*, London: Allen & Unwin

Powers, R, and Brothwell, D, 1988 Human bones – inhumations, in *An Anglo-Saxon cemetery at Alton, Hampshire* (V I Evison), Hampshire Field Club Mono **4**, 59–64

Preece, R C, and Bridgland, D R, 1998 *Late Quaternary environmental change in north-west Europe. Excavations at Holywell Coombe, south-east England.* London: Chapman and Hall

Prior, J, and Alvin, K L, 1983 Structural changes on charring wood of *Dichrostachys* and *Salix* from southern Africa, *IAWA Bulletin* n s **4**, 197–206

Pryor, F, 1974 *Excavation at Fengate, Peterborough, England: the first report* (Royal Ontario Museum Archaeol Mono **3**). Toronto: Royal Ontario Museum

Pryor, F, 1998 *Etton: excavations at a Neolithic causewayed enclosure near Maxey, Cambridgeshire, 1982–87*, English Heritage Archaeol Rep **18.** London: English Heritage

Rackham, O, 1977 Neolithic woodland management in the Somerset Levels: Garvin's, Walton Heath, and Rowland's tracks, *Somerset Levels Pap* **3**, 65–71

—, 1979 Neolithic woodland management in the Somerset Levels: Sweet track 1, *Somerset Levels Pap* **5**, 59–61

Rankine, W F, Rankine, W M, and Dimbleby, G W, 1960 Further excavations at a Mesolithic site at Oakhanger, Selborne, Hants. *Proceedings of the Prehistoric Society* **26**, 246–62

Rausing, G, 1990 *Vitis* pips in Neolithic Sweden, *Antiquity* **64**, 117–22

Raven, A M, van Bergen, P F, Stott, A W, Dudd, S N, and Evershed, R P, 1997 Formation of long-chain ketones in archaeological pottery vessels by pyrolysis of acyl lipids, *J Analytical Applied Pyrolysis* **40(1)**, 267–85

Rawlings, M N, 1994 Excavation and survey at Whitesheet Hill, Wiltshire, 1989/90, unpubl archive report, project no 33521, Salisbury: Wessex Archaeology

Rawlings, M, Allen, M J, and Healy, F, 2004 Investigation of the Whitesheet Down environs 1989–90: Neolithic causewayed enclosure and Iron Age settlement, *Wiltshire Studies* **97**, 144–96

Rayner, A, and Boddy, L, 1988 *Fungal decomposition of wood*, Chichester: Wiley

Renfrew, C, 1973 Monuments, mobilisation and social organisation in Neolithic Wessex, in *The explanation of culture change: models in prehistory* (ed C Renfrew), 539–58, London: Duckworth

Richards, J C, 1990 *The Stonehenge environs project*, English Heritage Archaeol Rep **16.** London: English Heritage

Richards, M P, 1998 *Palaeodietary studies of European populations using stable isotopes.* Unpublished DPhil thesis, University of Oxford

—, 2000 Human consumption of plant foods in the British Neolithic; direct evidence from bone stable isotopes, in *Plants in Neolithic Britain and beyond* (ed A Fairbairn), Neolithic Studies Group Seminar Papers **5**, 123–35, Oxford: Oxbow Books

—, 2003 Explaining the dietary isotope evidence for the rapid adoption of the Neolithic in Britain, in *Food, culture and identity in the Neolithic and early Bronze Age* (ed M Parker Pearson), 31–36, Brit Archaeol Rep Internat Ser **1117**. Oxford: British Archaeological Reports

Richards, M P, and Hedges, R E M, 1999 Stable isotope evidence for similarities in the types of marine foods used by late Mesolithic humans at sites along the Atlantic coast of Europe, *J Archaeol Sci* **26**, 717–22

Richards, M P, Mays, S, and Fuller, B, 2002 Stable carbon and nitrogen isotope values of bone and teeth reflect weaning at the mediaeval Wharram Percy site, Yorkshire, UK, *Amer J Physical Anthropol* 199, 205–10

Richmond, I, 1968 *Hod Hill volume 2. Excavations carried out between 1951 and 1958 for the Trustees of the British Museum*. London, Trustees of the British Museum

Riley, H, 1990 The scraper assemblages and *petit tranchet* derivative arrowheads, in Richards 1990, 225–28

Rival, L (ed), 1998 *The social life of trees*, Oxford: Berg

Roberts, C, and Manchester, K, 1997 *The archaeology of disease*, Stroud: Sutton

Robertson-Mackay, R, 1987 The Neolithic causewayed enclosure at Staines, Surrey: excavations 1961–63, *Proc Prehist Soc* **53**, 23–128

Robinson, M, 1988 Molluscan evidence for pasture and meadowland on the floodplain of the Upper Thames Basin, in *The exploitation of wetlands* (eds P Murphy and C French), Brit Archaeol Rep Brit Ser **186**, 101–12. Oxford: British Archaeological Reports

—, 2000 Further considerations of Neolithic charred cereals, fruit and nuts, in *Plants in Neolithic Britain and beyond* (ed A S Fairbairn), 85–90. Neolithic Studies Group Seminar Papers 5.Oxbow: Oxbow Books

Robledo, B, Trancho, G J, and Brothwell, D, 1995 Cribra orbitalia: health indicator in the late Roman population of Cannington (Somerset, Great Britain), *J Palaeopathology* **7(3)**, 185–93

Rodwell, J S, 1991 *British plant communities. Volume I: woodlands and scrub*, Nature Conservancy Council, Cambridge: Cambridge University Press

Roe F, 1999 The worked stone, in *Excavations alongside Roman Ermin Street, Gloucestershire and Wiltshire. The archaeology of the A419/A417 Swindon to Gloucester road scheme* (A Mudd, R J Williams and A Lupton), 414–21, Oxford: Oxford Archaeological Unit

—, 2000 Worked stone, in *Cadbury Castle, Somerset: the later prehistoric and early historic archaeology* (J C Barrett, P W M Freeman, and A Woodward), English Heritage Archaeol Rep **20**, 262–9

—, 2001 Whetstones, in *Fosse Lane, Shepton Mallet 1990: Excavation of a Romano-British roadside settlement in Somerset* (P Leach with C Jane Evans), Britannia Mono Series **18**, 235–7

Rogers, J, 1990 The human skeletal material, in *Hazleton North. The excavation of a long cairn of the Cotswold-Severn group, Gloucestershire, 1979–82* (A Saville), English Heritage Archaeol Rep **13**, 182–98. London: English Heritage

Rogers, J, and Waldron, T, 1994 *A field guide to joint disease in archaeology*, Chichester: Wiley

Rogers, J, Waldron, T, Dieppe, P, and Watt, I, 1987 Arthropathies in palaeopathology: the basis of classification according to most probable cause, *J Archaeol Sci* **14**, 179–93

Ross Williamson, R P, 1930 Excavations in Whitehawk Neolithic camp, near Brighton. *Sussex Archaeol Collect* **71**, 57–96

Rossen, J, and Olsen, J, 1985 The controlled carbonization and archaeological analysis of SE US wood charcoals, *J Field Archaeol* **12(4)**, 445–56

Rouse, A, and Evans, J G, 1993 Land molluscs, in A Neolithic downland monument in its environment: excavations at the Easton Down long barrow, Bishops Cannings, North Wiltshire (A Whittle, A J Rouse, and J G Evans), *Proc Prehist Soc* **59**, 197–239

Rouse, A, and Evans, J G, 1994 Modern land Mollusca from Maiden Castle, Dorset and their relevance to the interpretation of subfossil archaeological assemblages, *J Molluscan Studies* **60**, 315–29

Rowley-Conwy, P, 2000 Through a taphonomic glass darkly: the importance of cereal cultivation in prehistoric Britain, in *Taphonomy and interpretation in environmental archaeology* (eds J Huntley and S Stallibrass), Symposia of the Association for Environmental Archaeology **14**, 43–53, Oxford: Oxbow Books

RCHME, 1970 *An inventory of historical monuments in the county of Dorset. Volume 3: central Dorset*, London, HMSO

—, 1972 *An inventory of the historical monuments in the county of Dorset. Volume 4. North Dorset*, London, HMSO

—, 1977 *An inventory of the historical monuments in the county of Dorset. Volume 5. East Dorset*, London, HMSO

—, 1996 *Hambledon Hill, Child Okeford, Hanford and Iwerne Courtney or Shroton, Dorset. NMR numbers ST 81, SW 10 and 17. Request survey June–September 1996*, Cambridge: RCHME

Rozanski, K, Stichler, W, Gonfiantini, R, Scott, E M, Beukens, R P, Kromer, B, and van der Plicht, J, 1992 The IAEA ^{14}C intercomparison exercise 1990, *Radiocarbon* **34**, 506–19

Russell, M D, 1987a Bone breakage in the Krapina hominoid collection, *Amer J Phys Anthropol* **72**, 373–79

Russell, M D, 1987b Mortuary practices at the Krapina Neanderthal site, *Amer J Phys Anthropol* **72**, 381–97

Russell, M, and Rudling, D, 1996 Excavations at Whitehawk Neolithic enclosure, Brighton, East Sussex: 1991–93, *Sussex Archaeol Collect* **134**, 39–61

Salisbury, E J, and Jane, F W, 1940 Charcoals from Maiden Castle and their significance in relation to the vegetation and climatic conditions in prehistoric times, *J Ecology* **28**, 310–25

Sandars, H W, 1910 On the use of the deer-horn pick in the mining operations of the ancients, *Archaeologia* **62**, 101–24

Saunders, R L, 1998 The use of Old Red Sandstone in Roman Britain: a petrographical archaeological study, unpubl PhD thesis, Univ of Reading

Saville, A, 1973 A reconsideration of the prehistoric flint assemblage from Bourne Pool, Aldridge, Staffs, *S Staffordshire Archaeol Hist Soc* **14**, 6–28

—, 1978 Five flint assemblages from excavated sites in Wiltshire, *Wiltshire Archaeol Natur Hist Mag* **72/73**, 1–27

—, 1980 On the measurement of struck flakes and flake tools, *Lithics* **1**, 16–20

—, 1981a The flint and chert artefacts, in Excavations at Carn Brea, Illogan, Cornwall, 1970–73 (R J Mercer), *Cornish Archaeol* **20**, 101–52

—, 1981b *Grimes Graves, Norfolk, excavations 1971–72, vol 2: the flint* assemblage, Department of the Environment Archaeol Rep **11**, London: HMSO

—, 1982 Carrying cores to Gloucestershire: some thoughts on lithic resource exploitation, *Lithics* 3, 25–28

—, 1990a Recent research on flint assemblages from Hazleton, Gloucestershire and Hambledon Hill, Dorset, England, in *Le silex de sa genèse à l'outil* (eds M-R Séronie-Vivien and M Lenoir), Centre National de la Recherche Scientifique, Cahiers du Quaternaire **17**, 365–72, Paris

—, 1990b *Hazleton North: the excavation of a Neolithic long cairn of the Cotswold-Severn group*, English Heritage Archaeol Rep **13**. London: English Heritage

—, 1990c Fired clay, in Saville 1990b, 199–214.

—, 1991 Review of *Excavations at Grimes Graves, Norfolk, 1972–1976. Fascicule 3, Shaft X: Bronze Age flint, chalk and metal working* (I Longworth, A Herne, G Varndell and S Needham), *Antiq J* **71**, 272–74

—, 1997 The flint and chert artefacts, in The excavation of a Neolithic enclosure complex at Helman Tor, Lostwithiel, Cornwall (R J Mercer), *Cornish Archaeol* **36**, 39–52

—, 2002 Lithic artefacts from Neolithic causewayed enclosures: character and meaning, in *Enclosures in Neolithic Europe. Essays on causewayed and non-causewayed sites* (eds G Varndell and P Topping), 91–105, Oxford: Oxbow Books

Scaife, R G, 1982 Late Devensian and early Flandrian vegetation changes in southern England, in *Archaeological aspects of woodland ecology* (eds M Bell and S Limbrey), Brit Archaeol Rep Internat Ser **146**, 57–74. Oxford: British Archaeological Reports

—, 1991 Pollen investigation and vegetational history, in *Redeemed from the heath: the archaeology of the Wytch Farm oilfield (1987–90)* (P W Cox and C M Hearne), Dorset Natur Hist Archaeol Soc Mono **9**, 180–97. Dorchester: Dorset Natural History and Archaeology Society

—, 2003 Palynological analyses, in Archaeological and palaeo-environmental investigations of the upper Allen valley, Cranborne Chase, Dorset (1998–2000): a new model of earlier Holocene landscape development (C French, H Lewis, M J Allen, R G Scaife and M Green), *Proc Prehist Soc* **69**, 217–225

—, 2004 Pollen analysis, in Investigation of the Whitesheet Down environs 1989–90: Neolithic causewayed enclosure and Iron Age settlement (M Rawlings, M J Allen and F Healy), *Wiltshire Studies* **97**, 175–7

Schama, S, 1995 *Landscape and memory*, London: Harper & Collins

Scott, E M, Long, A, and Kra, R S (eds), 1990 Proceedings of the international workshop on intercomparison of radiocarbon laboratories, *Radiocarbon* **32**, 253–397

Scott, E M, Harkness, D D, and Cook, G T, 1998 Inter-laboratory comparisons: lessons learned, *Radiocarbon* **40**, 331–40

Schwarcz, H, and Schoeninger, M, 1991 Stable isotope analyses in human nutritional ecology, *Yearbook Phys Anthropol* **34**, 283–321

Schweingruber, F H, 1990a *Microscopic wood anatomy.* Birmensdorf: Swiss Federal Institute for Forest, Snow and Landscape Research

Schweingruber, F H, 1990b *Anatomy of European woods. An atlas for the identification of European trees, shrubs and dwarf shrubs*, Stuttgart: Paul Haupt

Schulting, R J, 1998 Slighting the sea: the Mesolithic-Neolithic transition in north-west Europe. Unpubl PhD thesis, Department of Archaeology, University of Reading

Scollar, I, 1975 Transformation of extreme oblique aerial photographs to maps or plans by conventional means or by computer, in *Aerial reconnaissance for archaeology* (ed D R Wilson), Counc Brit Archaeol Res Rep **12**, 52–9. London: Council for British Archaeology

Semenov, S A, 1964 *Prehistoric technology. An experimental study of the oldest tools and artefacts from traces of manufacture and wear. Translated, and with a preface by M W Thompson*, London: Cory, Adams & Mackay

Shackleton, C M, and Prins, F, 1992 Charcoal analysis and the 'principle of least effort' – a conceptual model, *J Archaeol Sci* **19**, 631–7

Sharples, N M, 1991 *Maiden Castle. Excavations and field survey 1985–6*, English Heritage Archaeol Rep **19**. London: English Heritage

—, 1994 Maiden Castle, Dorset, in *The Iron Age in Wessex: recent work* (eds A P Fitzpatrick and E L Morris), 91–94, Salisbury: Trust for Wessex Archaeology

Sharples, N, and Henderson J, 1991 Human bone in Sharples 1991, 151–2

Sheail, J, 1971 The formation and maintenance of water-meadows in Hampshire, England. *Biological Conservation* **3**, 101–6

Shepherd, W, 1972 *Flint: its origin, properties and uses.* London: Faber and Faber

Shotton, F W, 1978 Archaeological inferences from the study of alluvium in the lower Severn-Avon valleys, in *The effect of man on the landscape: the lowland zone* (eds S Limbrey and J G Evans), Counc Brit Archaeol Res Rep **21**, 27–32. London: Council for British Archaeology

Shvetsov, M S 1955 Visual diagrams for particle quantification (in translation), in Concerning additional aids in studying sedimentary formations (R D Terry and G V Chilingar), *J Sedimentary Petrology* **25**, 229–34

Silver, I A, 1969 The ageing of domestic mammals, in *Science in archaeology* (eds D Brothwell and E Higgs; second edition), 283–302, London: Thames and Hudson

Simmons, I, 1996 *The environmental impact of later Mesolithic cultures*, Edinburgh: Edinburgh University Press for the University of Durham

Simonds, J B, 1854 *The age of the ox, sheep and pig*, London: W S Orr

Smart, T L, and Hoffman, E S, 1988 Environmental interpretation of archaeological charcoal, in *Current palaeoethnobotany* (eds C A Hastorf and V S Popper), 167–205, Chicago and London: University of Chicago Press

Smith, C J, 1980 *Ecology of the English Chalk*, London: Academic Press

Smith, G H, 1987 The Lizard Project, landscape survey, 1978–1983, *Cornish Archaeol* **26**, 13–68

Smith, G, and Harris, D, 1982 The excavation of Mesolithic, Neolithic, and Bronze Age settlements at Poldowrian, St Keverne, 1980, *Cornish Archaeol* **21**, 23–62

Smith, I F, 1965 *Windmill Hill and Avebury: excavations by Alexander Keiller, 1925–1939*, Oxford: Clarendon Press

—, 1971 Causewayed enclosures, in *Economy and settlement in Neolithic and early Bronze Age Britain and Europe* (ed D D A Simpson), 89–112, Leicester: Leicester University Press

—, 1976 The pottery, in The Sweet Track: railway site (J M Coles and B J Orme), *Somerset Levels Pap* **2**, 34–65

—, 1981 The Neolithic pottery, in Excavations at Carn Brea, Illogan, Cornwall, 1970–1973 (R J Mercer), *Cornish Archaeol* **20,** 161–79

—, 1997 The Neolithic pottery, in Mercer 1997, 29–37

Smith, I F, and Darvill, T C, 1990 The prehistoric pottery, in *Hazleton North. The excavation of a long cairn of the Cotswold-Severn group, Gloucestershire, 1979–82* (A Saville), English Heritage Archaeol Rep **13**, 141–52. London: English Heritage

Smith, M, 1954 *The British amphibians and reptiles*, London: Collins

Smith, M J, and Brickley, M B, 2004 Analysis and interpretation of flint toolmarks found on bones from West Tump long barrow, Gloucesteshire, *Internat J Osteoarchaeology* **14**, 18–33

Smith, P S, 1987 Marine Mollusca, in The Roman villa site at Dicket Mead (T Rook), *Hertfordshire Archaeol* **9**, 170–2

Smith, R J C, 1997 Settlement. Iron Age, Roman and medieval, in Smith *et al* 1997, 299–306

Smith, R J C, Healy, F, Allen, M J, Morris, E L, Barnes, I, and Woodward, P J, 1997 *Excavations along the route of the Dorchester by-pass, Dorset, 1986–8*. Wessex Archaeol Rep **11**, Salisbury: Wessex Archaeology

Smith, R W, 1983 Everley Water Meadow, unpubl manuscript report

—, 1984 The ecology of Neolithic farming systems as exemplified by the Avebury region of Wiltshire, *Proc Prehist Soc* **50**, 99–120

—, 1985 Prehistoric human ecology in the Wessex chalklands with special reference to evidence from valleys, unpublished PhD thesis, University of Southampton

Sofranoff, S E, 1976 A petrological study of pottery of the so-called 'Windmill Hill' and 'Peterborough' traditions of the Wessex area of southern England, unpubl MPhil thesis, Univ of Southampton

Sparks, B W, 1953 The former occurrence of both *Helicella striata* (Müller) and *H geyeri* (Soòs) in England, *J Conchology* **23**, 372–78

—, 1961 The ecological interpretation of Quaternary non-marine Mollusca, *Proc Linnaean Soc London* **172**, 71–80

Spikins, P A, 2002 *Prehistoric people of the Pennines. Reconstructing the lifestyles of Mesolithic hunter-gatherers on Marsden Moor*. Leeds: West Yorkshire Archaeology Service

Sprugal, D G, 1991 Disturbance, equilibrium and environmental variability: what is 'natural' vegetation in a changing environment?, *Biological Conservation* **58**, 1–18

Stace, C, 1991 *New flora of the British Isles*, Cambridge: Cambridge University Press

Staines, S, 1991 Soils of Winterbourne Steepleton and the soil sections at Cowleaze and Loscombe, in Woodward 1991, 117–21

—, 1997 Prehistoric soil patterns in the Dorchester environs, in Smith *et al* 1997, 163–6

Steele, J, and Mays, S, 1995 Handedness and directional asymmetry in the long bones of the human upper limb, *Internat J Osteoarchaeology* **5**, 39–49

Stott, A W, Evershed, R P, Hedges, R E M, Bronk Ramsey, C, and Humm, M J, 2001 Radiocarbon dating of single compounds isolated from pottery cooking vessel residues, *Radiocarbon* **43**, 191–97

Straker, V, 1997 Charred plant remains, in Smith *et al* 1997, 184–90

Stuiver, M, and Kra, R S, 1986 Editorial comment, *Radiocarbon* **28(2B)**, ii

Stuiver, M, and Pearson, G W, 1986 High-precision calibration of the radiocarbon time scale, AD 1950–500 BC, *Radiocarbon* **28**, 805–38

Stuiver, M and Polach, H J, 1977 Discussion: reporting of ^{14}C data, *Radiocarbon*, **19**, 355–63

Stuiver, M, and Reimer, P J, 1986 A computer program for radiocarbon age calculation, *Radiocarbon* **28**, 1022–30

—, 1993 Extended ^{14}C data base and revised CALIB 3.0 ^{14}C age calibration program, *Radiocarbon* **35**, 215–30

Stuiver, M, Reimer, P J, Bard, E, Beck, J W, Burr, G S, Hughen, K A, Kromer, B, McCormac, F G, van der Plicht, J, and Spurk, M, 1998 INTCAL98 radiocarbon age calibration, 24,000–0 cal BP, *Radiocarbon* **40**, 1041–84

Summers, P G, 1941 A Mesolithic site near Iwerne Minster, Dorset, *Proc Prehist Soc* **7**, 145–6

Sumner H 1913, *The ancient earthworks of Cranborne Chase*, London

Tamers, M A, 1965 Routine carbon-14 dating using liquid scintillation techniques, in *Radiocarbon and tritium dating: proceedings of the sixth international conference on radiocarbon and tritium dating* (eds R M Chatters and E A Olson), 53–67, Washington D.C.

Taylor, C C, 1960 Report on soils from Hambledon Hill, unpubl report dated 14.5.60

Taylor, M, 1998 Wood and bark from the enclosure ditch, in Pryor1998, 115–59

Thomas, J, 1991 *Rethinking the Neolithic*, Cambridge: Cambridge University Press

—, 1996 Neolithic houses in mainland Britain and Ireland – a sceptical view, in *Neolithic houses in Northwest Europe and beyond* (eds T Darvill and J Thomas), 1–12. Oxbow Monograph 57, Neolithic Studies Group Seminar Papers 1. Oxford: Oxbow Books

—, 1999 *Understanding the Neolithic*, Cambridge: Cambridge University Press

—, 2003 Thoughts on the 'repacked' Neolithic revolution, *Antiquity* **77(295)**, 67–74

Thomas, K D 1982 Neolithic enclosures and woodland habitats on the South Downs in Sussex, England, in *Archaeological aspects of woodland ecology* (eds M G Bell and S Limbrey), Brit Archaeol Rep Internat Ser **146**, 147–70. Oxford: British Archaeological Reports

—, 1985 Land snail analysis in archaeology: theory and practice, in *Palaeobiological investigations: research design, methods and data analysis* (eds N R J Fieller, D D Gilbertson, and N G A Ralph), Brit Archaeol Rep Internat Ser **266**, 131–75. Oxford: British Archaeological Reports

Thomas, N, 1964 The Neolithic causewayed camp at Robin Hood's Ball, Shrewton, *Wiltshire Archaeol Natur Hist Mag* **59**, 1–27

Thompson, G B, 1984 Cefn Graeanog charcoals: A case study in intra-site spatial analysis, unpubl BSc dissertation, Institute of Archaeology, University College, London

Thorley, A, 1981 Pollen analytical evidence relating to the vegetation history of the chalk, *J Biogeography* **8**, 93–106

Thorpe, I J, 1984 Ritual, power and ideology: a reconstruction of earlier Neolithic rituals in Wessex, in *Neolithic Studies: A review of some current research* (eds R Bradley and J P Gardiner), Brit Archaeol Rep Brit Ser **133**, 41–60. Oxford: British Archaeological Reports

Thorpe, I J, and Richards, C, 1984 The decline of ritual authority and the introduction of Beakers into Britain, in *Neolithic studies: a review of some current research* (eds R Bradley and J Gardiner), (Brit Archaeol Rep Brit Ser **133**, 67–84. Oxford: British Archaeological Reports

Tieszen, L, and Fagre, T, 1993 Effect of diet quality and composition on the isotopic composition of respiratory CO_2, bone collagen, bioapatite and soft tissues, in *Prehistoric human bone: archaeology at the molecular level* (eds J Lambert and G Grupe), 121–55, Berlin and London: Springer-Verlag

Tilley, C, 1994 *A phenomenology of landscape: places, paths and monuments*, Oxford and Providence: Berg

Tingle, M, 1998 *The prehistory of Beer Head. Field survey and excavations at an isolated flint source on the south Devon coast*, Brit Archaeol Rep Brit Ser **270.** Oxford: British Archaeological Reports

Tite, M S, 1972 *Methods of physical examination in archaeology*, London: Seminar Press

Tomalin, D, 1982 The formal and textural characteristics of the Biconical Urn assemblage from Shaugh Moor Enclosure 15, and their implications, in The Shaugh Moor project: fourth report – environment, context and conclusion (N D Balaam, K Smith and G J Wainwright), *Proc Prehist Soc* **48**, 228–37

Trotter, M, and Gleser, G C, 1952 Estimation of stature from long bones of American whites and Negroes, *Amer J Phys Anthrop* **10(4)**, 463–514

—, 1958 A re-evaluation of estimation of stature based on measurements of stature taken during life and of long bones after death, *Amer J Phys Anthrop* **16(1)**, 79–123

Turner, C, 1993 Cannibalism in Chaco Canyon: the charnel pit excavated in 1926 at Small House Ruin by Frank H H Roberts Jr, *Amer J Phys Anthrop* **91**, 421–39

Ubelaker, D H, 1984 *Human skeletal remains*, Smithsonian Institution Manuals on Archaeology, Washington

Valentin, J, 1993 An early Iron Age hilltop settlement at Heron Grove, Sturminster Marshall, Dorset: first excavation report, *Proc Dorset Natur Hist Archaeol Soc* **115**, 63–70

van Beek, G C, 1983 *Dental morphology: an illustrated guide*, Bristol, London and Boston: Wright. PSG

van der Merwe, N J, and Medina, E, 1991 The canopy effect, carbon isotope ratios, and foodwebs in Amazonia, *J Archaeol Sci* **18**, 249–59

van der Plicht, J, 1993 The Gröningen radiocarbon calibration program, *Radiocarbon* **35**, 231–7

Varndell, G, 1991 The worked chalk, in Longworth, I, Herne, A, Varndell, G and Needham, S, *Shaft X: Bronze Age flint, chalk and metal working. Excavations at Grime's Graves Norfolk 1972–1976. Fascicule 3.* London, British Museum Press, 94–153

Vaquer, J, Geddes, D, Barbaza, M, and Errouzx, J, 1986 Mesolithic plant exploitation at the Balma Abeurador (France), *Oxford J Archaeol* **5(1)**, 1–18

Villa, P, Courtin, J, Helmer, D, Shipman, P, Bouville, C, and Mahieu, È, 1986 Un cas de cannibalisme au Néolithique; boucherie et rejet de restes humains et animaux dans la grotte de Fontbrégoua à Salernes (Var), *Gallia Préhistoire* **29**, 143–71

Vogt, E, 1937 Geflechte und Gewebe der Steinzeit, *Monographien zur ur- und frugeschichte der Schweiz* **B** and **I**, Basel

Wainwright, G J, 1972 The excavation of a Neolithic settlement on Broome Heath, Ditchingham, Norfolk, England, *Proc Prehist Soc* **38**, 1–97

—, 1979a *Mount Pleasant, Dorset: excavations 1970–1971*, Rep Res Comm Soc Antiq London **37**. London: Society of Antiquaries of London

—, 1979b *Gussage All Saints: an Iron Age settlement in Dorset.* Department of the Environment Archaeol Rep **10.** London: HMSO.

Wainwright, G J, with Longworth, I H, 1971 *Durrington Walls: excavations 1966–1968*, Rep Res Comm Soc Antiq London **29**. London: Society of Antiquaries of London

Waldron, T, 1988 The human bone, in A seventh-century inhumation cemetery at Shepherd's Farm, Ulwell, near Swanage, Dorset (P Cox), *Proc Dorset Natur Hist Archaeol Soc* **110**, 42–44

Wakely, J, 2006 Other marks, in The human remains (F Lee), in *A woodland archaeology. Neolithic Sites at Haddenham. The Haddenham project: volume 1* (C Evans and I Hodder). Cambridge: MacDonald Institute for Archaeological Research.

Wakely, J, Manchester, K, and Roberts, C, 1991 Scanning electron microscopy of rib lesions, *Internat J Osteoarchaeology* **1**, 185–9

Walne, P, 1974 *The culture of bivalve molluscs*, West Byfleet: Fishing News (Books) Ltd

Ward, G K, and Wilson, S R, 1978 Procedures for comparing and combining radiocarbon age determinations: a critique, *Archaeometry* **20**, 19–31

Ward, J O, Gillespie, R, and Hedges, R E M, 1984 Sample preparation for Accelerator-based dating, *J Archaeol Sci* **11**, 159–63

Ward, R, 1929 *Records of big game*, London: Rowland Ward

Waton, P V, 1982 Man's impact on the chalklands: some new pollen evidence, in *Archaeological aspects of woodland ecology* (eds M Bell and S Limbrey), Brit Archaeol Rep Internat Ser **146**, 75–91. Oxford: British Archaeological Reports

Wedlake, W J, 1958 *Excavations at Camerton, Somerset*, Camerton Excavation Club

Wells, L H, 1962 Report on the inhumation burials from the West Kennet barrow, in Piggott 1962, 79–89

Wheeler, R E M, 1943 *Maiden Castle, Dorset.* Rep Res Comm Soc Antiq London **12.** London: Society of Antiquaries of London

White, P S, 1979 Pattern, process, and natural disturbance in vegetation, *Botanical Review* **45(3)**, 229–99

Whitehead, B J, 1967 The management and land-use of water meadows in the Frome valley, Dorset, *Proc Dorset Natur Hist Archaeol Soc* **89**, 257–81

Whitehead, G K, 1964 *Deer of Great Britain and Ireland*, London Routledge & Kegan Paul

Whitley, M, 1943 Excavations at Chalbury Camp, Dorset, 1939, *Antiq J* **23**, 98–121

Whittle, A W R, 1977 *The earlier Neolithic of southern England and its continental background*, British Archaeological Reports Supplementary Series 35. Oxford: British Archaeological Reports

—, 1991 Wayland's Smithy, Oxfordshire: excavations at the Neolithic tomb in 1962–63 by R J C Atkinson and S Piggott, *Proc Prehist Soc* **57 (2)**, 61–101

—, 1997 *Sacred mound, holy rings. Silbury Hill and the West Kennet palisade enclosures: a later Neolithic complex in north Wiltshire*, Oxford: Oxbow Books

Whittle, A, and Pollard, J, 1999 The harmony of symbols: wider meanings, in Whittle *et al* 1999, 381–90

Whittle, A, and Wysocki, M, 1998 Parc le Breos Cwm transepted long cairn, Gower, West Glamorgan: date, contents, and context, *Proc Prehist Soc* **64**, 139–82

Whittle, A, Pollard, J, and Grigson, C, 1999 *The harmony of symbols: the Windmill Hill causewayed enclosure, Wiltshire*, Cardiff Studies in Archaeology, Oxford: Oxbow Books

Whittle, A, Davies, J J, Dennis, I, Fairbairn, A, and Hamilton, M, 2000 Neolithic activity and occupation outside Windmill Hill causewayed enclosure, Wiltshire: survey and excavation 1992–93, *Wiltshire Heritage Studies* **93**, 131–80

Williams, A, 1950 Excavations at Allard's Quarry, Marnhull, Dorset, *Proc Dorset Natur Hist Archaeol Soc* **72**, 20–75

Willock, E H, 1936 A Neolithic site on Haldon, *Proceedings of the Devon Archaeological Society* **2**(4), 255–63

Wilson, J E, 1997 Small sample high-precision ^{14}C dating, unpubl MPhil thesis, Queens Univ Belfast

Wilson, J E, McCormac, F G, and Hogg, A G, 1996 Small sample high-precision 14C dating: characterisation of vials and counter optimisation, in *Liquid scintillation spectrometry 1994* (eds G T Cook, D D Harkness, A B Mackenzie, B F Miller, and E M Scott), 59–65, Arizona

Winder, J M, 1992 A study of the variation in oyster shells from archaeological sites and a discussion of oyster exploitation, Unpubl Ph D thesis, Univ of Southampton

Woodward, P J, 1978 Flint distribution, ring ditches and Bronze Age settlement patterns in the Great Ouse valley. The problem, a field survey technique and some preliminary results', *Archaeol J* **135**, 32–56

—, 1991 *The South Dorset Ridgeway: survey and excavations 1977–84.* Dorset Natur Hist Archaeol Soc Mono **8**, Dorchester

Woodward, P J, and Bellamy, P, 1991 Artefact distribution, in Sharples 1991, 21–32

Wright, J F, Hiley, P D, Cooling, D A, Cameron, A C, Wigham, M E, and Berrie, A D, 1984 The invertebrate fauna of a small chalk stream in Berkshire, England, and the effect of intermittent flow, *Archive für Hydrobiologie* **99(2)**, 179–99

Wymer, J J (ed), 1977 *Gazetteer of Mesolithic sites in England and Wales*, Counc Brit Archaeol Res Rep **20.** London: Council for British Archaeology

Wysocki, M, 1998 The mortuary assemblages, in Whittle and Wysocki 1998, 147–65

Wysocki, M, and Whittle, A, 2000 Diversity, lifestyles and rites: new biological and archaeological evidence from British earlier Neolithic mortuary assemblages, *Antiquity* **74(285)**, 591–601

Index

Locators in **bold** refer to figures, those in *italic* refer to tables